E. C. S. Wade and A. W. Bradley

Constitutional and administrative law

Tenth Edition

By A. W. Bradley M.A., LL.B.
Professor of Constitutional Law in the University of Edinburgh

With T. St. J. N. Bates M.A., LL.B.
Senior Lecturer in Constitutional Law in the University of Edinburgh

and C. M. G. Himsworth B.A., LL.B.
Lecturer in Constitutional Law in the University of Edingburgh

Longman
London and New York

Longman Group Limited
Longman House, Burnt Mill, Harlow
Essex CM20 2JE, England
Associated companies throughout the world

Published in the United States of America
by Longman Inc., New York

© Longman Group Limited 1985, except Chapters 8 & 18 © T. St. J. Bates 1985,
and Chapter 25 © Longman Group Limited and T. St. J. Bates 1985

First Edition 1931
Second Edition 1935
Third Edition 1946
Fourth Edition 1950
Fifth Edition 1955
Sixth Edition 1960
Seventh Edition 1965
Eighth Edition 1970
Ninth Edition 1977
Third Impression, with revisions and corrections October 1980
Fourth Impression 1982
Tenth Edition 1985

British Library Cataloguing in Publication Data
Wade, E. C. S.
   Constitutional and administrative law. —
   10th ed.
   1. Great Britain — Constitutional law
   I. Title   II. Bradley, A. W.
   III. Bates, T. St. J. N.   IV. Himsworth, Chris
   344.102   KD3989

ISBN 0-582-49124-X csd
ISBN 0-582-49125-8 ppr

Library of Congress Cataloging in Publication Data
Wade, E. C. S. (Emlyn Capel Stewart), 1895–1978
  Constitutional and administrative law.

  Bibliography: p.
  Includes index.
1. Great Britain — Constitutional law. 2. Administrative
law — Great Britain.   I. Bradley, A. W. (Anthony
Wilfred)   II. Bates, T. St. J. N.   III. Himsworth, Chris.
IV. Title.
KD3930.W3 1985   342.41   84–4389
ISBN 0-582-49124-X   344.102
ISBN 0-582-49125-8 (pbk.)

Produced by Longman Group (FE) Limited
Printed in Hong Kong

Contents

Preface

Since the previous edition of this book was published in 1977, innumerable changes of greater or lesser importance have occurred in the detailed fabric of public law in the United Kingdom. Constitutional change is still needed, particularly in our manner of electing the House of Commons and in our arrangements for protecting human rights. Yet in 1985, the centennial of the first publication of Dicey's *Law of the Constitution*, it is chastening to reflect on the perishable quality of most books on constitutional law. How attractive it would be to the authors of such books (not to mention their families and their publishers) to create an analysis which required the minimum of revision from one decade to the next! As it is, this new edition seeks no immortality. The aim has been to take account of major developments of the last seven years within the structure adopted for the book in 1977. The most material change to this structure has affected chapters 34–36, but even so it will be apparent that we are still experiencing a process of rapid and sometimes confusing developments in administrative law. In this area at least, we must be prepared to re-assess and discard older precedents that are out of harmony with themes heard in the courts today.

Amongst the legislation which made extensive revision of the text necessary, the Police and Criminal Evidence Act 1984 presented a particular challenge, in part because it received the royal assent only shortly before proofs had to be returned to the printers, but mainly because it stops short of being a code of police powers yet makes many incursions into what has hitherto largely been an area of common law. Once the Act is in operation and new practice and case-law develop, further thought will need to be given to the presentation of police powers in chapter 26.

I completed the revision of chapter 19 before *The Attorney-General, Politics and the Public Interest* by Professor John Ll.J. Edwards became available. This important book adds immensely to our knowledge of the role of the law officers of the Crown in recent decades.

In this edition, as in 1977, I have sought to emphasise that English law is only one of three jurisdictions within the United Kingdom. But I have not been as helpful as I would have liked to readers of the book north of the border, since on some topics I have dealt much more fully with English law than with

the equivalent law in Scotland. Constraints of various kinds have led to several aspects of public law receiving less attention than they deserve (including Northern Ireland and the law relating to the economy, industry and the trade unions) and to the omission of the relationship between church and state.

I paid tribute to my predecessor Professor E. C. S. Wade, as author and editor of this book, in the preface to the 1977 edition, the preparation of which he had followed with great interest. His death occurred in April 1978, and an appreciation of his achievements may be found in the Proceedings of the British Academy for 1978. While Professor Wade did not wish a reference to his former colleague, the late G. Godfrey Phillips, to disappear from the title-page during his life-time, it was considered by the publishers as well as by several users of the book that a change in the designation of the book might now be appropriate.

For this edition, my Edinburgh colleague, T. St. J. N. Bates, has, as in the 9th edition, contributed chapters 8 (the EEC) and 18 (foreign affairs) and together we revised chapter 25. My colleague, C. M. G. Himsworth, undertook the revision of chapters 20 (the police), 21 (local government) and 31A (legislation against discrimination). I warmly appreciate their support, but they have no responsibility for aspects of the book falling outside the sections with which they have been concerned.

Many other people have rendered valuable assistance. For specific suggestions and advice I must thank Mr M. Bouchard, Dr A. G. Donaldson, Dr K. D. Ewing, Mr S. Horner and Professor H. W. R. Wade, and, for assistance with research, Mr A. R. Mowbray. Preparation of the book has been possible through access to the excellent facilities of Edinburgh University Library, whose staff have always been helpful. I owe a great debt of thanks to Miss Helen Dignan and Mrs Sheila Smith, who have again undertaken the secretarial and typing work.

The preparation of the manuscript for printing may be deemed to have been completed in December 1984, although most sections of the book were inevitably set in proof before this date and the main text must be read together with the notes on more recent developments to be found in Appendix B. For technical reasons, the tables of cases and statutes and the index do not include material in that appendix.

In principle case-citations are given to the main Law Reports (Appeal Cases, Chancery, Queen's Bench and Family) although these cases will also usually be found in *Weekly Law Reports* and *All England Law Reports*. Where a citation to the main Law Reports has not been possible, citations to All E.R. are given rather than to W.L.R. In the interest of saving space, abbreviated references are given to periodical articles and official publications; further details may be found in the periodicals concerned and in the annual index to government publications issued by H.M.S.O.

Old College,
Edinburgh

A. W. Bradley
January 1985

Table of Statutes

xviii

Statutes of other Parliaments

Australia

Canada

Ireland

Scotland

Table of Cases

xxvii

Abbreviations

Report — Report of Royal Commission on the Constitution, vol 1, Cmnd 5460 1973

Mackintosh, British Cabinet — J. P. Mackintosh, The British Cabinet

Maitland, Justice — F. W. Maitland, The Constitutional History of England

Marshall and Moodie — G. Marshall and G. C. Moodie, Some Problems of the Constitution

M.L.R. — Modern Law Review

M.P.R. — Report of Committee on Ministers' Powers Cmd 4060, 1932

N.I.L.Q. — Northern Ireland Legal Quarterly

P.L. — Public Law

S.I. — Statutory Instrument

S.O. — Standing Order

S.R. & O. — Statutory Rule and Order

S.L.T. — Scots Law Times

Smith and Hogan — J. C. Smith and B. Hogan, Criminal Law

Street, Freedom — H. Street, Freedom, the Individual and the Law

Farewell I Argument — Farwell L.argument, Dicing's Commentary & Bagg

Wilson, Cases — D. P. Wilson, Cases and Materials on Constitutional and Administrative Law

liv

Kilbrandon Report   Report of Royal Commission on the Constitution, vol. 1, Cmnd 5460, 1973

Mackintosh, *British Cabinet*   J. P. Mackintosh, *The British Cabinet*

Maitland, *History*   F. W. Maitland, *The Constitutional History of England*

Marshall and Moodie   G. Marshall and G. C. Moodie, *Some Problems of the Constitution*

M.L.R.   *Modern Law Review*

M.P.R.   Report of Committee on Ministers' Powers, Cmd 4060, 1932

N.I.L.Q.   *Northern Ireland Legal Quarterly*

P.L.   *Public Law*

S.I.   Statutory Instrument

S.O.   Standing Order

S.R. & O.   Statutory Rule and Order

S.L.T.   *Scots Law Times*

Smith and Hogan   J. C. Smith and B. Hogan, *Criminal Law*

Street, *Freedom, Individual and the Law*   H. Street, *Freedom, the Individual and the Law*

Taswell-Langmead   Taswell-Langmead, *English Constitutional History*

Wilson, *Cases*   G. P. Wilson, *Cases and Materials on Constitutional and Administrative Law*

Acknowledgements

We are grateful to the Controller of Her Majesty's Stationery Office for permission to reproduce extracts from *Red Lion Square Disorders June 15, 1974*, Cmnd 5919, and the *Report of the Metropolitan Police Commissioner for 1975*, Cmnd 6946.

Acknowledgements

We are grateful to the Controller of Her Majesty's Stationery Office for permission to reproduce extracts from Red Lion Square Disorder, June 15, 1974, Cmnd 5919; and the Report of the Metropolitan Police Commissioner for 1975, Cmnd 6496.

Chapter 1

Definition and scope of constitutional law

The starting-point for studying constitutional law should ideally be the same starting-point as for studying political philosophy, or the role of law and government in society. How is individual freedom to be reconciled with the claims of social justice? Is society founded upon a reciprocal network of rights and duties, or is the individual merely a pawn in the hands of state power?

These fundamental questions are often not pursued explicitly in the study of constitutional law. In fact constitutional law concerns the relationship between the individual and the state, seen from a particular viewpoint, namely the notion of law. As a historian has stated, 'It is inherent in the especial character of law, as a body of rules and procedures, that it shall apply logical criteria with reference to standards of universality and equity'.[1] Law is not merely a matter of the rules which govern relations between private individuals (for example between husband and wife, or between landlord and tenant). Law also concerns the structure and powers of the state. The constitutional lawyer is always likely to insist that the relations between the individual and the state should be founded upon and governed by law.

But law does not exist in a social and political vacuum. Within a given society, the legal rules that concern relations between husband and wife will reflect that society's attitude to marriage. So too the rules of constitutional law, that govern political relations, will within a given society reflect a particular distribution of political power. In a stable society, constitutional law expresses what may be a very high degree of consensus about the organs and procedures by which political decisions are taken. But when a community insists on taking political decisions by recourse to armed force or gang warfare, or by the might of industrial muscle, the rules of constitutional law are either non-existent, or at best are no more than a transparent cover for a power-struggle that is not conducted in accordance with anything deserving the name of law.

Within a stable democracy, constitutional law reflects the value that people attach to orderly human relations, to individual freedom under the law, and to institutions such as parliament, political parties, free elections, and a free press. Now the reality is often different from the rhetoric. Laws are the product

---

[1] E. P. Thompson, *Whigs and Hunters*, p. 262.

whole of new nations. There have indeed been periods of near political
upheaval culminating in the rebirth of certain institutions; for example the
revolution of 1688, which was the final act of the constitutional conflicts of the
17th century. Later there was the first major reform of the House of Commons
in 1832 and the disputes over the Lords which led to the Parliament Act of 1911.
There have too been the union of England and Scotland in 1707, the union
of Great Britain and Ireland in 1800, and the subsequent problems relating
to the government of Ireland. There was the abdication crisis affecting the
monarchy in 1936. And in 1972 the United Kingdom became a member of the
European Communities. But on none of these occasions was it necessary to
reconstruct the whole system of government. Instead legislation was passed
to translate into law the particular consequence of each major political or
a pragmatic approach has predominated at the expense of declaring British
political philosophy in terms of a law. Evidence of the same pragmatic approach
was provided by the Minority Report of the Royal Commission on the
Constitution, which concluded in 1973 that a codified and formal examination
of the whole constitution had not been undertaken and would not have been
practicable.

Nevertheless, numerous written constitutions have been framed for British
territories overseas, whether as colonies or on their attainment of independence. Such constitutions formed, stopped short of attempting to create fundamental political concepts in terms of law. They contained no written definition
of responsible government and did not guarantee the rights of the citizen.
Some of these older constitutions have stood the test of time virtually
unchanged, for example the constitution of the Commonwealth of Australia,
enacted in 1900. The Canadian constitution contained in the British North
America Act 1867 (now renamed the Constitution Act 1867), was amended
more frequently by the Westminster Parliament in meet requests from Canada,
but in 1982 the Canada Act passed at Westminster gave full powers of
constitutional amendment to Canada and also enacted the Canadian Charter
of Rights and Freedoms as part of the Canadian constitution. After 1945 a
different approach to constitution-making gradually became a usual
common form for guarantees of rights and declarations of broad political
purposes to be included in the constitutions of newly independent Commonwealth countries, as in 1979 when the colony of Rhodesia achieved independence as the republic of Zimbabwe.

Legal consequences of the unwritten constitution

Where there is a written constitution, the legal structure of government may
assume a wide variety of forms. Within a federal constitution, the tasks of
government are divided into two classes, those entrusted to the federal (or
central) organs of government, and those entrusted to the various states,
regions or provinces which make up the federation. Thus in countries such
as Canada, Australia or the United States, constitutional issues bind both the

Kilbrandon Report, para. 544. And see Ch. 29.

Zimbabwe Constitution Order, S.I. 1979 No. 1600, para. I.11 and see Stuart-Smith, The New
Constitutionalism in Commonwealth Ch. 2.

whole of government. There have indeed been periods of acute political upheaval culminating in the reform of certain institutions, for example the revolution of 1688, which was the final act of the constitutional conflicts of the 17th century. Later there was the first major reform of the House of Commons in 1832 and the crisis over the Lords which led to the Parliament Act of 1911. There have too been the union of England and Scotland in 1707, the union of Great Britain and Ireland in 1800, and the subsequent problems relating to the government of Ireland. There was the abdication crisis affecting the monarchy in 1936. And in 1973 the United Kingdom became a member of the European Communities. But on none of these occasions was it necessary to reconstruct the whole system of government. Instead legislation was passed to translate into law the particular consequences of each major political event. A pragmatic approach has predominated at the expense of declaring British political philosophy in terms of law. Evidence of the same pragmatic approach was provided by the Majority Report of the Royal Commission on the Constitution, which considered in 1973 that a root and branch examination of the whole constitution had not been intended and would not have been practicable.[4]

Nevertheless, numerous written constitutions have been framed for British territories overseas, whether as colonies or on their attainment of independence. Such constitutions formerly stopped short of attempting to enact fundamental political concepts in terms of law. They contained no written definition of responsible government and did not guarantee the rights of the citizen. Some of these older constitutions have stood the test of time virtually unchanged, for example the constitution of the Commonwealth of Australia, enacted in 1900. The Canadian constitution, contained in the British North America Act 1867 (now re-named the Constitution Act 1867), was amended more frequently by the Westminster Parliament to meet requests from Canada. But in 1982 the Canada Act passed at Westminster gave full powers of constitutional amendment to Canada and also enacted the Canadian Charter of Rights and Freedoms as part of the Canadian constitution.[5] After 1945, a different approach to constitution-making prevailed: it became almost common form for guarantees of rights and declarations of broad political purpose to be included in the constitutions of newly independent Commonwealth countries, as in 1979 when the colony of Rhodesia achieved independence as the republic of Zimbabwe.[6]

Legal consequences of the unwritten constitution

Where there is a written constitution, the legal structure of government may assume a wide variety of forms. Within a federal constitution, the tasks of government are divided into two classes, those entrusted to the federal (or central) organs of government, and those entrusted to the various states, regions or provinces which make up the federation. Thus in countries such as Canada, Australia or the United States, constitutional limits bind both the

---

[4] Kilbrandon Report, para. 14. And see ch. 24.
[5] App. A.
[6] Zimbabwe Constitution Order, S.I. 1979, No. 1600, part III; and see S. A. de Smith, *The New Commonwealth and its Constitutions*, ch. 5.

federal and state organs of government, which limits are enforceable as a matter of law. It may be desired to place certain rights of the citizen beyond reach of the organs of government created by the constitution; these fundamental rights may be entrenched by the device of requiring a special legislative procedure if they are to be amended, or even by rendering them unalterable, as in the Federal Republic of Germany.[7] Again, many written constitutions seek to avoid a concentration of power in the hands of any one organ of government by adopting the principle of separation of powers, vesting legislative power exclusively in the legislature, executive power in the executive and judicial power in the courts.[8]

Within the United Kingdom, there is no written constitution which can secure these objects or which can serve as fundamental law. In the absence of a constitution to serve as the foundation of the legal system, the vacuum is filled by the legal doctrine of the legislative supremacy of Parliament. The full significance of this doctrine will be examined later,[9] but the result is that formal restraints upon the exercise of power which exist elsewhere do not exist in the United Kingdom. For example, no truly federal system can exist so long as Parliament's legislative supremacy is maintained. Just as it was Parliament which passed the Government of Ireland Act 1920, devolving limited powers of self-government upon Northern Ireland, so in 1972 Parliament could suspend the operation of the Act of 1920 by re-imposing direct rule upon Northern Ireland.[10] For a federal system to be established a written constitution would be necessary, limiting the powers of the Westminster Parliament and thus preventing it from taking back the devolved powers into its own hands. Of course, if subordinate legislatures were to be established for Scotland and Wales, it might be politically difficult to abolish them: but their continued existence would be safeguarded by political factors rather than by constitutional law.

So too, in the absence of a written constitution, it is difficult to imagine how the courts could be entrusted with the function of protecting the rights of minorities and individual citizens against legislative infringement by Parliament. Moreover, the absence of a written constitution means that there is no special procedure prescribed for legislation of constitutional importance. Before the Republic of Ireland could join the EEC, a constitutional amendment had to be approved by referendum of the people. In the United Kingdom, while the European Communities Act 1972 was debated at length in Parliament, the Act was passed by essentially the same procedure as would apply to a Road Traffic Act or other legislation of purely domestic concern. British membership of the EEC was in 1975 confirmed by a consultative referendum; but this was a product of divisions in the Labour party, not a constitutional requirement. By contrast with written constitutions, which may be described as *rigid* because of the special procedure required if they are to be altered, the United Kingdom has what at least in form is an extremely *flexible* constitution. It would seem that there is no aspect of our consti-

---

[7]   Basic Law of the Federal Republic of Germany, articles 19(2) and 79(3).
[8]   Ch. 4.
[9]   Ch. 5.
[10]   Ch. 3.

promotion of the arts and sport. Many people still look to the courts for protection in the sphere of public order and the criminal law, but in the administration of the social services, and in the exercise of economic regulation, individuals more often come into contact with officials than with judges. When a dispute arises out of these activities, a citizen may ultimately wish to go to the courts to assert his rights. But he is likely first to seek redress of his grievances from his member of Parliament. Moreover administrative tribunals and the office of Ombudsman provide important means of redress for the citizen against official action with which he disagrees. Such bodies come within the scope of both constitutional and administrative law.

There is no precise demarcation between constitutional and administrative law in Britain. Administrative law may be defined as the law which determines the organisation, powers and duties of administrative authorities. Like constitutional law, administrative law deals with the exercise and control of governmental power. A rough distinction may be drawn by saying that constitutional law is mainly concerned with the structure of the primary organs of government, whereas administrative law is concerned with the work of official agencies in providing services and in regulating the activities of citizens. Within the vast field of government, the lawyer is chiefly concerned with the sources of administrative power, with the adjudication of disputes arising out of the public services and, above all, with the problem of securing a system of legal control over the services of government which takes account of both public needs and the private interests of the individual.

Constitutional law and public international law

Public international law is that system of law whose primary function it is to regulate the relations of states with one another. The system

presupposes the state, a territorial unit of great power, possessing within its own sphere the quality of independence of any superior, a quality which we are accustomed to call sovereignty, and possessing within that sphere the power and right to make law not only for its own citizens, but also for those of others.

International law thus deals with the external relations of a state with other states; constitutional law deals with the legal structure of the state and its mutual relations with its citizens and others present on its territory. But it is concerned with the problem of regulation by legal process and within the great power which states wield. In the dualist tradition, national and international law operate at two distinct levels, but both are concerned with state power and are necessarily connected. Thus one important branch of constitutional law is the national law relating to a government's power to enter into treaties with other states and thus to create new international obligations. So too the procedure of extradition, by which a criminal who escapes from one state to another may be sent back to the state in which his crime was committed, operates both in international and in constitutional law, the government of a

Ch. 37.
2. Oppenheim's International Law, pp. 125–6.
3. C. Parry, in Sources of Public International Law ed. J.P. Somerset, p. ...
4. Ch. 18 C.

promotion of the arts and sport. Many people still look to the courts for protection in the sphere of public order and the criminal law. But in the administration of the social services, and in the exercise of economic regulation, individuals more often come into contact with officials than with judges. When a dispute arises out of these activities, a citizen may ultimately wish to go to the courts to assert his rights. But he is likely first to seek redress of his grievance from his member of Parliament. Moreover administrative tribunals and the office of Ombudsman provide important means of redress for the citizen against official action with which he disagrees.[8] Such bodies come within the scope of both constitutional and administrative law.

There is no precise demarcation between constitutional and administrative law in Britain. Administrative law may be defined as the law which determines the organisation, powers and duties of administrative authorities.[9] Like constitutional law, administrative law deals with the exercise and control of governmental power. A rough distinction may be drawn by suggesting that constitutional law is mainly concerned with the structure of the primary organs of government, whereas administrative law is concerned with the work of official agencies in providing services and in regulating the activities of citizens. Within the vast field of government, the lawyer is chiefly concerned with the sources of administrative power, with the adjudication of disputes arising out of the public services and, above all, with the problem of securing a system of legal control over the activities of government which takes account of both public needs and the private interests of the individual.

Constitutional law and public international law

Public international law is that system of law whose primary function it is to regulate the relations of states with one another. The system

presupposes the state, a territorial unit of great power, possessing within its own sphere the quality of independence of any superior, a quality which we are accustomed to call sovereignty and possessing within that sphere the power and right to make law not only for its own citizens, but also for those of others.[10]

International law thus deals with the *external* relations of a state with other states; constitutional law deals with the legal structure of the state and its *internal* relations with its citizens and others present on its territory. Both are concerned with the problem of regulating by legal process and values the great power which states wield. In the dualist tradition, national and international law operate at two distinct levels, but both are concerned with state power and are necessarily connected. Thus one important branch of constitutional law is the national law relating to a government's power to enter into treaties with other states and thus to create new international obligations.[11] So too, the procedure of extradition, by which a criminal who escapes from one state to another may be sent back to the state in which his crime was committed, operates both in international and in constitutional law: the government of a

---

[8]   Ch. 37.
[9]   Ch. 32; and see Maitland, *History*, pp. 528–35.
[10]   C. Parry, in *Manual of Public International Law*, ed. M. Sorensen, p. 3.
[11]   Ch. 18 C.

state which is party to an extradition treaty must equip itself with the powers necessary in national law if the state is to be able to fulfil its treaty obligations.[12] International organisations have today established new forms of cooperation between states and have set standards of conduct for the international community. Increasingly international law has become concerned with the treatment of minority groups and individuals by states. These developments make it necessary to reconsider the nature of internal sovereignty which the national system of constitutional law ascribes to the state. Thus the European Convention on Human Rights, to which the United Kingdom is a party, imposes international obligations which directly affect our constitutional law.[13]

Constitutional law and the law of the European Communities

The European Communities were created and developed by means of treaties between the member states, but they are very different from other international organisations to which the United Kingdom has belonged. The Communities are equipped with legislative, administrative and judicial organs, which can exercise their powers with direct effect throughout the member states. The substantive rules of Community law in the economic and social fields, lie outside the scope of this book. But the main structure of the EEC will be outlined and the implications of membership for British constitutional law examined, including the relationship between Community law and national law.[14]

---

[12] Ch. 25 C.
[13] Ch. 31 B.
[14] Ch. 8.

had it down that no man should be punished except by the judgment of his peers or the law of the land, and that no issue should to none be bound, have been described as the origin of trial by jury and the writ of habeas corpus. Their basis may in fact be traced to another source, and their true origin may not yet have been proved, but these clauses embodied a protest against arbitrary punishment and asserted the right to a fair trial and to a just legal system. Today, few provisions of Magna Carta remain on the statute book. Its historical and symbolic value is greater than its current legal force.

Petition of Right

Another notable conflict between the English Parliament at a later period of constitutional conflict is the Petition of Right, 1628 embodied in the statute book (see Cm. 2.1.). This continued protest against taxation without consent of Parliament, arbitrary imprisonment, the use of commissions of martial law in time of peace and the billeting of soldiers upon private persons. To these protests the king yielded, though the effect of the concessions was weakened by the view Charles I held that his prerogative powers were not thereby diminished.

Bill of Rights and Claim of Right

The glorious revolution of 1688 brought about the downfall of James II of England and James VII of Scotland from his two thrones, and the vacated thrones of the monarchy of the two kingdoms in turn, laid down by the English and Scottish parliaments respectively. These terms were accepted by the incoming joint monarchs, William and Mary. In England it was the House of Lords and the Commons of Charles II's last parliament who in 1689 approved the Bill of Rights which was later confirmed by the post-revolution parliament. This laid the foundation of the modern constitution by abolishing of the more extravagant claims of the Stuarts to rule by prerogative right.

Its principal provisions (known as articles), many of which are still in force as part of English law, declared:

(1) That the pretended power of suspending of laws or the execution of laws by regal power without consent of Parliament is illegal.

(2) That the pretended power of dispensing with laws or the execution of laws by regal authority as it hath been assumed and exercised of late is illegal.

(3) That the commission for erecting the late court of commissioners for ecclesiastical causes, and all other commissions and courts of the like nature are illegal and pernicious.

(4) That the levying money for or to the use of the crown by pretence of prerogative without grant of Parliament for longer time or in other manner than the same is or shall be granted is illegal.

(5) That it is the right of the subjects to petition the king and all commitments and prosecutions for such petitioning are illegal.

(6) That the raising or keeping of a standing army within the kingdom in time of peace unless it be with consent of Parliament is against law.

(7) That election of members of Parliament ought to be free.

(8) That freedom of speech and debates or proceedings in Parliament ought not to be impeached or questioned in any court or place out of Parliament.

laid it down that no man should be punished except by the judgment of his peers or the law of the land, and that to none should justice be denied, have been described as the origin of trial by jury and the writ of habeas corpus. Trial by jury is in fact to be traced to another source, and the writ of habeas corpus had not yet been devised. But these clauses embodied a protest against arbitrary punishment and asserted the right to a fair trial and to a just legal system. Today few provisions of Magna Carta remain on the statute book. Its historical and symbolic value is greater than its current legal force.

Petition of Right

Another document enacted by the English Parliament at a later period of constitutional conflict is the Petition of Right 1628, enrolled on the statue book as 3 Car. 1 c. 1.[8] This contained protests against taxation without consent of Parliament, arbitrary imprisonment, the use of commissions of martial law in time of peace and the billeting of soldiers upon private persons. To these protests the king yielded, though the effect of the concessions was weakened by the view Charles I held that his prerogative powers were not thereby diminished.

Bill of Rights and Claim of Right

The 'glorious revolution' of 1688 brought about the downfall of James II of England and James VII of Scotland from his two thrones and the re-establishment of the monarchy in the two kingdoms on terms laid down by the English and Scottish parliaments respectively. These terms were accepted by the incoming joint monarchs, William and Mary. In England it was the House of Lords and the remnants of Charles II's last parliament who in 1689 approved the Bill of Rights which was later confirmed by the post-revolution parliament.[9] This laid the foundations of the modern constitution by disposing of the more extravagant claims of the Stuarts to rule by prerogative right.

Its principal provisions (known as 'articles'), many of which are still in force as part of English law, declared:

(1)   That the pretended power of suspending of laws or the execution of laws by regal authority without consent of Parliament is illegal.

(2)   That the pretended power of dispensing with laws or the execution of laws by regal authority as it hath been assumed and exercised of late is illegal.

(3)   That the commission for erecting the late court of commissioners for ecclesiastical causes and all other commissions and courts of like nature are illegal and pernicious.

(4)   That the levying money for or to the use of the crown by pretence of prerogative without grant of Parliament for longer time or in other manner than the same is or shall be granted is illegal.

(5)   That it is the right of the subjects to petition the king and all commitments and prosecutions for such petitioning are illegal.

(6)   That the raising or keeping of a standing army within the kingdom in time of peace unless it be with consent of Parliament is against law . . .

(8)   That election of members of Parliament ought to be free.

(9)   That the freedom of speech and debates or proceedings in Parliament ought not to be impeached or questioned in any court or place out of Parliament.

---

8   *Halsbury's Statutes*, vol. 6, p. 471.
9   Wilson, *Cases*, pp. 1–6.

(10) That excessive bail ought not be required nor excessive fines imposed nor cruel and unusual punishments inflicted.
(11) That jurors ought to be duly impannelled and returned. ...
(12) That all grants and promises of fines and forfeitures of particular persons before conviction are illegal and void.
(13) And that for redress of all grievances and for the amending, strengthening and preserving of the laws Parliaments ought to be held frequently.[10]

The Scottish Parliament enacted the Claim of Right in 1689. The contents of this measure followed those of the Bill of Rights of the English Parliament with certain modifications; for example the distinction between the suspending and dispensing powers was not made, but all proclamations asserting an absolute power to 'cass, annul or disable laws' were declared illegal.[11] Many provisions of the Claim of Right are still in force within Scotland.

The Act of Settlement
The Act of Settlement 1700, passed by the English Parliament, not only provided for the succession to the throne, but added important provisions complementary to the Bill of Rights, especially –

That whosoever shall hereafter come to the possession of this crown shall join in communion with the Church of England as by law established.
That in case the crown and imperial dignity of this realm shall hereafter come to any person, not being a native of this kingdom of England, this nation be not obliged to engage in any war for the defence of any dominions or territories which do not belong to the crown of England, without consent of Parliament.
That no person who has an office or place of profit under the King or receives a pension from the crown shall be capable of serving as a member of the House of Commons.
That ... judges' commissions be made *quamdiu se bene gesserint*, and their salaries ascertained and established, but upon the address of both Houses of Parliament it may be lawful to remove them.
That no pardon under the great seal of England be pleadable to an impeachment by the Commons in Parliament.[12]

The Bill of Rights and the Act of Settlement marked the victory of Parliament over the claim of kings to govern by the prerogative. There was, however, nothing in these statutes to secure the responsibility of the King's ministers to Parliament. That important principle of parliamentary government developed in the 18th century and later, a product of constitutional practice rather than legislation.[13]

Other statutes of constitutional importance
It is not intended to catalogue other principal statutes that form part of constitutional law. To illustrate that statute law is a vital source of constitutional law it is sufficient to mention the Act of Union with Scotland 1707,

---

[10] *Halsbury's Statutes*, vol. 6, p. 489. For judicial citation, see *Congreve* v. *Home Office* [1976] Q.B. 629 (art. 4) and *Williams* v. *Home Office* [1981] 1 All E.R. 1211 (art. 10).
[11] A. P. S. IX, 38.
[12] *Halsbury's Statutes*, vol. 6, p. 496.
[13] Ch. 7.

one another.[32] Two general approaches are intermittently followed by the courts. The literal approach to interpretation is based on the principle that it is the duty of the court to discover the true meaning of the words used by Parliament; this concentrates on the actual text of the legislation, and excludes consideration of legislative policy.[33] Another general approach is based on the principle that a court should endeavour to give effect to the policy of a statute and to the intentions of those who made it, a principle expressed in the mischief rule laid down in *Heydon's* case.[34] Whichever approach may be followed in a particular case, there is a firm rule that British courts may not look at Hansard (the record of debates in Parliament) to discover the meaning of legislation, although limited use may be made of documents such as the reports of royal commissions and parliamentary committees as an aid to identifying the mischief which legislation was intended to remedy.[35]

Certain presumptions of interpretation are of constitutional importance. In the past there has often been applied a presumption that Parliament does not intend to take away common law rights by mere implication, as distinct from express words. Thus the courts have presumed that Parliament does not intend to take away the property of a subject without compensation[36] or to deprive a subject of access to the courts[37] and have interpreted penal statutes strictly in favour of the citizen: thus a statute creating a criminal offence will not in the absence of express words be held to be retrospective.[38] These common law presumptions may not however be very reliable when applied to town and country planning law, where an essential object of the legislation is to restrict the common law rights of the landowner[39] or to social security legislation, which creates a whole scheme of rights and duties unknown to the common law.

British membership of the European Communities may well affect our traditional approaches to interpretation, since in most European legal systems both the methods of legislative drafting and the rules of statutory interpretation are very different from those in Britain. Where it is necessary for a provision of an EEC treaty or an EEC regulation to be interpreted in a British court, article 177 of the Treaty of Rome provides a procedure by which the question of interpretation may be settled by the European Court of Justice.[40]

Whatever the rules of interpretation may be within a given legal system, it is now recognised that many legal rules have what has been called an open texture.[41] As Professor Hart has said:

Even when verbally formulated general rules are used, uncertainties as to the form of

---

[32]   Report of the Law Commission, *The Interpretation of Statutes*, H.C. 256, 1968–9; G. Marshall, *Constitutional Theory*, ch. 4; R. Cross, *Statutory Interpretation*.
[33]   R. Cross, *Statutory Interpretation*, p. 13.
[34]   (1584) 3 Co. Rep. 71.
[35]   *Black-Clawson International Ltd* v. *Papierwerke AG* [1975] A.C. 591; *Davis* v. *Johnson* [1979] A.C. 264.
[36]   *Central Control Board* v. *Cannon Brewery Co.* [1919] A.C. 744, 752.
[37]   *Chester* v. *Bateson* [1920] 1 K.B. 829; Wilson, *Cases*, p. 387.
[38]   *Waddington* v. *Miah* [1974] 2 All E.R. 377.
[39]   *Westminster Bank Ltd* v. *Beverley Borough Council* [1971] A.C. 508.
[40]   Ch. 8.
[41]   H. L. A. Hart, *The Concept of Law*, p. 123.

behaviour required by them may break out in particular concrete cases . . . In all fields of experience, not only that of rules, there is a limit, inherent in the nature of language, to the guidance which general language can provide.[42]

However difficult the task of statutory interpretation may be, it is an essential principle of the concept of law that enacted laws should be interpreted by judicial bodies independent of the legislature which made the law: statutory provisions authorising the government to define the meaning of terms used in an Act of Parliament are contrary to basic legal principles.[43]

B. Non-legal rules of the constitution

Many important rules of constitutional behaviour, which are observed by the Sovereign, the Prime Minister and other ministers, members of parliament, judges and civil servants, are contained neither in Acts nor in judicial decisions. It will be shown below that disputes which arise out of these rules rarely lead to action in the courts and that judicial sanctions are not applicable if the rules are broken. Constitutional writers have applied a wide variety of names to these rules: the positive morality of the constitution,[1] the unwritten maxims of the constitution,[2] and 'a whole system of political morality, a whole code of precepts for the guidance of public men'.[3] Dicey referred to them as:

conventions, understandings, habits or practices which, though they may regulate the conduct of the several members of the sovereign power . . . are not in reality laws at all since they are not enforced by the courts.[4]

Under Dicey's influence, the most common name given to this phenomenon is constitutional convention.

This use of the word convention is quite different from its use in international law, where a convention is a synonym for a treaty, or binding agreement between states. But the notion of conventional conduct does include a strong element of what is customarily expected, in the sense of ordinary or regular behaviour. In common speech a person may be described as conventional or unconventional, depending on his capacity for conforming to or departing from accepted patterns of social behaviour and opinion. Most discussion of constitutional conventions has gone beyond description of conduct which is merely a customary practice and has suggested that conventions give rise to binding rules of conduct.[5] John Mackintosh described a convention as 'a generally accepted political practice, usually with a record

---

[42] *ibid.*
[43] Counter-Inflation Act 1973, sched. 3, para. 1(1); and *cf.* the *Black-Clawson* case, note 35.

[1] J. Austin, *The Province of Jurisprudence Determined*, p. 259.
[2] J. S. Mill, *Representative Government*, ch. 5.
[3] E. A. Freeman, *Growth of the English Constitution*, p. 109, quoted in Dicey, p. 418. And see O. Hood Phillips (1966) 29 M.L.R. 137.
[4] Dicey, p. 24.
[5] See *e.g.* J. D. B. Mitchell, *Constitutional Law*, p. 39; K. C. Wheare, *The Statute of Westminster and Dominion Status*, p. 10; and Marshall and Moodie, ch. 2.

of successful applications or precedents'[6] but other authors have described conventions as:

rules of constitutional behaviour which are considered to be binding by and upon those who operate the Constitution but which are not enforced by the law courts . . . nor by the presiding officers in the House of Parliament.[7]

Mackintosh here regards conventions as merely *descriptive* statements of constitutional practice, based on observation of what actually happens; the latter approach regards conventions as *prescriptive* statements of what should happen, based in part upon observation but also upon constitutional principle. We will return later to the choice between these two approaches[8]; but at present we will assume that conventions are concerned with matters of obligation, and will endeavour to explore the nature of that obligation.

In this section it is not possible to summarise all existing conventional rules; the aim is rather to discuss their general characteristics. Other chapters will examine the non-legal rules which apply to particular institutions alongside the appropriate legal rules. Some of the most important conventional rules will be discussed in the chapters dealing with responsible government, the Crown and the Cabinet. First, some examples will be given of non-legal rules and in each case relevant legal rules will be mentioned.

Non-legal rules of the constitution: some examples

1   It is a rule of common law that the royal assent must be given before a Bill which has been approved by both Houses of Parliament can become an Act of Parliament.[9] The manner in which the royal assent may be given is now regulated by statute and in certain circumstances the royal assent may be signified by others on behalf of the Sovereign.[10] These legal rules deal with a vital matter of legal form. But possibly an even more important conventional rule is that the royal assent is granted by the Sovereign on the advice of her ministers. It may be expected that where a Bill has been passed by both Houses of Parliament, the royal assent will be given as a matter of course. The Sovereign's legal power to refuse assent was last exercised by Queen Anne in 1708, when (apparently with the approval of her ministers and without objection by Parliament) the royal assent was refused to the Scottish Militia Bill.[11] In the Irish crisis of 1912–14, the Unionists suggested to George V that he should withhold assent from the Bill to give home rule to Ireland. The Liberal Prime Minister, Asquith, advised the King against this and the royal assent was granted.[12] While the Sovereign may not of her own initiative refuse the royal assent the position may be different if ministers themselves advise this course, although this advice would have to be defended in Parliament.

2   At common law the Sovereign has unlimited power to appoint whom she

---

6   Mackintosh, *The British Cabinet*, p. 13.
7   Marshall and Moodie, pp. 22–23.
8   Page 28 *post*.
9   Ch. 5 C.
10   Royal Assent Act 1967, Regency Acts 1937–1953; ch. 11 A.
11   W. E. Hearn, *The Government of England*, p. 61.
12   Jennings, *Cabinet Government*, pp. 395–400, and Wilson, *Cases*, pp. 23–30. Ch. 13 A.

pleases to be her ministers. Statutes provide for the payment of salaries to ministers, and limit the number of ministerial appointments which may be made from the House of Commons.[13] There is no rule of law which prevents the Sovereign appointing to ministerial office a person who is outside Parliament. But today all appointments are made by the Sovereign on the advice of the Prime Minister and the principle of ministerial responsibility[14] requires that a minister should belong to one or other House of Parliament. If a non-member is appointed to ministerial office, either he must receive a peerage, or he must fight an early by-election in order to win a seat in the Commons. Thus, after the general election in October 1964, Mr Frank Cousins and Mr Gordon Walker were each appointed ministers, the former not having stood for Parliament, the latter having stood unsuccessfully. In January 1965, Mr Cousins was successful at a by-election and continued in office; Mr Gordon Walker was defeated and forthwith resigned from the government. In 1983, when a Conservative minister (Mr Hamish Gray) was defeated at the general election, he became a life peer and continued to hold ministerial office.

The only exception to the general rule is that the two Scottish Law Officers (the Lord Advocate and the Solicitor-General for Scotland) may not always have seats in Parliament, although current practice (dating from 1969) is for the Lord Advocate to receive a life peerage when he is not a member of the Commons. While therefore there is a definite rule that ministers of the Crown should hold seats in Parliament, it is not absolute and limited exceptions are accepted.

3   Although the conduct of a general election is governed by detailed statutory rules,[15] there is no statutory rule which regulates the conduct of the Prime Minister when the result of the election is known. But there is a conventional rule that the government must have the confidence of a majority in the Commons. Therefore when it is clear from the election results that the Prime Minister on whose advice the election had been called has lost the election, he must now resign immediately without, as formerly, waiting for the new Parliament to meet.[16] Where however the result of the election gives no party an overall majority in the Commons, the Prime Minister may continue in office for such period as is necessary to discover whether he is able to form a coalition or to govern with the support of other parties. In February 1974, when this situation arose, a period of three days elapsed before Mr Heath decided to resign, having learned that the Liberal M.P.s would not support him. When on 28 March 1979, an Opposition motion of no confidence in the Labour government was carried by one vote, Mr Callaghan was forced to call an early general election. He resigned as Prime Minister as soon as it was clear that the Conservative party had won the election.

4   Superior judges in England and Wales hold their offices by statute during good behaviour, subject to a power of removal by the Sovereign on an address presented to her by both Houses; by statute they are disqualified from

---

13   Ch. 14 B.
14   Ch. 7.
15   Ch. 9 B.
16   Jennings, *Cabinet Government*, pp. 490–2.

membership of the Commons.[17] Before appointment as a judge, a lawyer may have been active in party politics but a conventional rule requires him on appointment to sever his links with the party which he had formerly supported. Although the legal tenure of judges in Scotland is different, the same conventional rule applies. In 1968, a Scottish judge, Lord Avonside, agreed to serve on a committee to consider the future constitution of Scotland which Mr Heath, then leader of the Opposition, had established. Within a few days, he resigned from the committee when his membership of the Conservative party's committee became a matter of public controversy.[18]

5   The office of Speaker of the House of Commons has been recognised by statute.[19] His election is the first business of a newly elected House. Before his first election to the post the Speaker will probably have been a member of the party then with a majority in the House. Once elected he is required to sever his links with that party and to carry out his duties with complete impartiality. If at a subsequent general election he is opposed in his constituency, he stands as the Speaker, not as a member of his former party.

6   When a person is appointed a minister, he must divest himself of such financial and business interests as would conflict with his duties as minister. The detailed rules which govern this matter were first laid down by Sir Winston Churchill when Prime Minister in 1952[20] and have been maintained by subsequent Prime Ministers. In 1962, a Conservative minister who was unable to divest himself of his interests in a family business having many contractual relations with the government had to resign soon after his appointment.[21]

Many more examples of non-legal rules of the constitution could be given. They serve a wide variety of constitutional purposes and vary widely in importance. Such rules develop under every system of government, whether a written constitution exists or not. Their special importance to the British constitution is that it is through these rules that the system of cabinet government has developed. In earlier times, non-legal rules were important in the process by which self-governing colonies in the British Empire attained dominion status.[22] When amendments to the Canadian constitution could be made only by Act of the Westminster Parliament, an elaborate system of conventions and practices evolved as to how the process of amendment should be set in motion.[23] Within the United Kingdom, conventional rules helped to secure the smooth working of the Government of Ireland Act 1920 so long as the Northern Ireland Parliament existed.[24] With such a diversity of subject matter, what general characteristics, if any, do these rules possess?

---

17   Ch. 19 A.
18   Page 336 *post.*
19   *E.g.* Parliament Act 1911, s.3.
20   H. C. Deb., 25 February 1952, cols. 701–3.
21   Ch. 14 B.
22   Ch. 24.
23.   App. A.
24   H. Calvert, *Constitutional Law in Northern Ireland*, Ch. 6.

General characteristics[25]

Although some long-established conventional rules (like the rule that the Queen's speech read at the opening of each session of Parliament is prepared on the advice of her ministers) have great authority and are universally known, many have developed out of a desire to avoid the formality, explicitness and publicity associated with changes in the law. The development of a regular practice may enable legislation on a point of principle to be avoided. The role of the Sovereign in the conduct of government has almost disappeared since the 18th century without a series of statutes removing one royal power after another. Conventional rules may be used for discreetly managing the internal relationships of government while the outward legal form is left intact.

The informality of non-legal rules is often accompanied by the fact that the rules themselves are not formulated in writing, for example, the rule that judges should not undertake party political activities. But this is not always the case. The government may give to the Commons an undertaking about the future use of its powers – for example, about the laying of treaties before the House to enable them to be debated[26] – or may convey to the House undertakings regarding future practice in the making of certain appointments by the Sovereign or Prime Minister. Such undertakings are publicly recorded.[27]

The development of unwritten rules is often an evolutionary process, one of growth rather than manufacture. In retrospect, it is now possible to identify the time when the royal assent to a Bill was last refused (1708), when the Lord Chief Justice of England was last appointed to a seat in the Cabinet (1806) and when a member of the House of Lords last held office as Prime Minister (1902). The fact that each of these events is highly improbable today, and would be regarded as contrary to good constitutional practice, does not mean that this has been so ever since the last occurrence. At a given moment of time, it may be impossible to tell whether practice on a certain matter has hardened into a rule, particularly where the practice is negative in character.

It is for these reasons, as well as the fact that they operate in a political context, that disputes may arise about the existence and content of conventional rules. Moreover, different rules are enforceable in different ways. While the Prime Minister is primarily responsible for interpreting and enforcing the rules regarding the financial interests of ministers, the rules which forbid a judge to undertake political activities are not primarily interpreted or applied by any person other than the judge himself, and depend on the force of public and political opinion at large. Disputes about the existence and content of legal rules are typically settled by judicial decision. If, as we have seen, many legal rules have an 'open texture',[28] how much more 'open' will be the texture of non-legal rules where there is no definite procedure for resolving disputes about existence and content.

---

[25]   A full discussion is to be found in the Supreme Court of Canada's decision cited in App. A; and see C. R. Munro (1975) 91 L.Q.R. 218; G. Marshall, *Constitutional Conventions*.

[26]   The so-called Ponsonby Rule: H.C. Deb., 1 April 1924, col. 2001; p. 321 *post*.

[27]   See H.C. Deb., 11 Dec. 1962, cols. 209–10 (appointment of Serjeant at Arms); and Cmnd 8323, 1981, para. 23 (Comptroller and Auditor General).

[28]   Page 18 *ante*.

In the past, accounts of constitutional conventions often concentrated on the rules by which powers legally vested in the Sovereign came to be exercised by ministers and other servants of the Crown. Dicey considered that conventions were 'rules intended to regulate the exercise of the whole of the remaining discretionary powers of the Crown'.[29] In fact many non-legal rules fall outside this category. It is more accurate to say that conventional rules regulate the conduct of those holding public office. Our constitutional system allots different roles to the Sovereign, ministers, judges, civil servants and so on. He who would play one of these roles effectively must observe the constitutional restraints which the system imposes on those who accept that office. Edward VIII was not willing to accept these constraints and was required to abdicate.[30] So too a minister who does not observe or does not accept the constraints of his office must resign. Hugh Dalton, when Chancellor of the Exchequer, inadvertently revealed Budget secrets to journalists as he entered the House to give his speech, and resigned from office.[31] Jeremy Bray, a junior minister in the Labour government in 1969, resigned from office in order to publish a book, permission for which had been refused by the Prime Minister. In 1982 Mr Nicholas Fairbairn, Solicitor-General for Scotland, resigned after making comments to the press which anticipated by one day an important statement being made to Parliament by the Lord Advocate.[32] Similar constraints operate at the institutional level. If the House of Lords does not accept its limited role when confronted with the determined will of the Commons, the House knows that it may lose its remaining legislative powers or be abolished.

Why are conventional rules observed?

Dicey, writing as a lawyer in a period dominated by Austinian jurisprudence according to which laws were observed because they could be enforced against the citizen by the coercive power of the state, said:

the sanction which constrains the boldest political adventurer to obey the fundamental principles of the constitution and the conventions in which these principles are expressed, is the fact that the breach of these principles and of these conventions will almost immediately bring the offender into conflict with the courts and the law of the land.[33]

To support this view, Dicey argued that Parliament meets at least once a year because the government would be compelled to act unlawfully if this did not happen. This argument has been shown to be much weaker than Dicey had supposed.[34] In any event, the rule which the supposed legal sanction supports is antiquated. Today Parliament is expected not merely to meet once a year but to be in session at Westminster for about 32 weeks in the year, interspersed with holidays and the long summer recess. During these weeks there is a customary pattern of parliamentary work to be done. The Provisional Collec-

---

29   Dicey, p. 426.
30   Ch. 13 A.
31   Report from Select Committee on the Budget Disclosure (H.C. 20, 1947–8).
32   H.C. Deb., 21 January 1982, col. 423.
33   Dicey, pp. 445–6.
34   *E.g.* by Jennings, *Law and Constitution*, pp. 128–9.

tion of Taxes Act 1968[35] imposes certain constraints upon the time-table of Parliament, but this in itself is inadequate to explain why Parliament continues to meet regularly throughout the year. That Parliament should do so is a fundamental expectation of politicians and citizens alike.

It is much nearer the mark to say, as did Sir Ivor Jennings, that conventions are observed because of the political difficulties which arise if they are not.[36] As these rules regulate the conduct of those holding public office, for such a person possibly the most acute political difficulty which can arise is that he should be forced out of that office. But an explanation merely in terms of political difficulties is inadequate since not every event which gives rise to political difficulties (for example an unpopular Bill) is a breach of a non-legal rule of the constitution. The Supreme Court of Canada has stated that the main purpose of conventions is to ensure that the legal framework of the constitution is operated in accordance with the prevailing constitutional values of the period.[37] On this basis, conventions are observed for the positive reason that they express prevailing constitutional values and for the negative reason of avoiding the difficulties that may follow from 'unconstitutional' conduct.

The meaning of 'unconstitutional'

Where a written constitution ranks as fundamental law, legislative or executive acts which conflict with the constitution may be held unconstitutional and thus illegal. In the United Kingdom, 'unconstitutional' has no defined legal content. The 19th century jurist, Austin, suggested that the sovereign was acting unconstitutionally when he infringed the maxims of government which with popular approval he generally observed – but by definition the Austinian sovereign could not act illegally.[38] For Freeman, unconstitutional conduct was conduct contrary to 'the undoubted principles of the unwritten but universally accepted constitution.'[39] It has been commented that 'for the Americans, anything unconstitutional is illegal, however right or necessary it may seem; for the British, anything unconstitutional is wrong, however legal it may be.'[40] The two senses of 'unconstitutional' were illustrated in the Canadian constitutional controversy of 1981–2, when the Supreme Court dealt separately with the issues of whether it would be (a) illegal and (b) in breach of convention for the Federal Parliament to adopt resolutions requesting amendments to the constitution which were opposed by eight of the ten provinces.[41]

While conduct may be unconstitutional without being illegal, illegal acts may also be unconstitutional. British politicians who instigated or covered up criminal offences for political ends would be in breach of the code of behaviour recognised by public opinion, as well as being in breach of the criminal law. Ministers are restrained from exceeding their powers not only by the likelihood of legal sanctions but also by the constitutional obligation on government to

---

[35]   Page 202 *post*.
[36]   *Law and Constitution*, p. 134.
[37]   *Reference re Amendment of the Constitution of Canada* (1982) 125 D.L.R. (3d) 1, 84; App. A.
[38]   Austin, *op. cit.*, pp. 257–60.
[39]   Freeman, *op. cit.*, p. 112.
[40]   J. R. Mallory, *The Structure of Canadian Government*, p. 2.
[41]   App. A.

conduct its affairs according to law.[42] When used concerning executive decisions, 'unconstitutional' implies that a decision is not merely incorrect in law
but also contrary to fundamental principle, for example where a policy of the
Inland Revenue involved 'taxation by self asserted administrative discretion
and not by law'.[43]

It is not however always easy to determine whether the boundary between
constitutional and unconstitutional conduct has been crossed, especially where
there turns out to be no universally accepted rule of conduct. Different politicians may well take opposing views of the constitutional propriety of the acts
of a government. Lawyers should be slow to condemn proposals for new legislation as unconstitutional – not only so that the coinage of constitutional
debate should not be debased, but also because lawyers are seldom unmoved
by other political considerations.[44] But there is no doubt that a Bill which
sought to destroy essential features of the electoral system could rightly be
described as unconstitutional.

The other difficulty in determining what is constitutional in a given situation is that there may be no relevant precedent. When in 1932 the Cabinet
of the National government agreed to differ on a major issue of economic
policy, an attack on the government for unconstitutional conduct was met by
the rejoinder:

Who can say what is constitutional in the conduct of a National Government? It is a
precedent, an experiment, a new practice, to meet a new emergency, a new condition
of things . . .[45]

In 1975, the open disagreement of the Labour Cabinet over Britain's
continued membership of the EEC was defended in similar terms.

Consequences of a breach of conventional rule

Various consequences may follow the breach of non-legal rules of the constitution. Loss of office or departure from public life would be the severest
consequence, but the force of public opinion or political controversy may
simply force the offender to think again: thus the Scottish judge who in 1968
joined a committee established by the Conservative party decided to resign
rather than prejudice the work of the committee.[46] In these instances, the
outcome reinforces the established rule. A less serious consequence would be
a reprimand or a reminder not to act similarly in the future, given by someone
in a position to enforce the rule: in November 1974 the Labour Prime Minister
reprimanded three leading ministers who had supported a motion passed by
the National Executive of the Labour Party sharply criticising the government's policy on South Africa. If no adverse consequences follow, the matter
becomes more open. Is it simply that it was politically expedient that, for
example, the Prime Minister should turn a blind eye to the acts of his

---

[42] Ch. 6.
[43] *Vestey* v. *Inland Revenue Comssrs* [1980] A.C. 1148, 1173.
[44] *Cf.* Jennings, *Law and Constitution*, pp. 316–17.
[45] Mr Baldwin, H. C. Deb., 8 February 1932, col. 535; Wilson, *Cases*, p. 58.
[46] Page 336 *post*.

colleagues, or has the application of the rule been modified or the rule itself abandoned?

As constitutional rules often give rise to reciprocal obligations, one consequence of a breach may be to release another office-holder from the normal constraints that would otherwise bind him. When Ian Smith's Cabinet in 1965 unilaterally declared Rhodesia's independence, the immediate response of the UK government, conveyed through the Governor-General of Rhodesia, was the dismissal of the entire Cabinet. In the event this dismissal proved purely nominal. Somewhat more significantly, the Southern Rhodesia Act 1965 was passed at Westminster to give the government full power to legislate for the domestic affairs of Rhodesia, thus overriding the previous convention that the Westminster Parliament would not exercise its sovereignty in such matters except with the agreement of the Rhodesian government.[47]

Another consequence may be the passing of legislation to avoid a similar breach in the future. When in 1909 the Lords rejected the Liberal government's Finance Bill, the crisis was resolved only by the Parliament Act 1911, which removed the power of the Lords to veto or delay money Bills. The 1911 Act contained other provisions intended to place the Lords–Commons relationship on a new footing.[48] These provisions led in turn to new conventional doctrine regarding the use by the House of Lords of its residual powers.

Should all constitutional rules be enacted as law?

In theory, all the non-legal rules of the constitution could be enacted in legal form by one or more Acts of Parliament. Written constitutions in the Commonwealth have adopted various means of incorporating conventions: express enactment of the main rules, wholesale adoption by reference to practice in the United Kingdom and so on.[49]

If a written constitution were to be drafted for the United Kingdom many hard decisions on these matters would have to be made. It would, for example, be very difficult to anticipate every possible eventuality in which the Sovereign might be required to invite a new Prime Minister to form a government. There would be no real difficulty in framing the main principles of responsible government, but this would make little difference if the principles continued to govern an essentially political relationship between government and Parliament: to make the doctrine of responsible government enforceable by the courts would be to change its character entirely.

While enactment might well be useful in the case of particular rules that need to be clarified, there is nothing to be said for 'codifying' the non-legal rules of the constitution. They cover so diverse an area, and they differ so much in character, that they could not sensibly be included within a single code. Even if the attempt were made, it would be impossible to stop the process by which formal rules are gradually modified by non-legal rules, principles and practices from starting over again.

It will be evident that there is often a very indistinct borderline between conduct which is a matter of habitual practice, and conduct which occurs as

---

[47]   *Cf. Madzimbamuto* v. *Lardner-Burke* [1969] A.C. 645, 723.
[48]   Ch. 11 B.
[49]   De Smith, *The New Commonwealth and its Constitutions*, pp. 78–87.

a result of what is felt to be constitutional obligation. Text-books on constitutional law often exaggerate the extent to which rules govern political life.

In 1963, by a procedure for which there was no precedent, the 14th Earl
of Home was chosen to follow Harold Macmillan as Prime Minister and forthwith renounced his title so that he could enter the House of Commons as Sir
Alec Douglas-Home. Commenting upon these events, the editor of *Public Law*
coined two aphorisms as an antidote against a convention-dominated view of
the constitution: 'the constitution is what happens' and 'if it works, it's
constitutional'. His comment concluded: 'So let us delete those pages in
constitutional textbooks headed Conventions, and talk about what happens
and why what happened yesterday may not happen tomorrow.'[50] In other
words, it is better to discuss why it would be politically impossible today for
a Prime Minister to govern from the House of Lords, then to try and read back
into past events a rule to this effect.

One reply to this approach involves considering the relation between the
reasons which give rise to a rule, and the rule itself. Legal rules, whether made
by the judges or by Parliament, may continue in force long after the original
reasons for a rule have been forgotten. In the constitutional field, the informality of many non-legal rules enables a rule to disappear or to alter in
character more readily as the underlying reasons for the rule change. This does
not mean that so long as the original reasons continue, there is no rule. Within
a stable political system, inherited experience can be expressed in the form of
precepts for present practice. Like her father, George VI, Elizabeth II has
been able to learn from the example of her uncle Edward VIII; subsequent
Cabinets have realised from the short life of the 'agreement to differ' in 1932
that such an agreement may create more difficulties than it solves; other judges
have been reminded by Lord Avonside's unhappy venture in 1968 that it is
prudent for judges to refrain from political activities. If constitutional experience is reduced to the level of sheer political expediency, short-term political
advantage might tempt a government to abuse its constitutional position.
There may be short-term advantage to a government in seeking to postpone
a general election falling due at an inconvenient time, but such a proposal
must be assessed in terms of constitutional principle. As Freeman wrote in
1872:

Political men may debate whether such and such a course is or is not constitutional,
just as lawyers may debate whether such a course is not legal. But the very form of
the debate implies that there is a Constitution to be observed, just as in the other case
it implies that there is a law to be observed.[51]

The motives for human conduct are often mixed. If we seek to understand the
behaviour of the Sovereign, a politician or a judge, we may discover both a
degree of enlightened self-interest and also a strong perception of constitutional
obligation. If that perception is shared by others in a similar position, as well

---

[50]   [1963] P.L. 401–2. For criticism of the distinction between law and convention, see Jennings,
        Law and Constitution, p. 132, and Mitchell, *Constitutional Law*, pp. 34–8; and in reply, Marshall,
        Constitutional Theory, pp. 7–12, O. Hood Phillips, (1964) 8 J.S.P.T.L. 60, and C. R. Munro
        (1975) 91 L.Q.R. 218.
[51]   *Op. cit.*, p. 112.

as by informed commentators, it is difficult to explain the behaviour in question without some reference to the perceived obligation. Without referring to the rules that differentiate the actors in their various roles at the opening of a new session of Parliament, it is difficult to explain why, for example, the Sovereign's speech is so different in character from the Prime Minister's speech in the ensuing debate in the House of Commons. The fact that non-legal rules and principles may change without formal amendment does not mean that they are irrelevant to constitutional behaviour.

The attitude of the courts

In this section it has been assumed that the rules under discussion are not capable of being enforced through the courts. If when a rule has been broken, a remedy is available in the courts for securing relief or imposing a sanction upon the wrongdoer, this would indicate that the rule has the quality of law. Where a non-legal rule has been broken, no remedy will be available in the courts. Often the citizen's only recourse will then be political action – a complaint to his Member of Parliament, a letter to the press, a public demonstration or protest. In view of the political nature of most conventional rules, the stress on political or parliamentary remedies is appropriate. Moreover, many conventional rules, for example those relating to the Cabinet system, do not affect a citizen's rights and interests closely enough for a judicial remedy to be justified.

It may however be necessary for a court to take into account the existence of a conventional rule in making its decision on a point of law. This is particularly likely to happen in administrative law cases where the court's decision on the extent of judicial control may be affected by the doctrine of ministerial responsibility. The courts have taken judicial notice of the fact that civil servants take decisions in the name of ministers and of the fact that ministers may be called to account by Parliament for the decisions.[52] The Australian High Court took account of the conventional rules which in practice restricted legislation by the UK Parliament for Australia before the rules were enacted in the Statute of Westminister 1931.[53] But on an appeal from Rhodesia following the unilateral declaration of independence, the Judical Committee, referring to the former convention by which the United Kingdom would not legislate for Rhodesia except at the request of the Rhodesian government, pointed out that the convention had no legal effect and that the Judicial Committee were concerned only with the legal powers of Parliament.[54]

The Crossman diaries case is an outstanding illustration of the inter-relation of legal and non-legal rules. As a last resort, an attempt was made by the Attorney-General in the public interest to prevent the breach of a conventional rule and to establish the existence of a legal obligation. The court held that former Cabinet ministers could be restrained by injunction from publishing confidential information which came to them as ministers, since there was a legal obligation to respect that confidentiality.[55] But it would be wrong to

---

[52] *Carltona Ltd* v. *Commissioners of Works* [1943] 2 All E.R. 560; p. 117 *post*.
[53] *Copyright Owners Reproduction Society Ltd* v. *E.M.I. (Australia) Pty Ltd*, (1958) 100 C.L.R. 597.
[54] *Madzimbamuto* v. *Lardner-Burke* [1969] A.C. 645.
[55] *A.-G.* v. *Jonathan Cape Ltd* [1976] Q.B. 752; p. 265 *post*.

simplify this decision by stating that the court was enforcing the convention of collective responsibility; that convention was no more than one factor taken into account by the judge in establishing the limits of the legal doctrine of confidence. In the different context of the Canadian constitution, the Supreme Court of Canada in 1981 gave an opinion on the existence of the conventions governing the process of constitutional amendment.[56] It is difficult to imagine circumstances in which the British courts would have jurisdiction to give a similar opinion.

While non-legal rules are not directly enforceable by the courts, it should be remembered that some legal rules too are not directly enforceable in the courts: for example, it is not possible to enforce in the courts the rules contained in Royal Warrants by which pensions are paid to former members of the armed forces or the duty of the Secretary of State for Education and Science to promote education and the progressive development of educational institutions.[57] Nor are all provisions contained in a written constitution necessarily suitable for judicial enforcement.[58]

C.   Other sources of the constitution

The law and custom of Parliament

While a distinction may be drawn between rules of the constitution which have the force of law and those which do not, it is difficult to classify the law and custom of Parliament under either heading. In earlier days, reference was often made to the 'High Court of Parliament'.[1] Each House has power over its own procedure and has certain privileges and immunities. The inherent authority of each House to control its own internal affairs is respected by the ordinary courts of law who seek to avoid interfering in these matters.[2] Many rules of constitutional importance are contained in the standing orders of the House of Commons, as well as in resolutions of the House and in other sources of the practice of the House, such as rulings by the Speaker.[3]

As well as the formal powers of each House, many informal practices and understandings are observed between the two main parties in the Commons, between the two front benches and the back-bench members, and between the main parties and the smaller parties. These practices are not contained in standing orders, nor are they often mentioned in that authoritative guide to the procedure of Parliament, Erskine May, but they directly affect the conduct of parliamentary business. These practices have many resemblances to the conventional rules of the constitution which apply outside Parliament. Departure from these conventional practices could lead to adverse political consequences within Parliament, for example the withdrawal of co-operation between government and opposition, and possibly to changes in the formal rules of parliamentary business.

---

56   App. A.
57   Education Act 1944, s.1; p. 637 *post.*
58   *Cf. Adegbenro* v. *Akintola* [1963] A.C. 614.

1   C. H. McIlwain, *The High Court of Parliament*, esp. ch. 2.
2   Ch. 12.
3   Erskine May, ch. 12.

Within Parliament, therefore, there are formal rules, informal rules, principles and practices; and the distinction between these various categories is often no more certain in Parliament than outside. In general the ordinary courts have no jurisdiction to apply and enforce the law of Parliament.

Legal and constitutional literature

In English law, it is a general rule that no legal text-book has intrinsic authority as a source of law: the authority of the most eminent text-book is confined to the extent to which a court considers that it accurately reproduces the law as enacted by the legislature or decided by earlier courts. 'Judges do not hesitate to differ from statements even in the most respected practice-books, if they consider them ill-founded.'[4] Where a statute has not yet been judicially interpreted, or where no court has pronounced authoritatively on a matter of common law, then the opinions of text-book writers and academic authors may be of great value to the legal profession, as well as to the court when a case arises for decision. Thus there can be no doubt that the late Professor de Smith's treatise, *Judicial Review of Administrative Action*, was a considerable influence upon the development of administrative law between 1959 and the author's death in 1974.

In Scots law, the position is very different as regards the past. A series of eminent legal authors who wrote between the mid-17th and early 19th centuries, including Viscount Stair, Professor John Erskine and Baron David Hume, are known as the institutional writers. Their work expounded the private law and criminal law of Scotland in a systematic manner which derived much from the institutional writers of Roman law: in the absence of other authority, a statement in their works is likely to be taken as settling the law.[5] Unfortunately none of the institutional writers dealt with constitutional law. The different approach of the Scottish legal system to the question of legal authority was seen in *Burmah Oil Co. v. Lord Advocate*,[6] relating to the Crown's prerogative: the case having reached the House of Lords on appeal from Scotland, counsel and judges referred extensively to the civilian writers of earlier centuries, in a manner untypical of the English common law.

Apart from their authority (or lack of it) in the courts, text-books on constitutional law are as valuable to the practitioner and the student as in other branches of law. Legal writers on the constitution are however handicapped by the unreality of many of the legal terms which they must sometimes employ.[7] Statements about the prerogative powers of the Crown often seem archaic, or to be conferring despotic powers upon the Sovereign, until it is realised that they concern powers of government exercised by ministers, civil servants and other Crown servants.[8]

In the field of the conventional rules of the constitution, books such as Sir Ivor Jennings's *Cabinet Government* and John Mackintosh's *The British Cabinet* are an invaluable record of constitutional practice. Since they are founded in part upon historical sources and in part upon contemporary political practice,

---

[4] C. K. Allen, *Law in the Making*, p. 279.
[5] D. M. Walker, *The Scottish Legal System*, p. 401.
[6] [1965] A.C. 75; Ch. 13 C.
[7] *Cf.* Bagehot, *The English Constitution*, pp. 99–100.
[8] See *Rogers* v. *Home Secretary* [1973] A.C. 388, for criticism of the term 'Crown privilege'.

in so far as it can be discovered, it is not surprising that such books are seldom unanimous in their description of controversial events (for example the differing interpretations of the political crisis in 1931 which led to the formation of the National government).[9] Rules of official secrecy, especially in Cabinet matters, make it unusually difficult to write about current practice. While most Cabinet papers are now made available in the Public Record Office after 30 years, the current structure of Cabinet committees is still regarded as secret.[10] Another problem is that historical precedents are often of doubtful relevance to present problems. Jennings, whose book was first published in 1936, was prepared to use constitutional precedents dating from 1841.[11] But the system of government has changed so much since 1841 (for example, concerning the role of the Sovereign and the House of Lords, and the electoral system) that precedents from before, say, the Liberal government of 1906 are probably today of no more than historical interest. In regard to aspects of the Cabinet system, 1906 is too early a date since, for example, a permanent Cabinet secretariat was not established until 1916.

In the field of parliamentary procedure, which is not affected by considerations of secrecy, an outstanding treatise which has especial authority is Erskine May's *Parliamentary Practice*. First published in 1844, this is revised regularly under the editorship of the Clerk to the House of Commons, and it summarises the collective experience of the Clerks of the House.[12] This work is essentially a means of reference to the original sources, which are found in standing orders, in resolutions passed by the House, and in rulings given by the Speaker and recorded in Hansard.

Finally, there is a more diverse source of information, namely the unending flow from government and Parliament of reports of such bodies as royal commissions, departmental committees, committees of Parliament and tribunals of inquiry. Many of these reports have concerned important constitutional topics (for example parliamentary privilege, telephone tapping and the interrogation of internees in Northern Ireland)[13] as well as matters of possible reform in public law (for example the law of official secrets and contempt of court).[14] Some reports, like those of tribunals of inquiry, are into specific events, like the inquiry into the collapse of the Vehicle and General Insurance Company.[15] Other reports come within series of publications by which parliamentary committees and other investigatory agencies regularly report on the operation of government. Since 1967 these have included the reports of the Parliamentary Commissioner for Administration, which give a more detailed insight into the methods of central departments than can be obtained from the law reports or Hansard alone. The importance of these publications is not that they reach heights of literary excellence, but that they provide information about the working of government which is not given by formal legal sources

---

9   See R. Bassett, *Nineteen Thirty-One*.
10   Ch. 14 A.
11   Jennings, *Cabinet Govt*, p. 9.
12   See the 20th ed., by Sir C. Gordon, 1983.
13   See respectively H.C. 34 (1967–68); Cmnd 283, 1957; and Cmnd 4823, 1971.
14   See Cmnd 5104, 1972 and Cmnd 5794, 1974.
15   H.L. 80, H.C. 133 (1971–2).

nor by private or political writings. Since 1973, British membership of the EEC has given rise to a new flow of official publications from the headquarters of the European Communities.

D. Constitutional government in Britain

Evolutionary development

The British constitution is flexible, not in the sense that it is unstable but in that its principles and rules can be changed by an Act of Parliament or the establishment of a new conventional rule. Perhaps because of this flexibility, the constitution has, at least since 1688, escaped those comprehensive and revolutionary convulsions which may occur in countries with more rigid constitutions but less stable political systems. Since the revolution settlement of 1688, there have been innumerable changes in the system of government, some freely conceded but many fought for by political action. The result has been a complete change from personal rule by the monarch to the collective ascendancy of the Prime Minister and Cabinet. Many of the older forms and organs have survived from earlier times, and these are tolerated or respected because they represent historic continuity. Writing in 1867, Walter Bagehot in *The English Constitution* distinguished between the *dignified* parts of the constitution 'which excite and preserve the reverence of the population' and the *efficient* parts, 'by which it, in fact, works and rules'.[1] Bagehot called it the characteristic merit of the constitution 'that its dignified parts are very complicated and somewhat imposing, very old and rather venerable; while its efficient part, at least when in great and critical action, is decidedly simple and rather modern.'[2] Certainly the apparent continuity of the constitution is misleading. Even the Royal Commission on the Constitution, who should have known better, were moved to say: 'The United Kingdom already possesses a constitution which in its essentials has served well for some hundreds of years',[3] a view of history which can scarcely be supported except by the most selective use of the evidence.

Constitutional monarchy and parliamentary government

Although the Queen is the head of the state, and government is carried on in her name, political responsibility for the acts of the government is borne by ministers of the Crown, who are answerable to and dependent for their offices upon the electorate and Parliament. After the settlement of 1688, it had to be established that the King could govern only through ministers who had the confidence of Parliament. Eventually executive powers came to be exercised by the Prime Minister and the Cabinet. Reforms of the electoral system after 1832 made the House of Commons more representative of the people, although universal adult suffrage was achieved only in 1929. The growth of the trade union movement and the Labour party enabled all the people to be directly represented in Parliament. This process of political evolution has avoided

---

[1] *The English Constitution*, p. 61.
[2] *Op. cit.*, p. 65.
[3] Kilbrandon Report, para. 395.

becoming a revolution, although there have been times of acute political and social unrest and there has been no simple, progressive improvement in democracy.

The party system

Parliamentary government cannot be explained solely in terms of legal and conventional rules. It depends essentially upon the political base which under-lies it, in particular on the party system around which political life is organ-ised. Given the present political parties and the electoral system, it is accepted that, following a general election, the party with a majority of seats in that House will form the government. As the British system of politics is strongly centralised, power to direct national affairs passes to the leadership of the party which, in popular terms, has won the general election. Except for February 1974, every general election held between 1931 and June 1983 produced an absolute majority in the Commons for one or other of the major parties. Even if that majority is counted in single figures (as it was in 1950–1, 1964–6 and after October 1974) it serves as a basis for the government's authority. In terms of the ability to govern for the time being, it is irrelevant that the majority of seats in the Commons may represent only a minority of votes cast by the electorate – as it has done in every election between 1906 and 1983, except in 1931 and 1935.

The British system therefore would seem to provide strong government, the continuance of the government in office being dependent mainly upon the ability of the governing party to retain its majority in the Commons. The concentration of power in the hands of the executive, including the direction of much of the economy, makes it necessary to emphasise that the British system is only tolerable because of the varied range of restraints upon govern-ment which exist. One restraint is the certainty of a general election, guar-anteed by law to occur at least every five years and likely by force of events to occur more frequently.

Another restraint is that government policies must run the gauntlet of criti-cism from opposition parties in Parliament. Another is that a government cannot ignore the force of public reaction to its measures; legislation which has passed through Parliament may not be enforceable unless it receives co-operation from the majority of those to whom it is intended to apply. Moreover, it is salutary to a government to know that its majority of members in the Commons (397 out of 650, after the election in 1983) was elected by only a minority of the electors (42.4% of the votes cast in 1983).

While there have been periods since the partition of Ireland when it has been possible to think of the United Kingdom as forming a single political system, dominated by two national parties, by 1983 this was no longer poss-ible. The Liberal party maintained its existence, and fought the 1983 election in harness with the Social Democratic party (formed in 1981), the alliance gaining 25.4% of the votes. A number of nationalist parties continued to exist in Wales, Scotland and Northern Ireland.[4] In 1953, an elder statesman of the

---

[4]   In *The Scottish Political System*, J. G. Kellas seeks to demonstrate 'the existence of a Scottish political system comprising a large number of actors engaged in a wide range of political activities' (p. 234).

Conservative party wrote:

the two-party system has been the normal type to which, after occasional interludes, we have regularly reverted, for the very reason that it has always centred round the business of maintaining a majority in Parliament for a Government or securing its displacement by another Government.[5]

Certainly the Conservative and Labour parties have a common interest in seeking to maintain a rigorous two-party system. But there is no reason to suppose that the constitutional structure of Britain rests upon that system, even if for many politicians the ideal state of affairs is one in which they hold office with their party commanding an absolute majority in the Commons, as the Conservatives did after the elections in 1979 and 1983. Periods of minority government, as occurred between February and October 1974, and again between 1976 and 1979, may well lead to adjustments in the arrangements of government, like the agreement between the Labour government and the Liberal party in 1977–8.[6] But there are no reasons based on constitutional principle for regretting such developments. Indeed, there would be evident advantage in a situation in which a government's legislative proposals and administrative performance came under more effective scrutiny in the Commons than is possible when that House is dominated by the government. Nor can coalitions, electoral pacts and unwritten understandings between the parties be regarded as unconstitutional.[7]

It is not possible in a book on constitutional law to give an account of the political system of the United Kingdom. The internal procedures of the parties are however often of constitutional importance – for example, the election of a leader, the relationship between the parliamentary party and other party organs, and the relationship between the party and other interests such as the trade unions. We will be examining electoral law, including such rules as there are on the financing of the parties.[8] As between the parties, however, this book must endeavour to apply the theory behind electoral law, namely that in a society which recognises the freedom of association for political purposes, the law should maintain conditions of neutrality between all contesting parties.

The leading role of the parties in political life is not without its critics. It has been argued that the party system serves not so much to enable public opinion to be represented in Parliament, as to restrict the scope for popular participation in the process of government. One advocate of this view submits that participation of the people will be enhanced if the electoral system is changed to one of proportional representation, and if the referendum becomes more widely used as a means of taking national decisions.[9] Before such developments are likely to occur, the Liberal and Social Democratic alliance will need to achieve greater success under the present electoral system than it did in June 1983.

---

[5] L. S. Amery, *Thoughts on the Constitution*, p. 43; and cf. Jennings, *Parliament*, pp. 23–4.

[6] See D. Steel, *A House Divided: the Lib-Lab Pact and the Future of British Politics*.

[7] See D. Butler (ed.), *Coalitions in British Politics*; D. Butler, *Governing without a Majority: Dilemmas for Hung Parliaments in Britain*; V. Bogdanor, *Multi-party Politics and the Constitution*.

[8] Ch. 9 B, III.

[9] V. Bogdanor, *The People and the Party System*.

Chapter 3

The structure of the United Kingdom

While the external identity of a state is a matter for international law, it is constitutional law which regulates the internal relationships of the various territories which make up the state. In the past, writers often used the word 'English' in referring to the constitution, a usage liable to give the false impression that English law prevailed throughout the United Kingdom. Dicey and Bagehot, for example, wrote about the English constitution when they were dealing with the British constitution, or, to be completely accurate, with what was then the constitution of the United Kingdom of Great Britain and Ireland. The active political consciousness of Ireland since the 19th century, and that of Scotland and Wales more recently, means that constitutional lawyers must now choose their geographical adjectives more carefully. When in 1969 a royal commission on the constitution was appointed, among its duties was 'to examine the present functions of the central legislature and government in relation to *the several countries, nations and regions* of the United Kingdom' and also to consider the constitutional and economic relationships between the United Kingdom and the Channel Islands and the Isle of Man.[1] While the appointment of the commission was a reminder that the unity of the United Kingdom should not be taken for granted, some of the deliberate vagueness of the words in italics was dispelled when the commission's report referred to England, Scotland, Wales and Northern Ireland as the four countries which make up the United Kingdom.

Legal definitions

In law, the expression 'United Kingdom' today refers to the United Kingdom of Great Britain and Northern Ireland; it does not include the Channel Islands or the Isle of Man.[2] For purposes of international relations, however, the Channel Islands and the Isle of Man are represented by the UK government.

---

[1] Ch. 22.

[2] Interpretation Act 1978, sch. 1. The British Nationality Act 1981, s.50(1) defines the United Kingdom as including the Channel Islands and the Isle of Man for purposes of nationality law.

So too are the colonies and other dependent territories of the United Kingdom overseas.[3]

The expression 'British Islands' is defined in the Interpretation Act 1978 as meaning the United Kingdom, the Channel Islands and the Isle of Man. The expression is occasionally used in legislation. Now that the Republic of Ireland is outside the United Kingdom[4] the British Islands do not in law include the Republic of Ireland.

The expression 'Great Britain' refers to England, Scotland and Wales: these first became a single kingdom by virtue of article 1 of the Treaty of Union between England and Scotland in 1707.

The Wales and Berwick Act 1746 provided that where the expression 'England' was used in an Act of Parliament, this should be taken to include the dominion of Wales and the town of Berwick on Tweed. But the Welsh Language Act 1967, section 4, provided that references to England in future Acts should not include the dominion of Wales. Concerning the boundary between Wales and England, a long standing controversy was brought to an end by the Local Government Act 1972, which declared that Monmouthshire was to be within Wales.[5]

The adjective 'British' is used in common speech to refer to matters associated with Great Britain or the United Kingdom. It seems to have no definite legal connotation and one authority has described the expression 'British law' as hopelessly ambiguous.[6] In legislation 'British' is sometimes used as an adjective referring to the United Kingdom, particularly in the context of nationality.[7]

Historical development of the United Kingdom

1 Wales[8] While it is not possible to summarise the lengthy history by which the kingdom of England became a single entity, it is worthwhile briefly to examine the historical formation of the United Kingdom. The military conquest of Wales by the English reached its culmination in 1282, when Prince Llywelyn was killed and his principality passed by conquest to King Edward I of England. Thereafter the principality (which formed only part of what is now Wales) was administered in the name of the Prince, but the rest of Wales was subjected to rule by a variety of local princes and lords; at this period English law was not extended to Wales, where the local customs, laws and language prevailed. From 1471, a Council of Wales and the Marches brought Wales under closer rule from England and the accession of the Tudors did much to complete the process of assimilation. In 1536, an Act of the English Parliament united Wales with England, establishing an administrative system

---

[3] Ch. 24.
[4] As to which, see K. Roberts-Wray, *Commonwealth and Colonial Law*, pp. 32–5.
[5] Ss. 1(12), 20(7) and 269; Interpretation Act 1978, sch. 1.
[6] Roberts-Wray, *op. cit.*, p. 69 *ff*.
[7] British Nationality Act 1981. Ch. 25 A.
[8] Kilbrandon Report, ch. 5, and J. A. Andrews (ed.) *Welsh Studies in Public Law*, esp. chs. 2 (D. Jenkins), 3 (H. Carter) and 4 (I. L. Gowan).

on English lines, requiring the English language to be used, and granting Wales representation in the English parliament.[9] In 1543, a system of Welsh courts (the Courts of the Great Sessions) was established to apply the common law of England. The Council of Wales and the Marches was granted a statutory jurisdiction which it exercised until its abolition in 1689. In 1830, the Courts of the Great Sessions were abolished and in their place were set up two new circuits to operate as part of the English court system. In the period after union with England, Acts of Parliament applying exclusively to Wales were rare.[10]

The mid-19th century saw the beginning of a political and educational revival, and occasional Acts of Parliament applying only to Wales began again to be passed.[11] In 1906 the Welsh Department of the Board of Education was established, the first central government department created specifically to administer Welsh affairs.[12] In 1914 was passed the Welsh Church Disestablishment Act which disestablished and disendowed the Church of England in Wales. Thereafter from time to time, the identity of Wales was recognised as new administrative arrangements were made. In 1949 a Council for Wales and Monmouthshire was established with the task of keeping the government informed of the impact of governmental activities on the life of the Welsh people: this Council gave way to the Welsh Economic Planning Council in 1966 and to the Welsh Council in 1968.[13] In 1964 following various limited ministerial experiments, the post of Secretary of State for Wales was established and the Welsh Office emerged as a department of the UK government. Wales and England share a common legal system but some statutes make special provision for Wales.[14] By the Welsh Language Act 1967, the Welsh language may be spoken in any legal proceedings within Wales, by any person who desires to use it; and ministers are authorised to prescribe the use of Welsh versions of any official document or form. The scheme of devolution proposed in the Wales Act 1978 will be outlined in chapter 22. In 1979 it was decisively rejected by the Welsh people in a referendum.

2 Scotland[15]   Unlike Wales, Scotland was able to maintain its national independence against English military and political pressures during the Middle Ages. Scotland retained its own monarchy and only in the 16th century did the two royal lines come closer together with the marriage to James IV of Scotland of Henry VII's daughter, Margaret. On the death of Elizabeth in 1603, James VI of Scotland, great-grandson of Henry VII, became James I of England. The union of the Crowns had the important legal consequence that persons born in England and Scotland after the union were citizens of both countries as they owed allegiance to the same King.[16] During the consti-

---

9   27 Hen. VIII, c.26. The Statute Law Revision Act 1948 called this Act the Laws in Wales Act 1535, but recent Welsh writers have called it the Act of Union of 1536: *Welsh Studies*, p. 28.
10   See *e.g.* Welsh Bible and Prayer Book Act 1563: *Welsh Studies*, pp. 38–9.
11   See *e.g.* Sunday Closing (Wales) Act 1881: *Welsh Studies*, p. 48.
12   *Welsh Studies*, p. 49.
13   *Welsh Studies*, pp. 62–3
14   *E.g.* Local Government Act 1972, Parts II and IV (p. 379 *post*).
15   Kilbrandon Report, ch. 4; see also G. Donaldson, *Scotland: James V–James VII*; W. Ferguson, *Scotland, 1689 to the Present.*
16   *Calvin's* case, (1608) 7 Co. Rep. 1a.

tutional conflicts of the 17th century, events took a broadly similar course in both countries and for a brief period under Cromwell, the Commonwealth of England, Scotland and Ireland was subject to a single legislature and executive. But apart from this, and despite the union of the Crowns, the constitutions of the two countries were not united and both the English and the Scottish Parliaments maintained their separate existences.[17] Following the ousting of James II/VII in 1688, the Scottish Parliament for the first time asserted independence of the royal will. There followed for some twenty years a contest of wills between the English and Scottish Parliaments, marked by religious disputation and by keen rivalry to profit from expanding ventures in world trade, against a deeply insecure European background. In 1704, the Scottish Parliament by the Act of Security went so far as to provide that if Anne died without heirs the Parliament would choose her successor, 'provided always that the same be not successor to the Crown of England', unless in the meantime acceptable conditions of government had been established between the two countries.[18] Following a strong initative from the English government, the English and Scottish Parliaments authorised negotiations between two groups of commissioners representing each Parliament but appointed by the Queen. The Treaty of Union was drawn up by them and was approved by Act of each Parliament together with an Act to maintain Presbyterian church government within Scotland.[19]

The Treaty of Union came into effect on 1st May 1707: it united the two kingdoms of England and Scotland into one by the name of Great Britain; the crown was to descend to the Hanoverian line after Anne's death; there was to be a Parliament of Great Britain including 16 Scottish peers and 45 elected members in the Commons. Extensive financial and economic terms were included in the Treaty. Guarantees were given for the continuance of Scottish private law (article 18) and the Scottish courts (article 19), as well as for the maintenance of the feudal jurisdictions in Scotland and the privileges of the royal burghs in Scotland. The Act to maintain the Presbyterian Church in Scotland was incorporated in the Treaty and also provided for the maintenance of the Scottish universities. While the Treaty was described as an incorporating union (*i.e.* it did not establish a federal system and did not maintain the previous Scottish and English legislatures for any purpose), it gave extensive guarantees to Scottish institutions. Guarantees of a similar kind for English institutions were not required as it was obvious that the English would be politically predominant in the new Parliament of Great Britain.[20]

In the years after 1707, the new unity of Great Britain was challenged by the Jacobite uprisings in 1715 and 1745 but without success. Various expedients were resorted to for governing Scotland from London and from time to time new laws were made for Scotland by the Parliament of Great Britain. Some of these, for example the abolition of the Scottish feudal jurisdictions in 1747, were considered in Scotland to be a breach of the Treaty of Union. The Scottish Privy Council having been abolished in 1708, for much of the 18th

---

[17] See G. Donaldson, *op. cit.*, ch. 15, and C. S. Terry, *The Scottish Parliament 1603–1707*.
[18] A.P.S. XI 136.
[19] Scottish Act: A.P.S. XI 406, English Act: 6 Anne c.11; *Halsbury's Statutes*, vol. 6, p. 501. For the making of the union, see P. W. J. Riley, *The Union of England and Scotland*.
[20] On the legal effect of these guarantees, see ch. 5 D.

and 19th centuries the Lord Advocate, the Crown's chief law officer in Scotland, occupied the primary role in politics and government, managing affairs in Scotland on behalf of the Crown. In 1885, a new post of Secretary for Scotland was created and in 1928 the post was raised to Cabinet status with the title of Secretary of State for Scotland. Demands for home rule for Scotland were expressed from the late 19th century onwards: the response of the government was to develop the Scottish Office as the department responsible for administering Scotland.[21] Political demands for a Scottish legislative assembly were firmly resisted, although greater use was made of committees of Scottish M.P.'s in the Commons. Since 1707, Parliament has often legislated separately for the English and Scottish legal systems. In particular, the structure of private law, courts, education and local government in Scotland has always differed from the English pattern. From the 1960s, there was a growing demand for greater devolution of government to Scotland; the rise and decline of this movement will be outlined in chapter 22. At a referendum in Scotland held in 1979, a narrow majority of those voting supported the scheme of devolution in the Scotland Act 1978; but there was considered to be insufficient support to justify the reform and the Act was repealed in 1979.

3 Northern Ireland[22]   The constitutional history of Northern Ireland is inextricably linked with the history of Ireland itself. As an entity Northern Ireland dates only from the partition of Ireland in the early 1920s. Ireland itself first came under English influence in the 12th century when Henry II of England became Lord of Ireland. As settlers came from England, courts modelled on those in England were established. While an Irish Parliament began to develop, some English legislation was extended to Ireland by ordinance of the King of England. In 1494, the Irish Parliament passed the statue known as Poyning's Law, which required that all Irish Bills should be submitted to the King and his Council in England; only such Bills as the English Council approved were to be returned for the Irish Parliament to pass. In 1541, the title of Lord of Ireland was changed to King of Ireland. During the 17th century, Ireland had its share of religious bitterness and conflict. William of Orange defeated the former King James II at the Battle of the Boyne in 1690. There followed a dispute over the power of the Irish House of Lords to hear appeals from Irish courts, and in 1720 the British Parliament by statue declared that it retained full power to legislate for Ireland and deprived the Irish House of Lords of all its judicial powers. Pressure from Ireland for greater autonomy led in 1782 to the repeal of the Declaratory Act of 1720, and to the recognition by the British Parliament of the Irish Parliament's legislative independence of Britain, although there was no change in the position of the monarchy.[23] But legislative independence was shortlived and after the rising of the United Irishmen in 1798, the British government proceeded to a legislative union with Ireland.

---

[21]   Ch. 22.

[22]   For the constitutional and legal history, see A. G. Donaldson, *Some Comparative Aspects of Irish Law*. For the 1920 Constitution of Northern Ireland, see H. Calvert, *Constitutional Law in Northern Ireland*, and Kilbrandon Report, ch. 6.

[23]   *Cf. In re Keenan* [1972] 1 Q.B. 533.

The Union agreement between the two Parliaments was broadly similar to the Union with Scotland, although fewer constitutional guarantees were given to Ireland than had been given to Scotland. Article 1 created the United Kingdom of Great Britain and Ireland, and articles 3 and 4 provided for Irish representation in the new Parliament of the United Kingdom. Article 5 provided for the (Protestant) United Church of England and Ireland, whose continuance was stated to be an essential and fundamental part of the Union. Within the enlarged United Kingdom, all trade was to be free; the laws in force in Ireland were to continue, subject to alteration by the UK Parliament from time to time. As with the Scottish union, the terms of the Union were separately adopted by Act of each of the two Parliaments concerned.[24]

The Irish Union with Britain was much less stable than the Anglo–Scottish Union of 1707. For much of the 19th century and on until the present day, the Irish question proved to be one of the most difficult political and constitutional issues within the United Kingdom. Catholic emancipation occurred in 1829, opening the way for political demands for further constitutional reform, often associated with militant action and acts of violence. The Irish Church was disestablished in 1869 despite the guarantee for its existence contained in the Act of Union.[25] Gladsone's two Home Rule Bills in 1886 and 1893 were both defeated in Parliament, the first in the Commons, the second in the Lords. After the Parliament Act 1911 had taken away the power of the House of Lords to veto legislation[26] the Government of Ireland Act 1914 became law, but it never came into effect because of the outbreak of world war; its parliamentary history had been marked by the extreme determination of Ulster protestants not to be separated from Britain.

The Easter rising in Dublin in 1916 was further evidence of the nationalist feeling in Catholic Ireland. In 1919 the Sinn Fein movement established a representative assembly for what was proclaimed to be the Irish Republic. In 1920 the Government of Ireland Act was passed by the UK Parliament, providing for two Parliaments in Ireland, one for the six northern counties and one for the remainder of Ireland, with co-operation between the two to be maintained by means of a Council of Ireland. The 1920 Act was ignored by Sinn Fein and after a period of bitter civil war, an Anglo–Irish Treaty was formally concluded in 1922. This recognised the emergence of the Irish Free State, on which Westminster conferred what was then described as the status of a self-governing dominion within the British Empire.[27] The six northern counties were excluded from the Irish Free State, acquiring their own government and Parliament under the 1920 Act.

While the position of the Irish Free State as a Dominion within the British Empire was not free from doubt, steps were taken by it in the 1930s to assert a more complete independence of the United Kingdom. The new Irish Constitution of 1937 declared that Eire was a sovereign independent state. During the second world war, Eire was neutral. In 1949, the state became the Republic of Ireland and the UK Parliament at long last recognised that Eire

---

24 For the Union with Ireland Act 1800, see *Halsbury's Statutes*, vol. 23, p. 832.
25 *Ex p. Canon Selwyn* (1872) 36 J.P. 54, and see Calvert, *op. cit.*, pp. 20–1.
26 Ch. 11 B.
27 Ch. 24.

had ceased to be part of Her Majesty's dominions although it was, perhaps anomalously, also declared by Parliament that Ireland was not to be regarded as a foreign country.[28]

The system of government established under the Act of 1920 in Northern Ireland survived in all essentials for the next half-century. Dissatisfaction with that system led to civil unrest from 1968 onwards. The UK government was required to intervene increasingly in the affairs of Northern Ireland until, in 1972, direct rule of Northern Ireland was resumed and the constitution of Northern Ireland was suspended.[29] In 1973, after a poll of the electorate had shown a clear majority in favour of Northern Ireland remaining part of the United Kingdom, the system of government under the 1920 Act was finally ended. In its place, a bold experiment was made to establish a new Assembly and a new form of executive based on the concept of power-sharing.[30] Elections for the Assembly were held in June 1973 and the executive came into office in January 1974. But the experiment failed after a few months. The Northern Ireland Act 1974 dissolved the Assembly, made temporary provision for the government of the province through the Secretary of State for Northern Ireland, and authorised the holding of an elected constitutional convention under the chairmanship of the Chief Justice of Northern Ireland. The convention met during 1975 but it failed to produce an agreed constitutional scheme[31] and direct rule from Westminster continued.

Of subsequent developments, mention may be made of the Anglo-Irish Inter-Governmental Council, established in 1981 by the governments of the United Kingdom and the Irish Republic for the discussion of matters of common concern; the increase in Northern Ireland's representation at Westminster from 12 to 17 seats;[32] and the re-activation in 1982 of the Assembly first created in 1973.[33] Under the Northern Ireland Act 1982, elections for the Assembly were held in October 1982. The Assembly was authorised to make proposals to the Secretary of State for a total or partial resumption of the devolution of powers authorised by the Act of 1973. It was also empowered to exercise a scrutinising function so long as direct rule continues, and for this purpose to establish a committee of Assembly members for each Northern Ireland department. The aim behind the 1982 Act was to bring together the parties of Northern Ireland, leaving to them the task of making further constitutional proposals. But in 1984 there was still no consensus on the future.

It follows that the Union with Ireland Act of 1800 is still in force as regards Northern Ireland, except as it has been amended by subsequent legislation, for example the disestablishment of the Episcopalian Church in 1869. The UK Parliament has pledged that no part of Northern Ireland should cease to be part of Her Majesty's dominions except after a poll of the electorate in Northern Ireland has approved such a proposal.[34]

---

28 Ireland Act 1949, s. 1(1) and 2.
29 Northern Ireland (Temporary Provisions) Act 1972.
30 Cmnd 5259, 1973; Northern Ireland Assembly Act 1973; Northern Ireland Constitution Act 1973.
31 H.C.1. (1975–6); Cmnd 6387, 1976.
32 House of Commons (Redistribution of Seats) Act 1979.
33 See Cmnd 8541, 1982; and C. Gearty [1982] P.L. 518.
34 Northern Ireland Constitution Act 1973, s. 1.

Three legal systems

For many purposes it would be correct to describe the United Kingdom as a unitary state, since there is no structure of federalism. But the aim of the brief historical outline given in this chapter has been to emphasise that constitutional and legal differences do exist within the United Kingdom, and that diversity, as well as political and economic unity, is found within the constitution. While the legislative competence of Parliament extends to all parts of the United Kingdom, three distinct legal systems exist, each with its own courts and legal profession, namely, (a) England and Wales (b) Scotland (c) Northern Ireland. A unifying influence is that the House of Lords is the final court of appeal from all three jurisdictions, except for criminal cases in Scotland. When Parliament legislates, it may legislate for the whole United Kingdom (for example, income tax or immigration law), for Great Britain (for example, social security or industrial relations law) or separately for one or more of the component countries within the United Kingdom. But such legal differences are not always of political significance. In 1984, direct rule in Northern Ireland continued and there was no prospect of a revival in the cause of Scottish or Welsh devolution. Nor were the English regions interested in devolution within England, despite the political and economic differences that exist between them.

The Channel Islands[35]

Neither the Channel Isles, nor the Isle of Man, form part of the United Kingdom, except for the purposes of the British Nationality Act 1981, but it is convenient to describe their position here. The islands are possessions of the Crown, and the British government is responsible for their defence and international relations. The laws of the Channel Islands are based on the ancient customs of the Duchy of Normandy, of which they formed part until 1204. The sovereignty of Her Majesty is admitted only in her right as successor to the Dukes of Normandy. These islands have never been colonies and enjoy wide autonomy for most domestic purposes, including taxation. They are subject to the legislative supremacy of the Westminster Parliament, in which they are not represented, but by a long-standing convention it is rare for Westminster to legislate directly for the Islands. Where this is intended it is usual for the Act of Parliament to authorise an Order in Council to be made applying the Act, as modified in the Order, to the Islands.

In Jersey the Sovereign is represented by the Lieutenant-Governor, who acts as the channel of communication between the UK government and the island authorities. He is entitled to sit but not to vote in the legislative body, the Assembly of the States, and also to sit in the Royal Court. The chief judicial and executive officer is the Bailiff who, like the Lieutenant-Governor, is appointed by the Crown. He presides over both the States and the Royal Court. The Assembly of the States consists of 12 senators, 12 constables and 28 deputies, chosen by various forms of election. The Assembly has power to make permanent laws, subject to their being approved by Orders of the Privy

---

[35] Kilbrandon Report, Part XI and H.L.E., vol. 6, pp. 371–7. And see *Re a debtor, ex p. Viscount of Royal Court of Jersey* [1981] Ch. 148.

Council registered in the Royal Court, and also to make subordinate regulations without such approval. Civil and criminal jurisdiction is exercised by the Royal Court, constituted by the Bailiff and 12 elected jurats.[36]

The Bailiwick of Guernsey is separate from, but in a similar position to that of Jersey. The Bailiff is the head of the administration as well as President of the States of Deliberation (the legislature) and the Royal Court. The legislature consists of 12 conseillers, 33 deputies, 10 douzaine representatives and two representatives of Alderney. The States of Guernsey legislate also for the adjoining islands of Alderney and Sark, subject in the former case to the consent of the local States, and in Sark to that of the Chief Pleas. As with Jersey, a law may be passed by the States but it must be sanctioned by an Order of the Privy Council, registered in the Royal Court.

There are separate Courts of Appeal for Jersey and Guernsey. The judges are the Bailiffs of Jersey and Guernsey and their deputies, together with persons appointed by the Queen from those who have held judicial office in the Commonwealth or are senior practitioners at the bar in any part of the United Kingdom, the Isle of Man, Jersey or Guernsey. From a decision of the Courts of Appeal in civil matters, appeal lies to the Judicial Committee of the Privy Council.[37]

The Home Secretary is the United Kingdom minister responsible for relations with the Channel Islands. Formal legislative business is transacted by a Committee of the Privy Council for Channel Islands matters. By a long standing practice, Orders in Council and Acts of Parliament which apply to the islands are registered in each Royal Court, but their legal effect does not derive from such registration. The Royal Courts may request reconsideration of an Order in Council but can in the last resort be compelled to register it.[38]

The Isle of Man[39]

The Isle of Man, an ancient kingdom, was until 1266 feudatory to the Kings of Norway: traces of this Norse heritage survive in Manx law and government. In the reign of Henry IV, the English claim to the island prevailed over that of Scotland and in 1405 the island was granted to the Earls of Derby with the title of King (later Lord) of Man. In 1765 the Lordship re-vested in the Crown. Tynwald, the ancient Manx legislature, consists of the Sovereign, represented by the Lieutenant Governor (appointed by the Crown), the Legislative Council and the elected House of Keys. The powers of the Manx authorities now extend to all domestic matters. In particular, by a series of Isle of Man Acts passed at Westminster since 1866 (in particular those of 1958 and 1979) Tynwald may regulate the island's finances, customs, harbours, civil service and police. In 1981, an Order in Council was made delegating to the Lieu-

---

[36]   For the system of criminal justice in the Channel Islands, see St.J. Robilliard [1979] Crim. L.R. 566.

[37]   Ch. 19 A. See *e.g. Vaudin* v. *Hamon* [1974] A.C. 569.

[38]   H.L.E., vol. 6, pp. 371–2. *cf.* F. de L. Bois [1983] P.L. 385, 389–91.

[39]   As well as the Kilbrandon Report, Part XI, see Report of the Joint Working Party on the Constitutional Relationship between the Isle of Man and the UK, 1969; H.L.E., vol. 6, pp. 377–9; and D. G. Kermode, *Devolution at Work: a Case Study of the Isle of Man.*

tenant Governor power to grant the royal assent to all internal legislation, except for particular measures that the Privy Council might reserve to itself. Executive power is divided between the Lieutenant Governor and Tynwald, but since 1981 the chairman of the Executive Council has been elected by Tynwald. A new Customs and Excise Agreement between the Manx authorities and the UK government took effect in 1980, replacing the former Common Purse Agreement. The Isle of Man has its own legal system and courts, from which an ultimate appeal lies to the Privy Council.

The Westminster Parliament may legislate for the Isle of Man, either directly or by extending Acts of Parliament by Order in Council: in practice this power is exercised only after consultation with the island authorities and mainly in relation to obligations of the United Kingdom arising under international treaties. During the 1960s, there was a prolonged dispute between Tynwald and the UK government over the control of broadcasting in the island and off its coast; the Marine etc. Broadcasting (Offences) Act 1967 was extended to the island by Order in Council against the wishes of Tynwald.[40]

British adherence to the European Convention on Human Rights caused difficulties when in *Tyrer* v. *United Kingdom*, the European Court of Human Rights held that judicial birching in the Isle of Man of a 15 year old boy constituted degrading punishment contrary to article 3 of the Convention.[41] Subsequently, at the request of the Isle of Man government, the UK government did not renew the right of individuals in the Isle of Man to petition under the Convention.[42]

Review by the Royal Commission on the Constitution

One specific task entrusted to the Royal Commission on the Constitution in 1969 was to consider whether any changes were desirable in the constitutional and economic relationships between the United Kingdom and the Channel Islands and the Isle of Man. This review took place against a background of negotiations for British membership of the EEC which the Islands feared would prejudice their existing advantages as tax havens and in other economic matters. In the event, special terms were negotiated for the Islands which were accepted by them and included in the Treaty of Accession. Under these terms, the Islands are included within the EEC for the purpose of free movement of industrial and agricultural goods, but the Islands are exempted from many provisions of the Treaty of Rome, including those relating to the harmonisation of taxation.[43] A major difficulty examined by the royal commission was the threat to the domestic autonomy of the Islands arising from international treaties entered into by the UK government which required the domestic law of both the United Kingdom and the Islands to be altered to give effect to the treaties.[44] The royal commission, rejecting proposals for clarifying or strengthening the position of the Islands, recommended the maintenance of existing

---

[40] Kilbrandon Report, pp. 429–32.
[41] (1978) 2 E.H.R.R.1; Ch. 31 B.
[42] H. C. Deb., 18 Mar. 1981, col. 98 (W.A.). And see *Teare* v. *O'Callaghan* (1982) 4 E.H.R.R. 232.
[43] Cmnd 4862–1 (1972), Protocol, No. 3.
[44] Kilbrandon Report, pp. 416–24.

relationships, subject to greater use of formal machinery for consultation between the Islands and the UK government. The commission suggested that, for consultation and conciliation, a body called 'The Council of the Islands' might be created, which would include independent members as well as representatives of all the Islands and of the UK government. But this suggestion was not adopted.

Chapter 4

The relationship between legislature, executive and judiciary

For purposes of constitutional analysis, the functions of government have often been divided into three broad classes — legislative, executive (or administrative) and judicial. It is not always easy, or indeed possible, to determine under which head a particular task of government falls, but the organs which mainly perform these functions are distinguishable. To give an example from one of the oldest tasks of government, that of taxation: the enactment of a law authorising a new tax is a legislative function; the provision of machinery for assessing and collecting the tax payable by each taxpayer is an executive (or administrative) function; the determination of disputes between the taxpayer and the tax-collector as to the tax due in a particular case is a judicial function, involving the interpretation of the law and its application to the facts. So too in criminal law: the creation of a new offence is a matter for legislation, the enforcement of the law is an executive function and the trial of alleged offenders is a judicial function. It is taken for granted in Britain that the imposition of a new tax and the creation of new offences are matters for Parliament, that the enforcement of the law is for the executive, and that the application of the law in individual cases is for the courts. But the tasks of government today are complex. The simple model afforded by taxation and criminal law is not easily applicable to many of the more elaborate processes of government.

In this chapter, it is intended to examine the two questions:

(a)   to what extent are the three functions (legislative, executive and judicial) distinguishable today?
(b)   to what extent are these three functions exercisable separately by the institutions of Parliament, the executive and the courts to which they are often attributed?

The legislative function
The legislative function involves the enactment of general rules determining the structure and powers of public authorities and regulating the conduct of citizens and private organisations. In the United Kingdom, legislative authority is vested in the Queen in Parliament: new law is enacted when, usually on the proposal of the government, it has been approved by Commons

and Lords and has received the royal assent. As this assent is given on the advice of the Cabinet, the royal assent has for practical purposes become a formality. Under the Parliament Acts of 1911 and 1949, legislation may be enacted even though it has been rejected by the House of Lords.[1] While the House of Lords remains part of the legislature, its power to amend measures passed by the Commons is limited; and it is politically subordinate to the elected House of Commons.

While legislative authority is vested in the Queen in Parliament, several qualifications need to be borne in mind.

(*a*)   By Act of Parliament, legislative powers may be conferred on other bodies — for example upon ministers, government departments and local authorities. While subordinate legislation of this kind is made under the authority of an Act, it follows that not all new legislation is directly made by Parliament.[2]

(*b*)   In the European Communities Act 1972, Parliament recognised that the organs of the European Communities could legislate in respect of the United Kingdom. In Community matters, legislative powers for the United Kingdom are exerciseable by the Council of Ministers and the Commission of the Communities.[3]

(*c*)   While one result of the 17th-century constitutional conflict was to impose very severe limits on the authority of the Crown to make new law without the approval of Parliament, certain legislative powers of the Crown have survived.[4]

(*d*)   While primary legislative authority is vested in Parliament, the two Houses have much work to do which does not involve legislating. In fact the time devoted by Parliament to the legislative programme seldom exceeds half the number of days in a session. The House of Commons especially serves an historic function as the 'grand inquest of the nation', where government policies are debated and the work of government departments is scrutinised.[5]

(*e*)   The great majority of Bills are prepared for Parliament by the government, which is also responsible for supervising their passage through each House and for implementing new Acts once they have received the royal assent. The executive therefore participates actively, and often decisively, in the process of legislation. When the government has a working majority in the Commons, no new legislation can be enacted by Parliament which is not approved also by the government.

(*f*)   Once a new law has been enacted by Parliament, the authoritative interpretation of that law is a matter for the courts. The interpretation of statutes is in one sense a vital part of the legislative process as it is only after judicial interpretation that it is known whether the intentions of those who framed the law have actually been carried into effect; but in this task the judges must not seek to compete with the political authority of the legislature.[6]

---

[1]   Ch. 11 B.
[2]   Ch. 33.
[3]   Ch. 8.
[4]   Ch. 13 C.
[5]   Ch. 11 C and D.
[6]   *Stock* v. *Frank Jones (Tipton) Ltd.* [1978] 1 All E.R. 948; *Duport Steels Ltd.* v. *Sirs* [1980] 1 All E.R. 529.

The executive function

It is more difficult to give a simple account of the executive function than of the legislative function. Broadly speaking the executive function comprises the whole corpus of authority to govern, other than that which is involved in the legislative functions of Parliament and the judicial functions of the courts. The general direction of policy includes the initiation of legislation, the maintenance of order, the promotion of social and economic welfare, administration of public services, and the conduct of the external relations of the state. The executive function has therefore a residual character, its techniques ranging from the formation of broad policy to the detailed management of routine services. Historically the executive was identified with the Sovereign, in whose name many acts are still performed by the Prime Minister, Cabinet and other ministers. But the executive today includes all those officials, public authorities and other agencies by which functions of government are performed. Within the executive are therefore to be included the civil service, the armed forces, the police, local authorities (who exercise executive functions within a defined locality) and independent statutory bodies. British membership of the European Communities has meant that the Council of Ministers and the Commission now exercise executive functions in relation to the United Kingdom.[7] Consequently the executive in Britain does not form a single structure with a simple organisation.

The judicial function

The primary judicial function is to determine disputed questions of fact and law in accordance with the law laid down by Parliament and expounded by the courts. This function is exercised mainly in the civil and criminal courts by professional judges. However, lay magistrates exercise many powers of criminal justice in the lower courts and ordinary citizens contribute to the administration of justice by serving on juries at criminal trials. The judicial function therefore is not assigned to the professional judiciary alone. Nor is it assigned to the civil and criminal courts alone. Many disputes which arise out of the conduct of government are entrusted to administrative tribunals. Today these tribunals are a recognised part of the machinery of justice; they operate subject to the supervision of the superior civil courts.[8]

As well as their primary function of settling legal disputes, the courts exercise certain legislative functions (for example the making of rules of court procedure) and administrative functions (for example the administration of the estates of deceased persons). Some work of the courts (for example the granting of an uncontested divorce) involves no dispute or controversy. Other tasks (for example the sentencing of criminals) are arguably not essential judicial functions, although they are traditionally the work of.judges. In matters of Community law, judicial functions are exercised for the United Kingdom by the European Court of Justice.

---

[7] Ch. 8.
[8] Ch. 37 A.

The doctrine of the separation of powers

To summarise the foregoing, it may be said that within a system of government based on law, there are legislative, executive and judicial functions to be performed; and that the primary organs for discharging these functions are respectively the legislature, the executive and the courts. A legal historian has remarked:

This threefold division of labour, between a legislator, an administrative official, and an independent judge, is a necessary condition for the rule of law in modern society and therefore for democratic government itself.[9]

Admittedly there is no clear-cut demarcation between some aspects of these functions, nor is there always a neat correspondence between the functions and the institutions of government. Historically there have been periods in Britain when in central government (for example, when the king governed through his Council, with its mixture of legislative, executive and judicial work) and at a local level (for example, when the justices in the English counties exercised a similar mixture of functions), there has been no clear differentiation of functions. Yet it may be argued that essential values of law, liberty and democracy are best protected if the three primary functions of a law-based government are discharged by three distinct institutions. Professor Robson described the doctrine of separation of powers as 'that antique and rickety chariot . . ., so long the favourite vehicle of writers on political science and constitutional law for the conveyance of fallacious ideas'.[10] But this does not do justice to the contribution which the doctrine has made to the maintenance of liberty and the continuing need by constitutional means to restrain abuse of governmental power.[11] The rest of this chapter will examine the doctrine and how far it applies in Britain today.

Locke and Montesquieu

In 1690, the Englishman John Locke wrote in his *Second Treatise of Civil Government*:

It may be too great a temptation to humane frailty, apt to grasp at power, for the same persons who have the power of making laws, to have also in their hands the power to execute them, whereby they may exempt themselves from obedience to the laws they make, and suit the law, both in its making and execution, to their own private advantage.[12]

The doctrine of the separation of powers was developed further by the French jurist, Montesquieu, who based his exposition on the British constitution of the early 18th century as he understood it. His division of powers did not closely correspond except in name with the classification which has become traditional; for, although he followed the usual meaning of legislative and

---

9   E. G. Henderson, *Foundations of English Administrative Law*, p. 5.
10   W. A. Robson, *Justice and Administrative Law*, p. 14.
11   See M. J. C. Vile, *Constitutionalism and the Separation of Powers*, for a valuable reassessment of the link between legal values, constitutionalism and separation of powers; also G. Marshall, *Constitutional Theory*, Ch. 5, and C. R. Munro [1981] P.L. 19.
12   Ch. XII, para. 143, quoted in Vile *op. cit.*, p. 62.

judicial powers, by executive power he meant only 'the power of executing matters falling within the law of nations', *i.e.* making war and peace, sending and receiving ambassadors, establishing order, preventing invasion.[13] He stated the essence of the doctrine thus:

When the legislative and executive powers are united in the same person, or in the same body of magistrates, there can be no liberty ... Again, there is no liberty, if the judiciary power be not separated from the legislative and executive. Were it joined with the legislative, the life and liberty of the subject would be exposed to arbitrary control; for the judge would then be the legislator. Were it joined to the executive however, the judge might behave with violence and oppression. There would be an end to everything, were the same man, or the same body, whether of the nobles or of the people, to exercise those three powers, that of enacting laws, that of executing the public resolutions, and of trying the causes of individuals.[14]

This statement emphasises that, within a system of government based upon law, the judicial function should be exercised by a body separate from legislature and executive. Montesquieu did not, it may be surmised, mean that legislature and executive ought to have no influence or control over the acts of each other, but only that neither should exercise the whole power of the other.[15]

In Montesquieu's observation of the British constitution in the 18th century, he saw that Parliament had achieved legislative dominance over the King with the passing of the Bill of Rights, and that the independence of the judiciary had been declared, but that the King still exercised executive power. Before the century was over, however, there had been established in Britain the Cabinet system, under which the King governed only through ministers who were members of Parliament and responsible to it. This system, with its emphatic link between Parliament and the executive, in a major respect ran contrary to Montesquieu's doctrine. It is in the United States constitution that his influence can best be seen.

Separation of powers in the US constitution

In the US constitution of 1787 the separation of powers was clearly expressed. The framers of the constitution intended that a balance of powers should be attained by vesting each primary constitutional function in a distinct organ. Possibly they were imitating the form of the British constitution but by that time in Britain executive power was passing from the Crown to the Cabinet. The US constitution vests legislative powers in Congress, consisting of a Senate and a House of Representatives (article 1), executive power in the President (article 2), and judicial power in the Supreme Court and such other federal courts as might be established by Congress (article 3). The President holds office for a fixed term of four years and is separately elected: he may therefore be of a different party from that which has a majority in either or both Houses of Congress. His powers, like those of Congress, are declared by the constitution. While the heads of the chief departments of state are known

---

13 But *cf.* Vile *op. cit.*, p. 87.
14 *De l'Esprit des Lois*, Book XI, ch. 6, quoted in Vile *op. cit.*, p. 90.
15 Jennings, *The Law and the Constitution*, app. 1; C. K. Allen, *Law and Orders*, ch. 1.

as the Cabinet, they are individually responsible to the President and not to Congress. This system of a presidential executive is quite different from that of Cabinet government in Britain.

Neither the President nor members of his Cabinet can sit or vote in Congress; they have no direct power of initiating Bills or securing their passage through Congress. The President may recommend legislation in his messages to Congress, but he cannot compel it to pay heed to his recommendations. While he has a power to veto legislation passed by Congress, this veto may be overridden by a two-thirds vote in each House of Congress. Treaties may be negotiated by the President, but must be approved by a two-thirds majority of the Senate. The President has power to nominate to certain key offices, including judges of the Supreme Court, but the Senate must confirm these appointments and may refuse to do so. The President himself is not directly responsible to Congress for his conduct of affairs: in normal circumstances he is irremovable from office, but the constitution does authorise the President to be removed from office by the process of impeachment at the hands of the Senate, 'for treason, bribery, or other high crimes and misdemeanours' (article 2(4)). (The prospect of such impeachment was the immediate cause of President Nixon's resignation from office in 1974 following his complicity in the Watergate affair.) Once appointed, the judges of the Supreme Court are independent both of Congress and the President, although they too may be removed from office by impeachment. Early in the history of the United States, the Supreme Court assumed the power, notably by the historic decision of Chief Justice Marshall in *Marbury* v. *Madison*,[16] of declaring both the acts of the legislature and the acts of the President to be unconstitutional.

Even in the US constitution, there is not a complete separation of powers between the executive, legislative and judicial functions, if by this is meant that each power can be exercised in complete isolation from the others. Indeed, having established the threefold allocation of functions as a basis, the constitution proceeds to construct an elaborate system of checks and balances designed to enable control and influence to be exercised by each branch upon the others. The Watergate affair showed not only the strong position of a President elected into office by popular vote: it also showed how a combination of constitutional powers exercised by Congress and the Supreme Court, as well as such forces as public opinion and the press, could combine to remove even the President from office.[17]

Separation of powers in other constitutions

Many other constitutions have been influenced by the separation of powers. In France, the doctrine has been of great importance but it has manifested itself very differently from the American version. Thus it is considered to flow from the separation of powers that the ordinary courts in France should have no jurisdiction to review the legality of acts of the legislature or executive. In place of the courts the Conseil d'Etat, structurally part of the executive, has developed a jurisdiction over administrative agencies and officials which is exercised independently of the political arm of the executive.[18]

---

[16]   (1803) 1 Cranch 137.
[17]   See *US* v. *Nixon* (1974) 418 U.S. 683.
[18]   L. N. Brown and J. F. Garner, *French Administrative Law*, pp. 28–31.

The constitutions of member states of the Commonwealth have been influenced by the doctrine of separation of powers in a variety of ways. Under the Australian constitution, for example, delegation of legislative powers to executive agencies has been accepted more readily than the delegation to them of judicial powers.[19] The former constitution of Sri Lanka was held to be based upon an implied separation of powers; legislation to provide special machinery for convicting and punishing the leaders of an unsuccessful coup was held to infringe the fundamental principle that judicial power was vested only in the judicature.[20] In countries with a written constitution based on an express or implied separation of powers, the courts may have to decide whether a particular statutory power should be classified as legislative, executive or judicial.[21] British courts do not have this task but have sometimes classified powers for such purposes as applying the law of contempt of court and the rules of natural justice.[22]

Meaning of separation of powers

As the strong contrast between the United States and France shows, the doctrine of separation of powers has a variety of meanings. The concept of 'separation' may mean at least three different things:

(*a*)　that the same persons should not form part of more than one of the three organs of government, for example that ministers should not sit in Parliament;
(*b*)　that one organ of government should not control or interfere with the work of another, for example that the judiciary should be independent of the executive;
(*c*)　that one organ of government should not exercise the functions of another, for example that ministers should not have legislative powers.

In considering each of these aspects of separation, it needs to be remembered that complete separation of powers is possible neither in theory nor in practice.

Legislature and executive

Writing in 1867, Bagehot described the 'efficient secret' of the constitution as 'the close union, the nearly complete fusion, of the legislative and executive powers'.[23] Bagehot's critics have rejected the concept of fusion, arguing that the close relationship between executive and legislature does not exclude the important constitutional distinction between the two. As Amery wrote:

Government and Parliament, however closely intertwined and harmonized, are still separate and independent entities, fulfilling the two distinct functions of leadership, direction and command on the one hand, and of critical discussion and examination on the other. They start from separate historical origins, and each is perpetuated in accordance with its own methods and has its own continuity.[24]

The three meanings of separation mentioned above will first be applied to the relationship between executive and legislature.

19　C. Howard, *Australian Federal Constitutional Law*, ch. 3 B.
20　*Liyanage* v. *R.* [1967] 1 A.C. 259.
21　*Hinds* v. *The Queen* [1977] A.C. 195 (appeal from Jamaica).
22　Page 604 *post*.
23　Bagehot, *The English Constitution*, p. 65.
24　L. S. Amery, *Thoughts on the Constitution*, p. 28: see also Vile, *op. cit.*, pp. 224–30.

(*a*) Do the same persons or bodies form part of both the legislature and executive? The form of the constitution shows the Sovereign as the head of the executive and also an integral part of the legislature. More important is the convention that ministers should be members of one or other House of Parliament. Their presence in Parliament helps to make a reality of their responsibility to Parliament. But it is often overlooked that there is a statutory limit on the number of ministers who may be members of the Commons.[25] Moreover, except for these ministers, the vast majority of persons who hold positions within the executive are disqualified from membership of the Commons, namely all members of the civil service, the armed forces, the police and the holders of many public offices. The House of Commons Disqualification Act 1975 and the rules which forbid civil servants and the police from taking part in political activities are evidence of a very strict separation of membership which is maintained between executive and legislature. Only ministers exercise a dual role as key figures in both institutions.

(*b*) Does the legislature control the executive or the executive control the legislature? This question goes to the heart of parliamentary government in Britain and no simple or brief answer can be adequate. In one sense, the Commons ultimately controls the executive, since the Commons can oust a government which has lost the ability to command a majority on an issue of confidence. The Commons did this to Mr Callaghan's minority government in March 1979. But so long as the Cabinet can retain the confidence of the Commons, it generally exercises a decisive voice in securing the passage of legislation. In 1978 the Select Committee on Procedure concluded that

the balance of advantage between Parliament and Government in the ·day to day working of the Constitution is now weighted in favour of the Government to a degree which arouses widespread anxiety and is inimical to the proper working of our parliamentary democracy.[26]

The period beginning with the Conservative government of 1970–4 has seen a developing willingness by M.P.s to use their voting power in the Commons to indicate when necessary their disapproval of particular government measures. This trend was at its height during the periods of minority government in 1974 and in 1976–9.[27] It can no longer be argued that a government must resign or call a general election whenever it is defeated on a policy issue, but where a government is elected with a secure and substantial majority, its prospects of being defeated are slight. In such circumstances, it has to be accepted that the government is able to use Parliament as a means of securing those changes in the law which it desires.

The close relationship between executive and legislature is not confined to legislation. It is also a function of the legislature to call the government to account for its administrative work. Control over administration is necessarily indirect, as neither House can take over the task of governing. But a variety of procedures exist, for example specialised committees and parliamentary

---

25 Page 165 *post.*
26 H.C. 588–1 (1977–8), p. viii.
27 See works by P. Norton: *Dissension in the House of Commons, 1945–74*; (same title) *1974–9*; *The Commons in Perspective*; and [1978] P.L. 360.

questions, by which Parliament informs itself about the activities of the executive. As means of control these procedures vary in effectiveness, but they make possible a measure of democratic scrutiny.

(*c*)   Do the legislature and the executive exercise each other's functions? The most substantial area in which the executive might appear to exercise functions belonging to the legislature is in respect of delegated legislation. In Britain there is no formal limitation on the power of Parliament to delegate legislative powers to the government. Provided that whenever possible the main principles of legislation are laid down in an Act of Parliament, there is advantage in ministers having power to implement those principles by detailed regulations. But it is often not easy to decide what is a matter of principle for Parliament and what is detail which should be left to ministerial discretion. It is therefore essential that parliamentary procedures should exist for scrutinising the use made of delegated power.[28]

Executive and judiciary

There must now be examined the relationship between the judiciary and the other two organs of government. Again the three questions may be asked:

(*a*)   Do the same persons form part of the judiciary and the executive? The courts are the Queen's courts, but judicial functions are exercised by her judges. The Judicial Committee of the Privy Council is in form an executive organ, but in fact it is an independent court of law.[29] The Lord Chancellor, who is a member of the Cabinet, is also head of the judiciary and is entitled to preside over the Lords, which is the final court of appeal from the courts of the United Kingdom. In fact, he rarely sits to hear appeals today and avoids hearing appeals in which a government department is involved as a party.

The law officers of the Crown (in particular the Attorney-General in England and the Lord Advocate in Scotland) have duties of enforcing the criminal law which are sometimes described as 'quasi-judicial'; it must be emphasised that the law officers are members of the executive, and are not judges.[30]

(*b*)   Does the executive control the judiciary or the judiciary control the executive? Although judges are appointed by the executive, judicial independence of the executive is secured by law, by constitutional custom and by professional and public opinion.[31] Since the Act of Settlement 1700, judges of the superior English courts have held office during good behaviour and not at the pleasure of the executive. One essential function of the judiciary is to protect the citizen against unlawful acts of government agencies and officials. It is the duty of the courts, if proper application is made to them by a citizen adversely affected, to check administrative authorities from exceeding their powers and to direct the performance of duties owed by officials to private citizens.[32] Only an independent judiciary can impartially perform these tasks

---

[28]   Ch. 33.
[29]   Ch. 19 A.
[30]   Ch. 19 C.
[31]   Ch. 19 A.
[32]   Chs. 34–6.

of administrative law. So too, within the EEC, it is the duty of the Court of Justice to ensure that the acts of the Community organs comply with the treaties on which the Community system is based.

(*c*)   Do the executive and judiciary exercise each other's functions? The value of an independent judiciary would be reduced if essential judicial functions, for example the conduct of civil and criminal trials, were removed from the courts and entrusted to administrative authorities. But many disputes which arise out of the administration of public services today are not suitable for decision by ordinary litigation. Many administrative tribunals are now entrusted with the task of resolving disputes between two citizens (for example rent tribunals) or between a citizen and a government department (for example social security tribunals). It is accepted that tribunals form part of the machinery of justice and should carry out their work independently of the departments concerned.[33] Tribunals therefore exercise judicial functions, even if they do so by procedures less formal than those used in the courts. There are nonetheless many matters which are entrusted not to tribunals but to government departments and ministers for decision. Procedures like the public inquiry have been established to maintain standards of fairness and openness but do not provide for a decision independent of the department concerned. It is because a decision is required in which full account may be taken of departmental policy, rather than a decision based on a judicial application of existing rules, that these matters remain subject to departmental or ministerial decision.[34]

It is not possible to draw a sharp distinction between decisions which should be entrusted to courts and tribunals on the one hand, and decisions which should be entrusted to administrative authorities on the other. When a new statutory scheme is introduced, a wide choice may be exercised between the different procedures available for deciding disputes likely to arise under the scheme. The separation of powers affords little direct guidance as to how particular categories of dispute should be settled, except to remind us that decisions which are to be made independently of political influence should be entrusted to courts or tribunals, and that decisions for which ministers are to be responsible to Parliament should be entrusted to government departments.

Local judges, such as the magistrates in England and the sheriffs in Scotland, still have administrative duties surviving from the days when they were the principal agents of local administration. While the exercise of administrative functions by inferior courts may cause uncertainty about the proper role of the court in dealing with local policy issues,[35] it has for so long been a feature of local government that it causes less controversy than would a corresponding confusion of roles at the national level.

In *Gouriet* v. *Union of Post Office Workers*, the House of Lords re-asserted the distinction between executive responsibility for enforcing the criminal law and the judicial function. In the Court of Appeal, Lord Denning M. R. had asked

---

[33]   Ch. 37 A.
[34]   Ch. 37 B.
[35]   *Glasgow Corpn.* v. *Glasgow Churches Council* 1944 S.C. 97; *Sagnata Investments Ltd* v. *Norwich Corpn* [1971] 2 Q.B. 614.

the rhetorical question (referring to a situation in which a trade union was instructing its members to commit a criminal offence), 'Are the courts to stand idly by?'. The House of Lords rejected this suggestion that the civil courts had some executive authority in relation to the criminal law.[36]

Judiciary and legislature

Finally, the relationship between the judiciary and the legislature:

(*a*) Do the same persons exercise legislative and judicial functions? All full-time judicial appointments disqualify for membership of the Commons. In the House of Lords, the Lord Chancellor presides over the House sitting in its legislative capacity; he is also entitled to preside over the Appellate Committee which discharges the judicial work of the House. The Lords of Appeal in Ordinary who sit as judges in the Appellate Committee occasionally take part in the legislative business of the House; but they do not sit as members of a political party and observe restraint in the topics they debate. Because of this, there is here no substantial infringement in practice of separation of powers. Lay peers by long-established convention do not take part in the hearing of appeals.[37]

(*b*) Is there any control by the legislature over the judiciary or by the judiciary over the legislature? By statute judges of the superior courts may be removed by the Crown on an address from both Houses, but only once since the Act of Settlement has Parliament exercised the power of removal.[38] The rules of debate in the Commons protect judges from certain forms of criticism. Apart from the lay magistracy in England, inferior judges have statutory protection against arbitrary dismissal by the executive. Under the Tribunals and Inquiries Act 1971, the members of tribunals are protected against removal from office by the appointing government department.[39]

While the courts may examine acts of the executive to ensure that they conform with the law, the doctrine of legislative supremacy denies the courts the power to review the validity of legislation. The judges are under a duty to apply and interpret the laws enacted by Parliament.[40] The effect of their decisions may be altered by Parliament both prospectively and also, if necessary, retrospectively. In one sense, therefore, the courts are constitutionally subordinate to Parliament, but the courts are bound only by Acts of Parliament and not by resolutions of each House, which may have no legal force.[41] The European Communities Act 1972 provides an outstanding example of the control which the legislature may exercise over the judiciary: by section 3, the courts are required to follow the case-law of the European Court of Justice in dealing with matters of Community law and to take full account of the reception of Community law into the United Kingdom.

(*c*) Do the legislature and judiciary exercise each other's functions? The judicial functions of the House of Lords have already been discussed. Each

---

36   [1978] A.C. 435; p. 662 *post.*
37   Page 327 *post.*
38   Page 334 *post.*
39   Ch. 37 A.
40   Note 6 *ante.*
41   *E.g. Bowles* v. *Bank of England* [1913] 1 Ch. 57; ch. 5.

House of Parliament has power to enforce its own privileges and to punish those who offend against them. This power might in some circumstances lead to a direct conflict with the courts.[42]

Because of the doctrine of precedent, the judicial function of declaring and applying the law has a legislative effect, whether in areas of common law or in statutory interpretation. But the scope for creating law by judicial decision is much narrower than the scope for legislation by Parliament; the courts have sometimes been criticised for creating new and uncertain criminal offences under the form of declaring the common law, for example the crime of conspiracy to corrupt public morals.[43] In the field of police powers, on which Parliament before 1984 had not legislated in a comprehensive way, not only have the courts had to apply ancient precedents to modern conditions[44] but in England the judiciary twice exercised a plainly legislative function in making the Judges' Rules, which were not rules of law in the strict sense but which gave authoritative guidance to the police in questioning and taking statements from suspects.[45] Indeed the improvised procedure by which new Judges' Rules were formulated in 1964 was open to criticism since it afforded no opportunity for democratic participation or consultation with interested parties.[46] The rules of precedent themselves are entirely judge-made, except where, as in the European Communities Act 1972, statute has intervened. In 1966 the House of Lords, sitting extra-judicially, announced that it would in future be prepared to depart from a former decision by the House when it appeared right to do so.[47]

As a source of law, judicial decision is particularly important in areas where government and Parliament are unwilling to legislate directly. This applies not only to the area of police powers and civil liberties, but also in administrative law. The executive is understandably slow to propose new measures exposing itself to more effective judicial control. In 1968, the House of Lords departed from a rule it had previously laid down in holding that the courts had power to overrule a claim by a government department to withhold a document from production as evidence in civil litigation on the ground of Crown privilege.[48] It is very unlikely that the government would have proposed to Parliament that the law should be amended in the manner thus declared judicially by the House of Lords. Many matters of government policy are best challenged and defended in Parliament, but judicial control of executive acts is a necessary complement to parliamentary control.

Summary

In the absence of a written constitution, there is no formal separation of powers in the United Kingdom. No Act of Parliament may be held unconstitutional on the ground that it seeks to confer powers in breach of the doctrine. While

---

[42] Ch. 12 A.

[43] *Shaw* v. *D.P.P.* [1962] A.C. 220; ch. 27 B.

[44] See *e.g. Ghani* v. *Jones* [1970] 1 Q.B. 695; p. 487 *post.*

[45] Ch. 26 C.

[46] The Royal Commission on Criminal Procedure recommended that the Judges' Rules be replaced by statutory rules: Cmnd 8092, 1981, pp. 107–8; p. 485 *post.*

[47] [1966] 3 All E.R. 77. Between 1898 and 1966, a contrary rule had prevailed: *London Street Tramways Co.* v. *LCC* [1898] A.C. 375.

[48] *Conway* v. *Rimmer* [1968] A.C. 910; p. 697 *post.*

the functions of legislative and executive are closely inter-related, and ministers are members of both, the two institutions of Parliament and government are distinct from each other. The formal process of legislation is different from the day-to-day conduct of government, just as the legal effect of an Act of Parliament differs from that of an executive decision. Practical necessity demands a large measure of delegation by Parliament to the executive of power to legislate. The independence of the judiciary is maintained, but many disputes which arise out of the process of government are entrusted not to the courts but to administrative tribunals: these tribunals are expected to observe the essentials of fair judicial procedure.

The effect of British membership of the European Communities is that the organs of the Communities may now exercise legislative, executive and judicial powers in respect of the United Kingdom. While judicial powers are exercisable by the European Court, whose independence is guaranteed, legislative authority is vested in the Council of Ministers, representing the governments of the member states. But in general this authority is not exercised except after extensive preparatory work by the Commission, and after consultation with the European Parliament.[49] Constitutional experience at a national level suggests that the excessive concentration of power in any single organ of government is a greater danger to liberty than departures from a formal separation of powers.

While the classification of the powers of government into legislative, executive and judicial powers involves many conceptual difficulties (for example, no sharp boundary can be drawn between judicial and administrative functions, or between legislation and administration), within a system of government based on law it remains important to distinguish in constitutional structure between the primary functions of law-making, law-executing and law-adjudicating. If these distinctions are abandoned, the concept of law itself can scarcely survive.

---

[49] Ch. 8.

Chapter 5

Parliamentary supremacy

A. The growth of the legislative authority of Parliament

Before examining the legal meaning of the supremacy of Parliament today, we may consider briefly the main stages by which the legislative dominance of Parliament came to be established.

It was recognised in the middle ages that an Act of Parliament could change the common law. With the Reformation there disappeared the idea that there were certain ecclesiastical doctrines that Parliament could not touch. Henry VIII and Elizabeth I made the Crown of England supreme over all persons and causes and used the English Parliament to attain this end. Even in the 17th century it was contended that there were certain natural laws which were immutable,[1] but the common lawyers were the allies of Parliament in the struggle with the Crown and, to defeat the Crown's claim to rule by prerogative, conceded that the common law could be changed by Parliament.[2]

The struggle for supremacy

Legislative supremacy involves not only the right to change the law but also that no one else should have that right. In many spheres the King's prerogative at the beginning of the 17th century was undefined and the King exercised through the Council a residue of judicial power which enabled him to enforce his prerogative powers. Acts of Parliament which purported to take away any of the inseparable prerogatives of the Crown were considered invalid[3] but this view of the royal prerogative could not survive the political challenge from Parliament.

1 Ordinances and proclamations A clear distinction between the statutes of the English Parliament and the ordinances of the King in Council was

---

[1] *Bonham's* case (1610) 8 Co. Rep. 114a; J. W. Gough, *Fundamental Law in English Constitutional History.*

[2] Dicey, Introduction by E. C. S. Wade (at page c.).

[3] 'No Act of Parliament can bar a King of his regality.': *The Case of Ship Money* (1637), 3 St. Tr. 825, Finch C. J., at 1235. A valuable account of the leading 17th century cases on prerogative is given in D. L. Keir and F. H. Lawson, *Cases in Constitutional Law*, ch. II.

lacking long after the establishment of the Model Parliament at the end of the 13th century. The Statute of Proclamations 1539 gave Henry VIII wide but not unlimited powers of legislating without reference to Parliament by proclamation, which had replaced the ordinance as a form of legislation. This statute did not give to the King and Council power to do anything that they pleased by royal ordinance, but was an attempt to deal with the obscure position of the authority possessed by proclamations. It safeguarded the common law, existing Acts of Parliament and rights of property, and prohibited the infliction of the death penalty for a breach of a proclamation.[4] 'Its chief practical purpose was undoubtedly to create machinery to enforce proclamations'.[5] Despite the repeal of this statute in 1547, Mary and Elizabeth continued to resort to proclamations. The judicial powers of the Council, and in particular of the Court of Star Chamber, were available to enforce proclamations. The scope of the royal prerogative to legislate remained undefined. James I made full use of this power, with the result that in 1611 Chief Justice Coke was consulted by the Council, along with three of his brother judges, about the legality of proclamations. The resulting opinion is to be found in the *Case of Proclamations*:

1 The King by his proclamation cannot create any offence which was not one before; for then he might alter the law of the land in a high point; for if he may create an offence where none is, upon that ensues fine and imprisonment.

2 The King hath no prerogative but what the law of the land allows him.

3 But the King for the prevention of offences may by proclamation admonish his subjects that they keep the laws and do not offend them upon punishment to be inflicted by law; the neglect of such proclamation aggravates the offence.

4 If an offence be not punishable in the Star Chamber, the prohibition of it by proclamation cannot make it so.[6]

A definite limit was thus put upon the prerogative, the full force of which was effective only when the Star Chamber and other conciliar tribunals were abolished in 1640. The gist of the *Case of Proclamations* is that the King's prerogative is under the law, and that Parliament alone can alter the law which the King is to administer.

2 Taxation The imposition of taxes is a matter for legislation. Inevitably taxation was a major issue between the Stuart Kings and Parliament. If the Crown could not levy taxes without the consent of Parliament, the will of Parliament must in the long run prevail. It had been conceded by the time of Edward I that the consent of Parliament was necessary for direct taxation. The history of indirect taxation is more complicated, since the regulation of foreign trade was a part of the royal prerogative in relation to foreign affairs. There was no clear distinction between the imposition of taxes by way of customs duties and the prerogative powers in relation to foreign trade and defence of the realm.

---

4 H.E.L., vol. IV, pp. 102–3.
5 G. R. Elton in E. B. Fryde and E. Miller, *Historical Studies of the English Parliament*, II, p. 206.
6 (1611) 12 Co. Rep. 74. This case was applied by the Court of Session in *Grieve* v. *Edinburgh and District Water Trustees* 1918 S.C. 700.

In the *Case of Impositions (Bate's Case)*,[7] John Bate refused to pay a duty on imported currants imposed by the Crown on the ground that its imposition was contrary to the statute 45 Edw. 3 c.4 which prohibited indirect taxation without the consent of Parliament. The Court of Exchequer unanimously decided in favour of the Crown. The King could impose what duties he pleased for the purpose of regulating trade, and the court could not go behind the King's statement that the duty was in fact imposed for the regulation of trade.

In the *Case of Ship Money*, (*R.* v. *Hampden*)[8] John Hampden refused to pay ship money, a tax levied by Charles I for the purpose of furnishing ships in time of national danger. Counsel for Hampden conceded that sometimes the existence of danger would justify taking the subject's goods without his consent, but only in actual as opposed to threatened emergency. The Crown conceded that the subject could not be taxed in normal circumstances without the consent of Parliament, but contended that the King was the sole judge of whether an emergency justified the exercise of his prerogative power to raise funds to meet a national danger. A majority of the Court of Exchequer Chamber gave judgment for the King.[9]

The decision was reversed by the Long Parliament,[10] and this aspect of the struggle for supremacy was concluded by the Bill of Rights, article 4 of which declared that it was illegal for the Crown to seek to raise money without Parliamentary approval.[11]

3 Dispensing and suspending powers The power of the Crown to dispense with the operation of statutes within certain limits may at one time have been necessary having regard to the form of ancient statutes and the irregular meetings of Parliament. So long, however, as the limits upon the dispensing power were not clearly defined, there was here a threat to the legislative supremacy of Parliament. In the leading case of *Thomas* v. *Sorrell*,[12] the court took care to define the limits within which the royal power to dispense with laws was acceptable. But in *Godden* v. *Hales* the court upheld a dispensation from James II to Sir Edward Hales excusing him from taking religious oaths and fulfilling other obligations imposed by the Test Act; it was held that it was an inseparable prerogative of the Kings of England to dispense with penal laws in particular cases and upon necessary reasons of which the King is sole judge.[13]

Fortified by the latter decision, James II proceeded to set aside statutes as he pleased, granting a suspension of the penal laws relating to religion in the Declarations of Indulgence in 1687 and 1688. These acts of James were an immediate cause of the revolution of 1688. The Bill of Rights abolished the Crown's alleged power of suspending laws and also prohibited the Crown's power to dispense with the operation of statutes, except where this was author-

---

7   (1606) 2 St. Tr. 371; G. D. G. Hall, (1953) 69 L.Q.R. 200.
8   (1637) 3 St. Tr. 825.
9   For a full analysis, see D. L. Keir (1936) 52 L.Q.R. 546.
10 Shipmoney Act 1640.
11 Page 14 *ante.*
12 (1674) Vaughan 330.
13 (1686) 11 St. Tr. 1165.

ised by Parliament.[14] Similar provision was made in the Scottish Claim of Right.[15]

4 The independence of the judiciary So long as the tenure of judicial office depended upon the royal pleasure there was a risk of the subservience of judges to the Crown. To ensure that English judges should not hold office at pleasure of the Crown, the Act of Settlement 1700 provided that they should hold office *quamdiu se bene gesserint* (during good behaviour) but subject to a power of removal upon an address from both Houses of Parliament.[16]

Growth of ministerial responsibility

The Bill of Rights and the Act of Settlement established the legislative authority of the English Parliament *vis-a-vis* the Crown, while preserving the prerogatives of the Crown in matters which had not been called in question. But it was not yet recognised that the responsibility of the King's ministers could best be achieved through their presence in Parliament. The process of impeachment was not too drastic to be used as the everyday method of ensuring that a minister should not disregard the will of Parliament. In the 18th century the nature of the struggle changed. The Crown and its ministers could not be allowed to govern without responsibility to Parliament in those matters which still fell within the royal prerogative. The first step was to ensure the individual responsibility of ministers to Parliament for their actions, and secondly, collective responsibility for general policy and for the actions of other ministers.[17]

The real point of transition to Cabinet government came with the accession of the House of Hanover in 1714. The absence of George I from meetings of the Cabinet made it essential that a minister should preside at these meetings. Here is to be found the beginning of the office of Prime Minister. Thereafter the leaders of the parties sought to exercise power by maintaining a majority of supporters in the Commons. The methods to which both Whigs and Tories resorted included the acquisition of pocket boroughs and the grant of pensions, sinecure offices and government contracts. During the period of personal rule by George III between 1763 and 1782, the same methods of maintaining support in Parliament were adopted but even these methods failed to maintain parliamentary support for royal policies on the loss of the American colonies and the fall of Lord North in 1782.

With the coming of parliamentary reform in 1832 it became no longer possible to govern by these means. Instead of reliance on influence and patronage, it came to be accepted that ministers must hold the same political views as the majority in Parliament and, as the electoral system was further reformed, that the executive must be responsive to the will of the electorate.

---

[14] Articles 1 and 2 of the Bill of Rights, p. 14 *ante*. The Bill of Rights did not curtail the prerogative of pardon nor the power to enter a *nolle prosequi*. Nor were all earlier dispensations declared invalid: Anson, vol. 1, p. 351. *Cf.* the present practice of granting extra-statutory concessions in taxation, p. 293 *post*.

[15] Page 15 *ante*.

[16] See now Supreme Court Act 1981, s.11(3). Ch. 19 A.

[17] Ch. 7.

The result of the constitutional conflict between Commons and Lords in 1909–1911 was to leave the House of Commons in a dominant position within Parliament. Thus the legislative authority of Parliament came to be based upon the political support of the electorate for the party with a majority of seats in the elected House.

B.   Meaning of legislative supremacy

In this brief historical summary, we have examined the rise of Parliament to be at the centre of our constitutional system. We now consider the legal doctrine of the legislative supremacy of Parliament. This doctrine is referred to by many writers, and notably by Dicey, as the sovereignty of Parliament. New constitutional developments are often debated in terms of their supposed effect on the sovereignty of Parliament. This was best seen in the debate about British membership of EEC; those opposed to British membership proposed, without success, an amendment to the Bill which became the European Communities Act 1972 declaring that British membership would not affect the sovereignty of Parliament.[1] Such debates are often confused because of the wide variety of meanings attributable to the sovereignty of Parliament. In this chapter, the expression legislative supremacy will be used, partly because, as a less familiar expression, its use should give rise to less misunderstanding; partly because it is less likely to be confused with the notion of sovereignty in international law; but mainly to avoid importing into constitutional law the jurisprudential doctrine of John Austin and his successors that in every legal system there must be a sovereign.[2]

By the legislative supremacy of Parliament is meant that there are no legal limitations upon the legislative competence of Parliament. Parliament here does not refer to the two Houses of Parliament individually, for neither House has authority to legislate on its own, but to the constitutional phenomenon known as the Queen in Parliament: namely the legislative process by which a Bill approved by Lords and Commons may receive the royal assent and thus become an Act of Parliament. Thus defined, Parliament, said Dicey, has 'under the English constitution, the right to make or unmake any law whatever; and further that no person or body is recognised by the law of England as having a right to override or set aside the legislation of Parliament'.[3] Now Dicey was writing at a time when England was often used as a loose synonym for Great Britain or the United Kingdom,[4] and today it is necessary to discuss whether the law on this matter is the same throughout the United Kingdom.[5] But the positive and negative aspects of the doctrine emerge clearly from Dicey's formulation, namely that power to legislate on any matter whatsoever is vested in Parliament and that there exists no competing authority with power either to legislate for the United Kingdom or to impose limits upon the legislative competence of Parliament.

---

[1] H.C. Deb., 5 Jul. 1972, cols. 556–644; H.L. Deb., 7 Aug. 1972, cols. 893–914.
[2] J. Austin, *The Province of Jurisprudence Determined*, Lecture 6.
[3] Dicey, pp. 39–40.
[4] Ch. 3.
[5] Section D, *post*.

Legal nature of legislative supremacy

It needs to be emphasised that this doctrine consists essentially of a rule which governs the legal relationship between the courts and the legislature, namely that the courts are under a duty to apply the legislation made by Parliament and may not hold an Act of Parliament to be invalid or unconstitutional. 'All that a court of law can do with an Act of Parliament is to apply it'.[6] In *Madzimbamuto* v. *Lardner-Burke*, which concerned the effect of the unilateral declaration of independence in 1965 by the Rhodesian government upon the Westminister Parliament's power to legislate for Rhodesia, it was said:

It is often said that it would be unconstitutional for the UK Parliament to do certain things, meaning that the moral, political and other reasons against doing them are so strong that most people would regard it as highly improper if Parliament did these things. But that does not mean that it is beyond the power of Parliament to do such things. If Parliament chose to do any of them, the courts could not hold the Act of Parliament invalid.[7]

While the legal content of legislative supremacy has great political significance, the legal rule is not to be confused with statements about the political dominance of the House of Commons or the Cabinet within the legislative process. Of course, it would be unacceptable politically if the House of Commons were today to be constituted as it was in the 18th century, if the Lords were today able freely to reject measures approved by the Commons, or if the Sovereign today were able to exercise a personal discretion in deciding whether or not to assent to Bills approved by both Houses. But the doctrine of legislative supremacy is not primarily concerned with the political process which goes on before a Bill receives the royal assent: it is confined to the much narrower question of the legal effect that should be assigned by the courts to an Act of Parliament.

Only an Act of Parliament is supreme

The courts ascribe to an Act of Parliament a legal force which they are not willing to ascribe to other instruments which for one reason or another fall short of being an Act of Parliament. Thus the courts do not attribute legislative supremacy to the following and will if necessary decide whether or not they have legal effect:

(*a*)   a resolution of the House of Commons;[8]

(*b*)   a proclamation or other document issued by the Crown under prerogative powers for which the force of law is claimed;[9]

(*c*)   a treaty entered into by the government under prerogative powers which seeks to change the law within territory subject to British jurisdiction;[10]

(*d*)   an instrument of subordinate legislation which appears to be issued under the authority of an Act of Parliament by a minister or a government depart-

---

[6]   D. L. Keir and F. H. Lawson, *Cases in Constitutional Law*, p. 1.

[7]   [1969] 1 A.C. 645, 723. And see *Manuel* v. *A.-G.* [1983] Ch. 77.

[8]   *Stockdale* v. *Hansard*, (1839) 9 A. & E. 1; *Bowles* v. *Bank of England* [1913] 1 Ch. 57.

[9]   *Case of Proclamations* (p. 61 *ante*).

[10]   *The Parlement Belge* (1879) 4 P.D. 129, 154; *A.-G. for Canada* v. *A.-G. for Ontario* [1937] A.C. 326. *Cf. Malone* v. *Metropolitan Police Commissioner* [1979] Ch. 344.

ment,[11] even though this has been approved by resolution of each House of Parliament;[12]

(e)   an act of a subordinate legislature within the United Kingdom;[13]

(f)   byelaws made by a public corporation or local authority.[14]

In all such cases, the courts must consider whether the document for which legislative force is claimed is indeed legally binding.

Position different under written constitution

The doctrine of legislative supremacy distinguishes the United Kingdom from those countries in which a written constitution imposes limits upon the legislature and entrusts the ordinary courts or a constitutional court with the function of deciding whether the acts of the legislature are in accordance with the constitution. In *Marbury* v. *Madison*, the US Supreme Court held that the judicial function vested in the court necessarily carried with it the task of deciding whether an Act of Congress was or was not in conformity with the constitution.[15] In a constitutional system which accepts judicial review of legislation, legislation may be held invalid on a variety of grounds: for example, because it conflicts with the separation of powers where this is a feature of the constitution,[16] or infringes human rights guaranteed by the constitution,[17] or has not been passed in accordance with the procedure laid down in the constitution.[18] By contrast, in the United Kingdom the legislative supremacy of Parliament appears to be the fundamental rule of constitutional law and this supremacy includes power to legislate on constitutional matters. In so far as constitutional rules are contained in earlier Acts, there seems to be no Act which Parliament could not repeal or amend by passing a new Act. The Bill of Rights could in law be abrogated by the same process as a Prevention of Damage by Pests Act, namely by a repealing measure passed in ordinary form.

Legislative supremacy illustrated

The apparently unlimited powers of Parliament may be illustrated by many Acts of constitutional significance. The Tudor Kings used Parliament to legalise the separation of the English church from the church of Rome: Sir Thomas More was executed in 1535 for having denied the authority of Parliament to make Henry VIII supreme head of the church. In 1715, Parliament passed the Septennial Act to extend the life of Parliament (including its own) from three to seven years, because it was desired to avoid an election so soon after the Hanoverian accession and the 1715 uprising in Scotland. In vain did opponents of the Act argue that the supreme legislature must be restrained 'from subverting the foundation on which it stands'.[19] Less controversially, the Parliament elected in December 1910 was dissolved in 1918, having five times

---

[11]   *E.g. Chester* v. *Bateson* [1920] 1 K.B. 829; ch. 33.

[12]   *Hoffmann-La Roche* v. *Sec. of State for Trade & Industry* [1975] A.C. 295.

[13]   *Belfast Corpn* v. *OD Cars Ltd* [1960] A.C. 490.

[14]   *E.g. Kruse* v. *Johnson* [1898] 2 Q.B. 91.

[15]   (1803) 1 Cranch 137.

[16]   *Liyanage* v. *R.* [1967] 1 A.C. 259; *Hinds* v. *The Queen* [1977] A.C. 195, p. 53 *ante*.

[17]   *E.g. Aptheker* v. *Secretary of State* 378 U.S. 500 (1964) (Act of U.S. Congress refusing passports to Communists held an unconstitutional restriction on right to travel).

[18]   *Harris* v. *Minister of Interior* 1952 (2) S.A. 428.

[19]   Quoted in G. Marshall, *Parliamentary Sovereignty and the Commonwealth*, p. 84.

extended its own existence, which had been limited to five years by its own enactment, the Parliament Act 1911. So too did the Parliament elected in 1935 prolong its own existence until 1945.[20]

Parliament has altered the succession to the throne (in the Act of Settlement 1700 and His Majesty's Declaration of Abdication Act 1936); removed prerogative powers from the Crown; reformed the composition of both Houses of Parliament; dispensed with the approval of the House of Lords for certain Bills (the Parliament Acts 1911 and 1949); given effect to British membership of the European Communities (the European Communities Act 1972); given effect to the Scottish and Irish Treaties of Union and has departed from those treaties;[21] altered the territorial limits of the United Kingdom[22] and so on. Parliament has even provided that certain provisions contained in an Act shall be subject to challenge in the courts as if they had merely been contained in subordinate legislation.[23]

Indemnity Acts and retrospective legislation

Moreover Parliament has exercised the power to legalise past illegalities and to alter the law retrospectively. This power has been used by an executive with a secure majority in Parliament to reverse inconvenient decisions of an impartial judiciary.[24] After the first world war, during which a number of illegal acts were committed in the interest of the prosecution of the war, two Indemnity Acts were passed; after the second world war, more limited retrospective legislation was passed.[25] Retrospective laws are, however,

prima facie of questionable policy and contrary to the general principle that legislation by which the conduct of mankind is to be regulated ought . . . to deal with future acts and ought not to change the character of past transactions carried on upon the faith of the then existing law . . . Accordingly the court will not ascribe retrospective force to new laws affecting rights unless by express words or necessary implication it appears that such was the intention of the legislature.[26]

Retrospective laws may not only confirm irregular acts but may also authorise what was lawful when done to be punished, or subjected to other adverse action by the executive. The Immigration Act 1971 was held to have conferred powers on the Home Office to deport Commonwealth citizens who had entered in breach of earlier immigration laws but against whom no such action could have been taken under those laws at the time the 1971 Act came into effect:[27] but the Act did not make punishable by criminal sanctions conduct which had occurred before the Act was passed.[28] Although article 7 of the European Convention on Human Rights, to which the United Kingdom

---

[20]   *E.g.* Prolongation of Parliament Act 1944.
[21]   Ch. 3, and Section D *post.*
[22]   Island of Rockall Act 1972.
[23]   National Insurance Act 1965, s. 116(2).
[24]   War Damage Act 1965 (*Burmah Oil Co.* v. *Lord Advocate* [1965] A.C. 75); Northern Ireland Act 1972 (*R.* (*Hume* et al.) v. *Londonderry Justices* 1972 N.I.L.R. 91); Education (Scotland) Act 1973 (*Malloch* v *Aberdeen Corpn* 1974 S.L.T. 253); National Health Service (Invalid Direction) Act 1980 (*Lambeth BC* v. *Secretary of State* (1980) 79 L.G.R. 61).
[25]   Indemnity Act 1920 and War Charges Validity Act 1925; Enemy Property Act 1953, ss. 1–3.
[26]   Per Willes J. in *Phillips* v. *Eyre* (1870) L.R. 6 Q.B. 1, 23.
[27]   *Azam* v. *Home Secretary* [1974] A.C. 18.
[28]   *Waddington* v. *Miah* [1974] 2 All E.R. 377.

is a party, provides that no one shall be held guilty of any criminal offence on account of conduct which did not constitute an offence at the time when it was committed,[29] Parliament has power to legislate retrospectively in breach of that provision: but, as Lord Reid has said, 'it is hardly credible that any government department would promote or that Parliament would pass retrospective criminal legislation'.[30] Legislation which authorises payments to be made to individuals in respect of past events is also retrospective, but plainly less objectionable.[31]

Legislative supremacy and international law

So far as British courts are concerned, the legislative supremacy of Parliament is not limited by international law. The courts may not hold an Act void on the ground that it contravenes general principles of international law.

The Herring Fishery (Scotland) Act 1889 authorised a fishery board to make byelaws prohibiting certain forms of trawling within the Moray Firth, an area which included much sea that lay beyond British territorial waters. The Danish master of a Norwegian trawler was convicted in a Scottish court for breaking these byelaws. The High Court of Justiciary held that its function was confined to interpreting the Act and the byelaws, and that Parliament had intended to legislate for the conduct of all persons within the Moray Firth, whatever might be the position in international law. 'For us an Act of Parliament duly passed by Lords and Commons and assented to by the King is supreme, and we are bound to give effect to its terms'.[32]

Nor may the courts hold an Act invalid because it conflicts with a treaty to which the United Kingdom is a party.

An assessment to income tax was challenged on the ground that part of the tax raised was used for the manufacture of nuclear weapons, contrary to the Geneva Convention Act 1957. It was held that the unambiguous provisions of a statute must be followed even if they are contrary to international law. Regarding an argument that tax had been imposed for an improper purpose, the judge said: 'What the statute itself enacts cannot be unlawful, because what the statute says and provides is itself the law, and the highest form of law that is known to this country'.[33]

So far as the British courts are concerned, there are no territorial restrictions on the legislative competence of Parliament. Generally Parliament legislates only in respect of its own territory or in respect of the conduct of its own citizens when they are abroad, but occasionally legislation is intended to operate outside the United Kingdom: thus the Continental Shelf Act 1964 vested in the Queen the rights of exploration and exploitation of the continental shelf; the Act also provided for the application of criminal and civil law in respect of conduct relating to any installations which are placed with the

---

[29] Ch. 31 B.
[30] [1974] 2 All E.R. 377, 379; and see *R.* v. *Home Secretary, ex p. Bhajan Singh* [1976] Q.B. 198.
[31] *E.g.* Employment Act 1982, s. 2 and sch. 1.
[32] Per Lord Dunedin in *Mortensen* v. *Peters* (1906) 8 F. (J.) 93, 100. The Trawling in Prohibited Areas Prevention Act 1909 later made it an offence to land in the UK fish caught in prohibited areas of the sea, thus limiting the extra-territorial effect of the earlier ban.
[33] Per Ungoed-Thomas J. in *Cheney* v. *Conn* [1968] 1 All E.R. 779, 782; and see *Inland Revenue Commissioners* v. *Collco Dealings Ltd* [1962] A.C. 1.

authority of a minister in the surface waters above the continental shelf.[34] A few serious crimes committed in a foreign state by UK citizens are justiciable in this country, such as treason, murder, manslaughter, bigamy and certain revenue offences.[35] But in general the United Kingdom makes very few of its criminal laws specifically applicable to its citizens while abroad, and the courts apply a rule of interpretation that statutes will not be given extra-territorial effect even as to UK citizens, unless this is expressly provided or necessarily implied.[36] By general principles of international law, the United Kingdom may not exercise jurisdiction in territory belonging to a foreign state. Sir Ivor Jennings suggested that Parliament could make it an offence to smoke in the streets of Paris, while recognising that only courts in the United Kingdom would be bound to take any notice of the new offence.[37] In practice Parliament refrains from passing laws which would be contrary to the comity of nations. Yet on a given matter the law in Britain may be inconsistent with Britain's international obligations. While the government by virtue of the royal prerogative has authority to enter into treaties, these treaties cannot themselves alter the law to be applied within the United Kingdom, but require to be approved or adopted by Act of Parliament if national law is to be altered.[38] While for some purposes international law may be part of national law, it yields to statute.[39]

British membership of the European Communities raises problems concerning the relationship between UK law and Community law which cannot be resolved by application of the general principles just discussed and which will be considered later.[40]

No legal limitations upon Parliament

It is therefore possible to give many illustrations of the use which Parliament has made of its legislative supremacy in legislating on constitutional matters, retrospectively, in breach of international law, and so on. It does not follow from a recital of this kind that the powers of Parliament are unlimited. As Professor Calvert has said,

No one doubts that the powers of the UK Parliament are extremely wide ... But that is not what is in issue. What is in issue is whether those powers are unlimited and one no more demonstrates this by pointing to a wide range of legislative objects than one demonstrates the contrary by pointing to matters on which Parliament has not, in fact, ever legislated.[41]

There is a great deal of evidence from the law reports that, at least since 1688, judges have been strongly inclined to accept the legislative omnicom-

---

34   See also Marine etc. Broadcasting (Offences) Act 1967, following *Post Office* v. *Estuary Radio* [1968] 2 Q.B. 740.

35   Law Commission, Report No. 91, 'Territorial and Extra-territorial Extent of Criminal Law', 1978, pp. 36–41.

36   *Treacey* v. *DPP* [1971] A.C. 537, 552. And see *R.* v. *Kelly* [1982] A.C. 665.

37   Jennings, *Law and Constitution*, pp. 170–1.

38   Note 10 *ante*.

39   Cases cited in note 33 *ante*.

40   Page 81 *post* and ch 8 B.

41   *Constitutional Law in Northern Ireland*, p. 14.

petence of Parliament. Yet this has not always been the judicial attitude. In his note on *Dr Bonham's* case, Coke C. J. said:

In many cases, the common law will control Acts of Parliament, and sometimes adjudge them to be utterly void: for when an Act of Parliament is against common right and reason, or repugnant, or impossible to be performed, the common law will control it, and adjudge such Act to be void.[42]

While English judges made similar statements only rarely after 1688,[43] it is not possible by legal logic alone to demonstrate that they have utterly lost the power to 'control' an Act of Parliament — or to show that a judge who is confronted with a statute fundamentally repugnant to moral principle (for example a law condemning all of a certain race to be executed) must either apply the statute or resign his office.[44]

Short of such an extreme situation, it is very unlikely that the courts would of their volition begin to exercise power derived solely from common law to review the validity of Acts of Parliament. Where in modern constitutional systems judicial review of legislation does take place, this is always derived from a written constitution. But in the United Kingdom, Parliament enjoys an unlimited power to legislate on constitutional matters. Is it therefore possible that, *on the initiative of Parliament itself*, the courts could begin to exercise a power of judicial review derived from constitutional legislation passed by Parliament? This possibility has often been dismissed out of hand by invocation of the principle that no Parliament may bind its successors. It has been said that the rule that the courts enforce without question all Acts of Parliament is the one rule of the common law which Parliament may not change.[45] But, it has been asked, 'Why cannot Parliament change that rule; since all other rules of the common law are subject to its sovereignty?'[46] It is to this difficult and fundamental question that we now turn.

C. The continuing nature of parliamentary supremacy

Within a modern legal system, enacted laws remain in force until they are repealed or amended, unless they are declared when enacted to have a limited duration.[1] It is inherent in the nature of a legislature that it should continue to be free to make new laws. The fact that legislation about, say, divorce or

---

[42]   (1610) 8 Co. Rep. 113b, 118a. And see S. E. Thorne, (1938) 54 L.Q.R. 543.

[43]   *E.g.* per Holt C.J., *City of London* v. *Wood* (1702) 12 Mod. 669, 687.

[44]   *Cf.* Jennings, *Law and Constitution*, pp. 159–60. For the attitude that British courts should take to foreign legislation which infringes fundamental rights, see *Oppenheimer* v. *Cattermole* [1976] A.C. 249 and F. A. Mann (1978) 94 L.Q.R. 512.

[45]   H. W. R. Wade, [1955] C.L.J. 172, 187–9.

[46]   E. C. S. Wade, Introduction to Dicey, p. lv; and see articles by Lord Hailsham, *The Times*, 12, 16, 19 and 20 May 1975.

[1]   This has always been the position in English law (S. G. G. Edgar, *Craies on Statute Law*, pp. 406–12). But in respect of Scottish Acts passed before 1707, by the doctrine of desuetude a statute may cease to be law through non-use and change of circumstances: see *M'Ara* v. *Magistrates of Edinburgh* 1913 S.C. 1059 and J. D. B. Mitchell, *Constitutional Law*, pp. 21–2. Even if the doctrine of desuetude applied to Acts of the UK Parliament, this would not seem materially to affect the legislative supremacy of Parliament. For a discussion of legislative obsolescence, see C. K Allen, *Law in the Making*, pp. 478–82.

slum-housing was enacted five or fifty years ago is no reason why fresh legislation on the same subject should not be enacted today: even if social
conditions have not changed, a newly elected legislature may favour a fresh
approach. If a legislature wishes to alter a law previously enacted, it is
convenient if the new Act expressly repeals the old law or states the extent to
which the old law is amended. Suppose that this is not done, and a new Act
is passed which conflicts with an older Act but does not expressly repeal it.
There now appear to be two inconsistent statutes on the statute-book. How
is the apparent conflict to be resolved? And by whom?

The doctrine of implied repeal

It is for the courts to resolve this conflict because it is their duty to decide the
law which applies to a given situation. Where two Acts conflict with each
other, the courts apply the Act which is later in time, and any earlier Act
inconsistent with the later Act is taken to have been repealed by implication:
leges posteriores priores contrarias abrogant.

> If two inconsistent Acts be passed at different times, the last must be obeyed, and if
> obedience cannot be observed without derogating from the first, it is the first which
> must give way . . . Every Act is made either for the purpose of making a change in the
> law, or for the purpose of better declaring the law, and its operation is not to be
> impeded by the mere fact that it is inconsistent with some previous enactment.[2]

This doctrine is to be found in all legal systems, but in Britain its operation
is sometimes considered to have special constitutional significance.

Before 1919, many public and private Acts of Parliament empowered public authorities
to acquire land compulsorily and laid down many differing rules of compensation. In
1919, the Acquisition of Land (Assessment of Compensation) Act was passed to provide
a uniform code of rules for assessing the compensation to be paid in future. Section 7(1)
provided: 'The provisions of the Act or order by which the land is authorised to be
acquired, or of any Act incorporated therewith, shall, in relation to the matters dealt
with in this Act, have effect subject to this Act, and so far as inconsistent with this Act
those provisions shall cease to have or shall not have effect'. The Housing Act 1925
sought to alter the 1919 rules of compensation by reducing the compensation payable
in respect of slum-housing. In *Vauxhall Estates Ltd* v. *Liverpool Corporation*,[3] it was held
that the provisions of the 1925 Act must prevail over the 1919 Act so far as they were
inconsistent with it. The court rejected the ingenious argument of counsel for the
owners whose slum property had been acquired that section 7(1) (and especially the
words 'or shall not have effect') had tied the hands of future Parliaments so that the
later Parliament could not (short of express repeal) legislate inconsistently with the
1919 Act. In a similar case, *Ellen Street Estates Ltd* v. *Minister of Health*, Maugham L. J.
said: 'The Legislature cannot, according to our constitution, bind itself as to the form
of subsequent legislation, and it is impossible for Parliament to enact that in a subsequent statute dealing with the same subject-matter there can be no implied repeal. If
in a subsequent Act Parliament chooses to make it plain that the earlier statute is being
to some extent repealed, effect must be given to that intention just because it is the will
of Parliament'.[4]

---

[2]   Lord Langdale, in *Dean of Ely* v. *Bliss* (1842) 5 Beav. 574, 582.
[3]   [1932] 1 K.B. 733.
[4]   [1934] K.B. 590, 597; Wilson, *Cases*, p. 260.

The correctness of these two decisions is not in doubt, for there were very weak grounds for suggesting that in 1919 Parliament had been attempting to bind its successors. But Maugham L. J. went far beyond the actual situation in saying that Parliament could not bind itself as to the *form* of subsequent legislation. He would have been closer to the facts of the case had he said that Parliament could not bind itself as to the *contents* of subsequent legislation.[5] However, these cases, which illustrate the doctrine of repeal by implication, have been used to support a much broader constitutional argument that Parliament may never bind its successors.[6]

Can Parliament bind its successors?

The rule that Parliament may not bind its successors (and that no Parliament is bound by Acts of its predecessors) is often cited both as a limitation upon legislative supremacy and as an example of it. To adopt for a moment the language of sovereignty: if it is an essential attribute of a legal sovereign that there should be no legal restraints upon him, then by definition the rules laid down by a predecessor in office cannot bind the present sovereign, for otherwise the present holder of the post would not be sovereign. Dicey, outstanding exponent of the sovereignty of Parliament, accepted this point:

The logical reason why Parliament has failed in its endeavours to enact unchangeable enactments is that a sovereign power cannot, *while retaining its sovereign character*, restrict its own powers by any parliamentary enactment. (italics supplied)[7]

Thus to state that no Parliament may bind its successors is to assume that all future Parliaments must have the same attribute of sovereignty as the present Parliament. But why must this be so? The problem is less intractable than the comparable conundrum of whether an omnipotent deity can bind itself[8] for even sovereign parliaments are human institutions; and there is nothing inherently impossible in the idea of a supreme Parliament having power to make fresh constitutional arrangements for the future. Merely to state that Parliament may not bind its successors leaves unclear both the nature of the obligation which a present Parliament is unable to impose on its successors, and also the meaning of 'successors'.[9] Indeed it may be shown that the doctrine that Parliament may not bind its successors is an over-simplification.

(*a*)   Some matters authorised by legislation are of such a kind that once done, they cannot be undone by further Act. Thus, over 60 years after Parliament approved the cession of Heligoland to Germany in 1890, Parliament repealed the statute by which cession was approved.[10] But in so doing, Parliament had no expectation that this would recover the territory for the United Kingdom. When Parliament confers independence upon a colony, as it has done on many occasions, it has been the practice since 1960 to provide that no future Act of

---

[5]   H. R. Gray, (1953) 10 Univ. of Toronto L.J. 54, 67.

[6]   *Cf.* H. W. R. Wade [1955] C.L.J. 172, 187 and E. C. S. Wade, Introduction to Dicey, p. xlix.

[7]   Dicey, p. 68.

[8]   *Cf.* H. L. A. Hart, *The Concept of Law*, p. 146; G. Marshall, *Parliamentary Sovereignty and the Commonwealth*, p. 13; and H. R. Gray, (1953) 10 Univ. of Toronto L.J. 54.

[9]   R. Stone, (1966) 26 Louisiana Law Rev. 753, 755.

[10]   Anglo–German Agreement Act 1890, repealed by Statute Law Revision Act 1953, s.1, sch. 1.

the UK Parliament 'shall extend or be deemed to extend' to the independent country as part of its law; and that the UK government should thereafter have no responsibility for the government of the country in question.[11] Earlier Independence Acts were less categorical in their terms, since it was thought that in some circumstances it might be convenient for the Westminster Parliament to continue to legislate for the territory at the request of the territory concerned.[12] In earlier times it was suggested that provisions conferring legislative independence could be revoked by the Westminster Parliament;[13] but the truer position is that conferment of independence is an irreversible process: 'freedom once conferred cannot be revoked'.[14] Thus, by ceding territory or conferring independence, Parliament may restrict the geographical area of effective legislation by future Parliaments. In the Canada Act 1982, which conferred full power of constitutional amendment upon Canada, it was provided that no subsequent Act of the UK Parliament 'shall extend to Canada as part of its law'.[15] If Westminster in future should seek to reverse the historical clock by attempting to legislate for Canada, the Canadian courts would ignore any such attempt, unless the Canadian Parliament had authorised them to give effect to the legislation from Westminster. But British courts would be bound to give effect to the Westminster legislation so far as it lay within their jurisdiction to do so.[16]

(b) In a different way, Parliament may bind future Parliaments by altering the rules for the composition of the two Houses of Parliament or the succession to the throne. Thus in 1832, when Parliament reconstituted the House of Commons to secure more democratic representation, later Parliaments were bound by that legislation inasmuch as the only lawful House of Commons was one elected in accordance with the 1832 Act. If it had been subsequently desired to revert to the pre-1832 composition of the House, this would have required the concurrence of the reformed House.[17] The same would be true of every occasion on which the composition of the Commons has been reformed since 1832. The same would also apply to legislative reform of the Lords (for example the introduction of life peerages in 1958) subject only to the possibility that under the Parliament Acts 1911 and 1949 any such reform could be reversed without the approval of the reformed House of Lords.[18] In 1936, His Majesty's Declaration of Abdication Act altered the line of succession to the throne laid down by the Act of Settlement 1700, by removing Edward VIII and his issue from the succession: if a later Parliament had wished the throne to revert to Edward VIII, the assent of the Sovereign for the time being (*i.e.* George VI or his descendant) would have been required, just as Edward VIII's assent was needed for the Abdication Act itself. In other words, the

---

[11] *E.g.* Kenya Independence Act 1963, s. 1; and see K. Roberts-Wray, *Commonwealth and Colonial Law*, p. 261.
[12] Statute of Westminster 1931, s. 4 and *e.g.* Ceylon Independence Act 1947, s. 1; ch. 24.
[13] *British Coal Corpn* v. *R.* [1935] A.C. 500, 520.
[14] *Ndlwana* v. *Hofmeyr* 1937 A.D. 229, 237; *Ibralebbe* v. *R.* [1964] A.C. 900, 923; *Blackburn* v. *A.-G.* [1971] 2 All E.R. 1380.
[15] App. A.
[16] *Manuel* v. *A.-G.* [1983] Ch. 77, 88.
[17] H. R. Gray, *op. cit.*, p. 63.
[18] Ch. 11 B.

supreme Parliament may alter the rules which determine who the successors of the component parts of the supreme Parliament are to be (and, it might be added, may abolish one of these component parts *e.g.* the House of Lords, though this issue deserves separate discussion below).

By contrast with these examples, an illustration may be given of the principle that a supreme Parliament may not bind its successors. Parliament may create subordinate legislatures, whether for parts of the United Kingdom or for colonies, without depriving itself of legislative authority for the territory concerned. Thus the Government of Ireland Act 1920, which established a legislature for the domestic affairs of Northern Ireland, did not (unlike earlier proposed schemes or home rule for Ireland[19]) affect the Westminster Parliament's continuing legislative authority for Northern Ireland. To avoid any doubt, whether legal or political, section 75 of the Act provided that the supreme authority of Parliament should remain undiminished in respect of Northern Ireland. The Westminster Parliament retained full authority to legislate for Northern Ireland and to abolish the legislature it had established:[20] this authority did not depend upon the inclusion of section 75 in the 1920 Act.[21] In respect of British colonies, the legislative supremacy of the UK Parliament was not abrogated by the mere existence of a colonial legislature, even though, for political reasons, its legislative authority would not normally be exercised. In the case of Rhodesia, the legislative authority of Westminster was exercised in 1965 after the unilateral declaration of independence by Ian Smith's government had caused a serious breach in the conventional relationship between Rhodesia and the United Kingdom, and again in 1979 when a settlement of the Rhodesian question was reached.[22]

The rule that Parliament may not bind its successors presents difficulties for certain forms of constitutional reform (for example, the creation of an entrenched Bill of Rights, to be discussed below). But it presents no obstacle to the adoption of a wholly new constitutional structure for the United Kingdom. As was said about Gladstone's first Home Rule Bill for Ireland, 'if the Irish Government Bill had become law the Parliament of 1885 would have had no successors'.[23] The object of securing that no subsequent Parliament enjoyed the attribute of legislative supremacy could be achieved in a variety of ways, for example by creating a federal system in the United Kingdom under which England, Scotland, Wales and Northern Ireland would each have its own legislature and executive; these bodies, together with a federal legislature and executive, would all be subject to the constitution as interpreted by a federal court. The creation of such a system would be inconsistent with the continuance of the legislative supremacy of Parliament. The legislative ground for the new constitution would be laid by the supreme Parliament before it ceased to exist.

With the possible exception of the Union between Scotland and England in 1707 and the Union between Ireland and Great Britain in 1800,[24] no actual

---

[19]   W. R. Anson, (1886) 2 L.Q.R. 427.
[20]   Northern Ireland (Temporary Provisions) Act 1972 and Northern Ireland Assembly Act 1973.
[21]   Neither the Scotland Act 1978 nor the Wales Act 1978 contained sections preserving the supremacy of Westminster, contrary to the original intention of the government.
[22]   Pages 430–3 *post.*
[23]   W. R. Anson, *op. cit.*, p. 436.
[24]   Ch. 3; and Section D *post.*

constitutional reforms have been intended to go as far as this. Instead, as with British accession to the European Communities,[25] problems have arisen only where the clear intention of Parliament to divest itself of legislative supremacy has not been manifested and where, therefore, it may be argued that the overriding rule of supremacy has not been affected. The question is not, 'May a supreme Parliament bind its successors?' but 'What must a supreme Parliament do (a) to express the definite intention that future Parliaments should not be supreme? and (b) to ensure (whether by positive direction or structural changes) that the courts will in future give effect to that intention?' The second part of the question is important: for if the matter were to rest merely on the intention of the present Parliament, it is likely that the courts would hold that a later Parliament would be free to depart from that intention. Moreover, it is only by subsequent judicial decisions, taken against the background of accompanying political developments, that it would be known whether or not the present (supreme) Parliament had successfully achieved its stated objective. To avoid the period of uncertainty that would otherwise ensue, it has been suggested as a simple form of entrenchment that the judges be required to take a fresh oath to observe the new scheme.[26] But if anything less than a completely new constitution were proposed, it would set a very undesirable precedent for Parliament to require the judges to take an oath to be loyal to a new piece of constitutional apparatus. Difficulties would arise if some judges refused to co-operate.

Before these matters are considered further, one question which has already been mentioned[27] needs to be more fully examined, namely the need for legal rules identifying the measures which are judicially accepted as Acts of Parliament.

What is an Act of Parliament?[28]

In an extremely simple community, where all powers within the human group are exercised by one man recognised as sovereign, no legal problems of identifying acts of the sovereign arise. But, as R. T. E. Latham said:

Where the purported sovereign is anyone but a single actual person, the designation of him must include the statement of rules for the ascertainment of his will, and these rules, since their observance is a condition of the validity of his legislation, are rules of law logically prior to him.[29]

Latham pointed out that Parliament, regarded only as an assembly of human beings, was not sovereign. 'It can only be sovereign when acting in a certain way prescribed by law. At least some rudimentary "manner and form" is demanded of it: the simultaneous incoherent cry of a rabble, small or large, cannot be law, for it is unintelligible.'[30]

In the absence of a written constitution to guide the courts in identifying stances a Bill may become an Act without having been approved by the Lords.

---

[25] Ch. 8.
[26] H. W. R. Wade, *Constitutional Fundamentals*, pp. 37–9.
[27] Page 65 *ante*.
[28] R. T. E. Latham, (1939) King's Counsel 152 and G. Marshall (1954) 2 Political Studies 193.
[29] *The Law and the Commonwealth*, p. 523; compare Hart's 'rule of recognition', *The Concept of Law*, (pp. 75, 245, and ch. 6).
[30] (1939) King's Counsel, 153, quoted in Heuston, *Essays*, pp. 7–8.

an Act of Parliament, the definition of an Act of Parliament is primarily a matter of common law.[31] The rule of English common law is that for a Bill to become law, it must have been approved by Lords and Commons and have received the royal assent. In the ordinary case, this simple test will be satisfied by a rapid inspection of the Queen's Printer's copy of an Act of Parliament which will bear at its head formal words of enactment.[32] When Acts of Parliament have been challenged on the ground of procedural defects during their passage through Parliament, the judges have laid down the 'enrolled Act' rule.

In *Edinburgh & Dalkeith Railway* v. *Wauchope*, a private Act which adversely affected Wauchope's rights against a railway company was challenged by Wauchope on the ground that notice of its introduction as a Bill into Parliament had not been given to him, as required by standing orders of the House of Commons. The court rejected this challenge. Lord Campbell said: 'All that a court of justice can do is to look to the Parliament roll: if from that it should appear that a Bill has passed both Houses and received the Royal Assent, no court of justice can inquire into the mode in which it was introduced into Parliament, or into what was done previous to its introduction, or what passed in Parliament during its progress in its various stages through both Houses'.[33] And in *Lee* v. *Bude & Torrington Railway Co.*, concerning similar facts, it was said: 'If an Act of Parliament has been obtained improperly, it is for the legislature to correct it by repealing it; but, so long as it exists as law, the courts are bound to obey it.'[34]

This principle was reaffirmed in 1974, when the House of Lords in *Pickin* v. *British Railways Board* held that a local or private Act of Parliament was binding whether or not the standing orders of each House of Parliament had been complied with.

Private Acts of 1836 and 1845 authorised the taking of land for a railway and provided that, if the line were ever abandoned, the land should vest in the owners of the adjoining land. In 1968, another private Act was passed, promoted by the British Railways Board, which abolished this rule. In 1969, Pickin bought a small piece of adjoining land and, when the railway was discontinued, claimed a declaration that under the 1836 and 1845 Acts he was entitled to a strip of the old line. He alleged that the board had fraudulently misled Parliament when promoting the 1968 Act, and had not complied with the standing orders of each House requiring individual notice to be given to owners affected by private legislation. Although the Court of Appeal held that these allegations raised a triable issue,[35] the House of Lords held that the courts had no power to disregard an Act of Parliament, whether public or private, nor had they any power to examine proceedings in Parliament to determine whether an Act had been obtained by irregularity or fraud.[36]

There are several reasons for this reluctance of the courts to inquire into the internal procedures of Parliament. One important reason is the privilege of each House to regulate its own proceedings.[37] There would be serious

---

31   Sir Owen Dixon, (1957) 31 A.L.J. 240. And see *Prince's Case* (1606) 8 Co. Rep. 1, 20b.
32   Interpretation Act 1978, s.3. And see *Manuel* v. *A.-G.* [1983] Ch. 77, 87.
33   (1842) 8 Cl. and F. 710, 725; Wilson, *Cases*, p. 243.
34   Per Willes J., (1871) L.R. 6 C.P. 577, 582.
35   [1973] Q.B. 219.
36   [1974] A.C. 765; Wilson, *Cases*, p. 244.
37   Ch. 12 A.

procedural difficulties if officers of Parliament were summoned before a court to give evidence about the internal proceedings of Parliament as well as a danger of the courts infringing article 9 of the Bill of Rights.[38] On many matters of parliamentary procedure, the courts have declined to intervene whether or not alleged breaches of statute were involved.[39] The rule that a Bill must be read three times in each House is not a requirement of the common law but is part of the *lex et consuetudo Parliamenti* and upon this the standing orders of each House are based. If one House wished to alter the requirement, say by abolishing the third reading, this change would not affect the validity of subsequent Acts.

But some comments must be made on the 'enrolled Act' rule. First, there is today no Parliament roll: in case of necessity, all that a court could inspect is the two vellum prints of an Act which since 1849 have been signed by the Clerk of Parliaments and preserved in the Public Record Office and the House of Lords library.[40] Secondly, the rule is reinforced by the rule in the Interpretation Act 1978 that every Act passed after 1850 shall be a public Act and judicially noticed as such, unless the contrary is expressly provided by the Act.[41] Thirdly, if it should appear that a measure has not been approved by one House, then (unless the Parliament Acts 1911–49 apply) the measure is not an Act.[42] Fourthly, where there is a written constitution, this may itself lay down the procedures which must be followed before a Bill can become an Act. Thus in South Africa, the constitution provided that certain entrenched rights could be revoked only by legislation adopted at a joint sitting of both Houses of the South African Parliament, voting by a two-thirds majority: where this procedure was not followed, the court held that the result was not a valid Act of Parliament.[43]

Could the 'enrolled Act' rule be changed by Act of Parliament? To an extent it has already been modified by statute. Thus the Regency Acts 1937–53 make permanent provision for the infancy, incapacity or temporary absence abroad of the Sovereign.[44] A regent appointed under these Acts may exercise all royal functions, including assenting to Bills, except that he may not assent to a Bill for changing the order of succession to the Crown or for repealing or altering the Act of 1707 securing Presbyterian Church Government in Scotland. If, which is unlikely, a regent did assent to a Bill for one of these purposes, there seems no reason why the courts should regard the resulting measure as an Act of Parliament.

Similarly, the Parliament Acts 1911–49[45] provide that in certain circumstances a Bill may become an Act without having been approved by the Lords.

---

38 Page 14 *ante*.
39 *Bradlaugh* v. *Gossett* (1884) 12 Q.B.D. 271; *Bilston* v. *Wolverhampton Corpn* [1942] Ch. 391; *Harper* v. *Home Secretary* [1955] Ch. 238; *Rediffusion (Hong Kong) Ltd* v. *A.-G. of Hong Kong* [1970] A.C. 1136, discussed by O. Hood Phillips in (1971) 87 L.Q.R. 321. And generally see B. Beinart, [1954] S.A.L.R. 135.
40 Heuston, *Essays*, p. 18; and Erskine May, p. 605.
41 For an explanation of this rule, see *Craies on Statute Law, op. cit.*, pp. 55–8.
42 *The Prince's Case* (1606) 8 Co. Rep. 1a; Erskine May, pp. 606–8.
43 *Harris* v. *Minister of Interior* 1952 (2) S.A. 428. For a full account, see G. Marshall, *Parliamentary Sovereignty and the Commonwealth*, Part 3.
44 Ch. 13 A.
45 Ch. 11 B.

The 1911 Act provides special words of enactment which refer to the Parliament Acts (section 4(1)) and also provide that the Speaker's certificate that the requirements of the Acts have been complied with shall be conclusive for all purposes (s. 3). But the Parliament Acts procedure does not apply either to a Bill to extend the life of Parliament or to private or local Bills. If it were attempted to extend the life of Parliament by a measure which had not been approved by the Lords, a court could decline to regard the result as an Act of Parliament: the 'conclusiveness' of the Speaker's certificate would not necessarily be enough to bar such a decision by the court.[46]

In respect both of the Regency Acts and the Parliament Acts, it has been argued that measures which become law thereunder are not Acts of the supreme Parliament but are Acts of a subordinate legislature to which the supreme Parliament has made a limited delegation of its powers; such measures are thus no more than delegated legislation.[47] But in other contexts, courts have been reluctant to apply the principle *delegatus non potest delegare* to a legislature[48] and a preferable view is that, for all but the purposes excluded, Parliament has provided a procedure for legislation which is alternative to the procedure of legislation by the supreme Parliament recognised at common law.[49] On this view, the legal definition of an Act of Parliament may already differ according to the circumstances, as it may where a written constitution requires special procedures or special majorities for certain purposes.[50]

There continues, however, to be doubt whether Parliament may by statute alter the legal rules for identifying an Act of Parliament. In *Pickin's* case, Lord Morris said:

It must surely be for Parliament to lay down the procedures which are to be followed before a Bill can become an Act. It must be for Parliament to decide whether its decreed procedures have in fact been followed.[51]

This statement needs to be read with great care. First, it was made in the context of an alleged departure from the standing orders of the House of Commons. Second, where there is a written constitution prescribing special legislative procedures for constitutional purposes, we have already seen that the enforcement of these procedures may be a matter for the courts. Third, Lord Morris's use of 'Parliament' is ambiguous. Are the procedures for legislation to be laid down by the Queen in Parliament (*i.e.* by statute) or by each House of Parliament separately (*i.e.* by standing orders and resolutions)? If the procedures for legislation were to be laid down by statute, so that a new statutory definition of an Act of Parliament (for all or some purposes) replaced the former common law rule, why should the courts continue to observe the former common law rule rather than the new statutory definition?

---

[46]   Section 3 of the 1911 Act requires that the Speaker's certificate shall be given 'under this Act'; in interpreting this section, a court might hold that the test of *ultra vires* had not been ousted: *cf. Minister of Health* v. *R.* [1931] A.C. 494 and *Anisminic Ltd* v. *Foreign Compensation Commission* [1969] 2 A.C. 147, p. 671 *post*.

[47]   O. Hood Phillips, *Constitutional and Administrative Law*, pp. 89–90; H. W. R. Wade, [1955] C. L. J. 172, 193–4 and *Constitutional Fundamentals*, pp. 27–8.

[48]   *R.* v. *Burah* (1878) 3 App. Cas. 889 and *Hodge* v. *R.* (1883) 9 App. Cas. 117 (power of colonial legislature to delegate).

[49]   P. Mirfield, (1979) 95 L.Q.R. 36, 47–50.

[50]   Note 43 *ante*.

[51]   [1974] A.C. 765, 790.

While it concerned a colonial legislature, the Judicial Committee's decision in *Attorney-General for New South Wales* v. *Trethowan*[52] may be of some relevance.

Under the Colonial Laws Validity Act 1865, the legislature of the state of New South Wales had full power to make laws respecting its own constitution, powers and procedure, provided that these laws were passed 'in such manner and form' as might from time to time be required by an Act of Parliament or other law for the time being in force in the state. In 1929 an Act provided that the upper House of the legislature should not be abolished until a Bill approved by both Houses had been approved by a referendum of the electorate; the requirement of a referendum applied also to amendments of the 1929 Act. Following a change of government, a Bill passed through both Houses which sought to abolish both the upper House and the requirement of a referendum. The government did not intend to submit the Bill to a referendum. An injunction was granted by the New South Wales court to restrain the government of New South Wales presenting the Bill to the Governor for the royal assent unless and until a majority of the electors had approved it. On appeal, the Judicial Committee held that the requirement of a referendum was binding on the legislature until it had been abolished by a law passed in the 'manner and form' required by law for the time being, *i.e.* with the approval of a referendum.

Two views may be held of *Trethowan's* case. The first is that the decision depended on the fact that the New South Wales legislature was a subordinate legislature, subject to the Colonial Laws Validity Act 1865 of the UK Parliament which, as stated, expressly laid down the 'manner and form' rule. On this view, the decision is not relevant to the present discussion.[53] The opposing view is that there is at common law a rule that legislation may be enacted only in such manner and form as is laid down by law and that the decision is therefore applicable to the UK Parliament.[54] While this may be so, *Trethowan's* case has little authority on this more general issue, since the decision of the Judicial Committee was expressly based on the effect of section 5 of the Colonial Laws Validity Act. In relation to the remedy of injunction granted by the Australian court, *Trethowan's* case presents problems that were not before the Judicial Committee. A British court might well hold that such a remedy was unavailable, because of section 21 of the Crown Proceedings Act 1947,[55] and inappropriate, because of the undesirability of judicial intervention in the relationship between ministers, Parliament and the Crown.[56] But there is nothing in *Trethowan* which diminishes the force of the argument that some kind of 'manner and form' rule to identify the acts of the legislature is essential within a legal system.

Summary
The argument so far may be summarised as follows. In principle a legislature must remain free to enact new laws on matters within its competence: if a conflict occurs between two laws enacted by Parliament, the courts apply the

---

52 [1932] A.C. 526, discussed in Marshall, *Parliamentary Sovereignty and the Commonwealth*, ch. 8, and W. Friedmann, (1950) 24 A.L.J. 103.
53 H. W. R. Wade [1955] C. L. J. 172, 183; E. C. S. Wade, Introduction to Dicey, pp. lxxiii–v.
54 *E.g.* Jennings, *Law and Constitution*, p. 153; Latham, (1939) King's Counsel 152, 161; Friedmann, (1950) 24 A.L.J. 103, 104; Dixon (1935) 51 L.Q.R. 590, 603.
55 Ch. 36.
56 G. Sawer, (1944) 60 L.Q.R. 83; see also *Rediffusion (Hong Kong) Ltd* v. *Attorney-General of Hong Kong* [1970] A.C. 1136, especially the comments of Dixon C.J. cited at p. 1156.

later of the two laws. The authority of Parliament includes power to legislate on constitutional matters, including both the composition of Parliament and the 'manner and form' by which new legislation may be made. While the courts may not of their own accord review the validity of the internal proceedings of Parliament, the scope for judicial decision could be extended if Parliament by statute altered the common law rules according to which the courts recognise or identify an Act of Parliament. The doctrine of parliamentary supremacy is no bar to the adoption of a written constitution for the United Kingdom which imposes judicially enforceable limits upon a future legislature, at least if such structural changes are made that the new legislative process appears radically different from the present process of legislation by Lords, Commons and royal assent. Much greater difficulty would arise if radical changes were *not* made in the structure of the legislature but the attempt was made to impose limits or restrictions upon the present legislature; in this situation, the courts might well not regard the purported limits or restrictions as being effective to oust the continuing legislative supremacy of Parliament. The matter therefore remains open. While Parliament could alter the 'manner and form' of the legislative process, such an attempt would not be effective if the courts still gave allegiance to the supreme Parliament defined in common law.

These general principles will now be discussed briefly in relation to some current constitutional problems.

1 Constitutional guarantees for Northern Ireland[57]   The United Kingdom of Great Britain and Ireland was established when the Irish Acts of Union took effect in 1801. An account is given elsewhere of the events by which Southern Ireland broke from the United Kingdom.[58] In the Ireland Act 1949, the UK Parliament recognised the republican status of Southern Ireland and its complete cessation from being part of the Crown's dominions. That Act also recognised the position of Northern Ireland within the United Kingdom by declaring in section 1(2):

that Northern Ireland remains part of His Majesty's dominions and of the United Kingdom and it is hereby affirmed that in no event will Northern Ireland or any part thereof cease to be part of His Majesty's dominions and of the United Kingdom without consent of the Parliament of Northern Ireland.[59]

The 1949 Act gave no express guarantee of the continued existence of the Parliament of Northern Ireland. That Parliament was suspended in 1972 and abolished in 1973 by Westminster. This made it necessary for the guarantee of Northern Ireland's status to be given a new form. The Northern Ireland Constitution Act 1973, section 1, provides that Northern Ireland shall not cease to be part of the United Kingdom without the consent of the majority of the people of Northern Ireland voting in a border-poll.[60] The guarantee is of great political significance. But has Parliament fettered itself from, say,

---

[57]   Calvert, *op. cit.*, pp. 23–33; Heuston, *Essays*, ch. 1.
[58]   Ch. 3.
[59]   For an analogous provision in Gladstone's First Home Rule Bill, see Marshall, *Parliamentary Sovereignty and the Commonwealth*, pp. 63–6.
[60]   See the Northern Ireland (Border Poll) Act 1972.

ceding Londonderry to the Republic of Ireland without first obtaining the consent of the majority of the people of Northern Ireland? Or could Parliament at a future date merely repeal the 1973 Act and provide nothing in its place? The strongest legal argument for the proposition that Parliament could not in law breach the 1973 guarantee is that for the purposes of legislating for the future status of Northern Ireland, Parliament has redefined itself so that an additional stage, namely approval by a border-poll, is required. But would the courts be disposed to hold that this intention had been sufficiently clearly expressed in the 1973 Act, and that a subsequent Parliament had lost the legal capacity to repeal the 1973 Act, either expressly or by implication? And would a court, whether in Northern Ireland or in Britain, assume jurisdiction in the matter? This would involve accepting also (a) that an individual had legal standing in the matter (*locus standi*) and (b) that the courts could grant effective relief (whether by way of injunction or a declaratory remedy). Probably the question of remedy is more problematic than that of *locus standi*: and issues that were not fully considered by the Judicial Committee in *Trethowan's* case would be relevant.[61] It has been suggested that the Northern Ireland guarantee is an example of a limitation which Parliament may impose on itself but which does not incapacitate Parliament from acting.[62] On this basis, presumably the 1973 Act is effective so long as it remains in force (in giving a continuing guarantee to the people of Northern Ireland) but the guarantee, like that in the 1949 Act, might in law be withdrawn by Parliament.

2 British membership of the European Communities A later chapter will outline the structure of the European Communities, and will discuss the relationship between UK law and Community law. Community law has been held by the European Court of Justice to prevail over any inconsistent provisions of the national law of the member states:

No provisions of municipal law, of whatever nature they may be, may prevail over Community law . . . lest it be deprived of its character as Community law and its very legal foundation be endangered.[63]

By the European Communities Act 1972, legal effect was given within the United Kingdom to those provisions of Community law which were, according to the European Treaties, intended to have direct effect within member states. This applied both to existing treaties and regulations and also to any future Community treaties or regulations. The Community organs therefore may legislate for the United Kingdom, as they do for other member states. While Britain remains a member of the Communities, the statement that only the Westminster Parliament has power to make new law for the United Kingdom is therefore untrue. Nor can Community law appropriately be described as delegated legislation.[64]

---

61 Marshall, *op. cit.*, pp. 105–13.
62 Mitchell, *Constitutional Law*, p. 81.
63 The *Internationale Handelsgesellschaft* case, (1972) 11 C.M.L.R. 255, 283. The translation quoted is by G. Bebr, (1971) 23 M.L.R. 481, 492. And see the *Simmenthal* case (1978) 3 C.M.L.R. 263, p. 121 *post*.
64 *Cf.* Cmnd 3301, 1967, para. 22.

In what other respects is the legislative supremacy of Parliament affected by British membership? Possibly the most important question is how in the future British courts will resolve any conflicts that there may be between Acts of Parliament passed after 1972 and EEC regulations issued after 1972. One view of the effect of sections 2(1), 2(4) and 3 of the 1972 Act is that the British courts have been required in any case of conflict to give effect to the EEC regulation as against any inconsistent UK statute. If this view is correct, then in 1972 Parliament did bind its successors as to the form of subsequent legislation, by altering the former doctrine of the *implied* repeal of statutes. How far, if at all, it has altered the doctrine of *express* repeal is a different question. Certainly Parliament could expressly repeal the 1972 Act in its entirety. But, short of that, has Parliament disabled itself from expressly legislating contrary to an EEC regulation? If such a situation arose, the attitude of the European Court is not in doubt: but a British court that failed to resolve the conflict by means of interpretation[65] would have a difficult choice to make between following the express provision of Parliament in the later Act or the doctrine of the European Court.[66]

3 A new Bill of Rights for the United Kingdom   The doctrine that Parliament may not bind its successors presents a major obstacle in the way of a new Bill of Rights in so far as this is intended to have any controlling effect upon later Parliaments. No such problem would arise if the Bill of Rights were to apply solely to subordinate legislation and administrative decisions,[67] but some have argued that it is essential to limit the power of future Parliaments to infringe human rights.[68] If a completely new constitutional structure for the United Kingdom were to be created, protection for fundamental rights could be included within it. Short of that, are there ways by which Parliament could entrench fundamental rights against infringement by Parliament? A select committee of the House of Lords, appointed to consider a Bill of Rights proposed by the Liberal peer, Lord Wade, gave a negative answer to this question in 1978. The committee's view was that:

there is no way in which a Bill of Rights could protect itself from encroachment, whether express or implied, by later Acts. The most that such a Bill could do would be to include an interpretation provision which ensured that the Bill of Rights was always taken into account in the construction of later Acts and that, so far as a later Act could be construed in a way that was compatible with a Bill of Rights, such a construction would be preferred to one that was not.[69]

It was on this basis that a Bill providing for the incorporation of the European Convention on Human Rights was approved by the House of Lords in 1979.[70] In brief, the Bill provided that the European Convention should prevail over any earlier enactments (clause 2); in the case of conflict between

---

[65]   *Garland* v. *British Rail Engineering Ltd.* [1983] 2 A. C. 751.
[66]   Ch. 8 B.
[67]   Ch. 31 C.
[68]   *E.g.* L. Scarman, *English Law – the New Dimension*, p. 15.
[69]   H.L. 176 (1977–8), para. 23.
[70]   H. L. Deb., 6 Dec. 1979, col. 915. Government opposition prevented the Bill making any progress in the Commons.

the Convention and any later enactment, the later Act was to be deemed to be subject to the Convention and must be so construed 'unless such subsequent enactment provides otherwise or does not admit of any construction compatible with the provisions' of the Convention (clause 3). Clause 3 thus recognised the possibility of express repeal in the future, and also of implied repeal whenever any later Act could not be interpreted in a manner compatible with the Convention.

In 1977, the Northern Ireland Standing Advisory Commission on Human Rights had recommended legislation that went further than this, namely that no subsequent Act that was inconsistent with the European Convention should have effect unless the later Act expressly declared that it should apply notwithstanding the Convention.[71] On this basis, implied repeal would have been totally barred. But in 1978 the select committee of the House of Lords stated that this solution was excluded by the *Vauxhall Estates* and *Ellen Street Estates* cases considered above.[72] Until government opinion moves in favour of creating a new Bill of Rights, the choice to be made about the legal form which it should take remains academic.[73] But the problem of entrenchment should not be seen as a constitutional technicality, since it raises fundamental questions about the future power of the courts to review legislation by Parliament.

4 Abolition of the House of Lords   In chapter 11B we will examine the present role of the House of Lords under the Parliament Acts 1911 and 1949. Here we will deal only with the issue of whether, as one of the component parts of the supreme legislature, the House of Lords can be abolished.[74] There would indeed be a significant change in fundamental legal doctrine if 'whatever the Queen, Lords and Commons enact is law' were to become 'whatever the Queen and Commons enact is law' If, as has been argued above, the former proposition is ultimately grounded upon decisions of the courts, the latter proposition would be authoritatively established only when the courts accepted the legislative supremacy of the Queen and Commons in place of the former supreme legislature. Arguably this change could be regarded as a legal revolution or a breach in legal continuity.[75] But this would not seem to be a significant description of the event if the courts had merely given effect to a constitutional change initiated and authorised by the former legislature.

Two issues of greater practical significance might arise. First, if the Act abolishing the House of Lords also included a Bill of Rights which was declared to be incapable of amendment by the new legislature (Queen and Commons), the courts would then have a choice between whether (a) to give effect to the stated intention of the former legislature, by holding that the Bill of Rights must prevail over any Acts passed by the new legislature or (b) to hold that the new legislature was as legislatively supreme as its predecessor.

---

[71]   Cmnd 7009, 1977.
[72]   Page 71 *ante*. And see the opinion given to the committee by D. Rippengal Q.C. (H.L. 81, 1977–8, pp. 1–10).
[73]   For a full discussion, see J. Jaconelli, *Enacting a Bill of Rights, the Legal Problems.*
[74]   For the main arguments, see P. Mirfield (1979) 95 L.Q.R. 36 and G. Winterton (1979) 95 L.Q.R. 386. And Dicey, pp. 64–70.
[75]   Mirfield, *op. cit.*, pp. 42–5.

Since the courts might not wish to create a legislative vacuum (i.e. a situation in which certain legislation is totally impossible), the outcome might depend on whether any procedure was provided in case of special need for encroachment upon the Bill of Rights.

Second, could the abolition of the House of Lords be lawfully carried out against the wishes of the House of Lords, by use of the procedures under the Parliament Acts 1911 and 1949? The answer depends essentially upon whether the legislative powers conferred by the Parliament Act 1911 on the House of Commons and the Crown are to be construed subject to implied limitations, over and above those that are expressed in the 1911 Act itself.[76] Since the analogy of delegated legislation does not seem a close one, it is submitted that an Act passed under the Parliament Act procedure could lawfully abolish the House of Lords; such a measure might be resisted on political grounds but not by challenge in the courts.[77]

D. The Treaty of Union between England and Scotland

In Section C, we have discussed the question whether the UK Parliament may impose legal limitations upon its successors. The Anglo-Scottish Union of 1707 raises the different question, 'was the UK Parliament born unfree?'[1] The main features of the Treaty of Union have already been outlined.[2] Now it is necessary to examine more closely those provisions of the Treaty concerning the power to legislate after the Union.

The Treaty clearly contemplated that the new Parliament of Great Britain would legislate both for England and Scotland; but no grant of general legislative competence to Parliament was made in the Treaty. Article 18 provided that the laws concerning regulation of trade, as well as customs and excise duties, should be uniform throughout Britain; subject to this, all other laws within Scotland were to remain in force

but alterable by the Parliament of Great Britain, with this difference betwixt the laws concerning public right, policy, and civil government, and those which concern private right; that the laws which concern public right, policy and civil government may be made the same throughout the whole united kingdom, but that no alternation be made in laws which concern private right except for evident utility of the subjects within Scotland.

By article 19, the Court of Session and the Court of Justiciary were to remain 'in all time coming' within Scotland as they were then constituted, and with the same authority and privileges as before the Union, 'subject nevertheless to such regulations for the better administration of justice as shall be made by the Parliament of Great Britain'. Other courts were to be subject to regulation and alteration by Parliament. No causes in Scotland were to be cognoscible (i.e. capable of being heard) by the Courts of Chancery, Queen's

---

[76]   Mirfield, op. cit., pp. 45–6 and Winterton, op. cit., pp. 390–2. And p. 192 post.
[77]   As suggested by Lord Denning in What Next in the Law, p. 320.

[1]   Mitchell, Constitutional Law, pp. 69–74; T. B. Smith, [1957] P.L. 99; D. N. MacCormick, (1978) 29 N.I.L.Q. 1.
[2]   Ch. 3.

Bench, Common Pleas or any other court in Westminster Hall. An Act for securing the Protestant religion and Presbyterian Church government in Scotland was passed at the same time by the English and Scottish Parliaments and was declared to be a fundamental and essential condition of the Treaty of Union 'in all time coming'.

There is therefore substantial evidence in the Treaty that, while the framers of the Union intended the new Parliament to be the sole legislature, they were at pains to distinguish between matters on which Parliament would be free to legislate, matters on which it would have a limited authority to legislate, and matters which were declared fundamental and unalterable. The Treaty made no provision for future amendment of itself, nor for future renegotiation of the terms of the Union. The former English and Scottish Parliaments ceased to exist. No machinery was provided for applying the distinction drawn in article 18 between the laws concerning 'public right, policy and civil government' and the laws concerning 'private right', nor, in the latter case, for ascertaining the changes in those laws that might be for 'evident utility' of the Scottish people.

The argument that the Union imposed limitations upon the new Parliament can be summarised as follows: the new Parliament entered upon its life by virtue of the Union; its powers were therefore limited by the guarantees in the Treaty, which guarantees had been enacted by the separate Parliaments before the united Parliament was born. The assertion that a sovereign Parliament may not bind its successors may be countered by the view that even if both the English and Scottish Parliaments were supreme before 1707,[3] they each committed suicide in favour of a common heir with limited powers. The Treaty of Union, concludes the argument, is a fundamental constitutional text which prevents the British Parliament from itself enjoying the attribute of legislative supremacy. When, as in *Cheney* v. *Conn*, an English judge remarks, 'what the statute says and provides is the highest form of law that is known to this country',[4] a Scots lawyer might reply, 'Not so: the Treaty of Union is a higher form of law and may prevail over inconsistent Acts of Parliament.'

This viewpoint is subject to both theoretical and historical difficulties. First, no legislature other than the British Parliament was created. If circumstances changed, and amendments to the Union became desirable, how could they be made except by Act of Parliament? Thus in 1748, the heritable jurisdictions were abolished and, when Scottish local government was reformed in 1975, the royal burghs were abolished.[5] In 1853, the Universities (Scotland) Act abolished the requirement that the professors of the ancient Scottish universities should be confessing members of the Church of Scotland, thus repealing an 'unalterable' provision of the Act for securing the Presbyterian Church. Secondly, the distinction between laws concerning 'public right, policy and civil government' and laws concerning 'private right' is a very difficult one. For example, power to tax private property or to acquire land compulsorily

---

[3] On whether the Scottish Parliament was supreme before 1707, see G. Donaldson, *Scotland: James V–James VII*, ch. 15; and A. V. Dicey and R. S. Rait, *Thoughts on the Union between England and Scotland*, pp. 19–22, 242–4.

[4] Page 68 *ante*.

[5] *Cf.* arts. 20 and 21 of the Treaty of Union.

for public purposes concerns both public and private right; and is the law of education or industrial relations a matter of public or private right? Thirdly, the test of 'evident utility' for changes in the law affecting private right is obscure: who is to decide – Scottish M.P.s, Scottish courts, public opinion or the opinion of Scottish institutions such as the General Assembly of the Church of Scotland?[6] Fourthly, after the Union the Westminster Parliament continued to conduct its affairs exactly as before, subject only to its enlargement by members from Scotland.[7] As the dominant partners in the Union, the English assumed that constitutional continuity from pre-Union days was unbroken. On a matter left silent by the Treaty of Union, the House of Lords in its judicial capacity has heard appeals from Scotland in civil cases since the case of *Greenshields* in 1711 (the House of Lords was not a court within Westminster Hall within the meaning of article 19 of the Union) but it still has no jurisdiction in Scottish criminal cases. Fifthly, even if the framers of the Union intended there to be legal limitations upon the British Parliament, this might not in itself be sufficient to vest jurisdiction in the courts to hold Acts of the UK Parliament invalid on the ground that they conflicted with the Treaty of Union. In Dicey's view, the subsequent history of the Union with Scotland 'affords the strongest proof of the futility inherent in every attempt of one sovereign legislature to restrain the action of another equally sovereign body'.[8]

These matters have been the subject of debate in two important Scottish cases.

In *MacCormick* v. *Lord Advocate*,[9] the Rector of Glasgow University challenged the Queen's title as 'Elizabeth the Second', on the grounds that this was contrary to historical fact and contravened article 1 of the Treaty of Union. At first instance, Lord Guthrie dismissed the challenge for the reason, *inter alia*, that an Act of Parliament could not be challenged in any court as being in breach of the Treaty of Union or on any other ground. In the Inner House of the Court of Session, the First Division dismissed the appeal against Lord Guthrie's decision, but on narrower grounds. After holding that MacCormick had no legal title or interest to sue in the matter, that the royal numeral was not contrary to the Treaty of Union, and that the Royal Titles Act 1953 was irrelevant, Lord President Cooper said: 'The principle of the unlimited sovereignty of Parliament is a distinctively English principle which has no counterpart in Scottish constitutional law'. He had difficulty in seeing why it should have been supposed that the Parliament of Great Britain must have inherited all the peculiar characteristics of the English Parliament but none of the Scottish Parliament. He could find in the Union legislation no provision that the Parliament of Great Britain should be 'absolutely sovereign' in the sense that it should be free to alter the Treaty at will. He reserved opinion on whether breach of such fundamental law as is contained in the Treaty of Union would raise an issue justiciable in the courts; in his view there was no precedent that the courts of Scotland or England had authority to determine 'whether a governmental act of the type here in controversy is or is not conform to the provisions of a

---

6   The court was prepared to find a statute to be of 'evident utility' in *Laughland* v. *Wansborough Paper Co.* 1921 1 S.L.T. 341, but *cf. Gibson* v. *Lord Advocate, post.*

7   See *e.g.* the comment by Bryce, *Studies in History and Jurisprudence*, vol. 1, p. 194, that, by fusing herself with Scotland in 1707, England altered the constitution of the enlarged state no further than by the admission of additional members to Parliament and the suppression of certain offices in Scotland.

8   Dicey, p. 65; and *cf.* Dicey and Rait, *op. cit.*, p. 252.

9   1953 S.C. 396; Wilson, *Cases*, p. 261.

Treaty, least of all when that Treaty is one under which both Scotland and England ceased to be independent States and merged their identity in an incorporating union'. Lord Russell, who concurred, stressed the limited functions of the courts in dealing with political matters, suggesting that a political remedy would be more suitable for MacCormick than a judicial remedy.

Although Lord Cooper's judgment went beyond what was necessary for decision of the case, the fundamental issues remain confused. In particular, the denial that the courts have jurisdiction to decide whether 'a governmental act of the type here in controversy' conformed to the Union must be read in relation to the disputed royal title. If the UK Parliament were to pass an Act which sought to deprive persons in Scotland of access to the Scottish courts in matters of private right, the courts would seem bound to decide whether to give effect to that Act.

In 1975, a Scottish fisherman unsuccessfully claimed in the Court of Session that British membership of the European Community was incompatible with the Treaty of Union.

In *Gibson* v. *Lord Advocate*, Gibson claimed that an EEC regulation granting EEC nationals the right to fish in Scottish waters, and the European Communities Act 1972, which gave this legal effect in Britain, were contrary to article 18 of the Union, since this was a change in the law concerning private right which was not for the 'evident utility' of the Scottish people. Lord Keith held that the control of fishing in territorial waters around Scotland was a branch of public law, which therefore might be made the same throughout the United Kingdom and was not protected by article 18. *Obiter*, Lord Keith said that the question whether an Act of Parliament altering Scots private law was or was not for the 'evident utility' of the Scottish people was not a justiciable issue. 'The making of decisions upon what must essentially be a political matter is no part of the function of the court'.[10] He considered the question of title to sue (*locus standi*) to be of secondary importance.

Both in *MacCormick* and in *Gibson* the question was held open of the validity of legislation seeking to abolish the Court of Session or the Church of Scotland, measures which would strike at the root of the Scottish institutions safeguarded by the Union. Short of such an extreme situation, the Scottish courts appear very reluctant to claim a power to review the validity of Acts of Parliament.

In 1872, an English court denied that it had any jurisdiction to determine the validity of an Act of Parliament, and rejected a challenge to the Irish Church Act 1869 on the ground that it was contrary to the Irish Acts of Union.[11] Whereas the turbulent course of Irish history would today make it difficult to base constitutional arguments upon the intended binding character of the Irish Union, the very different history of the Anglo-Scottish Union does not make the idea of a constitutional jurisdiction vested in the Court of Session with appeal to the House of Lords inherently absurd. If Scotland were to acquire its own legislative assembly, such a jurisdiction in respect of the measures passed by that assembly would almost certainly be necessary.[12]

---

10 1975 S.L.T. 134.
11 *Ex p. Canon Selwyn* (1872) 36 J.P. 54.
12 Ch. 22. And see *Smith* v. *Sillers* 1982 S.L.T. 539.

E. Conclusions

This chapter has examined the problem of whether there are any legal limits upon the legislative supremacy of Parliament, in particular whether there are, or could be, any limits capable of being enforced judicially. While British tradition has been strongly against the courts having power to review the validity of an Act of Parliament, the courts cannot escape the task of deciding whether a document for which legislative authority is claimed is in law an Act of Parliament. While the basic rule of legislative supremacy is a matter of common law, as well as being an important political fact, it cannot be demonstrated from existing precedents that under no circumstances could this rule be qualified by judicial decision – still less that the basic rule could not be changed by Act of Parliament. It is therefore not possible to assert dogmatically that the legislative supremacy of Parliament will continue for the future to be the primary rule of constitutional law in the UK. Indeed, closer relations between Britain and European institutions (through the EEC and the European Convention on Human Rights) make it more probable than not that the pure doctrine of legislative supremacy will not survive into the next century, if indeed it has survived British membership of EEC.[1]

Political significance of legislative supremacy

There are difficulties in attempting to assess the political significance of the legislative supremacy of Parliament. For one thing constitutional and legal rules tend to reflect political facts, but sometimes only with a considerable time-lag. Moreover, the doctrine of legislative supremacy has always been affected by a tinge of political unreality since it would apparently empower Parliament to do many unlikely, immoral or undesirable things which no-one wishes it to do. Does Parliament really need power to condemn all red-haired males to death or to make attendance at public worship illegal? Or to create criminal offences retrospectively? Regarding legislative omnipotence, Sir Robert Megarry has emphasised that validity in law must not be confused with practical enforceability.[2]

Yet it would be wrong to ignore the strong political argument for retaining supremacy, particularly when the wishes of a newly elected House of Commons can be clearly identified with the will of the people. The doctrine of legislative supremacy is well suited to a centralised, unitary system of government in which the needs of the political and administrative executive are closely linked with the dominant political voice in Parliament: and in which the judiciary exercise an important but subordinate role. Even in such a system, there are many political factors which limit the use to which the executive can put Parliament's legislative powers. Dicey suggested that political sovereignty, as opposed to legislative sovereignty, lay in the electorate, and that ultimately the will of the electorate was sure to prevail on all subjects to be determined by the British government.[3] Certainly, the electoral system serves as one limitation upon the use of legislative powers, but the control

---

[1]   See A. W. Bradley, in (ed. J. Jowell and D. Oliver), *The Changing Constitution*, ch. 2.
[2]   *Manuel* v. *A.-G.* [1983] Ch. 77, 89.
[3]   Dicey, p. 73.

which it provides is very generalised and sporadic in effect: and this effect depends in turn upon the political parties, on the media, on economic and social interest-groups, and on other means by which public opinion is formed and expressed. Moreover the voting system itself tends to produce an elected House of Commons which is a distortion of the spread of views amongst the electorate.[4]

Consultation of interests affected

The immense complexity of government makes it expedient that Parliament should exercise its powers only after the major interests affected by proposed legislation have been consulted. In the case of delegated legislation, statute often requires there to be consultation with interest-groups before the minister makes regulations.[5] In the case of legislation by Bill, there is no legal requirement of consultation but extensive consultation in practice nearly always occurs: such bodies as the Confederation of British Industries, the Trades Union Congress, the British Medical Association and local authority associations are frequently asked to make their views known to government departments on projected legislation. Consultation does not mean that the bodies whose advice is sought can dictate policy. It is for the government to weigh up that advice and to present its policy to Parliament. Many social reforms would not have taken place if government had permitted the interested organisation to veto changes; some reforms benefit citizens who are unable to participate in the process of of consultation. But other reforms may depend for their effectiveness upon the co-operation and support of those interest-groups most directly affected.

Parliament and the electorate

Under the British system, the electorate takes no direct part in legislative decision-making, save by electing the House of Commons. In some constitutions, for example the Republic of Ireland and the Commonwealth of Australia,[6] constitutional amendments may take effect only with the consent of the electorate obtained by a referendum. In other constitutions (for example Denmark and Switzerland) legislative proposals may be subject to a referendum. Until 1975, the British constitution found no place for the machinery of direct democracy, save in the case of the border-poll in Northern Ireland.[7] Where major political or constitutional issues have been concerned, the outcome of a general election may sometimes be taken as indicating the degree of popular support for any changes. In 1910, two elections were held because of the legislative veto of the Lords and the necessity to establish popular support for the constitutional changes involved. But this is the exception rather than the rule, since it is usually impossible to decide from the result of a general election the state of public opinion on particular issues. Since the party which wins a general election may be considered to have a popular mandate to implement its election manifesto, a government can scarcely be criticised

---

[4] Ch. 9 B, part V.
[5] Ch. 33.
[6] See Cmnd 5925, 1975, Annex B.
[7] Page 80 *ante.*

for seeking to carry out its election promises. But conversely a government may be criticised for proposing major reforms, particularly of a constitutional nature, which have never been before the electorate. The Conservative government elected in 1970 was criticised by those opposed to British membership of the European Communities for having completed the negotiations for membership, having signed the Treaty of Accession and having secured the passing of the European Communities Act 1972 without allowing the electorate the opportunity to vote on this major constitutional and political issue. For these reasons, but mainly because of the internal division of opinion within the Labour party, a referendum on Britain's membership of the Communities was held in 1975. In 1979, referendums were held in Scotland and Wales on whether devolution under the Scotland Act and Wales Act 1978 should take effect.[8] It may be argued that the referendum should be used in future for deciding other constitutional issues, such as the future of the House of Lords, and the creation of a new Bill of Rights. While advisory or consultative referendums do not directly affect the legislative authority of Parliament, if referendums were to be mandatory for certain constitutional reforms, this would affect the position of Parliament and it would be essential to define in law the limits of their use. It has been argued that referendums should be used 'as an extra check against government, an additional protection to that given by Parliament'.[9] This would give a form of entrenchment to certain matters against action by the elected majority in the Commons. Without all-party agreement on the matter, the selection of those aspects of the constitution to be protected would be very contentious. There is a case to be made for requiring a referendum whenever it is proposed to transfer the powers of Parliament;[10] as John Locke said, 'it being but a delegated power from the People, they who have it cannot pass it to others'.[11] In current circumstances, however, it may be doubted whether greater use of referendums would be as significant as electoral reform.

Conclusion

The view taken in this chapter has been that Parliament's legislative authority includes power to make new constitutional arrangements under which future Parliaments would not enjoy legislative supremacy. Those who would adhere to the doctrine of legislative supremacy at all costs must be prepared to demonstrate that the political system provides adequate safeguards against legislation which would be contrary to fundamental constitutional principle or the individual's basic rights. But it is doubtful whether the present system, which relies so heavily on political controls, always gives adequate protection to individuals or minority groups who may be vulnerable to legislative oppression. Moreover Parliament's importance within British government depends much less upon absolute legislative power, than upon its effectiveness as a political forum in expressing public opinion and in exercising control over government.

---

8   Ch. 22.
9   V. Bogdanor, *The People and the Party System*, p. 69.
10   Bogdanor, p. 77.
11   *Second Treatise on Civil Government*, quoted in Bogdanor, p. 77.

Chapter 6

The rule of law

During 1971, the IRA increased the ferocity of its campaign of violence in Northern Ireland, shooting soldiers and police and blowing up buildings. Early in August, the government of Northern Ireland, after consulting with the UK government, decided to exercise the power of internment available to it under the Civil Authorities (Special Powers) Act (Northern Ireland) 1922.[1] This power could be used against persons suspected of having acted or being about to act in a manner prejudicial to the preservation of peace or the maintenance of order. On 9 August, 342 men were arrested. By November 1971, when the total arrested had risen to 980, 299 of those arrested were being interned indefinitely; the remainder were held under temporary detention orders or had already been released.

The security forces saw in internment an opportunity of obtaining fresh intelligence about the IRA. In August 1971 twelve detainees and in October two more were interrogated in depth. The procedures of interrogation included keeping the detainees' heads covered with black hoods; subjecting them to continuous and monotonous noise; depriving them of sleep; depriving them of food and water, except for one slice of bread and one pint of water at six-hourly intervals; making them stand facing a wall with legs apart and hands raised. It was later held by a committee of inquiry that these procedures constituted physical ill-treatment.[2]

In November 1971, after these facts had been established, three Privy Councillors were asked to consider whether the procedures 'currently authorised' for interrogating persons suspected of terrorism needed to be changed. They produced two reports.[3] Two members, a former Lord Chief Justice and a former Conservative Cabinet minister, recommended that the procedures could continue to be used subject to certain safeguards, including the express authority of a UK minister for their use, the presence of a doctor with psychiatric training at the interrogation centre, and a complaints procedure. This report did not express any view on the legality of the interrogation procedures,

---

[1] See now Northern Ireland (Emergency Provisions) Act 1978, sch. 1 (detention of terrorists).
[2] Cmnd 4823, 1971 (Compton Report).
[3] Cmnd 4901, 1972 (Parker Report).

but stated that valuable information about the IRA had been discovered through the interrogation.

The minority report, by Lord Gardiner, a former Labour Lord Chancellor, held that the interrogation procedures had never been authorised:

> If any document or minister had purported to authorise them, it would have been invalid because the procedures were and are illegal by the domestic law and may also have been illegal by international law.

Should legislation be introduced enabling a minister in time of civil emergency to fix in secret the limits of permissible ill-treatment to be used in interrogating suspects? Lord Gardiner viewed with abhorrence any proposal that a minister should be empowered to make secret laws. Nor could he agree that a minister should fix secret limits without the authority of Parliament, 'that is to say illegally', and then if found out ask Parliament for an Act of Indemnity: that, he said, would be a flagrant breach of the whole basis of the rule of law and of the principles of democratic government.

The government accepted Lord Gardiner's report and abandoned the interrogation procedures. When those who had been interrogated sued the government for damages for their unlawful treatment, liability was not contested and substantial awards of damages were made. Subsequently the European Commission on Human Rights held that the interrogation procedures amounted to inhuman and degrading treatment and also torture, contrary to article 3 of the European Convention on Human Rights. When the Irish government referred the case to the European Court of Human Rights, the court held that the procedures were inhuman and degrading treatment but did not amount to torture.[4]

No clearer illustration could be given of the need to adhere to the rule of law if citizens are to be protected against arbitrary and harsh acts of government. However lawless may have been the acts of the IRA, and however seriously those acts infringed life and liberty, government must not retaliate with measures which are not only unlawful but are also of such a nature that it would be impossible on moral and political grounds to make them lawful. Controversial as the power of internment is, it was authorised by the legislature and its use was a matter of public knowledge and admitted political responsibility. But in law the power to intern does not include power to interrogate or to administer physical ill-treatment or torture.[5]

A. Historical development

For many centuries it has been recognised that the possession by the state of coercive powers that may be used to oppress individuals presents a fundamental problem both for legal and political theory.[1] Since the days of the Greek philosophers there has been recourse to the notion of law as a primary means of subjecting governmental power to control. Aristotle argued that

---

[4] *Ireland* v. *UK* (1978) 2 E.H.R.R. 25; and see ch. 31 B.
[5] For the report of the Bennett committee of inquiry into police interrogation procedures in Northern Ireland in 1975–8, see Cmnd 7497, 1979.

[1] See A. P. d'Entrèves, *The Notion of the State*. Also Heuston, *Essays*, ch. 2.

government by laws was superior to government by men.[2]

The legal basis of the state was developed further by Roman lawyers. In the middle ages, the theory was held that there was a universal law which ruled the world. As Gierke wrote, 'Medieval doctrine, while it was truly medieval, never surrendered the thought that law is by its origin of equal rank with the state and does not depend on the state for its existence'.[3] Bracton, writing in the 13th century, maintained that rulers were subject to law: 'The King shall not be subject to men, but to God and the law: since law makes the King'.[4] Justice according to law was due both to ruler and subject. Magna Carta and its subsequent confirmations expressed this theory in seeking to remedy the grievances of certain classes in the community. Renaissance and reformation in the 16th century weakened the idea of a universal natural law. Emphasis shifted to the national legal system as an aspect of the sovereignty of the state.[5] In Britain, the 17th-century contest between Crown and Parliament led to a rejection of the Divine Right of Kings and to an alliance between common lawyers and Parliament. The abolition in 1640 of the Court of Star Chamber ensured that the common law should apply to public as well as private acts, except as the common law was modified by Parliament.

The Bill of Rights in 1689 finally affirmed that the monarchy was subject to the law. Not only was the Crown thereby forced to govern through Parliament, but also the right of the individual to be free of unlawful interference in his private affairs was established.

In *Entick* v. *Carrington*, two King's Messengers were sued for having unlawfully broken and entered the plaintiff's house and seized his papers: the defendants relied on a warrant issued by the Secretary of State ordering them to search for Entick and bring him with his books and papers before the Secretary of State for examination. The Secretary of State claimed that the power to issue such warrants was essential to government, 'the only means of quieting clamours and sedition'. The court held that, in the absence of a statute or a judicial precedent upholding the legality of such a warrant, the practice was illegal. Lord Camden said: 'what would the Parliament say if the judges should take upon themselves to mould an unlawful power into a convenient authority, by new restrictions? That would be, not judgement, but legislation ... And with respect to the argument of State necessity, or a distinction that has been aimed at between State offences and others, the common law does·not understand that kind of reasoning, nor do our books take notice of any such distinction'.[6]

Such decisions stressed the value of personal liberty, and the necessity of protecting private property against official interference. At the same time, the remedy of habeas corpus was being developed. Formal adherence to the law was one of the public values of 18th century Britain, though not all the people gained equally from it.[7] Economic and social developments since 1765 have

---

[2] d'Entrèves, p. 71.

[3] Quoted in d'Entrèves, p. 83.

[4] d'Entrèves, p. 86; Maitland, pp. 100–4; C. H. McIlwain, *Constitutionalism Ancient and Modern*, ch. 4.

[5] For the rule of law in 16th-century England, see G. R. Elton, *Studies in Tudor and Stuart Politics and Government* vol. 1, p. 260.

[6] (1765) 19 St. Tr. 1030, 1067, 1073.

[7] E. P. Thompson, *Whigs and Hunters, the Origin of the Black Act*, pp. 258–69.

qualified the forthright declaration of Lord Camden that in the absence of precedent no common law powers of search and seizure will be recognised[8] but *Entick* v. *Carrington* still exercises considerable influence on judicial attitudes to the claims of government.

Dicey's exposition of the rule of law

One reason for this is to be found in the writings of A. V. Dicey, whose lectures at Oxford were first published in 1885 under the title, *Introduction to the Study of the Law of the Constitution.*[9] Dicey's aim was to introduce students to 'two or three guiding principles' of the constitution, foremost among these being the rule of law. The spirit of *Entick* v. *Carrington* seems to run through all Dicey's arguments, but he expressed the general doctrine of the rule of law in the form of several detailed statements describing the English constitution, some of them derived from authors who immediately preceded him.[10] Dicey gave to the rule of law three meanings:

It means, in the first place, the absolute supremacy or predominance of regular law as opposed to the influence of arbitrary power, and excludes the existence of arbitrariness, of prerogative, or even of wide discretionary authority on the part of the government . . .; a man may with us be punished for a breach of law, but he can be punished for nothing else.[11]

Thus none could be made to suffer penalties except for a distinct breach of law established before the ordinary courts. In this sense Dicey contrasted the rule of law with systems of government based on the exercise by those in authority of wide or arbitrary powers of constraint, such as a power of detention without trial.

Secondly, the rule of law meant:

equality before the law, or the equal subjection of all classes to the ordinary law of the land administered by the ordinary law courts.[12]

This implied that no one was above the law; that officials like private citizens were under a duty to obey the same law; and that there were no administrative courts to which were referred claims by the citizens against the state or its officials.

Thirdly, the rule of law meant:

that with us the law of the constitution, the rules which in foreign countries naturally form part of a constitutional code, are not the source but the consequence of the rights of individuals, as defined and enforced by the courts; that, in short, the principles of private law have with us been by the action of the courts and Parliament so extended as to determine the position of the Crown and of its servants; thus the constitution is the result of the ordinary law of the land.[13]

---

[8] Page 486 *post.* And see *Malone* v. *Metropolitan Police Commissioner* [1979] Ch. 344.
[9] Dicey's text is reprinted in the 10th ed. with introduction by E. C. S. Wade. And see R. A. Cosgrove, *The rule of law: Albert Venn Dicey, Victorian jurist.*
[10] H. W. Arndt, (1957) 31 A.L.J. 117.
[11] Dicey, p. 202.
[12] Dicey, pp. 202–3.
[13] Dicey, p. 203.

Therefore the rights of the individual were secured not by guarantees set down in a formal document but by the ordinary remedies of private law available against those who unlawfully interfered with his liberty, whether they were private citizens or officials.

Criticism of Dicey's views[14]

These three meanings of the rule of law raise considerable problems. In the first, for example, what is meant by 'regular law'? Does this include, for example, social security law, compulsory purchase of land or a statutory wages and income policy? Does 'arbitrary power' refer to powers of government which are so wide that they could be used for a wide variety of different purposes; powers which are capable of abuse if not subjected to proper control; or powers which directly infringe individual liberty (for example, power to detain a citizen without trial)?[15] If 'arbitrary power' and 'wide discretionary authority' alike are unacceptable, how are the limits of acceptable discretionary authority to be settled? If it is contrary to the rule of law that discretionary authority should be given to government departments or public officers, then the rule of law is inapplicable to any modern constitution. Today the state regulates national life in multifarious ways. Discretionary authority in most spheres of government is inevitable. While there are still certain powers which we are unwilling to trust to the executive (for example, the power to detain individuals without trial) except when national emergencies dictate otherwise,[16] our attention now has to be concentrated not on attacking the existence of discretionary powers but on establishing a system of legal and political safeguards by which the exercise of discretionary powers may be controlled.[17] Doubtless Dicey would have regarded as arbitrary many of the powers of government on which social welfare and economic organisation now depend.

Dicey's second meaning stresses the equal subjection of all persons to the ordinary law. Now the Fourteenth Amendment to the United States Constitution provides, *inter alia*, that no state shall 'deny to any person within its jurisdiction the equal protection of the laws', a provision which has been a fertile source of constitutional challenges to discriminatory state legislation.[18] Similar provisions are found in the constitutions of India and the Federal Republic of Germany.[19] In fact the legislature must frequently distinguish between categories of person by reference to economic or social considerations or legal status. Landlords and tenants, employers and employees, company directors and shareholders, British subjects and aliens, judges and tax officials – these and innumerable other categories are subject to differing legal rules. What a constitutional guarantee of equality before the law may achieve is to enable legislation to be invalidated which distinguishes between citizens on

---

[14] See Dicey, introduction by E. C. S. Wade; Jennings, *Law and Constitution*, ch. 2 and app. 2; F. H. Lawson, (1959) *7 Political Studies*, 109, 207; H. W. Arthurs, (1979) Osgoode Hall L.J. 1.

[15] *Cf.* Report of the Franks Committee, Cmnd 218, 1957, para. 29.

[16] Chs. 26 A and 29.

[17] K. C. Davis, *Discretionary Justice*.

[18] G. Marshall, *Constitutional Theory*, ch. 7; and P. G. Polyviou, *The Equal Protection of the Laws*.

[19] India, 1949 Constitution, art. 14; Federal Republic of Germany, Basic Law, art. 3; and see Canadian Bill of Rights 1960, s. 1.

grounds which are considered irrelevant, unacceptable or offensive (for example, improper discrimination on grounds of sex, race, origin or colour).[20] Dicey had in mind no such jurisdiction. The specific meaning he attached to equality before the law was that all citizens (including officials) were subject to the jurisdiction of the ordinary courts should they transgress the law which applied to them, and that there should be no separate administrative courts, as in France, to hear complaints of unlawful conduct by officials.[21] He believed that the *droit administratif* in France favoured the officials and that English law through decisions such as *Entick* v. *Carrington* gave better protection to the citizens. Dicey's influence on administrative law in Britain was felt for many years, and Britain still lacks separate administrative courts on the French model. But today it is accepted that the legal protection of the citizens against unlawful official conduct may be as well secured by separate administrative courts as by the ordinary courts in Britain.

Dicey's third meaning of the rule of law, which he summarised in the conclusion that the constitution is the result of the ordinary law of the land, expressed a strong preference for the principles of common law declared by the judges as the basis of the citizen's rights and liberties. Dicey had in mind the fundamental political freedoms – freedom of the person, freedom of speech, freedom of association. The citizen whose freedoms were infringed could seek a common law remedy in the courts and did not need to rely on formal constitutional guarantees. Dicey believed that the common law gave better protection to the citizen than a written constitution. The Habeas Corpus Acts, which made effective a remedy by which persons unlawfully detained might obtain their freedom were, said Dicey, 'for practical purposes worth a hundred constitutional articles guaranteeing individual liberty'.[22] Today it is difficult to share Dicey's faith in the common law as the primary legal means of protecting the citizen's liberties against the state. In the first place, the common law is subject to modification by Parliament: the most fundamental liberties may be removed by statute. Secondly, the common law does not assure the citizen's economic or social well-being. Thirdly, while it remains essential that legal remedies should be effective, the experience of many Western countries is that there can be value in imposing legal limits upon the legislature's power to infringe human rights; and the European Convention on Human Rights has shown the value of supra-national remedies.[23]

Much of the content which Dicey attributed to the rule of law is therefore based on a view of the British constitution which today seems in many respects outmoded. Nor did Dicey adequately resolve the potential conflict between the two notions of the rule of law and the supremacy of Parliament.[24] While Dicey's views have had an important influence upon subsequent attitudes to constitutional law in Britain, what follows in this chapter is an attempt to explore the main features of the rule of law within our constitution today, a discussion which should no longer be cast in the Diceyan mould.

---

[20] Ch. 31·A.
[21] See L. N. Brown and J. F. Garner, *French Administrative Law*; and Ch. 32.
[22] Dicey, p. 199.
[23] Ch. 31 B.
[24] Dicey, ch. 13.

B. Rule of law and its implications today

Emphasis will be placed upon three related but separate ideas. First, the rule of law expresses a preference for law and order within a community rather than anarchy, warfare and constant strife. In this sense, the rule of law is a philosophical view of society which in the western tradition is linked with basic democratic notions. Second, the rule of law expresses a legal doctrine of fundamental importance, namely that government must be conducted according to law, and that in disputed cases what the law requires is declared by judicial decision. Third, the rule of law refers to a body of political opinion about what the detailed rules of law should provide in matters both of substance (for example, whether the government should have power to detain citizens without trial) and of procedure (for example, the presumption of innocence in criminal trials, and the independence of the judiciary). While the second sense is founded on decisions of the courts, and expresses an existing legal doctrine, the third sense is more directly relevant to discussion in Parliament and elsewhere, when present law is criticised and proposals for new law are examined. Proponents of the rule of law are however likely to support constitutional protection for human rights by such means as a judicially enforceable Bill of Rights, so that legislation affecting fundamental rights may be subject to review in the courts.

(a) Law and order better than anarchy

In the limited sense of law and order, the rule of law may appear to be preserved by a dictatorship or a military occupation as well as by a democratic form of government. Under a government which is not freely elected, the courts of law may continue to function, settling disputes between private citizens and such disputes between a citizen and government officials as the régime permits to be so decided. Even in this restricted sense, the rule of law expresses some preference for human disputes to be settled by peaceful means without recourse to armed force, terrorism or other forms of physical might. But undue stress on law and order as social values readily leads to the restriction or suppression of political liberty. Political groups opposed to a régime dependent on physical might rather than popular consent may readily turn to the adoption of violent means to overthrow it. Constitutional experience in Britain and other western states, as well as Britain's experience as a colonial power, has shown that the maintenance of law and order and the existence of political liberty are not mutually exclusive, but mutually interdependent. As the Universal Declaration of Human Rights said, 'It is essential, if man is not to be compelled to have recourse, as a last resort, to rebellion against tyranny and oppression, that human rights should be protected by the rule of law.'[1] In a democracy, it must be possible by the exercise of political rights to change a government without threatening the existence of the state. Unless this possibility exists, the state becomes identified with the sheer force of coercive might and the role of law within the state is virtually emptied of moral content: for 'the State cannot be conceived in terms of force alone'.[2]

---

[1] Preamble, 3rd para.
[2] d'Entrèves, *The Notion of the State*, p. 69.

(b) Government according to law

It is a basic rule of constitutional law that the organs of government must themselves operate through law. If the police need to detain a citizen, or if taxes are to be levied, the officials concerned must be able to show legal authority for their actions. In Britain, they may be challenged to do so before a court of law, as in *Entick* v. *Carrington*. Acts of public authorities which are beyond their legal power may be declared *ultra vires* and invalid by the courts.[3] Thus the Home Secretary's discretionary power to cancel television licences may not be used to compel the citizen to pay an extra licence fee which is not authorised in law;[4] and an individual detained in a mental hospital is entitled to his freedom if he can establish that his detention was unlawful.[5] It is because of this fundamental principle of legality that legislation must be passed through Parliament if the police are to have additional powers to combat terrorism.[6] The rule of law thus serves as a buttress for the democratic principle, since new powers of government affecting individual liberty may be conferred only by Parliament.

The doctrine of government according to law requires that a person directly affected by government action must be able, if necessary, to challenge the legality of that action before a court, and not merely to register a complaint with the department concerned. In the British tradition, it is from the ordinary courts that a remedy for unlawful acts of government is to be obtained. In other countries, the ordinary courts often do not exercise jurisdiction in administrative matters: thus in Germany this jurisdiction is assigned to the Federal Administrative Court, and in France to the Conseil d'Etat. Today both approaches are recognised to be ways of maintaining the rule of law. Nor is the existence of specialised tribunals (for example for social security claims or rent control) contrary to the rule of law, providing there are adequate means of ensuring that the tribunals are subject to supervision by superior courts, and are independent of the government departments concerned.[7]

The rule of law does however require that public authorities and officials are subject to effective sanctions if they depart from the law. Often the sanction is that their acts are declared invalid by the courts. But another sanction is the duty to compensate citizens whose rights have been infringed. Today it is unlikely that the British Prime Minister would be sued for damages, not because she is immune from such action but because her political decisions do not normally have direct legal effect; but the Prime Minister of Quebec was in 1959 held liable in damages for having maliciously and without legal authority directed a liquor licensing authority to cancel the licence of a restaurant proprietor who had repeatedly provided bail for Jehovah's Witnesses accused of police offences.[8] In Britain, government departments came under a general liability to be sued for their wrongful acts only under the Crown Proceedings Act 1947.[9] That Act preserved the personal immunity of the

---

[3] Ch. 34.
[4] *Congreve* v. *Home Office* [1976] Q.B. 629; page 633 *post*.
[5] *R.* v. *Board of Control, ex parte Rutty* [1956] 2 Q.B. 109.
[6] Ch. 29 C.
[7] Ch. 37 A.
[8] *Roncarelli* v. *Duplessis* (1959) 16 **D.L.R. (2d.) 689.**
[9] Ch. 36.

Sovereign, an immunity which in other legal systems is enjoyed by the head of state. Thus in the USA, the President while in office is immune from liability for his unlawful acts. As the Watergate affair showed in 1974, when President Nixon resigned rather than face impeachment proceedings before a hostile Congress, the importance of impeachment is that it provides a constitutional means of removing a President, thus enabling him to be sued or prosecuted for unlawful acts which he may have committed while in office.[10] Even a President while in office is not at liberty to disregard the law.

In the course of criminal investigations into the Watergate affair, the special prosecutor appointed by the Attorney-General requested President Nixon to produce tape-recordings of discussions which the President had had with his advisers. When presidential privilege was claimed for the tapes, the US Supreme Court held that this claim had to be considered 'in the light of our historic commitment to the rule of law'. The court rejected the claim and ordered the tapes to be produced, since 'the generalised assertion of privilege must yield to the demonstrated, specific need for evidence in a pending criminal trial'.[11]

Limitations of the doctrine of government according to law The doctrine stresses the importance of legal authority and form for the acts of government. In a system in which Parliament is supreme, and in which the Cabinet is supported by a majority in the Commons, political decisions may readily be clothed with legality. In the absence of constitutional guarantees for individual rights, the need for legal authority does not protect these rights from legislative invasion. In South Africa, government may in form be conducted according to law:[12] but a political detainee's right to have recourse to a court for a ruling on the legality of his detention is of little value if the government has taken care to ensure that the detention order is within its statutory powers.

So too in the United Kingdom. Parliament may authorise the executive to exercise powers which drastically affect the liberty of the individual (for example, by authorising the deportation of citizens from the United Kingdom)[13] or which retrospectively alter judicial decisions.[14] If all that the rule of law means is that official acts must be clothed with legality, this gives no guarantee that more fundamental values are not infringed. These limitations on the doctrine of government according to law explain present demands for incorporating the European Convention on Human Rights in the law of the United Kingdom.

(c) The rule of law as a broad political doctrine
If the law is not to become merely a means of achieving whatever ends a particular government may favour, the rule of law must go beyond the principle of legality. The inherited experience and values of the legal system are

---

[10] R. Berger, *Impeachment*.
[11] *US* v. *Nixon* (1974) 41 L.Ed. 2d. 1039; for the power of the executive in Britain to withhold evidence, see ch. 36.
[12] *Cf.* D. V. Cowen, *The Foundations of Freedom*; O. D. Schreiner, *The Contribution of English Law to S. African Law, and the Rule of Law in South Africa*.
[13] Immigration Act 1971, ss. 3(5)(6), 5, 6.
[14] Page 67 *ante*.

relevant not only to the question, 'What legal authority *does* the government have for its acts?' but also to the question, 'What legal powers *ought* the government to have?' If, for example, the government is proposing to introduce criminal sanctions for conduct contrary to its economic or social policies, a lawyer will want the new legislation to respect accepted principles of fair criminal procedure. If a Bill seeks to depart from these principles (for example by abolishing the presumption of innocence) arguments invoking the rule of law are likely to be used in the debates on the Bill.

But for a number of reasons the opinion of lawyers may not be unanimous in invoking the rule of law in a legislative context. What *are* the essential values which have emerged from centuries of legal experience? Are they absolute values or may there be circumstances in which political necessity justifies the legislature in departing from them? For example, the rule of law requires that the power of interpreting statutes is vested in the courts, but is this power of the courts reduced if the courts look at the report of a government committee as an aid to interpreting a statute passed to give effect to the report?[15] Again, in the circumstances of Northern Ireland, physical liberty and trial by jury are two victims of the assault upon law and order.[16] Moreover the legal system exists within a social and political context; a legislator's perception of legal values is likely to be affected by his outlook on other social and political questions.[17] A Conservative lawyer in Parliament will be more inclined than a Labour lawyer to oppose measures which expropriate private property or confer immunities upon trade unions. A Labour lawyer is likely to oppose new police powers for dealing with public demonstrations (except, possibly, if they are meant to be used against groups with Fascist tendencies). A Liberal lawyer is likely to support proposals for a Bill of Rights and other means of protecting individuals and minorities.

Is the rule of law then in this broad political sense too subjective and uncertain to be of any value? Would discussion of new legislation be clearer if the rule of law were excluded from the vocabulary of debate? One attempt to ascertain certain values inherent in the system of law was made by Professor Lon Fuller, who argued, for example, that the enactment of secret laws would be contrary to the essential nature of a legal system, as would heavy reliance on retrospective legislation, or legislation imposing criminal sanctions for conduct which is not defined but may be deemed undesirable by an official.[18] But these views have not found universal favour with all legal philosophers.[19] Amongst the judges, there continues to be a vein of belief in certain values that should be upheld in a legal system.[20]

International movement to promote the rule of law

Since 1945, the rule of law, in parallel with the human rights movement, has

---

15 *Black-Clawson International Ltd* v. *Papierwerke AG* [1975] A.C. 591.
16 See *e.g.* Cmnd 5847, 1975 (Gardiner Report).
17 *Cf.* Jennings, *Law and Constitution*, p. 317: 'the "principles" of constitutional lawyers are always a dangerous foundation for the formation of policy.' But was not Lord Gardiner relying on constitutional principle in rejecting interrogation in depth (p. 92 *ante*)?
18 L. Fuller, *The Morality of Law*.
19 See H. L. A. Hart, (1958) 71 Harv. L.R. 593; *cf.* J. Raz, (1977) 93 L.Q.R. 195.
20 *E.g.* R. v. *Inland Revenue Comssrs., ex p. Rossminster Ltd.* [1980] A.C. 952, 1015 (dissent of Lord Salmon).

been a matter of much international discussion. The Universal Declaration of Human Rights, adopted by the United Nations in 1948, was followed by the European Convention on Human Rights, signed at Rome in 1950. The Convention recognised that European countries have 'a common heritage of political traditions, ideals, freedom and the rule of law' and sought to create machinery for protecting certain human rights.[21] In *Golder's* case, which concerned the right of a convicted prisoner in the United Kingdom to have access to legal advice regarding a possible civil action against the prison authorities, the European Court of Human Rights referred to the rule of law and said: 'in civil matters one can scarcely conceive of the rule of law without there being a possibility of having access to the courts'.[22]

Further developments have been stimulated by the International Commission of Jurists, an international organisation of lawyers.[23] The aim has been to formulate the rule of law as a basic idea which can inspire lawyers of many backgrounds to work to improve their own national systems. Thus at New Delhi in 1959, lawyers from 53 countries formally declared that the rule of law is a dynamic concept which should be employed to safeguard and advance the political and civil rights of the individual in a free society. The congress for the first time associated the concept with the establishment of social, economic, educational and cultural conditions under which the individual may realise his legitimate aspirations. On the one hand, the congress examined traditional safeguards required for the maintenance of the law: for example, the need for adequate controls against abuse of power by the executive, the essentials of fair criminal procedure and the maintenance of an independent judiciary. On the other, the congress stressed the need for an effective government capable of maintaining law and order and of ensuring adequate social and economic conditions. It was also emphasised that the legislature must be democratically organised and must not pass discriminatory laws in respect of individuals or minority groups, nor restrict the freedoms of religious belief, speech and assembly. Subsequent conferences dealt with such topics as the role of the legal profession in a changing society, and procedures for economic and social reform including the reform of land tenure, nationalisation and economic planning.[24]

Social and economic aspects of the rule of law

The rule of law movement has thus been broadened to include social and economic goals which lie far beyond the typical values associated with the legal profession and the practice of law. Such a broadening would be repugnant to those critics of the mixed economy and the welfare state who wish to see a return to the restricted functions of government in the 19th century. Thus Hayek has argued that economic planning in the sense of control of private enterprise by the state is inconsistent with the rule of law. In his view, government in all its actions must be 'bound by rules, fixed and announced beforehand – rules which make it possible to foresee with fair certainty how the authority will use its coercive powers in given circumstances, and to plan one's

---

[21] Ch. 31B.
[22] *Golder* v. *UK* (1975) 1 E.H.R.R. 524.
[23] N. S. Marsh, in (ed. Guest) *Oxford Essays in Jurisprudence*, ch. 9.
[24] International Commission of Jurists, *The Rule of Law and Human Rights – Principles and Definitions*, 1966. For the Declaration of Delhi see (1959) 2 Journal of the I.C.J., pp. 7–43.

individual affairs on the basis of this knowledge'.[25] Now certainty and predict-ability are values often associated with law; in a different context, Lord Diplock said in 1975, 'The acceptance of the rule of law as a constitutional principle requires that a citizen, before committing himself to any course of action, should be able to know what are the legal consequences that will flow from it'.[26] But however desirable it may be that some discretionary powers of government should be controlled by rules,[27] the certainty demanded by Hayek is not attainable so long as the state has such multifarious responsibilities for economic and social affairs. There is no reason why the rule of law cannot be maintained in the welfare state and the mixed economy[28] provided that new forms of control appropriate to the social and economic goals of the community are developed.

The welfare rights movement is a recent expression of the rule of law ideal which seeks to apply the legal concept of 'rights', traditionally associated with property and contracts, to the benefits distributed by the state under social security and other welfare schemes. Why should less legal protection be given to these benefits, on which many citizens depend for their daily subsistence, than to traditional rights of property?[29] One reason for tribunals is to ensure that official decisions awarding welfare benefits are made both fairly and with due regard to the social context. These tribunals are a modern attempt to subject government to the rule of law.[30] Indeed, the creation of immigration appeal tribunals, which hear appeals from the decisions of immigration officials, was based on the principle that 'it is fundamentally wrong and incon-sistent with the rule of law that power to take decisions affecting a man's whole future should be vested in officers of the Executive, from whose findings there is no appeal'.[31] Since the decisions of most tribunals can be challenged by appeal or review in the ordinary courts, the judges may determine the stan-dards of justice which tribunals must maintain.[32]

Conclusion

It is not possible to formulate a simple and clearcut statement of the rule of law as a broad political doctrine. As society develops, and as the tasks of government change, lawyers, politicians and administrators must be prepared to adapt the received values of law to meet changing needs.[33] It would be unfortunate if the new areas of governmental action were withdrawn from the scope of law, were considered to be of no more than administrative significance and were subjected only to such control as the political system might provide. Membership of the EEC has brought the United Kingdom within a new legal system, in part designed to exercise control over areas of economic activity

25   F. A. Hayek, *The Road to Serfdom*, p. 54. See also Hayek, *The Constitution of Liberty*.
26   *Black-Clawson International Ltd* v. *Papierwerke AG* [1975] A.C. 591, 638.
27   K. C. Davis, *Discretionary Justice*, ch. 3.
28   W. Friedmann, *Law in a Changing Society*, ch. 16; H. W. Jones, (1958) 58 Col. L.R. 143.
29   H. W. Jones, *op. cit.*; C. A. Reich, (1964) 73 Yale L.J. 733; *cf.* R. M. Titmuss, (1971) 42 *Political Quarterly* 113.
30   Ch. 37 A.
31   Report of Committee on Immigration Appeals, Cmnd 3387, 1967, p. 23; ch. 25 B.
32   *E.g. R.* v. *Preston Supplementary Benefits Tribunal, ex p. Moore* [1975] 2 All E.R. 807.
33   *Cf.* Sir. L. Scarman, *English Law – The New Dimension*.

(for example, the international business corporation) which previously were unregulated except at a national level. While the democratic base of the EEC needs to be strengthened, its organs are potentially capable of enlarging the effective scope of the rule of law, for example, by granting to the individual rights of legal protection against the governments of member states.[34]

In recent years there has been much discussion of the challenge to the rule of law presented by recent phenomena in our social life. Hi-jacking, urban terrorism, direct action by militant groups, campaigns of civil disobedience, student sit-ins, strikes, protests and demonstrations – all these are sometimes indiscriminately lumped together and described as a growing threat to the rule of law (by which may simply be meant in this context the authority and stability of established institutions). There are many important distinctions to be drawn between these different forms of political or criminal action.[35] But, if we leave aside acts of criminal violence at one end of the scale and law-abiding political expression at the other end, do acts of non-violent civil disobedience endanger the legal system? In particular, does the rule of law require complete obedience to the law from all citizens and organisations?[36] It would be to cast an impossible burden upon the courts to require them to base decisions as to whether certain conduct constitutes a criminal offence on the political motives of the accused.[37] It may be argued both that, in a democratic society, there are important reasons for obeying the law which do not exist in other forms of government, and also that there are some forms of limited disobedience which do not run counter to the democratic reasons for obedience, particularly those which are designed to improve the working of democratic procedures for political decisions.[38] Only rarely does the legislature recognise that citizens may feel compelled by their conscience to refuse to carry out a law, as in the provision made for conscientious objection to compulsory military service under the National Service Acts. What is the citizen to do if he believes that a certain law is unjust or immoral? Professor Hart has written:

What surely is most needed in order to make men clear sighted in confronting the official abuse of power is that they should preserve the sense that the certification of something as legally valid is not conclusive of the question of obedience, and that, however great the aura of majesty or authority which the official system may have, its demands must in the end be submitted to a moral scrutiny.[39]

But while this is so for the individual, there is a danger that group decisions to disobey particular laws for political reasons (particularly by trade unions and local authorities, who are not without political influence upon the legislative process) may cumulatively tend to suggest that there is no general

---

34   See the *Internationale Handelsgesellschaft* decision [1972] C.M.L.R. 255 and J. W. Bridge, in (ed. Bridge, Lasok *et al*) *Fundamental Rights*, ch. 20.
35   Passive resistance is contrary to the rule of law: *R.* v. *Chief Constable of Devon, ex p. Central Electricity Generating Board* [1982] Q.B. 458, 473 (Lawton L.J.).
36   Marshall, *Constitutional Theory*, ch. 9; R. Dworkin, *Taking Rights Seriously*, ch. 8; R. A. Wasserstrom, *The Obligation to Obey the Law*, repr. in *Essays in Legal Philosophy* (ed. Summers) p. 274.
37   *Cf. Chandler* v. *DPP* [1964] A.C. 763, p. 567 *post.*
38   P. Singer, *Democracy and Disobedience.*
39   H. L. A. Hart, *The Concept of Law*, p. 260.

obligation to obey the law, but only the law of which one approves. Our political system is not perfect and there are always many legislative reforms to be made. But the maintenance of life in modern society requires a willingness from most citizens for most of the time to observe the laws, even when individually they may not agree with them. American writings on the subject tend to suggest that state power is the great antagonist against which the rule of law must for ever be addressed.[40] But it deserves to be remembered that law, like the democratic process, may be used to protect the weak and underprivileged sections of society against those who can exercise physical, economic or industrial force.

---

[40]   H. W. Jones, cited in n.28, p. 144.

Chapter 7

Responsible government

Within a democratic state, those who govern should be accountable, or responsible, to those whom they govern. Since direct government by the people is impracticable, the constitution provides a framework within which the governors may be responsible to the representatives of the people. In ordinary speech, 'responsible' has a variety of meanings and responsibility takes a number of forms.[1] This chapter deals mainly with the political responsibility of the government to Parliament. Another important form of responsibility is the legal responsibility of ministers and officials for their acts. Whereas legal responsibility is enforced primarily through the courts, the responsibility of government to Parliament is a political relationship. As such, it is not a matter of precise definition and lawyers must resist the temptation to lay down rules for it.

Early origins of responsible government

So long as government was carried on by the King, the nature of monarchy made it extremely difficult to establish constitutional responsibility for acts of government. In medieval times, the practice developed by which the royal will had to be signified in documents bearing a royal seal, which would be applied by one of the King's ministers. Maitland detected in this practice 'the foundation for our modern doctrine of ministerial responsibility – that for every exercise of the royal power some minister is answerable'.[2] The minister who caused the seal to be applied was thereby endorsing the royal decision. With the responsibility of ministers came the rule that 'the King can do no wrong'. Today the use of the various seals or forms for recording decisions taken in the name of the Sovereign by ministers is regulated partly by statute and partly by custom.[3] The former significance of these details was that, at a time when the Sovereign could not be called personally to account, responsibility could be laid on those ministers who had carried out his decisions.

For a period, this responsibility was enforced by the English Parliament

---

[1] See *e.g.* A. H. Birch, *Representative and Responsible Government*, pp. 17–21.
[2] Maitland, *History*, p. 203. *Cf.* art. 64 of the Belgian Constitution of 1831.
[3] Anson, vol. II, part 1, pp. 62–72; H.L.E. vol. 8, pp. 719, 722, 739.

through impeachment. Holders of state office were liable to be impeached by the Commons at the bar of the House of Lords for the treason, high crimes and misdemeanours they were alleged to have committed in office. In the 17th century, impeachment became a political weapon wielded by Parliament for striking at unpopular royal policies.[4] Following the granting of a royal pardon to Danby in 1679 to forestall his impeachment, the Act of Settlement provided that a royal pardon could not be pleaded in bar of an impeachment. The last instance of a purely political impeachment came when the Tory ministers who in 1713 negotiated the Peace of Utrecht were later impeached by a Whig House of Commons. Thereafter only two impeachments occurred, of Warren Hastings between 1788 and 1795 for mis-government in India and of Lord Melville in 1804 for alleged corruption. The power of impeachment is still available to Parliament: but more modern means of achieving ministerial responsibility have rendered it an obsolete weapon.[5]

The legal responsibility of government

The principle that government must be conducted according to law has already been discussed.[6] The Sovereign may not personally be sued or prosecuted in the courts. But servants or officers of the Crown who commit crimes or civil wrongs are, and always have been, subject to the jurisdiction of the courts. Superior orders or the interest of the state are no defence to such proceedings.[7] Public authorities other than the Crown are at common law liable for the wrongful acts of their officials or servants.[8] The departments of central government become liable to be sued under the Crown Proceedings Act 1947.[9] While the legal control of government is important, and will be examined in Part III of this book, it is with political responsibility that the rest of this chapter is concerned.

Development of collective responsibility

After 1688 the doctrine of collective responsibility developed in fits and starts as the Cabinet system came into being.[10] For much of the 18th century, the Cabinet was a body of holders of high office whose relationship with one another was ill-defined; the body as a whole was not responsible to Parliament. Although the King rarely attended Cabinet meetings after 1717, it was the King's government in fact as well as in name and the King could and did act on the advice of individual ministers. Under Walpole, ministries were relatively homogeneous. Other Cabinets in the century were less united. Parliament could force the dismissal of individual ministers of whom they disapproved, but could not dictate appointments to the King. The King sometimes consulted those who were out of office without the prior approval of his ministers. There was no clear dividing line between matters dealt with by

---

4   Maitland, *History*, pp. 317–8; Taswell-Langmead, pp. 164–5, 353–4, 529–38; Clayton Roberts, *The Growth of Responsible Government in Stuart England*; R. Berger, *Impeachment*, ch. 1.
5   Cf. Dicey, p. 499.
6   Ch. 6.
7   Smith and Hogan, pp. 209–10; Dicey, pp. 302–6; *Entick* v. *Carrington*, page 93 *ante*.
8   *Mersey Docks and Harbour Board Trustees* v. *Gibbs* (1866) L.R. 1 H.L. 93.
9   Ch. 36.
10   Mackintosh, *British Cabinet*, ch. 2.

individual ministers and matters dealt with in the Cabinet. As late as 1806, it was debated in the Commons whether ministers must accept collective responsibility for the general affairs of government or whether only those ministers who carried policies into execution were individually responsible.[11]

By the early 19th century, as the scope for personal government by the Sovereign sharply declined, so did the tendencies towards the collective responsibility of the Cabinet become more marked. Soon after 1832, it became evident that the Cabinet must retain the support of the majority in the House of Commons if it was to continue in office. Just as it had earlier been recognised that a single minister could not retain office against the will of Parliament, so now it became clear that all ministers must stand or fall together in Parliament, if the Cabinet was to function effectively.

By the mid-19th century, ministerial responsibility was the accepted basis of Parliamentary government in Britain.[12] As the Victorian foundations of the system of government were laid, critics of the rule of Cabinet unity were reminded that 'the various departments of the Administration are but parts of a single machine . . . and that the various branches of the Government have a close connection and mutual dependence upon each other'.[13]

The meaning of collective responsibility

The doctrine of collective responsibility was stated in absolute terms by Lord Salisbury in 1878:

For all that passes in Cabinet every member of it who does not resign is absolutely and irretrievably responsible and has no right afterwards to say that he agreed in one case to a compromise, while in another he was persuaded by his colleagues . . . It is only on the principle that absolute responsibility is undertaken by every member of the Cabinet, who, after a decision is arrived at, remains a member of it, that the joint responsibility of Ministers to Parliament can be upheld and one of the most essential principles of parliamentary responsibility established.[14]

Yet it is difficult to control political behaviour in absolute terms. In the 19th century, the degree of political cohesion was variable. Cabinet unity could not always be achieved when mininsters held deeply divided opinions. Some subjects were regarded as 'open questions', for example Catholic emancipation before 1829 and women's suffrage between 1906 and 1914.[15] But it was regarded as a sign of political weakness if many issues were accepted as open questions. Except for open questions, ministers who did not wish to be publicly identified with Cabinet policies were expected to resign.

Today collective responsibility embodies a number of related aspects. Like other constitutional principles, it is neither static nor unchangeable and may give way before more pressing political forces.

1 The Prime Minister and other ministers are collectively responsible to Parliament, and to the Commons in particular, for the conduct of national

---

11   E. N. Williams, *The 18th Century Constitution*, pp. 123–5.
12   For a notable summary, see Earl Grey, *Parliamentary Government*, p. 4.
13   Grey, p. 57.
14   *Life of Robert, Marquis of Salisbury*, vol. II, pp. 219–20; Wilson, *Cases*, p. 57.
15   Jennings, *Cabinet Government*, pp. 277–9; H. J. Hanham, *The 19th Century Constitution*, pp. 79, 84–94; Grey, p. 116.

affairs. In practice, so long as the governing party retains its majority in the House, the Prime Minister is unlikely to be forced to resign or seek a dissolution of Parliament. At a general election, the Cabinet is seeking renewed electoral support for its policies.

2   When a Prime Minister dies or resigns office, then even if the same party continues in power, all ministerial offices are at the disposal of the new Prime Minister.

3   Although ministers are individually responsible to Parliament for the conduct of their departments, if members of the Commons seek to censure an individual minister for his policies, the government generally will rally to his defence: collective responsibility is a means of defending an incompetent or unpopular minister.

4   So long as a politician serves as a minister, he shares in the collective responsibility of all ministers in the sense that he may not publicly criticise or dissociate himself from government policy. A Cabinet minister may however ask for his dissent from a Cabinet decision to be recorded in the private minutes of Cabinet.[16] He is expected nonetheless to support the government by his vote in Parliament. Cabinet ministers who were also members of the National Executive of the Labour party were in 1974 told by the Prime Minister that they must observe the conventions of collective responsibility at Executive meetings.[17]

5   As a former Cabinet minister has said, an element of concealment is inherent in the concept of collective responsibility. 'Ministers must in the nature of things have differences, but they must outwardly appear to have none'.[18] Since all ministers are required to support government policy once it has been settled, a government generally considers it desirable that the process by which policy decisions are made should be kept secret. In principle, secrecy attaches to Cabinet discussions, Cabinet documents and the proceedings of Cabinet committees, except where the Cabinet or the Prime Minister decides that disclosure shall be made.[19] Exceptionally, where a minister resigns because of a disagreement over policy, he is permitted to explain the reasons for his resignation. Today leakages about the progress of controversial matters frequently occur and the principle of secrecy is under pressure to give way to a more open system of government.

6   Similarly, in principle secrecy attaches to communications between departments. Thus if a decision is taken to reject a proposal which would mean new expenditure, it may not be known whether this was primarily because the spending department does not favour the proposal or because the Treasury is not prepared to approve the expenditure involved: nor will it be disclosed whether the decision was taken by officials or at ministerial level. Thus collective responsibility reinforces the principle of the indivisibility of the executive.[20] Again an element of concealment is inherent in the principle: departments are

---

[16]   Mackintosh, *British Cabinet*, p. 534.
[17]   H. Wilson, *The Governance of Britain*, pp. 74–5, 191–3; and see D. L. Ellis [1980] P.L. 367, 379–83.
[18]   Gordon Walker, pp. 27–8.
[19]   Ch. 14 A.
[20]   H. Heclo and A. Wildavsky, *The Private Government of Public Money*, p. 116.

apparently expected to agree with each other because their ministerial heads are members of the same Cabinet. In real life, serious disagreements between departments occur, and often cannot be kept secret.

7 The collective decisions of the Cabinet are communicated by or on behalf of the Prime Minister to the Sovereign. Dissenting ministers have no access to the Sovereign to press their views upon her. Certain exceptions exist to the principle of collective responsibility for advice to the Sovereign. Thus, in advising the Sovereign on the prerogative of mercy, the Home Secretary or the Secretary of State for Scotland acts on his own responsibility.[21]

Collective responsibility thus serves a variety of political uses. As most governments are drawn from members of one party, it serves to reinforce party unity and to prevent back-bench M.P.s from inquiring too far into the processes of government. It helps to maintain the government's control over legislation and public expenditure and to contain public disagreements between departments. It reinforces the traditional secrecy of the decision-making process within government. It helps to maintain the authority of the Prime Minister.[22]

Some of the purposes for which the doctrine is maintained are controversial. Thus there is disagreement over the degree of protection which should be afforded to the secrecy of decision making, to the authority of the Prime Minister and to the need for external unanimity. In some more open processes of government, especially in the holding of public inquiries, it is now accepted that the separate views of government departments should be made public.[23] But there is an obvious political advantage in being able to maintain an outward appearance of unity, which is why some aspects of collective responsibility apply also to the 'shadow Cabinet' of the main opposition party in the Commons. The political authority of the Labour 'shadow Cabinet' was weakened when, in a Commons debate about denationalisation, two inconsistent policies were advocated by the leading speakers for the Opposition.[24]

An assessment of collective responsibility today must take account of the fact that not all important decisions of national policy are taken in full Cabinet. The decisions to manufacture the British atomic bomb,[25] to mount the Suez operation in 1956, to raise the bank rate in 1957[26] and to devalue the pound in 1967[27] were effectively taken by a few ministers meeting with the Prime Minister, subject at most to confirmation by the Cabinet. In such cases other members of the Cabinet are in little better position than ministers outside the Cabinet to influence the decision before it is taken. For much of the time, the size of modern Cabinets, as well as the heavy departmental burden of most of its members, would seem to preclude active participation by each minister in decisions. But much depends on the nature of the decision to be taken. While

21 Page 240 *post*.
22 *Cf.* Crossman's comment that collective responsibility had come to mean collective obedience to the Prime Minister (Introduction to Bagehot, p. 53). And see T. Benn (1980) 33 *Parliamentary Affairs* 7.
23 Ch. 37 B.
24 H. C. Deb., 10 Nov. 1981, cols. 438, 499.
25 Crossman, Introduction to Bagehot, pp. 54–5.
26 Cmnd 350, 1957; and R. A. Chapman (1965) 43 *Public Administration* 199.
27 H. Wilson, *The Labour Government 1964–70*, ch. 23.

the budget proposals are settled by the Chancellor of the Exchequer in consultation with the Prime Minister and not by the Cabinet, decisions about public expenditure economies are likely to be the subject of extended discussions between ministers, in Cabinet committees and in Cabinet.

Whether decisions are taken by the Cabinet or are merely reported to it, a minister may at any time resign in protest against decisions taken without his participation or with which he strongly disagrees. But by its nature a resignation does not affect decisions which have already been taken.[28]

Agreements to differ

In exceptional circumstances, it may be politically impossible for the Cabinet to maintain a united front. In 1932, the coalition or 'National' government, formed in 1931 to deal with the economic crisis, adopted an 'agreement to differ'. The majority of the Cabinet favoured the adoption of a general tariff of ten per cent, against the strong opposition of three Liberal ministers and one National Labour minister. It was announced that the dissenting ministers were to be free to oppose the proposals of the majority by speech and vote, both in Parliament and outside. When the Labour opposition criticised the government for violating 'the long-established constitutional principle of Cabinet responsibility', the motion of censure was defeated by an overwhelming majority.[29] Eight months later the dissenting ministers resigned on the cognate issue of imperial preference. This short-lived departure from the principle of unanimity has generally been regarded as demonstrating the virtues of that principle and justifiable, if at all, only in the special circumstances of a coalition government formed to deal with a national crisis.

In 1975, the Labour Cabinet agreed to differ over Britain's continued membership of EEC. Many in the Labour party were opposed to British membership. Party unity was maintained in the two general elections in 1974 by an undertaking from Mr Wilson to re-negotiate the terms of British membership and to submit the outcome to the people for decision, either at a general election or by referendum. When in April 1975 the re-negotiation of terms was completed, the Cabinet by a majority of 16–7 decided to recommend continued membership of EEC to the electorate. It was agreed that ministers who opposed this policy should be free to speak and campaign against it, but only outside Parliament.[30] When a junior minister, Mr Eric Heffer, insisted on opposing Britain's continued membership in the Commons,[31] he was required to resign from office. Other difficulties arose over the answering of parliamentary questions on EEC subjects by ministers opposed to British membership.[32]

In 1932 the agreement to differ occurred within a coalition between parties; in 1975, within the Labour party. Indeed, outside the Cabinet, majorities

---

[28]   *Cf.* R. K. Alderman and J. A. Cross, *The Tactics of Resignation.*
[29]   Jennings, *Cabinet Government*, pp. 279–81; Wilson, *Cases*, pp. 58–63.
[30]   See Cmnd 6003, 1975; H. C. Deb., 23 Jan. 1975, col. 1745; H. C. Deb., 7 Apr. 1975, col. 351 (W.A.). And see Wilson, *The Governance of Britain*, pp. 194–7.
[31]   H. C. Deb., 9 Apr. 1975, cols. 1325–32.
[32]   *E.g.* H. C. Deb., 5 May 1975, cols. 989–1015.

against Cabinet policy were recorded in the Parliamentary Labour Party, in the National Executive Committee and at a special party conference. Such agreements to differ on the part of the Cabinet give rise to many political difficulties, but neither in 1932 nor in 1975 did they lead to the downfall of the government. It is difficult to describe these rather desperate expedients as 'unconstitutional'. If conventions are observed because of the political difficulties which follow if they are not,[33] both in 1932 and 1975 it was less difficult to depart from Cabinet unanimity than to seek to enforce it. During a period of minority government, a free vote was allowed to the Labour party (including ministers) on the second reading of the European Assembly Elections Bill.[34] But there are other issues, notably capital punishment, on which it is universally accepted that ministers like all M.P.s are free to vote according to their conscience.[35]

Ministers not in the Cabinet

In any government there are more ministers outside the Cabinet than within it. Some have full departmental duties; others (for example, the parliamentary secretaries) merely assist in the work of their departments. These ministers are bound by Cabinet decisions and must refrain from criticising or opposing them in public.[36] On matters outside their departmental duties they are not consulted in advance, although some may participate in committees reporting to the Cabinet.

Because of the restraints on public activity which follow from a post in the government, some politicians prefer to remain on the back-benches rather than accept a ministerial post which offers no chance of participating in Cabinet decisions. In September 1969, Dr Jeremy Bray, Parliamentary Secretary at the Ministry of Technology, resigned from the government to publish a book on the management of the economy and the machinery of government. The Prime Minister, Mr Wilson, had refused him permission to publish the book and remain in office, stating that he had no alternative 'but to uphold the principles which every Prime Minister must maintain in relation to the collective responsibility of the Administration'; it had been open to Dr Bray to press his ideas from his position as a junior minister.[37] There is no reason to suppose that the publication of Dr Bray's book would have been a political embarrassment to the government. It is evident that collective responsibility is invoked to control the behaviour of ministers while they are in office and that this control is exercised by the Prime Minister. To this extent, the consequences of collective responsibility appear to be what the Prime Minister of the day chooses to make them. The obligation to support government policy on important issues now extends to the back-bench M.P.s who act as unpaid parliamentary secretaries to ministers.[38]

---

33 Page 25 *ante.*
34 H. C. Deb., 23 Mar. 1977, col. 1307; and see Ellis, [1980] P.L. 367, 388.
35 *E.g.* H. C. Deb., 13 July 1983, col. 972.
36 In 1981, a minister in the Ministry of Defence, Mr K. Speed, was dismissed for having spoken publicly against naval cuts; and see H. C. Deb., 19 May 1981, col. 151.
37 *The Times*, 26 and 29 Sep. 1969.
38 Mackintosh, *British Cabinet*, pp. 531–2.

The later development of individual responsibility

While it was established by the 18th century that ministers were individually responsible to Parliament for their policies, the activities of the central executive were still minute compared with those of modern government. The foundations of the present structure of government were laid only in the period of reform after 1832, when it became necessary to settle the relationship which should exist between Parliament and the new agencies which administered statutory schemes. It was to become increasingly difficult for ministers to supervise in detail the work of these agencies. In the mid-19th century a new class of administrators developed, whose energy did much to make possible the achievements of Victorian government: men like Edwin Chadwick, in the field of poor law and local government, Sir James Stephen at the Colonial Office and Sir John Simon in public health. The formal powers of these administrators derived from Acts of Parliament. Was Parliament to be able to supervise the use made of these powers?

For a period after 1832, powers were often vested in appointed public boards which were not directly responsible to Parliament.[39] Thus the Poor Law Commission between 1834 and 1847 consisted of three persons who were not answerable to Parliament for the manner in which they administered the reformed poor law. Dissatisfaction with such boards led to a strong parliamentary preference for administration to be conducted through a ministry, *i.e.* a department whose powers are vested in a single person who sits in Parliament and is responsible to Parliament for that department.[40] Thus in 1847 the Poor Law Commission was replaced by a ministry responsible to Parliament.[41] Procedures such as the parliamentary question developed which enabled members to obtain information about matters within the responsibility of ministers.[42] As the civil service was reformed following the Northcote-Trevelyan Report of 1854,[43] there developed as the corollary of ministerial responsibility the anonymity and permanence of the civil service. Nor was the scale of government yet too large for ministers to be able to supervise the work of their departments.[44]

In the 20th century, the tradition of ministerial responsibility was maintained. But in two ways the position changed. First, as the tasks of departments grew, civil servants continued to act in their minister's name, but the ability of the minister to supervise their work diminished. Secondly, the increase in the social and economic functions of government led to a new crop of boards and agencies which were deliberately created outside central government to avoid the full consequences of ministerial responsibility which would otherwise have attached to their work.[45]

The operation of individual responsibility today

According to the principle of individual responsibility, a minister must answer

---

39   F. M. G. Willson, (1955) 33 *Public Administration* 43, 44.
40   *Ibid.*
41   See Bagehot, p. 192.
42   D. N. Chester and N. Bowring, *Questions in Parliament*, ch. 2.
43   Ch. 15.
44   H. Parris, *Constitutional Bureaucracy*, ch. 3.
45   See chs. 14 B and 17 A.

to Parliament for the work of his department. Praise or blame for decisions must be addressed to the minister, not to the permanent officials. 'It would be a new and dangerous constitutional doctrine if ministers . . . could excuse the failure of their policies by turning upon the experts whose advice they have taken or upon the agents whom they have employed.'[46]

Much of the work of Parliament rests upon this basis. Thus government Bills are introduced into Parliament by ministers, who are responsible for the proposals they contain. In debates on the work of individual departments, the minister concerned replies to the criticisms raised and seeks usually to defend the department. A minister is expected to meet a member's reasonable requests for information and may not plead ignorance of a matter within his competence of which previous notice has been given. Question time in the House emphasises the responsibility of ministers.[47] Civil servants· may take part in parliamentary business only by appearing as witnesses before select committees. On these occasions civil servants may not be asked for their own views on the merits of departmental policies and their evidence does not absolve the minister of responsibility.[48]

The sanctions for individual responsibility

What are the sanctions which underlie this general practice of Parliament? The system assumes that ministers will fufil the parliamentary duties of their office, such as introducing legislation and answering questions. By a rota system, departments are assigned days for answering questions and a minister could not refuse to appear on the assigned day. But a minister cannot be compelled to answer a question if he considers that it does not fall within his responsi-bility, that it would be contrary to the public interest to answer the question[49] or that the expense of obtaining the information requested would be excessive. The position has been summarised by a Clerk of the House: 'The House wants the minister to answer a certain question, and he would be unwise not to do so unless supported by the government majority. There would be no legal saction'.[50] If therefore a minister persistently refused to provide information, and the Opposition moved a vote of censure upon him, the outcome would depend on whether the government could retain its majority in the House. While in the 18th century the House could secure the removal of a minister against the wishes of the Crown, it is most unlikely today that the House could in this way force a Prime Minister to remove an individual minister from office.

Ministerial responsibility for departmental maladministration[51]

Since parliamentary criticism of a department must be directed to a minister,

---

[46] *The Times*, 21 Nov. 1949. In 1963 the Prime Minister named a former Secretary to the Cabinet as responsible for not informing him of a warning given in the interests of state security as to private conduct which he had thought fit to give to a minister of Cabinet rank (H.C. Deb., 17 Jun. 1963, col. 59).

[47] Ch. 11 D. And see Chester and Bowring, *op. cit.*, pp. 251–68, and App. II.

[48] See Memorandum of guidance for officials appearing before select committees, H.C. 588–1 (1977–78) p. 38; p. 209 *post*.

[49] For the Commander Crabb case in 1956, in which the Prime Minister refused in the public interest to disclose information, see Wilson, *Cases*, pp. 150–5.

[50] H.C. 332–1 (1951–2) Minutes of Evidence, q. 337; Wilson, *Cases*, pp. 146–50.

[51] K. C. Wheare, *Maladministration and its Remedies*, ch. 3; Wilson, *Cases*, pp. 155–72.

then the minister may be said to be responsible to Parliament for the acts and omissions of the civil servants in his department. Two questions arise: (a) is the minister bound to take responsibility for every piece of maladministration within his department?; and (b) if serious maladmininstration is found to have occurred, is the minister under a duty to resign? In 1954, the Crichel Down affair gave rise to much discussion of these two issues.

Farm land in Dorset known as Crichel Down had been acquired under compulsory powers from several owners by the Air Ministry in 1937. After the war, the land was transferred to the Ministry of Agriculture, for whom it was administered by a commission set up under the Agriculture Act 1947. While the future of the land was being considered. Lieutenant-Commander Marten, whose wife's family had previously owned much of the land, asked that it be sold back to the family. Misleading replies and false assurances were given when this and similar requests were refused, and a seriously inaccurate report was prepared by a junior civil servant which led the ministry to adhere to a scheme which it had prepared for letting all the land to a single tenant. Inadequate financial information was supplied to the headquarters of the ministry. When Conservative M.P.s took up Marten's case with the Minister of Agriculture, Sir Andrew Clark Q.C. was appointed to hold an inquiry. His report established that there had been muddle, inefficiency, bias and bad faith on the part of some officials named in the report.[52] A subsequent inquiry to consider disciplinary action against the civil servants reported that some of the deficiencies were due as much to weak organisation within the ministry as to the faults of individuals.[53]

During a Commons debate on these reports, the Minister of Agriculture, Sir Thomas Dugdale, resigned. Speaking in the debate, the Home Secretary, Sir David Maxwell Fyfe, reaffirmed that a civil servant is wholly and directly responsible to his minister and can be dismissed at any time by the minister – a 'power none the less real because it is seldom used'. He went on to give a number of categories where differing considerations apply.

1   A minister must protect a civil servant who has carried out his explicit order.
2   Equally a minister must defend a civil servant who acts properly in accordance with the policy laid down by the minister.
3   'Where an official makes a mistake or causes some delay, but not on an important issue of policy and not where a claim to individual rights is seriously involved, the Minister acknowledges the mistake and he accepts the responsibility although he is not personally involved. He states that he will take corrective action in the Department.'
4   Where action has been taken by a civil servant of which the minister disapproves and has no previous knowledge, and the conduct of the official is reprehensible, there is no obligation on a minister to endorse what he believes to be wrong or to defend what are clearly shown to be errors of his officers. He remains however, 'constitutionally responsible to Parliament for the fact that something has gone wrong', but this does not affect his power to control and discipline his staff.[54]

This statement, and the implications of the Crichel Down affair, have been much discussed.[55] Between 1954 and 1982, no comparable instance of minis-

---

[52]   Cmd 9176, 1954.
[53]   Cmd 9220, 1954.
[54]   H. C. Deb., 20 Jul. 1954, cols. 1286–7.
[55]   See *e.g.* J. A. G. Griffith (1955) 8 M.L.R. 557; C. J. Hamson (1954) 32 *Public Administration* 383; D.N. Chester (1954) 32 *Public Administration* 389.

terial resignation occurred. While the above analysis is often quoted, it must be remembered that the responsibility of a minister to Parliament is a political relationship which does not fit within a neat code of rules. Moreover these four categories were intended to identify situations in which a minister must 'accept responsibility' without blaming civil servants. There is no suggestion in the statement that a minister has to resign if he does accept responsibility.

Subsequent events have confirmed that there is no duty upon a minister to resign when maladministration has occurred within his department. As Professor Finer has shown,[56] whether a minister may resign depends on a variety of political factors, including the attitude of the Prime Minister, the mood of the party, the temperament of the minister and other political factors. (Rather different considerations apply where the personal conduct of a minister is in issue: an inadvertent and harmless disclosure of a Budget secret led to the resignation of Hugh Dalton as Chancellor of the Exchequer in 1947;[57] and resignations occurred in 1963 of the Secretary of State for War for having lied to the Commons in a personal statement[58] and of ministers in 1973 because of personal improprieties.[59] Where no question of personal misconduct is involved, it may be considered desirable for a minister to resign to avoid a possible clash of interest between his public position and his private interests: Mr Maudling resigned as Home Secretary in 1972 after his name had been mentioned in connection with the Poulson group of companies, whose affairs were being investigated by the police.)

In 1964, when investigation by the Comptroller and Auditor-General revealed that there had been an over-payment of more than £4 million by the Ministry of Aviation to Ferranti Ltd in respect of work on defence contracts, and that this overpayment need not have occurred if two sections of the ministry had pooled their information, the minister, Julian Amery, explained to the House what had occurred and the steps taken to remedy the position, and displayed no intention of resigning: the Opposition motion of censure was defeated.[60] In 1968, when the first major investigation by the Parliamentary Commissioner for Administration established that there had been maladministration within the Foreign Office in the Sachsenhausen affair[61] the Foreign Secretary, Mr George Brown, assumed direct personal responsibility for the decisions of the Foreign Office, which he maintained were correct, while agreeing to provide compensation for the claimants. In the debate he said: 'We will breach a very serious constitutional position if we start holding officials responsible for things that are done wrong . . . If things are wrongly done, then they are wrongly done by ministers'.[62] This statement did not take full account of the duties of the Parliamentary Commissioner for Administration, whose investigation into departmental conduct must inevitably probe behind statements made for the department by the minister. But the creation

---

56   S. E. Finer, (1956) 34 *Public Administration* 377.
57   H.C.20 (1947–8).
58   H. C. Deb., 22 Mar. 1963, col. 809; 17 Jun. 1963, cols. 34–170. And see Cmnd 2152, 1963.
59   Cmnd 5367, 1973.
60   H. C. Deb., 30 Jul. 1964, col. 1801.
61   Page 726 *post*; and see G. K. Fry, [1970] P.L. 336.
62   H. C. Deb., 5 Feb. 1968, col. 112.

of the Parliamentary Commissioner did not mean a complete change in the relationship between minister and civil servant. As the Attorney-General, Sir Elwyn Jones, said on this matter in 1968:

It is only in exceptional cases that blame should be attached to the individual civil servant and it follows from the principle that the minister alone has responsibility for the actions of his department that the individual civil servant who has contributed to the collective decision of the department should remain anonymous.[63]

In terms of this statement, an 'exceptional case' was provided by the investigation into the affairs of the Vehicle and General Insurance company.

In March 1971, the company collapsed, leaving a million policy holders uninsured. The Department of Trade and Industry had statutory powers of supervision and control of insurance companies but it failed to exercise these powers in respect of the company. Following allegations of misconduct, the government appointed a statutory tribunal of inquiry[64] to inquire, *inter alia*, whether there had been negligence or misconduct by persons in the service of the Crown 'directly or indirectly responsible' for the government's statutory functions. The tribunal reported that Mr C. W. Jardine, under-secretary, and two named assistant secretaries were responsible for the failure to deal with the risk of the company's insolvency before 1971, and that the under-secretary's conduct fell below the standard which could reasonably be expected of an official in that position, and constituted negligence. The tribunal found that no other civil servants and no minister acted negligently. Under a scheme of delegation within the department, almost all the work allocated to a division was dealt with at the level of under-secretary or below. 'The responsibility for deciding whether or not to exercise the Department's powers lay with Mr Jardine as the Under-Secretary in charge of the Insurance and Companies Division.'[65] In the absence of a reference to them his superiors were entitled to assume that he did not feel in doubt as to the course to be pursued.

The significance of the report lies in the fact that, after a full public examination of administration within a very large department, the tribunal held that a single official should bear the entire responsibility for the department's inactivity. While the tribunal may have correctly described the facts which they had found, did this resolve the question of political responsibility to Parliament? If so, what is left of the principle that a minister takes the praise for the successes of his department and the blame for its failures? It is today a fiction that all decisions are taken by ministers. But unless some responsibility is borne by ministers for senior officials, the entire bureaucratic structure will have broken free from democratic control.[66] If a tribunal of inquiry had not been appointed in the Vehicle and General case, the Commons would scarcely have been disposed to accept a statement from the Secretary for Trade and Industry pillorying the luckless Mr Jardine.

In April 1982, the Argentine invasion of the Falkland Islands led to the resignation of the Foreign Secretary, Lord Carrington, and two Foreign Office ministers. The ministers stated that they accepted responsibility for the conduct of policy on the Falkland Islands, and insisted against the express wishes of the Prime Minister that they should resign. The resignation of the

---

63   H.C. 350 (1967–8) para. 24.
64   Under the Tribunals of Inquiry (Evidence) Act 1921: ch. 37 C.
65   H.L. 80, H.C. 133 (1971–2) para. 344.
66   See H. C. Deb., 1 May 1972, col. 34; and R. J. S. Baker, (1972) 43 *Political Quarterly* 340.

Defence Secretary, Mr Nott, was offered but refused by the Prime Minister on the ground that his department was not responsible for policy on the Falkland Islands. A committee of privy councillors later reviewed the way in which government responsibilities had been discharged before the invasion, and found that there had been a misjudgment of the situation within the Foreign Office and recommended changes in the intelligence organisation; but no blame could be attached to any individual, nor did the committee consider that criticism for the circumstances leading to the invasion could be attached to the government.[67] The report thus cleared the ministers who had resigned of any culpability, but the resignations had served a political purpose and may have helped to revive earlier notions of personal responsibility for institutional behaviour.

Relation between individual and collective responsibility
The relation between individual and collective responsibility is very close. As we have seen, if a minister is the subject of a vote of censure for his policies, he can expect to receive the support of his colleagues. A departmental minister has authority to make decisions which relate exclusively to the sphere for which he is responsible. But on many matters he has to consult with other departments. As there are few policy decisions which do not affect expenditure or civil service manpower, consultation with the Treasury is often essential. Policy decisions taken by English departments may involve consultation with the Scottish and Welsh Offices, and vice versa. Many decisions announced by a minister will have been taken or approved by Cabinet committees, whose existence and composition are usually not disclosed.[68] One reason for this secrecy is to avoid creating a level of responsibility intermediate between the minister's individual responsibility and the Cabinet's collective responsibility.

Ministerial responsibility and the courts
The responsibility of ministers to Parliament consists of a duty to account to Parliament for what they and their department are doing. The courts play no direct part in determining the extent of that duty or in enforcing it: but the duty is so essential to an understanding of British government that the courts have taken note of its existence. By legislative practice, administrative powers are usually vested in a specified minister. Does this mean in law that only the minister may exercise these powers?

In *Carltona Ltd* v. *Commissioners of Works*, an order to requisition a factory was issued under defence regulations by an assistant secretary in the Ministry of Works, and it was challenged on the ground that the First Commissioner of Works, who was the competent minister, had not personally considered the matter. The order was upheld by the court. Lord Greene M.R. said that government could not be carried on unless civil servants could take decisions on behalf of the minister. 'Constitutionally, the decision of such an official [*i.e.* the assistant secretary] is, of course, the decision of the minister. The minister is responsible. It is he who must answer before Parliament for anything that his officials have done under his authority'.[69]

---

67 Cmnd 8787, 1983.
68 Ch. 14 A.
69 [1943] 2 All E.R. 560, 563. And see *Lewisham MB* v. *Roberts* [1949] 2 K.B. 608; *Dalziel School Board* v. *Scotch Education Department* 1915 S.C. 234 and *R.* v. *Skinner* [1968] 2 Q.B. 700.

While therefore a minister's powers may in law be exercised on his behalf by civil servants, and it is not necessary to establish a formal delegation of authority to them (in the absence of an express statutory provision requiring such delegation),[70] the courts have maintained that the minister remains responsible to Parliament. However, there may be cases where from the nature of the power or for other reasons the general principle does not apply and powers must be exercised personally by the minister.[71] Where a statutory duty is vested in one minister, he may not adopt a policy whereby decisions are effectively made by another minister.[72]

Judicial discussion of ministerial responsibility has generally occurred when a citizen has sought a legal remedy against central government in respect of an act or omission which adversely affects him. In such cases, the courts have sometimes held that the remedy through Parliament which ministerial responsibility may provide is better suited to the citizen's complaint than a legal remedy. Thus in 1876, in denying a citizen a legal right to claim compensation out of a fund provided to the British government by the Emperor of China, Lord Coleridge C. J. said that, if there had been a failure by the government to administer the fund correctly, the failure was one which Parliament could and would correct.[73] In *Local Government Board* v. *Arlidge*, the House of Lords had to determine whether natural justice at common law bound a department in the procedure by which a decision was taken in the name of the minister following a public inquiry. In denying that the minister was bound to give a personal hearing to the citizen whose property was affected, the House stressed the minister's constitutional responsibility to Parliament, not only for his own acts but also for all that was done in his department.[74] In 1947, when a compulsory purchase order made by a minister was challenged, Lord Greene M. R. said: 'In a nutshell, the decision of the minister is a thing for which he must be answerable in Parliament, and his actions cannot be controlled by the courts'.[75]

Now this is a legitimate conclusion for a court to reach when it is satisfied that the minister's decision is not to be faulted on any legal grounds. But as an abstract statement of principle, the dictum is misleading if it implies that the courts *cannot* control a minister's decision *because* he is answerable to Parliament for it. This implication is not consistent with many decisions of the courts which will be considered in Part III of this book. In many areas of government, both the courts and Parliament have a role to play in controlling or influencing the use which departments make of their powers. In the past, judicial reliance on ministerial responsibility adversely affected the development of administrative law,[76] although as long ago as 1911, one judge doubted whether ministerial responsibility was 'more than the mere shadow of a

---

70   *Commissioners of Customs and Excise* v. *Cure & Deeley Ltd* [1962] 1 Q.B. 340.
71   *E.g.* Immigration Act 1971, in respect of exclusion or deportation orders: ss. 13(4), 14(3) and 15(4); and see de Smith, *Judicial Review*, pp. 307–9.
72   *Lavender and Son Ltd* v. *Minister of Housing* [1970] 3 All E.R. 871.
73   *Rustomjee* v. *R.* (1876) 2 Q.B.D. 69, 74.
74   [1915] A.C. 120; p. 645 *post*.
75   *Johnson and Co. (Builders) Ltd* v. *Minister of Health* [1947] 2 All E.R. 395, 400. And see *Liversidge* v. *Anderson* [1947] A.C. 206.
76   See J. D. B. Mitchell [1965] P.L. 95; and Dicey, App. 2.

name'.[77] Today, while many broad policy issues are not suitable for judicial decision, and while certain executive decisions are considered by the courts to be unsuitable for them to review,[78] it is widely accepted that judicial control and ministerial responsibility to Parliament serve complementary purposes, and are not mutually exclusive.

Conclusion

The principle of responsible government is broader and ultimately more important than ministerial responsibility. The British system has placed great weight upon the necessity of subjecting the departments of central government to control by ministers, who are the link between the executive and Parliament. Excessive devotion to the principle of ministerial responsibility today will mean inadequate supervision of departmental activities, unless parliamentary procedures are reformed to keep abreast of the scale of government. Yet the principle was invoked as an argument *against* constitutional developments (for example, the Parliamentary Commissioner for Administration and the use of specialist committees by the Commons) which opened up new ways of exerting democratic control over government and which threatened the working arrangements which had grown up between ministers and civil servants. While parliamentary government requires the continuance of the ministerial system, there is no reason for supposing that at a given moment. of time the boundaries of ministerial responsibility are drawn in the right places[79] or that new means of strengthening parliamentary control over government should not be found. Finally, since different forms of control over government serve different purposes, the existence of ministerial responsibility need not inhibit the development of an effective system of administrative law.

---

[77] *Dyson* v. *A.-G.* [1911] 1 K.B. 410, 422 (Farwell L.J.).

[78] E.g. *R.* v. *Home Secretary, ex p. Hosenball* [1977] 3 All E.R. 452; *Gouriet* v. *Union of Post Office Workers* [1978] A.C. 435.

[79] Fulton Report on the Civil Service, Cmnd 3638, 1968, para. 190.

Chapter 8

The United Kingdom and the European Communities

A. The EEC and Community law[1]

In 1973, the United Kingdom became a member of the European Economic
Community (EEC), the European Community for Atomic Energy (Euratom)
and the European Coal and Steel Community (ECSC).[2] This chapter is principally concerned with the legal implications of membership of the EEC.
Member states of the EEC have undertaken to establish a common market and
approximate their economic policies.[3] The objectives of the EEC include the
elimination of customs duties and quantitative restrictions on imports and
exports between themselves; the establishment of a common customs tariff and
common commercial policies towards non-member states; the abolition of
obstacles to freedom of movement of persons, services and capital within
member states; the creation of procedures to ensure that competition within
the common market is not distorted; such approximation of the laws of
member states as is necessary for the proper functioning of the common
market; and the establishment of common policies in such matters as agriculture and transport.[4] If such objectives are to be achieved Community law
must be applied in a uniform manner in the member states and this is most
easily achieved by treating Community obligations as separate from, and
prevailing over, national law. In the words of the Court of Justice of the
Communities,

The EEC Treaty has created its own legal system which [has become] an integral part
of the legal systems of the member states and which their courts are bound to apply.
By creating a Community of unlimited duration, having its own institutions, its own

---

[1] See: T. C. Hartley, *The Foundations of European Community Law*; P. S. R. F. Mathijsen, *A Guide to
European Community Law*; D. Lasok & J. W. Bridge, *Introduction to Law and Institutions of the
European Communities*; K. Lipstein, *The Law of the European Community*; P. J. G. Kapteyn & P.
Verloren Van Themaat, *Introduction to the Law of the European Communities*; A. Parry & S.
Hardy, *EEC Law*.

[2] The other member states are France, Germany, Italy, Belgium, Holland, Luxembourg,
Denmark, Republic of Ireland and Greece. For the establishment of the three Communities
see Mathijsen, *op. cit.*, ch. 2, Lasok & Bridge, *op. cit.*, ch. 1.

[3] EEC Treaty 1957 (Cmnd 5179–11, 1972) art. 2.

[4] *Ibid.*, art. 3.

personality, its own legal capacity ... and, more particularly, real powers stemming from a limitation of sovereignty or a transfer of powers from the states to the Community, the member states have limited their sovereign rights, albeit within limited fields, and have thus created a body of law which binds both their nationals and themselves. . . . The executive force of Community law cannot vary from one state to another in deference to subsequent domestic laws, without jeopardising the attainment of the objectives of the Treaty.[5]

By virtue of this principle, Community law thus prevails over the inconsistent domestic law of member states.

In *Costa* v. *ENEL*, Italy had nationalised the production and distribution of electricity and transferred the assets of private electricity undertakings to a new state body, ENEL. Costa, as a shareholder in one of the undertakings nationalised and as an electricity consumer, claimed before an Italian court that the 1962 Italian nationalisation legislation infringed provisions of the EEC Treaty. When the matter was considered by the Court of Justice of the Communities, the Italian Government argued that the Italian court was obliged to apply the Italian nationalisation legislation. However, the Court of Justice held *inter alia* that Community law prevailed over subsequent incompatible national law.[6]

Similarly, in the view of the Court of Justice, Community law prevails over the constitutional provisions of member states.

In the *Internationale Handelsgesellschaft* case, the plaintiff company obtained an export licence for maize on payment of a deposit which could be forfeited if the total quantity of maize specified was not in fact exported. The licence was issued under an EEC regulation. The company failed to export the specified quantity of maize and notice was served that the 'deposit would be forfeited. The company argued that the forfeiture would be contrary to the German Basic Law (constitution). The Court of Justice held that 'the validity of a Community instrument or its effect within a member state cannot be affected by allegations that it strikes at either the fundamental rights as formulated in a state's constitution or the principles of a national constitutional structure'.[7]

Community law is thus law within member states and prevails over national law. As Community law is part of the law of member states it is commonly described as 'directly applicable'. Some of these Community law provisions may also create rights and obligations for individuals which, by Community law, member states are bound to protect; such provisions of Community law are commonly described as 'directly effective'.[8] There is consequently a close relationship between the Community legal system and the legal system of member states, for Community law is applied and enforced by national courts subject to the jurisdiction of the Court of Justice.[9] This close relationship has

---

[5] *Costa* v. *ENEL* [1964] E.C.R. 585, 593.

[6] [1964] C.M.L.R. 425; see also the *Simmenthal* cases: [1977] 2 C.M.L.R. 1; [1978] 3 C.M.L.R. 263 and 670.

[7] [1972] C.M.L.R. 255, 283; see also *Re Export Tax on Art Treasures (No. 2)* [1972] C.M.L.R. 699.

[8] For further discussion see J. Winter [1972] 9 C.M.L. Rev. 425; D. Wyatt & A. Dashwood, *The Substantive Law of the EEC*, ch. 3; J. P. Warner [1979] 93 L.Q.R. 349.

[9] *E.g.* EEC Treaty, art. 177 (p. 133 *post*): art. 192 (enforcement of Community pecuniary obligations by national courts). In certain circumstances, the same facts may result in parallel actions under national and Community law: *e.g. Wilhelm* v. *Bundeskartallamt* [1969] C.M.L.R. 100.

posed difficulties for national courts.[10]

Membership of the European Communities clearly has important legal and constitutional consequences for the United Kingdom. However, before discussing these consequences, it is necessary to examine the institutions of the Community, the nature of Community law and the jurisdiction of the Court of Justice of the Communities.

The institutions of the Community

Four principal institutions serve the EEC, Euratom and the ECSC.[11] Their powers and functions differ somewhat under the Treaties establishing the three Communities. Here the powers and functions of the institutions under the EEC Treaty are considered.

1 The Commission. The Commission has wide executive powers and an important role in the Community legislative process. It consists of fourteen members who are appointed 'by common accord of the governments of the member states' for a renewable term of four years.[12] From among the Commissioners the governments also appoint a President and five Vice-Presidents of the Commission for renewable terms of two years.[13] The Commission must include among its members at least one national of each member state but no more than two.[14] Commissioners must be independent of the governments, and member states undertake not to attempt to influence the Commissioners in the performance of their duties.[15] The independence of the Commissioners is emphasised because it is an essential task of the Commission to represent the interests of the Community. It has been suggested that this independence would be enhanced if the President of the Commission were appointed by the governments of the member states and the remaining Commissioners appointed by the Commission President and the Council of Ministers, and if the European Parliament were given a role in the appointment of the Commission.[16]

Although the Commission takes decisions collectively, each Commissioner

---

[10]   E.g. France, *Directeur Général des Douanes* v. *Société des Cafés Jacques etc.* [1975] 2 C.M.L.R. 336, M. Simon, (1976) 92 L.Q.R. 85; in Belgium, *Le Ski* [1972] C.M.L.R. 330; in Germany, *Internationale Handelsgesellschaft* [1972] C.M.L.R. 177; in Italy, *Costa* v. *ENEL* [1964] C.M.L.R. 425, *Frontini* v. *Ministero delle Finanze* [1974] 2 C.M.L.R. 372.

[11]   Among other important Community institutions are (a) the Court of Auditors, established in 1977 to examine the accounts and financial management of the Community; (b) the European Investment Bank; (c) the Economic and Social Committee, which serves both the EEC and EURATOM and plays a significant role in the Community legislative process: see Lasok & Bridge, *op. cit.*, ch. 8.

[12]   Merger Treaty 1965, art. 11 (Cmnd 5179–11, 1972), as amended.

[13]   *Ibid.*, art. 14; and first Act of Accession, art. 16.

[14]   *Ibid.*, art. 10. In practice, two Commissioners are appointed from the nationals of each of the four larger member states (United Kingdom, France, Germany and Italy) and one from each of the others. In 1979, two studies suggested that a Commission consisting of just one Commissioner from each member state would increase efficiency: see *Proposals for Reform of the Commission of the European Communities and its Services* ('The Spierenburg Report') and *Report on European Institutions* ('The Three Wise Men's Report').

[15]   *Ibid.*, art. 10.

[16]   *Report on European Union, Bulletin of the European Communities*, Suppl. 1/76, pp. 31–2.

has responsibility for specific aspects of the Community's activities.[17] The Commission has a staff of approximately 9,000 divided into nineteen Directorates-General corresponding to the main functions of the Communities, for example, the Directorates-General for External Relations, Agriculture, and Regional Policy.[18] Each Directorate-General is the responsibility of a Director-General who in turn is responsible to a Commissioner.

One important function of the Commission is to ensure that Community law is obeyed.[19] Where the Commission considers that a member state has failed to fulfil its treaty obligations it may initiate proceedings which can lead ultimately to bringing the state before the Court of Justice.[20] The Commission may also challenge in that Court the legality of action taken by the Council of Ministers or its failure to act.[21]

The Commission plays an important role in the legislative process of the Communities. Normally it is the Commission which may initiate legislative proposals.[22] A common formula in the Treaty is that the Council of Ministers shall take action 'on a proposal of the Commission and after consulting the Assembly'. In some cases the Commission is obliged to submit a proposal, in others it has a discretion whether to do so. Failure by the Commission to submit a proposal to the Council within a time limit laid down in the Treaty could be challenged in the Court of Justice.[23]

In drawing up its proposals the Commission consults widely. There is frequent consultation with pressure groups, civil servants from member states, and the staff of the Council of Ministers.[24] After submission of a proposal to the Council of Ministers, the Commission may alter it 'as long as the Council has not acted'.[25] The Commission may, therefore, amend its proposal at any time prior to the adoption by the Council of legislation based on the proposal. Such amendments by the Commission may take account of the views of the Assembly or of deliberations within the Council itself. The position of the Commission in the Community legislative process is enhanced by the fact that where the Council acts on a Commission proposal it may only amend the proposal by unanimous vote.[26] Furthermore, where the Commission objects

---

[17] The Commission takes decisions by majority vote: Merger Treaty, art. 17(1). However, it is not always necessary for the Commission to meet as a body to take decisions. It may delegate authority to an individual Commissioner to take previously agreed action or it may simply circulate a proposal which in the absence of objections is taken as agreed policy. See *Re Noordwijks Cement Accoord* [1967] C.M.L.R. 77; E. Noel, *The European Community: How it works*, p. 66.

[18] There are also several 'service' departments such as the Secretariat General, the Statistical Office and the Legal Service; on the latter, see C.-D. Ehlermann, *The Role of the Legal Service of the Commission in the Creation of Community Law*.

[19] EEC Treaty, art. 155.

[20] *Ibid.*, art. 169, p. 131 *post*.

[21] *Ibid.*, arts. 173, 175, pp. 132–3 *post*.

[22] However, under art. 152, the Council of Ministers 'may request the Commission ... to submit to it any appropriate proposals'.

[23] EEC Treaty, arts. 175, 176.

[24] Merger Treaty, art. 15.

[25] EEC Treaty, art. 149.

[26] *Ibid.*

strongly to such a proposed amendment, the Commission may withdraw its proposal completely, thus making it impossible for the Council to act on it.

The Commission may itself legislate in certain fields[27] and the Council has delegated other legislative and executive functions to it.[28] The Commission also administers and implements the Community budget, maintains relations with international organisations and negotiates agreements on behalf of the Communities.[29]

2 The Council of Ministers.   The Council of Ministers has wide decision-making powers.[30] It is the Council, for example, which ultimately adopts most Community legislation,[31] lays down budgetary procedures[32] and concludes international agreements on behalf of the EEC.[33]

The Council is composed of a representative of each member state, who is normally a government minister.[34] The presidency of the Council is held by each member state in turn for a period of six months.[35] The Commission normally attends Council meetings.

Before the Council takes a decision on a Commission proposal, the proposal is examined by a committee or a working party of the Council and this is supervised by the Committee of Permanent Representatives (COREPER). COREPER consists of civil servants from each member state. It co-ordinates the attitudes of each state towards Commission proposals, thus enabling the Council to reach its decisions more easily.[36]

The EEC Treaty provides for complex voting procedures within the Council of Ministers. Decisions may require a unanimous vote, a qualified majority vote on a Commission proposal, a qualified majority vote where no Commission proposal is required or, where no other procedure is provided, a simple majority vote.[37]

For some years little use was made of these voting procedures, which were designed to balance the interests of the larger and smaller member states. One reason for this is that in 1966, after some months in which France had boycotted Community institutions, the Council of Ministers in the 'Luxembourg Agreement' accepted that where decisions were to be taken by majority vote on a Commission proposal in which 'very important interests of one or more partners' were at stake, member states should try to reach a unanimous decision. However, if a unanimous decision were not reached within a reasonable time, all the member states, except France, agreed that the normal voting

---

27   *E.g.* EEC Treaty, art. 48(3) (*d*).
28   *E.g. ibid.*, arts. 87, 79. See also *Bulletin of the European Communities*, 6/74, 122.
29   EEC Treaty, arts. 205, 228, 229–31.
30   *Ibid.*, art. 145.
31   *E.g. ibid.*, arts. 48, 49 (free movement of labour); 75 (transport policy).
32   *Ibid.*, art. 209.
33   *Ibid.*, art. 228.
34   *Ibid.*, art. 146; Merger Treaty, art. 2. Which ministers attend depends on the Council agenda *e.g.* agriculture ministers will usually attend Council meetings where agriculture is to be discussed. Council meetings may be held simultaneously to discuss different subjects.
35   Merger Treaty, art. 2.
36   On the work of COREPER see E. Noel, 5 *Journal of Common Market Studies* (1967) 219; E. Noel & H. Etienne, 6 *Government and Opposition* (1971) 447.
37   EEC Treaty, art. 148.

procedure should then apply; France considered that 'discussion must be continued until unanimous agreement is reached'.[38]

After the Luxembourg Agreement, there was a tendency for the Council to reach its decisions only by unanimity. As a result, particularly in the enlarged Community, the decision making process in the Council was frequently transformed into a rather slow process of negotiation. This may have contributed to the tendency of member states to take difficult political decisions closely connected with the development of the Communities outside the formal meetings of the Council of Ministers.[39]

More recently, member states have sought means of avoiding the constraints of reaching decisions by unanimity[40] and on one occasion in 1982 the Council of Ministers abandoned the concept of unanimity when the United Kingdom sought to apply the Luxembourg Agreement as part of its opposition to the adoption of Community agricultural prices.[41]

3 The Assembly. The Assembly, or the European Parliament as it is commonly called, exercises advisory and supervisory powers.[42] Until June 1979, the Assembly was composed of delegates designated by the parliaments of each member state from among their own members.[43] However, article 138 of the EEC Treaty requires the adoption of a uniform procedure for direct elections to the Assembly. To comply with the Treaty, the Council of Ministers decided in 1975 that the first direct elections would be held in 1979.[44] This Community legislation governed some aspects of the election. It stipulated, for instance, the number of members to be elected from each member state, eighty-one members in the case of the United Kingdom, and provided that members of the Assembly were to be elected for a renewable five-year term. It was not possible, however, to agree a uniform electoral procedure and much of the detailed procedure was left to the discretion of member states. In consequence, the UK Parliament enacted the European Assembly Elections Act 1978.[45] This Act divided Great Britain into seventy-eight constituencies, each constituency returning one member to the Assembly by simple majority vote; Northern Ireland formed a single constituency, returning three members by single transferable vote. In most respects, the procedure laid down in the Act followed that for domestic parliamentary elections.

The Assembly meets in plenary session some 12 to 14 times a year, for a few days on each occasion. Members of the Assembly sit and vote as political

---

38   For the text of the Luxembourg Agreement see *Bulletin of the European Communities*, 3/66, 5.
39   *E.g.* there are now regular meetings of the foreign ministers of member states and also of heads of government, the latter described as meetings of the 'European Council', which are independent of meetings of the Council of Ministers.
40   See *8th General Report on the Activities of the European Communities* (1975), p. 298; *11th General Report on the Activities of the European Communities* (1978), p. 23; E. Noel, *The European Community: How it Works*, p. 29.
41   *The Times*, 19 May 1982; (1982) 7 E. L. Rev. 145; (1982) 19 C. M. L. Rev. 371.
42   EEC Treaty, art. 137; in 1962, the Assembly adopted the title 'European Parliament': J.O. 1962, 1045.
43   EEC Treaty, art. 138.
44   O.J. 1976, L. 278: second Act of Accession 1979, art. 23. The Assembly has a total of 434 members.
45   See also the European Assembly Elections Act 1981; *Prince* v. *Younger* [1984] 1 C.M.L.R. 723.

rather than national groups. The Assembly has established *ad hoc* and standing committees. The standing committees each specialise in an area of Community activity. They examine Commission proposals within their sphere of competence and report on them prior to a debate in the Assembly. The Assembly committees maintain close contact with the Council and Commission and have become an important element in the supervision which the Assembly exercises over the other Community institutions.

The Assembly has a merely advisory role in the Community legislative process. The EEC Treaty commonly provides that the Council of Ministers must consult the Assembly on Commission proposals which have been submitted to it. This procedure is of limited political significance,[46] because neither the Commission nor the Council is obliged to amend a proposal in the light of the Assembly's opinions.[47]

In addition, the Assembly has a supervisory function. It may put both written and oral questions to the Commission and the Council.[48] In 1973, a 'question time' was introduced which allows for supplementary questions and some limited debate between members of the Assembly, the Commission and the Council. The Assembly also has the power to pass a motion of censure on the Commision.[49] If the motion of censure is passed the Commission is obliged to resign, but the Commissioners remain in office until they are replaced. A motion of censure may only be moved by a recognised political group within the Assembly or one-tenth of the current Assembly members. For the motion to be carried a 'two-thirds majority of the votes cast, representing a majority of the members' is required. Such motions of censure are extremely rare, possibly because the procedure has little utility.[50] For example, the Assembly may pass a motion of censure against the Commission as a whole, but not against an individual Commissioner. Moreover, the procedure does not give the Assembly any control over the Council nor over the appointment of the new Commission.[51]

Finally, the Assembly has limited powers over the Community budget.[52] The procedure for adopting the budget is complex but, in brief, the Assembly has ultimate control over the 'non-compulsory' part of the budget, which relates to the fuctioning of Community institutions and amounts to some 25 per cent of the total budget. The Council of Ministers has final control over

---

46   Failure to consult where it is obligatory to do so would be a ground for challenging the legality of the legislation: EEC Treaty, arts. 173, 190. See also *S. A. Roquette Frères* v. *EC Council* [1980] E.C.R. 3333.

47   Since 1975, there has been a conciliation procedure which may be invoked where the Council intends to depart from the opinion of the Assembly in adopting Community acts of general application which have appreciable financial implications: O.J. 1975, C89.

48   EEC Treaty, art. 140. The *European Parliament Rules of Procedure* provide for written questions, oral questions without debate and oral questions with debate. The Commission and the Council normally attend meetings of the Assembly.

49   EEC Treaty, art. 144; *European Parliament Rules of Procedure*, Rule 21.

50   See V. Herman & J. Lodge, *The European Parliament and the European Community*, p. 48 *et seq.*

51   However, the Assembly may bring an action in the Court of Justice where, in violation of the EEC Treaty, either the Commission or the Council has failed to act: art. 175.

52   *Ibid.*, art. 203, as amended; Budgetary Treaty 1970 (Cmnd 5179–11) arts. 1–9; Financial Provisions Treaty 1975 (O.J. 1977, L 359); P. J. G. Kapteyn (1972) 9 C.M.L. Rev. 386; C.–D. Ehlermann (1975) 12 C.M.L. Rev. 325.

the remainder of the budget, which relates to expenditure arising from the application of Community law, principally the common agricultural policy. However, the Assembly alone may formally adopt the budget and this tends to increase its influence. In 1980, for instance, the Assembly refused to adopt the draft budget for over six months in an attempt to persuade the Council to reduce expenditure on agriculture.[53]

It has been widely recognised that there is a serious lack of democratic control within the Community and there have been a number of proposals for increasing the Assembly's modest powers. Direct elections to the Assembly have stimulated demand for increased powers, but the nature of the powers which are granted to it will depend largely on the measure of political agreement on the future objectives and development of the Community.[54]

4 The Court of Justice.   The EEC Treaty provides that the Court of Justice 'shall ensure that in the interpretation and application of this Treaty the law is observed'.[55] The Court consists of eleven judges appointed by the governments of member states.[56] Judges are appointed for a renewable term of six years. Once appointed, a judge may only be removed from office if it is the unanimous opinion of the other judges and the advocates-general that 'he no longer fulfils the requisite conditions or meets the obligations arising from his office'.[57]

The judges are assisted by five advocates-general. The office of advocate-general has no parallel in the United Kingdom. His principal function is to consider the issues of each case independently of the judges and make a reasoned submission in open court after the parties to the case have completed their submissions. The advocate-general does not participate in the formulation of the judgement and his submissions are not binding on the Court. However, the Court frequently accepts his conclusions and refers to his submissions in its judgments.[58]

From amongst their own number the judges appoint a President of the Court.[59] The Court usually sits in plenary session but for certain purposes it may also sit in separate chambers of three or five judges.

The normal procedure of the Court includes both a written and an oral stage. Once a case is filed with the Court, the President appoints one of the judges as rapporteur. There follows an exchange of very full written pleadings by the parties. The pleadings are examined by the judge-rapporteur and the advocate-general assigned to the case, who both report on them to the Court.

---

[53]   See C. Sopwith (1980) 17 C.M.L. Rev. 315; J. Pipkorn (1981) 18 C.M.L. Rev. 141.
[54]   See *e.g. 6th General Report on the Activities of the European Communities* (1973); *The Enlargement of the Powers of the European Parliament* (H.M.S.O.: 1972); *Report on European Union, Bulletin of the European Communities*, Suppl. 1/76.
[55]   EEC Treaty, art. 164.
[56]   *Ibid.*, arts. 165, 167. In practice a national of each member state sits in the Court, the eleventh judgeship being held in rotation by nationals of the four larger member states, starting with a French judge: *Bulletin of the European Communities*, 1981–3, p. 63.
[57]   Statute of the Court (EEC), art. 6.
[58]   For an analysis of cases in which the Court has disagreed with the submissions of the Advocate-General see A. Campbell, *Common Market Law*, vols. 1 & 3, para. 6–33.
[59]   EEC Treaty, art. 167.

At this stage the Court usually decides whether *mesures d'instruction*, taking proof of the submissions made by the parties, will be required. There follows an oral stage in which the judge-rapporteur presents his report of the case, there is argument on behalf of the parties and the advocate-general makes his submission. Subsequently the Court delivers a single judgment in open court. The decision of the Court is final but it may, in limited circumstances, be revised or interpreted by the Court.[60]

The sources of Community law

1   Community treaties.   The principal sources of Community law are the treaties which established the three Communities and the treaties which have amended them. In many respects these treaties may be seen as the constitution of the Communities.[61] The EEC Treaty, for example, lays down the objectives of the Community and these objectives are used by the Court of Justice in interpreting the treaty.[62] The EEC Treaty also determines (a) the duties and powers of the Community institutions and (b) the rights and obligations of member states.In addition to these constitutional provisions, the EEC Treaty contains many, often detailed, substantive provisions which implement the objectives of the Community.

The treaties establishing the Communities are binding on member states and Community institutions. In certain circumstances the treaties may also create rights for individuals which may be enforced before national courts.

In *Van Gend en Loos* v. *Nederlandse Tariefcommissie*, an 8% duty was levied on a quantity of ureaformaldehyde imported into the Netherlands from Germany by the plaintiff company. The Netherlands had reclassified ureaformaldehyde for purposes of import duty after the EEC Treaty had come into force and as a result the level of duty increased from 3% to 8%. The company appealed to a Dutch customs tribunal against the level of duty imposed, arguing that the increase in duty was contrary to article 12 of the EEC Treaty, which requires member states not to increase customs duty already levied in their trade with each other. The Dutch tribunal sought a preliminary ruling from the Court of Justice on whether article 12 created rights for individuals enforceable before national courts. The Court of Justice held that article 12 did create such rights because (a) it imposed a clear and unconditional prohibition, (b) its implementation did not require legislation to be passed within member states, and (c) it could not be varied by such legislation. Although the obligation not to increase duty was laid on member states, private persons could benefit from this obligation.[63]

2 Community legislation.   An important secondary source of Community law is the legislation which Community institutions are empowered to make under Community treaties. Under the EEC Treaty, the Council and the Commission may make regulations, issue directives and take decisions.[64] This

---

[60]   Statute of the Court (EEC), arts. 40 & 41; Rules of Procedure of the Court, arts. 98–100, 102; see also L. N. Brown & F. G. Jacobs, *The Court of Justice of the European Communities*.

[61]   *Cf.* A. M. Donner (1974) 11 C.M.L. Rev. 127.

[62]   *E.g. Continental Can Case* [1973] C.M.L.R. 199, 224.

[63]   [1963] C.M.L.R. 105. For a list of articles of the EEC Treaty which the Court of Justice has held create rights enforceable by individuals before national courts, see Lasok & Bridge, *op. cit.*, pp. 275–7.

[64]   EEC Treaty, art. 189. The Commission and the Council may also make recommendations and deliver opinions, but usually they are not legally binding.

legislation must be reasoned, that is, it must indicate the authority by which it is made, the reasons for making it, and that any proposals or opinions of other Community institutions required by the Treaty have been obtained.[65]

A *regulation* made by the Council or Commission is of 'general application, . . . binding in its entirety and directly applicable in all member states'.[66] Regulations are intended as a means of ensuring the uniform application of Community law; normally they are binding in all member states without requiring implementation or adoption by national law.[67] Regulations prevail over inconsistent national law and may create rights enforceable by individuals before national courts.

In *Leonesio* v. *Italian Ministry of Agriculture*, EEC regulations were made to encourage the reduction of milk production in the Community. The regulations provided a cash premium for farmers who agreed to slaughter their dairy cows and not to engage in milk production for five years, The regulations also provided that each member state was to arrange for the administration of the scheme and be responsible for the payment of the cash premiums which were financed partly by the Community and partly by the member state. Signora Leonesio, an Italian farmer, slaughtered five dairy cows in accordance with the regulations but the Italian Ministry of Agriculture refused to pay the cash premium. The ministry argued that, although the relevant EEC regulations were law in Italy, the Italian constitution required legislation to be passed to authorise new expenditure by the government. Until this legislation had been passed, the Italian government argued that it could not finance its share of the payments due under the regulations and must postpone payment of the premium.

When an Italian court sought a preliminary ruling on the matter the Court of Justice held that (a) a regulation 'produces immediate effects and is, as such, apt to attribute to individuals rights which national courts must uphold'; (b) once the member state had made the required administrative arrangements and the farmer had satisfied the necessary conditions, these particular regulations 'attribute to the farmer the right to demand the payment of the premium, and the member state cannot invoke its own laws or its own administrative practice to oppose the payment'. The Court was not prepared to see farmers in Italy being treated less favourably than in other member states; to do so 'would be in defiance of the fundamental principle prescribing the uniform application of the regulations throughout the Community'.[68]

A *directive* is 'binding as to the result to be achieved, upon each member state to whom it is addressed'.[69] Unlike a regulation, a directive leaves member states a choice of the method by which the result required by the directive must be achieved. A directive normally contains a time-limit within which it must be implemented. Although directives are addressed only to states and not to individuals,[70] there may be circumstances in which directives create rights for individuals enforceable in national courts.

In *Van Duyn* v. *Home Office*, the UK government, having decided that the Church of

---

65 EEC Treaty, art. 190. If the legislation is not reasoned an action may be brought in the Court of Justice to review the legislation and annul it: EEC Treaty, arts. 173, 174.

66 *Ibid.*, arts. 189, 191.

67 A regulation may leave administrative arrangements to be implemented by member states; sometimes a regulation will only apply to one state.

68 [1973] C.M.L.R. 343; see also *Commission* v. *United Kingdom* [1979] 2 C.M.L.R. 45.

69 EEC Treaty, art. 189.

70 *Consten & Grundig* v. *Commission* [1966] C.M.L.R. 418, 468.

Scientology was socially harmful, announced in 1968 that it would use existing powers to prevent aliens entering the United Kingdom to work for the Church. In 1973 Miss van Duyn, a citizen of the Netherlands and a scientologist, was refused leave to enter the United Kingdom to work for the Church of Scientology. She sought a High Court declaration that this refusal was unlawful, being contrary to the EEC Treaty, article 48, and Directive 64/221. Article 48 provides for the free movement of workers within the Community but allows member states to limit this freedom on grounds of public policy. Directive 64/221 provides that measures taken on grounds of public policy 'shall be based exclusively on the personal conduct of the individual concerned'. The High Court sought a preliminary ruling from the Court of Justice on, *inter alia*, whether Directive 64/221 could confer rights on individuals enforceable in national courts.

The Court of Justice held that the provision of the directive in question (a) laid down an unconditional obligation which does not require implementation by Community institutions or member states; (b) was a derogation in favour of individuals from an exception to a fundamental principle of the treaty (freedom of movement for workers) and on grounds of legal certainty individuals should be able to rely on it. Consequently the directive created rights for individuals enforceable before national courts.[71]

A *decision* is 'binding in its entirety on those to whom it is addressed'.[72] It may be addressed either to member states, individuals or companies. It must be notified to the addressee and takes effect on notification.[73] A decision may be distinguished from a directive because it is 'binding in its entirety'; it may be distinguished from a regulation because it is normally only binding on the addressee; however a decision addressed to a member state may affect the rights of an individual.[74]

3 Other sources.   In addition to the Community treaties, other international agreements may be sources of Community law. The EEC Treaty gives the Community certain treaty-making powers.[75] Apart from these powers, the Court of Justice has held that the Community may conclude treaties on any matter within the objectives of the EEC, as laid down in the EEC Treaty.[76] Treaties concluded by the Community are binding on the Community and on member states.[77] The EEC Treaty also requires member states to negotiate with each other for specific purposes.[78] Treaties entered into by member states as a result of this provision may create obligations binding in international law which are different from Community obligations. It is not yet clear whether

---

[71]   [1975] Ch. 358. See also *Grad* v. *Finanzamt Traunstein* [1971] C.M.L.R. 1; *Commission* v. *Italy* [1973] C.M.L.R. 773; *Pubblico Ministero* v. *Ratti* [1980] 1 C.M.L.R. 96; *Becker* v. *Finanzamt Münster-Innenstadt* [1982] 1 C.M.L.R. 499.

[72]   EEC Treaty, art. 189.

[73]   *Ibid.*, art. 191.

[74]   E.g. *SACE* v. *Italian Ministry of Finance* [1971] C.M.L.R. 123.

[75]   EEC Treaty, art. 228; see also arts. 111, 113, 238. *Re the OECD Understanding on a Local Cost Standard* [1976] 1 C.M.L.R. 85.

[76]   *Re ERTA, Commission* v. *Council* [1971] C.M.L.R. 335.

[77]   EEC Treaty, art. 228. See also p. 322 *post*.

[78]   *Ibid.*, art. 220. See *e.g.* the Convention on Jurisdiction and the Enforcement of Judgments in Civil and Commercial Matters (O.J. 1972, L 299/32), incorporated into UK law by the Civil Jurisdiction and Judgments Act 1982.

such treaties are capable of altering existing Community law and should therefore be seen as a source of Community law.[79]

Decisions of the Court of Justice may also be treated as a source of Community law. Although the Court tends to follow its previous decisions, such decisions are treated as of persuasive rather than binding authority.[80] 'General principles common to the laws of the member states',[81] constitutional rights common to member states[82] and in certain circumstances, international law[83] may also be sources of Community law.

The jurisdiction of the Court of Justice

The jurisdiction of the Court of Justice is both complex and varied.[84] Perhaps the three most significant categories of its jurisdiction are: 1 actions against member states, 2 actions against Community institutions, 3 preliminary rulings.

1 Actions against member states. An action may be brought against a member state in the Court of Justice by other member states[85] or by the Commission.[86] Before one member state brings an action against another, the issue must be referred to the Commission. Such inter-state actions are extremely rare, partly because member states can usually rely on the Commission bringing an action wherever it would be appropriate and partly because the EEC depends on the continued co-operation of member states.[87]

Where the Commission considers that a member state has failed to fulfil its obligations under the Treaty, it may take action against that state. Initially, the Commission indicates that there has been a breach of a Community obligation and the member state is invited to submit its observations. If necessary, the Commission thereafter delivers 'a reasoned opinion' on the matter to the member state. If the state does not comply with this opinion within the period laid down by the Commission, the Commission may take the case to the Court of Justice. [88] In this event the reasoned opinion is of fundamental importance, because the case will be decided on the terms of that

---

79   *Krankenkasse etc.* v. *Van Dijk* [1966] C.M.L.R. 191, *cf. Re Tariff Quota on Wine* [1963] C.M.L.R. 347, 361–62 (Adv.-Gen. Roemer).
80   *E.g. de Haecht* (No. 2) [1973] E.C.R. 77, *cf. Bilger* v. *Jehle* [1974] 1 C.M.L.R. 382 and *Portelange* [1974] 1 C.M.L.R. 397.
81   *E.g.* EEC Treaty, art. 215; *CNTA* v. *Commission* [1975] E.C.R. 533; see also EEC Treaty, art. 164; *Internationale Handelsgesellschaft* [1972] C.M.L.R. 255; K. Lorenz (1964) 13 A.J.C.L. 1.
82   *E.g. Internationale Handelsgesellschaft, ante; Nold* v. *Commission* [1974] 2 C.M.L.R. 338; P. Pescatore, (1970) 18 A.J.C.L. 343: U. Scheuner (1975) 12 C.M.L. Rev. 171.
83   See EEC Treaty, arts. 37(5), 234; *Van Duyn* v. *Home Office* [1975] Ch. 358.
84   See G. Bebr, *Judicial Control of the European Communities*; L. J. Brinkhorst and H. G. Schermers, *Judicial Remedies in the European Communities*; L. N. Brown and F. G. Jacobs, *The Court of Justice of the European Communities*; A. J. Mackenzie Stuart, *The European Communities and the Rule of Law*; J. A. Usher, *European Court Practice*.
85   EEC Treaty, arts. 170, 93(2), 182, 219.
86   *Ibid.*, art. 169; see also art. 93(2) and *e.g. EC Commission* v. *UK* [1984] 1 All E.R. 353.
87   For an inter-state action see *France* v. *UK* [1980] 1 C.M.L.R. 6.
88   EEC Treaty, art. 169.

opinion and the facts at the time it was issued.[89] Where the Court finds that a member state has failed to fulfil a Community obligation, the state must take steps to comply with the judgment of the Court.[90]

2 Actions against Community institutions.   An action may be brought to annul Community legislation adopted by the Council or the Commission.[91] Such an action may be brought by a member state, the Commission, the Council, or, in limited circumstances, by a natural or legal person.[92]

The action to annul may be brought on four grounds. The first is lack of competence, where it is argued that the Community institution was not empowered by the treaty to take certain action.[93] Secondly, it may be argued that there has been an infringement of an essential procedural requirement, for example where the EEC Treaty requires the institution to give a reasoned decision and the reasons given were inadequate or there was a failure to give a hearing to a person whose interests were affected by the decision.[94] The third ground is the rather general one that there has been an infringement of the EEC Treaty 'or of any rule of law relating to its application'.[95] Finally, the action may be brought on the ground of a misuse of power, where it is argued that the institution has used a lawful power for an improper purpose.[96] Where an action for annulment is successful, the Court declares the Community legislation concerned to be void.[97]

An action for annulment must be instituted within two months of either the publication of the Community legislation or its notification to the plaintiff, or, in the absence of notification, two months of the plaintiff coming to know of it.[98] However, there are exceptions to this time limit. For example, at any time where a regulation is in issue before the Court of Justice a litigant may plead that the regulation is illegal on one of the grounds mentioned above.[99] This provision may only be relied on as a defence and does not provide an alternative means of challenging the acts of Community institutions.[1]

---

89   *Commission* v. *Italy* [1966] C.M.L.R. 97.
90   EEC Treaty, art. 171; *Procureur de la République* v. *Waterkeyn* [1983] 2 C.M.L.R. 145. Where a member state fails to comply with the judgment of the Court, the Commission may bring another action under act. 169 on the basis of the non-compliance, see *Re Export Tax on Art Treasures (No. 2)* [1972] C.M.L.R. 699.
91   EEC Treaty, arts. 173, 174. The action may be taken against any Community act which creates binding obligations, see *Re ERTA, Commission* v. *Council* [1971] C.M.L.R. 335; H. G. Schermers, *Legal Issues of European Integration*, (1975/2) 95.
92   EEC Treaty, art. 173; *Plaumann* v. *Commission* [1964] C.M.L.R. 29; *Compagnie Francaise Commerciale etc.* v. *Commission* [1970] C.M.L.R. 369, *cf. Bock* v. *Commission* [1972] C.M.L.R. 160.
93   *E.g.* delegation where the power to delegate did not exist: *Meroni* v. *High Authority* (1957–8) E.C.R. 133.
94   *E.g. Germany* v. *Commission* [1963] C.M.L.R. 347; *Sadolin & Holmblad* v. *Commission* [1974] 2 C.M.L.R. 459.
95   *E.g. August Töpfer & Co. GmbH* v. *Commission* [1978] E.C.R. 1019.
96   See *Fédération Charbonnière de Belgique* v. *High Authority* [1954–6] E.C.R. 245.
97   EEC Treaty, art. 174. The Court of Justice may declare a regulation or a decision void only in part.
98   *Ibid.*, art. 173, *cf. Commission* v. *France* [1970] C.M.L.R. 43.
99   EEC Treaty, art. 184; *Italy* v. *Council and Commission* [1969] C.M.L.R. 39; see also art. 177.
1   *Wohrmann* v. *Commission* [1963] C.M.L.R. 152.

Proceedings may also be taken in the Court of Justice against the Commission or the Council for infringing the EEC Treaty by failing to act where the Treaty imposes a duty to act. The Community institution concerned must first be called upon to act and if it 'has not defined its position' within two months, an action may be brought within a further period of two months.[2] The action may be brought by member states, other Community institutions and, in limited circumstances, by any natural or legal person.[3]

3 Preliminary rulings.[4] Under article 177 of the EEC Treaty a court or tribunal in a member state may, and in some circumstances must, refer certain questions of Community law to the Court of Justice for a preliminary ruling.[5] These are questions concerning the interpretation of the EEC Treaty, the validity and interpretation of acts of the Community institutions, including Community legislation which is adopted by the Council and Commission, and the interpretation of the statutes of bodies established by the Council.[6]

Before requesting such a preliminary ruling, it is for the national court to decide whether 'a decision on the question [of Community law] is necessary to enable it to give judgment'.[7] The national court may decide, for example, that the aspect of Community law in the case before it is clear and does not require interpretation.[8] In this sense all national courts and tribunals have a discretion on whether a question of Community law should be referred to the Court of Justice for a preliminary ruling. However, where a court decides that a decision on a question of Community law is necessary for it to give judgment and the court is also one 'against whose decisions there is no judicial remedy under national law', reference of the question to the Court of Justice for a preliminary ruling is mandatory.[9]

Once the Court of Justice has given a preliminary ruling under article 177, the case is referred back to the national court from which it originated and there the case is decided. It is an inherent aspect of the article 177 procedure that Community law is interpreted by the Court of Justice but applied by the

---

2 EEC Treaty, art. 175; A. G. Toth, *Legal Issues of European Integration*, (1975/2) 65; *Komponistenverband* v. *Commission* [1973] C.M.L.R. 902.

3 EEC Treaty, art. 175; *Mackprang* v. *Commission* [1972] C.M.L.R. 52; *Eridania* v. *Commission* [1969] E.C.R. 459.

4 See F. G. Jacobs and A. Durand, *References to the European Court: Practice and Procedure*.

5 The Court of Justice determines whether a body is a court or tribunal for the purposes of making a reference under EEC Treaty, art. 177: e.g. *Vaasen Göbbels* v. *Beambtenfonds etc.* [1966] C.M.L.R. 508.

6 This jurisdiction may be strictly construed, see *Caisse Régionale de Sécurité Sociale du Nord* v. *Torrekens* [1969] C.M.L.R. 377.

7 EEC Treaty, art. 177. A question may be referred for a preliminary ruling at any stage of the proceedings before national courts; once the preliminary ruling has been given it may be referred again for elaboration: *Milch, Fett etc.* v. *Hauptzollamt Saarbrucken* [1969] C.M.L.R. 390.

8 *E.g. Re Shell-Berre* [1964] C.M.L.R. 462; *cf. Da Costa* [1963] C.M.L.R. 224. This is commonly referred to as the *acte clair* doctrine; see M. Lagrange (1971) 8 C.M.L. Rev. 313. The danger of the doctrine is that a national court may not appreciate the complexity of the Community law question; see *C.I.L.F.I.T. Srl.* v. *Ministro della Sanita* [1983] 1 C.M.L.R. 472.

9 EEC Treaty, art. 177. However, where a question of Community law arises in interlocutory proceedings, in which the decision of the national court is final, there is no obligation to refer if the Community law question can be raised again in the main action: *Hoffmann-La Roche* v. *Centrafarm* [1977] 2 C.M.L.R. 334; see further F. G. Jacobs [1977] 2 E.L. Rev. 354.

national court. The Court of Justice has sought to maintain this differentiation of functions.[10] It will not, for example, apply its interpretation of Community law to the facts of the case;[11] nor will it determine whether a question referred to it is relevant to the case before the national court,[12] although it has refused to give preliminary rulings on questions which are *ex facie* irrelevant or hypothetical.[13] A preliminary ruling is, as a matter of Community law, binding in the case in which it is sought,[14] and may be binding *erga omnes*,[15] so the jurisdiction under article 177 provides a valuable means of encouraging the uniform application of Community law.[16] Indeed, it is under this procedure that many of the most important developments in Community law have been secured.

B. Community law and the United Kingdom[1]

With effect from 1 January 1973, the United Kingdom became a member of the three European Communities and a party to the treaties which had established them.[2] For the Treaty of Accession and other Community treaties to have legal effect in the United Kingdom, it was necessary for Parliament to pass legislation implementing them.[3] This was done by the European Communities Act 1972.

Despite the passage of that legislation, the political decision to join the Communities remained a controversial one. The Labour party election manifestos in 1974 declared that a Labour government would renegotiate the terms of UK membership. After the Labour government came into office in February 1974 there were extensive discussions with the other member states. In 1975, the Cabinet recommended that the United Kingdom should remain in the Communities. The question of continued UK membership was then put

---

[10] So the Court may redraft a question in more abstract terms before giving a preliminary ruling on it, *e.g. Otto Witt* v. *Hauptzollamt Lüneburg* [1971] C.M.L.R. 163. However, the Court may sometimes have to consider the facts of the case and national legislation in order to interpret Community law (*e.g. Van Duyn* v. *Home Office, ante*) and may take cognisance of a successful appeal within the national legal system against the reference of a question for a preliminary ruling *e.g. Chanel* v. *Capeha etc.* [1971] C.M.L.R. 403; *Belgische Radio etc.* v. *SABAM* [1974] 2 C.M.L.R. 238; *Firma Rheinmühlen Düsseldorf* v. *EVSt* [1974] 1 C.M.L.R. 523.

[11] *E.g. Salonia* v. *Poidomani and Baglieri* [1982] 1 C.M.L.R. 64.

[12] *E.g. Bosch* v. *de Geus* [1962] C.M.L.R. 1; *Van Gend en Loos, ante*.

[13] *Foglia* v. *Novella* [1981] 1 C.M.L.R. 45; *Foglia* v. *Novella (No. 2)* [1982] 1 C.M.L.R. 585; see also A. Barav (1980) 5 C.M.L. Rev. 443.

[14] *Milch, Fett, etc.* v. *Hauptzollamt Saarbrucken, ante*; *Benedetti* v. *Munari* [1977] E.C.R. 163.

[15] *International Chemical Corporation SpA* v. *Amministrazione Delle Finanze Dello Stato* [1983] 2 C.M.L.R. 593, *cf. Da Costa* [1963] E.C.R. 31, 42, 43 (Adv.-Gen. Lagrange). But the Court is not bound by its previous preliminary rulings and decisions.

[16] Thus the Protocol on the Statute of the Court, art. 20, entitles member states, the Commission and the Council of Ministers (where the act in dispute originates from the Council) to make submissions and observations to the Court on references for preliminary rulings.

[1] See L. Collins, *European Community Law in the United Kingdom*; Lasok & Bridge, *op. cit.*, ch. 12.

[2] By the Treaty of Accession 1972, art. 1, the United Kingdom became a member of the EEC and EURATOM and a party to the EEC and EURATOM Treaties. A Council of Ministers decision of 22 Jan. 1972 provided for UK accession to the ECSC Treaty.

[3] See ch. 18 C.

to the electorate in a national referendum;[4] 65% of the electorate voted in the referendum, 67.2% voting to remain in the Communities and 32.8% to leave.

The European Communities Act 1972[5]

This Act made the legislative changes necessary to enable the United Kingdom to comply with the obligations and exercise the rights of membership of the Communities arising under the Community treaties. The main constitutional objectives of the Act were achieved by sections 1 to 3 and the first two schedules.

The Community Treaties to which the Act relates are defined in section 1 and schedule 1. They include the original treaties establishing the three Communities, the Treaty of Accession, the Council decision relating to UK accession to the ECSC and certain other treaties entered into by the Communities prior to 22 January 1972, including those modifying the original treaties. Other treaties may be declared by Order in Council to be Community treaties for the purposes of the Act; where an Order declares that a treaty entered into by the United Kingdom after 22 January 1972 is such a Community treaty, a draft of the Order must be approved by each House of Parliament (section 1(3)).

The most important provision of the Act is section 2(1) which provides:

All such rights, powers, liabilities, obligations and restrictions from time to time created or arising by or under the Treaties, and all such remedies and procedures from time to time provided for by or under the Treaties, as in accordance with the Treaties are without further enactment to be given legal effect or used in the United Kingdom shall be recognised and available in law, and be enforced, allowed and followed accordingly; and the expression 'enforceable Community right' and similar expressions shall be read as referring to one to which this subsection applies.

The effective operation of Community law within the United Kingdom depends upon section 2(1). By this, all those provisions of Community law which, in accordance with Community law, are directly effective in the United Kingdom are given the force of law. The sub-section applies to Community law made both before and after the coming into force of the Act, whether contained in Community treaties, Community legislation or in the case law of the Court of Justice.

Community law may in some cases require implementation in member states. Sections 2(2) and 2(4), and schedule 2, of the Act give wide powers to the government to make delegated legislation to implement Community legislation; these powers are discussed below.

Section 2(2) also authorises persons entrusted with any statutory power or duty to have regard in exercising it to the objects of the Communities and to Community rights and obligations. The very broad effect of this is that Community objectives and Community law may be taken into account where powers are exercised under other UK legislation.

Section 2(3) charges on the Consolidated Fund, or the National Loans Fund, all amounts required to be paid by the UK government to meet its

---

[4]   Referendum Act 1975; R. E. M. Irving (1975–6) 1 E.L. Rev. 3.
[5]   See G. Howe (1973) 49 *International Affairs*, 1: J. Forman (1973) to C.M.L. Rev. 39.

Community obligations, whether to one of the Communities or to other member states. Permanent authority is thus given for such payments and it is unnecessary for Parliament to approve annually the payment of these sums.[6]

Section 3 relates to decision on, and proof of, Community treaties and Community legislation in proceedings before UK courts. By section 3(1), questions as to the meaning of any of the Community treaties, or as to the validity, meaning or effect of any Community legislation shall be treated as questions of law and, if not referred to the Court of Justice, are to be decided in accordance with the principles laid down by and relevant decisions of that Court.[7] Section 3(2) requires UK courts to take judicial notice of the Community treaties, the Official Journal of the Communities and of any decision or opinion of the Court of Justice on Community law. The remainder of section 3 relates to the proof in UK courts of instruments issued by Community institutions, including judgments or orders of the Court of Justice.

Section 4 and schedules 3 and 4 provide for the repeal and amendment of UK legislation consequent upon UK membership of the Communities. Other sections make provision for complying with Community rights and obligations, such as the common customs tariff (section 5), the common agricultural policy (section 6) and the first directive on harmonisation of company law (section 9). Also in pursuance of a Community obligation, section 11 makes it an offence in the United Kingdom to give false evidence on oath before the Court of Justice or to disclose classified information from EURATOM to unauthorised persons.

Some of the major constitutional implications of UK membership of the Communities will now be considered.

I. Parliamentary supremacy and Community law[8]

Within the Community legal system, Community law prevails over inconsistent provisions of the national law of member states. In the event of a conflict between Community law and an Act of Parliament, the Court of Justice would give preference to Community law.

In the United Kingdom, the legislative supremacy of Parliament is a fundamental doctrine of constitutional law. However, the European Communities Act 1972, section 2(1), has given legal effect to Community law within the United Kingdom, including the doctrine of the primacy of Community law over inconsistent national law. As a result of Community membership, a potential conflict now exists in the United Kingdom between these two doctrines of legal supremacy. This could arise between various forms of national law (for example, legislation, delegated legislation, or a judgment of a UK court) and Community law (for example, a provision of a Community treaty, a regulation, directive, decision or a judgment of the Court of Justice).

---

[6] See ch. 16.
[7] See *R.* v. *Goldstein* [1983] 1 All E.R. 434.
[8] A. Martin (1968–9) 6 C.M.L. Rev. 7; N. M. Hunnings, *ibid.*, 50; S. A. de Smith (1971) 34 M.L.R. 597; H. W. R. Wade (1972) 88 L.Q.R. 1; J.D.B. Mitchell *et al.* (1972) 9 C.M.L. Rev. 134; F. A. Trinidade (1972) 35 M.L.R. 375; G. Winterton (1976) 92 L.Q.R. 591; and ch. 5C *ante.*

It may involve national or Community law adopted before or after the United Kingdom became a member of the Communities.

To some extent the terms of the European Communities Act seek to minimise the potential conflict, but it must be recognised that the 1972 Act is itself subject to the doctrine of parliamentary supremacy. Although it deals largely with delegated legislation, section 2(4) is particularly relevant in this respect.[9] It states:

The provision that may be made under subsection (2) above includes, subject to Schedule 2 to this Act, any such provision (of any such extent) as might be made by Act of Parliament, *and any enactment passed or to be passed, other than one contained in this Part of this Act, shall be construed and have effect subject to the foregoing provisions of this section*; but, except as may be provided by any Act passed after this Act, Schedule 2 shall have effect in connection with the powers conferred by this and the following sections of this Act to make Orders in Council and regulations. [Emphasis supplied.]

The 'foregoing provisions' mentioned include section 2(1), which provides that Community law shall be given legal effect in the United Kingdom. Thus it would seem that any enactment, whether passed prior to the Act or subsequently, must be 'construed and have effect' subject to Community law.

The italicised clause in section 2(4) has not yet come directly before the courts and discussion of its meaning must remain speculative, but it is open to a variety of applications:

(*a*) With respect to UK legislation enacted before the 1972 Act, the courts could hold that the 1972 Act authorises the modification of existing UK law by existing Community law and recognises that future Community law may modify UK law. Thus, by virtue of sections 2(1) and 2(4) of the 1972 Act, Community law whenever adopted would prevail over clearly inconsistent UK legislation enacted prior to the European Communities Act.

(*b*) The clause could be treated as establishing a new principle of interpretation, that *wherever possible* UK courts should seek to interpret all UK legislation, whether enacted before or after the 1972 Act, in a manner which would avoid conflict with Community law. Such a principle of interpretation could also be given a special status; it might, for example, be treated as prevailing over other principles of interpretation.

This does not, however, exhaust the possible constitutional effects of the clause. A conflict might arise between UK legislation and Community law which could not be avoided by mere interpretation. In such circumstances, the clause may be considered to have other effects.

(*c*) The clause could be treated as being entrenched against *implied* repeal or amendment by later UK legislation. Thus, by virtue of section 2(4), effect would be given to subsequent UK legislation only to the extent that it was in accordance with Community law.

(*d*) A more extreme position would be to treat the clause as entrenching sections 2(1) and 2(4) against *express* repeal or amendment in a later statute.

In seeking to reconcile conflicts between UK legislation and Community

---

[9] And so, as legislative guidance to the courts, is s. 3 (1) *ante*.

law, UK judges have inevitably adopted a cautious and pragmatic approach to the implications of section 2(4). English courts and tribunals have certainly recognised that, as a general principle, English law must be applied subject to Community law.[10]

In cases where inconsistency has been established between Community law and UK legislation, courts and tribunals have applied Community law, and have done so even in preference to post-accession UK legislation. A 1971 EEC regulation, for instance, has been held to prevail over the Social Security Act 1975,[11] and a 1968 EEC regulation has been applied in preference to an inconsistent 1979 UK statutory instrument.[12]

However, judicial recognition of the supremacy of Community law over inconsistent post-accession UK legislation is not unqualified. It has been suggested that, should a UK statute expressly declare that it prevailed over Community law, English courts would apply the domestic legislation in preference to Community law. In *Macarthys Ltd.* v. *Smith*, Lord Denning, M. R., stated,

if the time should come when our Parliament deliberately passes an Act with the intention of repudiating the Treaty or any provision in it or intentionally of acting inconsistently with it and says so in express terms then I should have thought that it would be the duty of our courts to follow the statute of our Parliament.[13]

Secondly, although English courts have sought to interpret ambiguous UK legislative provisions to avoid inconsistency with Community law, they may not be prepared to strain unduly the domestic rules of statutory interpretation to avoid such inconsistencies. In *Garland* v. *British Rail Engineering Ltd*, Lord Diplock raised the question whether, in the light of section 2 (4),

anything short of an express positive statement in an Act of Parliament passed after 1 January 1973 that a particular provision is intended to be made in breach of an obligation assumed by the United Kingdom under a Community treaty would justify an English court in construing that provision in a manner inconsistent with a Community treaty obligation of the United Kingdom however wide a departure from the prima facie meaning of the language of the provision might be needed in order to achieve consistency.[14]

Thus, in terms of the range of possible applications of section 2(4) outlined above, it may be said that at present English courts are willing to apply (a) and (b),[15] are willing to adopt (c) with some qualification, but are not willing to accept the more extreme constitutional implications of (d).

---

[10] *E.g. Esso Petroleum Co. Ltd* v. *Kingswood Motors Ltd* [1974] 1 *Q.B.* 142; *Shields* v. *E. Coomes (Holdings) Ltd* [1979] 1 All E.R. 456, 460; *Macarthys Ltd* v. *Smith* [1979] 3 All E.R. 325.

[11] *Re an Absence in Ireland* [1977] 1 C.M.L.R. 5; *Re Medical Expenses Incurred in France* [1977] 2 C.M.L.R. 317.

[12] *MacMahon* v. *Department of Education* [1982] 3 C.M.L.R. 91.

[13] [1979] 3 All E.R. 325, 329; *cf.* Customs and Excise Duties (General Reliefs) Act 1979, s. 2(1).

[14] [1982] 2 All E.R. 402, 415.

[15] The supremacy of Community law over pre-accession UK legislation has been accepted by implication in *e.g. R.* v. *Goldstein* [1983] 1 All E.R. 434.

II. Parliament, the Executive and the Communities

Parliament and Community policies

Membership of the Communities did not only affect the position of Parliament as the source of legislation. It also led to a considerable increase in the powers of the executive, for it is through government ministers that the United Kingdom is represented at meetings of the Council of Ministers. Since UK accession, procedures have been gradually established by which Parliament may examine Community policy and legislative proposals before they are adopted, and express a view on them.[16] Conventions are also evolving with respect to the accountability of the government to Parliament for Community policies and legislation.

The government provides Parliament with information on Community activities. Thus all documents published by the Commission for submission to the Council of Ministers, are made available to the two Houses, with an explanatory memorandum prepared by the government on each document. The government also makes monthly forecasts of the agenda for Council of Ministers meetings. Ministerial statements are usually made in Parliament after meetings of the Council and every six months the government publishes a white paper on developments within the Communities. Six days are allocated in each parliamentary session for debating Community affairs and there is a place for EEC questions in the rota for parliamentary questions. However, there are limitations on the information supplied to Parliament by the government. The government has, for example, been reluctant to provide information to Parliament on Commission proposals before they are published, although the proposals may have been the basis of widespread consultation.[17]

The Commission proposals received by Parliament are examined by two committees, established for the purpose in 1974. Those committees are the House of Lords Select Committee on the European Communities and the House of Commons Select Committee on European Secondary Legislation. The committees report on the proposals to their respective Houses and may recommend that a proposal be debated. By virtue of a House of Commons resolution, no UK minister will consent to a Community legislative proposal in the Council of Ministers until such a debate has taken place, unless there are special reasons for doing so. If the minister decides that there are special reasons for agreeing to the proposal in the Council before a debate, he must explain his reasons to the House 'at the first opportunity thereafter'.[18] The debates are taken on the floor of the House or, in the Commons, in standing committee.[19]

---

[16] See T. St. J. N. Bates (1975–6) 1 E.L. Rev. 22.

[17] However, the government has agreed to inform Parliament of substantial amendments made to Commission proposals of UK interest after they have been submitted to the Council of Ministers; H. C. Deb., 3 Nov. 1975, cols. 36–8, 106–7.

[18] H. C. Deb., 30 Oct. 1980, cols. 843–4. The select committee may also recommend a Community legislative proposal for debate but indicate that agreement to the proposal need not be withheld prior to the debate: *ibid.* For a government undertaking to the House of Lords in similar terms, see H.L. Deb., 9 Dec. 1974, col. 490.

[19] For the standing committee procedure see H.C. Deb., 3 Nov. 1975, cols. 28–113.

The extent to which the government is responsible to Parliament for Community policies and legislation is not always clearly defined. The Foreign Secretary has overall responsibility to Parliament for ensuring that the government complies with its undertakings to supply information on Community affairs.[20] The government must in principle be accountable to Parliament where a Commission proposal has been adopted in the Council of Ministers before there has been a parliamentary debate on the proposal, where such a debate was recommended.[21] Whether the government is bound to comply with a parliamentary resolution on a Commission proposal is disputed. The government considers that such a resolution is merely indicative of opinion and is not binding. However, some M.P.s take the view that a resolution of the Commons should limit the government's freedom of action on a Commission proposal; on this basis failure to comply with the terms of the resolution would be a serious breach of ministerial responsibility. In fact a resolution critical of a Commission proposal imposes no formal restriction on executive action but, as one minister said, the government would 'ignore the decision of the House at its peril'.[22] Once Community legislation or a Community policy has been adopted by the Council of Ministers, the government is responsible for informing Parliament of the Council's decision. Ministers have generally been unwilling to indicate the positions adopted by member states during the negotiations in the Council leading to a decision, and this unwillingness extends to the negotiating position of the United Kingdom.[23]

The hesitant development of conventional rules relating to the responsibility of the government for its policy towards Community affairs may be attributed to several factors. The parliamentary procedures which have been established are directed to examining Community proposals rather than the policy of the government towards them. Furthermore, Commission proposals often have economic and foreign policy implications, so that formulating government policy towards them involves a number of departments. It may thus be difficult to make individual ministers responsible for such a policy and the policy therefore attracts a more diffuse collective responsibility. The enforcement of responsibility is also rendered more difficult because of the limited information which is available on the negotiations within the Council of Ministers and by the fact that, in practice, many Council decisions are reached by consensus. However, the government remains responsible to Parliament for fulfilling its obligations to provide information on Community affairs, and, in principle, for its actions on Community matters.

Parliament and the implementation of Community legislation

Some Community legislation requires implementation within member states. In the United Kingdom, such Community legislation is commonly imple-

---

20   H.C. Deb., 2 May 1974, col. 524 (W.A.).
21   See *e.g.* H.C. Deb., 27 Feb. 1975, cols. 847–8. *Cf.* H.C. Deb., 3 Jul. 1974, col. 471.
22   First Report, Select Committee on Procedure, H.C. 294 (1974–5), Minutes of Evidence, Q. 166 (Mr Short).
23   However, the government has declared itself willing to provide, 'in particular cases', *ex post facto* explanations of a failure to reserve its position on a proposal in the Council where there would normally have been a parliamentary debate on the proposal prior to its adoption: Select Committee on European Secondary Legislation, Minutes of Evidence, H.C. 87–1 (1974–5), p. 11, *cf.* note 17, *ante.*

mented by statutory instrument, but may be implemented by statute or simply by administrative action. To facilitate the use of statutory instruments for this purpose, the European Communities Act provides that Orders in Council and regulations by designated ministers may be made to implement Community obligations, to enable Community rights to be exercised and to deal with matters arising out of such rights or obligations; it also provides that any other statutory power or duty may be exercised for the same purposes.[24]

Such subordinate legislation made under section 2(2) may include 'any such provision (of any such extent) as might be made by Act of Parliament'.[25] However, it may not (a) impose or increase taxation, (b) have a retrospective effect, (c) subdelegate the power to legislate except the power to make rules of procedure for any court or tribunal, or (d) create any new criminal offence punishable by more than two years imprisonment or, on summary conviction, by more than three months imprisonment or a fine of more than £1000 or £200 per day.[26] A statutory instrument made under section 2(2) either requires approval in draft by each House, or is subject to annulment by either House.[27] The choice of procedure rests with the government.

Delegated legislation implementing Community legislation, in common with other delegated legislation, is scrutinised by parliamentary committees.[28] These committees examine, and have reported adversely on, the drafting and procedural aspects of delegated legislation implementing Community legislation. However, although the committees consider whether such delegated legislation is *intra vires* the enabling Act, they do not normally examine the Community legislation which the delegated legislation purports to implement unless there is *prima facie* evidence that the Community legislation has not been satisfactorily implemented.

III. United Kingdom courts and Community law

There is, as we have seen, a close relationship between Community law and the legal systems of member states. Community law is developed by the Court of Justice of the Communities, both in cases brought before it directly and in preliminary rulings sought by national courts under article 177 of the EEC Treaty. However, Community law is applied primarily by the national courts of member states, and it is important that they apply it in a uniform manner.

In the United Kingdom, issues of Community law have arisen frequently before a wide variety of courts and tribunals, from VAT tribunals and magistrates' courts to the House of Lords. Initially, there were some judicial misunderstandings over the nature of Community law and mistakes in its application.[29] A number of factors contributed to this. First, it was perhaps

---

24 S. 2(2).
25 European Communities Act, s. 2(4); p. 137 *ante*, and p. 614 *post*.
26 Sch. 2, para. 1(1); see also para. 1(2).
27 Sch. 2, para. 2(1) (2) as amended, p. 618 *post*.
28 Ch. 33.
29 Some courts and tribunals assumed that all provisions of the EEC Treaty were directly effective (*e.g. Schorsch Meier GmbH* v. *Hennin* [1975] Q.B. 416; but see now *e.g. Shields* v. *E. Coomes (Holdings) Ltd* [1979] 1 All E.R. 456) and some were uncertain about the direct effect of regulations, directives and decisions. See J. W. Bridge (1975–6) 1 E.L. Rev. 13 and (1981) 19 *Journal of Common Market Studies* 351.

less easy for a state which joined the Communities in 1973 to adapt speedily to the complexities of Community law than for the original six member states, which were able to adapt more gradually as Community law itself developed. Moreover, Community law was developed by the original member states who shared a similar legal tradition, a tradition not shared to the same extent by English law. Secondly, UK courts were encouraged by some judges to emulate the Court of Justice and interpret Community law broadly. Lord Denning, M. R., for example, expressed the view that Community regulations and directives give only an outline plan. 'The details are to be filled in by the judges'.[30] Thirdly, the dangers inherent in encouraging the broad interpretation of Community law were compounded by a cautious approach to the use of the article 177 procedure.[31]

This cautious approach was reflected in *H. P. Bulmer Ltd* v. *J. Bollinger S. A.*[32] In that case, two English companies brought an action against two representative French companies producing champagne. The English companies thereby sought declarations that they were entitled to manufacture drinks described as 'champagne cider' and 'Champagne perry'. The French companies argued, *inter alia*, that the use of the word 'champagne' in connection with a beverage other than wine produced in the Champagne district of France was contrary to Community law, and they asked the court of first instance to refer two questions of Community law to the Court of Justice for a preliminary ruling. The request was refused and the French companies appealed against the refusal to make a reference under article 177. In the Court of Appeal, Lord Denning, M. R. suggested 'guidelines' by which a court could determine whether a decision on a question of Community law was 'necessary for it to give judgement'. As we have seen, this is an essential condition for making a reference under article 177 and a matter which the Court of Justice leaves largely to be determined by the national court making the reference. Lord Denning suggested that it would not be necessary to refer a question of Community law to the Court of Justice (a) where it would not be conclusive of the case,[33] (b) where the same question, or substantially the same question, had previously been decided by the Court of Justice,[34] (c) where the court asked to refer the question considers 'the point reasonably clear and free from doubt'[35] or (d) where the facts of the case had not been decided.[36] Lord Denning also suggested that a court which has a discretion whether to seek a preliminary ruling should consider in exercising that discretion such matters

---

30   *H. P. Bulmer Ltd* v. *J. Bollinger S. A.* [1974] Ch. 401, 426.
31   At the time of UK accession, some English judges emphasised in extrajudicial pronouncements that inferior courts and tribunals should make article 177 references sparingly: e.g. Lord Diplock (1972) *Journal of Association of Law Teachers*, 3; Lord Denning, *The Times, Forward into Europe*, Pt. 1, 2 Jan 1973; Lord Hailsham, speech to magistrates, extract appended to Home Office Circular No. 149/1973 (CS 18/1973).
32   [1974] Ch. 401; for comment see J. D. B. Mitchell (1974) 11 C.M. L. Rev. 351; F. G. Jacobs (1974) 90 L.Q.R. 486; E. Freeman (1975) 28 C.L.P. 187.
33   However, it may be difficult to decide when such a question is conclusive of the case. *Cf.* Stephenson L. J. at 428–29; *Van Duyn* v. *Home Office* [1974] 3 All E.R. 178, 186 (Pennycuick V.-C.); *EMI Records Ltd* v. *CBS United Kingdom Ltd* [1975] 1 C.M.L.R. 285, 296(Graham J.); *Re an Illness In France* [1976] 1 C.M.L.R. 243, 248 (Mr J. G. Monroe).
34   Except where the English court considers that the decision of the Court of Justice was wrong, or where it wishes to bring new factors to the attention of that court: at 422.

as the wishes of the litigants,[37] the expense and delay of seeking a ruling and the possibility of overloading the Court of Justice.[38]

These guidelines were not intended by Lord Denning to be binding and were viewed with caution by his brother judges,[39] yet they remain influential and have been refined and developed in subsequent cases. Clearly such guidelines may have an inhibiting effect on a UK court considering whether to make an article 177 reference.[40] However, national appellate courts may not limit the wide discretion granted to courts and tribunals to refer questions of Community law under article 177.[41]

The use of the article 177 procedure could be further inhibited by restrictive interpretation in the United Kingdom of the category of courts and tribunals 'against whose decisions there is no judicial remedy under national law'. Article 177(3) provides that where a question of Community law arises before such a court and it is a question on which a decision is necessary to enable it to give judgment, that court is obliged to refer the question to the Court of Justice. In the *Bulmer* case, Lord Denning considered that within the English legal system article 177(3) would only apply to the House of Lord.[42] However, article 177(3) would also apply to the Court of Appeal where it is declared by statute to be the final court of appeal,[43] and may apply to cases before the Court of Appeal where leave to appeal to the House of Lords is refused[44] and possibly to tribunals from whose decisions there is only a discretionary judicial remedy.[45]

---

[35]   In *Garland* v. *British Rail Engineering Ltd* [1982] 2 All E.R. 402, the House of Lords emphasised the dangers of misconstruing Community law by adopting this approach, which is a formulation of the *acte clair* doctrine (p. 133 *ante*). For illustrations of the danger see *R.* v. *Secchi* [1975] 1 C.M.L.R. 383, *Schorsh Meier GmbH* v. *Hennin* [1975] Q.B. 416 and *Miliangos* v. *Frank (Textiles) Ltd* [1976] A.C. 443 at 465, 477, 498.

[36]   See also *R.* v. *Henn and Darby* [1980] 2 All E.R. 166, 229; *Church of Scientology of California* v. *Commissioners of Customs and Excise* [1981] 1 All E.R. 1035.

[37]   See also *English Speaking Union of the Commonwealth* v. *Commissioners of Customs and Excise* [1981] 1 C.M.L.R. 581.

[38]   On whether the latter possibility is an appropriate consideration, *cf. Van Duyn* v. *Home Office*, *ante*, at 187 (Pennycuick V.-C.).

[39]   *H. P. Bulmer Ltd* v. *J. Bollinger SA*, *ante*, at 427 (Stamp L.J.), 430 (Stephenson L. J.).

[40]   See *e.g. R.* v. *Plymouth JJ.*, *ex p. Rogers* [1982] 3 C.M.L.R. 221; *Burton* v. *British Railways Board* [1982] Q.B. 1080; *cf. Commissioners of Customs and Excise* v. *ApS Samex* [1983] 1 All E.R. 1042. However, UK courts have also been influenced by other considerations. Thus they have perhaps been more willing to make a reference when it is known that there are parallel actions in other member states (*e.g. E.M.I. Records Ltd* v. *CBS (UK) Ltd* [1975] 1 C.M.L.R. 285) and unwilling to make a reference when the request for a reference is considered to be a procedural tactic (e.g. *British Leyland Motor Corpn Ltd* v. *T. I. Silencers* [1980] 1 C.M.L.R. 598, 601–2).

[41]   On the procedural rules made in the United Kingdom relating to art. 177 references, see F. G. Jacobs and A. Durand, *References to the European Court*; Collins, *op. cit.*, pp. 88–90; *Firma Rheinmühlen Düsseldorf* v. *EVST* [1974] 1 C.M.L.R. 523, 575 (Adv.–Gen. Warner). See also Collins, *op. cit.*, p. 116; Lasok and Bridge, *op. cit.*, pp. 351–2.

[42]   *H. P. Bulmer Ltd* v. *J. Bollinger SA*, *ante* at 421; *cf.* Stephenson L.J. at 430. See also *Miliangos* v. *Frank (Textiles).Ltd* [1976] A.C. 443, 465.

[43]   *E.g.* Bankruptcy Act 1914, s. 108(2)(a).

[44]   See *Hagen* v. *Fratelli D. & G. Moretti SNC* [1980] 3 C.M.L.R. 253.

[45]   See Jacobs and Durand, *op. cit.*, p. 163; E. Freeman, (1975) 28 C.L.P. 176, 184–6; Lasok and Bridge, *op. cit.*, pp. 338–40; *cf. Re a Holiday in Italy* [1975] 1 C.M.L.R. 184. Courts in other parts of the United Kingdom may fall within art. 177(3), e.g. the High Court of Justiciary in Scotland.

Chapter 9

Composition of Parliament

Parliament consists of the Queen, the House of Lords and the House of Commons. Although both Houses meet in the palace of Westminster, they sit separately and are constituted on entirely different principles. The process of legislation is however a matter in which both Houses take part and the two-chamber structure is an integral part of the British parliamentary system. Within Parliament the House of Commons is the dominant House. Under the Parliament Acts of 1911 and 1949, the formal power of the Lords in legislation is limited to imposing a temporary veto upon government Bills, a power which may sometimes be an effective check upon party legislation. The role of the Lords as a revising chamber is more important, especially for securing amendments to Bills which have been subjected to closure in the Commons,[1] and the House serves certain other constitutional purposes.

A. House of Lords

The most striking feature of the House of Lords is that its composition depends in no way upon methods of direct or indirect election or upon the principle of geographical representation. All members achieve their place either by virtue of the hereditary principle or by virtue of appointment by the Crown. The House consists of over 1,100 temporal, and 26 spiritual, Lords of Parliament. The temporal peers are:

(a) Hereditary peers and peeresses in their own right of the United Kingdom,[2] who include holders of titles created in the peerage of England before the Union with Scotland in 1707 and in the peerage of Great Britain from 1707 to 1801 when the Union of Great Britain and Ireland took effect. In December 1982, there were 766 peers who sat by succession and 33 hereditary peers of the first creation.[3] No hereditary peerages were created between

---

[1] Ch. 11 A.

[2] Princes of the Blood Royal sit in the House only by virtue of hereditary peerages conferred upon them by the Sovereign, with the exception of the heir apparent who, unless a minor, sits as Duke of Cornwall.

[3] *Dod's Parliamentary Companion*, 1983.

1964 and 1983, when the practice was revived by the Prime Minister, Mrs Thatcher.

(*b*)   Hereditary peers of Scotland created before the Union of 1707 and not also members of the peerage of the United Kingdom.

(*c*)   Not more than eleven Lords of Appeal in Ordinary appointed by the Crown on statutory authority to perform the judicial duties of the House and holding their seats for life.

(*d*)   Life peers: by the Life Peerages Act 1958 the Crown may confer a life peerage upon a man or a woman without limitation as to the number of creations.

Creation of hereditary peers

Hereditary peerages may be created by the Queen on the advice of the Prime Minister; they are peerages of the United Kingdom and carry with them the right to a seat in the Lords. Between 1964 and 1983, all Prime Ministers pursued a policy of not advising the creation of hereditary peerages. Some of the oldest surviving hereditary peerages were created by the issue of a writ of summons to the House, followed by the taking of his seat by the recipient of the writ. In modern times, all peerages have been created by letters patent from the Sovereign.[4] A peerage created by letters patent descends according to the limitation expressed in the letters patent, which is almost always to the heirs male of the body of the grantee, *i.e.* to and through the male line in direct lineal descent from the grantee. A peerage created by writ of summons descends to the heirs general of the grantee, *i.e.* to his heirs male or female, lineal or collateral. Thus in the absence of a special limitation in the letters patent, it is only a peerage created by writ of summons which ever devolves upon a female. Where there is only one female heir, she becomes a peeress in her own right. Where, however, there are two or more female descendants of equal degree, the elder is not preferred to the younger, and both or all inherit as co-parceners. In such cases a peerage falls into abeyance. Such an abeyance may, on the advice of the Committee for Privileges of the House of Lords, which decides claims to exixting peerages, be terminated by the Crown in favour of one co-heir, or in process of time may become vested in one descendant of the last holder of the peerage.[5] A dispute as to the right of a newly-created peer to sit is determined by the House itself, acting through the Committee for Privileges.

A peerage cannot be alienated nor, apart from disclaimer for life under the Peerage Act 1963, be surrendered,[6] nor has a peerage any connection with the tenure of land.[7] It was decided in the *Wensleydale Peerage* case[8] that the Crown, although able to create a life peerage, could not create such a peerage carrying with it the right to a seat in the House. The conferment of life peerages upon

---

4   For an example, see [1964] 2 Q.B. 257, 271. And see the Crown Office Rules Orders of 1927 (S.R. and O.425) and 1958 (S.I. 1250).
5   On the termination of abeyances, see H.L. (1926) 189 and H.L. Deb. 6 July 1927, col. 222, 7 July 1927, col. 285.
6   *Re Parliamentary Election for Bristol South East* [1964] 2 Q.B. 257.
7   *Berkeley Peerage* case (1861) 8 H.L.C. 21.
8   (1856) 5 H.L.C. 958.

those appointed to judicial office in the House had therefore to be authorised by statute.

Disqualifications

An alien may not receive a writ of summons to the House of Lords nor may a writ of summons be issued to a bankrupt peer or to a person under 21 years of age.[9] It was decided in the case of *Viscountess Rhondda's Claim*[10] that the Sex Disqualification (Removal) Act 1919 did not enable a peeress in her own right to receive a writ of summons to Parliament. The Peerage Act 1963, section 6, now allows a peeress in her own right to take her seat. This change was not in fact of benefit to many women, since the great majority of hereditary peerages are restricted to male heirs. A peer who is a civil servant was formerly debarred by Treasury Minute from speaking or voting, but since 1973 such a peer is obliged only to exercise a general caution in entering any political controversy.

Creation of peers to coerce the Lords

The right of the Crown to create new peers without limit was in the past an important weapon to enable the Crown on the advice of the Prime Minister to compel the Lords to give way to the Commons in case of conflict. In 1712, Queen Anne appointed 12 new peers to secure a majority for the Tory administration. The Peerage Bill of 1719 attempted to limit the power of the Crown to create new peers, but the proposal was rejected. The passing of the Reform Bill in 1832 and the Parliament Bill in 1911 was procured by a statement that the King had consented to create peers in sufficient numbers to secure a majority for the government in the Lords. It seems improbable that this prerogative will again be invoked; the passing of the Parliament Act 1911 was thought at the time to reduce the likelihood of this.[11]

The peers of Scotland and Ireland

No new Scottish peerages have been created since the Union of 1707. The Peerage Act 1963, section 4, admitted all surviving peers of Scotland to the Lords. Formerly when a new Parliament was summoned the Scottish peers elected sixteen of their number to represent them in the House.

Irish peers have fared differently. The Act of Union with Ireland in 1800 provided that the Irish peerage might be maintained to the number of a hundred. The last creation was in 1898. Formerly the peers of Ireland elected 28 of their number to represent Ireland in the House for life; the last surviving elected peer died in 1961.[12] All holders of Irish peerages are now entitled to be elected to the Commons and to vote at parliamentary elections.[13]

---

9   H.L. Standing Order 2, which dates from 1685.
10 [1922] 2 A.C. 339.
11 Ch. 11 B.
12 *Earl of Antrim's Petition* [1967] 1 A.C. 691, which decided against any new election since Ireland had as a whole ceased to exist politically under the legislation of 1922 which created the Irish Free State (now the Republic of Ireland). And see Lord Dunboyne [1967] P.L. 314 and C. E. Lysaght, (1967) 18 N.I.L.Q. 277.
13 Peerage Act 1963, s. 5.

The Lords of Appeal in Ordinary
The 11 peers appointed by virtue of statute to perform the judicial functions of the House of Lords are styled Lords of Appeal in Ordinary. They have the right to sit and vote for life, notwithstanding resignation from their judicial appointment. To be qualified for appointment, they must have held for two years high judicial office in the United Kingdom, or have practised at the Bar in England, Scotland or Northern Ireland for fifteen years.[14]

Life peers
The Life Peerages Act 1958 both strengthened the Lords and weakened the hereditary principle. The Act enabled the Queen, by letters patent, to confer a peerage for life with a seat in Parliament upon a man or woman. It did not restrict the power of the Crown to confer hereditary peerages although its existence enabled the creation of such peerages to cease between 1964 and 1983. The object was partly to enable the Labour party's representation to be increased, and partly to bring in new members, particularly from outside the ranks of party politicians, without creating more hereditary titles. In December 1982, 283 peers and 44 peeresses appointed under the 1958 Act were in the House.

The Lords Spiritual
The Lords Spiritual are 26 bishops of the Church of England; they hold their seats in the Lords until they resign from their episcopal office. The Archbishops of Canterbury and York and the Bishops of London, Durham and Winchester have the right to a seat. The remaining 21 spiritual lords are the 21 other diocesan bishops having seniority of date of appointment.[15] When such a bishop dies or resigns, his place in the House is taken by the next senior diocesan bishop. Since 1847, whenever a new diocesan bishopric has been created, it has been enacted that the number of bishops sitting in Parliament should not be increased in consequence.[16]

Disclaimer of titles
The Peerage Act 1963 enables hereditary peers other than those of the first creation to renounce their titles for life by disclaimer. The primary purpose of granting such a right was to enable hereditary peers to sit in the Commons. This reform was the direct result of the action of Mr Anthony Wedgwood Benn, then Viscount Stansgate by succession, in challenging the existing law which disqualified members of the Lords from standing for election to Parliament.[17] Under the 1963 Act, disclaimer is irrevocable and binds a wife, but the courtesy titles of children are not affected, nor has a disclaimer any effect on the succession of the heir. If a sitting member of the Commons succeeds to a title he has one month after the death of his predecessor in which to disclaim, or, if the death occurs during an election campaign, one month from

---

14 Ch. 19 A.
15 The Bishop of Sodor and Man is excepted and cannot take a seat.
16 Ecclesiastical Commissioners Act 1847, s. 2; Bishoprics Act 1878, s. 5; and *e.g.* The Bishoprics of Southwark and Birmingham Act 1904.
17 Note 6 *ante*.

the declaration of the poll in favour of a successful peer. Existing peers were given twelve months from the royal assent to the Act, 31 July 1963, in which to exercise their power to disclaim; peers who succeed thereafter have twelve months from succession or their coming of age. These time limits are extended to cover any period when Parliament is not sitting or a peer is disabled by sickness from making his choice. Subsequent to a disclaimer there can be no restoration of an hereditary peerage, but there is nothing in the Act to prohibit a peer who has disclaimed from subsequently being created a life peer under the Life Peerages Act 1958, as has happened both to Lord Home and to Lord Hailsham. One unforeseen sequel of the Peerage Act 1963 was that during the period allowed for disclaimer by peers who were already members of the House, the Conservative Prime Minister (Macmillan) resigned because of ill-health and it was possible for the 14th Earl of Home to disclaim his title upon being appointed Prime Minister. Such a move from the Lords to the Commons has not been possible since the expiry in 1964 of the transitional period for disclaimer by existing peers.

Attendance

A summons to Parliament cannot be withheld from a peer who is entitled to it, and individual writs of summons are issued to both the temporal and spiritual lords for each new Parliament. In order to secure that only those peers interested in the work of Parliament shall in practice attend and record their votes, the House adopted in June 1958 a new standing order (now S.O. 20) relating to leave of absence. This order emphasises the obligation on Lords of Parliament to attend the sittings of the House in accordance with the writ of summons, but enables a peer to apply for leave of absence at any time during a Parliament for the remainder of that Parliament. A peer who has been granted leave of absence is expected not to attend the sittings of the House during the period of his leave. In this way it is presumably expected to eliminate the influence of the so-called 'backwoodsman'. Provision is made for a peer who wishes to terminate his leave of absence to give a month's notice. But the House of Lords has no power to prevent the attendance of a peer who, having received a writ of summons, does not observe the leave of absence rules.[18]

Apart from the law lords, who receive a salary so long as they perform their judicial work, members of the House do not receive a salary as such. But since 1957, a daily attendance allowance has been paid and travel to the House is also paid for. Attending peers also receive allowances for necessary overnight stays away from home, and secretarial and research assistance. In 1979, the average daily attendance of peers was 292, compared with 95 in 1955, 140 in 1963 and 265 in 1971.

B. House of Commons

The laws which govern the composition of the House of Commons are of fundamental political importance, for they provide the structure of the elec-

---

[18]   See H.L. (1955–6) 7, 66–1, 67, paras. 37–8.

toral system that determines which political party has the right to govern the country. Under a written constitution, the basic rules for electing the Commons would probably be contained in the constitution and possibly given some degree of entrenchment. But in the United Kingdom, these fundamental rules are contained in Acts of Parliament which may be amended by ordinary process of legislation. Whereas the composition of the Lords may be altered without upsetting the balance of political power, politicians are well aware that any change in the legal composition of the Commons is likely to benefit one or other of the political parties: constitutional arguments about proposed changes can be thin veils for the political calculations upon which the position of the parties is based. In Britain today there is general agreement over many essential rules of the electoral system, for example, universal adult suffrage and the secret ballot. Other aspects of the electoral system are not universally accepted, for example, the 'first past the post' system of counting the vote, the distribution of constituencies, the laws which regulate the financing of the parties and the use of broadcasting. Except for the controversy about proportional representation, these points of continuing controversy are less fundamental than the long and serious conflicts by which the unrepresentative House of Commons of the 18th century was transformed into the democratically elected assembly of today.

The composition of the House of Commons will be discussed under the following headings:

I.   The franchise
II. The arrangement of constituencies
III. The conduct of the election campaign
IV. Membership of the House of Commons
V.   Electoral systems

I. The franchise

Before 1918, the right to vote was largely dependent upon the ownership or occupation of property. It was also affected by the ancient distinction between counties and boroughs. For more than five centuries after Simon de Montfort's Parliament of 1265, the English people were represented in the Commons by two knights from every county and by two burgesses from every borough. Before the Reform Act of 1832, the franchise was exercisable in the counties by those men who owned freehold land worth 40 shillings per year. In the boroughs, the franchise varied according to the charter of the borough and to local custom. In fact many seats in the House before 1832 were controlled by members of the landowning aristocracy who had sufficient influence by purchasing votes or other means to nominate the successful candidates. Acts for widening the franchise were passed in 1832, 1867, 1884, 1918, 1928, 1948 and 1969 until today the total electorate is over 40 million. The details of the earlier Acts have passed into history. In 1918 a uniform franchise based on residence was established for county and borough constituencies.[1]

---

[1]   See D. E. Butler, *The Electoral System in Britain since 1918*.

Votes for women over 30 were introduced in 1918 and in 1928 for women over 21. After 1918, various categories of persons had the right to vote more than once either by reason of occupying land for business purposes or because of the right of graduates to vote in separate constituencies representing the universities. These last elements of plural voting were abolished in 1948.

The present franchise

The law is now contained in Part I of the Representation of the People Act 1983, which consolidated earlier legislation, notably the Representation of the People Act 1949 as subsequently amended (for example, when the voting age was lowered to 18 in 1969). By section 1 of the 1983 Act, the right to vote at parliamentary elections is exerciseable by all Commonwealth citizens (which in law includes all British citizens and British subjects)[2] and citizens of the Republic of Ireland, who (a) are of full age (*i.e.* who have attained the age of 18 years by the date of the election); (b) are resident in a parliamentary constituency on the qualifying date; (c) are not subject to any legal incapacity to vote; and (d) whose names are recorded in the official register of electors.

Although aliens are not entitled to vote, the right to vote extends to citizens of all Commonwealth countries, and also to citizens of the Republic of Ireland who, though neither aliens nor Commonwealth citizens, are expressly entitled to vote by the 1983 Act.

No person qualified by nationality may vote unless he is resident in a constituency on the qualifying date, 10 October, which each year serves as the basis on which the electoral register is prepared. Before 1948, a qualifying period of residence was required but this requirement now applies only to elections for the Westminster Parliament in Northern Ireland constituencies, where the elector must have been resident in Northern Ireland (not necessarily in a particular constituency) during the period of three months ending on the qualifying date, 15 September.

The meaning of residence for electoral purposes was considered in *Fox* v. *Stirk*[3], where university students at Bristol and Cambridge were held to be resident on 10 October in their hall of residence and college respectively and therefore entitled to register for those constituencies. Applying the dictionary definition of 'reside' as meaning 'to dwell permanently or for a considerable time, to have one's settled or usual abode, to live in or at a particular place', the Court of Appeal held that the stay of the students at their university addresses displayed a considerable degree of permanence. A person's residence at his normal home address is not affected by temporary absence from that address, whether because of holidays, business duties[4] or other reasons. While a person may be held to be resident at more than one address, and may therefore be registered in more than one constituency, he may not vote more than once at the same parliamentary election.[5] Ownership of a country cottage as a second home is not enough to make the owner resident there if on the facts his use of it is incidental to his main home.[6]

---

2   See British Nationality Act 1981, s. 37; and ch. 25 A. See also App. B.
3   [1970] 2 Q.B. 463, discussed by S. Maidment in [1971] P.L. 25.
4   Representation of the People Act 1983, s. 5(2)(*a*).
5   1983 Act, s.1(4) and s.61(2)(a).

Special rules apply for determining the residence of mental patients, whose rights were widened in 1982.[7] In brief, a person detained under statutory powers because of mental disorder cannot be treated as resident in the hospital where he is detained. A voluntary patient resident in a mental hospital may complete a declaration entitling him to be registered as resident at an address elsewhere, for example his home; in this case he may vote by post in the relevant constituency.

The register of electors

It is a condition precedent to exercising the vote that the elector should be placed upon the register of electors. The register is prepared once a year by the registration officer of each constituency, who in England and Wales is appointed by the council of each district or London borough, as the case may be.[8] A new register comes into force on 16 February each year.[9] The register is prepared after a house to house canvass or other inquiries have been made of all householders. It is first published in a provisional form on or before 28 November, to allow for claims and objections.

A separate register which is compiled on information obtained from service declarations contains the names of members of the forces, whether serving at home and abroad, and of other Crown servants and British Council staff who are employed abroad together with the names of their spouses resident with them. The principle of registration is that a service voter shall be registered as if he were living at the address at which but for his service he would normally be resident.[10]

Any Commonwealth citizen or Irish citizen may claim to be placed upon the register, and any registered elector may object to such claims. An appeal lies from the decision of a registration officer to the county court (in Scotland to the sheriff) and thence on a point of law to the Court of Appeal (in Scotland to the Electoral Registration Court of three senior judges). The decision of the county court may also be reviewed on jurisdictional grounds.[11] Once placed upon the register, any person not suffering from a legal incapacity, such as infancy or insanity, is entitled to vote, the register being conclusive on such questions as whether a person was on the qualifying date resident at the address shown. But while a person registered cannot be excluded from voting he may incur penalties if he records a vote while subject to a legal incapacity.[12] Additions or alterations to the register may be ordered by the High Court[13] and may also be made by the registration officer.[14]

---

6   *Scott* v. *Phillips* 1974 S.L.T. 32, following *Ferris* v. *Wallace* 1936 S.C. 561: s. 5(1) of the 1983 Act requires the courts to have regard to principles established by judicial decisions on the former requirement of a qualifying period of residence, even though that requirement has disappeared in Britain.

7   1983 Act, s.7.

8   1983 Act, s. 8(2) (a).

9   1983 Act, s. 13.

10   1983 Act, ss. 14–17.

11   *R.* v. *Hurst, ex p. Smith* [1960] 2 Q.B. 133.

12   1983 Act, ss. 49 and 61(1).

13   *E.g. R.* v. *Hammond, ex p. Nottingham Council, The Times,* 10 Oct. 1974. For Scotland, see *John Ferguson,* 1965 S.C. 16.

14   1983 Act, s. 11.

Disqualification for the franchise

The franchise may not be exercised by:

(*a*)   aliens;

(*b*)   persons who have not attained the age of 18 by the date of the poll;[15]

(*c*)   those who, for reasons such as mental illness, subnormality, drunkenness, and infirmity, lack the capacity at the moment of voting to understand what they are about to do. It is for the presiding officer at the poll to take the decision of refusing to allow such persons to vote;

(*d*)   peers and peeresses in their own right (but Irish peers may vote);[16]

(*e*)   convicted persons during the time that they are detained in a penal institution in pursuance of a sentence;[17]

(*f*)   persons convicted of corrupt or illegal practices at elections, the period and geographical extent of disqualification depending on the offence.[18]

Voting procedure

Responsibility for the official conduct of the election in each constituency rests upon the returning officer, who in England and Wales in the case of a county constituency wholly contained within the area of a county council is the sheriff, and in the case of a borough constituency wholly contained within a local government district is the chairman of the district council.[19] Most functions of the returning officer are however discharged by the registration officer or by a deputy appointed by him. Certain matters, for example the declaration of the poll, may be reserved to the returning officer. The official costs of an election, as distinct from the expenses of the candidates, are paid out of public funds in accordance with a scale prescribed by the Treasury.

Normally voting takes place in person at the polling station assigned to the area in which the elector is resident. Certain exceptions exist. Thus service voters may vote by proxy or by post. Since 1948, other classes of voter have also been able to vote by post. This right may be claimed by an elector unable to vote in person on a number of grounds (for example, the general nature of his occupation, service or employment; his employment on election duties; physical incapacity; no longer residing at his qualifying address)[20] but not for absence on holiday.

The nomination of candidates, the form of the ballot papers, the secrecy of the ballot and the counting of votes are governed in detail by the Representation of the People Acts. It is only since 1969 that the ballot-paper may include words describing the political affiliation of candidates. The first proposal to Parliament was that a register of political descriptions should be created and maintained by the Registrar of Friendly Societies. This would have required political parties to register for electoral purposes. But the difficulties inherent in that proposal[21] led to a simpler solution being adopted by which each candidate may give a description of himself in up to six words, which may include a statement of his political allegiance.[22]

---

15   1983 Act, s. 1(1)(c).
16   *Beauchamp* v. *Madresfield* (1872)8 C.P.245; Peerage Act 1963, ss. 5 and 6. And see [1983] P.L. 393.
17   1983 Act, s. 3.
18   1983 Act, s. 160.
19   1983 Act, s. 24(1).
20   1983 Act, s. 19(1).
21   *Cf.* A. P. Herbert, *Uncommon Law*, ch. 10 ('Which is the Liberal Party?').
22   1983 Act, sch. 1, rule 6.

In the past, office-holders who conducted elections did not always exercise their functions impartially. In the great case of *Ashby* v. *White*, the Mayor of Aylesbury as returning officer wrongfully refused to allow Ashby to vote and Ashby sued him for damages. The House of Lords upheld the view of Chief Justice Holt (dissenting in the Queen's Bench) that the remedy of damages should be given. In Holt's words, 'To allow this action will make public officers more careful to observe the constitution of cities and boroughs, and not to be so partial as they commonly are in all elections . . .'[23] Today, officials concerned with the conduct of elections are required to carry out their duties impartially and are subject to criminal penalties if they do not, but they cannot now be sued for damages if breach of official duty is alleged.[24]

II. Distribution of constituencies

Before 1832, the unreformed House of Commons was composed on the general principle that every county and borough in England and Wales was entitled to be represented by two members. A similar principle applied to Scottish representation in the Westminster Parliament, subject to the limit of numbers imposed in the Treaty of Union which led to the grouping of certain shires and royal burghs for this purpose. Representation thus depended on the status of the territorial unit of local government and bore no regard to population. Before 1832 counties such as Cornwall, which contained many tiny boroughs, were grossly over-represented by comparison with areas of rapidly growing industrial population. From the Reform Act 1832 onwards, successive measures of redistributing constituencies to remove glaring differences were undertaken, usually at the same time as reforms in the franchise were made.[1] Only in this century has there come to be general acceptance of the principle of broad mathematical equality in the size of constituencies,[2] and only since 1945 has there been permanent machinery to enable boundaries to be adjusted from time to time to take account of shifting population and to avoid excessive disparities developing between constituencies. The legislation has sought to establish impartial machinery, but in practice the system has not operated without controversy. The system does not seek to achieve strict arithmetical equality between constituencies, but lays emphasis also on the territorial aspect of representation, on the link between the elected member and his constituency and on the desirability of parliamentary boundaries not clashing with local government boundaries. The degree of discretion built into the system of electoral apportionment makes it particularly necessary to ensure that the machinery is impartial and charges of gerrymandering are avoided.

Machinery for determining constituency boundaries
By the House of Commons (Redistribution of Seats) Acts 1949 and 1958, there are four permanent boundary commissions, for England, Wales, Scotland and Northern Ireland. The Speaker is the chairman of each commission, and a

---

23 (1703) 2 Ld. Raym. 938, 956.
24 1983 Act, s. 63.

1 Butler, *The Electoral System in Britain since 1918*, app. II.
2 Report of Speaker's Conference, Cd 8463, 1917; Report of Committee on Electoral Machinery, Cmd 6408, 1943.

judge from the appropriate High Court (in Scotland, from the Court of Session) is appointed deputy chairman of each commission. Each commission includes two other members, those for England being appointed by the Home Secretary and the Secretary of State for the Environment. Each commission has two official assessors, those for England being the Registrar General and the Director General of Ordnance Survey. Each commission must undertake a general review of constituencies in that part of the United Kingdom assigned to it, at intervals of not less than ten or more than fifteen years; changes in particular constituencies may be proposed from time to time when necessary. Notice must be given to the constituencies affected by any provisional recommendations. If objections are received from an interested local authority or from a body of at least 100 electors, a local inquiry must be held into the recommendations. Having received a report on the inquiries, a commission must submit its report to the Secretary of State. The 1949 Act, by section 2(5), imposes a duty on the Secretary of State, 'as soon as may be after a Boundary Commission have submitted a report', to lay the report before Parliament together with a draft Order in Council for giving effect, with or without modifications, to the recommendations in the report (reasons must be given to Parliament for any modifications). The draft Order must be approved by resolution of each House before the final Order can be made by the Queen in Council. The validity of any Order in Council which purports to be made under the 1949 Act and recites that approval was given by each House is not to be called into question in any legal proceedings.[3]

Rules for redistribution of seats

The 1949 and 1958 Acts also contain the rules which the commissions must observe in redistributing seats. Scotland must be represented by not less than 71 seats, Wales by not less than 35, Northern Ireland by from 16 to 18 seats,[4] and Great Britain by 'not substantially greater or less than 613'. These rules are not easy to apply, particularly in the case of England, but their effect is that Scotland and Wales on a population basis are represented more generously than England. Thus in 1981 the average electorate in English constituencies was 67,961, compared with 58,753 in Wales and 54,725 in Scotland. Northern Ireland was formerly represented at Westminster by only 12 members, since until 1973 it had its own Parliament at Stormont for devolved matters; but with direct rule continuing, increased representation was granted in 1979.

The legislation provides for the calculation of a separate electoral quota for each of the four countries (namely, the total electorate in each country divided by the number of constituencies existing when each commission starts on its general review). Each commission must secure that the electorate of a constituency shall be as near the relevant electoral quota as is practicable, having regard to certain other rules, for example, that parliamentary constituencies shall as far as practicable not cross certain local government boundaries. Strict application of these principles may be departed from if special geographical

---

[3]   1949 Act, s. 3(7).
[4]   House of Commons (Redistribution of Seats) Act 1979.

considerations make it desirable; and account must be taken of inconveniences that may follow the alteration of constituencies and of local ties that might be broken by alteration. The commissions thus have a broad discretion to decide how much priority should be given to achieving arithmetical equality between constituencies.[5]

Boundary review in practice

General reviews were completed by the four commissions in 1954, 1969 and 1982. In 1954, the review resulted *inter alia* in the abolition of six constituencies and the creation of eleven new ones, all in England, to bring the membership of the House up to 630. As well as other difficulties experienced by the English commission,[6] the method of calculating the electoral quota for England under the 1949 Act resulted in the draft orders in Council being challenged in the courts.

In *Harper* v. *Home Secretary*, two electors in Manchester sought an injunction to restrain the Home Secretary from submitting the draft Order in Council, already approved by both Houses of Parliament, to the Queen in Council. The injunction was granted by Roxburgh J. but was discharged by the Court of Appeal, which held that the English commission had not departed from the statutory rules which vested a wide discretion in them. 'In so far as the matter was not within the discretion of the commission, it was certainly to be a matter for Parliament to determine', said Evershed M. R., who reserved his position on the power of the court to intervene where the commission had made recommendations which were manifestly in complete disregard of the Act.[7]

In 1954, the government gave effect without modification to the recommendations of the four commissions. But events took a different turn in 1969 when the next general review was completed. The commission for England proposed major changes to 271 constituencies and five new constituencies for England bringing the total in the House to 635.

At the time the commissions submitted their reports, a radical reorganisation of local government in England (outside Greater London) and in Wales was in train and the Labour government decided that revision of parliamentary boundaries should wait until local government had been reorganised. The government therefore delayed laying the commissions' reports in Parliament and instead introduced a Bill which sought to give effect to the changes affecting Greater London, and a few abnormally large constituencies elsewhere, and postponed the general changes. The government thus sought by legislation to depart from its obligations under the Acts of 1949 and 1958. The Bill passed the Commons against severe criticism but was drastically amended by the Lords and was abandoned by the government when that House in October 1969 refused to give way to the Commons. An elector for the borough of Enfield then sought an order of mandamus from the High Court requiring the Home Secretary to perform his duty under the 1949 Act of laying before

---

[5]   *R.* v. *Boundary Commission for England, ex p. Foot* [1983] Q.B. 600.
[6]   Butler (1955) 33 *Public Administration* 125; Wilson, *Cases*, pp. 106–23.
[7]   [1955] Ch. 238, 251. See also Marshall and Moodie, ch. 5; and S. A. de Smith, (1955) 18 M.L.R. 281.

Parliament the commission reports together with draft Orders in Council.[8]
Thereupon the Home Secretary laid before Parliament the reports and the
draft Orders in Council, but invited the Commons to reject them, using the
government majority for this purpose.

By this rather tangled course of events, the Labour government succeeded
in postponing the much-needed adjustment of constituency boundaries until
after the 1970 general election, following which the new Conservative government promptly secured parliamentary approval to the changes recommended
in 1969. In the debate, some M. P.s complained that Parliament had fettered
its hands by setting up the boundary commissions and argued that Parliament
must retain the constitutional right to make the final decisions. But the
Conservative Home Secretary considered it 'enormously important' that
Parliament should comply with the impartial recommendations of the four
commissions.[9] In 1983, the general review again led to extensive changes in
constituencies, with seats in Great Britain being increased by ten, and the total
in the House rising to 650.[10] When the Conservative government took step to
implement the reports, the Labour party leader challenged the English
changes in the High Court, but with no success.[11]

The boundary commission procedure, which derives from Act of Parliament, is certainly liable in law to be set aside by a later Act and this may tempt
a government to seek to do this if it should think that this will benefit its own
electoral interests. But, as the late Aneurin Bevan said, 'I can think of nothing
that could undermine the authority of Parliament more than that people
outside should feel that the constitutional mechanism by which the House of
Commons is elected has been framed so as to favour one party in the State'.[12]
In the United States, the Supreme Court has acted to protect the value of the
individual elector's vote in state elections, holding that the voter has a plain,
direct and adequate interest in maintaining the effectiveness of his vote which
falls within the 'equal protection of the laws' guaranteed in the US constitution.[13] In Britain the process of boundary review is more likely to be blocked
in Parliament than to be set aside by the courts.

III.   The conduct of elections

The Representation of the People Act 1983 also regulates the behaviour of
candidates and their supporters. The object of Part II of the Act is to eliminate
corrupt and illegal practices and other means by which one candidate could

---

[8]   *R.* v. *Home Secretary, ex p. McWhirter, The Times,* 20 Oct. 1969. The application was dismissed in
view of the Home Secretary's action in Oct. 1969 in laying the reports and draft Orders in
Parliament. Previously on 19 Jun. 1969 the reports alone had been laid in Parliament 'by
Command' of the Crown rather than 'by Act', a distinction which it was difficult for the
Home Secretary to sustain in view of the principle in *A.–G.* v. *De Keyser's Royal Hotel Ltd*
[1920] A.C. 508, (chap. 13 C) and which was shown to be non-existent in *R.* v. *Immigration
Appeals Tribunal, ex p. Joyles* [1972] 3 All E.R. 213.

[9]   H.C. Deb., 28 Oct. 1970, col. 241 *ff.*

[10]   See the commission reports for Scotland, England and Wales, respectively Cmnd 8794, 8797
and 8798 (1983).

[11]   Note 5 *ante.*

[12]   H.C.Deb., 15 Dec. 1954, col. 1872.

[13]   *Baker* v. *Carr* (1962) 369 U.S. 186; *Reynolds* v. *Sims* (1964) 377 U.S.

obtain an unfair advantage over another. The context within which the election is controlled is an individual candidate's campaign within his constituency. Every candidate must appoint an election agent but a candidate may appoint himself to act in that capacity.[1] The most important control is a ban on expenditure being incurred with a view to promoting the election of a candidate on account of holding public meetings or issuing advertisements or circulars, or otherwise presenting the candidate or his views to the electorate, except with the authority of the candidate or his agent.[2] It is a corrupt practice to incur expenditure in breach of this ban. A maximum limit is imposed on the expenditure which may be incurred in respect of the conduct or management of the election on behalf of a candidate[3] and it is an illegal practice for a candidate or agent knowingly to exceed the limit. Certain forms of expenditure are prohibited, for example, payment to an elector for the display of posters unless payment is made in the ordinary course of the elector's business as an advertising agent; and payment to canvassers.[4] Corrupt practices include bribery, treating and undue influence, which includes the making of threats and attempts to intimidate an elector.[5]

The rules on election expenses are in practice strictly enforced, and inadvertent departures from the rules require to be formally excused by the courts,[6] but the scope of the rules is limited. While they may secure equality in many respects between candidates in their constituency campaigns, the rules are not designed to deal with the national expenditure of the parties before or during a general election, nor with national political advertising in the press.

In *R. v. Tronoh Mines Ltd*, just before a general election, the defendant company advertised in *The Times* urging the nation to save Britain from the perils of socialism. Both the company and the publishers of *The Times* were charged with unlawfully incurring expenses in the Westminster constituency in breach of section 63 of the 1949 Act (now section 75 of the 1983 Act). McNair J. held that the section aimed at expenditure on advertisements which sought to promote the cause of a candidate at a particular election, and not at those which supported the interest of one party generally in all constituencies, 'even though that general political propaganda does incidentally assist a particular candidate amongst others'.[7]

The broad effect of this decision is that Part II of the 1983 Act does not control expenditure on advertising in the national press during a general election. The 1983 election was the first at which the Labour and Conservative parties incurred such expenditure on a large scale, the Conservative party having greater resources for this purpose. It is anomalous that national advertising escapes control while local expenditure is subject to strict limits. The problem of election material which is aimed against, rather than for, a candidate was re-considered in 1976.

In *D.P.P.* v. *Luft*, in three constituencies an anti-fascist group had distributed pamphlets urging voters not to vote for the National Front candidate, there being at

---

[1]   1983 Act, s. 67(2).
[2]   1983 Act, s. 75(1): see *Grieve* v. *Douglas-Home, post* (1965 S.C. 315).
[3]   1983 Act, s. 76 as varied subsequently by order of the Home Secretary.
[4]   1983 Act, ss. 109 and 111.
[5]   1983 Act, s. 115.
[6]   1983 Act, s. 167.
[7]   [1952] 1 All E.R. 697, 700: Wilson, *Cases*, p. 128.

least three other candidates in each constituency. Members of the group were prosecuted under what is now section 75 of the 1983 Act for incurring expenditure with a view to promoting the election of a candidate without authority from an election agent. The House of Lords held that the offence had been committed, since it was sufficient for the prosecution to establish an intention on the part of the accused to *prevent* the election of a candidate, and not necessary to prove an intention to promote the election of one particular candidate: a dictum to the contrary by McNair J. in the *Tronoh Mines* case was disapproved.[8]

Broadcasting and elections

Political broadcasting at election times has also given rise to difficulties. It is an illegal practice for any person to procure the use of transmitting stations outside the United Kingdom with intent to influence voters at an election.[9] The Independent Broadcasting Authority is under a statutory duty to secure that news programmes are accurate and impartial and that due impartiality is preserved in political programmes.[10] Political advertising is banned on ITV and on local radio stations.[11]

Since 1945, time has been regularly provided both on radio and television for party political broadcasts. The allocation of time is made by agreement between the BBC, the IBA and the major parties and at general elections a special allocation of time is made. There is no statutory control of this allocation. Thus the Scottish National Party has complained about the arrangements without success, both in the Court of Session and to the Parliamentary Commissioner for Administration.[12] But once agreement on the broadcasts has been reached, the broadcasting authorities may be under a contractual liability to transmit the programme at the agreed time.[13] Do the costs of such broadcasts rank as election expenses?

In *Grieve* v. *Douglas-Home*, an unsuccessful Communist candidate petitioned against the election of the Conservative leader, Sir Alec Douglas-Home, at the general election in 1964, on the ground that the expenses of the party broadcasts in which he had appeared fell within the then section 63 of the 1949 Act. The Election Court held that no election offence had been committed since the dominant motive of the broadcasting authorities had been the intention to transmit information of public importance and not to procure Douglas-Home's election. The court considered it inevitable that an allocation of time for party broadcasts must exclude some of the minor parties.[14]

While the allocation of party broadcasts remains unregulated by law, section 75 of the 1983 Act now makes it clear that the broadcasting authorities, like the press, are free to incur expenditure in disseminating matter relating to the election, other than advertisements.[15] In 1969, the broadcasting of items about particular constituencies was also brought under control: in brief, if a candi-

---

8   [1977] A.C. 962.
9   1983 Act, s. 92.
10   Broadcasting Act 1981, ss. 4(1)(b), 4(1) (f). The BBC, which exists under royal charter, seeks to maintain due impartiality although it is not subject to statutory restrictions. And see note 18 *post*.
11   Broadcasting Act 1981, sch. 2, rule 8.
12   *Scotsman*, 27 May 1970 (refusal of interdict by the Court of Session); Report of P.C.A. for 1971, p. 6 (investigation discontinued because complaint 'political'), H.C. 116 (1971–2).
13   *Evans* v. *BBC and IBA, The Times*, 27 Feb. 1974 (C.A.).
14   1965 S.C. 315.
15   1983 Act, s. 75(1)(c)(i).

date takes part in an item about a constituency election, the item may not be broadcast without his consent; and it is an offence for a candidate to take part in such an item for the purpose of promoting his own election unless the broadcast has the consent of every other candidate for the constituency.[16] To 'take part' in a constituency item means to participate actively, for example in an interview or discussion; a candidate may not prevent the BBC from filming him while campaigning in the streets.[17] The duty of the Independent Broadcasting Authority to maintain a proper balance in its programmes was enforced by the Court of Session in 1979, when the IBA was barred before the devolution referendum in Scotland from transmitting a series of party political broadcasts, three in favour of devolution and one against.[18]

In 1968 the Speaker's Conference on electoral law recommended that there should be a ban on broadcasting or publishing opinion polls and betting odds relating to an election within 72 hours before the holding of the poll but this recommendation was not accepted.[19]

Funds of the political parties

While electoral law seeks to achieve equality between candidates in respect of constituency-based expenditure during the election campaign, the law does nothing to secure equality between national political expenditure nor to control constituency expenditure outside the election campaign. Political funds are not ranked as charitable and do not therefore receive the fiscal benefits which are enjoyed by charitable bodies.[20] Many but not all trade unions exercise their right under the Trade Union Act 1913 to maintain political funds which are used to support the Labour party and other political activities, but individual members may 'contract out' of subscribing to the political fund. A member's complaint that the political fund rules have been broken may be heard by an impartial official, the Certification Officer.[21]

For tax purposes, a company may deduct certain political contributions from its assessable profits[22] but companies must disclose details of their contributions for political purposes in excess of £200, including direct payments to political parties and indirect support of political activities.[23] Individual shareholders and company employees may not 'contract out' of such contributions.

In 1975, when the parties were in financial difficulties caused by two general elections in 1974 and the effects of inflation, the government appointed a committee to consider whether support should be given to the parties out of public funds, as happens in Germany, Finland and Sweden. In 1976, a majority of the Houghton committee recommended the introduction of a system of state aid for political parties, to take the form of annual Exchequer grants to the central organisations of the parties, the amounts to depend on

---

16 1983 Act, s. 93(1).
17 *Marshall* v. *BBC* [1979] 3 All E.R. 80. And see *McAliskey* v. *BBC* [1980] N.I. 44.
18 *Wilson* v. *IBA* 1979 S.C. 351.
19 Cmnd 3550 and 3717, 1968.
20 Cf. *Conservative and Unionist Central Office* v. *Burrell* [1982] 2 All E.R. 1; and *Re Grant's Will Trusts* [1979] 3 All E.R. 359.
21 Trade Union Act 1913, s. 3. For a full account, see K. D. Ewing, *Trade Unions, the Labour Party and the Law*.
22 *Morgan* v. *Tate and Lyle Ltd* [1955] A.C. 21.
23 Companies Act 1967, s. 19; Wilson, *Cases*, p. 133.

the extent of each party's support at the previous general election, and, at local level, a limited reimbursement of the election expenses of candidates. The scheme was estimated to cost about £2¼ million a year. Four members of the committee dissented, on the ground that direct state aid would breach the established British practice that organisation for political ends is a strictly voluntary activity.[24] This difference of opinion represented a division of views between the parties, and the recommended scheme has not been adopted. A non-governmental commission inquired into the financing of the parties in 1981: it concluded that the public interest justified support for the parties from public funds, in the form of matching payments being made to the head-quarters of a party for every individual contribution of £2 made to a constituency party. This proposal opened up the issue of closer legal regulation of parties, and it has not been adopted.[25] Public funds are now used to assist opposition parties with their work in Parliament, since it is recognised that ministers enjoy an immense advantage in Parliament through being able to call on all the resources of the civil service. In 1983, annual payments were made to opposition parties at a scale of £1,080 for every seat won at the preceding general election, plus £2.26 for every 200 votes then cast for it, up to a maximum of £325,000 for any party.[26]

Disputed elections

If elections are to be conducted according to law there must be effective machinery for investigating alleged breaches of the law and for imposing appropriate sanctions. Since the House of Commons has a direct interest in its own composition, it formerly claimed as a matter of privilege[27] to determine questions of disputed elections. The Commons exercised the right to determine such questions from 1604 to 1868; and objected, not always with success, to breaches of election law being raised in the ordinary courts.[28] From 1672, election disputes were decided by the whole House but the growth of party government resulted in disputes being settled by purely party voting. In 1868, Parliament entrusted the duty of deciding disputed elections to the courts.

The procedure is now regulated by the Representation of the People Act 1983, Part III. Within 21 days of the official return of the result of an election, an election petition complaining of an undue election may be presented by a registered elector for the constituency in question, by an unsuccessful candidate or by any person claiming to have been validly nominated as a candidate. The petition may raise a wide variety of issues, including the improper conduct of the election by officials,[29] the legal qualification of the successful candidate to be a member of the Commons,[30] and the commission of election offences such as unauthorised election expenditure.[31] The petition is heard by an Election Court consisting of two judges of the Queen's Bench Division in England or of the Court of Session in Scotland. The

---

[24] Cmnd 6601, 1976.
[25] Hansard Society, *Paying for Politics*; V. Bogdanor, (1982) 35 *Parliamentary Affairs* 367.
[26] H.C. Deb., 8 Mar. 1983, col. 809.
[27] Ch. 12 A.
[28] *Ashby* v. *White* (1703) 2 Ld. Raym. 938; *R.* v. *Paty* (1704) 2 Ld. Raym. 1105.
[29] E.g. *Re Kensington North Parliamentary Election* [1960] 2 All E.R. 150.
[30] E.g. *Re Parliamentary Election for Bristol South East* [1964] 2 Q.B. 257.
[31] E.g. *Grieve* v. *Douglas-Home* 1965 S.C. 315.

Election Court has a wide range of powers, including power to order a recount or a scrutiny of the votes. The court determines whether the person whose election is complained of was duly elected and whether any corrupt or illegal practices at the election were proved. If the court finds the candidate to have been disqualified from membership of the House, the court may, if satisfied that the cause of disqualification was known to the electorate, deem the votes cast for him to be void and declare the runner-up to have been elected.[32] If the election has not been conducted substantially in accordance with the law, or if there have been irregularities which have affected the result, the court must declare the election void and require a fresh election to be held.[33] The decision of the court is notified to the Speaker and is entered upon the journals of the House of Commons. The House must then give the necessary directions for confirming or altering the return or for issuing a writ for a new election, as the case may be.[34] In recent years, there has been an almost total disappearance of petitions in respect of parliamentary elections. The last instance of a successful candidate being unseated for election practices arose after the general election in December 1923.[35] Election petitions are more frequent in respect of local elections, where the procedure for challenging an irregular election is broadly the same.[36]

IV. Membership of the House of Commons

The following are the main categories of persons who are disqualified from sitting and voting in the House of Commons.[1]

(a) Both by common law and by statute, aliens are disqualified; citizens of the Republic of Ireland are not disqualified.[2]

(b) Persons under 21.[3]

(c) Mental patients. Under the Mental Health Act 1983, section 141, when a member is ordered to be detained on grounds of mental illness, the detention must be reported to the Speaker. The Speaker obtains a medical report from two medical specialists, followed by a second report after six months. If the member is still detained and suffering from mental illness, his seat is vacated.

(d) Peers and peeresses in their own right, other than those who have disclaimed under the Peerage Act 1963; peers of Ireland are eligible.

(e) Clergy who have been episcopally ordained (in the Church of England and Church of Ireland), ministers of the Church of Scotland,[4] and priests of the Roman Catholic Church.[5]

---

32   As in the *Bristol South East* case.
33   *Morgan* v. *Simpson* [1975] Q.B. 151; *Ruffle* v. *Rogers* [1982] Q.B. 1220 (local election cases).
34   1983 Act, s. 144 (7).
35   Butler, *The Electoral System in Britain since 1918*, p. 57.
36   Note 33 *ante*.

1   For greater detail, see Erskine May, ch. 3.
2   British Nationality Act 1981, sch. 7, first item.
3   Parliamentary Elections Act 1695, s. 7, was expressly preserved by the Family Law Reform Act 1969, sched. 2, para. 2, when the age of majority was reduced to 18. And see P. Norton [1980] P.L. 55.
4   House of Commons (Clergy Disqualification) Act 1801: *Re MacManaway* [1951] A.C. 161; Report of Select Committee on Clergy Disqualification, H.C. 200 (1952–3).
5   Roman Catholic Relief Act 1829, s. 9.

(*f*) Bankrupts. Under the Bankruptcy Acts, a debtor who is adjudged bankrupt is disqualified from membership while so adjudged and for five years after discharge, unless the discharge is accompanied by a certificate that bankruptcy was not caused by the bankrupt's misconduct.

(*g*) Persons guilty of corrupt or illegal practices, under the Representation of the People Act 1983. Various forms of disqualification exist; depending on the offence the period may last from five to ten years, and the disqualification may be universal or limited to a particular constituency.[6]

(*h*) Under the Forfeiture Act 1870, a person convicted of treason is disqualified from membership until expiry of the sentence or receipt of a pardon. The effect of the Criminal Law Act 1967 was that other criminal convictions, even where a substantial prison sentence was imposed, did not disqualify from the House. Thus prisoners convicted of terrorist offences in Northern Ireland could be nominated and elected to the Commons, though they were unable to attend at Westminster.[7] Since 1981, a person convicted of an offence and sentenced to prison for more than a year by a court in the United Kingdom or elsewhere is, while he is detained in the British Isles or in the Republic of Ireland or is unlawfully at large, disqualified from being nominated and from being a member. If he is already a member his seat is vacated.[8] It is within the disciplinary powers of the House to expel a member, but expulsion does not prevent him from being re-elected.[9]

Formerly a person who held contracts with the Crown for the public service was disqualified from membership. But this disqualification was abolished in 1957 along with the disqualification which formerly attached to the holding of a pension from the Crown. There continue to be rules and customs of the Commons regarding the declaration by members of their financial interests in matters under debate.[10]

Disqualification of office-holders

Until 1957, the law governing the disqualification which arose from the holding of public offices could only be described as 'archaic, confused and unsatisfactory'.[11] That law had grown out of ancient conflicts between Crown and Commons. During the early 17th century, the House secured recognition of the right to control its own composition. In particular, the House asserted the principle that a member could not continue to serve when appointed by the Crown to a position the duties of which entailed prolonged absence from Westminster. After 1660, the House feared that the Crown would exercise excessive influence over it by the use of patronage, and sought to avert a situation in which members held positions of profit at pleasure of the Crown. This fear led in 1700 to a provision in the Act of Settlement to the effect that no-one who held an office or place of profit under the Crown should be capable

---

6   1983 Act, ss. 159, 160, 173, 174.
7   See G. J. Zellick [1977] P.L. 29.
8   Representation of the People Act 1981; and see C. P. Walker [1982] P.L. 389.
9   Page 218 *post*.
10   Ch. 12 B.
11   H.C. 120 (1940–1) and H.C. 349 (1955–6).

of serving as a member of the House. This provision, which would have excluded ministers from the Commons, was repealed before it took effect. In its place, the Succession to the Crown Act 1707 enabled certain ministers to retain their seats in the House, subject to re-election after appointment, but excluded those who held office of a non-political character, for example in what today would be regarded as the civil service. But much elaborate legislation was necessary to establish the modern distinction between ministerial, or political, office holders, who were eligible for membership, and non-political office-holders, who were excluded. Moreover, it became necessary to restrict the number appointed to ministerial office from the Commons, to avoid returning to a situation where the executive (now in the form of the Prime Minister) exercised excessive control by patronage over the House. For a member appointed to ministerial office loses his status as a back-bencher and becomes subject to the constraints of collective responsibility.[12]

The House of Commons Disqualification Act 1957 replaced disqualification for holding 'an office or place of profit under the Crown' by disqualification attached to the holding of specified offices. There are three broad reasons for disqualification: (1) the physical impossibility for certain office-holders of attendance at Westminster, (2) the risk of patronage and (3) the conflict of constitutional duties. In 1975, the law re-enacted in an Act of the same name; references given are to the 1975 Act. The disqualifying offices fall under section 1 into six categories.

(a)   A great variety of judicial offices, listed in schedule 1 of the Act, including judges in the High Court and the Court of Session, circuit judges in England and Wales, sheriffs in Scotland, resident magistrates in Northern Ireland and stipendiary magistrates. The principle is that no person may hold full-time judicial office and be a practising politician. Lay magistrates are not affected.
(b)   Employment in the civil service of the Crown, whether in an established capacity or temporarily, whole-time or part-time. The disqualification extends to members of the civil service of Northern Ireland and the diplomatic service. Civil servants who wish to stand for election to Parliament are required by civil service rules to resign before becoming candidates.[13]
(c)   Membership of the regular armed forces of the Crown. Members of the reserved and auxiliary forces are not, as formerly, disqualified on embodiment for active service. Nor are officers on the retired or emergency lists of any of the regular forces (section 3).

Members of the armed forces, like civil servants, must resign before becoming candidates for election to Parliament and they may apply for release to contest parliamentary elections. A spate of such applications in 1962 caused the appointment of a select committee on parliamentary elections, whose recommendations resulted in the appointment of an advisory committee of seven members to examine the credentials of applicants and to test the sincerity of their desire to enter Parliament.[14]

---

[12]   Ch. 7.
[13]   Servants of the Crown (Parliamentary Candidature) Order 1960; and ch. 15.
[14]   H.C. 111 and 262 (1962–3); H.C. Deb., 18 Feb. 1963, col 163.

(*d*)   Membership of any police force maintained by a police authority.
(*e*)   Membership of the legislature of any country or territory outside the Commonwealth. This disqualification was first imposed in 1957. Except in the case of the Republic of Ireland, it is likely that members of such legislature would be debarred by their status as aliens from membership of the Commons.
(*f*)   A great variety of disqualifying offices arising from membership of commissions, boards, administrative tribunals, chairmanship or membership of a number of public authorities and undertakings; in a few cases the disqualification attaches only to particular constituencies (schedule 1, parts 2–4). As these offices cover such a wide range, each office is specified by name. Provision is made for amendment of the schedule by Order in Council pursuant to a resolution approved by the House of Commons. This power obviates the need for amendment by statute as and when new offices are created (section 5). The Queen's Printer is authorised to print copies of the 1975 Act as it is amended by subsequent Orders in Council.

For one purpose alone acceptance of an office of profit continues to disqualify. From early times a member of the House has in law been unable to resign his seat, and acceptance of an office of profit under the Crown was the only legal method of release from membership. The offices commonly used for this purpose were the office of Steward or Bailiff of the Chiltern Hundreds or of the Manor of Northstead. Under the Act of 1975 these offices are disqualifying offices (section 4). Appointment to them is made by the Chancellor of the Exchequer on the request of the member concerned.

Effects of disqualification

If any person is elected to the House while disqualified by the 1975 Act, the election is void (section 6(1)) and this could be so determined on an election petition. If a member becomes disqualified subsequent to election, his seat is vacated and the House may so resolve. Before 1957, it was the practice for Parliament to pass an Act of Indemnity in favour of members who had unwittingly become subject to disqualification. But today, the House may direct by order that a disqualification under the 1975 Act which existed at the material time be disregarded if it has already been removed (for example, by the member's resignation from the office in question) (section 6(2)). Thus a new election is unnecessary where the House itself has dispensed with the consequences of the disqualification, but no such order can affect the proceedings on an election petition (section 6(3)).

Determination of claims

Disputed cases of disqualification are in general determined by the House after consideration by a select committee. Thus in 1961, the Committee of Privileges reported adversely on the claim of Anthony Wedgwood Benn, who had succeeded to his father's peerage while a member of the House of Commons, to retain his membership.[15] While disputes under the 1975 Act as to disqualifying offices arise rarely, the Judicial Committee of the Privy Council has jurisdiction to declare whether a person has incurred a disqualification under that

---

[15]   H.C. 142 (1960–1).

Act (section 7). Any person may apply to the Judicial Committee for a declaration of disqualification but must give security for costs. Issues of fact may on the direction of the Judicial Committee be tried by the High Court in England, the Court of Session in Scotland or the High Court in Northern Ireland (section 7(4)). A declaration may not be made if an election petition is pending or if one has been tried in which disqualification on the same grounds was in issue, nor where the House has given relief by order (section 7(5)). This jurisdiction of the Judicial Committee replaces the former procedure by which a common informer could sue a disqualified member for financial penalties; it gives persons outside Parliament a means of seeking to enforce the Act. Only in the case of members disqualified by the House of Commons (Clergy Disqualification) Act 1801 does the common informer procedure still survive.

Another procedure open where there is a dispute over disqualification is for the Commons to petition the Crown to refer the matter to the Judicial Committee of the Privy Council for an advisory opinion on the law.[16]

Limitation of number of ministers in Commons

British constitutional practice requires that the holders of ministerial office should be members of either the Commons or the Lords and that the great majority should be drawn from the Commons. But it has long been found necessary for statutory limits to be imposed on the number of ministers who may sit in the Commons, lest excessive powers of patronage should be exercised by the Prime Minister over the House. The present law is to be found partly in the House of Commons Disqualification Act 1975 and partly in the Ministerial and other Salaries Act 1975. Section 2 of the former Act allows not more than 95 holders of ministerial office (whether paid or unpaid, it would seem) to sit and vote in the Commons; this limit had been 70 between 1957 and 1964, being raised to 91 in 1964[17] and to 95 in 1974.[18] If more members of the Commons are appointed to ministerial office than are allowed by law, those appointed in excess must not sit or vote in the House until the number has been reduced to the permitted figure (section 2(2)).

The Ministerial and other Salaries Act sets out the salaries payable to various categories of ministerial office, these salaries being subject to revision by Order in Council (section 1(4)). Schedule 1 of the Act also imposes limits upon the total number of such salaries payable at any one time to the various categories. Thus, to category 1 (holders of posts in the Cabinet apart from the Lord Chancellor) not more than 21 salaries are payable. Not more than 50 salaries are payable to posts in category 1 taken together with category 2 (ministers of state and departmental ministers outside the Cabinet). Not more than 83 salaries are payable to posts in categories 1, 2 and 3 (parliamentary secretaries) taken together. In addition salaries may be paid to the four law officers of the Crown, to five Junior Lords to the Treasury (governmental whips in the Commons) and to seven assistant whips in the Commons, as well as to various political posts in the royal household, some of which may be held

---

[16]   Under the Judicial Committee Act 1833, s. 4; and see *Re MacManaway* [1951] A.C. 161.
[17]   Ministers of the Crown Act 1964 noted by A.E.W. Park (1965) 28 M.L.R. 338.
[18]   Ministers of the Crown Act 1974.

only by members of the Lords.

The growth of central government has led to modern governments being larger than their predecessors. Statutory limits imposed on grounds of constitutional principle may seem irksome to a new Prime Minister, who may resort to various devices for by-passing these limits until they can be raised by legislation. Sometimes there are strong reasons for a particular increase to be made; thus the assumption of direct rule in Northern Ireland by the UK government made it necessary for extra ministers to be appointed. But the present limits are not ungenerous in relation to the size of the Commons, especially as there are also some 20 to 30 parliamentary private secretaries, who hold no statutory office but are close supporters of the government. The result is that a Prime Minister has at his disposal approximately 120 parliamentary appointments and in practice relatively few of these posts are given to members of the House of Lords.

V.   Electoral systems

Under the present electoral system in the United Kingdom, each constituency returns a single member. Each elector can vote for only one candidate and the successful candidate is the one who receives the highest number of valid votes. This system of 'first past the post' is known as the relative majority system since whenever there are more than two candidates in a constituency, the successful candidate may not have an absolute majority of votes but merely a majority relative to the vote of the runner-up.[1] This system is simple, but as a means of providing representation in Parliament it is very crude. It makes no provision for the representation of minority interests nor does it ensure that the distribution of seats in the Commons is at all proportionate to the national distribution of votes. In Britain, the general tendency of the system has been to exaggerate the representation of the two largest parties and to reduce that of the smaller parties; but even for the larger parties there is no consistent relation between the votes and the seats which they obtain. Thus in 1979, the Conservative party won 44.9% of the votes and 339 (53%) of the 635 seats; in 1983, 42.4% of the votes and 397 (61%) of the 650 seats. In 1979, the Labour party won 37.8% of the votes and 269 (42%) of the seats; in 1983, 27.6% of the votes and 209 (32%) of the seats. Ever since the Liberals became the third party in 1923, they have been regularly under-represented in relation to their national vote. Most strikingly, in 1983 the Liberal-Social Democratic alliance won 25.4% of the votes and only 23 (3·5%) of the seats. Similar anomalies occur for areas within the United Kingdom. Thus in Scotland in 1983, the Labour party won 35.1% of the votes but 41 (57%) of the 72 seats. The same voting system is used in Great Britain in direct elections for the European Parliament; in 1979, the Conservatives won 50.6% of the votes in Great Britain and 60 (77%) of the 78 seats.

The advantages claimed for the system include the simplicity of the voting method, the close links which develop between the member and his constituency, and its tendency to produce an absolute majority of seats in the House out of a large minority of votes. In defence of the system it is claimed that the

---

[1]   In the 1983 general election, 52% of the successful candidates lacked absolute majorities.

function of a general election is to elect a government as well as a Parliament, and that the system produces strong government. But this last claim needs to be examined with care, since a relatively small change of political support in a few constituencies may be exaggerated into an apparent change of mind from one party to the other by a majority of the electorate.

Other voting systems

For over a century, other electoral systems have been devised with a view to securing better representation of minorities and a distribution of seats which bears a less haphazard relation to the votes cast. Many different systems are used in other countries.[2] One method, the alternative vote system, retains single-member constituencies but allows the elector to express his choice of candidates in order of preference. If no candidate has an absolute majority of first preferences, the lowest on the list is eliminated and his votes are distributed according to the second preferences shown on the voting papers. The procedure continues until one candidate obtains an absolute majority. This system eliminates the return of a candidate on a minority vote when account is taken of second and later preferences but it does not necessarily secure representation in the Commons proportional to the first preferences of the electorate.

Other systems have been designed to secure representation in Parliament directly proportional to the national voting strengths of the parties. Thus by the list system, as used in Israel, voting for party lists of candidates takes place in a national constituency, with each party receiving that number of seats which comes closest to its national vote; this system does not provide for any local links between voters and their representatives. In the Federal Republic of Germany, a mixed system is used by which each elector has two votes, one to elect a candidate in a single member constituency, the other to vote for a party list; the list seats are assigned to parties to compensate for disproportionate representation arising from the constituency elections, but a party must record 5% of the national vote or win 3 constituencies to gain any list seats.

The system which is likely to produce a reasonably close relationship between votes and seats while maintaining a local basis for representation is that of the single transferable vote. This method has been used within the United Kingdom for several purposes.[3] It would require the country to be divided into multi-member constituencies, each returning between three and, say, seven members. Each elector would have a single vote but would vote for candidates in order of preference. Any candidate obtaining the quota of first preferences necessary to guarantee election would be immediately elected, the quota being calculated by a simple formula: in a five-member constituency, the quota would be one vote more than one-sixth of the total votes cast. The surplus votes of any successful candidate would be distributed to other candidates proportionately according to the second preferences expressed; any candidate then obtaining the quota would be elected and a similar distribution

---

[2]   V. Bogdanor, *The People and the Party System*, parts III–V; and D. Oliver [1983] P.L. 108.

[3]   *E.g.* for university constituencies between 1918 and 1948; in Northern Ireland for elections to Stormont in 1922–8, to the Assembly in 1973 and 1982, to the Constitutional Convention in 1975, and to the European Parliament.

of his surplus would follow. If at any count no candidate obtained the quota figure, the candidate with the lowest number of votes would be eliminated and all his votes distributed amongst the others.

Under this scheme, parties would both nationally and locally be likely to secure representation according to their true strength; minority parties and independent candidates would stand a better chance of election; and the number of ineffective votes would be reduced. Within the constituency, electors could in their order of preference choose between candidates from the same party and could base their choice of candidates on non-party considerations. A probable consequence is that one party would be less likely to secure an absolute majority of seats in the Commons than at present; and Britain would become used to periods of minority or coalition government.[4] But this would not necessarily lead to instability nor to a proliferation of small parties. Nor would the quality of government be necessarily impaired. Parties which benefit from the present system are likely to oppose any change, and existing M.P.s may resist the idea of multi-member constituencies. But it is not obvious why an elector is better represented in Parliament by a single member whose election he opposed rather than by a team of members the choice of which he has directly influenced, even if the candidate of his first preference has not been elected.

The case for proportional representation has been examined many times. A royal commission in 1910 rejected proportional representation but recommended the alternative vote.[5] In 1917, the Speaker's Conference on Electoral Reform recommended the adoption of proportional representation by the single transferable vote,[6] but Parliament after some vacillation refused to accept either this or the alternative vote. Following an all-party conference in 1929–30,[7] a Bill which sought to introduce the alternative vote passed the Commons but was abandoned when the Labour government fell in 1931. The Speaker's Conference on Electoral Reform in 1944 rejected by large majorities proposals for change, as did a similar conference in 1967.[8] But in 1973, the Royal Commission on the Constitution considered voting methods in relation to elected assemblies for Scotland and Wales and recommended the adoption of the single transferable vote. The commission considered that an overriding requirement for the assemblies was to ensure the proper representation of minorities, but emphasised that it was not concerned with elections to the Westminster Parliament.[9] Nonetheless the Labour government supported by a majority in the Commons decided that the 'first past the post' system should be used for the assemblies that were to have been created under the Scotland Act and Wales Act 1978.[10] The introduction of direct elections for the European Parliament at a time of minority government and the Callaghan-Steel pact gave an opportunity for the adoption of proportional representation in Great Britain, but the House of Commons defeated the

---

[4]   Page 35 *ante*.
[5]   Cd 5163, 1910.
[6]   Cd 8463, 1917. And see Butler, *The Electoral System in Britain since 1918*, Part I.
[7]   Cmd 3636, 1930.
[8]   Cmd 6534, 1944; and Cmnd 3202, 1967.
[9]   Kilbrandon Report, paras. 779–88.
[10] Cmnd 6348, 1975, p. 9; and ch. 22.

proposal for a regional list system on a vote in which the Labour and Conservative parties were divided.[11]

Forms of proportional representation have been advocated by two non-governmental commissions. In 1976, a commission appointed by the Hansard Society (chairman, Lord Blake) recommended a system by which three-quarters of the Commons could be elected in single-member constituencies, the remainder to be allocated to parties within voting regions so that the seats won by parties might be brought closer to the proportion of votes. In 1982, a joint Liberal-Social Democratic commission on constitutional reform recommended a scheme of 'community proportional representation'; this was mainly based on the single transferable vote in multi-member constituencies but the alternative vote was also used in a few single-member constituencies retained for geographical reasons.[12] The results of the general election in 1983 strengthened the case for electoral reform but may also have stiffened the resolve of the Labour and Conservative parties to continue their opposition to it.

Speaker's Conference on electoral law

One constitutional device which has been used from time to time for discussing the reform of electoral law has been a conference of party leaders meeting in private under the impartial chairmanship of the Speaker. One reason for these conferences is to secure all-party support wherever possible for reforms in electoral law. While the aim is laudable, the device is not suitable for resolving matters of major controversy, such as proportional representation. The conferences are conducted in private, not in public, and reasons for agreed recommendations are not usually published. The proceedings may lead to allegations of a private bargain having been reached between the party leaders, and to subsequent recriminations when one party adopts a different position.[13] Nor are the recommendations of such a conference binding on the government, which remains responsible for the detailed changes which it lays before Parliament.[14]

In 1948, Winston Churchill said:

It has become a well-established custom that matters affecting the interests of rival parties should not be settled by the imposition of the will of one side over the other, but by an agreement reached either between the leaders of the main parties or by conferences under the impartial guidance of Mr Speaker.[15]

Even if this is accepted as a statement of the ideal, in practice the situation falls far short of it and it is doubtful whether a Speaker's Conference is suitable to bear the strain of serious disagreement between the parties, as there was in 1948. On less controversial matters, the purposes served by a Speaker's Conference might be served as well by more familiar procedures such as a royal commission or a select committee of the Commons.

---

[11] Cmnd 6768, 1977; H. C. Deb., 13 Dec. 1977, col. 417; and ch. 8.

[12] *Electoral Reform: Fairer Voting in Natural Communities*, 1982.

[13] The controversy in 1948 is discussed by Butler, *op. cit.*, pp. 109–22. And see Wilson, *Cases*, p. 134.

[14] After the Speaker's Conference reported in 1968, the government published its decisions on the recommendations: Cmnd 3550 and 3717, 1968.

[15] H.C. Deb., 16 Feb. 1948, col. 859. And see D. Butler in (ed. D. Butler and A. H. Halsey) *Policy and Politics*, ch. 2.

Chapter 10

Meeting of Parliament

Frequency and duration of Parliaments

In law, a new Parliament is summoned by the Sovereign by means of a royal proclamation. It is by the Sovereign that Parliament is prorogued, which occurs when a session of Parliament is terminated, and dissolved, which brings the life of one Parliament to an end. These powers of the Sovereign are prerogative powers, that is they are derived from the common law powers of the Crown, not from statute.[1] They were used as political weapons by the Stuart kings during their struggles with Parliament in the 17th century; since then, they have been subjected to both legal and political controls, originally to ensure that the King could not govern without Parliament. In 1689, article 13 of the Bill of Rights provided that 'for redress of all grievances, and for the amending, strengthening and preserving of the laws, Parliaments ought to be held frequently'.[2] In 1694, the Meeting of Parliament Act (formerly known as the Triennial Act) supplemented this rather vague demand by requiring that Parliament should meet at least once every three years, a requirement which still forms part of the law. Although there is no rule of law expressly requiring this, in practice Parliament has met annually ever since 1689. One reason for this is that since that time it has been the practice for some essential legislation, including authority for certain forms of taxation and expenditure, to be passed only for a year at a time; this legislation must therefore be renewed annually if lawful government is to be maintained. So too the legislative authority for the maintenance of the army has been continued in force annually, although this is done today by resolution of Parliament and not by Act.[3] In fact the many pressures upon government to maintain a flow of legislation through Parliament and the expectation of all politicians that Parliament should meet regularly combine to ensure that, subject to customary periods of holiday, Parliament is in constant session.

The Meeting of Parliament Act 1694 also regulated the life of a Parliament: no Parliament was to last for more than three years and, unless sooner

[1] Ch. 13 C.
[2] Ch. 2 A.
[3] Ch. 23.

dissolved, was then to expire by lapse of time. The Septennial Act 1715 extended the life of Parliament to seven years but the Parliament Act 1911 reduced the period to five years. In practice, apart from the two world wars, when the life of Parliament was extended annually to avoid the holding of a general election during war-time, all modern Parliaments have been dissolved by the Sovereign, rather than expiring by lapse of time. The length of recent Parliaments has varied: that elected in February 1974 lasted only until October 1974; by contrast, the Parliament elected in October 1959 lasted for almost the full period of five years.

Modern practice is that the same proclamation both dissolves Parliament and summons a new one. The new Parliament can be summoned to meet not less than 20 clear days after the date of the proclamation,[4] although a longer interval is usually allowed. Between general elections, a session of Parliament usually runs from late October or early November for about one year. After the long summer adjournment of both Houses, there is usually a short resumption of the two Houses to complete necessary legislative business. Parliament is then prorogued, and a new session opens a few days later.

General elections and by-elections

After the summoning of Parliament by proclamation, individual writs are issued to the members of the Lords, and writs are issued to returning officers commanding an election of members of the Commons to be held.[5] When a vacancy occurs in the House during a Parliament, for example by the death of a member, the Speaker may by warrant authorise the issue of a writ for the holding of a by-election. When the House is sitting, the Speaker issues the warrant upon the order of the House.[6] By long-established custom of the House, the motion for the issue of a writ is moved by the Chief Whip of the party which held the seat before the vacancy occurred. There is no time-limit for filling the vacancy. While the constituency party concerned may need time to select a new candidate, there have been delays of as long as nine months before the motion for the writ is moved, especially in the case of seats held by the government party, which for tactical reasons may wish to postpone the by-election for as long as possible. To avoid abuse of this position, a statutory time-limit seems necessary. In 1973, the Speaker's Conference on electoral law recommended that the writ for a by-election should normally be moved within three months of the vacancy occurring.[7]

Dissolution

Parliament continues for five years unless it is sooner dissolved by the Sovereign on the advice of the Prime Minister. Save in exceptional circumstances, the Sovereign is obliged to give effect to the Prime Minister's request. It is today not necessary that the Cabinet should have decided in favour of dissolution, although the Prime Minister may have discussed the desirability of a

---

[4] Representation of the People Act 1918, s. 21(3).
[5] Ch. 9 B.
[6] By the Recess Elections Act 1975, which re-enacted an Act of 1784, the Speaker may himself order the issue of a writ during a recess caused by prorogation or adjournment.
[7] Cmnd 5500, 1973.

dissolution with the Cabinet or with selected colleagues.[8] The opportunity to choose the timing of a general election is an important power at the disposal of the Prime Minister; thus he may choose a time when there is a revival in the economy or when the government's popularity is rising. It is sometimes said that the right to request a dissolution is a powerful weapon in the hands of a Prime Minister to compel recalcitrant supporters in the Commons to conform. Where government policies are challenged by major national interests, the Prime Minister may take the dispute to the electorate in the hope of getting renewed support, as happened in February 1974 when Mr Heath called a general election because the miners' strike challenged his economic policy. But dissolution is too ultimate a deterrent to be a convenient means of bringing pressure to bear on government members of the Commons, since a general election at an unfavourable time may mean that the government party goes out of office sooner than it otherwise would have done. While the utility of the weapon may be exaggerated, the possibility of a dissolution before the statutory life of a Parliament has run its course leaves the executive with a definite means of controlling Parliament which would not be available if the law were changed to require an election of a new Parliament at prescribed intervals (for example, once every four years). The personal role of the Sovereign in respect of a dissolution will be examined later.[9]

Demise of the Crown

Since the Representation of the People Act 1867 the duration of Parliament has been independent of the life of the Sovereign. If however Parliament should be prorogued or adjourned when the Sovereign dies, Parliament must reassemble at once without a summons.[10] Should the Sovereign die after a dissolution, but before the day fixed for the meeting of the new Parliament, the former Parliament must, according to an ancient statute, immediately assemble and sit for six months or until sooner dissolved.[11] But today there seems no good reason why the election of the new Parliament and its first meeting should be thus interrupted.

Prorogation and adjournment

Prorogation brings to an end a session of Parliament. Today Parliament is prorogued not by the Sovereign in person but by a royal commission, through whom the prorogation speech reviewing the work of the session is delivered to Parliament. Parliament may be recalled by proclamation at one day's notice during a prorogation, if this should prove to be necessary.[12] Prorogation terminates all business pending in Parliament, with the exception of the judicial work of the House of Lords. Any public Bills which have not passed through all the stages in both Houses lapse. In the case of private Bills a resolution may be passed before prorogation directing that a Bill be held over till the next session.

---

[8]   Jennings, *Cabinet Government*, pp. 417–9; Mackintosh, *The British Cabinet*, pp. 452–5.
[9]   Ch. 13 A.
[10]   Succession to the Crown Act 1707, s. 5.
[11]   Meeting of Parliament Act 1797, s. 3.
[12]   Parliament (Elections and Meetings) Act 1943, s. 34.

It is within the power of each House to adjourn for such time as it pleases, but this does not put an end to any uncompleted business. The Sovereign may call upon Parliament to meet before the conclusion of an adjournment intended to last for more than fourteen days.[13] The standing orders of each House authorise an adjournment of either House to be terminated at short notice, should the Lord Chancellor or the Speaker be satisfied on the request of the government that the public interest requires it. Parliament must be recalled within 5 days if a state of emergency is declared or the reserve forces are called out during an adjournment or prorogation.[14] In several recent sessions the House of Lords has resumed its sittings after the long summer adjournment earlier than the Commons to deal with a backlog of Bills considered by the Commons earlier in the session.

Opening of Parliament

After a dissolution or a prorogation, Parliament is opened by the Sovereign in person or by royal commissioners. When a new Parliament meets, the House of Commons first elects a Speaker, for which purpose the member of the House who has the longest continuous period of membership and is not a minister of the Crown presides over the proceedings.[15] After this the House adjourns until the following day when the election of the Speaker is announced to the Lord Chancellor in the House of Lords. The Lords take the oath of allegiance as soon as Parliament has been opened, and the Commons as soon as the Speaker has been formally approved by the Sovereign and has himself taken the oath.[16]

At the beginning of every session, the first business is the debate on the speech from the Throne. This speech, for which the Cabinet is responsible, announces in outline the government's plans for the principal business of the session. It is delivered in the House of Lords, to which the Commons are summoned to hear the speech read by the Sovereign or by the Lord Chancellor. In each House an address is moved in answer to the speech, and the debate provides an opportunity for a general discussion of national affairs, lasting some four or five days. Before the address is moved, the ancient right of Parliament to deal with matters not brought before it by the Crown is asserted by the formal first reading of a dummy Bill; in the Lords this is the Select Vestries Bill, in the Commons the Outlawries Bill.

Lord Chancellor

The Lord Chancellor presides over the House of Lords as its Speaker. He has many important functions outside the House as a member of the Cabinet, responsible for many aspects of the machinery of justice, and as head of the judiciary.[17] In contrast with the impartial position occupied by the Speaker in the Commons, the Lord Chancellor is free to take part in debates. He is often the principal spokesman for the government; while speaking, he vacates

---

13 Meeting of Parliament Act 1870, amending the Meeting of Parliament Act 1799.
14 Emergency Powers Act 1920 (ch. 29 B); Reserve Forces Act 1966, s. 5(2).
15 H.C. Standing Order 124, and see H.C. 111 (1971–2).
16 Under the Oaths Act 1978, s. 5, members may make a solemn affirmation in lieu of the oath.
17 Ch. 19 C.

the Woolsack temporarily by stepping aside from it. That part of the Lord Chancellor's salary which is paid in respect of his duties as Speaker in the Lords is charged on the House of Lords vote.[18] In order that their official salaries may be paid, the Lord Chancellor must in cases of doubt decide which peers are the Leader of the Opposition and the Chief Opposition Whip in the Lords.[19]

In the absence of the Lord Chancellor, the duties of Deputy Speaker are undertaken by the Lord Chairman of Committees. A member of the House is elected each session to this salaried office, which carries with it extensive duties relating to private Bills, as well as the duty to preside in committee of the whole House.

The Speaker

The chief officer of the House of Commons is the Speaker. Except when the House is in committee, he is its chairman and is responsible for the orderly conduct of debate. It is through the Speaker that the House communicates with the Sovereign. Today, although not always in the past, the Speaker is expected to carry out his duties with complete impartiality between the parties and to preserve the right of minorities in the House.[20] He has the duty of determining whether a Bill is a money Bill within the meaning of the Parliament Act 1911.[21] He is chairman of each of the four boundary commissions which review the distribution of seats,[22] although he does not attend their meetings. He has many duties to perform which affect the business of the House, for example he must decide whether to accept for debate a question raised as an important matter that should have urgent consideration by the House,[23] and he has an important discretion to exercise in selecting amendments to Bills for debate.[24] His rulings on procedure are an important source of Commons practice and if given in the House have always been recorded in Hansard. Since 1981, his private rulings that are of general interest or likely to become precedents are also published in Hansard.[25]

The Speaker is a member of the House elected to be Speaker whenever a vacancy in the office occurs and at the beginning of each new Parliament. It is customary for the party with a majority in the House to select a candidate from amongst its own number. The selection is usually made after consultation with the other parties, in order that the selection may be the unanimous choice of the House. In 1971, when Mr Selwyn Lloyd, a former Conservative Cabinet minister, was elected as Speaker, many members felt that there had been inadequate consultation; subsequently certain changes in procedure were made.[26] It is customary for the previous Speaker to be re-elected when a new Parliament meets. In 1972, it was proposed that a Speaker who had decided

---

[18] Ministerial and other Salaries Act 1975, s. 1(2).
[19] Ministerial and other Salaries Act 1975, s. 2(3).
[20] See P. Laundy, *The Office of Speaker.*
[21] Ch. 11 B.
[22] Ch. 9 B.
[23] H.C. Standing Order 10.
[24] Ch. 11 A.
[25] H. C. Deb., 5 Nov. 1981, col. 113; and see e.g. H. C. Deb., 9 Dec. 1981, col. 970.
[26] Note 15 *ante.*

to retire should do so during the life of a Parliament, and not wait until dissolution: this occurred in 1976 when Mr George Thomas was elected, but Mr Thomas himself retired at the dissolution in 1983.

The Speaker may not continue in office in a new Parliament unless he has been re-elected for his constituency, but his duty to abstain from party political activities prevents him from fighting his seat as a member of his former party. At one time, the Speaker's seat was not contested by other parties at a general election, but in recent years Labour and Liberal candidates have stood against the Speaker. While the Speaker is unable to represent his constituency's interests in debate, he is able to take up individual grievances of constituents privately with the departments concerned. The Speaker's salary is payable out of the Consolidated Fund. When he retires, he will receive a peerage and a statutory pension. If a Speaker dies in office, all business of the House comes to an end until a successor is appointed.

Deputy Speaker

When the House of Commons is in committee, the chair is taken by the Chairman (or one of the two Deputy Chairmen) of Ways and Means, or by one of a Chairmen's panel of not less than ten members nominated by the Speaker for the purpose of providing chairmen of standing committees. Thus one of these officers will preside when a Bill is taken in committee by the whole House.[27] The Chairman of Ways and Means is the Deputy Speaker, but the duties of Deputy Speaker may also be performed by the two Deputy Chairmen of Ways and Means.[28] Unlike the office of Speaker, new appointments as Chairman of Ways and Means and Deputy-Chairman may be made on a change of government. By custom of the House the holders of these offices do not take an active part in debates but may resume their normal political activities after they have resigned from these posts.

Permanent officers of Parliament

The chief permanent officer of the House of Lords is the Clerk of the Parliaments, appointed by the Crown and removable only by the Crown on address from the House. His duties include the endorsement of every Act of Parliament with the date on which it received the royal assent, and the custody of one copy of every Act printed on vellum. Under the Clerk of the Parliaments are a Clerk Assistant and a Reading Clerk appointed by the Lord Chancellor, who may be removed only upon an address from the House. The Lord Chairman of Committees is assisted in his detailed work on private legislation by a lawyer appointed as Counsel to the Chairman of Committees.

The Clerk of the House of Commons is appointed by the Crown; two Clerk Assistants are appointed by the Crown on the nomination of the Speaker. These officers may be removed only upon an address from the House. The Clerk of the House is responsible for the records and journals of all proceedings in the Commons, endorsing all Bills sent to the Lords, and laying documents on the table of the House. He is the Accounting Officer for House of Commons expenditure. The Speaker's Counsel advises the Speaker and officers of the

---

27 Ch. 11 A.
28 The Deputy Speaker Act 1855; H.C. Standing Order 125.

House on matters of law, and his duties include the oversight of private legislation and the scrutiny of statutory instruments. The Serjeant at Arms, appointed by the Crown, is responsible for enforcing the orders of the House, including warrants issued by the Speaker for commitment for contempt or breach of privilege. The question was raised in 1962 whether the Crown was under a duty to consult the House of Commons before making an appointment to the office of Serjeant at Arms. After consultation with the Queen, the Prime Minister announced that on any future occasion when the office of Serjeant at Arms should fall vacant the Queen would, before exercising her prerogative of appointment, initiate informal discussions with the Speaker as had been done in the past. It is for the Speaker to take soundings at his discretion to inform the Sovereign of any feelings there may be in the House before the appointment is made.[29]

The administration of Parliament

The Palace of Westminster was formerly controlled on the Sovereign's behalf by the Lord Great Chamberlain but in 1965, with the consent of the Queen, control of the Palace (except for Westminster Hall) passed to the two Houses. Control of that part of the Palace occupied by the House of Lords is vested in the Lord Chancellor, and is exercised by the House of Lords Offices Committee; and of that part occupied by the Commons in the Speaker, who is advised by the Select Committee on House of Commons (Services). Arrangements for the management of the work of the Commons were reformed with the establishment of a new House of Commons Commission under the House of Commons (Administration) Act 1978.[30] The commission consists of the Speaker, the Leader of the House, a member nominated by the Leader of the Opposition and three other members appointed by the House. The commission is responsible for the staff of the House (appointments, salaries, pensions and conditions of service), for preparing annual estimates of House expenditure, and for supervising the system of departments into which the work of the House is organised. In practice the commission delegates many of its staffing functions to the Speaker and other officers of the House. Underlying these arrangements are such problems as how much should be paid to service the activities of the House, what these activities should be, and whether the government should control the House's expenditure.

---

[29] H.C. Deb., 11 Dec. 1962, cols. 209–10.
[30] Largely based upon the Bottomley report (H.C. 624, 1974–5).

Chapter 11

Functions of Parliament

We have already examined the relationship between Parliament, the executive and the judiciary, and the principle of responsible government. In looking more closely at the principal functions of Parliament, we will focus attention upon the House of Commons, since it is the composition of the Commons that determines which party will form the government, it is from the Commons that most ministers are drawn, and it is the House of Commons alone that has power by withdrawing its support to cause the Prime Minister either to resign or to seek a dissolution. But the work of the House of Commons must not be exaggerated beyond its institutional context. First, the role of the House of Lords in the work of Parliament, especially in legislation, is not trivial or insignificant, although in political terms the role of the House is definitely secondary to that of the Commons. Second, the political authority of the House of Commons does not extend to its undertaking the work of government itself. Most members of the House of Commons are not members of the government. Nor is the House organised in a manner that would enable it to take over the direction of national affairs.

A classic statement of both the importance of parliamentary control of government and its limitations was made by the Victorian political philosopher, John Stuart Mill:

There is a radical distinction between controlling the business of government, and actually doing it. The same person or body may be able to control everything, but cannot possibly do everything; and in many cases its control over everything will be more perfect, the less it personally attempts to do . . . It is one question, therefore, what a popular assembly should control, another what it should itself do . . . Instead of the function of governing, for which it is radically unfit, the proper office of a representative assembly is to watch and control the government; to throw the light of publicity on its acts; to compel a full exposition and justification of all of them which anyone considers questionable; to censure them if found condemnable, and, if the men who compose the government abuse their trust, or fulfil it in a manner which conflicts with the deliberate sense of the nation, to expel them from office, and either expressly or virtually appoint their successors.[1]

---

[1] J. S. Mill, *Representative Government*, ch. 5.

Mill also stressed that a no less important function of the Commons was to be a sounding-board for the nation's grievances and opinions, 'an arena in which not only the general opinion of the nation, but that of every section of it . . . can produce itself in full light and challenge discussion'.[2]

This high-principled analysis is still of value, even though the strength of the executive power today, the present electoral and party system, and the fact that economic and industrial power is located outside the House of Commons, together present a formidable challenge to the political authority of the House itself. If it is a duty of the House to find out about, scrutinise and influence the many acts of government agencies, two consequences follow: first, the House needs procedures and resources that match the scale of the task; second, the members of the House who do not hold ministerial office need the political will to do more than simply sustain the government in office while voting through the measures laid before it. The creation by the House of Commons in 1979 of a system of specialist committees to scrutinise the main departments of government was a notable reform,[3] but the committees must operate within a House which for many tasks still adopts an adversary approach to politics in its proceedings.[4]

Many writers have sought to list the principal functions of Parliament. Bagehot in *The English Constitution* included within the functions of the House of Commons the expressive function (expressing the opinion of the people), the teaching function, and the informing function ('it makes us hear what otherwise we should not'),[5] as well as the functions of legislation and finance. In 1978, the House's Select Committee on Procedure, whose report led directly to the reform of the select committee system in 1979, considered that the major tasks of the Commons fell into four main categories: legislation, the scrutiny of the activities of the executive, the control of finance, and the redress of grievances.[6] Inevitably these categories overlap and the list does not include the broader political functions of the House that underly its more detailed tasks. In the present chapter, the work of Parliament will be examined under four headings: (a) legislation; (b) conflict between the Houses; (c) financial procedures; and (d) scrutiny of administration.[7] The redress of collective grievances is related to all these headings; the redress of individual grievances is an aspect of the scrutiny of administration, and also relevant is the Parliamentary Commissioner for Administration (the ombudsman), whose work will be considered in chapter 37 D.

A. Legislation

In chapter 5, it was shown that the legislative supremacy of Parliament does not mean either that the whole work of legislating is carried on within Parliament, or that the parliamentary stage is always the most formative stage in

---

2   *Ibid.*
3   Section D *post*.
4   *Cf.* S. E. Finer (ed.), *Adversary Politics and Electoral Reform.*
5   Bagehot, p. 153. And see P. Norton, *The Commons in Perspective*, ch. 4.
6   H.C. 588–1 (1977–8), p. viii.
7   See also S. A. Walkland and M. Ryle (ed.), *The Commons Today*; S. A. Walkland (ed.), *The House of Commons in the Twentieth Century*; and P. Norton, *The Commons in Perspective.*

the process of legislation. In practice about half of the time of the Commons is devoted to legislative work. Many government policies can be achieved within the framework of existing legislation: for example, by the provision of more money for certain purposes or by the use of existing powers to guide and direct local authorities. But other government policies require legislation and most legislation is initiated by the government. The scope for legislative initiatives by individual M.P.s is severely limited, both because of restricted parliamentary time and of the tight hold which the government maintains over departmental responsibilities. The process by which government policies are turned into law falls into three broad stages:

(a)   before publication of the Bill;
(b)   the passage of the Bill through Parliament;
(c)   after the Bill has received the royal assent.

In this section, emphasis is placed on the second of these stages. But stages (a) and (c) are both important to an understanding of the legislative process.

The pre-Bill stage
The life-history of a Bill usually has begun long before it is laid before Parliament. The source of a Bill may be in a party's political programme or in the efforts of a pressure-group to get the law reformed. Public authorities may have experienced difficulties in administering the existing law and may seek wider powers. A royal commission, a departmental committee or the Law Commissions may have published reports recommending reform. Economic problems or the action of terrorists may have made it necessary for government to take preventive measures. A decision of the courts may have shown the need for amending legislation. The government may have entered into a treaty which imposes an obligation to change the domestic law of the United Kingdom. Whatever the situation in which the need for legislation arises, before a Bill can be introduced into Parliament by the minister of the sponsoring department, it must be adopted into the government's legislative programme. Approval for this will be given by one or more committees of the Cabinet concerned with the legislative programme in Parliament, who will supervise the drafting of government Bills and determine the order of their introduction into Parliament.[1]

Within the limits of Cabinet approval, it is for the department primarily concerned to decide what the Bill should contain and these instructions are conveyed to the official draftsmen, Parliamentary Counsel, who are responsible for drafting all government Bills. While a Bill is being drafted, extensive consultation may take place with other departments affected and successive revisions of the draft Bill are circulated confidentially within government. There may also be consultation with organisations outside government representing the interests primarily affected, but it is not usual for the draft Bill itself to be disclosed. If more open consultation is desired, the government may publish a consultative document, for example a 'green paper', which states the government's provisional views, or a 'white paper', which while stating the

---

[1]   In 1976 there was a single Legislation Committee of the Cabinet for these purposes: H. Wilson, *The Governance of Britain*, p. 129. And see ch. 14 A.

government's decided position may leave certain matters open for further discussions. Where green or white papers are published, they are sometimes debated in Parliament, but the pre-Bill stage is essentially an administrative and political process which is carried on within government and behind the closed doors of Whitehall. More than once, committees of the Commons have recommended the wider use of pre-legislation committees of Parliament, so that M.P.s may be more closely associated with the stage when legislative policies are being settled. Occasionally select committees have been established for this purpose.[2] The system of select committees created in 1979 has enabled some committees to act as pre-legislation committees by receiving evidence from interested quarters and recommending changes in the law. Introduction of a Bill into Parliament by the responsible minister means that the form of the legislation has been settled. While lobbying and consultation may continue, subsequent changes to the Bill can be made only by formal amendment: this will involve persuading the government to admit publicly that it has had second thoughts. Only rarely will a government Bill leave a choice between alternative proposals to be made by Parliament, but as a result of the Liberal/Labour pact in 1977, the choice of voting systems was left to the Commons in the Bill which became the European Assembly Elections Act 1978.

Public Bill procedure

The process of legislation, like most aspects of parliamentary procedure, is complicated.[3] A distinction must be drawn between public and private Bills. A public Bill seeks to alter the general law and is introduced into Parliament under the standing orders of the two Houses relating to public business. A private Bill is a Bill relating to a matter of individual, corporate or local interest and is subject to separate standing orders relating to private business.[4] A private Bill must not be confused with a public Bill introduced by a private member, which is known as a private member's Bill.[5] In the case of government Bills, the sponsoring minister presents the Bill to the Commons; the Bill receives a formal first reading and is then printed and published. There follows the second reading of the Bill, when the House may debate the general proposals contained in the Bill. If the second reading is opposed, a division may take place on an Opposition amendment to postpone the second reading for three or six months, or on a reasoned amendment opposing the Bill. For a government Bill to be lost on second reading would be a serious political defeat, a setback which has been avoided by most modern governments. In the Commons, a whole day (*i.e.* from 3.30 p.m. to 10 p.m.) may be set aside for the second reading of a major Bill, but many Bills are debated for less than two hours and two or more days may be allotted to the debate of Bills of exceptional political importance.[6] Where a Bill involves new public expendi-

---

2 See H.C. 538 (1970–1) paras. 7–9 and app. I, part IV and H.C. 588–1 (1977–8), p. xii. Select committees considered proposals for corporation tax in 1970–1, for tax credit in 1972–3, and for wealth tax in 1974–5.

3 For detailed information, see H.C. 538 (1970–1), J. A. G. Griffith, *Parliamentary Scrutiny of Government Bills*, Erskine May, and D. R. Miers and A. C. Page, *Legislation*.

4 Page 189 *post*.

5 Page 184 *post*.

6 Griffith, *op. cit.*, ch. 2.

ture or new taxation, the Commons must approve a financial resolution on the proposal of a minister before the clauses concerned may be considered in committee; the financial resolution is approved immediately after a Bill's second reading.[7]

Second reading committees

Some Bills may receive a second reading without any debate in the whole House. Where a Bill relates exclusively to Scotland, the Bill may, unless at least ten members object, be referred on the proposal of a minister to the Scottish Grand Committee, which consists of the 71 members for Scottish constituencies. The Scottish Grand Committee considers the principle of the Bill and, unless the Opposition wishes to divide the House, the Bill may be deemed to have had a second reading.[8] In the case of other public Bills, a minister may propose that a Bill be referred to a second reading committee, subject to objection by at least twenty members. In this case a committee is appointed *ad hoc* to consider whether the Bill ought to be read a second time and to recommend accordingly to the House.[9] Where a second reading debate takes place in committee, the general merits of the Bill are debated, but any vote on the Bill is taken in the whole House. These procedures are therefore not suitable for major or controversial Bills.

Committee stage

After Second Reading, a Bill is normally referred for detailed consideration to a standing committee, consisting of between 16 and 50 members nominated by the Committee of Selection.[10] In nominating these members, the Committee of Selection must have regard to the qualifications of those members and to the composition of the House, which means in practice that the parties are represented as nearly as possible in proportion to their representation in the House. Despite its name, a standing committee is today constituted afresh for each Bill. The chairman of a standing committee is a member of the chairmen's panel appointed by the Speaker. Not more than two standing committees may be appointed for the committee stage of Bills which relate exclusively to Scotland.[11]

Instead of referring a Bill to a standing committee, the House may commit the Bill to a committee of the whole House,[12] for which purpose the Speaker leaves the chair and his place is taken by the Chairman of Ways and Means or one of the deputy chairmen. In practice this happens only on the proposal of the government, sometimes for minor Bills on which the committee stage is purely formal, but sometimes for Bills of outstanding political or constitutional importance, or for Bills which the government wishes to see become law as soon as possible. Major Bills taken in committee of the whole House have included the Bills for the Industrial Relations Act 1971, the European

---

[7]   Page 198 *post*. Erskine May, ch. 30; G. Reid, *The Politics of Financial Control*, pp. 84–92.

[8]   H.C. Standing Orders (S.O.) 70, 71.

[9]   H.C. S.O. 69; Griffith, *op. cit.*, ch. 2.

[10]   H.C. S.O.s 42, 63, 65; Griffith, *op. cit.*, ch. 3.

[11]   H.C. S.O. 72. For consideration of a public Bill relating exclusively to Wales, the standing committee includes all members for Welsh constituencies (S.O. 65(2)).

[12]   H.C. S.O. 42(1).

Communities Act 1972, the Scotland Act 1978, the Wales Act 1978, the European Assembly Elections Act 1978, and the Northern Ireland Act 1982, as well as the Parliament (No. 2) Bill 1969, which sought unsuccessfully to reform the House of Lords. Such Bills require a great deal of time if they are to be adequately considered. Until 1967, the annual Finance Bill, which embodies the changes in taxation proposed in the Chancellor of the Exchequer's Budget speech, was referred to a committee of the whole House but the Bill is now divided, certain major clauses being taken before the whole House, the remainder being referred to a standing committee.[13]

Whether a Bill is considered in standing committee or in committee of the whole House, the object of the committee stage is to give consideration to the individual clauses of the Bill and to enable amendments to be made. While general approval has been given to the Bill on second reading, members opposed to the Bill may use the committee stage to propose amendments seeking to narrow the scope of the Bill or in other ways to render it more acceptable to them. Members may be able to persuade the minister in charge of the Bill to reconsider a specific point, but the government expects to maintain its majority in committee and it is infrequent for an amendment to be made against the wishes of the government. As one member remarked, 'The most difficult thing in the world is to get any government, of whatever complexion, to change the major structure of a Bill once it has been presented'.[14] In committee, members may speak any number of times supporting or opposing amendments. After the amendments to a clause have been considered, there may take place a further debate on the motion that the clause, or the clause as amended, should stand part of the Bill. The chairman of the committee has wide powers of regulating committee proceedings: thus he must decide whether amendments are admissible or out of order and he exercises an important discretion in selecting and grouping the amendments which are to be moved.[15] While civil servants are present, and assist ministers in dealing with points raised in debate, they are not allowed to address the committee.

Exceptionally, when it is desired that a small number of members should investigate in detail the need for a Bill and the merits of its clauses, a Bill after second reading may be referred to a select committee of the Commons, or to a joint committee of Lords and Commons. Such a committee has power to take evidence from persons and organisations whether within government or outside. While committees on procedure have recommended the more regular use of select committees, it has not been the practice to use select committees for Bills which are strongly supported by government departments and which seek to give effect to settled government policies.[16]

---

[13]   H.C. S.O. 42(3); Griffith, *op. cit.*, pp. 34–7.

[14]   Peter Emery M.P., quoted in Griffith, *op. cit.*, p. 115. In this book, Griffith presents statistics which indicate the fate of all amendments proposed to government Bills during the three sessions 1967–68, 1968–69 and 1970–71.

[15]   H.C. S.O.s 34 and 68(3). By S.O.s 50 and 68, the chairman may refuse to allow debate of the motion that a clause 'stand part' of the Bill if he is of opinion that the principle of the clause has been adequately discussed in the debate on the amendments. Griffith, *op. cit.*, ch. 3.

[16]   H.C. 538 (1970–71), paras. 27–9; Griffith, *op. cit.*, pp. 248–52; and H.C. 588–1 (1977–8), pp. xv–xix.

In the 1980–1 session, three government Bills (those which became the Criminal Attempts Act 1981, the Education Act 1981 and the Deep Sea (Mining) Act 1981) were referred to 'special standing committees'. Before considering the Bills clause by clause, the committees took evidence for up to three sittings of $2\frac{1}{2}$ hours each. The experiment was welcomed by those M.P.s who took part, and enabled experts and interest groups to give public evidence. In the 1981–2 session the procedure was applied to the Mental Health (Amendment) Act 1982.[17]

Report and third reading

When a Bill has completed its committee stage, it is reported as amended to the whole House. On the report stage, further amendments may be made to the Bill on the proposal of ministers, sometimes to give effect to undertakings which they have given in committee, sometimes to remove amendments made in committee but not accepted by the government. The Opposition may also use the report stage to urge further amendments upon the government, although it is rare for these amendments to succeed and the Speaker has the discretion to select the amendments which will be debated.[18] A Bill committed to the whole House and not amended in committee is not considered by the House on report, a practice which probably influenced the government to resist all amendments in committee to the European Communities Bill 1972. Bills which were referred to a second reading committee or to the Scottish Grand Committee may be referred to a standing committee for the report stage, but there has been reluctance to deprive the whole House of its opportunity to consider Bills on report.[19]

After a Bill has been considered on report, it receives its third reading; only verbal amendments may be made to a Bill at this stage and there will be a debate only if at least six members request this.[20] Such debates as there are tend to be brief and formal, although with a controversial Bill the Opposition may wish once more to vote against it.

Allocation of time

In the legislative work of the Commons, the time factor is always of importance both to the government, which wishes to see its Bills pass through Parliament without delay, and to the Opposition and individual members, who may seek to prolong proceedings as a means of persuading the government to make concessions. Exceptionally, as in the case of the Commonwealth Immigrants Act 1968 and the Northern Ireland Act 1972, the government may see the passage of legislation as being of extreme urgency. But even in matters which are not themselves urgent, the more time which one Bill takes, the less time is available in the House for other legislation. As well as the power of the Speaker or chairman to require a member to discontinue his speech who persists in irrelevance or tedious repetition,[21] various methods of curtailing

---

[17]   See H.C. 588–1 (1977–8), p. xviii–xix; and H. J. Beynon [1982] P.L. 193.
[18]   H.C. S.O. 34(1).
[19]   H.C. S.O. 78; Griffith, *op. cit.*, ch. 4; H.C. 588–1 (1977–8), p. xx.
[20]   H.C. S.O. 58.
[21]   H.C. S.O. 23.

debates have been adopted by the House. The simplest method is that known as the closure, by which any member (in practice usually a government whip) may, either in the House or in Committee, move 'that the question be now put'. The chairman may refuse to put the motion on the ground that it is an abuse of the rules of the House or an infringement of the rights of the minority, but, if the chairman does not so refuse, the closure motion must be put forthwith and it is voted upon without debate. It can be carried in the House only if not less than 100 members vote for the motion; if so carried, the debate cannot be resumed and the motion under discussion must then be voted upon.[22]

A second method, which has already been mentioned, is the power of the chairman at the committee stage and of the Speaker at the report stage to select from amongst the various amendments proposed those which are to be discussed; this power is exercised more strictly at the report stage than in committee. A third and more drastic method is the 'guillotine', by which a minister may move an allocation of time order in the House to allot a specified number of days or portions of days to the consideration of a Bill in committee of the whole House or on report. The guillotine motion may be debated for no more than three hours. If it is carried it is the duty of the Business Committee, which consists of the Chairman of Ways and Means and up to eight other members nominated by the Speaker, to divide the Bill into parts and to allot to each part a specified period of time.[23] A similar procedure exists by which the House may allocate time for the proceedings of a standing committee on any Bill; the detailed allocation of time is then made by a Business sub-committee.[24] The effect of an allocation of time order is that at the end of each allotted period, the portion of the Bill in question is voted upon without further discussion. Compulsory timetabling of this kind can have the result that substantial parts of a Bill have not been considered at all by the Commons before it is sent to the Lords. In practice, the two sides in the House often agree through the usual channels (*i.e.* through the respective whips) on the voluntary timetabling of a Bill; where such informal agreement is not available, an imposed timetable is necessary if the government wishes to maintain its legislative programme against pressure from the Opposition. The proposal that a formal timetable should be established for all public Bills has not been favoured.[25] The minority Labour government of 1976–9 failed to secure a guillotine for the Scotland and Wales Bill in 1976–7, and the Bill lapsed; with support from Liberal and Nationalist M.P.s, the guillotine was imposed on the devolution legislation in 1977–8.

Private members' Bills
Although the bulk of the legislative programme is taken up by government Bills, a small but significant part of the programme consists of Bills introduced by backbench M.P.s. Standing orders generally give precedence to government business but they set aside ten Fridays in each session on which private

---

[22] H.C. S.O.s 31, 32.
[23] H.C. S.O.s 45, 46. For a historical account, see Jennings, *Parliament*, pp. 241–6.
[24] H.C. S.O. 81.
[25] H.C. 538 (1970–71), Part III; H.C. 588–1 (1977–8), pp. xxii–xxv; Griffith, *op. cit.*, p. 20–3.

members' Bills have priority. On the first six of these Fridays, precedence is given to the second reading of Bills presented by members who have secured the best places in the ballot for private members' Bills held at the beginning of each session. On the remaining four Fridays, precedence is given to the later stages of those Bills which received their second readings earlier in the session.[26] One of the standing committees is used primarily for the committee stage of private members' Bills, but these Bills may instead be referred to other standing committees which are not occupied with government Bills; it is usual for the composition of a standing committee on a private member's Bill to reflect the voting of the House on second reading, so that the supporters of the Bill form a majority. Private members' Bills are used for a variety of purposes[27] including matters of social reform (for example, abortion and divorce law reform) on which public opinion may be too sharply divided for the government to wish to take the initiative, matters of special interest to minority groups (for example, animal welfare), and topics of law reform which may be useful but have too low a priority to find a place in the government's programme. A private member may not propose a Bill the main object of which is the creation of a charge on the public revenue;[28] where a Bill proposes charges on the revenue which are incidental to its main object, a financial resolution moved by a minister is needed before the financial clauses can be considered in committee. It is not the practice for the government to use its majority to defeat a private member's Bill by applying the whips.[29] Where a government is sympathetic to a Bill, it may offer the services of a draftsman to the member concerned and other assistance from the departments affected; the government may also provide extra time for the later stages of a Bill for which there is substantial parliamentary support. Such assistance may be vital for a measure such as the Chronically Sick and Disabled Persons Act 1970 which was initiated by a private member but which affected the work of twelve government departments.[30] Not all private members' Bills become law: many are talked out by their opponents. The guillotine is not applied and the closure of debate needs the support of 100 members, which may not be easy to achieve on a Friday. A Bill which has not become law by the end of the session lapses.

In addition to the ballot for Bills at the beginning of each session, there are two other procedures by which a private member's Bill may be introduced. A member may simply present a Bill for its first reading, after giving notice but without previously obtaining the leave of the House.[31] Under the 'ten-minute rule' procedure, on Tuesdays and Wednesdays a private member may seek leave to bring in a Bill; he may speak briefly in support of the Bill and an opponent may reply and the House may thereupon divide on the issue.[32] Under each of these procedures the chances of a Bill proceeding further

---

[26] H.C. S.O. 6.
[27] See P. G. Richards, *Parliament and Conscience* and (same author) *The House of Commons in the Twentieth Century* (ed. S. A. Walkland) ch. 6; P. A. Bromhead, *Private Members' Bills in the British Parliament*; and H.C. 538 (1970–1).
[28] H.C. S.O. 111.
[29] Richards, *Parliament and Conscience*, p. 27, describes this as a 'strong convention'.
[30] H.C. 538 (1970–1), evidence of Alfred Morris, M.P., pp. 57–62.
[31] H.C. S.O. 39.
[32] H.C. S.O. 15.

depend on whether it is completely unopposed or on whether some time can be found for a second reading debate and later stages, either by the government or on a Friday devoted to private members' business. While it is a hazardous business for a backbencher to be in charge of a Bill in its passage through the House, without the resources available to a minister, private members' initiatives form a small but valuable part of the whole legislative work of Parliament.

Consolidation Bills

Where Parliament has legislated frequently on a particular subject (for example, rent control, social security or housing), the legislation may become unwieldy and very difficult to consult, since numerous Acts must be consulted to discover the law on that subject. It is desirable that such legislation should be consolidated, that is, re-enacted in the form of a comprehensive Act, thus enabling all the earlier Acts on the subject to be repealed. As no new law is being made, consolidation Bills may become law with the minimum time being spent on them. For this purpose a Joint Committee on Consolidation Bills is appointed each session, consisting of twelve members of each House; the purpose of the committee is to provide sufficient control to guard against abuse of the procedures by which consolidating Bills pass through the two Houses without full scrutiny. The main categories of Bill referred to the committee are (a) pure consolidation Bills; (b) Bills which, as well as consolidation, make corrections and minor improvements to the law under the Consolidation of Enactments (Procedure) Act 1949; (c) Bills which consolidate the law together with amendments recommended by the English or Scottish Law Commissions under the Law Commissions Act 1965; (d) Bills which repeal obsolete enactments; and (e) draft Orders in Council under the Northern Ireland Act 1974 which consolidate the law in Northern Ireland.[33] Bills approved by the joint committee pass through curtailed proceedings thereafter and, in so far as they consolidate the existing law or make minor improvements under the 1949 Act, are immune from amendment. The effect of these procedures is that consolidation is not delayed by the need for parliamentary time, only by such practical considerations as the shortage of draftsmen.

Procedure in the House of Lords

Except as provided by the Parliament Acts 1911 and 1949, which are considered below, a Bill may be presented for the royal assent only when it has been approved by both Houses. After a public Bill has had its third reading in the Commons, it will be introduced into the Lords. The various stages in the Lords are broadly similar to those in the Commons, although they are governed by separate standing orders. The main differences are that there are no standing committees and the committee stage is usually taken in committee of the whole House. Occasionally Bills are referred to public Bill committees consisting of 12 or 14 members.[34] In committee, there is no provision for the selection of amendments so that any amendments tabled may be moved. Even if no

---

[33]   H.C. S.O. 102. Cmnd 6053 (1975), chs. 4 and 14; Lord Simon of Glaisdale and J. V. D. Webb [1975] P.L. 285.
[34]   Griffith, *op. cit.*, pp. 226–8.

amendments are made in committee, there may be a Report stage; unlike the position in the Commons, there is no limitation on the amendments which may be moved at the third reading.

While many Bills are approved by the Lords without debate or without amendment, proceedings in the House enable further amendments to be made to the Bill. This opportunity is particularly valuable when the effect of the guillotine has been that only part of a Bill has been considered in detail by the Commons. The government itself tables many amendments in the Lords, sometimes in response to undertakings given in the Commons. The passage of a Bill through the Lords thus enables the drafting of Bills to be improved as well as substantial amendments to be made and new material to be introduced.[35]

Where a Bill approved by the Commons has been amended in the Lords, the Bill in its amended form is sent back to the Commons so that the Lords' amendments may be approved or rejected. If all the amendments are approved, the House of Commons sends a message notifying the Lords of this fact. If not, the message will contain reasons for disagreement and possibly counter-amendments. It then is for the Lords to decide whether to persist in its earlier decisions or to give way to the views of the Commons. Usually the Lords may be expected to give way; but if the House insists on maintaining its position, the disagreement between the two Houses must be resolved in some way if the Bill is to receive the royal assent. The ultimate resolution of these conflicts is governed by the Parliament Acts 1911–49.[36]

Distribution of Bills between the Houses

While the foregoing account has assumed that Bills are always introduced in the Commons, in principle Bills may originate in either House. The major exception is that by ancient privilege of the Commons, Bills of 'aids and supplies', *i.e.* those which relate to national taxation and expenditure or to local rates and charges upon them, must begin in the Commons.[37] Moreover, the representative character of the Commons and the fact that most ministers are members of the Commons mean that Bills of major political importance start there.

These factors have often meant that early in a session the Lords have too little legislative work, and have too much later in the session when a load of Bills approved by the Commons reaches them. In 1972, a new standing order was adopted by the Commons which relaxed the extent of the Commons' financial privilege in the case of government Bills and made it easier for Bills with financial provisions to begin in the Lords.[38]

In the Lords, any peer may present a Bill without notice and without seeking leave to do so. In practice not many private members' Bills pass through the Lords before they have passed through the Commons, but Bills on controversial subjects are sometimes discussed in the Lords in one session

---

[35] Griffith, *op. cit.*, pp. 228–31.
[36] Section B *post*.
[37] Erskine May, ch. 32; H.C. 538 (1970–1) paras. 19–21. And see M. Ryle in *The House of Commons in the Twentieth Century* (ed. S. A. Walkland), pp. 355–9.
[38] H.C. Deb., 8 Aug. 1972, col. 1656; Erskine May, p. 846; H.C. S.O. 61.

before similar Bills are introduced into the Commons by private members in the following session.[39]

The royal assent

Parliament cannot legislate without the concurrence of all its parts, and therefore the assent of the Sovereign is required after a Bill has passed through both Houses. Although the Sovereign may still in law attend Parliament to assent in person, an Act of 1541 authorised the giving of the assent by commissioners in the presence of Lords and Commons, and this became the invariable practice. Formerly the business of the Commons was interrupted to enable the Commons to attend the Lords for the purpose. But by the Royal Assent Act 1967, the assent, having been signified by letters patent under the Great Seal signed by the Sovereign, is notified separately to each House by its Speaker.[40] The traditional procedure is preserved, however, and it is used for Bills assented to at the prorogation ceremony. In giving the royal assent ancient forms are used.[41] A public Bill, unless dealing with finance, as also a private Bill other than one of a personal nature, is accepted by the words '*La Reyne le veult*'. A financial Bill is assented to with the words '*La Reyne remercie ses bons sujets, accepte leur benevolence et ainsi le veult*'. The formula for the veto was '*La Reyne s'avisera*'. The right of veto has not been exercised since the reign of Queen Anne. The veto could now only be exercised on ministerial advice, and no government would wish to veto Bills for which it was responsible or for the passage of which it had afforded facilities through Parliament.[42]

The consent of the Sovereign is requested before legislation which affects any matter relating to the royal prerogative is debated. Although the seeking of such consent may today be no more than an act of courtesy so far as government Bills are concerned, the need for this consent does present an obstacle for a private member's Bill which seeks to abolish one of the Sovereign's prerogatives.

After the royal assent

While the royal assent concludes the formal process by which Bills become law, it would be wrong to assume that the assent also marks the end of the legislative process. The giving of the royal assent may bring the Act into force immediately,[43] but it is very common for the operation of all or part of an Act to be suspended by provisions in the Act itself. Thus the Act may specify a later date on which it is to come into force or may give power to the government by order in Council or to a minister by statutory instrument to specify when the Act, or different parts of it, will operate. Moreover many Acts confer powers on the government to regulate in detail topics which are indicated only in outline in the Acts. While some Acts are complete in themselves, others,

---

[39]   Between 1962 and 1970 on average three Bills a year became law after being introduced into the Lords by a private member: J. P. Morgan, *The House of Lords and the Labour Government 1964–1970*, pp. 58–63.

[40]   See H.L. Deb., 2 Mar. 1967, col. 1181.

[41]   See Crown Office Rules Order 1967, S.I. 802.

[42]   See pp. 20 *ante* and 242 *post*.

[43]   Acts of Parliament (Commencement) Act 1793 and Interpretation Act 1978, s. 4. (Acts deemed in force at beginning of day on which royal assent given, if no other provision made)

particularly those affecting complex social services, cannot take effect until the powers of delegated legislation which they confer are exercised. The exercise of these powers is primarily a matter for the executive, subject to control and scrutiny by Parliament.[44]

Parliamentary interest in what happens after a Bill becomes law is not confined to delegated legislation, but traditional procedures are not well designed for enabling M.P.s to keep in touch with later developments. In 1971, the Select Committee on Procedure of the Commons recommended that much greater use should be made of 'post-legislation' committees. These committees would examine the working of a statute within a short period of its enactment, and would consider whether there was a need for early amending legislation to deal with difficulties arising in the administration of the Act, for example difficulties of interpretation.[45] Select committees are from time to time appointed to review the working of a particular Act (the Abortion Act of 1967 has been the subject of several such reviews) and the specialist select committees created in 1979 may also review the effects of legislation, but no general scheme of post-legislation committees has been adopted.

Private Bills

A private Bill is a Bill to alter the law relating to a particular locality or to confer rights on or relieve from liability a particular person or body of persons (including local authorities and statutory undertakers, for example British Railways). The procedure for private legislation is regulated by the standing orders of each House relating to private business.[46] When the objects of the Bill have been advertised and plans and other documents have been displayed in the locality concerned, a petition for the Bill together with the Bill itself must be deposited in Parliament by 27 November each year. Landowners and others whose interests are directly affected are separately notified by the promoters and they may petition against the Bill. The second reading of the Bill does not determine its desirability, as in the case of a public Bill, but merely that, assuming the facts stated in the preamble to the Bill to be true, it is unobjectionable from the point of view of national policy. If read a second time, the Bill is committed to a committee of four members in the Commons or of five members in the Lords.

The committee stage is usually the most important stage in the passage of a private Bill, particularly if there are many petitions of objection to the Bill. The committee procedure has some of the attributes of a quasi-judicial proceeding. The promoters and opponents of the Bill are usually represented by counsel and may call evidence in support of their arguments. The views of relevant government departments are made known to the committee. The committee first consider whether or not the facts stated in the preamble, which sets out the special reasons for the Bill, have been proved. If the preamble is accepted, the clauses are taken in order and may be amended. If the preamble is rejected, the Bill is dead. After the committee stage the Bill is reported to the House and its subsequent stages are similar to those of a public Bill. When

---

[44] Ch. 33.
[45] H.C. 538 (1970–1), pp. vii–ix; and H.C. 588–1 (1977–8) p. xxvii.
[46] See O. C. Williams, *History of Private Bill Procedure*, vol. I; and Erskine May, chs. 35–9.

a private Bill is opposed, the procedure is expensive, each side having to bear the fees of their counsel, expert witnesses and parliamentary agents and the expense of preparing and publicising the necessary documents. Unopposed Bills are scrutinised closely by officers of each House. This method of obtaining special statutory powers is useful to individual local authorities who seek wider powers than are generally conferred or who have special needs for which the general law does not provide. One reason for the elaborate procedure is to ensure that Parliament does not inadvertently take away an individual's private rights.[47] But there are other means of obtaining statutory authority for the exercise of special powers, and ministerial orders are of more general importance today.[48]

A hybrid Bill has been defined as 'a public Bill which affects a particular private interest in a manner different from the private interests of other persons or bodies of the same category or class'.[49] Thus a Bill to confer general powers on the Secretary of State to acquire land for the construction of airports is not a hybrid Bill since all landowners are potentially affected: but the Bill which became the Maplin Development Act 1973 was a hybrid Bill since it sought to confer power on the Secretary of State to acquire land and construct works at Maplin for the purposes of a new airport for London. After its second reading, a hybrid Bill is referred to a select committee and those whose legal rights are adversely affected by the Bill may petition against the Bill and bring evidence in support of their objections.

After the petitioners have been heard by the select committee, the Bill then passes through the committee stage and later stages as if it were an ordinary Bill. Whether a public Bill is hybrid and therefore subject to the standing orders for private business is a matter decided initially by the Examiners of Petitions for Private Bills, usually before the second reading. In 1976, after a government Bill to nationalise the aircraft and shipbuilding industries had completed a lengthy committee stage in the Commons, the Speaker ruled that the Bill was *prima facie* a hybrid Bill: rather than submit the Bill to a select committee to enable petitions against the Bill to be considered and evidence received, the government proposed and the Commons resolved that the standing orders relative to private business should not be applied to the Bill, a reminder that the House is master of its own procedure.[50] When the Bill reached the Lords, the offending clauses were rejected; in the next session, the Bill was found by the Lords to be hybrid in respect of the clauses affecting ship-repairers. In 1977 the government withdrew these clauses rather than cause further delay to the Bill.

B.   Conflict between the two Houses

The background to the Parliament Acts 1911.–49

No account has yet been given of the processes available for resolving disputes

---

[47]   *Cf. Pickin* v. *British Railway Board* [1974] A.C. 765, p. 76 *ante.*
[48]   Pages 383–5 *post.*
[49]   Erskine May, p. 896, and also pp. 588–93, 908–11.
[50]   The complex saga, which ran its course amongst great political excitement, may be followed at H.C. Deb., 25 May 1976 (col. 299), 26 May (col. 445), 27 May (col. 632), 29 June (col. 218) and 20 July (col. 1527).

between the two Houses which cannot be settled by consultation and compromise while the Bill is passing to and fro between the Houses. Today it is generally assumed that the will of the elected House should ultimately prevail. In the 19th century, the only means of coercing the Lords available to a government was to advise the Sovereign to create enough new peers to obtain a majority for the government in the Lords. Thus in 1832 the Lords abandoned their opposition to the Reform Bill when William IV eventually agreed to accept Grey's advice to create peers. Thereafter a rather uncertain convention developed that the Lords should give way in the event of a deadlock between the two Houses, whenever the will of the people was clearly behind the Commons, as it had been in 1832. This proved unsatisfactory for the Liberal party, since it gave the Lords a virtual claim to decide when a general election should be held to test the will of the people. Somewhat more definite rules applied to Bills relating to public finance. Since the 17th century, the Commons had asserted privilege in proposals for taxation and public expenditure: it was clear that the Lords might not *amend* such Bills, for this would trespass upon the exclusive right of the Commons to grant or refuse supplies to the Crown. But, however contradictory to that exclusive right it seems to us today, it was still asserted by the Lords that they had the right to *reject* financial Bills.[1] With the widening of the electoral system, the growth of the Liberal party and the appearance of a perpetual Conservative majority in the Lords, the surviving powers of that House were bound to cause conflict. This conflict became an acute problem for the Liberal government after 1906. The Lords rejected measures of social reform which had been approved by the Commons; and in 1909 the Lords rejected the Finance Bill based on the budget which Lloyd George had presented to the Commons.

The Commons had in 1907 resolved that the powers of the Lords should be restricted by law to secure that within the limits of a single Parliament the final decision of the Commons should prevail. This principle of a suspensory veto became law in the Parliament Act 1911, passed after a prolonged constitutional crisis. This crisis was resolved only when, after two general elections in 1910, the Liberal government made known George V's willingness on the Prime Minister's advice to create over 400 new Liberal peers to coerce the Lords into giving way.[2]

The 1911 Act, which did not alter the composition of the upper House, made three main changes: (a) it reduced the life of Parliament from seven to five years; (b) it removed the power of the Lords to veto or delay money Bills; and (c) in the case of other public Bills, apart from a Bill to prolong the life of Parliament, the veto of the Lords was abolished and there was substituted a power to delay legislation for two years. The Act enabled the Welsh Church Act 1914 and the Government of Ireland Act 1914 to become law. But the period of delay which the Lords could impose meant that in the fourth and fifth years of a Parliament the Lords could hold up a Bill knowing that it could not become law until after a general election. After 1945, faced with a massive

---

[1]   In 1860 the Lords rejected the Bill to repeal the paper duty. The Commons challenged the propriety of this rejection and from 1861 all the government's proposals for taxation were included in a single Finance Bill: Taswell-Langmead, pp. 548–9.

[2]   See R. Jenkins, *Mr Balfour's Poodle*; H. Nicolson, *King George V*, chs. 9 and 10; Jennings, *Cabinet Government*, pp. 428–48.

programme of nationalisation which it wished to get through Parliament, the Labour government proposed to reduce the period of delay from two years to one year. After extensive discussions on the reform of the House of Lords, which broke down on the period of delay, the Parliament Act 1949 became law under the 1911 Act procedure.

The present law

The Parliament Acts 1911–1949 provide that in certain circumstances Bills may receive the royal assent after having been approved only by the Commons. There are two situations in which this may happen: (a) if the Lords fail within one month to pass a Bill which, having passed the Commons, is sent up at least one month before the end of the session and is endorsed by the Speaker as a money Bill;[3] or (b) if the Lords refuse in two successive sessions, whether of the same Parliament or not, to pass a public Bill (other than a Bill certified as a money Bill or a Bill to extend the maximum duration of Parliament beyond five years) which has been passed by the Commons in those two sessions, provided that one year has elapsed between the date of the Bill's second reading in the Commons in the first of those sessions and the date of its third reading in that House in the second of those sessions.[4]

A money Bill is a public Bill which, in the opinion of the Speaker, contains only provisions dealing with: the imposition, repeal, remission, alteration or regulation of taxation; the imposition of charges on the Consolidated Fund or the National Loans Fund, or on money provided by Parliament for the payment of debt or other financial purposes or the variation or repeal of such charges; supply; the appropriation, receipt, custody, issue or audit of public accounts; or the raising or guarantee or repayment of loans. Bills dealing with taxation, money or loans raised by local authorities or bodies for local purposes are not certifiable as money Bills.[5] This definition has been so strictly interpreted that most annual Finance Bills have not been endorsed with the Speaker's certificate.[6] Before giving his certificate, the Speaker must, if practicable, consult two members appointed from the chairmen's panel each session by the Committee of Selection of the House of Commons.

Where a Bill is presented for the royal assent under section 2 of the 1911 Act, it must be endorsed with the Speaker's certificate that section 2 has been complied with. As the Speaker must certify that it is the same Bill which has been rejected in two successive sessions, there are strict limits on the alterations which may be made to a Bill between the first and second sessions. But the Bill in the second session may include amendments which have already been approved by the Lords and, in sending up the Bill in the second session, the Commons may accompany it with further suggested amendments without inserting them into the Bill.[7]

Any certificate of the Speaker given under the 1911 Act 'shall be conclusive

---

[3]   1911 Act, s. 1. For the Act, see Wilson, *Cases*, p. 239.
[4]   1911 Act, s. 2, as amended by the 1949 Act.
[5]   1911 Act, s. 1, as amended by National Loans Act 1968.
[6]   Erskine May, pp. 853–7; and Jennings, *Parliament*, pp. 416–9.
[7]   1911 Act, s. 2(4). The procedure was used in relation to the Bill which became the Trade Union and Labour Relations (Amendment) Act 1976.

for all purposes, and shall not be questioned in any court of law',[8] a formula which seeks to exclude any challenge to the validity of an Act passed under the Parliament Acts based on alleged defects in procedure.

The Parliament Acts do not apply to Bills which seek to extend the maximum duration of Parliament beyond five years, nor to local and private legislation, nor to public Bills which confirm provisional orders. Nor do they apply to delegated legislation: here the formal powers of the Lords will depend on whether the parent Act expressly empowers the Lords to approve or disapprove of the delegated legislation in question.[9]

As well as the Welsh Church Act 1914 and the Government of Ireland Act 1914, only the Parliament Act 1949 has become law under the Parliament Act procedure. Under Labour governments after 1945, it was the general practice of the Lords to give way when Lords' amendments to government Bills were rejected by the Commons, if only to avoid the constitutional confrontation which might otherwise arise. In the late 1960s the Lords, strengthened by the appointment of life peers, adopted a more resolute policy, causing the Labour government in 1969 to abandon the House of Commons (Redistribution of Seats) (No. 2) Bill.[10] In the 1974–5 session, failure to reach agreement between the Commons and Lords meant that the Trade Union and Labour Relations (Amendment) Bill did not become law. In the 1975–6 session, the Labour government invoked the Parliament Acts procedure but a much amended Bill was in March 1976 accepted by the Lords. The Bill which become the Aircraft and Shipbuilding Industries Act 1977 was similarly delayed by opposition from the Lords until the government abandoned the proposal to nationalise certain ship-repairing firms.[11]

The infrequency with which the Acts have been called into operation is in one respect fortunate since the procedure they provide is not without its difficulties (for example, on the question of when the Speaker may deem a Bill to have been not passed by the Lords in the second of the two sessions). The statutory method of calculating the one year's delay means that the effective period of delay may be considerably less than twelve months.

Professor Hood Phillips has argued that the Parliament Act 1949 is invalid since the Parliament Act procedure was never intended to be used for amending the 1911 Act itself and since a delegate may not use his delegated authority to increase the scope of his authority.[12] While there are indeed limits on the Bills which may become law under the Parliament Act procedure, the argument that the 1949 Act is invalid depends essentially upon the view that measures passed by the Commons and the Crown alone should be regarded as delegated legislation: yet the interpretation of Commonwealth constitutions suggests that a legislature is not subject to the limitations implied by the maxim '*delegatus non potest delegare*'.[3] While the 1911 Act was not intended to provide a final solution to the House of Lords question, it is doubtful whether

---

[8]   1911 Act, s. 3.
[9]   Ch. 33.
[10]   Ch. 9 B II
[11]   Page 190 *ante*.
[12]   *Constitutional and Administrative Law*, pp. 89, 143; *Reform of the Constitution*, pp. 18–9, 91–3.
[13]   *R.* v. *Burah* (1878) 3 App. Cas. 889; *Hodge* v. *R.* (1883) 9 App. Cas. 117.

the scope of the Act should be subject to implied constitutional limitations; if so, it would follow that, for example, a Bill to reform the Lords or to vary the succession to the throne could not become law under the Parliament Act procedure.[14]

House of Lords reform

The preamble to the 1911 Act looked forward to the creation of a new second chamber constituted on a popular instead of a hereditary basis and with its own powers, but this promise has never been fulfilled. In 1918, an all-party conference chaired by Viscount Bryce agreed that the primary functions of the second chamber included (a) the examination and revision of Bills brought from the Commons; (b) the initiation and discussion of non-controversial Bills; (c) 'the interposition of so much delay (and no more) in the passing of a Bill into law as may be needed to enable the opinion of the nation to be adequately expressed upon it'; and (d) full and free discussion of current issues of policy which the Commons might not have time to consider. Yet the Bryce conference did not reach unanimity on the composition of the House, although many members favoured indirect election of the second chamber by the House of Commons. Disputes between the Houses could, it was suggested, be settled by a joint conference of 60 members, chosen equally from each House, meeting in secret.[15]

At an inter-party conference in 1948, extensive agreement was reached on broad questions such as the need for a second chamber which should complement and not rival the Commons; the need to secure that a permanent majority was not assured to any one party; the admission of women; and the ending of admission based solely on succession to an hereditary peerage. The conference broke down through disagreement over the Lords' delaying powers: the Labour government would have accepted a delay of twelve months from second reading in the Commons or nine months from third reading, whichever was the longer, but the Conservatives insisted upon eighteen months from second reading or twelve months from third reading.[16] In the event the Parliament Act 1949 became law. No general reform of the House of Lords took place thereafter, although the Life Peerages Act 1958 and the Peerage Act 1963 appreciably modified its composition.[17]

Another all-party conference was convened by the Labour government in November 1967: this was very near the point of reaching complete agreement when the Lords in June 1968 rejected a government order continuing sanctions against the Rhodesian government.[18] This caused the government to break off the conference and to propose a comprehensive scheme for the reform of the House, which was later embodied in the Parliament (No. 2) Bill 1968–69.[19] This sought to eliminate the hereditary basis of membership, and to ensure that the House would not in future contain a permanent Conservative

---

[14] And see p. 84 *ante*.
[15] Cd 9038, 1918. See also Jennings, *Parliament*, ch. 12 and P. A. Bromhead, *The House of Lords and Contemporary Politics 1911–1957*.
[16] Cmd 7390, 1948.
[17] Ch. 9 A.
[18] Page 619 *post*, and see J. P. Morgan, *The House of Lords and the Labour Government 1964–70*.
[19] Cmnd 3799, 1968; Morgan, *op. cit.*, chs. 7 and 8.

majority. It proposed two tiers of members. The 'voting' members, entitled to vote and speak, would comprise life peers and hereditary peers of first creation; but they would be expected to attend at least one-third of the sittings in each session and would retire at the end of the Parliament in which they became 72 years old; serving or retired law lords and a reduced number of Anglican bishops would also be voting members. The second tier of members, entitled to speak and take part in committees (except on legislation) but not to vote, would comprise created peers who were not able to attend the House regularly or had retired because of age from voting membership; and also, as a transitional measure, existing peers by succession who wished to stay in the House. Initially there would be about 250 voting members. New life peers would be created at the start of each new Parliament if this was necessary to give the government party approximately 10% more members than the other parties in the House. Thus the balance of power would be retained by those voting peers who sat on the cross-benches and were not allied to any party. The creation of peers was to remain in the hands of the Prime Minister. No legal limits on the creation of peers were to be imposed but the government proposed that an advisory committee should review periodically the composition of the House, for example to consider how far the House included members with direct knowledge of Scotland, Wales, Northern Ireland and English regions.

Regarding the powers of the House, no change was proposed in respect of money Bills. In place of section 2 of the Parliament Act 1911, the reformed House was to have power to delay a Commons Bill for six months from the date on which the Lords had rejected the Bill, had insisted on maintaining amendments to which the Commons were opposed or had failed within 60 sitting days to make progress on a Bill sent up from the Commons. When the six months had elapsed, the Commons could then resolve that the Bill be submitted for the royal assent without the Bill needing to pass again through the Commons. The Bill could be sent for the royal assent in this way even though during the six month delay Parliament had been prorogued or dissolved. As regards delegated legislation, the Commons were to have power to override any rejection of a statutory instrument by the Lords.

While this scheme had the general support of Labour, Conservative and Liberal leaders, and of the House of Lords, it was not popular with back-benchers in the Commons and it moved so slowly through its committee stage in the House that the government eventually abandoned the Bill. The objections raised to the scheme included the wide patronage left to the Prime Minister; the artificial arrangements for ensuring that the government had a majority over other parties after each general election (which assumed that the government would always have an absolute majority in the Commons); the doubtful value of having a large number of non-voting members; the failure to make satisfactory provision for representation of the parts and regions of the United Kingdom; and failure to declare what should be the essential functions of the Lords. But the scheme had some advantages and its failure has meant that, while a second chamber is needed to serve a number of legislative purposes, the present House is restricted by its composition from exercising its powers effectively.

Within a federal system, the upper House normally has a role to play in

representing the component parts of the federation, whereas the lower House may be elected on a population basis. In 1973 the majority report of the royal commission on the constitution rejected the idea of a regional structure for the Lords[20] and in 1978 the Labour government's scheme of devolution to Scotland and Wales did not include reform of the Lords.[21]

No political consensus on the House of Lords existed in 1984. The Labour party conference in 1977 had called for 'the total abolition of the House of Lords and the reform of Parliament into an efficient single chamber legislating body without delay'. In its 1983 election manifesto, the party undertook to abolish the House as quickly as possible and in the interim to remove all the House's legislative powers, except for those relating to the life of Parliament. In 1978, a review committee appointed by the Conservative party considered the retention of a second chamber essential for the review of legislation and as a constitutional safeguard against an 'elected dictatorship'. It proposed a House of some 400 members, one-third appointed on the advice of the Prime Minister after consultation with a committee of Privy Councillors, two-thirds elected by proportional representation. The House's power to delay legislation would be based on the Parliament Act 1911, and a joint mediation committee would seek to resolve differences between the two Houses. The powers of the reformed second chamber would be incapable of amendment except with that House's consent.[22]

C. Financial procedure[1]

No government can exist without raising and spending money. In the Bill of Rights 1689, article 4, the levying of money for the use of the Crown without grant of Parliament was declared illegal. Relying on the principle that the redress of grievances preceded supply, the Commons could thereafter insist that the Crown pursued acceptable policies before granting the taxes or other revenue which the Crown needed. It has been said of the financial procedure of Parliament that the Crown demands money, the Commons grant it and the Lords assent to the grant.[2] Today a government regards it as a condition of holding office that its financial proposals should be accepted by the Commons. While a government may sometimes accept that its Bills should be amended in Parliament against its wishes, it is unlikely that any government would accept that the Commons should modify its expenditure proposals. A government which failed to ensure supply would have to resign or to seek a general election.[3]

---

20 Kilbrandon Report, p. 322; *cf.* vol. II, Memorandum of Dissent, pp. 116–9.
21 Ch. 22.
22 *The House of Lords*: report of the Conservative review committee, chairman Lord Home.

1 See also ch. 16, with which this section must be read.
2 Erskine May, p. 750.
3 Hence the necessity for a general election after the Lords had rejected the Liberal government's Finance Bill in 1909. In 1975, the Governor-General of Australia dismissed the Prime Minister of Australia, Mr Whitlam, after his government had failed to get the approval of the Senate to two Appropriation Bills. The Governor-General applied the principle that if a Prime Minister cannot get supply, he must resign or advise an election. Unlike the House of Lords, the Australian Senate is authorised by the Australian constitution to reject Appropriation Bills. Page 242 *post.*

The requirement of statutory authority before a government can impose charges on the citizen is a fundamental legal principle which gives the citizen protection in the courts against unauthorised charges.[4] Another fundamental principle is that no payment out of the national Exchequer may be made without the authority of an Act, and then only for the purposes for which the statute has authorised the expenditure. By contrast with the rule on taxation, this is unlikely to give rise to litigation in the courts since the rights of individuals are not in issue if it is broken. But on this principle is based an elaborate formal system of controlling expenditure in which both the government, through the Treasury, and the Commons play a part. The system still owes much to reforms linked with Gladstone's tenure of office as Chancellor of the Exchequer in the 1860s, when the scale of government was very much less than it is today. While the formal controls ensure that legal and financial proprieties are observed, they were not designed to cope with the present scale of public expenditure; since 1961 new procedures have been developed in an attempt to control public expenditure more effectively, and these will be considered in chapter 16.

There are various roles which the Commons may play in respect of taxation and expenditure. First, since the level of public expenditure largely depends on the policies which governments pursue, the House can by public discussion of policies influence the choices to be made between conflicting objectives (for example, improved social services as against lower taxation). Second, since the Commons cannot administer departments, M.P.s can as external critics scrutinise the administrative performance of the departments, and find out whether they are effectively administered within the broad policies decided by government and Parliament. Third, in the watch-dog role, the Commons may scrutinise the government's activities to check that departments are observing the formal rules of public accounting. Fourth, the Commons may scrutinise the details of tax legislation, just as they do in the case of other legislation. Since not all these functions are best discharged by the whole House, the House makes considerable use of committees for various financial purposes.

Basic rules of financial procedure
The financial procedures of the Commons are intricate and can only be outlined here. According to Erskine May, three rules underly present procedures.[5] For the purpose of these rules, the word 'charge' includes both charges upon the public revenue, *i.e.* expenditure, and charges upon the people, *i.e.* taxation.

1   A charge does not become fully valid until authorised by legislation; it must generally originate in the Commons, and money to meet authorised expenditure must be appropriated in the same session of Parliament as that in which the relevant estimate is laid before Parliament.

2   A charge may not be considered by the Commons unless it is proposed or recommended by the Crown. The financial initiative of the Crown is expressed

---

[4] Page 290 *post*.

[5] Erskine May, ch. 28. A fourth rule, that no more than one stage of certain money Bills may be taken on the same day in the Commons, now seems obsolete: *cf.* Erskine May, p. 763. For discussion of earlier forms of the rules, see G. Reid, *The Politics of Financial Control* and M. Ryle in (ed. S. A. Walkland), *The House of Commons in the Twentieth Century*, ch. 7.

in a standing order of the Commons which in part dates from 1713: 'This House will receive no petition for any sum relating to public service or proceed upon any motion for a grant or charge upon the public revenue ... unless recommended from the Crown'.[6] This rule gives the government formal control over almost all financial business in the Commons and severely restricts the ability of Opposition and backbenchers to propose additional expenditure or taxation.

3   A charge must first be considered in the form of a resolution which, when agreed to by the House, forms an essential preliminary to the Bill or clause by which the charge is authorised. Before 1967, these resolutions had to be passed by the whole House sitting as the Committee of Supply, in the case of expenditure, or as the Committee of Ways and Means, in the case of taxation. These committees no longer exist[7] and the resolutions are now passed by the House itself. Certain financial Bills must be preceded by a Commons resolution before they can be read a second time. But for most Bills, whether the main object or an incidental object is the creation of a public charge, the financial resolution normally follows the second reading and must be proposed by a minister.[8] In 1938 written instructions were given by the Prime Minister to departments and parliamentary draftsmen to draft financial resolutions in wide terms in order that the committee stage of Bills might not be unduly confined by the resolutions.[9]

The work of the Commons is conducted on a sessional basis, each session usually running for a year from early November. However, the government's financial year begins on 1 April (the income tax year begins on 6 April). The result is a rather complex annual financial cycle, which will now be described – first in relation to the authorisation of expenditure (supply), second in relation to taxation.

Consideration of estimates

By a long-standing principle of financial procedure, the estimates of departmental expenditure must be approved by resolutions of the Commons to enable the necessary money to be appropriated from the Exchequer. Each year, during March or at the latest on the day of the Budget speech by the Chancellor of the Exchequer, the departmental estimates of expenditure for the year commencing in April are presented to Parliament and published. The estimates will have been prepared by the departments themselves in the previous autumn and will have been revised by and agreed with the Treasury, in accordance with current Cabinet policy.[10]

In the 19th century and until 1967, the estimates were considered by the House sitting in the Committee of Supply, which could reduce but not increase a departmental vote. In fact, by 1900 consideration of the estimates had become little more than a peg on which to hang a debate of some aspect of

6   For the history of S.O. 109, see Reid, *op. cit.*, pp. 35–45.
7   For the reasons for their abolition, see H.C. 122 (1965–6).
8   H.C. S.O. 111.
9   Jennings, *Parliament*, pp. 260–67; Erskine May, pp. 769, 818.
10 Ch. 16.

government policy. As was said in 1966, 'the forms of procedure by which the House considers and votes Supply have . . . come to be mainly used not for truly financial purposes but as a means of controlling administration'.[11] By convention of the House, the subjects debated were chosen by the Opposition. The tradition of supply business for a time survived the abolition of the Committee of Supply. Between 1967 and 1982, 29 'supply days' were assigned for debate on topics chosen by the Opposition, taken during the session at times which enabled the main estimates to be formally approved before 5 August, and other matters (supplementary estimates, votes on account and excess votes) to be approved by two earlier fixed dates. In 1982, the House severed the connection between debates initiated by the Opposition and formal consideration of the estimates.[12] In each session, 19 days in the whole House are now at the disposal of the Leader of the Opposition,[13] it being understood that some part of this time will be made available to the smaller Opposition parties. A significant innovation is that, by a separate standing order, three days each session are allotted for the consideration of estimates, and must be taken before 5 August.[14] The particular estimates to be debated are selected by the Liaison Committee, which comprises the chairmen of the House's select committees.[15] Standing orders also require that the House should be asked to approve (without debate) the winter supplementary estimates and votes on account not later than 6 February; the spring supplementary estimates, excess votes, and votes relating to the numbers in the defence services not later than 18 March; and all outstanding estimates not later than 5 August.[16] If the House makes good use of the three days allotted for consideration of the estimates, M.P.s are likely to demand an increased amount of time for this purpose. Scottish M.P.s are already well placed in this respect: estimates for the Scottish departments are referred to the Scottish Grand Committee, with a limit of six days for debate.[17]

An important political opportunity for debating government plans for expenditure over the next five years arises each year in the spring when the government white paper on public expenditure is published.[18] This debate does not however form part of the annual cycle by which the House gives formal authority to the government's spending on a yearly basis.

Consolidated Fund and Appropriation Acts
Once the formal supply resolutions have been approved by the Commons, they must be embodied in legislation. Where this authorises the issue of money from the Consolidated Fund, it is known as a Consolidated Fund Act; where it also gives authority for the appropriation of money to the purposes contained in

---

[11]   H.C. 122 (1965–6). And see Balfour's speech in 1896, in Reid, *op. cit.*, pp. 69–70.
[12]   See H.C. 118 (1980–1) and H.C. Deb., 19 July 1982, col. 117.
[13]   H.C. S.O. 6(2). In addition, the government has undertaken to provide eight or nine days for topics (such as the armed forces and the EEC) which by custom were debated each year on supply days.
[14]   H.C. S.O. 19.
[15]   H.C. S.O. 101.
[16]   H.C. S.O. 19.
[17]   H.C. S.O. 73.
[18]   Page 291 *post.*

the estimates, as with the main estimates that must be adopted in July or early August, it is known as an Appropriation Act. By custom of the House, debate on Consolidated Fund or Appropriation Bills had become an opportunity for backbench M.P.s to debate subjects of their own choice. In 1982 the House decided that the various stages of these Bills should be taken formally and without debate; but on the day when such a Bill passes through the House, a series of private members' debates commences on a motion for the adjournment of the House that can continue through the night until 9 a.m. on the next day.[19] The object of this strange procedure is to preserve for private members opportunities for debate which they had previously exercised while essential financial legislation was passed.

Votes on account and supplementary estimates

Although no expenditure can be incurred without parliamentary authorisation, the Appropriation Act is not passed until July or August. Since each financial year begins on 1 April, the government must have interim authority for its expenditure. For this purpose, in the preceding February or March, votes on account of the civil and defence departments are submitted, and these are incorporated in one or more Consolidated Fund Bills passed before 1 April. The sum formally authorised by the Appropriation Act is the total expenditure voted for the year less the sum already authorised by Consolidated Fund Acts.

Where a department considers that it will need to exceed its estimated expenditure during the current financial year, whether because of unforeseen circumstances or new policy decisions, a supplementary estimate must be introduced. Supplementary estimates are submitted in July, November and February. The resolutions authorising the withdrawal from the Consolidated Fund of the sums so voted are embodied in the next Consolidated Fund Act to be passed or, in the case of the summer supplementary estimates, in the Appropriation Act.

Other forms of authorisation

(*a*)   The need for an *excess vote* arises when a department has incurred expenditure beyond the amount granted to it but has not been able to present a supplementary estimate to cure the excess before the end of the financial year. The excess votes are examined each year by the Public Accounts Committee on a report from the Comptroller and Auditor General[20] before they are granted in the March Consolidated Fund Bill.

(*b*)   In times of grave emergency there may be voted a lump sum not allocated to any particular object. Such votes are known as *votes of credit*. By this means the extraordinary expenditure in time of world war was in the main voted. The method involved relaxation of the usual methods of Treasury control.

(*c*)   The estimates for *appropriation in aid* appear side by side with the estimates of expenditure, though only the net amount of the latter is voted. Appropriations in aid are sums received by departments and retained to meet departmental expenditure.

(*d*)   Expenditure by a department may be needed for purposes not covered

---

[19]   H.C. S.O. 113.
[20]   Ch. 16.

by its existing legislation. In cases of urgent or temporary expenditure, it is accepted that the general provision made for the department in the Appropriation Act may be sufficient authority: but this is not acceptable for expenditure which is meant to continue indefinitely; nor is it acceptable if the Appropriation Act is thereby used to override limits imposed by existing legislation.[21]

Money may also be spent in anticipation of express statutory authority when by a supplementary estimate expenditure is proposed for purposes to be authorised by a future Act. In 1967, the government was strongly criticised for paying the salaries of the Parliamentary Commissioner for Administration designate and his staff before the Bill to create this office had become law: the money had in fact come out of the Civil Contingencies Fund, a statutory reserve fund to meet items of expenditure which could not have been foreseen.[22] The maximum capital in the Fund, now re-named the Contingencies Fund, has been fixed at an amount equal to 2% of the authorised supply expenditure for the previous year:[23] it may not now be drawn upon for any purpose for which legislation is necessary until a second reading has been given to the Bill in question. The existence of the Fund, which by 1981 had increased to over 1 billion pounds, is a striking exception to the principle that parliamentary authority should be obtained before expenditure is incurred.[24]

Taxation
While many forms of revenue, such as customs and excise duties, are raised under Acts which continue in force from year to year, some major taxes, notably income tax and corporation tax, are authorised from year to year. In fact the machinery for the collection of these taxes is permanent but Parliament must approve each year the rates of tax. Early in April, the Chancellor of the Exchequer presents his Budget. The Budget speech now includes a survey of the national economy as well as a financial survey of the year which has just ended; the total estimated expenditure having been published, the Chancellor announces his proposals for taxation and for detailed amendments to the revenue legislation. The contents of the speech are closely guarded secrets until the speech is delivered. While the government is collectively responsible for the Budget speech and the Chancellor will have prepared it in close consultation with the Prime Minister, the contents are made known to the Cabinet only on the previous day, or even on the morning of the Budget speech. 'The Budget is seen, not as a simple balancing of tax receipts against expenditure, but as a sophisticated process in which the instruments of taxation and expenditure are used to influence the course of the economy'.[25] In periods of economic instability, the Chancellor may find it necessary to announce changes in indirect taxation and expenditure decisions at other times in the year. In recent years, he has made an autumn statement outlining

---

21 Erskine May, p. 791.
22 H.C. 257, 326 (1966–7); H.C. Deb., 7 Feb. 1967, col. 1357.
23 Miscellaneous Financial Provisions Act 1946; Contingencies Fund Act 1974.
24 H.C. 118–1 (1980–1), p. xiv. And H.C. 137 (1981–2), app. 20; H.C. 24–1 (1982–3), p. xliii.
25 Plowden Report, Cmnd 1432, 1961, para. 10.

expenditure plans and reviewing the economy. But the spring Budget is still an important stage of the annual financial cycle on the revenue side.

Budget resolutions

As soon as the Chancellor's speech is completed, the House passes formal resolutions which enable immediate changes to be made in the rates of existing taxes and duties and give renewed authority for the collection of the annual taxes. These resolutions are confirmed by the House at the end of the Budget debate. The taxing resolutions are later embodied in the annual Finance Act. The effect of any changes made by the Finance Act may be made retrospective to the date of the Budget or any selected date.

It was for long the practice to begin at once to collect taxes under the authority of the Budget resolutions alone. This practice was challenged in *Bowles* v. *Bank of England*,[26] in which Bowles successfully sued the Bank for a declaration that it was not entitled to deduct any sum by way of income tax from dividends, until such tax had been imposed by Act of Parliament. This decision illustrates the principle maintained in *Stockdale* v. *Hansard*[27] that no resolution of the House of Commons can alter the law of the land. But the decision made it necessary to pass a law which has now been re-enacted in the Provisional Collection of Taxes Act 1968. This Act gives statutory force for a limited period to resolutions of the House varying an existing tax or renewing a tax imposed during the preceding year. Under the 1968 Act, the Finance Bill which embodies the resolutions must be read a second time within 25 sitting days of the resolutions having been approved by the House; and an Act confirming the resolutions must become law within four months from the date of the resolution or by 5 August in the same year if voted in March or April. As now amended, the Act applies to resolutions for the variation or renewal of income tax, value added tax, customs and excise duties, car tax and petroleum revenue tax.[28]

Because the Finance Bill must become law by 5 August, the government must ensure that the Bill has passed the Commons and is sent to the Lords as early in July as possible.[29] Now that the committee stage of the Bill is divided between the whole House and a standing committee, this presents fewer problems than formerly. If the House of Lords wished to be obstructive, the Finance Bill would have to be certified as a 'money Bill' for the purposes of the Parliament Act 1911[30] and be sent to the Lords not later than 4 July to ensure that the Bill could receive the royal assent by 5 August. In practice, the Lords do not obstruct Finance Bills, most of which are not certified as money Bills.[31]

Estimates and Expenditure Committees

We have seen that the formal machinery for control of the government's esti-

---

[26]   [1913] 1 Ch. 57.
[27]   (1839) 9 A. & E. 1; p. 216 *post*.
[28]   For details, see Erskine May, pp. 832–3.
[29]   H.C. 276 (1970–71).
[30]   Section B *ante*.
[31]   H.C. 276 (1970–71).

mates by the Commons has traditionally been used for broader political purposes. The decision in 1982 to allot three days in the House for debate of selected estimates was an attempt to provide a limited opportunity to the whole House to give attention to aspects of departmental expenditure. Before the creation of the present system of select committees in 1979,[32] the House had appointed a succession of committees to examine government expenditure. During the two world wars, select committees on national expenditure were appointed. After 1945, the House each year appointed a committee to examine such of the estimates presented to the House as it saw fit, 'and to report what, if any, economies consistent with the policy implied in those Estimates (might) be effected therein'. But it came to be realised that the detailed examination of estimates with a view to proposing economies was a task for the Treasury and that a parliamentary committee had a broader duty to inquire into the effectiveness of the work of government departments; thus the Estimates Committee 'became an instrument of general administrative review and scrutiny, and a major source of information about how the departments operate'.[33] In 1965, the committee's sub-committees began to specialise in particular areas of government activity as the demand was raised for the appointment of specialised investigatory committees by the House. In 1971, the Estimates Committee gave way to a new Expenditure Committee consisting of 49 members; its remit was 'to consider any papers on public expenditure presented to this House and such of the estimates as may seem fit to the Committee and in particular to consider how, if at all, the policies implied in the figures of expenditure and in the estimates may be carried out more economically'.[34]

The Committee, which was composed of backbench members, carried out its work through six sub-committees, concerned respectively with: general expenditure policy; defence and external affairs; the environment; trade and industry; education, the arts and Home Office affairs; social services and employment. Within these broad areas, each sub-committee inquired into a particular topic of departmental activity. The aim of the committee was to inform the House about particular areas of the government's work so that they might be better debated in Parliament and outside. As with many committees of the Commons, the Expenditure Committee sought to avoid working in an atmosphere of party politics and to produce unanimous reports. Although the estimates when laid before the House were referred to the committee, there was no direct link between the work of the committee and the formal supply business of the House. The committee's work extended into matters that might seem to have no financial implications, but this scrutiny of the work of government derived directly from the constitutional function of the Commons in authorising the government's total expenditure. The Expenditure Committee was abolished in 1979, when the present system of select committees was established, but its work between 1970 and 1979 prepared the way for the more comprehensive scheme described in the next section.

---

[32] Section D *post.*
[33] N. Johnson, *Parliament and Administration: the Estimates Committee 1945–65*, p. 128.
[34] For a full study, see A. Robinson, *Parliament and Public Spending: The Expenditure Committee 1970–76.*

D. Scrutiny of administration

In chapter 7, the principle of responsible government was discussed. We are now concerned with the procedures within the Commons by which the conduct of administration may be scrutinised by the House. The legislative and financial procedures of Parliament have strongly influenced the means by which Parliament finds out about the administrative work of government. But certain procedures have an importance which is not related either to legislation or to finance.

Parliamentary questions[1]

At the start of each day that the House is sitting, except on Fridays, 45 to 55 minutes are set aside to enable members to question ministers. As well as receiving oral answers to written questions of which prior notice has been given, members may ask oral supplementary questions on matters arising out of the minister's reply to the written question. Members may also ask questions for written answer at any time, and the written answers are printed in Hansard. According to Erskine May, 'the purpose of a question is to obtain information or press for action'; questions to ministers 'should relate to the public affairs with which they are officially connected, to proceedings pending in Parliament, or to matters of administration for which they are responsible'.[2] Because of the existence of question-time, matters concerning their constituencies may be raised by members privately in correspondence with ministers, who know that an unsatisfactory reply may lead to the tabling of a question. For this reason questions are used more for concentrating public attention on topics of current concern than for securing the redress of individual grievances. Civil servants are aware that action which they take in their departments may result in a parliamentary question. While ministers customarily answer those questions which have been accepted as being in order by the clerks of the House, acting under the Speaker's direction, it is for the minister himself to decide whether and how to reply to questions. There are a number of grounds on which the information sought may be withheld, for example, if the cost of obtaining the information would be excessive or if it would be contrary to the public interest for the information to be given (for example matters relating to confidential Cabinet proceedings or to the security services). 'An answer to a question cannot be insisted upon, if the answer be refused by a Minister'.[3] Question-time, it has been said, is 'pre-eminently a device for emphasizing the individual responsibility of ministers'.[4] Thus questions may be ruled out of order or refused an answer if they relate to matters for which ministers are not responsible: for example, decisions by local authorities, the BBC, courts and tribunals, the universities, trade unions and so on, for which no minister is directly responsible, or matters concerning the day-to-day administration of a nationalised industry.[5]

---

[1]   D. N. Chester and N. Bowring, *Questions in Parliament*; D. N. Chester in (ed. S. A. Walkland and M. Ryle), *The Commons Today*, ch. 8; H.C. 198 (1969–70); H.C. 393 (1971–2); Erskine May, pp. 331–47.

[2]   Erskine May, pp. 336–7.

[3]   Erskine May, p. 343.

[4]   Chester & Bowring, *op. cit.*, p. 287.

[5]   Ch. 17.

The pressure on question-time is such that departmental ministers attend for questioning by rota, although the Prime Minister is allotted fifteen minutes every Tuesday and Thursday. Members may not ask more than two starred questions (*i.e.* questions for oral answer) on any day, nor more than eight in any period of ten sitting days. Notice of starred questions cannot be given more than ten sitting days in advance.[6] Starred questions which are not reached during question-time receive a written answer. While question-time dramatises the personal responsibility of ministers to the House for government policy and departmental action, its effectiveness as a means of securing information is limited. The form which the twice-weekly questioning of the Prime Minister now takes is better for the media than it is for serious politics, but the use of 'open' questions (for example, asking the Prime Minister to list her engagements for the day) as a device for enabling a supplementary question to be asked is to continue.[7] A member who is dissatisfied with a reply may take the matter further, for example by raising the matter in an adjournment debate.

Debates

At the end of every day's public business, when the adjournment of the House is formally moved, half an hour is made available for a private member to raise a particular issue and for a ministerial reply to be given.[8] Members periodically ballot for the right to initiate an adjournment debate and advance notice of the subject is given so that the relevant minister may reply. While this gives more time for discussion of an issue than is possible in question-time, the member is not able to challenge the minister's reply, which often consists of a reasoned defence of the department's decision. During the debate, incidental reference to the need for legislative action may be permitted by the Speaker.[9] These brief debates are not followed by a vote of the House.

Although there is usually no lack of business for the House, provision is made for debates to be held at short notice on motions for the adjournment of the House for the purpose of discussing a specific and important matter that should have urgent consideration. The Speaker must be satisfied that the matter is proper to be discussed under the urgency procedure and either the request must be supported by at least 40 members, or leave for the debate must be given by the House, if necessary upon a division. In deciding whether the matter should be debated, the Speaker must consider the extent to which it concerns the administrative responsibilities of ministers or could come within the scope of ministerial action, but he does not give reasons for his decision.[10] In practice, few requests for such debates are granted.

Other occasions on which members may debate the administration of government departments occur on Opposition days, in debates on the Queen's Speech and in the all-night adjournment debate which follows the passage of a Consolidated Fund Bill. All such debates are limited by the adversary framework in which they are held and individual members have no means of probing behind the statements made by ministers, who will often seek to justify depart-

---

[6] H.C. S.O. 8.
[7] H.C. Deb., 3 Feb. 1983, col. 427.
[8] H.C. S.O. 1(7).
[9] H.C. S.O. 18.
[10] H.C. S.O. 10.

mental decisions. It is these limitations that have given rise to demands for other procedures by which the House may inform itself more directly of the work of government departments. Where it is alleged that maladministration by a department has caused injustice to individual citizens, a member may refer the citizen's complaint for investigation to the Parliamentary Commissioner for Administration.[11] Another method of investigating an issue is for the matter to be examined by a select committee.

Select committees

Select committees were much used to investigate social and administrative problems in the 19th century. A small group of M.P.s would examine a topic of current concern, with power on behalf of the House to take evidence from witnesses with firsthand knowledge and experience of the issues. Their report, published with the supporting evidence, might convince the House of the need for legislative reforms. The use of select committees declined as departments grew in strength and resources, as the primary initiative for legislation moved to the government, and as the party system established stricter control over back-bench M.P.s. The experience of the select committee that inquired into the Marconi scandal, when Liberal ministers were accused of reaping financial rewards through their prior knowledge of a government contract, showed that a select committee was not appropriate for investigations directly involving the reputation of Cabinet ministers.[12] However, the Public Accounts Committee has since 1861 had the task of reporting to the House on the financial and accounting practices of department.[13] In the period after 1945, little use was made of committees for scrutinising administration, apart from the work of the Estimates Committee described in Section C above, the technical scrutiny of delegated legislation by the committee on statutory instruments,[14] and (from 1956) the work of the Select Committee on Nationalised Industries.[15] One obstacle to the development of committees in other areas of government was the fear that their investigations would interfere with the running of departments and conflict with ministerial responsibility. Thus in 1959 the Select Committee on Procedure rejected a proposal for a permanent committee on colonial affairs, on the ground that this was 'a radical constitutional innovation': 'there is little doubt that the activities of such a committee would be aimed at controlling rather than criticising the policy and actions of the department concerned. It would be usurping a function which the House itself has never attempted to exercise'.[16]

By the mid 1960s, the mood of the Commons had changed. In 1965, a report of the Committee on Procedure declared that lack of knowledge of how the executive worked was the main weakness of the House.[17] After some hesitation by the Labour government, two new specialised committees were

---

[11] Ch. 37 D.
[12] F. Donaldson, *The Marconi Scandal*; and ch. 37 C.
[13] Ch. 16.
[14] Ch. 33.
[15] Ch. 17.
[16] H.C. 92–1 (1958–9), para. 47; B. Crick, *The Reform of Parliament* ch. 7.
[17] H.C. 303 (1964–5).

created in 1966, one to consider the activities of a department (the Ministry of Agriculture, Fisheries and Food), the other to consider the subject of science and technology. In the event the Committee on Science and Technology was regularly re-appointed in later sessions, but the Committee on the Ministry of Agriculture was appointed for only two sessions. Other committees established at this period included 'departmental' committees to examine the activities of the Department of Education and Science and the Ministry of Overseas Development; committees were also appointed to examine Scottish affairs, race relations and immigration, and the reports of the Parliamentary Commissioner for Administration.[18]

At the same time as these piecemeal developments occurred, the sub-committees of the Estimates Committee had since 1965 begun to specialise, and in 1970 the Estimates Committee was converted into an enlarged Expenditure Committee.[19] Thereafter, between 1970 and 1979, the select committees which scrutinised the work of departments fell into three broad categories:

(*a*)   committees serving specialised constitutional purposes in respect of all departments (the Public Accounts Committee, the committees on statutory instruments and the Parliamentary Commissioner for Administration),
(*b*)   the Expenditure Committee and its sub-committees, and
(*c*)   committees specialising in various subjects (nationalised industries, overseas development, race relations and immigration, science and technology).

In 1978 an influential report by the Select Committee on Procedure recommended a complete reorganisation of the committees in categories (b) and (c) to produce a more rational structure.[20] The minority Labour government was divided on the proposals[21] but the main recommendations were adopted by the House of Commons soon after the Conservative government had been elected in 1979.[22] The new scheme meant an end to the Expenditure Committee, along with the committees in category (c).

Now embodied in the House's standing orders,[23] the present system of select committees in directly related to the principal government departments. Fourteen committees are appointed for the life of a Parliament to examine the 'expenditure, administration and policy' of the main departments as follows: agriculture; defence; education, science and the arts; employment; energy; environment; foreign affairs; home affairs; industry and trade; Scottish affairs; social services; transport; Treasury and civil service; Welsh affairs. Each committee has either 9 or 11 members, except for the Scottish Affairs Committee with 13 members. Three committees have power to appoint a sub-committee: the Foreign Affairs Committee (whose sub-committee deals with overseas development); the Home Affairs Committee (whose sub-committee deals with race relations and immigration); and the Treasury and Civil Service Committee (whose sub-committee has dealt mainly with civil service matters).

---

[18]   See A. Morris (ed.), *The Growth of Parliamentary Scrutiny by Committee*; and J. P. Mackintosh, *Specialist Committees in the House of Commons – have they failed?*
[19]   See H.C. 410 (1968–9); and Cmnd 4507, 1970. And section C *ante*.
[20]   H.C. 588–1 (1977–8), chs. 5–7.
[21]   H.C. Deb., 19 and 20 Feb. 1979, cols. 44, 276.
[22]   H.C. Deb., 25 June 1979, col. 33.
[23]   H.C. S.O. 99.

As well as examining the work of the principal department(s) specified for the committee, each committee has power to look at 'associated public bodies', that is, public corporations, boards and advisory bodies in the relevant field (thus the work of the Commission for Racial Equality has been examined by the Home Affairs Committee). Not including Wales and Scotland, 228 public bodies associated with government departments have been identified by the committees.[24] These public bodies include the boards of the nationalised industries, and certain committees may jointly appoint a sub-committee to investigate a matter that affects two or more industries.[25]

Only back-bench M.P.s serve on the committees. Each committee has a majority of members from the government side of the House, but some committee chairmen are Opposition members. The committees are serviced by House of Commons clerks, and they may appoint specialist advisers. Within its subject-area, each committee may choose the topics for investigation, subject only (through the Liaison Committee) to the avoidance of duplication with other committees. The topics investigated vary widely in scope, ranging from major subjects that may take a year or longer to complete, to the latest departmental estimates and issues of topical concern which a committee may seek to influence by holding one or two hearings and publishing the evidence with a brief report. This freedom for a committee to decide for itself what to investigate is very important, and no government approval is needed. Thus the Foreign Affairs Committee chose to explore the role of the Westminster Parliament in the Canadian constitutional controversy at a time when the government had indicated that its policy was to accept without question any proposals coming from the Canadian government in Ottawa; the committee came to a different conclusion, after studying the matter in much greater depth than the Foreign and Commonwealth Office had done.[26]

The Home Affairs Committee has investigated a series of important topics including proposed immigration rules, race relations and the 'sus' law, deaths in police custody, police complaints procedures and electoral law.[27] The Treasury and Civil Service Committee has published many strongly-argued reports, dealing with the government's budgetary and monetary policies, financial procedure, financing of the nationalised industries, and a notable report on efficiency and effectiveness in the civil service.[28]

The committees exercise an important critical function even if they cannot change government decisions. When the Foreign Affairs Committee investigated the decision to increase university fees for overseas students in Britain, the committee considered the decision to have been ill-considered and hasty, adding: 'If "ill-considered" seems a harsh epithet to apply to policy, it is one well supported by the evidence'.[29] For such criticism to be made, it must have been supported in the committee by one or more M.P.s from the government

---

[24] H.C. 92 (1982–3), p. 13.
[25] H.C. S.O. 99(4). But no such sub-committee has been appointed; H.C. 92 (1982–3), p. 16.
[26] H.C. 42 and 295 (1980–1); Cmnd 8450, 1981; H.C. 128 (1981–2). And see App. A.
[27] H.C. 434, 559, 631 (1979–80); H.C. 98 (1981–2); H.C. 32 (1982–3).
[28] The reports include H.C. 163, 325, 348 (1980–1) and H.C. 236 (1981–2).
[29] H.C. 553 (1979–80); and see in reply Cmnd 8010, 1980.

side of the House. The committee's report contains only the majority view; but the extent of unity or division is revealed in minutes of committee proceedings that are published with the report.

In June 1979, some M.P.s were unconvinced of the value of specialised committees, believing that they might detract from the adversary quality of parliamentary procedure, might develop an undue form of consensus politics, might lead to too close a relationship between a committee and the department concerned, and so on. These fears have not been borne out in practice. But the 1979 reform of committees did not transform overnight the power-relationship between government and Parliament. The government has undertaken to cooperate fully with the committees[30] but it lays down the rules by which civil servants may give evidence; these rules seek *inter alia* to protect from scrutiny the process of decision-making within government.[31] Where civil servants are unable to answer a committee's questions, a minister from the department may attend for questioning. While evidence is usually heard in public, departments may ask for private sittings and for sections of the evidence to be deleted from the published report, on grounds of the public interest.

In reporting on the first three years of the committees (1979–82), the Liaison Committee stated that the scheme had markedly improved the flow of information from departments to the House, and that the long and regular appearances of ministers for questioning by the committees had become a valuable feature of parliamentary life.[32] Of some 180 substantive reports published by the committees, only five had been the subject of a set debate in the Commons, but 33 had been debated on other occasions: there continues to be a need for more regular debates of committee reports.[33]

---

[30] H.C. Deb., 25 June 1979, col. 45; and 16 Jan. 1981, col. 1697.
[31] H.C. 588–1 (1977–8), App. D. This significant constitutional document was revised by May 1980: H.C. 92 (1982–3), p. 17.
[32] H.C. 92 (1982–3); and see H.C. Deb., 16 Jan. 1981, col. 1651.
[33] H.C. 92 (1982–3), pp. 20–1.

Chapter 12

Privileges of Parliament

If legislative bodies are to be able to perform their constitutional functions effectively, they must have freedom to conduct their own proceedings without improper interference from outside bodies. Parliamentary privilege does not exist for the personal benefit of members of Parliament. 'The sole justification for the present privileges of the House of Commons is that they are essential for the conduct of its business and maintenance of its authority'.[1] The privileges of each House have both external and internal aspects: they restrain interference with the House from outside, thus restricting the freedom of speech and action which those outside the House would otherwise have; they also protect the House from internal attack, for example, from the conduct of members which is an abuse of their position.

Privilege is an important part of the law and custom of Parliament. In so far as privilege may affect the legal position of those outside the House, questions as to the existence and extent of privilege must be settled by the courts. In this sense, except when a privilege has been created by statute, privilege is part of the common law. Since neither House can separately exercise the legislative supremacy of Parliament, neither House can by its own resolution create new privileges. Where a dispute arises as to a matter of privilege, the courts will not enquire into the exercise of privilege, nor into the internal proceedings of either House; but the courts will not allow a House to extend its privileges at the expense of the rights of the citizen. Today the most difficult disputes are likely to involve the issue of whether a particular application of privilege in a new set of circumstances is to be categorised *either* as the legitimate exercise of an existing privilege in changed circumstances *or* as an attempt to create a new privilege; in the latter case, an Act of Parliament is needed if the law is to be changed.[2]

---

[1] Memorandum by Sir Barnett Cocks, in Report from Select Committee on Parliamentary Privilege, H.C. 34 (1966–7), p. 12. See also Erskine May, chs. 5–11; and G. Marshall, in (ed. S. A. Walkland) *The House of Commons in the Twentieth Century*, ch. 4.

[2] Cocks, *op. cit.*, p. 3: *cf.* the position of prerogative powers, p. 254 *post*.

A. House of Commons

There have for several centuries been attached both to the House and its members certain privileges and immunities. At the opening of each Parliament, the Speaker formally claims from the Crown for the Commons 'their ancient and undoubted rights and privileges', and in particular: 'freedom of speech in debate, freedom from arrest, freedom of access to Her Majesty whenever occasion shall require; and that the most favourable construction should be placed upon all their proceedings'. The privileges of individual members are primarily freedom from arrest and freedom of speech; other privileges are the collective privileges of the House, for example, the right of access to the Sovereign which is exercised through the Speaker.

Freedom from arrest[3]

This ancient privilege developed to enable individual members to attend meetings of the House. It protects a member from arrest in connection with civil proceedings for the customary period of from forty days before to forty days after a session of Parliament. But M.P.s have no privilege from arrest in connection with criminal or quasi-criminal proceedings.

As regards civil arrest, the privilege has become of small importance since the virtual abolition of imprisonment for civil debt. A member is protected against committal for contempt of court where his imprisonment is sought to compel performance of a civil obligation.[4] Under the Parliamentary Privilege Act 1770, members have no general immunity from having civil actions brought against them,[5] but members retain certain privileges in regard to civil litigation. It is a contempt of the House for any person to seek to serve a writ or other legal process upon a member within the precincts of the House.[6] A subpoena addressed to a member to give evidence in a civil court probably cannot be enforced by the High Court while the House is in session, but the House may grant a member leave of absence to attend as a witness in the courts. Members are not protected from proceedings under the Bankruptcy Acts, but are exempt from jury service.[7]

As regards the criminal law, members have no privilege from arrest. Nor are they protected in cases of refusal to give surety to keep the peace or security for good behaviour, nor against committal for contempt of court where contempt has a criminal character.[8] An M.P. was held in preventive detention under defence regulations during the second world war,[9] although detention as a result of words spoken in Parliament would be a violation of the privilege of freedom of speech. The House has always insisted on receiving immediate information of the imprisonment or detention of a member, together with

---

[3] Erskine May, ch. 7.
[4] As in *Stourton* v. *Stourton* [1963] P. 302.
[5] *Re Parliamentary Privilege Act 1770* [1958] A.C. 331.
[6] H.C. 221 (1969–70) and H.C. 144 (1972–3)
[7] Juries Act 1974, s. 9 and sch. 1.
[8] Ch. 19 B.
[9] H.C. 164 (1939–40) (Captain Ramsay's case).

reasons for the detention. In 1970, the Committee of Privileges inquired into the rights of members who were detained in prison whether awaiting trial or after conviction. The committee reported that a member awaiting trial could carry out many of his duties as a constituency representative but that a member who had been convicted could do so only if granted exceptional concessions under prison rules. The committee considered that no special advantages in the conditions of detention should be granted to members.[10]

Freedom of speech[11]

Freedom of speech is today the most substantial privilege from which members and the House benefit. Its essence is that no penal or coercive action should be taken against a member for what he has said or done in Parliament. The privilege has a venerable history. Haxey's case in 1397–99 is sometimes regarded as the first recognition of parliamentary freedom of speech; and in 1512, after Richard Strode, a member of Parliament, had been imprisoned by the Stannary Court of Devon for having introduced a Bill to regulate the tin mines of that county which were within that court's jurisdiction, an Act was passed to nullify the Stannary Court's decision and to protect freedom of speech in Parliament against similar interference by courts thereafter.[12] The right of the Commons to criticise the King's government was called in question in 1629 when Eliot, Holles and Valentine were convicted by the Court of King's Bench for seditious words spoken in the Commons and for tumult in the House.[13] This judgment was in 1668 reversed by the House of Lords on the ground that words spoken in Parliament could be judged only in Parliament. In article 9 of the Bill of Rights 1689 it was declared, 'that the freedom of speech and debates or proceedings in Parliament ought not to be impeached or questioned in any court or place out of Parliament'.[14]

The main effect of this historic declaration is that no member may be made liable in the courts for words spoken in the course of parliamentary proceedings. Thus members may speak in the House knowing that they are immune from the law of defamation.[15] Nor can what is said in Parliament be examined by a court for the purpose of deciding whether it supports a cause of action in defamation which has arisen outside Parliament: 'a member must have a complete right of free speech in the House without any fear that his motives or intentions or reasoning will be questioned or held against him thereafter'.[16] What a minister says in the House explaining an executive decision may not be cited in court to support an application for judicial review of the decision.[17] Moreover, since 1818 leave of the House has been required before clerks or officers of the House may give evidence in court of proceedings in the House. In 1980, the House relaxed its practice to the extent of permitting reference to be made in court to Hansard and to the published evidence and reports of

---

[10]   H.C. 185 (1970–1). And see G. J. Zellick [1977] P.L. 29.
[11]   Erskine May, ch. 6. And P. M. Leopold [1981] P.L. 30.
[12]   Erskine May, pp. 78–9.
[13]   *Eliot's* case (1629) 3 St. Tr. 294.
[14]   And see *Re Parliamentary Privilege Act 1770* (n. 5 *ante*)
[15]   E.g. *Dillon* v. *Balfour* (1887) 20 L.R. Ir. 600. And *Lake* v. *King* (1667) 1 Saunders 131.
[16]   *Church of Scientology of California* v. *Johnson-Smith* [1972] 1 Q.B. 522, 530 (Browne J.).
[17]   *R.* v. *Secretary of State for Trade, ex p. Anderson Strathclyde plc* [1983] 2 All E.R. 233.

committees, without special leave from the House.[18] This change did not diminish the continuing force of Article 9 of the Bill of Rights, nor did it alter the rule that Hansard may not be used in court as an aid to statutory interpretation.[19]

The protection of members for words spoken extends to criminal as well as civil liability. It seems that members could not be prosecuted for an alleged conspiracy to make untrue statements in Parliament to the injury of a third party[20] although such conduct might make the members liable to the disciplinary jurisdiction of the House. Again, subject to the same possibility of disciplinary action by the House, disclosures made in Parliament either by speeches or questions may not be made the subject of a prosecution under the Official Secrets Acts 1911–39; this was so ruled in the case of Duncan Sandys M.P. in 1938, when he included information in a draft parliamentary question which had been obtained in breach of the Official Secrets Acts.[21] Speeches or questions in Parliament may be in breach of the House's own *sub judice* rule if they concern pending judicial proceedings, but may not be held to be in contempt of court.[22]

The meaning of 'proceedings in Parliament'

Protection for members is not confined to debates in the House. It covers the asking of questions and giving written notice of questions, and also 'everything said or done by a member in the exercise of his functions as a member in a committee in either House, as well as everything said or done in either House in the transaction of parliamentary business'.[23] On this broad view, protection extends to clerks and other officials of the House acting in the course of their duties, as well as to witnesses giving evidence to committees of the House. It may be that privilege is not confined to words spoken or acts done within the precincts of the House and includes words spoken outside Parliament, for example, a conversation between a minister of the Crown and a member on parliamentary business in a minister's office. Conversely, it may not extend to a casual conversation within the House on private affairs. The posting by a citizen of alleged libels to members in the House on matters unconnected with proceedings in the House is not protected.[24]

In 1957, the difficult question of whether a member's letter to a minister concerning a nationalised industry is a 'proceeding in Parliament' arose in the London Electricity Board case.

G. R. Strauss M.P. had written to the minister responsible in the Commons for the electricity industry (the Paymaster-General) complaining of the methods of disposal of scrap cable followed by the board, a regional unit of the Central Electricity Board. The minister referred the letter to the board, who protested to Mr Strauss about its contents. Finally the solicitors to the board informed the member that they had instructions to

---

18 H.C. Deb., 3 Dec. 1979, col. 167 and 31 Oct. 1980, col. 879; and H.C. 102 (1978–9).
19 Page 19 *ante. Cf.* P.M. Leopold [1981] P.L. 316.
20 *Ex parte Wason* (1869) L.R. 4 Q.B. 573.
21 H.C. 101 (1938–9).
22 *E.g.* the disclosure of Colonel B's identity on 20 April 1978: H.C. 667 (1977–8) and 222 (1978–9); and p. 338 *post.*
23 H.C. 101 (1938–9).
24 *Rivlin* v. *Bilainkin* [1953] 1 Q.B. 485.

sue him for libel unless he withdrew and apologised. Mr Strauss drew the attention of the House to the correspondence, and the matter was referred to the Committee of Privileges. The most important question was whether the original letter from the member to the Paymaster-General was a 'proceeding in Parliament' within the meaning of the Bill of Rights. The committee concluded that Mr Strauss was engaged in a proceeding in Parliament; accordingly the threat by the board to sue for libel was in respect of statements made by the member in Parliament and therefore threatened to impeach or question his freedom in a court or place outside Parliament. Thus the board and their solicitors had acted in breach of privilege. However, the committee recommended the House to take no further action in the matter. On 8 July 1958, the House decided on a free vote (218 to 213) to disagree with the committee, and thereupon resolved that the original letter was not a proceeding in Parliament and that nothing in the subsequent correspondence constituted a breach of privilege. The threat to sue for libel was then withdrawn.[25]

In support of the majority view, it was argued that members should not seek to widen the scope of absolute parliamentary privilege under the Bill of Rights and should be content to rely on the defence of qualified privilege in the law of defamation. There is no doubt that a complaint addressed by a member of Parliament to a minister on an issue of public concern in which the minister has an interest has the protection of qualified privilege.[26] But qualified privilege may be rebutted by proof of express malice and it might possibly be held to constitute malice in this sense if a member passed on to a minister without any inquiry a letter from a constituent containing defamatory allegations.

In support of the view that a member's letter to a minister should be regarded as a proceeding in Parliament, it is certain that if a member tabled a parliamentary question instead of writing to the minister, he would be absolutely protected. Today it seems both desirable and inevitable that many matters should be raised in correspondence with ministers and not immediately become the subject of questions. A complicating factor in the London Electricity Board case was that Mr Strauss's complaint might have been regarded as raising a matter of day-to-day administration for which the minister was not responsible to Parliament, in which case a parliamentary question might not have been accepted.[27]

One important issue that was taken for granted in the parliamentary discussion was whether the commencement of proceedings for defamation against a member in respect of a proceeding in Parliament amounts in itself to a breach of privilege. For example, an action for libel based on remarks spoken in the course of a debate cannot succeed. It has been argued very strongly that members should be content to leave it to the courts to reject such an action and that the House should not treat the action itself as a breach of privilege.[28]

In 1967 a select committee appointed to review the law of parliamentary privilege remarked that the decision of the Commons in the London Electricity

---

[25]   H.C. 305 (1956–7); *Re Parliamentary Privilege Act 1770* [1958] A.C. 331; H.C. 227 (1957–58). Also S. A. de Smith (1958) 21 M.L.R. 465; D. Thompson [1959] P.L. 10.

[26]   *Beach* v. *Freeson* [1972] 1 Q.B. 14 (M.P. forwarding constituent's complaint about solicitors to Law Society and Lord Chancellor); and p. 503 *post*.

[27]   Ch. 17 A.

[28]   S. A. de Smith, (1958) 21 M.L.R. 465, 468–75.

Board case was binding neither upon the House nor upon the courts. The committee recommended that legislation should be introduced to extend absolute privilege to letters written by a member to a minister: 'such communications are today part of the ordinary way in which members perform their parliamentary functions or are inextricably mixed up with them'.[29] Other committees have also urged that the meaning of 'proceeding in Parliament' should be defined in legislation.[30]

Publication of parliamentary proceedings outside Parliament

The House has always maintained the right to secure privacy of debates in the House. Thus in wartime the House has occasionally excluded the press and the public to enable matters to be discussed in secret for security reasons. The House also formerly maintained the right to control publication of its debates outside Parliament. By a resolution of 3 March 1762 any publication in the press of speeches made by members was declared a breach of privilege. In modern times breach of privilege was occasionally raised in cases of misreporting of speeches in the press. But on 16 July 1971 the House resolved that in future it would entertain no complaint of contempt or breach of privilege in respect of the publication of debates in the House or its committees, except when the House or a committee sat in private session. The House has thus retained the power to permit select committees and sub-committees to meet in private.[31] While select committees have increasingly taken evidence in public, their deliberations, especially when a draft report is being considered, still take place in private. Premature reporting of these proceedings constitutes a serious breach of privilege,[32] but the reporting of evidence taken at public sittings of committees is no longer restricted.[33]

The public interest in the publication of reports of parliamentary proceedings is recognised in the law of defamation; unless a defamed person can prove malice, a fair and accurate unofficial report of proceedings in Parliament is privileged, as in an article founded upon such proceedings, provided it is an honest and fair comment upon the facts.[34] The interest of the public in discovering what was said in Parliament outweighs the inconvenience or discomfort which may be caused to individuals mentioned in Parliament. The common law defence of qualified privilege protects a 'parliamentary sketch', that is an impressionistic and selective account of a debate,[35] but not reports of detached parts of speeches published with intent to injure individuals, nor the publication of a single speech which contains libellous matter. Thus a member who repeats outside Parliament what he has said in Parliament is liable if the speech contains defamatory material.[36] It is doubtful if qualified privilege attaches to the publication of a member's speech for the information of his constituents.[37]

---

[29] H.C. 34 (1966–7) para 91.
[30] H.C. 261 (1969–70), pp. 8–12; Cmnd. 5909 (1975), p. 51; H.C. 417 (1976–7), p.v.
[31] H.C. 34 (1966–7) paras. 116–29.
[32] *E.g.* H.C. 357 (1967–8), debated on 24 Jul. 1968; H.C. 185 (1969–70); H.C. 180 (1971–2); and H.C. 22 (1975–6), debated on 16 Dec. 1975.
[33] H.C. Deb., 31 Oct. 1980, col. 917; and H.C. Standing Order 94.
[34] *Wason* v. *Walter* (1868) L.R. 4 Q.B. 73.
[35] *Cook* v. *Alexander* [1974] Q.B. 279.
[36] *R.* v. *Creevey* (1813) 1 M. and S. 278.
[37] *Cf. Davison* v. *Duncan* (1857) 7 E. & B. 229.

After long discussion within Parliament and an experimental period in 1975, regular sound broadcasting of proceedings in both Houses began in 1978.[38] The BBC and IBA have full editorial control to select what is broadcast, but the use of recorded extracts for the purposes of light entertainment or political satire is excluded. The Commons appoints a select committee on sound broadcasting, that may meet with a similar committee from the Lords. It would seem that qualified privilege at common law protects the BBC and IBA against liability for the broadcasting of speeches containing defamatory material but it has been suggested that the BBC and IBA should be granted absolute privilege in respect of live broadcasting.[39] A proposal for televising proceedings in the House of Lords was adopted in 1984.[39a]

Parliamentary papers

A difficult question at common law concerned the authority of the House to publish outside Parliament accounts of debates, reports of select committees, and so on. In 1839, after a protracted dispute between the House and the courts, it was established that at common law the authority of the House was no defence when defamatory material was published outside the House and, more fundamentally, that the House could not create a new privilege by its own resolution.

In *Stockdale* v. *Hansard*,[40] Hansard had by order of the Commons printed and sold to the public a report by the inspectors of prisons which stated that an indecent book published by Stockdale was circulating in Newgate prison. The first action in defamation raised by Stockdale against Hansard was decided for Hansard on the ground that the statement in the report was true. When Stockdale brought a second action, after the report had been re-published, Hansard was ordered by the House to plead that he had acted under an order of the House of Commons, a court superior to any court of law, whose orders could not be questioned; and further that the House had declared that the case was a case of privilege; that each House of Parliament was the sole judge of its own privileges; and that a resolution of the House declaratory of its privileges could not be questioned in any court. The Court of Queen's Bench rejected the defence, holding that only the Queen and both Houses of Parliament could make or unmake laws; that no resolution of either House could place anyone beyond the control of the law; and that, when it was necessary in order to decide the rights of private individuals in matters arising outside Parliament, courts of law should determine the nature and existence of privileges of the Commons. It was held further that there was no privilege of the House which permitted the publication outside the House of defamatory matter.

One sequel to *Stockdale* v. *Hansard* was the *Case of the Sheriff of Middlesex*, which concerned the power of the House to commit for contempt and will be considered below. The other sequel was the passing of the Parliamentary Papers Act 1840. By section 1, this enacted that any civil or criminal proceedings arising out of the publication of papers, reports etc. made by the authority of either House must be stayed on the production of a certificate of such authority from

---

[38] See H.C. 376 (1981–2) for an historical account of the broadcasting of debates.
[39] H.C. 261 (1969–70); H.C. 376 (1981–2). [39a] See H.L. 299 (1983–4).
[40] (1839) 9 A. & E. 1. For the background, see P. & G. Ford (ed.), *Luke Graves Hansard's Diary 1814–1841*.

an officer of the House. Thus Parliament as a whole gave the protection of absolute privilege to parliamentary papers. The official report of debates in the House (Hansard) is covered by absolute privilege under the 1840 Act, and so are documents in the series of House of Commons papers. But Command papers as such are not considered to be covered; if the report of an inquiry may contain defamatory material, a minister will move an order calling for the report to be produced to Parliament, so bringing it within the 1840 Act.[41] Section 3 of the 1840 Act also protected in the absence of malice the publication of fair and accurate extracts from, or abstracts of, papers published under the authority of Parliament: thus press reports of parliamentary papers are protected by qualified privilege, and the same privilege now applies to broadcast reports.[42] This defence of qualified privilege is unusually advantageous to the plaintiff, since the Act places upon the defendant the negative burden of proving that there has been no malice.

Right to control internal proceedings

The House has the right to control its own proceedings and to regulate its internal affairs without interference by the courts. This important principle helps to explain why the courts refuse to investigate alleged defects of parliamentary procedure when the validity of an Act of Parliament is challenged on this ground.[43] The courts will not consider whether the report of a select committee of the House is invalid because of procedural defects[44] and will not issue an injunction to restrain a local authority from breaking a contractual obligation not to oppose in Parliament a Bill being promoted by another local authority.[45]

The House is also considered to have the right to provide for its own proper constitution as established by law.[46] At one time this included the right to determine disputed elections; today by statute election disputes are decided by the courts.[47] But the House retains (a) the right to regulate the filling of vacancies by ordering the issue of a warrant by the Speaker for the issue of a writ for a by-election;[48] (b) the right to determine whether a member is qualified to sit in the House and to declare a seat vacant if, for example, a member has succeeded to an hereditary peerage and does not disclaim the title within the statutory month; and (c) the right to expel a member whom it considers unfit to continue as a member. When the House expels a member, he is not thereby disqualified from re-election to the House. Subject to this, expulsion is the ultimate disciplinary sanction which the House can exercise over its members.

---

41   H.C. 261 (1969–70); Cmnd. 5909 (1975), p. 55; Erskine May, p. 266. *Mangena* v. *Lloyd* (1908) 98 L.T. 640 is of doubtful authority.

42   Defamation Act 1952, s. 9.

43   *Pickin* v. *British Railways Board* [1974] A.C. 765; *cf. Harper* v. *Home Secretary* [1955] Ch. 238, p. 155 *ante*.

44   *Dingle* v. *Associated Newspapers Ltd* [1961] 2 Q.B. 162.

45   *Bilston Corporation* v. *Wolverhampton Corporation* [1942] Ch. 391.

46   Erskine May, p. 118.

47   Ch. 9 B III.

48   Page 171 *ante*.

In 1947, Mr Allighan M.P. published a press article which accused members of the House of disclosing for reward or under the influence of drink the proceedings of confidential party meetings held in the precincts of the House but not forming any part of the formal business of Parliament. It was held by the House, after investigation by the Committee of Privileges, that the article was a gross contempt of the House; other grave contempts had been committed by Mr Allighan since he had himself corruptly accepted payment for disclosing information and, except for a single case, he had been unable to substantiate any of the charges against his fellow-members. The House voted to expel Mr Allighan.[49]

By contrast with the position in the United States[50] no court in Britain has jurisdiction to review the legality of a resolution of the House to exclude or expel a member. One safeguard against abuse of this power by the House is that a constituency may re-elect an expelled member, as in the case of John Wilkes in the 18th century. Today the House would generally prefer a member to resign rather than be expelled.

In 1975, the conduct of John Stonehouse M.P., who had disappeared after feigning death in a drowning accident in the USA and was later arrested by the police in Australia where he was living under an assumed name, gave rise to the question of whether he should be expelled by the House. While he was refusing to return to Britain to stand trial, it was argued that expulsion would be justified since he could not perform his parliamentary duties. Eventually the House decided to take no action pending the outcome of the criminal charges against him.[51] After Mr Stonehouse's return to Britain, he was in 1976 convicted of serious crimes involving fraud, was imprisoned for seven years and resigned from the Commons.

While the House has power to enforce the attendance of members at Westminster, this power is not now used.[52]

The right of the House to regulate its own proceedings includes the right to maintain order and discipline during debates. A member guilty of disorderly conduct who refuses to withdraw may, on being named by the Speaker, be suspended from the service of the House either for a specified time or for the remainder of the session.[53] While in *Eliot's* case[54] the question of whether the courts could deal with an assault on the Speaker committed in the House was expressly left open when the judgment was declared illegal by resolutions of both Houses, in principle criminal acts within the Palace of Westminster (for example theft or assault) may be dealt with in the ordinary courts. In the case of a statutory offence, it will be necessary to show that the statute in question applies to the Palace of Westminster: an attempt to convict members of the Kitchen Committee of the House for breaches of licensing law failed, primarily on the ground of the right of the House to regulate its internal affairs.[55]

Breaches of privilege and contempt of the House

The House has inherent power to protect its privileges and to punish those

---

[49]   H.C. 138 (1946–7).
[50]   *Powell* v. *McCormack* (1970) 395 U.S. 486.
[51]   See H.C. 273, 357, 373, 414 (1974–5) and H.C. Deb., 11 Jun. 1975, col. 408.
[52]   Erskine May, pp. 221–2.
[53]   H.C. Standing Orders 24–6.
[54]   Page 212 *ante*.
[55]   *R.* v. *Graham-Campbell, ex p. Herbert* [1935] 1 K.B. 594.

who violate its privileges or commit contempt of the House. The penal powers of the House include power to order the offender to be reprimanded or admonished by the Speaker. Members may be suspended or expelled; officials of the House may be dismissed from its service; and non-members such as lobby correspondents, who are granted certain facilities in the Palace of West-minister, may have those facilities withdrawn.[56] Although the House is considered to have no power to impose a fine, it has power to commit any person to the custody of its own officers or to prison for contempt of the House or breach of its privileges. Such commitment cannot last beyond the end of the session.

In parliamentary speech, the term 'breach of privilege' has often been used as synonymous with contempt of the House. But this usage can lead to confusion. While most breaches of privilege are likely to be contempts, a person may be adjudged to be guilty of a contempt who has not infringed any existing privilege of the House. Thus in *Allighan*'s case[57] the Committee of Privileges reported that the unfounded imputation in regard to the proceedings of party meetings held in private at Westminster involved an affront to the House: but information about such meetings was not in itself a breach of privilege. Contempt of the House, like contempt of court, is a very wide concept. In Erskine May's words,

any act or omission which obstructs or impedes either House of Parliament in the performance of its functions, or which obstructs or impedes any member or officer of such House in the discharge of his duty, or which has a tendency, directly or indirectly, to produce such results may be treated as a contempt even though there is no precedent of the offence.[58]

Contempt has been held by the House to include: disorderly conduct by members or strangers within the precincts of the House;[59] refusal of a person to give evidence to a committee of the House; giving false evidence to a committee; inteference with the giving of evidence by others to a committee;[60] obstruction of a member in coming to and from the House;[61] inclusion by a member in a personal statement to the House of words which were known by him to be untrue; bribery and corruption, or attempts thereat, in relation to the conduct of members as such;[62] molestation of a member on account of his conduct in the House (for example, publication of a newspaper article inviting readers to telephone a member at his home to express their views about a parliamentary question which he had tabled);[63] publication of material which is derogatory of the House or its members (for example, an allegation of drunkenness amongst members);[64] an allegation that members 'have surrendered

---

56   *Cf.* H.C. 22 (1975–6).
57   Page 218 *ante*.
58   Erskine May, p. 143; and see H.C. 34 (1967–8) pp. xi–xviii and 95–101.
59   For the precedents and full references, see Erskine May, ch. 10 A.
60   The House resolved in 1688 that all witnesses summoned to the House should have the privilege of the House 'in coming, staying and returning'; and see the Witnesses (Public Inquiries) Protection Act 1892.
61   *Cf. Papworth* v. *Coventry* [1967] 2 All E.R. 41.
62   And see Section B *post*.
63   The *Daily Graphic* case, H.C. 27 (1956–7).
64   *Duffy's* case, H.C. 129 (1964–5) and see H.C. 302 (1974–5).

for money their freedom of action as parliamentarians';[65] calling in a news-paper for the arrest of a member described as an arch-traitor;[66] the service of writs on members within the precincts of the House;[67] premature disclosure of the proceedings of a committee of the House;[68] obstructing or assaulting an officer of the House while in the execution of his duty; and disruption of a meeting at Essex University of a sub-committee of the Select Committee on Education and Science when it was receiving evidence about student rela-tions.[69] But it has been held not to constitute a contempt for pressure to be brought to bear upon a citizen to withdraw his complaint of a grievance which he had asked his M.P. to raise in Parliament.[70] The fact that certain action may be a contempt of the House does not mean that the House will always wish to take action against the offender. In 1967 it was recommended that the House should be restrained in the exercise of its penal jurisdiction, which should be used:

only when the House is satisfied that to do so is essential to provide reasonable protection for the House, its members or its officers, from such improper obstruction or attempt at or threat of obstruction as is causing or is liable to cause, substantial interference with the performance of their respective functions.[71]

The courts and contempt of the House

While the courts assert jurisdiction to decide the existence and extent of privi-leges of the House, what constitutes a contempt of the House is essentially a matter which only the House itself can decide. If a contempt issue arises relating to the internal proceedings of the House, the courts will decline to interfere. But whether in relation to events inside or outside the House, the courts have long recognised the power of the House to detain persons for contempt. Do the courts have power to review the House's decision when the rights of an individual are in issue?

In *Paty's* case, which arose after five electors of Aylesbury had sued returning officers for the malicious refusal of their votes and thereby had annoyed the Commons, Chief Justice Holt in a dissenting judgment held that a writ of habeas corpus would go to release any one committed for contempt by the House, where the cause of committal stated in the return to the writ was insufficient in law.[72] This view of the law is accepted today. But if only the bald statement of contempt of the House is shown in the return, the court will not make further inquiry into the reasons for the committal. As Lord Ellenborough said in *Burdett* v. *Abbot*, 'If a commitment appeared to be for contempt of the House of Commons generally, I would neither in the case of that court nor of any other of the superior courts enquire further.'[73] This prin-

---

65   *Ashton's* case, H.C. 228 (1974).
66   The *Protestant Telegraph* case, H.C. 462 (1966–7) ('Why does Ulster's rebel leader go free? Arrest the Fenian Fitt.').
67   Note 6 *ante*.
68   Note 32 *ante*.
69   H.C. 308 (1968–9).
70   *Stevenson's* case, H.C. 112 (1954–5).
71   H.C. 34 (1967–8), para. 15.
72   (1704) 2 Lord Raymond 1105.
73   (1811) 14 East 1.

ciple was applied in the *Case of the Sheriff of Middlesex*.

As a sequel to *Stockdale* v. *Hansard*, the sheriffs attempted to recover for Stockdale by execution on Hansard's property £600 damages awarded in the third action of the series. The money recovered from Hansard was in the hands of the sheriffs when the parliamentary session of 1840 opened; they were aware of the resolutions of the Commons. The House first committed Stockdale and then, on the sheriffs refusing to refund the money to Hansard, also committed the two sheriffs for contempt, without expressing the reason for the committal. In habeas corpus proceedings it was held that the court had to accept the statement by the House that the sheriffs had been committed for contempt.[74]

Thus the House of Commons, like the superior courts, has power to commit persons for contempt for whatever conduct it adjudges to amount to contempt, and may not be required to state the nature of the contempt. Fortunately the power of the House to commit for contempt has not been exercised since 1880. If the House were to have power to impose fines for contempt, the power to imprison for contempt could be abolished.[75]

The courts and parliamentary privilege[76]

Questions of privilege used to be a potential source of conflict between the Commons and the courts. The House claimed to be the absolute and sole judge of its own privileges. But the court in *Stockdale* v. *Hansard* resolutely maintained the right to determine the nature and limit of parliamentary privilege, should it be necessary to decide these questions in adjudicating upon the rights of individuals outside the House. Another illustration of the relationship between courts and Parliament is provided by the Bradlaugh affair in the 1880s.

Bradlaugh, an atheist, was elected to Parliament as member for Northampton on successive occasions. The House took the view that as an atheist he could not sit or vote, as he could not properly take the oath as required by existing statue law. At one stage Bradlaugh was allowed by resolution of the House, subject to any legal penalties he might incur, to affirm instead of taking an oath. In an action brought against him by a common informer for penalties for sitting and voting without taking the oath, the Court of Appeal held that the Parliamentary Oaths Act 1866 and other statutes did not authorise him to affirm.[77]

Later, following his re-election to Parliament, Bradlaugh required the Speaker to call upon him to take the oath. The Speaker refused to do so. The House then by resolution authorised the Serjeant at Arms to exclude Bradlaugh from the House. Bradlaugh sought an injunction against the Serjeant at Arms to restrain him from carrying out this resolution. In *Bradlaugh* v. *Gossett*, it was held that, this being a matter relating to the internal management of the procedure of the House, the court had no power to interfere. As Lord Coleridge C. J. said, 'If injustice has been done, it is injustice for which the courts of law afford no remedy.'[78] The Act of 1866 permitted certain persons to affirm instead of taking an oath. The dispute in *Clarke* v. *Bradlaugh* had been whether or not Bradlaugh was a person entitled to affirm; any person making an affirmation otherwise than as authorised by the Act could be sued for certain penalties. Stephen J. in *Bradlaugh* v. *Gossett* emphasised that, if the House had by resolution stated that

---

[74] (1840) 11 A. & E. 273.
[75] H.C. 417 (1976–7).
[76] Erskine May, ch. 11.
[77] *Clarke* v. *Bradlaugh* (1881) 7 Q.B.D. 38. And see W. L. Arnstein, *The Bradlaugh Case*.
[78] (1884) 12 Q.B.D. 271, 277.

Bradlaugh was entitled to make the statutory declaration, such a resolution would not have protected him against an action for penalties:

'We should have said that, for the purpose of determining on a right to be exercised within the House itself, and in particular the right of sitting and voting, the House, and the House only could interpret the statute; but that, as regarded rights to be exercised out of and independently of the House, such as a right of suing for a penalty for having sat and voted, the statute must be interpreted by this court independently of the House.'[79]

It has therefore been said that 'there may be at any given moment two doctrines of privilege, the one held by the courts, the other by either House, the one to be found in the Law Reports, the other in Hansard'.[80] But this dualism must not be exaggerated. On the one hand, new privileges, for example, the absolute privilege which an M.P. has in forwarding a citizen's complaint to the Parliamentary Commissioner for Administration[81] must be created by statute and not by resolution of the House. On the other hand, the courts recognise the control which the House has over its own proceedings. Today it is extremely unlikely that the House would wish to use its power to commit for contempt so as indirectly to create a new privilege when it was not willing to do this by process of legislation.[82] While the House needs to be able to protect itself against external attack, the House should not use its powers lightly or abuse its powers for political ends.

Procedure

How does the House exercise its power when a complaint of breach of privilege or contempt is raised? Before 1978, members were expected to raise a privilege complaint in the House at the earliest opportunity, whereupon the Speaker had 24 hours to consider whether there had been a *prima facie* breach of privilege. The procedure was changed in 1978, to enable complaints to be considered under less pressure and trivial complaints to receive less publicity.[83] A member must now give written notice of a privilege complaint to the Speaker as soon as is reasonably practicable after the event in question. The Speaker then has a discretion to decide if the complaint should have precedence over other Commons business. If not, he informs the member by letter, who may then if he wishes seek to bring the matter to the House by other means. If the Speaker decides that the complaint should have priority over other business, he announces this decision to the House, whereupon the member may table a motion for the next day proposing that the matter be referred to the Committee of Privileges or other appropriate action. The motion is then debated and voted upon by the House. The Committee of Privileges consists of 17 of the most senior members of the parties in the House. It is for the committee to decide on the procedure for investigating the complaint. It is not the practice of the House to authorise the person responsible for the alleged

---

[79]   (1884) 12 Q.B.D. 271, 282.
[80]   D. L. Keir and F. H. Lawson, *Cases in Constitutional Law*, p. 255; Erskine May, p. 203.
[81]   Parliamentary Commissioner Act 1967, s. 10(5); ch. 37 D.
[82]   *Cf.* the argument by Mr L. A. Abraham that use of the contempt power can never have the effect of creating a new privilege: H.C. 34 (1967–8), pp. 97–8.
[83]   H.C. 417 (1976–7); H.C. Deb., 6 Feb. 1978, col. 1155; and H.C. Deb., 29 Apr. 1981, col. 789.

breach to be represented by counsel. After examining witnesses and being advised by the Clerk of the House on relevant precedents, and if necessary by the Attorney-General on matters of law, the committee reports its conclusions to the House, and may recommend the action that the House should take. The House need accept neither the conclusions nor the recommendations. The party whips are not applied on privilege issues.

This procedure has been criticised, in particular on the ground that the individual against whom the complaint is made has inadequate procedural safeguards: thus he does not have the right to be heard or to be legally represented, to have notice of the charge against him, to cross-examine witnesses or call evidence, or to receive legal aid. In 1967 the Select Committee on Parliamentary Privilege recommended improvements in the procedure which went some way to meeting these criticisms but these proposals were not adopted.[84] It would only be possible to meet the major criticism, that the House is judge in its own cause, if power to decide questions of privilege were vested in a body outside the House. This the House has not been prepared to do. Today the House is likely to make restrained use of its powers. In the case of a minor breach of privilege, the House may decide that no further action should be taken and will not automatically follow the committee's advice: in 1975, when the Committee on Privileges had recommended that the editor of the *Economist* and a political correspondent should be denied access to the House for six months, the House voted that no further action be taken.[85]

B. The financial interests of members

It is one thing to maintain the formal constitutional principle that M.P.s should have complete freedom of speech in debates and to declare, as the House has done, that bribery of members in relation to the work of the House is a breach of privilege. It is another thing to ensure that members are in fact able to do their work free of undue influence from financial, industrial and business interests outside the House. Moreover the notion of undue influence is far from clearcut. This is not a new problem. By the creation of sinecure offices and the use of patronage, control over the House was maintained in the 18th century. Today pressure groups proliferate. They seek in a wide variety of ways and from a wide variety of motives to influence government decisions and to ensure that the interests and causes which they support are not without spokesmen in Parliament.[1] While the House gains from having within it members from many different backgrounds, serious problems arise if the speeches and acts of members come to be directly governed by policies laid down outside the House by bodies from which members derive financial advantage. A member's allegiance to his party is a matter of public knowledge and responsibility, but in an extreme case this known allegiance might have less influence on a member's actions in Parliament than his secret, financial relationships.

---

[84]   H.C. 34 (1967–8); and H.C. 417 (1976–7).
[85]   H.C. Deb., 16 Dec. 1975, cols. 1303–56.

[1]   There is an extensive literature on pressure groups: see *e.g.* S. E. Finer, *Anonymous Empire*, J. D. Stewart, *British Pressure Groups*.

Payments and rewards to members of Parliament

It is only since 1911 that members not holding ministerial office have received a salary. Payment of salaries to members became essential after the House of Lords in *Osborne* v. *Amalgamated Society of Railway Servants* had held that the use of trade union funds for political purposes was *ultra vires* and illegal,[2] thus preventing trade unions from paying salaries to those Labour M.P.s whom they supported. Today, in addition to their salary, members receive allowances for secretarial assistance, travel between Westminster and their constituencies, necessary overnight stays away from home, as well as the benefit of a contributory pension scheme.[3] Advice on the level of members' salaries is regularly given by the Review Body on Top Salaries, but it is difficult to keep members' salaries fairly related to salaries outside the House and to government policy. In 1983, when the government's refusal to accept the review body's advice was unpopular with many M.P.s, a compromise solution was reached on present and future salary increases.[4]

Apart from those public offices which disqualify from membership of the House,[5] members are free to take up paid employment outside the House, to practise in the professions for which they may be qualified, to earn fees from journalism and broadcasting, and to accept advisory and consultancy posts with commercial and other organisations. Many members regard their parliamentary and constituency duties as occupying all their time, others merely as a useful background to a successful career outside Parliament. Constitutional problems arise as soon as the payments or rewards which are received from outside sources relate to work done by the member in his capacity as such.[6]

In 1695, the House resolved that 'the offer of money, or other advantage, to a member of Parliament for the promoting of any matter whatsoever depending or to be transacted in Parliament is a high crime and misdemeanour'. And in 1858, the House resolved that it was improper for any member to promote or advocate in the House any proceeding or measure in which he had acted or was acting for pecuniary reward. In 1945, the Committee of Privileges considered that, in accordance with the resolution of 1695, it would be a breach of privilege for an offer of money or other advantage to be made to a member, or to his local political party or to a charity, to induce him to take up a question with a minister.[7] While specific offers or payments of this kind are improper, some members receive regular payments from outside organisations in return for giving advice on political and parliamentary matters. Two main problems arise:

1   Is the contract between the member and the outside organisation improper, in that it limits or restricts the member's freedom of action in Parliament?
2   If the contract itself is acceptable, is it to be regarded as an improper threat to the member's freedom of action if the organisation seeks to bring the arrangement to an end?

---

2   [1910] A.C. 87. Under the Trade Union Act 1913, unions may pay the expenses of sponsored M.P.s from separate political funds, p. 159 *ante*.
3   For the detailed history of members' salaries, see Erskine May, ch. 1.
4   H.C. Deb., 19 July 1983, cols. 267–352.
5   Ch. 9 B IV.
6   The account which follows draws upon the Report from the Select Committee on Members' Interests (Declaration), H.C. 57 (1969–70).
7   *Henderson's* case, H.C. 63 (1944–5).

In 1947, W. J. Brown M.P. held an appointment as Parliamentary General Secretary of the Civil Service Clerical Association. The agreement, which provided Brown with substantial financial benefits, stated *inter alia* both that he would be entitled to engage in his political activities with complete freedom and that he should deal with all questions arising in the work of the association which required parliamentary action. After political disagreements arose between Brown and the association, the latter's executive agreed to propose that the appointment should be terminated on terms to be agreed. The Committee on Privileges reported that while it would be improper for a member to enter into any arrangement fettering his complete independence as a member, and also for an organisation to seek to punish a member pecuniarily because of his actions as a member, the agreement in Brown's case was not in itself improper; any member who entered such an agreement must be taken to have accepted its possible termination as a matter which would not influence him in his parliamentary duties. The House accepted this report, and resolved that it was improper for a member 'to enter into any contractual agreement with an outside body, controlling or limiting the Member's complete independence and freedom of action in Parliament or stipulating that he shall act in any way as the representative of such outside body in regard to any matters to be transacted in Parliament.'[8]

From the circumstances in the Brown case, it is evident that the question of where the line should be drawn between propriety and impropriety is very difficult. Although the terms on which trade unions sponsor M.P.s in the House today do not closely resemble those in the Brown case,[9] more than once since 1947 questions of privilege have arisen when branches or members of a trade union have become dissatisfied with the political work of those members whom they sponsor.[10] The 1947 resolution of the House seems to have been more concerned with the formal provisions in sponsorship contracts rather than with the intangible effect on the member's conduct of being a party to an agreement which may bring him very substantial rewards. In 1969 it was suggested that the distinction to be drawn is between advocacy of a cause in Parliament for a fee or retainer, which is improper, and the advancement of an argument by a member 'who through a continuing association with an industry, service or concern from which he may obtain some remuneration, is able to draw upon specialist knowledge of the subject under debate'.[11] And it was doubted whether the old resolution of 1695 covered new kinds of benefit, such as free travel and holidays or lavish hospitality, which are offered to members in return, say, for influencing the opinion of members in favour of a particular regime in a foreign country.[12]

Voting and declarations of interest
Members of local authorities are subject to statutory rules enforceable in the courts regarding the declaration of their interests and excluding them from voting on matters which affect their interests.[13] But no comparable statute

---

[8] H.C. Deb., 15 Jul. 1947, col. 284; H.C. 118 (1946–7). See also *Robinson's* case, H.C. 85 (1943–4).

[9] In H.C. 57 (1969–70), appendix III, D. Houghton M.P. surveyed the nature and extent of sponsorship in 1968.

[10] See *e.g.* H.C. 50 (1971–2), H.C. 634 (1974–5) and H.C. 512 (1976–7).

[11] H.C. 57 (1969–70), p. xxxii.

[12] H.C. 57 (1969–70), p. xi.

[13] Local Government Act 1972, ss. 94–98; and ch. 21.

applies to the Commons. By an old rule of the House, no member who has a direct pecuniary interest in a question may vote upon it. In 1811, Mr Speaker Abbot declared that the rule applied only where the interest was a 'direct pecuniary interest and separately belonging to the persons . . . and not in common with the rest of His Majesty's subjects, or on a matter of State policy'. In fact the rule was applied only to private legislation and a vote on a public Bill has never been disallowed.[14] A declaration of interest is formally required only at the committee stage of opposed private Bills. However, by custom of the House, members are required to declare their personal pecuniary interest when speaking in a debate in the House or in Standing Committees, but the custom has not applied to Question Time. In 1940, a member was criticised for having failed to disclose that his private interests were affected by action which he was urging upon the House, the Treasury and members of whom he wrote.[15] The duty to disclose private interests was placed on a more formal footing and its scope extended when on 25 May 1974 the House resolved:

That in any debate or proceedings of the House or its Committees or transactions or communications which a member may have with other members or with Ministers or servants of the Crown, he shall disclose any relevant pecuniary interest or benefit of whatever nature, whether direct or indirect, that he may have had, may have or may be expecting to have.

This resolution governs parliamentary proceedings and dealings which an M.P. may have with government departments but does not in terms apply to dealings with local authorities, public corporations or foreign governments.

Register of members' interests
Today a more systematic method of making members' interests publicly known is required than the former custom of the House provided. In 1967 the Liberal party began a voluntary register open to the public on which were shown the business and professional interests of Liberal members. In 1969, a select committee had recommended against a register, preferring to improve and extend the traditional practice of the House. But on 12 June 1975, the House resolved to establish a compulsory register of members' interests.[16] The aim is to provide information of any pecuniary interest or other material benefit 'which a member may receive which might be thought to affect his conduct as a member or influence his actions, speeches or vote in Parliament', a test which means that the member's own judgment of what affects him is not decisive. The register comprises nine categories of interest, including company directorships, employment, trade, profession or vocation; the names of clients for whom professional services are provided related to membership of the House; financial sponsorships, whether as a parliamentary candidate (*i.e.* election expenses) or as a member; overseas visits arising out of membership of the House and not wholly paid for by the member or out of public funds; payments, material benefits or advantages received from foreign governments

---

[14]   H.C. 57 (1969–70), p. xii; Erskine May, pp. 411–6.
[15]   *Boothby's* case, H.C. 5 (1940–1).
[16]   See H.C. 57 (1969–70) and H.C. 102 (1974–5).

or organisations; land or property of a substantial value; and the names of companies in which the member (with his spouse and infant children) owns more than 1% of the issued share capital.

The register is maintained by a senior clerk of the House as Registrar and a select committee supervises the operation of the register. The only sanction envisaged for failure to register interests or for supplying false information is the power of the House to regard such conduct as contempt. In 1983 the register revealed that every member had sent in a return of his interests except for one, Mr Enoch Powell.[17] Registration of an interest has been declared to be sufficient disclosure by the member for the purpose of voting, but a member must still declare a relevant interest in debate or in committee proceedings, even though it has been registered.

While the systematic disclosure of interests on the register was an important step, it is unlikely to be a complete answer to the problems which arise on the border-line between the private and public interests of politicians. In 1976, a royal commission on standards of conduct in public life, under the chairmanship of Lord Salmon, expressed the view that neither the statute law nor the common law on corruption applied to the bribery or attempted bribery of an M.P. in respect of his parliamentary duties; although such acts were subject to the penal jurisdiction of the Commons, the commission recommended consideration of the need for legislation to extend the criminal law to these matters.[18] No such legislation has been brought forward, and Professor Zellick has argued that the existing criminal law is not as powerless as Lord Salmon's commission supposed.[19]

The importance of full disclosure of interests and the problems that arise when M.P.s combine promotional activities on behalf of a business organisation with parliamentary work, were illustrated in a report by a select committee that inquired into the conduct of M.P.s in relation to the Poulson group of companies. The group's activities in the 1960s gave rise, after Poulson's bankruptcy in 1972, to many prosecutions for corruption concerning public authorities, but none were brought against M.P.s. The events covered by the report occurred before the present rules on declaration of interests were introduced.

The report examined the activities of three M.P.s, each of whom had received payments from the Poulson group of companies for a variety of legitimate business activities. In the case of Mr J. Cordle, the committee found that he had committed a contempt of the House by promoting a matter in Parliament (namely, an adjournment debate advocating more government aid to Gambia, from which Poulson companies would benefit) without declaring his interest. It was found that Mr R. Maudling, while a member of the shadow Cabinet, had taken part in a debate and other proceedings relating to Malta, without declaring his interest in a Poulson company that was actively seeking a hospital contract in Malta. Mr A. Roberts was found to have written letters outside the House for Poulson's benefit without disclosing his interest. On a subsequent debate of the report, after Mr Cordle had resigned his seat, the House resolved not to

---

17   H.C. 172 (1982–3). See H.C. 677 (1974–5) for rulings by the select committee; and Erskine May, pp. 435–9. Also H.C. Deb., 30 Jan. 1984, col. 24.

18   Cmnd 6524, 1976.

19   G. J. Zellick [1979] P.L. 31.

'agree with' the report so far as it related to Mr Maudling and Mr Roberts but to 'take note of' the report; motions seeking the expulsion or suspension of Mr Maudling were defeated.[20]

The House's reaction to the report was in several respects unsatisfactory. It may be hoped that the present rules on disclosure of interests will give clearer guidance for the future.

C. House of Lords

Questions of privilege very rarely arise in relation to the House of Lords. In outline, the privileges of the House and of peers are:

1 Freedom from civil arrest for peers.   In *Stourton* v. *Stourton*[1] a peer was held to be privileged from a writ of attachment for civil contempt following his failure to send his wife her property under a court order. The judge found that arrest was being sought to compel performance of a civil obligation. This privilege may be claimed by an individual peer at any time, but the House claims privilege only 'within the usual times of privilege of Parliament'.[2]

2 Freedom of speech.   Article 9 of the Bill of Rights applies to the Lords as it does to the Commons; a speech made in the House is not privileged if published separately from the rest of the debate.[3]

3 Freedom of access to the Sovereign.   This privilege exists for the House collectively and by virtue of privilege of peerage for each peer individually.

4 The right to commit for contempt.   The Lords can commit a person for a definite term, and the imprisonment is not terminated by prorogation of Parliament. The Lords also have power to impose fines and to order security to be given for good conduct.

5 The right to exclude disqualified persons from the proceedings of the House.   The House itself decides, through the Committee for Privileges, the right of newly created peers to sit and vote. Claims to old peerages are referred by the Crown to the House, and are also decided by the Committee for Privileges.[4] That body is not bound by its own previous decisions.

---

[20] H.C. Deb., 26 July 1977, col. 332; and G. J. Zellick, [1978] P.L. 133.

[1] [1963] P. 302.

[2] H.L. Standing Order 78. For the effect of this privilege on detention under the Mental Health Act 1983, see H.L. 254 (1983–4).

[3] *R.* v. *Lord Abingdon* (1795) 1 Esp. 226.

[4] See *e.g. the Ampthill Peerage* [1977] A.C. 547.

Chapter 13

The Crown and the prerogative

Article II of the United States Constitution declares that, 'The executive power shall be vested in a President of the United States of America'. On this formal declaration of law is based the system of a presidential executive. By contrast, where the British system of cabinet government is practised, the formal statement that the executive power is vested in the Crown[1] corresponds much less closely with the reality of government. The Sovereign may reign, but it is the Prime Minister and other ministers who rule. Yet within the executive in Britain, it is not possible to dismiss the position of the Sovereign as a legal archaism since the Sovereign as head of state performs some essential constitutional functions. The fact that central goverment is carried on in the name of the Crown has left its mark on the law. Our law has never developed a notion of 'the state': the judges have been opposed to the idea of allowing interests of the state to override common law rights.[2] Although it is common to speak of state schools, state ownership and so on, legislation rarely refers to the state as such.[3] Instead, the Crown has developed as 'a convenient symbol for the State'.[4] Because of this development, it is usual to refer to 'the Sovereign' in matters concerning the personal conduct or decisions of the monarch, and to 'the Crown' as the collective entity which in law may stand for central government.

We have already seen that the functions of the executive are more diverse than those of the legislature and the judiciary, having acquired a residual character after legislature and judiciary had become separated from the main work of governing.[5] The functions of the executive include 'the execution of law and policy, the maintenance of public order, the management of Crown property and nationalised industries and services, the direction of foreign

---

[1] See *e.g.* for Canada, the Constitution Act 1867, s. 9; for Australia, ch. II of the Constitution; and *cf.* Blackstone, *Commentaries*, vol. 1, pp. 249–50; and H.L.E. vol. 8, para. 931.

[2] *Entick* v. *Carrington* (1765) 19 St. Tr. 1030, p. 93 *ante*.

[3] *Cf. Chandler* v. *DPP* [1964] A.C. 763.

[4] G. Sawer's phrase, quoted in P. W. Hogg, *Liability of the Crown*, p. 10; and see G. Marshall, *Constitutional Theory*, ch.2.

[5] Ch. 4.

policy, the conduct of military operations, and the provision or supervision of such services as education, public health, transport and national insurance'.[6] Today such a catalogue is far from complete. To perform all the tasks of government the executive must comprise a wide array of officials and agencies. These include the Sovereign, the Prime Minister and other ministers, government departments, the civil service, the armed forces, and also the police, who are outside the direct hierarchy of central government but exercise a vital executive function. Outside central government, but closely linked to it, are the local authorities and nationalised industries, which may be considered to perform executive functions, albeit confined to one locality or one economic activity.

Unlike the work of Parliament and the courts, much of the work of the executive is carried on behind closed doors. British government still seeks to maintain secrecy on matters which it believes to affect its own vital interests.[7] This secrecy often masks a divergence between the legal form and the political substance. Thus in exercising some of the Crown's powers, the Sovereign may exercise a personal discretion; others are exercised by the Sovereign on the advice of ministers; and many powers are exercised directly by ministers and civil servants, although they are exercised on behalf of the Crown. Whether a statutory power is conferred upon the Queen in Council or directly in a named minister, the government is responsible to Parliament for the decisions taken. Since it is rare in legislative practice for statutory powers to be vested in the Cabinet or the Prime Minister,[8] decisions taken in Cabinet or by the Prime Minister usually have to be translated into the appropriate legal form before they can take full effect. In view of this interplay of legal form and conventional practice, study of the executive in the United Kingdom must begin with the legal position of the Sovereign.

A. The Sovereign

Title to the Crown

In 1689 the Convention Parliament (that had been summoned by Prince William of Orange at the request of an improvised assembly of notables) filled the constitutional vacuum which arose on the departure of James II by declaring the throne vacant and inviting William of Orange and his wife Mary jointly to accept the throne.[1] These events finally confirmed the power of Parliament to regulate the succession to the Crown as it should think fit.[2] Today title to the Crown is derived from the Act of Settlement 1700, subsequently extended to Scotland in 1707 and to Ireland in 1800 by the Acts of Union. By the Act of Settlement, the Crown shall 'be remain and continue to the said most excellent Princess Sophia' (the Electress of Hanover, granddaughter of James I) 'and the heirs of her body being Protestant'.[3] The

---

6   H.L.E., vol. 8, para. 814.
7   E.g. A.-G. v. Jonathan Cape Ltd [1976] Q.B. 752; ch. 14 A.
8   But see Police Act 1976, s. 1 and National Heritage Act 1983, sch. 1, para. 2.
1   Maitland, History, pp. 283–5; Taswell-Langmead, pp. 443–8.
2   Taswell-Langmead, p. 504.
3   See A.-G. v. Prince Ernest Augustus of Hanover [1957] A.C. 436, for construction of Princess Sophia Naturalization Act 1705 (repealed by British Nationality Act 1948) which entitled to British nationality all non-Catholic lineal descendants of Princess Sophia.

limitation to the heirs of the body, which has been described as a parliamentary entail, means that the Crown descends in principle as did real property under the law of inheritance before 1926.[4] That law *inter alia* gave preference to males over females and recognised the right of primogeniture. The major exception to the common law rules of inheritance is that for practical reasons the right of two or more sisters to succeed to real property as coparceners does not apply: as between sisters, the Crown passes to the first-born.[5] The Act of Settlement disqualifies from the succession Roman Catholics and those who marry Roman Catholics; the Sovereign must swear to maintain the Churches of England and Scotland and must join in communion with the former Church. Since 1714, when the Hanoverian succession took effect under the Act of Settlement, the line of hereditary succession has been altered only once: it was provided by His Majesty's Declaration of Abdication Act 1936 that the declaration of abdication by Edward VIII should have effect; that the member of the royal family then next in succession to the throne should succeed (whereby Edward VIII's brother became King George VI); and that Edward VIII, his issue, if any, and the descendants of that issue should not thereafter have any right to the succession.

The eldest son of a reigning monarch is the heir apparent to the throne; he is Duke of Cornwall by inheritance and is invariably created Prince of Wales. When the Sovereign has no son, the person next in succession (for example, the eldest daughter of the Sovereign or, if the Sovereign is childless, his younger brother) is known as heir or heiress presumptive: his or her right to succeed may be displaced by the subsequent birth of a son to the Sovereign. It is probable that this principle applies even if the subsequent birth is post-humous. To take an extreme case, should a future King die leaving a daughter and a pregnant wife but no son, it would seem that the daughter as heiress presumptive succeeds to the Crown upon his death, but with a qualified title which is set aside if a son is posthumously born.[6]

Style and titles

The style and titles of the Crown are determined by royal proclamation under the great seal issued under statutory authority from time to time. The Royal Titles Act 1953 authorised the adoption by the Queen, for use in relation to the United Kingdom and all other territories for whose foreign relations the UK government is responsible, of such style and titles as the Queen may think fit. Under this Act in 1953 the present title was proclaimed:

Elizabeth II by the Grace of God of the United Kingdom of Great Britain and Northern Ireland and of Her other Realms and Territories Queen, Head of the Commonwealth, Defender of the Faith.

Before the 1953 Act, the royal style and titles had rested on the indivisibility of the Crown throughout the Commonwealth. The Preamble to the Statute of Westminster 1931 had declared that it would be in accord with the estab-

---

[4] On which, see R. E. Megarry and H. W. R. Wade, *The Law of Real Property*, pp. 509–12.
[5] Blackstone, *Commentaries*, I, p. 193; Chitty, *Prerogatives of the Crown*, p. 10.
[6] See Megarry and Wade, *op. cit.*, p. 512 and *e.g. Richards* v. *Richards* (1860) Johns. 754. *Cf.* Regency Act 1830, ss. 3–5, and views of Lyndhurst L. C. at H.L. Deb., 15 Nov. 1830, col. 505; and 6 Dec. 1830, col. 764.

lished constitutional position of the members of the Commonwealth in relation to one another that any alteration in the law or the succession to the throne or the royal style and titles should require the consent of the Parliaments of all the Dominions.[7] By 1952, when the Commonwealth already included the Republic of India, a meeting of Prime Ministers agreed that in future it would be for each member state within the Commonwealth to enact its own form of title.[8] In the result the only description of the Sovereign common to all states within the Commonwealth is 'Head of the Commonwealth'. The Crown itself is no longer single and indivisible but 'separate and divisible' for each self-governing territory within the Commonwealth.[9]

In *MacCormick* v. *Lord Advocate*[10] the proclamation of the Queen as Elizabeth II was challenged in Scotland on the ground that this contravened the Treaty of Union between England and Scotland (since there had never been an Elizabeth I of Scotland). The Court of Session considered that the royal numeral did not derive from the Royal Titles Act 1953 but from the proclamation of the Queen at her accession in 1952, and found nothing in the Treaty of Union which prohibited the adoption of the style 'Elizabeth II'. The court also held that no citizen had, under Scots law, title or interest to challenge the legality of the royal numeral.

Royal marriages

The archaic Royal Marriages Act 1772, by restricting the right of a descendant of George II to contract a valid marriage without the consent of the Sovereign, seeks to guard against undesirable marriages which might affect the succession to the throne. Until the age of twenty-five the Sovereign's assent is necessary, except in respect of the issue of princesses who have married into foreign families. After that age a marriage may take place without consent after a year's notice to the Privy Council, unless Parliament expressly disapproves.[11]

Accession and coronation

There are two ceremonies which mark the accession of the new Sovereign. Immediately on the death of his predecessor the Sovereign is proclaimed by the Accession Council, a body which comprises the Lords Spiritual and Temporal and other leading citizens, and is a survival of an old assemblage which met to choose and proclaim the King. The proclamation is afterwards approved at the first meeting of the new Sovereign's Privy Council. Later there follows the coronation, the ancient ceremony which, before the hereditary principle was established, gave religious sanction to title by election and brought to a close the interregnum between the death of one King and the election of his successor. Today there is no interregnum and the main legal significance of the coronation is the taking of the oath by the Sovereign of his duties towards his subjects. The form of the oath was prescribed by the Coronation Oath Act 1688 as amended by the Acts of Union.[12] In place of the formal declaration against transubstantiation required by the Bill of Rights and the

---

[7]   Ch. 24.

[8]   Cmd 8748, 1953; and see S. A. de Smith (1953) 2 I.C.L.Q. 263.

[9]   *R.* v. *Foreign Secretary, ex p. Indian Assn of Alberta* [1982] Q.B. 892; and ch. 24.

[10]   1953 S.C. 396, p. 86 *ante*.

[11]   See C. d'O. Farran (1951) 15 M.L.R. 53 and C. Parry (1956) 5 I.C.L.Q. 61.

[12]   For the oath taken by Elizabeth II, see H.L.E., vol. 8, para. 861.

Act of Settlement, the Accession Declaration Act 1910 substituted a modified declaration of adherence to the Protestant faith; this declaration is made when the new Sovereign first opens Parliament or at the coronation, whichever is earlier. The oath to preserve the Presbyterian Church in Scotland was taken by Elizabeth II at the first Privy Council held after her accession.

Minority and incapacity

The Regency Acts 1937–53 make standing provision for the Sovereign's minority, incapacity and temporary absence from the realm. Until the Sovereign attains the age of 18, the royal functions are to be exercised by a regent, who will also act in the event of total incapacity of an adult Sovereign. Normally the regent will be the next person in the line of succession who is not excluded by the Act of Settlement and is a British subject domiciled in the United Kingdom. If the heir apparent or heir presumptive is to be regent, he or she must have attained the age of 18; if another person, the age of 21.[13] Regency is automatic on the succession of a minor; but in the case of total incapacity a declaration has to be made by the wife or husband of the Sovereign, the Lord Chancellor, the Speaker, the Lord Chief Justice and the Master of the Rolls, or any three of them, that they are satisfied by evidence (including that of physicians) that the Sovereign is by reason of infirmity of mind or body incapable of performing the royal functions, or that for some definite cause he is not available for the performance of those functions. This declaration must be made to the Privy Council and communicated to the other governments of the Commonwealth. A regency on these grounds may be ended by a similar declaration. A regent may exercise all the royal functions, except that he may not assent to a Bill for changing the order of succession to the Crown or for repealing or altering the Scottish Act of 1706 for securing the protestant religion and presbyterian church government.[14]

Illness and temporary absence

In the event of illness which does not amount to total incapacity or of absence or intended absence from the United Kingdom, the Sovereign may appoint Counsellors of State to exercise such of the royal functions as may be conferred upon them by letters patent. There may not be delegated the power to dissolve Parliament otherwise than on the express instructions of the Sovereign (which may be conveyed by telegraph), or to grant any rank, title or dignity of the peerage. The Counsellors of State must be the wife or husband of the Sovereign, the four persons next in line of succession to the Crown (excluding any persons (a) disqualified from being regent, or (b) being absent or intending to be absent from the United Kingdom during the period of delegation) and Queen Elizabeth, the Queen Mother. The heir apparent or heir presumptive may be a Counsellor of State, if not under 18 years of age.[15] The functions of Counsellors of State during absence of the Sovereign from the United Kingdom do not extend to those functions which in relation to a Dominion are normally exercised by the Sovereign in person.

---

[13] The Regency Act 1953, s. 1 provided for the Duke of Edinburgh to be regent in circumstances that now can scarcely arise.

[14] Regency Act 1937, s. 4; p. 77 *ante*.

[15] Regency Act 1937, s. 6.

Demise of the Crown

Formerly the death of the Sovereign involved the dissolution of Parliament and the termination of the tenure of all offices under the Crown. The duration of Parliament is now independent of the death of the Sovereign.[16] The Demise of the Crown Act 1901 provided that the holding of any office should not be affected by the demise of the Crown and that no fresh appointment should be necessary. When in 1936 effect was given to Edward VIII's abdication by His Majesty's Declaration of Abdication Act 1936, it was enacted that there should be a demise of the Crown upon the Act receiving the royal assent. Before Edward VIII signed the declaration of abdication, the King's intention had been communicated informally to the Dominion governments by the Prime Minister. Upon signature the declaration was formally communicated to the Dominion governments.[17]

Financing the monarchy

In the 17th century, when the Sovereign himself carried out the functions of government, the revenue from the taxes which Parliament authorised was paid over to the Sovereign and merged with the hereditary revenues already available to him. Today a separation is made between the expenses of government and the expenses of maintaining the monarchy. Since the time of George III, it has been customary at the beginning of each reign for the Sovereign to surrender to Parliament for his life the ancient hereditary revenues of the Crown, including the income from Crown lands.[18] Provision is then made by Parliament for meeting the salaries and other expenses of the royal household. This provision, known as the Civil List, was granted to the Queen for her reign and six months after, by the Civil List Act 1952. In 1952 the total annual amount paid was £475,000 but following an inquiry into the financial position of the monarchy by a select committee of the House of Commons,[19] the amount was raised to £980,000 by the Civil List Act 1972. The 1972 Act also provided that the annual sum might be increased by means of a Treasury Order subject to annulment by the House of Commons. The idea behind the Civil List used to be that Parliament should not be asked to vote money for the expenses of the royal household each year, and the 1972 Act provided for a periodic report from the Royal Trustees on the state of the royal finances. But because of continuing inflation, the Civil List Act 1975 empowered the Treasury to make payments to the Royal Trustees for supplementing any of the sums payable under the Queen's Civil List and abolished the procedure of periodic reports. The select committee of the Commons in 1971 had rejected a proposal that the royal household should be placed on the footing of a government department to receive an annual payment voted by normal budgetary procedures, but the 1975 Act was a step in that direction.[20] Cer-

---

16   Ch. 10.
17   Page 422 *post.*
18   Under Crown Estate Act 1961, the Crown Estate Commissioners are responsible for administering the Crown Estate: for the history see H.C. 29 (1971–2), app. 18.
19   H.C. 29 (1971–2).
20   In 1982–3, over £2.9 m. was paid to the Royal Trustees under the 1975 Act, s. 1(1) to supplement the direct payment for the Civil List from the Consolidated Fund: Supply Estimates 1982–3. Class XIII. 4. And see H.C. 183 (1983–4).

tain expenses in connection with the royal household (for example, the cost of overseas visits, the royal yacht and the Queen's Flight) are met out of departmental allocations.

The Act of 1952, as amended in 1972, also makes provision for the Duke of Edinburgh, the Queen's younger children and other members of the royal family. The justification for this is stated to be that these members of the royal family take a share in the burden of work placed on the Sovereign and are, by reason of their relationship to the Sovereign, unable to earn a living in ways open to the rest of the community.[21] The Prince of Wales enjoys separate provision out of the revenues of the Duchy of Cornwall.

The Sovereign also holds private property in a personal capacity and derives income from this. In 1971 the select committee of the Commons were assured that suggestions that the Queen owned private funds in the region of £50 million were 'wildly exaggerated' but no estimate of their actual value was given to the committee. Apart from the Balmoral and Sandringham estates, which under the Crown Private Estates Act 1862 are liable to pay local rates, the Sovereign benefits from the principle that the Crown is not liable to pay taxes unless Parliament says so either expressly or by necessary implication.[22]

Duties of the Sovereign

No attempt can be made to list the full duties which fall to the Sovereign to perform in person.[23] Many formal acts of government require her participation. Many state documents require her signature and she receives copies of all major government papers, including reports from ambassadors abroad and their instructions from the Foreign Office, and also minutes of Cabinet meetings and other Cabinet papers. 'There is therefore a continuing burden of unseen work involving some hours reading of papers each day in addition to Her Majesty's more public duties'.[24] About ten meetings of the Privy Council are held each year. She gives frequent audiences to the Prime Minister and visiting ministers from the Commonwealth, receives foreign diplomatic representatives, holds 14 investitures each year and personally confers honours and decorations. She receives state visits to this country by the heads of foreign and Commonwealth states, and makes state visits to countries overseas. She attends numerous state occasions, for example to deliver the Queen's Speech at the opening of each session of Parliament. Her formal consent is needed for appointments made by the Crown on the advice of the Prime Minister, the Lord Chancellor and other ministers.

A catalogue of official duties does not reveal what influence, if any, the Sovereign has on the political direction of the country's affairs. In general, the Sovereign is bound to act on the advice of the Prime Minister or other appropriate minister, for example, the Home Secretary or the Secretary of State for Scotland in respect of the prerogative of mercy. The Sovereign cannot reject the final advice which ministers offer to her without the probable consequence

---

[21] H.C. 29 (1971–2), para. 31.
[22] H.C. 29 (1971–2), App. 12; and pp. 693–4 *post*.
[23] See H.C. 29 (1971–2), paras. 16–17, and evidence by the Queen's Private Secretary, pp. 30–41 and app. 13.
[24] H.C. 29 (1971–2), para. 17.

of bringing about their resignation and their replacement by other ministers, thereby bringing the future of the monarchy into controversy. But to what extent may the Queen offer them guidance from her own fund of experience in public affairs? Bagehot described the Sovereign's rights as being the right to be consulted, the right to encourage and the right to warn.[25] While this may entitle the monarch to express personal views on political events to the Prime Minister, these views may have little influence over the whole range of the government's work.[26] This was so even in relation to the later years of Queen Victoria, whose attitude to Gladstone was, by the standards of her successors, not that to be expected of a constitutional monarch. Much light was thrown upon the tasks performed by the Sovereign in the 20th century by Sir Harold Nicolson's biography of George V and by Sir John Wheeler-Bennett's biography of George VI. Thus it appears that the Sovereign, even before the days when Cabinet conclusions were regularly recorded by the Cabinet secretariat, could insist on the advice of the Cabinet being given in written form, if he felt that it was dangerous or opposed to the wishes of the people. This was so that the King could record in writing the misgivings and reluctance with which he followed the advice of his Cabinet.[27] The clear impression is given in these two biographies that the monarch is far from being a mere mouthpiece of his constitutional advisers. But it would be wrong to suppose that the right to be consulted, to encourage and to warn apply to all areas of policy-making, in many of which the Sovereign will have had no relevant experience. Such rights can be understood better in relation to those powers of the Sovereign where she may be required to exercise a personal discretion; they will be discussed below under the heading, the personal prerogatives of the Sovereign.

Private Secretary to the Sovereign

The Private Secretary to the Sovereign plays a significant role in conducting communications between the Sovereign and her ministers and, in exceptional circumstances where this is constitutionally proper, between the Sovereign and other political leaders. This office is filled on the personal selection of the Sovereign; usually it goes to a member of the royal household who has extensive experience in the service of the Court. It is through the Private Secretary that communications from the government to the Sovereign are sent. Inevitably, the secretarial function demands much discretion in selecting the information which should be brought to the personal notice of the Sovereign, and in obtaining confidential advice for the Sovereign from independent sources should this be necessary.[28] The Private Secretary must belong to no political party. He is made a member of the Privy Council.

Personal prerogatives of the Sovereign

1 The appointment of a Prime Minister.[29]   In appointing a Prime

---

25 *The English Constitution*, p. 111.
26 Jennings, *Cabinet Government*, ch. 12; Mackintosh, *The British Cabinet*, chs. 4, 9, 17 and 19.
27 H. Nicolson, *George V*, p. 115.
28 Wheeler-Bennett, *George VI*, app. B and H.C. 29 (1971–2), pp. 30–41.
29 See Jennings, *Cabinet Government*, ch. 2; Marshall and Moodie, ch. 3; Wilson, *Cases*, pp. 7–17; and R. Brazier [1982] P.L. 395.

Minister the Sovereign must appoint that person who is in the best position to receive the support of the majority in the House of Commons. This does not involve the Sovereign in making a personal assessment of leading politicians since no major party could today fight a general election without a recognised leader. Where an election produces an absolute majority in the Commons for one party, the leader of that party will be invited to become Prime Minister, or if he already is Prime Minister, he will continue in office. By modern practice, a defeated Prime Minister resigns from office as soon as a decisive result of the election is known. Where after an election no one party has an absolute majority in the House (as in 1923, 1929 and February 1974), the Prime Minister in office may decide to wait until Parliament resumes to see whether he can obtain a majority in the new House with support from another party (as did Baldwin after the 1923 election, only to find that he could not) or he may resign without waiting for Parliament to meet (as did Baldwin in 1929 and Heath in 1974). When he has resigned, the Queen will send for the leader of the party with the largest number of seats (as in 1929 and 1974) or with the next largest number of seats (as in January 1924 after Baldwin had been defeated by combined Labour and Liberal votes). Thus, where the election produces a clear majority for one party, the Sovereign has no discretion to exercise. Where an election does not produce a conclusive result, the Sovereign has no discretion except where the procedure described still fails to establish a government in office; in this case, the Sovereign would have to initiate discussions with and between the parties to discover, for example, whether a government could be formed by a politician who was not a party leader or whether a coalition government could be formed.[30]

Where a Prime Minister resigns because of ill-health or old age, or dies while in office, a new leader of the governing party must be found. Formerly, in the case of the Liberal and Conservative parties, this was a situation in which the Sovereign was required to exercise a discretion, namely to invite a person to be Prime Minister who would command general support within the governing party. Sometimes the successor might be clear (as in 1955 when Eden followed Churchill) and the retiring Prime Minister could advise the Sovereign of this fact, although he was not required to give advice to the Sovereign about his successor. Where there were two or more possible successors, the Sovereign was entitled to consult with senior members of the party concerned to discover which person would command most support within the party. This was the case in May 1923 when the choice lay between Baldwin and Curzon, and Baldwin was chosen. In 1957, when Eden resigned because of illness, he left two possible successors, Butler and Macmillan; the Queen consulted with Sir Winston Churchill, a former Prime Minister, and with Lord Salisbury, to whom the views of the Cabinet ministers were known. This established that Macmillan commanded much the greater support, and he was invited by the Queen to be Prime Minister. While Sir Ivor Jennings stated that the Queen in this instance 'had a genuine choice',[31] in fact her decision gave effect to the definite preference of those influential in the Conservative party.[32]

---

[30] See D. Butler, *Governing without a Majority: Dilemmas for Hung Parliaments in Britain*, ch. 5.
[31] *Cabinet Government*, p. 28.
[32] Mackintosh, p. 425.

In 1963, when Macmillan announced his imminent resignation because of ill-health, he organised rapid consultations with different sections of the Conservative party. On the basis of these consultations, he advised the Queen that the Earl of Home, as he then was, had the greatest support. The Queen then invited Home to see whether he could form a government, on the understanding that if successful he would disclaim his peerage. Although he succeeded and was appointed Prime Minister, some criticism was expressed of the Queen's part in having acted so promptly that those who favoured Butler had no time in which to organise support for him: but there seems no reason why the Queen was not entitled to act on the definite advice of Macmillan.[33]

After the events in 1957 and in 1963, it was realised that if the Sovereign was merely expected to invite as next Prime Minister the person whom the Conservative party wished to lead it, it would be better for the party to have its own procedure for electing a leader. This the Parliamentary Labour Party already had. The present position is that the Conservative party rules provide for a series of up to three secret ballots, in which only the M.P.s may vote. Consultation must take place with sections of the party outside the Commons. New candidates may be nominated after the first ballot. The written rules do not expressly require that candidates are members of the Commons. In the case of the Labour party, the right to vote in the election of leader was formerly confined to Labour M.P.s, but in 1981 the party changed its constitution and standing orders to provide for the leader and deputy leader to be elected at a party conference. Candidates must be Labour M.P.s. The electoral college is in three sections, Labour M.P.s and constituency parties each having 30% of the votes, and affiliated trade unions having 40%. Successive ballots with open voting are· held until one candidate has more than half the votes so apportioned. When Labour is in opposition, an election shall be held at each annual conference. When Labour is in government and the party leader is Prime Minister, an election takes place only if required by a majority of the conference on a card vote. While both parties have used these procedures to elect leaders while in opposition (the Conservatives in 1965 and 1975; Labour in 1983), new ground was broken in 1976 when Harold Wilson announced his intention of resigning as Prime Minister. He remained in office until (under the party's former rules) Labour M.P.s elected their new leader, Mr Callaghan. Mr Wilson then resigned and Mr Callaghan became Prime Minister.

Thus the Labour and Conservative parties have their own procedures for electing a new leader, and so do the Liberal and Social Democratic parties. Does this mean that the Sovereign has no residual discretion to exercise in appointing a Prime Minister? First, since the election of a new leader may take some weeks, the appointment of an acting Prime Minister might well be needed if, unlike the position in 1976, the outgoing Prime Minister had died or was too ill to continue in office. Presumably a senior member of the Cabinet would be so appointed.[34] Moreover, there could well be circumstances in

---

[33]   Mackintosh, pp. 426–7; and R. Brazier [1982] P.L. 395, 396.

[34]   *Cf.* R. Brazier [1982] P.L. 395, 406. By Labour party standing orders, when the leader becomes 'permanently unavailable', the deputy leader automatically becomes leader to serve until a new leader is elected. But if Labour were in office, would the deputy leader become acting Prime Minister if, as in 1968–70, he was not then a member of the government?

which reliance on normal party procedures would not produce an immediate solution: for example, where a party holding office broke up after serious internal dissension; or where no party had a majority in the House and there was a deadlock between the parties as to who should form a government; or where a coalition agreement had broken down. In such situations, the Sovereign could not avoid taking initiatives to enable a new government to be formed, for example by initiating inter-party discussions. In 1931, when Ramsay MacDonald and the Labour Cabinet resigned because of serious disagreement within the Cabinet over the steps that should be taken to deal with the financial crisis, George V, after consulting with Conservative and Liberal leaders invited MacDonald to form a 'National Government' with Liberal and Conservative support. The extreme bitterness which MacDonald's defection caused in the Labour party led to criticism of George V's conduct as unconstitutional, but such criticism seems unjustified.[35]

While therefore under stable political conditions the Sovereign will not need to exercise a personal discretion in selecting a Prime Minister, it might become necessary for the Sovereign to do so. There are no grounds for supposing that a monarch is less capable of impartially exercising such a discretion, should it become necessary, than an elected president or the Speaker of the House of Commons.[36]

2 Dissolution of Parliament.[37] In the absence of a regular term for the life of Parliament fixed by statute, the Sovereign may by the prerogative dissolve Parliament and cause a general election to be held. The Sovereign normally accepts the advice of the Prime Minister and grants a dissolution when this is requested. Since 1918, it has become established practice that a Cabinet decision is not necessary before the Prime Minister may seek a dissolution, although members of the Cabinet may be consulted before the Prime Minister makes his decision.[38] The refusal of a dissolution when the Prime Minister had requested it would probably be treated by him as tantamount to a dismissal. Are there circumstances in which the Sovereign would be justified in refusing a dissolution or is it automatic that the Sovereign should grant a dissolution when requested?

It is doubtful whether there can be grounds for the refusal of a dissolution to a Prime Minister who commands a clear majority in the Commons.[39] Our political practice accepts that a Prime Minister may choose his own time for a general election within the five-year life of Parliament prescribed by the Parliament Act 1911. If a Sovereign did refuse dissolution to a Prime Minister who commanded a majority in a House, and the Prime Minister then resigned

---

[35] A full account is in R. Bassett, *1931: Political Crisis*. See also Mackintosh, pp. 419–20 and K. Middlemas and J. Barnes, *Baldwin*, ch. 23.

[36] *Cf.* D. Butler, *Governing without a Majority*, pp. 84–8.

[37] E. A. Forsey, *The Royal Power of Dissolution in the British Commonwealth*; B. S. Markesinis, *The Theory and Practice of Dissolution of Parliament*.

[38] Jennings, *Cabinet Government*, pp. 417–19; Mackintosh, pp. 453–5; Markesinis, *op. cit.*, ch. 5 A.

[39] Markesinis, *op. cit.*, pp. 84–6; Forsey, *op. cit.*, p. 269. If an opportunist Prime Minister decided to take advantage of the death of the leader of the Opposition to seek an immediate dissolution, knowing that the rules of the opposition party required the election of a new leader to take a month, could the Sovereign insist on delaying the election so that the parties could campaign on more equal terms?

from office with the other ministers, any other politician invited to be Prime Minister (for example, the leader of the Opposition) would presumably have no prospect of a majority at Westminster until an election had been held. The Sovereign would therefore be faced with an early request for a dissolution from the new Prime Minister and with inevitable criticism for political bias if he granted this request. Where a minority government holds office, the position is more complicated but here again it is for the Prime Minister rather than the Sovereign to choose the time for an election. Much would depend on the circumstances in which the minority government had come about and on how recently a general election had been held. Thus a Prime Minister who had been granted one dissolution and failed to get a majority at the ensuing election, could scarcely request a second dissolution immediately. His duty would be to resign and to give the leader of another party the opportunity of forming a government. Where a Prime Minister had been in office for a considerable period (for example, some months) since the previous election, and was then defeated on an issue of confidence in the House, he would then have a choice between resigning or, as MacDonald did in 1924, seeking a dissolution.

In 1950, during discussion of the problems caused by the Labour government's small majority after the 1950 election, it was submitted by the Private Secretary to George VI that the Sovereign could properly refuse a dissolution if he were satisfied that (a) the existing Parliament was still 'vital, viable, and capable of doing its job', (b) a general election would be detrimental to the national economy and (c) he could rely on finding another Prime Minister who could carry on his government for a reasonable period with a working majority.[40] It will be seldom that all these conditions can be satisfied, and it might be argued that these are eminently matters for the Prime Minister in office to decide. It might be particularly difficult for the Sovereign to be reasonably certain that another Prime Minister could command a working majority in the House. Yet the Sovereign would be strongly criticised if having refused a dissolution to one Prime Minister he was faced with an early request from his successor for dissolution.

In the last 100 years there are no instances of the Sovereign having refused a dissolution in the United Kingdom, but there are two leading illustrations of the problem from the former Dominions where the prerogative was exercisable by the Governor-General. In 1939 the Governor-General of South Africa refused a dissolution to the Prime Minister, General Hertzog, whose proposal that South Africa should be neutral in the second world war had been defeated in Parliament, and he invited General Smuts to form a government which remained in power thereafter. But in 1926, the Governor-General of Canada, Lord Byng, refused a dissolution to the Liberal leader, Mackenzie King, and instead invited Meighen, the Conservative leader, to form a government believing that Meighen would be supported by a third party which held the balance of power. When that support failed within a matter of days, Meighen sought a dissolution of Parliament which was granted by Lord Byng: the ensuing election was won by the Liberals and the Governor-General was

---

[40]   For his pseudonymous letter to *The Times*, see Wilson, *Cases*, p. 22; Markesinis, *op. cit.*, pp. 87–8 and app. 4.

much criticised for his decisions.[41]

The controversy between the 'automatic' and 'discretionary' views of the prerogative of dissolution was raised again in 1969. Although at that time Labour had a clear majority in the Commons, there were press reports of Labour dissension within the party. The question was raised whether a Prime Minister could use the weapon of dissolution to defend his own position against attempts within the party to dislodge him.[42] In 1974, after the election in February 1974, when no party had an absolute majority, the question was raised whether Mr Wilson as Prime Minister was entitled to a dissolution if his government were defeated in the Commons by a combined opposition vote. Certain Labour M.P.s, who feared that a Liberal-Conservative coalition might be formed to govern the country, urged that the Sovereign was both consti- tutionally and morally bound to grant dissolution whenever the Prime Minister requested it. In reply, the Lord President of the Council, Mr Short, told them: 'Constitutional lawyers of the highest authority are of the clear opinion that the Sovereign is not in all circumstances bound to grant a Prime Minister's request for dissolution'; it was impossible to define in advance the circumstances in which the Sovereign's discretion to refuse a request for a dissolution might be exercised.[43] There the matter had to rest, since the government refused to allow the matter to be debated in the Commons. In the event, when Mr Wilson sought a dissolution in September 1974, this was granted without question by the Sovereign.

That the Sovereign should not refuse a Prime Minister's request for dissol- ution except for very strong reason is obvious. In practice, the political signifi- cance of the Prime Minister's power to decide when Parliament should be dissolved is much greater than the possibility of the Sovereign's refusal of a dissolution. But the view that the Sovereign's reserve power may serve to restrain a Prime Minister who otherwise might be tempted to abuse his position is an argument for maintaining the reserve power as a potential weapon, not for abolishing it.

3 The dismissal of ministers.   The refusal of a Prime Minister's request for a dissolution is but one aspect of a larger question, namely whether the Sovereign may ever reject the advice of the Prime Minister on a major issue, for example, by refusing to make an appointment to ministerial office which the Prime Minister had recommended, by refusing to give the royal assent to a Bill which has passed through both Houses or by insisting that a general election is held before the royal assent is given. In 1910 George V insisted that a general election be held on the Liberal proposal to remove the veto of the House of Lords, before he would create enough new Liberal peers to pass the Parliament Bill through the Lords against Conservative opposition; this deci- sion was accepted by the Prime Minister, Asquith. But in other situations a

---

[41]   Forsey, *op. cit.*, gives a detailed commentary; and see J. R. Mallory, *The Structure of Canadian Government*, pp. 50–2.

[42]   Markesinis, *op. cit.*, app. 4. Earlier in 1969, Captain O'Neill, Prime Minister of Northern Ireland, had been granted a dissolution of the Northern Ireland Parliament at a time when members of the Unionist party were growing restive at O'Neill's measures of reform.

[43]   *The Times*, 11 May 1974.

refusal by the Sovereign to accept advice could be seen as a direct challenge to the authority of the Prime Minister and might mean his immediate resignation. The underlying question is whether the Sovereign is merely part of the formal apparatus of government, and thus incapable of taking an independent position on a point of constitutional principle, or whether the monarchy provides some kind of safeguard against potential abuses of power by the Prime Minister and Cabinet.

The last occasion on which it was seriously urged that the Sovereign should intervene to ensure that a general election should be held against the wishes of the government was during the crisis over Home Rule for Ireland between 1912 and 1914.[44] After the Parliament Act 1911 had become law, the Liberal government intended that the Government of Ireland Bill should be passed under the Parliament Act procedure. Opposition leaders regarded the relationship between the Liberal party and the Irish Nationalists as 'a corrupt Parliamentary bargain'. They urged George V to insist that an election be held before the Bill became law or to withhold the royal assent. Asquith, the Prime Minister, reminded George V of the constitutional limitations upon the Sovereign, of the principle of ministerial responsibility, and of the value for the Sovereign of having no personal responsibility for the acts of executive and Parliament. The King concluded that he should not adopt the extreme course of withholding the royal assent from the Bill 'unless there is convincing evidence that it would avert a national disaster, or at least have a tranquillizing effect on the distracting conditions of the time'.[45]

Where the question is that of assent to a Bill which has passed through Parliament, it would scarcely be prudent for the Sovereign to challenge the wishes of a majority in the House of Commons. Yet the relationship between Sovereign and Prime Minister is bilateral in the sense that both persons hold office subject to some principles of constitutional behaviour, however vague these principles often appear to be. If the Prime Minister steps outside those principles (as for example, Ian Smith, Prime Minister of Rhodesia, did in 1965 when with his Cabinet he unilaterally declared Rhodesia independent of the United Kingdom),the Sovereign may respond by dismissing his ministers and by taking steps to ensure the maintenance of constitutional government. In 1975, the Labour government of Australia was failing to get essential financial legislation through the Canberra Parliament because of opposition from the Senate, whose approval to the legislation was required. When Sir John Kerr, the Governor-General, had satisfied himself that Prime Minister Whitlam was not willing to hold a general election to resolve the deadlock, he dismissed Whitlam and invited the Opposition leader, Fraser, to form an interim government and hold an election. The election was won by Fraser, but the acts of the Governor-General gave rise to controversy of a kind which might be more damaging to a hereditary monarchy than to a Governor-General with a limited tenure of office.[46]

British government depends to a large extent upon implicit agreement

---

[44]   See Nicolson, *George V*, ch. 14; Jennings, *Cabinet Government*, ch. 13.
[45]   Draft letter by George V, 31 Jul. 1914; Wilson, *Cases*, p. 30.
[46]   The literature includes G. Evans (ed.) *Labour and the Constitution 1972–5*. J. Kerr, *Matters for Judgment*, G. Sawer, *Federation under Strain* and G. Whitlam, *The Truth of the Matter*.

between the parties and their leaders about the rules and understandings of the political contest. If in a particular situation it were clear that one party or its leader had seriously departed from the accepted rules, personal inter- vention by the Sovereign could in those circumstances be justified on consti- tutional grounds. But a plain instance of flagrant abuse is less likely than a situation which is not covered by existing rules and understandings, and in which it may be difficult to determine what are the constitutional require- ments.[47] While the Sovereign may have a sensitive role to play in enabling a constitutional deadlock to be resolved, the main lesson of British history is that personal government by the Sovereign is excluded. Indeed, the Sovereign needs the co-operation of ministers even for the purpose of dissolving Parlia- ment and causing a new general election to be held.[48] The political impotence of a monarch who cannot find ministers willing to hold office explains why, as a 'far-sighted precaution' at an early stage of the abdication crisis in 1936, Prime Minister Baldwin ensured that other political leaders would not be willing to form a government if he were forced to resign.[49]

B. The Queen in Council

The Tudor monarchs governed mainly through the Privy Council, a select group of royal officials and advisers, having recourse to Parliament only when legislative authority was considered necessary for matters of taxation or to give effect to royal policies. The Privy Council survived the 17th century conflicts, although its judicial arm, the Court of Star Chamber, was abolished in 1641. But in the 50 years after the restoration of the monarchy in 1660, the Privy Council lost its position as the main political executive and its numbers grew, many becoming members because of other offices which they held. As the Cabinet system developed, so did the English Privy Council lose its policy- making and deliberative role.[1] Soon after the union of England and Scotland in 1707, the Scottish Privy Council was abolished and its functions were assumed by the Privy Council for Great Britain. In a formal sense the Council remained at the centre of the administrative machinery of government, but despite an attempt by Parliament in the Act of Settlement to insist that the Privy Council should exercise its former functions, the Council had lost its political authority. Significantly, politicians began to remain members of the Council after they had ceased to be ministers, a practice which has continued until today.

Office of privy councillor
Membership of the Privy Council is today a titular honour. Appointments are made by the Sovereign on ministerial advice. By convention all Cabinet ministers become privy councillors. Members of the royal family and holders of certain high offices of a non-political character such as Archbishops and Lords Justices of Appeal, are appointed members of the Council. So in recent years

---

[47]   Page 27 *ante*.
[48]   Jennings, *Cabinet Government*, pp. 412–17; Markesinis, *op. cit.*, p. 56.
[49]   Middlemas and Barnes, *Baldwin*, p. 999.
[1]   For the history of this period, see Mackintosh, ch. 2.

has been the leader of the Liberal party. The office is a recognised reward for public and political service, and appointments to it figure in the honours lists. The Council now numbers about 330 members. Members are entitled to the prefix, 'Right Honourable'. They take an oath on appointment which binds them not to disclose anything said or done 'in Council' without the consent of the Sovereign. As all members of the Cabinet are also privy councillors it has been considered that it is this oath which, in addition to their obligations under the Official Secrets Acts 1911–39, binds to secrecy all present and past Cabinet ministers, who may only disclose Cabinet proceedings and other confidential discussions if so authorised by the Sovereign; but little reliance was placed on this oath in the *Crossman Diaries* case[2] and its wording does not seem apt to include Cabinet proceedings. Aliens are disqualified, but on naturalisation an alien becomes qualified for membership.[3]

Functions of Privy Council

Despite the many powers conferred by statutes on individual ministers, the Order in Council remains a principal method of giving the force of law to acts of the government, especially the more important executive orders. A royal proclamation is issued when it is desired to give wide publicity to the action of the Queen in Council, as for the purpose of dissolving a Parliament and summoning its successor. Nowadays Orders in Council are approved by the Sovereign at a meeting of the Council to which only four or five members are summoned. No discussion takes place and the acts of the Council are purely formal. Orders are made either under the prerogative, as for the dissolution of Parliament, or under an Act of Parliament, for example, orders which make regulations under the Emergency Power Act 1920 after a state of emergency has been proclaimed.[4] Statutory Orders in Council are generally subject to the Statutory Instruments Act 1946.[5]

A few traces remain of the Council's former advisory functions: the Committee for Channel Islands business is a survivor of the old standing committees appointed by the King at the beginning or in the course of his reign. Other committees are the Judicial Committee of the Privy Council,[6] a committee to consider grants of charters to universities and the committee for the Scottish universities.[7] Issues of constitutional importance are sometimes referred to *ad hoc* committees of the Privy Council, as, for example, the legal basis of the practice of telephone tapping and matters affecting state security.[8] A committee of six Privy Councillors reviewed British policy towards the Falkland Islands leading up to Argentina's invasion in 1982; after the Prime Minister had consulted with five former Prime Ministers to secure their consent, the committee had access to the papers of previous governments and secret intelligence assessments.[9]

---

2   *A.-G.* v. *Jonathan Cape Ltd* [1976] Q.B. 752; for the oath, see H.L.E. vol. 8, p. 708.
3   *R.* v. *Speyer* [1916] 2 K.B. 858.
4   Ch. 29 B.
5   Ch. 33.
6   Ch. 19 A.
7   Universities (Scotland) Act 1889, s. 9.
8   Page 254 *post* and ch. 30.
9   H.C. Deb., 1 Jul. 1982, col. 1039 and 8 Jul. 1982, col. 469; Cmnd 8787, 1983; and ch. 14 A.

The functions of the Privy Council are quite distinct from those of the Cabinet. The first gives legal form to certain decisions of the government; the second exercise the policy-making function of the executive in major matters. The Cabinet is summoned by the Prime Minister; the Council is convened by the Clerk of the Council, whose office dates back to the 16th century. The Lord President of the Council is usually a senior member of the Cabinet. As he has no onerous departmental duties, he often acts as chairman of Cabinet committees. Where Privy Council business concerns the activities of a department, responsibility for that business is borne by the minister of that department; thus the Secretary of State for Education and Science is responsible for decisions of the Privy Council regarding university charters, although this responsibility tends to be obscured by the dignified facade of Privy Council formality.

C. The royal prerogative

Both the Sovereign, as head of state, and the government, as personified for many purposes by the Crown, need powers to be able to perform their constitutional functions. The rule of law requires that these powers are grounded in law, and are not outside or above the system of law which the courts administer. In Britain the powers of the Sovereign and the Crown must either be derived from Act of Parliament or must be recognised as a matter of common law, for there is no written constitution to confer powers on the executive. In the 17th-century constitutional settlement, it was established that the powers of the Crown were subject to law and that there were no powers of the Crown which could not be taken away or controlled by statute. Once that position had been achieved against the claims of the Stuarts, the courts thereafter accepted that the Sovereign and the Crown enjoyed certain powers, rights, immunities and privileges which were necessary to the maintenance of government and which were not shared with private citizens. The term prerogative is used as a collective description of these matters. Blackstone referred to prerogative as 'that special pre-eminence which the King hath, over and above all other persons, and out of the ordinary course of the common law, in right of his royal dignity'.[1] A modern definition would stress that the prerogative has been maintained not for the benefit of the Sovereign but to enable the government to function, and that prerogative is a matter of common law and does not derive from statute. Thus Parliament may not create a new prerogative, although it may confer on the Crown new rights or powers which may be very similar in character to prerogative power, for example, the statutory power to deport aliens from the United Kingdom whose further presence is considered undesirable,[2] or the statutory power to create life peerages.

History of the prerogative[3]

The mediaeval King was both feudal lord and head of the kingdom. He thus

---

[1] Blackstone, *Commentaries*, I, p. 239. *Cf.* H. W. R. Wade, *Constitutional Fundamentals*, pp. 45–53.
[2] Ch. 25 B.
[3] A valuable account is in D. L. Keir and F. H. Lawson, *Cases in Constitutional Law*, Part II, on which this section has drawn. See also Heuston, *Essays*, ch. 3.

had all the rights of a feudal lord and certain exceptional rights above those of other lords. Like other lords the King could not be sued in his own courts; as there was no lord superior to the King, there was no court in which the King could be sued. In addition the King had powers accounted for by the need to preserve the realm against external foes and an 'undefined residue of power which he might use for the public good'.[4] We have already seen that mediaeval lawyers did not regard the King as being above the law.[5] Moreover certain royal functions could be exercised only in certain ways. The common law courts were the King's courts and only through them could the King decide questions of title to land and punish felonies. Yet the King possessed a residuary power of doing justice through his Council where the courts of common law were inadequate.

In the 17th century, the main disputes arose over the undefined residue of prerogative power claimed by the Stuart kings.[6] Those common lawyers who allied with Parliament in resisting the Stuart claims asserted that there was a fundamental distinction between what was called the ordinary as opposed to the absolute prerogative. The ordinary prerogative meant those royal functions which could only be exercised in defined ways and involved no element of royal discretion. Thus the King could not himself act as a judge; he must dispense justice throught his judges.[7] And he could make laws only through Parliament.[8] By contrast, the absolute or extraordinary prerogative meant those powers which the King could exercise in his discretion. They included not only such powers as the right to pardon a criminal or grant a peerage, but also the King's undoubted powers to exercise discretion in the interest of the realm, especially in times of emergency. It was these powers on which Charles I relied in seeking to govern without Parliament. The conflict was resolved only after the execution of one King and the expulsion of another. But the particular disputes often gave rise to cases in the courts, in which the rival political theories were expressed in legal argument. Where the judges accepted the Crown's more extreme claims, their decisions had subsequently to be reversed by Parliament. As well as the cases on taxation and the dispensing power, which have already been discussed,[9] another outstanding case was *Darnel's* or *The Five Knights' Case*,[10] where it was held that it was a sufficient answer to a writ of habeas corpus to state that a prisoner was detained *per speciale mandatum regis* (by special order of the King). Thus the King was entrusted with a power of preventive arrest which could not be questioned by the courts and which in *Darnel's Case* was used to enforce taxation levied without the consent of Parliament. This arbitrary power of committal was declared illegal by the Petition of Right 1628, and in 1640 the subject's right to habeas corpus against the King and his Council was guaranteed by statute.[11]

---

[4]   Keir and Lawson, *op. cit.*, p. 70.
[5]   Ch. 6.
[6]   Ch. 5 A.
[7]   *Prohibitions del Roy* (1607) 12 Co. Rep. 63; ch. 19 A.
[8]   *The Case of Proclamations* (1611) 12 Co. Rep. 74; p. 61 *ante*.
[9]   Pages 61–2 *ante*.
[10] (1627) 3 St. Tr. 1.
[11] Habeas Corpus Act 1640.

The problem of the prerogative was solved in two stages. The first was that of the 17th century struggle culminating in the Bill of Rights 1689 which declared illegal certain specific uses and abuses of the prerogative.[12] The second stage was the growth of responsible government and the establishment of a constitutional monarchy.[13] It became established that prerogative powers could only be exercised through and on the advice of ministers responsible to Parliament.

The prerogative today

Today the greater part of government depends on statute. But certain powers, rights, immunities and privileges of the Sovereign and of the Crown, which vary widely in importance, continue to have their legal source in the common law. Where these powers or rights are common to all persons, including the Crown (for example, the power to own property or enter into contracts), they are not described as matters of prerogative; but the term royal prerogative is properly applied to those legal attributes of the Crown which the common law recognises as differing significantly from those of private persons. Thus the legal relationship between the Crown and Crown servants is an aspect of the prerogative since it differs markedly from the normal contractual relationship between employer and employee; the same applies to the power of the Crown in certain circumstances to override contracts to which it is a party.[14]

Except in those special instances where prerogative powers involve the personal discretion of the Sovereign, prerogative powers are exercised by or on behalf of the government of the day. For their exercise, just as for the use of statutory powers, ministers are responsible to Parliament. Thus questions may be asked of ministers about the exercise of prerogative powers. Where a matter does not fall within the province of a departmental minister, questions may be addressed to the Prime Minister. To this rule there are certain exceptions: thus it has been ruled that the Prime Minister may not be questioned in the Commons as to the advice that he may have given to the Sovereign regarding the grant of honours or the ecclesiastical patronage of the Crown.[15] Nor could a question to the Home Secretary about the exercise of the prerogative of mercy in a sentence involving capital punishment be raised while the sentence was pending,[16] but questions are asked about the prerogative of mercy in non-capital cases.[17]

Although Parliament may abolish or curtail the prerogative by statute, the prior authority of Parliament is not required for the exercise of a prerogative power. For example, the Crown may recognise a new foreign government or enter into a treaty without first informing Parliament. Parliament may criticise ministers for their action and for the consequences; but Parliament has no right to be consulted in advance, except to the extent that a conventional practice has

---

12 Ch. 2 A.
13 Ch. 7.
14 Ch. 36.
15 Erskine May, p. 338.
16 Cmd 8932, 1953, paras. 37–41, and G. Marshall [1961] P.L. 8.
17 A. T. H. Smith [1983] P.L. 398, 436.

developed of assuring the opportunity for such consultation.[18] Certain prerogatives could of course be exercised only if the government were assured of subsequent support from Parliament. The Crown may declare war, but Parliament alone may vote the supplies which enable war to be waged. Again, where a treaty envisages changes in our domestic law, Parliament could frustrate the treaty made by the Crown if it subsequently refused to pass the necessary legislation.

Although the extent of prerogative powers depends largely upon history, they have survived because for one reason or another they are essential to government. While some prerogatives, for example, the grant of honours, may not be considered suitable for discussion in Parliament, other aspects of the prerogative (for example, foreign affairs and defence) are eminently suitable for political debate. One consequence of the survival of the prerogative is that a particular power may not be subject to parliamentary or judicial safeguards that would be considered appropriate if the power was being conferred afresh by legislation. Why, for example, should Parliament not have a formal right to approve treaties which the government has concluded? And why should the prerogative power to issue and withdraw passports not be subject to legal safeguards for the citizen? It has evidently been more convenient for successive governments to retain prerogative powers in their ancient form than to modernise them.

The extent of the prerogative today

Because of the diverse subjects covered by prerogative, and because of the uncertainty of the law in many instances where an ancient power has not been used in modern times, it is not possible to give a comprehensive catalogue of prerogative powers.[19] Instead the main areas where the prerogative is used today will be mentioned briefly; most of these are discussed more fully in other chapters.

1 Powers relating to the legislature. By virtue of the prerogative the Sovereign summons, prorogues and dissolves Parliament. The prerogative power to create hereditary peers could still be used on the advice of a government to ensure the passage of a Bill through the Lords but the Parliament Acts 1911–49 and the Life Peerages Act 1958 together make this unlikely. It is under the prerogative that the Sovereign assents to Bills. The Crown retains certain powers to legislate under the prerogative by Order in Council or by letters patent. Formerly this was important in respect of the colonies,[20] but the power is still sometimes used in respect of the civil service.[21] While the Crown may not create new criminal offences or impose new obligations upon citizens,[22] it may under the prerogative create schemes for conferring benefits upon citizens provided that Parliament appropriates the necessary money to

---

[18] For the 'Ponsonby rule' in relation to treaties, see ch. 18 C.
[19] For an account which was authoritative in its day, see Chitty, *Prerogatives of the Crown*; and see B. S. Markesinis, [1973] C.L.J. 287.
[20] K. Roberts-Wray, *Commonwealth & Colonial Law*, ch. 5.
[21] *E.g.* Servants of the Crown (Parliamentary Candidature) Order 1960; p. 277 *post*.
[22] *The Case of Proclamations* (1611) 12 Co. Rep. 74.

pay for these benefits; thus concerning the Criminal Injuries Compensation scheme, set up by means of a non-statutory document notified to Parliament, Diplock L. J. said:

It may be a novel development in constitutional practice to govern by public statement of intention made by the executive government instead of by legislation. This is no more, however, than a reversion to the ancient practice of government by royal proclamation, although it is now subject to the limitations imposed on that practice by the development of constitutional law in the 17th century.[23]

2 Powers relating to the judicial system.[24] While the Crown may still have a prerogative power to establish courts to administer the common law[25] new courts are now established by statute. Through the Attorney-General in England and the Lord Advocate in Scotland, the Crown exercises many functions in relation to criminal justice. Thus in England prosecutions on indictment may be stopped by the Attorney-General entering a *nolle prosequi*. The Crown may pardon convicted offenders or remit or reduce a sentence on the advice of the Home Secretary or the Secretary of State for Scotland. It is under the prerogative that the Crown grants special leave to appeal from colonial courts to the Judicial Committee of the Privy Council, where the right of appeal to the Privy Council has not been abolished.[26] In civil matters the Attorney-General represents the Crown as '*parens patriae*' to enforce matters of public right.[27]

3 Powers relating to foreign affairs.[28] The conduct of foreign affairs by the government is carried on mainly by reliance on the prerogative, for example, the making of treaties, the declaration of war and the making of peace. The prerogative includes power to acquire additional territory; thus by royal warrant in 1955, the Crown took possession of the island of Rockall, subsequently incorporated into the United Kingdom as part of Scotland by the Island of Rockall Act 1972. It is doubtful whether the Crown may by treaty cede British territory without the authority of Parliament and modern practice is to secure parliamentary approval[29] but it seems that the prerogative includes power to declare or to alter the limits of British territorial waters.[30] The phrase 'act of state' is often used to refer to acts of the Crown in foreign affairs: while these acts would often fall within the scope of the prerogative, there is an argument for confining the concept of the prerogative to powers of the Crown exercised in relation to its own subjects and not applying the concept to acts of the Crown performed in foreign territory in relation to aliens, over which British courts have no jurisdiction.[31]

---

23 *R.* v. *Criminal Injuries Compensation Board, ex p. Lain* [1967] 2 Q.B. 864, 886; *cf.* H. W. R. Wade, *Constitutional Fundamentals*, pp. 47–8.
24 Ch. 19.
25 Page 332 *post.*
26 Ch. 24.
27 *Gouriet* v. *Union of Post Office Workers* [1978] A.C. 435, p. 662 *post.*
28 Ch. 18.
29 Anson, II, ii, pp. 137–42; and Roberts-Wray, *op. cit.*, ch. 4.
30 *R.* v. *Kent JJ, ex parte Lye* [1967] 2 Q.B. 153; cf. W. R. Edeson (1973) 89 L.Q.R. 364.
31 See *In re Ferdinand, Ex-Tsar of Bulgaria* [1921] 1 Ch. 107, 139; the varying opinions on the application of prerogative abroad in *Nissan* v. *A.-G.* [1970] A.C. 179; and ch. 18 B.

The Crown has power under the prerogative to restrain aliens from entering the United Kingdom; but it is uncertain whether the Crown has a prerogative power to expel aliens who have been permitted to reside here. Today, powers over aliens are exercised under the Immigration Act 1971, although that Act expressly reserves such prerogative powers as the Crown may have (section 33(5)). The issue of passports to citizens is based on the prerogative.[32] At common law the Crown could restrain a person from leaving the realm when the interests of state demanded it by means of the writ *ne exeat regno*, but it is doubtful whether the power should today be exercised except in circumstances governed by the Debtors Act 1869;[33] in time of war the Crown may possibly under the prerogative restrain a British subject from leaving the realm or recall him from abroad, but during modern wars entry and exit have been controlled by statutory powers.

4 Powers relating to the armed forces.[34]   Both by prerogative and by statute the Sovereign is commander-in-chief of the armed forces of the Crown. The Bill of Rights 1689 prohibited the keeping of a standing army within the realm in time of peace without the consent of Parliament; thus the authority of Parliament is required for the maintenance of the army, the Royal Air Force and other forces serving on land. Although many matters regarding the armed forces are regulated by statute, their control, organisation and disposition are within the prerogative and cannot be questioned in a court.[35] But members of the armed forces and the Ministry of Defence may be held liable for unlawful acts which infringe the rights of individuals.

5 Appointments and honours.[36]   On the advice of the Prime Minister or other ministers, the Sovereign appoints ministers, judges, magistrates and many other holders of public office, including the members of royal commissions to inquire into matters of controversy. Appointments to the civil service are appointments to the service of the Crown. The Sovereign is the sole fountain of honour and alone can create peers, confer honours and decorations, grant arms and regulate matters of precedence.[37] Honours are generally conferred by the Sovereign on the advice of the Prime Minister, who is advised by three Privy Councillors acting as a Political Honours Scrutiny Committee on the character and antecedents of those whom it is proposed to honour for political services.[38] Certain honours, namely the Order of the Garter, the Order of the Thistle, the Royal Victoria Order (for personal services to the Sovereign) and the Order of Merit are in the personal gift of the Sovereign.

6 Immunities and privileges.   The Crown benefits from the principle of interpretation that statutes do not bind the Crown unless by express statement

---

[32]   Ch. 25 A.
[33]   J. W. Bridge (1972) 88 L.Q.R. 83; *Parsons* v. *Burk* [1971] N.Z.L.R. 244; and *Felton* v. *Callis* [1969] 1 Q.B. 200.
[34]   Ch. 23.
[35]   *China Navigation Co. Ltd* v. *A.-G.* [1932] 2 K.B. 197; *Chandler* v. *DPP* [1964] A.C. 763; Crown Proceedings Act 1947, s. 11.
[36]   Jennings, *Cabinet Government*, ch. 14; P. G. Richards, *Patronage in British Government*, ch. 10.
[37]   A. Wagner and G. D. Squibb (1973) 80 L.Q.R. 352.
[38]   Cmd 1789, 1922; Honours (Prevention of Abuses) Act 1925.

or necessary implication it is evident that Parliament intends this to be the case. Thus tax is not payable on income received by the Sovereign as such, nor in respect of Crown property, nor on income received on behalf of the Crown by a servant of the Crown in the course of official duties.[39] Many of the privileges and immunities of the Crown in civil litigation were removed by the Crown Proceedings Act 1947, but the Crown and central departments still have certain privileges. For example, under the 1947 Act the remedies of injunction and specific performance are not available against the Crown. The 1947 Act also preserved the personal immunity of the Sovereign from being sued.[40]

7 The prerogative in time of emergency. The extent of the prerogative in times of grave emergency cannot be precisely stated. That prerogative powers were wide was admitted by Hampden's counsel in the *Case of Ship Money*, nor, save in regard to taxation, were they abridged by the Bill of Rights. In 1964, Lord Reid said: 'The prerogative certainly covers doing all those things in an emergency which are necessary for the conduct of war'; but he added that there was difficulty in relating the prerogative to modern conditions since no modern war had been waged without statutory powers.

The mobilisation of the industrial and financial resources of the country could not be done without statutory emergency powers. The prerogative is really a relic of a past age, not lost by disuse but only available for a case not covered by statute.[41]

According to the old law, in time of sudden invasion or insurrection, the King might demand personal service within the realm.[42] Either the Crown or a subject might invade the land of another to erect fortifications for the defence of the realm.[43] But it is not certain whether this should be regarded as an aspect of the prerogative since it was a duty shared by the Crown with all its subjects. The difficulty of applying the old common law in modern circumstances was evident in *Burmah Oil Company* v. *Lord Advocate*.[44]

In 1942 extensive oil installations were destroyed by British troops in Rangoon, not accidentally as a result of fighting but deliberately so as to prevent the installations falling into enemy hands. One day later, the Japanese army entered Rangoon. After receiving some £4 million from the British government as an *ex gratia* payment, the company sued the Lord Advocate representing the Crown in Scotland for over £31 million. It was agreed that the destruction had not been ordered under statutory authority and the company claimed compensation for the lawful exercise of prerogative power. The House of Lords held (a) that, as a general rule, compensation was payable by the Crown to the subject who was deprived of his property for the benefit of the state, by prerogative act in relation to war and (b) that the destruction of the refineries did not fall within the 'battle damage' exception to the general rule. But the House left open the basis on which compensation should be assessed.

---

39 *Bank voor Handel en Scheepvaart NV* v. *Administrator of Hungarian Property* [1954] A.C. 584; and p. 235 *ante*.

40 Ch. 36.

41 *Burmah Oil Co. Ltd* v. *Lord Advocate* [1965] A.C. 75, 101; and see ch. 29 B.

42 Chitty, *Prerogatives of the Crown*, p. 49.

43 *The Case of the King's Prerogative in Saltpetre* (1607) 12 Co. Rep. 12.

44 [1965] A.C. 75, discussed by A. L. Goodhart (1966) 82 L.Q.R. 97; T. C. Daintith (1965) 14 I.C.L.Q. 1000; and in (1966) 79 *Harvard Law Review* 614.

This decision established that where private property was taken under the prerogative, the owner was entitled at common law to compensation from the Crown; but the War Damage Act 1965 retrospectively provided that no person should be entitled at common law to receive compensation in respect of damage to or destruction of property caused by lawful acts of the Crown 'during, or in contemplation of the outbreak of, a war in which the Sovereign is or was engaged'. This Act prevented the Burmah Oil Company's claim from succeeding but its effect was limited to acts of the Crown which destroyed property during or in contemplation of a war; the principle that the Crown is obliged to pay compensation for property taken under the prerogative for use of the armed forces still seems to apply.[45]

The principle that compensation may be payable for lawful acts of the prerogative was already known before the *Burmah Oil* case. Thus the Crown may under prerogative requisition British ships in time of urgent national necessity, but compensation is payable, as it was in 1982 when British ships were requisitioned for use in the recapture of the Falkland Islands.[46] By the right of angary, the Crown may in time of war appropriate the property of a neutral which is within the realm where necessity requires, but compensation must be paid.[47] In both world wars, statutory powers of requisitioning property have been conferred on the Crown, and compensation has been paid. But if, for example, an emergency arose in which it was necessary for the armed forces to take immediate action against terrorist action within the United Kingdom, it is possible both that private property needed for this purpose could be occupied under prerogative and that compensation would at common law be payable to the owners.

8 Miscellaneous prerogatives.   Other historic prerogative powers, concerning matters which are today largely regulated by statute, relate to: the creation of corporations by royal charter; the guardianship of infants (a prerogative jurisdiction exercised through the High Court and not excluded by the statutory powers of local authorities);[48] the right to mine precious metals; coinage; the grant of franchises, for example markets, ferries and fisheries; the right to treasure trove;[49] the sole right of printing or licensing others to print the Authorised Version of the Bible,[50] the Book of Common Prayer and state papers.[51]

The effect of statutes upon prerogative powers

Parliament may expressly abolish or restrict prerogative rights, whether or not

---

45   *E.g. Nissan* v. *A.-G.* [1970] A.C. 179, 229 (Lord Pearce).
46   Requisitioning of Ships Order 1982 (printed in *Statutory Instruments 1982*, p. 1693). And see *Crown of Leon* v. *Admiralty Commissioners* [1921] 1 K.B. 595; W. S. Holdsworth (1919) 35 L.Q.R. 12.
47   *Commercial and Estates Co. of Egypt* v. *Board of Trade* [1925] 1 K.B. 271. And see W. I. Jennings (1927) 3 C.L.J. 1.
48   *In re M.* [1961] Ch. 328.
49   Treasure trove, *i.e.* gold or silver objects which have been hidden and of which no owner can be traced, is the property of the Crown; *A.-G. of Duchy of Lancaster* v. *G. E. Overton (Farms) Ltd.* [1982] Ch. 277.
50   *Universities of Oxford and Cambridge* v. *Eyre & Spottiswoode Ltd* [1964] Ch. 736 (royal prerogative did not extend to New English Bible).
51   Copyright Act 1956, s. 39.

coupling this with the grant of statutory powers in the same area of government. But often Parliament has not expressly abolished prerogative rights but has merely created a statutory scheme dealing with the same subject. Where this is the case, must the Crown proceed under the statutory powers or may it rely instead upon the prerogative?

In *Attorney-General* v. *De Keyser's Royal Hotel*[52] an hotel was required for housing the administrative staff of the Royal Flying Corps during the First World War. The Army Council offered to hire the hotel at a rent, but, negotiations having broken down, a letter was sent on the instruction of the Army Council stating that possession was being taken under the Defence of the Realm Acts and Regulations. A petition of right was later brought against the Crown claiming compensation as of right for the use of the hotel by the authorities.

It was argued for the Crown that there was a prerogative to take the land of the subject in case of emergency in time of war; that no compensation was payable as of right for land so taken; and that this power could be exercised, notwithstanding provisions of the Defence Act 1842 which had been incorporated into the Defence of the Realm Acts and provided for statutory compensation as of right to the owners. The argument for the owners of the hotel was that the Crown had taken possession under the statutes and so could not fall back on the prerogative.

The House of Lords rejected the argument of the Crown, holding that on the facts the Crown had taken possession under statutory powers. The House also held that the prerogative had been superseded for the time being by the statute. The Crown could not revert to prerogative powers when the legislature had given to the Crown statutory powers which covered all that could be necessary for the defence of the nation, and which were accompanied by important safeguards to the individual. Thus for the duration of the statutory powers, the prerogative was in abeyance. The House therefore did not have to decide whether the Crown had a prerogative power to requisition land in time of war without paying compensation, but serious doubts were expressed about this claim.[53]

The principle in this case, namely that the conferment of statutory powers upon the Crown[54] may prevent the Crown from using prerogative powers which otherwise would have been available to it, applies only when Parliament has not given an express indication of its intention. Thus the Immigration Act 1971 provided that the powers which it conferred should be additional to any prerogative powers (section 33(5)), as did the Emergency Powers (Defence) Act 1939.[55] The question whether a prerogative power has been swallowed up by a wider statutory power may depend on whether the statute has imposed conditions or restrictions on the power to which the court attaches significance.[56]

The prerogative and the courts

Some prerogative acts are unlikely to give rise to the possibility of challenge in the courts, for example the conferment of an honour or the dissolution of Parliament. But where an act purporting to be done under the prerogative directly affects the rights of an individual, the courts may be asked to determine the following issues:

---

[52] [1920] A.C. 508.
[53] See the *Burmah Oil* case, *ante.*
[54] And possibly even upon other public authorities: *In re M.* [1961] Ch. 328.
[55] Ch. 29 B.
[56] *Sabally and Njie* v. *A.-G.* [1965] 1 Q.B. 273, per Russell L. J.

1 The existence and extent of a prerogative power. In principle the courts will not recognise the existence of new prerogative powers. In *Entick* v. *Carrington*, in which the court held that the mere plea of state necessity would not protect anyone accused of an unlawful act, Lord Camden C. J. said, 'If it is law, it will be found in our books. If it is not to be found there, it is not law'.[57] And in 1964 Diplock L. J. said,

it is 350 years and a civil war too late for the Queen's courts to broaden the prerogative. The limits within which the executive government may impose obligations or restraints on citizens of the United Kingdom without any statutory authority are now well settled and incapable of extension.[58]

But some prerogative powers are very wide and difficulties arise when the courts are asked to decide whether an ancient power applies in a new situation; for example, whether the Crown's power to act in situations of grave national emergency justifies action to deal with a wholly new form of terrorist activity which threatens the nation, or whether the prerogative right to intercept postal communications justifies the tapping of telephones.[59] In these situations, it may be difficult to distinguish between creating a new prerogative and applying an old prerogative to new circumstances. Do the courts have power to rule that an ancient prerogative has become so unsuited to modern conditions that it can no longer be relied on by the Crown? In general, rules of common law do not lapse through desuetude.[60] But it is difficult to see why a court should be required to give new life to an archaic power which offends modern constitutional principles, merely because its existence had been recognised several centuries ago

2 Whether a public authority or official is entitled to benefit from the prerogative. Central government departments, ministers and civil servants may usually act for the Crown. But what of public corporations, nationalised industries, hospital boards and so on? Often the parent Act states expressly whether an authority is entitled to benefit from immunities or privileges of the Crown. Where this is not the case, the courts have to decide the question.[61]

3 Whether statute has affected the existence or exercise of a prerogative power. This has already been discussed.

4 Whether official action was taken under prerogative or statute. This had to be decided in the *De Keyser's Royal Hotel* case.

5 Whether the exercise of prerogative imposes a duty on the Crown to compensate the citizen. As the *Burmah* Oil case showed, there are

57 (1765) 19 St. Tr. 1030, 1066: p. 93 *ante. Entick's* case was distinguished in *Malone* v. *Metropolitan Police Commissioner* [1979] Ch. 344 (no evidence of unlawful act in tapping telephones); p. 572 *post.*
58 *BBC* v. *Johns* [1965] Ch. 32, 79.
59 *Cf.* Cmnd 283, 1957; ch. 30. In *Malone's* case (*ante*, n. 57), no claim of prerogative power was made.
60 Maitland, *History*, p. 418; cf. *Nyali Ltd* v. *A.-G.* [1956] 1 Q.B. 1 and *McKendrick* v. *Sinclair* 1972 S.C. (H.L.) 25, 60–1.
61 For the case-law, see pp. 302–3 *post.*

various prerogative powers which, when exercised against private property, give rise at common law to a right in the owner to receive compensation.[62]

Although the courts have power to decide these five issues, in general they may not go further and review on its merits the exercise of an admitted prerogative power. It is not for a judge to substitute his own view of what the public interest requires for the decision of a government department, acting within its powers. Thus, since the disposition of the armed forces is a matter for the Crown, the courts may not consider whether the Crown's discretion has been wisely exercised;[63] nor is it for the courts to say whether the government should enter into a particular treaty[64] or whether the Home Secretary has properly advised the Sovereign regarding the prerogative of mercy.[65] In *Chandler* v. *DPP*, Lord Devlin said, 'The courts will not review the proper exercise of discretionary power but they will intervene to correct excess or abuse'.[66] 'Excess' means action which exceeds the limits of the prerogative (see 1 above). But what would constitute an abuse of the prerogative? In the case of a statutory power, the courts may quash action taken for improper purposes or in bad faith, *i.e.* where the motives or reasons for the action fall outside the purposes which Parliament is held to have had in mind when conferring the power.[67] In the case of a prerogative power, it would presumably be necessary to show analogous vitiating factors before abuse of the prerogative could be established.

In *Laker Airways Ltd* v. *Department of Trade*, the Court of Appeal held *inter alia* that the Crown's prerogative action in cancelling the designation of an airline under a treaty made in 1946 with the USA was unlawful, since the cancellation nullified a licence granted earlier under statutory powers.[68] This decision rested essentially on the principle in the *De Keyser's Royal Hotel* case, and thus is an instance of excess rather than abuse. In the *Laker* case, Lord Denning MR went further, saying that the use of prerogative power could be examined by the courts just as any other power that is vested in the executive. However, in respect of the Attorney-General's discretion in giving consent to the bringing of relator actions, the House of Lords held in *Gouriet* v. *Union of Post Office Workers* that the courts may not review the exercise of that discretion.[69] In the absence of case-law illustrating the notion of abuse of prerogative, caution is required, but it is submitted that *Gouriet's* case does not apply to all prerogative powers, and that judicial protection against abuse of power should extend to prerogative as well as to statutory powers. In 1984, the House of Lords accepted such arguments in principle, but held that a prerogative decision based on national security could not be reviewed.[70]

---

62 Page 251 *ante*.
63 Note 35 *ante*.
64 *Blackburn* v. *A.-G.* [1971] 2 All E.R. 1380.
65 *Hanratty* v. *Lord Butler* (1971) 115 S.J. 386, discussed by A.T.H. Smith [1983] P.L. 398, 432.
66 [1964] A.C. 763, 810.
67 Ch. 34 A.
68 [1977] Q.B. 643, p. 628 *post*.
69 [1978] A.C. 435, p. 662 *post*.
70 For the GCHQ case, see p. 283 *post*.

Chapter 14

The Cabinet, ministers and government departments

A. Cabinet and Prime Minister

As organs of government, the Cabinet and the office of Prime Minister have evolved together since the 18th century. Their existence is recognised in occasional statutes (for example, the Ministerial and other Salaries Act 1975) but their powers of government derive neither from statute nor from common law administered in the courts. Parliament could confer powers directly upon the Prime Minister or upon the Cabinet. In practice this rarely happens, statutory powers being conferred either upon named ministers or upon the Queen in Council. Yet the Prime Minister and the Cabinet occupy key places at the heart of the political and governmental system.[1] As the Prime Minister provides the individual leadership of the majority party in the House of Commons, so the Cabinet provides the collective leadership of that party.[2] If national affairs are to be directed in any systematic way, if deliberate choices in government between competing political priorities are to be made, these decisions can be made only by the Prime Minister and the Cabinet. In the past, descriptions of the British system of government often labelled it Cabinet government. As L. S. Amery wrote,

The central directing instrument of government, in legislation as well as in administration, is the Cabinet. It is in Cabinet that administrative action is co-ordinated and that legislative proposals are sanctioned. It is the Cabinet which controls Parliament and governs the country.[3]

But recently more emphasis has been placed on the role of the Prime Minister and less on the Cabinet itself. In 1963, when he had not yet served as a Cabinet minister, Richard Crossman wrote: 'The post-war epoch has seen the

---

[1] Bagehot's celebrated description of the Cabinet in *The English Constitution*, pp. 65–9 must still be read, though his definition of the Cabinet as 'a committee of the legislative body selected to be the executive body' is misleading. For general accounts, see Jennings, *Cabinet Government*; Mackintosh, *The British Cabinet*; P. Gordon Walker, *The Cabinet*; H. Daalder, *Cabinet Reform in Britain 1914–1963*; and H. Wilson, *The Governance of Britain*.

[2] Gordon Walker, p. 56.

[3] *Thoughts on the Constitution*, p. 70.

final transformation of Cabinet government into Prime Ministerial government', arguing that the Cabinet had joined the Crown and the House of Lords as one of the 'dignified' elements in the constitution.[4] There is no doubt that the Prime Minister commands a formidable range of political and governmental powers, but it would be wrong to suppose that he therefore can govern without recourse to the Cabinet. Even in the earlier accounts of Cabinet government, the leader's role was stressed: thus Amery cited Morley's description of the Prime Minister as the 'keystone of the Cabinet Arch', and added:

It is his Cabinet and he has in large measure created it; he can at any time change its composition; his is the decisive voice in bringing it to an end by dissolution or resignation.[5]

Having served in the Cabinets of Eden and Macmillan, Lord Home said, 'if the Cabinet discusses anything it is the Prime Minister who decides what the collective view of the Cabinet is'.[6] Different styles of political leadership exist but Cabinet and Prime Minister depend upon each other. Moreover it must be stressed that the Cabinet system today refers not merely to a meeting once or twice a week of some 20 leading ministers but to a complex structure for the co-ordination of the activities of departments and for the formulation of the collective policies of the government.

Composition of the Cabinet

A modern Cabinet usually consists of between 18 members (Mr Heath's Cabinet in 1970) and 24 members (Mr Callaghan's in 1979). No statute regulates the composition of the Cabinet, but there are both administrative and political constraints on the Prime Minister's freedom of choice. Thus in peace-time it is impossible to exclude certain offices, such as the Home Secretary, the Foreign Secretary, the Lord Chancellor and the Secretary of State for Scotland. In addition to the Secretaries of State and ministers in charge of the major departments, every Cabinet includes two or three members with few if any departmental responsibilities, for example, the Lord President of the Council, who is often also Leader of the House of Commons; the Lord Privy Seal, often also Leader of the House of Lords; and the Chancellor of the Duchy of Lancaster. These ministers may assist the Prime Minister on special issues or co-ordinate different aspects of a single problem, and they often serve as chairmen of Cabinet committees. Since 1951, the government chief whip in the Commons, whose formal title is Parliamentary Secretary to the Treasury, has regularly attended Cabinet[7] but only rarely, as in 1975, has he been a member of it. The Law Officers of the Crown[8] are not appointed to the Cabinet but, like other ministers outside the Cabinet, the Attorney-General and his Scottish counterpart, the Lord Advocate, may attend Cabinet meetings for particular matters.

---

4 Introduction to Bagehot, pp. 51, 54. See also H. Berkeley, *The Power of the Prime Minister*, and Mackintosh, ch. 24; *cf.* A. H. Brown [1968] P.L. 28, 96.
5 Amery, *op. cit.*, p. 73.
6 Quoted in Mackintosh, p. 628.
7 Gordon Walker, p. 104.
8 Ch. 19 C.

The size of the Cabinet is primarily determined by practical and political considerations. But the number of salaried Cabinet posts is limited by statute: apart from the Prime Minister and the Lord Chancellor, not more than 20 salaries may be paid to Cabinet ministers at one time.[9] Political necessity requires that all members of the Cabinet are members of the Commons or the Lords, unless a minister is actively seeking election to the Commons at a by-election or is to be created a life peer.[10] In practice at least two Cabinet officers (Lord Chancellor and Leader of the House of Lords) will be held by peers but more may be appointed. In all modern governments there have been some ministers with departmental responsibilities who are outside the Cabinet. They may serve on Cabinet committees, will see Cabinet papers relating to their departments and may be asked to attend Cabinet meetings. The amalgamation of departments to form larger departments which took place during the 1960s[11] meant that all major departments were placed under the supervision of a Cabinet minister.

During the two world wars, the normal Cabinet was superseded by a small War Cabinet to take charge of the conduct of the war. In 1916 the War Cabinet consisted of five, later six, senior ministers, of whom only the Chancellor of the Exchequer had departmental duties. The War Cabinet of 1939–45 was larger, varying between seven and ten, including several senior departmental ministers.[12]

The Prime Minister

Like the Cabinet, the office of Prime Minister has evolved as a matter of political expediency and constitutional practice rather than of law. Though he did not recognise the title, Robert Walpole is now regarded as having been the first Prime Minister when he was First Lord of the Treasury, from 1721 to 1742. William Pitt the younger did much to create the modern office of Prime Minister in the years after 1784. In fact the post acquired its present form only with the advent of the modern party system and the creation of the present machinery of government. For most of its history, the office of Prime Minister has been held together with a recognised post, usually that of First Lord of the Treasury. Between 1895 and 1900 Lord Salisbury was both Prime Minister and Foreign Secretary, and between 1900 and 1902 he was Prime Minister and Lord Privy Seal; during these years A. J. Balfour was First Lord of the Treasury and Leader of the Commons. Since 1902, the offices of Prime Minister and First Lord of the Treasury have always been held together by a member of the Commons. In 1905, by act of the prerogative, the Prime Minister was given precedence next after the Archbishop of York[13] and his existence is recognised by occasional statutes.[14] Since 1937, statutory provision of a salary and a pension has assumed that the Prime Minister is also First

---

9   Ministerial and other Salaries Act 1975.
10   Page 21 *ante*.
11   Page 272 *post*.
12   For the War Cabinet, see 8th ed. of this book, 1970, pp. 201, 203–7; Jennings, *Cabinet Government*, ch. 10; and Mackintosh, ch. 14 and pp. 490–99.
13   *London Gazette*, 5 Dec. 1905.
14   *E.g.* Chequers Estate Act 1917; Chevening Estate Act 1959; Ministerial and other Salaries Act 1975. And see n. 8, p. 230 *ante*.

Lord of the Treasury. In the latter capacity, the Prime Minister is one of the Treasury ministers, although the financial and economic duties of the Treasury are borne primarily by the Chancellor of the Exchequer. Exceptionally, the Prime Minister may decide also to hold another office: Ramsay MacDonald was both Prime Minister and Foreign Secretary in the first Labour government in 1924. During World War II, Churchill assumed the title of Minister of Defence, although without a separate ministry and without his duties being defined. When the Civil Service Department was established in 1968,[15] the Prime Minister became the minister for the department, although another Cabinet minister undertook the regular administration of the department on the Prime Minister's behalf.

The approval of the Prime Minister is required for appointment of the most senior civil servants *i.e.* the permanent heads and deputy heads of departments and principal finance and establishment officers. The most important Crown appointments are filled on his nomination, for example, the senior judges, the bishops, the chairman of the BBC and the Parliamentary Commissioner for Administration. He also advises the Sovereign on new peerages, on appointments to the Privy Council and the grant of honours,[16] and the filling of those chairs in English universities which are in the gift of the Crown. In respect of these appointments, the Prime Minister's freedom of action may to a greater or lesser extent be restricted by conventions requiring prior consultation with the interests affected. Nonetheless, the Prime Minister's extensive patronage can be used for political purposes, particularly in appointing to the boards of nationalised industries and other public corporations.[17]

Powers of Prime Minister in relation to the Cabinet

Although each Prime Minister must adopt his or her own style of leadership, the Prime Minister is in a position to exercise a dominant influence over the Cabinet since he has powers which other ministers do not have, however senior and experienced they may be.

1   He effectively makes all appointments to ministerial office, whether within or outside the Cabinet. He may ask ministers to resign, recommend the Sovereign to dismiss them or, with their consent, move them to other offices. In June 1962, in an attempt to regain popularity for his administration, Harold Macmillan removed from office seven ministers out of a Cabinet of 20 members. The Prime Minister settles the order of precedence in the Cabinet. He may if he wishes name one of the Cabinet to be Deputy Prime Minister[18] or First Secretary of State. These powers are exercised in a political context. In forming his first Cabinet, a new Prime Minister will be expected to appoint from the senior members of his party; and a leading politician may be able to stipulate the Cabinet post which he is prepared to accept. But the

---

15   Ch. 15.
16   Some honours are granted on the advice of other ministers, *e.g.* the Foreign Secretary and the Defence Secretary. Some appointments are made on the recommendation of other ministers, *e.g.* High Court judgeships on the recommendation of the Lord Chancellor.
17   See T. Benn (1980) 33 *Parliamentary Affairs* 7.
18   In 1951, George VI refused to appoint Anthony Eden to this 'non-existent' office: Wheeler-Bennett, *King George VI*, p. 797.

refusal of an individual to serve under a Prime Minister or the resignation of a minister may be merely a gesture of dissociation from the Prime Minister and his policies or mode of government, and is seldom a real threat to him.

2   The Prime Minister controls the machinery of central government in that he decides how the tasks of government should be allocated to the different departments and whether departments should be created, amalgamated or abolished. Thus in 1981 Mrs Thatcher abolished the Civil Service Department and divided its duties between the Treasury and a new Management and Personnel Office.[19]

3   The Prime Minister is able to take interest in different areas of government from time to time and may indeed carry out his policy through the agency of a minister whom he has appointed. Most Prime Ministers must take a special interest in foreign affairs, the economy and defence. The Prime Minister may intervene personally in major industrial disputes and other pressing issues. In consultation with individual ministers he may take decisions or authorise them to be taken without waiting for a Cabinet meeting. When a Cabinet committee is dealing with a problem, the Prime Minister may take the chair and report on action taken to a later Cabinet meeting.

4   By presiding at Cabinet meetings, the Prime Minister is able to control Cabinet discussions and the process of decision-making by settling the order of business, deciding which items are to be discussed[20] and by taking the sense of the meeting rather than by counting the votes of Cabinet members. While the Cabinet Secretariat provides services for the whole Cabinet, it owes a special responsibility to the Prime Minister; disputes over minutes are if necessary settled by him.

5   Compared with other ministers, the Prime Minister has a more regular opportunity to present and defend the government's policies in Parliament. He is available for questioning in the Commons on Tuesdays and Thursdays at 3.15 p.m. and he may choose when to intervene in debates. He is also in a position to control the government's communications to the press and to disclose information about government decisions and Cabinet business.[21]

6   Alone among Cabinet ministers, he has regular meetings with the Sovereign and is responsible for keeping the Sovereign informed of the Cabinet's handling of affairs. In particular, he may recommend to the Sovereign that a general election be held, and he is not required to discuss this first with the Cabinet.[22]

It does not follow from this accumulation of powers that the Prime Minister can assume the detailed direction of all departments of government. Departmental ministers are expected to deal with their own business. Nor can a Prime Minister ensure continued support from his party, from the Commons or from the electorate. But his position at the centre of government is unique. In 1889, it was said, 'The flexibility of the Cabinet system allows the Prime Minister

---

[19]   Ch. 15.
[20]   Mackintosh, p. 449, asserts that the Prime Minister can keep any item off the agenda indefinitely but the examples he gives do not support this. *Cf.* H. Wilson, *The Governance of Britain*, p. 47.
[21]   See J. Margach, *The Abuse of Power*.
[22]   Ch. 13 A.

in an emergency to take upon himself a power not inferior to that of a dictator, provided always that the House of Commons will stand by him'.[23] In 1984, the indications were that the Prime Minister, Mrs Thatcher, had since 1979 gained authority at the expense of her Cabinet. The Cabinet and the system of departments still provide the framework for much of the business of government; nor could a Prime Minister continue in office if Cabinet ministers withdrew their support. But Mrs Thatcher's government was by no means the first in which many important decisions were made outside the Cabinet, whether by the Prime Minister alone or in consultation with a few senior ministers, or by Cabinet committees.

Cabinet committees[24]

The increase in the scale of government since 1900 has not been accompanied by a corresponding increase in the size of the Cabinet. Few problems of government can be solved by a single department acting on its own, if only because most policy decisions have expenditure and manpower implications (hence the interest of the Treasury in all new policies). The Cabinet could not have kept abreast of its work had there not developed under its umbrella a complicated structure of committees. In the 19th century, Cabinet committees were appointed for particular purposes (for example, to keep under review the conduct of the Crimean War). They were used much more frequently after 1918. Two main factors led to the appointment of a system of permanent committees. The first was the creation of the Committee of Imperial Defence in 1903, which showed the value of a permanent committee charged with a major policy area;[25] the second was the experience in two world wars of a system of specialised committees to deal with defined policy areas which operated under the authority of a small War Cabinet. In 1945, the Labour government decided to adapt the war-time system to the problems of peace. Since then, a structure of standing committees has remained an important feature of the Cabinet system.

Successive governments have sought to keep secret the functions, composition and even the existence of most Cabinet committees. Various reasons have been advanced for this: that the existence of the committees is not intended to affect the collective responsibility of the whole Cabinet; that public knowledge of the existence and composition of committees would give rise to inconvenient public criticism and lobbying; and so on.[26] Yet the terms of reference and composition of the Committee on Defence and Overseas Policy have been published.[27] In 1973, the Conservative Cabinet was surmised to have 16 named committees, including committees on home and social policy, economic policy, prices and incomes, regional and environmental policy, industrial relations, European relations, agriculture, broadcasting, immigra-

---

23   From Morley, *Walpole*, pp. 154–60 quoted in H. J. Hanham, *The Nineteenth-Century Constitution, 1815–1914*, p. 90.
24   Jennings, *Cabinet Government*, pp. 255–61; Mackintosh, pp. 521–9; Gordon Walker, pp. 38–47; H. Wilson, *The Governance of Britain*, pp. 62–8.
25   Jennings, *op. cit.*, ch. 10; Daalder, *op. cit.*, ch. 9.
26   For a personal minute by Mr Callaghan, when Prime Minister, see *New Statesman*, 10 Nov. 1978. *Cf. The Times*, 3 May 1973.
27   Cmnd 2097, 1963.

tion and community relations.[28] In addition *ad hoc* committees of a more or less temporary nature may be appointed to deal with problems of home or overseas policy or proposals for new developments in government. In 1979, Mrs Thatcher stated that she had established four standing committees of the Cabinet: a defence and overseas policy committee and an economic strategy committee, both under her chairmanship; a home and social affairs committee chaired by the Home Secretary; and a legislation committee chaired by the Lord Chancellor. But she refused to give more information than this, apart from adding that sub-committees and other committees would be set up as required.[29] During the Falkland Islands campaign in 1982, British policies were directed by a committee comprising the Prime Minister and four other Cabinet ministers.

One function of Cabinet committees is to secure co-ordination between different departments concerned with the same problem. A committee composed of ministers, who need not all be Cabinet members, is often paralleled by a committee of officials from the same departments.[30] The duty of a committee is often to prepare a subject for decision by the Cabinet, defining the common ground between departments and the issues still in dispute. But a Cabinet committee may be authorised to take decisions on behalf of the Cabinet. In 1967, Mr Wilson ruled that matters were to be taken to the Cabinet from a committee only with the agreement of the committee's chairman, a ruling which reduced the pressure on Cabinet business but also restricted the right of an individual minister to obtain a decision by the full Cabinet.[31] Where a committee is appointed to direct the government's actions in an urgent situation, for example, the Suez operation in 1956, the committee is exercising the authority of the full Cabinet and has been described as a 'partial' Cabinet,[32] but it is difficult to see why a 'partial' Cabinet has greater authority to act than a Cabinet committee.

In March 1968, the Wilson government established what was called the Parliamentary Committee of the Cabinet, consisting of about ten members of the Cabinet. This was intended to discuss political and parliamentary problems raised with the Committee by the Prime Minister. This committee was referred to by its progenitor as a management committee or inner Cabinet[33] and its existence enabled meetings of the full Cabinet to be held less frequently. In April 1969, the Home Secretary, Mr Callaghan, was removed from this committee because he had expressed disagreement with the government's industrial relations policy. While in any Cabinet the Prime Minister is likely to turn to a few ministers for close discussion and political advice, it is unusual for the group of advisers to be identified in this way.

---

28   *The Times*, 3 May 1973. See also Gordon Walker, pp. 174–5; R. Crossman, *The Diaries of a Cabinet Minister*, vol. I, pp. 198 and 280.

29   H.C. Deb., 24 May 1979, col. 179 (W.A.). See also H.C. Deb., 29 Nov. 1979, col. 540 (W.A.) and *The Times*, 10 Feb. 1981.

30   After Crossman had discovered the existence of these official committees, he commented, 'This is the way in which Whitehall ensures that the Cabinet system is relatively harmless': *op. cit.*, p. 198.

31   Gordon Walker, p. 44; J. P. Mackintosh, *The Times*, 21 Jun. 1968.

32   Gordon Walker, pp. 87–9.

33   H. Wilson, *op. cit.*, pp. 663, 811, 816; Mackintosh, *The Times*, 21 Jun. 1968.

The Cabinet Office[34]

Before 1917, there was no regular machinery for preparing the agenda for Cabinet meetings, circulating documents or recording decisions. Each Prime Minister sent his own accounts of Cabinet meetings to the Sovereign and members of the Cabinet took note of matters requiring action by their departments. On a major constitutional issue, for example, the creation of peers to coerce the House of Lords into approving the Parliament Bill in 1911, the Sovereign could require the Cabinet's advice to be recorded in writing. But in general there was often uncertainty about the actual decisions. In 1917, to enable the War Cabinet and its system of committees to function efficiently, a Secretary to the Cabinet was appointed to be present at meetings of the Cabinet and its committees, to circulate minutes of the conclusions reached, to communicate decisions rapidly to those who had to act on them and also to circulate papers before meetings. The first Secretary was Sir Maurice Hankey, who applied to the Cabinet methods which he had developed as Secretary of the Committee of Imperial Defence. The secretariat has been maintained ever since, sometimes in an uneasy relationship with the Treasury. It is headed by the Secretary of the Cabinet, who in 1984 was also Permanent Secretary to the Management and Personnel Office and Head of the Home Civil Service.

The conclusions prepared by the Secretary to the Cabinet and circulated to the Sovereign and Cabinet ministers are the only official record of Cabinet meetings. This account is designed to record agreement and not controversy. Differences of opinion in discussion are not attributed to individuals, although the arguments for and against a decision may be summarised: 'behind many of the decisions lay tensions and influences which are not reflected in the official records'.[35]

The Cabinet Office has no executive functions like those of a department. It seeks to secure inter-departmental co-ordination by circulating documents before meetings and providing a formal record of decisions. While the Cabinet Office is responsible to the Prime Minister, it does not seek to operate as a 'Prime Minister's Department', although on one recent view, everything that a Prime Minister could create 'is already there to hand in the Cabinet Office'.[36] Within the Cabinet Office there are also the Central Statistical Office and the chief scientific adviser to the government. From time to time other units are created for co-ordinating government policy on key issues, for example, negotiations regarding British entry into the EEC in 1970–2 and devolution policy in 1975–7.

In 1970 there was established within the Cabinet Office a small multi-disciplinary unit, known as the Central Policy Review Staff (or 'think-tank'). Its task was to enable ministers collectively to work out the implications of

---

[34] Jennings, *Cabinet Government*, pp. 242–5; Gordon Walker, pp. 47–55; R. K. Mosley, *The Story of the Cabinet Office*; S. S. Wilson, *The Cabinet Office to 1945; The Times*, 8 Mar. 1976; H. Wilson, *The Governance of Britain*, ch. 4.

[35] S. S. Wilson, *op. cit.*, p. 4. At p. 142 are printed instructions on minute-taking current in 1936. Crossman's comment 30 years later was that the minutes 'do not pretend to be an account of what actually takes place in the Cabinet' (*op. cit.*, p. 198).

[36] H. Wilson, *The Governance of Britain*, p. 82. *Cf.* R. Clarke, *New Trends in Government*, ch. 2.

their basic strategy in terms of policy in specific areas, to identify areas of policy in which new choices might be exercised and to ensure that the implications of alternative policies were fully analysed.[37] As well as advising ministers on more immediate issues, the CPRS produced studies in depth of issues requiring major policy decisions. Subjects included the organisation of government sponsored research, the Concorde project, government support for a British-owned computer industry and the future of the British car industry; not all the reports were published. In 1982 Mrs Thatcher abolished the CPRS. During her period in office, she appointed within the Cabinet Office specialist advisers on foreign and economic affairs. In 1979 she had also appointed Sir Derek Rayner as a part-time adviser on the elimination of waste and the improvement of civil service efficiency. The Rayner unit, as it was known, was a small team consisting mainly of civil servants reporting to the Prime Minister on reviews made of departmental administration. In 1981, the influence of the Cabinet Office was extended when the Civil Service Department was abolished and some of its functions were assigned to the Management and Personnel Office, with the Secretary to the Cabinet as the permanent head of the new Office.

Outside the Cabinet Office but relating closely to it are the Prime Minister's private secretaries, drawn from the civil service, and a team of political advisers.[38]

Cabinet secrecy

The operation of the Cabinet system is surrounded by considerable secrecy.[39] Most Cabinet papers are made available for public inspection in the Public Record Office after 30 years or such other period as the Lord Chancellor may direct.[40] Many Cabinet decisions are notified to Parliament or otherwise made public, but the doctrine of collective responsibility throws a heavy veil over the process of decision-making in Cabinet. It is inevitable that ministers often disagree as to the right course of action before a decision is made. One justification for Cabinet secrecy commonly supported by those with experience of the system is the view that anything which damages the collective unity and integrity of the Cabinet damages the good government of the country.[41] Certainly the public interest in national security requires that some information about defence and external relations must be kept secret by those in government. But the 'good government' argument goes very much further than national security since it seeks to preserve the process of decision-making within government from scrutiny by those outside. Some critics argue, to the contrary, that 'good government' in a democracy requires that more light should be thrown on political decision-making, and that government should

---

37 Cmnd 4506, 1970, paras. 44–8.
38 See G. W. Jones in (ed. J. A. G. Griffith) *From Policy to Administration*, ch. 1.
39 D. Williams, *Not in the Public Interest*, ch. 2; Gordon Walker, pp. 26–33, 164–8; Report on Section 2 of Official Secrets Act 1911, Cmnd 5104, 1972, ch. 11; Report on Ministerial Memoirs, Cmnd 6386, 1976.
40 Public Records Act 1958, s. 5, amended by Public Records Act 1967.
41 Cmnd 5104, 1972, p. 68.

be more open.[42] In fact newspapers frequently contain speculation about the Cabinet's deliberations, some of which may be based on unauthorised disclosures of Cabinet proceedings by ministers who wish to make their points of view known.

In law, Cabinet documents are protected from production as evidence in litigation by a rule which authorises non-disclosure of documents which it would be injurious to the public interest to disclose[43] and from examination by the Parliamentary Commissioner for Administration;[44] they are also protected by the Official Secrets Acts.[45] Political sanctions also operate: a serving Cabinet minister would be liable to lose his office if he could be shown to have revealed the details of Cabinet discussions to the press. But is a former Cabinet minister, who may be subject to no political sanction, under a legal obligation not to reveal such secrets? The question arose for decision in *Attorney-General* v. *Jonathan Cape Ltd.*[46]

Richard Crossman kept a political diary between 1964 and 1970 while a Labour Cabinet minister. After his death in 1974, his diary for 1964–6 was edited for publication and, as was customary, submitted to the Secretary to the Cabinet. He refused to consent to publication, since the diary contained detailed accounts of Cabinet discussions, reports of the advice given to ministers by civil servants and comments about the suitability of senior civil servants for promotion. When Crossman's literary executors decided to publish the diary, the Attorney-General sought an injunction to stop them. Lord Widgery C. J. held that the court had power to restrain the improper publication of information which had been received by a Cabinet minister in confidence, and that the doctrine of collective responsibility justified the court in restraining the disclosures of Cabinet discussions; but that the court should act only where continuing confidentiality of the material could clearly be shown. On the facts, he held that publication in 1975 of Cabinet discussions during the period 1964–6 should not be restrained. In this decision, no reliance was placed either upon the Privy Counsellor's oath of secrecy or upon the Official Secrets Acts.

This decision established the power of the court to restrain publication of Cabinet secrets but gave no clear guidance as to when the power should be exercised. The problems of memoirs of ex-Cabinet ministers were subsequently considered by a committee of privy councillors.[47] The committee distinguished between secret information relating to national security and international relations, on which an ex-minister must accept the decision of the Cabinet Secretary, and other confidential material about relationships between ministers or between ministers and civil servants. In the latter case there should be no publication within 15 years, except with clearance from the Cabinet Secretary, but in the event of a dispute it must in the last resort be for the ex-

---

[42] The evidence given to the Franks Committee on section 2 of the Official Secrets Act 1911 contained a wide range of opinions on the proper extent of Cabinet secrecy *e.g.* from senior civil servants, former ministers, academics and journalists.

[43] Ch. 36.

[44] Parliamentary Commissioner Act 1967, s. 8(4); ch. 37 D.

[45] Ch. 30.

[46] [1976] Q.B. 752; H. Young, *The Crossman Affair*.

[47] Cmnd 6386, 1976.

minister himself to decide what to publish. Advice given by a civil servant to a minister should not be revealed while the adviser was still a civil servant. The committee recommended against legislation, preferring to suggest a clear working procedure which would be brought to the attention of every minister on assuming office. The committee's recommendations were accepted by the government in 1976 and, it may be assumed, have been maintained by subsequent governments.

One important convention is that the ministers in one government do not have access to the papers of an earlier government of a different political party. The convention applies to papers of the Cabinet and ministerial committees, as well as departmental papers that contain the private views of ministers and advice given by officials. The main reason for the convention is to prevent a minister from one party having access to 'matters that the previous Administration had been most anxious to keep quiet'.[48] Former ministers retain the right of access to documents which they saw in office. Before access to Cabinet papers or other ministerial documents of a former government can be given to third parties, the present Prime Minister must seek the agreement of the former Prime Minister concerned, or the current leader of his party. Thus, when a committee of privy councillors was appointed to review British policy towards the Falkland Islands before the Argentine invasion, five former Prime Ministers agreed to the relevant documents being seen by the committee.[49]

B. Ministers and departments

Ministerial offices: the background

Some ministerial offices have a much longer history than the office of Prime Minister, others have been created more recently. The office of Lord Chancellor goes back to the reign of Edward the Confessor and was of great political and judicial significance for several centuries after the Norman conquest. The office of Lord Privy Seal dates from the 14th century and in a later period was often held by leading statesmen; but the historic duties in respect of the Privy Seal were abolished in 1884 and the office now carries no departmental responsibilities. The office of Lord President of the Council was created in 1497 and became of great importance during the period of government through the Council under the Stuarts.

The office of Secretary of State has almost as long history, acquiring its political significance in the Tudor period, particularly during the tenure of the Cecils under Elizabeth I. It came to be recognised as the means by which communications could take place between citizens and the Sovereign.[1] From the 17th century, two and sometimes three Secretaries of State were appointed, who divided national and foreign affairs between them. In 1782, a different division of functions vested in one Secretary of State responsibility for domestic affairs and the colonies, and in the other Secretary responsibility for foreign affairs. Thus were created the offices of Home Secretary and

---

[48]   H.C. Deb., 8 July 1982, col. 474 (Mr M. Foot).
[49]   H.C. Deb., 1 July 1982, col. 1039; 8 July 1982, col. 469. See Lord Hunt of Tanworth [1982] P.L. 514.
[1]   For the history of the Secretaries of State, see Anson, vol. II, 1, pp. 172–84.

Foreign Secretary. In 1794 a Secretary of State for War was appointed, and thereafter from time to time additional Secretaryships (for example, for the colonies, for India, for Scotland) were created and abolished as need arose. In 1984 there were 13 Secretaries of State who between them headed nearly all the major departments. When statutory powers are conferred on a Secretary of State, it is usual for the statute to designate him as 'the Secretary of State' but it will usually be obvious from the context which Secretary of State is intended to exercise the new functions.[2] In law the duties of Secretaries of State are interchangable but in practice each Secretary limits his functions to those related to his own department. One Secretary of State may be named by the Prime Minister as First Secretary; while this makes no legal difference to the office, it determines precedence in the Cabinet and the First Secretary may deputise for the Prime Minister in the latter's absence.

Ministers of the Crown

According to one statutory definition, minister of the Crown means 'the holder of any office in Her Majesty's Government in the United Kingdom, and includes the Treasury, . . . and the Defence Council'.[3] In a less technical sense, ministers are those members or supporters of the party in power who hold political office in the government. They are all appointed by the Crown on the advice of the Prime Minister and their offices are at the disposal of an incoming Prime Minister. They do not include members of the civil service or the armed forces, who continue in office despite a change of government; nor personal advisers of ministers, who may be paid salaries and are temporarily attached to departments but who lose their position when a minister leaves office; nor members of public boards, regulatory bodies and so on. Unlike all these other office holders, ministers are not disqualified from membership of the House of Commons

There are various grades of ministerial appointment today, but they may be grouped into three broad categories: (a) Cabinet ministers, who may or may not have departmental responsibilities; (b) departmental ministers and ministers of state who are outside the Cabinet, the duty of a minister of state being to share in the administration of a department headed by a Cabinet minister;[4] and (c) parliamentary secretaries, whose duty it is to assist in the parliamentary work of a department and who may also have some administrative responsibility. The four Law Officers of the Crown are within category (b) but the government whips, who have no departmental responsibilities, may be allotted amongst the categories according to their status and seniority.

By exercise of the prerogative, new posts in the Crown's service can be created, for example, extra Secretaries of State. But when a new ministry is formed, there is often legislation to create the minister a corporation sole, thus giving him legal capacity, and providing in broad terms for his functions.[5]

---

[2] By the Interpretation Act 1978, unless the contrary intention appears, 'Secretary of State' means 'one of Her Majesty's Principal Secretaries of State'. See *Agee* v. *Lord Advocate* 1977 S.L.T. Notes 54.

[3] Ministers of the Crown Act 1975, s. 8(1).

[4] *Cf.* House of Commons Disqualification Act 1975, s. 9(1).

[5] *E.g.* Secretary of State (New Departments) Order 1974, S.I. No. 692.

There are no legal limits on the number of ministers which the Crown may appoint, assuming that the appointees are not to receive a salary and do not sit in the House of Commons, but there are statutory limits on the number of ministers who may be members of the Commons and on the number of salaries payable to holders of ministerial office.[6]

Ministerial salaries

The maximum salaries payable to the Prime Minister, the Lord Chancellor, other Cabinet ministers, ministers of state, parliamentary secretaries and the Law Officers of the Crown are prescribed by the Ministerial and other Salaries Act 1975, as varied by subsequent Orders in Council. The making of such an Order in Council is subject to the prior approval of the Commons being given to the draft Order. Ministerial salaries are in practice increased only after their level has been considered by the Review Body on Top Salaries, at the same time as the salaries of M.P.s are reviewed.[7] In January 1984, the statutory salary of the Prime Minister was £51,050, of a Cabinet minister in the Commons £40,930 and of a parliamentary secretary in the Commons £26,780.[8]

All ministerial salaries are maximum salaries and less may be paid;[9] thus the House of Commons may still exercise its traditional right to move the reduction of a minister's salary in order to call attention to a grievance or censure the conduct of a department.[10]

While these are not ministerial salaries, the Act of 1975 also provides for the Speaker's salary and salary to the leader of the Opposition in the Commons, who is defined as being the leader of the party in opposition to the government having the greatest numerical strength in the House; the Speaker has power to resolve doubts as to who this is. Salaries are also paid under the Act to the chief opposition whip in the Commons and in the Lords to the leader of the Opposition and the chief opposition whip. The salaries of the Speaker and opposition officers are charged on the Consolidated Fund and are thus not subject to reduction by vote of the Commons.

Ministers in Parliament

It is a convention that ministerial office-holders should be members of one or other House of Parliament. Such membership is essential to the maintenance of ministerial responsibility. There is, however, no law that a minister must be in Parliament. The statutory limit on the number of ministers receiving salaries who may sit at one time in the Commons ensures indirectly that there should be ministerial representation in the Lords. When a Prime Minister appoints to ministerial office someone who is not already in Parliament, a life peerage is usually conferred on him.

---

6   Pages 165–6 ante.
7   E.g. Cmnd 8881, 1983; and p. 224 ante.
8   See H.C. Deb., 21 July 1983, cols. 180–4 (W.A.) for salaries payable under the 1975 Act in 1983–7.
9   Ministerial and other Salaries Act 1975, s. 4.
10   In 1976, helped by a mix-up in voting, the Opposition carried a resolution calling for a reduction of £1,000 in the salary of the Secretary of State for Industry; this was overridden a week later (H.C. Deb., 11 and 17 Feb. 1976).

Financial interests of ministers

Because of their office, many ministers are in a position to take decisions which have a direct financial effect on particular business, sections of industry and land values. They also have access to confidential information about future decisions which could be put to financial profit. The Marconi affair of 1912 involved three leading members of the Liberal government who were alleged to have made use of secret information about an impending government contract to make an investment in Marconi shares: an inquiry by a parliamentary committee established that they had bought shares not in the company to which the contract was about to be awarded but in a sister company.[11] In 1948 the Lynskey Tribunal of Inquiry reported on allegations that ministers and other public servants had been bribed in connection with the grant of licences by the Board of Trade; a junior minister, who later resigned from Parliament, was found to have received presents of wine and spirits and other gifts, knowing that they had been made to secure favourable treatment by the department of applications for licences.[12] While such conduct could give rise to criminal proceedings, additional safeguards are required if ministers are to avoid suspicion. In 1952, rules were laid down by the Prime Minister which have been in force since then.[13] The overriding principle is that ministers must ensure that no conflict arises, or appears to arise, between their private interests and their public duties. This conflict could arise if a minister took any active part or had a financial interest in any undertaking which had contractual or other relations (for example, receiving a licence or a subsidy) withe his department. Under the 1952 rules, ministers should on assuming office resign any directorships which they may hold and should dispose of controlling interests in any company which could give rise to conflict of interest. In cases of doubt, for example as to the propriety of retaining certain shares in a company, the Prime Minister must be informed and is the final judge. In 1962, a junior minister in the Ministry of Aviation, Mr B. de Ferranti, resigned a few months after accepting office as he had found it impossible to divest himself of his interests in a family business having extensive contractual relations with the Ministry.[14]

In 1982, the Secretary of State for Trade, Lord Cockfield, declined to take a decision on whether to approve a majority report of the Monopolies and Mergers Commission about a controversial takeover bid, since he had a small shareholding in the bidding company. The decision was instead taken by the minister of state in the same department. On becoming a minister, Lord Cockfield had in accordance with the rules on financial interests deposited the relevant share certificates with his bank, instructing the bank not to deal in them so long as he held ministerial office.[15] Ministers who are members of the Commons are expected to disclose all relevant interests in the register which that House maintains;[16] but the House of Lords does not keep a similar register.

---

11 See F. Donaldson, *The Marconi Scandal*.
12 Cmd 7616, 1949.
13 H.C. Deb., 25 Feb. 1952, col. 701; and 20 Mar. 1980, col. 293 (W.A.)
14 *The Times*, 31 Oct. 1962.
15 H.C. Deb., 21 Dec. 1982, col. 821 and 22 Dec. 1982, col. 955; and *R.* v. *Secretary of State for Trade, ex p. Anderson Strathclyde plc* [1983] 2 All E.R. 233.
16 Ch. 12 B. In practice, most ministers submit a nil return.

There are also rules which govern the conditions on which ministers may while in office contribute to the press or undertake other literary work. A minister may not become a regular columnist for a newspaper nor, as Dr Jeremy Bray discovered in 1969, may he publish a book on matters related to his ministerial work.[17]

Departments

While the term 'government department' has no precise meaning in law, in relation to central government it usually refers to those branches of the central administration which are staffed by civil servants, paid for out of Exchequer funds and headed by a minister responsible to Parliament. A single minister may be responsible for more than one department: thus the Chancellor of the Exchequer is responsible for the Treasury and the two revenue departments (Inland Revenue; Customs and Excise), as well as for a group of executive departments closely associated with the Treasury, for example the Public Works Loan Board. Exceptionally, there are departments which for constitutional reasons do not have a ministerial head: thus the National Audit Office is headed by the Comptroller and Auditor General.[18] For the purposes of legal proceedings against the Crown, a list of departments is maintained under the Crown Proceedings Act 1947.[19] For the purposes of investigation by the Parliamentary Commissioner for Administration, a statutory list of departments is maintained and this is revised as new departments are established.[20]

There are many public bodies with governmental functions which are not regarded as government departments. They include local authorities; boards of nationalised industries and other public corporations; regulatory bodies such as the Commission for Racial Equality and the Civil Aviation Authority; grant-giving bodies such as the Arts Council and the research councils established under the Science and Technology Act 1965; advisory councils and committees, such as the Council on Tribunals, and other bodies which may report to ministers but are not directly controlled by them (for example, the English and Scottish Law Commissions). Often such bodies are financed from central Exchequer funds.

Government departments are much affected by the principle of ministerial responsibility. In the 19th century, administrative tasks were often entrusted to boards which did not include a minister responsible to Parliament.[21] But strong emphasis was later laid on the principle of ministerial responsibility for government departments. In 1968, the report of the Fulton Committee on the Civil Service considered the effect of ministerial responsibility in relation to the variety of departments and other agencies which then existed, and said: 'we see no reason to believe that the dividing line between activities for which ministers are directly responsible and those for which they are not, is necessarily drawn in the right place today'.[22] The committee recommended that

17 *The Times*, 26–9 Sept. 1969.
18 Ch. 16.
19 Ch. 36.
20 Ch. 37 D.
21 F. M. G. Willson (1955) 33 Public Administration 43; H. Parris, *Constitutional Bureaucracy*, ch. 3.
22 Cmnd 3638, 1968, p. 61.

further consideration be given to the scope for 'hiving-off' areas of governmental work to autonomous or relatively autonomous agencies. One form of
hiving-off was applied in 1969 when the Post Office Corporation was established; this took postal and telephone services away from a government department and entrusted them to a public corporation similar to those which ran
the nationalised industries.[23] Other lesser forms of hiving-off have involved
establishing agencies within government departments charged with specific
managerial tasks: for example, the Property Services Agency within the
Department of the Environment, which provides government departments
with the accommodation which they need, and the Procurement Executive
within the Ministry of Defence, which obtains the weapons and equipment
needed by the armed forces. Many tasks formerly performed by the Department of Employment are now entrusted to the Manpower Services
Commission and to the Health and Safety Commission, subject to ministerial
control.[24]

The organisation of central government
In 1918 was published the report of the Machinery of Government Committee
presided over by Lord Haldane. This committee had been appointed to inquire
into the responsibilities of central government departments and 'to advise in
what manner the exercise and distribution by the Government of its functions
should be improved'.[25] It recommended that the business of government
should be distributed into ten main divisions by reference to their functions:
finance; national defence; external affairs; production; transport and
commerce; employment; supplies; education; health; and justice. The report
also favoured a small Cabinet of up to twelve members and the retention of
a permanent Cabinet secretariat. Except for the last recommendation, the
structure of central government after 1918 was not reorganised on the Haldane
lines, although today the scope of some departments (for example, Ministry
of Defence, Foreign Office, Department of Employment) closely resembles the
division of functions recommended in 1918.

The Haldane report is notable for having been the only occasion in the 20th
century on which the structure of government has been reviewed by an independent committee. Although Cabinet committees have sometimes been
appointed to review the organisation of government, this has been recognised
as a responsibility of successive Prime Ministers. Changes have usually
occurred piecemeal.[26] Between 1968 and 1981, the Civil Service Department
was concerned with the machinery of government, and this responsibility is
now exercised by the Management and Personnel Office.[27]

To enable changes in the structure of government to be carried out quickly,
there have since 1946 been statutory powers by which new needs can be met
without recourse to Acts of Parliament. The Ministers of the Crown Act 1975
now authorises the Crown, by Order in Council, to transfer to any minister

---

[23] Ch. 17. And see British Telecommunications Act 1981.
[24] Employment and Training Act 1973, s. 1; Health and Safety at Work etc. Act 1974, s. 10.
[25] Cd 9230, 1918. See also H. Daalder, *Cabinet Reform in Britain 1914–1963*, ch. 17; and R. G. S.
      Brown, *The Administrative Process in Britain*, ch. 10.
[26] See F. M. G. Willson, *The Organization of British Central Government 1914–64*.
[27] Ch. 15.

functions previously exercised by another minister; to provide for the dissolution of a government department and for the transfer to other departments of the functions previously exercised by that department; and to direct that functions shall be exercised concurrently by two ministers. Consequential steps may also be authorised, such as the transfer of property from one department to another and changes in the title of ministers. Orders in Council under the 1975 Act are subject to parliamentary scrutiny. The powers conferred by the 1975 Act are in addition to the Crown's prerogative powers, which may still be exercised to make some governmental changes.[28]

One constant problem of government is to secure adequate co-ordination between different departments while maintaining ministerial responsibility to Parliament and the representation of departmental interests in the Cabinet. The small Cabinets used in war-time were able to concentrate on directing the war while leaving other matters to Cabinet committees. But in peace-time there is strong pressure for representation in the Cabinet of the major spending departments. In 1951, when Churchill became Prime Minister, he appointed two ministers out of a Cabinet of 16 as co-ordinating ministers, and he excluded departments such as education and agriculture from representation in the Cabinet. The co-ordinating ministers were both peers (they promptly became 'the Overlords') and the idea proved unpopular with the Labour opposition in the Commons. There was confusion as to the responsibility to the Commons of the ministers whose departments had been placed under a co-ordinating minister.[29] The experiment did not last long: its failure may help to explain why subsequent governments have not disclosed their arrangements for co-ordination through Cabinet committees.

While the organisation of government often depends on short-term political factors, steps were taken during the 1960s for grouping related functions of government in larger departments. These steps led by 1970 to the emergence of five 'giant' departments, namely the Foreign and Commonwealth Office, Defence, Trade and Industry, Health and Social Security, and Environment,[30] each having been formed from an amalgamation of ministries. These large departments had certain advantages (for example, it became possible for all departments to be represented in the Cabinet; and greater co-ordination between related activities could take place within the larger department) but also disadvantages: thus it became necessary for the larger departments to have two or more permanent secretaries, and for a team of ministers to be formed to lead each department. Nonetheless in 1984 the Foreign and Commonwealth Office, the Ministry of Defence and the Department of Health and Social Security still survived intact; but, without mentioning intervening changes, Energy was in 1984 separate from Trade and Industry, and Transport separate from the Environment. No final scheme for the allocation of tasks between departments will ever emerge. The relevant political and administrative factors are often in conflict with each other. As R. G. S. Brown remarked, 'there is no simple relationship between administrative functions and the focal points of ministerial responsibility'.[31]

---

28   1975 Act, s. 5. And see S.I. 1981 No. 1670.
29   Wilson, *Cases*, pp. 42–7; Jennings, *Cabinet Government*, pp. 78–81; Daalder, *op. cit.*, ch. 7.
30   See R. Clarke, *New Trends in Government*; and Cmnd 4506, 1970.
31   *Op. cit.*, p. 214.

Chapter 15

The civil service

What is a civil servant?

The departments of central government are staffed by administrative, professional, technical and other officials who constitute the civil service. For the purposes of inquiry by royal commissions, civil servants have been defined as: 'Servants of the Crown, other than holders of political or judicial offices, who are employed in a civil capacity and whose remuneration is paid wholly and directly out of moneys voted by Parliament'.[1] This definition excludes ministers of the Crown, members of the armed forces (who are Crown servants but are not employed in a civil capacity), the police, and those employed in local government, the National Health Service, and the nationalised industries, even though they are all engaged in public services. A somewhat similar definition of an officer of the Crown is contained in section 2(6) of the Crown Proceedings Act 1947, which limits proceedings against the Crown in tort (or in Scots law, delict) to the act, neglect or default of an officer who 'has been directly or indirectly appointed by the Crown and was at the material time paid in respect of his duties as an officer of the Crown' wholly out of the national exchequer.[2]

Whatever the precise legal nature of the civil servant's relationship with the Crown, it is an important constitutional principle that those concerned with the administration of government departments should in fact enjoy a tenure of office by which they may serve successive ministers of different political parties. Particularly since 1979, the size and expense of the civil service have become a matter of political controversy. But without the service, the achievements of modern government would have been impossible.

Structure of the civil service

'The Home Civil Service today is still fundamentally the product of the 19th century philosophy of the Northcote-Trevelyan Report'.[3] This was the view

---

[1] Report of the Committee on the Civil Service (Fulton Report), Cmnd 3638, 1968, App. A.
[2] Ch. 36.
[3] Cmnd 3638, p. 1. For a perceptive history of the civil service, see H. Parris, *Constitutional Bureaucracy*. For a critical assessment of the civil service by the Expenditure Committee, see H.C. 535 (1976–7).

in 1968 of the Fulton committee, who considered that that philosophy had encouraged the cult of the amateur in the processes of administration. In 1854, the Northcote-Trevelyan report had condemned the incompetence of a system based on nepotism and patronage, pointing out that government could not be carried on 'without the aid of an efficient body of permanent officers, occupying a position duly subordinate to that of the ministers who are directly responsible to the Crown and to Parliament, yet possessing sufficient independence, character, ability and experience to be able to advise, assist and, to some extent, influence those who are from time to time set over them'.[4] The 1854 report gave rise to the system of competitive entry into the civil service based on intellectual merit. To promote this, the Civil Service Commission was established in 1855, and in 1870 open competition became the normal method of recruitment for all classes of the service. While the selection of candidates was entrusted to the impartial discretion of the Civil Service Commission, free of political interference, Treasury ministers were responsible to Parliament for the regulations prescribed by the commission. Because of the cost of salaries, the Treasury was already concerned with the size of staff in the departments. After 1870 the Treasury increasingly issued general instructions to the departments on staffing matters. In 1919, the Treasury was reorganised to make better provision for establishment and staffing matters and the Permanent Secretary to the Treasury was recognised as Head of the Civil Service.[5] In 1956, two Permanent Secretaries to the Treasury were appointed, one to deal with finance and the economy, the other to deal with staffing and management questions. In 1968, as recommended by the Fulton committee, civil service matters were separated from the financial and economic work of the Treasury and the Civil Service Department was created.[6]

The department's immediate task was to carry through many of the reforms recommended in the Fulton report (for example, to substitute a broader system of grading posts for the former system of classes within which civil servants were confined). But the department's prestige and vigour waned thereafter. When government control of public expenditure became a foremost political priority, the department's responsibility for the control of civil service manpower (including the costs of salaries) was seen to be divorced from control by the Treasury of the rest of government expenditure.

In 1981, the Civil Service Department was abolished and its functions divided between the Treasury and a new Management and Personnel Office.[7] The functions transferred to the Treasury included control of civil service manpower and costs, the pay and superannuation of civil servants, and similar powers in respect of the armed forces. The functions vested in the Management and Personnel Office included management systems, cost-cutting and the review of effectiveness and efficiency,[8] personnel management (including senior civil service appointments), recruitment policy and training, public appoint-

---

[4] Cmnd 3638, app. B (which reprints the 1854 report), p. 108.
[5] Lord Bridges, *The Treasury*, p. 173.
[6] See S.I. 1968 No. 1656; and S.I. 1971 No. 2099.
[7] See H.C. Deb., 12 Nov. 1981, col. 658, and 20 Jan. 1982, col. 367; S.I. 1981 No. 1670. *Cf.* Cmnd 8170, 1981.
[8] See Cmnd 8293, 1981; and H.C. 236 (1981–2).

ments, and the machinery of government. The Prime Minister continues to be Minister for the Civil Service, although day-to-day responsibility for the Management and Personnel Office is borne by another Cabinet minister. A minister of state in the Treasury also has responsibility for civil service matters. The Secretary to the Cabinet is Permanent Secretary to the Management and Personnel Office and in 1984 he was also Head of the Home Civil Service. The Civil Service Commission comes under the Management and Personnel Office, although in selecting recruits to the service the commission is independent of political control.

The Diplomatic Service, which secures overseas representation of the Crown, is not part of the Home Civil Service. The scope of the service includes the staffing of embassies and high commissions in foreign and Commonwealth states, as well as consular and trade mission services, and oversight of the few remaining colonies. The service comes under the Secretary of State for Foreign and Commonwealth Affairs, whose office is responsible for organisation, training, promotion and security. The Permanent Under-Secretary at the Foreign and Commonwealth Office is Head of the Diplomatic Service.

Tenure of appointment

Except where statute provides otherwise, all civil servants hold office in law at the pleasure of the Crown. This means that a civil servant may in law be dismissed at pleasure and has no common law remedy for wrongful dismissal, even when he has been promised employment for a stated period of years.[9] However, he probably does have an action in respect of salary due to him in respect of a period of service before his dismissal.[10] Employment legislation now extends to civil servants such forms of protection as the right to union membership and the remedy of appealing to an industrial tribunal against unfair dismissal, but these rights may be revoked on grounds of national security.[11]

In practice, a civil servant's tenure bears little relation to the common law and is very much more secure than most other forms of employment: the Fulton committee drew attention to the very rare use made of the power to dismiss or to require early retirement in the interests of efficiency.[12] Departmental rules lay down the procedures which must be followed before adverse action is taken against a civil servant: they provide for notice to be given to him of what is alleged against him and grant him the right to present his case and also to appeal, in cases of dismissal or premature retirement, to a Civil Service Appeals Board independent of the department concerned. While the salary scales of all civil servants are published, they are not fixed by statute and only the total sums required for salaries appear in the annual estimates of the departments laid before Parliament. Formerly the detailed provisions of civil service pension schemes were included in Acts of Parliament but the Superannuation Act 1972 authorised a more flexible arrangement whereby pension schemes may be made by the Minister for the Civil Service. These

---

9 *Dunn* v. *R.* [1896] 1 Q.B. 116; and see ch. 36.
10 *Kodeeswaran* v. *A.-G. of Ceylon* [1970] A.C. 1111.
11 Employment Protection (Consolidation) Act 1978, s. 138; p. 283 *post*.
12 Cmnd 3638, p. 43.

schemes for the civil service are not contained in statutory instruments and are merely required to be laid before Parliament; thus they are not subjected to the degree of parliamentary scrutiny considered appropriate for other branches of the public service (for example, the local government service, teachers and the health service).[13] Before 1972, the former Superannuation Acts were interpreted as conferring no right which the civil servant could enforce in the courts to secure payment of his pension.[14] The 1972 Act includes no provision directly excluding the jurisdiction of the courts; it distinguishes between mandatory and discretionary pension allowances and, while decisions of the Minister for the Civil Service on pension questions are stated to be final, provision is made for questions of law to be decided in the superior civil courts.[15] The civil servant therefore has an entitlement to his pension which did not exist before 1972. Pensions are increased annually to support their purchasing power, a benefit which civil servants share with others in public employment (including judges, the police, teachers and university lecturers).[16] Pension rights may be forfeited where a civil servant or former civil servant is convicted of offences under the Official Secrets Acts 1911 to 1939 and sentenced to at least 10 years in prison, or is convicted of an offence related to his employment which was gravely injurious to the state or liable to lead to serious loss of confidence in the public service.[17]

While departmental grievance procedures enable a civil servant to pursue a complaint about the way he has been treated, allegations of maladministration relating to appointments, promotion, discipline, pay and other personnel matters may not be investigated by the Parliamentary Commissioner for Administration, a restriction which has been maintained contrary to the view of the House of Commons committee on the Parliamentary Commissioner.[18]

Regulation of the civil service

While certain statutes affect the position of the civil servant, management of the civil service is conducted by reliance on the Crown's common law powers as employer, and where necessary on the royal prerogative, exercised through Orders in Council and supporting regulations. The Civil Service Order in Council 1982, which is a prerogative act, authorises the Minister for the Civil Service 'to make regulations or give instructions for controlling the conduct of the Home Civil Service, and providing for the classification, remuneration and other conditions of service' of its members. The civil service is also governed by circulars, minutes and instructions which come to departments from the Treasury and the Management and Personnel Office. Although these instruments are binding on those whom they affect, they are not generally enforceable in the courts[19] and it is therefore sometimes said that they cannot

---

13 Superannuation Act 1972, ss. 1, 2(11) and 12(6). For the 1972 Act schemes, see H.L.E., vol. 8, pp. 811–30.
14 *E.g. Nixon* v. *A.-G.* [1931] A.C. 184.
15 Superannuation Act 1972, s. 2(6)–(8).
16 Pensions (Increase) Act 1971; Superannuation Act 1972, s. 25.
17 I.P.C.S. Handbook (n. 20 *post*) p. 347.
18 Parliamentary Commissioner Act 1967, sched. 3, para. 10; ch. 37 D.
19 *Rodwell* v. *Thomas* [1944] K.B. 596. *Cf. Sutton* v. *A.-G.* (1923) 39 T.L.R. 294; L. Blair [1958] P.L. 32 and (1958) 21 M.L.R. 265.

be law. Indeed, the customary approach of British government has been that the courts should be excluded from interfering in the internal management of the service. But there are certain prerogative Orders in Council, such as the Servants of the Crown (Parliamentary Candidature) Order 1960 which, while seeking primarily to regulate the conduct of Crown servants, have a wider constitutional effect; they also have a strong claim to be regarded as law. The texts of these Orders in Council, the principal civil service regulations and the pensions schemes are public documents, but many of the subordinate instruments and circulars are not published. Nor does the government publish the official collection of these rules, known as the Civil Service Pay and Conditions of Service Code, although its contents are not secret or confidential.[20]

In the management of the civil service, governments make wide use of both formal and informal means of collective bargaining. Negotiations as to conditions of service are conducted through a complex scheme of Whitley Councils and arbitration procedures. But the government retains final control and embodies the agreements or awards in official circulars or minutes.[21] The Civil Service National Whitley Council, which dates from 1919, is composed equally of senior departmental officers (the official side) representing the Crown as employer, and representatives of civil servants appointed by the recognised staff associations and unions (the staff side). The Council is based on the system of joint councils of workers and employers for settling employment disputes which was recommended in 1918 by a commission presided over by J. H. Whitley.

The civil servant within his department

The senior civil servant within a department is the Permanent Secretary. According to the Fulton committee, he has four functions:

He is the Minister's most immediate adviser on policy; he is the managing director of the day-to-day operations of the department; he has the ultimate responsibility for questions of staff and organisation; as the Accounting Officer (in nearly every department), he also has the ultimate responsibility for all departmental expenditure.[22]

In the larger departments, a second Permanent Secretary may be appointed. Beneath the Permanent Secretary, the affairs of the department will be handled by a number of divisions or branches, controlled (in descending order of seniority) by deputy secretaries, under-secretaries, and assistant secretaries. The work of these senior civil servants often brings them into close contact with ministers and Parliament. When the Fulton committee was established in 1966, the Prime Minister stated that the government was not intending to alter the basic relationship between ministers and civil servants. 'Civil servants, however eminent, remain the confidential advisers of Ministers, who alone are answerable to Parliament for policy'.[23] In fact the Fulton committee found that the constitutional framework of government had a strong influence

---

[20]   Lengthy extracts from the code are reprinted in the informative Handbook of the Institution of Professional Civil Servants.

[21]   See *Dudfield* v. *Ministry of Works, The Times*, 24 Jan. 1964.

[22]   Cmnd 3638, p. 58. And see ch. 16.

[23]   Cmnd 3638, app. A.

over the way in which the work was transacted, and that much of the parliamentary work done by civil servants, for example, in preparing legislation and drafting answers to parliamentary questions, had no counterpart outside the government service.

Operating policies embodied in existing legislation and implementing policy decisions take up most of the time of most civil servants. There are taxes to be collected, employment and social security offices to be run. There is a mass of individual case-work both in local offices and in the central departments of state. There are major programmes to be arranged and controlled, such as the planning and engineering of motorways from their initial location and design to the finished construction.[24]

The Fulton committee found that, while the position of a civil servant within his hierarchy was usually clear, departments did not find it easy to allocate to individual officers or units the authority to take decisions. The principles of ministerial responsibility meant that decisions often had to be referred to a higher level than their difficulty or importance merited; and many decisions involved other departments. 'For these reasons clear delegation of authority is particularly difficult in the Civil Service'.[25] Since the Fulton committee reported in 1968, some measures designed to improve this position have been adopted. For example, in areas of mainly executive work where there is less need for detailed supervision by ministers, agencies have been set up within departments, managed by an executive head to whom authority is delegated and who has a degree of managerial independence from the department.[26]

Where schemes of delegation exist within a department, they do not generally affect the legal position of the department or of outsiders dealing with it. Where the power to make a discretionary decision affecting an individual is vested in a minister, an official within the department may in general take that decision on behalf of the minister. In a criminal case in which it was claimed that the Home Secretary had never approved a breathalyser device as required by the Road Safety Act 1973, Widgery L. J. said: 'The minister is not expected personally to take every decision entrusted to him by Parliament. If a decision is made on his behalf by one of his officials, then that constitutionally is the minister's decision'.[27] Except where the express delegation of authority is required by a particular statute, the civil servant's authority flows from the general nature of his administrative work and not from a formal delegation scheme.[28] Although a letter sent from a department may be signed by a particular civil servant, it cannot be assumed that he personally made the decision expressed in the letter, since the matter may have been referred to a more senior official or to a minister for decision or approval.

Since for these reasons no citizen can be expected to know the limits of a civil servant's authority, difficulties may arise when a civil servant exceeds his actual authority within the department but does not exceed the legal authority of the department, or when he exceeds the authority of his department but

---

24   Cmnd 3638, p. 15.
25   Cmnd 3638, p. 50.
26   Report of C.S. Department 1971–3, p. 2; and see ch. 14 B.
27   *R. v. Skinner* [1968] 2 Q.B. 700, 707. And see ch. 7.
28   *Cf. Commissioners of Customs and Excise* v. *Cure and Deeley Ltd* [1962] 1 Q.B. 340.

does not exceed the legal authority of the Crown. Such conduct is likely to be an act of maladministration and where it causes injustice to the citizen may be investigated by the Parliamentary Commissioner for Administration.[29] But is the department or the Crown legally bound by the civil servant's action?

In *Robertson* v. *Minister of Pensions*, an army officer had written to the War Office inquiring whether a physical disability of his would be considered as attributable to military service and thus qualify him for a war pension. A reply came from the War Office stating that the case had been duly considered and the disability had been accepted as attributable to military service. The officer relied on this letter, not knowing that administration of such claims had been transferred from the War Office to the Ministry of Pensions. Later the Ministry of Pensions denied that the Crown was bound by the War Office letter. Denning J. held that the Crown was estopped by the letter, *i.e.* barred, from seeking to show that the officer's disability was not attributable to military service; the officer was entitled to assume that other departments that might be concerned had been consulted by the War Office.[30]

While the House of Lords in a later case disapproved the principle that a citizen is entitled to rely on an official having the authority which he assumes, at least for the purposes of the criminal law,[31] the law should not be powerless to provide an appropriate remedy to the individual who has suffered loss through relying on an official's assurance.[32]

Anonymity of civil servants

Civil servants take part in a process of institutional decision-making in which, while their names may be known to the citizens primarily affected, they may not be identified with the policies or decisions which emerge. Indeed, the civil servant's anonymity is typically the corollary of ministerial responsibility. The Fulton committee found that the administrative process was surrounded by too much secrecy, criticising the convention that only ministers should explain departmental policies in public; the committee predicted that the traditional anonymity of civil servants would increasingly be eroded by the pressures of press and broadcasting.[33] In fact, while most departments employ press and public relations officers, the major burden of defending publicly departmental policies and decisions is still borne by ministers. At public inquiries, for example into motorway proposals, civil servants may be required to give evidence about departmental policy but they may not be asked questions directly relating to the merits of government policy.[34] Senior civil servants frequently attend before parliamentary committees to give evidence about the work of their departments, but they may not be asked for their individual views on governmental policies.[35] The published reports of the Parliamentary Commissioner on his investigations into alleged maladministration customarily respect the anonymity of the civil servants concerned; the select committee of

---

29   Ch. 37 D.
30   [1949] 1 K.B. 227. And see ch. 34 C.
31   *Howell* v. *Falmouth Boat Construction Co. Ltd* [1951] A.C. 837.
32   Ch. 34 C.
33   Cmnd 3638, pp. 93–4.
34   Ch. 37 B.
35   See H.C. 588–1 (1977–8). App. D (and p. 209 *ante*).

the Commons which considers these reports has claimed the right to ask for individual civil servants to give evidence before it, but the right was not conceded by the government.[36] The veil of official anonymity is liable to be pierced when a major inquiry is held into a piece of administration which has run into political criticism, as in the inquiries relating to Crichel Down and the Vehicle and General Insurance Company.[37] In these exceptional situations, it is right that the individual responsibility of officials should be made known but this should not be done without adequate procedural safeguards for the officials in question. In the Crossman Diaries case, one important issue was the extent to which former ministers could make known the advice given to them by civil servants in their department. In that case this question was overshadowed by the issue of Cabinet secrecy, and the extent to which the courts will protect the confidentiality of such advice is uncertain.[38] Yet the desirability of maintaining confidential relationships between ministers and civil servants has often been stressed; former civil servants who wish to publish books about their work in the public service are subject to restraints which may be greater than those which bind former ministers.[39]

Financial interests of civil servants

We have seen that ministers are subject to rules enforced by the Prime Minister that are intended *inter alia* to ensure that they do not profit improperly from their public position.[40] Civil servants are fully subject to the criminal law, including the Prevention of Corruption Acts 1906 and 1916. Internal rules of the service provide that no civil servant may engage in any occupation which might conflict with the interests of his department or with his position as a public servant; nor must he put himself in a position (for example, by dealing in shares or land) where his duty to the public service might conflict with his private interests. Moreover there are strict rules about the acceptance of gifts or hospitality from those with whom civil servants have official dealings.[41] The integrity of the civil service is also protected by established procedures for the awarding of contracts and the disposal of surplus property, breaches of which are subject to investigation by the Comptroller and Auditor General.[42] Complaints of bias in the use of discretionary powers may be investigated by the Parliamentary Commissioner for Administration.[43]

The public interest in integrity is not confined to what civil servants do while in post, but extends in some cases to their actions after leaving the service. The rules that govern the taking up of private business appointments by former civil servants recognise the desirability of experienced administrators entering the private sector; but an official of the rank of under-secretary

---

[36] See, arising out of the *Sachsenhausen* case, (p. 726 *post*) H.C. 350 (1967–8).

[37] Pages 114–6 *ante*.

[38] *A.-G.* v. *Jonathan Cape Ltd* [1976] Q.B. 752, 772. Lord Widgery L.C.J. later stated that he had not intended to lay down a general rule that the confidentiality of advice given by civil servants to ministers could never be protected (*ibid.*).

[39] Cmnd 6386, 1976, Pt. IV; and p. 265 *ante*.

[40] Ch. 14 B.

[41] See I.P.C.S. Handbook (n. 20 *ante*) pp. 17, 23 and see Cmd 3037, 1928.

[42] Ch. 16.

[43] Ch. 37 D.

or above (or who has held certain technical posts) must obtain government approval if within two years of leaving the service he wishes to accept employment with certain companies (for example, those which have government contracts, or receive official subsidies or loans, or have a special relationship with departments). These rules are not statutory and do not seem to be legally enforceable, having regard to the common law doctrine regarding contracts in restraint of trade, and to the civil servant's present entitlement to superannuation.[44] A House of Commons committee in 1981 recommended that the rules should be applied more consistently and their scope extended, for example to include the taking of appointments with foreign governments.[45]

Political activities of civil servants

Servants of the Crown are prohibited from parliamentary candidature and disqualified from membership of the Commons. But should civil servants be subject to additional limitations, to secure the political impartiality of the civil service as a whole? The present scheme, first brought into force in 1954,[46] recognises that the political neutrality of the civil service is a fundamental feature of British government, but that the rules need not be the same for all members of the service. Three categories exist. Participation in national political activities (for example, holding office in a political party; expressing public views on matters of national political controversy) is barred to the senior administrative grades and to those in executive or clerical grades whose work is associated with those giving advice to ministers or who administer services directly to the public (for example, staff in social security offices); this 'restricted' category may with permission take part in local political activities (for example, candidature for local authorities) but must act with moderation and discretion, particularly in matters affecting their own departments. A second 'intermediate' category may with leave of their departments take part in all political activities, both local and national, except parliamentary candidature, subject to observing a code of discretion (for example, they may discuss national policies but should avoid personal attacks on ministers and should avoid causing embarrassment to their departments). The third 'politically free' category combines industrial staff and the non-industrial staff in minor and manipulative grades: they are free to engage in all political activities, national and local, except when on duty or on official premises or while wearing uniform. But like all civil servants they are subject to the rules of the Official Secrets Acts on unauthorised disclosure of information gained from official sources.[47] The restrictions on political activity, especially in the first category, are severe; in particular, they limit the ability of individual officials to contribute publicly to debate on controversial issues. But there are other forms of employment, both public and private, where comparable limitations exist.

The scheme was fully reviewed by the Armitage committee in 1978, in response to requests from the civil service unions for much greater political freedom for civil servants. The committee re-asserted the constitutional

[44] Page 276 *ante*.
[45] H.C. 216 (1980–1), and see C. R. Munro [1981] P.L. 310.
[46] See Cmd 7718, 1949 and Cmd 8783, 1953; Wilson, *Cases*, pp. 72–5.
[47] Ch. 30.

importance of the political neutrality of the civil service. It recommended that the existing scheme should continue subject to substantial changes in its operation, the effect of which would be to reduce the number of civil servants in the 'restricted' category from about 26% of the civil service to 3%.[48] In 1984, these recommendations were adopted after extensive discussion between government and the civil service unions.[49]

Civil servants, unlike the police and armed forces, have full freedom of association for purposes of collective bargaining, except when this is withdrawn on security grounds. In law civil servants are as free to withdraw their services when collective bargaining breaks down, as are employees in the private sector. Civil service unions are likely to affiliate to the Trades Union Congress, but not to the Labour party.

Security measures in the civil service[50]

Provided that a civil servant observes the restrictions on political activities which apply to him and carries out his duties properly, his political beliefs are generally of no concern to those in authority over him. But since 1948, because of the threat to the state which has been considered to arise from Communist or Fascist activities, and because of the danger to national security caused by foreign espionage, there have been special security measures which affect those engaged in work vital to the security of the state, whether they are employed in the public service or by government contractors. One procedure, the purge procedure, applies to all civil servants concerned with work the nature of which is vital to state security: its aim is to discover whether any of these persons are, or have recently been, members of the Communist party or Fascists, sympathetic to Communism or Fascism, associated with Communists or Fascists, or susceptible to Communist or Fascist pressure. If any civil servant is found to be within one of these categories he may be transferred to other work or dismissed from the civil service. Before a final decision is taken, the civil servant may ask for his case to be referred to a panel of three advisers before whom he will have a right to an informal hearing and certain other limited procedural rights. By another procedure, positive vetting, civil servants who are being considered for promotion to the rank of under-secretary or who are employed on exceptionally secret work may be subject to a special investigation into their character and circumstances, which goes far beyond political beliefs or associations.[51] These procedures are also applied to government contractors engaged on secret work, and may be used to withhold facilities (for example, access to official establishments) from Communists and others holding office in civil service staff associations and trade unions. Security measures inevitably lead to restrictions being imposed on some individuals but without any such measures a government's activities would be very vulnerable to certain forms of external influence. The Official Secrets Acts apply to all civil servants and a civil servant will have the right to defend himself if a pros-

---

[48] Cmnd 7057, 1978.
[49] H.C. Deb., 26 Mar. 1981, col. 1186; 4 Mar. 1982, col. 503; 19 Jul. 1984, col. 272 (W.A.).
[50] See also ch. 30; and Wilson, *Cases*, pp. 89–98.
[51] For recent reports on positive vetting, see Cmnd 8540, 1982; Cmnd 8876, 1983; and H.C. 242 (1982–3).

ecution is brought under those Acts. But apart from this the civil servant has no recourse to the courts should adverse action be taken against him under security procedures,[52] and there is no effective form of parliamentary control of these procedures.

Interests of national security brought about controversial action by the government in 1984 which inter alia took away from staff at Government Communications Headquarters, Cheltenham, the freedom to join a trade union and the right to seek remedies from an industrial tribunal for unfair dismissal. These measures, ordered by the Prime Minister in her capacity as Minister for the Civil Service, took the form of (a) statutory certificates exempting GCHQ staff from the Employment Protection (Consolidation) Act 1978, and (b) instructions under the prerogative laying down new conditions of service for the future that excluded union membership.[53] The civil service unions failed to persuade the government to change its mind, and action in the English courts also failed. Glidewell J. held that while the government had power to take the measures in question, the GCHQ staff should have been consulted before being deprived of their right of union membership. But the Court of Appeal held that action taken under the prerogative on grounds of national security was not subject to judicial review; even if acts of the prerogative were subject to review, prior consultation by the government with the staff would have served no useful purpose. In November 1984, an appeal to the House of Lords against this decision was rejected.[54]

---

52   *Cf. R.* v. *Home Secretary, ex p. Hosenball* [1977] 3 All E.R. 452, p. 457 *post.*
53   See H.C. Deb., 25 Jan. 1984, col. 917; 31 Jan. 1984, col. 119 (W.A.); 1 Feb. 1984, col. 209; 27 Feb. 1984, col. 25; and 1 Mar. 1984, col. 387. And see H.C. 238 (1983–4).
54   *The Times,* 23 Nov. 1984.

Chapter 16

Public finance, taxation and the economy

Government policies for taxation and public expenditure have long been liable to give rise to legal and constitutional disputes. In the 20th century, the responsibilities of central government have widened to include not just raising and spending the proceeds of taxation to meet the costs of government but also the tasks of overseeing the national economy, maintaining policies on employment and the social services, and securing a sound external balance of payments. In chapter 11 C, an account was given of the financial procedures of Parliament. The present chapter deals in outline with the main financial procedures of government. These matters are mostly the responsibility of the Treasury which, with the Cabinet Office, is at the centre of the structure of government.

The Treasury[1]

Since 1714, the ancient office of Lord High Treasurer has always been in commission; that is, its duties have been entrusted to a board of commissioners. Today the commissioners are the First Lord of the Treasury, an office held by the Prime Minister; the Chancellor of the Exchequer; and the Junior Lords of the Treasury, who are the assistant government whips in the House of Commons. The Treasury Board never meets, individual members of the board being responsible for the Treasury's business. Treasury warrants are usually signed by two of the Junior Lords.

The Chancellor of the Exchequer's responsibilities cover the whole range of Treasury business, including the control of public expenditure and the direction of economic and financial policy. He is invariably a member of the Commons. The other Treasury ministers include the Chief Secretary to the Treasury, who has since 1961 dealt with all matters of public expenditure, including the scrutiny of departmental estimates, and is often a member of the Cabinet; the Financial Secretary to the Treasury, who by custom is charged with handling the government's financial business in the Commons, including the passage of the Finance Bill;[2] and the Economic Secretary to the Treasury.

---

[1]   See Lord Bridges, *The Treasury*; H. Roseveare, *The Treasury*; and J. Barnett, *Inside the Treasury*.
[2]   By convention of the House, his initials are required before a financial resolution may be placed on the order paper: Bridges, *op. cit.*, p. 35; and p. 181 *ante*.

The Parliamentary Secretary to the Treasury acts as the government's chief whip in the Commons and has had no connection with Treasury business since political patronage in the civil service disappeared in the 19th century. The duties of Paymaster-General are purely formal: payments on account of the public service are made to the Paymaster-General by the Bank of England and the money is then paid out in his name to the departments and other persons authorised to receive it. In practice the Paymaster-General may serve as a minister without portfolio, or may be assigned ministerial duties in the Treasury or in another department.

Functions of the Treasury
The Treasury's functions were formerly concerned primarily with financial matters, including the imposition and regulation of taxation, the control of expenditure and the management of the government's funds and accounts. But in the 20th century, except for two periods when a separate department for economic affairs was established (for some months in 1947 and between 1964 and 1969), the Treasury has also become an economic policy department. A recent official description of its tasks states simply that the Treasury is responsible for the overall management of the economy.[3] Its work was in 1982 organised into four main sectors (a) the public services sector, responsible for public expenditure in aggregate and for most of the departmental spending programmes, including civil service manpower and pay; (b) the economy sector, concerned with fiscal, monetary and counter-inflation policies, and the oversight of industrial policy, including expenditure on industry and agriculture; (c) the overseas finance sector, concerned with the balance of payments, the management of the reserves, international monetary co-operation, the overseas aid programme, and matters connected with British membership of the EEC; (d) the chief economic adviser's sector, that prepares economic forecasts and gives specialist advice on macro-economic policies. The Treasury has a strong complement of the most senior civil servants. In 1982, as well as the Permanent Secretary to the Treasury, there were three Second Permanent Secretaries (each leading one of the first three sectors mentioned) and the Chief Economic Adviser to the Treasury.

A variety of other agencies and boards enable the Treasury's tasks to be performed. Thus the administration of taxation is vested in the Board of Inland Revenue and the Board of Customs and Excise. They come under the general direction of the Chancellor of the Exchequer, who is responsible to Parliament for their work; but this responsibility does not include responsibility for tax assessments made in respect of individual taxpayers.[4] Other subordinate departments placed under the control of the Treasury include the Royal Mint and the Public Works Loans Board, which 'advances money to local authorities for capital expenditure.

We have already seen that, during the life of the Civil Service Department between 1968 and 1981, that department exercised responsibilities for the civil service which before 1968 had been vested in the Treasury. In 1981, the Treasury again became responsible for the numbers and grading of posts in

---

[3]   *Civil Service Yearbook 1982.*
[4]   Page 292 *post.*

the civil service, and for the pay, allowances and superannuation of the civil service and the armed forces.[5]

The Bank of England

The Bank of England was first established in 1694, mainly to provide loans to meet the needs of the Crown; it eventually became the government's bankers for all purposes. It was taken into public ownership under the Bank of England Act 1946, although the Treasury had for many years been able to control its policies. Under the 1946 Act, the Bank of England remains a separate institution from the Treasury and it is not a government department. But the Governor and directors of the Bank are appointed by the Crown, and the Treasury is empowered to issue formal directions to the Bank.[6] In practice, the Bank undertakes many tasks in the financial field (for example, control of the monetary system, regulation of borrowing by the commercial banks) which are entrusted by formal or informal delegation to the Bank by the Treasury. The close relations between Treasury and Bank are indicated by the fact that the Treasury's statutory power to issue formal directions to the Bank has never been exercised,[7] but the Bank may still give independent advice to the Treasury.[8] Between 1969 and 1979, the Bank was in some of its activities subject to investigation by the select committee on nationalised industries of the House of Commons.[9] Since 1979, the Bank has come within the sphere of the Treasury and Civil Service Committee of the Commons, as one of the 'associated public bodies' related to the Treasury.[10]

The revenue and expenditure cycle

The annual cycle of revenue and expenditure that was established in the 19th century depended on a highly centralised system of financial procedure built up by a combination of statutory and parliamentary rules, Cabinet conventions and administrative practices. In chapter 11 C we saw that without the formal authority of Parliament the Crown could neither raise money by taxation nor incur expenditure. While permanent authority was given by statute for some forms of expenditure and revenue, authority for much expenditure and taxation was given by Parliament strictly on an annual basis. This led to the system by which each year the Treasury co-ordinated the various expenditure needs of the departments. While the annual cycle ensured that Parliament should regularly approve the government's financial proposals, the government in fact retained a firm control over the House; thus by a standing order of the House dating from 1713, the House could not consider new charges on the public revenue or new taxes except on the recommendation of the Crown signified by a Minister.[11] This emphasised that the government bore the primary responsibility for all taxation and expenditure.

---

[5] Ch. 15.
[6] Bank of England Act 1946, s. 4.
[7] T. C. Daintith (1976) 92 L.Q.R. 62, 74; and Bridges, *op. cit.*, pp. 68–9.
[8] M. Moran (1981) 59 *Public Administration* 47.
[9] Ch. 17 A and see H.C. 258 (1969–70).
[10] Ch. 11 D.
[11] Ch. 11 C.

Consolidated Fund and other funds

This centralised system required that all the revenue collected for the national exchequer be paid into a single fund and that all payments for public purposes should come from the same fund. With certain exceptions, all revenue derived from taxation is paid into the Consolidated Fund.[12] In the case of receipts which arise in the course of a department's business (for example, sales or fees for services provided) these may be appropriated in aid of the department's estimate of the money which it will need, thereby reducing the provision which would otherwise have to be made by Parliament; but any surplus over the estimated figure must be paid into the Consolidated Fund.[13] Formerly all money lent by the government came from the Consolidated Fund but in 1968 a separate account with the Bank of England was established, named the National Loans Fund, through which all borrowing by central government and most domestic lending transactions now pass. The operations of the two funds are very closely linked: thus sums needed to meet charges on the National Loans Fund must be paid into it from the Consolidated Fund and a process of daily balancing takes place between the funds.[14]

The annual cycle of financial provision by Parliament proved unsuitable as a means of financing activities of government which were in the nature of trading or business undertakings. In 1973 it was provided that certain government services (for example, the Royal Mint, the Royal Ordnance Factories, Her Majesty's Stationery Office and other similar services) could be financed by means of a trading fund established with public money, instead of by means of annual votes and appropriations from Parliament; the initial capital would normally be provided by way of loan from the National Loans Fund and a financial target for the service would be set by the Treasury.[15] The aim is to improve the accountable management of the undertaking: its staff remain civil servants and ministerial responsibility continues.

Consolidated Fund and Supply services

The expenditure of central departments may be classified under two heads, namely Consolidated Fund services and supply services. The Consolidated Fund services are payments under statutes which provide continuing authority for the payments in question: the customary statutory phrase is that such payments 'shall be charged on and paid out of the Consolidated Fund'. As this authority continues from year to year, it is not necessary for the payments to be voted each year by the Commons. The principal expenditure under this heading is the provision which is made *via* the National Loans Fund for paying the interest on the national debt. There are also charged on the Consolidated Fund other payments which for constitutional reasons are considered inappropriate for annual review and authorisation by Parliament. These include the Civil List,[16] and the salaries of the Speaker, the judiciary, the Comptroller

---

12 Consolidated Fund Act 1816. Certain payments are made to special funds *e.g.* the National Insurance Fund in the case of social security contributions (Social Security Act 1975, s. 134).
13 Public Accounts and Charges Act 1891.
14 National Loans Act 1968, s. 18.
15 Government Trading Funds Act 1973.
16 Ch. 13 A.

and Auditor General and the Parliamentary Commissioner for Administration. This means that there is no regular annual opportunity of discussing in Parliament the work of these officers. This practice tends purposely to preserve their independence, but the constitutional justification for it loses some of its force during rapid inflation when the Civil List and public salaries may need to be increased or supplemented annually. A different example of a charge on the Consolidated Fund was created by the European Communities Act 1972: section 2(3) gives continuing authority for payment from the Consolidated Fund or National Loans Fund of any amounts required to meet Community obligations, whether these payments are to be made to Community organs, to other member states or to the European Investment Bank. While it was argued by the government in 1972 that such continuing authority was an essential feature of British membership of EEC,[17] it is politically convenient for the government to have continuing authority to pay over the large sums concerned, without seeking fresh approval from Parliament each year.

By contrast, supply services involve charges for purposes stated by the statutes which authorise them to be payable 'out of money to be provided by Parliament'. This statutory phrase means that an estimate must be presented to Parliament in each year that the expenditure is to be incurred and payment appropriated to it by an Appropriation Act. The great bulk of departmental expenditure is voted annually on this basis, through the procedure of supply already described.[18]

Comptroller and Auditor General[19]

An essential aspect of parliamentary control of expenditure is that the House of Commons should be able to ensure that public money is used for the purposes for which it has been voted. The Comptroller and Auditor General is head of the National Audit Office, known before 1984 as the Exchequer and Audit Department. Like senior judges, he holds office during good behaviour, subject to a power of removal by the Crown on an address from both Houses of Parliament. His duties are two-fold. First, as Comptroller, he ensures that all revenue is duly paid into the Consolidated Fund and the National Loans Fund, and his authority to the Bank of England is required before the Treasury may withdraw money from the Funds; in this capacity, he must see that the total limits of expenditure authorised by Parliament are not exceeded. Second, as Auditor General, he and a staff of over 600 officials are responsible for examining the accounts of departments annually. The purpose was originally to ensure that money had been spent only for the purpose intended by Parliament and, when required, with the authority of the Treasury.[20] In practice, from the 19th century the audit also sought to discover instances of waste and extravagance. Express authority for 'value for money' and 'efficiency' auditing was given by the National Audit Act 1983.[21] The Comptroller and Auditor

---

[17]   H.C. Deb. 22 Feb. 1972, col. 1137 and 8 Jun. 1972, col. 813.

[18]   Ch. 11 C.

[19]   Exchequer and Audit Departments Acts 1866–1957; National Audit Act 1983; E.L. Normanton, *The Accountability and Audit of Governments*; D. Henley (and others), *Public Sector Accounting and Financial Control*, chs. 2, 7.

[20]   Exchequer and Audit Departments Act 1921, s. 1.

[21]   For the background, see Cmnd 7845, 1980; H.C. 115 (1980–1), discussed by G. Drewry, [1981] P.L. 304; and Cmnd 8323, 1981.

General may under that Act carry out examinations into the economy, efficiency and effectiveness with which a department has used its resources in
discharging its functions; but he may not question the merits of the policy
objectives set for a department. His powers extend not only to central departments but also to the National Health Service and to other bodies or institutions (such as the universities) which are wholly or mainly supported from
public funds and to whose records and accounts he has access for inspection
purposes.[22]

The Comptroller and Auditor General reports on his investigations to the
Committee of Public Accounts of the Commons. This committee has 15
members and its chairman is always a senior opposition M.P. who has held
ministerial office, often as a Treasury minister. For each department the
Treasury appoints an Accounting Officer, who is usually the Permanent
Secretary of the department. The practice of the Public Accounts Committee
is to follow up selected audit reports by calling the Accounting Officer before
the committee to explain publicly the actions of the department. In exceptional circumstances, where a particular item of expenditure has been incurred
by decision of a minister against the written advice of the Permanent
Secretary, the minister himself may have to account to the committee for that
item. The committee's work depends essentially on the investigations made by
the staff of the Comptroller and Auditor General. This may reveal misuse of
funds that was unknown to the department concerned, as in 1963 when serious
overcharging by contractors on the Bloodhound missile contracts was discovered.[23]

In 1981–2, matters examined by the committee included a government guarantee of
up to £200 million given to International Computers Ltd; the sale of shares in British
Aerospace, British Petroleum and other publicly owned companies; the escalation to
£1,000 million in the costs of the Chevaline improvement to the Polaris missile system,
and failure to disclose these costs to Parliament; fraud and irregularities in the Property
Services Agency; and the refusal by British Leyland to permit the Comptroller and
Auditor General to inspect documents held by the company relating to the sale of a
tractor assembly line by Leyland Vehicles Ltd to a private purchaser.[24]

The reports made to the Commons by the Public Accounts Committee are
debated annually by the House. The government is expected to reply to criticisms and to act on them. The published rulings made by the Committee and
the related Treasury Minutes are an authoritative guide to the main rules of
financial accountability.[25]

Important changes in the status of the Comptroller and Auditor General
were made by the National Audit Act 1983. In particular, appointments to
the office are no longer made by the Crown on the advice of the Prime
Minister, but by the Crown upon a resolution of the House of Commons,
moved by the Prime Minister with the approval of the chairman of the Public
Accounts Committee (section 1 (1)). The Comptroller and Auditor General

---

[22]   National Audit Act 1983, ss. 6–8.
[23]   H.C. 183 (1963–4) and H.C. Deb., 29 Apr. 1964, col. 408.
[24]   See respectively H.C. 17, 189, 269, 382 and 407 (1981–2).
[25]   Epitome of Reports from the Committee of Public Accounts 1857–1937 and 1938–69, H.C.
       154 (1937–8) and 187 (1969–70).

is declared to be an officer of the House of Commons (section 1 (2)), a statutory change which confirmed the assumption made since 1866 that he exercises his powers on behalf of the House. While he has complete discretion in exercising his functions, he must take into account proposals regarding his investigations that may be made by the Public Accounts Committee (section 1 (3)). The aim behind these reforms was to strengthen still further the authority and independence of the audit system, and to improve the ability of the Commons to ensure the proper use of public funds, both by central departments and by many bodies that receive public funding. But no system of public audit can guarantee that controversial political decisions involving heavy expenditure will not be made (for example, the costly development of the Concorde aircraft)[26] and economies for their own sake are not always popular, either with politicians or civil servants.[27]

Control of public expenditure

The annual cycle of estimates and supply backed up by public accounting provided a structure within which Treasury control of expenditure was formerly exercised.[28] In addition to the approval of a department's estimates, Treasury consent was needed for new services and for any new policies which involved an increase in expenditure.[29] Another aspect of the system has been the rule laid down by successive Prime Ministers that, except in cases of extreme urgency, no memorandum involving any financial issue may be circulated to the Cabinet or a Cabinet committee unless it has been seen and discussed by the Treasury. The system of Treasury control depended ultimately on the Chancellor's political authority within the Cabinet. Significantly, three Treasury ministers resigned in January 1958 when they had failed to persuade Mr Macmillan's Cabinet to restrict expenditure.[30]

One limitation of the system of Treasury control was that individual policy decisions could be taken on a piecemeal and unplanned basis, commitments being accepted for political reasons without regard for the implications for total government spending. Another limitation was that decisions were made within a system related to cash provision for one financial year at a time, whereas many modern programmes (for example, motorway construction, hospital building and defence procurement) may take many years to be planned and brought into operation. Moreover, the supply procedure applied only to a part of total public expenditure (namely the supply services) and not to the Consolidated Fund services, nor to such matters as the payment of social security benefits from the National Insurance Fund, nor to expenditure by local authorities and nationalised industries.

In 1961, the Plowden report recommended that regular surveys should be made of public expenditure as a whole, over a period of years ahead and in

---

[26]   See H.C. 335 (1972–3) and C. C. Turpin, *Government Contracts*, ch. 2.
[27]   *Cf.* L. Chapman, *Your Disobedient Servant*. For the cautionary tale of the Crown Agents, see G. Ganz [1980] P.L. 454.
[28]   For the system as it used to be, see S. H. Beer, *Treasury Control* and B. Chubb, *The Control of Public Expenditure*.
[29]   See H.C. 251–1 (1957–8) p. 3.
[30]   For the relationship between Chancellor and Cabinet see H. Heclo and A. Wildavsky, *The Private Government of Public Money*, ch. 4.

relation to prospective resources; and that decisions involving substantial future expenditure should be taken in the light of those surveys.[31] This influential report led to the creation of a new system of public expenditure control,[32] but changes in that system became necessary in the 1970s as economic growth declined and the control of expenditure broke down during the period of rapid inflation in 1973–5.

Unlike the supply estimates, the public expenditure survey system covers all forms of public expenditure, including expenditure by local authorities and nationalised industries. The survey is made annually by the spending departments in consultation with the Treasury, under the supervision of the Public Expenditure Survey Committee (PESC), a committee of officials chaired by the Treasury and including the principal finance officers of the departments. Each summer a report on the survey is submitted to the Cabinet, showing the effect of continuing present policies over the next three to four years. This report is the basis for Cabinet decisions about the future size and content of expenditure programmes, taking account of existing commitments, political priorities and economic factors. Eventually, not later than the date of the Chancellor's Budget statement to the Commons, a white paper is published embodying the government's decisions. If time permits, this will be considered by the Treasury and Civil Service Committee of the Commons before it is debated in the House.[33]

The most significant change in the PESC system made during the 1970s was probably the introduction of cash limits in 1976.[34] Before then, public expenditure was essentially planned in 'volume terms'; that is, it was based on the volume of approved spending programmes (for example, so many new miles of motorway). As wages and prices of materials increased with inflation, the programmes were not themselves affected and the necessary cash requirement was automatically increased. In 1976, cash limits were applied by the Labour government to counter this automatic increase in cash provision. The method was adopted and extended by the Conservative government after 1979 as a primary means of restraining public expenditure and of managing the economy. Thus, cash limits have been used to limit pay-increases within the public sector and to control the numbers of those so employed.[35] Cash limits are applied to as many spending programmes as possible, including the rate support grant paid to local authorities, but they do not apply to programmes which are 'demand determined', such as social security payments, which must be paid to every person who becomes entitled to them. Since 1979, cash limits have been related directly to the supply estimates, and as such are approved by Parliament. Nationalised industries and water authorities are subject to 'external financing limits', which limit the resources these industries may receive apart from their own revenues. The system of annual cash limits was

---

[31]   Cmnd 1432, 1961.
[32]   For early accounts of PESC see Cmnd 4071, 1969 and H.C. 549 (1970–71); R. Clarke, *New Trends in Government* ch. 2; and Heclo and Wildavsky, *op. cit.*, ch. 5.
[33]   See *e.g.* for 1983, Cmnd 8789 and H.C. 204 (1982–3).
[34]   Cmnd 6440, 1976; H.C. 274 (1977–8); M. Elliott (1977) 40 M.L.R. 569; and J. A. Likierman, *Cash Limits and External Financing Limits*.
[35]   See P. K. Else and G. P. Marshall (1981) 59 *Public Administration* 253, and G. Bevan, K. Sisson and P. Way (1981) 59 *Public Administration* 379.

extended to medium-term control by cash planning from 1981.[36] Despite these and other changes in financial procedures, proposals have been made for remodelling the budgetary system and for closer parliamentary scrutiny of the government's financial policies.[37]

Taxation

While the control of public expenditure remains an urgent constitutional problem, lawyers' skills are probably less relevant to it than they are to the process of taxation by which funds are obtained from the citizen to pay for the expenditure incurred on his behalf. It is not necessary here to outline the principal forms of direct and indirect taxation which Parliament has authorised. The Commissioners of Inland Revenue are charged with the administration and management of such taxes as income tax, corporation tax and capital gains tax.[38] While the rates of these taxes are fixed from year to year by the Finance Act, permanent authority for the machinery of tax-collection is contained in such Acts as the Income and Corporation Taxes Act 1970 and the Taxes Management Act 1970. These Acts provide for the appointment of the Commissioners of Inland Revenue, who are all civil servants: under their direction, a citizen's liability to tax is assessed by inspectors of taxes and the assessed tax is collected by collectors of taxes. In the performance of their duties the Commissioners of Inland Revenue are subject to the authority, direction and control of the Treasury.[39] Where a taxpayer does not accept that he has been correctly assessed for income tax by an inspector of taxes, he has a right of appeal to an independent tribunal which may, depending on the circumstances, be either the General Commissioners of Income Tax or the Special Commissioners of Income Tax.[40] From these tribunals, appeals on points of law lie to the High Court in England or to the Court of Session in Scotland, and thence further appeals may reach the House of Lords.

The principal forms of indirect taxation, such as value added tax, customs and excise duties, and gaming and betting duties, are administered by the second revenue department, the Commissioners of Customs and Excise,[41] whose position closely resembles that of the Inland Revenue Commissioners. As with income tax, customs and excise duties must be collected in accordance with the law and assessments are subject to an appeal to an administrative tribunal (for example, the value added tax tribunal) or to a court. The detailed rules of these forms of taxation are contained in continuing Acts of Parliament, but the rates of duty may be subject to variation from time to time by the Treasury or by a Secretary of State under the authority of an Act of Parliament.[42] Many of the duties administered by the Commissioners of Customs and Excise are directly affected by obligations which arise from British membership of the EEC.

---

[36] Treasury, *Economic Progress Report* No. 139, Nov. 1981.
[37] See W. Armstrong (ed.), *Budgetary Reform in the UK*; and H.C. 24 (1982–3).
[38] See A. Johnston, *The Inland Revenue*, and annual reports of the Commissioners.
[39] Inland Revenue Regulation Act 1890, s. 2.
[40] Ch. 37 A.
[41] Customs and Excise Act 1952; J. Crombie, *Her Majesty's Customs and Excise*.
[42] *E.g.* Import Duties Act 1958; Finance Act 1961, s. 9.

Taxation and the courts

Whenever a government department demands payment of a tax or other charge from the citizen, the citizen may challenge the legality of the demand in the courts but he may first be required to appeal to the relevant tribunal. When such a dispute reaches the court, the court may take into account the ancient principle expressed in the Bill of Rights that the authority of Parliament must be shown to exist if any tax or charge on the citizen is to be lawful.[43] Thus it has been held that a tax may not be imposed in reliance on a resolution of the House of Commons alone, in the absence of a statute giving legal effect to the resolution.[44] Subordinate legislation which infringes the Bill of Rights principle may be declared invalid by the courts.[45] When in 1975 the television licence fee was increased, it was held unlawful for the Home Office to use a discretionary power to revoke licences so as to prevent viewers from receiving the benefit of an overlapping licence bought at the lower rate just before the increased fee became operative.[46] The courts control the legality not only of the taxes which may be demanded from the citizen but also of administrative steps leading to a tax assessment: thus in *Dyson* v. *Attorney-General*[47] the court declared that certain information demanded by the Commissioners of Inland Revenue on threat of a £50 penalty could not lawfully be required of the citizen.

Although the assessment of tax is governed by law, certain areas of tax administration escape judicial control. Thus the revenue authorities may exercise their discretion not to enforce payment against an individual taxpayer or a class of taxpayers; only in very exceptional circumstances could another taxpayer complain of such a decision to the courts.[48] The revenue authorities may also issue extra-statutory concessions by which they announce that tax due will be waived in certain circumstances. While such concessions have received judicial criticism,[49] it is difficult for a court to take direct notice of them and they do not affect the payment that in law is due. However, these concessions may as a matter of policy come under the scrutiny of the Comptroller and Auditor General. An individual's complaint about the refusal of a concession in his case may be investigated by the Parliamentary Commissioner for Administration on a complaint of maladministration causing injustice to the citizen.[50]

Management of the economy

Power to control public expenditure and the imposition of taxes are only two of the means by which governments seek to manage the economy. In a vast area of governmental power, which public lawyers are now beginning to explore,[51] other means include monetary policy and control of borrowing,

---

43 Page 14, *ante*.
44 *Bowles* v. *Bank of England* [1913] 1 Ch. 57; p. 202 *ante*.
45 *Commissioners of Customs and Excise* v. *Cure and Deeley Ltd* [1962] 1 Q.B. 340; ch. 33.
46 *Congreve* v. *Home Office* [1976] Q.B. 629.
47 [1912] 1 Ch. 158.
48 Pages 666–7 *post*.
49 *Vestey* v. *Inland Revenue Cmssrs.* [1980] A.C. 1148; ch. 33.
50 Ch. 37 D; see *e.g.* Annual Report of PCA for 1970, H.C. 261 (1970–1) p. 36.
51 *E.g.* V. Korah (1976) 92 L.Q.R. 42; T. C. Daintith (1976) 92 L.Q.R. 62, (1979) 32 C.L.P. 41, and (1982) 9 Jl. of Law and Society 191; A. C. Page (1982) 9 Jl. of Law and Society 225.

control over consumer transactions, prices and incomes, and financial assistance to business and industry. The special powers which economic difficulties
during the 1970s forced governments to take to deal with inflation were usually
limited in duration; they enabled governments to intervene much more extensively in private economic transactions than had previously been possible in
peace-time. The legislative sequence included the Counter-Inflation (Temporary Provisions) Act 1972, the Counter-Inflation Act 1973, the Remuneration,
Charges and Grants Act 1975, the Price Commission Act 1977 and the
Dividends Act 1978. Most of the continuing provisions of this legislation were
repealed by the Competition Act 1980, the Conservative government preferring to use different means of achieving its economic policies.

In an economic crisis, a government may be forced to take exceptional steps
and the legislation had a number of novel aspects. Thus the Price Commission,
a regulatory body set up under the 1972 Act, could under the 1973 Act issue
orders or notices to employers and businesses. Breach of these could create
criminal liability, yet the orders or notices themselves might define expressions
used in the Act under which they were issued.[52] The 1975 Act was notable
for the manner in which the 'social contract' approved by the trade unions as
a basis for voluntary wage restraint was given a measure of statutory effect and
provision made for a new policy document to take its place.[53] One consequence
of the need to continue an incomes policy after the 1975 'social contract'
expired came in the Chancellor of the Exchequer's 1976 Budget proposals:
certain increases in personal tax allowances were made conditional upon the
agreement of the trade unions being obtained to an incomes policy. This agreement was duly obtained and the allowances were included in the Finance Act
1976, but some critics considered that this development diminished the
authority of both government and Parliament.[54]

A far more controversial development occurred between 1976 and 1978
when the minority Labour government, having laid down non-statutory guidelines on pay, sought to enforce these against employers by means that included
the blacklisting of companies which breached the guidelines. The sanctions
used by the government included the withholding of government contracts, the
refusal of industrial assistance and export credit guarantees, and the inclusion
of a pay-limits clause in new government contracts.[55] While the government's
use of the Crown's contractual capacity to achieve its policies would seem to
have been legal, it is less certain that the government could lawfully use powers
under industrial assistance and export credits legislation to impose pressure
upon companies to confirm with non-statutory pay limits. Before the issue was
decided by a court, the government's pay-policy was itself defeated in the
House of Commons and the blacklisting of companies was abandoned.[56]

---

[52] Counter-Inflation Act 1973, sched. 3, para. 1(1), discussed by Korah, *op. cit.*, p. 44.
[53] Remuneration, Charges and Grants Act 1975, s. 1.
[54] *E.g. The Times*, 7 Apr. 1976 (editorial).
[55] R. B. Ferguson and A. C. Page (1978) 128 N.L.J. 515; G. Ganz [1978] P.L. 333.
[56] H.C. Deb., 13 Dec. 1978, col. 673 and 14 Dec. 1978, col. 920.

Chapter 17

Public boards and advisory bodies

We have already considered the constitutional position of government departments, and have seen that they are staffed by civil servants and headed by ministers who are responsible to Parliament for their activities. When functions are entrusted to local authorities,[1] the administrative structure is very different from that in central government, yet political responsibility for the policies and decisions of local councils is borne by the elected councillors. Today many public tasks are entrusted not to central or local government, but to a wide variety of official boards, commissions and other agencies. Some are well known, such as the BBC, the British Railways Board and the University Grants Committee. Many of them operate in obscurity, known only to a few civil servants and specialists in the area concerned. It is difficult to generalise about such diversity, but these bodies have one feature in common, namely that the members of these boards and agencies are not publicly elected. Instead, these members have all been appointed to their posts, in the vast majority of cases by central government (that is, by the minister of the department concerned with the activity in question). Thus, while ministers do not directly administer the affairs of these bodies, ministers have an underlying but indirect responsibility to Parliament for their continued efficiency and effectiveness. Many of these bodies were created by means of legislation and many are wholly or mainly supported by public funds. If one of these bodies antagonises public opinion, overspends the funds available to it, is badly administered or has outlived its usefulness, then the minister can be asked in Parliament to introduce legislation abolishing the body or reforming its powers, to appoint a new governing body, or to take other steps for improving the position.[2] Moreover, because of the economic, financial and social significance of some boards (in particular those concerned with the nationalised industries), strategic decisions concerning their activities are inevitably affected by government policies.

---

[1] Ch. 21.
[2] For an outstanding example, see the ill-fated Crown Agents, whose affairs led to the Fay committee of inquiry, (H. C. 48, 1977–8), a judicial tribunal of inquiry (H.C. 364, 1981–2), and the Crown Agents Act 1979; and see G. Ganz [1980] P.L. 454.

During the 1970s, the increasing scale and costs of government helped to bring these appointed bodies into public debate and controversy. Some critics objected to the fact that their functions were being undertaken by the state at all; others to their undemocratic nature and to the amount of patronage that ministers exercised in making appointments to them; and others to the lack of adequate accountability for their activities. One problem was to find a generic name for such diverse bodies. Within government they were described by such terms as 'fringe bodies' and 'non-departmental public bodies'. One unofficial term applied to them was 'quangos', that originally stood for 'quasi non-governmental organisations'.[3] However imprecise, this term entered the language of politics.[4] After its election in 1979, the Conservative government's programme of cutting back the size and activities of the state included the pruning of quangos. A detailed survey by Sir Leo Pliatzky did much to clarify the various purposes served by many non-departmental public bodies and laid down principles to be observed in their creation and supervision,[5] but relatively few of the agencies were abolished. Indeed, bodies created since 1979 include the National Heritage Memorial Fund Trustees, the Welsh Fourth Channel Authority, the Merseyside and London Docklands Urban Development Corporations, the Audit Commission (for local government finance), the Mental Health Act Commission and a body known as 'Food from Britain' to promote agricultural exports.[6]

Mainly because there is no single agreed definition of the bodies concerned, it is not possible to state accurately how many exist. According to one official but incomplete list,[7] there were in April 1982 over eight hundred separate entities, falling within four broad categories: (a) nationalised industries and similar commercial organisations; (b) non-departmental public bodies that have executive or regulatory functions; (c) non-departmental public bodies that have solely advisory functions; and (d) tribunals, licensing and appeal bodies. In this chapter, we will examine some general questions relating to the public boards that fall within categories (a) and (b). Emphasis will be given to issues that have arisen in relation to the nationalised industries, but important constitutional issues also arise regarding, for example, the control of broadcasting, the financing of the universities, and the enforcement of anti-discrimination policies. We will also consider briefly the many advisory bodies in category (c). The constitutional position of tribunals and other bodies in category (d) will be examined later.[8]

---

[3] See D. C. Hague, W. J. M. Mackenzie and A. Barker (ed.), *Public Policy and Private Interests*; and A. Barker (ed.), *Quangos in Britain*.

[4] See *e.g.* P. Holland, *The Governance of Quangos*, and G. Drewry [1982] P.L. 384.

[5] Cmnd 7797, 1980; and see *Non-Departmental Public Bodies: A Guide for Departments* (HMSO 1981).

[6] See respectively National Heritage Act 1980, Broadcasting Act 1980, Local Government, Planning and Land Act 1980, Local Government Finance Act 1982, Mental Health Act 1983, Agricultural Marketing Act 1983.

[7] *Public Bodies 1982* (HMSO 1983). This list excluded National Health Service bodies, agricultural marketing boards, several 'unique' corporations (*e.g.* the BBC) and companies in which government had substantial holdings (*e.g.* British Aerospace, Rolls Royce).

[8] Ch. 37A.

A. Public boards

History

The creation of specialised public agencies which are not government departments is nothing new. In the 18th century, there were innumerable bodies of commissioners created by private Acts, which exercised limited powers for such purposes as police, paving, lighting, turnpikes and local improvements. Through the curtailment of the powers of the Privy Council in the previous century, they were free from any effective administrative control by central government, but in England they were subject to legal control by means of the prerogative writs issued by the Court of King's Bench. These bodies were essentially local in character. Later, in the period of social and administrative reform which followed the reform of Parliament in 1832, experiments were made in setting up national agencies with administrative powers covering the whole country. One of the most notable experiments occurred in 1834 when the English poor law was reformed. The Poor Law Commissioners enforced on the local administration of poor relief strict central control by means of rules, orders and inspection. Yet no minister answered for the commissioners in Parliament, to defend them against political attack or to control their decisions. In 1847 the experiment gave way to a system based on a minister responsible to Parliament but similar experiments occurred, such as the General Board of Health in 1848. Administration by the board system was much used in Scotland and in Ireland. By the late 19th century, it was accepted that the vesting of public powers in departments of central government had the great constitutional advantage of securing political control through ministerial responsibility.[1] As Chester has remarked, the House of Commons has never found a way of making anybody other than ministers accountable to it.[2]

In the 20th century, the state acquired vast new social and economic powers. Particularly as a result of the nationalisation programme followed by the Labour government from 1945 to 1951, the United Kingdom became and has remained a mixed economy, in which privately owned and publicly owned industrial enterprises co-exist. Extensive schemes of social regulation and welfare have been accepted by all political parties. These developments have not only meant an increase in the tasks entrusted to government departments. There has also been a widespread creation of public boards and other agencies that are classifiable neither as government departments, nor as local authorities. Reacting against these trends, the Conservative government after 1979 sought both to abolish unnecessary public agencies and through 'privatisation' to return profitable public undertakings to private ownership, either wholly or in part. By 1984, changes in the boundary between the public and private sectors had occurred, but most public boards continued to exist.

---

[1] See also Ch. 7 and, for rise and fall of the board system, F. M. G. Willson (1955) 33 *Public Administration* 43 and H. Parris, *Constitutional Bureaucracy*, ch. 3.

[2] D. N. Chester (1979) 57 *Public Administration* 51, 54.

Reasons for the creation of public corporations[3]

Public corporations serve a wide variety of purposes but most of them have a number of characteristics in common. First, they have corporate status, *i.e.* legal capacity to act in their own name, to own property, to make contracts and so on. Second, their existence usually derives directly from an Act of Parliament, although some (for example, the BBC) have been set up by royal charter. Third, they are not government departments, but the members of the boards are appointed by the relevant minister or by the Crown on the advice of ministers. Fourth, because many corporations undertake commercial and industrial activities, their revenue may be largely derived from the charges made to consumers for the services they provide, not from taxation. Fifth, while the boards themselves are entrusted with control of the corporation's activities, the relevant minister retains responsibility for major policy issues, for example approval of programmes of capital expenditure. Sixth, their activities fall within the public sector and are not carried on for private profit.[4]

In theory, the tasks entrusted to public boards could be undertaken directly by civil servants working in government departments, although this would mean a vast increase in the civil service and the adoption by it of new methods. Indeed, before the Post Office was established in 1969 as a public corporation, postal and telephone services had been for very many years provided by the Post Office as a government department. But the existence of so many public corporations affords strong evidence for the view that departmental administration of major industries is likely to be less efficient and less flexible than management by a public board. The post-war nationalisation legislation sought to apply the concept of the public corporation associated with the late Herbert Morrison.[5] This aimed at a combination of vigorous and efficient business management with an appropriate measure of public control and accountability. Civil service methods, Treasury control, and complete accountability to Parliament were considered unsuited to the successful running of a large industry. In the 1945–51 period, when major public utilities, transport and energy undertakings were acquired by the state, they were entrusted not to departments but to new statutory boards. The relevant ministers were given important powers relating to the boards but were not expected to become concerned with the day-to-day management of the industries. Similar reasoning also led to the creation of public corporations to take over certain activities formerly performed by departments, for example the Atomic Energy Authority (1954) and the British Airports Authority (1965).

Another reason for establishing public corporations is to entrust an activity to an autonomous body and thereby reduce the scope for direct political control. The existence of the BBC and the Independent Broadcasting Authority separate from the government is necessary if ministers are not to be responsible for every programme broadcast. The same reason explains why many grant-giving bodies have been established to distribute funds provided

---

[3]   The extensive literature includes: D. N. Chester, *The Nationalisation of British Industry 1945–51*; A. H. Hanson, *Parliament and Public Ownership*; W. A. Robson, *Nationalised Industries and Public Ownership*; W. Friedmann and J. F. Garner (ed.) *Government Enterprise*; J. F. Garner, *Administrative Law*, ch. 10.

[4]   For the position of mixed enterprises, see p. 309 *post*.

[5]   See his book, *Government and Parliament*, ch. 12.

by Parliament. The government is responsible for the total grants made to such bodies as the research councils, the arts councils and the University Grants Committee, but not for the detailed allocation of these funds. The aim of enabling discretionary decisions to be made by an agency without regard to short-term political considerations explains also the existence of the Commission for Racial Equality and the Equal Opportunities Commission, which enforce social legislation designed to reduce racial and sexual discrimination. However, as has been emphasised above, ministers may not absolve themselves of broad responsibility for the existence, activities, funding and composition of such agencies. Nor have all attempts to take a sensitive area of administration 'out of politics' by entrusting it to an appointed board been successful.[6]

The device of a public board for the marketing of agricultural products (for example, the Milk Marketing Board) enables the producers' interests to be represented in the membership of the board. In the case of the National Health Service, a complex structure of boards and other agencies enables various branches of the medical profession to be directly involved in administering the hospitals and other health services but reduces the scope for democratic control of the service.[7]

Since the Fulton report on the civil service in 1968,[8] new managerial structures have been developed within government departments. Some functions have been 'hived off' to new public corporations outside the department, but others have been entrusted to new agencies within a department, for example the Manpower Services Commission within the Department of Employment. While the existence of such a commission has certain advantages (thus the MSC enables experienced persons from both sides of industry to be involved in developing the use of employment services), it is unlikely that these developments in managerial structure will lead to the supersession of existing public corporations.

Classification of public boards

The wide range of activities exercised by public boards and the fact that they have nearly all been created under different Acts of Parliament make it difficult to classify them. But by reference to the main tasks entrusted to them, a number of broad groups may be seen.[9]

1   The major nationalised boards, for example, the National Coal Board and the British Railways Board, which administer industries that were formerly in private ownership. This group also includes bodies such as the Atomic Energy Authority, the Post Office and British Telecommunications, which exercise functions previously vested in government departments, and also bodies such as the regional water authorities, which administer public utilities that were formerly organised on a local basis.[10]

---

6   As with financial relief for the unemployed in 1934: see J. D. Millett, *The Unemployment Assistance Board.*
7   National Health Service Act 1977 and National Health Service (Scotland) Act 1978.
8   Ch. 15.
9   *Cf.* Garner, *op. cit.*, ch. 10; A. H. Hanson and M. Walles, *Governing Britain*, ch. 8.
10   For a list of such boards, see National Audit Act 1983, sch. 4.

2   A closely related group includes various public corporations which provide important national services, for example, the Bank of England, which was taken wholly into public ownership in 1946,[11] and the BBC, incorporated under royal charter and operating under licence from the government.[12]

3   Undertakings created to enable the state to promote economic and industrial development and to take part in commercial activities, including the former National Enterprise Board, the British National Oil Corporation, and the Scottish and Welsh Development Agencies, all established in 1975.

4   Agencies which provide certain social services, for example, the health authorities which administer the national health service; the Housing Corporation and the Scottish Special Housing Association; and the new town development corporations and the Commission for the New Towns.

5   Agencies whose functions are essentially regulatory, for example, the Civil Aviation Authority, which licenses domestic air-services and maintains safety standards; the Independent Broadcasting Authority, which licenses the independent television companies and local radio stations; and the Commission for Racial Equality and the Equal Opportunities Commission, each enforcing legislative policies against discrimination.[13]

6   Agencies which distribute funds provided by Parliament for cultural, educational, and scientific purposes, for example the arts councils and the research councils at home, and the British Council abroad.

7   Agencies which have a very close relationship with a particular government department and which may directly administer a part of that department's work, for example, the Manpower Services Commission, the Health and Safety Commission and the Forestry Commission.

This classification is neither perfect nor complete. The inclusion of two corporations within the same group does not mean that they are the same in all respects: thus the Bank of England's relationship with the government is quite different from the BBC's. Moreover, these groups do not include the agricultural marketing boards, nor the many statutory bodies which regulate professions and occupations by means of licensing, registration and disciplinary means.

Legal structure

There is no uniform legislative framework for the national industries. The structure of the British Railways Board is however typical. The board was established by the Transport Act 1962 under a reorganisation of nationalised transport by which it took over responsibility for the railways from the British Transport Commission. The chairman and between 9 and 15 other members of the board are appointed by the Secretary of State for Transport from among persons appearing to him to have wide experience of transport, industry, finance and other relevant matters.[14] They are paid such salaries or allowances as the Secretary of State may with Treasury approval determine. They are disqualified from membership of the House of Commons. It is the duty of the

---

[11]   Ch. 16.
[12]   Ch. 27 C.
[13]   Ch. 31 A.
[14]   Transport Act 1962, part I and sched. 1, as amended, and S.I. 1981, No. 238.

board to provide railway services in Great Britain and the board may provide other services and facilities in connection with the railway services. The board has power to develop its land, to construct and operate pipe-lines and to manufacture anything required for the purposes of its business or its subsidiaries. The board may acquire other undertakings and with the consent of the Secretary of State may acquire securities in any body corporate. Certain broad financial duties are laid on the board, but many of the board's financial powers (for example, to incur capital expenditure) require the consent of the Secretary of State, given with the approval of the Treasury. The board's borrowing powers are restricted by statute and the main source of borrowing is the National Loans Fund, from which funds may be drawn with the approval of the Secretary of State and the Treasury. The board must keep proper accounts and when audited they are to be sent to the Secretary of State for laying before Parliament. After consultation with the board, the Secretary of State may give 'directions of a general character as to the exercise and performance by the Board of their functions . . . in relation to matters which appear to him to affect the national interest';[15] when given, these directions must be observed by the board. The Secretary of State may also give directions to the board in the interests of national defence. The board must give such information to the Secretary of State about its activities as he may require and the board must make an annual report to him for laying before Parliament. The 1962 Act also provided for the appointment of a Central Transport Consultative Committee, intended to express the views of those who make use of transport services, and of area consultative committees; these latter committees must be consulted, and must consider objections from the public, regarding the closure of passenger services on any railway line.

According to this structure, the management of the railways is vested in the British Railways Board. Neither the members of the board nor the board's employees are civil servants. The board has no private share capital; for new capital it looks to the government and for revenue to the charges it makes on the users of its services. In place of the control which shareholders may exercise over the directors of a company, the government through the Secretary of State and the Treasury may exercise extensive control, particularly in relation to matters of major policy. In furtherance of the Conservative government's policy of privatisation, the Transport Act 1981 gave powers to the board to dispose of its property, assets and subsidiary undertakings, with the consent of the Secretary of State. Under the same Act, the Secretary of State may require the board to form subsidiary companies to facilitate the disposal of its property and activities to private purchasers.

A broadly similar structure is found for other nationalised industries but the Acts are far from uniform. Thus, while the relevant minister usually has power to give directions to the board, the power takes different forms. In the case of the Bank of England, the Treasury's power is 'to give such directions to the Bank as, after consultation with the Governor of the Bank, they think necessary in the public interest'.[16] It has sometimes been proposed that the

---

[15] Transport Act 1962, s. 27(1).
[16] Bank of England Act 1946, s. 4(1).

minister should have power to give both general and specific directions to a board when this would be in the public interest.[17] In 1978, the Labour government expressed agreement with this,[18] but the necessary amendments were not made to the legislation. It seems from recent legislation that the Conservative government in 1983 was opposed to a power to give specific directions except to promote privatisation.[19]

The detailed rules governing the composition of each board depend on the Act in question, but essentially they leave appointments to the discretion of the relevant minister. A departure from the normal pattern is the British National Oil Corporation, where the statute requires that two places on the board are held by members of the civil service. The government's practice is to appoint senior civil servants from the Department of Energy and the Treasury respectively who are concerned with the oil industry. However the two official members are not entitled to vote and do not receive additional remuneration.[20]

While most nationalised industries are administered by statutory boards this is not the invariable pattern. Public ownership may take the form of state ownership of shares in an existing company. Thus it was by purchase of shares that the aero-engine manufacturing business of Rolls-Royce was acquired in 1971.[21] In these situations the legal structure of the company is governed by the Companies Act 1948, although as sole shareholder the government has effective control. The form of a limited company is particularly suitable for an enterprise that is partly in private and partly in public ownership. The creation of companies in the public sector has recently been encouraged to facilitate the policy of privatisation.[22]

Legal status

Except where statutes provide otherwise, departments of central government share in the legal status of the Crown and may benefit from certain privileges and immunities which are peculiar to the Crown.[23] But local authorities, statutory bodies set up for local commercial purposes and privately owned companies do not benefit from Crown status.[24] Into which category do the nationalised industries fall?

In *Tamlin* v. *Hannaford*, it had to be decided whether, after nationalisation of the railways, a dwelling-house owned by the British Transport Commission was subject to the Rent Restriction Acts or was exempted from them by virtue of being Crown property. After examining the Transport Act 1947, the Court of Appeal rejected the view that the commission was the servant or agent of the Crown, even though the Ministry of

---

[17] H.C. 371–I (1967–8), ch. 13; and National Economic Development Office, *A study of UK Nationalised Industries.*
[18] Cmnd 7131, 1978; *cf.* Cmnd 4027, 1969.
[19] *E.g.* British Telecommunications Act 1981, s. 6.
[20] Petroleum and Submarine Pipe-Lines Act 1975, s. 1 and sched. 1.
[21] Rolls-Royce (Purchase) Act 1971; and see British Leyland Act 1975.
[22] *E.g.* Civil Aviation Act 1980, s. 3; Transport Act 1981, Parts I, II; Oil and Gas (Enterprise) Act 1982, Part I.
[23] Ch. 13 C.
[24] *Mersey Docks and Harbour Trustees* v. *Gibbs* (1866) L.R. 1 H.L. 93, p. 677 *post.*

Transport had wide statutory powers of control over the commission. 'In the eye of the law, the corporation is its own master and is answerable as fully as any other person or corporation. It is not the Crown and has none of the immunities or privileges of the Crown. Its servants are not civil servants and its property is not Crown property . . . It is, of course, a public authority and its purposes, no doubt, are public purposes, but it is not a government department nor do its powers fall within the province of government.'[25]

It would seem that this decision governs the status of other public corporations, especially in the nationalised industries, unless they are expressly made to act by and on behalf of the Crown or are directly placed under a minister of the Crown, as in the case of the health authorities, which are means of enabling the. Secretary of State to perform his statutory duty to provide health services.[26] In *Pfizer Corporation* v. *Ministry of Health*, it was held that, since a hospital board was acting on behalf of the then Minister of Health, the treatment of patients in NHS hospitals was a government function and thus the use of drugs was use 'for the services of the Crown'; the Crown could therefore make use of its special rights under patent law for importing drugs.[27] By contrast, in *BBC* v. *Johns*, the BBC were held not to be entitled to benefit from the Crown's immunity from taxation since broadcasting had not become a function of the central government.[28] It was strange that financial considerations led the BBC in this case to argue its close dependence upon the Crown and central government, whereas usually the BBC is anxious to stress its independence.

It is today usual for the statute which creates a new public corporation to make express provision for its status. Thus the Health and Safety Commission and the Health and Safety Executive, created in 1974 to exercise functions previously exercised by departments, are stated to perform their functions on behalf of the Crown.[29] But the National Heritage Memorial Fund, British Telecommunications, and the Welsh Fourth Channel Authority are declared not to have Crown status, except as may be otherwise stated in the legislation.[30] Where a public corporation does not benefit from Crown immunities, it is subject to the criminal law.[31] For the purposes of the law relating to corruption, the boards of nationalised industries are 'public bodies', since they have public duties to perform which they carry out for the benefit of the public and not for private profit.[32]

---

[25] [1950] 1 K.B. 18, 24 (*per* Denning L.J.). The Transport Act 1962, s. 30, makes express provision to the same effect for the British Railways Board.
[26] Note 7, *ante*.
[27] [1965] A.C. 512.
[28] [1965] Ch. 32.
[29] Health and Safety at Work Act 1974, s. 10(7).
[30] National Heritage Act 1980, sch. 1; British Telecommunications Act 1981, sch. 1; Broadcasting Act 1981, sch. 5.
[31] For the Scarcroft case, in which the Yorkshire Electricity Board was prosecuted, see A. H. Hanson, *Parliament and Public Ownership*, p. 69. The Post Office has been convicted for breach of the Weights and Measures Act 1963: *The Times*, 10 Jul. 1971.
[32] *R.* v. *Manners* [1978] A.C. 43.

Judicial control of public corporations

As public corporations do not generally benefit from immunities of the Crown, in carrying out their operations they are fully subject to the law as are industrial enterprises in private ownership. In fact many corporations provide public utility services which were subject to statutory control long before the era of nationalisation. To provide these services special powers are needed (for example, to enter private property for the purpose of reading gas or electricity meters) which private businesses do not have. So far as the principal powers and duties of the nationalised corporations are concerned, these are usually expressed in such general terms in the parent Acts that it is doubtful whether they could be enforced by legal process.

In *Charles Roberts and Co. Ltd* v. *British Railways Board*[33] a company which manufactured railway tank wagons sought a declaration that the board were not authorised to manufacture such wagons for sale to an oil company for use on railways in Britain. *Held* that the court should not interfere with the board's *bona fide* decision that such manufacture was an efficient way of carrying out the board's business within its statutory powers and duties; the judge declined to consider the economic effect which the board's policies might have on private manufacturers.

It would similarly be difficult by action in the courts to enforce the general duties of a board, as this seems to be left by the statutes to the minister concerned and judicial enforcement is sometimes expressly excluded.[34] But public corporations are subject to the jurisdiction of the courts if they commit a tort or a breach of contract, if they exceed their powers, or if they fail to observe statutory procedures or to perform specific statutory duties.[35]

Ministerial control of public corporations

Public ownership of an industry has usually come about because of the need for greater public control than can be obtained by means of legal restrictions imposed on privately owned undertakings. If there is to be public control of a corporation, this must be achieved primarily through the relevant minister, for it is he who appoints the chairman and members of the board, who has power to call for information and give directions to the board, who approves the board's external financing limits, and who receives the board's accounts and annual report. This does not mean that a minister should be responsible for every act of day-to-day administration, but he must at least have power to intervene on strategic matters which by the legislation are subject to his approval. In turn, ministerial responsibility to Parliament requires that ministers should account to Parliament for the use that they make of their statutory powers.

Whatever the framers of the nationalisation Acts in 1945–50 may have intended, ministers have in fact exercised very considerable control over the

---

[33] [1964] 3 All E.R. 651.
[34] *E.g.* British Telecommunications Act 1981, s. 3(4). *Cf. British Oxygen Co.* v. *South of Scotland Electricity Board* 1956 S.C. (H.L.) 113, 1959 S.C. (H.L.) 17.
[35] *Warwickshire CC* v. *British Railways Board* [1969] 3 All E.R. 631; *Booth & Co. (Holdings) Ltd.* v. *National Enterprise Board* [1978] 3 All E.R. 624; *Grunwick Processing Laboratories Ltd.* v. *ACAS* [1978] A.C. 655; *Home Office* v. *Cmssn for Racial Equality* [1982] Q.B. 385.

industries and have often intervened in their affairs. One reason for this has been that while for some periods some nationalised industries have been financially profitable, many of the industries have gone through periods when they have made heavy losses and have needed financial support from the government. Another reason is that the nationalised industries play a substantial part in the national economy, as employers, as providers of basic means of communication and energy, and in their investment programme: management of the nationalised industries has become an aspect of the management of the economy. Many of the industries' decisions have widespread social and economic repercussions, for example the level of prices charged to the consumer, wage rates for their employees, purchasing decisions (for example, whether British Airways should buy British aeroplanes) the closure of unprofitable activities (for example, railway-lines and coal-mines) and employment policies. It is impossible to insulate such decisions from the political process, but it is extremely difficult to strike the right balance. As was said by a committee of the House of Commons which made a special study of the subject.

If control is incorrectly exercised – too much or too little or in the wrong directions or by the wrong ... methods – then the wrong effects are liable to be created in the industries themselves. Ministers may fail to achieve what the public interest requires and the industries may be frustrated in providing economically the goods and the services their consumers desire.[36]

The report of this committee, published in 1968, stressed that control was not confined to the exercise of ministers' statutory powers – indeed very few formal directions whether general or particular had ever been issued by ministers – and that ministerial control included extra-statutory powers and influence. The defect of informal control and influence was not that it existed but that the extent of its exercise was generally not known. While different ministers and departments had different approaches to the industries, the general tendency until 1968 had been for government intervention to increase. 'If intervention is pressed too far, the whole concept of a public corporation is brought under strain'.[37] The 1968 report thus advocated an 'arm's length' relationship between boards and ministers, with political intervention being confined to a few key points.

During the 1970s, successive governments frequently intervened in the nationalised industries. Thus for some years prices to the consumer were kept down and the industries were compensated for the losses incurred.[38] In 1976 a report by the National Economic Development Office argued that the public policy issues affecting the industries were too wide-ranging to be left to the management of the industries, and urged that strategic planning must be a combined operation between the boards, the government and other interests (such as the trade unions and the consumers).[39] The government endorsed this

---

[36]   H.C. 371–I (1967–8) p. 3.
[37]   H.C. 371–I (1967–8) p. 32.
[38]   Statutory Corporations (Financial Provisions) Acts 1974 and 1975.
[39]   Note 17 *ante.*

approach,[40] emphasising its right to determine the financial objectives to be achieved in pricing policies, pay decisions and so on. These objectives, combined with the external financing limits set for the industries, have restricted capital investment and for some industries have led to larger price increases than would otherwise have been imposed. Under the Conservative government since 1979, ministers have sought to ensure that the industries give effect to the policy of privatisation.

Parliamentary control

Parliamentary control of the nationalised industries must take account both of the role of the departments concerned and of the boards themselves. If an adequate measure of parliamentary control is to be achieved, a variety of procedures must be used.[41]

In the first place, it is by the use of Parliament's legislative powers that most corporations have been established; amending legislation is needed if an industry is to be reorganised. So too legislation may be needed if borrowing limits are to be raised, if accumulated deficits are to be written off or if other major policies are to be implemented. Such legislation provides an occasion for the state of the industries to be debated. Secondly, there are other opportunities in the Commons for debates (for example, on opposition days, in the Queen's Speech debate and in adjournment debates) when the industries may be discussed.

Thirdly, M.P.s have wished to use question-time as a means of securing information about the industries. There is no doubt that ministers may be questioned about the use which they have made or are proposing to make of their own statutory powers, for example, the appointment of members to a board. But inevitable difficulties have been encountered by M.P.s in seeking information from ministers about matters within the competence of the corporations, since one reason for entrusting the industries to appointed boards was to eliminate the detailed scrutiny which may be exercised by parliamentary questioning over the work of civil servants. Ministers have often refused to answer questions about matters within the day-to-day administrative tasks of the boards, but have undertaken to answer questions seeking statistical information on a national basis. A minister's refusal to answer questions on a particular topic normally leads to the clerks in the House refusing to accept similar questions, but in relation to the nationalised industries the Speaker is prepared to accept questions on matters about which information has been previously refused if in his opinion they raise matters of urgent public importance.[42] In 1960 it was stated that, while ministers could not encroach upon the managerial functions of the boards, they would be prepared to answer questions which related to ministerial responsibilities for matters of general policy.[43] Today the questioning of ministers gives rise to fewer problems. An

---

[40]   Cmnd 7131, 1978.
[41]   W. A. Robson, *Nationalised Industries and Public Ownership*, chs. 7 and 8; H. A. Hanson, *Parliament and Public Ownership*.
[42]   Erskine May, p. 341.
[43]   H. C. Deb., 25 Feb. 1960, col. 577; D. N. Chester and N. Bowring, *Questions in Parliament*, pp. 301-5.

M.P. who is in doubt about ministerial responsibility for a certain matter can ask whether the minister intends to issue a direction to the board on the subject.

Select committees and accountability

The difficulties encountered by M.P.s in obtaining information about the industries, together with the lack of adequate procedures for dealing with the reports and accounts laid annually before Parliament, led in the early 1950s to various attempts to use select committees of the Commons to establish greater parliamentary control. In 1954–5, the House appointed a committee to inform Parliament about the current policy and practice of the industries, but excluded from its terms of reference matters which involved a minister's responsibility to Parliament or were matters of day-to-day administration. Not surprisingly, this left the committee with insufficient scope to do anything useful.[44] In 1956 there was set up for the first time a select committee with the duty of examining the reports and accounts of the nationalised industries.[45] The committee was regularly re-appointed until 1979. By then its terms of reference had been widened to include powers in respect of other public undertakings, such as the Independent Broadcasting Authority and the Bank of England, except for certain of the Bank's activities which were reserved from inquiry.

Between 1956 and 1979 this all-party committee made a series of searching and sometimes highly critical inquiries into the performance of the industries and their relationships with the government. The inquiries started from the published reports and accounts of the industry under review but much evidence was taken from the industry, the department concerned and other interested parties.

The committee sought to discover how far the industries were subject to informal ministerial control and to ensure that ministers were responsible to Parliament for the influence which they in fact exercised, especially when ministerial pressure had prevailed against the commercial judgment of the boards. As well as inquiring periodically into each industry, the committee reported on topics of more general concern, for example, ministerial control of the industries (in 1968), and capital investment procedures (in 1974). These informative reports contributed much to the development of policies relating to the nationalised industries and of parliamentary attitudes towards them. The success of the committee on a non-partisan basis also contributed to the spread of specialised parliamentary committees into other areas of governmental activity.[46] The committee's success, however, brought about its own demise. When in 1979 the present scheme of select committees was set up, each committee was empowered to examine the expenditure, administration and policy of the principal departments and their 'associated public bodies'.[47] This was considered to leave no place for the nationalised industries committee. Standing orders allow a sub-committee to be set up from time to time to

---

[44]   H.C. 120 (1955–6).
[45]   D. Coombes, *The Member of Parliament and the Administration.*
[46]   Ch. 11 D.
[47]   H.C. S.O. 99(1); ch. 11 D.

consider matters affecting two or more industries, but by 1983 that power had not been exercised.[48] The resulting gap in scrutiny has been filled in part by the work of committees such as the Treasury and Civil Service Committee, the Industry and Trade Committee and the Transport Committee.[49] Some aspects of the industries' finances have been considered by the Public Accounts Committee, but that committee is under the difficulty that although the accounts of the industries are laid annually in Parliament, the Comptroller and Auditor General has no power to inspect the books of the industries themselves.[50] Although the National Audit Act 1983 extended the Auditor General's power to examine the economy, efficiency and effectiveness of government departments and related bodies, the nationalised industries, the BBC, the IBA and the regional water authorities were expressly excluded from the scope of the Act.[51]

One reason for this exclusion was that since 1980 the government has had power to refer to the Monopolies and Merger Commission questions relating to the efficiency and costs of the nationalised industries, the services provided by them and any possible abuse by them of their monopoly position.[52] Under this procedure, the commission may probe deeply into the conduct of the industries and has been sharply critical of the quality of management within certain industries.[53] In 1981, the government announced that it proposed to make up to six references on aspects of the industries each year to the Monopolies and Merger Commission. With increased resources, the commission is thus the main instrument for external scrutiny of the industries.[54]

Consumer consultation

In Parliament are represented both the taxpayers, who underwrite the nationalised industries, and the consumers of the services which they provide. But the legislation has often provided formal machinery for consultation between the industries themselves and the consumers and users of their services. Consumer councils and consultative committees have been created at different times for electricity, gas, coal, rail and air transport, iron and steel, and the Post Office. Thus the Post Office Act 1969 made provision for a Post Office Users' National Council (and also similar councils for Scotland, Wales and Northern Ireland) appointed by the minister. The National Council must consider any matters relating to Post Office services which are the subject of representation by any users of the services, or which are referred to it by the minister or by the Post Office, or which the Council itself thinks it ought to consider; and the Council must be consulted before the Post Office put into effect any major proposals relating to its main services, for example, a general increase in postal charges.[55] Such consultative committees provide a means for

---

48   H.C. 92 (1982–3), p. 16.
49   See respectively H.C. 348 (1980–1), H.C. 758 (1979–80) and H.C. 390 (1981–2).
50   H.C. 115 (1980–1).
51   National Audit Act 1983, s. 7(4) and sch. 4; p. 288 *ante*.
52   Competition Act 1980, ss. 11, 12.
53   See, on the inner London letter post, H.C. 515 (1979–80) and, on the Central Electricity Generating Board, H.C. 315 (1980–1); and M. R. Garner (1982) 60 *Public Administration* 409.
54   H.C. Deb., 30 Nov. 1981, col. 48.
55   Post Office Act 1969, ss. 14, 15.

the expression of the views of the more articulate consumers, including opinions on the quality of services. They also provide a channel by which dissatisfied consumers may seek redress for grievances regarding the services they have received. But the existence of these consultative bodies is not widely known, and in 1976 it was suggested that an ombudsman be established for the industries to be an impartial investigator of consumer complaints.[56]

The mixed enterprise

Not all of the state's industrial activities take the form of a statutory corporation. As already mentioned, public enterprise may take the form of government ownership of shares in a limited company. The government or a public corporation may sometimes own all the shares in a company, but majority and minority shareholdings by the government are also found. A mixed enterprise may be described as an enterprise, a substantial part of whose capital is privately subscribed, which has the form of a company subject to the Companies Acts, and in which the government itself or a public corporation has a substantial financial interest, together with power to exercise a measure of internal control, either by way of voting power conferred by the ownership of shares or by the possession of a right to nominate directors or both.[57] Possibly the best known mixed enterprise in British history was the Suez Canal Company in which £4 million worth of shares were brought by Disraeli for the government in 1875. One which has survived from Britain's imperial past into the present day is British Petroleum (BP) in which the government is the largest single shareholder[58] and appoints to the board two directors who have the right of veto over many matters of general policy (for example, matters affecting foreign or defence policy or relating to naval contracts). In practice the veto is never exercised and the company seeks to compete fully with other oil companies.[59]

Government participation in mixed enterprises may arise for a variety of reasons, for example because a company's activities are too important in the national interest for it to be allowed to cease operations or because of the grave social consequences of the extinction of a large business. The extension of government participation was a controversial feature of the Labour government's policy after 1974, both relating to industry generally and to the North Sea oil programme in particular.[60] Such public action raises novel questions that cannot be answered from the experience of the nationalised industries alone, for example, the effect on the competitors of a mixed enterprise of discriminatory government backing.[61] The Conservative government has since 1979 pursued a policy of reducing the industrial activities of the state. For this

---

[56] Report by Justice, *The Citizen and Public Agencies: Remedying Grievances.* See also W. A. Robson, *op. cit.*, ch. 10; H.C. 514 (1970–1) and Cmnd 5067, 1972; and H.C. 334 (1978–9).

[57] T. C. Daintith, in Friedmann and Garner (ed.), *Government Enterprise*, p. 56, and in W. Friedmann (ed.), *Public and Private Enterprise in Mixed Economies*, ch. 5.

[58] At the end of 1983, after several sales of shares to the public, the government holding was just under 32% of the share capital.

[59] Daintith, in *Government Enterprise*, pp. 66–7; H.C. 298 (1967–8), pp. xvi–xviii.

[60] See Industry Act 1975 and Petroleum and Submarine Pipe-lines Act 1975.

[61] See T. Sharpe (1979) 95 L.Q.R. 205 and *Booth and Co. (International) Ltd* v. *NEB* [1978] 3 All E.R. 624.

reason, the more profitable nationalised industries have been required by legislation to establish companies in which their assets and undertakings could be vested, thus enabling shares in those companies to be sold to the public. In some cases the undertaking may pass completely into private ownership, subject if necessary to legislation imposing 'public service' obligations upon the company; in others a pattern of mixed ownership may be maintained. It remains to be seen whether the BP model will be appropriate to other instances of joint ownership.

B. Advisory bodies

We have seen that public corporations provide services or manage undertakings themselves, subject to a degree of control by ministers and departments. Where a department wishes to retain all decision-making and management in its own hands, it may seek through advisory bodies to receive expert advice and assistance from persons outside government. Such advisory bodies can take many different forms. In April 1982, nearly 400 advisory bodies existed in the United Kingdom,[1] but many others are appointed for a particular purpose and have a temporary existence. Some advisory bodies are primarily concerned with considering the need for fresh legislation; others are concerned with the choice of policies under existing laws. Some are appointed because an Act of Parliament says that they must be; others are appointed simply because the government wishes to seek information and advice from wherever it can find it.

Royal commissions and departmental committees

The appointment of a royal commission or a departmental committee is an act of the executive which requires no specific parliamentary approval although often it may be a response to political demands. When an issue of public policy or a possible change in the law requires thorough examination, and the government is not already politically committed to a definite policy, the task may be entrusted to an invited group of persons from outside the relevant departments. A departmental committee is appointed by one minister or by several ministers acting jointly. For substantial matters where greater formality is considered appropriate and where time is not of the essence, a royal commission may be appointed instead. This requires a royal warrant to be issued to the commissioners by the Sovereign on the advice of a Secretary of State. Apart from the formality and greater prestige of a royal commission, both commissions and departmental committees carry out their inquiries in a similar manner. The commission or committee will usually call for evidence, from individuals and organisations outside government as well as from public authorities, and it may undertake its own programme of research. Usually a royal commission hears the main evidence in public and copies of the oral and written evidence received are published; the commission's report is invariably published and laid before Parliament. A departmental committee is more likely to receive evidence in private and it is less common for its evidence to be

---

[1]   *Public Bodies 1982* (HMSO, 1983).

published. But both the Committee on Ministers' Powers (1929–32) and the Committee on Administrative Tribunals and Inquiries (1955–7) took evidence in public and this was later published.[2] The reports of departmental committees are usually but not always published.

Detailed study has shown that 24 royal commissions and over 600 departmental committees were appointed between 1945 and 1969. The average life of a royal commission was $2\frac{1}{2}$ years, compared with an average for royal commissions and major departmental committees of $1\frac{1}{2}$ years; not surprisingly, royal commissions were normally more expensive than the committees.[3] Major examples of royal commissions include the Kilbrandon Commission on the Constitution (which sat between 1969 and 1973 and cost over £480,000) and the Benson Commission on Legal Services (which sat between 1976 and 1979 and cost over £1.2 million). No less important topics are often entrusted to departmental committees, for example, the Fulton Committee on the Civil Service (1966–8), the Finer Committee on One-parent Families (1969–74) and the Layfield Committee on Local Government Finance (1974–6). Neither royal commissions nor departmental committees have power to compel the attendance of witnesses, unlike tribunals of inquiry appointed under the Tribunals of Inquiry (Evidence) Act 1921 by authority of Parliament.[4] The choice of the chairman of a commission or committee is important since he must ensure that the commission or committee carries through its work efficiently and he will seek to achieve a unanimous report where possible.[5] Usually the commission or committee disbands when it has reported but committees or commissions may be appointed on a more permanent basis and will produce a series of reports (for example, the Royal Commission on Environmental Pollution, first appointed in 1970).

When the investigating body has delivered its report, it is for the minister or the government to decide how far its recommendations are acceptable and if so in what form they should be carried out, for example by the preparation of a Bill to amend the law. A departmental committee should not be confused with a statutory public inquiry such as those held in connection with appeals under town planning legislation, where the department concerned is required to make a decision under existing law on the specific matters considered at the inquiry.[6] Nor should it be confused with the innumerable committees and working parties which exist within government and are usually manned exclusively by ministers or civil servants.

Consultative committees

The practice of consultation between government departments and organisations outside government is a widespread phenomenon of British government today. Consultation serves to meet the needs of the administrator for expert information and advice on scientific, technical or industrial matters. It also is

---

[2] Ch. 32.

[3] T. J. Cartwright, *Royal Commissions and Departmental Committees in Britain.*

[4] Ch. 37 C; *cf.* Cartwright, *op. cit.*, pp. 142–5.

[5] Report of Balfour Committee on Procedure of Royal Commissions, Cd 5235, 1910; and see Lords Benson and Rothschild (1982) 60 *Public Administration* 339.

[6] Ch. 37 B.

an important means by which those in government seek to maintain the continuing consent of the governed, and it thus serves important political purposes. Where consultative committees and advisory councils exist, they enable the practice of consultation to be placed on a regular and structured footing. Consultative committees are used over the whole range of government. They have proved particularly useful in the process by which new delegated legislation is prepared, but their use is not confined to projected legislation. In some cases there is a statutory obligation on a minister to consult a standing committee or named association, though the advisory body may be unable to take the initiative in discussing a subject without the matter being referred to it by the minister. Very many advisory bodies are appointed and consulted at the discretion of the minister or department concerned, and their discussions are often regarded as confidential.

An illustration of a statutory body which ministers must consult is the Police Negotiating Board for the United Kingdom. Regulations relating to the government, administration and conditions of service in police forces can be made under the Police Act 1964, and the equivalent Acts for Scotland and Northern Ireland, only after the Secretary of State has consulted the Board, on which sit representatives of local police authorities and of all ranks of the police.[7] The Social Security Advisory Committee gives advice and reports to the Secretary of State for the Social Services on his functions under the Social Security and Supplementary Benefits Acts. In particular, where the Secretary of State proposes to make regulations about social security benefits the proposal must be referred to the committee; when the regulations are laid before Parliament, the Secretary of State must inform Parliament of the committee's views and, if he has not given effect to the committee's recommendations, of the reasons for this.[8]

Another example of an advisory body appointed under statute is the Lord Chancellor's advisory committee on legal aid to which is referred the annual report of the Law Society on the civil legal aid scheme.[9] The Council on Tribunals, appointed to oversee the operation of tribunals and inquiries, is essentially a body which advises and is consulted by government departments; like most advisory bodies it has no executive functions, but its watchdog role includes consideration of complaints about particular tribunals and inquiries.[10]

Consultative bodies influence both fundamental reforms and the continuing work of departments. As well as enabling informed opinion to be expressed, they serve as a source of expert knowledge on technical matters. Research and the collection of information within departments thereby benefit from the assistance of outside organisations.

---

[7]   Police Negotiating Board Act 1980.
[8]   Social Security Act 1980, ss. 9–11.
[9]   Legal Aid Act 1974, s. 21.
[10]   Ch. 37.

Chapter 18

Foreign affairs

The conduct of the foreign affairs of the United Kingdom is the responsibility of the executive[1] and in this sphere the executive normally acts under prerogative powers.[2] Executive action taken under the prerogative includes the recognition of states and governments, the conclusion of treaties, the declaration of war, making peace and, subject to some limitations, the annexation and cession of territory. Such executive action is subject to constitutional controls. The executive is naturally responsible to Parliament for the manner in which it conducts the foreign affairs of the United Kingdom. Executive action in relation to foreign affairs, and the actions of other states, may also come before the courts.

The extent to which the courts assume jurisdiction over such matters is an important but difficult question. Various considerations tend to inhibit the courts in assuming jurisdiction. Inter-state relations are subject to international law and international law is not, in the main, administered by national courts. The courts have also shown awareness of the difficulties inherent in encroaching upon an executive function of such a highly political nature as the conduct of foreign affairs. A further consideration has been the efficacy of assuming jurisdiction, for enforcing judgment outside the territorial jurisdiction of the court may be impossible, particularly against the property or the representatives of a foreign state.

Whether jurisdiction is assumed largely depends upon the manner in which the issue is raised before the court. First, it may arise simply as a question of fact. The question could be, for example, whether or not a state had been recognised by the United Kingdom. Here the court may seek a certificate or declaration from the executive and the response is treated as conclusive of the fact that recognition has or has not been accorded.

Secondly, the court may be faced with claims against the executive or another state. Whether the court assumes jurisdiction over such an issue is

---

[1] In law, the executive is the Crown; in practice action is taken, or the action of others is authorised or adopted, by ministers acting in the name of the Crown *e.g.* the Foreign Secretary. For convenience the term 'executive' is generally used in this chapter.

[2] See ch. 13 C.

determined by the law governing the plea of act of state.

Finally, executive acts in relation to foreign affairs may come before the courts where it is necessary to determine the consequences which flow from them in the domestic law of the United Kingdom. Here the courts exercise a much wider jurisdiction. The consequences of executive acts are determined either by statute or by the common law; the particular consequences depend upon the executive act concerned. In *Rustomjee* v. *R.*[3], for instance, an Anglo-Chinese peace treaty provided that the Emperor of China should pay three million dollars to the Crown in settlement of outstanding debts owed to British subjects by Chinese merchants. Rustomjee, a British subject to whom such a debt was due, claimed a portion of the money paid to the Crown under the treaty, basing his claim on the provisions of the treaty. It was held that the making of the treaty was a prerogative act and could not be the source of a right enforceable in English law.

Executive certificates, acts of state, and the effect in English law of the conclusion of treaties and acts of recognition by the executive[4] are now considered more fully.

A. Executive certificates[1]

In certain circumstances the courts may seek a certificate or declaration from the executive on matters relating to foreign affairs.[2]

In *R.* v. *Bottrill ex parte Kuechenmeister*[3] a German citizen who was interned under war-time regulations applied for a writ of habeas corpus some months after the unconditional surrender of Germany in 1945. A certificate from the Foreign Secretary stated, *inter alia*, 'No treaty of peace or declaration of the Allied Powers having been made terminating the state of war with Germany, His Majesty is still in a state of war with Germany, although as provided in the declaration of surrender, all active hostilities have ceased.' The Court of Appeal held that as a state of war still existed with Germany the applicant was an enemy alien and therefore not entitled to a writ of habeas corpus against the executive.

Certificates may also be sought to determine, for example, whether (a) a person is an independent sovereign,[4] (b) a state or government has been

---

[3]   (1876) 2 Q.B.D. 69.

[4]   Other executive acts in relation to foreign affairs may also have domestic legal effects. A declaration of war, for example, affects trading and contractual rights with persons of enemy character, affects the rights within the United Kingdom of citizens of enemy states and makes the acquisition of the nationality of an enemy state by a British subject treasonable (*R.* v. *Lynch* [1903] 1 K.B. 444). See further Lord McNair and A. D. Watts, *The Legal Effects of War.*

[1]   For the history of executive certificates see W. S. Holdsworth (1941) 41 Col. L.R. 1313, 1322–5; see also H. Lauterpacht (1939) 20 B.Y.I.L. 125, and A. B. Lyons (1946) 23 B.Y.I.L. 240.

[2]   Certificates are now normally issued by the Foreign and Commonwealth Office, but have in the past been issued by other departments *e.g.* the Colonial Office. See also *Dalmia Dairy Industries Ltd* v. *National Bank of Pakistan* [1978] 2 Lloyds Rep. 223. *Cf. Reel* v. *Holder* [1981] 3 All E.R. 321 and *Spinney's Ltd* v. *Royal Ins. Co.* [1980] 1 Lloyd's Rep. 406.

[3]   [1947] K.B. 41; *cf. Willcock* v. *Muckle* [1951] 2 K.B. 844.

[4]   *Mighell* v. *Sultan of Johore* [1894] 1 Q.B. 149.

recognised by the United Kingdom, (c) a person or entity has a status which attracts immunity from the jurisdiction of the courts, for example whether a person is a diplomat, and (d) to ascertain the extent of the jurisdiction of the Crown.[5]

The practice of seeking certificates from the executive has been justified on various grounds. In certain circumstances an executive certificate may provide the best evidence,[6] or alternatively the most authoritative statement,[7] of a fact. Perhaps more controversially, it has been suggested that the executive certificate allows the courts and the executive to adopt the same view on matters of foreign affairs. In the words of Lord Atkin, 'our state cannot speak with two voices on such a matter, the judiciary saying one thing, the Executive another'.[8]

These various approaches are reflected in the judicial attitude to the content of executive certificates. They are treated as conclusive as to the facts they certify[9] and a court would be entitled to use other evidence only where the executive declined to answer the questions put to it.[10] Consequently argument questioning the conclusions of fact reached in the certificate will not be permitted by the court, even where the argument is restricted solely to information contained in the certificate.[11] However, the court will examine a certificate to see that the proper matters have been considered by the appropriate ministers.[12]

Although executive certificates are conclusive of the facts contained in them, theoretically they are not conclusive as regards the legal consequences which flow from these facts. However, judicial practice varies. Courts have sometimes determined important questions of law solely by construing the certificate, even where the certificate contained an express disclaimer that it was intended to be conclusive on questions of law,[13] while sometimes courts have shown a marked independence in determining the legal consequences which flow from the facts contained in an executive certificate.[14] The Privy Council has warned that were courts to seek guidance from the executive on general questions of law, 'what may begin by guidance as to the principles to be applied may end in cases being decided irrespective of any principle in accordance with the view of the Executive as to what is politically expedient'.[15]

---

5   *The Fagernes* [1927] P. 311; see also ch. 13 C.
6   *The Fagernes* [1927] P. 311, 324.
7   F. Vallat, *International Law and the Practitioner*, p. 54.
8   *The Arantzazu Mendi* [1939] A.C. 256, 264; *cf. Kawasaki Kisen* v. *Bantham Steamship Co. Ltd* [1939] 2 K.B. 544, 552.
9   *Duff Development Co. Ltd* v. *Government of Kelantan* [1924] A.C. 797, *cf. The Zamora* [1916] 2 A.C. 77. Some statutes expressly provide that where a certificate pertaining to the legislation is issued, it is conclusive evidence of certain facts (*e.g.* Diplomatic Privileges Act 1964, s. 4) or of certain questions of fact and international law (*e.g.* State Immunity Act 1978, s. 21).
10 *Duff Development Co. Ltd* v. *Government of Kelantan, ante*, 825.
11 *Ibid*, 807.
12 *Sayce* v. *Ameer Ruler, Bahawalpur State* [1952] 2 Q.B. 390, 397.
13 *The Arantzazu Mendi* [1939] A.C. 256; *Gdynia Ameryka Linie* v. *Boguslawski* [1953] A.C. 11.
14 *Carl Zeiss Stiftung* v. *Rayner and Keeler Ltd* (No.2) [1967] 1 A.C. 853; *Re Al-Fin Corporation's Patent* [1970] Ch. 160. In respect to the recognition of governments, this independence may be reinforced by the change in UK practice in 1980, p. 323 *post*.
15 *The Phillipine Admiral* [1977] A.C. 373, 399.

B. Act of state[1]

An act of state has been described as 'an act of the Executive as a matter of policy performed in the course of its relations with another state, including its relations with the subjects of that state, unless they are temporarily within the allegiance of the Crown'.[2] As this description suggests, the term act of state may be used in a number of senses. In its broadest sense act of state is used to describe an 'exercise of sovereign power'.[3] Secondly, act of state may be used to describe the exercise of prerogative power in relation to foreign affairs. Thirdly, act of state may be used in a procedural sense. In this sense the plea of act of state is to be distinguished from a plea that action has been taken under a prerogative power. A plea that action taken was an exercise of prerogative power is an assertion of a lawful authority for taking the action. The limits of the prerogative power may be uncertain, for example the extent to which the power may be exercised extra-territorially,[4] but it is for the court to determine whether the prerogative provides authority for the action taken. A plea of act of state, on the other hand, is an assertion that the court does not have jurisdiction to determine whether the act was performed with lawful authority. Where a plea of act of state is successful,

the court does not come to any decision as to the legality or illegality, or the rightness or wrongness, of the act complained of: the decision is that because it was an act of state the court has no jurisdiction to entertain a claim in respect of it.[5]

It is in this third sense that the term act of state is used in this chapter.

A successful plea of act of state thus ousts the jurisdiction of a court to determine the legality of an act authorised or adopted[6] by the executive which might otherwise have been a tortious or criminal act.[7] Such a plea may substantially diminish the rights of the private litigant.

In *Buron* v. *Denman*,[8] a British naval officer, with general instructions to suppress the slave trade, exceeded his instructions by setting fire to buildings belonging to a Spanish slave owner and liberating his slaves. This action, which occurred in West Africa outside British territory, was subsequently adopted by the executive in Britain. The

---

[1] Studies of act of state include: W. Harrison Moore, *Act of State in English Law*; E. C. S. Wade (1934) 15 B.Y.I.L. 98; W. S. Holdsworth (1941) 41 Col. L. R. 1313; M. Zander (1959) 53 A.J.I.L. 826; J. G. Collier [1968] C.L.J. 102; D. R. Gilmour [1970] P.L. 120; *cf.* P. Cane (1980) 29 I.C.L.Q. 680.

[2] E. C. S. Wade (1934) 15 B.Y.I.L. 98, 103; the description was cited with approval in *Nissan* v. *A.-G.* [1968] 1 Q.B. 327, 347; *cf.* [1970] A.C. 179, 212, 231.

[3] *Salaman* v. *Secretary of State for India* [1906] 1 K.B. 613, 639 (Fletcher Moulton L.J.).

[4] *E.g. Nissan* v. *A.-G.* [1968] 1 Q.B. 286; [1970] A.C. 179, 213, 229. See also D.R. Gilmour, *op. cit.*, pp. 141–3.

[5] *Nissan* v. *A.-G.* [1970] A.C. 179, 237 (Lord Pearson).

[6] *Buron* v. *Denman* (1848) 2 Ex. 167.

[7] J. F. Stephen, *History of the Criminal Law of England*, vol. II, pp. 61–5. The plea of act of state may also be available with respect to an act authorised by a foreign State and performed within the jurisdiction of that state; *e.g. Carr* v. *Fracis Times & Co.* [1902] A.C. 176; *R.* v. *Lesley* (1860) Bell C.C. 220; *Buttes Gas & Oil Co.* v. *Hammer* [1975] Q.B. 557, 580–81. Nevertheless, in limited circumstances, the courts will consider such acts: *In re claim by Helbert Wagg & Co. Ltd* [1956] Ch. 323, 345–6; *Oppenheimer* v. *Cattermole* [1976] A.C. 249.

[8] (1848), 2 Ex. 167.

slave owner sought damages for trespass but it was held that the naval officer's actions, having been adopted by the executive, were acts of state and no action could lie against the officer in respect of them.

However, where an act of state is pleaded, the mere fact of the plea does not oust the jurisdiction of the court. The court must examine the facts and determine whether, all other circumstances being satisfied, the action of the executive is an act of state.[9] 'The courts are not bound to accept the *ipse dixit* of the executive but have the right to decide for themselves whether the act is, in this sense, an act of state'.[10]

In *Nissan* v. *Attorney-General*,[11] the plaintiff was a citizen of the United Kingdom and colonies whose hotel in Cyprus was occupied by British troops invited, under an agreement between the British and Cypriot governments, to assist in restoring peace during a period of civil strife on the island. Later, the British troops continued to occupy the hotel as an element of a UN peacekeeping force. The plaintiff brought an action against the Crown for, *inter alia*, compensation for the requisitioning of the hotel and the use of its contents, on the grounds that the requisitioning was an exercise of the prerogative and compensation was therefore payable. The case was determined on preliminary issues, in particular the plea by the Crown that the actions of the British troops with respect to that claim were acts of state. On this point it was held by the House of Lords that the occupation and use of the hotel were not acts of state and were therefore justiciable.

No comprehensive test has been adopted by the courts in deciding whether an act of the executive is an act of state, but a variety of factors have been considered persuasive. One such factor is the importance of the executive act as a matter of policy; the executive act to be an act of state must be 'something exceptional'.[12] However, it may be undesirable for a court to deny a plea of act of state solely on this ground. 'The act may appear to be of a routine or trivial character. But in a delicate situation there may be discussion and decision at the highest level about such acts, and the decision to do such an act may be a decision of high policy'.[13] The apparent intention of the executive may also be persuasive. 'The intention is to be inferred from words and conduct and surrounding circumstances'[14] but 'the court cannot inquire into or ask the Crown to disclose the reason why the act was done'.[15] On occasion, the courts in determining whether an executive act is an act of state have been influenced by its close connection, causal or temporal, with an accepted act of state.[16]

---

9   *Entick* v. *Carrington* (1765) 19 St. Tr. 1030; *Salaman* v. *Secretary of State for India, ante.*
10 *Nissan* v. *A.-G.* [1970] A.C. 179, 231–2 (Lord Wilberforce).
11 [1970] A.C. 179.
12 *Nissan* v. *A.-G.*, 237 (Lord Pearson); *cf. Salaman* v. *Secretary of State for India, ante,* 640.
13 *Nissan* v. *A.-G.*, 212 (Lord Reid).
14 *Nissan* v. *A.-G.*, 238 (Lord Pearson); *Secretary of State for India* v. *Kamachee etc.* (1859) 13 Moo. P.C.C. 22; *Salaman* v. *Secretary of State for India, ante.*
15 *Nissan* v. *A.-G., ante,* 212 (Lord Reid). It is arguable however that where an executive act has been taken in purported exercise of a legal right the executive has submitted to the jurisdiction of the courts: *ibid.*
16 *Salaman* v. *Secretary of State for India, ante; Nissan* v. *A.-G., ante,* 216–17, 227.

Circumstances in which act of state may be pleaded

The plea of act of state is only available in certain circumstances and the availability of the plea depends largely on (a) whether the executive act took place within the territories of the Crown or outside them and (b) whether or not the litigant owes allegiance to the Crown.[17] The concept of 'the Crown' is an imprecise one in relation to the colonies and the Commonwealth[18] and it poses problems in modern constitutional law which could not have been anticipated in the 19th century cases on which many of the rules governing act of state rest. The widest interpretation of the territories of the Crown (and the more archaic 'dominions of the Crown') would be all territories under the sovereignty of the Crown, that is all Commonwealth states including the United Kingdom and colonies, which recognise the Queen as head of state and not merely as head of the Commonwealth. Similarly the widest interpretation of those owning allegiance to the Crown would be citizens of states recognising the Queen as head of state, and aliens on whom a duty of allegiance is imposed by the law of those states. It may be desirable, but it is not yet the law, that in the context of act of state the concept of 'the Crown' should be more restrictively interpreted. The rules outlined below govern the availability of the plea before courts in the United Kingdom. It is therefore arguable that the concept of 'the Crown' should here be limited to the Queen as head of state in the United Kingdom. For the purposes of these rules, 'the territories of the Crown' would thus be limited to the United Kingdom and colonies. Similarly, those 'owing allegiance to the Crown' would be those owing allegiance to the Queen as head of state in the United Kingdom, that is, principally citizens of the United Kingdom and colonies and residents therein.[19]

1   Executive acts in the territories of the Crown.   Where an executive act occurs within the territories of the Crown act of state may be pleaded only against very limited categories of litigant. It will not succeed against a British subject[20] or a resident friendly alien.[21]

In *Walker* v. *Baird*,[22] the commander of a British warship, acting merely under executive instructions to enforce a treaty between Great Britain and France, seized a lobster factory in Newfoundland owned by a British subject. It was held by the Privy Council that in such circumstances act of state was not a defence to the action. In *Johnstone* v.

---

[17]   On allegiance, see ch. 25 A. A further rationale which is sometimes suggested, that act of state is not available as a defence against those who rely on the diplomatic protection of the Crown, cannot be sustained. As will be seen, act of state may not be available against aliens who would be entitled to the diplomatic protection of their own states, but in certain circumstances it is possibly available against UK citizens who have no diplomatic protection against the Crown; *cf. Johnstone* v. *Pedlar* [1921] 2 A.C. 262, 281.

[18]   See ch. 24.

[19]   This aspect of the argument was recognised but not resolved in *Nissan* v. *A.-G., ante.*

[20]   Given the present case-law, it is not possible to state whether in the context of act of state in modern English law, British subject means (a) British citizen; (b) British Dependent Territories citizen; (c) British Overseas citizen; (d) citizen of any Commonwealth country which recognises the Queen as head of state; (e) citizen of every Commonwealth state. See British Nationality Act 1981 and also ch. 24 and 25 A.

[21]   It is possible that act of state may not succeed against a friendly alien who is merely *present* within the territories of the Crown: *Kuchenmeister* v. *Home Office* [1958] 1 Q.B. 496.

[22]   [1892] A.C. 491.

Pedlar,[23] a cheque and money found on a United States citizen were seized by the police when he was arrested in Dublin, which was then within the United Kingdom. In an action for the return of the property it was argued that the seizure, which had been approved by the executive, was an act of state. It was held by the House of Lords that the defence of act of state was not available in respect of an executive act done within the territory of the Crown to a citizen of a friendly state.

There may be some circumstances in which the plea of act of state is available where the executive act was committed within the territories of the Crown. It is commonly asserted that the defence of act of state is available with respect to such executive acts taken against enemy aliens.[24] However, the cases usually cited in support of this proposition are better explained on the grounds of the prerogative power of the Crown in relation to enemy aliens. Where executive action is taken against property situated within the territories of the Crown which is owned by a friendly alien resident abroad, the owner, although he does not owe allegiance to the Crown, is surely entitled to the protection of the courts and the defence of act of state should not be available.[25] *A fortiori*, where the owner is a friendly alien who does owe allegiance to the Crown, his property should also be protected.[26] In general, as a successful plea of act of state ousts the jurisdiction of the court, it seems desirable that the categories of person or property within the territory of the Crown against which it is available should be restrictively interpreted.

2 Executive acts abroad. Act of state is available in respect of executive action taken abroad against aliens who do not owe allegiance to the Crown.[27]

The extent to which act of state is available in respect of executive action taken abroad against British subjects is however unclear. On the one hand, in *Johnstone* v. *Pedlar* the view was expressed, *obiter*, that the doctrine of act of state 'has no application to any case in which the plaintiff is a British subject',[28] and *Walker* v. *Baird*[29] was cited in support of this proposition. On the other hand, there are a number of cases in which the plea of act of state was successful with respect to executive action taken abroad against litigants who seem to have been British subjects.[30] It is possible to explain these

---

23 [1921] 2 A.C. 262.
24 *R.* v. *Vine Street Police Station ex p. Liebmann* [1916] 1 K.B. 268; *Netz* v. *Ede* [1946] Ch. 224; *R.* v. *Bottrill ex p. Kuechenmeister* [1974] K.B. 41. In respect of friendly aliens whose permission to remain within the territories of the Crown has been expressly withdrawn, see *Johnstone* v. *Pedlar, ante*, 284–5, *cf.* 293–4.
25 *Commercial & Estates Co. of Egypt* v. *Board of Trade* [1925] 1 K.B. 171, 290, 297. See also E. C. S. Wade (1934) 15 B.Y.I.L. 98, 99; *cf.* G. Williams (1948) 10 C.L.J. 54, 64–5.
26 For circumstances in which a friendly alien who is abroad may owe allegiance to the Crown, see *Joyce* v. *DPP* [1946] A.C. 347; *Re P. (G.E.) (an infant)* [1965] Ch. 568. See further, ch. 25A.
27 *Buron* v. *Denman, ante.*
28 [1921] 2 A.C. 262, 272 (Visc. Finlay).
29 [1892] A.C. 491.
30 *E.g. Rustomjee* v. *R.* (1876) 2 Q.B.D. 69; *West Rand Central Gold Mining Co.* v. *R.* [1905] 2 K.B. 391; *Salaman* v. *Secretary of State for India* [1906] 1 K.B. 613; *Civilian War Claimants Association* v. *R.* [1932] A.C. 14. The facts of nationality are not always clear from the reports, see *Nissan* v. *A.-G.* [1968] 1 Q.B. 286, 320–1.

apparently conflicting lines of authority on the basis that the latter cases do not truly relate to the plea of act of state since, unlike *Johnstone* v. *Pedlar* and *Walker* v. *Baird*, they were attempts to establish a right against the Crown on the basis of a prerogative act.

The position might have been clarified by the House of Lords in *Nissan* v. *Attorney-General* but it was not. Lord Reid considered that a British subject 'can never be deprived of his legal right to redress by any assertion . . . that the acts of which he complains were acts of state';[31] Lord Wilberforce found it 'impossible to accept the broad proposition that in no case can the plea of act of state . . . be raised against a British subject'[32] and the rest of the court expressed varying degrees of doubt or left the question open.[33] Although the legal position remains unclear it may at least be said that the majority in *Nissan* v. *Attorney-General* had reservations about the proposition that, with regard to executive acts committed abroad, the plea of act of state would always fail against a British subject. However the uncertainties surrounding act of state may be resolved, it is submitted that the same rules should apply to aliens owing allegiance to the Crown in right of the United Kingdom as to citizens of the United Kingdom.[34]

C.   Treaties[1]

A treaty has been defined as an 'international agreement in written form . . . concluded between two or more States or other subjects of international law and governed by international law'.[2] States usually become parties to a treaty by the process of signing followed by ratification, that is, formal acceptance of the terms of the treaty. Under international law treaties are binding on the parties to them. In the United Kingdom, subject to obligations arising from membership of the European Communities which are considered below, the conclusion of treaties is a prerogative power exercised by the executive[3] which will not be impugned by the courts.[4] Unless limited by statute,[5] the executive may therefore enter into treaty obligations which are binding on the United Kingdom in international law.

There is no constitutional requirement that the terms of a treaty must be approved by Parliament before it is concluded by the executive.[6] However, the executive is responsible to Parliament for the conduct of foreign affairs; and

---

[31]   [1970] A.C. 179, 213.

[32]   *Ibid.*, 235.

[33]   *Ibid.*, 221, 227, 240.

[34]   Arguably they should also be applied to British protected persons; see British Nationality Act 1981, ss. 38, 50 and K. Polack (1963) 26 M.L.R. 138, L.L. Kato [1969] P.L. 219.

[1]   See generally Lord McNair, *Law of Treaties*, pp. 81–97.

[2]   *Yearbook of International Law Commission*, 1962, ii, p. 161. Such an international agreement is commonly designated as a treaty but other designations, such as convention, covenant, pact or charter, may be used. 'Other subjects of international law' which may conclude treaties include some international organisations.

[3]   Blackstone, *Commentaries*, vol. I, p. 257; Anson, II, 1, p. 65.

[4]   *Blackburn* v. *A.-G.* [1971] 2 All E.R. 1380, 1383; *McWhirter* v. *A.-G.* [1972] C.M.L.R. 882, 886–7.

[5]   *E.g.* European Assembly Elections Act 1978, s. 6.

by virtue of a constitutional usage, 'the Ponsonby rule', Parliament is informed of the terms of most treaties before they are ratified by the executive. The Ponsonby rule provides that where a treaty requires ratification the executive will not ratify it until 21 parliamentary days after the text of the treaty has been laid before both Houses of Parliament.[7] This procedure was introduced in 1924, abandoned,[8] and re-introduced in 1929. It has operated since that date although occasional exceptions to it have been made where there have been urgent reasons for ratifying a treaty within the 21 day period.[9]

However, although the executive has a largely unfettered power to enter into treaty obligations, normally such obligations need to be implemented by domestic legislation before they will be enforced as law by courts in the United Kingdom.[10] Consequently the executive, before entering into treaty obligations which will require legislative implementation, usually protects itself by seeking parliamentary approval of the treaty or securing the passage of the implementing legislation before ratification.

The general rule that 'the making of a treaty is an executive act, while the performance of its obligations, if they entail alteration of the existing domestic law, requires legislative action'[11] may be subject to exceptions. It is sometimes argued that peace treaties may have domestic legal effect without legislative implementation. In *Walker* v. *Baird* it was argued that a treaty of peace or a treaty to prevent war may, without statutory implementation, alter the private rights of the subject. The point was left undecided but it would not appear to be well founded in the light of subsequent practice.[12] It is possible that the cession of territory by treaty could also have domestic legal effect without legislative implementation.[13] However it is doubtful whether, in the absence of legislation, such a treaty could deprive the subject of his nationality or his property or contractual rights.[14] In any event, the cession of territory is now always effected by statute rather than by treaty.

---

6   However, occasionally a treaty may provide that it will not come into force until the parties to it have obtained legislative approval of its terms (*e.g.* Anglo-Portuguese Commercial Treaty Act 1914) or that it may lapse if a party to it is prevented by domestic legislation from giving full effect to its provisions (*e.g.* Anglo-American Liquor Treaty 1924). It is more usual for a treaty to provide that it should be ratified by intending parties 'in accordance with their respective constitutional requirements' (*e.g.* Treaty of Accession to the EEC and EURATOM 1972, art. 2). In the United Kingdom, such a provision would not necessarily impose a duty on the executive to obtain parliamentary approval before ratification.

7   The rule has its origin in a Foreign Office minute dated 1 Feb. 1924, and was later announced in the Commons: H.C. Deb., 1 Apr. 1924, cols. 2001–4. See also Erskine May, p. 267; E. Lauterpacht (1957) 6 I.C.L.Q. 578 and (1958) 7 I.C.L.Q. 121.

8   (1925) 6 B.Y.I.L. 188.

9   *E.g.* Nuclear Test Ban Treaty 1963: E. Lauterpacht, *British Practice in International Law*, 1963, p. 137.

10   *The Parlement Belge* (1879) 4 P.D. 129; *Walker* v. *Baird* [1892] A.C. 491; *A.-G. for Canada* v. *A.-G. for Ontario* [1937] A.C. 326.

11   *A.-G for Canada* v. *A.-G. for Ontario, ante*, 347 (Lord Atkin).

12   *E.g.* Treaty of Peace Act 1919; Treaties of Peace (Italy, Rumania, Bulgaria Hungary and Finland) Act 1947; and see Lord McNair, *op. cit.*, p. 86.

13   *Damodhar Gordhan* v. *Deoram Kanji* (1876) 1 App. Cas. 332, 373–4; see also K. O. Roberts-Wray, *Commonwealth and Colonial Law*, ch. 4; H.L.E., vol. 6, pp. 474–5, 486.

14   Anson, II, ii, pp. 137–42; W. S. Holdsworth (1942) 58 L.Q.R. 175.

The provisions of a treaty cannot be the source of legal rights enforceable in the United Kingdom.[15] The issue has arisen where, by treaty, territory has been ceded to, or annexed by, the Crown, or the Crown has received compensation for loss suffered by British subjects. In concluding such a treaty the Crown cannot be taken to be acting as an agent or trustee of one of its subjects,[16] at least in the absence of an express declaration to that effect.[17] Where a treaty provides that compensation is payable to the Crown for losses suffered by British subjects, the allocation of the sums received may be delegated to an independent statutory body, the Foreign Compensation Commission.[18] Although a statutory appeal now lies to the courts against a Commission determination on a point of law or on the grounds of a violation of the rules of natural justice, a claimant cannot obtain a judicial declaration that he is entitled to a specific sum.

Although treaties are normally not a source of legal rights and obligations enforceable in the United Kingdom, nevertheless judicial consideration may be given to their provisions. The courts, for example, have referred to the provisions of a treaty as an aid to the interpretation of the statute which implemented it,[19] and also as an aid to the interpretation of other statutes.[20] On occasion, treaties to which the United Kingdom was not a party have been used as an aid to interpretation.[21] However, the use of treaties in statutory interpretation must always be qualified by the rule that, although there is a rebuttable presumption that Parliament will not seek to legislate inconsistently with the treaty obligations of the United Kingdom, if there is a clear inconsistency the statute must prevail.[22]

Treaties and British membership of the European Communities[23]

British membership of the European Communities affects UK law regarding treaties in two important respects: (a) it limits the prerogative power of the executive to enter into treaties, and (b) it qualifies the general principle that treaty obligations must normally be implemented by domestic legislation before they will be enforced as law by courts in the United Kingdom.

The EEC and EURATOM treaties expressly empower the two Communities to enter into treaties with non-member states and international organisations for certain purposes.[24] However, their treaty-making capacity is not limited to these express powers. The Court of Justice of the Communities has

---

15   *Malone* v. *Metropolitan Police Commissioner* [1979] Ch. 344.
16   *Rustomjee* v. *R.* (1876) 2 Q.B.D. 69; *Administrator of German Property* v. *Knoop* [1933] Ch. 439.
17   *Civilian War Claimants Association Ltd* v. *R.* [1932] A.C. 14, 26–7.
18   Foreign Compensation Acts 1950 and 1969; see also *Anisminic Ltd* v. *Foreign Compensation Commission*, p. 671 *post*.
19   *Salomon* v. *Commissioners of Customs and Excise* [1967] 2 Q.B. 116; *Post Office* v. *Estuary Radio Ltd* [1968] 2 Q.B. 740. Implementing legislation may require courts to refer to the treaty in interpreting the statute, *e.g. Fothergill* v. *Monarch Airlines* [1981] A.C. 251.
20   *Waddington* v. *Miah* [1974] 2 All E.R. 377, 379; *R.* v. *Home Secretary, ex p. Bhajan Singh* [1976] Q.B. 198; *cf. Surjit Kaur* v. *Lord Advocate* [1980] 3 C.M.L.R. 79.
21   *Fenton Textile Association Ltd* v. *Krassin* (1921–2) 38 T.L.R. 259; *The Phillipine Admiral* [1977] A.C. 373.
22   *Cheney* v. *Conn* [1968] 1 All E.R. 779.
23   See ch. 8 A.

held that this capacity may also be implied where Community institutions are empowered to legislate for member states in respect of common policies, whether this internal legislative competence has been exercised or not.[25] Where the Communities have an express treaty-making capacity,[26] and possibly where there is an implied capacity,[27] the capacity is exclusive and consequently deprives member states of their capacity to enter into treaties for the same purposes.

Membership of the Communities thus limits the prerogative power of the executive in the United Kingdom to enter into treaties. This limitation may be understood in terms of domestic constitutional law as having come about directly through the exercise of that prerogative power. For the United Kingdom became a member of the EEC and EURATOM on the ratification of the Treaty of Accession by the executive. The executive thereby accepted the limitation on its treaty-making capacity which is inherent in Community law as interpreted by the Court of Justice.

The treaties establishing the Communities also provide the legal basis for Community legislation which, in certain circumstances, may be directly enforced in member states. Some of the provisions of Community treaties may themselves be similarly enforced in member states. As we have already seen, under the European Communities Act 1972, section 2(1), the 'rights, powers, liabilities, obligations and restrictions from time to time created or arising by or under the [Community] Treaties . . . as in accordance with the Treaties are to be given legal effect . . . in the United Kingdom . . . shall be recognised and available in law'.[28] This provision gives legal effect within the United Kingdom to those Community treaties which are intended under Community law to be the source of legal rights enforceable within the United Kingdom; the detailed rules governing that effect are themselves matters of Community law.

D. Recognition and immunities

By prerogative, the executive may recognise a foreign state or government. States are in practice expressly recognised, but since 1980 the executive has not expressly recognised governments. Instead, following the practice of many other states, it decides 'the nature of our dealings with regimes which come to power unconstitutionally in the light of our assessment of whether they are able of themselves to exercise effective control of the territory of the state

---

24   EEC Treaty, arts. 113, 238, *cf.* arts. 229–31; EURATOM Treaty, art. 101, *cf.* art. 103; *cf.* ECSC Treaty, arts. 6, 71, 93–4, and the Convention on the Transitional Provisions. See also P.M. Leopold (1977) 26 I.C.L.Q. 54. It is also possible for both European Community and individual member states to be parties to a treaty, where only some aspects of the treaty are within the treaty-making capacity of the Community.

25   *Commission* v. *Council* (ERTA) [1971] E.C.R. 263; *Kramer* [1976] E.C.R. 1279.

26   Opinion 1/75, *Re Export Credit Guarantee* [1975] E.C.R. 1355.

27   Opinion 1/76, *Re Laying-up Fund for Inland Waterway Vessels* [1977] E.C.R. 741.

28   Ch. 8B. Community treaties are defined in section 1, under which other treaties may be designated as Community treaties by Order in Council. See also M. Maresceau (1979) 28 I.C.L.Q. 241.

concerned and seem likely to continue to do so'.[1] Possibly with the assistance of executive certificates, UK courts will have to determine whether the nature of these 'dealings' signifies implied recognition.

The act of recognition has a number of important legal consequences in the United Kingdom. A recognised state or government, but not one which is unrecognised, has *locus standi* in the courts.[2] Where it is necessary for British courts to consider foreign law, it is usually the law of a recognised state or government which is considered.[3] Finally, recognised states and governments may be immune from the jurisdiction of the courts, and their diplomats also enjoy a similar immunity.

State immunity

Until 1978, under the common law, recognised states were granted a wide immunity from legal process in UK courts. This immunity had come to extend to commercial activities conducted by or under the close regulation of states, their governments and other public agencies.[4] Such immunity could operate to the substantial injustice of the private litigant who had, for example, entered into a commercial contract with a foreign state agency and was unable to sue on the contract in a UK court. For this and for international economic reasons, this immunity was given a new basis by the State Immunity Act 1978.[5]

Under this Act, foreign states, their governments and other entities which are exercising sovereign authority have immunity from the jurisdiction of UK courts.[6] However, this immunity is subject to a wide range of exceptions. Matters which do not attract immunity include commercial transactions;[7] contracts which fall to be performed in the United Kingdom;[8] tortious actions in respect of death, personal injury or tangible property in the United Kingdom;[9] actions relating to immoveable property in the United Kingdom[10] and Admiralty proceedings against ships and their cargoes used for commercial purposes.[11] Furthermore, an entity which is distinct from the executive organs of the government of a foreign state and which is not exercising sovereign authority cannot claim immunity.[12]

---

[1]   H.L. Deb. 28 Apr. 1980, cols. 1121–2; H.L. Deb. 23 May 1980, cols. 1097–8; C.R. Symmons [1981] P.L. 249.

[2]   *City of Berne* v. *Bank of England* (1804) 9 Ves. Jun. 347.

[3]   *A.M. Luther* v. *James Sagor & Co.* [1921] 1 K.B. 456, [1921] 3 K.B. 532; *Adams* v. *Adams* [1971] P. 188. *Cf. Carl Zeiss Stiftung* v. *Rayner & Keeler (No. 2)* [1967] 1 A.C. 853; *Hesperides Hotels* v. *Aegean Holidays Ltd* [1979] Q.B. 205, 218; Z.M. Nedjati (1981) 30 I.C.L.Q. 388.

[4]   For the previous common law position, see *e.g. The Phillipine Admiral* [1977] A.C. 373; *Trendtex Trading Corp.* v. *Central Bank of Nigeria* [1977] Q.B. 529.

[5]   I. Sinclair (1980-II) 167 *Hague Recueil*, 113; C. Lewis, *State and Diplomatic Immunity*. The Act is not retrospective: s. 23; *Hispano Americana Mercantil S.A.* v. *Central Bank of Nigeria* [1979] 2 Lloyd's Rep 277. *Cf.* s. 12; *Planmount Ltd* v.*Republic of Zaire* [1981] 1 All E.R. 1110.

[6]   Sections 1, 14. Immunity is lost if they submit to the jurisdiction of the courts: s. 2.

[7]   Sections 3; *Alcom Ltd* v. *Republic of Colombia* [1984] 2 All E.R. 6.

[8]   Section 3. For contracts of employment, see s. 4; *Sengupa* v. *Republic of India* [1983] I.C.R. 221.

[9]   Section 5.

[10]   Section 6; *cf.* s. 16(1) and *Intpro Properties (U.K.) Ltd* v.*Sauvel* [1983] Q.B. 1019.

[11]   Section 10.

[12]   Section 14(2).

Diplomatic immunity

The privileges and jurisdictional immunities of diplomats are now largely governed by the Diplomatic Privileges Act 1964.[13] The Act divides members of a diplomatic mission into three categories: (a) members of the diplomatic staff and their families[14] who are granted, with some limited exceptions, full personal immunity from the jurisdiction of the courts in both civil and criminal actions; (b) members of the administrative and technical staff who are given full immunity in respect of their official acts, although they attract civil, but not criminal, liability for acts performed outside the course of their duties; (c) members of the domestic service staff who have full immunity for their official acts but attract both civil and criminal liability for acts performed outside their official duties. The Act provides that these immunities may be withdrawn or partially withdrawn, by Order in Council, from diplomats or a state which accords less extensive immunities to British diplomats.[15] The Act also provides that a certificate of the Foreign Secretary is conclusive as to whether any person is entitled to any privileges or immunity under the Act,[16] but it is not conclusive on other facts or on points of law.[17] Diplomatic immunity may be waived by the diplomat's state or the head of his diplomatic mission.[18] The waiver must be express[19] and may not be retrospective.[20] A waiver of immunity from the jurisdiction of the court does not include a waiver of immunity from execution of the judgment of the court, for which a separate waiver would be necessary.[21]

Similar privileges and immunities are extended to heads of recognised states in their private capacity,[22] consuls,[23] certain international organisations and persons connected with them, and to representatives attending various international conferences in the United Kingdom.[24]

Community law grants substantial immunity from the jurisdiction of the courts of member states to members of the European Parliament, to representatives of member states taking part in the work of Community institutions and to officials and other servants of the Communities, including the judges, advocates-general and certain other officials of the Court of Justice.[25]

---

[13] The 1964 Act implemented most of the provisions of the Vienna Convention on Diplomatic Relations 1961 (Cmnd 1368). See also the Diplomatic Immunities (Commonwealth Countries and Republic of Ireland) Act 1952.

[14] P.J. O'Keefe, (1976) 25 I.C.L.Q. 329.

[15] Sections 3, 6(1).

[16] Section 4.

[17] *E.g. Empson* v. *Smith* [1966] 1 Q.B. 426; *Agbor* v. *Metropolitan Police Commissioner* [1969] 2 All E.R. 707; *R.* v. *Governor of Pentonville Prison ex p. Teja* [1971] 2 Q.B. 274; and questions of waiver of immunity and submission to the jurisdiction.

[18] Diplomatic Privileges Act 1964, s. 2(3); *cf. Re Suarez* [1918] 1 Ch. 176; *R.* v. *Madan* [1961] 2 Q.B. 1.

[19] Diplomatic Privileges Act 1964, sch. 1, art. 32(2).

[20] *R.* v. *Madan, ante.*

[21] Diplomatic Privileges Act 1964, sch. 1, art. 32(4); *cf. Re Suarez, ante.*

[22] State Immunity Act 1978, s. 20.

[23] Consular Relations Act 1968; Diplomatic and other Privileges Act 1971, s. 4.

[24] *E.g.* International Organisations Act 1968; Diplomatic Immunities (Conferences with Commonwealth Countries and Republic of Ireland) Act 1961.

[25] Protocol on the Privileges and Immunities of the European Communities 1965, arts. 8–12, 16, 18, 21, 22.

Chapter 19

The courts and the machinery of justice

In chapter 4 the broad relationship between the judiciary, the legislature and the executive was examined. This chapter will consider the major constitutional aspects of the courts and the machinery of justice. After the barest catalogue of the civil and criminal courts, the House of Lords, the Privy Council and certain specialised courts will be briefly discussed.[1] It must be stressed that there are in the United Kingdom three distinct court systems: in England and Wales, in Scotland, and in Northern Ireland. The judiciaries in the three systems are quite separate from each other except that judges and senior practitioners in each system are eligible for appointment to the House of Lords as Lords of Appeal in Ordinary. They are also eligible for appointment to the Court of Justice of the EEC and to those specialised courts and tribunals (such as the Restrictive Practices Court) which have jurisdiction throughout the United Kingdom.

A. The courts and the judiciary

The courts of civil and criminal jurisdiction

In England and Wales, civil jurisdiction is exercised by the High Court, the judges of which sit in three divisions (Queen's Bench, Chancery and Family) and, on appeal, by the Court of Appeal, Civil Division. Together the High Court, the Court of Appeal and the Crown Court form the Supreme Court. From the Court of Appeal, and in some cases direct from the High Court, appeals lie with leave to the House of Lords, sitting as a court. A limited civil jurisdiction is exercised by the county courts and on a few subjects (for example, certain matrimonial disputes) by the magistrates' courts. Criminal jurisdiction is exercised at first instance in summary trials by the magistrates' courts and in jury trials by the Crown Court, created by the Courts Act 1971,

---

[1] For accounts of the English legal system, see R. M. Jackson, *The Machinery of Justice in England*; G. Wilson, *Cases and Materials on the English Legal System*. For Scotland, D. M. Walker, *The Scottish Legal System*, and H.M.S.O., *The Legal System of Scotland*.

which sits in London and in over 90 provincial centres. In the Crown Court the judge may be a High Court judge, a circuit judge or a part-time recorder. Criminal appeals lie, depending on the nature and grounds of the appeal, to the Queen's Bench Divisional Court of the High Court (composed of two or three judges sitting together) or to the Court of Appeal, Criminal Division. A further appeal in criminal cases on matters of law may lie, with leave, to the House of Lords.

In Scotland, civil jurisdiction is exercised by the ancient Court of Session. Single judges sit in the Outer House for trials at first instance; eight senior judges form the Inner House, sitting in two divisions for mainly appellate purposes. A wide civil jurisdiction is exercised by the sheriff court, from which appeals may lie to the Inner House of the Court of Session. Criminal jurisdiction, for jury trials and appeals, is exercised by the High Court of Justiciary, which comprises the same judges as sit in the Court of Session; and also by the sheriff court, both for summary trials and jury trials. The district courts, established by the District Courts (Scotland) Act 1975, have a summary criminal jurisdiction which is less extensive than magistrates' courts in England. Appeals from Scotland in civil cases, but not in criminal cases, lie to the House of Lords.

In Northern Ireland, jurisdiction is exercised by the High Court, the Crown Court and the Court of Appeal, forming the Supreme Court of Northern Ireland. Civil jurisdiction is exercised by the High Court (with Queen's Bench, Chancery and Family divisions) and the Court of Appeal. Criminal jurisdiction is exercised by the Crown Court (in which sit the judges of the Court of Appeal and the High Court, and the county court judges), by the Queen's Bench side of the High Court, and by the Court of Appeal, including the High Court judges. At an intermediate level, civil jurisdiction is exercised by the county courts. At a local level, civil and criminal jurisdiction is exercised by magistrates' courts, presided over by resident magistrates. Civil and criminal appeals from the Court of Appeal and, in specified cases, from the High Court, lie to the House of Lords.

The House of Lords

For practical purposes, the House of Lords sitting as the final court of appeal is distinct from the House in its legislative capacity, although judicial business is governed by standing orders of the House. The sittings of the House for judicial business used to be ordinary sittings of the House. After *O'Connell's* case,[2] in which the presence of lay peers was ignored by the Lord Chancellor, it was a conventional rule that no lay peer should take part in appellate work. Because of a shortage of peers who held judicial office, the Appellate Jurisdiction Act 1876 provided for the appointment of two Lords of Appeal in Ordinary, for whom the statutory qualification was to have held high judicial office in the United Kingdom or to have been a practising barrister (or advocate in Scotland) for 15 years. The Act declared that appeals should not be heard unless there were present at least three from the following: the Lord

---

[2] *O'Connell* v. *R.* (1844) 11 Cl. & Fin. 155, 421–6.

Chancellor, the Lords of Appeal in Ordinary, and such peers as held or had previously held high judicial office (*i.e.* in a superior court in the United Kingdom). The Lords of Appeal in Ordinary, of whom up to eleven may now be appointed, are salaried and under an obligation to sit for appellate work; the other qualified peers serve voluntarily. There is a convention, but no more than a convention, that an ex-Lord Chancellor in receipt of a pension should serve when requested to do so by the Lord Chancellor. Usually appeals are heard by five judges but in exceptional cases seven judges may sit.[3]

In 1948, as a temporary measure, the House of Lords authorised the hearing of appeals by an appellate committee. This practice became permanent: appeals are now heard by the Law Lords sitting as one or two appellate committees of the House. Judgment is still delivered by members of a committee in the full Chamber, but since 1963 the speeches of the individual members have not been delivered orally but are handed to the parties and their counsel already printed. As the sittings of the appellate committees often clash with those of the whole House, the Lord Chancellor rarely sits for judicial business: he is entitled to preside when he does so. The appellate committees may sit for the purpose of hearing appeals when Parliament has been prorogued or dissolved or during an adjournment of the House. Standing orders also provide for two appeals committees which consider and report to the House on petitions for leave to appeal.

Being at the apex of the hierarchy of courts in the United Kingdom, except that it has no jurisdiction in Scottish criminal cases, the House of Lords has great authority in influencing the development of the law through the system of precedent.[4] For many years the House regarded itself as bound by its own previous decisions[5] but in 1966 the Lords of Appeal in Ordinary made through the Lord Chancellor a statement modifying that doctrine and accepting that too rigid adherence to precedent might lead to injustice in a particular case and unduly restrict the proper development of the law.[6] The House of Lords now treats its former decisions as normally binding but is prepared to depart from a previous decision when it appears right to do so.[7]

Judicial Committee of the Privy Council

Although in 1640 the Long Parliament abolished the jurisdiction of the King in Council at home, the power of the Council to receive petitions from the Channel Islands and the Isle of Man survived. From the late 17th century onwards, an increasing number of petitions by way of appeal were brought from the colonies and other overseas possessions of the Crown. In 1833 the Judicial Committee of the Privy Council was set up by statute to exercise the jurisdiction of the Council in deciding appeals from colonial, ecclesiastical and

---

[3]   *E.g. R.* v. *National Insurance Commissioner, ex p. Hudson* [1972] A.C. 944.

[4]   For studies of its work, see L. Blom-Cooper and G. Drewry, *Final Appeal*; A. Paterson, *The Law Lords*; R. Stevens, *Law and Politics*.

[5]   *London Street Tramways Co.* v. *LCC* [1898] A.C. 375.

[6]   Note [1966] 3 All E.R. 77; and see Paterson, *op. cit.*, ch. 6.

[7]   For use made of this freedom in public law cases, see *e.g. Conway* v. *Rimmer* [1968] A.C. 910, *Hudson's* case (*ante*), *Knuller Ltd* v. *DPP* [1973] A.C. 435 and *R.* v. *Home Secretary, ex p. Khawaja* [1984] A.C. 74.

admiralty courts. In the heyday of the British Empire, the Judicial Committee was indeed an imperial court exercising what was potentially a vast jurisdiction over much of the globe. Today its role as an appeal court within the Commonwealth has much declined.[8] Apart from this, it has a miscellany of judicial functions. The Judicial Committee is still the final court of appeal from the Channel Islands and the Isle of Man. It lost much of its appellate jurisdiction in Church of England matters when in 1963 new appellate courts were created within the church, but appeals may still be taken to it in faculty cases from the consistory courts. An appeal lies to the Judicial Committee from various professional disciplinary boards, including the disciplinary committees of the General Medical Council and the Dental Council.[9] By section 4 of the Judicial Committee Act 1833, the Crown may refer any matter to the Committee for an advisory opinion: this unusual power has been used infrequently, to obtain advisory opinions on matters of some public concern and legal difficulty which cannot otherwise be brought conveniently before the courts, including matters relating to disqualification from the House of Commons and parliamentary privilege.[10] Under section 5 of the Government of Ireland Act 1920, which formed the constitution for Northern Ireland until 1972, the government was empowered to refer to the Judicial Committee questions as to the interpretation of the Act; while this provided a procedure for obtaining a judicial decision on whether measures passed by the Northern Ireland Parliament were within their legislative competence, only one reference under this procedure was made to the Judicial Committee in 50 years.[11] The scheme of legislative devolution proposed for Scotland in 1978 included procedure enabling the Judicial Committee to decide issues relating to the powers of the Scottish Assembly.[12]

The composition of the Judicial Committee is governed by the 1833 Act: usually three or five Lords of Appeal in Ordinary sit but the Committee also includes the Lord President of the Council (who does not sit), the Lord Chancellor, the Lord Justices of Appeal, such members of the Privy Council as hold or have held high judicial office in the United Kingdom or have been judges in the superior courts of the Commonwealth states from which appeals still lie to the Committee, or of any colony that may be determined by Order in Council. In theory the Judicial Committee does not deliver judgment. It advises the government who acts on its report and issues an Order in Council to give effect to the advice. Until 1966 the opinion of the majority alone was given but dissenting opinions are now permissible.[13] Although the Committee is in form merely giving advice to the government, 'in substance, what takes place is a strictly judicial proceeding'.[14]

---

8   Ch. 24. For the background, see L. P. Beth [1975] P.L. 219.
9   Medical Act 1978, s. 11; Dentists Act 1957, s. 29. For the scope of the appeal, see *e.g. Libman* v. *General Medical Council* [1972] A.C. 217.
10 *In re MacManaway* [1951] A.C. 161; *In re Parliamentary Privilege Act 1770* [1958] A.C. 331, and see H.L.E., Vol. 10, pp. 362–3.
11 *Reference under the Government of Ireland Act 1920* [1936] A.C. 352; H. Calvert, *Constitutional Law in Northern Ireland*, pp. 298–301.
12 Scotland Act 1978, s. 19, and sch. 12; ch. 22.
13 Judicial Committee (Dissenting Opinions) Order 1966 (*Statutory Instruments 1966*, Part I, 1100).
14 *Hull* v. *McKenna* [1926] I.R. 402.

It has been suggested that the work of the Judicial Committee and the appellate jurisdiction of the House of Lords should be amalgamated as most of the work is carried out by the same judges anyway. To abolish the Judicial Committee and transfer its jurisdiction to the Lords would present no real difficulties except that it might be unpopular with those few overseas territories and Commonwealth states from which appeals may still be brought to London. To transfer the judicial work from the House of Lords to the Judicial Committee would be a greater upheaval in constitutional terms.[15] It has not been shown that the present arrangements produce serious inconvenience.

Courts of specialised jurisdiction

The judicial system is not confined to the courts of general civil and criminal jurisdiction. The numerous administrative tribunals, in whose proceedings judges of the civil and criminal courts rarely play a part, will be examined in chapter 37. Rather than creating such tribunals, Parliament has sometimes created specialised courts which are solely composed of judges of the superior courts (for example, the election court [16] or the Patents Appeal Tribunal) or which include both judges and lay members. The Restrictive Practices Court was established by the Restrictive Trade Practices Act 1956 and its jurisdiction has been subsequently enlarged.[17] As a superior court of record, it has a status co-ordinate with that of other superior courts in the United Kingdom. The court consists of five judges and not more than ten other members, being persons who appear to the Lord Chancellor to have knowledge or experience of industry, commerce or public affairs. Of the five judges, three are drawn from the English High Court, one from the Court of Session and one from the Supreme Court of Northern Ireland. The court is concerned with the enforcement of the legislation against restrictive trade practices, trading agreements and retail price maintenance. Restrictive agreements are brought before the court by the Director-General of Fair Trading, who acts as registrar of restrictive trading agreements; they are deemed to be contrary to the public interest unless the court is satisfied that one or more of the statutory circumstances which may justify an agreement are proved to exist.

The short-lived National Industrial Relations Court from 1971 to 1974 had a similar form to that of the Restrictive Practices Court. As well as its controversial powers in relation to industrial disputes, appeals could be brought to it from industrial tribunals. In its place in 1975 was created the Employment Appeal Tribunal to hear appeals on points of law from industrial tribunals, for example on claims against employers for unfair dismissal. The tribunal is composed of one or more judges from the English Supreme Court nominated by the Lord Chancellor and at least one judge from the Court of Session nominated by the Lord President, who sit together with persons having special knowledge of industrial relations as representatives of employers and of workers. Despite its name, the tribunal is a superior court of record. It may sit anywhere in Great Britain. Parties to appeals may be represented by

---

[15]   Blom-Cooper and Drewry, *Final Appeal*, p. 411.
[16]   Ch. 9 B, III.
[17]   Resale Prices Act 1976, Restrictive Trade Practices Act 1976, Restrictive Practices Court Act 1976, Competition Act 1980.

counsel, solicitors, trade union officials or any other person. Appeals from the tribunal lie on points of law, with leave, to the Court of Appeal or to the Inner House of the Court of Session.[18]

The Sovereign and the courts

According to Blackstone, 'All jurisdictions of courts are either indirectly or immediately derived from the Crown. Their proceedings are generally in the King's name; they pass under his seal, and are executed by his office', but it is 'impossible as well as improper that the King personally should carry into execution this great and extensive trust'.[19] The notion of the Sovereign as the fountain of justice was important in feudal times in helping to ensure that a single system of justice prevailed over competing jurisdictions. The early kings delivered justice in their own courts. But the delegation of this duty to judges was an inevitable result of the growth of the business of government and the development of a system of law requiring specialised knowledge. In England it was enacted in 1328 by the Statute of Northampton that the royal command should not disturb or delay common justice and that, although such commands had been given, the judges were not therefore to cease to do right in any point.

In Scotland, the Court of Session, which was placed on a permanent basis in 1532, more than once had to resist royal interference in the course of justice and issued a notable rebuff to James VI in 1599.[20] In 1607, James, who had by then also become King James I of England, claimed the right in England to determine judicially a dispute between the common law courts and the ecclesiastical courts. In the case of *Prohibitions del Roy*, it was decided by all the common law judges headed by Coke that the right of the King to administer justice no longer existed.[21] In a famous passage, Coke declared:

that the King in his own person cannot adjudge any case, either criminal, as treason, felony, etc., or betwixt party and party, concerning his inheritance, chattels, or goods, etc., but this ought to be determined and adjudged in some Court of Justice, according to the law and custom of England; . . . true it was, that God had endowed His Majesty with excellent science, and great endowments of nature; but His Majesty was not learned in the laws of his realm of England, and causes which concern the life, or inheritance, or goods, or fortunes of his subjects, are not to be decided by natural reason, but by the artificial reason and judgment of law, which law is an act which requires long study and experience, before that a man can attain to the cognizance of it: that the law was the golden met-wand and measure to try the causes of the subjects; and which protected His Majesty in safety and peace.

This declaration may not have been supported by all Coke's precedents[22] but it served to establish a fundamental constitutional principle. This principle was reinforced by provisions in the Bill of Rights 1689 and the Scottish Claim of

---

[18]   Employment Protection (Consolidation) Act 1978, ss. 135, 136 and schedule 11. For industrial tribunals, see ch. 37 A.
[19]   1 *Commentaries*, Book 1, ch. VII.
[20]   *Bruce* v. *Hamilton*, recounted in (1946) 58 J.R. 83; and see *Earl of Morton* v. *Fleming* (1569) Morison 7325.
[21]   (1607) 12 Co. Rep. 63.
[22]   *Cf.* Dicey, p. 18.

Right which restricted royal interference in the course of justice. Certain prerogative powers in relation to the administration of justice have survived and will be examined later in this chapter. But the Crown can no longer by the prerogative create courts to administer any system of law other than the common law.[23] This restriction had its roots in the common lawyers' distrust of the prerogative courts of the Star Chamber and the High Commission. Its effect today is that new courts and tribunals may be created only by Act of Parliament, but this does not prevent the Crown under prerogative power from establishing a body to administer a scheme for conferring financial benefits upon individuals.[24]

Judicial independence

The primary judicial function is to determine disputes, whether between private persons or between a private person and a public authority. Judges must apply the law and are bound to follow the decisions of the legislature as expressed in statutes. In interpreting statutes and applying decided cases they do however to a large extent make, as well as apply, law. In countries where there is a written constitution which cannot be overridden by ordinary legislation (for example, the United States of America), the judges are guardians of the constitution and may declare a statute to be unconstitutional and invalid. In the United Kingdom, the chief constitutional function of the judiciary is to ensure that government is conducted according to law and thus in an important sense to secure the observance of the rule of law.[25] If this function is to be adequately performed, independence of the judiciary must be maintained. Like other constitutional principles, judicial independence has many facets, only some of which are expressed in definite legal rules. Clearly it must be possible for a judge to decide a case without fear of reprisals, whether from the executive, a wealthy corporation, a powerful trade union, or a group of terrorists. But there is no reason why judges should be totally immune from public opinion and the free discussion of current issues in the media. Judicial independence does not mean isolation of the judge from the society in which he exercises his office.

Appointment of judges

Judicial appointments in the United Kingdom are a matter for the executive. The Queen's judges are appointed on the advice of the Queen's ministers. There is no formal machinery, such as a Judicial Service Commission, to insulate judicial appointments from executive control. Nor is there, as in the USA, any requirement that the executive's nominees should be subject to scrutiny and confirmation by the legislature. Appointments to the House of Lords and to the most senior judicial posts in England (including Lord Justice of Appeal, Master of the Rolls, President of the Family Division and Lord Chief Justice) are made by the Crown on the advice of the Prime Minister. High Court judges, circuit judges and recorders are appointed by the Crown on the

---

23   *In re Lord Bishop of Natal* (1864) 3 Moo. P.C. (N.S.) 115.
24   *R. v. Criminal Injuries Compensation Board, ex p. Lain* [1967] 2 Q.B. 864, p. 249 *ante*.
25   Ch. 6.

advice of the Lord Chancellor.[26] Magistrates, who except for stipendiary magistrates are not required to be legally qualified, are appointed to the commission of the peace by the Lord Chancellor. Judges of the Court of Session are appointed by the Crown on the advice of the Secretary of State for Scotland, who by convention forwards to the Crown nominations submitted to him by the Lord Advocate.

By statute, minimum qualifications for appointment must be observed. Thus judges of the High Court must be of ten years' standing as a barrister; Lord Justices of Appeal, who sit in the English Court of Appeal, must be of 15 years' standing as a barrister or already be a High Court judge.[27] For appointments to the Court of Session there is a rule of five years' standing as a member of the Faculty of Advocates.[28] There are also rules of standing for the inferior judiciary: a recorder must be a barrister or solicitor of ten years' standing; a circuit judge must be of ten years' standing as a barrister or have held the office of recorder for five years.[29] In Scotland a sheriff must be of ten years' standing as advocate or solicitor.[30]

In practice appointments to the superior courts are made only from successful practitioners at the bar, and the average experience of those appointed is well above the legal minimum.[31] There can be little doubt that extensive consultations take place between the Lord Chancellor and senior judges (for example, the Lord Chief Justice) before new appointments are made and that the Lord Chancellor submits to the Prime Minister nominations for the highest judicial posts. In Britain there is not as in some other legal systems a career service of judges. It is rare for inferior judges, such as the circuit judges or the sheriffs, to be promoted to the superior courts, but an ambitious judge of the High Court does have the prospect of further advancement to the Court of Appeal or the House of Lords. Despite the lack of formal machinery to guard against this, judicial appointments are not made by the government in power as a reward for political services. Today the Attorney-General has no claim to be appointed Lord Chief Justice when a vacancy occurs in that post. But neither in England nor in Scotland do political activities disqualify an otherwise well qualified barrister or advocate, at least if they are within the mainstream of British politics. Scotland appears to have seen the last of the unhappy convention by which the Lord Advocate nominated himself whenever a vacancy occurred in the two senior posts of Lord President and Lord Justice Clerk. But it is usual for a Lord Advocate to become a judge in due course.

Tenure of judges

Judges of the High Court and Court of Appeal hold their offices during good behaviour, subject to a power of removal by the Queen on an address

---

26 Supreme Court Act 1981, s. 10.
27 *Ibid*, s. 10(3).
28 Treaty of Union 1706, art 19.
29 Courts Act 1971, s. 16(2).
30 Sheriff Courts (Scotland) Act 1971, s. 5.
31 In Scotland, average practice at the bar on appointment to the Court of Session has been 29 years: I. D. Willock, 1969 J.R. 193, 202.

presented to the Queen by both Houses of Parliament.[32] A similar provision applies to Lords of Appeal in Ordinary.[33] These statutory rules clearly prevent a judge being removed at the pleasure of the Crown, but their meaning is not wholly certain. The wording of the provision in the Act of Settlement from which these rules derived[34] suggests that the intention of Parliament was that, while a judge should hold office during good behaviour, Parliament itself should enjoy an unqualified power of removal. Assuming that there was no intention to alter the effect of the Act of Settlement by the revised wording now contained in the Supreme Court Act 1981, it is theoretically possible for a judge to be dismissed not only for misconduct but for any other reason which might induce both Houses to pass the necessary address to the Crown. It is, however, extremely unlikely that Parliament would be willing to pass an address from any motive other than to remove a judge who had been guilty of misconduct.

But what would constitute misconduct sufficient to justify removal? It is not the case that any conviction for a criminal offence will lead to the removal of a judge, although arguably any conviction is misconduct. In 1975 a High Court judge pleaded guilty to driving with more than the permitted degree of alcohol in his blood;[35] and he continued in office. Since the Act of Settlement, only one judge has been removed from office by means of an address to the Crown from both Houses: in 1830, Jonah Barrington, an Irish judge, was found to have misappropriated money belonging to litigants and to have ceased to perform his judicial duties many years previously.[36] It would seem that the address to the Crown must originate in the Commons. The accused judge is entitled to be heard at the Bar of the House or before a select committee; if the facts of misconduct are disputed, witnesses may be called to give evidence.

Before 1959, judicial appointments were made for life, but there are now statutory ages for retirement (for example, 75 for a High Court judge, 72 for a circuit judge). Although Parliament could by passing an Act alter the tenure of existing judges, in 1959 judges already in office who wished to remain on tenure for life were permitted to do so.[37] In 1973, a statutory procedure for the compulsory retirement of judges was introduced to deal with the difficult but unusual situation where a judge is permanently incapacitated from carrying out his judicial duties and is also incapacitated from resigning. In this situation, the Lord Chancellor may declare the judge's post to be vacant, subject to medical evidence and to the approval of the relevant senior judge.[38]

Inferior judges receive a lesser degree of protection. Circuit judges may be removed from office by the Lord Chancellor, if he thinks fit, for incapacity or misbehaviour.[39] Lay magistrates may be removed from the commission of the

---

[32] Supreme Court Act 1981, s. 11(3).
[33] Appellate Jurisdiction Act 1876, s. 6.
[34] Page 15 *ante*.
[35] *The Times*, 2 Sep. 1975.
[36] D. M. R. Esson, 1972 J.R. 50.
[37] See now Judicial Pensions Act 1981, sch. 2, para. 1(1).
[38] See now Supreme Court Act 1981, s. 11(8)(9).
[39] Courts Act 1971, s. 17(4). And see *Ex p. Ramshay* (1852) 18 Q.B. 173. In 1983, a circuit judge was dismissed for misbehaviour after a conviction for smuggling quantities of whisky and cigarettes from the Channel Islands to England.

peace at the discretion of the Lord Chancellor, though in practice a magistrate is not removed unless he has been arrested for a criminal offence of some gravity or for persistent minor offences, or has in some other way ceased to uphold the law, for example, by taking part in a civil disobedience compaign.[40]

In Scotland, the historic tenure on which judges hold office is *ad vitam aut culpam, i.e.* they cannot be removed except on grounds of misconduct.[41] Judges of the Court of Session still hold office on this basis, subject to the retiring age of 75 for appointments made after 1959. The Act of Settlement procedure involving a resolution from both Houses of Parliament does not apply to them. Should the need arise, a procedure for removal by the Crown for misconduct would have to be devised: it might well be prudent for the Crown to seek the support of the two Houses for its action. Sheriffs have greater protection than do circuit judges in England: a sheriff may be removed from his office only after an inquiry, conducted jointly by the Lord President of the Court of Session and the Lord Justice-Clerk, has established unfitness for office by reason of inability, neglect of duty or misbehaviour, and only by means of an order of removal made by the Secretary of State for Scotland and laid before Parliament.[42] This procedure was used in 1977 to dismiss Sheriff Peter Thomson, who despite a warning had persisted in using his judicial position to promote political activities, namely a campaign for government by plebiscite. An attempt by some M.P.s to persuade the House of Commons to grant the judge a hearing was unsuccessful; he had earlier declined to make use of the statutory rules entitling him to a hearing.[43]

Judicial salaries

Salaries are an aspect of tenure. The Act of Settlement provided that judicial salaries should be 'ascertained and established'. This was interpreted as requiring that judicial salaries should be fixed by Act of Parliament and not left to the discretion of the executive. By long-standing practice, judicial salaries are charged on the Consolidated Fund, which means that the authority for payment is permanent and does not have to be reviewed by Parliament each year.[44] In 1931, consternation was caused to some English judges when the National Economy Act 1931 authorised the Crown by Order in Council to make economies in the remuneration of persons in the service of the Crown, and an Order in Council was made reducing the salaries of judges (which had been £5,000 per annum since 1832) by 20%. A deputation of judges complained to the Lord Chancellor but a petition of right against the cuts which MacNaghten J. threatened to bring never materialised, even though the judges had some strong legal arguments on their side.[45]

In a period of rapid inflation, the need is not so much to guard against reductions in the statutory salaries as to provide machinery to enable salaries

---

40   *Cf.* Jackson, *The Machinery of Justice in England*, pp. 296–8.
41   Claim of Right 1689, art. 13; *Mackay and Esslemont* v. *Lord Advocate*, 1937 S.C. 860.
42   Sheriff Courts (Scotland) Act 1971, s. 12.
43   H.C. Deb., 25 Nov. 1977, col. 922 (W.A.), 30 Nov. 1977, col. 245 (W.A.), and 6 Dec. 1977, col. 1288.
44   Supreme Court Act 1981, s. 12(5); and see ch. 16.
45   R. F. V. Heuston, *Lives of the Lord Chancellors 1885–1940*, pp. 513–19, and see W. S. Holdsworth (1932) 48 L.Q.R. 25.

to be increased to keep pace with other public salaries. The Judges' Remuneration Act 1965 gave authority for judicial salaries to be increased, but not reduced, by means of Orders in Council, subject to the approval of both Houses of Parliament. A further step was taken in 1973 when the Lord Chancellor (or, in the case of the Court of Session, the Secretary of State for Scotland) was authorised to increase judicial salaries, acting with the approval of the Prime Minister.[46] There is now no requirement of express parliamentary approval but, at the request of the government, judicial salaries may be examined by the advisory Review Body on Top Salaries.[47] The highest paid judge in the United Kingdom is the Lord Chief Justice, whose salary in 1984 was £64,000; in the second highest bracket come the Lords of Appeal in Ordinary, the Master of the Rolls and the Lord President of the Court of Session (£58,500). Judges of the High Court in England were in 1984 paid £51,250.

Use of judges for extra-judicial purposes

Judges are frequently called on by the government to preside over royal commissions, departmental committees and inquiries conducted under the Tribunals of Inquiry (Evidence) Act 1921. From 1953 to 1973, not including judges who served on permanent committees for law reform, 79 such appointments were made.[48] Many judges are well suited for this work but there are potential dangers to judicial independence in the practice, particularly when matters of acute political controversy are referred to a judge for an impartial opinion. Examples may be found in the inquiries by Lord Wilberforce in 1970 and 1972 into industrial disputes and in the regular use of judges (including Lords Radcliffe, Diplock and Bridge) to chair the Security Commission which investigates shortcomings in the work of British intelligence services.[49] Particularly controversial references were the investigations conducted by Lord Denning on the request of the Prime Minister into the security aspects arising out of the resignation of a minister (J. Profumo) in 1963 and by the Lord Chief Justice, Lord Widgery, in 1972 into the Londonderry riot deaths.[50] Such references may give rise to allegations that the government of the day is using the judiciary for its own ends; and they may expose the judge in question, particularly if he is the sole member of the inquiry, to political criticism by those who disagree with his report. It needs to be stressed that such work is not the primary task of the judges and that the government may not assume that the services of a judge will be available whenever an awkward political situation might be eased by an impartial inquiry.

While the government may invite judges to take part in inquiries into current problems, the political parties are not entitled to ask judges to assist them in the preparation of their policies.

In 1968, the leader of the Opposition, Mr Heath, appointed a committee to consider

---

46   See now Supreme Court Act 1981, s. 12.
47   See *e.g.* Cmnd 9254, 1984; and H.C. Deb., 7 Jun. 1984, col. 221 (W.A).
48   H.C. Deb., 7 Dec. 1973, col. 478 (W.A.). And see J. A. G. Griffith, *Politics of the Judiciary*, ch. 2 and G. Zellick [1972] P.L. 1.
49   Ch. 30.
50   See respectively Cmnd 2152, 1963 and H.C. 220 (1971–2).

possible changes in the constitutional position of Scotland. Included in the committee, which was chaired by a former Conservative Prime Minister, Sir Alec Douglas-Home, was a judge of the Court of Session, Lord Avonside, nominated at the request of Mr Heath by the Lord President of the Court of Session. In the ensuing controversy, the Lord Advocate maintained that the nomination of a judge to this committee was in breach of 'a long-standing constitutional convention' by which the judiciary did not participate in the activities of a political party. When the Scottish National Party asked the Lord President to nominate a judge to serve on that party's constitutional committee, the Lord President declined. Lord Avonside thereupon resigned from the Douglas-Home committee, while denying that a judge in Scotland could be bound against his will to eschew party politics.[51]

Despite the judge's assertions to the contrary, these unusual events reinforced the strong constitutional convention that a judge should not become involved in party political activities. All salaried judges are disqualified from membership of the Commons. While the Lords of Appeal in Ordinary and other senior judges are members of the House of Lords, they sit on the cross-benches and do not take part in the legislative work of the House as party supporters.

Parliamentary criticism of the judiciary

The work of the courts should not be outside the scope of political discussion. There is however a convention that members of the executive, whether ministers or civil servants, do not criticise judicial decisions. The government may say that a judicial decision differs from the legal advice upon which it had acted or that it proposes to bring in amending legislation, but ministers are not expected to state that a court's decision is wrong. Nonetheless in 1982 the Prime Minister stated that she found the decision of a judge to impose a suspended prison sentence for rape of a six year old girl incomprehensible, and informed the House of Commons of action taken by the Lord Chancellor requiring trials for rape to be conducted only by senior judges.[52] As individuals, back bench M.P.s are not subject to the restraints that apply to ministers, but there is a long-standing rule of the House that unless the discussion is based on a substantive motion, reflections must not be cast upon the conduct of judges, nor upon judges generally.[53] The effect of these rules was seen in 1973 when the National Industrial Relations Court and its president, Sir John Donaldson, an English judge, became the subject of acute controversy.

The court had been set up under the Conservative government's Industrial Relations Act 1971, and its jurisdiction in industrial disputes was bitterly opposed by trade unions. The Amalgamated Union of Engineering Workers disregarded an order of the court and were fined £100,000 for contempt. The court directed that funds of the union be sequestrated to pay the fine, action which was later defended by Sir John Donaldson in the course of an after-dinner speech. Over 180 Labour M.P.s signed a motion calling for Sir John's dismissal as High Court judge, but this was not supported by opposition leaders. When the Commons debated a motion calling for the repeal of the 1971 Act, and regretting the involvement of the court in matters of political controversy, the Speaker ruled that it could be argued in debate that a judge's decision was wrong,

---

51   *The Times* and *The Scotsman*, 26 Jul.–6 Aug. 1968.
52   H.C. Deb., 14 Dec. 1982, Col. 123; 15 Dec. 1982, col. 285.
53   Erskine May, pp. 378 and 431.

and the reasons for this view could be given. But no reflections on a judge's character or motives could be raised except on a motion for his dismissal.[54] In the event, the motion calling for the judge's dismissal was never debated, since neither the government nor the opposition wished to provide time for the purpose. The Speaker ruled that the ancient Articles of Charge procedure, if it were still available, could not be given precedence over the ordinary business of the House.[55]

On subsequent occasions, when judges have made controversial remarks or decisions, M.P.s have been quick to raise these matters in the Commons and to show their disapproval. Thus in January 1978, Judge McKinnon conducted a trial at the Old Bailey of charges of incitement to racial hatred and in his summing-up called into question the policy behind the race relations legislation. After these remarks had been criticised in Parliament, the Lord Chancellor discussed the criticisms with the judge, who indicated that he did not wish to conduct further trials for similar offences.[56] Concern was also expressed over remarks by Melford Stevenson J. about the law on homosexuality, which remarks were 'strongly deprecated' by the Lord Chancellor,[57] and remarks by Judge King-Hamilton criticising a jury's decision to acquit defendants at an 'anarchist' trial.[58]

In 1977, motions were tabled for the dismissal of three judges who in the Court of Appeal had reduced a sentence for rape.[59] A judge who described a victim of rape as having been guilty of 'contributory negligence' was also criticised.[60] Instant political reaction to events such as these may sometimes be ill-informed or exaggerated, but a corrective is needed when judges are seriously insensitive to changing social opinion. Criticism of the historical role of the judiciary was expressed in 1977, when Mr Michael Foot, while holding a senior Cabinet post, told a trade union rally that the British people, especially trade unionists, would have 'precious few' freedoms if these had been left to the good sense and fair mindedness of the judges.[61]

Another parliamentary rule seeks to protect the principle of a fair trial rather than the status of the judges: by the *sub judice* rule, matters awaiting the adjudication of a court may not be raised in debate. The rule applies to matters pending decision both in criminal and civil cases; but in regard to civil cases, the Speaker has a discretion to permit reference to matters awaiting adjudication where they relate to ministerial decisions which can be challenged in court only on grounds of misdirection or bad faith, or to issues of national importance, such as the national economy, the essentials of life or public order.[62] The reason for this relaxation is to permit some parliamentary discussion of ministerial decisions or other major issues of public concern, notwithstanding the fact that a civil action may have been instituted.[63] The *sub*

---

54   H.C. Deb., 4 Dec. 1973, col. 1092. And see H.C. Deb., 19 Jul. 1977, col. 1381.
55   H.C. Deb., 10 Dec. 1973, col. 42.
56   *The Times*, 7 and 14 Jan. 1978.
57   *The Times*, 6 Jul. 1978.
58   *The Times*, 20 and 21 Dec. 1979, 17 Jan and 1 Feb. 1980.
59   H.C. Deb., 23 Jun. 1977, col. 1748.
60   *The Times*, 6 and 12 Jan. 1982.
61   *The Times*, 16 May 1977.
62   Erskine May, p. 429; H.C. Deb., 23 Jul. 1963, col. 1417; 28 June 1972, col. 1589.
63   See *e.g.* debate on the thalidomide cases, H.C. Deb., 29 Nov. 1972, col. 432.

judice rule has been described as a self-denying ordinance, created by the Commons so that Parliament should not influence or seem to be influencing the administration of justice.[64] It does not affect the power of Parliament to legislate: thus the War Damage Act 1965 altered the law retrospectively while litigation against the government was in process.

Judicial immunity from civil action

Just as the public interest in free debate in Parliament justifies the rule of absolute privilege for things said in the course of parliamentary debates, so the public interest in the administration of justice justifies similar protection for judicial proceedings. At common law no action will lie against a judge for any acts done or words spoken in his judicial capacity in a court of justice.

It is essential in all courts that the judges who are appointed to administer the law should be permitted to administer it under the protection of the law independently and freely, without favour and without fear. This provision of the law is not for the protection or benefit of a malicious or corrupt judge, but for the benefit of the public, whose interest it is that the judges should be at liberty to exercise their functions with independence and without fear of consequences.[65]

It seems from the authorities that the judge of a superior court is not liable for anything done or said in the exercise of his judicial functions, however malicious, corrupt or oppressive are the acts or words complained of.[66] A similar immunity to that of judges attaches to the verdict of juries, [67] and to words spoken by parties, counsel and witnesses in the course of judicial proceedings.[68] In *Rondel* v. *Worsley*, it was held that a barrister is not liable to be sued for the negligent conduct of a client's case in court.[69] The immunity of judges is reinforced by the Crown Proceedings Act 1947, section 2(5), which absolves the Crown from liability for the conduct of any person 'while discharging or purporting to discharge any responsibilities of a judicial nature vested in him' or in the execution of judicial process. But immunity does not extend to the acts or words of a judge in his private capacity.

Judicial immunity also applies to the work of inferior courts, for example, county courts and magistrates' courts,[70] and acts within the jurisdiction of these courts are protected from liability. But difficult problems may arise in relation to the extent of this immunity, in particular concerning the liability of an inferior judge for acts committed outside his jurisdiction.[71] It was formerly held that the judge in an inferior court was liable for acts committed in his judicial capacity if they were outside his jurisdiction;[72] but where the excess of jurisdiction occurred because of an erroneous finding of fact, he was liable only where he knew or could reasonably have known the true facts.[73]

---

[64] H.C. Deb., 29 Jul. 1976, col. 882; and see H.C. 222 (1978–9).
[65] *Scott* v. *Stansfield* (1868) L.R. 3 Ex. 220, 223 per Kelly C.B.
[66] *Anderson* v. *Gorrie* [1895] 1 Q.B. 668.
[67] *Bushell's* case (1670) 6 St. Tr. 999.
[68] *Munster* v. *Lamb* (1883) 11 Q.B.D. 588.
[69] [1969] 1 A.C. 191. But see *Saif Ali* v. *Sydney Mitchell & Co.* [1980] A.C. 198.
[70] *Scott* v. *Stansfield* (*ante*), *Law* v. *Llewellyn* [1906] 1 K.B. 487.
[71] De Smith, *Judicial Review*, pp. 121–3, 337–9; and A. Rubinstein, *Jurisdiction and Illegality*, ch. 6.
[72] *Houlden* v. *Smith* (1850) 14 Q.B. 841.
[73] *Calder* v. *Halket* (1839) 3 Moo. P.C. 28, 77.

On this basis, the immunity of judges in superior courts was greater than that of judges in inferior courts. It was also uncertain whether the latter were liable for acts done within jurisdiction but motivated by malice and bad faith.[74] The liability of justices of the peace was especially complex, since this rested in part upon the obscurely drafted Justices' Protection Act 1848.[75] The decision of the Court of Appeal in *Sirros* v. *Moore* in 1974 went a long way to solve these complexities by assimilating the position of judges in inferior courts to that of judges in the superior courts. In that case a circuit court judge was held immune from liability for damages after he had by a wholly erroneous procedure ordered a Turkish citizen to be detained by the police.[76] The Court of Appeal considered that no distinction should be drawn in principle between the protection given to superior court judges and that given to inferior courts. According to Lord Denning M. R. and Ormrod L. J., every judge, including a justice of the peace, was entitled to be protected from liability in respect of what he did while acting judicially and in the honest belief that his acts were within his jurisdiction.[77]

While the judges in *Sirros* v. *Moore* considered it an adequate remedy for the plaintiff that he had recovered his liberty by means of habeas corpus, their decision meant that he had no right to be compensated for having suffered an unlawful detention. It is indeed doubtful whether there is yet an adequate framework of legal rules for enabling individuals to be compensated from public funds who suffer loss through defects in the administration of justice. Possibly the United Kingdom has something to learn from the law of Trinidad and Tobago. That country's written constitution declares the fundamental rights of the individual and also provides that the High Court may grant redress to an individual whose rights have been infringed. In *Mararaj* v. *Attorney-General of Trinidad (No. 2)* the Judicial Committee held that these provisions did not impose personal liability on a judge who had committed Maharaj to prison for contempt of court (by an order that was later held to be invalid), but that the constitution imposed a duty on the state to compensate Maharaj out of public funds for the infringement of his right to liberty.[78] This example suggests that it would be possible to maintain the personal immunity of the judges in the United Kingdom, while providing by legislation an enforceable right to compensation for plaintiffs such as Sirros.[79]

To what extent does immunity extend to the members of administrative tribunals, some of whose duties may be judicial, others of which may be administrative or 'ministerial'? Here there may be immunity for judicial acts, but liability for 'ministerial' acts, such as refusal to perform a definite duty which permits of no discretion.[80] When a licensing body does not have the attributes of a court, even though for some purposes it may be required to act

---

[74] De Smith, *Judicial Review*, p. 338.
[75] D. Thompson (1958) 21 M.L.R. 517; *O'Connor* v. *Isaacs* [1956] 2 Q.B. 288; Justices of the Peace Act 1979, Part V.
[76] [1975] Q.B. 118, discussed by M. Brazier [1976] P.L. 397.
[77] *Cf.* the approach of Buckley L.J. [1975] Q.B. at p. 137.
[78] [1979] A.C. 385.
[79] Such a right is required by article 5(5), European Convention on Human Rights; ch. 31B.
[80] *Ferguson* v. *Earl of Kinnoull* (1842) 9 Cl. & F. 251.

judicially, words spoken in the course of its proceedings are privileged only in the absence of malice.[81] But where a statutory inquiry was held in Scotland into a teacher's dismissal, by an adversary procedure modelled on that of a court and conducted before a lawyer appointed by the Secretary of State, the witnesses were held to be protected by absolute privilege.[82]

Other safeguards

Despite their immunities, it would be wrong to suppose that professional judges are uncontrolled despots. For one thing, laymen make a significant contribution to the administration of justice: the role of the jury in major criminal trials is an important constitutional safeguard against an oppressive judiciary; removal of the right to trial by jury is a matter of grave concern.[83] So too is interference with the freedom of the jury, whether it takes the form of criminal conduct or 'jury-vetting'.[84] Lay magistrates in England and Wales discharge a heavy burden of adjudication. Non-lawyers have a significant role to play in courts of specialised jurisdiction and in administrative tribunals.

There are also many legal rules which serve to maintain the quality of justice in the courts. The law of contempt of court is considered in the next section. The written rules of court procedure as well as the unwritten rules of natural justice seek for each litigant a fair and orderly hearing before an unbiased judge.[85] The statutory schemes for legal aid from public funds seek to ensure that it is not only the wealthy who benefit from legal representation in the courts. The rules of evidence, particularly in criminal trials before a jury, exclude material which might be unfairly prejudicial to the accused. Most judges carry on their work knowing that their decisions may be subject to scrutiny and criticism by a higher court on appeal.

In principle all trials are conducted in open court, and may be fully reported in the press. In a few exceptional cases, the court may sit in camera, and press and public are then excluded.[86] These exceptions include cases in which the court is asked to preserve the secrecy of an industrial process or invention; proceedings brought under the Official Secrets Acts 1911–39, for example for spying, where the public interest so requires; certain domestic and juvenile court hearings; and proceedings for an offence against morality or decency when evidence is being given by children or young persons.[87] But the court may not hear a case in camera merely in the interests of decency.[88] The rule of public hearing does not apply when a judge sits in chambers, nor in cases concerning wards of court or mentally disordered persons. When an appeal is brought against the decision of a court which had power to sit in

---

81   *Royal Aquarium Society Ltd* v. *Parkinson* [1892] 1 Q.B. 431.
82   *Trapp* v. *Mackie* [1979] 1 All E.R. 489; N. V. Lowe and H. F. Rawlings [1982] P.L. 418, 431–40.
83   See Cmnd 5185, 1972; and Northern Ireland (Emergency Provisions) Act 1978 s. 7(1).
84   Page 358 *post*.
85   Ch. 34 B.
86   Both by statute and by judicial discretion, reporters may sometimes be present when the public are excluded: *e.g.* Children and Young Persons Act 1933, s. 47(2) and *R.* v. *Waterfield* [1975] 2 All E.R. 40.
87   Children and Young Persons Act 1933, s. 37.
88   *Scott* v. *Scott* [1913] A.C. 417.

private, the appellate court has the same power to sit in private during all or part of the appeal, but the decision and the reasons for it must in general be given in public.[89]

Where judicial proceedings take place in open court in the United Kingdom, the press may be present and may publish reports of the proceedings which, if fair and accurate reports, will be privileged in the law of defamation.[90] But Parliament has imposed various restrictions on reporting of judicial proceedings. Newspapers may not publish details of the evidence in matrimonial cases, but may only publish the names of parties, a statement of the issues, submissions on points of law and the judgment.[91] There are also reporting restrictions relating to the identity of children and young persons.[92] The law relating to committal proceedings, at which magistrates in England determine whether or not an accused person shall be tried on indictment before judge and jury, was amended in 1981: if full committal proceedings take place, the evidence is heard in open court, but reporting restrictions prevent publication of the evidence unless the accused asks for the restrictions to be lifted.[93]

B. Contempt of court[1]

The law on contempt of court was developed by the judges as a means whereby the courts may prevent or punish conduct that tends to obstruct, prejudice or abuse the administration of justice, whether in a particular case or generally.[2] This branch of the law operates in the interests of all who take part in court proceedings, as judges, counsel, parties or witnesses. But it also imposes restraints upon many persons, particularly on the press, whose freedom to report news about the administration of justice is sometimes severely limited by the law of contempt. Significant reforms were made by the Contempt of Court Act 1981, which sought to strike a fresh balance between the need of the judicial system to be protected against improper attack, and the public interest in maintaining freedom of speech and discussion.

Civil contempt

Contempt of court may take two forms. Civil contempt is the failure to obey the order of a superior court of record which prescribes certain conduct upon a party to a civil action. A civil judge has power to commit to prison anyone who disregards an order addressed to him. In this way, decrees of specific

---

[89] Domestic and Appellate Proceedings (Restriction of Publicity) Act 1968, s. 1.
[90] Law of Libel Amendment Act 1888, s. 3; Defamation Act 1952, ss. 7–9; and in Scots law *Drew v. Mackenzie* (1862) 24 D. 649.
[91] Judicial Proceedings (Regulation of Reports) Act 1926; Magistrates' Courts Act 1980, s. 71.
[92] Children and Young Persons Act 1933, s. 39.
[93] Magistrates' Courts Act 1980, s. 8. For the position when there are two or more accused, see Criminal Justice (Amendment) Act 1981, s. 2.

[1] See G. Borrie and N. Lowe, *The Law of Contempt*; C. J. Miller, *Contempt of Court*; A. Arlidge and D. Eady, *The Law of Contempt*; Report of the Phillimore Committee on Contempt of Court, Cmnd 5794, 1974.
[2] Phillimore Report, p. 2.

performance and injunctions, as well as the writ of habeas corpus and other judicial orders, may be enforced by the High Court. The power of courts to enforce their orders against litigants is not, however, available against the Crown or against government departments; the constitutional assumption is that the government will always observe the law as it is declared by courts.[3] Where a civil contempt is committed, the court may commit the wrongdoer to prison for a fixed period, may fine him or may order his property to be sequestrated. The short-lived National Industrial Relations Court exercised all these powers when trade unions opposed to the Industrial Relations Act 1971 refused to observe its jurisdiction. The Official Solicitor to the Supreme Court is required to review all cases of persons committed to prison for contempt and may intervene to secure their release.[4] The Crown may not grant a pardon in cases of civil contempt since this would be to intervene in litigation between parties.

Criminal contempt

Conduct which is calculated to interfere with the due administration of justice or to bring the courts into disrepute gives rise to proceedings which are in the nature of criminal proceedings, although both civil and criminal courts may exercise the jurisdiction. Criminal contempt may take various forms, including:

1   contempt in the face of the court;
2   publications prejudicial to a fair criminal trial;
3   publications prejudicial to civil proceedings;
4   scandalising the court; and
5   other acts which interfere with the course of justice.[5]

1 Contempt in the face of the court.   All superior courts have power to punish summarily by fine or imprisonment violence committed or threats uttered in face of the court. Thus the judge may punish an attack on himself or anyone in court, or restrain the use of threatening words or scurrilous abuse. The issue whether an act constitutes a contempt is for the judge alone. If the act is committed in his court, he is in a sense prosecutor, chief witness, judge and jury.

In *Morris* v. *Crown Office*,[6] a group of students demonstrated in support of the Welsh language by interrupting a sitting of the High Court in London, where they sang, shouted slogans and scattered pamphlets. After order was restored, the trial judge sentenced some of the students to prison for three months and fined others £50 each. On appeal, the Court of Appeal, Civil Division, held that a High Court judge still had power at common law to commit instantly to prison for criminal contempt; and that the requirement under the Criminal Justice Act 1967 that prison sentences under six months be suspended did not apply to committal for contempt. The court did not consider the prison sentences to be excessive, but, having regard to all the circum-

---

3   Ch. 36.
4   *Churchman* v. *Joint Shop Stewards' Committee* [1972] 3 All E.R. 603; Borrie and Lowe, *op. cit.*, ch. 11 and Miller, *op. cit.* ch. 14; *Enfield BC* v. *Mahoney* [1983] 2 All E.R. 901.
5   This classification derives from Borrie and Lowe.
6   [1970] 2 Q.B. 114.

stances, allowed the appeal against sentence and bound over the appellants to be of good behaviour for one year.

Contempt in the face of the court includes insulting behaviour, disregard of a judge's ruling and refusal by a witness to give evidence or to answer questions which he is required to answer.

In *Attorney-General* v. *Mulholland and Foster*,[7] two journalists refused to disclose their sources of information to a tribunal of inquiry appointed after an Admiralty clerk, Vassall, had been convicted of espionage. The tribunal had by statute the powers of the High Court in examining witnesses.[8] On appeal against a prison sentence imposed by the High Court, to whom the tribunal had reported the journalists, it was held that journalists had no legal privilege to refuse to disclose sources of information given to them in confidence, where the information was relevant and necessary to the trial or inquiry.

So too, in *British Steel Corporation* v. *Granada Television Ltd*,[9] the House of Lords ordered the Granada company to reveal the name of an employee of the corporation who had passed secret documents to Granada that were then used in a programme about the corporation. Although failure by Granada to comply with this order would have constituted contempt, the matter was resolved when the employee concerned made his identity known. In 1981, the power of the court to demand information was limited by Parliament. The court may not now request a person to disclose the source of information contained in a publication for which he is responsible unless the court is satisfied that disclosure is necessary in the interests of justice or national security or for the prevention of disorder or crime.[10] If cases such as *Mulholland* and *British Steel Corporation* were to occur today, the statutory test of necessity would have to be applied before the court decided to require disclosure, but the outcome might still be the same.

Magistrates and county court judges do not have inherent power to deal with those who interrupt proceedings in their courts. But they have statutory power to impose penalties upon anyone who wilfully insults those concerned in the proceedings, or who interrupts the proceedings or otherwise misbehaves.[11]

2 Publications prejudicial to a fair criminal trial. An outstanding example of a publication likely to jeopardise the possibility of a fair criminal trial occurred in 1949 when the *Daily Mirror* described a man accused of murder as a 'vampire' and named other murders which he had committed: the court fined the proprietors £10,000 and sent the editor to prison for three months.[12] And in 1967 the publishers of the *Sunday Times* were fined £5,000

---

7   [1963] 2 Q.B. 477. And see *Senior* v. *Holdsworth* [1976] Q.B. 23.
8   Ch. 37 C.
9   [1981] A.C. 1096.
10 Contempt of Court Act 1981, s. 10; *Secretary of State for Defence* v. *Guardian Newspapers Ltd* [1984] Ch. 156 (return of secret document ordered in interests of national security).
11 Contempt of Court Act 1981, s. 12; County Courts Act 1984, s. 118.
12 *R.* v. *Bolam, ex p. Haigh* (1949) 93 Sol. Jo. 220.

after publishing the picture of a man awaiting trial on a charge under the Race Relations Act 1965, with a caption which described him as a 'brothel-keeper, procurer and property racketeer'.[13]

One reason for the seriousness with which such contempts are treated is the principle that a jury must not hear before a trial anything of the past character or record of the accused, and must give its verdict on the basis of evidence heard at the trial. Newspapers must observe strict rules in this respect. When a trial is pending they may not publish interviews with witnesses or alleged confessions by the accused. They may not publish a photograph of the accused where a question of identity is likely to arise and publication may prejudice a fair trial.[14]

Difficult issues regarding contempt of court may arise from investigative journalism, particularly when a press campaign seeks to establish that fraudulent or corrupt practices have occurred.

After a press campaign about the dubious affairs of an insurance company, its prime mover Savundra was interviewed on television by David Frost. Soon after, charges of fraud were brought against Savundra. When Savundra appealed against his conviction claiming that this interview had prevented him receiving a fair trial, the Court of Appeal considered that the object of the interview had been to establish Savundra's guilt at a time when 'it must surely have been obvious to everyone' that fraud charges were about to be brought. 'Trial by television', said Salmon L.J., 'is not to be tolerated in a civilized society'.[15]

This dictum may not take adequate account of the public benefit to be derived from investigative journalism (for example, in exposing police corruption), but it emphasises that the media should not seek to prejudice the outcome of criminal proceedings nor make it impossible for a person to receive a fair trial. In one Scottish case, a television programme broadcast shortly before the trial of a nurse for alleged mercy-killing led to the prosecution being withdrawn.[16]

3 Publications prejudicial to civil proceedings. Civil proceedings, no less than criminal proceedings, should be conducted fairly and free of prejudice. When a matter is *sub judice*, public discussion may need to be restricted even though the subject is of public concern.[17] But the law of contempt applies differently to civil proceedings, partly because a citizen's liberty is unlikely to be in issue and partly because most civil proceedings do not involve a jury. Thus an article in the *Daily Telegraph* which argued that sherry could come only from Spain was held not to be likely to prejudice the fair trial of a pending action regarding the propriety of descriptions such as 'Cyprus Sherry'.[18] In 1973, a newspaper campaign to secure adequate compensation for the thalido-

---

13   *R* v. *Thomson Newspapers, ex p. A.-G.* [1968] 1 All E.R. 268.
14   *Stirling* v. *Associated Newspapers Ltd* 1960 J.C. 5.
15   *R.* v. *Savundranayagan* [1968] 3 All E.R. 439, 441: note that this was an appeal against conviction, not proceedings for contempt.
16   *Atkins* v. *London Weekend Television Ltd* 1978 S.L.T. 76; *cf. Hall* v. *Associated Newspapers Ltd* 1978 S.L.T. 241.
17   For the *sub judice* rule in Parliament, see p. 338 *ante.*
18   *Vine Products Ltd* v. *Green* [1966] Ch. 484.

mide victims caused the law of contempt to be considered by the House of Lords.

Nearly 400 claims against Distillers Ltd, the manufacturers of thalidomide, were pending when the *Sunday Times* published an article which *inter alia* urged the company to make a generous settlement. Later it proposed to publish an article examining the precautions taken by the company before the drug was sold. On the Attorney-General's request, the Divisional Court granted an injunction to restrain publication of the article, holding that it would create a serious risk of interference with the company's freedom of action in the litigation. The Court of Appeal discharged the injunction, on the grounds that the article commented in good faith on matters of outstanding public importance and did not prejudice pending litigation since the litigation had been dormant for some years. The House of Lords restored the injunction, holding that it was a contempt to publish an article prejudging the merits of an issue before the court where this created a real risk that fair trial of the action would be prejudiced; the thalidomide actions were not dormant, since active negotiations for a settlement were going on. It was a contempt to use improper pressure to induce a litigant to settle a case on terms to which he did not wish to agree, or to hold a litigant up to public obloquy for exercising his rights in the courts.[19]

Thereafter the *Sunday Times* claimed that the decision of the House of Lords infringed the freedom of expression protected by article 10 of the European Convention on Human Rights. Before the European Court of Human Rights, the main issue was whether, under article 10, the ban on publication was 'necessary in a democratic society ... for maintaining the authority and impartiality of the judiciary'. By 11 to 9 votes, the court held that the ban had not been shown to be necessary for this purpose.[20]

The decision of the House of Lords had been based on the view that the media must not prejudice a civil court's decision by seeking to persuade the public that one party to litigation is right and the other wrong. The contrary view of the European Court caused the British government to undertake to introduce legislation amending the law on contempt, so as to make it more consistent with the requirements of the European Convention. This led to the passing of the Contempt of Court Act 1981, whose main provisions are considered below.[21]

The application of the *sub judice* rule to statutory tribunals of inquiry[22] has caused extra difficulties, since a tribunal of inquiry is appointed only on matters of outstanding public interest, such as the Aberfan disaster in 1966. In 1969, the Salmon committee on the law of contempt in relation to tribunals of inquiry recommended that the law should continue to apply to tribunals of inquiry but in a modified form. There should be no prohibition on newspaper comment at any time on the subject-matter of the inquiry, but after the appointment of the tribunal of inquiry it should be contempt if any person said or did anything 'in relation to any evidence relevant to the subject-matter of

---

[19]   *A.-G.* v. *Times Newspapers Ltd* [1974] A.C. 273; *cf. Schering Chemicals Ltd* v. *Falkman Ltd* [1982] Q.B. 1.

[20]   *Sunday Times* v. *U.K.* 26 Apr. 1979 (No. 30) 2 E.H.R.R. 245.

[21]   Page 349 *post*.

[22]   Ch. 37 C.

the inquiry' which was intended or likely to alter, destroy or withhold that evidence from the tribunal.[23] This recommendation has not been adopted, but changes in the law made by the Contempt of Court Act 1981 were applied also to statutory tribunals of inquiry.[24]

4 Scandalising the court. The law protects courts and judges from criticism which might undermine public confidence in the judiciary, in particular scurrilous abuse and attacks upon the integrity or impartiality of a judge. Criticism of a court's decision may be a contempt if it imputes unfairness and partiality to a judge in the discharge of his duties.

In 1928, the *New Statesman*, commenting on a judgment in a libel action given against Dr Marie Stopes, a known advocate of birth control, concluded, 'an individual owning to such views as those of Dr Stopes cannot apparently hope for a fair hearing in a court presided over by Mr Justice Avory – and there are so many Avorys'. Three colleagues of the judge in question, though they imposed no fine on the editor, adjudged him guilty of contempt.[25]

Yet it is clearly in the public interest that there should be public discussion and criticism of judicial decisions and the work of the courts. When a colonial newspaper had discussed a variation in sentences in two apparently similar cases, suggesting that this was due to the personal attitudes of the judge, the Privy Council set aside the conviction for contempt. The judgment of the Judicial Committee was given by Lord Atkin, who said:

But whether the authority and position of an individual judge, or the due administration of justice, is concerned, no wrong is committed by any member of the public who exercises the ordinary right of criticising, in good faith, in private or public, the public act done in the seat of justice. The path of criticism is a public way: the wrong-headed are permitted to err therein: provided that members of the public abstain from imputing improper motives to those taking part in the administration of justice, and are genuinely exercising a right of criticism, and not acting in malice or attempting to impair the administration of justice, they are immune. Justice is not a cloistered virtue: she must be allowed to suffer the scrutiny and respectful, even though outspoken, comments of ordinary men.[26]

Discussion of the legal merits or social implications of judicial decisions is therefore not contempt, even where a Queen's Counsel chooses to make sweeping and inaccurate criticisms of the Court of Appeal in the columns of *Punch*.[27] Potentially this aspect of the law might deter a critic who sought to show that the judges were biased politically or socially or that a particular court was failing to administer justice. But today the scope of permissible criticism has widened, to judge by the sharp controversy over the National Industrial Relations Court between 1971 and 1974, and by the attacks made

23 Cmnd 4078, 1969; Borrie and Lowe, *op. cit.*, ch. 10.
24 Page 721 *post*.
25 *R. v. New Statesman (Editor), ex p. DPP* (1928) 44 T.L.R. 301.
26 *Ambard v. A.-G. for Trinidad and Tobago* [1936] A.C. 322, 335.
27 *R. v. Metropolitan Police Commissioner, ex p. Blackburn (No. 2)* [1968] 2 Q.B. 150. Probably the most savage criticism of a British court ever published was N. J. D. Kennedy, *The Second Division's Progress*, (1896) 8 J.R. 268.

on some of Lord Denning's decisions before his retirement in 1982. The Phillimore committee recommended that this branch of contempt should be replaced by an offence of publishing matter which imputes improper judicial conduct with the intention of impairing confidence in the administration of justice,[28] but this recommendation has wisely not been adopted.

5 Other acts interfering with the course of justice.

The categories of contempt are not closed. A wide variety of other acts are punishable as contempts, some of them also being criminal offences in their own right, for example, attempts to pervert the course of justice or interference with witnesses. A prison governor who, acting under prison rules, obstructed a prisoner's communication to the High Court was held to be in contempt.[29] It is contempt to punish or victimise a witness for evidence which has already been given, even in proceedings which have concluded, since this might deter potential witnesses in future cases.[30] So too it is contempt for a newspaper to disregard a judge's direction that the names of prosecution witnesses in blackmail cases should not be published.[31]

Such directions have not always been easy to enforce.

In *Attorney-General* v. *Leveller Magazine Ltd* a magazine published the name of a prosecution witness at an official secrets trial, who had been described in court as Colonel B. The House of Lords held that it was contempt to publish a witness's name if this interfered with the administration of justice. But on the facts no contempt had occurred, since (*inter alia*) no clear direction against publication had been given by the magistrates; and Colonel B's identity could have been discovered from evidence given in open court.[32]

The uncertainties left by this decision were lessened by the Contempt of Court Act 1981. By section 11, where a court has power to withhold evidence from the public (although the court is sitting in public) and allows the name of a witness or other matter to be withheld, the court may restrict publication accordingly.[33] Under earlier legislation, it is contempt to publish details of certain judicial proceedings that are held in private (for example, proceedings relating to the adoption or custody of infants, national security or industrial secrets).[34]

Interference with the work of a jury may constitute contempt, whether before, during or after a trial. But in 1980 a magazine article disclosing aspects of the jury's deliberations during the trial of Mr Jeremy Thorpe was held not to be a contempt of court.[35] The law was changed in 1981 when it became a contempt of court to solicit, obtain or disclose details of any statements made

---

[28] Phillimore Report, pp. 69–71.
[29] *Raymond* v. *Honey* [1983] A.C. 1.
[30] *A.-G.* v. *Butterworth* [1963] 1 Q.B. 696; *Moore* v. *Clerk of Assize, Bristol* [1972] 1 All E.R. 58. And see Law Commission, Report No. 96, *Offences relating to interference with the course of justice.*
[31] *R.* v. *Socialist Worker Ltd, ex p. A.-G.* [1975] Q.B. 637.
[32] [1979] A.C. 440; and see C. Aubrey, *Who's Watching You?*, ch. 5.
[33] The restriction must be in writing: *Practice Note* [1983] 1 All E.R. 64.
[34] Administration of Justice Act 1960, s. 12; and see *Re F (a minor)* [1977] Fam. 58.
[35] *A.-G.* v. *New Statesman Publishing Co.* [1981] Q.B. 1.

or votes cast by jurors during their deliberations in any legal proceedings.[36]

A sharp conflict between freedom of expression and the due administration of justice arose in *Home Office* v. *Harman*.

A prisoner challenged the legality of a Home Office decision to set up a 'control unit' for prisoners considered to be troublemakers. An order for discovery of documents being made against the Home Office, a large number of official documents were made available to the prisoner's solicitor.[37] She undertook that the documents would be used only for the case in hand, but she later allowed a journalist to see documents which had been read out in open court. The journalist published an article based on these documents. The House of Lords held (by 3-2) that although the documents had been read in court, and could have been reported by journalists present, the solicitor was guilty of contempt since she had used the documents for a purpose which was not necessary for the conduct of her client's case, and had broken her implied undertaking to the court that had ordered discovery.[38]

As with the earlier *Sunday Times* case, this decision was taken up under the European Convention on Human Rights as an alleged breach of the freedom of expression guaranteed by article 10.[39]

The strict liability rule

One controversial aspect of the law before 1981 was the strict liability rule, defined in the Contempt of Court Act 1981 as 'the rule of law whereby conduct may be treated as tending to interfere with the course of justice in particular legal proceedings regardless of intent to do so'.[40] The 1981 Act narrowed the scope of this rule. It is now limited to publications (including broadcasts and other forms of communication to the public) which create a 'substantial risk' that the course of justice in the proceedings in question will be 'seriously impeded or prejudiced'.[41] This test differs significantly from the test of pre-judgment applied by the House of Lords in the *Sunday Times* case. Moreover the 1981 Act requires that the proceedings in question must be 'active', and lays down in detail when civil or criminal proceedings begin to be active and when they are concluded. Thus criminal proceedings become active when an individual is arrested or orally charged, or when a warrant for his arrest is issued. Civil proceedings become active not when the writ is served but when the action is set down for trial.[42]

Other changes in the strict liability rule were made in 1981. It is now a statutory defence to strict liability if the person responsible for the publication can prove that, having taken all reasonable care, he did not know that relevant legal proceedings were active.[43] It is not contempt to publish contempor-

---

[36] Contempt of Court Act 1981, s. 8.
[37] *Williams* v. *Home Office* [1981] 1 All E. R. 1151; and see ch. 36.
[38] *Home Office* v. *Harman* [1983] A.C. 280.
[39] Ch. 31 B.
[40] Contempt of Court Act 1981, s. 1; and see *e.g. R.* v. *Odhams Press* [1957] 1 Q.B. 73.
[41] Contempt of Court Act 1981, s. 2(2).
[42] Contempt of Court Act 1981, s. 2(3) and sch. 1.
[43] Contempt of Court Act 1981, s. 3.

aneously and in good faith a fair and accurate report of legal proceedings held in public; but a court has power to order that publication of reports be delayed where necessary for avoiding a substantial risk of prejudice to the administration of justice.[44] This power may be exercised even in respect of committal proceedings that are not subject to statutory reporting restrictions.[45] There is now no contempt in respect of a publication made as part of a discussion in good faith of public affairs if the risk of prejudice to legal proceedings is merely incidental to the discussion.[46] Proceedings for contempt under the strict liability rule may be initiated in England only with the consent of the Attorney-General or on motion of a court.[47] None of these changes in the law affect liability for conduct that is *intended* to prejudice the administration of justice.[48]

The scope of contempt of court

Many legal disputes today are determined not by the civil and criminal courts but by administrative tribunals.[49] These bodies have no inherent power to deal with conduct which prejudices their proceedings, but the High Court has power to punish conduct that is in contempt of inferior courts.[50] Are tribunals to be classified as inferior courts for this purpose? In 1980, the House of Lords held that, despite its name, a local valuation court that hears appeals against rating valuations was not a court, since its functions were essentially administrative; it was thus not protected by the law of contempt.[51] The government's response to this decision was to propose that contempt of court be extended to all tribunals, but neither this nor a proposal to list tribunals for this purpose was accepted in Parliament.[52] The Contempt of Court Act 1981 thus does not deal with the matter, although section 19 defines 'court' as including 'any tribunal or body exercising the judicial power of the State'. The effects of this definition in the framework of the Act are far from clear, although tribunals within the definition now appear to have power under section 9 to control the use of tape recorders in proceedings before them, and possibly under section 11 to direct that certain matters be not published.

Procedure in contempt cases

In English law contempt is treated as a common law misdemeanour. Unlike other crimes it may be dealt with by a superior court in summary proceedings and without a jury. An indictment before judge and jury is possible but unusual. Criminal contempts may be punished by a fine or by a prison sentence. A two year prison sentence is now the maximum that may be

---

[44] Contempt of Court Act 1981, s. 4.
[45] *R.* v. *Horsham Justices, ex p. Farquharson* [1982] Q.B. 762.
[46] Contempt of Court Act 1981, s. 5, applied in *A.-G.* v. *English* [1983] A.C. 116.
[47] Contempt of Court Act 1981, s. 7.
[48] Contempt of Court Act 1981, s. 6(c).
[49] Ch. 37 A.
[50] R.S.C. Order 52, rule 1.
[51] *A.-G.* v. *B.B.C.* [1981] A.C. 303. See *Badry* v. *D.P.P. of Mauritius* [1982] 3 All E.R. 973, and N. V. Lowe and H. F. Rawlings [1982] P. L. 418.
[52] H.L. Deb., 9 Feb. 1981, col. 163; H.C. Deb.,16 Jun. 1981, col. 917.

imposed by a superior court.[53] Inferior courts may imprison for up to one month or impose a fine up to £500. All orders for committal must now be for a fixed term, but the court may order release at an earlier date.[54] While the superior courts need to be able to exercise summary powers, the normal safeguards of criminal process should not be absent from contempt proceedings. In 1960 a general right of appeal was provided in cases of criminal contempt[55] and legal aid became available in 1981.[56] Regarding contempts in the face of the court, the Phillimore committee recommended that the alleged offender should have an opportunity of denying or explaining the contempt; and that except in trivial cases there should.be some delay between determining the issue of contempt and imposing the penalty. It has been left to the courts themselves to develop their practice in accordance with these principles.

Scots law
The law of contempt of court serves the same broad purposes both in England and Scotland. But the law is distinct and there are many procedural differences. Thus Scots law does not recognise the distinction between civil and criminal contempts and the law of contempt is regarded as *'sui generis'*.[57] The contempt jurisdiction may be exercised by the Court of Session, the High Court of Justiciary and the sheriff court. Reliance is placed for some purposes upon the residual authority, or *nobile officium*, of the Court of Session and the High Court, to whom a petition and complaint alleging a contempt may be presented with the consent of the Lord Advocate. Appeal lies either by normal channels of appeal or through a petition to the *nobile officium*. In some instances the law has been more strictly applied in Scotland than in England.[58] The Phillimore committee considered that the law applying to the press and broadcasting should be the same in the two jurisdictions; consequently the Contempt of Court Act 1981 for the most part applies both in England and Scotland, including the reforms in the strict liability rule discussed above.

Conclusion
The law of contempt of court has certain resemblances to the power of the two Houses of Parliament to punish for contempt. Both are considered necessary to protect the working of major organs of the constitution. Both have been criticised in the past for making excessive inroads into freedom of discussion and physical liberty. The reforms made by the Contempt of Court Act 1981 were extensive, but uncertainties remain.[59] In particular it remains to be seen whether contempt law as reformed now conforms with the minimum standards of freedom of expression and judicial procedure guaranteed by the European

---

53 The county court ranks as a superior court for this purpose: County Courts (Penalties for Contempt) Act 1983, overruling *Peart* v. *Stewart* [1983] 2 A.C. 109.
54 See *e.g. Enfield BC* v. *Mahoney* [1983] 2 All E.R. 901.
55 Administration of Justice Act 1960, s. 13.
56 Contempt of Court Act 1981, s. 13.
57 G. H. Gordon, *Criminal Law*, ch. 51
58 *E.g. Stirling* v. *Associated Newspapers Ltd* 1960 J.C. 5; and consider *Wylie* v. *H.M. Advocate* 1966 S.L.T. 149 *Royle* v. *Gray* 1973 S.L.T. 31 and *Cordiner* v. *Cordiner* 1973 S.L.T. 125.
59 See N. V. Lowe [1982] P.L. 20.

Convention on Human Rights. The possibility of recourse to the Convention organs should ensure that British judges remember, in the words of Lord President Normand,

that the greatest restraint and discrimination should be used by the court in dealing with contempt of court, lest a process, the purpose of which is to prevent interference with the administration of justice, should degenerate into an oppressive or vindictive abuse of the court's powers.[60]

C. The executive and the machinery of justice

The court system is part of the framework by which our society is governed and it cannot be totally separated from the executive. Such questions as what courts we should have, in what buildings they should be housed, and how the court system should be paid for, are questions which cannot be decided by the judges and the legal profession. Many countries have a Ministry of Justice to administer the court system. This was proposed for the United Kingdom in 1918 by the Haldane committee on the machinery of government[1] but a Ministry of Justice by that name has never been established. Instead the duties that would fall to such a ministry are in England and Wales exercised principally by the Lord Chancellor and the Home Secretary, and in Scotland by the Secretary of State for Scotland and the Lord Advocate.

Lord Chancellor[2]

The Lord Chancellor is concerned with virtually all judicial appointments in England and Wales, appointing to the magistracy himself, formally advising the Crown on new circuit and High Court judges, and informally advising the Prime Minister on the most senior judicial appointments. He is entitled to preside over the House of Lords in its judicial work and the Judicial Committee of the Privy Council, although today Lord Chancellors do not sit frequently. He is titular head of the Supreme Court; within the High Court, he is president of the Chancery Division, although the duties of this office are performed by the Vice-Chancellor. The administrative business of the Supreme Court and the appointment of court officials are in the hands partly of the Lord Chancellor and partly of the judges, primarily the presidents of the various divisions of the court. Rules of the Supreme Court are made by the Rule Committee, consisting of the Lord Chancellor and other judges together with practising barristers and solicitors. The secretariat comes from the Lord Chancellor's department. The Lord Chancellor is responsible for the administration of the county court system; thus he may alter the boundaries of county court districts and the groupings of county courts into circuits. He appoints the County Court Rule Committee and may alter or disallow the rules which it prepares. By the Courts Act 1971, the Lord Chancellor assumed responsibility for setting up

---

[60] *Milburn, Petitioner*, 1946 S.C. 301, 315.

[1] Cd 9230, 1918.

[2] For accounts of his duties, see Haldane Report, Cd 9320, ch. 10; Lord Schuster (1949) 10 C.L.J. 175; R. F. V. Heuston, *Lives of the Lord Chancellors 1885–1940*, Introduction; R. M. Jackson, *The Machinery of Justice in England*, ch. 7.

a unified service to administer the courts and acquired power to issue direc-
tions regarding sittings of the High Court outside London. Rules for the Crown
Court are made by the Lord Chancellor together with the Crown Court Rule
Committee.

The Lord Chancellor's department has a growing responsibility for administrative tribunals, especially since the Tribunals and Inquiries Act 1958. The
Council on Tribunals is appointed jointly by the Lord Chancellor and the
Lord Advocate and reports to these ministers. The Lord Chancellor appoints
the chairmen of many tribunals; dismissal of a chairman or member of a tribunal usually requires the approval of the Lord Chancellor. The Lord Chancellor
has also important duties in connection with the solicitors' profession, for example, power to regulate the rates of remuneration.[3] He is the minister responsible
for the legal aid schemes; and it is through his department that central funds are
provided for neighbourhood law centres. The Lord Chancellor also has broad
responsibility for the Land Registry and the Public Trustee. The Public Record
Office was placed under his direction by the Public Records Act 1958; there is an
advisory committee on public records of which the Master of the Rolls is chairman.

The Lord Chancellor is also Speaker of the House of Lords and a member
of the Cabinet. He has no greater security of tenure than any other minister,
although the post is less vulnerable to Cabinet re-shuffles and Lord Chancellors tend to remain in post longer than other Cabinet ministers. The office is
a bridge between the judicial and the political worlds. Despite its judicial
responsibilities, the office must be classed as political. A previous political
career is not an essential qualification, but all modern Lord Chancellors have
had extensive and successful experience of practice at the English bar; some
before becoming Lord Chancellor have already held judicial appointments,
others have been law officers of the Crown. Despite the heavy departmental
duties of the Lord Chancellor, no junior ministers are appointed to his department, although the Attorney-General and the Solicitor-General may act for
him if required in the House of Commons. When in 1979 the present scheme
of select committees related to government departments was created by the
Commons, neither the Lord Chancellor's department nor the law officers'
departments were brought within it, although this would have been a valuable
means of informing M.P.s about the problems of administering the system of
justice.[4]

Responsibilities for law reform

As well as his responsibility for the judicial system, the Lord Chancellor has
a general responsibility for law reform in England and Wales. Many branches
of law are the responsibility of particular departments (thus housing and town
planning law is a matter for the Department of the Environment; company
law for the Department of Trade) and the Home Secretary has the primary
responsibility for reform of the criminal law. The Lord Chancellor is therefore
mainly concerned with those areas of civil law which are not looked after by
particular departments. The Law Commissions Act 1965 was essentially the
work of Lord Gardiner, then Lord Chancellor; this established the Law

---

[3] See *Bates* v. *Lord Hailsham* [1972] 3 All E.R. 1019.
[4] See ch. 11 D; H.C. 588–1 (1977–8), p. lv; and H.C. Deb., 25 Jun. 1979, cols. 118, 230.

Commission (for England) and the Scottish Law Commission to keep under review all the law with which each is concerned 'with a view to its systematic development and reform', including codification and generally the simplification and modernisation of the law.[5] Members of the Law Commission in England are appointed by the Lord Chancellor for terms not exceeding five years. They are qualified for appointment through holding judicial office (the chairman of the Commission is always a judge seconded from the High Court) or having professional or academic experience of the law. Programmes of work prepared by the Commission and approved by the Lord Chancellor are laid before Parliament; the Lord Chancellor may ask the Commission to report on particular topics. While the Law Commissions consult widely with the legal profession, government departments and other interested parties, they exercise an independent judgment in preparing recommendations for reform. The two Law Commissions must consult with each other and they may produce joint reports. Very many Law Commission reports have been directly followed by legislation, but pressure on parliamentary time and a lack of political interest may still be obstacles to reform.

The Lord Chancellor is also advised by three standing committees on law reform, the Law Reform Committee, the Statute Law Committee and the Committee on Private International Law.

Home Secretary

While the appointment of judges to administer the criminal law is a matter for the Lord Chancellor, the Home Secretary, as the minister responsible for law and order, has a general responsibility for the system of criminal justice, including the police and the administration of prisons and other penal institutions. In 1959 the Home Secretary set up the Criminal Law Revision Committee, consisting of a small number of judges, barristers, solicitors and academic lawyers, to examine such aspects of the criminal law as he might refer to them from time to time. In 1972, the committee, whose earlier work had led to the passing of the Theft Act 1968, produced a controversial report on the rules of evidence in criminal trials.[6] The Home Secretary has also some responsibility for the magistrates' courts. Thus the administrative arrangements for the metropolitan courts are under his control and the Home Office must confirm the appointments of justices' clerks which are made by local magistrates' courts committees. Magistrates' courts are not subject to control by the executive in the exercise of their judicial functions. The Home Office however seeks to foster uniformity by means of advisory circulars on such topics as the collection of fines, and sometimes the interpretation of new legislation. It is important in terms of constitutional principle that such circulars should be publicly available and not become a means for giving secret instructions to the magistrates. The training of lay magistrates is now compulsory, but this is supervised not by the Home Office but by the Lord Chancellor's department.[7]

---

[5]   Law Commissions Act 1965, s. 3. See also Cmnd 2573, 1965 and J. H. Farrar, *Law Reform and the Law Commission.*

[6]   Cmnd 4991, 1972. On the work of the Committee, see Glanville Williams (1975) 13 J.S.P.T.L. 183.

[7]   Justices of the Peace Act 1979, s. 63.

The law officers of the Crown[8]

The law officers of the Crown in respect of England and Wales are the Attorney-General and Solicitor-General. Their historic role is to represent the Crown in the courts. They now act as legal advisers to the government on important matters which cannot be left to the lawyers in the civil service who advise the departments on day-to-day matters. The English law officers are today invariably members of the House of Commons and of the English bar; as ministers they support the government of the day. Their duties require them to fill a wide variety of roles, which include leading for the Crown in major prosecutions (especially in trials involving state security) or in major civil actions to which the Crown is a party. They are assisted by junior counsel to the Treasury, who are practising barristers and hold no political office. Representing the Crown, the law officers take part in many judicial or quasi-judicial proceedings relating to the public interest, such as statutory tribunals of inquiry[9] and contempt of court proceedings.[10] The Attorney-General's consent is needed for relator actions: his decisions granting or refusing consent are not subject to review by the courts.[11] They also have parliamentary responsi-bilities, helping to see legal and fiscal Bills through the Commons and giving advice to the Committee on Privileges. The Attorney-General is responsible for the work of the Treasury Solicitor, and for the parliamentary counsel who draft most government Bills; but Bills that relate exclusively to Scotland or Northern Ireland are prepared by parliamentary draftsmen for Scotland and Northern Ireland respectively. The Attorney-General is leader of the English bar. He has sometimes been a member of the Cabinet but in view of his duties in connection with prosecutions, it is regarded as preferable that he should remain outside the Cabinet as the government's chief legal adviser, attending particular Cabinet meetings only when summoned. Many law officers receive further advancement to judicial or political posts, but it is clear that the Attorney-General has no claim to become Lord Chief Justice when a vacancy in that office occurs: the development of any such claim was effectively stifled by the disastrous and unsavoury elevation of Sir Gordon Hewart as Lord Chief Justice in 1922.[12] In 1974, the Labour law officers declined the knighthoods that have customarily gone with their jobs.[13]

Where a law officer has given advice to a minister on a matter upon which the minister has subsequently acted, the opinion is treated as confidential and not laid before Parliament or quoted from in debate; but if a minister considers it expedient to do so, he may make the advice known to Parliament and there is no absolute rule of confidentiality.[14]

The machinery of justice in Scotland

Except for his membership of the House of Lords and for his part in nomi-nating the two Lords of Appeal in Ordinary who by custom are appointed

---

8   J. Ll. J. Edwards, *The Law Officers of the Crown.*
9   Ch. 37 C.
10 Section B *ante.*
11 *Gouriet* v. *Union of Post Office Workers* [1978] A.C. 435; pp. 359, 662 *post.*
12 Edwards, *op. cit.* ch. 15.
13 *Cf.* Edwards, *op. cit.*, pp. 282–5.
14 Edwards, *op. cit.*, pp. 256–61.

from Scotland, the Lord Chancellor has no jurisdiction in Scotland. The Secretary of State for Scotland has a wide responsibility for Scotland's internal affairs. Under him, the Scottish Home and Health Department is responsible for the police and the penal system. The department also has many responsibilities for the legal system, including legal aid. In 1971, the Secretary of State was placed under a general duty to secure the efficient organisation of the sheriff courts, and was equipped with ample powers of issuing administrative directions, re-organising the sheriffdoms, providing court-houses and so on.[15] His duties are discharged through the Scottish Courts Administration. The Secretary of State appoints the justices of the peace who sit in the district courts. In respect of law reform the Secretary of State has general oversight of all branches of the law which are not the specific responsibility of other government departments or of the Lord Advocate.[16]

The law officers for Scotland are the Lord Advocate and the Solicitor-General for Scotland. They represent the Crown's interests before the Scottish courts and they advise the government on matters of Scots law. But their position is not identical with their English counterparts. It has not always been possible to fill these offices from the House of Commons[17] and the head of the Scottish bar is the elected Dean of the Faculty of Advocates, not the Lord Advocate. The two major differences in function are, first, that the Lord Advocate, assisted by the Solicitor-General, controls the system of public prosecutions throughout Scotland. Secondly, the Lord Advocate discharges machinery of justice and law reform functions which in England are performed by the Lord Chancellor. These now include the appointment of the Scottish Law Commission, and responsibility for the reform of branches of the law relating to evidence and civil procedure.[18] The Lord Advocate is responsible for the parliamentary draftsmen who draft Bills applying to Scotland.

Functions which in England are performed by the Lord Chancellor as head of the judiciary are in Scotland entrusted to the Lord President of the Court of Session: these include the making of rules of court procedure, which in Scotland is directly under the control of the judges, and the appointment and removal of tribunal personnel.

Control of prosecutions in England and Wales[19]

In principle, private persons may institute prosecutions in English law for any criminal offence unless by statute this has been excluded.[20] In practice the great majority of criminal prosecutions are instituted by the police; others are instituted by government departments (for example, revenue departments for evasion of tax) or local authorities (for example, for breach of bye-laws). Certain prosecutions may by statute be instituted only with the consent of the

---

15   Sheriff Courts (Scotland) Act 1971; *cf.* I. D. MacPhail, 1971 S.L.T. 80, 104.
16   H.C. Deb., 21 Dec. 1972, col. 456 (W.A.).
17   For the difficulties of the first Labour government, see J. P. Casey (1975) 26 N.I.L.Q. 18.
18   Note 16, *ante.*
19   See Report of Royal Commission on Criminal Procedure, Cmnd 8092, 1981, Part II and the description of the existing system in Cmnd 8092–I, ch. 5.
20   For the procedural rights of a private prosecutor, see *R.* v. *George Maxwell (Developments) Ltd* [1980].2 All E.R. 99.

Attorney-General, for example, for certain offences against the state, under the Official Secrets Acts or the Public Order Act 1936, and for obscenity in dramatic productions under the Theatres Act 1968.

Since most prosecutions are brought by the police, the decision to prosecute is essentially made by the local police forces, acting under the control of the chief constable. In 1879 the present office of Director of Public Prosecutions was created.[21] The Director, a barrister or solicitor, is appointed by the Home Secretary and works under the general supervision of the Attorney-General, who has made regulations for the conduct of his work. Although the title might suggest otherwise, the office is not that of a general prosecutor. He prosecutes only in certain types of case when the regulations require him to do so, for example, in all murder cases; when so directed by the Attorney-General; and when it appears to the Director himself that he ought to take over a particular case because of its importance or difficulty.[22] He is required to prosecute for election offences under the Representation of the People Act 1983. He may be consulted by chief officers of police on any matter of difficulty. The Director has power to take over a prosecution begun by someone else if he considers this desirable. He has no direct power to stop a prosecution, but occasionally he takes over a case and then offers no evidence, so that an acquittal automatically follows. The Attorney-General may however exercise the prerogative power to stop a prosecution on indictment by issuing a *nolle prosequi*. This power is rarely used today: abuse of the power would be subject to criticism in Parliament, but may not be reviewed by the courts.[23]

The decision whether to prosecute or not may involve difficult questions of law and proof. It may also involve questions of prosecuting policy. Prosecuting is not a judicial function but an executive function; it has been called a quasi-judicial function, although what that signifies is not very clear. But a prosecutor is well advised to consider how his case will stand up to the adversary process in court. Most difficult for the prosecutor may be to decide when the public interest requires that a case which would probably lead to a conviction should nonetheless not be prosecuted.[24] Under the English system, different police forces may follow different prosecuting policies, according to the view of the chief constable. In the case of prosecutions instituted by the Director of Public Prosecutions or the Attorney-General, what political control is there over the discretion that may have been exercised? Can the Prime Minister or the Cabinet control or influence the Attorney-General's decision? What is the Attorney-General's responsibility to Parliament for prosecution decisions?

These difficult questions were raised by the Campbell case in 1924, which brought down the first Labour government.[25] In brief, the Attorney-General, Sir Patrick Hastings, who was experienced in advocacy but not in ministerial work, authorised the prosecution of J. R. Campbell, acting editor of a

---

21   For a historical account, see Edwards, *op. cit.*, chs. 16 and 17.
22   Prosecution of Offences Act 1979; and Prosecution of Offences Regulations S.I. 1978 No. 1357 (as amended by S.I. 1978 No. 1846).
23   *R. v. Allen* (1862) 1 B. & S. 850.
24   See Cmnd 8092, pp. 128–9.
25   Edwards, *op. cit.*, chs. 10 and 11; F. H. Newark (1969) 20 N.I.L.Q. 19; Wilson, *Cases* p. 515, For the censure debate, see H.C. Deb., 8 Oct. 1924, col. 581.

Communist weekly, for having published an article which apparently sought to seduce members of the armed forces from their allegiance to the Crown. A few days later, the prosecution was withdrawn in circumstances which suggested that improper political pressure had been brought to bear on the Attorney-General. The true facts are not easy to establish, but the Cabinet minutes record a decision by the Cabinet on 6 August 1924 that '*no public prosecution of a political character should be undertaken without the prior sanction of the Cabinet being obtained*'; the Cabinet also agreed to adopt the course indicated by the Attorney-General *i.e.* to withdraw the Campbell prosecution.[26]

Whatever the faults of the different actors in the Campbell affair, and the precedents were less clear than the critics of the Labour government stated, there can be no doubt that the Cabinet decision in the words italicised was asserting a right to interfere in prosecuting decisions which was excessive and constitutionally improper, as well as being seriously vague.[27] The decision was promptly rescinded by the next Cabinet. The present doctrine is something like this: the Attorney-General is required to take his own prosecuting decisions, and must not receive directions from the Cabinet or any ministerial colleague; in his decisions he must not be influenced by considerations of party advantage or disadvantage; but if he considers that a particular case involves wider questions of public interest or state policy, he may seek information from ministerial colleagues and also their opinions.[28] It is not possible to know whether it is present-day practice for such information or opinions to be sought at meetings of the Cabinet, but this seems unlikely.

Since current practice emphasises that the Attorney-General must make his decisions personally, it follows that he bears personal responsibility to Parliament for these decisions; and that there is no collective responsibility for his decisions, except to the extent that the Prime Minister could be criticised for allowing an incompetent Attorney-General to remain in office. It is in order for questions to be asked in the Commons about particular decisions made by the Attorney-General: how much information the Attorney-General gives in reply is a matter for his own discretion.[29]

With oversight of the Director of Public Prosecutions, the Attorney-General is able to exercise extensive and often secret influence over criminal justice. Thus in 1975 the Attorney-General issued guidelines to the police about jury-vetting which became public knowledge by accident during an Official Secrets Act trial in 1978.[30] Divergent judicial views were expressed about the legality of jury-vetting,[31] and revised guidelines were published in 1980.[32] In *Gouriet*

---

26 Newark, *op. cit.*, p. 35.
27 What *is* a public prosecution of a political character? It might refer to (a) prosecution of a politician for an ordinary criminal offence, (b) prosecution of a politician for offences related to his political activities *e.g.* corruption or election offences, (c) prosecution of an individual for his political beliefs, (d) prosecution for criminal conduct committed in the course of a strike or political demonstration, (e) prosecution for offences against the security of the state, etc.
28 See the Shawcross statement in the debate on the gas strikers, H.C. Deb., 29 Jan. 1951, col. 681 (Wilson, *Cases*, p. 516); and H.C. Deb., 16 Feb. 1959, col. 31.
29 *Cf.* Edwards, *op. cit.*, p. 261.
30 H.C. Deb., 1 Aug. 1980, col. 1929; M. D. A. Freeman [1981] C.L.P. 65; H. Harman and J. A. G. Griffith, *Justice Deserted*.
31 *R.* v. *Sheffield Crown Court, ex p. Brownlow* [1980] Q.B. 530; *R.* v. *Mason* [1981] Q.B. 881.
32 Note [1980] 3 All E.R. 785.

v. *Union of Post Office Workers*, the House of Lords held that the courts could not review decisions of the Attorney-General taken in the enforcement of public rights.[33] While the case concerned relator proceedings, the many discretionary decisions taken by the Attorney-General affecting criminal justice are also immune from judicial review, although a positive decision to prosecute will be tested in court at the ensuing trial.[34] The House of Commons itself has no effective machinery for ensuring due accountability to the House for the Attorney-General's decisions, the assumption being that both he and the Director of Public Prosecutions should be free from extraneous political interference in their work. In 1983, the government decided to introduce a general, more centralised system for conducting prosecutions in England and Wales.[35] Such a reform is bound to mean an increase in the powers exercisable by the Attorney-General and the Director of Public Prosecutions.

Control of prosecutions in Scotland

In England the Attorney-General has hitherto been concerned only with a few exceptionally difficult or sensitive prosecutions and there is no system of public prosecution. In Scotland, the Lord Advocate is responsible for virtually all criminal proceedings, assisted by the Solicitor-General for Scotland and a number of Advocates-Depute, who are practising advocates retained to act for the Crown. The work is conducted through the Crown Office in Edinburgh and by procurators-fiscal who serve in every part of Scotland. The police make no prosecuting decisions, reporting every case to the procurator-fiscal, who may decide what to do himself or may refer a case to the Crown Office for the decision of an·Advocate-Depute or a law officer. Prosecution policies are laid down by the Lord Advocate and are binding on all procurators-fiscal. Some of these policies are publicly known: thus it was considered unnecessary for the Sexual Offences Act 1967, which in England legalised homosexual conduct between consenting adult males in private, to be extended to Scotland since it was already Crown Office policy not to prosecute in such cases.[36] While this is not an adequate way of reforming the law, the Scottish system seems preferable to the reliance in England upon local police discretion. In Scotland private prosecutions are virtually unknown, although in law a private citizen may prosecute if he has a personal and peculiar interest in the case and gets the permission of the High Court of Justiciary, which is rarely granted.[37] Such permission was given in the much-publicised Glasgow rape case in 1982, in which prosecution by the Crown was barred because of an earlier statement of behalf of the Lord Advocate that no further proceedings would be taken.[38] What has been said earlier about the personal responsibility of the Attorney-General and his freedom from political direction applies equally to the Lord Advocate, but is of even greater significance under the Scottish system than in England. In 1982, a judicial inquiry into events related to the Meehan case

---

[33] Note 11 *ante*.
[34] See for the difficulties arising at one Official Secrets Act trial, C. Aubrey, *Who's Watching You?*
[35] Cmnd 9074, 1983. And see App. B.
[36] The law on homosexuality in Scotland was changed in Criminal Justice (Scotland) Act 1980, s. 80.
[37] *J. & P. Coats Ltd* v. *Brown* 1009 S.C. (J.) 29; *McBain* v. *Crichton* 1961 J.C. 25.
[38] *H.* v. *Sweeney* 1983 S.L.T. 48. And see H.C. Deb., 21 Jan. 1982, col. 423.

held (*inter alia*) that mistakes had been made by the Crown Office, particularly in failing to co-ordinate the extensive investigations involved; but such an inquiry is a very rare event.[39]

The prerogative of pardon[40]

The royal prerogative of pardon is exercised by the Crown on the advice of the Home Secretary in cases from England and Wales and, in cases from Scotland, by the Secretary of State for Scotland. Each minister acts on his individual responsibility in giving his advice to the Crown. A royal pardon could in law be used as a bar to a criminal prosecution being brought (as was the effect of the blanket pardon given by President Ford to ex-President Nixon in 1974). But in British practice, a pardon is granted only after conviction when there is some special reason why a sentence should not be carried out or why the effects of a conviction should be expunged. Now that the right of an appeal in criminal cases is recognized, a pardon is not normally granted in respect of matters that could be raised on an appeal. Pardons under the prerogative are of three kinds: (a) an absolute or free pardon, which sets aside the sentence but not the conviction;[40a] (b) a conditional pardon, which substitutes one form of punishment for another (for example, the substitution of life imprisonment for the death penalty, which occurred when the prerogative of mercy was exercised in the days of capital punishment);[41] and (c) a remission, which reduces the amount of a sentence without changing its character, and has been used to enable a convicted spy to be exchanged for a British subject imprisoned abroad. The prerogative power of pardon may not be used to vary the judgment of the court in matters of civil dispute between citizens. Under the Act of Settlement 1700, a pardon may not be pleaded in bar of an impeachment by the Commons, nor under the Habeas Corpus Act 1679 may the unlawful committal of any person to prison outside the realm be pardoned.

Extensive use of the power of pardon could come close to being an attempt to exercise the royal power to dispense with laws which was declared illegal in the Bill of Rights 1689. The Home Secretary is answerable to Parliament for the advice which he gives to Parliament. Before the abolition of the death penalty, questions could not be raised in the House of Commons regarding a case while it was still pending.[42]

By section 17 of the Criminal Appeal Act 1968, the Home Secretary may, at any time after a conviction on indictment, (a) refer the whole of a case to the Court of Appeal, and the case will then be treated as if the convicted person had appealed or (b) if he desires the assistance of the court on any point arising in the case, refer that point alone for the court's opinion.[43]

The Treasury Solicitor

The Treasury Solicitor is the head of the government legal service. His depart-

---

[39] H.C. 444 (1981–2) pp. 1257–63.
[40] See A. T. H. Smith [1983] P.L. 398; also the report 'Miscarriages of Justice' H.C. 421 (1981–2) and, for the position in Scots law, C. H. W. Gane 1980 J.R. 18.
[40a] *R.* v. *Foster* [1984] 1 All E. R. 679.
[41] P. Brett (1957) 20 M.L.R. 131.
[42] G. Marshall [1961] P.L. 8.
[43] Smith, *op. cit.*, pp. 405–8; *cf.* Criminal Procedure (Scotland) Act 1975, s. 263.

ment carries out legal work for the Treasury and for all government departments which do not have their own solicitors or, as in the case of the Foreign Office, their own legal advisers. The department undertakes conveyancing work for the government; it also undertakes most of the litigation to which the Crown or a department is a party in the superior courts. The Solicitor to the Secretary of State for Scotland serves a similar function in relation to the Scottish departments.

Chapter 20

The police

The preservation of law and order and the prevention and detection of crime are matters of great importance to the maintenance of organised government. The police constable is an officer with powers long known to the common law and some of the powers of the modern police officer still derive from the old common law. But the professional police forces we know today date only from the 19th century.[1] How they exercise their powers and how they are controlled are matters which directly affect the quality of life and liberty in the community. While the executive has a strong interest in maintaining an effective police system, the central government does not itself undertake the policing of the country. In 1962, a royal commission which inquired into the constitutional position of the police in Great Britain examined the arguments for and against establishing a national police force. The commission rejected the view that a national force would lead to a totalitarian 'police state', considering that a national force in Britain would be subject to the law and to the authority of Parliament. But, except for a notable and incisive dissenting opinion from Dr A. L. Goodhart, the commission concluded that the police should not be brought under the direct central control of the government and that the police should continue to be linked with local government; provided that the responsibilities of central government and the controls from the centre were made more explicit, a system of local police forces should be continued.[2] The commission's report led to the Police Act 1964 which, as amended subsequently, now contains the main legal framework of the police system in England and Wales. Similar but not identical statutory provisions are contained in the Police (Scotland) Act 1967.[3] These Acts provide a structure of the police which is 'sui generis': while police forces have connections with local government, the police system is not a typical local government service; nor is it in form a central government service, although its operation is supervised by central government. This legislation does not contain the powers, for

---

[1] See T. A. Critchley, *A History of the Police in England and Wales*.

[2] Cmnd 1728, 1962, ch. 5; *cf.* memorandum of dissent by A. L. Goodhart. And see G. Marshall, *Police and Government*, and J. Hart [1963] P.L. 283.

[3] For the former position in Scotland, see J. D. B. Mitchell, 1962 J.R. 1.

example of arrest and search, which the police use in dealing with crime and maintaining public order: these powers will be considered in later chapters.

Local police authorities

In 1962, there were 125 separate police forces in England and Wales, including the Metropolitan Police and the City of London Police, and 33 in Scotland. Since 1975, due partly to the reform of local government and partly to a policy of amalgamating forces, there have been 41 forces in England and Wales and 8 in Scotland. There is still no national police force although the Criminal Investigation Department of the Metropolitan Police aids local forces in many problems of detection; and there are many forms of co-operation and common services, including a central Criminal Record Office, police colleges in England and Scotland, the police national computer and regional crime squads.

The Metropolitan Police was created in 1829 as the first modern British force: it is the only police force for which the Home Secretary is directly responsible as the police authority. It is subject to the Metropolitan Police Acts which have been passed since 1829 and to some provisions of the Police Act 1964. The chief officer is the Commissioner of Police for the Metropolis who is appointed by the Crown on the advice of the Home Secretary, together with Assistant Commissioners. The Commissioner appoints constables and has powers of suspension and dismissal; he has power to make orders for the general government of the force, subject to the Home Secretary's approval. The City of London Police are a separate force; the chief officer, the Commissioner, is appointed by the police authority, the Court of Common Council, subject to the approval of the Home Secretary.

Elsewhere in England and Wales, a police force is maintained by every county council as defined by the Local Government Act 1972,[4] except where a combined area has been constituted by an amalgamation of forces. The police authority for a county force is a committee of the county council known as the police committee. Two-thirds of the committee are county councillors appointed by the council; one-third are magistrates appointed by the magistrates' courts committee. Where two or more county areas have been combined, a combined police authority is appointed, two-thirds of its members being members of the constituent county councils and one-third being magistrates. It may be argued that, in view of their judicial duties, magistrates should not be members of a police authority; probably magistrates are still included on police committees as a safeguard against certain forms of political bias.

Under the Police Act 1964, it is the duty of a police authority to secure the maintenance of an adequate and efficient police force for the area; subject to the approval of the Home Secretary, it appoints the chief constable and deputy or assistant chief constables, and provides the requisite premises and equipment (section 4). But a police force is under the direction and control of the chief constable or in his absence, a deputy (sections 5(1), 6(1)); it is not for operational purposes under the control of the police authority. The police authority has power to require the chief constable, and any deputy or assistant

---

[4] Ch. 21.

chief constable to retire in the interests of efficiency (sections 5(4), 6(5)). In this the police authority must act with the approval of the Home Secretary, who may himself take the initiative in requiring the police authority to retire the chief constable (section 29(1)). The chief constable must be given an opportunity to make representations to the police authority or the Home Secretary before he can be required to retire (sections 5(5), 29(2)). The police authority may exercise disciplinary powers over the chief constable, including dismissal, subject to an appeal to the Home Secretary (section 33(3)).[5] The police authority is the paymaster for local police expenditure, though salaries are fixed according to national scales.

The police authority is thus made responsible for ensuring an efficient force and it exercises a measure of supervision over the chief constable. But its powers are in reality very limited, since general standards of policing are laid down by the Home Secretary, and the chief constable has operational control of the force. The police authority have no power to give instructions to the chief constable regarding the use of the police, but the authority may serve as a means of communication between the public and the police. At county council meetings, members of a police authority can be questioned by county councillors about the discharge of the authority's functions (section 11).[6] A police authority receives the annual report of the chief constable and, subject to a power in the chief constable with the support of the Home Secretary to withhold information which in the public interest ought not to be disclosed, the authority may request the chief constable to make a report on specific matters connected with the policing of the area (section 12). The police authority must also keep itself informed about the manner in which complaints about the police from the public are dealt with by the chief constable (section 50), a vague provision which may not in practice achieve very much.[7]

In Scotland, under the Local Government (Scotland) Act 1973, the police authorities are the regional councils, except where joint authorities are created by the amalgamation of forces. Magistrates are not required to be appointed to membership of police committees. The powers of the authority in relation to the chief constable are broadly the same as in England, except that the police authority does not have the general duty to secure the maintenance of an adequate and efficient police force and its functions are in law even more closely controlled by central government, in the person of the Secretary of State for Scotland, than are those of an English authority.[8]

Chief constables

Before the Police Act 1964, there was much uncertainty about the legal position of the chief constable, which for historical reasons differed between county and borough forces.[9] The importance of his position is that the hierarchy of command within a police force runs from the police constable on the beat to

5   *Cf. Ridge* v. *Baldwin* [1964] A.C. 40, p. 648 *post*, which concerned the dismissal of a chief constable under the pre-1964 legislation.
6   But see *R.* v. *Lancashire Police Authority, ex p. Hook* [1980] Q.B. 603, p. 386 *post*.
7   For the Home Office view in 1968, see H.C. 350 (1967–8) p. 58. The section has been replaced by the Police and Criminal Evidence Act 1984, s. 95.
8   Police (Scotland) Act 1967, s. 2. And see P. Gordon, *Policing Scotland*.
9   Cmnd 1728, pp. 25–8; Marshall, *op. cit.*, chs. 4 and 5.

the chief constable, and no further. The royal commission in 1962 went so far as to say, 'The problem of controlling the police can . . . be re-stated as the problem of controlling chief constables'.[10] The Police Act 1964 places each police force under the chief constable's direction and control. Subject to the powers of the police authority already mentioned (for example, in regard to finance), all appointments and promotions to ranks below that of assistant chief constable are made by the chief constable. He is also the disciplinary authority for these ranks and, subject to an appeal to the Home Secretary (not, it should be noted, to the police authority), he may impose disciplinary penalties, including dismissal or suspension. The chief constable also appoints police cadets and special constables and decides what special police services (for example, to a football club for policing the terraces) are to be provided in return for payments to the police authority.[11] Certain duties are imposed on the chief constable by the 1964 Act, for example, to report annually to the Home Secretary and the police authority, to make special reports when requested by either, and to submit criminal statistics as required by the Home Secretary (sections 12, 30, 54). He may be required to enter into collaboration agreements with other police forces or to provide extra constables or other assistance in aid of another force (sections 13, 14). He also has important duties in regard to complaints against the police.[12] A chief constable must himself observe police discipline and may be dismissed for misconduct or required to resign in the interests of efficiency; but it seems that neither the police authority nor the Home Office may direct him as to the use of his police force. In England and Wales, his extensive autonomy is especially important because, subject to the position of the Director of Public Prosecutions, most prosecuting decisions are made by the police.[13]

In Scotland, the authority of the chief constable over members of his police force is made even more explicit than in English law: 'The performance by a constable of his functions under this or any other enactment or under any rule of law shall be subject to the direction of the appropriate chief constable'.[14] This leaves no doubt that the chain of command within a police force may control the use by a constable of both his statutory and his common law powers. The major difference from the position in England is that in relation to the investigation of offences, the chief constable must comply with all lawful instructions which he may receive from the public prosecutor and also with instructions from the Lord Advocate regarding the reporting of alleged offences for prosecution.[15] The chief constable must also observe all lawful instructions which he may receive from the sheriff principal, who is the senior judge in a sheriffdom, but such instructions are rare today.

Functions of the Home Secretary
Within the Metropolitan area, the Home Secretary is himself the police

10 Cmnd 1728, p. 34.
11 1964 Act, s. 15; *cf. Glasbrook Brothers Ltd* v. *Glamorgan CC* [1925] A.C. 270.
12 Page 371 *post*.
13 Ch. 19C.
14 Police (Scotland) Act 1967, s. 17(2).
15 Police (Scotland) Act 1967, s. 17(3); Criminal Procedure (Scotland) Act 1975, s. 9.

authority. While some of his powers in this capacity derive from the Police Act 1964, he has a long-standing and close relationship with the Metropolitan Police Commissioner which is not governed solely by that Act. In the past, Home Secretaries accepted a wide responsibility for the general policies followed by the Metropolitan Police, while not directing the detailed operations of the force.[16] More recently, the official Home Office view, which convinced the Parliamentary Commissioner for Administration in 1967, is that the Home Secretary as police authority has no power to give instructions to members of the Metropolitan Police as to the manner in which they should carry out their duties as constables.[17] In 1968, Salmon L. J. said: 'Constitutionally it is clearly impermissible for the Home Secretary to issue any order to the police in respect of law enforcement',[18] but this forthright view is not in full accord with the history of the Metropolitan Police.

Apart from the special position of the Metropolitan Police, the Home Secretary has very many statutory powers affecting the police. He must approve the appointment of a chief constable and has the ultimate power to dismiss him or to require his resignation. He may require a chief constable to submit a report on any specific matter connected with the policing of his area and in cases of dispute must decide how much information the chief constable should give to the police authority (sections 30(1), 12(3)). The Home Secretary may set up a local inquiry into any matter connected with the policing of an area (section 32).[19] By section 33, the Home Secretary may make regulations for the government, administration and conditions of service of the police forces, in particular with respect to ranks, qualifications for appointment and promotion, probationary service, voluntary retirement, discipline, duties, pay, allowances, clothing and equipment. Many of these regulations can be brought into force only after a draft has been submitted to the Police Advisory Board for England and Wales; the Home Secretary must take into consideration any representations made by that board (section 46). There is a similar board for Scotland. The advisory boards are constituted in such form as the Secretary of State may determine after consulting bodies representing police authorities and police officers. Those regulations which relate to pay, hours of duty, leave and pensions must be shown in draft to the Police Negotiating Board for the United Kingdom, a body which represents police authorities and the members of police forces.[20]

Under the Aviation Security Act 1982, the Secretary of State has power by statutory instrument to order the policing of a designated civil airport to be taken over by a local police force if he considers this necessary in the interests of preserving peace and preventing crime.

As well as these wide legislative powers, the Home Secretary has always exercised considerable financial control. Since 1856, a grant has been made from the Exchequer towards the police expenses of local authorities. Payment

---

[16] Critchley, *op. cit.*, p. 268; Marshall, *op. cit.*, pp. 29–32.
[17] H.C. 6 (1967–8), p. 25; H.C. 350 (1967–8) pp. xiii, 56–68.
[18] *R.* v. *Metropolitan Police Commissioner, ex p. Blackburn* [1968] 2 Q.B. 118, 138; p. 370 *post.*
[19] See *e.g.* the reports by Lord Scarman into the Red Lion Square disorders, Cmnd 5919, 1975, and into the Brixton disorders, Cmnd 8427, 1981.
[20] Police Negotiating Board Act 1980.

of the grant, which is now one-half of all approved expenses, is by statute conditional on the Home Secretary's certificate that a police force is efficient, co-operates adequately with other police forces, and is properly equipped and administered. No police authority could afford to forgo its certificate of efficiency. Both the Metropolitan and City of London Police receive similar grants, the balance of expenditure in the case of the former being contributed by the councils who are within the Metropolitan police district. Her Majesty's Inspectors of Constabulary have proved powerful instruments in maintaining the efficiency of police forces: they are appointed by and report to the Home Secretary (section 38).

The royal commission in 1962 recommended that the Home Secretary should have a general statutory duty to ensure the efficiency of the police in England and Wales. This recommendation was not adopted. Instead, section 28 of the 1964 Act states that the Home Secretary 'shall exercise his powers under this Act in such manner and to such extent as appears to him to be best calculated to promote the efficiency of the police'. The effect of these words needs to be considered with care. First, they do not provide the Home Secretary with a residual source of powers. Second, it may be commented that the concept of police efficiency is not always a simple one: is a police force efficient if it exercises its powers rigorously but at the cost of local goodwill? Or if its chief constable disagrees with advice which he has received from the Home Office? Or if it mishandles a major public demonstration?[21] Section 28 leaves it to the Home Secretary to decide by what criteria police efficiency is to be assessed. The subjective wording of the section would make it very difficult for a chief constable who had been retired in the interests of efficiency to seek judicial review of the Home Secretary's decision. Thus, far from imposing a legally enforceable duty on the Home Secretary, section 28 serves to protect his decisions against challenge in the courts.[22]

In addition to the Home Secretary's statutory powers, the Home Office and the Inspectors of Constabulary exercise much informal influence over local policing, for example, by convening conferences of chief constables and by issuing advisory circulars to police forces.

In Scotland the powers of the Secretary of State are no less extensive than those of the Home Secretary. There is no equivalent in the Police (Scotland) Act 1967 to section 28 of the 1964 Act but this seems to make no difference in practice.

Legal status of a police officer

The courts have not always found it easy to define the precise status of a police officer. There is no doubt at common law that a constable is personally liable to be sued for damages in respect of wrongful or unlawful acts which he commits while a constable. 'The powers of a constable *qua* peace officer, whether conferred by common or statute law, are exercised by him by virtue of his office, and cannot be exercised on the responsibility of any person but

---

21 *Cf.* Marshall, *op. cit.*, pp. 51, 85.
22 *Cf.* page 673 *post*.

himself'.[23] Indeed in the past it was found necessary to protect constables by statute against certain risks of liability, as was done in the Constables' Protection Act 1750. The individual liability of the constable continues today and it is no defence to an action for trespass or false imprisonment that the constable had been ordered by a superior officer to act.

As modern police forces grew in professionalism, organisation and resources, citizens who suffered from improper police action sought to make the local police authority vicariously liable for the wrongful acts of the constables. These attempts were unsuccessful. In *Fisher* v. *Oldham Corporation*, a borough council which maintained a police force was held not to be the employer of a constable sued for wrongful arrest, though the council's watch committee was at that time responsible for appointing, paying and dismissing the constables.[24] The court explained that in making an arrest, a police officer was 'a servant of the State, a ministerial officer of the central power'; and that in the absence of power to control his acts, the local authority could not be held vicariously liable for them. It is true that when he is first appointed a police officer swears to serve the Sovereign as a constable. And in *Lewis* v. *Cattle*, which concerned the unauthorised publication of confidential police information, a police officer was held to be 'a person holding office under Her Majesty' for the purpose of the Official Secrets Acts.[25] But in relation to vicarious liability, at common law a constable was not in the employment of the Crown since he was neither appointed nor paid by the Crown, and this was not affected by the Crown Proceedings Act 1947. In the absence of legal liability, police authorities might decide to stand behind individual constables and to pay any damages and costs awarded against them. But this remained a matter for their discretion until Parliament changed the law.

By section 48 of the Police Act 1964, liability for the wrongful acts of constables is placed upon the chief constable in respect of torts committed in the performance of their functions by constables under his direction and control, in the same way as a master is liable for torts committed by his servants in the course of their employment. Any damages and costs awarded against the chief constable for vicarious liability are paid out of the local police fund, as is any sum required to settle a claim against the chief constable where the police authority approves the settlement. The police authority has also a statutory discretion to pay damages or costs awarded against a constable, whether or not the chief constable has been sued.[26]

Notwithstanding this change in the law, there are still legal contexts in which it is important that the police constable holds a public office and is not employed under a contract of employment. The constable's tenure of office is essentially statutory and can be terminated only in accordance with the regulations.[27] Indeed, legislation restricts the freedom of a police officer in a

---

23 *Enever* v. *R.* (1906) 3 C.L.R. 969, 977.
24 [1930] 2 K.B. 364. For Scotland see *e.g. Muir* v. *Hamilton Magistrates* 1910 1 S.L.T. 164. On a related legal issue, see *Metropolitan Police Receiver* v. *Croydon Corporation* [1957] 2 Q.B. 154.
25 [1938] 2 K.B. 454, criticised by Sir Ivor Jennings in (1938) 2 M.L.R. 73.
26 Similar liability in reparation has been imposed in Scotland: Police (Scotland) Act 1967, s. 39, on which see H.C. Deb., 22 May 1973, col. 429.
27 *E.g. Ridge* v. *Baldwin* [1964] A.C. 40; *Chief Constable of North Wales* v. *Evans* [1982] 3 All E.R. 141.

way in which no employer could by a contract of employment. Thus police officers are not allowed to be members of a trade union or of any association which seeks to control or influence the pay or conditions of service of any police force; instead, there are Police Federations for England and Wales and for Scotland which represent police officers in all matters of welfare and efficiency, other than questions of discipline and promotion affecting individuals.[28] Police regulations impose a great many restrictions upon the private life of serving police officers, including one of constitutional importance, namely that a police officer 'shall at all times abstain from any activity which is likely to interfere with the impartial discharge of his duties or which is likely to give rise to the impression amongst members of the public that it may so interfere; and in particular (he) shall not take any active part in politics'.[29]

Parliamentary control of the police

The constitutional structure within which the police operate in Great Britain provides few overt opportunities for political control of police decisions either at a local or a national level. Whether in the field of maintaining public order or in the work of detecting and prosecuting crime, police decisions constantly involve the exercise of discretion, choice between alternative courses of action and the setting of priorities for the use of limited resources. In a stable society it is easier for the police to seek to play an impartial and a non-political role but even this role has latent political significance. In less stable conditions, issues of law and order acquire a more immediate political content. It is both inevitable and desirable that there should be parliamentary interest in the work of the police. One problem which has often faced M.P.s wishing to raise police subjects in Parliament has been that there is no direct ministerial responsibility either for the acts of the police or for the decisions of police authorities. The position of London has always been exceptional since it has long been recognised in the Commons that the Home Secretary accepts what has been described as an extremely wide and detailed responsibility for the Metropolitan Police.[30] The royal commission in 1962 proposed additional powers for the central government which, the commission considered, would make the Secretaries of State accountable to Parliament for the efficient policing of the whole country. The Police Act 1964 did not go as far in this direction as the royal commission recommended, but the extent of ministerial responsibility for police outside London was undoubtedly widened by the Act. Thus M.P.s who wish to raise a matter of local policing may now ask the appropriate Secretary of State whether he is proposing to call for a report on the matter from the chief constable, institute an inquiry into the matter, to require the chief constable to resign in the interests of efficiency, and so on. But the fact that such a question may be asked does not mean that as full an answer will be given as the M.P. would like. The Home Secretary will not give to Parliament details of police work which he considers should not be publicly disclosed. Nor does the jurisdiction of the Parliamentary Commissioner for

---

[28] Police Act 1964, ss. 44, 47.

[29] Police Regulations 1979, S.I. 1470, sch. 2; Police (Scotland) Regulations 1976, S.I. 1073, sch. I.

[30] Marshall, *op. cit.*, p. 30.

Administration include power to investigate complaints against the police.[31] On specific matters of great political concern, however, the Secretary of State may be willing to order an inquiry to be held[32] or to lay before Parliament the report received from a chief officer of police.[33] More general police subjects are suitable for examination by the Home Affairs Committee of the House of Commons.[34]

Judicial control of police policies

Relying on the time-worn but inaccurate sentiment that a policeman possesses few powers not enjoyed by the ordinary citizen, and is only 'a person paid to perform, as a matter of duty, acts which if he were so minded he might have done voluntarily', the royal commission in 1962 came to an astonishing conclusion: 'The relation of the police to the courts is not . . . of any greater constitutional significance than the relation of any other citizen to the courts'.[35] The corrective was supplied in *R. v. Metropolitan Police Commissioner, ex p. Blackburn*.[36]

Under the Betting, Gaming and Lotteries Act 1963, certain forms of gaming were unlawful, and gaming clubs in London sought to avoid the Act. After legal difficulties in enforcing the Act had arisen, the Police Commissioner issued a secret circular to senior officers giving effect to a policy decision that no proceedings were to be taken against a gaming club for breach of the law, unless there were complaints of cheating or it had become the haunt of criminals. Blackburn sought a mandamus against the commissioner which in effect ordered him to reverse that policy decision. The circular was withdrawn before the case was concluded, but the Court of Appeal held that every chief constable owed a duty to the public to enforce the law. That duty could if necessary be enforced by the court. Although chief officers had a wide discretion with which the court would not interfere, the court would control a policy decision which amounted to a failure of duty to enforce the law. The court left open whether Blackburn had a sufficient interest in the matter to ask for mandamus. In a later case brought by Blackburn to enforce the obscenity laws, the court held on the merits that the Police Commissioner was doing what he could to enforce the existing laws with the available manpower and no more could reasonably be expected.[37]

Obvious difficulties are presented by the proposal that a court should direct a chief constable in the performance of his duties at the instance of a member of the public. It is one thing for a court to strike down instructions by a chief constable which are plainly illegal; it is another for the court to impose its own views on the priorities for the use of police manpower. Given that the courts must allow the police discretion in carrying out their work, a capable chief constable with some appreciation of the law should have little difficulty in keeping within the permissible bounds. Rather than relying to the extent that

---

[31] Note 17 *ante.*
[32] Note 19 *ante.*
[33] *E.g.* H.C. 351 (1974), report from Metropolitan Police Commissioner on the Lennon case.
[34] *E.g.* Race relations and the 'sus' law, H.C. 559 (1979–80); Deaths in police custody, H.C. 631 (1979–80); Police complaints procedures, H.C. 98 (1981–2).
[35] Cmnd 1728, p. 34.
[36] [1968] 2 Q.B. 118.
[37] *R. v. Metropolitan Police Commissioner, ex p. Blackburn (No. 3)* [1973] Q.B. 241. See also *R. v. Chief Constable of Devon and Cornwall, ex p. CEGB* [1982] Q.B. 458.

we have come to do upon the autonomy and professional judgment of the chief officer to solve difficult questions of social policy for us, and then looking to the courts to control their decisions, it might be better to re-assess the proper scope for political direction and parliamentary discussion of police policies.

Complaints against the police

The handling of complaints against the police has for many years been viewed as an important factor in maintaining good relations between the police and the public, but it has been difficult to establish the right machinery. Since 1964 there have been three different systems.

Under the Police Act 1964, the handling of complaints was left almost entirely to the senior officers in individual forces subject only to some scrutiny of complaints by the Director of Public Prosecutions. The Director could decide whether or not criminal proceedings should be taken against the officer concerned and he provided the only measure of independent supervision. Critics of the 1964 Act argued that public confidence in the police required the substantial strengthening of independent review.

This concern led to the second phase, with the creation by the Police Act 1976 of the Police Complaints Board. This provided an independent review of the outcome of all investigations of complaints in England and Wales, but it did little to stem the tide of concern about the system as a whole. In particular, it did not resolve the central problem of public confidence, because it did not end the investigation of complaints against the police by the police. Moreover, the board adopted a view of its functions which prevented its intervention in cases in which criminal proceedings had been considered.[38] The board's first triennial report in 1980 proposed the investigation of serious complaints not by serving police officers but by a separate body of investigating officers seconded from their forces and responsible to an independent layman.[39] This theme was developed in Lord Scarman's report on the Brixton disorders in 1981.[40] One of his principal findings was of widespread public dissatisfaction with complaints procedures. For minor complaints they were too formal and too cumbersome and tended to widen the rift between police and community. Their impartiality and fairness were also in doubt. Lord Scarman first recommended the creation of an informal conciliation procedure. Secondly, accepting that completely independent investigation of all formal complaints might be impractical, he recommended that all serious complaints be investigated by officers of another force under the active supervision of the chairman of the complaints board or his representative.

In 1981–2 the Home Affairs Committee of the House of Commons confirmed the need both for reconciliation procedures and for the independent supervision of investigations of serious complaints.[41] Reforms on these lines were proposed in a White Paper in 1982.[42] The Police and Criminal Evidence Act 1984 establishes a three-tier system for the investigation of complaints

---

[38] See *R. v. Police Complaints Board, ex p. Madden* [1983] 2 All E.R. 353.
[39] Cmnd 7966, 1980. See also Cmnd 8193, 1981.
[40] Cmnd 8427, 1981.
[41] H.C. 98 (1981–2).
[42] Cmnd 8681, 1982. See also Cmnd 8853, 1983.

against the police. The principal structural change is the abolition of the Police Complaints Board and its replacement by a Police Complaints Authority whose chairman is appointed by the Crown with at least eight further members including two deputy chairmen appointed by the Secretary of State.[43]

Under the 1984 Act, complaints made by or on behalf of a member of the public against a police officer are submitted to the chief officer of the force concerned. It is his first duty to take steps to obtain or preserve relevant evidence. The procedure thereafter depends on whether or not the complaint concerns a senior officer (that is, above the rank of chief superintendent). The main difference is that investigation of complaints about senior officers is the duty of the police authority, while other complaints are handled by the chief officer. What follows outlines the procedure to be adopted by a chief officer. Having established that he rather than the police authority is responsible, he records the complaint. Thereafter three levels of complaint are distinguished and treated differently.

(a) At the lowest level is a new category of complaint suitable for informal resolution: it is the chief officer's duty to decide, with the help of an inquiry by a chief inspector if necessary, whether a complaint falls into this category. The complaint cannot be dealt with informally unless the complainant consents and the chief officer is satisfied that the conduct complained of, even if proved, would not justify a criminal or disciplinary charge.[44] The actual arrangements for informal resolution may vary but will include discussion with the complainant and, in some cases, a meeting between the complainant and the accused officer.[45]

(b) If a complaint is not suitable for informal resolution, the chief officer must arrange for it to be investigated either by an officer (of at least chief inspector rank) from his own force or from another area. When he receives the report of the investigation, the chief officer must send a copy to the Director of Public Prosecutions in all cases where there is an indication that a criminal offence may have been committed and the officer ought to be charged with it. The Director then decides whether criminal proceedings should be taken against the officer concerned.[46] If there is a criminal prosecution, whether it ends in conviction or acquittal, there can be no disciplinary charge for an offence which is in substance the same.[47] Different considerations apply where the Director decides against prosecution, in which case disciplinary proceedings may be brought, although the Home Office advises that special care be taken in cases where the Director's decision is based on the insufficiency of evidence. Disciplinary proceedings are conducted by the chief constable and must allow a fair hearing. If an officer is found guilty of an offence, penalties range from dismissal to a caution. The more serious penalties of dismissal, requirement to resign or reduction in rank may not however be awarded unless the officer has been given the prior opportunity of electing to be legally represented at the

---

[43]   1984 Act, s. 83 and sch. 4.
[44]   1984 Act, s. 85.
[45]   On this and the new system in general, see Cmnd 9072, 1983 and regulations to be made under the 1984 Act, s. 99.
[46]   1984 Act, s. 90.
[47]   1984 Act, s. 104.

hearing.[48] There is a right of appeal to the Home Secretary who must refer most appeals for consideration by a three-person inquiry. An officer may be legally represented at this stage.[49]

This procedure for handling of complaints is subject to some supervision by the Police Complaints Authority. Reports on investigations must be sent by chief officers to the Authority, which may require a report to be referred to the Director of Public Prosecutions. It may also recommend, and in the last resort direct, that disciplinary charges be brought. In exceptional circumstances, the Authority may require that a charge shall be heard not by the chief constable alone but by a disciplinary tribunal consisting of the chief constable and two members of the Authority.[50] In the exercise of their powers, both chief officers and the Complaints Authority must have regard to guidance given to them by the Home Secretary.[51]

(c) The Authority's role is much stronger in relation to the third category of complaint. If a complainant alleges that the conduct of a police officer has been the cause of a death or serious injury, the complaint must be referred to the Authority before investigation begins. In addition, the Authority may call in any other complaint. A chief officer may refer to the Authority other complaints, and other matters which are not the subject of a complaint but which indicate a criminal or disciplinary offence and, by reason of their gravity or exceptional circumstances, ought to be so referred. In all these cases the Authority does not merely monitor the outcome of an investigation but supervises the investigation itself. The Authority has to approve the appointment of the investigating officer and it may, thereafter, give instructions on the conduct of the investigation. Once the investigation is complete, however, the outcome is processed as in other cases.[52]

In Scotland, there has not been the same pressure for independent supervision of the handling of complaints and there is no equivalent of the Police Complaints Authority. On the other hand an independent element does exist in the procurator-fiscal, who must be notified of all complaints from which it might be inferred that a constable has committed an offence.[53] A citizen may, moreover, complain to him directly.

Police accountability – the continuing debate

The police complaints machinery has in recent years been under almost perpetual review, but this is only one indication that the central issue of the accountability of the police has not been satisfactorily resolved. Despite changing circumstances, the arguments in the royal commission report of 1962 are still relied upon, and few would deny that police organisation and accountability should be treated as a special case. There is no apparent increase in enthusiasm for a 'national' force directly responsible to a minister. On the

---

[48] 1984 Act, s. 102. For the previous exclusion of legal representation, see *Maynard* v. *Osmond* [1977] Q.B. 240.
[49] 1984 Act, s. 103.
[50] 1984 Act, ss. 90–4.
[51] 1984 Act, s. 105.
[52] 1984 Act, ss. 87–9.
[53] Police (Discipline) (Scotland) Regulations 1967, S.I. 1021.

other hand, the lack of public confidence in the police which has affected complaints procedures has cast doubt on their accountability, particularly at the local level. Problems about police reaction to racial violence, the increased use of computers, the use of firearms, and a more flamboyant and idiosyncratic approach adopted by some chief constables have contributed to the concern.[54]

One response has been a move to make chief officers directly responsible to their police authorities, but this has not attracted government support.[55] A less radical approach draws heavily upon the recommendations of Lord Scarman in the report of his inquiry under section 32 of the Police Act 1964 into the Brixton disorders.[56] The breakdown of order in the social, and particularly racial, conditions of Brixton led Lord Scarman to substantial criticisms of the police and their relations with the community. He recommended that, without the sacrifice of independence, police accountability should be improved. He argued that police authorities should take more seriously their existing powers under the Police Act 1964 to require reports from the chief constable and to ensure that close co-operation between authority and chief officer is maintained. In addition, procedures for systematic liaison between committees representative of local communities and the police at divisional level should be introduced. Lord Scarman considered this to be particularly important in London where there was no local police authority, a point argued with force by the Greater London Council. To ensure the adoption of the liaison committee principle, legislation would be necessary.[57]

The Police and Criminal Evidence Act 1984 makes provision for a modest measure of consultation and liaison.[58] It requires police authorities (in London the Metropolitan Commissioner under the guidance of the Home Secretary) to make arrangements for obtaining the views of people in their area about the policing of it and for obtaining their co-operation in crime prevention. The authority must consult with its chief constable as to the appropriate arrangements.

---

[54]   On police accountability generally see *e.g.* R. Baldwin and R. Kinsey, *Police Powers and Politics*; G. Marshall, in (ed. D. Butler and A. H. Halsey) *Policy and Politics*, ch. 5; D. E. Regan, (1983) 61 *Public Administration* 97. For contributions by chief police officers, see J. C. Alderson, *Policing Freedom*; Sir Robert Mark, *In the Office of Constable*.

[55]   *E.g.* the unsuccessful Police Authorities (Powers) Bill (1979–80).

[56]   Cmnd 8427, 1981.

[57]   Scarman Report, paras. 5.55–5.71.

[58]   1984 Act, s. 106.

Chapter 21
Local government

The responsibility of the central government for the economic and social well-being of the country as a whole does not mean that central government itself must provide all the public services and exercise all the regulatory powers which may be needed. Nor does the fact that the major political responsibility for government depends on the outcome of national elections mean that there is no place for the exercise of political power at a lower level. The organs of local government serve two broad purposes: (a) they enable many public services to be provided at a level nearer the people whom the services benefit, and (b) they enable local political opinion to be organised and expressed. The extensive reforms of local government which took place in Great Britain in the 1970s were designed to improve the effectiveness of local government to meet both these purposes. There would have been very little support for a proposal to do away with local government and instead make a massive increase in the functions performed directly by central government. But since the reforms there has developed an increasing tendency for central government to restrict the freedom of local authorities to decide their own policies. And in 1984 the future of central-local relations was a burning political issue.

Development of local government[1]
More than once in modern times, the structure of local government has been recast by Parliament, but its development has always been influenced by strong local feelings which have grown up around local institutions. Indeed historical forms have often survived after they have outlived their usefulness. Often reform has kept old names and titles in being (county, borough, parish, sheriff) while giving new functions to the institutions to which they refer. One feature of English local government which lost its main significance only when the Local Government Act 1972 took effect was the historical distinction between the boroughs, which were incorporated by charters from the Crown

---

[1] K. B. Smellie, *A History of Local Government*; J. Redlich and F. W. Hirst, *The History of Local Government in England*; P. G. Richards and B. Keith-Lucas, *A History of Local Government in the Twentieth Century*. Note that in the titles of statutes cited in the footnotes to this chapter, 'L.G.' stands for 'Local Government'.

and endowed with powers of self-government, and the counties, which until late in the 19th century were largely governed by the justices of the peace meeting in quarter sessions. During the 19th century, borough government had been reorganised by the Municipal Corporations Acts of 1835 and 1882, mainly concerned with internal structure and the administration of corporate property. In the counties the Local Government Act 1888 created elected county councils and transferred to them the administrative powers of the county justices. This Act conferred on the larger boroughs the status of 'county borough', exempting them from the jurisdiction of the new county councils. As a result of the 1888 Act and other legislation, there was set up in England and Wales a complex pattern of local government by which there was single-tier government in the county boroughs, two-tier government in the non-county boroughs and urban districts, and three-tier government in the rural districts of the counties, the third tier consisting of parish councils and parish meetings. The sharp division between town and country which this structure involved eventually proved inimical to effective local government.

Another aspect of the development of local government is the tension and sometimes conflict which there has been between multi-purpose and *ad hoc* authorities. *Ad hoc* authorities are established when a particular function of government (for example, the poor law, education, electricity, the hospitals, water) is thought to require its own organisational structure, separate from both central and local government. By contrast, multi-purpose local authorities provide a wide variety of services within the same framework. The stronger the system of local government, the better able is it to resist arguments for the creation of *ad hoc* agencies. In the 20th century, these arguments have been but one aspect of the challenge to local government coming from central government. Obviously certain activities, for example the supply of gas and electricity and the maintenance of social security, cannot be carried on efficiently within a local system. But many other public services and controls could be entrusted to local government, to *ad hoc* authorities or to central government itself. There is no hard-and-fast dividing line between central and local services. Even where major services such as education or housing have been kept within local government, there has been a growing tendency on the part of central government to superimpose central controls on local decisions. One reason for this is financial, since local government has come increasingly to depend on grants from central government. Local government expenditure is also of considerable economic significance, and central government has claimed power to intervene in numerous local decisions that in aggregate may affect the national economy.

From the 1950s onwards, weaknesses in local government became increasingly evident in the face of an expanding and shifting population, increased human mobility and the higher standards set for public services, which required larger units of government able to support more specialised and professional work. Piecemeal reform of local boundaries was attempted in England and Wales under the Local Government Act 1958. Only in Greater London was a thorough reform achieved, by the London Government Act 1963, largely based on the work of a royal commission which reported in 1960.[2] Be-

---

[2]   Cmnd 1164, 1960.

tween 1966 and 1969, a royal commission chaired by Lord Redcliffe-Maud examined the whole structure of local government in England in relation to its existing functions. Its report recommended what was basically a single-tier system for England, apart from three conurbations based on Birmingham, Liverpool and Manchester, in which a new two-tier system was proposed.[3] In the event, reform in England and Wales was achieved by the Local Government Act 1972, but in a very different way from that recommended for England by the Redcliffe-Maud report.

In Scotland, the local government system has always been distinct from that in England and Wales and has been generally subject to separate legislation.[4] While the historical origins of local government were different, the influences on the development of English local government already mentioned have been felt in Scotland, for example the distinction between the burghs and the counties, the challenge from *ad hoc* agencies, the growing influence of central government and the increasing financial dependence of local government on the centre. A royal commission on local government in Scotland under the chairmanship of Lord Wheatley sat at the same time as the Redcliffe-Maud commission.[5] Its report led to the Local Government (Soctland) Act 1973.

Proposals by the Conservative government for further reforming local government in the six 'metropolitan counties' and Greater London were before Parliament in the 1984–5 session; these are outlined in appendix B.

The present structure of local government[6]

1 England (outside Greater London). The Local Government Act 1972 established what is essentially a two-tier system of local government throughout England. The upper tier is composed of the county councils, the lower tier of district councils. The Act defined the boundaries of the counties, some of which follow ancient divisions between counties, others of which are quite new. The allocation of functions between the tiers differs between the six 'metropolitan counties' (Greater Manchester, Merseyside, South Yorkshire, Tyne and Wear, West Midlands and West Yorkshire) and the 39 non-metropolitan counties. In the non-metropolitan counties, the major responsibilities of the county councils are education, transport planning and highways, the personal social services, refuse disposal, libraries, consumer protection and (subject to amalgamation schemes) fire and police; the main responsibilities of the district councils are housing, environmental health, clean air, building regulations, refuse collection, levying rates and the making of byelaws. Important town planning functions are vested in both county and district councils, and they have concurrent powers in matters such as museums, parks and recreation. In the metropolitan counties, the district councils and not the counties

---

3   Cmnd 4040, 1969.
4   For the position before reform in Scotland, see J. Bennett Miller, *Administrative and Local Government Law in Scotland*.
5   Cmnd 4150, 1969.
6   For accounts of the law of local government in England and Wales, see C. A. Cross, *Principles of Local Government Law* and K. Davies, *Local Government Law*. See also T. Byrne, *Local Government in Britain*, A. Alexander, *The Politics of Local Government in the United Kingdom*, and H. Elcock, *Local Government*.

are responsible for education, the personal social services and libraries, but the division of functions is otherwise broadly the same. For each county and district, there is an elected body of councillors, who annually elect the chairman of the council. Under the 1972 Act, a district council may on the advice of the Privy Council be granted a royal charter: the charter confers on the district the status of a borough and the chairman of the council is then termed mayor. Under the prerogative, the Crown may grant the status of a city or royal borough or confer the style of lord mayor.

In addition to the two principal tiers of local government, there is in many parts of England a third tier which consists of parish meetings and parish councils, either in the former rural districts or in smaller urban areas which had previously been boroughs or urban districts. The 1972 Act provided a procedure by which new parish councils might be constituted. The council of a parish may resolve to adopt the status of town, in which case the parish council is known as a town council and its chairman as the town mayor. The functions vested in parish councils are minor in comparison with those of the principal councils, but include the management of parish property, the acquisition of land, and the provision of amenities such as recreation grounds and village halls; they have a statutory right if they so wish to be informed of applications for planning permission affecting their parish.[7] To enable historic privileges, dignities and ceremonies to be maintained, the 1972 Act provided for former cities and boroughs which were merged in the new districts and did not become separate parishes to form a new body corporate known as the Charter Trustees of the city or town. Consisting of the district councillors for the wards in the area concerned, the trustees may each year elect a city or town mayor.[8]

2 Greater London. The vast resources and population of Greater London and its position as the national centre of government and commerce present great administrative problems; these formerly were accentuated by local boundaries which had not kept pace with the physical growth of London. The boundaries of the Metropolitan Board of Works, created in 1855, became those of the London County Council in 1888. They remained unchanged until the London Government Act 1963, by which time less than half the population of Greater London lived within the administrative county of London. The Act of 1963 established the Greater London Council (GLC) and 32 London borough councils. The principle embodied in the 1963 Act was to confer as many functions as possible on the boroughs and to vest in the GLC only vital powers which concerned the whole area, in respect of traffic regulation, highways, town planning, housing, sewage disposal and other regulatory and licensing functions. The boroughs also have important highways, traffic and planning functions and they are the primary authorities for housing, environmental health and the personal social services. For education the Inner London Education Authority exists within the GLC for the 12 inner boroughs; the outer boroughs are themselves the local education authorities.

---

[7] L.G. Act 1972, sch. 16, para. 20.
[8] L.G. Act 1972, s. 246.

Certain services for London are provided by *ad hoc* authorities, for example, the Metropolitan Police and the Port of London Authority. The Transport (London) Act 1969 established a new public corporation, the London Transport Executive, whose relationship with the GLC was intended to be broadly similar to that between the board of a nationalised industry and central government. The special nature of that relationship was one of the difficulties in the controversy over fares in London in 1981.[9]

The City of London stands apart. It was unaffected by the Municipal Corporation Acts and shares with the Inns of Court the privilege of being a medieval corporation which has never undergone reform from without. The city is still largely governed under its old charters. Some local government functions are exercised by the city corporation for its area of barely one square mile: environmental health, police, housing, open spaces and parks, libraries and markets. Other services are provided in the city by the GLC. Town planning functions are exercised both by the city and the GLC. The city corporation comprises three courts, whose composition is linked directly with the ancient city companies: the Court of Common Hall, the Court of Aldermen and the Court of Common Council. The last body, the major governing body of the corporation, consists of the Lord Mayor, aldermen and councillors. The aldermen and councillors are elected at the wardmotes, the former for life, the latter annually, by the local government electors of the ward.

3 Wales. A reformed structure of local government for Wales was provided by the Local Government Act 1972. It follows broadly the same lines as for England outside the metropolitan counties. One major difference is that the district councils exercise certain functions which in England are reserved to county councils, including refuse disposal, libraries and aspects of consumer protection. Another difference is that, as the third tier of local government, community councils take the place of the parish councils in England.

4 Scotland. Local government in Scotland was reformed by the Local Government (Scotland) Act 1973. Except for three islands areas (Orkney, Shetland and the Western Isles) which are each governed by an all-purpose authority, a two-tier system was established throughout Scotland, the upper tier consisting of 9 regional councils and the lower tier consisting of 53 district councils. The allocation of functions between the two tiers is broadly equivalent to that which is made in the non-metropolitan counties in England: thus education, social work, highways, transport, water, sewerage, police and fire are assigned to the regional councils; housing, building control and public health are the main duties of the district councils; planning functions are vested both in regional and in district councils, except in three regions where planning powers are vested solely in the regional council. [10] The major difference in structure between the English and Scottish systems is that there are

---

9   See *Bromley BC* v. *GLC* [1983] 1 A.C. 768, p. 636 *post*; and also Transport Act 1983.
10   Some adjustments affecting planning powers and removing most concurrent powers were made by the L.G. and Planning (Scotland) Act 1981. See also Cmnd 8115, 1981 and Cmnd 9216, 1984.

no parish councils in Scotland, but a scheme of community councils must be established within each district and islands area. Although these Scottish bodies share their name with the third tier authorities in Wales, they are not intended to become a third tier of local government but to be organs for co-ordinating and expressing local opinion on any matters affecting services provided by public authorities in their communities and for taking such action in the interests of their communities as appears 'expedient and practicable'. The structure and composition of the community councils within each district are settled by the district council, subject to the approval of the Secretary of State for Scotland.[11]

Local government elections

The local franchise formerly rested on the occupation of land or premises but since 1945 those registered as parliamentary electors have also had the right to vote as local government electors. A non-resident property qualification for local elections was abolished in 1969. Thus the main qualification for registration as a local government elector is residence on the qualifying date within the area concerned.[12] Service voters may vote in local as in parliamentary elections. Peers and peeresses in their own right may vote at local elections.

The conduct of local elections is governed by the Representation of the People Act 1983. With modifications, for example a much lower limit for permitted expenses, local elections are conducted in the same manner as parliamentary elections. The ballot is secret, there are penalties for corrupt and illegal practices, and the results of elections can be challenged by way of election petition to the court.[13]

The Local Government Act 1972 established the principle that councillors should be elected for four-year terms. In the case of county councils, the county areas are divided into single-member divisions and all the councillors retire together every four years. In the metropolitan districts, one-third of the members retire in each year in which there is no county council election. Other district councils were given by the 1972 Act a choice between simultaneous retirement every four years and the system of one-third retiring at a time. Members of parish councils in England and community councils in Wales are also elected for four-year periods. To avoid the expense of separate elections, provision is made for members of these councils to be elected at the same time as the relevant district councillors.[14] Apart from elections to fill casual vacancies, all local elections in England and Wales are held on the first Thursday in May unless another day is fixed by the Home Secretary. In Scotland, members of both regional and district councils are elected for four-year periods and all members of a council retire simultaneously; regional and district elections are held in alternation every two years. There is no fixed pattern for community councils.[15]

Whereas candidates for parliamentary elections may stand for any consti-

---

11   L.G. (Scotland) Act 1973, Pt. IV.
12   For the parliamentary franchise see ch. 9. BI.
13   *E.g. Morgan* v. *Simpson* [1974] Q.B. 344; ch. 9 BIII.
14   Cross, *op. cit.*, ch. 13.
15   L.G. (Scotland) Act 1973, s. 4.

tuency, candidates at local elections have to satisfy a test of local connection. A British, Commonwealth or Irish citizen aged 21 or more is qualified to be nominated and elected only if (a) he is and continues to be a local government elector for the area of the council; or (b) if for one year before nomination and election days, he has occupied as owner or tenant any land or premises in that area; or (c) if throughout that year his principal or only place of work has been in that area; or (d) if throughout that year he has resided in that area. When the successful candidate does not fulfil any of these conditions, his election may be challenged by election petition and declared void. In the case of parish councils in England and community councils in Wales, residence for one year within three miles of the parish or community is a qualification.[16]

As with the House of Commons there are a number of grounds on which a person otherwise qualified may be disqualified from membership.[17] They include bankruptcy, a sentence of imprisonment for not less than three months without option of fine in respect of a criminal offence, and conviction for corrupt or illegal practices at elections. Disqualification also arises from the holding of any paid office or employment (other than the office of chairman of the council, vice-chairman or a deputy chairman), appointments to which are made or confirmed by the local authority, by a committee or sub-committee of the authority, by a joint board or committee on which the authority is represented, or by any person holding office or employment under the authority. Thus employees of a county council, such as school teachers, are disqualified from membership of that council but may be elected to a district council. Disqualification may also be declared by the court for a stated period when expenditure exceeding £2,000 has been declared to have been incurred contrary to law and the person responsible is a member of a local authority.[18]

Once elected, councillors must show at least some interest in the affairs of their council: a member who fails throughout six consecutive months to attend any meeting of the authority, including committees, ceases to be a member of the authority unless his absence is due to a reason approved by the council within the six month period.[19]

Local Government Boundary Commissions

No system of local government boundaries can expect to survive indefinitely. But in the past it has been found difficult to make satisfactory provision for revising boundaries to keep them adjusted to changes in population and other physical developments.[20] The 1972 Act established Local Government Boundary Commissions for England and for Wales. The English commission is required to make at intervals of between 10 and 15 years a general review of the areas of counties, metropolitan districts, London boroughs and the boundaries between Greater London and the adjoining counties. But this

---

16 L.G. Act 1972, s. 79; and *cf.* L.G. (Scotland) Act 1973, s. 29.
17 L.G. Act 1972, s. 80; and see L.G. (Scotland) Act 1973, s. 31.
18 L.G. Finance Act 1982, s. 20.
19 L.G. Act 1972, s. 85; *cf.* L.G. (Scotland) Act 1973, s. 35.
20 *Cf.* the review of parliamentary constituencies, discussed in ch. 9 BII.

general duty may be varied by directions from the Secretary of State for the
Environment. The commission also keeps under general review the areas of
non-metropolitan districts and it may make specific reviews of particular areas.
In advising the Secretary of State on boundary changes which should be made,
the commission must act in 'the interests of effective and convenient local
government'.[21] The Secretary of State may order changes to be made in local
areas by means of statutory instruments, which may give effect with or without
modifications to the commission's advice. The commission for England also
has certain responsibilities relating to parish boundaries and the electoral areas
within counties and districts. A similar commission has been established for
Scotland.[22] Because of the existence of the commissions, local authorities are
prohibited from promoting private legislation to alter local government areas.[23]

Powers of local authorities

Local authorities, although representative bodies chosen by popular election,
have not the autonomy of Parliament; indeed, they are dependent on Parliament for their powers. The powers of a local authority derive either expressly
or by implication from statute and they are exercised subject to the rules of
ultra vires. The application of these rules in disputed cases is a matter for the
courts and no local authority can determine the extent of its own powers. But
within the limits of its powers, and subject to the performance of statutory
duties laid upon it, a local authority has a discretion in deciding how it is to
administer the services for which it is responsible. In practice this discretion
is subject to many forms of direct and indirect pressure from central
government.

The working of the *ultra vires* doctrine will be examined later.[24] The doctrine
applies to local authorities for several reasons. Many local services involve
interference with the citizen's common law rights, for which statutory authorisation is needed. Again, the courts have always been concerned to ensure that
money raised from local taxation is spent only on lawful objects. Subject to
a financial limit, a local council may now incur expenditure for any purpose
not covered by other statutory authority which in its opinion is in the interests
of its area or of the inhabitants of the area.[25] Finally, all local authorities
except the corporation of the city of London are statutory corporations, *i.e.*
they are incorporated by virtue of statute and have legal capacity only in
relation to the purposes for which they are incorporated. The Local Government Act 1972 did not bestow unlimited legal competence on local authorities,
but it does provide that a local authority has power to do anything 'which is
calculated to facilitate, or is conducive or incidental' to the discharge of any
of its functions;[26] this enactment probably adds little to the common law of

---

[21] *Enfield BC* v. *L.G. Boundary Commission* [1979] 3 All E.R. 747.
[22] For the English and Welsh commissions, see L.G. Act 1972, Pt. IV and schs. 7–11. For the
Scottish commission, see L.G. (Scotland) Act 1973, Pt. II and schs. 4–6.
[23] L.G. Act 1972, s. 70; L.G. (Scotland) Act 1973, s. 22.
[24] Ch. 34 A.
[25] L.G. Act 1972, s. 137; L.G. (Scotland) Act 1973, s. 83.
[26] L.G. Act 1972, s. 111 and L.G. (Scotland) Act 1973, s. 69; *cf.* Cmnd 4040, 1969, p. 84 and
Cmnd 4150, 1969, p. 153. And see *McColl* v. *Strathclyde Council* 1983 S.L.T. 616.

implied powers but it may be useful when a local council wishes to undertake an activity subsidiary to one of its main functions.

The limitations on the corporate powers of a local authority mean that a contract entered into by an authority for a purpose beyond its powers is void and of no legal effect.[27] Formerly local authorities like other corporations could contract only under their common seal, an inconvenient formality which was often ignored. Contracts now bind a local authority regardless of formality, provided only that they would be valid if made in the same form between private persons, and that they are entered into by a person acting with express or implied authority.[28]

Legislation affecting local authorities

As well as constituent legislation like the Local Government Act 1972, which establishes the authorities, regulates their composition, authorises them to appoint committees and so on, most legislation applying to local government enables a particular service to be carried on and for this purpose vests powers and duties in a named class of local authority. Examples are the Education Act 1944 and the Town and Country Planning Act 1971. These powers are available to the local authority without any formality or procedural step. But some powers, contained in what are known as adoptive Acts, are available to a council only when it has gone through a stated procedure (for example, passing a special resolution and seeking the approval of central government).

In the 18th and 19th centuries, local or private Acts were the means by which local initiatives in public enterprise could be taken at a time when few general powers were conferred by Parliament. Parliamentary procedures developed to safeguard private interests against excessive powers being granted to new authorities; this was essential for, by virtue of the supremacy of Parliament, the provisions of a local Act are as binding as those of a public general Act.[29] The need for local legislation is less today than in the past. But a larger local authority may still consider it worthwhile to promote its own Bill, either for acquiring a variety of additional powers which are needed in the locality or for obtaining power to carry through a single project which will involve large capital expenditure, the acquisition of land and the construction of works. The parliamentary aspects of private Bill legislation have been described above.[30] All local authorities except parish and community councils are empowered to promote legislation, provided that they comply with the statutory requirements, which involve a special resolution being adopted and later confirmed at specially convened meetings of the council.[31] The existence of local Act powers causes difficulty when general legislation is passed relating to the same subject-matter (does a local authority continue to enjoy its former special powers, where these differ from those conferred by the new general law?) and also when local government boundaries are reorganised (are the

---

27   *Rhyl UDC* v. *Rhyl Amusements Ltd* [1959] 1 All E.R. 257; *Triggs* v. *Staines UDC* [1969] 1 Ch. 10.
      N. W. Leicestershire DC v. *E. Midlands Housing Association Ltd.* [1981] 3 All E.R. 364.
28   Corporate Bodies' Contracts Act 1960.
29   *Pickin* v. *British Railways Board* [1974] A.C. 765; ch. 5 C.
30   Ch. 11 A.
31   L.G. Act 1972, s. 239; L.G. (Scotland) Act 1973, s. 82.

former special powers applied to the new boundaries, retained to operate only within the old boundaries, or abolished?). In such circumstances, the expedient is often adopted of conferring on the appropriate minister power by order to modify or to repeal the local Acts concerned. This is one of the exceptional situations in which a minister may justifiably be granted power to amend an Act of Parliament by order.[32] The Local Government Act 1972, section 262, authorised local legislation to remain in force in the areas to which it already applied, subject to a ministerial order extending it to the whole of a new area. The Act also provided that, except where a local Act was continued in force by ministerial order, all existing local Acts were to cease to operate in metropolitan counties in 1979 and in non-metropolitan counties in 1984, a period intended to allow time for the new councils to seek the re-enactment of essential local laws.[33]

In addition to promoting local Bills, there are other ways by which local authorities may obtain special statutory powers. By the provisional order procedure, an order is made by a minister on the request of a council under power conferred by an enabling Act. The provisional order must be confirmed by Parliament before it takes effect. Confirmation is given by a Provisional Order Confirmation Bill, a public Bill introduced by the minister concerned. If any objections are put forward by interested parties, a public inquiry may be held before the minister makes the order. Again, when the confirmation Bill is pending before Parliament, petitioners may be heard before the select committee to which the Bill is referred. A modified version of this procedure is used under the Private Legislation Procedure (Scotland) Act 1936 as the means whereby local councils in Scotland may obtain additional powers without promoting private Bills.

When a provisional order is opposed, the procedure is almost as cumbrous as private Bill procedure. By contrast, a ministerial order comes into effect simply by ministerial action. This type of order is often made by a minister to confirm a scheme put before him by a local authority, for example for the compulsory purchase of land, after a public inquiry at which the reasons for the scheme and objections to it are publicly presented. Under the Acquisition of Land Act 1981, the order takes effect as soon as the minister's confirmation is announced and thereafter it can be challenged in the courts on the ground of *ultra vires*, but only within six weeks.[34] This procedure allows opponents of the order no opportunity of putting their case before a committee in Parliament if the minister should overrule the objections presented at the public inquiry. Under the New Towns Act 1981, the minister's confirmation may exceptionally be subject to approval or rejection by Parliament.[35]

Another procedure, known as special parliamentary procedure, was provided by the Statutory Orders (Special Procedure) Act 1945. This preserves the right of interested parties to be heard at a public inquiry and before a parliamentary committee on detailed objections; it also enables M.P.s to debate in the House itself questions of general policy. The procedure applies

---

[32] Page 614 *post.*
[33] *Cf.* L.G. (Scotland) Act 1973, ss. 225, 229. And see Civic Government (Scotland) Act 1982.
[34] Page 669 *post.*
[35] New Towns Act 1981, s. 77; *cf.* p. 647 *post.*

to any statutory power to make orders granted after 1945 where the power is stated to be subject to special parliamentary procedure. By the use of this formula, certain types of land (for example, land held inalienably by the National Trust) are protected against compulsory purchase by ministerial decision alone.[36]

Byelaws

No local authority has a residual power to make local laws affecting the public at large, but district councils and London borough councils may make byelaws 'for the good rule and government' of their areas and 'for the prevention and suppression of nuisances'.[37] There are also more specific powers to make byelaws conferred by such legislation as the Public Health Acts.[38] The byelaw making power is controlled in various ways. The maximum penalty for breach of a byelaw is fixed in the enabling statute. Byelaws come into force only after confirmation by central government, usually by the Department of the Environment or by the Home Office. In consequence of this central control, it is the practice to adopt, with or without modification, model sets of byelaws drawn up by the confirming department. Byelaws are subject to review in the courts: the courts may declare a byelaw invalid on the grounds of *ultra vires*, uncertainty, inconsistency with the general law, and even unreasonableness,[39] but a byelaw made by a public authority will not readily be condemned by a court on this ground.[40] In some fields the byelaw making power has given way to centrally made regulations: thus building standards are now regulated by ministerial regulations, no longer by byelaws.[41]

Members of local councils

County and district councils may pay to their chairmen and vice-chairmen such allowances for enabling them to meet the expenses of their office as the council think reasonable. Members of these councils are entitled to receive reasonable travelling and subsistence allowances and also to receive an attendance allowance, which must not exceed a maximum amount laid down by central government. Certain councillors are entitled to special responsibility allowances but they do not receive a salary as such.

Before 1933 a person was disqualified from membership if he had directly or indirectly a share or interest in any contract with the council. The rule is now that if a member has 'any pecuniary interest, direct or indirect, in any contract, proposed contract or other matter', and is present at a council meeting or committee when the matter is being considered, he must disclose his interest and thereafter take no part in the discussion nor vote.[42] Many

---

36 Acquisition of Land Act 1981. ss. 17–20.
37 L.G. Act 1972, s. 235; and see L.G. (Scotland) Act 1973, s. 201.
38 See Cross, *op. cit.*, app. 5.
39 *Powell* v. *May* [1946] K.B. 330; *Cinnamond* v. *British Airports Authority* [1980] 2 All E.R. 368; *Burnley BC* v. *England* (1978) 77 L.G.R. 227.
40 *Kruse* v. *Johnson* [1898] 2 Q.B. 91.
41 Public Health Act 1961.
42 L.G. Act 1972, s. 94; and L.G. (Scotland) Act 1973, s. 38. A councillor may give a general notice declaring his own and his spouse's interests in employment, business, rented property etc.

councils in their standing orders require a member who cannot thus take part in a discussion to withdraw from the meeting until the decision is made. Certain interests which members may have as ratepayers, as members of the public, or as consumers of public utilities, are not affected, but a councillor who holds shares in a company which may contract with the council has an indirect pecuniary interest which must be disclosed; in the case of certain minority shareholdings with a nominal value of less than £1,000, ownership must be disclosed but voting and discussion are not affected. Disclosure has generally to be made of the interests of the councillor's spouse. The council must appoint an officer to keep a record of all interests disclosed. Breach of these rules does not in itself affect the validity of the council's decision,[43] but is a criminal offence, subject to summary prosecution on the decision of the Director of Public Prosecutions, with a maximum penalty of £200. The Secretary of State has power to remove the ban on discussion and even that on voting if so many members of the council are affected by an interest that the business of the council is impeded. The definition of 'interest' has been interpreted stringently,[44] but no pecuniary interest is relevant which is so remote or insignificant that it cannot reasonably be regarded as likely to influence a member in considering the particular contract or other matter.[45] Councillors who are tenants of council houses have been granted a general dispensation permitting them to speak and vote on matters of general housing policy.[46]

The problem of corruption in local government became of acute concern in the light of the Poulson disclosures in the early 1970s. A committee chaired by Lord Redcliffe-Maud reported in 1974 that the law regarding councillors' financial interests should be tightened up, that it should become a criminal offence to use for private gain information received through membership or employment in local government, and that a register of councillors' interests should be maintained by each council for public inspection, which should contain such details as employment held by a councillor, land owned in the area of the local authority and tenancies of council property.[47] On the recommendation of the committee and with the support of local authority associations and government departments, in October 1975, a Code of Conduct for local government was issued.[48] When a broader inquiry was conducted by a royal commission under Lord Salmon into standards of conduct in public life generally, the commission endorsed the recommendations of the Redcliffe-Maud Report regarding local government.[49]

In order that they may be able to discharge their duties, councillors have a right to inspect documents in the possession of the council. This right, however, extends only to documents about which a councillor needs to know in order to perform his functions. He has no general right of access to his authority's files and the council may deny access if it is not related to the coun-

---

[43]   But see *R. v. Hendon RDC, ex p. Chorley* [1933] 2 K.B. 696, p. 645 *post.*
[44]   *Brown v. DPP* [1956] 2 Q.B. 369; *Rands v. Oldroyd* [1959] 1 Q.B. 204.
[45]   L.G. Act 1972, s. 97(5); L.G. (Scotland) Act 1973. s. 41(5).
[46]   Cmnd 5636, 1974, app. F.
[47]   Cmnd 5636, 1974.
[48]   Circulars 94/75 (Dept. of Environment) and 95/75 (Scottish Development Dept.).
[49]   Cmnd 6524, 1976.

cillor's legitimate interests.[50]

Internal administration of local councils

The structure of administration in local government is very different from that in departments of central government where a hierarchy of civil servants is placed under the control and direction of a minister. Local government has instead made wide use of committees and sub-committees of councillors to enable a single authority to administer many diverse services. Usually every item of business which comes to the full council meeting has already been considered by a committee and many matters of business are dealt with finally by committees. Every council has power to appoint committees, which in turn may appoint sub-committees.[51] Except for a committee which controls the finance of the authority, up to one-third of the members of a committee may be persons from outside the council. Certain committees are obligatory: education committees must be appointed by local education authorities under the Education Act 1944, according to schemes of membership approved by the Secretary of State for Education and Science; social services committees and police committees must also be appointed by the appropriate councils. But the aim in the 1972 Local Government Act was to leave the committee structure to the discretion of each local authority. In general, local authorities may 'arrange for the discharge of any of their functions' by their committees, sub-committees, or officers or by other local authorities; but only the council itself may levy a rate or borrow money.[52] This statutory power appears to allow wide scope for delegation to committees and officials; and matters which are not delegated may be referred to committees or officials for their recommenendations. Moreover a committee to which powers have been delegated may itself arrange for the discharge of its functions by a sub-committee or an officer, a statutory provision which overrides the principle of *delegatus non potest delegare*.[53] Two or more councils may appoint joint committees. Where a council delegates functions to a committee, the decisions of the committee are binding on the council; but a council retains the power to act itself, may revoke the authority of a committee at any time and may also remove a single member from membership of a committee.[54]

County and district councils must hold an annual meeting and such other meetings as each council may determine. Council meetings and meetings of council committees and joint committees (but not sub-committees) are required to be open to the public, except when the council or a committee resolves to exclude the public during consideration of a particular matter for which publicity would be prejudicial to the public interest.[55] Representatives

---

50 See *R.* v. *Barnes BC, ex p. Conlan* [1938] 3 All E.R. 226; *R.* v. *Lancashire Police Authority, ex p. Hook* [1980] Q.B. 603; *City of Birmingham DC* v. O. [1983] 1 A.C. 578.
51 L.G. Act 1972, s. 102; L.G. (Scotland) Act 1973, s. 57.
52 L.G. Act 1972, s. 101; L.G. (Scotland) Act 1973, s. 56.
53 L.G. Act 1972, s. 101(2), *cf.* L.G. (Scotland) Act 1973, s. 56(2); p. 634 *post.*
54 *Manton* v. *Brighton Corporation* [1951] 2 K.B. 393.
55 Public Bodies (Admission to Meetings) Act 1960; L.G. Act 1972, s. 100; L.G. (Scotland) Act 1973, s. 44. The duty of a local authority is to provide reasonable accommodation for the public, not to accommodate an unexpectedly large number of persons: *R.* v. *Liverpool City Council, ex p. Liverpool Taxi Fleet Operators Association* [1975] 1 All E.R. 379.

of the press are entitled to be present while the public is there and reasonable facilities and information about the business of the meeting must be supplied to them. Press reports of proceedings, so long as they are fair and accurate, are protected by qualified privilege from liability for defamation.[56]

Local authorities must appoint such officers as they think necessary for the proper discharge of their functions;[57] when appointed they hold office on such reasonable terms and conditions as the employing authority thinks fit.[58] Local government officers are not Crown servants and in general each authority as the employer has full powers of appointment and dismissal. The appointment of some chief officers is required by statute: thus chief education officers, chief fire officers, inspectors of weights and measures, and directors of social services must be appointed by the appropriate councils. Subject to any particular statutory provisions the relationship between officer and authority is governed by the general law of contract, unlike that between the Crown and its servants. Under the principle laid down in *Mersey Docks and Harbour Board Trustees* v. *Gibbs*,[59] local authorities are vicariously liable for the tortious acts of their servants.[60] But a local authority is not liable when an officer whom it has appointed commits a tort while performing duties laid directly on him by central government.[61] The individual officer is personally liable for any torts which he commits and may not be required to obey an unlawful order, for example, to make a wholly illegal payment from the general rate fund.[62]

In carrying out their work, local government officers are subject to control and direction exercised through the appropriate committee. But many local officials have to deal directly with the public, and difficult problems may arise when a private individual relies upon a statement made or assurance given by an official with apparent authority, which turns out to be incorrrect. Is the statement or assurance binding on the council, and if not does the individual have any other remedy, for example an action for damages?[63] Now that councils have power to arrange for any of their functions to be discharged by officers, it might have been thought more likely that outsiders could rely upon the statements and assurances of officials. But the Court of Appeal has emphasised that any delegation scheme must be made with due formality by the council.[64] The aggrieved person may in any event be able to make a complaint of maladministration to the local government ombudsmen.

As part of the reform of local government in the 1970s, ombudsmen were appointed for local government to investigate citizens' complaints of injustice caused by acts of maladministration committed by local authorities. The jurisdiction of the Commissioners for Local Administration will be considered in chapter 37, section D.

---

[56]   Defamation Act 1952, s. 7; and see *Horrocks* v. *Lowe* [1975] A.C. 135.
[57]   L.G. Act 1972, s. 112; L.G. (Scotland) Act 1973, s. 64.
[58]   *Cf. Roberts* v. *Hopwood* [1925] A.C. 578.
[59]   (1866) L.R. 1 H.L. 93.
[60]   Ch. 36. Of recent cases, see in particular *Anns* v. *Merton BC* [1978] A.C. 728.
[61]   *Stanbury* v. *Exeter Corporation* [1905] 2 K.B. 838.
[62]   *A.-G.* v. *De Winton* [1906] 2 Ch. 106.
[63]   Ch. 34C.
[64]   *Western Fish Products Ltd* v. *Penwith DC* [1981] 2 All. E.R. 204.

Relationship with central government[65]

In the British tradition, local government implies a measure of local *self* government. Authorities do not operate as mere agents of central departments subject to the latter's full direction and control. On the other hand, it would be inaccurate to imagine that local authorities are immune from adjustments to their structure and powers made by Parliament at the behest of government; or to suppose that authorities can discharge their functions without regard to departmental views. Because of central government's responsibility for national policies, some of which (education and housing, for instance) depend utterly upon local implementation, claims are made by central departments to supervise or control local authority activities, both for the overall maintenance of standards of service and reasons of national economic policy. The relationship which results from these central claims and from the desire of local government for some autonomy is sometimes (perhaps optimistically) described as a 'partnership'. To be more precise is notoriously difficult. Some central powers of control (such as default powers to compel local authorities to discharge their reponsibilities) are less significant in practice than the statute book suggests. Again, in some local services close supervision is maintained but on an informal, non-statutory basis. Many accounts of the relationship are directed more towards what ought(constitutionally) to be the case than towards what is the case at present. And it is difficult to weigh the relaxation of some forms of central control against the imposition of others. Recent trends symbolised by the Local Government, Planning and Land Act 1980,[66] and the Local Government Finance Act 1982 have been towards the repeal of many provisions requiring the Secretary of State's consent to individual local authority actions, but the strengthening of his controls over total levels of local spending and, therefore, over the scale of local authority programmes as a whole. Together with more recent government policies, the net result for local councils is a severe loss of freedom.

The department of central government primarily concerned with the general health of local government in England is the Department of the Environment; the specific responsibilities of the department have included housing, new towns, town planning, public health, water, transport and highways as well as local government finance and boundary reform. The department was formed in 1970, its predecessors from 1951 onwards having been the Ministry of Housing and Local Government and a separate Ministry of Transport. In September 1976, a separate Department of Transport was again created, under its own Secretary of State. It must be realised that the Department of the Environment does not control a number of important services within local government and has no special responsibility for co-ordinating them. Thus it is the Secretary of State for Education and Science who seeks to secure the execution by local authorities of a national policy for education; the Home Secretary is concerned with the police and fire services, local government elections and byelaws; and the Secretary of State for the Social

---

[65] See J. A. G. Griffith, *Central Departments and Local Authorities*; M. J. Elliott, *The role of law in central-local relations*; Central Policy Review Staff, *Relations between Central Government and Local Authorities*.

[66] Implementing recommendations in Cmnd 7634, 1979.

Services has an oversight of the social services performed by local government.

In the case of Wales, the place of the Department of the Environment and of the Department of Education and Science is taken by the Welsh Office. In Scotland, the Scottish Development Department has functions equivalent to those of the Department of the Environment, but the Scottish Education Department and the Home and Health Department are also concerned with local authority services.[67]

Methods of central control

Although they are not the sole factor in determining the whole central-local relationship, the methods of control available to central departments are extremely important. They may be categorised under three overlapping heads.

1 Legislation. As local authority powers and procedures are dependent on statute, the departments responsible for initiating legislation exercise general control over local government law. In many local services, the enabling Act confers on the Secretary of State power to make detailed regulations which, as subordinate legislation, are binding on local authorities. Byelaws made by local authorities are subject to central confirmation. Under the provisional order procedure, confirmation of the order requires the co-operation of the ministry concerned. In theory but not always in practice, influence over the general legislative policies of central government is exercised by the local authority associations, which may be extensively consulted by the central departments when new legislation is being considered.

2 Finance. To control their finances is to control the activities of local authorities as a whole and, as we shall see below, central government has wide powers of financial supervision. Levels of revenue and capital expenditure are today subject to centrally imposed limits. Local authority accounts are subject to inspection by the Audit Commission – a body under the supervision of the Secretary of State.

3 Policy and standards. Central departments have an inevitable interest in the implementation of local policies and the standards maintained. Occasionally this is made explicit by statute – the Secretary of State for Education and Science, for example, has a general duty 'to promote the education of the people of England and Wales'.[68] Central financial controls are also very important in the determination of local policies. But beyond these, a range of administrative controls ensure a more detailed form of supervision. Recent statutory changes have extricated central departments from many of the minutiae of local government administration. Authorities are now assumed to be staffed by councillors and officials competent to make their own decisions locally and, with the exception of chief constables, the hiring and firing of officers is no longer centrally controlled. On the other hand, there is provision

---

[67] Chs. 3 and 22.
[68] Education Act 1944, s. 1.

for central approval of local authority schemes or programmes (for instance, in town planning, transport and education) often associated with approval of capital expenditure plans. Some services (education, fire and police) are subject to routine central inspection. In others, notably town planning, local decisions may be taken on appeal to the Secretary of State. Some specific decisions such as to make a compulsory purchase order require confirmation by a minister. Occasionally, where a local authority refuses to implement a statutory policy or to comply with central wishes, central government will deploy statutory reserve powers to compel an authority to perform its functions.[69]

Local government finance

There can be no doubt that, in recent years, the most troublesome issue in local government has been that of finance. In part, the problems are technical and result from successive attempts to modernise a system devised for an earlier age. More importantly, however, they are constitutional and political since, as we have seen, finance is at the core of the relationship between central and local government. In 1974, following concern over the level of expenditure and the burden which this imposed on the tax system, the Secretaries of State for the Environment, Scotland and Wales jointly appointed a committee under the chairmanship of F. H. Layfield Q.C. to inquire into local government finance. The Layfield report, published in 1976, remains the most comprehensive and systematic treatment of the subject, although many of its recommendations aimed at reducing the dependence of local authorities upon central assistance, creating new forms of local revenue, clarifying central and local responsibilities and improving local accountability for expenditure have not been implemented. The brief account of the subject which follows deals with the position in England and Wales except where otherwise stated; emphasis will be placed on (a) the rating system (b) capital expenditure (c) central government grants and (d) audit procedures.[70]

The rating system

Local authorities are obliged to raise through local taxation the revenue which they need to meet their estimated expenditure after account has been taken of government grants and of fees and charges for services supplied, for example, rents for council houses, income from markets and other corporate property. The only form of tax available to councils comes from the rating system.[71] Rates are charged on the occupation of land and buildings. Some kinds of property, for example, places of public worship, are exempted from rating altogether; property occupied by charitable or other voluntary organisations is subject to a reduction in the amount of rates paid. The inherent limitations of a tax based simply on the value of the land or building, without regard to the means of the occupier, have led to various expedients being devised to protect some types of property against excessive burdens; thus

---

[69]   *R. v. Secretary of State for Environment, ex p. Norwich City Council* [1982] Q.B. 808, but see *Secretary of State for Education v. Tameside MB* [1977] A.C. 1014, p. 634 *post.*

[70]   For the Layfield Report, see Cmnd 6453, 1976; and Cross, *op. cit.*, chs. 7–9.

[71]   Rating law was consolidated in the General Rate Act 1967.

agricultural land and buildings are exempt from rating. Provision is made to restrict the rates paid by the occupiers of dwelling-houses. Since 1966, rate-payers of low income have been able to claim rate rebates in respect of private dwellings.[72] Although rates are in principle based on the occupation of property, rating authorities now have limited powers of rating the owners of unoccupied property.[73]

A rate is assessed on the annual value of land or buildings, and statute prescribes how this value may be calculated. The annual value in theory represents the rent at which the property might reasonably be expected to be let from year to year, less the annual cost of repairs, insurance and other expenses. The law thus assumes the existence of a hypothetical tenant, and calculates what sum he would be prepared to pay for a lease on such terms. Special methods are provided for calculating the value of large undertakings, such as waterworks and harbours, and also for assessing the liability to pay rates, or sums in lieu of rates, of the nationalised industries. Properties occupied for the purposes of the Crown are exempt from rating; in practice the Treasury makes a contribution in lieu of rates to the appropriate local authorities, based on a special valuation of Crown properties.

The valuation of property for rating purposes is undertaken by the Commissioners of Inland Revenue.[74] A valuation officer of the Inland Revenue prepares and publishes a valuation list, containing the individual values attributed to all properties in the rating area. If objections are made, the valuation officer can himself revise the list or an appeal may be taken to the local valuation court, a special tribunal of three persons drawn from a local valuation panel, and thence to the Lands Tribunal.[75] In principle, revaluation takes place every five years but individual proposals to alter the list may be made at any time. Because of the unpopularity of increased assessments and the work involved in a full revaluation, such revaluations are frequently deferred.[76]

The rating authorities are the borough and district councils. County councils, parish councils and joint boards precept on the rating authorities for the sums required. The rate is a uniform amount in the £ on the assessment of each rating unit of land and buildings, levied twice a year by the rating authority, but ratepayers have the opportunity of payment by instalments. The amount of the rate is fixed by relating the total sum needed to the total rateable value of the area.

Although rates are an unpopular tax, and although the law on rating is complex and artificial, the Layfield committee in 1976 considered that rating had certain advantages and should continue to be used as a local tax, subject to extensive reforms (for example, the capital value of dwelling-houses should be used as the basis for valuation). Of other possible forms of local taxation, the committee considered that only a local income tax would be practicable.[77]

---

72   See now Social Security and Housing Benefits Act 1982, Part II.
73   General Rate Act 1967, s. 17 and L.G. Act 1974, ss. 15, 16.
74   In Scotland, valuation is undertaken by assessors employed by regional and islands councils; appeals lie to valuation appeal committees: L.G. (Scotland) Act 1975, s. 4.
75   Page 709 *post*. And see *R.* v. *Paddington Valuation Officer, ex p. Peachey Property Corporation* [1966] 1 Q.B. 380.
76   No domestic revaluation is likely in the 1980s. See Cmnd 9008, 1983.
77   Cmnd 6453, ch. 11.

By 1984, however, no move in this direction had been made. Successive governments have retained the rate as the only substantial source of local authority revenue. Government attention has focussed instead upon attempts to curb rate income in order to limit local authority expenditure as a whole. A power to levy supplementary rates midway through the year has been removed and in 1984 major changes designed to impose rate income restraints (both selective and general) upon high spending authorities were made by the Rates Act.[78]

Capital expenditure

Although councils may pay for some items of capital expenditure out of their current income, in general they finance capital expenditure by borrowing money which they are required to repay over a fixed period of years, subject generally to a maximum of 60 years. The security offered is in part that of the fund formed by the council's future revenue and its property and in part the statutory control which is exercised over local borrowing. The general power to borrow money for their statutory purposes is given to local authorities by the Local Government Act 1972 and is exercised subject to the sanction of the Secretary of State for the Environment. The procedure of loan sanction was originally set up to guard against financial improprieties, but then became important as a means of control by central government over local decisions (for example, the building of a new school or road) and more recently as an instrument of economic management. In further support of control by loan sanction the Secretary of State may now determine directly the upper limit of capital expenditure for each authority for each year. Thus local authorities are given annual expenditure allocations sub-divided into blocks related to the housing, education, transport, personal social services, and other services they administer. Subject, however, to a limited power in the Secretary of State to earmark certain parts of the allocation for projects of national or regional importance, a local authority is free to aggregate and reallocate the five blocks to purposes of its choice. Authorities are authorised to borrow up to the limit of their annual gross allocation.[79] Scottish local authorities are required by statute to obtain the consent of central government before they incur any capital expenses.[80]

Local authorities may borrow from the Public Works Loan Board (created in 1817 for the purpose of advancing money to municipal bodies from funds coming out of the national exchequer), or from independent sources of finance, including the raising of loans and the issuing of bonds in the domestic capital market and the borrowing of money from abroad: access to these forms of borrowing is regulated by the Treasury and the Bank of England.

Central government grants

When local government was simply a matter for local initiative, and the interests of the ratepayers dictated the services undertaken, the rates could be

---

[78]   See Cmnd 8449, 1981 and Cmnd 9008, 1983. For Scotland, where powers to curb rates already existed, see Cmnd 9018, 1983. And see App B.

[79]   See Circular 9/83, Department of the Environment.

[80]   L.G. (Scotland) Act 1973, s. 94 and, for borrowing powers, L.G. (Scotland) Act 1975, sch. 3.

regarded as payment for benefits received. Today, the introduction of new services at the instance of the central government, the desire to maintain national standards, the disparity between the resources and needs of different local authorities and the limitations of the rating system, are all reasons why grants should be made to local councils from the national exchequer.

Government grants take two main forms:

(*a*)   the specific grant in aid of a particular service, usually calculated as a fixed proportion of the costs of the service, for example, 50% of police expenditure, 90% of mandatory student grants for first-degree courses. In 1984, the largest specific grants were made for the police, housing improvement and area improvement grants, magistrates, courts, probation and after care service, the urban aid programme and slum clearance. This form of grant is usually accompanied by close control over the services in question, for example by inspection or by regulations which leave local councils with little or no discretion. Supplementary grants are made for transport subsidies and national parks.

(*b*)   the general grant to increase a local council's income. With a general grant, first made in 1929, there should be less detailed control of particular services, although the degree of central control over total levels of local spending which results from a heavy dependence upon grant has been one of the most politically explosive issues in recent years.

The grant system has been recast several times since 1929 and it underwent a very substantial overhaul with the implementation of the Local Government, Planning and Land Act 1980. This Act continued the name of the grant used since 1966 – the rate support grant – but altered the way in which it was to be calculated. It is a grant fixed annually by the Secretary of State for the Environment (with the consent of the Treasury) following consultation with local authority associations. The Secretary of State makes a rate support grant report which contains details of the proposed grant and which has to be approved by resolution of the House of Commons.[81] Calculation of the amount of grant to be paid to individual authorities is done in a series of steps. The Secretary of State first determines, in the light of national economic conditions and the likely levels of local government spending, the aggregate level of Exchequer assistance to local authorities. From this total are deducted amounts payable to authorities in housing subsidies and specific grants. This produces an aggregate amount of rate support grant which is divided into two parts. One – the domestic rate relief grant – consists of an amount payable to all rating authorities to enable them to reduce the level of rates to be levied on domestic ratepayers. The other, much larger limit is the block grant which is payable to all local authorities and is for allocation in a manner intended to achieve two main purposes: (a) the grant formula aims to compensate those authorities with below average income of their own from rates i.e., with a low aggregate of rateable values in their areas; (b) the formula enables those authorities whose spending needs (measured in terms of the functions they perform and the populations they serve) are high to enjoy a higher level of grant. The actual grant paid to an authority then depends upon the level of

---

[81]   See e.g. H.C. 149 (1982–3).

spending it determines (the higher the rate, the higher the lack of grant) but the Secretary of State is empowered to build in further individual adjustments including reduction in grant to penalise high spenders.[82]

Audit

Every council must arrange for the proper administration of its financial affairs and appoint one of its officers to be responsible for this.[83] As well as employing their own qualified staff to maintain proper accounts, all councils are subject to the safeguard of external audit of their accounts. Until 1983 councils made their own choice between two forms of audit: (a) audit by approved auditors, who are qualified accountants in private practice approved by the Secretary of State for the purpose; (b) district audit, a form of public audit comparable with that carried out by the Comptroller and Auditor General in relation to central government. Most councils chose district audit.

With effect from 1983, however, the organisation of external audit for local authorities was substantially changed. A new Audit Commission for Local Authorities in England and Wales consisting of between 13 and 17 members appointed by the Secretary of State now has overall responsibility for the audit process. The commission appoints its own staff headed by the Controller of Audit. However, the appointment of the first Controller was made by the Secretary of State (thereafter by the commission but with his approval) and he also has the power to give directions to the commission as to the discharge of its functions.[84]

The audit of the accounts of an individual authority is undertaken either by an officer on the commission's staff or by accountants in private practice. The appointment is made by the commission after consultation with the authority. Once appointed an auditor has to comply with a code of audit practice prepared by the commission but otherwise he performs an independent and quasi-judicial function of his own. He must satisfy himself that the accounts have been prepared in the proper form, and that the council has made proper arrangements for securing economy, efficiency and effectiveness in its use of resources. All persons interested are entitled to inspect the accounts and any local government elector may object before the auditor to items in the accounts or may question the auditor about the accounts. The auditor must report on matters arising from the accounts which should in the public interest be made known. Where an auditor considers that an item of expenditure in the accounts is contrary to law he may, except where it has been sanctioned by the Secretary of State, apply to the court for a declaration accordingly. The court may then, if it grants the declaration, order the person or persons responsible for incurring the expenditure to repay it to the council and, if the expenditure exceeds £2,000 and the person responsible is a councillor, order him to be disqualified from membership of a council for a stated

---

82 L.G. Finance Act 1982; *R.* v. *Secretary of State, ex p. Brent BC* [1982] Q.B. 593; *R.* v. *Secretary of State, ex p. Hackney BC* [1984] 1 All E.R. 956. For Scotland, see L.G. and Planning (Scotland) Act 1982.
83 L.G. Act 1972, s. 151; L.G. (Scotland) Act 1973, s. 95.
84 L.G. Finance Act 1982, Part III. Scotland has a separate system of audit under the Commission for Local Authority Accounts: L.G. (Scotland) Act 1973, ss. 96–106.

period; but repayment and disqualification must not be ordered if the court is satisfied that he 'acted reasonably or in the belief that the expenditure was authorised by law'.[85] In the case of a loss or deficiency exceeding £2,000 caused by the wilful misconduct of any councillor, disqualification for a period of 5 years must be ordered.

The auditor may exercise these powers when there has been such excessive expenditure on lawful objects that the excess becomes unlawful.[86] External audit is not the only safeguard against unlawful expenditure by a local authority. The High Court may grant an injunction to restrain a council from incurring expenditure or a declaration that the expenditure is unlawful.[87] If such a remedy is sought, the prior consent of the Secretary of State to the expenditure will be no justification. If necessary, the Audit Commission may order an extraordinary audit of an authority's accounts either on application from an elector or on its own initiative. Such an audit must be held if the Secretary of State so directs.

---

[85]   L.G. Finance Act 1982, s. 19(3).
[86]   *Roberts* v. *Hopwood* [1925] A.C. 578, p. 636 *post*.
[87]   *Prescott* v. *Birmingham Corporation* [1955] Ch. 210.

Chapter 22

Devolution of government

We have already considered the historical structure of the United Kingdom and forms of government within it such as central departments, public boards and local government.[1] During and after the mid-1960s there developed a movement to secure the devolution of government within the United Kingdom, in particular to Scotland and Wales. This movement has given rise to complex constitutional, political, administrative, economic and financial issues. Devolution has been defined as 'the delegation of central government powers without the relinquishment of sovereignty',[2] but this definition is too wide to be very helpful, since the powers of government are numerous, many different methods of delegation are possible, and powers could be delegated to many different recipients. According to another authority, devolution consists of three elements: 'the transfer to a *subordinate elected body* on a *geographical basis*, of *functions at present exercised by Parliament*'.[3] But this is incomplete, since devolution also involves the transfer to a subordinate political executive of functions at present exercised by the central government. In the United Kingdom, devolution has come to be associated with proposals for conferring a measure of domestic self-government or 'home rule' on the various parts of the kingdom. Some have proposed a federal system as the best way to meet the demand for devolution, yet most proposals for devolution must be distinguished from federalism. Under devolution, while legislative and executive powers may be conferred by the centre upon subordinate bodies, the central organs retain residual constitutional authority, even if in practice the exercise of that authority is restricted so long as the scheme of devolution continues. But in a federal system, the powers of government at the two levels are determined by the constitution, which regulates the formal relations between the two tiers of government.

The position of Ireland apart, the United Kingdom has been governed

---

[1] In chs. 3, 14, 17 and 21.
[2] Kilbrandon Report, para. 543. On aspects of devolution, see H. Calvert (ed.), *Devolution*; J. P. Grant (ed.), *Independence and Devolution, the Legal Implications for Scotland*; V. Bogdanor, *Devolution*; T. Dalyell, *Devolution, The End of Britain?*
[3] Bogdanor, *op.cit.*, p. 2.

during the 20th century by a single Parliament and a single executive, within one political and administrative system. Local government has been reformed more than once, but most proposals for extending local government upwards so that it may become elected regional government have been resisted.[4] In fact, *ad hoc* regional structures have developed for administrative purposes within government departments, nationalised industries and services such as the National Health Service. In the 1960s, when much emphasis was placed on economic planning, regional economic planning boards and councils were established throughout Great Britain.[5] In 1972, much of the town planning work of the Department of Environment was decentralised to six regional offices. But these diverse developments fell far short of a system of regional government.

In the late 19th and early 20th centuries, the burning issue of Ireland led to proposals for 'home rule all round'. Bills proposing home rule for Scotland and in some cases for Wales were introduced in Parliament before and after the first world war.[6] An inconclusive Speaker's Conference on devolution was held in 1919.[7] Thereafter, except for the Liberals, who were a rapidly declining force, the major parties were interested primarily in controlling the British system of government from the centre. Scotland and Wales were regarded as presenting administrative rather than political problems; efforts were concentrated on developing suitable administrative arrangements, first for Scotland and later for Wales.

The Scottish Office system[8]

By 1939 the structure of the Scottish Office was fully established. Headed by a Cabinet minister, the Secretary of State for Scotland, its four functional departments were based in Edinburgh but were expected to co-operate closely with their Whitehall counterparts. The officials concerned were all part of the British civil service. After 1945 there was a tendency to transfer additional functions to the Scottish Office, although economic and industrial powers were retained by British departments. This system was reproduced on a smaller scale when in 1964 the Welsh Office was established in Cardiff, with its own Secretary of State, a step which built on earlier Welsh forms of administration.[9]

Under this system, many functions of domestic government have been entrusted to Scottish and Welsh departments. Other functions, such as inland

---

[4]   In Scotland, where regional councils were created by the Local Government (Scotland) Act 1973, these councils form the upper tier of a system of local government. The provincial councils recommended by the Redcliffe-Maud Commission on Local Government in England (Cmnd 4040, 1969) were never established. And see ch. 21.

[5]   See J. P. Mackintosh, *The Devolution of Power*, ch. 6.

[6]   See J. N. Wolfe (ed.), *Government and Nationalism in Scotland*, ch. 1 (G. Donaldson).

[7]   Cmd 692, 1920.

[8]   D. Milne, *The Scottish Office*; J. G. Kellas, *The Scottish Political System*, ch. 3; M. J. Keating and A. Midwinter, *The Government of Scotland*; N. and H. M. Drucker, (ed.) *Scottish Government Yearbook* 1980, ch. 8 (M. Macdonald and A. Redpath). And see Cmd 5563, 1937; and Cmd 9219, 1954.

[9]   See J. A. Andrews (ed.), *Welsh Studies in Public Law*, ch. 4 (I. L. Gowan).

revenue and social security, have been exercised in Scotland and Wales by British departments. In 1984, the functions of the five Scottish departments[10] included agriculture and fisheries, the arts, crofting, education (except universities and research), electricity, the environment, fire service, forestry, health, housing, industrial assistance, legal functions, local government, police, prisons, roads, rural and urban development, social work, sport, transport (except road freight and rail), tourism and town planning.[11] As well as being directly responsible for these matters to Parliament, the Secretary of State has an indirect interest in all matters affecting Scotland. He is able to represent Scottish interests to other departmental ministers individually, and in the Cabinet to ministers collectively. An important change in the control of public expenditure occurred in 1978, when the system of reviewing Scottish and Welsh expenditure by direct comparison of particular programmes (such as housing and education) with the English equivalents, gave way to one in which total Scottish and Welsh Office expenditure is determined, with each Secretary of State enjoying greater freedom to allocate funds within that total. Scottish and Welsh expenditure is now shown in separate territorial programmes in the annual survey of public expenditure.[12]

This system, which has sometimes but not very aptly been called 'administrative devolution', has many administrative and some political advantages. Under it much Scottish and Welsh business may be dealt with by civil servants familiar with the two countries. It enables uniform social and economic policies to be applied throughout Great Britain when this is felt to be desirable; but in Scotland and Wales it also enables some administrative initiatives to be taken and policies to be varied to take account of special needs. The fact that all new legislation passes through Westminster ensures strong central control. Separate laws are often made for Scotland, but these have to be fitted into Westminster's legislative programme and the Scottish legal system sometimes suffers because of this. The system also has political disadvantages. There is no political forum to consider Scottish and Welsh affairs, except what has been devised at Westminster in the form of the Grand Committees for Scotland and Wales, the standing committees for Scottish legislation, and since 1979 the Select Committees on Scottish and Welsh Affairs.[13] Politically the system is awkward when, as in 1970–4 and since 1979, the majority of M.P.s from Wales and Scotland are in the opposition at Westminster. But the system has (for those in charge of it) the great advantage of maintaining unified control within the executive and Parliament. The competing claims of England, Scotland and Wales are either not thought of in those terms or, if they are, they may be resolved within the system, rather than by negotiation or disputation between two or more governments.

---

[10] Agriculture and Fisheries; Development; Education; Home and Health; Industry. Another section of the Scottish Office is concerned with central services, including personnel, management and finance.

[11] The functions of the Welsh Office, which forms a single department, do not include electricity, fire service, legal functions, police and prisons; in agriculture and education, its functions are narrower than those of the Scottish Office.

[12] D. McCrone, (ed.) *Scottish Government Yearbook 1983*, Ch. 8 (R. Parry). And see ch. 16.

[13] See ch. 11 A, D.

The Stormont system

The Scottish Office system may be contrasted with that which obtained in Northern Ireland for over 50 years. Under the Government of Ireland Act 1920, Northern Ireland possessed her own executive (Governor, Prime Minister, Cabinet and civil service departments) and a legislature of two Houses, the Senate and the House of Commons, which sat at Stormont. Northern Ireland retained representation at Westminster, although on a reduced scale, and was subject to Westminster's legislative supremacy. By the 1920 Act, certain subjects were reserved exclusively for the United Kingdom authorities. These included laws in respect of the Crown, treaties and foreign relations, the armed forces and defence, coinage, nationality, merchant shipping, wireless telegraphy, aerial navigation, the postal services, customs and excise and income tax. Subject to these matters, the Stormont Parliament had power 'to make laws for the peace, order and good government of Northern Ireland'.[14] Constitutional issues might be referred for decision to the Judicial Committee of the Privy Council[15] but an Act of the Northern Ireland Parliament which exceeded its legal competence (for example, by legislating with respect to the armed forces)[16] could be held void by the ordinary courts. Certain taxing powers were exercised by Stormont, but in practice Northern Ireland became heavily dependent on the United Kingdom for financial support. On many matters, such as the social security system, the apparent legislative freedom of Stormont was illusory, since the agreed policy was that Northern Ireland should be entitled to the same benefits as were available in Great Britain. This led to much identical legislation being passed in Stormont and at Westminster. The legal limits on the powers of Stormont proved to be of no great significance, since Westminster frequently found it convenient to legislate for Northern Ireland, whether or not a matter had been transferred to Stormont. The courts were rarely called on to interpret the Act of 1920, and when they were, they seemed reticent in matters of constitutional interpretation. Even in respect of religious matters, where the 1920 Act sought to ensure religious equality, little use was made of the courts.[17] In political conditions under which the Unionist party remained in power throughout the life of Stormont, the majority of the people in Northern Ireland (but not the permanent minority) were able to exercise more influence on the government of their own affairs than if Northern Ireland had been ruled directly from London.[18] The relationship between the United Kingdom and Northern Ireland under this system has sometimes been described as quasi-federal. It lacked the essential qualities of a federal relationship, since at any time Westminster could legislate in derogation of the transfer of powers to Stormont. The Stormont system came to an end, not because in the abstract it was a bad system, but because of deep seated political issues in Ireland, which it had contained for 50 years but could not solve.

---

14   Government of Ireland Act 1920, s. 4(1). And see H. Calvert, *Constitutional Law in Northern Ireland*.
15   Government of Ireland Act 1920, s. 51.
16   *R. (Hume et al.)* v. *Londonderry Justices* [1972] N.I.L.R. 91; Northern Ireland Act 1972.
17   Government of Ireland Act 1920, s. 5; and Calvert, *op. cit.*, ch. 14.
18   *Cf.* R.J. Lawrence, *The Government of Northern Ireland*, ch. 10. And see D. Birrell and A. Murie, *Policy and Government in Northern Ireland: Lessons of Devolution*.

Royal Commission on the Constitution 1969–73

Increased electoral support for the Welsh and Scottish nationalist parties from the mid-1960s made it necessary for both Conservative and Labour parties, and the English generally, to reconsider the position of Scotland and Wales. In 1968, a Scottish Constitutional Committee was appointed by Mr Heath, then Leader of the Conservative opposition. The report of the committee, published in 1970, recommended the creation of a directly elected Scottish Convention, to which would be transferred the main stages of Scottish legislation from Westminster. But the Convention was not to have independent legislative powers, nor was a separate executive responsible to the Convention for Scottish administration to be created.[19]

In 1969, the Labour government appointed a royal commission on the constitution. With wide but vague terms of reference, the commission's primary duty was 'to examine the present functions of the central legislature and government in relation to the several countries, nations and regions of the United Kingdom'. The commission's majority report (known as the Kilbrandon report after Lord Kilbrandon, the commission's second chairman) together with a long memorandum of dissent signed by two members, were published in 1973.[20] The report examined the general reasons for public dissatisfaction with government in the United Kingdom but concentrated its attention on the position of Scotland, Wales and the English regions. Rejecting separatism and federalism, the latter after a somewhat cursory examination, the report examined possible forms of devolution.

Three forms of devolution were identified: (a) administrative devolution (the Scottish Office system); (b) executive devolution, under which directly elected regional assemblies might be responsible for devising regional policies and administering regional affairs, in accordance with laws and general policies made in London; and (c) legislative devolution (broadly the Stormont system) under which power to legislate, to settle policies and to administer might be devolved on elected assemblies in respect of specified subjects, with Westminster retaining ultimate power to legislate on all matters. Even amongst the eleven who signed the majority report, there were many differences of opinion in their positive recommendations for the future. Eight members favoured legislative devolution for Scotland; only six favoured legislative devolution for Wales. The report recommended that the two assemblies should be elected by proportional representation, that executive powers should be vested in ministers drawn from the assemblies, that the representation of Scotland and Wales in the Commons should be reduced to a number proportionate to their population,[21] and that the Secretaries of State for Scotland and Wales should disappear. The new assemblies were to be financed from the United Kingdom exchequer, the amount of an annual block grant being settled by an independent exchequer board. As regards England, the majority favoured the creation of regional co-ordinating and advisory councils, in part appointed by local authorities and in part nominated by central government.

---

[19] *Scotland's Government*, 1970 (the Douglas-Home report).
[20] Cmnd 5460 and 5460-I, 1973, discussed by T. C. Daintith (1974) 37 M.L.R. 544.
[21] For Scotland, a reduction from 71 to 57; for Wales, from 36 to 31.

The memorandum of dissent, by Lord Crowther-Hunt and Professor Peacock, adopted a broader approach to the question of constitutional reform. Stressing the importance of establishing a uniform system of government throughout Great Britain, it recommended directly elected assemblies for Scotland, Wales and five English regions, to be responsible for the execution of social and economic policies for their areas, within a framework of national laws. It also recommended other changes, such as revised parliamentary procedures and a reformed House of Lords.

Despite the differences of opinion within the commission, the Kilbrandon report brought nearer the prospect of some form of devolution to elected assemblies in Scotland and Wales. Demands for changes in the government of Scotland and Wales were made, which it seemed could not be met by further development of the Scottish Office system. It fell to the Labour government of 1974–9 to decide how to implement the Kilbrandon recommendations. The government's approach to the matter was influenced by the fact that after 1976 its continuance in office depended on the support of the Liberal party and of nationalist M.P.s from Scotland and Wales. The future prospect of a Labour government at Westminster might also depend on Labour's continued representation from Scotland and Wales.

The Scotland Act 1978 and the Wales Act 1978

In September 1974, the government announced that it accepted the broad conclusion in the Kilbrandon report that a further measure of devolution was desirable, and undertook to establish elected assemblies in Scotland and Wales. But the government departed from the Kilbrandon report on many points. Thus the Scottish but not the Welsh assembly was to have legislative powers; the assemblies were to be elected by the traditional voting system, not by proportional representation; the Secretaries of State for Scotland and Wales were to continue, retaining important powers in branches of government which were not devolved, and also providing the constitutional link between the new assemblies and the UK government and Parliament; the two assemblies were to be financed by a block grant determined annually by the government and voted by the Westminster Parliament; Welsh and Scottish representation at Westminster was not to be reduced. The government stated that its concern was 'to foster democratic control over the increasingly complex processes of modern government and to bring government closer to the people'.[22]

In 1975, under increasing pressure from supporters and opponents of devolution, the government described in more detail what it called a 'massive handover to the new elected Assemblies of responsibility for the domestic affairs of Scotland and Wales, within the firm continuing framework of the United Kingdom'.[23] The proposals first took legislative form in the Scotland and Wales Bill 1976. This cumbrous and poorly-drafted Bill ran into immediate difficulties in the Commons. After ten days in committee, only three clauses had been examined. The government's 'guillotine' motion, seeking to allocate 20 more days for the Bill to pass through the Commons, was defeated

---

[22]   Cmnd 5732, 1974, p. 10.
[23]   Cmnd 6348, 1975, p. 1. And see Cmnd 6585, 1976.

by 312–283,[24] a defeat which led to the shelving of the Bill.

In the 1977–8 session, two Bills were laid in the Commons providing separately for Scotland and Wales. This time the government succeeded in carrying a motion to allocate time for the two Bills in the Commons. After protracted proceedings in both Houses, both Bills received the royal assent on 31 July 1978.

The Scotland Act 1978[25] proposed to devolve legislative powers on Scottish domestic affairs to an assembly, and executive powers to a Scottish executive. The single-chamber assembly was to consist of about 150 members, elected every four years, although by a two-thirds majority of its members the assembly could seek an earlier dissolution. The electoral system was to be broadly the same as that for parliamentary elections, and proportional representation was not adopted. The legislative measures of the assembly were to be known as Scottish Assembly Acts when they had been passed by the assembly and approved by the Queen in Council. The legislative competence of the assembly was limited to matters devolved by the Act. The Act provided for review of assembly Bills by the Judicial Committee of the Privy Council on grounds of *vires*; once a Scottish Assembly Act had been approved by the Queen in Council, its validity could be reviewed by the courts or the Judicial Committee, again on grounds of *vires*. The assembly was to have power to legislate on twenty-five groups of devolved matters including health, social welfare, education, housing, local government, land use, pollution, the countryside, transport, roads, harbours, agricultural land, fisheries, water, fire services, tourism, licensing, the courts and legal profession, tribunals and inquiries and matters of civil and criminal law. The Act laid down in great detail the precise extent of these powers, doing this often by reference to provisions in existing statutes. Not only was it extremely difficult to understand why certain matters of detail were devolved and others were not, but it was impossible to believe that the assembly could have exercised real legislative authority when faced with so many restrictions.

The Scottish Executive was to consist of the First Secretary and other Secretaries (in effect ministers) appointed from the party or parties which commanded a majority in the assembly. The office of Secretary of State for Scotland was to continue as a member of the British Cabinet, shorn of most administrative responsibilities (except for reserved matters, such as the police) but gaining oversight of the assembly and executive. For example, the Secretary of State was to have residual power to override Scottish Acts and executive decisions when this seemed necessary to maintain essential UK interests; any such intervention was to be subject to confirmation by the Westminster Parliament. The devolved services were to be paid for entirely by a block grant from the UK Consolidated Fund, and the assembly had no power of its own for raising revenue by taxation. The staff of the executive was to consist of civil servants transferred from the Scottish Office but remaining members of the UK civil service.

---

24   H. C. Deb., 22 Feb. 1977, col. 1362.
25   Bogdanor, *op.cit.*, ch. 7; and see the annotations in *Current Law Statutes* 1978.

The Wales Act 1978 sought to create a Welsh assembly, a body of 80 members elected every four years. The assembly was to perform a variety of executive functions previously vested by statute in the Secretary of State for Wales and other ministers, relating to such matters as local government, education, housing, fire services, health and social services, pollution, land use, tourism, transport and highways. Unlike the Scottish assembly, the Welsh assembly was to have no power to amend Acts of Parliament. The assembly's affairs were to be conducted by a system of committees. The financial arrangements were to be similar to those for the Scottish assembly. The Secretary of State for Wales was to continue but with much reduced administrative duties. Like his Scottish counterpart, he was to have specific power (subject to confirmation by Parliament) to override decisions of the assembly.

The Labour government had intended that devolution to Scotland and Wales should come into operation only after an advisory referendum had been held in both countries. Against the wishes of the government, the Commons included what came to be known as the 40% rule, intended to guard against the possibility of a very low turn out in each referendum. By sections 85 of the Scotland Act and 80 of the Wales Act, the Secretary of State was required to lay before Parliament a draft order for the repeal of the legislation if it appeared to him that either those voting 'No' had been in the majority or that less than 40% of those entitled to vote had voted 'Yes'. The final decision on whether devolution would take effect was to be made by Parliament. Voting took place on 1 March 1979. In Wales, the result was a resounding 'No' vote: 58% of the electorate voted, and of those 79% voted 'No' and less than 21% voted 'Yes'. In Scotland, there was a small majority in favour of devolution (32.9% voted 'Yes', and 30.8% voted 'No') but over one-third of the electorate did not vote and the 40% rule was far from being satisfied. When the Scottish National Party failed to persuade the Labour government to seek an immediate vote in the Commons on the future of the 1978 Act, the S.N.P. withdrew its support from the government, a direct result of this being the government's defeat on a confidence motion on 28 March 1979. After the general election, at which the nationalists in Scotland and Wales polled badly, the incoming Conservative government offered no more than a nebulous prospect of all-party talks: the repeal of the Scotland and Wales Acts was approved by Parliament during June 1979.

The repeal of both Acts meant that devolution on the lines considered in the Kilbrandon report was unlikely to be attempted again for some time. One response later in 1979 to the needs of Scotland and Wales was the creation of two committees dealing with Scottish and Welsh affairs respectively, as part of the new system of select committees set up by the House of Commons.[26] These committees provide a useful means of assisting M.P.s to scrutinise the administration of Scotland and Wales but do not in themselves lead to any dispersal of the power to govern.

As was realised during the home rule debates in the late 19th century,[27] proposals for devolution raise many difficult questions, including (a) the

[26]   Ch. 11 D.
[27]   Bogdanor, *op.cit.*, ch. 2.

problem, once an elected assembly is created for part of the United Kingdom, of determining what the future representation of that part should be at Westminster; (b) whether the subordinate assembly should have its own power of raising revenue; and (c) the relationship between the legislative power vested in a subordinate assembly and the legislative supremacy of Westminster. The 1978 Acts did not provide adequate answers to these questions, the Labour government claiming that it was possible to change the machinery of government in Scotland and Wales without changing 'the firm continuing framework of the United Kingdom'.[28]

In 1984, the cause of devolution to Scotland was supported by the Labour party and by the Liberal/Social Democratic alliance, which favoured a general decentralisation of government throughout the United Kingdom. But the Conservative government remained firmly opposed to all proposals for political devolution.

Devolution and the regions of England

Although the Kilbrandon report had recommended regional co-ordinating councils for England, in a consultative document published in 1976[29] the government rejected the idea of an English assembly and of regional legislative assemblies. To allay English alarm at the prospect of Scottish and Welsh assemblies, the government argued that the range of controls over economic, financial and industrial matters which would be retained at the centre meant that devolution for Scotland and Wales would not in any way prejudice economic prospects for the English regions. The government suggested that the effective choice in England lay between the creation of elected regional assemblies with administrative functions (which could be done only by drawing away powers from central government, from local government or possibly from regional bodies such as water authorities), or the strengthening of regional advisory bodies, such as the regional economic planning councils, to improve communication between central departments and local authorities. Neither prospect was attractive to established interests in central and local government.

---

28 Cmnd 6348, 1975, p.l.
29 See *Devolution: The English Dimension*, 1976.

Chapter 23

The armed forces

In the interests of constitutional government and the rule of law, the exercise of the physical might of the modern state must be subject to democratic control. Experience of government at the hands of Cromwell's army led after the restoration of the monarchy in 1660 to a declaration by Parliament in the Militia Act 1661 that

the sole supreme government, command and disposition of the militia and of all forces by sea and land is, and by the laws of England ever was, the undoubted right of the Crown.

Subsequent attempts by Charles II and James II against parliamentary opposition to maintain their own armies led to the declaration in the Bill of Rights that

the raising or keeping of a standing army within the Kingdom in time of peace, unless it be with consent of Parliament, is against law.

This declaration remains important today, not because there is now any possibility that Parliament would withdraw authority for the continued maintenance of an army but because it asserts that the armed forces are constitutionally subordinate to Parliament.

Legislative authority for the armed forces[1]

The armed forces of the Crown include the army, the Royal Navy, the Royal Air Force, the women's services and the reserve forces. Since the Bill of Rights, statutory authority for the maintenance of armed forces on land during peacetime has never been granted on a permanent basis but only for limited periods. Statutory authority has been needed for three reasons: to overcome the Bill of Rights provision; to provide funds to pay for the armed forces; and to authorise discipline within the armed forces to be enforced by rules which differ from common law. Statutory authority was not needed to authorise the

---

[1] For the history of the legal position of the armed forces, see Maitland, pp. 275–80, 324–9, 447–62; Anson, vol. II(2), ch. 10.

maintenance of the navy, which had not aroused the suspicion of Parliament and therefore was not included in the prohibition in the Bill of Rights against a standing armed force. But naval discipline was from 1661 authorised by statute and the appropriation of funds by Parliament to maintain the navy has long been authorised annually on the same basis as for the other armed forces.

After the Bill of Rights, it became the custom of Parliament each year to pass a Mutiny Act, which gave authority for one year only to the Crown to maintain armed forces up to the limit of manpower stated in the Act and to enforce rules of discipline. Eventually what had become a lengthy and detailed collection of rules of military law was codified in the Army Act 1881. This code was until 1955 continued in force from year to year by the passing of an Act known until 1917 as the Army (Annual) Act and thereafter as the Army and Air Force (Annual) Act. Amendments to the 1881 Act could be made when necessary by the annual Act. When a separate Air Force was constituted in 1917, its discipline was governed by the Army Act 1881 with modifications.

By 1955 it had come to be accepted that parliamentary approval of the size of the armed forces was granted through parliamentary consideration of the defence estimates and the formal procedure for appropriating supply to the armed forces. Following a series of reports from Select Committees of the House of Commons[2] there were enacted the Army Act 1955 and the Air Force Act 1955. Each Act was in the first instance limited to a duration of twelve months but for a period of five years, it could be continued in force from year to year by resolution of each House of Parliament. At the end of the five years a further Act would be needed.[3]

The effect of this has been to use the constitutional requirement for regular approval of the armed forces as a device whereby the Commons may scrutinise periodically the rules and procedures of service discipline. The Acts which have been needed each quinquennium (the Armed Forces Acts of 1966, 1971, 1976 and 1981) have revised the disciplinary codes of the forces and related legislation. One feature of the procedure has been that each Armed Forces Bill has after second reading been referred to a select committee of the Commons, which has examined the Bill thoroughly, has made many constructive proposals for revising the law and has visited military prisons.[4] In 1971, the Naval Discipline Act 1957, which previously had been a permanent Act, was brought within the same system. There has been a tendency to make similar provision for the main matters of discipline in each of the armed forces.

In 1976, a proposal by the government to discontinue the need for annual resolutions of each House within the five-year period was not accepted by a select committee of the Commons; the committee wished the government to continue to provide an annual opportunity for a debate on the continuance of the Acts, even though in some years the resolution is approved without a debate.[5]

Legislative authority for maintaining the armed forces does not confer

---

[2] H.C. 244 and 331 (1951–2), 289 (1952–3) and 223 (1953–4).
[3] For an argument that these arrangements do not overcome the Bill of Rights prohibition on a standing army, see (1981) 4 *State Research* 149; *cf. The Times* 17 Jun. 1981.
[4] See *e.g.* H.C. 253 (1980–1), and see P. Rowe (1981) 44 M.L.R. 693.
[5] H.C. 429 (1975–6).

power on the executive to conscript citizens into the forces. Recruitment for the navy by impressment under the prerogative is now only a matter of history. In both world wars conscription was authorised by Parliament. After the second world war, conscription was continued under the National Service Act 1948 until its operation was brought to an end in 1960.[6] Like earlier legislation, the 1948 Act made special provision for conscientious objectors to military service.

As well as the full-time regular forces of the Crown, the reserve forces are maintained under statutory authority. The legislation makes provision for the recall of the reserve forces, in some circumstances by notice from the Secretary of State for Defence but, in the case of imminent national danger or great emergency, by an order of the Sovereign, signified by the Secretary of State and notified to Parliament; if Parliament is not sitting at the time, it must meet within five days.[7]

Ulster Defence Regiment

Following the report of an advisory committee set up in 1969 under Lord Hunt to advise on the police in Northern Ireland,[8] the Ulster Defence Regiment Act 1969 created a new part-time military force (in effect, in replacement of the Ulster Special Constabulary) called the Ulster Defence Regiment. The 1969 Act established the force as part of the armed forces of the Crown and provided for the control of its size by Parliament. It is a disciplined force, under the command of the General Officer Commanding, Northern Ireland, and liable to be called out, when needed, for emergency service in Northern Ireland in defence of life or property there against armed attack or sabotage.[9]

Central organisation for defence

Like other branches of central government, the armed forces are placed under the control of ministers of the Crown, who are in turn responsible to Parliament for them. Formerly each of the main services had its own ministerial head. Between the two world wars all three service ministers were usually in the Cabinet. Today the responsibility for a unified defence policy rests upon the Secretary of State for Defence, whose office has undergone several changes since the post of Minister of Defence was created and occupied by Winston Churchill in the second world war. In 1964, the Ministry of Defence became a unified ministry for the three services and absorbed the Admiralty, the War Office and the Air Ministry.[10] The present ministerial structure dates from May 1981, when the junior minister for the navy was dismissed after publicly criticising proposed reductions in Britain's naval strength. The Prime Minister promptly abolished the separate junior ministerial posts for the three services. The Ministry was in 1984 headed by the Secretary of State for Defence, with (a) a minister of state and a parliamentary under-secretary responsible for all the armed forces, and (b) a minister of state and a parliamentary under-secretary responsible for defence procurement and equipment.

---

6   For details, see 8th ed. of this work, pp. 394–6.
7   Reserve Forces Act 1980, s. 10.
8   Cmd 535, 1969 (Northern Ireland).
9   Reserve Forces Act 1980, ss. 24, 25.
10 Cmnd 2097, 1963.

All statutory powers for the defence of the realm which formerly were vested in the separate service ministers were in 1964 vested in the Secretary of State.[11] Within the Ministry of Defence, there is a Defence Council, which in 1984 consisted of the defence ministers, the Chief of the Defence Staff, the three service chiefs of staff, the Vice Chief of the Defence Staff, the Chief Scientific Adviser, the Chief of Defence Procurement and two Permanent Under-Secretaries of State. Beneath the Defence Council there are separate boards for the navy, the army and the air force, to whom is delegated management of the three services, including formal powers in relation to the regulation and discipline of each service. The chiefs of staff are the professional heads of the armed forces; through the Chiefs of Staff Committee, they give professional advice to the government on strategy and military operations and on the military implications of defence policy.

The creation of a unified Ministry of Defence was necessary because it had been found inadequate for a Minister of Defence to seek to control defence policy by coordinating the policies of three departments responsible to separate ministers. A unified ministry was also essential if the defence budget was to strike a proper balance between the commitments, resources and roles of the three services.

In 1971 there was established within the Ministry of Defence a Procurement Executive, with the duty of procuring supplies of defence equipment needed by the three services; the executive also has certain duties with which other ministries are concerned, in relation to aerospace and space procurement. The executive was established in the interests of accountable management; it was intended to work closely with other sections of the Ministry of Defence, and not to become an autonomous agency.[12] In 1984, further integration occurred when a unified central Defence Staff was created. There were also established an Office of Management and Budget and a single Equipment Policy Committee.[13]

Major questions of defence policy cannot be decided in purely military terms without reference to the government's financial and economic policies, that affect the size, disposition and equipment of the armed forces. The collective responsibility of the government for defence is exercised primarily through the Cabinet's Committee on Defence and Overseas Policy under the chairmanship of the Prime Minister. This includes the Foreign Secretary, the Chancellor of the Exchequer, the Home Secretary and the Secretary of State for Defence. In attendance on this committee are the Chief of the Defence Staff and the chiefs of staff of each of the three services if the business so requires. Senior civilian officials such as the Permanent Under-Secretary of State or the Chief Scientific Adviser may also attend.[14]

Parliamentary control of the armed forces

We saw in chapter 20 that the chain of command within the police stops with the chief constable and that neither local police authorities nor central government may give him instructions on the operational use of the police. This is

---

[11] Defence (Transfer of Functions) Act 1964.
[12] Cmnd 4641, 1971.
[13] Cmnd 9315, 1984.
[14] Cmnd 2097, 1963.

not the case with the armed forces. In the case of the army, for example, the line of command runs upwards from the private soldier, through his commanding officer and higher levels of command to the Chief of Staff for the army, the Chief of the Defence Staff and the Secretary of State for Defence. During active operations of course, many immediate decisions have to be taken by soldiers in the field. But there can be no doubt that the tasks which are undertaken by the armed forces, the objectives which they are set, and the manner in which they carry out these tasks are matters for which the government is accountable to Parliament – whether it be the conduct of troops in Northern Ireland, the use of the army to empty dustbins during a prolonged strike by local authority workers (as in Glasgow in 1975), the making of a controversial public speech by a high-ranking army officer, or the sinking of the Argentinian ship *General Belgrano* during the Falklands conflict in 1982. The full range of parliamentary procedures which are available in respect of other branches of central government may be used in respect of defence and the armed forces. Thus the Public Acccounts Committee has often investigated cases of excessive spending by the services. Since 1979 the Defence Committee of the House of Commons has regularly examined the Ministry of Defence's annual statement on the defence estimates. It has also conducted major inquiries into strategic nuclear weapons policy, the handling of press and public information during the Falklands conflict, and the future defence of the Falkland Islands.[15] Defence policies and expenditure are often matters of keen political debate in the House. As mentioned earlier, military law has received close scrutiny from select committees appointed to consider the Armed Forces Bills. Members of the forces are entitled under service regulations to communicate with M.P.s on all matters, including service matters, so long as they do not disclose secret information, but it is the policy of the Ministry of Defence that wherever possible servicemen should pursue the normal channels of complaint open to them through superior officers.[16] While allegations of maladministration on the part of the Ministry of Defence may be referred by M.P.s for investigation by the Parliamentary Commissioner for Administration, it is outside his jurisdiction to investigate action relating to appointments, pay, discipline, pensions, or other personnel matters affecting service in the armed forces; nor may he investigate complaints relating to the conduct of judicial proceedings under military law.[17] A proposal for a military ombudsman has not received very much support.[18]

The nature of military law[19]

Military law is the internal law of the armed forces, administered by officers with appropriate authority, by courts-martial and on appeal by the Courts-Martial Appeal Court. It is made by Parliament and, under the authority of Parliament, by the defence authorities by means of Queen's Regulations.

---

15   See respectively H.C. 35, 130 (1980–1), H.C. 17–I (1982–3) and H.C. 154 (1982–3).
16   Erskine May, p. 168; Army Act 1955, ss. 180–1. *Cf.* the Stevenson case, H.C. 112 (1954–5).
17   Parliamentary Commissioner Act 1967, sched. 3, paras. 6, 10.
18   Cmnd 4509, 1971, app. 5.
19   See the Manual of Military Law for a complete account, and J. Stuart-Smith (1969) 85 L.Q.R. 478 for a lucid introduction.

There is also power to make rules of procedure for the administration of military law. Military law must be distinguished from 'martial law', a term used to describe the situation which arises when the normal processes of law and justice have broken down and the military exercise *de facto* authority over the public at large.[20] Strictly speaking, military law applies to the army alone. In fact air force law was founded upon the army's scheme of discipline and closely resembles it. Discipline within the navy derived from quite separate statutes but is today being brought closer to army and air force law.

Military law is the basis of discipline in the armed forces, for a disciplined force could not be run with reliance on the ordinary law applicable to civilians. For example, an employee's misconduct in private employment may lead to his being dismissed, as when he refuses to obey an instruction which the employer is contractually entitled to give him. Misconduct by a soldier may eventually lead to his discharge, but a citizen who has agreed to enter the armed forces necessarily gives up the freedom to walk out on the job which a private employee has. In the case of a conscript, his freedom of decision has been taken from him by the legislator.

The Army Act 1955, and its counterparts for the air force and the navy, create a large number of offences, including mutiny, insubordination, disobedience to orders, desertion, absence without leave, malingering, and, by section 69, a residual offence of 'any act, conduct or neglect to the prejudice of good order and military discipline'. It is also an offence against the Army Act, section 70, for any person subject to military law to commit, whether in the United Kingdom or elsewhere, a civil offence *i.e.* an offence punishable by English criminal law or which, if committed in England, would be so punishable.

Because of the loss of freedom involved in military service, it is important that, in the absence of conscription, enlistments into the forces are voluntary. The formal process of enlistment is laid down by the Army Act. The terms of engagement upon which members of the forces are enlisted are governed by regulations made by the Defence Council; it is provided that the statutory rights of existing members of the forces are not to be varied or revoked by a change of regulations except with their consent.[21] The former scheme of recruitment to the army through the boy-soldiers scheme was criticised on the ground that it made inadequate provision for a soldier on coming of full age to change his mind from the original consent given while under age.[22]

Courts-martial
The Army Act regulates the constitution and proceedings of the military courts. A commanding officer has power to dispose of many charges summarily (his power to order detention for an offence was increased from 28 to 60 days by the Armed Forces Act 1976) or in more serious cases to investigate the charge with a view to determining whether or not to send the accused for trial by court-martial. Courts-martial are convened by a senior military officer to try a particular charge. The court is always constituted of serving officers.

---

[20]   Ch. 29 A.
[21]   Armed Forces Act 1966, s. 2.
[22]   Cmnd 4509, 1971 (the Donaldson report).

Trial by court-martial is generally held in public and in many respects (for example, with regard to the rules of evidence and the presumption of innocence) it resembes a trial in an ordinary criminal court. There is however no jury and the president of the court is not a professional judge. To minimise the chances of an unjust result, a finding of guilt and the sentence of the court are both subject to confirmation by higher military authority. A person sentenced by a court-martial may also petition higher authority for a review of the sentence.

The proper administration of military law by courts-martial is supervised by the Judge Advocate General, who is a barrister or advocate of ten years' standing appointed by the Crown on the recommendation of the Lord Chancellor. He may be removed from office only for inability or misbehaviour.[23] Amongst his duties, which do not include the task of prosecuting, is to provide a legally qualified judge advocate to attend the more important courts-martial. The judge advocate's function at a court-martial is to give expert and independent advice to the court on the law and to summarise the evidence; although he must act judicially, he is not a member of the court and does not retire with the court when it is considering its findings. The proceedings of all courts-martial are reviewed in the office of the Judge Advocate General to detect miscarriages of justice.

Courts-Martial Appeal Court

An important link between military courts and the ordinary judicial system was formed in 1951 when the Courts-Martial Appeal Court was established. The court and its jurisdiction are now governed by the Courts-Martial (Appeals) Act 1968. The judges of the court are the Lord Chief Justice, the judges of the Court of Appeal, and such of the judges of the Queen's Bench Division of the High Court and the corresponding judges for Scotland and Northern Ireland as may be nominated for the purpose, together with such other persons of legal experience as the Lord Chancellor may appoint. The court is constituted by an uneven number of judges, not less than three sitting; it normally sits in London. A person convicted by a court-martial may appeal to the court against his conviction, but leave to appeal must be obtained from the court itself. Only one application for leave to appeal may be made.[24] Before he can apply for leave to appeal, a convicted person must first await confirmation of the sentence and, unless he is under sentence of death, must petition the Defence Council for the quashing of his conviction. In deciding whether to grant leave to appeal, the court must have regard to any opinion of the Judge Advocate General on whether the case is a fit one for appeal. In deciding an appeal, the court must consider whether a conviction is in all the circumstances unsafe or unsatisfactory or involves a mistake of law or whether a material irregularity occurred during the court-martial. A further appeal to the House of Lords lies by leave of the court or of the House on a point of law of general public importance.[25]

---

[23]   Courts-Martial (Appeals) Act 1951, ss. 29–32. For the history of the Judge Advocate General, see Stuart-Smith, *op. cit.*

[24]   *R.* v. *Grantham* [1969] 2 Q.B. 574.

[25]   *E.g. Cox* v. *Army Council* [1963] A.C. 48 and *R.* v. *Warn* [1970] A.C. 394.

Judicial control of military jurisdiction

Courts-martial are limited to the powers conferred on them by statute. The prerogative orders of certiorari or prohibition lie, at the discretion of the Queen's Bench Divisional Court, to control the limits of jurisdiction of a court-martial, just as they lie to control all inferior courts or tribunals on jurisdictional matters.[26] Where as a result of a decision by a court-martial a person is detained in prison, he may recover his freedom by habeas corpus if he can show that the decision was outside the jurisdiction of the court-martial, for example, because he was not a person subject to military law.[27] These remedies were especially important before the creation of the Courts-Martial Appeal Court. In fact the Divisional Court had come to take a narrow view of the extent to which it could intervene in imposing proper standards of justice upon courts-martial and was inclined to intervene only when there was a clear excess of jurisdiction and not when serious procedural errors had occurred.[28]

This disinclination to intervene in the decisions of courts-martial may have stemmed from a wider reluctance on the part of the courts to become involved in disciplinary grievances for which military channels of redress exist. This reluctance was seen at work in cases in which former soldiers sought to recover damages from the military authorities or from individual officers who had been concerned with disciplinary proceedings against them. In one such case, *Heddon* v. *Evans*,[29] McCardie J. drew a distinction between liability (a) for an act done in excess of or without jurisdiction by the military tribunal, which amounts to an assault, false imprisonment or other common law wrong and (b) for an act which, though within jurisdiction and in the course of military discipline, is alleged to have been done maliciously and without reasonable or probable cause. Only in the former case would the military officers be held liable. The problem resembles that which we have already encountered in relation to the individual liability of magistrates and the members of other inferior tribunals.[30] In the present context, it seems that it is still open to the House of Lords to decide whether an action will lie for the malicious abuse of military authority without reasonable and probable cause.[31] Probably the major obstacle which faces a former soldier in seeking to recover damages in respect of his dismissal from the service of the Crown is that at common law a soldier serves at the pleasure of the Crown.[32]

Who is subject to military law?

It is not only serving members of the armed forces and reservists undergoing training who are subject to military law. Various classes of civilians are also subject to military law. As well as civilian employees of the Ministry of Defence who accompany the armed forces when they are on active service, the Army

---

[26]   *Grant* v. *Gould* (1792) 2 H.Bl. 69; and see ch. 35.

[27]   *R.* v. *Governor of Wormwood Scrubs, ex p. Boydell* [1948] 2 K.B. 193.

[28]   *E.g. R.* v. *Secretary of State for War, ex p. Martyn* [1949] 2 All E.R. 242, and see D. C. Holland [1950] C.L.P. 173; de Smith, *Judicial Review*, p. 146.

[29]   (1919) 35 T.L.R. 642. And see *Dawkins* v. *Paulet* (1869) L.R. 5 Q.B.D. 94.

[30]   Ch. 19 A.

[31]   *E.g. Fraser* v. *Balfour* (1918) 34 T.L.R. 502.

[32]   Ch. 36.

Act 1955 makes subject to military law, albeit with modifications, civilians who are employed outside the United Kingdom within the limits of the command of any officer commanding a body of the regular forces. Also subject to military law are the families of members of the armed forces who are residing with them outside the United Kingdom, and even relatives merely staying with a service family on holiday.[33] The main effect of this is to make the families of British servicemen in Germany and elsewhere subject to be tried under military law for 'civil offences', defined by section 70 of the 1955 Act as acts or omissions punishable under English law or which, if committed in England, would be so punishable. In *Cox* v. *Army Council*,[34] it was held that a 'civil offence' for this purpose included the offence of careless driving on a public road in Germany. In view of various difficulties which had been encountered in entrusting such extensive jurisdiction over civilians to courts-martial (for example, how were juvenile offenders to be dealt with?) the Armed Forces Act 1976 authorised the Secretary of State for Defence with the approval of the Lord Chancellor to specify areas abroad to be served by a Standing Civilian Court. The court deals with the less serious offences committed by civilians in the area concerned. It consists of a legally qualified magistrate, appointed by the Lord Chancellor to the staff of the Judge Advocate General; for dealing with juvenile offenders, he sits with two other persons.

Dual jurisdiction

A person subject to military law continues to be subject to the ordinary criminal law and to the jurisdiction of the criminal courts in the United Kingdom. In the context of military law, by a somewhat confusing usage which will be followed here, the ordinary criminal courts are referred to as 'civil courts' to distinguish them from military courts. Except so far as Parliament provides otherwise, the soldier's obligations under the Army Act and Queen's Regulations are in addition to his duties as a citizen. As we have already seen, section 70 of the Army Act provides that a civil offence committed by a person subject to military law may be dealt with as an offence against military law; but certain serious crimes (including treason, murder, manslaughter and rape) must, if committed in the United Kingdom, be tried by the competent civil court. In practice most criminal offences committed by members of the armed forces in the United Kingdom are dealt with in peace time by the civil courts. The decision rests with the civil prosecutor: offences affecting the person or property of a civilian will usually be prosecuted in the civil courts.[35]

Where a person subject to military law has been tried for an offence by court-martial or has been dealt with summarily by his commanding officer, a civil court is debarred from trying him subsequently for an offence which is substantially the same as that offence.[36] Apart from this there is no restriction on a civil court trying a member of the armed forces for an offence under criminal law. A person tried by a civil court in the United Kingdom or elsewhere is not liable to be tried again under military law in respect of the same

---

[33]   Army Act 1955, s. 209 and sch. 5. And see G. J. Borrie (1969) 32 M.L.R. 35.
[34]   [1963] A.C. 48.
[35]   Stuart-Smith, *op. cit.*, p. 492.
[36]   Armed Forces Act 1966, s. 25.

offence.[37] In general, a person who has ceased to be subject to military law is liable to be tried under military law for offences committed while he was so subject, but only within prescribed time limits after he ceased to be subject to military law (three months in the case of summary proceedings and six months in the case of trial by court-martial).[38]

Conflict of duty

Does the dual jurisdiction of the military and civil courts lead to a possible conflict of duty for the soldier? In theory there is no conflict since military law is part of the law of the land and a soldier is only required to obey orders which are lawful.[39] If an order involves a breach of the general law, a soldier is not only under no obligation to obey it but is under an obligation not to obey it. But in practice, particularly when troops are operating in a peace-keeping role within the United Kingdom at a time when the civil courts are functioning, as now in Northern Ireland, the soldier may be placed in an awkward position. He is not trained, nor may he have time, to assess the legality of an order. But if, for example, unlawful injuries are inflicted on a citizen as the result of compliance, the soldier may be liable to an action for damages or to a criminal prosecution.[40] In principle, the defence of obedience to the order of a superior is not accepted by the civil courts if the order is unlawful. But if a soldier disobeys an order claiming that it is unlawful, a court-martial may hold that it was lawful. The practical difficulty for the soldier is only partially eased by the possibility of an appeal to the Courts-Martial Appeal Court, whose judges are in a position to ensure that military law and the ordinary law do not conflict; indeed their duty is to use their powers 'so far as they think it necessary or expedient in the interests of justice'.[41] But it may be better to leave the soldier in a position of some difficulty, and for the circumstances to be relied on in mitigation of a criminal offence, than to place him and thus the army outside the ordinary law.

There is little direct authority on the matter. In *Keighley* v. *Bell*, Willes J. expressed the opinion that if a prosecution results from obedience to an order, the soldier who obeys it is not criminally liable unless the order was necessarily or manifestly illegal.[42] This opinion was followed during the Boer War by a special court in South Africa which acquitted of murder a soldier who had shot a civilian in obedience to an unlawful order given to him by his officer,[43] a decision which today seems an alarming one in view of the facts. It would seem that for the defence to succeed the mistaken belief in the legality of the order must be reasonable, and this would be a matter for the jury to decide. In a Scottish case, *Her Majesty's Advocate* v. *Hawton and Parker*, when a naval officer

---

37 Army Act 1955, s. 134.
38 Army Act 1955, s. 132(3), amended by Armed Forces Act 1981, s. 6. The time limit does not apply to mutiny, desertion nor, with the consent of the Attorney-General, offences committed outside the UK.
39 Army Act 1955, s. 34.
40 In the case of injuries to another soldier, protection against civil liability is given by the Crown Proceedings Act 1947, s. 10: ch. 36.
41 Courts-Martial (Appeals) Act 1968, s. 1(3).
42 (1866) 4 F. & F. 763, 790.
43 *R.* v. *Smith* (1900) 17 Cape of Good Hope S.C.R. 561.

and a marine were charged with killing a fisherman on a trawler which was being intercepted by a naval vessel, Lord Justice General McNeill said: 'it was the duty of the subordinate to obey his superior officer, unless the order given by his superior was so flagrantly and violently wrong that no citizen could be expected to obey it'.[44] This test is materially different from that proposed by Willes J. but there was in the Scottish case no order to kill. In the circumstances in which British troops have been used in Northern Ireland, the question of criminal liability for the death or injury of a civilian will normally depend not on the legality of army orders but on whether a soldier's use of firearms is reasonably justifiable in the immediate circumstances.[45] When in 1971 unlawful interrogation methods were used against certain internees in Northern Ireland,[46] civil liability to compensate for the injuries was accepted by the military authorities but the interrogators were not prosecuted; the question of legality seems not to have been considered at the time by those responsible.

The issue is not solely of importance within national law. In respect of the violation of the rules of international law relating to the conduct of war, the defence of superior orders had for many years been recognised by the Manual of Military Law, which contains the official view on the laws and usages of war. In 1944 the Manual was amended and it is now stated to be no defence for a person accused of a war crime to plead obedience to the orders of a government or of a superior, whether military or civil, or obedience to a national law. The plea of superior orders may however be put in mitigation of punishment. The amendment made in 1944 conforms with the Articles of the Nuremburg Charter of 1945 under which the International Military Court tried enemy leaders accused of major war crimes.[47]

Visiting Forces Act 1952

Just as it is necessary for British military jurisdiction to be exercised when British forces are stationed abroad, so it is necessary that foreign troops stationed in the United Kingdom should be able to enforce their own military law. This would be unlawful without the authority of Parliament. The Visiting Forces Act 1952 gave effect to an agreement reached between parties to the North Atlantic Treaty on the legal status of the armed forces of one state when stationed in the territory of another.[48] It also applies to forces from member states of the Commonwealth which are stationed in the United Kingdom, and it may be extended to forces from other countries by Order in Council. Under Part I of the Act, the service courts and service authorities of visiting forces may exercise in the United Kingdom all the jurisdiction given to them by their own national law over all persons (including civilians accompanying the visiting forces) who may be subject to their jurisdiction; the death penalty may

---

44   (1861) 4 Irvine 58, 69.
45   The case of Marine Bek, *The Times*, 31 Mar. 1971; *A.-G. for Northern Ireland's Reference (No. 1 of 1975)* [1977] A.C. 105; *Farrell* v. *Secretary of State for Defence* [1980] 1 All E.R. 166. And see ch. 29 A.
46   Ch. 6.
47   Arts. 7 and 8 (Cmd 6668, 1945).
48   Cmd 8279, 1951.

not, however, be carried out in the United Kingdom unless under United Kingdom law the death sentence could have been passed (section 2). The Act excludes the jurisdiction of criminal courts in the United Kingdom over members of visiting forces only if the alleged offence (a) arises out of and in the course of military duty; or (b) is one against the person of a member of the same or another visiting force, for example, murder or assault; or (c) is committed against property of the visiting force or of a member thereof (section 3). The service authorities of the visiting force may however waive jurisdiction over such an offence. A member of a visiting force who has been tried by his own service court cannot be put on trial in a United Kingdom court for the same offence (section 4). Police powers of arrest, search etc. in respect of offences against United Kingdom law may still be exercised notwithstanding the jurisdiction of the visiting service authorities, but the police may deliver an arrested member of a visiting force into the custody of that force (section 5). The 1952 Act also makes provision for the settlement by the Secretary of State for Defence of certain civil claims in respect of acts or omissions of members of visiting forces (section 9).

In Part II of the 1952 Act, section 13 confers important powers on the police and on United Kingdom courts to arrest and hand over into the custody of the appropriate visiting force persons who are deserters or absentees without leave from the forces of any country to which the Act applies. In *R. v. Thames Justices, ex parte Brindle,*[49] the Court of Appeal held that this power could be exercised in respect of any person who had deserted from any of the forces of a country to which the Act applied, and was not restricted to persons who had deserted from visiting forces while they were serving in the United Kingdom; thus a United States citizen who deserted from a unit of the US army in Germany and came to England could be handed over to the US authorities in England, who might then return him in custody to the USA.

---

[49] [1975] 3 All E.R. 941. And see *R. v. Tottenham Magistrates' Court, ex p. Williams* [1982] 2 All E.R. 705.

Chapter 24

The United Kingdom and the Commonwealth

It is difficult to imagine a bigger contrast of legal and constitutional styles than that between the EEC and the Commonwealth. We saw in chapter 8 that the EEC derives its existence from treaties entered into by the member states. It was created specifically for purposes stated in the treaties, primarily to further the economic interests of a group of adjoining states in Western Europe. Its machinery, which depends on a unique system of law enforceable in the courts of member states, includes organs exercising legislative, executive and judicial functions; and since 1979, there has been an elected parliament for the Community. By contrast, the Commonwealth evolved uncertainly and was never created; as an international organisation, it has a fragile existence, based on mutual understandings rather than legal formality; it provides a loose framework for international association and co-operation in various economic, cultural and educational activities. The members of the Commonwealth are drawn with remarkable heterogeneity from across the world, sharing only the historical and often haphazard qualification of having had some part to play in Britain's imperial past. As a friendly, inter-racial association of young and old nations, representing a quarter of the world's population, the Commonwealth enables bridges to be built between the continents, but its political foundations could not support a massive organisational edifice.

For two reasons this chapter is short, shorter indeed than the political significance of the subject deserves. First, much of what was previously to be described as the constitutional law of the colonies and the Commonwealth has become of historic interest only, so far as the law of the United Kingdom is concerned.[1] Second, the structure of the Commonwealth is scarcely a matter of law at all. Written constitution it has none, nor has it organs of government in any formal sense.

Dependence and independence

The end of the British Empire was brought about by a protracted historical process in which the United Kingdom's colonies and other dependent terri-

---

[1] The main current works are K. Roberts-Wray, *Commonwealth and Colonial Law* and W. Dale, *The Modern Commonwealth*. See also K. C. Wheare, *The Constitutional Structure of the Commonwealth* and S. A. de Smith, *The New Commonwealth and its Constitutions*.

tories overseas first received some kind of representative legislature; then acquired responsible self-government in domestic matters while still being subject to the overriding authority of Westminster and Whitehall, particularly in matters of defence, external relations and other matters affecting the imperial power; and then in due course achieved national independence. The conferring of independence means that the territory becomes a separate entity in international law, having its own organs of government with power to determine its own policies, even if for political or economic reasons it may not in fact be a very strong nation. While imperial rule continued, there was a great body of law relating to the powers and duties of the colonial authorities: the rule of law was far from being a notion confined to the internal affairs of the United Kingdom.[2] Superimposed on the body of colonial law, in the late 19th and early 20th centuries, came to be a rich layer of conventional rules and practices out of which grew the concept of dominion status. The Statute of Westminster 1931 gave legislative effect to some of these conventions; in the case of the older dominions (Australia, New Zealand, Canada, South Africa), this marked the legal transformation from colonial to dominion status. The period after the second world war saw the rapid progress of numerous other territories from dependence to independence: and dominion status in turn gave way to the status of member of the Commonwealth. In 1984, in addition to the United Kingdom, there were some 48 member states of the Commonwealth.[3]

While there continue to be some dependent territories of the United Kingdom overseas, the list is short. In 1984, it included Anguilla, Bermuda, the Cayman Islands, the Falkland Islands, Gibraltar, Hong Kong, Montserrat, and other small islands. Under the West Indies Act 1967, several Caribbean islands ceased to be colonies and received the status of associated states, the British government remaining responsible only for their defence, external affairs and other reserved matters.[4] But by 1984 the associated states had all become wholly independent, except that Anguilla, which previously had formed an associated state with St. Kitts–Nevis, had under the Anguilla Act 1980 resumed colonial status.

Since most of the former dependent territories of the United Kingdom have moved from dependence to independence, it is not proposed to summarise the various legal rules which applied to different forms of dependent territory: but some general legislative aspects of the development of the Commonwealth will now be examined.

The Colonial Laws Validity Act 1865

The system of colonial government which the British usually pursued involved the creation of legislative, executive and judicial organs for a colony. Inevitably differences of opinion on matters of policy could arise between those holding office in the colony and in the imperial government. So too conflicts of law could arise between the laws made locally and the laws made in Westminster.

---

[2]   A perceptive study of the relationship between law and political development is given in Y. P. Ghai and J. P. W. B. McAuslan, *Public Law and Political Change in Kenya.*

[3]   The youngest members were Dominica, the Solomon Islands and Tuvalu (1978); Kiribati, St. Lucia and St. Vincent (1979); Vanuatu and Zimbabwe (1980); Antigua and Belize (1981); the Maldives (1982); St. Kitts-Nevis (1983).

[4]   M. Broderick (1968) 17 I.C.L.Q. 368; and K. R. Simmonds (1972) 21 I.C.L.Q. 151.

In practice it was usually found convenient for the power to create institutions of government in the dependent territories to be exercised by the Crown, whether under prerogative powers or under powers conferred on the Crown by statute (for example, the British Settlements Acts 1887 and 1945; the Foreign Jurisdiction Acts 1890 and 1913).[5] Where the Crown had created a legislature for a colony under the prerogative, the Crown could not still legislate for the colony unless in the grant of the legislature it had reserved the right to do so.[6] But the legal doctrine of the legislative supremacy of the imperial Parliament was not affected by the existence of subordinate legislatures. Thus the Westminster Parliament could if it wished legislate for the territories overseas, although it did so rarely in matters affecting the internal affairs of a colony which had its own legislature. Doubts arose in the mid-19th century concerning the powers of colonial legislatures to legislate contrary to English statutes or to the common law in England, mainly because of a series of decisions in South Australia by Mr Justice Boothby.[7] The Colonial Laws Validity Act 1865, 'An Act to remove doubts as to the validity of colonial laws', was passed to make it clear that the authority of a colonial legislature within its own sphere was not subordinate to the law in England, but only to Acts of the imperial Parliament applying to the colony.

The 1865 Act defined a colonial legislature as 'the authority, other than the Imperial Parliament or Her Majesty in Council, competent to make laws for any colony'; and a representative legislature as a colonial legislature comprising a legislative body of which one-half of the members were elected by the inhabitants of the colony. The Act applied only to colonies possessing legislatures. *Inter alia*, it enacted:

(*a*)   that an Act of the imperial Parliament extended to a colony only when it was made applicable to the colony 'by the express words or necessary intendment' of the Act (section 1);

(*b*)   that a colonial law which was in any respect repugnant to an Act of the imperial Parliament extending to the colony should be read subject to such Act and to the extent of such repugnancy, but not otherwise, should be void and inoperative (section 2);

(*c*)   that no colonial law should be void by reason only of repugnancy to the law of England, *i.e.* the common law as opposed to statute law (section 3); and

(*d*)   that every colonial legislature should have power to establish courts of judicature and every colonial representative legislature should have full power to make laws respecting the constitution, powers and procedure of its own body, provided that such laws were passed in such manner and form as might from time to time be required by any Act of Parliament, letters patent, Order in Council, or colonial law for the time being in force in the colony (section 5).

Thus, while the supremacy of the UK Parliament remained unchallenged, henceforth a colonial legislature could depart from the rules of the common law without fear of challenge in the courts, and was not required to observe

---

[5]   Roberts-Wray, ch. 5.

[6]   *Campbell* v. *Hall* (1774) 1 Cowp. 204, discussed by Roberts-Wray, pp. 157–63; and see *Sammut* v. *Strickland* [1938] A.C. 678.

[7]   See D. P. O'Connell and A. Riordan, *Opinions on Imperial Constitutional Law*, pp. 60–74.

Acts passed at Westminster unless expressly or by necessary implication they applied to the colony. It was the use by the New South Wales legislature of its powers under section 5 of the 1865 Act which gave rise to the case of *Attorney-General for New South Wales* v. *Trethowan*.[8] The 1865 Act still applies to the legislature of Hong Kong but the courts will not act to prevent a Bill passing through that legislature even though it may prove to be 'void and inoperative' by reason of section 2.[9]

Dominion status and the Statute of Westminster 1931[10]

Dominion status developed in the late 19th century as certain of the colonies (in particular Canada, New Zealand and Australia) began to move towards full nationhood. From 1887 there were periodic conferences of colonial governments meeting under the chairmanship of the Prime Minister of the United Kingdom. At the imperial conference in 1907, the term dominion was used in contrast with the term colony. After the First World War, the dominions had complete internal freedom from interference; they had been conceded the right of separate diplomatic representation in foreign countries; they acquired in 1923 the right to make separate treaties with foreign countries in the name of the Crown; and they were separate members of the League of Nations. The imperial conference in 1926, in words drawn up by a committee chaired by Lord Balfour, declared that Great Britain and the dominions were

autonomous Communities within the British Empire, equal in status, in no way subordinate one to another in any aspect of their domestic or external affairs, though united by a common allegiance to the Crown, and freely associated as members of the British Commonwealth of Nations.[11]

This important statement of equality of status and free association was not matched by the law, which had not kept pace with the development of constitutional convention. In law the dominions still had the status of colonies and were subject to the Colonial Laws Validity Act 1865. This gave rise to various limitations upon their legislative autonomy. These limitations included the obsolete power of the Crown to disallow legislation; the power of a dominion government to reserve Bills for the views of the UK government; the fact that dominion legislation would be void if repugnant to Acts of the imperial Parliament applying to a dominion; the supposed inability of the dominion legislatures to pass legislation having extraterritorial effect;[12] and the continuing power of the Westminster Parliament to legislate for the dominions, which however by convention was exercised only at the request and with the consent of a dominion. As an example of the subordinate legislative position

---

8   [1932] A.C. 526, p. 79 *ante.*
9   *Rediffusion (Hong Kong) Ltd* v. *A.-G. of Hong Kong* [1970] A.C. 1136; p. 79 *ante.*
10   K. C. Wheare, *The Statute of Westminster and Dominion Status*; G. Marshall, *Parliamentary Sovereignty and the Commonwealth*; Dale, *op. cit.*, part. 1. The older and more general meaning of 'dominion' in the phrase, 'Her Majesty's dominions', denotes all territories belonging to the Crown, including the UK and colonies: Roberts-Wray, *op. cit.*, pp. 23–29.
11   Cmd 2768, 1926, p. 14; Dale, *op. cit.*, p. 21.
12   *MacLeod* v. *A.-G. for New South Wales* [1891] A.C. 455; *Croft* v. *Dunphy* [1933] A.C. 156; Roberts-Wray, pp. 387–96; D. P. O'Connell (1957) 75 L.Q.R. 318; P. Wesley-Smith [1980] P.L. 150.

of the dominions, it was held that the Canadian Parliament lacked power to abolish appeals from Canadian criminal courts by special leave to the Privy Council.[13]

These limitations were mainly dealt with by the Statute of Westminster 1931, which sought to give effect to resolutions of imperial conferences of 1926, 1929 and 1930.[14] A notable feature of the Statute is a lengthy preamble, which records the background to the passing of the Statute and also contains declarations of principle and statements of conventional practice. Referring to the Crown as the symbol of the free association of the members of the British Commonwealth of Nations, united by a common allegiance to the Crown, the preamble stated that it would be in accord with the established constitutional position that any alteration in the law dealing with the succession to the throne or the royal style and titles should thereafter require the assent of the dominion parliaments as well as of the UK Parliament. The effect of this was seen in relation to the abdication of Edward VIII in 1936, when different courses of action were taken by the dominion governments and parliaments in assenting to the abdication.[15] After the accession of Elizabeth II in 1952, the royal style and titles were reconsidered by the monarchies within the Commonwealth and each formulated its own title.[16]

In the Statute of Westminster, the dominions were defined by enumeration: Canada, Australia, New Zealand, South Africa, the Irish Free State and Newfoundland.[17] Section 2 provided that the Colonial Laws Validity Act 1865 should cease to apply to the dominions (and to the provinces of Canada); that a dominion Parliament should have power to amend or repeal Acts of the UK Parliament in so far as they formed part of the law of that dominion; and that no law passed by a dominion Parliament should be void on the ground of repugnancy to an Act of the UK Parliament or to the law of England. By section 3, dominion Parliaments were declared to have full power to make laws having extra-territorial operation. Section 4 stated:

No Act of Parliament of the United Kingdom passed after the commencement of this Act shall extend, or be deemed to extend, to a Dominion as part of the law of that Dominion, unless it is expressly declared in that Act that that Dominion has requested, and consented to, the enactment thereof.

The meaning and effect of these provisions have been much discussed. Sections 2 and 3 enabled dominion Parliaments if they so chose (and subject to any limitations on legislative competence contained in their own constitutions) to abolish completely appeals to the Judicial Committee of the Privy Council.[18] Section 4 did not specify how a dominion was to 'request and consent' to the

---

13 *Nadan* v. *R.* [1926] A.C. 482; p. 429 *post*.
14 Cmd 2768, 1926; Cmd 3479, 1930; and Cmd 3717, 1930.
15 See K. H. Bailey (1937–8) 3 *Politica* 1, 147.
16 Wheare, *The Constitutional Structure of the Commonwealth*, pp. 164–8; p. 231 *ante*.
17 Only the first three are now members of the Commonwealth. The Irish Free State became the Republic of Ireland and left the Commonwealth in 1949; South Africa left the Commonwealth in 1961; and Newfoundland became a province of Canada in 1949.
18 *Moore* v. *A.-G. of Irish Free State* [1935] A.C. 484; *British Coal Corporation* v. *R.* [1935] A.C. 500; *A.-G. for Ontario* v. *A.-G. for Canada* [1947] A.C. 127.

passing of legislation at Westminster extending to the dominion: but in relation to Australia, section 9(3) provided that the request and consent should be given both by the Australian government and Parliament.[19]

Concerning section 4, Lord Sankey L. C. stated in the *British Coal Corporation* case:

it is doubtless true that the power of the imperial Parliament to pass on its own initiative any legislation that it thought fit extending to Canada remains unimpaired. Indeed, the imperial Parliament could, as a matter of abstract law, repeal or disregard section 4 of the Statute. But that is theory and has no relation to realities.[20]

Contrary views have been expressed by an eminent Australian constitutional lawyer.[21] And the Supreme Court of South Africa said, 'freedom once conferred cannot be revoked'.[22] While courts in the United Kingdom would be bound to observe legislation by Parliament which disregarded section 4, it is unlikely that Australian, Canadian or New Zealand courts would feel themselves under the same obligation to give effect to any such legislation from Westminster.

In dealing with the legal relationship between the dominions and the UK Parliament, the Statute of Westminster was also likely to affect the written constitutions of the dominions which were to be found in Acts of the United Kingdom Parliament (for example, the British North America Act 1867, the Commonwealth of Australia Act 1900, and the South Africa Act 1909). Was it intended that each dominion legislature should after 1931 be able to override the constitution under its new power to amend or repeal UK Acts in so far as they were part of the law of that dominion? In the case of Canada, section 7 provided that the Statute did not apply to the repeal or amendment of the British North America Acts 1867–1930 and that the legislative powers conferred by the Statute were confined to matters already within the competence of the dominion and provincial legislatures in Canada. This meant that it was still necessary for the UK Parliament to legislate if the Acts of 1867–1930 were to be amended. In 1949, the British North America (No. 2) Act 1949 empowered the Canadian Parliament to amend the constitution except on certain matters which included the exclusive powers of the provincial legislatures and the two official languages. Eventually, after many years of constitutional discussion in Canada, the Canada Act 1982 was passed at Westminster to give effect to the request of the Canadian parliament (against the wishes of the province of Quebec) that the Canadian constitution be 'patriated' to Canada.[23] This removed the necessity for there to be any further legislation at Westminster on Canadian affairs.

---

[19] *E.g.* Christmas Island Act 1958, which is one of very few instances of legislation by the UK Parliament under s. 4.

[20] [1935] A.C. 500, 520.

[21] Sir Owen Dixon (1935) 51 L.Q.R. 590, 611; and see *Copyright Owners Reproduction Society* v. *EMI (Australia) Pty Ltd* (1958) 100 C.L.R. 597.

[22] *Ndlwana* v. *Hofmeyr* 1937 A.D. 229, 237; the reasoning in this case was overruled by *Harris* v. *Minister of the Interior* 1952 (2) S.A. 428 A.D. but not with reference to this dictum. And see *Blackburn* v. *A.-G.* [1971] 2 All E.R. 1380.

[23] See App. A.

In the case of Australia and New Zealand, neither of whom wanted the Statute of Westminster to be applied to them immediately, it was provided that the legislative powers conferred by the Statute were not in any event to confer any new power to alter the Australian and New Zealand constitutions.[24] In the case of South Africa, no express saving was made for the South Africa Act 1909. Whatever may have been intended by the South African government in 1931, in *Harris* v. *Minister of the Interior* it was held by the South African court in 1952 that the Statute of Westminster did not enable the South African Parliament by ordinary legislative process to override the entrenched clauses of the 1909 Act; the Union of South Africa was a sovereign state, but this did not prevent her Parliament from being subject to the written constitution which had created it.[25]

Post-1945 independence

It was envisaged in 1931 that there might be subjects on which the United Kingdom would continue to legislate on behalf of one or more dominions. When after 1945 independence was granted to India, Pakistan, Ceylon, Ghana and many other territories, the position had changed in various respects since 1931. First, it was accepted in 1949, in relation to India, that an independent state might remain a member of the Commonwealth even if it became a republic. Second, the term dominion passed out of fashion in favour of 'member of the Commonwealth'. Third, the nature of independence had become clearer and it was realised that it would be anomalous for Westminster to retain a reserve power to legislate for independent states. By 1960 it became the practice for legislation which conferred independence to go further than the Statute of Westminster. Thus it was provided, for Nigeria in 1960, that from the date of independence:

(a)   the UK government should have no responsibility for the government of Nigeria or any part thereof;
(b)   the Colonial Laws Validity Act 1865 should not apply to any law made thereafter by the Nigerian legislature;
(c)   the Nigerian legislature should have full power to make laws repugnant to the law of England and to the legislation of the UK Parliament (including the Independence Act itself), and to make laws having extra-territorial operation; and
(d)   no Act of the UK Parliament passed thereafter should extend or be deemed to extend to Nigeria as part of the law thereof.[26]

These categorical statements of legislative independence indicated clearly that both government and Parliament of the United Kingdom had given up all power to govern and legislate for the territory in question. Even Dicey had accepted the view that a sovereign Parliament could surrender its powers.[27]

---

24   Sections 8 and 9(1). Australia adopted the Statute of Westminster in 1942, New Zealand in 1947: Wheare, *Statute of Westminster, op. cit.*, chs. 8, 9. Today the New Zealand Parliament has full powers of constitutional amendment, but the federal Australian Parliament does not.

25   1952 (2) S.A. 428. For a full account, see Marshall, *Parliamentary Sovereignty and the Commonwealth*, ch. 11. See also D. V. Cowen (1952) 15 M.L.R. 282 and (1953) 16 M.L.R. 273; and E. C. S. Wade, Introduction to Dicey, pp. lxxxiii–xcii.

26   Nigeria Independence Act 1960, s. 1(2) and sch. 1.

27   Dicey, p. 68; p. 72 *ante*.

Membership of the Commonwealth

Independence of the United Kingdom and membership of the Commonwealth are not the same. The granting of independence to a dependent territory of the United Kingdom is a matter for the UK government to decide, taking account of the wishes of the territory concerned and, as in the case of Rhodesia before its unilateral declaration of independence in 1965, the suitability of the government in the territory to have independence conferred upon it. But the admission of a new member to the Commonwealth requires the agreement of existing members. It would be contrary to the nature of the Commonwealth for the United Kingdom to attempt by its own action to confer such membership.

In 1971, it was declared by the heads of Commonwealth governments meeting at Singapore:

The Commonwealth of Nations is a voluntary association of independent sovereign states, each responsible for its own policies, consulting and co-operating in the common interests of their peoples and in the promotion of international understanding and world peace.[28]

There are no written rules of membership.[29] Probably the most significant change in the basis of membership occurred in 1949 when India announced her intention of becoming a republic. Before then, as the Balfour Declaration of 1926 had stated, all members owed a common allegiance to the Crown. In 1949, the response of other governments to India's intention was, in the Declaration of London, to note India's desire to continue her full membership of the Commonwealth and her acceptance of the British Sovereign 'as the symbol of the free association of its independent member nations and as such the Head of the Commonwealth'. Since 1949, while some states have adopted republican status after becoming independent, others have become republics at the moment of independence or have become monarchies with their own royal head of state. In 1984, only a minority of Commonwealth states owed allegiance to the Crown, but all states recognised the British Sovereign in the symbolic role of Head of the Commonwealth. Symbolism has its importance, but the role involves the Sovereign in no specific duties and requires her to undertake no governmental functions.

Most states which have become independent of the United Kingdom since 1945 have considered it worthwhile to become members of the Commonwealth. Cyprus did not become a member until 1961 although it became independent in 1960. In 1961, when South Africa had decided to become a republic, the government withdrew its application to remain in membership rather than have it rejected. After the civil war in Pakistan, Pakistan left the Commonwealth in 1972 and Bangladesh was admitted.[30] There is no doubt that a member state may decide to leave the Commonwealth at any time (secession is too strong a word for the act of withdrawal) and, although the

---

[28] Commonwealth Declaration, 22 Jan. 1971 (Dale, *op. cit.*, p. 41).

[29] For the practice, see Dale, *op. cit.*, ch. 3.

[30] See for consequential legislation in the UK, Pakistan Acts of 1973 and 1974 and the Bangladesh Act 1973.

event has not occurred, it seems likely that a member could be expelled against its wishes. The lack of rigid rules has made it possible for the category of Special Member to be devised for certain very small territories (including Nauru, a former dependent territory of Australia, Tuvalu, St Vincent and the Maldives) which have the right to participate in all functional activities of the Commonwealth but not to attend meetings of heads of Commonwealth governments.[31] Membership is however reserved for independent states. Thus Hong Kong and Gibraltar are within the Commonwealth since they are colonies of the United Kingdom which is a member: but they are not members of the Commonwealth in their own right.

Meetings of heads of Commonwealth governments

The imperial conferences held between 1907 and 1937 gave way from 1944 to meetings of Commonwealth Prime Ministers. These were held in London and were presided over by the British Prime Minister; the secretariat for the meetings was provided by the British government. These meetings gave way in turn to what are now called meetings of heads of Commonwealth governments since, in 1971, ten out of 31 Commonwealth states did not have Prime Ministers. They no longer meet only in London. Thus meetings have been held also in Lagos, Singapore, Lusaka, Melbourne and New Delhi, when the head of government of the host country has presided. In 1965, the meeting of Prime Ministers agreed to establish a Commonwealth Secretariat, headed by a Secretary-General. The headquarters are in London but the secretariat is responsible for servicing Commonwealth conferences wherever they may be held. The secretariat serves as a clearing house for information on international questions of common concern and has oversight of many forms of practical Commonwealth co-operation. The Secretary-General has an important diplomatic role on international issues that directly affect the Commonwealth. Under the Commonwealth Secretariat Act 1966, an Act of the United Kingdom Parliament, the secretariat is a body corporate and its members, from many Commonwealth countries, are entitled to diplomatic immunities and privileges. The secretariat has a number of divisions including those concerned with development, aid and planning; finance, trade and commodities; international affairs; education; and legal matters.

Since the enlargement of the Commonwealth, the nature of the heads of government meetings has changed. While they provide an umbrella for various forms of practical co-operation, the meetings themselves are mainly concerned with contentious issues of world politics – Suez, the Vietnam war, South Africa. In 1964 it was said that the Prime Ministers' meetings observed three conventions: they did not make any formal decisions or seek to lay down common policies; they did not discuss the internal affairs of a member state except at that member's request; and they did not discuss disputes between members, except at the request of both the parties.[32] But not all these conventions have survived the larger-scale diplomacy which now characterises Commonwealth meetings. In 1971, the Singapore conference produced the

---

[31]   Dale, *op. cit.*, p. 62.
[32]   Lord Normanbrook (1964) 45 *Jl. of Parliaments of the Commonwealth* 248, 251.

Commonwealth Declaration, which defined the nature of the Commonwealth, stressed the diversity of its membership and also stated the principles which were held in common by the members. In 1977, the heads of governments meeting in Britain issued a statement of a common policy on apartheid in sport, known as the Gleneagles Agreement. In 1979, the Lusaka Declaration concerned racism and racial prejudice.[33]

Other aspects of Commonwealth membership

As independent sovereign states, members of the Commonwealth do not observe any uniform constitutional pattern in their own systems of government. While most of them entered on independence with constitutions drafted under the guiding influence of Westminster and Whitehall, many of these gave way to new constitutions after independence or were pushed aside by political or military coups and civil war. While South Africa could not today be a member of the Commonwealth in view of its policy on apartheid, the brutality of President Amin's rule in Uganda did not lead to Uganda's expulsion from the Commonwealth. In the case of those members which are monarchies and owe allegiance to the Queen, a governor-general is appointed by the Queen, on the advice of the government of the state in question, to carry out the functions of head of state. Usually he is an eminent citizen of the state concerned. While formerly the doctrine of the indivisibility of the Crown was maintained, in those states which acknowledge the Queen as their monarch, the Queen today reigns over a kingdom which has that status in its own right. Thus obligations towards the Indian people of Canada which had been assumed by George III in 1763 and in subsequent treaties are owed by the Crown in right of Canada and not in right of the United Kingdom.[34]

There was formerly uncertainty as to whether the constitutional powers of a governor-general were the same as those of the Sovereign in the United Kingdom. After the controversial action in 1926 of Lord Byng, Governor-General of Canada, in refusing a dissolution to one Prime Minister and granting one to the next, the imperial conference in 1926 laid down that the governor-general held the same position in relation to the affairs of the dominion as the Sovereign did in the United Kingdom and that he was not the representative or agent of the UK government.[35] It must however be remembered that, for example, Canada and Australia have written constitutions which are very different from the unwritten constitution in the United Kingdom. Accordingly situations may arise in which the governor-general is entitled or required to exercise a personal discretion and which could not arise in the same form in the United Kingdom.[36]

Formerly the United Kingdom's relations with other Commonwealth members were carried on by the Secretary of State for Commonwealth Relations: but in 1968 the Commonwealth Relations Office was merged with the Foreign Office. The practice has survived however that member states are

---

[33]   Dale, *op. cit.*, ch. 1.
[34]   *R. v. Foreign Secretary, ex p. Indian Association of Alberta* [1982] Q.B. 892.
[35]   Cmd 2768, 1926, p. 7. And see H. V. Evatt, *The King and his Dominion Governors.*
[36]   As in Australia in 1975, when the governor-general, Sir John Kerr, dismissed the Labour Prime Minister; p. 196 *ante.*

represented diplomatically in other member states by high commissioners; high commissioners do not have the title of ambassador but they are members of the diplomatic service of their own state and they are equal in rank and status to ambassadors. Members of the Commonwealth conduct their own defence and foreign policies and have their own treaty-making capacity. The UK government may conclude an international treaty on behalf of the United Kingdom and its own dependent territories but it has no power to bind other member states. Equally the UK government has no power to make peace or declare war on behalf of member states. At the outbreak of the second world war, formal declarations of war were made on different dates by members of the Commonwealth.[37] By comparison with the EEC, which has a definite existence as an entity in international law and can make treaties on behalf of its member states, the position of the Commonwealth in international law is uncertain.[38] Some Commonwealth states in accepting the jurisdiction of the International Court of Justice have excluded disputes between members of the Commonwealth. This is almost all that survives of what was known as the 'inter se' doctrine, by which relations between member states were carried on without reliance on the normal rules of international relations.

Before 1967, the law regarding fugitive offenders within the Commonwealth was governed by the Fugitive Offenders Act 1881. It became increasingly unsuited to the modern Commonwealth (for example, there was no exclusion for political offenders) and following a conference of Commonwealth representatives, the UK law was reformed by the Fugitive Offenders Act 1967.[39] History also left its mark on the laws of nationality and citizenship. Citizens of other Commonwealth countries were formerly under UK law regarded as British subjects but are now described as 'Commonwealth citizens'.[40] This allows them to exercise political rights if they are resident in the United Kingdom but does not now entitle them to enter the United Kingdom. When Ireland, South Africa and Pakistan left the Commonwealth, legislation was necessary to deal with matters of nationality.[41]

Appeals to the Privy Council
In deciding appeals from the courts of the colonies and other dependent territories of the United Kingdom, the Judicial Committee of the Privy Council exercises the ancient jurisdiction of the King in Council to hear appeals from the overseas dependencies of the Crown.[42] This jurisdiction was based on 'the inherent prerogative right and, on all proper occasions, the duty of the King in Council to exercise an appellate jurisdiction, with a view not only to ensure . . . the due administration of justice in the individual case, but also to preserve the due course of procedure generally'.[43] This jurisdiction was given statutory form by the Judicial Committee Acts of 1833 and 1844.

---

[37]   E.g. UK on 3 Sep. 1939; South Africa on 6 Sep. 1939 and Canada on 10 Sep. 1939.
[38]   J. E. S. Fawcett, *The British Commonwealth in International Law*; Dale, *op. cit.*, ch. 6.
[39]   Ch. 25C.
[40]   British Nationality Act 1981, s. 37; ch. 25A.
[41]   Ireland Act 1949, South Africa Act 1962, Pakistan Act 1973.
[42]   Page 328 *ante*; Roberts-Wray, *op. cit.*, pp. 433–63; Dale, *op. cit.*, p. 128.
[43]   *R. v. Bertrand* (1867) L.R. 1 P.C. 520, 530.

Where the jurisdiction survives, appeals may be brought without special leave of the Privy Council or with special leave. Appeals without special leave, available mainly in civil cases, are regulated by legislation applying to the territory in question. This legislation lays down the conditions for appeal (for example, the amount which must be at stake, the requirement that only a final judgment may be appealed) and states whether the local court may exercise a discretion in deciding whether a question is involved which because of its public or general importance ought to be decided by the Privy Council. In such cases, an intending appellant must apply to the local appellate court for a decision on whether the statutory requirements are satisfied. The Judicial Committee may itself interpret legislation regulating the right of appeal.[44]

Appeals with special leave of the Privy Council apply mainly in criminal cases: special leave may be granted by the Judicial Committee where the local court has no power to grant an appeal or, exceptionally, has in the exercise of its discretion decided not to grant it.[45] The Judicial Committee is not a court of criminal appeal in the usual sense of the term. Appeals are allowed with special leave only where there has been a clear departure from the requirements of justice and it is shown that by a disregard of the forms of legal process or by some violation of the principles of natural justice, or otherwise, substantial and grave injustice has been done.[46] Thus an appeal was allowed where a judge in Ashanti, sitting without a jury, convicted and sentenced a man to death for murder without considering the possibility of manslaughter,[47] and where it was shown after a conviction that a member of the jury did not understand the language in which the trial was conducted.[48]

In the case of colonies and other dependent territories, the local legislature may under its constitution have power to regulate the conditions on which appeals lie to the Privy Council; it will not have power to legislate contrary to the provisions of a UK Act applying to the territory.[49] Thus it cannot abolish the power of the Judicial Committee to grant special leave to appeal. The conferring of independence on a colony does not in itself have the effect of terminating appeals to the Privy Council[50] unless of course the independence Act so provides. When independence has been conferred, any state may legislate to abolish or curtail appeals to the Privy Council.[51] Most Commonwealth states have in fact abolished appeals to the Privy Council, but jurisdiction continues in respect of certain appeals from Australia, the Bahamas, Barbados, Belize, Fiji, the Gambia, Jamaica, Malaysia, Mauritius, New Zealand, Singapore and from Trinidad and Tobago. In the case of Australia, a combination of circumstances (section 74 of the Commonwealth Constitution of 1900;[52] judicial reluctance to allow the Privy Council to decide issues relating to the federal distribution of powers; and federal legislation in 1968)

---

[44]   *Davis* v. *Shaughnessy* [1932] A.C. 106.
[45]   *Cf. Thomas* v. *R.* [1980] A.C. 125.
[46]   *Ibrahim* v. *R.* [1914] A.C. 599; *Prasad* v. *R.* [1981] 1 All E.R. 319.
[47]   *Knowles* v. *R.* [1930] A.C. 366.
[48]   *Ras Behari Lal* v. *R.I.* (1933) 50 T.L.R. 1.
[49]   Colonial Laws Validity Act 1865, s. 2.
[50]   *Ibralebbe* v. *R.* [1964] A.C. 900.
[51]   Note 18 *ante*.
[52]   On which see *e.g. Dennis Hotels Pty Ltd* v. *State of Victoria* [1962] A.C. 25.

has in effect excluded all appeals on matters of federal law and jurisdiction and the interpretation of the constitution, and has limited appeals, whether from the High Court of Australia or from state courts, to issues purely of state law.[53] In the case of Malaysia, which has its own monarchy, the application for leave to appeal goes to the head of state, who then refers it to the Judicial Committee.

It is evident that the legal link between Commonwealth states which arises from the provision of appeals to the Judicial Committee has worn thin. In the past, the Judicial Committee exercised an important role as a constitutional court, especially in regard to Canada; it helped to develop the common law in jurisdictions outside the British Isles; and it sought to preserve certain fundamentals of criminal justice when the local legal system had departed from them. From time to time proposals have been made for re-constituting the Judicial Committee as a travelling Commonwealth court of appeal, but these have never attracted much support.[54] The Committee's role is now of special significance in relation to those constitutions which include protection for fundamental human rights, but the degree of protection which the Committee has given in this role has been very uneven.[55] Yet it still provides an ultimate court of appeal for the smaller jurisdictions in the Commonwealth.

The Rhodesian revolution

Since 1945, the British have generally sought to confer independence rather than have it wrested from them. Southern Rhodesia became a colony in 1923 and thereafter exercised a large measure of self-government.[56] An unsuccessful experiment was made in establishing a Central African Federation which included Southern Rhodesia between 1953 and 1963. After the federation had broken up, independence was in 1964 granted to the other two members of the federation, Malawi (Nyasaland) and Zambia (Northern Rhodesia). In 1961 a new constitution had been granted to Southern Rhodesia by Order in Council; while it gave the colony 'an extraordinary degree of autonomy' in respect of its domestic affairs,[57] it included a declaration of rights and certain provisions which could be altered only by an amending Order in Council and others which could be altered by special legislative process in Rhodesia. On 11 November 1965, the Prime Minister, Ian Smith, and the other Rhodesian ministers proclaimed a new constitution for the people of Rhodesia, which declared that Southern Rhodesia was no longer a colony and sought to confer full legislative powers on the Rhodesian legislature, to abolish appeals to the

---

53   See C. Howard, *Australian Federal Constitutional Law*, pp. 197–9. On the difficult question of the complete abolition of appeals from Australian courts to the Privy Council, which might require an Act of the UK Parliament to be passed, see G. Nettheim (1965) 39 A.L.J. 39.

54   Roberts-Wray, *op. cit.*, pp. 461–3; and J. E. S. Fawcett, in J. D. B. Miller, *Survey of Commonwealth Affairs: Problems of Expansion and Attrition 1953–1969*, p. 429.

55   Cf. *e.g. Maharaj* v. *A.-G. of Trinidad and Tobago (No. 2)* [1979] A.C. 385 and *Ong Ah Chuan* v. *Public Prosecutor* [1981] A.C. 648 (severely criticised in D. Pannick, *Judicial Review of the Death Penalty*).

56   C. Palley, *The Constitutional History and Law of Southern Rhodesia 1888–1965*.

57   de Smith, *The New Commonwealth and its Constitutions*, p. 42. For the constitution, see S.I. 1961 No. 2314 and Cmnd 1399, 1961.

Privy Council and to protect the validity of the 1965 constitution from being questioned in the courts. This proclamation and the unilateral declaration of independence were clearly unlawful. The response of the UK government was to instruct the Governor-General of Rhodesia to dismiss the Rhodesian ministers. Parliament passed the Southern Rhodesia Act 1965, which declared that Rhodesia continued to be part of Her Majesty's dominions and gave the Queen in Council wide power to legislate for the colony; by Order in Council it was declared that laws for Rhodesia that were made without the authority of an Act of Parliament were void and that the Secretary of State could exercise all powers of government vested by the 1961 constitution in officers of the Rhodesian government.[58]

Thereafter the Smith government continued to govern Rhodesia. In *Madzimbamuto* v. *Lardner-Burke*, an appeal with special leave was heard by the Privy Council challenging the legality of Madzimbamuto's detention under emergency regulations made in 1966.[59] By a majority, the Judicial Committee held that the detention was unlawful because the Smith government was not lawfully in office and the emergency regulations were void. The Southern Rhodesia Act 1965 and the Order in Council made under it had the force of law. The granting of the 1961 constitution could not be regarded as a grant of limited sovereignty which in any way prevented the UK Parliament from legislating for Rhodesia. Whether or not there was a doctrine of necessity, by which the courts could recognise the need to preserve law and order in territory controlled by a usurper, the UK Parliament's right to legislate for Rhodesia prevailed. Dissenting, Lord Pearce held that acts done by those actually in control in Rhodesia might be recognised as valid where they were required for the orderly running of the state, did not impair the rights of citizens under the 1961 constitution and were not intended directly to help the usurpation of authority contrary to the policy of the lawful sovereign; Lord Pearce thus applied the principle of necessity, or implied mandate from the lawful sovereign, which took account of the effective seat of governmental power in Rhodesia, without accepting that the Smith regime was lawful.

In the Rhodesian courts, a very different view of the law had been taken by the Rhodesian judges from that taken by the Privy Council, although it fell short of recognising that the Smith government had *de iure* authority.[60] In fact the Rhodesian government did not recognise the decision of the Privy Council as having any legal effect. The majority in the Privy Council had accepted the historical fact that 'there are now regimes which are universally recognised as lawful but which derive their origins from revolutions or *coups d'état*'[61] but considered that the British government acting for the lawful sovereign was still taking steps to regain control of the government of Rhodesia. But in *Dhlamini* v. *Carter*, the Appellate Division of the Rhodesian High Court refused to stay the execution of applicants who had earlier lodged appeals against their death sentence to the Privy Council as the court considered that whatever judgment

---

58 S.I. 1965 No. 1952.
59 [1969] 1 A.C. 645. *Cf. Mutasa* v. *A.-G.* [1980] Q.B. 114.
60 *Madzimbamuto* v. *Lardner-Burke* 1968 (2) S.A. 284.
61 [1969] 1 A.C. at 724; *cf. The State* v. *Dosso* [1958] 2 P.S.C.R. 180 (Pakistan) and *Uganda* v. *Commissioner of Prisons, ex p. Matovu* [1966] E.A. 514.

the Privy Council might give would be wholly ineffective in Rhodesia.[62] In *R.* v. *Ndhlovu* the same court ruled that the 1965 constitution had become the only lawful constitution of Rhodesia.[63] Thereafter it was no longer possible for any Rhodesian judge to claim that he was still acting under the 1961 constitution: indeed Fieldsend J. and Dendy Young J. resigned during 1968 on the constitutional issue and new judges were appointed in their place by the Smith government. In 1969 the Rhodesian parliament adopted a new republican constitution. So far as Rhodesian law was concerned the revolution was complete.

Yet African opinion and successive British governments refused to accept that the revolution had been politically successful. The Southern Rhodesia Act 1965 remained on the statute-book in the United Kingdom, although the power to make Orders in Council under it was used more to resolve legal difficulties which would otherwise have ensnared ordinary citizens in the United Kingdom than to seek to govern Rhodesia.[64] There were repeated attempts by the UK government to negotiate a settlement of the Rhodesian question: one which reached the point of a conditional agreement between the two governments failed because the settlement proposed was not acceptable to the majority of the Rhodesian people.[65] Thereafter diplomatic pressures on the government of Rhodesia continued and guerilla warfare within the country intensified. In 1978 the Smith government reached an agreement with certain African leaders, the country was re-named Zimbabwe/Rhodesia, and in April 1979 multi-racial elections were held. Between September and December 1979, a constitutional conference in London laid the basis for a return to legality and for a short period of direct rule by Britain while fresh elections were held. In April 1980, under the authority of the Westminster Parliament, independence was conferred on Zimbabwe. The enabling legislation also authorised a general amnesty, both as regards the unlawful acts of the Smith government following UDI, and for acts done in opposition to that government.[66]

An extensive literature was published dealing with the aftermath of UDI: much of it has concentrated on the behaviour and reasoning of the Rhodesian judges in a revolutionary situation[67] but difficult questions in the law of treason have also arisen.[68] One conclusion which emerged is that doctrines of legal philosophy are more helpful in analysing what has happened after the event than in providing authoritative guidance for judges at the moment when cases

---

[62] 1968 (2) S.A. 464 (and see 445 and 467).

[63] 1968 (4) S.A. 515.

[64] *Adams* v. *Adams* [1971] P. 188 (validity of post-UDI divorces in Rhodesia) and *Franklin* v. *A.-G.* [1974] Q.B. 185 (and the sequels at 202 and 205) led respectively to S.I. 1972 No. 1718 and S.I. 1973 No. 1226. See also *In re James* [1977] Ch. 41, discussed by P. Mirfield [1978] P.L. 42.

[65] See Cmnd 4835, 1971 and Cmnd 4964, 1972.

[66] See Cmnd 7758, 1979 and Cmnd 7802, 1980; Southern Rhodesia Act 1979; Zimbabwe Act 1979; S.I. 1979 No. 1600.

[67] See *e.g.* R. W. M. Dias (1968) 26 C.L.J. 233; J. M. Eekelaar (1967) 30 M.L.R. 156; S. Guest [1980] P.L. 168; L. J. Macfarlane [1968] P.L. 325; C. Palley (1967) 30 M.L.R. 263, [1968] P.L. 293; R. S. Welsh (1967) 83 L.Q.R. 64.

[68] B. A. Hepple, P. O'Higgins and C. C. Turpin [1966] Crim. L.R. 5; O. Hood Phillips [1966] Crim. L.R. 68; and A. Wharam [1967] C.L.J. 189.

come before them in such extreme circumstances. As has been said of the Rhodesian judgments in *Madzimbamuto's* case, 'the overall picture that emerges is of a *melée* of arguments advanced, not for their persuasive power, but rather as respectable cover for personal attitudes'.[69] It is unlikely that the Rhodesian judges could have diverted the Smith government from its chosen course: but it is unfortunate that they did not adhere unequivocally to the principles enshrined in the 1961 constitution.

---

[69] R. W. M. Dias (1968) 26 C.L.J. 233, 239.

Part II

The citizen and the state

Chapter 25

Citizenship, immigration and extradition

A. Citizenship
Nationality[1]
In both constitutional and international law, nationality is a significant, but not necessarily conclusive, factor in such matters as immigration, deportation and diplomatic protection abroad. The nationality law of the United Kingdom is now largely contained in the British Nationality Act 1981.[2] However, this Act can only be fully understood with some knowledge of the previous legislation on nationality and also of immigration law.[3]

Prior to 1949, there was a common statutory code which had governed most aspects of the status of British subjects throughout the British Empire. The status of British subjects in the United Kingdom and its colonies was governed by the Nationality and Status of Aliens Act 1914. The terms of this UK statute were substantially enacted in those dominions (Australia, Canada, New Zealand and South Africa) which at that time had legislative competence to enact separate nationality legislation. This common code was based on the principle of a common allegiance to the Crown and was amended only after consultation and agreement between the governments concerned. This arrangement became less appropriate when the dominions wished to enact nationality legislation which was more closely related to a local allegiance than to a common allegiance to the Crown. After the second world war, it was agreed that each independent Commonwealth country would determine its own nationality law, but that all Commonwealth countries would recognise citizenship of any Commonwealth country as a sufficient qualification for a new common status of Commonwealth citizen, or British subject.[4]

To implement this agreement, the United Kingdom enacted the British Nationality Act 1948 which created a new citizenship of the United Kingdom and Colonies and provided that such citizens and citizens of independent Commonwealth states had the status of Commonwealth citizens in the United

---

[1] I. A. MacDonald & N. Blake, *The New Nationality Law*. For the former law, see C. Parry, *Nationality and Citizenship Laws of the Commonwealth*; J. M. Jones, *British Nationality Law*.
[2] See also the British Nationality (Falkland Islands) Act 1983.
[3] Section B, *post*.
[4] Cmd 7326, 1948.

Kingdom. Under the 1948 Act, citizens of the United Kingdom and Colonies and citizens of other Commonwealth countries enjoyed the same legal rights in the United Kingdom. Over the years this coincidence between a category of citizenship and legal rights and duties was substantially eroded, principally by the statutory control of immigration to the United Kingdom and by the rights and obligations which flowed from UK membership of the European Communities. Thus some citizens of the United Kingdom and Colonies, some citizens of other Commonwealth countries, and some aliens had the right of abode in the United Kingdom while others in each category did not. The government considered that categories of citizenship should correspond more closely to rights under immigration law and for this and other reasons the British Nationality Act 1981 was enacted.[5]

The Act of 1981 replaced citizenship of the United Kingdom and Colonies with three new categories of citizenship: British citizenship, British dependent territories citizenship and British overseas citizenship. Almost all those who, immediately before the 1981 Act took effect on 1 January 1983, were citizens of the United Kingdom and Colonies and had a right of abode in the United Kingdom under the Immigration Act 1971 became British citizens.[6] Those who were citizens of the United Kingdom and Colonies by virtue of a connection with a British dependent territory (such as Hong Kong) but did not have a right of abode in the United Kingdom became British dependent territories citizens.[7] Those citizens of the United Kingdom and Colonies who did not qualify for either British citizenship or British dependent territories citizenship became British overseas citizens.[8] In addition, the Act provided for two residual categories of citizenship, British subjects under the Act,[9] and British protected persons.[10] All British citizens, British dependent territories citizens,

---

[5]   Although the 1981 Act was concerned with the rights of citizens to enter and remain in the United Kingdom, it does not deal with other rights and duties which flow from citizenship, such as allegiance, the right to vote and jury service, nor does it deal adequately with the issue of who are UK nationals for the purposes of European Community law (p. 461 *post*). It does, however, allow citizenship to be acquired through both the male and female line in most eases, whereas under previous legislation acquisition was usually permitted only through the male line.

[6]   1981 Act, s. 11(1). There are two exceptions to this: s. 11(2), (3).

[7]   1981 Act, s. 23, sch. 6. The status of British dependent territories citizen does not carry with it a right to enter and remain in the United Kingdom or any dependent territory. Although there will often be a right of abode in the territory with which the person is connected, such a right does not flow from the 1981 Act.

[8]   1981 Act, s. 26. The rights of a British overseas citizen are extremely limited. In normal circumstances they do not extend beyond the right of diplomatic protection by the UK government. However, if such a citizen were not allowed to remain in any other state, the UK government would be under a duty in international law to admit him to the United Kingdom (p. 448 *post*).

[9]   A British subject under the Act is a person who (when the 1948 Act came into force) was a British subject and potentially a citizen of a Commonwealth country (including the United Kingdom) or the Republic of Ireland, but had not become such a citizen: 1981 Act, ss. 30, 31. The status is lost if any other citizenship or nationality is acquired: s. 35.

[10]   A British protected person is one who is granted the status by Order in Council by virtue of a connection with a protectorate, protected state, or a UK trust territory as defined in the 1948 Act, or is such under the Solomon Islands Act 1978. The status is not granted to those who are citizens of an independent Commonwealth state which now includes such a territory: 1981 Act, ss. 38, 50(1), (12), sch. 3.

British overseas citizens, British subjects and citizens of scheduled independent Commonwealth countries have the status of Commonwealth citizens in the United Kingdom.[11]

Acquisition of British citizenship[12]

British citizenship as defined in the 1981 Act may be acquired by birth or adoption, descent, registration or naturalisation.

1 Birth or adoption   A child born legitimately in the United Kingdom[13] becomes a British citizen if, at the time of the birth, one of its parents is either a British citizen or is 'settled' in the United Kingdom.[14] Prior to the 1981 Act, with few exceptions, a person born in the United Kingdom became a UK citizen by birth. The 1981 Act made the acquisition of British citizenship by birth contingent in many cases on the status of a parent in immigration law, a status which may well be a matter of legal dispute. For, under the 1981 Act, to be 'settled' in the United Kingdom a person must be 'ordinarily resident . . . without being subject under the immigration laws to any restriction on the period for which he (or she) may remain';[15] and no-one can be ordinarily resident for the purposes of the Act who is in breach of the immigration laws.[16] The change in the law was made because the government considered it undesirable that a child born in the United Kingdom of transient parents should acquire a right of abode. However, the difficulties which are likely to ensue where a person's citizenship is in doubt because of a parent's unresolved immigration status are somewhat ameliorated by provisions which, in limited circumstances, entitle those born in the United Kingdom to be registered as British citizens.[17]

A minor who is adopted becomes a British citizen from the date of the order authorising the adoption, if the order is made by a UK court and either adoptive parent is a British citizen at that date.[18]

2 Descent   A person born outside the United Kingdom becomes a British citizen by descent if either parent is a British citizen, unless the parent is also a British citizen by descent.[19] Like British citizenship by birth, to determine

---

[11] 1981 Act, s. 37.

[12] For transitional arrangements for acquiring British citizenship, see 1981 Act, ss. 7–10. For the acquisition of British dependent territories citizenship, see ss. 15–22, schs. 1, 2. Apart from transitional arrangements (ss. 27, 28) there is no provision in the 1981 Act for the acquisition of British overseas citizenship other than at its entry into force.

[13] The 'United Kingdom' for the purposes of the 1981 Act includes the Channel Islands and the Isle of Man: s. 50(1) (*cf.* ch. 3 *ante*). A child may be deemed to have been born in the United Kingdom: *e.g.* s. 50(7) (birth on UK registered ship or aircraft).

[14] 1981 Act, s. 1(1). An illegitimate child may acquire citizenship only through its mother, unless legitimated by the subsequent marriage of its parents: ss. 50(9), 47. Special provision is made for those born after the death of a parent (s. 48), or who have a parent with diplomatic immunity (s. 50(4)), or who would otherwise be stateless (s. 36, sch. 2), and for abandoned new-born infants (s. 1(2)).

[15] 1981 Act, s. 50(2), *cf.* s. 50(3) (4).

[16] 1981 Act, s. 50(5).

[17] 1981 Act. s. 1(3)(4).

[18] 1981 Act, s. 1(5).

[19] 1981 Act, s. 2.

whether a person is a British citizen by descent may involve questions of status under immigration law.[20] Where the parent is a British citizen by descent, British citizenship is acquired as of right only if the parent is employed outside the United Kingdom in Crown service under the UK government, in similar designated service, or in service under a European Community institution.[21]

3 Registration   Various categories of person are entitled to be registered as British citizens if certain statutory conditions are satisfied. A common condition is a period of residence in the United Kingdom, which again involves questions of status under immigration law.

Some children born in the United Kingdom who do not acquire citizenship by birth are entitled to be registered. A child is, for instance, entitled to be registered as a British citizen at any time after the age of ten, if he has not been absent from the United Kingdom for more than 90 days in each of his first ten years;[22] and a child is similarly entitled if, while a minor, one of his parents becomes either a British citizen or settles in the United Kingdom.[23] Some children born outside the United Kingdom are also entitled to be registered if certain conditions are satisfied.[24] British dependent territories citizens, British overseas citizens and British protected persons who satisfy a 5 year residence requirement in the United Kingdom are also entitled to be registered.[25]

In certain cases, registration is at the discretion of the Secretary of State (that is, the Home Secretary): for instance, the Secretary of State may register any minor as a British citizen.[26]

4 Naturalisation   Those who do not benefit from other provisions of the 1981 Act and wish to become British citizens must apply to be naturalised. Naturalisation is granted at the discretion of the Secretary of State, who must be satisfied that applicants have completed a five year UK residence requirement (which involves questions of status under immigration law), are of good character, have sufficient knowledge of English, Welsh or Gaelic, and, if naturalised, intend to have their principal home in the United Kingdom or alternatively pursue one of the types of employment specified in the Act.[27] Less stringent conditions apply where the applicant is the spouse of a British citizen.[28]

---

20   1981 Act, s. 14.
21   Recruitment to the service must have taken place in the United Kingdom or, in the case of service under a Community institution, in a Community member state: 1981 Act, s. 2(1)(b)(c).
22   1981 Act, s. 1(4).
23   1981 Act, s. 1(3).
24   1981 Act, s. 3(2)(5).
25   1981 Act, s. 4. Those who have a sufficient connection with Gibraltar do not have to satisfy the residence requirement: s. 5.
26   1981 Act, s. 3(1).
27   1981 Act, s. 6(1), sch. 1, paras. 1, 2. Service at the date of application outside the United Kingdom under the UK government can be substituted for the residence requirement: sch. 1, para. 1(1)(a), (3).
28   1981 Act, s. 6(2), sch. 1, paras. 3, 4.

It will be noted that in many cases the acquisition of British citizenship is closely associated with status under immigration law. Moreover, decisions on all naturalisation and some registration applications are subject to the discretion of the Secretary of State. It is perhaps surprising, therefore, that the British Nationality Act does not create mechanisms for appeal against refusal of citizenship,[29] comparable to appeals under the Immigration Act 1971. Where British citizenship is a matter of right, an unfavourable decision may be the subject of an application for judicial review to the High Court; if it can be established that the statutory requirements have been satisfied, a declaration of the citizenship or entitlement to citizenship may be obtained.[30] However, where a decision is at the discretion of the Secretary of State, he cannot be required to give reasons for his decision and his decision is not subject to appeal or review by any court.[31]

Renunciation and deprivation of British citizenship[32]

A person may, by declaration, renounce British citizenship.[33] Renunciation is normally effective once the declaration has been registered.[34] However, it cannot be registered unless the Secretary of State is satisfied that after registration the person will have or will acquire some other citizenship or nationality;[35] the Secretary of State may also withhold registration of a declaration made while the United Kingdom is at war.[36] A person who has renounced British citizenship is entitled in limited circumstances to resume British citizenship by registration;[37] otherwise resumption of citizenship is by registration at the discretion of the Secretary of State.[38]

A naturalised or registered British citizen may be deprived of citizenship where the Secretary of State is satisfied that the citizenship was obtained by fraud, false representation or concealment of any material fact.[39] A naturalised British citizen, or a British citizen who obtained citizenship by registration under the 1981 Act, may be deprived of citizenship where the Secretary of State is satisfied that the citizen (a) has been disloyal or disaffected, (b) has traded or communicated with, or assisted, the enemy, or (c) unless deprivation would render him stateless, has been sentenced to not less than 12 months

---

29 See however 1981 Act, s. 40.

30 1981 Act, s. 44(3); Rules of the Supreme Court, Order 53, and Order 15, rule 16; ch. 35.

31 1981 Act, s. 44(2). But it is possible that the criteria on which a decision is based may be reviewable: see T. St. J. N. Bates [1982] P.L. 179. The Secretary of State must exercise his discretion without regard to the race, colour or religion of any person who may be affected (s. 44(1)) and breach of this would be reviewable.

32 For the renunciation, resumption and deprivation of other forms of citizenship, see ss. 24, 29 and 40(10).

33 1981 Act, s. 12(1).

34 1981 Act, s. 12(2).

35 1981 Act, s. 12(3). If the person does not acquire another citizenship or nationality within six months of the date of registration, he is deemed to have remained a British citizen: *ibid*.

36 1981 Act, s. 12(4).

37 1981 Act, s. 13(1)(2).

38 1981 Act, s. 13(3).

39 1981 Act, s. 40(1) (2). These provisions apply to those naturalised or registered under the 1981 Act, and also those who acquired citizenship by registration under the British Nationality Acts 1948–64 or by naturalisation under any previous legislation. See also *R.* v. *Home Secretary, ex p. Parvaz Akhtar* [1981] Q.B. 46, *R.* v. *Home Secretary, ex p. Sultan Mahmood* [1981] Q.B. 58.

imprisonment in any country within five years of registration or naturalisation.[40] In all cases, the Secretary of State may deprive a person of British citizenship only where he is satisfied that it is not conducive to the public good that the person should continue to be a citizen.[41] Where he intends to deprive a citizen of citizenship he must give the citizen notice and the citizen is entitled to have the case considered by an independent committee of enquiry.[42]

Where a former dependent territory has become an independent Commonwealth country, or where a country has left the Commonwealth, statutory provision has been made for the consequent loss, acquisition or retention of UK citizenship; for example, in the Kenya Independence Act 1963 and the Pakistan Act 1973.

Aliens

For all statutory purposes, an alien is a person who is neither a Commonwealth citizen nor a British protected person nor a citizen of the Republic of Ireland.[43] So long as they are permitted to remain in the territorial jurisdiction of the Crown, aliens enjoy the protection of the Crown, owe allegiance and are in general amenable to the ordinary law.[44] Aliens were, however, subject to a range of disabilities under the common law; where these disabilities still exist the common law has been largely superseded by statute.

Aliens do not have the right of abode in the United Kingdom. They may only enter and remain with permission and are subject to the Immigration Act 1971.[45] An alien may not be a member of the Privy Council or of either House of Parliament, nor hold an office under the Crown in the United Kingdom unless a certificate is issued by the responsible minister with the consent of the Minister for the Civil Service.[46] Aliens are not entitled to vote at parliamentary or local elections.[47] Aliens are also subject to certain occupational and proprietary disabilities, although as regards citizens of EEC states such disabilities operate subject to the provisions of Community law.[48]

---

[40] 1981 Act, s. 40(3), (5)(b). Those who were registered as UK citizens under previous legislation are not affected by these provisions (s. 40(4)).

[41] 1981 Act, s. 40(5)(a).

[42] 1981 Act, s. 40(7), (8), (9). There were only 12 cases of deprivation of citizenship between 1948 and 1981; no appeal was successful (H.C. Deb., 7 May 1981, col. 1841 W.A.).

[43] 1981 Act, ss. 50(1), 51(4); the class of Commonwealth citizens includes all British citizens, British dependent territories citizens, British overseas citizens and British subjects under the 1981 Act (s. 37(1)).

[44] For allegiance and protection, see *post*. There are some special offences related to aliens (*e.g.* Aliens Restriction (Amendment) Act 1919, s. 3) and certain categories of alien may not be subject to the jurisdiction of the ordinary courts (*e.g.* those to whom the Visiting Forces Act 1952 applies).

[45] See Section B.

[46] Act of Settlement 1700, s. 3; Aliens Employment Act 1955, s. 1(1)(b),(2). See also the Army Act 1955, s. 21 and the Air Force Act 1955, s. 21. By prerogative order, a person with alien parents may be refused employment under the Crown: see B. A. Hepple, *Race, Jobs and the Law*, pp. 270–2.

[47] Representation of the People Act 1983, ss. 1(1), 2(1); Status of Aliens Act 1914, s. 17.

[48] *E.g.* an alien may not own a British ship (Status of Aliens Act 1914, s. 17) and, subject to exceptions, is not qualified to own an aircraft registered in the UK (Air Navigation Order S.I. 1980 No. 1965). Some such restrictions have been removed, *e.g.* Solicitors (Amendment) Act 1974, s. 1. The EEC Treaty, art. 7 prohibits discrimination against nationals of member states; *cf.* ch. 31A.

In wartime, a legal distinction is drawn between alien friends and alien enemies.[49] An alien enemy is a national of a state at war with the Crown.[50] Such alien enemies may be interned or expelled under the prerogative power.[51] However, if allowed to remain in the United Kingdom, an alien enemy has an implied licence to protect his interests before the courts.[52] The term 'alien enemy' may also be used to describe a person of any nationality carrying on business, or voluntarily resident, in any enemy or enemy-occupied state.[53] Alien enemies in this sense may not raise or pursue an action in UK courts;[54] but if actions are brought against them, they may defend the action and appeal against an adverse decision.[55] Trading with such enemy aliens, unless by licence of the Crown, is prohibited by the common law,[56] which has been supplemented by statute.[57] The Crown may confiscate enemy property in wartime either under prerogative or statutory power;[58] such property is usually vested in a custodian of enemy property.

Allegiance and protection[59]

The duty of allegiance at common law is owed to the Crown by British subjects at all times, whether or not they are within the realm.[60]Although the British Nationality Acts of 1948 and 1981 do not refer to allegiance, it may be supposed that the duty of allegiance is today owed by all categories of citizenship in UK law, except Commonwealth citizens whose citizenship is derived from a country which does not recognise the Queen as head of state. A friendly alien within the jurisdiction of the Crown also owes allegiance.[61] A friendly alien outside the jurisdiction of the Crown who 'has still a call on the protection of the Crown' owes allegiance.[62] Such a case may arise where a friendly alien is abroad but his family or effects are still within the realm, or where a friendly alien abroad has a British passport or travel document.[63] Alien enemies within the realm with the express or implied licence of the Crown owe allegiance. Consequently, interned alien enemies owe alle-

---

49 See McNair and A. D. Watts, *The Legal Effects of War*, chs. 2, 3.
50 *Sylvester's* case (1703) 7 Mod. Rep. 150.
51 *R. v. Vine St. Police Station Superintendent, ex p. Liebmann* [1916] 1 K.B. 268 (internment); *Netz* v. *Ede* [1946] Ch. 224, *R. v. Bottrill, ex p. Kuechenmeister,* [1947] K. B. 41 (deportation).
52 *Re Duchess of Sutherland* (1915) 31 T.L.R. 248, and *cf. R. v. Bottrill, ex p. Kuechenmeister, ante,* 56–7.
53 *Porter* v. *Freudenberg* [1915] 1 K.B. 867–9. The term also applies to a company carrying on business in such circumstances: *Daimler Co.* v. *Continental Tyre and Rubber Co.* [1916] 2 A.C. 307.
54 *Janson* v. *Driefontein Consolidated Mines Ltd* [1902] A.C. 484; but the right of action revives on peace being restored *cf.* McNair and Watts, *op. cit.,* p. 86.
55 *Porter* v. *Freudenberg, ante.*
56 *E.g. The Hoop* (1799) 1 C. Rob. 196.
57 Trading with the Enemy Act 1939; Emergency Laws (Miscellaneous Provisions) Act 1953.
58 Trading with the Enemy Act 1939; Emergency Laws (Miscellaneous Provisions) Act 1953, s. 2, sch. 2. The prerogative is preserved by s. 16 of the 1939 Act.
59 See H. Lauterpacht (1947) 9 C.L.J. 330; G. L. Williams (1948) 10 C.L.J. 54.
60 *R. v. Casement* [1917] 1 K.B. 98.
61 *Cf. R* v. *Owen* (1615) 1 Roll Rep. 185.
62 *Re P.(G.E.) (An Infant)* [1965] Ch. 568, 585.
63 *Joyce* v. *DPP* [1946] A.C. 347; *Re P.(G.E.) (An Infant), ante.*

giance but not an alien enemy coming to invade the realm.[64] The allegiance owed by an alien does not cease when the British territory in which he is resident is occupied by enemy forces and the protection of the Crown is temporarily withdrawn.[65]

In the modern law, the practical consequences of owing allegiance to the Crown are liability to the offence of treason, certain procedural consequences in actions against the Crown and an entitlement to some level of protection by the Crown.[66] This protection consists of physical protection by the Crown, at a normal but not exceptional[67] level, within the realm;[68] diplomatic protection;[69] and, in the case of a child who owes allegiance and is made a ward of court, judicial protection.[70]

Passports and the right to travel[71]

The citizen has a general common law right to leave the United Kingdom,[72] although the right is subject to common law and statutory exceptions.[73] Theoretically this right is not affected by possession of a passport issued by the United Kingdom. In law, it is possible to leave the United Kingdom without a passport. A passport merely provides *prima facie* evidence of status from which the duty of allegiance and possibly the protection of the Crown may flow.[74] In fact, travel abroad is extremely difficult without a passport or an equivalent document, and the lack of a passport effectively deprives the citizen of his right to travel.

In the United Kingdom passports are issued by the Foreign and Commonwealth Office under the royal prerogative. A passport may be refused, withdrawn or revoked by the Crown at its absolute discretion.[75] There is no judicial

---

64   *Calvin's case* (1608) 7 Co. Rep. 1a; as to prisoners of war see McNair and Watts, *op. cit.*, pp. 60–1.

65   *De Jager* v. *A.-G. of Natal* [1907] A.C. 326.

66   See ch. 18B and *Mutasa* v. *A.-G.* [1980] Q.B. 114.

67   *Glasbrook Bros* v. *Glamorgan CC* [1925] A.C. 270.

68   *China Navigation Co.* v. *A.-G.* [1932] 2 K.B. 197.

69   *Joyce* v. *DPP, ante.*

70   *Re P.(G.E.) (An Infant), ante.* See also ch. 18B.

71   K. Diplock (1947) 32 Grot. Soc. Trans. 42; G.L. Williams (1948) 10 C.L.J. 54; H. W. R. Wade, *The Times*, 7 Aug. 1968; *Going Abroad: A Report on Passports* (Justice, 1974); D. W. Williams (1974) 23 I.C.L.Q. 642; D. Turack, *The Passport in International Law.*

72   Blackstone, *Commentaries*, 1, 265. Under Community law, the UK is under an obligation to allow its nationals to leave the UK to take work in another EEC member state: Council directives 68/360, art. 2; 73/148, art. 2.

73   *E.g.* the common law writ *ne exeat regno* restraining the citizen from leaving the realm: *Felton* v. *Callis* [1969] 1 Q.B. 200 *cf. Parsons* v. *Burk* [1971] N.Z.L.R. 244 (an attempt to prevent the 'All Blacks' rugby team leaving New Zealand to tour Southern Africa). Under the Foreign Enlistment Act 1870 it is an offence for a British subject to enlist in the armed forces of a foreign state which is at war with a foreign state at peace with the Crown, or to leave the Crown's dominions for that purpose (ss. 4, 5). A committee of Privy Counsellors appointed to inquire into the recruitment of mercenaries in the UK recommended that these provisions should be repealed: Cmnd 6569, 1976.

74   See *ante.*

75   The police are not entitled to retain a passport against the wishes of its holder merely because they believe there is a serious risk that its holder may leave the country if it is returned (*Ghani* v. *Jones* [1970] 1 Q.B. 693), although a court in England may require the surrender of a passport as a condition of bail (Bail Act 1976, s. 3).

review of this discretion and no other formal appellate or review procedure.[76] Exercise of the discretion by the Foreign Secretary does attract ministerial responsibility, so that it has been suggested that the 'only action open to one aggrieved would be in fact to defeat the Government'.[77] However, under Community law the United Kingdom is under a qualified obligation to issue a passport to a citizen, although this obligation may not create a legal right enforceable by the individual citizen.[78]

The prerogative power to refuse, withdraw or revoke passports is in practice only exercised in a limited number of situations.[79] A passport may be denied (a) to a person for whom an arrest warrant has been issued in the United Kingdom, (b) to a person who has been repatriated at the public expense, until the debt is paid, and (c) to a minor in certain circumstances, such as where a journey is known to be contrary to parental wishes, and (d) on grounds of public interest, to a person whose past or present activities are demonstrably undesirable.

The prerogative power to deny a passport is little used for political purposes.[80] However, while the denial of a passport clearly prejudices the citizen's ability to travel, it does not prevent him leaving the country, either in law, or, for the determined person informed of his legal rights, in practice.[81] Thus this prerogative power represents a potentially substantial restriction on the freedom of movement, yet when it is exercised, it may fail to achieve its primary objective. For such reasons there is force in the suggestion that there should either be a statutory procedure for appeal or review where a passport is denied, or that the citizen should have a statutory right to a passport.[82]

B. Immigration and deportation[1]

Legislative background to the Immigration Act 1971

The development of immigration law is inextricably linked with the background of nationality law described in section A. The history of the Commonwealth has left problems for British immigration policy which today may be identified but have not been solved. British immigration law is often accused of being inspired by racial motives: but economic self-interest may afford a more accurate explanation. Since 1973 British membership of the EEC has imposed additional requirements on immigration law.

It is one of the classic attributes of national sovereignty that a state is entitled to control entry into its territory by citizens or nationals of another state. At common law, the Crown had power under the prerogative to prevent

---

[76] *Secretary of State* v. *Lakdawalla* [1972] Imm. A.R. 26.

[77] H. L. Deb., 16 June 1958, col. 862 (Lord Wilmot).

[78] See Council directives, 68/360, arts. 2(2), 10; 73/148, arts. 2(2), 8.

[79] See H. C. Deb., 15 Nov. 1974, col. 265 (W.A.); H. C. Deb., 27 June 1968, cols. 126–30 (W.A.).

[80] 27 passports were denied on political grounds between 1945 and 1973; *Going Abroad: A Report on Passports, op. cit.*, para. 29.

[81] See *Going Abroad: A Report on Passports, op. cit.*, para. 7; Cmnd 6569, 1976, para. 21.

[82] *E.g. Going Abroad: A Report on Passports, op. cit.*, paras. 45–55. *Cf.* H. L. Deb., 6 May 1976, cols. 697–720, H. L. Deb., 22 Jan. 1981, col. 558 (W.A.).

[1] See I. A. MacDonald, *Immigration Law and Practice*, and J. M. Evans, *Immigration Law*.

aliens from entering the United Kingdom and an alien had no right to be admitted into the Sovereign's realms and territories.[2] As Widgery L. J. said in *Schmidt* v. *Home Secretary*,

when an alien approaching this country is refused leave to land, he has no right capable of being infringed in such a way as to enable him to come to this court for the purpose of assistance . . . In such a situation the alien's desire to land can be rejected for good reason or bad, for sensible reason or fanciful or for no reason at all.[3]

At common law, though no definite authority existed, it was possible that the Crown had power to expel friendly aliens who had been previously admitted into the United Kingdom.[4] Such prerogative powers as the Crown may have in respect of aliens have been expressly preserved in being.[5] But for most of the 20th century, the executive has relied upon statutory powers for controlling the entry of aliens and for enabling aliens here to be deported. The Alien Immigration Act 1905 enabled the government to prevent the entry of certain undesirable classes of alien. Wider powers of control were exercised under the Aliens Restriction Act 1914 and these powers, including power to deport, were kept in being by the Aliens Restriction (Amendment) Act 1919. It was under the 1914 and 1919 Acts that the Aliens Order 1953 was later made containing a code of powers for controlling aliens.

By contrast with aliens, British subjects both before and after the British Nationality Act 1948[6] had full right to enter and remain in the United Kingdom without restriction and the Crown had no prerogative power to prevent their admission, to deport them or to prevent their departure.[7] These rights became available to the citizens of all member states of the Commonwealth who, under the British Nationality Act 1948, were British subjects. Their right to enter the United Kingdom was not affected by the fact that many Commonwealth states imposed their own restrictions on entry by British subjects from other parts of the Commonwealth, including the United Kingdom.

The right of all British subjects to enter the United Kingdom was severely restricted by the Commonwealth Immigrants Acts of 1962 and 1968. The 1962 Act, passed primarily to check immigration from the West Indies, India and Pakistan, subjected all British subjects to immigration control, except for those born in the United Kingdom and those who were citizens of the United Kingdom and Colonies and held passports issued by the UK government.[8] The 1962 Act also authorised the deportation from the United Kingdom of Commonwealth citizens (but not holders of UK passports) who had been

---

2   *Musgrove* v. *Chun Teeong Toy* [1891] A.C. 272; *cf. Poll* v. *Lord Advocate* (1899) 1 F. 823.
3   [1969] 2 Ch. 149, 172.
4   See C. Parry (ed.) *British Digest of International Law*, vol. 6, pp. 83–98; *A.-G. for Canada* v. *Cain* [1906] A.C. 542, 547; and Dicey, pp. 224–7.
5   Immigration Act 1971, s. 33(5), which ousts the principle in *A.-G.* v. *De Keyser's Royal Hotel Ltd* [1920] A.C. 208 (ch. 13C).
6   Section A, *ante*.
7   *Cf.* D. W. Williams (1974) 23 I.C.L.Q. 642, who argues that the Crown has or had a prerogative power to restrain citizens from leaving the UK; p. 444 *ante*.
8   Passports issued by governments of colonial territories did not entitle holders to enter the UK: *R.* v. *Home Secretary, ex p. Bhurosah* [1968] 1 Q.B. 266.

convicted of offences punishable with imprisonment and recommended by a court for deportation.

The Commonwealth Immigrants Act 1968 was passed in great haste to forestall what was feared might become a mass exodus to Britain from Kenya of those persons of Asian origin who, when Kenya had become independent in 1963, had chosen to continue as citizens of the United Kingdom and Colonies rather than to become citizens of Kenya. Since they held passports issued by the UK government, they were not subject to the controls established by the 1962 Act.[9] The 1968 Act was notable because it took away from a non-resident citizen of the United Kingdom and Colonies the right of entry into the United Kingdom unless he, or at least one of his parents or grandparents, had a prior UK connection (for example, through having been born, adopted or naturalised in the United Kingdom). The 1968 Act thereby prevented citizens of the United Kingdom and Colonies from entering the United Kingdom, even though they were subject to expulsion from the state in which they had been residing and were entitled to enter no other country. The UK government subsequently came under great pressure to admit other UK citizens in similar circumstances and, notwithstanding the 1968 Act, did admit many of the Asians expelled from Uganda in 1972.[10]

The Acts controlling immigration vested wide discretionary powers in the Home Secretary; these powers were mainly exercised by immigration officers acting under his direction. The Home Secretary was responsible to Parliament for the use of these powers. Immigration decisions were in principle subject to review by the courts on grounds of legality, but before 1969, the individual had no right of appeal against an official decision excluding him from the United Kingdom. Implementing the recommendations of the Wilson committee on immigration appeals,[11] the Immigration Appeals Act 1969 created a two-tier system of tribunals to hear appeals from immigration decisions.

The Immigration Act 1971 and after

The Immigration Act 1971 continued in being the system of appeals, but in other respects the Act provided a new and extensive code for the control of immigration. On 1 January 1973, when the 1971 Act came into operation, the distinction between aliens and Commonwealth citizens lost much of its significance for purposes of immigration control. The earlier legislation dealing separately with aliens and Commonwealth immigrants ceased to have effect, but this did not mean a relaxation in the system of control.

Under the 1971 Act, the most important distinction drawn was between those who had the right of abode in the United Kingdom and those (whether aliens or Commonwealth immigrants) who were subject to immigration control and needed permission to enter and reside in the United Kingdom.

---

[9] For the controversy over whether, during negotiations for Kenyan independence in 1963, the UK government intended Asians who chose to retain UK citizenship to have the right to enter the UK, see H. C. Deb., 27, 28 Feb. 1968; H. L. Deb., 29 Feb. 1968; D. Steel, *No Entry*; and Evans, *op. cit.*, pp. 64–8.

[10] *Cf. R.* v. *Immigration Officer at Heathrow, ex p. Thakrar* [1974] Q.B. 684.

[11] Cmnd 3387, 1967.

The fact that an intending immigrant might be a citizen of the United Kingdom and Colonies or of a Commonwealth country did not confer the right of entry. The 1971 Act created a new legal concept, patriality, to identify those British subjects who had a sufficient connection with the United Kingdom to entitle them to the right of abode in the United Kingdom. Thus under the 1971 Act, section 2, the class of patrials included those who were citizens of the United Kingdom and Colonies by reason of their birth, adoption, naturalisation or registration in the United Kingdom or in the Islands (i.e. the Isle of Man and the Channel Islands); citizens of the United Kingdom and Colonies who had been settled and ordinarily resident in the United Kingdom or Islands for five years or more without being in breach of immigration law; Commonwealth citizens who were born to or adopted by a parent who at the time of the birth or adoption was a UK citizen by virtue of his own birth in the United Kingdom or Islands; and also women who were Commonwealth citizens and married to patrials. Depending on the category of patriality, the status of patrial could be acquired in a variety of ways (for example, by birth, marriage, residence and so on). Those claiming to be patrial and wishing to enter the United Kingdom could prove their status by obtaining a certificate of patriality (section 3(9)). In *R.* v. *Home Secretary, ex p. Phansopkar*, the Court ordered the Home Secretary to hear and determine the application for such a certificate made by an Indian woman, who had married a man who had become a UK citizen by registration. The court held that the woman's right to a certificate could not be withheld by arbitrary delay on the part of the Home Office.[12]

The elaborate concept of patriality was considered necessary because of the divergence that had developed between the law of British nationality and immigration policy. The concept was subject to criticism on various grounds. Foremost was the criticism that patriality did not extend to many persons who, like the East African Asians, were citizens of the United Kingdom and Colonies and had no country to which they might go other than the United Kingdom. It was for this reason that the UK government has been unable to ratify the Fourth Protocol to the European Convention on Human Rights, which declares that 'no-one shall be denied the right to enter the territory of which he is a national'.[13] The concept of patriality was also subject to the criticism that it included many citizens of other Commonwealth countries, namely those of whom at least one parent had been born in the United Kingdom; this extension of patriality was likely to favour Commonwealth citizens who were of British origin, thus affording some basis for those critics who saw a racial motivation behind the 1971 Act.

The desire to bring the law of nationality into conformity with immigration policy and to reform the law to take account of changes in the Commonwealth since 1948 was the main reason for the passing of the British Nationality Act 1981. As we have seen in section A, the 1981 Act created a new category of British citizen, the rules defining which were in essence derived from the rules of patriality contained in the Immigration Act 1971. This change enabled the

---

12   [1976] Q.B. 606; *cf. R.* v. *Home Secretary, ex p. Akhtar* [1975] 3 All E.R. 1087.
13   See ch. 31B; and *cf. R.* v. *Home Secretary, ex p. Thakrar*, criticised by M. B. Akehurst (1975) 38 M.L.R. 72.

concept of patriality as such to disappear from the legislation on 1 January 1983 when the 1981 Act came into effect. But despite the change in legal form, the essence of the notion of patriality is kept alive in the new definition of British citizen, and many of the earlier criticisms of the 1971 scheme remain applicable to the 1981 Act. What follows is a brief outline of the present structure of immigration control, which is now founded upon the Immigration Act 1971 as amended by the British Nationality Act 1981.

Immigration control

At the risk of over-simplifying a very complex branch of the law, the following are the main categories of persons for the purposes of immigration control.

(*a*)   British citizens, as defined in the Act of 1981. They have the right of abode in the United Kingdom and do not need leave to enter or reside in the United Kingdom.

(*b*)   British dependent territories citizens, British overseas citizens, British subjects and citizens of other Commonwealth countries (all as defined in the 1981 Act). In general they do not have the right of abode in the United Kingdom and are subject to immigration control. But certain Commonwealth citizens who under the 1971 Act were patrials and as such had the right of abode in the United Kingdom, continue to have that right and are treated as if they were British citizens.[14]

(*c*)   Citizens of the Republic of Ireland, who benefit from the 'common travel area' for immigration purposes formed by the United Kingdom, the Isle of Man, the Channel Islands and the Republic of Ireland.[15] They may in principle enter the United Kingdom from Ireland without passing through immigration control, but they are subject to deportation from the United Kingdom under the Immigration Act 1971 and also to exclusion under the Prevention of Terrorism (Temporary Provisions) Act 1976.[16]

(*d*)   Those aliens who, as nationals of other EEC countries, are subject to immigration control, but benefit from certain rights of movement within the EEC conferred by Community law and in respect of whom the powers of the UK authorities are subject to restrictions imposed by Community law.[17]

(*e*)   Those aliens who, as nationals of non-EEC countries, are subject to immigration control. In the same category may be placed British protected persons, who do not come within the groups mentioned in paragraph (b) above.

Under the 1971 Act, as amended, those who as British citizens have the right of abode in the United Kingdom are free 'to live in, and to come and go into and from, the United Kingdom without let or hindrance' except such as may be required under the Act to enable their right to be established (section 1(1)). The 1971 Act also provides that those who are not British citizens and do not have the right of abode shall not enter or remain in the United Kingdom unless leave is given to them in accordance with the Act.

---

[14]   Immigration Act 1971, s. 2(1)(b) and (2), as substituted by British Nationality Act 1981, s. 39(2).

[15]   Immigration Act 1971, s. 1(3).

[16]   Ch. 29 C.

[17]   Page 460 *post*.

Such leave may be given for a limited or an indefinite period. Where a person is given a limited leave to enter or remain, this leave may be given subject to conditions restricting his employment or occupation in the United Kingdom, or requiring him to register with the police, or both (section 3(1)); where indefinite leave to remain is given, no such conditions may be imposed (section 3(3)). Even though a person has indefinite leave to remain, he remains liable to be deported.[18] A person's leave to enter or remain may lapse when he goes outside the common travel area and fresh leave may be needed on his return (section 3(4)).

The 1971 Act exempts certain groups of non-British citizens from the need to get individual leave to enter and remain. These groups include those non-British citizens who were in the United Kingdom when the Act came into force and were then settled here; that is, were ordinarily resident here and were not subject to any restriction on the period for which they might remain.[19] By section 1(5), an assurance was given that Commonwealth citizens settled in the United Kingdom when the Act came into force, and their wives and children, would not be rendered by immigration rules less free to come into and go from the United Kingdom than if the 1971 Act had not been passed. But in *Azam* v. *Home Secretary*, the House of Lords held that the powers of removal granted by the 1971 Act could be exercised retroactively against those who had unlawfully entered the United Kingdom in breach of the Commonwealth Immigrants Act 1968, even though by the lapse of time they had ceased to be subject to criminal proceedings under the 1968 Act.[20]

Other groups exempted from the need to get individual leave to enter and remain include citizens of the Republic of Ireland, crew members of a ship or aircraft coming temporarily to the United Kingdom, diplomats and others entitled to diplomatic privilege, and members of certain military forces.[21]

So that immigration control might be enforced, the 1971 Act equipped the Home Secretary and immigration officers with a wide variety of powers, including power to examine persons arriving or leaving the United Kingdom, power to remove persons from the United Kingdom who are refused leave to enter or have entered unlawfully or have outstayed a limited leave to remain, and power to detain persons pending examination or removal.[22] Part III of the Act created many criminal offences including illegal entry, outstaying a limited leave to enter or remain, failure to observe a condition of a limited leave, assisting or harbouring illegal entrants, failure without reasonable excuse to submit to examination on arrival into or departure from the United Kingdom, and failure to observe a condition requiring a person to register with the police. Extensive legislation creating such offences was considered necessary because before the 1971 Act, Commonwealth citizens who managed to

---

18 Page 454 *post*.
19 Immigration Act 1971, s. 1(2) and (inserted by British Nationality Act 1981) s. 33(2A); *R.* v. *Home Secretary, ex p. Mughal* [1974] Q.B. 313.
20 [1974] A.C. 18. In 1974, the government granted an amnesty from removal to Commonwealth citizens in the *Azam* category: H. C. Deb., 11 Apr. 1974, col. 637 and Macdonald, *op. cit.*, p. 398.
21 Immigration Act 1971, s. 8; Macdonald, *op. cit.*, ch. 4.
22 For judicial review of decisions on illegal entrants, see p. 458 *post*.

avoid immigration control when they entered the United Kingdom did not commit criminal offences by remaining here.[23] The House of Lords held that the criminal offences created by the 1971 Act were not retrospective in effect.[24] The offence of remaining in the United Kingdom beyond the time limit for which leave to enter was granted is not a continuing offence, but prosecutions must be brought within three years of the offence being committed.[25] As well as granting wide powers of deportation and compulsory removal, the Act also authorises the Home Secretary to meet the expenses of repatriation in the case of a non-British citizen (and his family or household) who wishes to leave for a country where he intends to reside permanently, when it is shown that it is in the person's interest to leave the United Kingdom (section 29).

Immigration rules

The policies followed by the immigration authorities are contained not in the 1971 Act itself but in immigration rules which the Home Secretary from time to time lays down as to the practice to be followed in the administration of the Act (section 3(2)). Statements of these rules must be laid before Parliament. If a statement of the rules is disapproved by a resolution of either House passed within 40 days of the laying, the Home Secretary shall 'as soon as may be' make such changes in the rules as appear to him to be required in the circumstances.[26] The status of the rules is difficult to define. They are not technically statutory instruments[27] but, since they contain rules made by the Home Secretary which are binding on those who hear immigration appeals, they are nonetheless a form of delegated legislation, and they are far from being mere administrative circulars.[28] They must be interpreted sensibly, according to the natural meaning of the words used.[29]

The current rules, which took effect in February 1983, deal separately with control *on* entry and control *after* entry.[30] In all cases immigration control is to be exercised without regard to a person's race, colour or religion. The rules dealing with control on entry deal *inter alia* with: the requirement that a person arriving in the United Kingdom must produce a valid national passport or other satisfactory evidence of his identity and nationality; the need for persons seeking admission to produce an entry clearance (that is, an entry certificate in the case of Commonwealth citizens or a visa in the case of certain aliens)[31]; and the admission of persons coming for temporary purposes (as visitors,

---

23   *DPP* v. *Bhagwan* [1972] A.C. 60.
24   *Waddington* v. *Miah* [1974] 2 All E.R. 377.
25   Immigration Act 1971, ss. 24(1)(c), 24(3) and 28; *Gurdev Singh* v. *R.* [1974] 1 All E.R. 26; *Grant* v. *Borg* [1982] 2 All E.R. 257.
26   New rules made by the government were disapproved by the Commons on 22 Nov. 1972 and again on 15 Dec. 1982; in each case revised rules were later approved by the Commons. And see p. 619 *post*.
27   Ch. 33.
28   *R.* v. *Chief Immigration Officer, ex p. Salamat Bibi* [1976] 3 All E.R. 843, 848; *R.* v. *Home Secretary, ex p. Hosenball* [1977] 3 All E.R. 452, 459, 463; *Pearson* v. *Immigration Appeal Tribunal* [1978] Immigration Appeal Reports 212, 224.
29   *Alexander* v. *Immigration Appeal Tribunal* [1982] 2 All E.R. 766.
30   H.C. 169 (1982–3); and see H. C. Deb., 15 Feb. 1983, col. 180.
31   On the nature of entry clearance, see *Alexander's* case, *ante*.

students[32] or au pair girls). A person arriving for employment must normally hold a work permit issued by the Department of Employment, but work permits are not needed for certain forms of employment (for example, ministers of religion, doctors, exchange teachers). Nationals of EEC countries are admitted without a work-permit, in accordance with Community law, to take or seek employment, to set up in business or to become self-employed. A Commonwealth citizen who can prove that one of his grandparents was born in the United Kingdom, does not need a work permit and if he holds appropriate entry clearance he is granted indefinite leave to enter. Young Commonwealth citizens may be admitted for extended working holidays of up to 2 years. The rules also govern the admission for settlement of a spouse, children under 18 and other relatives of persons who are settled here. In the case of a husband or fiancé of a woman who is settled in the United Kingdom, entry will be refused unless the entry clearance officer is satisfied that the primary purpose of the marriage or intended marriage was not to gain admission to the country; but this rule against 'marriages of convenience' does not apply to a wife or fiancée seeking to join a man settled in the United Kingdom.[33]

The rules for control after entry deal with the variation of leave to enter or remain, for example where a person admitted as a visitor seeks leave to remain as a student. They also deal with the position of children born in the United Kingdom who, because of the British Nationality Act 1981, are not British citizens;[34] in principle, they are to be given leave to remain with their parents. As regards refugees, the criterion for the grant of political asylum is that a person should not be required to leave the United Kingdom 'if the only country to which he can be removed is one to which he is unwilling to go owing to well-founded fear of being persecuted for reasons of race, religion, nationality, membership of a particular social group or political opinion'.

As will be evident from this outline of the immigration rules, important changes of policy can be made by alteration of the rules, subject to the express constraints contained in the Immigration Act 1971.[35] The way in which the rules are framed leaves important discretionary decisions to be made by the immigration authorities. The scheme therefore depends a greal deal upon the scope for appealing against immigration decisions.

Immigration appeals[36]

As has already been mentioned, the Immigration Appeals Act 1969 established a two-tier system of appeals which was continued in being by the Immigration Act 1971. The lower tier consists of adjudicators appointed by the Home Secretary; their duties are allocated to them by the chief adjudicator, and individual adjudicators sit to hear appeals at the ports of entry. The upper tier

---

32 On students, see *e.g. R.* v. *Immigration Appeal Tribunal, ex p. Shaikh* [1981] 3 All E.R. 29; and *Alexander's* case, *ante.*

33 And see *R.* v. *Immigration Appeal Tribunal, ex p. Weerasuriya* [1983] 1 All E.R. 195.

34 Page 439 *ante.*

35 *E.g.,* Immigration Act 1971 s. 1(5), (rules not to restrict freedom of Commonwealth citizens settled in the UK on 1 Jan. 1973 to enter and leave the UK).

36 Evans, *op. cit.,* ch. 7; Macdonald, *op. cit.,* ch. 11. See also Home Office, *Review of Appeals under the Immigration Act 1971: a discussion document.*

consists of the Immigration Appeal Tribunal, appointed by the Lord Chancellor, whose president must be a lawyer of not less than seven years standing. Both the adjudicators and the Tribunal are subject to the supervision of the Council on Tribunals. In 1982, 15 full-time adjudicators and 56 part-time adjudicators heard over 11,000 cases. The Tribunal, sitting in four divisions of three members each, decided 476 appeals and dealt with nearly 4,500 applications for leave to appeal.[37]

The 1971 Act does not confer a general right of appeal against every official decision that may affect an immigrant. For example, there is no right of appeal against the refusal of a work permit by the Department of Employment,[38] nor against the refusal of a special entry voucher,[39] nor against the Secretary of State's refusal to naturalise an alien or register a Commonwealth citizen as a British citizen.[40] Apart from deportation matters, which are discussed below, an appeal lies against (a) the refusal of entry (b) the refusal of a certificate of entitlement (replacing the former certificate of patriality) or an entry certificate (c) conditions of admission, variations of limits imposed on leave to enter and refusals to make such variations.[41] Written notice to the individual must be given of any decision that may be appealed against, together with the reasons for it.[42] These rights of appeal are subject to important restrictions. In particular, a person may not appeal against a refusal of leave to enter so long as he is in the United Kingdom, unless he was refused such leave at a port of entry at a time when he held a current entry clearance or a current work permit (section 13(3)). This means that many appeals can be brought only after the appellant has left the United Kingdom, and thus they will be decided in his absence. Appeals against the refusal of an entry certificate will also generally be heard in the appellant's absence. There is no appeal against a refusal of leave to enter if the Home Secretary certifies that he has personally directed that a person be refused entry on the grounds that his exclusion is conducive to the public good (section 13(5)). Where a person who has a limited leave to remain in the United Kingdom applies before the expiry of that leave for an extension in the time limit, his leave to remain is deemed to be extended until 28 days after the Home Secretary's decision on the application.[43'] If he appeals against that decision to an adjudicator, he cannot be required to depart from the United Kingdom so long as his appeal is pending; but if he does not apply for an extension in the time limit until his original leave has expired, he has no right of appeal against a refusal by the Home Secretary to extend the period of his leave.[44]

Assuming that an appellant manages to exercise a right of appeal, what are the powers of the adjudicator or the Immigration Appeal Tribunal to review

---

[37]   Annual Report of Council on Tribunals 1982–3, p. 36; and see ch. 37 B.
[38]   *Pearson's* case, *ante* note 28.
[39]   *Amin* v. *Entry Clearance Officer, Bombay* [1983] 2 All E.R. 864.
[40]   British Nationality Act 1981, s. 44.
[41]   Immigration Act 1971, ss. 13 and 14; and see *R.* v. *Immigration Appeal Tribunal, ex p. Coomasaru* [1983] 1 All E.R. 208.
[42]   For appeals procedure, see S.I. 1972 No. 1684.
[43]   See S.I. 1976 No. 1752, made to alter the effect of *Suthendran* v. *Immigration Appeal Tribunal* [1977] A.C. 359.
[44]   Immigration Act 1971, s. 14(1); and *Suthendran's* case, *ante*.

the decision appealed against? By section 19 of the 1971 Act, an adjudicator is required to allow an appeal in two situations: first, if he considers that the decision was not in accordance with the law or with the relevant immigration rules (for this purpose he may review questions of fact); and second, if he considers, where the decision involved the exercise of a discretion, that the discretion should have been exercised differently. But otherwise he must dismiss the appeal. No decision which is in accordance with the immigration rules is to be treated as having involved the exercise of discretion merely because the Home Secretary was asked by the appellant to depart from the rules and refused to do so (section 19(2)). These statutory rules are also binding on the Immigration Appeal Tribunal, to whom an appeal may lie with leave from the adjudicator's decision. Selected decisions by the Immigration Appeal Tribunal are published and bind adjudicators. There thus exists a framework of rules and principles within which the exercise of administrative discretion may be reviewed by tribunals without, from the Home Office point of view, creating too great a risk of decisions that cut across the day-to-day pattern of control. Indeed, the system of appeals has been criticised for being under excessive Home Office influence; adjudicators are said to be too ready to accept statements made by the immigration authorities, and to reject evidence given on behalf of immigrants. In 1981, only one in every eight appeals to adjudicators was successful.[45]

There is no further appeal from decisions of the Immigration Appeal Tribunal, but these may be reviewed in the High Court by means of an application for judicial review.[46]

Deportation and removal from the United Kingdom[47]

The power to deport a person is a drastic power which needs to be subject to close political and judicial safeguards. Under the Aliens Order 1953, an alien could be deported *either* after conviction for a criminal offence punishable with imprisonment, and a recommendation for deportation by the court *or* if the Secretary of State deemed it conducive to the public good that he should be deported. It was the latter power which proved the more controversial, since the Home Secretary's broad discretion could be used for a wide variety of purposes. Attempts to control the discretion by recourse to the courts were unsuccessful. Thus it was held that the alien need not be given a hearing before he was deported, although in practice he often was;[48] that, while the Home Secretary could not name the country to which an alien must go, he could achieve the same result by placing him on a specified ship or aircraft;[49] and that the Home Secretary need not give reasons for his decision to deport.[50] In the most controversial case under the Aliens Order 1953, an attempt by the

---

45   For a critique of the system, see Evans, *op. cit.*, pp. 362–74.
46   Page 665 *post*.
47   Evans, *op. cit.*, ch. 5; Macdonald, *op. cit.*, ch. 13.
48   *R. v. Leman Street Police Inspector, ex p. Venicoff* [1920] 3 K.B. 72; *R. v. Governor of Brixton Prison, ex p. Soblen* [1963] 2 Q.B. 243.
49   *R. v. Home Secretary, ex p. Chateau Thierry* [1917] 1 K.B. 922.
50   *Soblen's* case *ante*.

American, Dr Soblen, to prevent his deportation to the USA failed, even though the US government had requested the British government that Dr Soblen, who had been convicted in the USA of an espionage offence, should be returned to the USA: in other words, by use of the deportation power the Home Secretary could achieve a 'disguised extradition' of Dr Soblen to the US authorities, though in law the Home Secretary had no power to extradite him for an espionage offence.[51]

In 1962, Commonwealth citizens were for the first time made subject to deportation but only upon the recommendation of a court for conviction of a criminal offence. Under the Immigration Act 1971, all non-British citizens are in principle subject to the same powers of deportation. By that Act, a non-British citizen may be deported in four circumstances: (a) if, having only a limited leave to remain, he breaks a condition attached to the leave or remains beyond the time permitted; (b) 'if the Secretary of State deems his deportation to be conducive to the public good'; (c) if another person to whose family he belongs is ordered to be deported;[52] or (d) if, being 17 years old or more, he is convicted of an offence for which he is punishable with imprisonment and on his conviction is recommended for deportation by the court.[53] If a deporttation order is made, it requires the person named to leave the United Kingdom and prohibits him from returning until the order has been revoked; but the order ceases to have effect if the person named becomes a British citizen or if, in case (c) above, the person ceases to belong to the family of the orginal deportee (for example, on becoming 18). Under case (d), a court may not recommend a convicted person for deportation unless he has first been given seven days' written notice of the proposal (section 6(2)); and the convicted person has a right of appeal against the recommendation to a higher court (section 6(5)).[54]

Certain exemptions from deportation were given to Commonwealth citizens and citizens of the Republic of Ireland who were ordinarily resident in the United Kingdom on 1 January 1973. By section 7, a Commonwealth citizen or Irish citizen who has been ordinarily resident in the United Kingdom continuously since 1 January 1973 may not be deported on ground (b) above; and if he was ordinarily resident here on that date and has been so resident for the five years preceding the Home Secretary's decision or the conviction by the court, he may not be deported on any ground.[55]

Under the 1971 Act, there are also powers for removal of illegal entrants and others refused entry, which may be exercised without a deportation order.[56] These powers of removal have become of increased importance since the courts have held that illegal entry is not confined to clandestine entry (that is, the complete avoidance of immigration control) but also includes entry by

---

[51] *Soblen's* case, *ante*, criticised by P. O'Higgins (1964) 27 M.L.R. 521. For extradition, see section C *post*.
[52] For this purpose, a man's family means his wife and his or her children under 18; a woman's family means her children under 18. And see Immigration Act 1971, s. 15(6).
[53] Immigration Act 1971, s. 3(5)(6); and see ss. 57 and sch. 3.
[54] For the criteria to be applied, see *R. v. Nazari* [1980] 3 All E.R. 880.
[55] For this purpose, 'ordinarily resident' has a special meaning: s. 7(2).
[56] Immigration Act 1971, sch. 2, paras. 8–10; Macdonald, *op. cit.*, pp. 404–8.

deception through the use of false documents, the making of false representations and in some circumstances non-disclosure of material facts.[57]

Appeals against deportation

In view of the wide discretion that may be exercised in a deportation case,
there are evident difficulties in conferring a full right of appeal to a tribunal
against a deportation decision. Under the Immigration Appeals Act 1969,
however, when the Home Secretary decided that it was conducive to the public
good that an alien should be deported, the alien had in general a full right of
appeal to an adjudicator and to the Immigration Appeal Tribunal. The only
exception was that, where it appeared to the Home Secretary that the original
decision had been taken in the interest of national security, the appeal lay to
a special panel of the Immigration Appeal Tribunal, appointed by the Home
Secretary and the Lord Chancellor jointly. The decision of the tribunal was
stated to be advisory only and the tribunal was allowed to hear evidence in
the absence of the appellant if the Home Secretary certified that considerations
of national security so required.[58] This awkward hybrid procedure was used
only once, in the case of Rudi Dutschke, the German student leader, when the
Home Secretary decided that Dutschke's continued presence for postgraduate
research at Cambridge was undesirable. The tribunal's advisory decision
rejecting the appeal was based on evidence given by the security service in the
absence of Dutschke and his representatives; and the decision itself had many
controversial implications.[59]

Since the 1969 Act procedure pleased neither side, the 1971 Act made a
fresh attempt to reconcile the interests of justice, political discretion and
national security. The complicated provisions for appeals against deportation
decisions may be summarised in this way.

(a)   Where a court has recommended deportation after a conviction for a
criminal offence, appeal against the recommendation lies to a higher criminal
court, not to the immigration appeals system. There is no appeal against a
decision by the Home Secretary to accept the recommendation.

(b)   Where the Home Secretary has decided to deport a person on grounds
of breach of an entry condition or exceeding the time-limit of leave to remain,
appeal lies to an adjudicator and a further appeal lies to the Immigration
Appeal Tribunal.[60] This right of appeal is, however, subject to (c) and (e)
below.

(c)   Where a person is to be deported because he or she belongs to the family
of a person who is being deported, his or her appeal lies direct to the Immigration Appeal Tribunal; and where such an appeal is related to an appeal
against deportation on the grounds stated in (b) above, both appeals go direct
to the Appeal Tribunal.[61]

---

57   Macdonald, *op. cit.*, ch. 14; Evans, *op. cit.*, ch. 6; *R.* v. *Home Secretary, ex p. Zamir* [1980] A.C.
930 and *R.* v. *Home Secretary, ex p. Khawaja* [1984] A.C. 74; p. 459 *post*.
58   Immigration Appeals Act 1969, s. 9. *Cf.* Cmnd 3387, 1967, p. 49.
59   See B. A. Hepple (1971) 34 M.L.R. 501.
60   Immigration Act 1971, s. 15(1).
61   Immigration Act 1971, s. 15(7).

(*d*)   Where the ground of the decision is that the deportation is conducive to the public good, appeal lies direct to the Appeal Tribunal (subject to (*e*) below).

(*e*)   There is, however, no right of appeal if the ground of the decision is that deportation is conducive to the public good 'as being in the interests of national security or of the relations between the United Kingdom and any other country or for other reasons of a political nature.'[62]

In the latter case, in lieu of an appeal, the individual may be given a private hearing before a panel of three advisers of the Home Secretary. The reason for this informal and non-statutory procedure was stated by the Home Secretary in 1971 to be that deportation decisions on national security grounds 'are decisions of a political and executive character which should be subject to Parliament and not subject to courts, arbitrators and so on'.[63] The procedure was tested in 1977.

Deportation orders in the interests of national security were made by the Home Secretary against two American journalists, Philip Agee and Mark Hosenball. The Home Secretary claimed that they had sought to obtain and publish information harmful to the security services. When they were given a hearing before the panel of three advisers, the Home Office gave no further particulars of the allegations, nor of the evidence against the journalists, nor was the panel's report on the appeal seen by the deportees. When Hosenball challenged the validity of his deportation, the Court of Appeal upheld the deportation, holding that normal issues of natural justice must give way to the interests of state security; the Home Secretary was responsible to Parliament for the decision and for holding the balance between national security and individual freedom.[64]

While the problem of achieving an acceptable balance between these conflicting interests seems as intractable as ever, in one respect the Immigration Act 1971 made an important reform in the law of deportation. Under the Aliens Order 1953, as we saw in the case of Dr Soblen, the Home Secretary could order the deportee to be placed on a named ship or aircraft and thus in effect order him to be taken to a particular destination. There is however a very strong argument that the essence of the power to deport is to ensure that the individual leaves this country, not that he should be sent to another. Under the Act of 1971, section 17, where directions are given for an individual's removal from the United Kingdom, either on being refused leave to enter or in pursuance of a deportation order, the individual may in all cases, even in those affecting national security, appeal to an adjudicator and thence to the Immigration Appeal Tribunal against the directions on the ground that he ought to be removed to a different country or territory specified by him. Subject to this right of appeal, the Home Secretary may direct a deportee's removal either to a country of which he is a citizen or to a country to which there is reason to believe that he will be admitted.[65] The deportee has no absolute right to go to the country of his choice, even if that country is willing

---

62   Immigration Act 1971, s. 15(3).
63   H. C. Deb., 15 Jun. 1971, col. 375.
64   *R.* v. *Home Secretary, ex p. Hosenball* [1977] 3 All E.R. 452.
65   Immigration Act 1971, sch. 3, para. 1.

to admit him, but nonetheless his right of appeal should help to reduce the risk of deportation being used as 'disguised extradition'.

Judicial review of immigration decisions[66]

In principle, decisions under the 1971 Act are subject to review in the superior civil courts. Where the decision of an immigration officer or the Home Secretary is subject to appeal to an adjudicator or to the Appeal Tribunal, an individual will normally be expected to appeal rather than to have direct recourse to the courts.[67] But the remedies obtainable by application for judicial review, which are discretionary in their nature, are available where either there is no right of appeal or where the right of appeal is subject to restrictions (for example, the requirement that the applicant must first leave the United Kingdom) sufficient to persuade the court that it should intervene to assist the applicant.[68] Moreover, in the view of Lord Denning, the creation of an appeals system did not take away the individual's right to seek habeas corpus, which is not a discretionary remedy.[69] The decisions of the adjudicators or Immigration Appeal Tribunal are themselves subject to judicial review.[70]

The grounds on which immigration decisions may be reviewed include a breach of duty by the Home Office,[71] failure to exercise a discretion properly,[72] and an abuse of power. For example, if it could be shown that a deportation order was made for an improper purpose or was a 'mere sham', the order could be quashed by the courts, but the burden of establishing this is a heavy one.[73] The official interpretation of a statutory provision may be reviewed by the courts and so may interpretation of the immigration rules.[74]

Difficult questions may arise as to whether findings made by the immigration authorities are supported by the evidence. Under the 1971 Act, section 3(8), the burden of proving that a person is a British citizen or is entitled to any exemption under the Act is placed on the person asserting it. But it may be difficult to determine the truth of events in the past, particularly where an intending immigrant has not always told the same story,[75] or to decide the true nature of his future intentions.[76] The approach of the courts in reviewing findings made by the immigration authorities has fluctuated a great deal. Some courts have been willing to intervene only when there are no grounds upon which the authorities could reasonably have come to a particular conclusion, a test derived from *A.P. Picture Houses Ltd* v. *Wednesbury Corporation*.[77] In 1980

---

66   For judicial review in general, see chs. 34, 35.

67   *R.* v. *Chief Immigration Officer, Heathrow, ex p. Salamat Bibi* [1976] 3 All E.R. 843, 850.

68   As in *R.* v. *Home Secretary, ex p. Phansopkar* [1976] Q.B. 606; page 657 *ante*.

69   *R.* v. *Governor of Pentonville Prison, ex p. Azam* [1974] A.C. 18, 31 (C.A.). *Cf.* the view that habeas corpus does not lie when a would-be immigrant is free to leave the country at a moment's notice: [1976] Q.B. 606, 611.

70   See *e.g. R.* v. *Immigration Appeals Tribunal, ex p. Khan (Mahmud)* [1983] 2 All E.R. 420 (failure to give adequate reasons).

71   Note 68 *ante*.

72   *Alexander* v. *Immigration Appeal Tribunal* [1982] 2 All E.R. 766.

73   *Soblen's* case, note 48 *ante*.

74   *E.g. Alexander's case ante.*

75   *R.* v. *Home Secretary, ex p. Mughal* [1974] Q.B. 313.

76   *R.* v. *Immigration Appeals Adjudicator, ex p. Khan* [1972] 3 All E.R. 297.

77   [1948] 1 K.B. 233, p. 630 *post*.

the House of Lords applied this test in upholding a decision that a Pakistani citizen, Zamir, should be deported as an illegal entrant, who at the time of entry had not revealed that he had married after receiving an entry certificate.[78] In 1983, the House of Lords adopted a significantly different approach in *Khawaja's* case, holding that the question whether an individual is an illegal entrant is a 'precedent fact', which has to be established to the satisfaction of the court.[79] Only when this fact can be established on the available evidence, does the discretionary power to remove the individual arise. The approach adopted in *Khawaja's* case is essential if the courts are to give adequate protection to the individual against executive decisions that affect his liberty. Thus, if the Home Secretary decided to deport someone whom he wrongly believed to be a non-British citizen, the question of citizenship must be decided by the court in habeas corpus proceedings; and the court should not confine itself to deciding whether the Home Secretary's belief was in the circumstances reasonable.

To what extent can immigration decisions be challenged on grounds of natural justice?[80] Under the former Aliens Order, the Home Secretary was not required to give a hearing to an alien before deciding to deport him nor before deciding that an alien should leave the United Kingdom.[81] The extension of immigration control to all non-British citizens and the creation of an appeals system has broadened the scope for judicial application of natural justice. In *Re H. K.*, which concerned the investigation by an immigration officer into the question of whether an intending immigrant was under 16 and the son of a Commonwealth citizen settled in England, the court held that the officer was bound to act impartially and fairly; to that extent he was bound to observe the rules of natural justice, but he need not hold any fullscale inquiry nor adopt judicial procedure.[82] In the case of citizens from EEC countries, the United Kingdom is not free to adopt whatever procedure it likes. In *R. v. Home Secretary, ex p. Santillo*, the deportation of an Italian citizen, who had been convicted of serious sexual offences and recommended for deportation by a British court, was challenged unsuccessfully on grounds of natural justice. However, the judgment of the European Court of Justice which was obtained in the case established that Community law, on which Santillo was entitled to rely, may impose procedural requirements (including the right of representation and defence before an independent authority) greater than those imposed by national law.[83] As we shall see below, the immigration authorities are required to observe Community law in decisions applying to citizens of EEC countries. But, despite a difference of judicial opinion, it seems that immigration officers are not required to have regard to the European Convention on Human Rights.[84]

---

[78]   *R. v. Home Secretary, ex p. Zamir* [1980] A.C. 930.
[79]   *R. v. Home Secretary, ex p. Khawaja* [1984] A.C. 74. And see ch. 26 B.
[80]   Ch. 34 B.
[81]   *Soblen's* case *ante*; *Schmidt* v. *Home Secretary* [1969] 2 Ch. 149.
[82]   [1967] 2 Q.B. 617.
[83]   *R. v. Home Secretary, ex p. Santillo* [1981] Q.B. 778.
[84]   *R. v. Chief Immigration Officer, Heathrow, ex p. Salamat Bibi* [1976] 3 All E.R. 843 *cf. R.* v. *Home Secretary, ex p. Bhajan Singh* [1976] Q.B. 198, 207 and *R.* v. *Home Secretary, ex p. Phansopkar* [1976] Q.B. 606, 626; and see ch. 31 B.

Parliamentary control

There is wide political interest in immigration. The practice and policies of the immigration authorities are often controversial. When changes are made to the immigration rules, a statement of the changes must be laid before Parliament and either House may resolve to disapprove the statement within 40 days of the laying.[85] Immigration statistics are published annually to Parliament. Individual decisions, particularly in deportation cases, may give rise to questioning or debate in Parliament.[86] Despite the system of appeals, M.P.s are often anxious to raise with the Home Secretary the personal circumstances of individuals who are refused permission to stay in the United Kingdom. Political pressure may be exercised to persuade the Home Secretary to·depart from the immigration rules in favour of an individual, a matter that is beyond the powers of the adjudicator or the Immigration Appeal Tribunal.[87] Such political intervention seems essential to mitigate distress and hardship caused by over-rigid administration of the law.[88] Complaints of maladministration in immigration matters may be sent by M.P.s to the Parliamentary Commissioner for Administration, although he may not investigate a complaint where it was reasonable for the individual to exercise a right of appeal to an adjudicator or tribunal.[89]

Between 1968 and 1979, the House of Commons appointed a select committee on race relations and immigration, which investigated several aspects of the immigration system.[90] Since 1979, these matters have come within the remit of the Home Affairs Committee, which in practice appoints a sub-committee to investigate matters affecting race relations and immigration.[91]

Immigration law and the EEC

An essential aim of the EEC is to establish 'the free movement of persons, services and capital'.[92] Since the EEC Treaty is concerned primarily with individuals from an economic viewpoint, it seeks to create free movement of workers and the right of individuals and companies to set up business and to supply services within all member states. By article 7 of the Treaty, any discrimination on grounds of nationality is prohibited. By article 48, any discrimination based on nationality between workers of member states as regards employment, remuneration and other labour conditions must be abolished. Nationals of member states are therefore entitled to accept offers of employment made within the EEC, to move freely within the EEC for this purpose, to remain in a member state for employment, and to remain in a state after having been employed there. When a worker exercises his freedom of movement, he must not thereby be prejudiced as to his social security rights (for

---

85   Immigration Act 1971, s. 3(2); and see p. 451 *ante.*
86   See *e.g.* adjournment debate on deportation of Serge Descubes, H. C. Deb., 19 May 1971, col. 1422.
87   Immigration Act 1971, s. 19(2).
88   See e.g. R. Moore and T. Wallace, *Slamming the Door.*
89   Ch. 37 D.
90   *E.g.* H.C. 303 (1977–8).
91   *E.g.* H.C. 434 (1979–80) and H.C. 90 (1981–2); ch. 11D.
92   Article 3(*c*), EEC Treaty; and see Evans, *op. cit.*, ch. 4.

example, to a retirement pension). A wage earner's right of entry extends to his spouse, children who are under 21 or dependent on him ,and the dependent parents or grandparents of the wage-earner and spouse.[93] To give effect to these rights, the rules made under the Immigration Act 1971 enable EEC nationals and their families to enter the United Kingdom to take up employment, to set up homes and so on.[94]

No summary of Community law on these matters can be given here, but two points in particular may be noted. First, the declaration by the UK government defining UK nationals for purposes of Community law was annexed to the final Act of the Treaty of Accession when it was signed in 1972. The declaration provided that UK nationals for Community law purposes were (a) citizens of the United Kingdom and Colonies, and also British subjects who were not citizens of any Commonwealth country, who in either case had a right of abode in the United Kingdom and were therefore exempt from UK immigration control; and (b) persons who were citizens of the United Kingdom and Colonies by birth, naturalisation or registration in Gibraltar (or whose father was). Thus, the declaration did not include all those who were citizens of the United Kingdom and Colonies nor all those who were patrial under the Immigration Act 1971. It excluded (a) citizens of Commonwealth countries (other than the United Kingdom) who were patrial and (b) UK citizens and Commonwealth citizens who were settled as resident in the United Kingdom, but not patrial. For special reasons, those who held UK citizenship by virtue of a connection with the Channel Islands or the Isle of Man were also excluded from the benefit of freedom of movement in Community law.[95] It is not certain whether the 1972 declaration may be unilaterally amended by the United Kingdom (as it was noted but not formally adopted by the other states which were parties to the Treaty of Accession), but unilateral amendment is probably competent.[96] In this event, the British Nationality Act 1981 has made the application of the 1972 declaration uncertain,[97] since it replaced citizenship of the United Kingdom and Colonies with three new categories of citizenship and also redefined the right of abode for purposes of the Immigration Act 1971. These changes could affect those who would be entitled to benefit from Community law under the 1972 declaration.

Second, the provisions of Community law which provide for the free movement of wage-earners and other persons are directly applicable within the national law of member states[98] and they thereby restrict the powers which the UK government would otherwise be able to exercise under the Immigration Act 1971. For example, the power of the Home Secretary to exclude an alien on the ground that his presence would not be conducive to the public good, and his power to deport aliens on the same ground, have been limited by EEC Directive 64/221 which in part provides '1. Measures taken on grounds of public policy or public security shall be based exclusively on the

---

93   EEC Regulation 1612/68, art. 10.
94   See H.C. 169 (1982–3), paras. 66–72, 139–47.
95   Treaty of Accession, Protocol 3, Arts. 2, 6.
96   The provisions cited in note 95 were agreed by the other states party to the Treaty of Accession and may not be varied unilaterally.
97   For the position of Gibraltarians, see British Nationality Act 1981, s. 5.
98   Ch. 8 A.

personal conduct of the individual concerned. 2. Previous criminal convictions shall not in themselves constitute grounds for the taking of such measures'.

In *Van Duyn* v. *Home Office*, a Dutch scientologist offered employment at a college of scientology in England, was denied entry, the Home Secretary having decided that it was undesirable to grant anyone leave to enter the United Kingdom for such employment. On a reference under article 177 of the EEC Treaty, the European Court of Justice held that the provision in the EEC directive quoted above was directly applicable and that the voluntary act of an individual in associating with a particular organisation could be regarded 'as a matter of personal conduct'. The ban on persons entering the United Kingdom to take employment with the college of scientology did not therefore conflict with the EEC directive.[99]

These restrictions on the Home Secretary's powers in respect of EEC nationals may be enforced through the British courts. Although in *Van Duyn* v. *Home Office* the plaintiff sued in the English High Court, the directly applicable provisions of Community law are binding also upon adjudicators and upon the Immigration Appeal Tribunal.[100] For example, an EEC national who was refused entry could exercise the statutory right of appeal against the immigration officer's decision claiming that the decision was not in accordance with Community law.

C.   Extradition[1]

Extradition is the formal surrender by one state to another of a person who, being found in the former state, is accused or has been convicted of an offence committed within the jurisdiction of the latter. It is a procedure which is widely accepted by states as a means of ensuring that fugitive criminals do not avoid the consequences of serious crime. An alternative procedure is for states to adopt extra-territorial jurisdiction in respect of specific serious crimes. A number of modern multilateral treaties, for instance, require a state to prosecute anyone who has allegedly committed certain crimes in another state, if they are found within its jurisdiction and not extradited.[2]

In the United Kingdom, extradition procedure is regulated by statute. Extradition to and from foreign non-Commonwealth states, other than the Republic of Ireland, is subject to the Extradition Acts 1870–1935; extradition to and from other Commonwealth states and UK dependencies must comply with the Fugitive Offenders Act 1967. The return of fugitive criminals between the Republic of Ireland and the United Kingdom is effected under a simpler procedure in the Backing of Warrants (Republic of Ireland) Act 1965. All three types of extradition procedure are subject to the Suppression of Terrorism Act 1978.

---

99   [1975] Ch. 358. See also *R.* v. *Bouchereau* [1977] 2 C.M.L.R. 800; *R.* v. *Saunders* [1979] 2 All E.R. 207, C.J.E.C.: *cf. R.* v. *Secchi* [1975] 1 C.M.L.R. 383.

100   *R.* v. *Home Secretary ex p. Sandhu* [1982] Imm. A.R. 36.

1   See V. E. Hartley-Booth, *British Extradition Law and Practice*; S. D. Bedi, *Extradition in International Law and Practice*; A. Shearer, *Extradition in International Law.*

2   *E.g.* European Convention on the Suppression of Terrorism, art. 1; Suppression of Terrorism Act 1978, s. 4. *Cf.* Criminal Jurisdiction Act 1975: p. 470 *post.*

I. Extradition: foreign states

Extradition between the United Kingdom and foreign states takes place under extradition arrangements, usually bilateral or multilateral treaties,[3] made in accordance with the Extradition Acts[4] and to which that legislation has been applied by order.[5] The Extradition Acts lay down the procedure for the extradition of fugitives who have been accused or convicted[6] of an extradition crime within the jurisdiction of a foreign state.[7] An extradition crime is one which (a) is a crime in the state requesting extradition, (b) if it had been committed within the jurisdiction, would be a crime in English law and (c) is one of the crimes described in schedule 1 of the Extradition Act 1870.[8] An extradition treaty may contain provisions which are more restrictive than those in the Extradition Acts. Where a request for extradition is made under such a treaty, the treaty restrictions will prevail. An extradition treaty may, for example, provide for a more limited list of extradition offences than that contained in the Extradition Act 1870 or, unlike the Extradition Acts, prohibit or restrict the extradition of nationals.[9] Thus, 'to justify a committal, the offence for which the accused is committed must come within the language both of the treaty and the Extradition Act'.[10]

In *Re Arton (No. 2)*, Arton had been accused of *faux* (forgery) in France; under an extradition treaty the French government requested his extradition from the United Kingdom. At the committal proceedings, the magistrate decided that there was no evidence that Arton had committed the English offence of forgery although there was sufficient evidence of the English offence of fraudulent falsification of accounts and that offence amounted to *faux* (forgery) in French law. Both the English law offences and the French law offence were extradition crimes under the extradition treaty. Arton was committed to prison pending extradition and sought a writ of habeas corpus. It was held that the following conditions must be fulfilled before extradition: '(1) the imputed

---

3   *E.g.* Convention on the Physical Protection of Nuclear Material; Nuclear Material (Offences) Act 1983, s. 5(2). On the prerogative power to surrender and request the surrender of fugitive criminals see *Barton v. Commonwealth of Australia* (1974) 131 C.L.R. 477, 485; D. Brown (1975) 24 I.C.L.Q. 127.

4   Extradition Act 1870, s. 4.

5   Extradition Act 1870, ss. 2, 5. The rules of Community law regarding the free movement of workers do not apply to extradition: *R. v. Governor of Pentonville Prison, ex p. Budlong* [1980] 1 All E.R. 701, 715–7, *cf. R. v. Saunders* [1980] Q.B. 72.

6   On what amounts to a conviction see Extradition Act 1870, s. 26; *R. v. Governor of Brixton Prison, ex p. Caborn-Waterfield* [1960] 2 Q.B. 498; *Royal Government of Greece v. Governor of Brixton Prison* [1971] A.C. 250, 267; *R. v. Governor of Pentonville Prison, ex p. Zezza* [1983] A.C. 46.

7   The offence need not have been committed within the territory of the state requesting extradition: *R. v. Godfrey* [1923] 1 K.B. 24. On diplomatic immunity, see *R. v. Governor of Pentonville Prison, ex p. Teja* [1971] 2 Q.B. 274. For the procedure where a fugitive is extradited to the UK see: Extradition Act 1870, s. 19; *R. v. Corrigan* [1931] 1 K.B. 527; *R. v. Smith* (1975) 120 Sol. J. 63; *R. v. Kerr* (1975) 62 Cr. App. R. 210; *R. v. Davidson* (1976) 64 Cr. App. R. 209.

8   Additions have been made to the crimes listed in schedule 1: *e.g.* Genocide Act 1969, s. 2(1)(a); Internationally Protected Persons Act 1978, s. 3(1). An attempt to commit a scheduled crime is also an extradition crime (Suppression of Terrorism Act 1978, s. 3(1)(c)). See also *R. v. Governor of Holloway Prison ex p. Jennings* [1983] A.C. 624.

9   *E.g. Re Arton* [1896] 1 Q.B. 108; *Re Arton (No. 2)* [1896] 1 Q.B. 509; *Wan Ping Nam v. Minister of Justice of Federal German Republic* 1972 J.C. 43. And see D. N. Schiff [1979] P.L. 353.

10   *Re Arton, ante,* 112.

crime must be within the Treaty; (2) it must be a crime against the law of the country demanding extradition; (3) it must be a crime within the . . . Extradition Acts . . . and (4) there must be such evidence before the committing magistrate as would warrant him sending the case for trial, if it were an ordinary case in this country'; as the alleged offence was 'a crime against the law of both countries, and is, in substance, to be found in each version of the Treaty, although under different heads, we are bound to give effect to the claim for extradition'.[11]

The extradition procedure is initiated by a request from a foreign state to the UK government for the surrender of a fugitive criminal who is believed to be in the United Kingdom. A Secretary of State, in practice the Home Secretary, may then instruct a metropolitan magistrate to issue a warrant for the arrest of the fugitive.[12] Such a warrant is issued where there is evidence which would, in the opinion of the magistrate, justify issuing the warrant if the crime had been committed, or the fugitive convicted, in England.[13] Alternatively, where there is sufficient evidence, a metropolitan magistrate or any justice of the peace may issue a provisional warrant for the arrest of a fugitive prior to receiving instructions from the Home Secretary.[14] On arrest, the fugitive is normally brought before the metropolitan magistrate at Bow Street, who decides whether the fugitive should be committed to prison pending his extradition or discharged.[15] The magistrate may only order committal where, in addition to other requirements, (a) there is evidence which in English law would be sufficient either to justify committal for trial, had the crime been committed in England, or to prove the alleged conviction[16] and (b) extradition is not prohibited by the Extradition Acts or the relevant extradition treaty.[17]

A fugitive who is committed to prison pending extradition has a statutory period of fifteen days in which to apply to the High Court for a writ of habeas corpus[18] and cannot be extradited during that time.[19] The High Court will grant such an application (a) where the magistrate had no jurisdiction to order the committal, or (b) where there was no evidence on which, if properly directing himself, he could have committed, or (c) where the extradition offence is either one of a political character or one which falls within the terms of the Suppression of Terrorism Act 1978, section 2(1).[20] However, the High Court will not re-examine facts which were before the magistrate nor, except for limited

---

11 [1896] 1 Q.B. 509.
12 Extradition Act 1870, s. 7.
13 1870 Act, s. 8.
14 Extradition proceedings cannot proceed further on provisional warrant without instructions from the Home Secretary.
15 1870 Act, s. 10.
16 However, evidence by foreign police officers obtained other than in accordance with the Judges' Rules is admissible (*Beese* v. *Governor of Ashford Remand Centre* [1973] 3 All E.R. 689) and the magistrate may not consider whether a foreign conviction is nullified by breach of natural justice (*Atkinson* v. *US* [1971] A.C. 197, 213); *US Govt* v. *McCaffery* [1984] 2 All E.R. 570; *Govt of Denmark* v. *Nielsen* [1984] 2 All E.R. 81.
17 1870 Act, s. 10.
18 1870 Act, s. 11; *cf. Wan Ping Nam* v. *Federal German Republic, ante.*
19 If an application for a writ of habeas corpus is made the fugitive cannot be extradited until the court has reached a decision.
20 See general restrictions on surrender, *post; Armah* v. *Government of Ghana* [1968] A.C. 192, 208.

purposes, allow fresh evidence to be adduced.[21] There is an appeal, with leave, to the House of Lords from the decision of the High Court.[22] After the completion of proceedings arising out of a habeas corpus application, the Home Secretary may at his absolute discretion issue a warrant for the surrender of the fugitive to the requesting state.[23] The Home Secretary may thus consider other matters, such as fresh evidence which was not before the magistrate at the committal proceedings, before allowing the extradition to proceed.[24] If, without reasonable cause, a fugitive has not been removed from the United Kingdom two months after his committal to prison (or where there was an application for habeas corpus, after the High Court decision on the writ) he may, on giving reasonable notice to the Home Secretary, apply to the High Court for his release.[25]

General restrictions on surrender

In addition to these procedural safeguards, other statutory rules restrict the surrender of fugitive criminals.[26] Of special importance is the rule, subject to qualifications which will be considered below, that there may be no extradition for an offence 'of a political character'.[27] Where this restriction applies, the Home Secretary may refuse to instruct that an arrest warrant be issued, or may order the discharge of the fugitive at any stage of the extradition proceedings, if he considers that the request for extradition relates to a political offence.[28] Similarly, the metropolitan magistrate will not commit the fugitive to prison where there is evidence that the offence is of a political character; and, as we have seen, the political character of the offence is a ground for application for habeas corpus.

There is no statutory definition of an offence 'of a political character',[29] and it has not been the subject of exhaustive judicial definition. In some leading cases it has been suggested that an exhaustive definition would be undesirable and the nature of a political offence 'must always be considered according to the circumstances at the time'.[30] Nevertheless, a political offence does 'represent an idea which is capable of description and needs description if it is to form part of the apparatus of a judicial decision'.[31] Several factors appear to be influential in determining whether an offence is an offence of a political character. An important element is the nature of the offence and the circum-

---

21 *Schtraks* v. *Government of Israel* [1964] A.C. 556, 605; *cf. Re Nobbs* [1978]3 All E.R. 390.
22 Administration of Justice Act 1960, s. 15.
23 Extradition Act 1870, s. 11.
24 See also *Atkinson* v. *US, ante,* 232–3.
25 Extradition Act 1870, s. 12. For extradition procedure in Scotland, see W. Finnie, 1983 S.L.T. (News) 25, 41.
26 Thus, the Extradition Act 1870 prohibits surrender unless provision is made that the fugitive may only be tried for the extradition offence proved by the facts on which surrender is grounded (s. 3(2)), and also where the fugitive is accused of another offence in England or is undergoing sentence for a conviction in the UK (s. 3(3)).
27 1870 Act, s. 3(1); C. F. Amerasinghe (1965) 28 M.L.R. 27; J. G. Castel & M. Edwardh (1975) 13 Osgoode Hall L.J. 89.
28 1870 Act, s. 7.
29 Genocide, however, cannot be an offence of a political character: Genocide Act 1969, s. 2(2).
30 *R.* v. *Governor of Brixton Prison, ex p. Kolczynski* [1955] 1 Q.B. 540, 549 (Cassels J.).
31 *Schtraks* v. *Government of Israel, ante,* 589 (Visc. Radcliffe).

stances in which it was committed. In some early cases it was suggested that a political offence must be an 'overt act in the course of acting in a political matter, a political rising, or a dispute between two parties in the State as to which is to have the government in its hands'.[32] In more recent cases the nature and circumstances which may establish an offence as a political offence have not always been so restrictively interpreted. In *Schtraks*, for example, Lord Reid suggested that a political offence could include acts of underground resistance movements as well as acts of open insurrection and need not necessarily involve an attempt to overthrow the government or to achieve power. He also suggested that the use of force, and even the disturbance of public order, were not essential characteristics of a political offence.[33]

The motive of the fugitive 'must be relevant and may be decisive'[34] in establishing the political character of an offence. An offence committed for a private motive cannot be a political offence.[35] In the early cases the necessary motive was considered to be the furtherance of, or assistance in, a political uprising. In *Schtraks* Lord Reid stated that only in the most exceptional cases would an offence be of a political character if the motive of the fugitive was not 'to force or ... promote a change of government, or ... a change of government policy or to achieve a political objective'.[36] However, the motive of the fugitive may be difficult to determine,[37] and other problems remain. For example, must the political motive be the sole or predominant motive to establish an offence as political?[38] How remote may the political objective of the offence be?[39] To what extent may the political objectives of an organisation be attributed to one of its members who commits an offence?[40]

The attitude of the state requesting extradition has also been considered in determining whether an offence is a political offence. In a number of cases it has been suggested that to establish the political character of an offence there must be an element of political opposition between the fugitive and the requesting state. For example, Viscount Radcliffe suggested that 'if the central government stands apart and is concerned only to enforce the criminal law', the crime, whatever the motive of the fugitive, would lack the element of political conflict and would not be a political offence.[41] Arguments that a state requesting extradition for one offence in fact seeks the surrender of the fugitive for another political offence have been accepted in some cases[42] but not in others.[43]

---

32   *Re Castioni* [1891] 1 Q.B. 149, 156 (Denman J.); *Re Meunier* [1894]2 Q.B. 415.

33   *Schtraks* v. *Government of Israel, ante*, 583–4; *cf. Cheng* v. *Governor of Pentonville Prison* [1973] A.C. 931 and *R.* v. *Pentonville Prison Governor, ex p. Rebott* [1978] L. S. Gaz, R. 43.

34   *Schtraks* v. *Government of Israel, ante*, 583 (Lord Reid).

35   *Re Castioni, ante.*

36   *Schtraks* v. *Government of Israel, ante*, 584. *Cf. Kolcznyski's* case, *ante*; *re Grass, ex p. Treasury Solicitor* [1968] 3 All E.R. 804; *Cheng's* case, *ante.*

37   *E.g. Cheng's* case, *ante.*

38   *ibid.*, 954 (Lord Simon).

39   *ibid.*, 945 (Lord Diplock); *R.* v. *Pentonville Prison Governor, ex p. Budlong* [1980] 1 All E.R. 701.

40   *Cf. Re Castioni* and *Re Meunier, ante*; *R.* v. *Governor of Winson Green Prison, ex p. Littlejohn* [1975] 3 All E.R. 208.

41   *Schtraks* v. *Government of Israel, ante*, 592.

42   *E.g. Re Arton, ante, Cheng's* case, *ante.*

43   *E.g. R.* v. *Governor of Brixton Prison, ex p. Kolczynski, ante*, 549 (Lord Goddard, C.J.); *Schtraks* v. *Government of Israel, ante*, 581 (Lord Reid), 587–8 (Visc. Radcliffe).

A significant narrowing in the exclusion from extradition of offences of a political character was made by the Suppression of Terrorism Act 1978. By section 1, where a state which is a party to the European Convention on the Suppression of Terrorism requests the extradition of a fugitive in respect of an extradition offence listed in schedule 1 of the Act, such an offence is not to be regarded as being of a political character.[44] In this event, an alternative restriction on surrender applies. The fugitive may not be surrendered (a) where extradition is requested in order to try or punish him on account of his race, religion, nationality or political opinions; or (b) where, by reason of the same factors, he might if surrendered be prejudiced at his trial, punished, detained or restricted in his personal liberty.[45] Courts have been cautious in attributing such motives to the authorities of a requesting state in other contexts and, although this alternative restriction may be necessary in an increasingly violent world, it does not provide as great a protection to the fugitive at odds with a requesting state as the restriction on surrender for offences of a political character.

The provisions of the Suppression of Terrorism Act may be extended to states with which the United Kingdom has extradition arrangements but which are not parties to the European Convention.[46] Other crimes have been added to those in schedule 1 of the Act which cannot be regarded as political offences.[47]

II.   Extradition: Commonwealth countries and UK dependencies

The surrender of fugitive criminals between the United Kingdom and other designated Commonwealth countries or UK dependencies is subject to the Fugitive Offenders Act 1967.[48] The Act provides for the extradition of a person found in the United Kingdom who is accused of a 'relevant offence' in a Commonwealth country, or who is unlawfully at large after conviction for such an offence.[49] A relevant offence is one punishable by at least 12 months imprisonment which, however it is described in the law of the requesting country, falls within the description of any offence in schedule I of the Act and would constitute an offence in the United Kingdom if it took place within UK jurisdiction.[50] However, extradition for a relevant offence is prohibited on a number of grounds. The principal grounds[51] are those contained in section

---

[44]   Schedule 1 of the Act includes common law offences, such as murder, manslaughter, rape and kidnapping, statutory offences against the person and property, and offences relating to explosives, firearms, abduction and the protection of aircraft.

[45]   Suppression of Terrorism Act 1978, s. 2(1); *cf.* Fugitive Offenders Act 1967, s. 4(1), *post.*

[46]   Suppression of Terrorism Act 1978, s. 5(1), *cf.* s. 5(2)(3).

[47]   See *e.g.* Taking of Hostages Act 1982, s. 3(2).

[48]   Commonwealth countries and UK dependencies are designated by Order in Council (s. 2). The 1967 Act replaced the Fugitive Offenders Act 1881, which lacked important safeguards for the fugitive; see *e.g. R.* v. *Governor of Brixton Prison, ex p. Enahoro* [1963] 2 Q.B. 455.

[49]   Fugitive Offenders Act 1967, s. 1.

[50]   *ibid.*, ss. 3(1)(4), 16(1); *R.* v. *Governor of Brixton Prison, ex p. Gardner* [1968] 2 Q.B. 399; *R.* v. *Governor of Brixton Prison, ex p. Rush* [1969] 1 All E.R. 316; *R.* v. *Governor of Pentonville Prison, ex p. Khubchandani* (1980) 71 Cr. App. R. 241.

[51]   See also s. 4(2) (3). For restrictions on extradition to the UK see ss. 14, 15.

4(1), which provides that extradition is prohibited if in the view of the court of committal, the High Court or the Secretary of State:

(*a*)   the relevant offence is of a political character;[52] or
(*b*)   the extradition request, although purporting to be made for a relevant offence, is in fact made for the purpose of punishing or prosecuting the fugitive on account of race, religion, nationality or political opinions;[53] or
(*c*)   the fugitive, if returned, might be prejudiced at his trial, or punished, detained or restricted on the same grounds as in (*b*).[54]

The statutory procedure for extradition to other Commonwealth countries is broadly similar to that under the Extradition Act 1870. On receiving an extradition request and certain documentary evidence from a Commonwealth country, the Secretary of State may issue an authority to proceed to a metropolitan magistrate,[55] unless he considers that, under the Act, an order surrendering the fugitive would be unlawful or would not in fact be made.[56] The magistrate may then issue a warrant for the arrest of the fugitive on evidence which, in his view, would be sufficient to issue a warrant if within his jurisdiction a person were accused of a corresponding offence or unlawfully at large after conviction.[57]

Once arrested, the fugitive is brought before the metropolitan magistrate.[58] The magistrate may commit to prison a fugitive accused of a relevant offence on evidence which would be sufficient to commit for trial if the alleged offence had been committed within the jurisdiction of the court and extradition is not otherwise prohibited.[59] A fugitive who is committed to prison has a fifteen day period in which to apply to the High Court for a writ of habeas corpus;[60] he may not be extradited within that period or while habeas corpus proceedings are pending.[61] By virtue of section 8(3), the High Court may discharge the fugitive if in all the circumstances it would be unjust or oppressive to extradite him on one of three grounds: (a) the triviality of the extradition offence,[62] (b) the passage of time since the alleged offence or conviction,[63] or (c) because the

---

52   Neither an offence against the life or person of the Queen (s. 4(5)), genocide (Genocide Act 1969, s. 2(2)) nor an offence within the Suppression of Terrorism Act 1978, s. 1, can be of a political character.
53   *R.* v. *Governor of Pentonville Prison, ex p. Teja* [1971] 2 Q.B. 274 (the political opinions must have been expressed).
54   *R.* v. *Governor of Pentonville Prison, ex p. Fernandez* [1971] 2 All E.R. 24 (there must be substantial grounds for believing that the fugitive will be so prejudiced.)
55   In Scotland the functions of the metropolitan magistrate vest in the Sheriff of Lothian and Borders.
56   1967 Act, s. 5(3).
57   1967 Act, s. 6(1)(a), (2). For provisional warrants, see s. 6(1)(b), (3).
58   1967 Act, s. 7(1).
59   1967 Act, s. 7(5); *Government of Australia* v. *Harrod* [1975] 2 All E.R. 1, *R.* v. *Governor of Pentonville Prison, ex p. Kirby* [1979] 2 All E.R. 1094, *R.* v. *Governor of Gloucester Prison, ex p. Miller* [1979] 2 All E.R. 1103.
60   Or in Scotland, an application to the High Court of Justiciary for review of the committal order: s. 8(1); *cf. Wan Ping Nam* v. *Federal German Republic, ante.*
61   1967 Act, s. 8(2).
62   *Cf. Re Clemeston,* (1955) 7 *British International Law Cases,* 1115.
63   *Teja's* case *ante; Higginson* v. *Secretary of State for Scotland* 1973 S.L.T. (Notes) 35; *Union of India* v. *Narang* [1978] A.C. 247; *Kakis* v. *Government of Cyprus* [1978] 2 All E.R. 634; *R.* v. *Governor of Pentonville Prison, ex p. Tarling* [1979] 1 All E.R. 981.

accusation against the fugitive was not made in good faith in the interests of justice.[64] After the statutory fifteen day period or the completion of habeas corpus proceedings, the Secretary of State may order the surrender of the fugitive, subject to certain restrictions.[65] In particular, surrender is prohibited if the Secretary of State considers that the restrictions imposed in sections 4(1) and 8(3) are applicable.[66] The fugitive, after giving reasonable notice to the Secretary of State, may apply to the High Court for his discharge, if he is still in custody in the United Kingdom without sufficient cause two months after he could have been surrendered under the Act, or one month after the Secretary of State had issued the order for surrender.[67]

III. Extradition: Republic of Ireland

The Backing of Warrants (Republic of Ireland) Act 1965 provides for the arrest and return of fugitives who have been accused or convicted of offences under the law of the Republic of Ireland and are found in the United Kingdom.[68] Under the Act, warrants for arrest issued in the Republic are indorsed by a justice of the peace in the United Kingdom and, once indorsed, a warrant operates as if it had been issued in the United Kingdom.[69] Unlike the procedures for extradition to other foreign states and to Commonwealth countries, this indorsement procedure does not require a *prima facie* case to be established against the fugitive.[70] Where an application for indorsement is properly made, a justice of the peace must indorse the warrant if it relates to an indictable offence or, subject to certain conditions, a summary offence punishable by six months imprisonment.[71]

When arrested on an indorsed warrant, the fugitive is brought before a magistrate who, subject to the provisions of the Act, must order him to be delivered into the custody of the police of the Irish Republic;[72] again, the magistrate is not required to determine whether there is a *prima facie* case against the fugitive.[73] There are certain restrictions on making an order for the surrender of the fugitive.[74] For example, an order must not be made where (a) there is no offence within that part of the United Kingdom in which the court has jurisdiction which corresponds with the offence specified in the

---

[64] The applicant is limited to these three grounds in establishing that his extradition would be unjust or oppressive: *Union of India* v. *Narang, ante.*

[65] 1967 Act, s. 9.

[66] 1967 Act, s. 9(1)(3).

[67] 1967 Act, s. 10; *Re Shuter* [1960] 1 Q.B. 142; *R.* v. *Governor of Brixton Prison, ex p. Enahoro, ante* (cases under the Fugitive Offenders Act 1881).

[68] The Extradition Act 1965 (No. 17) is the corresponding legislation in the Irish Republic.

[69] Backing of Warrants (Republic of Ireland) Act 1965, s. 1(4).

[70] *Re Arkins* [1966] 3 All E.R. 651.

[71] Backing of Warrants (Republic of Ireland) Act 1965, s. 1(1), (2). Additional conditions apply where the warrant is for the arrest of a fugitive who has been convicted of an offence: s. 1(3).

[72] *ibid.*, s. 2(1).

[73] *Keane* v. *Governor of Brixton Prison* [1972] A.C. 204, 211.

[74] Backing of Warrants (Republic of Ireland) Act 1965, s. 2(2). Where the Suppression of Terrorism Act 1978, s. 1 applies, s. 2(2) of that Act imposes a restriction similar to that referred to in respect of the Extradition Act 1870, *ante.*

indorsed warrant,[75] (b) the offence specified is an offence of a political character,[76] or (c) there are substantial grounds for believing that the fugitive will be prosecuted or detained for an offence of a political character, if returned to the Irish Republic.

Where the magistrate orders his surrender the fugitive may apply to the High Court for a writ of habeas corpus;[77] an appeal lies from the decision of the High Court, with leave, to the House of Lords. Fifteen days after the magistrate has ordered his surrender, or after any consequential habeas corpus proceedings, the fugitive must be delivered into the custody of the Irish police.[78] If, without reasonable cause, he has not been surrendered one month after the magistrate's order was made, the fugitive may apply to the High Court to be discharged.[79]

In the context of the serious conflicts in Northern Ireland, the extradition procedures contained in the Backing of Warrants (Republic of Ireland) Act and the corresponding Irish legislation have not proved to be effective. The Criminal Jurisdiction Act 1975 with its corresponding Irish legislation established an alternative procedure to extradition in an attempt to bring to trial persons who in recent years have committed serious crimes of violence for apparently political motives.[80] The Act extends the jurisdiction of the courts in Northern Ireland to enable them to try offences committed in the Republic of Ireland; these offences are termed 'extra-territorial offences'.[81] Extra-territorial offences include acts or omissions occurring in the Irish Republic which, if they took place in Northern Ireland, would constitute one of the offences described in schedule 1 of the Act. The schedule includes various common law offences, such as murder, manslaughter and arson, and statutory offences relating to such matters as malicious damage, explosive substances and offences against the person. Hijacking a vehicle in the Irish Republic and escaping from detention in the Irish Republic are other examples of extra-territorial offences.[82] A person accused in Northern Ireland of an extra-territorial offence may choose to be tried in the Republic of Ireland.[83] The Act also provides for witnesses to be examined in one jurisdiction for the purposes of the trial of an extra-territorial offence in the other.[84] Legislation in the Republic of Ireland gives the courts there similar jurisdiction over extra-territorial offences committed in Northern Ireland.[85]

---

[75] Re Arkins, ante; Keane's case, ante; cf. The State (Furlong) v. Kelly and A.-G. [1971] I.R. 132.
[76] R. v. Governor of Winson Green Prison, Birmingham, ex p. Littlejohn [1975] 3 All E.R. 208; Keane's case, ante; Re Nobbs, ante; cf. (Irish) Extradition Act 1965 (No. 17) s. 50 and Bourke v. A.-G. [1972] I.R. 36.
[77] Backing of Warrants (Republic of Ireland) Act 1965, s. 3(1)(b).
[78] 1965 Act., s. 2(1).
[79] 1965 Act, s. 6(1); see also s. 6(2).
[80] The Criminal Jurisdiction Act 1975 implements the recommendations in the Report of the Law Enforcement Commission: Cmnd 5627, 1974.
[81] Criminal Jurisdiction Act 1975, s. 1(3).
[82] 1975 Act, ss. 2, 3.
[83] 1975 Act., sch. 3, para. 2(1). Schedule 3 also contains various procedural safeguards for those accused, in Northern Ireland, of an extra-territorial offence.
[84] 1975 Act, sch. 4.
[85] Criminal Law (Jurisdiction) Act 1976.

Chapter 26

Freedom of person and property

The constitutional structure of the United Kingdom provides for no formal guarantees of liberty. The declarations of rights contained in the ancient charters and the restrictions on the powers of the Crown imposed by the Bill of Rights 1689 have a symbolic rather than a practical significance, and they may at any time be overridden by Act of Parliament. We have already seen that Dicey's influential view of the rule of law[1] relied upon the role of the judges in applying the ordinary law (of property, civil liability and so on) and on the political assumption that Parliament would not grant to the organs of the state such wide powers that the individual's liberties were destroyed. This traditional approach has always involved an over-simplification; problems of public powers have not been resolved by simply applying the rules and procedures of the 'ordinary' law, whatever that may mean. Nor has the political process always provided individuals and minorities with effective protection. Moreover, from the viewpoint of those whose task it is to enforce the law, in particular the police, the law has not kept pace with the increasing pressures that criminal behaviour creates in society today. While the powers of the police have never been unlimited, the legal limits on their action have for long been uncertain and often unworkable.

The present outlook for individual liberties is one of rapid change and adjustment. In recent years, with greater awareness of the United Kingdom's obligations under the European Convention on Human Rights, some protection has been given to the individual against acts of public power which conform with the law inside the United Kingdom, but may infringe rights guaranteed by the Convention. New forms of protection against certain forms of discrimination have been developed and it continues to be argued that we need a new constitutional framework for protecting fundamental rights.[2] Another recent development has been the emergence of a political willingness to consider whether the law on police powers is satisfactory. Until 1984 the powers of the police had never been the subject of broad legislative review.

---

[1] Ch. 6.
[2] Ch. 31.

In 1929 a royal commission on police powers and procedure, reviewing the practice of the police in searching the dwelling of a person for whose arrest a warrant had been issued, expressed the concern that police 'in the discharge of their essential duties, should have to rely on powers of which the legality seems doubtful'.[3] But the law was not reformed and in 1960 an eminent judge wrote: 'The police power of search under English law is haphazard and ill-defined'.[4] The comment was almost equally true of the law of arrest. In 1978, a royal commission was set up by the Labour government to review the powers and duties of the police in the investigation of offences and the process of the prosecution of crime. The commission was required to have regard 'both to the interests of the community in bringing offenders to justice and to the rights and liberties of persons suspected or accused of crime'. Its report sought within the criminal justice system 'to define a balance between the rights of individuals and the security of society and the state'.[5] Many of the changes recommended by the report were controversial, but there could be little disagreement with the commission's main finding that there was a strong need to bring the law up to date. Existing police powers were 'found in (or extracted with difficulty from) a mixture of statute law, common law, evidential law, and guidance to the police from the judges and the Home Office'; the law regulating police investigation needed 'to be reformulated and restated in clear and coherent terms that have regard to contemporary circumstances'.[6]

This broad conclusion was accepted by the Conservative government. There resulted the Police and Criminal Evidence Act 1984, which received the royal assent late in 1984 after long and hard-fought proceedings in both Houses of Parliament. The Act provides what is a very extensive (although not comprehensive) code of police powers. When the Bill is brought into force, the law affecting individual liberty in this area will have been transformed, new powers being conferred on the police, and new safeguards being imposed on their exercise. Where Parliament has plainly authorised police interference with an individual's liberty in the public good, no remedy will be available in English law, since the courts have no power to override the plain wishes of Parliament. In this situation, the individual's right of recourse to the European Commission of Human Rights acquires added significance.

It is not possible here to summarise all the law that is relevant to the individual's liberties, although many branches of law (for example, concerning the rights of trade union members, the rights of parents over their children, trial by jury and the presumption of innocence in criminal trials) are of great practical significance.[7] Nor is it possible to deal with the complex schemes of social legislation which ensure the individual a minimum standard of welfare and grant him access to the social services. Emphasis will be placed on the

---

[3]   Cmd 3297, 1929, p. 45.
[4]   P. Devlin, *The Criminal Prosecution in England*, p. 53.
[5]   Cmnd 8092, 1981 (the Philips report on criminal procedure), p. 8. For comment, see M. Inman [1981] Crim. L.R. 469; K. W. Lidstone [1981] Crim. L.R. 454; D. McBarnet [1981] Crim. L.R. 445; and B. Smythe [1981] P.L. 184, 481.
[6]   Cmnd 8092, p. 110.
[7]   For much source material, see S. H. Bailey, D. J. Harris and B. L. Jones, *Civil Liberties, Cases and Materials*, and P. O'Higgins, *Cases and Materials on Civil Liberties*.

main powers which exist for taking away an individual's liberty or property
and on the main remedies relevant to these powers.

While the approach to civil liberties is essentially the same in Scotland and
Northern Ireland as in England and Wales, it is not possible in this and
succeeding chapters to deal with the law of Scotland and Northern Ireland as
well as English law. One reason for this is that in Scotland the common law
background is quite distinct from that in England, and recent legislative
reform (the Criminal Justice (Scotland) Act 1980) has taken its own course.[8]
In Northern Ireland, although the common law background is the same as in
England, the abnormal strains that have been imposed on civil liberties since
1968 have produced a different legislative response. Statements of the law must
therefore be taken as referring only to England and Wales, except where
express mention is made of another jurisdiction.

In Section A below, the main features of the Police and Criminal Evidence
Act 1984 are outlined against the common law background which the Act
seeks to change. Since by section 121 of the Act the Home Secretary may bring
provisions of the Act into operation at different times, it must not be assumed
from this or other chapters that any part of the Act is already in operation.

A. Personal freedom and police powers

There are two main aspects of the law relating to individual liberty: first, the
grounds on which an individual may be deprived of his physical liberty;
second, the remedies which an individual has if he wishes to contest the
legality of such a deprivation.

Grounds for lawful detention
The principal grounds for lawful detention are:

(*a*) Arrest and detention pending trial on a criminal charge, and detention
for other purposes concerned with the investigation of offences.

(*b*) Sentence of imprisonment or detention (for example, in youth custody)
imposed after conviction by a court on a criminal charge.

(*c*) Imprisonment for non-payment of maintenance orders and taxes.[1]

(*d*) Imprisonment for contempt of court[2] and for contempt of Parliament.[3]

(*e*) Detention of mental patients.

(*f*) Detention of a child in need of care or control under the Children and
Young Persons Acts 1933 to 1969.

(*g*) The exercise of parental authority over an infant.[4]

(*h*) Detention of persons under the Extradition Act 1870, the Fugitive
Offenders Act 1967 and the Immigration Act 1971 (for example, pending a
decision by the Home Secretary on whether an individual is to be deported

---

[8] See K. D. Ewing and W. Finnie, *Civil Liberties in Scotland.*

[1] Administration of Justice Act 1970, ss. 11, 12.

[2] Ch. 19 B. For the role of the Official Solicitor, see p. 343 *ante.*

[3] Ch. 12 A.

[4] A husband may not detain his wife: *R. v. Jackson* [1891] 1 Q.B. 671.

or extradited).[5]

(*i*)   Detention of persons subject to military law by the service authorities and detention under the Visiting Forces Act 1952.[6]

(*j*)   Detention of persons and restrictions on movement imposed under emergency powers and anti-terrorist legislation.[7]

Of these grounds of detention, that relating to mental patients will be considered briefly; arrest and related police powers will be considered more fully.

Detention of mental patients

Compulsory admission to hospital of those suffering from acute mental disorder is governed in England and Wales by the Mental Health Act 1983, which consolidated earlier legislation, notably the Mental Health Act 1959 and the Mental Health (Amendment) Act 1982.[8] Under Part II of the 1983 Act, compulsory admission (whether for assessment or for treatment) generally requires an application to have been made by the nearest relative of the patient or an approved social worker, and to be supported by the recommendation of two medical practitioners, one of whom must have had special experience in the diagnosis or treatment of mental disorder. In an acute emergency, admission for up to 72 hours may be based upon only one medical recommendation. Voluntary patients already in hospital may be detained from leaving for up to six hours on the decision of a mental nurse, and for up to 72 hours on the decision of a hospital doctor. Under Part III of the 1983 Act, the criminal courts may make hospital and restriction orders for the compulsory admission of those suffering from mental disorder who have been convicted of, or in some cases merely charged with, criminal offences.

Since 1959, compulsorily detained patients have been able to seek their release by applying to mental health review tribunals, which exist for each hospital area. The members of the tribunals are appointed by the Lord Chancellor; the chairman must be a lawyer and one of the other two members must be a doctor. The powers of the tribunals were extended in 1982. Thus the detention of some categories of patient must be reviewed at stated intervals, whether or not a patient is seeking to be released; and the tribunals may now order the release of patients on whom the courts had imposed restriction orders, a power which only the Home Secretary had exercised before 1982.[9] Legal aid is available for representation of patients before the tribunals.

A patient who is detained not only loses his physical liberty but also becomes potentially vulnerable to abuse, neglect and ill-treatment.[10] Concern at this vulnerability led in 1982 to additional legal protection being given to patients. Part IV of the 1983 Act governs the consent needed for various forms of medical treatment; for the most serious forms of treatment (for example, psycho-surgery) both the patient and a second doctor must consent. Hospital

---

[5]   Ch. 25.

[6]   Ch. 23.

[7]   Ch. 29.

[8]   See Cmnd 8405, 1981; also B. Hoggett [1983] P.L. 172, and M.J. Gunn (1983) 46 M.L.R. 318.

[9]   The former law was held to be in breach of the European Convention of Human Rights in *X. v. UK* (1981) 4 E.H.R.R. 188; and see L. O. Gostin [1982] Crim. L.R. 779.

[10] See *e.g.* L. O. Gostin, *A Human Condition*.

authorities must inform patients of their rights under the Act, and a hospital's power to interfere with patients' correspondence is restricted.[11] If a patient wishes to bring proceedings against hospital staff or other persons concerned with his admission or treatment, he needs leave from the High Court to bring civil proceedings, or from the Director of Public Prosecutions to bring criminal proceedings. In each case the defendant is liable only if he acted in bad faith or without reasonable care; but the rules for gaining consent are less stringent than before 1982, and hospital authorities are not now protected in this way.[12]

Separate legislation exists in Scotland,[13] and mental health review tribunals have not been created. An application for compulsory admission to hospital must be founded on two medical reports and must be approved by a sheriff; a compulsorily detained patient may appeal to the sheriff against continued detention.

The law relating to arrest[14]

Powers of arrest are not exclusive to the police and some may be exercised by any person. But today the very great majority of arrests are undertaken by the police. The significance of the act of arrest is that it is at that moment that an individual loses his liberty and, if the arrest is lawful, becomes subject to lawful detention. Arrests are of two kinds (a) with a warrant and (b) without a warrant.

(a) Arrest with a warrant. Most arrests relate to the initiation of proceedings in the criminal courts. Under the Magistrates' Courts Act 1980, section 1, proceedings may be initiated either by the issue of a summons, requiring the accused to attend court on a certain day, or in more serious cases by a warrant of arrest, naming the accused and the offence with which he is charged. A warrant is obtained from a magistrate after a written application (information) has been substantiated on oath. In issuing a warrant for arrest, the magistrate may endorse it for bail.[15] A warrant may be executed anywhere in England or Wales by a police constable. If the warrant is to arrest a person charged with an offence, it may be executed even when a constable does not have it in his possession, but the warrant must be shown, on his demand, to the arrested person as soon as possible.[16] Despite judicial *dicta* to the contrary[17] a person arrested would seem entitled to know that he is being arrested under a warrant (for if not, how can he demand to see it?). Where a constable in good faith executes a warrant that seems valid on its face, he is protected from liability for the arrest by the Constables Protection Act 1750 if it should turn

---

[11] Mental Health Act 1983, ss. 132, 134.
[12] Mental Health Act 1983, s. 139. On the former law, see *Carter* v. *Metropolitan Police Commissioner* [1975] 2 All E.R. 33, *Pountney* v. *Griffiths* [1976] A.C. 314 and *Ashingdane* v. *U.K.* (1982) 4 E.H.R.R. 590.
[13] Mental Health (Scotland) Act 1960; Mental Health (Scotland) (Amendment) Act 1983.
[14] Royal Commission on Criminal Procedure, *The Investigation and Prosecution of Criminal Offences in England and Wales: the Law and the Procedure*, Cmnd 8092–1, 1981. See also Bailey, Harris and Jones, *op. cit.*, ch. 2; L. H. Leigh, *Police Powers in England and Wales*, chs. 2–5.
[15] Magistrates' Courts Act 1980, s. 117.
[16] Magistrates' Courts Act 1980, s. 125(3); and *cf. R.* v. *Purdy* [1975] Q.B. 288. And see Police and Criminal Evidence Act 1984, s. 33.
[17] *R.* v. *Kulynycz* [1971] 1 Q.B. 367, 372.

out that the warrant was beyond the jurisdiction of the magistrate who issued it. The requirement that the warrant be issued by a magistrate is thus as much a safeguard for the police as it is for the person named on it. When an arrest warrant has been issued, a constable may enter and search premises to make the arrest, using such reasonable force as is necessary.[18]

General warrants[19]

The practice of issuing general warrants to arrest unspecified persons and to search property is said to have originated with the Court of Star Chamber. It was obviously a powerful weapon to assist the executive to obtain material upon which to formulate charges against persons suspected of hostility towards the government. The practice was authorised by the Licensing Act 1662 for use by a Secretary of State to prevent publication of unlicensed material but it continued after the lapse of that Act in 1695. In the 1760s the general warrant cases arose out of the attempts of George III's government to stifle the political activities of John Wilkes and others, and publications such as the *North Briton*. Three cases decided the illegality of general warrants: *Leach* v. *Money*, that a general warrant to arrest unnamed persons (the printers and publishers of the *North Briton*) against whom no charge had been formulated was illegal;[20] *Wilkes* v. *Wood*, that the papers of an unnamed person could not be seized on such a warrant;[21] and *Entick* v. *Carrington*, that there was no inherent power in the Secretary of State to order an arrest except for treason, and that a general search warrant purporting to give authority to the King's Messengers to take all Entick's books and papers was illegal.[22] These decisions established the fundamental principle that state necessity does not justify a wrongful act. General warrants are similarly unlawful by the law of Scotland.[23] In 1979, when Inland Revenue officials had conducted very extensive searches for documents related to alleged tax frauds, the House of Lords, overruling the Court of Appeal, held that the warrants in question met the relevant statutory requirements and that the general warrant cases were irrelevant.[24]

(b) Arrest without a warrant.   The law on arrests without a warrant has hitherto been a complicated mixture of common law and statutory powers.[25] The Police and Criminal Evidence Act 1984 takes further reform of the law which was begun when the Criminal Law Act 1967, section 2, abolished the distinction between felonies and misdemeanours and created a new category of arrestable offences. The effect of the 1984 Act is that powers of arrest without warrant fall into four main divisions.

(1)   For the most serious offences, the category of arrestable offences now comprises: (a) all offences for which the sentence is fixed by law (for example,

---

18   Police and Criminal Evidence Act 1984, ss. 17, 117.
19   P. G. Polyviou, *Search and Seizure*, ch. 1.
20   (1765) 19 St. Tr. 1002.
21   (1763) 19 St. Tr. 1153.
22   (1765) 19 St.Tr. 1030.
23   *Webster* v. *Bethune* (1857) 2 Irv. 596; *Bell* v. *Black and Morrison* (1865) 5 Irv. 57, 3 M. 1026.
24   *R.* v. *Inland Revenue Comssrs, ex p. Rossminster Ltd* [1980] A.C. 952. *Cf.* criticism of searches by immigration officers, I. A. Macdonald, *Immigration Law and Practice*, pp. 328–30.
25   For the position in Scots law, see G. H. Gordon, *Renton and Brown's Criminal Procedure*, ch. 5.

life imprisonment in the case of murder); (b) all offences for which a first offender over 21 may be sentenced to five years imprisonment or more; and (c) certain other specified offences (under such legislation as the Official Secrets Acts 1911–20, the Sexual Offences Act 1956, and the Theft Act 1968), even though they do not carry prison sentences of five years or longer.[26]

Any person (whether a constable or not) may arrest without warrant one who is, or whom he reasonably suspects to be, in the act of committing an arrestable offence. Where such an offence has actually been committed, any person may arrest anyone who is with reasonable cause suspected to be guilty of the offence, or is guilty of it. Where there is merely reasonable cause to suspect that an arrestable offence has been committed, a constable has the additional power of arresting any person whom he reasonably suspects of having committed it: but a private person does not have this additional power and may be liable in damages to the person arrested if it should turn out that no arrestable offence has been committed by anyone.[27] A constable may also arrest any person whom with reasonable cause he suspects to be about to commit an arrestable offence. For the purpose of arresting a person for an arrestable offence, a constable may enter (if need be by force) and search any place where he reasonably suspects that person to be.[28]

(2)   As well as this general power in respect of arrestable offences, at common law a constable (and any other person) may arrest at the time anyone who commits a breach of the peace in his presence or whose conduct causes a breach of the peace to be reasonably apprehended.[29] Breach of the peace involves an element of actual or apprehended violence to person or property.[30] By an old common law rule, any passer-by may be called on to assist a constable who has seen a breach of the peace committed by two or more persons or who has been assaulted or obstructed in making an arrest and has reasonable necessity in calling others to assist him. To refuse assistance in these circumstances is an offence.[31]

(3)   A general power of arrest created by the Police and Criminal Evidence Act 1984, section 25, applies to any offence (other than an arrestable offence) which has been or is being committed or attempted, and it seems to a constable impracticable or inappropriate to rely on the service of a summons at a later date. Such an arrest may be made when any of the 'general arrest conditions' is satisfied. These conditions include situations in which the constable does not know and cannot ascertain the name of the relevant person; where the constable reasonably doubts whether the name given by the person is his real name; where the person has not provided a satisfactory address for service of a summons; and where the constable reasonably believes that arrest

---

26   Police and Criminal Evidence Act 1984, s. 24, replacing Criminal Law Act 1967, s. 2.
27   Police and Criminal Evidence Act 1984, s. 24(4)–(6), which maintains the rule in *Walters* v. *W.H. Smith & Son Ltd* [1914] 1 K.B. 595.
28   Note 18 *ante*. And see *Swales* v. *Cox* [1981] Q.B. 489.
29   *R.* v. *Howell* [1982] Q.B. 416, *Albert* v. *Lavin* [1982] A.C. 546. Police and Criminal Evidence Act 1984, ss. 17(6), 25(6).
30   *R.* v. *Howell* (*ante*).
31   *R.* v. *Brown* (1841) Car. & M. 314. For the constable's liability if he fails to act, see *R.* v. *Dytham* [1979] Q.B. 722.

is necessary to prevent the person causing physical harm, damage to property, an offence against public decency or obstruction of the highway. This broad power makes possible the repeal of very many statutory powers of arrest both for such general offences as unauthorised possession of controlled drugs, having an offensive weapon in a public place, acting in a disorderly manner at a public meeting and so on, and also for many miscellaneous local offences, such as street nuisances under the Metropolitan Police Act 1839.[32]

(4)   In addition to these general powers, some specific statutory powers of arrest are continued in force.[33] These include the power to arrest someone apparently driving a car while unfit through drink or drugs, and persons reasonably suspected of various offences including absence without leave from the armed forces, entering and remaining on property under the Criminal Law Act 1977, illegal entry under the Immigration Act 1971, and offences under the Public Order Act 1936. The police may also arrest and detain prisoners who are unlawfully at large, children who are neglected, exposed to moral danger or absent without authority from a place of safety, and persons liable to be examined or removed from the United Kingdom under the Immigration Act 1971.

The police have no general power to arrest for obstruction of a constable in the execution of his duty.[34] However, an arrest at common law may occur for this offence when breach of the peace is involved, and an arrest may be made under the 1984 Act when one of the 'general arrest conditions' mentioned in (3) above is satisfied.

Where by statute an arrest may be made when a constable has reasonable cause to suspect the commission of a particular offence, reasonable suspicion justifying arrest is less than *prima facie* proof of guilt.[35] Even where a statute appears to suggest that a power of arrest is conditional upon a certain offence having in fact been committed, the legality of an arrest depends on whether at the time the constable honestly believed on reasonable grounds that an offence had been committed; the arrest does not become unlawful if the arrested person is later acquitted, or set free without having been charged.[36]

Under the Criminal Law Act 1967, section 3, a person may use such force as is reasonable in the circumstances in the prevention of crime and in effecting or assisting in the lawful arrest of offenders, actual or suspected, or of persons unlawfully at large. Thus excessive force makes an arrest unlawful. Where a person is arrested otherwise than by being told that he is under arrest, the arrest is lawful only if he is told this as soon as practicable thereafter.[37]

No arrest is lawful unless the arrested person is informed of the ground for the arrest at the time or as soon as practicable after the arrest.[38] The origin of this important rule may be found in *Christie* v. *Leachinsky*, where the Liverpool

---

[32]   Police and Criminal Evidence Act 1984, s. 26(1); and see Cmnd 8092−1, 1981, app. 9.

[33]   Police and Criminal Evidence Act 1984, s. 26(2) and sch. 2.

[34]   *Gelberg* v. *Miller* [1961] 1 All E.R. 291; *Wershof* v. *Metropolitan Police Commissioner* [1978] 3 All E.R. 540.

[35]   *Hussien* v. *Chong Fook Kam* [1970] A.C. 942; and see J. L. Lambert [1973] P.L. 285.

[36]   *Wills* v. *Bowley* [1983] 1 A.C. 57.

[37]   Police and Criminal Evidence Act 1984, s. 28(1). *Cf. R.* v. *Inwood* [1973] 2 All E.R. 645 and *Wheatley* v. *Lodge* [1971] 1 All E.R. 173.

[38]   Police and Criminal Evidence Act 1984 s. 28(3).

police had purported to exercise a local Act power of arrest when they knew that the conditions for this were not met. When the officers concerned were later sued for wrongful arrest and false imprisonment, it was argued that the arrest was lawful because at the time they had information about Leachinsky which would have justified his arrest for another offence. The House of Lords held that the arrest was unlawful, since it was a condition of lawful arrest that the man arrested should be entitled to know the reason for it. An actual charge need not be formulated at the time of arrest, but 'the arrested man is entitled to be told what is the act for which he is arrested'.[39] In *R.* v. *Kulynycz*, an unlawful arrest occurred when a constable arrested the accused without telling him why, but soon after at the police station Kulynycz was told that he had been arrested on suspicion of handling stolen drugs in King's Lynn: this was held to be sufficient information to make his continued detention lawful, even though the charges later brought against him were for unauthorised possession of controlled drugs in Cambridge.[40]

Powers associated with arrest

Where a person is arrested by a constable at a place other than a police station, he must be brought to a police station as soon as practicable after the arrest, though this may be delayed if his presence elsewhere is necessary for immediate investigations.[41] He may then be formally charged and, if arrested without a warrant, either he may be released on bail by the police in accordance with the Bail Act 1976, or if kept in custody, he must be brought before a magistrates' court as soon as is practicable and in any event, with certain exceptions, on the day following the charge.[42] At common law a constable could search a person on arrest and take possession of articles which might be evidence connected with the offence charged, or which might help the arrested person to escape or cause harm. However, the police had a discretion to exercise and could not apply an automatic rule of searching every person arrested.[43] Under the Police and Criminal Evidence Act 1984, a person arrested away from a police station may be searched if he is reasonably believed to present a danger to anyone or to have anything concealed on him which might help him to escape or might be evidence relating to an offence.[44] Once taken to a police station, he may be searched to ascertain the property which he has with him. This property may be retained by the police, but clothing and personal effects may be retained only on certain grounds (for example, if they might be used to cause injury, to damage property or to interfere with evidence).[45] Intimate searches (that is, examination of a person's body orifices) may be conducted only if a police superintendent reason-

---

[39] [1947] A.C. 573, 593 (Lord Simonds). And see *Pedro* v. *Diss* [1981] 2 All E.R. 59.

[40] [1971] 1 Q.B. 367; *cf. R.* v. *Holah* [1973] 1 All E.R. 106, where a stricter test was applied in a breath-test case.

[41] Police and Criminal Evidence Act 1984 s. 30. *Cf. John Lewis & Co. Ltd* v. *Timms* [1952] A.C. 676; *Dallison* v. *Caffery* [1965] 1 Q.B. 348.

[42] Police and Criminal Evidence Act 1984, s. 46. For the former law, see *R* v. *Malcherek* (1981) 73 Cr. App. R. 173, and C. R. Munro [1982] P.L. 210.

[43] *Lindley* v. *Rutter* [1981] Q.B. 128; *Brazil* v. *Chief Constable of Surrey* [1983] 3 All E.R. 537.

[44] Police and Criminal Evidence Act 1984, s. 32.

[45] Police and Criminal Evidence Act 1984, s. 54.

ably believes that the person may have concealed on him (a) an article that could be used to cause physical injury to himself or others, or (b) certain unlawful drugs. Intimate searches must in general be made only by a doctor or nurse, but if this is not practicable, a search for articles within category (a) may be made by a constable of the same sex as the person searched.[46]

It was formerly the law that a magistrates' court order was required to enable the police to take the fingerprints of a person who was not less than 14 years old and was charged with a criminal offence, where he did not consent.[47] Under the 1984 Act, a police superintendent may, without recourse to a court, order the fingerprints of a person detained at a police station to be taken, subject to procedural safeguards.[48]

Another power associated with arrest was that at common law the police might search premises in the arrested person's immediate control and occupation at the time of arrest, and take away property which might be used as evidence relating to the offences for which the arrest was made.[49] But the precise extent of this power was very doubtful, although as long ago as 1929 the police often searched the dwelling of a person for whose arrest a warrant had been issued. In *Jeffrey* v. *Black*, the court held that the police acted unlawfully in searching Black's home when he had been arrested for stealing a sandwich from a public house.[50] Under the 1984 Act, in general on the authority of an inspector or above, the police may enter and search premises occupied or controlled by a person who is under arrest for an arrestable offence, if they reasonably suspect that there is evidence on the premises that relates to that offence or to a connected or similar arrestable offence.[51]

'Stop and search' powers[52]

At common law, the police have no general power to search a person before arresting him. But search before arrest may be authorised by statute. Thus under the Misuse of Drugs Act 1971, section 23, a constable who on reasonable grounds suspects that a person is in unlawful possession of a controlled drug may search him, and may detain him for the purpose of searching him; there is a similar power to stop and search vehicles for drugs. Other stop and search powers are granted by the Firearms Act 1968 and the Aviation Security Act 1982. By section 1 of the Police and Criminal Evidence Act 1984, a constable (who must be in uniform to stop a vehicle) may in a place to which the public have access stop and search any person or vehicle for stolen goods or 'prohibited articles'. The latter include offensive weapons and articles made or intended for use in the course of theft and other property offences. No search

---

46 Police and Criminal Evidence Act 1984, s. 55.
47 Magistrates' Courts Act 1980 s. 49; *Callis* v. *Gunn* [1964] 1 Q.B. 495 and *R.* v. *Jones* [1978] 3 All E.R. 1098.
48 1984 Act, s. 61. See also ss. 62, 63 (taking of intimate and other samples) and 64 (destruction of fingerprints and samples).
49 *Dillon* v. *O'Brien* (1887) 16 Cox C.C. 245 (Ir.).
50 [1978] Q.B. 490 (but cannabis found at the house was admissible as evidence, p. 489 *post*).
51 1984 Act, s. 18.
52 Cmnd 8092–1, 1981, apps. 1–3, Leigh, *op. cit.*, ch. 7; Police and Criminal Evidence Act 1984, part I.

may occur unless the constable reasonably suspects that he will find stolen or prohibited articles. If during a search he discovers such articles, they may be seized. Before exercising these powers, a constable must (*inter alia*) inform the person to be searched of his name and police station and of his grounds for the search. He must subsequently record details of the search, and if required a copy must be supplied to the person searched. Reasonable force may be used by the police, but during any search made before arrest, a person may not be required to remove any clothing in public except for an outer coat, jacket or gloves.[53].

The police in London have had power since 1839 to stop and search persons and vehicles reasonably suspected of having stolen property on them.[54] But there are potential dangers in granting wide stop and search powers to the police. In the past the power to stop and search for controlled drugs has caused controversy, since it has sometimes involved indignity and intrusion upon personal privacy.[55] A proposal to limit this wide discretion by excluding certain factors (such as a person's physical appearance) from being taken into account in relation to drugs was made unsuccessfully in 1970.[56] It is to be hoped that the detailed safeguards contained in the 1984 Act will ensure that the police do not abuse their powers, for example by harassing a particular ethnic section in the community. In law, a constable who stops and searches a person for stolen or prohibited articles without reasonable grounds for suspecting that he will find them is liable in damages for the unlawful search; in practice, such liability can be very difficult to establish. Since the exercise of such powers may intrude upon an individual's privacy, police officers must have a precise knowledge of the relevant statutory rules or they may be held to have acted outside the course of their duty.[57] Even where the power to stop and search is not expressly restricted to persons in a public place, such a power will not be interpreted as giving the police a power of entry into private premises.[58]

Under the Road Traffic Act 1972, section 159, a constable in uniform may require a person driving a vehicle to stop. The Police and Criminal Evidence Act 1984, section 4, authorises the police to set up road checks when it is believed that there is or about to be in the locality during the period of the check someone who has committed or witnessed a serious arrestable offence,[59] someone who is intending to commit such an offence or an escaped prisoner.

Police questioning

Apart from powers given by anti-terrorist legislation,[60] the police did not before 1984 have express power to detain suspects for further investigations

---

[53] 1984 Act, s. 2(9). This restriction now applies to all statutory stop and search powers.
[54] Metropolitan Police Act 1839, s. 66; *Pedro* v. *Diss* [1981] 2 All E.R. 59.
[55] Home Office Advisory Committee on Drug Dependence, *Powers of Arrest and Search in Relation to Drug Offences, 1970*; and Lord Scarman, *Report into the Brixton Disorders*, Cmnd 8427, 1981, paras. 4·37–41, 5·37, 7·2.
[56] Home Office Advisory Committee, note 55 *ante*.
[57] *Wither* v. *Reid* 1979 S.L.T. 192.
[58] *Cf. Morris* v. *Beardmore* [1981] A.C. 446.
[59] Page 483 *post*.
[60] Ch. 29 C.

to be carried out, nor did they have a general power to detain individuals for questioning, whether as suspects or potential witnesses.[61] In practice the police sometimes acted as if they had such powers. The royal commission on criminal procedure recommended in 1981 that extra powers to detain suspects for questioning should be given to the police, with safeguards to ensure that those powers were not abused.[62] The Police and Criminal Evidence Act 1984 gives effect to this recommendation and its provisions are outlined below against the background of the earlier law.

While individuals may have a moral or social duty to assist the police, they do not at common law have a legal duty to answer their questions. In *Rice* v. *Connolly*, a man who refused in a Grimsby street late at night to give his full name and address to a constable was held not guilty of obstructing the police in the execution of their duty, since the police had no right to compel him to answer.[63] In *Kenlin* v. *Gardner*, where two boys were stopped by constables in plain clothes and asked why they were going from door to door, it was held that the boys were justified in using reasonable force to get away.[64] But where a constable had tapped a man on the shoulder in the street to persuade him to stop and speak to him about an alleged offence, a blow struck at the constable with force was held an assault on the constable in the execution of his duty.[65]

An important principle in criminal procedure is the privilege of a suspected or accused person to remain silent; the burden is on the police to obtain evidence of guilt, not on a suspect to clear himself. The main control over abuse at the stage of questioning has been exercised by the criminal courts. It has long been established that a confession or statement by an accused person is not admissible in evidence at his trial unless it is voluntary, in the sense that it has not been obtained from him by fear of prejudice or hope of advantage, exercised or held out by a person in authority, or by oppression.[66] Moreover in 1912 and again in 1964,[67] the judges of the Queen's Bench Division drew up rules to govern the taking of statements from those being questioned by the police. The Judges' Rules did not have the force of law, but voluntary statements taken in accordance with the rules were usually admitted in evidence at a trial, and statements taken in serious breach of the rules might be excluded.[68] The 1964 Judges' Rules required that a person being questioned should be cautioned as soon as a police officer had evidence which afforded reasonable grounds for suspecting that he had committed an offence. When a person was charged with an offence, he had again to be cautioned; thereafter only for special reasons might further questions be put to him.

In issuing the rules, the judges emphasised that the rules were not to affect certain principles, including the principle that every person at any stage of an

---

[61]   But see *Mohammed-Holgate* v.*Duke* [1984] A.C. 437.

[62]   Cmnd 8092, 1981, ch. 4.

[63]   [1966] 2 Q.B. 414; and see M. Bennun in (ed.) D. Lasok *et al.*, *Fundamental Duties*, ch. 11.

[64]   [1967] 2 Q.B. 510.

[65]   *Donnelly* v. *Jackman* [1970] 1 All E.R. 987, and see J. M. Evans (1970) 33 M.L.R. 438.

[66]   E.g. *Ibrahim* v. *R.* [1914] A.C. 599.

[67]   *Judges' Rules and Administrative Directions to the Police*, Home Office Circular No. 89/1978; Cmnd 8092–1, app. 12.

[68]   See *e.g. R.* v. *Prager* [1972] 1 All E.R. 1114.

investigation should be able to consult privately with a solicitor (provided that no unreasonable hindrance was thereby caused to the investigation); and that a person should be charged with an offence as soon as there was enough evidence to do this.[69]

The Judges' Rules were much criticised. On one side, it was argued that they hampered police inquiries, for example by the requirement of two cautions. On the other side, it was argued that the rules paid lip-service to such matters as the right to consult privately with a solicitor,[70] and failed to prevent improper police methods. In 1972, the Criminal Law Revision Committee reviewed the law of criminal evidence, proposing that the right of silence should be restricted, in the sense that at a trial it should be possible to draw adverse inferences from an accused's failure to defend himself or to explain his conduct.[71] This report was extensively criticised and it did not become the basis of legislation. The royal commission on criminal procedure in 1981 did not recommend changes in the right to silence, but proposed that the police should have an express power to question suspects who had been arrested but not yet charged.

The 1984 Act does not directly affect the right to silence nor does it impose a duty to answer police questions, but in Parts IV and V it establishes elaborate rules to govern the detention of arrested persons. At every police station that is designated for such detention, there must be a custody officer of the rank of sergeant or above. He must ensure that the rules of detention are observed; he must decide if there is sufficient evidence on which a person should be charged, and he has recourse to a superintendent should he disagree with the views of an officer in charge of the investigation who is senior to himself. Where there is insufficient evidence for a person to be charged, the custody officer may authorise him to be kept in detention if this is considered necessary to secure or preserve evidence relating to the offence in question, or 'to obtain such evidence by questioning him'.[72] Detention for questioning must be reviewed six hours after the detention was first authorised, and thereafter at nine hour intervals, although a review may be postponed if a review would interrupt the questioning and this would prejudice the investigation.[73]

In principle, a person may not be kept in detention for more than 24 hours without being released or charged, but a superintendent or above may authorise continued detention for questioning for up to 36 hours, where the offence in question is a 'serious arrestable offence'.[74] Serious arrestable offences are stated to include murder, manslaughter, rape, kidnapping, and other arrestable offences which are likely to have consequences such as serious harm to state security or public order, or death, serious injury or serious financial loss to any person.[75]

---

[69] See *R. v. Holmes, ex p. Sherman* [1981] 2 All E.R. 612; and note 42, *ante*.

[70] *R. v. Lemsatef* [1977] 2 All E.R. 835.

[71] Cmnd 4991, 1972. And see B. MacKenna [1972] Crim. L.R. 605, R. Cross [1973] Crim. L.R. 329 and A.A.S. Zuckerman (1973) 36 M.L.R. 509.

[72] Police and Criminal Evidence Act, 1984 s. 37(2).

[73] 1984 Act, s. 40(4).

[74] 1984 Act, s. 42(1).

[75] 1984 Act, s. 116 and sch. 5.

When serious arrestable offences are concerned, the period of 36 hours may be extended for up to 96 hours in total, if a magistrates' court on application by the police is satisfied that further detention is justified to secure or preserve evidence or to obtain evidence by questioning the detainee.[76] The detainee must be notified of the application to the magistrates and may be legally represented at the hearing. If the court does not authorise further detention, he must be released or charged.[77] Thus, from the time an arrested person reaches the police station, he may be detained for questioning by the police in connection with a serious arrestable offence for no less than 96 hours.

Once charged, the individual is no longer being detained for questioning, and if not released on bail, he is entitled to be brought to court as soon as is practicable.[78]

What safeguards are there to govern these extensive powers? As well as the duty of the custody officer to record in detail all stages in a detainee's custody, various rights are granted to the detainee by the 1984 Act.

(a)   A detainee is entitled to have a relative, friend or other person told of his arrest and detention. In the case of serious arrestable offences, this right to inform may be delayed by a police superintendent, for example if he believes that to let the information be sent might hinder the recovery of property or lead to interference with evidence. But except for those detained under anti-terrorist legislation,[79] the detainee's right to have someone informed cannot be delayed after the first 36 hours of detention.[80]

(b)   Where a child or young person is detained, his parent or guardian must be informed as soon as is practicable.[81]

(c)   A person held in police custody is entitled if he so requests to consult a solicitor privately at any time. In the case of serious arrestable offences, this right is subject to delay authorised by a superintendent for up to 36 hours on the same grounds as in (a).[82]

(d)   The 1984 Act does not require that the 'interviews' at which detainees are questioned shall be tape-recorded, but the Home Secretary must issue a code of practice for tape-recording interviews and may by order require the procedure to be used for all or some specified offences.[83]

(e)   The common law relating to the admissibility of confessions is replaced by very different statutory rules. In brief, confessions are declared admissible so far as they are relevant to issues at a trial, except that no confession may be admitted where a relevant objection is taken by the defence, unless the prosecution proves to the court beyond reasonable doubt (1) that the confession was not obtained by oppression (which includes torture, inhuman or degrading treatment, and the use or threat of violence)[84] and (2) that nothing

---

[76]   1984 Act, s. 43.
[77]   But see 1984 Act, s. 43(16).
[78]   Note 42, *ante*.
[79]   Ch. 29 C. And see 1984 Act, ss. 56 (11), 65.
[80]   1984 Act, s. 56(3).
[81]   1984 Act, s. 57.
[82]   1984 Act, s. 58. For legal aid. see s. 59.
[83]   1984 Act, s. 60.
[84]   *Cf.* European Convention on Human Rights, art. 3.

was said or done when the confession was obtained that was likely to make it unreliable.[85]

In 1981 the royal commission on criminal procedure considered it necessary 'to replace the vagueness of the Judges' Rules with a set of instructions which provide strengthened safeguards to the suspect and clear and workable guidelines for the police'.[86] Under Part VI of the 1984 Act, the Home Secretary must issue codes of practice for the detention, treatment, questioning and identification of persons, search and seizure of property, and stop and search powers. These codes must be laid before Parliament in draft and may be brought into effect by the Home Secretary with the approval of each House. Failure by a police officer to observe a code of practice makes him liable to disciplinary proceedings,[87] but not of itself to civil or criminal proceedings. Where it is relevant to proceedings before a court, the code of practice must be taken into account, but breach of a code (for example, an improper search) does not in itself make inadmissible the evidence so obtained. As a form of subordinate legislation, the codes of practice cannot run counter to Acts of Parliament and may not extend police powers at the expense of individual rights. If they are faithfully observed, the codes will set standards for police questioning more effectively than did the Judges' Rules. If they are not so observed, the prospect of police officers making full use of their powers under the 1984 Act is not an attractive one.

Powers of entry, search and retention of property

The effect of the general warrant cases was that, except for the power to search for stolen goods, for which a warrant could be obtained at common law from a magistrate,[88] statutory powers were needed if the police were to be authorised to enter and search private premises. 'By the laws of England', said Lord Camden, 'every invasion of private property, be it ever so minute, is a trespass. No man can set his foot upon my ground without my licence, but he is liable to an action though the damage be nothing'.[89] This principle was applied in *Davis* v. *Lisle*, where it was held that two police officers, who had entered a garage to make inquiries about a lorry which had been obstructing the highway, became trespassers when the occupier told them to leave.[90] A common sense view of the law of trespass was taken in *Robson* v. *Hallett*, which held that a police officer, like other members of the public coming to a house on lawful business, has an implied licence from the householder to walk to the front door and to ask whether he can come inside; and that he must be allowed a reasonable time to leave the premises before he becomes a trespasser.[91] Moreover, at common law a constable may enter private premises to suppress a breach of the peace which is in progress.[92] We have already seen that the police may enter to make an arrest under warrant or for an arrestable

---

[85] 1984 Act, s. 76. And see s. 77 (confessions by mentally handicapped persons).
[86] Cmnd 8092, 1981, p. 107.
[87] 1984 Act, s. 67(8); and ch. 20.
[88] Now see Theft Act 1968, s. 26.
[89] *Entick* v. *Carrington* (1765) 19 St. Tr. 1030, 1066.
[90] [1936] 2 K.B. 434.
[91] [1967] 2 Q.B. 939.
[92] *Thomas* v. *Sawkins* [1935] 2 K.B. 249; *Robson* v. *Hallett* [1967] 2 Q.B. 939.

offence.[93] But once an arrest has been completed, the police at common law have no right to enter the arrested person's home, even to search for the instrument by which a crime was committed.[94]

In view of the position at common law, many statutory powers of entry for purposes of inspection or search have been granted to the police and other authorities. Thus Inland Revenue officials have wide powers of entry, search and seizure in connection with alleged tax frauds, subject to a warrant being granted by a circuit judge.[95] These powers have been described by Lord Scarman as 'a breath-taking inroad on the individual's rights of privacy and right of property'.[96] Customs and excise officers have long exercised similar powers without warrant in respect of smuggled goods under the so-called 'writ of assistance'.[97] By the Misuse of Drugs Act 1971, section 23(3), a search warrant may be obtained if a constable satisfies a magistrate that there are reasonable grounds for suspecting that controlled drugs are in the unlawful possession of a person on any premises. Very wide powers of search are conferred by the Official Secrets Act 1911, section 9: a magistrate may issue a warrant authorising the search of named premises and persons found there, and the seizure of 'anything which is evidence of an offence under this Act having been or being about to be committed'; where the interests of the state require immediate action, a police superintendent may himself authorise such a search. This power is all the wider because the scope of offences under the Official Secrets Act 1911 is very extensive.[98] Under the Incitement to Disaffection Act 1934, section 2, there are similar powers but the warrant must be issued by a High Court judge.[99] The existence of these numerous express powers of entry is one reason why the courts are reluctant to hold that a statutory power to arrest or search a person carries with it an implied power to enter premises against the wishes of the occupier.[1]

Despite these statutory powers, difficult questions of common law have arisen regarding police powers to search for and to retain private property for use as evidence, In view of the public interest in the investigation of crime, the courts have found it impossible to maintain the view of the common law that was taken by Lord Camden in *Entick* v. *Carrington*.[2] Rather than conclude that the police were acting unlawfully, the courts have recognised powers of search and seizure for which there was no precedent but which were considered to be reasonable in the public interest.

Thus in *Elias* v. *Pasmore*, when the organiser of an unemployed workers' movement was arrested under warrant while he was at the movement's headquarters, Horridge J. held that the 'interests of the State' justified the police in seizing material that was relevant to the prosecution for any crime of any

---

93   Pages 476–7 *ante*.
94   *McLorie* v. *Oxford* [1982] Q.B. 1290.
95   Taxes Management Act 1970, s. 20c, inserted by Finance Act 1976.
96   *R.* v. *Inland Revenue Cmssrs, ex p. Rossminster Ltd* [1980] A.C. 952, 1022; and see Cmnd 8822, 1983.
97   Customs and Excise Management Act 1979, s. 161; and see [1983] P.L. 1, 345.
98   Ch. 30.
99   Ch. 27 B.

1   *Morris* v. *Beardmore* [1981] A.C. 446. See now Transport Act 1981, s. 25.
2   Note 89, *ante*.

person, not only of the person being arrested.[3] With poor logic, Horridge J.
argued that although it may at the time have been improper to seize the
material, its later use as evidence justified the seizure. This principle of retrospective justification was disapproved by the Court of Appeal in two more
recent cases.

In *Chic Fashions (West Wales) Ltd* v. *Jones*, while the police were executing
a search warrant for certain stolen goods, they took away other goods which
they reasonably believed to have been stolen. When the owner sued for trespass to goods, the Court of Appeal held that in executing a search warrant
for stolen goods, a constable may seize other goods 'which he believes on
reasonable grounds to have been stolen and to be material evidence on a
charge of stealing or receiving against the person in possession of them or
anyone associated with them'.[4] A wider question arose in *Ghani* v. *Jones*: while
investigating a suspected murder, police officers wished to retain the passports
of the victim's close relatives (who were from Pakistan) and some letters
belonging to them. The Court of Appeal ordered the police to return the passports and letters to the relatives, since it had not been shown that they were
material evidence to prove the commission of the murder nor that the police
had reasonable grounds for believing that the relatives were in any way
implicated in a crime. The court laid down certain principles which it considered to apply when the police need to take private property in the course of
an investigation: the police must have reasonable grounds for believing (a) that
a serious crime has been committed, (b) that the article is the instrument by
which the crime was committed or is material evidence to prove commission
of the crime, and (c) that the person in possession of the article is implicated
in the crime 'or at any rate his refusal (of consent to the police) must be quite
unreasonable'; moreover (d) the police must not keep the article longer than
is reasonably necessary; and (e) the lawfulness of the conduct of the police
must be judged at the time and not (as in *Elias* v. *Pasmore*) by what happens
afterwards.[5] In a different context, it has been held that the police may obtain
an injunction to stop a person accused of forgery from withdrawing sums from
a bank account which contained the proceeds of the crime.[6]

In 1981, the royal commission on criminal procedure proposed that the
powers of the police to enter private premises should be made statutory, and
that the police should have power to search under warrant for evidence
relating to grave offences.[7] Broad effect is given to these proposals by the Police
and Criminal Evidence Act 1984.

(*a*) Under the Act, a justice of the peace may issue a warrant authorising a
constable to enter and search premises for material specified in the warrant
which is likely to be of value as evidence in relation to a serious arrestable
offence.[8] Such a warrant may be issued if, for example, entry to premises will
not be granted without a warrant, or if a search will be frustrated unless a

[3] [1934] 2 K.B. 164. and see E.C.S. Wade (1934) 50 L.Q.R. 354.
[4] [1968] 2 Q.B. 299, and see Theft Act 1968, s. 26(3).
[5] [1970] 1 Q.B. 693. *Cf. Frank Truman (Export) Ltd* v. *Metropolitan Police Cmssr* [1977] Q.B. 952.
[6] *Chief Constable of Kent* v. *V.* [1983] Q.B. 34.
[7] Cmnd 8092, 1981, pp. 33–6.
[8] 1984 Act, s. 8. For the meaning of serious arrestable offence see p. 483 *ante*.

constable arriving at the premises can have immediate entry. But a justice's warrant may not be used in respect of certain forms of evidentiary material, namely (1) material subject to legal privilege as defined in the Act (notably communications between a lawyer and his client, when they are in the possession of someone entitled to possess them),[9] (2) 'excluded material' and (3) 'special procedure material'.

(b)   'Excluded material' comprises three categories:

(1)   personal records acquired by a person in the course of any business, profession or other occupation, or for the purposes of any office, and which he holds in confidence; the records must relate to an individual's health, to spiritual or social counselling, or to other forms of counselling or assistance relating to his personal welfare;[10]

(2)   human tissue or tissue fluid taken for diagnosis or medical treatment and held in confidence;

(3)   journalistic material (as defined in the Act) consisting of documents or records and held subject to an obligation of confidence.[11]

(c)   'Special procedure material' comprises other forms of journalistic material, and also other material that is held in confidence or subject to an obligation of secrecy and has been acquired in the course of any business, profession or other occupation, or for the purposes of any office.[12]

(d)   In respect of excluded material and special procedure material, a circuit judge may in certain circumstances order the individual who possesses it to disclose it to the police; in other circumstances the judge may grant an entry and search warrant to the police.[13] Moreover, the 1984 Act applies the protection that it gives to excluded and special procedure material to all existing statutory powers under which the police may search premises.[14]

(e)   The Act places on a statutory basis entry and search for the purpose of making arrests[15] and also entry to save life or prevent serious damage to property. Entry to deal with breaches of the peace is not affected but, apart from this, all common law rules authorising a constable to enter premises without a warrant are abolished.[16]

(f)   The principle laid down in the *Chic Fashions* case[17] is given a new form. A police officer who is lawfully on any premises may now seize anything which he reasonably believes is evidence relating to any offence (or has been obtained as the result of any offence) and which must be seized to prevent its concealment, loss or destruction.[18] This power includes power to obtain material held on a computer. The only exception from this power of seizure is of items subject to legal privilege as defined in the Act. All forms of excluded and special procedure material may be seized if the police come across them in the

---

9   1984 Act, s. 10.
10   1984 Act, s. 11(1)(a) and s. 12.
11   1984 Act, s. 11(1)(c), (3) and s. 13.
12   1984 Act, s. 14.
13   1984 Act, s. 9 and sch. 1.
14   1984 Act, s. 9(2) and sch. 1, para. 3(b).
15   Page 476 *ante.*
16   1984 Act, s. 17.
17   Note 4, *ante.*
18   1984 Act, ss. 19–22.

course of a lawful search. Any article so seized may be retained for use as evidence, for forensic examination or, if it is reasonably believed that it has been obtained by means of an offence, to establish the lawful owner.

(g) Finally, the 1984 Act introduces safeguards relating to the granting of warrants and the conduct of searches. Thus a warrant authorises an entry on one occasion only.[19] Entry and search must generally take place at a reasonable hour. A copy of a warrant must be given to the occupier. After a warrant has been executed (or if not executed, after a month) the warrant must be returned to the court, where it may on demand be inspected by the occupier.[20]

Admissibility of unlawfully obtained evidence

If the police carry out an unlawful search, whether of a person or premises, may they use in evidence articles which they come across during the search? In the United States, unlawfully obtained evidence has been excluded by the Supreme Court.[21] A conflict of principles is likely to arise on this question. On one hand, the citizen needs to be protected against unlawful invasion of his liberties by the police; on the other hand, if justice is to be done at a trial, relevant evidence should not be excluded on merely formal or technical grounds.[22] In Scots law, irregularity in the obtaining of evidence does not necessarily render it inadmissible, but it may do so; and whether unlawfully obtained evidence is admitted is a matter for the trial judge, who may deem it inadmissible, if it has been obtained in circumstances of unfairness to the accused.[23] In English common law, the test of admissibility is whether the evidence is relevant to the matters in issue; 'if it is, it is admissible and the court is not concerned with how the evidence was obtained'.[24] The trial judge has a discretion to exclude evidence which is admissible, if its prejudicial effect would outweigh any probative value that it might have. But the House of Lords held in 1979 that a trial judge has no discretion to exclude evidence on the ground that it was obtained by improper or unfair means, or as the result of an illegal search.[25]

The royal commission on criminal procedure in 1981 reported against automatic exclusion of evidence for breach of the rules of search and seizure. The commission doubted whether such exclusion would deter police misconduct, and preferred to see effective disciplinary sanctions applied within the police. But the commission did recommend the automatic exclusion of evidence obtained as a result of any violence, threats of violence, torture or inhuman or degrading treatment by the police; and that a trial court should be prepared to treat an individual's confession as unreliable where the police had not observed the code of practice for interviewing suspects.[26] These matters were fully debated when the Police and Criminal Evidence Bill was

---

[19] 1984 Act, s. 15(5); *cf. R.* v. *Adams* [1980] Q.B. 575.
[20] 1984 Act, s. 16.
[21] *Weeks* v. *US* (1914) 232 U.S. 383, *Mapp* v. *Ohio* (1961) 367 U.S. 643.
[22] See *Lawrie* v. *Muir* 1950 J.C. 19, 26 (Lord Cooper).
[23] *H.M. Advocate* v. *Turnbull* 1951 J.C. 96, *Fairley* v. *Fishmongers of London* 1951 J.C. 14; *cf. Miln* v. *Cullen* 1967 J.C. 21 and *H.M. Advocate* v. *Hay* 1968 J.C. 40.
[24] *Kuruma* v. *R.* [1955] A.C. 197, 203; and *King* v. *R.* [1969] 1 A.C. 304.
[25] *R.* v. *Sang* [1980] A.C. 402; and see *R.* v. *Adams (ante)* and *Jeffrey* v. *Black* [1978] Q.B. 490.
[26] Cmnd 8092, 1981, pp. 112–8; and see 1984 Act, ss. 67(11), 76; p. 484 *ante*.

before Parliament. A defeat for the government in the Lords forced the government to adopt a clause permitting judges to exclude unfair evidence, and this provision of the 1984 Act is outline in appendix B.

Remedies for infringement of freedom

Wrongful interference with a person's freedom or property gives rise to various forms of remedy.

1   The person injured may be able to bring a civil action for damages against the person responsible (for example, for assault, false imprisonment, or trespass to property or goods) or an action for return of the property, as in *Ghani* v. *Jones*. An action for malicious prosecution may be maintained by any person who is prosecuted for a criminal offence maliciously and without reasonable and probable cause; but it is difficult to win such an action against the police.[27] In principle civil actions may be brought both against private citizens and public officials alike. But special protection is given to some officials against certain liabilities.[28]

2   In the case of injury to the person, a prosecution may be instituted for assault. In England the possibility of a prosecution of a police officer being initiated by a private citizen is sometimes a valuable means of legal protection: in 1963, it was a private prosecution of police officers in Sheffield which led to an official inquiry into the 'rhino tail' assaults.[29]

3   Where the wrong-doer is a police officer, the citizen may make a formal complaint to the police which may cause criminal or disciplinary proceedings to be taken against him.[30]

4   At the time of the interference with person or property, the citizen may well have some right of self-defence, and this can affect both civil and criminal liability. Thus the occupier of land may use reasonable force to remove or keep out a trespasser.[31] The Criminal Law Act 1967, section 3, provided *inter alia* that a person may use such force as is reasonable in the circumstances in the prevention of crime, which would include an assault upon himself.[32] But under the Police Act 1964, section 51, it is an offence to assault, resist or wilfully obstruct a constable in the execution of his duty. There are therefore risks and hazards in the way of a citizen who uses force to resist what he believes to be an unlawful arrest by police, whether of himself or of a close relation.[33] 'The law does not encourage the subject to resist the authority of one whom he knows to be an officer of the law'.[34] Although in *Kenlin* v. *Gardiner*, two boys were entitled to use reasonable force to escape from two constables who were seeking to question them,[35] in general it is inexpedient by self-defence to resist

---

[27]   *E.g. Glinski* v. *McIver* [1962] A.C. 726; *Wershof* v. *Metropolitan Police Cmssr* [1978] 3 All E.R. 540. *Cf. Hunter* v. *Chief Constable of West Midlands Police* [1982] A.C. 529.
[28]   *E.g.* Constables Protection Act 1750, and note 12, p. 475 *ante*.
[29]   Cmnd 2176, 1963.
[30]   Ch. 20.
[31]   *E.g. Vaughan* v. *McKenzie* [1969] 1 Q.B. 557; *cf. Robson* v. *Hallett* [1967] 2 Q.B. 939.
[32]   The effect on the law of self-defence is uncertain: C. Harlow [1974] Crim. L.R. 528.
[33]   *R.* v. *Fennell* [1971] 1 Q.B. 428.
[34]   *Christie* v. *Leachinsky* [1947] A.C. 573, 599 (Lord du Parcq)
[35]   [1967] 2 Q.B. 510. And see *e.g. Lindley* v. *Rutter* [1981] Q.B. 128 and *Pedro* v. *Diss* [1981] 2 All E.R. 59.

arrest by a police officer because, if the arrest is lawful, the assault on the constable is aggravated because he is in execution of his duty. The offence of obstructing a constable in execution of his duty has been widely interpreted in English law;[36] the equivalent offence in Scotland has been interpreted as limited to some physical interference with the police.[37]

5   The remedy of habeas corpus, which is available in English law to a person who has been deprived of his liberty, will be considered in the next section.

B. Habeas corpus

The remedy of habeas corpus has been one of the most distinctive contributions of English law to the international vocabulary of constitutional law. Unlike broad concepts such as the rule of law and 'the right to liberty and security of person',[1] it gives effect to a definite principle which is expressed in the European Convention on Human Rights thus:

Everyone who is deprived of his liberty by arrest or detention shall be entitled to take proceedings by which the lawfulness of his detention shall be decided speedily by a court and his release ordered if the detention is not lawful.[2]

If an individual is wrongfully deprived of his liberty, it is not sufficient that he should be able to sue his gaoler for damages under the ordinary civil law. Whether he is detained by an official or by a private individual, it would be wrong that his detention should continue while the process of civil litigation takes its normal lengthy course. English law provides in the writ of habeas corpus a means by which a person detained without legal justification may secure prompt release. The person responsible for the detention is not thereby punished, but the person imprisoned is set free and may pursue such further remedies for compensation or punishment as may be available.

In view of the proud claims often made for habeas corpus, it is chastening for an English lawyer that the question has more than once arisen under the European Convention on Human Rights whether habeas corpus in fact meets the requirement from that Convention quoted above.[3] Fortunately, after a period in which the effectiveness of the remedy declined, the House of Lords in 1983 reached a decision in an immigration case which should do much to reverse the trend.[4]

History of habeas corpus[5]
Blackstone called habeas corpus 'a high prerogative writ . . . running into all parts of the King's dominions; for the King is at all times entitled to have an account, why the liberty of any of his subjects is restrained, wherever that

---

36   R. C. Austin [1982] C.L.P. 187; J. C. Smith and B. Hogan, *Criminal Law*, pp. 362–71.
37   Police (Scotland) Act 1967, s. 41; *Curlett* v. *McKechnie* 1938 J.C. 176.

1   European Convention on Human Rights, art. 5(1).
2   Art. 5(4).
3   See *X.* v. *UK* (1981) 4 E.H.R.R. 188, *Caprino* v. *UK* (1980) 4 E.H.R.R. 97.
4   *R* v. *Home Secretary, ex p. Khawaja*, p. 494 *post*.
5   H.E.L. IX, 108–25; W. Forsyth, *Cases and Opinions in Constitutional Law*, ch. 16. For a comprehensive account of history and modern law, see R. J. Sharpe, *The Law of Habeas Corpus*.

restraint may be inflicted'.[6] In its modest origin, the writ of habeas corpus merely enabled a court of common law to bring before itself persons whose presence was necessary for some pending legal proceeding. In the 15th and 16th centuries, the courts of King's Bench and Common Pleas used habeas corpus to assert their authority against local courts and other rival courts, and to release persons imprisoned by order of such a court in excess of its jurisdiction. The form of writ known as habeas corpus *ad subjiciendum* came to be a writ by which persons unlawfully imprisoned could be released. In the 17th century, parliamentarians were quick to use the writ to check arbitrary arrest by the King or by the King's Council.[7] In 1640 the Act which abolished the court of Star Chamber provided that, where any detention was ordered by the King or the King's Council, the common law courts must issue a writ of habeas corpus and inquire into and rule upon the true cause of the detention.

In 1679, the Habeas Corpus Act was passed to secure that persons detained on criminal charges were brought speedily to trial and to ensure that the power to detain persons on criminal charges was not abused. The Act of 1679 applied only to detention for 'any criminal or supposed criminal matter'. It imposed a duty on the Lord Chancellor or any of the judges of the superior courts in term or in vacation to issue the writ of habeas corpus, unless the prisoner had been committed on conviction of a crime or by some legal process; breach of this duty exposed a judge to a penalty of £500 at the suit of the prisoner. Strict rules were laid down for the number of days within which the gaoler must deliver a return to the writ and produce the prisoner before the court. No person released by habeas corpus could be re-committed. Provision was made for the speedy trial of persons charged with treason or felony. Evasion of habeas corpus by transfer of a prisoner to another gaol or to a place outside the jurisdiction of the court (for example, to Scotland, Ireland or into any 'islands or places beyond the seas') was prohibited, on pain of heavy penalties.

Sections of the Act are still in force, although its operation has been much affected by reforms of the courts and of the criminal law.[8] While the Act sought to encourage the granting of bail, it did not deal with the problem of excessive bail being required as a condition of release: the Bill of Rights ten years later therefore declared that 'excessive bail ought not to be required'. The Act of 1679 did not grant the court express power to examine the truth of a return to a writ of habeas corpus, nor did the Act apply to detention for non-criminal matters. During the 18th century, the writ was used in its common law form to secure relief from detention by private persons (for example, of infants or lunatics) or on non-criminal charges (for example, impressment for military service). Reforms were proposed in 1758 but only in 1816 was another Habeas Corpus Act passed. By this Act, provisions like those in the 1679 Act were applied to persons deprived of their liberty otherwise than by reason of a charge of crime, unless they were imprisoned for debt or on process in a civil suit. In civil cases the 1816 Act gave the judge power to inquire summarily into the truth of the facts stated in a return, even though the return was 'good

---

6   3 *Commentaries* (10th ed.) p. 131.
7   For *Darnel's* case and the Petition of Right 1628, see p. *246 ante.*
8   *E.g.* Criminal Law Act 1967, Courts Act 1971, Bail Act 1976.

and sufficient in law'.[9] This provision was not applied to criminal cases by the Act but the judges came to relax the strict rule of incontrovertibility.[10]

After *Anderson's* case, in which the Court of Queen's Bench issued habeas corpus in respect of a detention in Canada,[11] the Habeas Corpus Act 1862 provided that the writ was not to issue from a court in England into any colony or foreign dominion of the Crown where there were courts having authority to grant habeas corpus and with power to ensure its execution. So today the writ cannot be issued by the English High Court to any member state of the Commonwealth or to any colonial territories where the local courts are competent.

Present scope of habeas corpus[12]

As a means of checking the legality of various forms of official detention, habeas corpus is sought mainly by convicted prisoners, those detained in custody pending trial, and those held by the police during criminal investigations;[13] those awaiting deportation or otherwise detained under the Immigration Act 1971; those awaiting extradition, or removal under the Fugitive Offenders Act 1967; and mental patients. The writ may be used as a means of determining disputes over the custody of children but these cases are dealt with by the Family Division of the High Court and because of other procedures recourse to habeas corpus is seldom necessary. We have seen that the Bill of Rights declared that excessive bail ought not to be required: legislation today encourages the magistrates to give bail to persons awaiting trial whenever possible, and there is a right of appeal to a High Court judge or to the Crown Court against a refusal of bail by magistrates. But a person who claims that excessive bail has been required of him may have a residual right to apply to the Divisional Court for habeas corpus.[14]

The writ is available to all persons within the Queen's protection, including aliens within the jurisdiction. As an exception, it has been held not to be available to an enemy prisoner of war nor to an interned enemy alien, nor can a notice of internment of an enemy alien be challenged by application for the writ.[15] Habeas corpus was sought in the English High Court by two internees in Northern Ireland but detention in Northern Ireland is a matter within the jurisdiction of the courts in Northern Ireland.[16] Habeas corpus may be issued from the English High Court to the Isle of Man or the Channel Islands but not to Scotland.[17]

Habeas corpus is described as a writ of right which is granted *ex debito justitiae*. This means that a *prima facie* case must be shown before it is issued

---

9   See *e.g. R.* v. *Board of Control, ex p. Rutty* [1956] 2 Q.B. 109.
10   H.E.L. IX, pp. 119–22.
11   *Ex p. Anderson* (1861) 3 El. & El. 487; K. Roberts-Wray, *Commonwealth and Colonial Law*, pp. 612–5. *Cf. In re Mwenya* [1960] 1 Q.B. 241.
12   H.L.E., XI, pp. 768–801; de Smith, *Judical Review*, app. 2; Sharpe, *op. cit.*
13   *E.g. R.* v. *Holmes, ex p. Sherman* [1981] 2 All E.R. 612.
14   See *Ex p. Thomas* [1956] Crim. L.R. 119 and *Ex p. Goswami* (1966) 111 S.J. 17.
15   *R.* v. *Vine Street Superintendent, ex p. Liebmann* [1916] 1 K.B. 268 and *R.* v. *Bottrill, ex p. Kuechenmeister* [1947] K.B. 41.
16   *Re Keenan* [1972] 1 Q.B. 533; *In re McElduff* [1972] N.I.L.R. 1.
17   *R.* v. *Cowle* (1759) 2 Burr. 834, 856.

but it is not a discretionary remedy and it may not be refused merely because an alternative remedy exists: thus in *Azam's* case, the court had jurisdiction to decide on a habeas corpus application whether three Commonwealth citizens were liable to be removed as illegal entrants under the Immigration Act 1971; the issue of whether they were illegal entrants could have been decided on a statutory appeal brought under the 1971 Act, but only if they had first left the United Kingdom.[18] Persons who are serving sentences following a conviction may apply for habeas corpus, and if they are not otherwise legally represented may be assisted by the Official Solicitor, but they may not use the writ as a means of appealing against conviction or sentence.[19]

Habeas corpus is a remedy against *unlawful* detention: clearly an order for detention issued by an inferior tribunal or an executive body is unlawful if it is *ultra vires*, that is, if the tribunal or body had no jurisdiction to issue it. But is habeas corpus a remedy for correcting every error made by an inferior tribunal? The question of how far the High Court will go in reviewing the validity of an order for detention which appears to be lawful cannot be answered simply, 'for the case-law is riddled with contradictions'.[20] In *Rutty's* case, habeas corpus issued to release a high-grade mental defective who had been detained eight years before by order of a magistrate: the High Court exercised its power under the 1816 Act to examine the truth of the facts stated in the return and established that there was no evidence before the magistrate on which a valid order could have been made.[21] In *Greene's* case, a war-time internment case, the Home Secretary was not required to give the grounds for his belief that the applicant was of hostile origin and association, and the internment order was upheld without further inquiry into the facts.[22]

Similar difficulties have arisen in cases concerning immigration law. In one line of cases during the 1970s, the courts placed the burden on the would-be immigrant of disproving findings of fact made by the immigration authorities.[23] The reluctance to make effective use of habeas corpus culminated in *Zamir's* case, in which the House of Lords laid down that the executive decision that someone was an illegal entrant could be questioned by a court only if no reasonable person could have reached that conclusion or if there was no evidence to support it.[24] Within three years, the House of Lords reversed its approach, holding in *Khawaja's* case that, both in habeas corpus cases and on applications for judicial review, the court must itself be satisfied that the applicant was on the facts an illegal immigrant, since this matter was a 'precedent fact' on which the power to deport depended.[25] Lord Scarman considered in that case that the Habeas Corpus Act 1816 imposed a duty on the court

---

[18] *R.* v. *Governor of Pentonville Prison, ex p. Azam* [1974] A.C. 18, 31 (C.A.).

[19] *Re Wring* [1960] 1 All E.R. 536; *Ex p. Hinds* [1961] 1 All E.R. 707.

[20] De Smith, *Judical Review*, p. 606; and see A. Rubinstein, *Jurisdication and Illegality*, pp. 105–16, 176–86.

[21] Note 9 *ante*.

[22] *Greene* v. *Home Secretary* [1942] A.C. 284, following *Liversidge* v. *Anderson* [1942] A.C. 206.

[23] See *e.g. R.* v. *Home Secretary, ex p. Mughal* [1974] 1 Q.B. 313, *Re Wajid Hassan* [1976] 2 All E.R. 123, *R.* v. *Home Secretary , ex p. Choudhary* [1978] 3 All E.R. 790. Also C. Newdick [1982] P.L. 89.

[24] *R.* v. *Home Secretary, ex p. Zamir* [1980] A.C. 930.

[25] *R.* v. *Home Secretary, ex p. Khawaja* [1984] A.C. 74 and p. 459 *ante*.

to examine the truth of the facts set out by the executive, where an individual's liberty is in issue.

Regarding habeas corpus applications under the Extradition Act 1870 and the Fugitive Offenders Act 1967, it is similarly difficult to lay down the limits to which the High Court can go in reviewing the magistrate's order, for such an application is less than an appeal but is not confined to narrow issues of validity; moreover both the 1870 and 1967 Acts expressly require the High Court to be satisfied that the return of an offender is not being sought for a political offence.[26]

Procedure[27]

Normally the person detained will apply for habeas corpus but any relative or other person may do so on his behalf if there is good reason why the person detained cannot do so. Application is made *ex parte* (that is, without notice to the other side) supported by an affidavit to the Divisional Court or in vacation to a single judge. If *prima facie* grounds are shown, the court or judge ordinarily directs that notice of motion be given or an originating summons be issued to the person having physical control of the person detained (for example, a prison governor) but notice may also be served on a minister (for example, the Home Secretary) who is responsible for the detention. On the day named in the notice or summons, argument on the merits of the application takes place. If the court decides that the writ should issue, it orders the release of the prisoner and this order is sufficient warrant for the release. Under this practice there is no need to produce the prisoner in court at the hearing (only exceptionally is an applicant allowed to present his case in person)[28] and no return to the writ is actually made as the writ itself has not yet been issued. In exceptional cases, the court may order the issue of the writ on the *ex parte* application, for example if there is danger of the person detained being taken outside the jurisdiction; in these cases, argument as to the legality of the detention takes place on the return to the writ. Disobedience to the writ is punishable by fine or imprisonment for contempt of court and there may also be penalties under the Act of 1679.

Appeals

The right of appeal on habeas corpus cases was formerly restricted in two ways: first, where a court granted an application and released the applicant from detention, the gaoler had no right of appeal;[29] secondly, in criminal cases there was no right of appeal from the High Court's decision. The lack of an appeal was to some extent redressed by rights granted by the Habeas Corpus Act 1679 to a prisoner whose first application was refused to make successive applications before different courts and judges.[30] The right of appeal is now

---

26   See *e.g. Schtraks* v. *Government of Israel* [1964] A.C. 556 and *R.* v. *Governor of Pentonville Prison, ex p. Sotiriadis* [1975] A.C. 1, 29–30; and ch. 25 C.

27   See R.S.C. Ord. 54; and Sharpe, *op. cit., chs* 9, 10.

28   *Re Wring* [1960] 1 All E.R. 536.

29   *Secretary of State* v. *O'Brien* [1923] A.C. 603.

30   But see the three *Re Hastings* cases: [1958] 1 All E.R. 707, [1959] 1 Q.B. 358, and [1959] Ch. 368; and Heuston, *Essays*, ch. 5.

governed by the Administration of Justice Act 1960. It depends on whether the application is a civil matter (for example, internment or deportation) or a criminal matter (for example, extradition).[31]

(a)   On an application for habeas corpus in a *civil* matter, an appeal to the Court of Appeal (and thence with leave to the House of Lords) may be brought by either side against the decision of the High Court (section 15(1)). If the High Court has granted the application, the individual remains at liberty whatever the outcome of an appeal (section 15(4)).

(b)   On an application for habeas corpus in a *criminal* matter, a single judge of the High Court may grant the application but may not refuse it (section 14(1)) and no appeal lies against a single judge's decision to grant the application (section 15(2)). A criminal application may be refused or granted by a Divisional Court of the Queen's Bench Division, to whom the single judge must refer any application which he is not prepared to grant. Against a decision of the Divisional Court, either side may appeal to the House of Lords with leave either of the Divisional Court or of the House (section 15(3)). If the Divisional Court grants an application for habeas corpus and leave for appeal is then sought, the Divisional Court may order the continued detention of the prisoner or his release on bail pending the outcome of the appeal (section 5(1)).[32] Where the Divisional Court does not so order, the prisoner will be released under the decision of the Divisional Court on the habeas corpus application and is not liable to be again detained if the House of Lords reverses that decision (sections 5(5) and 15(4)).

Under the 1960 Act, no person may make successive applications for habeas corpus, whether to the same court or judge or to any other court or judge, without fresh evidence[33] and no application for habeas corpus may be made to the Lord Chancellor (section 14(2)).[34]

Safeguards in Scotland

The writ of habeas corpus has no direct counterpart in Scots law, but there is statutory provision to ensure the speedy trial of a person who is held in custody on a criminal charge. This is based on the Act of the Scottish Parliament of 1701 for preventing wrongful imprisonment and undue delay in trials. The Act of 1701 set time limits on the length of time within which a person committed for trial could be held in custody and introduced the '110 day rule'.

The law is now found in the Criminal Procedure (Scotland) Act 1975, section 101, as amended by the Criminal Justice (Scotland) Act 1980, section 14. An accused shall not be tried on indictment for any offence unless the trial is commenced within 12 months from his first appearance in court, although this period may for cause shown be extended by a sheriff or judge of the High Court. By the 80 day rule, an accused may not be detained for more than 80 days under a warrant committing him for trial for any offence, without being

---

31   On the civil/criminal distinction, see *Amand* v. *Home Secretary* [1943] A.C. 147, 156 and *R.* v. *Southampton Justices, ex p. Green* [1976] Q.B. 11.

32   By s. 5(4), release on bail may not in general be ordered for a prisoner detained under Pt. III, Mental Health Act 1983.

33   See *Ex p. Schtraks* [1964] 1 Q.B. 191.

34   See *In re Kray* [1965] Ch. 736.

served with an indictment; if an indictment is not served within this period, he must be liberated forthwith unless the period has 'for any sufficient cause' been extended. If so liberated, he may have to stand trial later, but he may not spend further time in custody awaiting trial. By the 110 day rule, an accused may not be detained for more than 110 days under a warrant committing him for trial without being placed on trial. If the trial has not started within this period, 'he shall be liberated forthwith and thereafter he shall be for ever free from all question or process for that offence' (section 101(3)). The court may extend the 110 day limit if the delay is due to the illness of the accused or judge, the absence or illness of any necessary witness or to 'any other sufficient cause which is not attributable to any fault on the part of the prosecutor' (section 101(4)).[35] By section 19 of the 1975 Act, a person arrested on a criminal charge is entitled to notify a solicitor and to obtain a delay of 48 hours in his examination before the sheriff to enable the solicitor to have a private interview with him.

As regards civil detention, the Court of Session has jurisdiction to order the release of any person who is unlawfully detained. If no other more convenient remedy is available (for example, by a suspension and interdict), the detained person may petition the Inner House of the Court of Session for his release in the exercise of the *nobile officium* of the court.

C. Enjoyment of property rights

Public control of land

In Section A of this chapter, we examined the powers of the police to enter upon private property for the purposes of making arrests, searching for evidence of criminal offences and so on. The enjoyment of private property rights is subject to many other incursions of an economic or social character. The right to enjoy property has long been subject at common law to private obligations which are owed to neighbours and others and arise out of the law of nuisance, negligence, trespass, easements, restrictive covenants and leases. Today the owner's private rights are subjected to a wide variety of statutory controls and obligations which Parliament has imposed upon owners and occupiers in the public interest. The effect on the owner is sometimes dramatic.

In *Hutton* v. *Esher Urban District Council*, the local authority proposed to lay a large pipe leading into the river Thames for the purpose of draining away surface water from the area and flood water from a tributary of the Thames. The line of the pipe ran through the plaintiffs' bungalow and the pipe could not be laid without demolition of the bungalow. Megarry J. held that the council's power under the Public Health Act 1936, section 15, to construct a public sewer 'in, on or over any land, after giving reasonable notice' did not include power to demolish a building. He said, 'Parliament could, of course, provide that once any council resolves on the line on which a public sewer is to be constructed, this constitutes the sewer a juggernaut, and authorises the demolition or removal of all that stands in its way, whether factories, offices, houses or anything else'. But Megarry J. did not consider that Parliament had shown an intention so to provide.[1]

---

[35] See *H.M. Advocate* v. *Bickerstaff* 1926 J.C. 65 and *H.M. Advocate* v. *McTavish* 1974 J.C. 19.

[1] [1972] Ch. 515.

The Court of Appeal reversed this decision, holding that the council's power to construct a sewer 'in, on or over' land applied also to buildings and that power to demolish the bungalow was 'just part and parcel' of the power to lay the sewer. The council had a public duty to provide an effective drainage system for its district and it was bound to bear the entire cost of reconstructing the bungalow.[2]

This case is notable not just because it illustrates the limitations on private rights which may be necessary in the public interest, but because of the simple procedure (resolution of the council, plus reasonable notice to the owner) laid down in the Public Health Act for the exercise of such a wide power. Indeed, the council could have achieved its object by making a compulsory purchase order of the bungalow, in which case the owners would have had the chance to contest the scheme at a public inquiry.

Public control over privately owned land and buildings takes several forms. Under the Town and Country Planning Acts, an owner is required to obtain planning permission from the local planning authority before he can develop his land by building on it or by changing the use of existing buildings (for example, from flats to offices). From the local authority's decision there is a right of appeal to the Secretary of State, but at both levels the official decision is based on matters of planning policy and the owner cannot claim that he should be free to do what he likes with his own land. That claim has, in fact, worn very thin in view of the many other controls over land besides planning, which serve a wide variety of social and economic purposes: thus the owner's rights in respect of his property are affected by legislation passed in the interests of good race relations, the health and safety of employed persons, protection of tenants of rented accommodation against their landlords, social policies of controlling gambling, the sale of alcohol and so on.

Public acquisition of private property

The most extreme form of interference with the rights of property occurs when the owner's property is acquired by the state, or expropriated. Expropriation takes two main forms: (a) nationalisation of industrial undertakings and other property, and (b) compulsory purchase of land. Statutory authority is necessary for both forms of expropriation.[3] Nationalisation Acts since 1945 have typically taken an entire industry into public ownership, in some cases by acquisition of the physical assets (for example, land, buildings, plant) being used for the industry but more usually by acquisition of the shares held in all companies engaged in the industry. When the assets or shares have been acquired they are usually vested in a public board created to run the industry.[4] The decision to nationalise an industry is always a matter of major government policy which must receive the legislative approval of Parliament. It has been the invariable practice of Parliament when it defines the assets or securities which are to be nationalised also to lay down the terms on which compensation is payable.

---

2   [1974] Ch. 167.
3   For the Crown's prerogative to take land needed for the defence of the realm, see ch. 13 A. Today land is acquired for defence purposes under statute: see Defence Acts 1842–73 and Land Powers (Defence) Act 1958.
4   Ch. 17 A.

Compulsory purchase of land was known in the 18th century when it was invariably brought about by private Acts of Parliament, which specified the land to be purchased and the purposes for which it was to be used.[5] Today most public authorities have power, with ministerial approval, to acquire land compulsorily which is needed for their statutory functions; even where general powers are not available, an authority may promote a private Bill in Parliament for the acquisition of specified land. Under the Town and Country Planning Act 1971, section 112, local planning authorities have wide powers of acquiring land to secure its development or redevelopment or for a purpose necessary in the interests of proper planning. Some powers of acquisition are available to commercial undertakings: thus by the Pipe-lines Act 1962 an oil company may be authorised to acquire land compulsorily for constructing a pipe-line.

Where powers are available for the compulsory purchase of land, the standard procedure is by compulsory purchase order confirmed by the Secretary of State under the Acquisition of Land Act 1981 or the equivalent Scottish Act. Parliamentary approval is needed only when special classes of land, for example common land or National Trust property, are affected.[6] Before the Secretary of State confirms a compulsory purchase order, it is common for a public inquiry to be held so that all relevant information may be available and the views of the interested parties made known before the order is confirmed.[7] The role of the courts in this context is to ensure that the acquiring authority keeps within its statutory powers and that the correct procedures have been observed; the decision whether particular land should be acquired compulsorily is a government decision for which there is political responsibility to Parliament.

Where a statute authorises the compulsory acquisition of property, it is the invariable practice to provide for the payment of compensation. Parliament could authorise the taking of property without payment but express words would be needed for a statute to have this effect.[8] It is important that statute should provide not only rules for assessing compensation, as in the Land Compensation Act 1973, but also machinery for securing an impartial assessment of compensation in accordance with the rules. Where the owner and the acquiring authority cannot agree as to the amount of compensation payable, the dispute is referred to the Lands Tribunal, which in effect is a specialised court for the valuation of land.[9] The rules for assessing compensation on compulsory purchase are contained in complex legislation which has frequently been amended for political reasons. The rights of landowners therefore depend to a large extent on the latest legislative policies.

These policies have fluctuated sharply in accordance with the differing

---

[5] See F. A. Mann (1959) 75 L.Q.R. 188 and for the modern law, K. Davies, *Law of Compulsory Purchase and Compensation*.

[6] Page 385 *ante*.

[7] Ch. 37 B.

[8] *Newcastle Breweries* v. *R.* [1920] 1 K.B. 854. For what constitutes taking of property, see *France Fenwick and Co.* v. *R.* [1927] 1 K.B. 458, and *Belfast Corporation* v. *O.D. Cars Ltd* [1960] A·C. 490. On statutory immunity for nuisance arising from works authorised by statute, see *Allen* v. *Gulf Oil Refining Ltd* [1981] A.C. 1001.

[9] Ch. 37 A.

views of Labour and Conservative governments. Thus Labour's Community Land Act 1975, which sought to ensure the development of land to meet public needs and to secure to the community the increase in the value of land which arises from development, was repealed by Conservative legislation before it came into full effect. So too, in relation to economic and industrial activities, the Conservative government after 1979 embarked on a policy of privatisation involving the sale to private purchasers of public undertakings. Once rights under such sales are acquired, further legislation will be needed before they can be compulsorily re-vested in public ownership.

Parliament therefore may legislate to modify, sometimes with drastic effect, private rights of property. Such legislation now must take account of the European Convention on Human Rights.[10] The Convention does not primarily seek to protect economic rights. But article 6(1) of the Convention guarantees to everyone, in the determination of civil rights and obligations, a fair and public hearing by an impartial court or tribunal. By article 1 of the First Protocol to the Convention, everyone is entitled to the peaceful enjoyment of his or her possessions, subject only to (a) expropriation in the public interest, in accordance with general principles of international law, and (b) the right of the state to control the use of property in the general interest. In *Ringeisen* v. *Austria*, the European Court of Human Rights held that the rights guaranteed by article 6(1) applied to legislation requiring official approval to be given to the sale of land.[11] The court has also held by a majority that expropriation permits granted in Stockholm for planning purposes, which prohibited all development of the land but were cancelled many years later, involved infringements both of article 6(1) and article 1 of the First Protocol.[12] In 1983, the European Commission on Human Rights declared admissible applications from the United Kingdom concerning the adequacy of compensation for nationalisation under the Aircraft and Shipbuilding Industries Act 1977 and the deprivation of rights under the Leasehold Reform Act 1967.[13] This growing European case-law indicates that the power of Parliament to legislate about private property rights is not absolute.

---

[10] Ch. 31 B.
[11] (1971) 1 E.H.R.R. 455.
[12] *Sporrong and Lönnroth* v. *Sweden* (1982) 5 E.H.R.R. 35.
[13] *Lithgow* v. *UK* (1983) 5 E.H.R.R. 491; *Trustees of Duke of Westminster's Estate* v. *UK* (1983) 5 E.H.R.R. 440.

Chapter 27

Liberty of expression

Within the United Kingdom liberty of expression is both protected and restricted by the law. The law takes for granted what is declared in the European Convention on Human Rights, namely that 'Everyone has the right to freedom of thought, conscience and religion' (article 9). The right to freedom of expression, in the words of article 10 of the Convention, includes freedom to hold opinions, 'and to receive and impart information and ideas without interference by public authority and regardless of frontiers'. This freedom is fundamental to the individual's life in a democratic society. In the first place, it has a specific political content. The freedom to receive and express political opinions, both publicly and privately, is linked closely with the freedom to organise for political purposes and to take part in free elections.

Without free elections the people cannot make a choice of policies. Without freedom of speech the appeal to reason which is the basis of democracy cannot be made. Without freedom of association, electors and elected representatives cannot bind themselves into parties for the formulation of common policies and the attainment of common ends.[1]

So does freedom of expression closely affect freedom of religion. Lawyers remember *Bushell's* case in 1670 as having established the right of the jury to acquit an accused 'against full and manifest evidence', and against the direction of the judge: they should also remember that Bushell was foreman of the jury which acquitted the Quakers William Penn and William Mead on charges of having preached to a large crowd in a London street contrary to the Conventicle Act.[2] Moreover liberty of expression is an integral part of artistic, cultural and intellectual freedom – the freedom to publish books or produce works of art, however disconcerting they may be to the prevailing orthodoxy.

In this broad field, as with other freedoms of the individual, English law has relied 'on the principle that what is not prohibited is permitted and ... therefore on keeping within acceptable limits, and providing precise definitions

---

[1] Jennings, *Cabinet Government*, p. 14.
[2] *R. v. Penn and Mead* (1670) 6 St. Tr. 951.

of, the restrictictions imposed by the civil and criminal law' on the individual's
freedom.[3] Several comments may be made on this view. First, restrictions on
liberty of expression there must be, unless the rights of others are to suffer.
A person's freedom to preach religion to his neighbours is limited by their right
to tell him to get away from their front doors and leave them in peace. Fervent
belief in a good cause does not avoid the need for planning permission before
the enthusiast puts up an advertisement hoarding in his garden. The freedom
to express political or religious opinions may have to be restrained if social
harmony is to be maintained. The bold assertion of freedom of expression in
the European Convention on Human Rights, article 10, is stated to be subject

to such formalities, restrictions or penalties as are prescribed by law and are necessary
in a democratic society, in the interests of national security, territorial integrity or
public safety, for the prevention of disorder or crime, for the protection of health or
morals, for the protection of the reputation or rights of others, for preventing the
disclosure of information received in confidence, or of maintaining the authority and
impartiality of the judiciary (article 10(2)).[4]

Second, the restrictions on freedom of expression have often been imprecise
and entrusted to the subjective judgment of those administering the law. As
Dicey remarked, 'Freedom of discussion is, then, in England little else than
the right to write or say anything which a jury, consisting of twelve shopkeepers, think it expedient should be said or done'.[5] Today juries are composed
rather differently but in several areas of the law, such as obscenity, they retain
power to decide contested cases. Third, the principle that what is not prohibited is permitted may suggest that freedom of expression is no more than
the residue left when all restrictions have taken effect. Yet in many situations of
legal restriction, a process of balancing occurs whereby the public interest in
freedom of expression is weighed against other public interests such as the
administration of justice or the protection of confidentiality.[6]

In this chapter, a sketch will be given of the principal restrictions on
freedom of expression imposed by the civil law (notably the law of defamation)
and by the criminal law (including sedition and obscenity), and also of the law
relating to the principal media of communication. Contempt of court was
considered in chapter 19B. Limits on free speech which relate to public meetings and demonstrations will be considered in chapter 28, and the Official
Secrets Acts in chapter 30. This chapter does not deal with freedom of
association, without which freedom of expression is often ineffective, nor with
the law relating to the churches and the organisation of education.

A.   Civil restraints upon freedom of expression

The law of defamation

The law of defamation seeks to resolve the conflict between the freedom of
speech and publication, and the right of the individual to maintain his

---

3   Report of Committee on Privacy, Cmnd 5012, 1972, p. 10.
4   For interpretation of these provisions, see *Sunday Times* v. *UK* (1979) 2 E.H.R.R. 245 and
     Handyside v. *UK* (1976) 1 E.H.R.R. 737.
5   Dicey, p. 246.
6   An approach perceptively explored in A. Boyle [1982] P.L. 574.

reputation against improper attack.[1] Possibly because of this, defamation law is one of the most complex branches of civil liability. In principle the law provides a remedy for false statements which expose a person to 'hatred, ridicule or contempt' or which tend to lower him 'in the estimation of right-thinking members of society generally'.[2] Defamation takes two main forms (a) slander (defamation in a transitory form by spoken word or gesture) and (b) libel (defamation in a permanent form such as the written or printed word). By statute, words used in the course of broadcasting and of public performances in a theatre are treated as publication in permanent form.[3] With certain exceptions, slander is actionable only when the plaintiff can prove special damage as a result of the slander, whereas libel is actionable without such proof. Actions for defamation are one of the few surviving forms of civil action where either party has a right to insist on trial by jury. When the judge rules that a statement is capable of being regarded as defamatory, it is the jury which decides whether the plaintiff has been defamed and if so the damages that he should recover. Substantial damages may be awarded for injury to reputation and may include exemplary damages.[4] In fact many claims are settled out of court and newspapers often publish notes of correction or apology to persons whom they have unintentionally defamed.

The law of defamation is often directly relevant to government and the working of democratic procedures. In *Beach* v. *Freeson*, an M.P. was sued by a firm of solicitors concerning whom the M.P. had received complaints from a constituent which he had forwarded with covering letters to the Lord Chancellor and the Law Society: it was not disputed that the letters were defamatory, but the publication of the letters to their recipients was held to be protected by qualified privilege.[5] In *Church of Scientology of California* v. *Johnson-Smith*, another M.P. was sued for remarks about scientology made on television: when the plaintiffs sought to rely on what the M.P. had at other times said in Parliament in order to show express malice on his part, it was held that what was said in Parliament was absolutely privileged from being used as evidence in a libel action, even to support a cause of action which arose outside Parliament.[6] Local councillors are more vulnerable. In *Horrocks* v. *Lowe*, a Labour councillor at Bolton was sued by a Conservative councillor for slander on account of a speech at a council meeting in which the defendant had made critical but inaccurate remarks about the plaintiff: the council meeting being an occasion of qualified privilege, the House of Lords held that however prejudiced the defendant had been, or however irrational in leaping to conclusions unfavourable to the plaintiff, he honestly believed in the truth of what he had said, and the defence of qualified privilege succeeded.[7] But where a disgruntled ratepayer had written and distributed at a public meeting a pamphlet which made a strong and abusive attack upon his local council and some members

---

[1]   For fuller accounts of the law of defamation, see textbooks on the law of tort and also Street, *Freedom, the Individual and the Law*, ch. 7 and Report of Committee on Defamation (chairman Faulks J.) Cmnd 5909, 1975.

[2]   *Sim* v. *Stretch* (1936) 52 T.L.R. 669, 671 (Lord Atkin).

[3]   Defamation Act 1952, s. 1; and Theatres Act 1968, s. 4.

[4]   *Broome* v. *Cassell and Co. Ltd* [1972] A.C. 1027.

[5]   [1972] 1 Q.B. 14, p. 214 *ante*.

[6]   [1972] 1 Q.B. 522, p. 212 *ante*.

[7]   [1975] A.C. 135.

of it, the local council was awarded £2,000 damages: Browne J. held that the council had a 'governing' reputation which it was entitled to defend by an action for libel and no privilege protected the ratepayer's pamphlet.[8]

Absolute and qualified privilege

As these cases have shown, publication of statements that would otherwise be defamatory may be protected if made in circumstances of absolute or qualified privilege. Absolute privilege applies to, *inter alia*, (a) statements made during judicial proceedings;[9] (b) statements made during parliamentary proceedings and statements in the official reports of debates or in other papers published by order of either House of Parliament;[10] (c) statements made by one officer of state to another in the course of his official duty, a privilege which in absolute form applies only to certain communications at a high level;[11] and (d) reports by and statements to the Parliamentary Commissioner for Administration.[12]

Qualified privilege, unlike absolute privilege, is destroyed as a defence if the plaintiff proves express malice on the part of the defendant; but carelessness, impulsiveness or irrationality does not amount to malice.[13] Such privilege arises in a wide variety of circumstances, which include: (a) statements made in pursuance of a duty (legal, social or moral) or in protection of an interest, to a person who has a corresponding duty or interest to receive them;[14] (b) fair and accurate reports of judicial proceedings, whether or not published in newspapers and whether or not published contemporaneously with the proceedings (contemporaneous newspaper reports of court proceedings in the United Kingdom have a statutory privilege),[15] (c) fair and accurate reports of parliamentary debates and extracts from parliamentary papers.[16] The Defamation Act 1952 established many new instances of qualified privilege for newspaper and broadcast reports. These reports fall into two categories. Category (a), reports privileged without any explanation or contradiction, includes fair and accurate reports of the proceedings of international organisations and courts, and of certain Commonwealth courts and legislatures. Reports in category (b) are privileged only if the newspaper or broadcasting authority agrees if requested to publish a reasonable letter or statement by way of explanation or contradiction. Category (b) includes fair and accurate reports of proceedings at any public meeting (defined as a meeting *bona fide* and lawfully held for a lawful purpose and for the discussion of any matter of public

---

[8] *Bognor Regis UDC* v. *Campion* [1972] 2 Q.B. 169, aptly criticised by A. J. Weir [1972] C.L.J. 238.

[9] Ch. 19 A; and see *Addis* v. *Crocker* [1961] 1 Q.B. 11 (disciplinary committee of Law Society); and *Trapp* v. *Mackie* [1979] 1 All E.R. 489 (statutory inquiry into teacher's dismissal).

[10] Ch. 12 A.

[11] *E.g. Chatterton* v. *Secretary of State of India* [1895] 2 Q.B. 189. Other official communications are more likely to be protected by qualified privilege.

[12] Parliamentary Commissioner Act 1967, s. 10(5); ch. 37 D.

[13] *Horrocks* v. *Lowe, ante.*

[14] As *e.g.* in *Beach* v. *Freeson* and *Horrocks* v. *Lowe, ante ;cf. Blackshaw* v. *Lord* [1983] 2 All E.R. 311 (no qualified privilege at common law for newspaper report about 'inefficient' civil servant).

[15] Law of Libel Amendment 1888, s. 3;and see *Webb* v. *Times Publishing Co. Ltd* [1960] 2 Q.B. 535 (report of foreign judicial proceedings).

[16] Ch. 12 A.

concern, whether admission is general or restricted); meetings of local authorities and their committees; statutory tribunals and inquiries; and general meetings of public companies.[17] Category (b) also includes 'any notice or other matter issued for the information of the public' by a government department, local authority lord or chief constable, but a newspaper article that included information given by a government press officer to a reporter engaged in investigative journalism does not enjoy this form of qualified privilege.[18]

As regards defamatory statements published by or on behalf of candidates in parliamentary or local elections, such a statement is not protected by qualified privilege on the ground that it was material to a question in issue at the election.[19] But a fair and accurate newspaper report of an election meeting at which defamatory statements were made, would be protected by qualified privilege under the 1952 Act.

Other defences in defamation law

Certain other defences are available. The defendant may seek to justify the defamatory statement, that is, to prove at the trial that what he said was true. Not every detail of the statement need be shown to be literally true, provided that the defendant shows it to be true in substance. By the Defamation Act 1952, section 5, where an action contains a number of distinct charges against the plaintiff, a defence of justification does not fail because the truth of every charge is not proved, provided that the words not proved to be true do not materially injure the plaintiff's reputation having regard to the truth that has been established.[20]

The defence of 'fair comment' protects expressions of opinion on matters of public interest. The comment itself can be quite outspoken, and even unfair, provided that the comment could have been made by an honest man holding strong, exaggerated or even prejudiced views. It is also important that the comment does not contain any incorrect allegations of fact,[21] that the subject of the comment is a matter of public interest, and that malice on the part of the defendant is not shown. The policies and acts of politicians are clearly of public interest. In *Silkin* v. *Beaverbook Newspapers Ltd*, described by Diplock J. as an important case since it concerned 'the right to discuss and criticise the utterances and actions of public men', a former Cabinet minister sued the *Sunday Express* over remarks by a political columnist which pointed to inconsistencies between the plaintiff's speeches in Parliament and his business interests: the jury decided that the defence of fair comment had been established.[22] In *Slim* v. *Daily Telegraph Ltd*, fair comment was a defence to an action brought concerning two letters which criticised a company and its legal adviser over the use for cars of a riverside footpath; Lord Denning M. R. said,

[17] Defamation Act 1952, s. 7 and sched. And *see Khan* v. *Ahmed* [1957] 2 Q.B. 149.
[18] *Blackshaw* v. *Lord ante.*
[19] Defamation Act 1952, s. 10, reversing *Braddock* v. *Bevins* [1948] 1 K.B. 580.
[20] But the value of s. 5 is limited: see *e.g. Speidel* v. *Plato Films Ltd* [1961] A.C. 1090. The Rehabilitation of Offenders Act 1974, s. 8 restricts the use of justification as a defence in respect of statements imputing spent convictions to ex-offenders.
[21] See Defamation Act 1952, s. 6.
[22] [1958] 2 All E.R. 516.

'When a citizen is troubled by things going wrong, he should be free to "write to the newspaper": and the newspaper should be free to publish his letter. It is often the only way to get things put right'.[23] In both these cases, the court stressed that the facts on which the comment was based were correctly stated.

To mitigate the strictness of the law, the Defamation Act 1952, section 4, introduced a limited defence of unintentional defamation. By this defence, one who has published words defamatory of another may claim that the words were published 'innocently' in relation to that other person and make a formal offer of amends (for example, an offer to publish a correction and an apology). If a suitable offer is not accepted, it will provide the basis of a defence to any proceedings which the person defamed may bring. Words are published innocently in relation to a person if, for example, the defendant did not intend the statement to refer to him and did not know of circumstances by which they might be understood to refer to him. In practice, this defence is little used because of its complexities; the Faulks Committee recommended that a simplified version of the defence be introduced.[24]

The press and the law of defamation
There is no doubt that the press and the broadcasting authorities have constantly to be aware of the law of defamation. The important role of the press in reporting on current events of public interest has been recognised more than once by Parliament. As we have seen, the Law of Libel Amendment Act 1888 and the Defamation Act 1952 extended the protection of privilege to various classes of report published in a newspaper or broadcast. For this purpose, the 1952 Act defined a newspaper as any paper containing public news or observations thereon, or consisting wholly or mainly of advertisements, printed for sale and published in the United Kingdom either periodically or in parts at intervals not exceeding 36 days. Beyond this the law of defamation makes little special provision for the press,[25] although by the so-called 'newspaper rule', a newspaper which is pleading privilege or fair comment in defence of an action for libel is not required on discovery to disclose the source of its information. This rule is confined to defamation proceedings and does not confer on the press and broadcasting authorities a general immunity from disclosure of their sources.[26]

The position of the press is very different in the USA, where, by the First Amendment to the Constitution, 'Congress shall make no law ... abridging the freedom of speech, or of the press' and, by the Fourteenth Amendment, 'No State shall make or enforce any law which shall abridge the privileges or immunities of citizens of the United States'. The effect of Supreme Court decisions on the freedom of the press has been to create a new law of libel concerning matters of public or general interest under which the press has much greater freedom to publish information and comment than under English law: thus, on a matter of public or general interest, the plaintiff must

---

23   [1968] 2 Q.B. 157.
24   Cmnd 5909, 1975, ch. 9.
25   But see the Law of Libel Amendment Act 1888, s. 8, p. 515, *post*.
26   *British Steel Corpn* v. *Granada Television Ltd* [1981] A.C. 1096. But see p. 344, *ante*.

prove that the publication was false and that it was published either with knowledge of its falsity or with serious doubts as to its truth.[27] It has been suggested in Britain that there should be no liability for statements made on matters of public interest when the publisher believes the statement of fact to be true and has exercised all reasonable care in relation to the facts.[28] What underlies such a proposal is the view that British newspapers are inhibited by the law of defamation from publishing reports (for example, exposing corruption in high places) which should be available to the public. At the same time, many hold the view that the intrusion by the press into matters involving personal privacy should be more closely restricted than at present and that a new general right of privacy should be created.[29]

In 1975 the Faulks committee did not favour the creation of new rights for the press on the lines of the United States law, on the ground that this would in many cases deny a just remedy to defamed persons.[30] The committee recommended many less radical changes in the law, including the abolition of exemplary damages and the restriction of jury trials in defamation cases, but these recommendations had not been implemented by 1984.

Other civil restraints upon free expression

The restraints which arise from contempt of court and contempt of Parliament have already been considered.[31] The law of copyright lies outside the scope of this book: but under the Copyright Act 1956, section 6(2), fair dealing with a literary work is not an infringement of copyright if it is for purposes of criticism or review and is accompanied by a sufficient acknowledgement.[32]

In the law of defamation, the courts are reluctant to ban publication of a book or article before trial of the action; in particular, the courts do not restrain publication of a work, even though it is defamatory, when the defendant intends to plead justification or fair comment on a matter of public interest and it is not manifest that such a defence is bound to fail.[33] In actions for breach of confidence, however, damages may be recovered but emphasis is laid on the power of the court by issuing an injunction to prohibit publication which would be in breach of confidence. Breach of confidence is a rapidly developing branch of the law, and there is uncertainty as to its legal basis.[34] But the law has been much influenced by the equitable doctrine that a person should not knowingly take unfair advantage of the plaintiff's confidence, for example, by publication of information received in confidence. Thus in the early case of *Prince Albert* v. *Strange*, the defendant was prohibited from publishing etchings made by Prince Albert and Queen Victoria and a catalogue describing the etchings based on information which had been obtained

---

27   Cmnd 5909, 1975, ch. 23 and see *New York Times* v. *Sullivan* (1964) 376 U.S. 254.
28   Report by Justice, *The Law and the Press*, 1965; *cf.* Cmnd 5909, pp. 53–5, and Street, *Freedom, the Individual and the Law*, p. 186.
29   See report of the committee on privacy, Cmnd 5012, 1972, ch. 23; Justice, *Privacy and the Law*, 1970; and G. D. S. Taylor (1971) 34 M.L.R. 288.
30   Cmnd 5909, p. 169.
31   Chs. 12 A and 19 B.
32   See *Hubbard* v. *Vosper* [1972] 2 Q.B. 84 (attempt to ban book criticising scientology).
33   *Fraser* v. *Evans* [1969] 1 Q.B. 349.
34   For a full analysis by the Law Commission, see Cmnd 8388, 1981.

in breach of confidence.[35] The action has been used mainly to protect commercial and industrial secrets but in *Argyll* v. *Argyll*, the Duke of Argyll and a Sunday newspaper were barred by injunction from publishing articles which sought to reveal marital confidences entrusted to the Duke by his wife during a former marriage.[36] The same action was invoked in 1975 by the Attorney-General in his attempt to restrain publication of the Crossman diaries. While in that case an injunction was not granted, Lord Widgery C. J. ruled that publication of information received by a Cabinet minister prejudicial to the collective responsibility of the Cabinet would be restrained if the public interest clearly required this.[37] It must be emphasised that the label of 'confidential' applied to a document, whether by a public authority or not, does not mean that the court will restrain publication of it should a copy reach a newspaper. In *Fraser* v. *Evans*, the court refused to ban publication of a confidential report which Fraser, a public relations consultant, had prepared for the Greek government, when the *Sunday Times* had obtained a copy of it from Greek sources: Fraser's contract with the Greek government required him but not the government to keep it confidential.[38]

The action for breach of confidence may not be used to suppress disclosure of material that should in the public interest be made known, such as dishonest trading practices.[39] But severe difficulties are encountered in defining the relation between a private duty of confidence, the public interest in the protection of confidence and the public interest in information being made known. In 1981, the Court of Appeal granted a drug company an injunction to restrain the making of a television documentary about the company's public relations methods, on the basis that the giving of confidential information in a commercial context imposed an obligation of confidence upon the recipient of the information.[40] In *British Steel Corporation* v. *Granada Television Ltd*, the House of Lords granted the corporation an order requiring Granada to disclose the name of the corporation's employee who had passed confidential documents to the company.[41] The English Law Commission in 1981 recommended legislation to abolish the present action for breach of confidence, to replace it by a new tort of breach of confidence, to define the circumstances in which a duty of confidence would arise, and to provide for the public interest in confidentiality to be balanced against the public interest in disclosure of information.[42] While such legislation would clarify the doctrinal basis of breach of confidence, the judges would still have to make difficult and far-reaching choices in exercising their discretionary powers of control.

A discretionary power to ban publication of a book on novel grounds of private interest was firmly rejected by the Court of Appeal in 1975. In *Re X* (*a minor*), the stepfather of a girl of 14 sought an order making her a ward of

---

[35] (1849) 1 Mac. & G. 25.
[36] [1967] Ch. 302.
[37] *A.-G.* v. *Jonathan Cape Ltd* [1976] Q.B. 752; ch. 14 A.
[38] [1969] 1 Q.B. 349.
[39] *Initial Services Ltd* v. *Putterill* [1968] 1 Q.B. 396; and see Cmnd 8388, 1981, pp. 41–51.
[40] *Schering Chemicals Ltd* v. *Falkman Ltd* [1982] Q.B. 1, criticised by M. W. Bryan [1981] P.L. 459.
[41] [1981] A.C. 1096.
[42] Cmnd 8388, 1981; M. W. Bryan [1982] P.L. 188.

court, and an injunction to stop publication of a book which he claimed would do psychological harm to her, as the book in part described her dead father's sexual activities, his excessive drinking and so on. Lord Denning M. R. stated that the limits on the freedom of the press were already staked out by rules of law, and added: 'It would be a mistake to extend these so as to give the judges a power to stop publication of true matter whenever the judges – or any particular judge – thought that it was in the interests of a child to do so' [43]

B. Criminal restraints upon freedom of expression

Control of printing
Public control over the printing of books may take two main forms: (a) a system of censorship or licensing of printers and books, whereby official approval is given to a book before it is printed and it is an offence to publish a book without such approval; (b) post-publication control exercised by the courts, whereby those who have published material which infringes the criminal law may be prosecuted and the book destroyed. From the time of the Tudors, printed matter in England was licensed before publication, control being carried out by the executive under the prerogative. In 1556, the monopoly of all printing in England was granted by the Crown to the Stationers' Company, the company being required to seek out and suppress printers of seditious and heretical works. In 1586 and again in 1637, regulations for printing and bookselling were issued by the court of Star Chamber; they established a scheme of censorship enforced by the court. Star Chamber was abolished in 1640 but control over printing continued. By the Licensing Act 1662, Parliament authorised a scheme of censorship which was maintained intermittently until 1695, when Parliament allowed the Licensing Act to expire, mainly because the licensers' control over printing and importation of books had become irksome and ineffective. Thereafter the emphasis shifted to post-publication control by means of the criminal law of libel in its various forms, particularly seditious libel. The ecclesiastical courts still exercised jurisdiction in respect of heresy and obscenity. As Blackstone emphasised, 'The Liberty of the Press is indeed essential to the nature of a free State; but this consists in laying no *previous* restraints upon publication, and not in freedom from censure for criminal matter when published'.[1]

History of the law of libel
The law of seditious libel developed at a period when it was considered that adverse criticism of the monarch and his authority was injurious to the public good and deserved punishment. As government became more a matter for the King's ministers, and less a matter of the King's personal decision, the view that those exercising authority should not be criticised was maintained. In 1704 Holt C. J. remarked, 'it is very necessary for all governments that the

---

[43] [1975] Fam. 47.

[1] *Commentaries*, 9th edn. IV, 151. See also H.E.L. VI, 360–78 and VIII, 333–78; L. Hanson, *Government and the Press 1695–1763*; D. Thomas, *A Long Time Burning*; P. O'Higgins, *Censorship in Britain*; G. Robertson, *Obscenity*.

people should have a good opinion of it'.[2] For much of the 18th century Parliament sought to prevent publication of its debates and it was contempt of court to publish a report of legal proceedings without leave of the judge. The campaign of John Wilkes in the 1760s made some notable advances but in 1792 Tom Paine's *Rights of Man* was prosecuted as a seditious libel.

Because the criminal law of libel had derived from the jurisdiction of Star Chamber, the duties of the jury at a trial for libel in the 18th century were very limited. It was the judges who decided in cases of seditious and other libel the character of the publication as a matter of law; the jury was restricted to delivering a verdict on the fact of whether the accused had published the work in question. After a long controversy on this matter[3] Fox's Libel Act 1792 enabled the jury in a prosecution for criminal (including a seditious) libel to return a verdict on the general issue and thus to decide whether or not the publication had the character alleged by the prosecution. The measure coincided with fears of revolution spreading from France. At first convictions of radical pamphleteers were as readily obtained from 'twelve shopkeepers' as from a bench of judges, but later the new machinery established liberty of discussion within the framework of the common law. The old law of libel has now given way to a number of distinct offences – sedition, blasphemy, obscenity and criminal libel. But it is still the jury's verdict which determines the character of the publication in question and provides a safeguard against repressive prosecutions.[4]

Sedition

It is an offence at common law to publish a seditious libel or to utter seditious words. In 1886, at a trial of Socialist leaders for speeches made at a demonstration in Trafalgar Square which had been followed by disorder, a seditious intention was defined very widely as

an intention to bring into hatred or contempt, or to excite disaffection against the person of, Her Majesty . . . or the government and constitution of the United Kingdom, as by law established , or either House of Parliament, or the administration of justice, or to excite Her Majesty's subjects to attempt, otherwise than by lawful means, the alteration of any matter in Church or State by law established, or to raise discontent or disaffection amongst Her Majesty's subjects, or to promote feelings of ill-will and hostility between different classes of such subjects.[5]

But at the same time it was explained that it is not seditious to point out errors or defects in the government or constitution of the United Kingdom, or to seek to bring about changes in church or state by lawful means or, with a view to their removal, to draw attention to matters which were tending to produce ill-will or hostility between classes of Her Majesty's subjects. In two leading prosecutions for seditious libel in the 20th century, the element of incitement to

---

[2]   *R.* v. *Tutchin* (1704) 14 St. Tr. 1095, 1128; *cf.* the 'good government' argument against publication of Cabinet discussions (p. 264 *ante*).

[3]   H.E.L. X, 676–88.

[4]   *Cf. Joshua* v. *R.* [1955] A.C. 121.

[5]   *R.* v. *Burns* (1886) 16 Cox C.C. 355, citing Stephen's *Digest of Criminal Law.* And see H. Street, *Freedom, the Individual, and the Law*, ch. 9 and D. G. T. Williams, *Keeping the Peace*, ch. 8.

violence was stressed. In *R.* v. *Aldred*, a journal advocating independence for India published articles which commended political assassination soon after an assassination by an Indian nationalist had occurred in London: Coleridge J. told the jury that sedition implied violence or lawlessness in some form, and said, 'the test is this: was the language used calculated, or was it not, to promote public disorder or physical force or violence in a matter of State?' Aldred, editor of the journal was convicted.[6] The test of whether the words were *calculated* (that is, likely) to promote violence was not followed in *R.* v. *Caunt*, where Birkett J. directed the jury that proof of *intention* to promote violence was an essential part of the offence.

At a time shortly before the creation of the state of Israel, when British troops in Palestine were being subjected to terrorist atrocities and soldiers had been murdered, the editor of the *Morecambe and Heysham Visitor* published a leading article attacking British Jews in virulent terms and calling for Jews to be ostracised. The article ended with a suggestion that violence might be the only way to bring British Jews to the sense of their responsibility to the country in which they lived. Notwithstanding these words, the jury acquitted the editor of having published a seditious libel.[7]

Such a case provided a severe test for the principle of free speech. A possible comment on the outcome is that the jury shared the editor's views, or at least did not find his anti-Semitism so abhorrent to them that he should be punished for having published them. On the other hand, given the judge's direction on the law of seditious libel, the jury may not have been satisfied beyond reasonable doubt that the editor was intending to incite his readers to violence: in evidence he had denied any such intention, while adhering to the words of his article. It is fundamental in such a case that a jury does not give reasons for its verdict nor need the jurors each come to their decision by the same route.

The scope of sedition has therefore changed. The prosecution must now shown an intention to promote violence and disorder over and above the strong criticism of public affairs.[8] A pamphlet which advocated civil disobedience in support of a political objective would not be regarded today as seditious: but the permissible limits would be exceeded by a pamphlet which incited violence against the authorities or against private people. It would be more difficult to categorise a speech which, without directly inciting violence, was phrased in extreme terms which were likely to promote violence between sections of the community. On the test applied in *R.* v. *Caunt*, this would not be seditious, but the circumstances of publication might cause a jury to reject a defence of no intention to promote violence. One reason why prosecutions for sedition are extremely rare is that statutory offences have been created which, from the prosecution's point of view, are easier to handle. If a local newspaper published an anti-Semitic article today, it could be prosecuted for incitement to racial hatred.[9] In 1977, the Law Commission formed the provisional view that there is no need to retain the offence of sedition because of the existence of other offences.[10]

---

6 (1909) 22 Cox C.C. 1; Wilson, *Cases*, p. 724.
7 See *An Editor on Trial*, 1948; and E. C. S. Wade (1948) 64 L.Q.R. 203.
8 Smith and Hogan, pp. 783–7; *cf. Boucher* v. *R.* [1951] 2 D.L.R. 369.
9 Page 513 *post*.
10 Working Paper No. 27, *Treason, Sedition and Allied Offences*.

Incitement to disaffection[11]

Parliament has on several occasions legislated to prevent the spread of disaffection, mainly to protect members of the armed forces, who might otherwise be exposed to attempts to persuade them to disobey their orders. The Incitement to Mutiny Act 1797, passed following the Nore mutiny, made it a felony maliciously and advisedly to endeavour to seduce members of the armed forces from their duty and allegiance to the Crown, or to incite members to commit any act of mutiny. The Aliens Restriction (Amendment) Act 1919, section 3, prohibits an alien from causing sedition or disaffection among the civil population as well as among the armed forces; and it is a summary offence for any alien to promote or interfere in an industrial dispute in any industry in which he has not been *bona fide* engaged in the United Kingdom for at least two years preceding an alleged offence. The Police Act 1964, section 53, replacing legislation passed in 1919 at a time of serious unrest within the police, prohibits acts calculated to cause disaffection among police officers or to induce them to withhold their services or commit breaches of discipline. The Incitement to Disaffection Act 1934, which passed through Parliament against severe criticism from a variety of quarters,[12] sought without repealing the 1797 Act to provide a modern version of it. Under the 1934 Act, it is an offence maliciously and advisedly to endeavour to seduce a member of the armed forces from his duty or allegiance. The Act contains stringent provisions for the prevention and detection of the offence, including wide powers of search on reasonable suspicion, but a warrant may be issued only by a High Court judge. Moreover, it is an offence for any person, with intent to commit or to aid, counsel or procure commission of the main offence, to have in his possession or under his control any document of such a nature that the distribution of copies among members of the forces would constitute that offence. Notwithstanding the safeguards in the Act, it does restrain certain forms of political propaganda; and it could be used to suppress or interfere with the distribution of pacifist literature. Prosecutions under the Act in England require the consent of the Director of Public Prosecutions. This consent was given between 1973 and 1975 for prosecution of members of a campaign for the withdrawal of British troops from Northern Ireland in respect of leaflets which they had prepared. One conviction was upheld by the Court of Appeal.[13] The accused has a right to jury-trial: it would be a matter for the jury to decide whether a leaflet which gave information to a soldier about procedures for leaving the army and his rights as a soldier was an attempt to seduce him from his duty or allegiance to the Crown.

Incitement to racial hatred

It has long been recognised that the preservation of public order justifies the imposition of criminal sanctions on those who utter threats, abuse or insults

---

[11] Street, *op.cit.*, ch. 8; Williams, *op. cit.*, ch. 8; T. Young, *Incitement to Disaffection*; T. Bunyan, *The Political Police in Britain*, pp. 28–36.

[12] See *e.g.* W. I. Jennings, *The Sedition Bill Explained.*

[13] *R.* v. *Arrowsmith* [1975] Q.B. 678; and see *Arrowsmith* v. *UK* (1978) 3 E.H.R.R. 218 (no infringement of European Convention on Human Rights).

in public places which are likely to give rise to a breach of the peace.[14] In 1965, when Parliament first created machinery to deal with racial discrimination,[15] an offence of incitement to racial hatred was created which was not dependent on proof of an immediate threat to public order. The reason for this was the belief that racial hatred itself contains the seeds of violence.[16] Under what is now section 5A of the Public Order Act 1936 (enacted by the Race Relations Act 1976, section 70), it is an offence for any person *either* to publish or distribute written matter (including a sign or visible representation) which is threatening, abusive or insulting *or* to use in any public place or at a public meeting words which are threatening, abusive or insulting, where (in either case) in all the circumstances hatred is likely to be stirred up against any racial group in Great Britain. 'Racial group' means a group of persons defined by reference to colour, race, nationality or ethnic or national origins.[17] It is no offence to publish a fair and accurate report of proceedings in Parliament or of proceedings in a court or tribunal, provided in the latter case that the report is published contemporaneously with the proceedings or as soon as is reasonably practicable. Nor is it an offence if the publication of written matter is restricted to members of an association of which the person publishing it is a member. It is not now necessary, as it was under the 1965 Act, to prove that the accused intended to stir up racial hatred: in practice, such proof had been too stringent a requirement for the law to be an effective restraint upon racialist propaganda.[18] No prosecution in England and Wales may occur without the consent of the Attorney-General. The issue of whether spoken or written matter is 'threatening, abusive or insulting' is likely to be decided with reference to precedents interpreting the same words in the Public Order Act.[19]

Under the 1965 Act there were few prosecutions but they included persons from both the anti-black and the anti-white extremes.[20] It was held that to leave pamphlets in the porch of an M.P.'s house was not evidence of distribution to a section of the public.[21] The Act conferred no right upon a citizen to seek an injunction against the BBC to restrain allegedly racialist broadcasts.[22] The Theatres Act 1968, section 5(1), made it an offence for any person, with intent to stir up racial hatred, to present or direct the public performance of a play which included the use of threatening, abusive or insulting words, if the performance taken as a whole was likely to stir up racial hatred.

The offence of incitement to racial hatred is justifiable primarily because a serious threat to public order is inherent in certain forms of political and

---

[14] Ch. 28.
[15] Ch. 31 A.
[16] See D.G.T. Williams [1966] Crim. L.R. 320; A. Lester and G. Bindman. *Race and Law*, ch. 10; and P.M. Leopold [1977] P.L. 389.
[17] 1976 Act, s. 3. Religion is not mentioned, but Sikhs in Britain form an ethnic group under the Act: *Mandla* v. *Dowell Lee* [1983] 2 A.C. 548. See also *King-Ansell* v. *Police* [1979] 2 N.Z.L.R. 531.
[18] See comments of Scarman L.J. in Cmnd 5919,1975, p. 38.
[19] Ch. 28.
[20] See A. Dickey [1968] Crim. L.R. 489 and *R.* v. *Malik* [1968] 1 All E.R. 582.
[21] *R.* v. *Britton* [1967] 2 Q.B. 51.
[22] *Thorne* v. *BBC* [1967] 2 All E.R. 1225.

social expression. There are evident dangers to liberty in the imposition of criminal penalties for the publication of unpopular opinions. The requirement that the words must be 'threatening, abusive or insulting' is important; for it means both that the offence is unlikely to be committed by those who make use of reasoned argument and also that the issue of whether truth is a defence does not arise. Since 1976, many difficulties have been experienced in the prosecution of incitement to racial hatred, and it has been argued that the law on incitement needs to be reformulated and more effectively enforced.[23] But changes in legislation alone will not necessarily reduce the occurrence of racial violence and harassment in the streets.

Blasphemy

While it continues to be a common law offence to utter or publish blasphemous words and writings, the old precedents which held that it is blasphemy to deny the truth of the Christian religion or the existence of God have ceased to be helpful. 'If the decencies of controversy are observed, even the fundamentals of religion may be attacked without the writer being guilty of blasphemy'.[24] In the absence of modern authorities, it became unclear what the essentials of the offence were. But in *R. v. Lemon*, the publishers of *Gay News* were in 1977 convicted by a jury of publishing a blasphemous libel, in the form of a poem by James Kirkup that linked homosexual practices with the life and crucifixion of Christ. The House of Lords held by 3–2 that it was sufficient for the prosecution to prove that blasphemous material had been published, and not necessary to prove that the defendants intended to blaspheme. In the view of the House, a blasphemous libel was material calculated to outrage and insult a Christian's religious feelings; it is not an element of the offence that the publication must tend to lead to a breach of the peace.[25] In 1981 the Law Commission formed the provisional view that the criminal law was not an appropriate means of enforcing respect for religious beliefs and that the common law offence of blasphemy should be abolished; if there were to be a statutory replacement for blasphemy, it should not be restricted to attacks upon Christianity.[26] The Commission believed that there should continue to be a statutory offence aimed at offensive conduct which disturbs public worship.[27] Where insulting behaviour directed at members of a religious group is likely to lead to a breach of the peace, those responsible can be prosecuted under the Public Order Act 1936, section 5.[28]

Criminal libel[29]

To publish defamatory material in writing became a criminal offence punishable by the common law courts after the abolition of Star Chamber in 1640.

---

23 See R. Cotterrell [1982] P.L. 378.
24 *R. v. Ramsay and Foote* (1883) 15 Cox C.C. 231, 238 (Coleridge C.J.). See also *Bowman* v. *Secular Society* [1917] A.C. 406; and *R.* v. *Gott* (1922) 16 Cr. App. Rep. 87.
25 *R.* v. *Lemon* [1979] A.C. 617. And see *Gay News Ltd* v. *UK* (1982) 5 E.H.R.R. 123.
26 Working Paper No. 79, *Offences against Religion and Public Worship*; and see St. J. Robilliard (1981) 44 M.L.R. 556.
27 *Cf. Abrahams* v. *Cavey* [1968] 1 Q.B. 479 (political interruption of church service held to be 'indecent behaviour').
28 Ch. 28.
29 J. R. Spencer [1977] Crim. L.R. 383 and (1979) 38 C.L.J. 60.

The justification for treating libel as a criminal offence was considered to be the threat to the preservation of the peace which some libels presented. Today criminal proceedings are rarely instituted for libel. If they are, it is not necessary to prove that the libel was likely to cause breach of the peace,[30] but a criminal libel must be a serious libel to justify invoking the criminal law. At common law, truth was no defence to a prosecution for libel but by the Libel Act 1843, truth is a defence if the accused also proves that the publication was for the public benefit. By the Law of Libel Amendment Act 1888, section 8, no prosecution may be commenced in respect of a libel in a newspaper without the order of a High Court judge. Prosecutions are rare but in 1976, Wien J. gave an order enabling a private prosecution to be brought by Sir James Goldsmith against the publishers of *Private Eye* in respect of repeated allegations that Goldsmith was the ringleader of a conspiracy to obstruct the course of justice; the judge said that the press does not have licence to publish scandalous or scurrilous matter which is wholly without foundation.[31] In 1982, the Law Commission's provisional view was that criminal libel at common law should be abolished and replaced by a much narrower statutory offence, aimed at a person who publishes a deliberately defamatory statement, which he knows or believes to be untrue, and is likely to cause the victim significant harm.[32] But it has been argued that the criminal law should be excluded from the area of defamation.[33]

Obscene publications: before the Act of 1959

It resulted from the development of the law concerning the printing of books that, as with seditious, blasphemous and other libels, it became an offence punishable by the common law courts to publish obscene material. This jurisdiction was exercised for the first time in *Curll's* case when the court held that it was an offence to publish a book which tended to corrupt morals and was against the King's peace.[34] The flourishing business of pornography in the Victorian underworld led to the Obscene Publications Act 1857. This Act gave the police power to search premises, seize obscene publications kept for sale and bring them before a magistrates' court for destruction. The Act did not define 'obscene' but its sponsor, Lord Campbell, stated that it was to apply 'exclusively to works written for the single purpose of corrupting the morals of youth, and of a nature calculated to shock the common feelings of decency in any well regulated mind.'[35]

In 1868, in *R.* v. *Hicklin*, Cockburn C. J. declared the test for obscenity to be

whether the tendency of the matter charged as obscenity is to deprave and corrupt those whose minds are open to such immoral influences and into whose hands a publication of this sort may fall.[36]

---

[30] *R.* v. *Wicks* [1936] 1 All E.R. 384; *Gleaves* v. *Deakin* [1980] A.C. 477.

[31] *Goldsmith* v. *Pressdram Ltd.* [1977] Q.B. 83. And see *Desmond* v. *Thorne* [1982] 3 All E.R. 268.

[32] Law Commission, Working Paper No. 84, *Criminal Libel*. See also J. R. Spencer [1983] Crim. L.R. 524 and Cmnd 5909, 1975, ch. 16.

[33] G. Robertson [1983] P.L. 208.

[34] (1727) 17 St. Tr. 153; G. Robertson, *Obscenity*, ch. 2.

[35] H.L. Deb., 25 Jun 1857, col. 329.

[36] (1868) L.R. 3 Q.B. 360, 371.

This test came to dominate the English law of obscenity. It required account to be taken of the circumstances of publication: in *Hicklin's* case Cockburn C. J. said that immunity for a medical treatise depended upon these circumstances, since the publication of some medical details would not be fit for boys and girls to see. But the test did not permit the author's intention to be taken into account. Although the tendency to deprave and corrupt was often assumed from the character of a book, who might the potential readers be? In 1954, in *R.* v. *Reiter*, the Court of Criminal Appeal took the view that a jury should direct their attention to the result of a book falling into the hands of young people.[37] But a few months later, in *R.* v. *Secker Warburg Ltd*, Stable J. asked: 'Are we to take our literary standards as being the level of something that is suitable for the decently brought up young female aged 14?' He continued:

A mass of literature, great literature from many angles, is wholly unsuitable for reading by the adolescent, but that does not mean that the publisher is guilty of a criminal offence for making those works available to the general public.[38]

Other difficulties in the law included the lack of authority establishing that the publication of matter *prima facie* obscene might nonetheless be for the public good; the use of the 1857 Act against serious literature; the failure of the 1857 Act to enable a publisher or author to defend a work against destruction; and the tendency of prosecutors to take selected passages of a book out of context. A lengthy campaign by publishers and authors led to the Obscene Publications Act 1959.[39]

The Obscene Publications Acts 1959 and 1964
The 1959 Act, which did not apply to Scotland, sought both to provide for the protection of literature and to strengthen the law against pornography. For the purposes of the 1959 Act (but not of other Acts in which the word 'obscene' is used)[40]

an article shall be deemed to be obscene if its effect or (where the article comprises two or more distinct items) the effect of any one of its items[41] is, if taken as a whole, such as to tend to deprave and corrupt persons who are likely, having regard to all relevant circumstances, to read, see or hear the matter contained or embodied in it (section 1(1)).

A wide definition of 'article' (section 1 (2)) includes books, pictures, films, records and such things as film negatives used in producing obscene articles,[42] and video cassettes.[43] It is an offence to publish an obscene article, whether for gain or not, or to have obscene articles in one's possession, ownership or control for the purpose of publication for gain or with a view to such publi-

---

[37] [1954] 2 Q.B. 16.
[38] [1954] 2 All E.R. 683, 686 (Kauffman's *The Philanderer*.)
[39] See H.C. 123 (1957–8); and Robertson, *op. cit.*, pp. 40–4.
[40] *R.* v. *Anderson* [1972] 1 Q.B. 304, 317 (*Oz, School Kids Issue*).
[41] On the item by item test, see *R.* v. *Anderson*, at 312.
[42] 1964 Act, s. 2, the sequel to *Straker* v. *DPP* [1963] 1 Q.B. 926.
[43] *A.-G's Reference (No. 5 of 1980)* [1980] 3 All E.R. 816.

cation,[44] whether for sale within Britain or abroad.[45] The definition of 'publishing' includes distributing, circulating, selling, hiring and, for example, showing pictures or playing records; but it excludes television and sound broadcasting.[46] No person may be prosecuted for an offence at common law consisting of the publication of an article when the essence of the offence is that the matter is obscene.[47]

It is a defence to prove that publication of an obscene article is justified 'as being for the public good on the ground that it is in the interests of science, literature, art or learning or other objects of general concern'. Expert evidence on the literary, artistic, scientific or other merits of an article is admissible to establish or negative the defence of public good.[48]

The 1954 Act, section 3, confers search, seizure and forfeiture powers similar to those in the 1857 Act. A warrant may be obtained by a constable or the Director of Public Prosecutions[49] from a magistrate for the search of specified premises, stalls or vehicles, where there is reasonable suspicion that obscene articles are kept for publication for gain. When a search is made, articles believed to be obscene and also documents relating to a trade or business may be seized. The seized articles must be brought before a magistrate. When notice has been given to the occupier of the premises to show cause why the articles should not be forfeited, the magistrates' court may order forfeiture if satisfied that the articles are obscene and were kept for publication for gain. The owner, author or maker of the articles may also appear to defend them against forfeiture. The defence that publication is for the public good is available, and expert evidence relating to the merits of the articles may be called. In these proceedings there is no right to the decision of a jury but there are rights of appeal to the Crown Court or by case stated to the High Court.

Because of certain defects in the 1959 Act, the Act of 1964 was passed to strengthen the law against publishing obscene matter. *Inter alia*, the Act made it an offence to have an obscene article for publication for the purposes of gain,[50] and authorised a forfeiture order to be made following a conviction under the 1959 Act.

Obscenity law today[51]

The best-known outcome of the 1959 Act was the trial and acquittal of Penguin Books Ltd for publishing *Lady Chatterley's Lover* in 1960.[52] The verdict did not reveal whether the jurors considered the book not to be obscene, or considered the book to be obscene but its publication to be for the public good in the

---

44 1959 Act, s. 2(1) as amended in 1964.
45 *Gold Star Publications Ltd* v. *DPP* [1981] 2 All E.R. 257; and see (1983) 5 E.H.R.R. 591.
46 1959 Act, s. 1(3), as amended by Criminal Law Act 1977, s. 53.
47 1959 Act, s. 2(4). This does not prevent a prosecution for conspiracy to corrupt public morals: p. 520, *post*. In the case of cinema performances, such prosecution is excluded by 1959 Act, s. 2(4A), inserted by Criminal Law Act 1977, s.53.
48 1959 Act, s. 4.
49 Criminal Justice Act 1967, s. 25.
50 *Cf. Mella* v. *Monahan* [1961] Crim. L.R. 175.
51 See report of Williams committee on obscenity and film censorship, Cmnd 7772, 1979; and G. Robertson, *Obscenity*, chs. 3–6.
52 See C. H. Rolph, *The Trial of Lady Chatterley*.

interests of literature, art or learning. But the Act had clearly achieved one of its main objects. Since then many difficulties have arisen out of the legislation. The confusion and perplexities were discussed in *R. v. Metropolitan Police Commissioner, ex parte Blackburn*:[53] the Court of Appeal was satisfied that, despite the powers of the police, hard-core pornography was freely on sale in central London and that 'moderately obscene' publications were generally available. The court considered that the cause of the ineffectiveness of police efforts lay largely with the legal framework in which the police had to operate. In fact some of the difficulties are inherent in the legal problem of defining obscenity; others are attributable to features of the 1959 Act; and some were due to police corruption.

One difficulty is the 1959 Act's definition of obscenity as 'a tendency to deprave and corrupt'. The definition makes it impossible to rely on such synonyms as 'repulsive', 'filthy', 'loathsome' or 'lewd'[54] and requires the jury to consider whether the effect of a book is to tend to deprave and corrupt a significant proportion of those likely to read it. 'What is a significant proportion is entirely for the jury to decide'.[55] Lord Wilberforce has said, 'An article cannot be considered as obscene in itself: it can only be so in relation to its likely readers'.[56] Experienced police officers may for practical purposes not be susceptible of being depraved and corrupted[57] but it seems that a man may be corrupted more than once.[58] Although the circumstances in which articles are sold are relevant, it is no defence for booksellers to prove that most of their sales are made to middle-aged men who are already addicted to pornography; articles may 'deprave and corrupt' the mind without any overt sexual activity by the reader resulting.[59] Obscenity is not confined to sexual matters: a book dealing with the effects of drug taking may be obscene[60] and so may cards depicting scenes of violence when sold with chewing gum to children.[61]

Other difficulties have been caused by the defence of public good. Expert evidence relating to literary and other merits may not deal with the issue of whether the article is obscene,[62] except when the jury needs to be informed of the likely effect of an article upon children,[63] and is not admissible to establish that obscene articles may have a therapeutic effect on some individuals.[64] The jury must be directed to balance the number of readers who would tend to be corrupted by a book, and the nature of that corruption, against the literary or other merits of the book, and then decide whether on balance

---

53   [1973] Q.B. 241.
54   *R. v. Anderson* [1972] 1 Q.B. 304; *cf.* the perceptive analysis by Windeyer J. in *Crowe v. Grahame* (1968) 41 A.J.L.R.402, 409
55   *R. v. Calder & Boyars Ltd* [1969] 1 Q.B. 151, 168.
56   *DPP v. Whyte* [1972] A.C. 849, 860.
57   *R. v. Clayton and Halsey* [1963] 1 Q.B. 163.
58   *Shaw v. DPP* [1962] A.C. 220, 228 (C.C.A.).
59   *DPP v. Whyte* [1972] A.C. 849, 867.
60   *Calder (Publications) Ltd v. Powell* [1965] 1 Q.B. 509.
61   *DPP v. A. & B.C. Chewing Gum Ltd* [1968] 1 Q.B. 159.
62   *R. v. Anderson (ante).* And see *R. v. Stamford* [1972] 2 Q.B. 391.
63   Note 61 *ante.*
64   *DPP v. Jordan* [1977] A.C. 699; and see *A.-G. 's Reference (No. 3 of 1977)* [1978] 3 All E.R. 1166.

publication is for the public good.[65] The need for such a balancing act springs from the structure of the 1959 Act. As Geoffrey Robertson has said, 'Instead of one clause enabling a court to weigh all aspects of the publication in one decision, the two-tier approach set up an illogical and unworkable dichotomy between "obscenity" and "artistic merit".'[66]

Other legislation on indecency and pornography

Fewer legal difficulties arise in the exercise of other powers of censorship on moral grounds. Under the Customs Consolidation Act 1876, section 42, and the Customs and Excise Management Act 1979, section 49, customs officers may seize and destroy 'indecent or obscene' books and other articles being imported into the United Kingdom; and the Post Office Act 1953, section 11, seeks to prevent the postal service being used for the dispatch of 'indecent or obscene' articles.[67] These statutes do not provide a defence of publication for the public good and the test appears to be whether an article offends current standards of propriety.[68] The concept of indecency is no doubt as subjective as obscenity, but it implies a less serious judgment and in practice is easier to apply than obscenity. There is also the Vagrancy Act 1824, section 4, which makes it an offence to expose to view in any public place 'any obscene print, picture or other indecent exhibition'; and similar clauses are in many local Acts. The Children and Young Persons (Harmful Publications) Act 1955 seeks to prevent the circulation of 'horror comics'. These are books and magazines likely to fall into the hands of children and consisting wholly or mainly of stories told in pictures which portray the commission of crimes, acts of violence or cruelty, or incidents of a repulsive or horrible nature and do so in such a way that the work as a whole would tend to corrupt a child or young person. Under the Act it is a summary offence to print, publish or sell such publications. Prosecutions in England and Wales require the consent of the Attorney-General.

The Protection of Children Act 1978 tightened up the law with regard to indecent photographs (including films and video recordings) involving children under 16. Offences under the Act include the taking of indecent photographs of children, the distribution or showing of such photographs, and the advertisement of such photographs. Prosecutions require the consent of the Director of Public Prosecutions. The Indecent Displays (Control) Act 1981 deals with the public nuisance aspect of pornography. The Act makes it an offence to display publicly any indecent matter, where the display is visible from a public place. A public place is a place to which the public have access except either in payment for the display or within a shop where the public have passed a warning notice, provided in each case that entry is limited to persons over 18. The exceptions to the Act include television broadcasts by the BBC and the IBA, displays in art galleries or museums that are not visible from

---

[65] Note 55 *ante*.

[66] *Obscenity*, p. 163.

[67] See *Derrick* v. *Commissioners of Customs and Excise* [1972] 2 Q.B. 28; C. Manchester [1981] Crim. L.R. 531, [1983] Crim. L.R. 64.

[68] *R.* v. *Stamford ante.* On the conformity of this power of customs officers with Community law, see *R.* v. *Henn* [1981] A.C. 850.

outside the premises, and matter contained within the performance of plays and films. Since the Act contains no definition of indecency, 'indecent' will probably receive the same interpretation as in the customs and post office legislation.[69] In 1982 district councils were authorised to license sex shops and sex cinemas, by resolving to introduce a licensing scheme.[70] The grounds on which a council may refuse a licence include the reason that the existing number of such establishments in the area is equal to or exceeds the number which the council considers to be appropriate. Finally, the Video Recordings Act 1984, which is outlined in appendix B, established a new system of censorship.

Conspiracy to corrupt public morals

The specific objectives of these recent Acts prevent them from being a grave restriction upon the liberty of expression. The same cannot be said of the common law offence of conspiracy to corrupt public morals.

In *Shaw* v. *DPP*, the appellant had published the *Ladies' Directory*, an illustrated magazine containing names, addresses and other details of prostitutes and their services. The House of Lords upheld Shaw's conviction for the offence of conspiracy to corrupt public morals. Lord Simonds accepted that the law must be related to the changing standards of life, having regard to fundamental human values and the purposes of society; he said that 'there remains in the courts of law a residual power to enforce the supreme and fundamental purpose of the law, to conserve not only the safety and order but also the moral welfare of the State'.[71] It was the jury which provided a safeguard against the launching of prosecutions to suppress unpopular or unorthodox views. Lord Reid, dissenting, rejected the view that the court was guardian of public morals.

This controversial decision derived in part from the supposed offence of conspiracy to effect a public mischief, which was later held not to be part of criminal law.[72] Although Shaw was also convicted for having published an obscene book, contrary to the 1959 Act, *Shaw's* case enabled prosecutions to be brought at common law for conspiracy rather than for breaches of the 1959 Act. Thereafter the Law Officers assured the House of Commons that a conspiracy to corrupt public morals would not be charged so as to circumvent the 'public good' defence in the 1959 Act.[73]

In *Knuller Ltd* v. *DPP*, the House of Lords reaffirmed the decision in *Shaw's* case. The appellants had published a magazine which contained advertisements by male homosexuals seeking to meet other homosexuals. The Lords upheld a conviction of the appellants for conspiracy to corrupt public morals, rejecting a defence based on the Sexual Offences Act 1967 by which homosexual acts between adult males in private had ceased to be an offence. A second conviction for conspiracy 'to outrage public decency' was quashed on the ground of misdirection, but a majority of the House held that at common

---

69   See J. L. Lambert [1982] P.L. 226 and R.T.H. Stone (1982) 45 M.L.R. 62.
70   Local Government (Miscellaneous Provisions) Act 1982, s.2 and sch. 3.
71   [1962] A.C. 220, 268. See D. Seaborne Davies (1962) 6 J.S.P.T.L 104, J. E. Hall Williams (1961) 24 M.L.R. 626, and Robertson, *op. cit.*, ch 8.
72   *DPP* v. *Withers* [1975] A.C. 842.
73   H.C. Deb., 3 Jun. 1964, col. 1212.

law it was an offence to outrage public decency and also to conspire to outrage public decency; and that such a conspiracy could take the form of an agreement to insert outrageously indecent matter on the inside pages of a magazine sold in public. Lords Reid and Diplock did not agree that 'outraging public decency' was an offence; Lord Reid said, 'To recognise this new crime would go contrary to the whole trend of public policy followed by Parliament in recent times'.[74]

The common law of conspiracy was reformed by the Criminal Law Act 1977, which created a new statutory offence of conspiracy. But the abolition of common law conspiracy is not to affect conspiracy that involves an agreement to engage in conduct which tends to corrupt public morals or outrages public decency.[75] However, few prosecutions for conspiracy to corrupt public morals or to outrage public decency have been brought since *Knuller's* case.[76]

The law of obscenity and indecency was reviewed by a Home Office committee (chairman, Professor Bernard Williams) which reported in 1979.[77] The committee analysed the purposes for which legal regulation of obscenity was justified. It considered that the existing law in this area should be scrapped and a fresh start made with a comprehensive new statute. In particular, terms such as 'obscene', 'indecency', 'deprave and corrupt' should be abandoned as having outlived their usefulness. The government did not accept these recommendations. Since 1979, as we have seen, Parliament has legislated in a piecemeal manner that in important respects runs contrary to the Williams report.[78]

C. Law and the media[1]

External restraints imposed by the courts are only one form of control over the exercise of the liberty of expression. Editors exercise much greater power over what is transmitted to the public than do judge and jury, who merely exercise an intermittent veto. But who then appoints and controls the editors? In a mixed economy, the media are controlled by a mixture of public and private powers. Where there is public intervention, one danger is that the government of the day may seek to influence the medium in question. Yet most of us do not wish broadcasting to be left solely in the hands of private business. This section deals only with some aspects of the present law. The law relating to advertising is not mentioned, except briefly in relation to broadcasting; nor is state patronage of the arts.

Theatres

For many years dramatic and operatic performances in Great Britain were subject to the prior censorship of the Lord Chamberlain, an officer of the royal

---

74 *Knuller Ltd* v. *DPP* [1973] A.C. 435, 459.
75 Criminal Law Act 1977, s. 5(3); *cf.* s. 53(3).
76 Robertson, *op.cit.*, pp. 219, 223.
77 Cmnd 7772, 1979.
78 And see app. B.

1 Street, *Freedom, the Individual and the Law*, chs. 3 and 4; O'Higgins, *Censorship in Britain*, ch. 4; G. Robertson, *Obscenity*, ch. 9.

household. The Theatres Act 1968 abolished the requirement that plays should receive a licence before being performed.[2] Theatres are now licensed by local authorities but only in regard to such matters as public health and safety. In place of censorship, rules against obscenity similar to those in the Obscene Publications Act 1959 are applied to the performance of plays, subject to a defence of public good. Other criminal restraints placed upon theatrical performances are in respect of incitement of racial hatred (section 5) and the use of threatening, abusive or insulting words or behaviour intended or likely to occasion a breach of the peace (section 6). Prosecutions for these various offences, including obscenity, require the consent of the Attorney-General in England and Wales. There may be no prosecution at common law for any offence the essence of which is that a performance of a play is 'obscene, indecent, offensive, disgusting or injurious to morality' nor may there be prosecutions under various statutes relating to indecency (section 2(4)), an important safeguard against moral censorship. However, in 1982 a private prosecution of the director of the National Theatre's production of *The Romans in Britain* was withdrawn after the judge had decided that the Sexual Offences Act 1956, section 13 (relating to gross indecency between males) could apply to simulated homosexual acts on stage.[3]

Cinemas[4]

Censorship of films originated unintentionally with the Cinematograph Act 1909, which authorised local authorities to license cinemas in the interests of public safety, mainly against fire. In fact, with the approval of the courts,[5] local authorities extended the scope of licensing to other matters including power to approve the films shown in licensed cinemas. In the Cinematograph Act 1952, Parliament confirmed the power of licensing the films shown and required licensing authorities to impose conditions restricting children from seeing unsuitable films. Licensing authorities are now the district councils and the Greater London Council: they may delegate their powers to a committee or to the local magistrates. The main work of censorship of films is undertaken by the British Board of Film Censors, a non-statutory body set up in 1912 with the approval of central and local government, by the film industry. The board is responsible for the classification of films with special reference to the admission of young children and others under 18. Although a licensing authority normally allows the showing of films which have been classified by the board, the authority may not transfer its functions to the board and must retain power to review decisions of the board.[6] Thus it may refuse a local showing to a film classified by the board; it may vary the board's classification; or it may grant permission to a film refused a certificate by the board. Powers of local censorship are not popular with the film industry, and were not supported by the Williams committee in 1979, but a case can be made for maintaining some local option on issues of public morality.

---

2   For the background, see H.C. 503 (1966–7)
3   *The Times*, 19 Mar. 1982.
4   N. M. Hunnings, *Film Censors and the Law*; Williams report on obscenity and film censorship, Cmnd 7772, 1979.
5   *E.g. LCC* v. *Bermondsey Bioscope Ltd* [1911] 1 K.B. 445.
6   *Ellis* v. *Dubowski* [1921] 3 K.B. 621; *Mills* v. *LCC* [1925] 1 K.B. 213.

The relationship between the system of film censorship and the law of obscenity and public indecency has caused many difficulties. Before 1977, the Obscene Publications Act 1959 did not apply to the public showing of films,[7] but the Cinematograph Acts did not protect licensed films against prosecution at common law.[8] In 1976 the Court of Appeal held the licensing policy followed by the Greater London Council to be unlawful since it applied only a test of obscenity (that is, whether a film would tend to deprave and corrupt those likely to see it) and excluded from consideration issues of public decency.[9] By the Criminal Law Act 1977, section 53, the public showing of films was brought within the Obscene Publications Act, subject to a defence that showing a film is for the public good in the interests of drama, opera, ballet or any other art, or of literature or learning. The consent of the Director of Public Prosecutions is required for prosecution and forfeiture of films of not less than 16 millimetres in width. Under the 1977 Act, the common law of obscenity, indecency, and conspiracy to corrupt public morals does not now apply to cinematographic exhibitions. In 1982, the Cinematograph Acts were extended to profit-making clubs that had previously been exempted from licensing; but certain members' societies are still exempt from those Acts.[10] Importers of films remain subject to the power of customs officers to exclude foreign films that are considered to be indecent or obscene.

The press
The historic freedom of the press means that, subject to the civil and criminal restraints upon publication which have already been considered, any person or company may publish a newspaper or magazine without getting official approval in advance. For economic reasons, this liberty is unlikely to be exercised effectively except by a very few newspaper publishers. Fears of a movement towards monopoly conditions in sectors of the press led, after an inquiry by a royal commission[11] to the enactment in what is now the Fair Trading Act 1973, sections 57–62, of provisions to ensure that newspaper mergers above a certain scale do not take place in a manner contrary to the public interest.[12] In 1975 and 1976, the freedom of the press was considered by some to be endangered by the Labour government's Bill to give further protection to the closed shop in industry; a determined action was fought, mainly in the House of Lords, to protect the press against potential abuse of their position by trade unions. In the result, the Trade Union and Labour Relations (Amendment) Act 1976, section 2, provided for a charter on press freedom to be drawn up by newspaper proprietors, editors and trade unions representing journalists. The Act authorised the Secretary of State to prepare and issue such a charter, if the newspaper industry failed to do so within 12 months. The industry failed to draw up such a charter within the time, and the Secretary of State for Employment embarked on the task.[13] But

---

[7] Section 1 (3) and *A.-G.'s Reference (No. 2 of 1975)* [1976] 2 All E.R. 753.
[8] G. Zellick [1971] Crim. L.R. 126; and H.C. 176 (1975–6), pp. 84–103.
[9] *R. v. Greater London Council, ex p. Blackburn* [1976] 3 All E.R. 184.
[10] Cinematograph (Amendment) Act 1982.
[11] Cmnd 1811, 1962.
[12] For the report on *The Observer* transfer see H.C. 378 (1980–1).
[13] See Cmnd 6810, 1977, ch. 17; and H.C. Deb., 18 May 1978, col. 810.

the statutory provisions for a press charter were repealed when the law on the closed shop was amended by Conservative legislation.[14]

Freedom of expression, no less than trade union power, is capable of being abused. Sensational reporting, intrusive investigations and careless editing may cause unjustified distress to private individuals. The Press Council was established in 1953 by the newspaper industry: it was reconstituted in 1963, and again in 1973 and 1978. In addition to the chairman, who is always an eminent lawyer, the council now has 36 members, half nominated by sections of the press, and half appointed from outside the industry. The council seeks to preserve the freedom of the British press, to maintain the highest professional and commercial standards and to consider complaints about the conduct of the press. Before the Press Council will accept a complaint, the individual must first have tried to obtain redress from the editor of the newspaper. No complaint will be accepted for consideration if the complainant is also bringing legal proceedings against the newspaper, for example, for defamation. The council has no power to impose sanctions: should it uphold a complaint, the newspaper is expected to publish a statement of the complaint and the council's ruling. The published decisions of the council have built up an extensive system of precedent,[15] and in 1977 a royal commission on the press recommended that a code of press conduct should be prepared. Declarations of principle had been issued on cheque-book journalism and on privacy but, in the commission's view, the council needed to be more vigilant in protecting the public 'against the danger of partisan opinion exacerbated by factual inaccuracy'.[16]

Broadcasting

In the case of broadcasting, technical reasons have so far prevented access to the medium being open to all comers as in the case of the press. Even if all broadcasting were to be provided by privately owned companies, it would still be necessary for a regulatory agency to allocate channels and wave-lengths to them. Until 1954, the British Broadcasting Corporation enjoyed a public monopoly of all broadcasting in the United Kingdom, and it still provides the major share of broadcasting services. The BBC is a corporation set up by royal charter, and its chairman and governors are appointed by the Crown on the advice of the Prime Minister. It transmits broadcasts throughout the United Kingdom under licence from the government issued under the Wireless Telegraphy Acts.[17] Although the BBC is mainly financed by a grant from the Exchequer, equivalent to the net revenue of television licence fees, the structure of the BBC seeks to maintain its independence of the government of the day. Certain duties are imposed on the BBC: it must broadcast a daily account of the proceedings in Parliament and any minister of the Crown may require announcements to be broadcast. The minister responsible for broadcasting (now the Home Secretary) may require the BBC not to broadcast certain

---

[14]   Employment Act 1980, s. 19.
[15]   For which see H. P. Levy, *The Press Council*.
[16]   Cmnd 6810, 1977, ch. 20; and *cf.* G. Robertson, *The People against the Press*.
[17]   For the charter, see Cmnd 8313, 1981 and for the licence and agreement, Cmnd 8233, 1981. And see *BBC* v. *Johns*, p. 303 ante.

matters. The BBC may not broadcast its own opinions about current affairs or matters of public policy, and may not broadcast party political programmes except those broadcast by agreement with the major parties.[18] Ministers may broadcast statements explaining legislation or policies on which there is general consensus, but on national issues involving political controversy, the opposition in Parliament has a right of reply.[19] In emergency the government may take over the BBC's broadcasting facilities. Apart from these specific powers, the government may not control the BBC's programmes, yet it is responsible for the structure of broadcasting as well as for financing the BBC. The Annan committee on the future of broadcasting sought in 1977 to reconcile the independence of the broadcasters with the government's ultimate responsibility, arguing that the solution was to be found in the accountability of government and broadcasting authorities to Parliament.[20] In fact the BBC is bound to take account of current opinion and to seek mass audiences for many of its television broadcasts. One danger is that minority groups with unpopular views may find it difficult to get opportunity to express them. Another is the great pressure that the government may bring to bear on the BBC, particularly at a time of emergency such as the Falklands campaign.[21]

Television and local radio services financed by advertising are now governed by the Broadcasting Act 1981. The Independent Broadcasting Authority is a public corporation, whose members are appointed by the Home Secretary, to provide television and local radio services additional to the BBC's, 'as a public service for disseminating information, education and entertainment' (section 2). The actual programmes are provided by contractors, in the choice and control of whom very extensive discretion is exercised by the IBA.[22] The high standards to which the service must attain are stated in the 1981 Act in general terms. By section 4, the IBA must satisfy itself *inter alia* that, so far as possible, (a) 'nothing is included in the programmes which offends against good taste or decency or is likely to encourage or incite to crime or to lead to disorder or be offensive to public feeling'; (b) all news is presented with due accuracy and impartiality; and (c) due impartiality is preserved in respect of matters of political or industrial controversy or relating to current public policy. The opinions of the IBA and the programme contractors may not be broadcast. The 1981 Act contains strict rules on advertising: thus no advertisements may be directed to religious or political ends or relate to any industrial dispute.[23] The IBA may be required by a minister of the Crown to broadcast particular items if it appears to the minister 'to be necessary or expedient to do so in connection with his functions' but the IBA may announce the ministerial origin of the item; the IBA may be required by a minister not to broadcast certain items (section 29). Use of these powers by the government is and should be a matter for public knowledge and criticism.

---

[18] Page 158 *ante*.
[19] BBC, *Annual Report and Handbook* 1984, p. 178.
[20] Cmnd 6753, 1977, p. 10 and ch. 5.
[21] On the handling of press and public information during the Falklands conflict, see H.C. 17 (1982–3) and Cmnd 8820, 1983. On the protection of military information in general, see Cmnd 9112, 1983.
[22] See N. Lewis [1975] P.L. 317; and H.C. 465 (1971–2).
[23] 1981 Act, sch. 2, para. 8; and see s. 9 (code of advertising standards).

The IBA may be under a duty to satisfy itself that programmes comply with the statutory standards, but is this duty legally enforceable?

In *Attorney-General, ex rel. McWhirter* v. *IBA*, McWhirter, a member of the public, sought an injunction against the IBA to stop a film being shown about Andy Warhol which according to press reports contained matter offending against good taste and decency. An interim injunction was granted by the Court of Appeal at a time when members of the IBA had not seen the film. Some days later, the injunction was lifted since the court was then satisfied that the IBA had performed its statutory duty and there were no grounds on which the court should interfere with the IBA's decision. Lawton L. J. said, 'In the realm of good taste and decency, whose frontiers are ill-defined, I find it impossible to say that the (IBA) have crossed from the permissible into the unlawful.'[24] Although the interim injunction had been sought by McWhirter in his own name, the court ruled that such proceedings required the consent of the Attorney-General, since the individual had no *locus standi* to apply for the injunction himself.[25]

While the case lays down the admirable principle that the IBA like everyone else is required to observe the law, and that the IBA's decisions are subject to judicial review, the court did not show a desire to assume the role of censor, nor indeed would such a role be appropriate.[26]

Neither the BBC nor the IBA are subject to the jurisdiction of the Press Council. After the two bodies had separately devised procedures for handling complaints from the public, a statutory Broadcasting Complaints Commission was created in 1980.[27] Appointed by the Home Secretary, the commission adjudicates upon complaints of unjust or unfair treatment in sound or television broadcasts, and of 'unwarranted infringement of privacy' in the obtaining of material for broadcast programmes. An individual's complaint need not be considered by the commission if he has a remedy in a court of law and it is not appropriate in the circumstances for the commission to consider it. Complaints may not be considered by the commission when the matter complained of is the subject of court proceedings.[28] The commission sits in private to hear the persons directly concerned. It may direct the broadcasting authority to publish a summary of the complaint together with the commission's findings.[29]

Current developments in technology, such as direct broadcasting by satellite and cable systems, will have profound effects on the established broadcasting and telecommunications authorities. Increasing diversity in the systems of communication and a greater reliance on private financing are making necessary new forms of regulation.[30]

---

[24] [1973] Q.B. 629, 659.
[25] Page 661 *post*. For the position in Scots law, see *Wilson* v. *IBA* 1979 S.C. 351, p. 159 *ante*, p. 674 *post*. And see *R.* v. *IBA, ex p. Whitehouse, The Times*, 14 Apr. 1984.
[26] For the legal and other constraints upon broadcasting, see C.R. Munro, *Television, Censorship and the Law*.
[27] Now see Broadcasting Act 1981, part III and sch. 7.
[28] *R.* v. *Broadcasting Complaints Cmssn, ex p. Thames Television Ltd, The Times*, 8 Oct. 1982.
[29] And see *e.g.* H.C. 33 (1983–4).
[30] See Cmnd 8679, 1982; Cmnd 8866, 1983; Telecommunications Act 1984; Cables and Broadcasting Act 1984.

Chapter 28

Meetings, protest and public order

On a Saturday afternoon in June 1974, public order broke down in central London. The occasion was a march to Red Lion Square by the National Front which was bitterly opposed by left-wing organisations. The march and the counter-march were kept apart by the police but clashes between police and left-wing protesters took place during which one student died and policemen and members of the public were injured. The Home Secretary appointed Lord Scarman to conduct an inquiry into these events. In his report, the judge discussed the principles which in his view underlie such events.

Amongst our fundamental human rights there are, without doubt, the rights of peaceful assembly and public protest and the right to public order and tranquillity. Civilised living collapses ... if public protest becomes violent protest or public order degenerates into the quietism imposed by successful oppression. But the problem is more complex than a choice between two extremes – one, a right to protest whenever and wherever you will and the other, right to continuous calm upon our streets unruffled by the noise and obstructive pressure of the protesting procession. A balance has to be struck, a compromise found that will accommodate the exercise of the right to protest within a framework of public order which enables ordinary citizens, who are not protesting, to go about their business and pleasure without obstruction or inconvenience. The fact that those who at any one time are concerned to secure the tranquillity of the streets are likely to be the majority must not lead us to deny the protesters their opportunity to march: the fact that the protesters are desperately sincere and are exercising a fundamental human right must not lead us to overlook the rights of the majority.
... Indiscipline among demonstrators, heavy-handed police reaction to disorder are equally mischievous: for each can upset the balance. Violent demonstrators by creating public disorder infringe a fundamental human right which belongs to the rest of us: excessively violent police reaction to public disorder infringes the rights of the protesters. The one and the other are an affront to civilised living.[1]

Not all would agree with every aspect of this analysis. Some would, for example, argue that a march by the National Front in the streets of London is itself an affront to civilised living and would seek to change the laws which

---

[1] Report on Red Lion Square Disorders of 15 Jun. 1974, Cmnd 5919, 1975, pp. 1–2.

permit such a march to take place. Others might argue that there should be less emphasis on the tranquillity of the streets and that we should express more concern about the evils and inequalities in society. But in this field as in others, liberty in society is a matter of constant compromise and adjustment between competing interests.

Since 1974, the tranquillity of streets in some urban areas in Britain has been disturbed more than once. While the vast majority of processions and demonstrations continued to be orderly, 'a style of aggressive street politics emerged which caused growing concern'.[2] In 1977–80 disorder occurred in Lewisham, Birmingham, Leicester, Southall and Bristol. In April 1981 the Brixton riots took place, followed in July by rioting in Southall, Liverpool (Toxteth), Manchester (Moss Side) and the West Midlands. Industrial disputes led to severe clashes between police and mass pickets in July 1977 in north London (the Grunwick dispute)[3] and in November 1983 in Lancashire (the *Warrington Messenger* dispute). Serious political and social concerns underlay all these events, and they also made prominent the law by which public order is maintained.[4]

This chapter examines the principal features of that law.[5] If there were for the United Kingdom a written constitution which guaranteed fundamental rights, it is likely that it would include protection for the freedom of association, although this protection would probably be subject to extensive qualifications.[6] In deciding cases involving meetings and demonstrations, the courts would no doubt interpret and apply the relevant provisions of the constitution. In the absence of such a basis for their decisions, the courts in Britain sometimes ignore the constitutional dimension in the cases coming before them.[7] According to Dicey, 'the right of assembling is nothing more than a result of the view taken by the courts as to individual liberty of person and individual liberty of speech'.[8] This approach does not recognise a guaranteed right of collective protest, but it does ensure that criminal or civil restrictions on the freedom of people to meet together must be shown to derive from the existing law. It may be debated whether this approach provides a firm enough foundation for such freedom, at a time when that freedom is under heavy pressure from competing interests.

Freedom of association

In principle the law imposes no restrictions upon the freedom of individuals to associate together for political purposes. One exception is provided by those branches of the public service (for example, the civil service and the police)

---

[2] Report of Home Affairs Committee, *The Law Relating to Public Order*, H.C. 756–I (1979–80), p. vii.

[3] See J. Rogaly, *Grunwick*; and Cmnd 6922, 1977.

[4] See Cmnd 7891, 1980; H.C. 756–I (1979–80); Law Commission, *Offences Relating to Public Order*, H.C. 85 (1983–4).

[5] See M. Supperstone, *Brownlie's Law of Public Order and National Security*; Bailey, Harris and Jones, *Civil Liberties: Cases and Materials*, ch. 3; T. A. Critchley, *The Conquest of Violence*; H. Street, *Freedom, the Individual and the Law*; D. G. T. Williams, *Keeping the Peace*; Wilson, *Cases*, ch. 14.

[6] See *e.g.* art. 11, European Convention on Human Rights.

[7] Notably in *Duncan* v. *Jones* [1936] 1 K.B. 218. *Cf. Papworth* v. *Coventry* [1967] 2 All E.R. 41.

[8] Dicey, p. 271.

where the terms of employment exclude political activities.[9] Moreover organisations which are registered as charities under the Charities Act 1960, and thereby enjoy valuable tax advantages, run into danger of losing that status if they embark upon political activities. But in general, individuals are free to form themselves into political parties, action groups, campaign committees and so on without any official approval or registration. In the interests of public order, however, paramilitary organisations are banned. At a time when a serious threat to public order was posed by the activities of fascists and communists, the Public Order Act 1936, section 2, made it an offence (a) to organise or train the members or supporters of any association for the purpose of enabling them to be used in usurping the functions of the police or the armed forces, or (b) to organise and train (or equip) them, either for enabling them to be employed for the use or display of physical force in promoting any political object, 'or in such manner as to arouse reasonable apprehension that they are organised and either trained or equipped for that purpose'. In 1963, the leaders of a movement known as Spearhead, whose members wore uniforms and exchanged Nazi salutes, were convicted under this section, even though there was no evidence of specific training for attacks on opponents.[10] The organisers of a volunteer force intended to be available for maintaining order in emergencies would run some risk of contravening this section, even if their avowed aim was to lend support when needed to the police or armed forces.[11] In 1974, several organisations of this kind started by former army officers were severely criticised on such grounds.

In Northern Ireland the authorities have had for many years power to ban organisations with unlawful or seditious objectives[12] but in Great Britain only since 1974 has the IRA been a proscribed organisation.[13]

Another restriction on the freedom of association is that under the Public Order Act 1936, section 1, it is an offence for any person in a public place or at a public meeting to wear uniform signifying his association with a political organisation or with the promotion of any political object. On ceremonial or other special occasions, however, a chief constable may, with the consent of the Secretary of State, permit the wearing of such a uniform if it is not likely to involve risk of public disorder. The word uniform is not defined in the Act but the coloured shirts worn by political groups in the 1930s were undoubtedly uniforms for this purpose. The wearing of black berets by a group marching in London under the banner of the Provisional Sinn Fein constituted an offence, since the berets were worn to indicate association with a political body.[14]

Freedom of meeting

This freedom arises essentially from the fact that no permission is needed from any public authority or official before a meeting of individuals is held to discuss

---

9   Chs. 15 and 20. And see p. 159 *ante*.
10   *R.* v. *Jordan and Tyndall* [1963] Crim. L.R. 124; D. G. T. Williams [1970] C.L.J. 96, 102–4.
11   *Cf.* Supperstone, *op. cit.*, p. 185.
12   See *McEldowney* v. *Forde* [1971] A.C. 632; Wilson, *Cases*, p. 395; and Northern Ireland (Emergency Provisions) Act 1978, s. 21 and sch. 2.
13   Ch. 29 C.
14   *O'Moran* v. *DPP* [1975] Q.B. 864.

a matter of common concern. Nor do public authorities have power to ban in advance the holding of meetings.[15] Such meetings may be in private and restricted to invited individuals or be open to the public or a section of the public (for example, all students) and advertised publicly. The major practical restriction on the organisation of meetings is the necessity to find premises for them. The organisers of an unpopular cause may find it difficult to hire suitable halls, whether these are owned by private individuals or by public authorities such as the local council. Subject only to the constraints of anti-discrimination legislation,[16] it would appear that local councils may exercise an absolute discretion in deciding to whom to let their halls. Under the Representation of the People Act 1983, sections 95 and 96, however, candidates at local and parliamentary elections are entitled to the use of schools and other public rooms for the purpose of holding election meetings. It may be argued that local authorities should be under a general duty to make their halls available to all groups, whether popular or unpopular, without discriminating between them on political or other grounds.[17] In 1981, the Home Affairs Committee of the House of Commons recommended that the right of candidates to use school rooms and other halls for election meetings should be subject to a power to require a meeting to be held elsewhere, when serious public disorder or serious disruption to the normal life of the community was reasonably apprehended as a result of a proposed meeting.[18]

The so-called right of public meeting is often applied to meetings held in the open air in places to which members of the public have free access. Here also it is usually necessary to get the prior consent of the owners of the land. Many local authorities have made byelaws governing the use of parks, beaches etc. for various purposes, including public meetings; breach of these byelaws is a criminal offence, unless the court is prepared to hold the byelaw to be *ultra vires*,[19] and a civil remedy may also be available to restrain persistent breach of the law.[20] In the case of Trafalgar Square in London, statutory regulations have been made under which application for the holding of public rallies must be made to the Department of the Environment; while permission is a matter of discretion, the Secretary of State for the Environment is responsible to Parliament for the decisions taken.[21] Similarly in the case of Hyde Park, no meetings may be held as of right[22] although Speakers' Corner is available for any who care to speak there.

Although the law does not confer on the organiser of a meeting a right to hold it in any particular place, it does give protection against certain forms of interruption. By the Public Meeting Act 1908, passed at a time of suffragette

15 *M'Ara* v. *Edinburgh Magistrates* 1913 S.C. 1059. And see E. R. H. Ivamy [1949] C.L.P. 183.
16 Ch. 31 A.
17 Street, *Freedom, the Individual and the Law*, p. 56. And see *Verrall* v. *Great Yarmouth BC* [1981] Q.B. 202.
18 H.C. 756–1 (1979–80), p. xxvi.
19 *De Morgan* v. *Metropolitan Board of Works* (1880) 5 Q.B.D. 155; *Aldred* v. *Miller* 1925 J.C. 21.
20 *Cf. Llandudno UDC* v. *Woods* [1899] 2 Ch. 705.
21 S.I. 1952 No. 776; Supperstone, *op. cit.*, p. 348; Bailey, Harris and Jones, p. 142. And see *Ex p. Lewis* (1888) 21 Q.B.D. 191.
22 *Bailey* v. *Williamson* (1873) 8 Q.B.D. 118; Royal and other Parks and Gardens Regulations, S.I. 1977 No. 217.

activity, it is a summary offence at a lawful public meeting to act in a disorderly manner for the purpose of preventing the transaction of the business for which the meeting was called. Moreover the chairman of the meeting may request a constable who reasonably suspects any person of committing the summary offence to require the latter's name and address and in default to arrest him.[23] Similar provisions apply to election meetings.[24] In practice these powers are not very effective in dealing with organised interruptions to meetings. Whether heckling would be a breach of the Act would depend on the nature of the meeting and on the intensity of the heckling.

Meetings on the highway

At common law, the highway is land dedicated to the public use for the primary purpose of passing and re-passing. There are many legitimate uses of the highway incidental to this primary purpose (for example, conversation with friends, unloading goods or passengers from vehicles, the distribution of leaflets to passers-by, reasonable rest by the roadside during a journey[25]) many of which are today subject to statutory restriction. But these secondary uses do not appear to include the use of the highway for holding a public meeting[26] just as they do not include the right to sell hot dogs from a van.[27] The attitude of the courts has been that no person may claim to be exercising the right of passage by standing still on the highway and making a speech which attracts a crowd. Use of the highway for an improper purpose may constitute a trespass against the owners of adjoining property, in whom at common law the soil of the highway is vested,[28] or against the highway authority in whom the surface of the highway is vested. Obstruction of the public right of passage is also a public nuisance, which may be prosecuted as an indictable offence at common law[29] or give rise to a civil action for an injunction brought in the public interest by the Attorney-General. If the obstruction interferes with the private rights of an adjoining occupier or causes special injury to him, it may give rise to a private action in nuisance. In practice civil proceedings are not often used to restrain the holding of public meetings or other protests upon the highway.[30] For there to be criminal liability for a public nuisance, the use of the highway in question, if *prima facie* lawful, must have been unreasonable in the circumstances.[31]

Under the Highways Act 1980, section 137, it is an offence 'if a person without lawful authority or excuse in any way wilfully obstruct the free passage

---

[23] Added to the 1908 Act by the Public Order Act 1936, s.6. Under the 1908 Act, a meeting on the highway may be a 'lawful public meeting': *Burden* v. *Rigler* [1911] 1 K.B. 337. But see now Police and Criminal Evidence Act 1984, ss. 25, 26(1) and sch. 7, pt. I.

[24] Representation of the People Act 1983, s. 97 (amended by 1984 Act cited in n. 23 *ante*).

[25] *Rodgers* v. *Ministry of Transport* [1952] 1 All E.R. 634; and see Supperstone, *op. cit.*, pp. 42–50.

[26] Ex p. Lewis (1888) 21 Q.B.D. 191, 197; *M'Ara* v. *Edinburgh Magistrates* 1913 S.C. 1059, 1073; A. L. Goodhart (1937) 6 C.L.J. 161.

[27] *Nagy* v. *Weston* [1965] 1 All E.R. 78.

[28] *Harrison* v. *Duke of Rutland* [1893] 1 Q.B. 142; *Hickman* v. *Maisey* [1900] 1 Q.B. 752.

[29] *E.g. R.* v. *Clark (No. 2)* [1964] 2 Q.B. 315; Wilson, *Cases*, p. 706; and see Smith and Hogan, *Criminal Law*, pp. 746–50.

[30] But see *Hubbard* v. *Pitt* [1976] Q.B. 142, *post*.

[31] *R.* v. *Clark (No. 2) (ante)*.

along a highway'.An obstruction in this sense is caused when a meeting is held on the highway. It is no defence that the obstruction affected only part of the highway leaving the other part clear.[32] Nor that a defendant believed that she was entitled to hold meetings at the place in question or that other meetings had been held there.[33]

Neither the highway authority nor the police have power to authorise meetings on the highway. In practice, meetings are sometimes held in the street with the tacit approval of the police, if no serious obstruction is caused and if they are not likely to lead to a breach of the peace. A person who attempts to address a meeting on the highway, and refuses to move on when requested to do so by the police, may be guilty of obstructing a police officer in the execution of his duty.[34] Those who sit down on the highway as an act of protest are obstructing the highway and may also be guilty of obstructing the police.

Picketing

The right of peaceful picketing is important both in the law of industrial disputes and in the law of public order. As now provided by statute,

It shall be lawful for a person in contemplation or furtherance of a trade dispute[35] to attend
(a) at or near his own place of work; or
(b) if he is an official of a trade union, at or near the place of work of a member of that union whom he is accompanying and whom he represents
for the purpose only of peacefully obtaining or communicating information or peacefully persuading any person to work or abstain from working.[36]

This provision, like its predecesssors, gives certain immunities in the law of conspiracy and nuisance to picketing which relates to an industrial dispute. It also means that the mere presence of the pickets on a highway may not be treated as an obstruction. But if the police think it reasonably necessary to prevent a breach of the peace, they may decide how many pickets should be allowed at the entrance to a factory[37] and, if they consider it necessary in the interests of preventing disorder, may even form a cordon to keep the pickets away from vehicles coming to or leaving the premises.[38] The purpose of picketing is to enable the pickets peacefully to impart information or opinions to those entering or leaving the premises, but the pickets are not entitled physically to obstruct the highway. When the organiser of a picket had directed 40 pickets to walk in a circle in the highway near a factory entrance, this was held to be an obstruction of the highway and not protected by

---

32   *Homer* v. *Cadman* (1886) 16 Cox C.C. 51.
33   *Arrowsmith* v. *Jenkins* [1963] 2 Q.B. 561; Wilson, *Cases*, p. 705. *Cf. Cambridgeshire CC* v. *Rust* [1972] 2 Q.B. 426.
34   *Duncan* v. *Jones*, p. 543, *post.*
35   For the meaning of the last eight words, reference may be made to works on labour law, and see *e.g. Duport Steels Ltd* v. *Sirs* [1980] 1 All E.R. 529.
36   Trade Union and Labour Relations Act 1974, s. 15, as amended by Employment Act 1980, s. 16; and see Code of Practice on Picketing issued under Employment Act 1980, s. 3; H.C. Deb., 13 Nov. 1980, col. 647.
37   *Piddington* v. *Bates* [1960] 3 All E.R. 660.
38   *Kavanagh* v. *Hiscock* [1974] Q.B. 600.

statute.[39] In *Broome* v. *DPP*, the House of Lords held that the Industrial Relations Act 1971, section 134, did not entitle a picket to stop a vehicle for the purpose of talking to the driver. Such an interpretation, said Lord Salmon, would involve reading into the Act words which would seriously diminish the liberty of the subject.

Everyone has the right to use the highway free from the risk of being compulsorily stopped by any private citizen and compelled to listen to what he does not want to hear.[40]

The courts therefore have interpreted the protection for peaceful picketing as granting an immunity against certain liabilities, not as conferring a positive right. While the trade union movement wishes to see greater protection given to peaceful picketing, for example, by allowing picketing to stop vehicles for a brief period to talk to the driver, no such extension of peaceful picketing could accommodate mass picketing by strikers whose object is to make it impossible by force of numbers for goods or materials to be moved on the highway. Such mass picketing is unlawful as an obstruction of the highway, if for no other reason.[41] The Employment Act 1980 restricted lawful picketing to the place of work, confined it to the workers and union officials directly involved by a dispute, and thus excluded secondary picketing.[42]

So far picketing has been considered solely in relation to industrial disputes. Is picketing lawful for other purposes?

In *Hubbard* v. *Pitt*, a community action group organised a peaceful picket outside the offices of estate-agents in Islington, distributing leaflets and displaying placards to protest against the firm's part in improving property at the expense of working-class residents. On the issue of whether an interim injunction should be issued to the firm against the picket, Forbes J. held that the picketing was unlawful since it was not in contemplation or furtherance of a trade dispute and was inconsistent with the public right to use the highway for passage and repassage. But in the Court of Appeal, the majority upheld the interim injunction on quite different grounds, holding only that the plaintiffs had a real prospect of establishing at the eventual trial that the protesters were committing a private nuisance against them and that the balance of convenience lay in favour of the picketing being stopped until the main action was heard. Lord Denning M. R. dissented, holding that the use of the highway for the picket was not unreasonable and did not constitute a nuisance at common law; he considered that picketing other than for trade disputes was lawful so long as it was done merely to obtain or communicate information or for peaceful persuasion.[43]

While the law remains uncertain, in practice peaceful picketing of embassies and other public buildings in London often occurs and is not stopped by the police. In *Papworth* v. *Coventry*, however, a vigil of seven persons in Whitehall to draw attention to the situation in Vietnam was stopped by the police on the ground that it infringed directions issued by the Commissioner of Metro-

---

[39] *Tynan* v. *Balmer* [1967] 1 Q.B. 91.
[40] [1974] A.C. 587, 603. And see *British Airports Authority* v. *Ashton* [1983] 3 All E.R. 6.
[41] See Conspiracy and Protection of Property Act 1875, s. 7.
[42] See B. Bercusson (1980) 9 I.L.J. 215, 220–32.
[43] [1976] Q.B. 142.

politan Police under the Metropolitan Police Act 1839, which sought to keep the streets leading to the Houses of Parliament free of obstruction: the court held that the vigil was in breach of the directions only if its effect was to give rise to obstruction of the streets leading to Parliament or to disorder of the kind likely to lead to a breach of the peace.[44] In relation to picketing, as with other forms of protest, much in practice turns on the attitude of the police. As Wills J. put it in the 19th century, 'Things are done every day in every part of the kingdom, without let or hindrance, which there is not and cannot be a legal right to do, and not infrequently are submitted to with a good grace because they are in their nature incapable, by whatever amount of user, of growing into a right'.[45] The existence of wide police discretion has both advantages and disadvantages, since policies for dealing with political protesters may change rapidly without any legislative authorisation.

Processions

By contrast with static meetings on the highway, at common law a procession in the streets is *prima fàcie* lawful, being no more than the collective exercise of the public right to use the highway for its primary purpose.[46] This does not mean that it would be a reasonable use of the highway for a dozen demonstrators to link arms and proceed down a street so as to interfere with the right of others to use the highway or for a large group of demonstrators to decide to obstruct a street: a procession would become a nuisance 'if the right was exercised unreasonably or with reckless disregard of the rights of others'.[47] Because processions were *prima facie* lawful, statutory powers were needed if the police were to control them. Some local Acts provide special powers over processions but general powers are contained in the Public Order Act 1936, passed at a time when fascist marches in the East End of London were a serious threat to order. By section 3 of the Act, if a chief officer of police, having regard to the time, place and route of an actual or proposed procession, has reasonable ground for apprehending that the procession may occasion serious public disorder, he may issue directions imposing on the persons organising or taking part in the procession such conditions as appear to him to be necessary for the preservation of public order, including conditions prescribing the route of the procession and prohibiting it from entering any public place specified; but he may not restrict the display of flags, banners or emblems unless this is reasonably necessary to prevent risk of a breach of the peace. Breach of the conditions is an offence against the 1936 Act.[48] If these powers are insufficient to prevent serious public disorder being occasioned by the holding of processions in any urban area, the chief officer of police may apply to the district council for an order prohibiting all or any class of public processions for a period not exceeding three months; such an order may be made by the council only with the approval of the Secretary of State. In the

---

44   *Papworth* v. *Coventry* [1967] 2 All E.R. 41.
45   *Ex p. Lewis* (1888) 21 Q.B.D. 191, 197.
46   A.L. Goodhart (1937) 6 C.L.J. 161, 169.
47   *Lowdens* v. *Keaveney* [1903] 2 I.R. 82, 90 (Gibson J.); and see *R.* v. *Clark (No. 2)*, n. 29, *ante*.
48   See *Flockhart* v. *Robinson* [1950] 2 K.B. 498.

case of London, the Commissioner of Metropolitan Police may himself, with the approval of the Home Secretary, issue a prohibition order. The need for the approval of the Secretary of State makes it likely that the matter will be raised in Parliament if M.P.s disagree with the ban.

While effective to meet the immediate purposes for which it was enacted, section 3 of the 1936 Act needs to be considered with care. Only *processions* are subject to control: the Public Order Act gives no power to the police or anyone else to forbid the holding of a meeting or other form of protest. The Act does not however exclude the common law powers of the police to deal with situations in which there is a reasonable apprehension of a breach of the peace, and these powers can be exercised in respect of any kind of gathering.[49] The key phrase in section 3 is the apprehension that an actual or intended procession 'may *occasion* serious public disorder'. The italicised word was chosen to avoid problems that would arise from use of the word 'cause'.[50] It would seem that 'serious public disorder' refers to breaches of the peace and not the disruption of traffic, but is there a risk of 'serious'disorder if hundreds of police officers must at considerable cost be brought in to maintain order? The directions must be given by the chief officer personally,[51] but must they be in writing? Under the Act organisers are not required to give prior notice of a procession although this is required by some local Acts.[52] In practice, particularly in London, the police have encouraged organisers to inform them in advance of the intended route of a procession.[53] The practical advantage of this is that the police may then accompany the procession along the agreed route. Although the reason for a ban may be a proposal for one controversial procession, a chief officer of police may recommend a general ban on all processions, even if this means that processions that present no threat to public order must be cancelled.[54]

Under the Metropolitan Police Act 1839, section 52, the Metropolitan Police Commissioner may make regulations for preventing obstruction of the streets in the metropolitan area and for the route to be observed by all persons 'in all times of public processions', and may give directions to constables for preventing obstruction of the streets. This power was used in September 1961 in respect of an anti-nuclear demonstration in central London after a 24-hour ban on processions imposed under the Public Order Act 1936 with the approval of the Home Secretary had expired.

In 1980, the Home Affairs Committee of the House of Commons examined the operation of the Public Order Act, and inter alia recommended (a) that serious disruption to the normal life of the community should become an additional ground on which the police may give directions to the organisers of processions, but not a ground for banning processions; (b)that the organisers of a procession should be required to give the police 72 hours notice of

---

49 *Post*, p. 540.
50 *Beatty* v. *Gillbanks*, *post*, p. 538.
51 See s. 9(4), Public Order Act 1936.
52 E.g. Greater Manchester Act 1981, s. 56; see also Civic Government (Scotland) Act 1982, s. 62.
53 As in the case of the two marches upon Red Lion Square, Cmnd 5919, pp. 4–5.
54 *Kent* v. *Metropolitan Police Commissioner*, *The Times*, 15 May 1981.

their plans or (in cases of urgency) to do so 'as soon as reasonably practicable after that time'; (c) that the organisers of static demonstrations on the highway should be required to give the same notice to the police and that the police should have the same power to give directions to the organisers as in the case of processions; and (d) that bans imposed on processions should in practice be given only for the time, area and class of procession in relation to which a clear case for banning had been established.[55]

Riot and unlawful assembly[56]

As well as the rules relating to meetings and processions, there are several ways in which breaches of public order may be dealt with. Various ancient common law offences may be committed at times of disorder, in particular the offences of riot and unlawful assembly. For there to be a riot, at least three persons, sharing a common purpose, with an intent to help one another by force if necessary against any person who may oppose them, must actually execute or begin to execute that common purpose, using force or violence in such a manner as to alarm at least one person of reasonable firmness and courage.[57] When a riot is in progress, the police and other citizens may use such force as is reasonable in the circumstances for suppressing the riot.[58] Prosecutions for riot are rare today although in Scotland an unsuccessful prosecution for the offence in Scots law of mobbing and rioting occurred after incidents during the miners' strike in 1972, when strikers used force to prevent supplies of coal reaching a power station.[59] The legal elements of a riot may be considered when a claim is brought against the police authority under the Riot (Damages) Act 1886, which enables owners to recover compensation for damage to property done by rioters.[60] Although compensation has been paid for damage done by those celebrating the end of a world war and by football enthusiasts seeking to climb into a football ground, a claim by a firm of jewellers for compensation following a robbery by four men failed because the robbery did not involve a tumultuous disturbance of the public peace.[61]

Another ancient offence against the peace is affray, which consists of unlawful fighting or a display of force by one or more persons in a public place or on private premises, involving a degree of violence calculated to terrify persons present who are of reasonably firm character.[62]

An unlawful assembly at common law is an assembly of three or more persons meeting for purposes forbidden by law (for example, to commit a crime by open force) or with intent to carry out any common purpose, lawful

---

55   H.C. 756–1 (1979–80); and see Cmnd 7891, 1980.
56   Law Commission, *Offences Relating to Public Order*, H.C. 85(1983–4).
57   *R.* v. *Graham and Burns* (1888) 16 Cox C.C. 420; *Field* v. *Metropolitan Police Receiver* [1907] 2 K.B. 853. And see *Devlin* v. *Armstrong* [1971] N.I.L.R. 13.
58   Criminal Law Act 1967, s. 3. The Riot Act 1714 has now been repealed, both for England and Scotland.
59   See P. T. Wallington (1972) 1 I.L.J. 219.
60   *Field* v. *Metropolitan Police Receiver (ante)*; *Munday* v. *Metropolitan Police Receiver* [1949] 1 All E.R. 337. In Scotland, compensation is payable under the Riotous Assemblies (Scotland) Act 1822, s. 10.
61   *J. W. Dwyer Ltd* v. *Metropolitan Police Receiver* [1967] 2 Q.B. 970.
62   *Button* v. *DPP* [1966] A.C. 591; *Taylor* v. *DPP* [1973] A.C. 964.

or unlawful, in such a manner as to endanger the public peace or to give firm and courageous persons in the neighbourhood reasonable grounds to apprehend a breach of the peace in consequence of it.[63] There is however disagreement as to precisely what constitutes the offence today.[64] The history of unlawful assembly is an important part of the history of the law of public order. After the lapse of the Seditious Meetings Act 1817, it fell to the courts to develop the definition of an unlawful assembly, upon which depended the powers of the police to control or disperse such assemblies. An assembly was unlawful if it met for the commission of a crime involving violence or breach of the peace. The courts extended the offence to gatherings for a lawful purpose if those present at the meeting, whether speakers or audience, acted in such a way 'as to give firm and rational men, having families and property there, reasonable ground to fear a breach of the peace'.[65] Accordingly, a meeting which begins as a lawful gathering may become an unlawful assembly if disorder takes place, weapons are produced of if language inciting an offence is used by speakers. When this transformation occurs, do persons present who do not share the unlawful purpose become guilty of unlawful assembly? The law seems to be that it is no defence to plead ignorance of the fact that the meeting was or became unlawful, if steps were taken to let bystanders know that the meeting was convened for a criminal object.[66] Once a riot or unlawful assembly is in progress, it is the duty of every citizen to assist in restoring order, for example by dispersing or by going to the assistance of the police.[67]

Prosecutions for unlawful assembly have been rare in modern times but when serious disorder occurred at a demonstration protesting against a Greek dinner at the Garden House Hotel, Cambridge (at a time when the Greek government was unpopular in left-wing circles) students in the forefront of the disorder were convicted of riot and unlawful assembly.[68] In *Kamara* v. *DPP*, students from Sierra Leone occupied the Sierra Leone High Commission in London, locking the staff in a room and threatening them with an imitation gun. Their conviction for, *inter alia*, unlawful assembly was upheld by the House of Lords, which ruled that it was not necessary to show that an unlawful assembly had occurred in a public place. The essential requirement was the presence of innocent third parties, since it was the danger to their security which constituted the threat to public peace necessary to the commission of the offence.[69]

In 1983, the Law Commission recommended that the common law offences

---

63   Hawkins, *Pleas of the Crown*, c. 65, s. 9.
64   See *e.g. R.* v. *Chief Constable of Devon, ex p. CEGB* [1982] Q.B. 458; and H.C. 85 (1983–4), p. 38.
65   *R.* v. *Vincent* (1839) 9 C. & P. 91, 109.
66   *R.* v. *Fursey* (1833) 6 C. & P. 80.
67   *Charge to the Bristol Grand Jury* (1832) 5 C. & P. 261; *R.* v. *Brown* (1841) Car. & M. 314,. And see *Devlin* v. *Armstrong* (*ante*).
68   *R.* v. *Caird* (1970) 54 Cr. App. R. 499. And see *The Listener*, 8 Oct. and 26 Nov. 1970. An extraordinary myth surrounds this case; see *e.g.* B. Cox, *Civil Liberties in Britain*, p. 12: 'In 1970, Cambridge students were arrested and gaoled merely for taking part in a demonstration'.
69   *Kamara* v. *DPP* [1974] A..C. 104. For unlawful assembly during an industrial dispute, see *R.* v. *Jones* (1974) 59 Cr. App. R. 120.

of riot and affray should be abolished and replaced by statutory offences bearing the same names; and that the offence of unlawful assembly should be abolished and replaced by two offences, namely an offence of violent disorder (where three or more persons are present together using or threatening unlawful violence) and an offence, where three or more persons are present together, of using threatening, abusive or insulting words or behaviour, where this is intended or likely to cause fear of violence, or to provoke violence.[70] These proposals for making a clean break with the history of unlawful assembly are well justified.

Responsibility for causing disorder

One reason why for many years few prosecutions were brought for unlawful assembly was the difficult question of deciding who was responsible for causing disorder when the disorder arose through a clash between those organising a meeting or procession, and those opposed to it. To put the problem in a modern setting, in the Garden House affair at Cambridge, disorder would not have occurred if the hotel had not decided to hold a Greek dinner. And the Red Lion Square disorders in 1974 would not have occurred if there had been no march by the National Front, which led the left-wing protesters to attempt to break through a police cordon. But are we to conclude that in the one case it was the hotel proprietors and in the other the National Front which *caused* the disorder, even though they might have provided the occasion for it? The answer to the question was given in a decision which has not always been regarded with favour but which seems essentially correct.

In *Beatty* v. *Gillbanks*, which arose out of opposition to the Salvation Army in its early days, the Salvationists at Weston-super-Mare insisted in marching through the streets despite violent opposition from the 'Skeleton Army' and despite an order from the magistrate that they should not march. In an attempt to stop the Salvationist marches, the police sought to have their leaders bound over to keep the peace on the ground that they had committed an unlawful assembly. If the Salvationists had not marched, there would clearly have been no disturbance of the peace. As previous processions had led to disorder, the Salvationists knew that similar consequences were likely to ensue. The Divisional Court held that the acts of the Salvation Army were lawful and that it was not a necessary and natural consequence of these acts that disorder should have occurred. The court did not accept that a man might be punished for acting lawfully if he knew that his so doing might lead another man to act unlawfully.[71]

The court in effect instructed the police that they could not disperse an otherwise lawful assembly simply because of opposition from another body, and that they should direct their attention to dealing with the counter-demonstration. The decision certainly seems correct in the allocation of criminal liability but it was to cause difficulties for the authorities in dealing with disorder. In principle *Beatty* v. *Gillbanks* still stands today,[72] but its operation has been modified in three main ways.

---

[70] H.C. 85 (1983–4); and see p. 539 *post*.
[71] (1882) 9 Q.B.D. 308; Wilson, *Cases*, p. 689. And see H. L. A. Hart and A. M. Honoré, *Causation in the Law*, pp. 333–5.
[72] *Howard E. Perry & Co.* v. *British Railways Board* [1980] 2 All E.R. 579.

First, as we have seen, the powers of controlling processions under the Public Order Act 1936, section 3, may be exercised when a procession is likely to *occasion* disorder: a ban may be imposed on those who have no other intention but to march without violence through the streets if their marches are likely to be the occasion for serious disorder caused by their opponents.

Second, the courts have recognised that while the police have no power to ban meetings in advance, there may be situations of actual disorder when, if order is to be restored swiftly, the police are entitled to stop someone doing what he would otherwise be entitled to do. In *Humphries* v. *Connor*, where an action for assault was brought against a policeman, the Irish court held that the policeman was entitled to remove an orange lily from the plaintiff's clothes since this was necessary to prevent a breach of the peace amongst a crowd in whom the emblem aroused animosity.[73] And in *O'Kelly* v. *Harvey*, a magistrate was held entitled to disperse a lawful meeting since he had reasonable grounds for supposing that Orangemen opposed to the meeting would use violence and that there was no other way in which the peace could be preserved.[74] Neither of these two Irish cases, it should be stressed, involved any question of the criminal liability of those against whom the action of the policeman and the magistrate was directed.

Third, a court may hold certain words or conduct to be provocative and insulting and not worthy of protection under the *Beatty* v. *Gillbanks* principle. Thus in *Wise* v. *Dunning*, a Protestant 'crusader' was bound over to keep the peace after he had repeatedly insulted the Roman Catholic faith in Catholic areas of Liverpool and breaches of the peace had occurred: on the facts, the magistrates were entitled to regard the hostile response by the Catholics as the natural consequence of Wise's insulting conduct.[75]

Threatening, abusive and insulting behaviour

In *Wise* v. *Dunning*, Wise had before being bound over already been convicted several times under a local Act which prohibited insulting and abusive behaviour. These offences were made of general application by the Public Order Act 1936, section 5, which as amended now provides:

Any person who in any public place or at any public meeting –
(*a*) uses threatening, abusive or insulting words or behaviour, or
(*b*) distributes or displays any writing, sign or visible representation which is threatening, abusive or insulting,
with intent to provoke a breach of the peace or whereby a breach of the peace is likely to be occasioned, shall be guilty of an offence.

The offence is punishable summarily.[76] It has often been charged against those who interrupt a lawful meeting. In 1963, however, the main speaker at a rally in Trafalgar Square, Colin Jordan, was convicted under this section because his speech was provocative 'beyond endurance' to the Jews, coloureds and ex-

---

[73] (1864) 17 Ir. C.L.R. 1; Wilson, *Cases*, p. 693.
[74] (1883) 15 Cox C.C. 435; Wilson, *Cases*, p. 695.
[75] [1902] 1 K.B. 167; Wilson, *Cases*, p. 697.
[76] Criminal Law Act 1977, s. 15 and sch. 1, item 5. For the statutory offence of incitement to racial hatred, see p. 512 *ante*.

servicemen in the crowd. The court rejected the argument that the test was the effect the words would have had on 'a hypothetical audience of ordinary, reasonable citizens', holding that the test was whether the words used to the audience in question were likely to provoke a breach of the peace.[77] Lord Parker C. J. suggested that to insult meant 'to hit by words' but the need to find synonyms for the words threatening, abusive and insulting was rejected in a later case, *Brutus* v. *Cozens*.

During a Wimbledon match, Brutus and other anti-apartheid protesters went on to the court, distributed leaflets and sat down. The spectators strongly resented the interruption of play. Brutus was prosecuted for using insulting behaviour whereby a breach of the peace was likely to be occasioned. The justices dismissed the charge, finding that the conduct was not insulting. On appeal by the prosecutor, the Divisional Court directed the justices that behaviour was insulting if it affronted other people and evidenced a disrespect or contempt for their rights, and thereby was likely to cause the resentment which the spectators had expressed at Wimbledon. The House of Lords unanimously allowed an appeal by Brutus against this direction, holding that 'insulting' was to be given its ordinary meaning and that the question of whether certain behaviour had been insulting was one of fact for the justices to determine. Lord Reid pointed out that section 5 of the 1936 Act did not prohibit *all* speech or conduct likely to occasion a breach of the peace. Vigorous, distasteful and unmannerly speech was not prohibited. There could be no definition of insult: 'an ordinary sensible man knows an insult when he sees or hears it'.[78]

It is submitted that the last remark was not intended to cast doubt on the principle in *Jordan* v. *Burgoyne* that the speaker takes his audience as he finds them. Lord Reid's 'ordinary sensible man' is the lay magistrate, able to decide for himself whether words or conduct are insulting without having to apply the Divisional Court's elaborate attempt to stretch the Act to cover conduct which is merely annoying. Even where conduct is considered to be insulting, the prosecution must also prove intent to provoke a breach of the peace or that a breach of the peace is likely.[79]

Preventive powers of police and the courts

We have already seen, as in *Humphries* v. *Connor* and *O'Kelly* v. *Harvey*, that in circumstances of actual disorder the priority for police action is to adopt whatever course of action seems necessary for restoring order. An argument may be made for bringing these powers of the police forward in time so that the police may prevent disturbance occurring. Yet the trouble with this is that it may have the effect of enabling a prior ban to be imposed on an activity that is, on the *Beatty* v. *Gillbanks* principle, quite lawful. It is one thing for the police to bring a meeting to an end because of severe disturbances caused by protesters. It is another thing for the police to be entrusted with the power to ban similar events in the future. Three forms of preventive authority will be discussed: 1 binding over to keep the peace, 2 entry into meetings, 3 obstruction of the police.

---

77   *Jordan* v. *Burgoyne* [1963] 2 Q.B. 744.
78   [1973] A.C. 854, 862.
79   *Parkin* v. *Norman* [1983] Q.B. 92.

1 Binding over to keep the peace[80] Magistrates in England and Wales have a wide power to order any person to enter into a recognisance (undertaking), with or without sureties, to keep the peace or to be of good behaviour, either in general or towards a particular person.

At a time of suffragette militancy, when many acts of damage to property were being committed, George Lansbury made speeches encouraging the militants to continue. The magistrate required him to give undertakings to be of good behaviour in the sum of £1,000 and to find sureties for his good behaviour, or in default to go to prison for 3 months. The Divisional Court upheld the order, holding that a person could be bound over for inciting breaches of the peace even though no particular person was threatened.[81]

The origin of this power is obscure: it may rest upon the Justices of the Peace Act 1361 or it may be inherent in the commission of the peace held by magistrates. A magistrate may bind a person over whenever it is apprehended that he is likely to commit a breach of the peace or do something contrary to law, but he need not have committed any criminal offence and it is not necessary to show that anything has been done calculated to lead to acts of personal violence.[82] If a person refuses to give an undertaking to be of good behaviour, a magistrates' court may commit him to prison for a term not exceeding six months.[83] There is a right of appeal to the Crown Court against an order binding a person over, though the making of an order does not constitute a conviction.[84] Natural justice requires that a person may not be bound over until he has been at least told what is passing through the magistrate's mind and given a chance of answering.[85]

Although the power to bind over could not be used against the Salvationists in *Beatty* v. *Gillbanks*, it may be used to restrain those organising a public demonstration in the course of which they intend breaches of the law to occur. In 1961, when a large demonstration against nuclear arms had been planned, Bertrand Russell and other members of the Committee of 100 were summoned for having incited the public to obstruct the highway in Parliament Square: those who declined to be bound over were imprisoned for between 7 days and 2 months.[86]

The apprehension of a breach of the peace is important both in binding over and for other purposes in the criminal law, but the concept of breach of the peace at common law is not completely clear-cut.[87] English law does not recognise a substantive offence of breach of the peace. By contrast, in Scots law there is a very broad common law offence of breach of the peace, which

---

[80] Williams, *Keeping the Peace*, ch. 4 and [1977] Crim L.R. 703; A.D. Grunis [1976] P.L. 16.
[81] *Lansbury* v. *Riley* [1914] 3 K.B. 229.
[82] *R.* v. *Sandbach, ex p. Williams* [1935] 2 K.B. 192; *cf. R.* v. *Aubrey-Fletcher, ex p. Thompson* [1969] 2 All E.R. 846.
[83] Magistrates' Courts Act 1980, s. 115; Justices of the Peace Act 1968, s. 1(7).
[84] Magistrates' Courts (Appeals from Binding Over Orders) Act 1956, amended by Courts Act 1971.
[85] *Sheldon* v. *Bromfield JJ.* [1964] 2 Q.B. 573.
[86] *The Times*, 13 Sep. 1961.
[87] See *R.* v. *Howell* [1982] Q.B. 416, 426 and *R.* v. *Chief Constable of Devon, ex p. CEGB* [1982] Q.B. 458, 471; H.C. 85 (1983–4), pp. 46–9.

includes the use of violent and threatening language in public, breaches of public order and decorum and even the making of indecent suggestions in private to young persons[88] but not the peaceful singing of hymns at a prayer meeting in the street.[89] The broad nature of this offence probably explains why, on facts very similar to those in *Beatty* v. *Gillbanks*, the Scottish court convicted the local leaders of a Salvation Army procession of breach of the peace.[90]

2 Entry into meetings.   In a public place like Trafalgar Square, there can be no doubt of the power of the police to be present and to deal with outbreaks of disorder if they occur. Where a public meeting is held on private premises, the power of the police to attend is less certain. At one time the official view of the Home Office was that except when the promoters of a meeting asked the police to be present in the meeting, they could not go in, unless they had reason to believe that an actual breach of the peace was being committed in the meeting.[91]

This view was stated after disorder occurred at a fascist meeting at Olympia in London, when the stewards inflicted physical violence on dissentients in the audience. No police were stationed on the premises, though large numbers had been assembled in nearby streets. Within a year, the court disapproved of the Home Office view of the law.

In *Thomas* v. *Sawkins*[92] a meeting had been advertised in a Welsh town (a) to protest against the Incitement to Disaffection Bill which was then before Parliament and (b) to demand the dismissal of the Chief Constable of Glamorgan. Admission to the meeting was open to the public without payment, and the police arranged for some of their number to attend. The promoter requested the police officers to leave. A constable committed a technical assault on the promoter thinking that the promoter was on the point of employing force to remove a police officer from the room. There was no allegation that any criminal offence had been committed at the meeting or that any breach of the peace had occurred. When the promoter prosecuted the constable for assault, the finding in the magistrates' court was that the police had reasonable grounds for believing that if they were not present at the meeting there would be seditious speeches and other incitement to violence and that breaches of the peace would occur; that the police were entitled to enter and remain in the hall throughout the meeting; and that consequently the constable did not unlawfully assault the promoter. In the Divisional Court these findings were upheld. Lord Hewart C. J. was of opinion that the police have power to enter and to remain on private premises when they have reasonable grounds for believing that an offence is imminent or likely to be committed; nor did he limit this statement to offences involving a breach of the peace. In the opinion of Avory J., 'the justices had before them material on which they could properly hold that the police officers in question had reasonable grounds for believing that, if they were not present, seditious speeches would be made and/or that a breach of the peace would

---

88   *Ferguson* v. *Carnochan* (1889) 2 White 278; *Dougall* v. *Dykes* (1861) 4 Irv. 101; *Young* v. *Heatly* 1959 J.C. 66.
89   *Hutton* v. *Main* (1891) 19 R. (J.) 5.
90   *Deakin* v. *Milne* (1882) 10 R. (J.) 22.
91   H. C. Deb., 14 June 1934, col. 1968.
92   [1935] 2 K.B. 249; Wilson, *Cases*, p. 635. See A.L. Goodhart (1936) 6 C.L.J. 22.

take place. To prevent any such offence or a breach of the peace the police were entitled to enter and to remain on the premises'.[93]

Although the second objective of the meeting in *Thomas* v. *Sawkins* was admittedly provocative to the local police, it did not suggest an incitement to violence which is a necessary element in the offence of sedition. Nor need a protest against a Bill involve a breach of the peace. It is unclear whether Lord Hewart's opinion is confined to public meetings on private premises or whether it also applies to private meetings and other activities on private premises. May the police enter any private premises if they reasonably believe that any offence is imminent or is likely to be committed?

The judgments in the case gave scant consideration to the argument that as soon as the promoter asked the police to withdraw from the premises, this rescinded the open invitation given to the public (including the police) to attend. Did not this make the officers trespassers on private premises from that point onwards?[94] It may be that, as the evidence of the fascist rallies in the 1930s suggests, it is in the public interest that the police should be entitled to enter and remain in any public meeting: but why should a similar right apply to private meetings? Doubts as to the width of *Thomas* v. *Sawkins* are resolved by the Police and Criminal Evidence Act 1984, which preserves the power of the police to enter premises to deal with or prevent a breach of the peace, but otherwise abolishes all common law powers of the police to enter premises without a warrant.[95]

3 Obstruction of the police. The statutory offence of obstructing the police in the execution of their duty has already been considered in relation to the law of arrest.[96] It is no less important in the law of public order, especially in regard to the preventive powers of the police. In *Beatty* v. *Gillbanks*, for example, could the Salvationists have been convicted of obstructing the police in the execution of their duty? It has been suggested that in the 19th century such an offence would have been proved only if the Salvationists had been committing the offence of unlawful assembly.[97] The decision in *Duncan* v. *Jones* in 1936 gave rise to fears about the uses to which the offence of obstructing the police could be put.

Mrs Duncan, a woman speaker, was forbidden by Jones, a police officer, to hold a street meeting at a place opposite a training centre for the unemployed. She refused to hold the meeting in another street 175 yards away. Fourteen months previously Mrs Duncan had held a meeting at the same spot, which had been followed by a disturbance in the centre attributed by the superintendent of the centre to the meeting. Mrs Duncan mounted a box on the highway to start the meeting but was arrested and charged with obstructing a police officer in the execution of his duty. There was no allegation of obstruction of the highway or of inciting any breach of the peace. The lower court found

---

93   [1935] 2 K.B. at 256.
94   *Davis* v. *Lisle* [1936] 2 K.B. 434, *Robson* v. *Hallett* [1967] 2 Q.B. 939; ch. 26 A.
95   1984 Act, s. 17(5)(6); p. 488 *ante*.
96   Police Act 1964, s. 51; ch. 26 A. And see R. C. Austin [1982] C.L.P. 187, T. Gibbons [1983] Crim. L.R. 21, K. W. Lidstone [1983] Crim. L.R. 29.
97   T. C. Daintith [1966] P.L. 248, 252.

(a) that Mrs Duncan must have known of the probable consequences of her holding the meeting, *viz.* a disturbance and possibly a breach of the peace, and was not unwilling that such consequences should ensue, (b) that Jones reasonably apprehended a breach of the peace, (c) that in law it therefore became his duty to prevent the holding of the meeting, (d) that by attempting to hold the meeting Mrs Duncan obstructed Jones when in the execution of his duty. The Divisional Court upheld the conviction. Humphreys J. remarked that on the facts as found, Jones reasonably apprehended a breach of the peace; it then became his duty 'to prevent anything which in his view would cause that breach of the peace'.[98]

The decision raises many difficulties. On one view, it would give a policeman power to prevent the holding of a lawful meeting if he suspected not that the meeting itself might be disorderly but that breaches of the peace might occur as a result of the meeting, whether committed by supporters or opponents of the speakers at the meeting. The reasoning of Humphreys J. brings forward in time and widens the preventive powers of the police to a degree that could lead to intolerable restrictions upon the liberty of meeting.On this basis the police could forbid a meeting in the students' union of a college from taking place merely because a 'disturbance' had previously occurred in the college after a similar meeting.

It may be that the finding of fact that Mrs Duncan must have known of the probable consequences of holding the meeting and was not unwilling that such consequences should ensue limits the authority of *Duncan* v. *Jones* to those cases where it can be shown that the defendant has caused disorder on a previous occasion. But if so speakers are being penalised for their previous conduct, irrespective of whether they have committed an offence on the current occasion. Moreover, the test of causation seems vague. Concerning *Duncan* v. *Jones*, Professor Goodhart remarked:

At first sight it may seem unreasonable to say that a police officer cannot take steps to prevent an act which, when committed, becomes a punishable offence. But it is on this distinction between prevention and punishment that freedom of speech, freedom of public meeting and freedom of the press are founded.[99]

Duncan v. *Jones* therefore cannot be accepted as authority for the exercise of such wide preventive powers by the police in relation to public meetings in general. Under the doctrine of precedent, the authority of a case depends not upon the statements of the judges read in abstract but on these statements read in relation to the material facts of the case. Probably the most important single fact in *Duncan* v. *Jones* is that the meeting was to be held on the highway; an obstruction to the highway must inevitably have resulted from Mrs Duncan's meeting even though the police did not in the case rely on evidence of such obstruction. It is submitted that *Duncan* v. *Jones* has authority only in respect of meetings on the highway and has no application to public meetings on private property. If a hall had been hired for Mrs Duncan's meeting opposite the unemployed training centre, it is not conceivable that events would have taken the turn they did. Still less does *Duncan* v. *Jones* have any authority in

---

98   [1936] 1 K.B. 218, Wilson, *Cases*, p. 701; E. C. S. Wade (1937) 6 C.L.J. 175.
99   (1936) 6 C.L.J. 22, 30.

respect of private meetings on private property.

Even this interpretation does not deal with all the difficulties of *Duncan* v. *Jones*. It has been persuasively shown that the decision broke new ground when compared with the 19th century view that the police could interrupt a meeting only when it had become an unlawful assembly.[1] The new reasoning may however be accepted to this extent: namely, that if, on the basis of *Humphries* v. *Connor* and *O'Kelly* v. *Harvey*, the police at the scene of actual disorder adopt a course of action which on reasonable grounds appears to be the only practicable means of restoring order, those who obstruct that action commit the offence of obstructing the police in the execution of their duty.[2] In the context of public order, the courts have not been quick to overrule the view of a police officer that certain action was required: in other fields of police power, it is clearly established that disobedience to a policeman does not always amount to the offence of obstructing a police officer in the execution of his duty.[3]

Sit-ins, squatting and forcible entry

In recent years the expression of protest has frequently taken the form of squatting in unoccupied houses, occupation by students of university property and occupation by industrial workers of factories threatened with closure. These forms of direct action have given rise to difficult problems both in civil and criminal law. In *Chandler* v. *DPP*, an attempt by nuclear disarmers to enter and sit down on an RAF base was held to be a conspiracy to commit a breach of the Official Secrets Act 1911, section 1(1), which makes it an offence for any purpose prejudicial to the safety of the state to approach or enter 'any prohibited place'.[4] But most forms of property are not protected in this way. In *Kamara* v. *DPP*, the House of Lords held that, although trepass is a civil wrong and not a criminal offence, a group of Sierra Leoneans who occupied the Sierra Leone High Commission offices in London were guilty of a criminal conspiracy: not every agreement between two or more persons to commit a trespass to land would amount to such a conspiracy, but circumstances such as the invasion of a publicly owned building or an embassy or the intention to use force or violence would give rise to liability for conspiracy.[5] The ancient offences of forcible entry and forcible detention of land were for a time revived to deal with forms of squatting.[6] Civil procedure for the recovery of possession may now be taken against unknown squatters and others in unauthorised occupation of premises.[7]

Although serious breaches of the peace may occur in connection with the forcible taking or defence of property, in many cases of squatting and occupation of buildings (for example, by students or factory workers) the police

---

[1]   Note 97 *ante*.
[2]   *Cf.* Daintith, *op. cit.*, pp. 258–61.
[3]   *E.g. Rice* v. *Connolly* [1966] 2 Q.B. 414; ch. 26 A.
[4]   [1964] A.C. 763; Wilson, *Cases*, p. 713; ch. 30.
[5]   [1974] A.C. 104. Certain forms of trespass are criminal offences in Scotland: Trespass (Scotland) Act 1865.
[6]   *R.* v. *Robinson* [1971] Q.B. 156, *R.* v. *Mountford* [1972] 1 Q.B.28, *R.* v. *Brittain* [1972] 1 Q.B. 357, *McPhail* v. *persons unknown* [1973] Ch. 447.
[7]   R.S.C. Order 113; *Warwick University* v. *De Graaf* [1975] 3 All E.R. 284, *University of Essex* v. *Djemal* [1980] 2 All E.R. 742.

have refrained from intervening in what they consider to be essentially domestic or civil disputes. Indeed, the use of police in such circumstances may intensify a situation of potential conflict. But the police are prepared to protect a residential occupier from being dispossessed.[8]

These various forms of direct action go far beyond what can be regarded as included within the liberty of expression and public meeting, since they involve direct interference with the rights of others. On the recommendation of the English Law Commission,[9] the Criminal Law Act 1977 made an extensive reform of the law. The old offences of forcible entry and forcible detainer were abolished and conspiracy to commit a civil trespass, as in *Kamara* v. *DPP*, ceased to be a criminal offence (sections 1(1), 5(1), 13). Part II of the 1977 Act created various offences relating to entering and remaining on property. These include (a) without lawful authority, to use or threaten violence for the purpose of securing entry into any premises on which another person is present, and against the will of that person (section 6); (b) to remain on residential premises as a trespasser after being required to leave by or on behalf of a displaced residential occupier of the premises (section 7); (c) without lawful authority, to have offensive weapons on premises after having entered them as a trespasser (section 8); (d) to enter as a trespasser any foreign embassies and other diplomatic premises (section 9); and (e) to resist or obstruct a sheriff or bailiff seeking to enforce a court order for possession (section 10).

---

8   And see *R.* v. *Chief Constable of Devon, ex p. CEGB* [1982] Q.B. 458.
9   Report on Conspiracy and Criminal Reform, H.C. 176 (1975–6).

Chapter 29

Emergency powers

In times of grave national emergency, normal constitutional principles may have to give way to the overriding need to deal with the emergency. In Lord Pearce's words, 'the flame of individual right and justice must burn more palely when it is ringed by the more dramatic light of bombed buildings'.[1] The European Convention on Human Rights, article 15, permits a member state to take measures derogating from its obligations under the Convention 'in time of war or other public emergency threatening the life of the nation'. The UK government has exercised the right of derogation in respect of events in Northern Ireland. But even under such circumstances no derogation is permitted from article 2 (which protects the right to life) except in the case of deaths resulting from lawful acts of war, article 3 (which prohibits the use of torture), article 4(1) (which prohibits slavery) and article 7 (which bars retrospective criminal laws). Thus even in grave emergencies there are limits beyond which a state may not go. This chapter examines the role of the armed forces and the use of statutory emergency powers during war and peace, and includes an account of recent anti-terrorist legislation. Emphasis must be both on the increased powers of the state in emergencies and on the continuing limits on state action.

A. Use of the armed forces

In chapter 28 we examined the main powers available to the police in maintaining public order. In the 20th century in Great Britain, the police, with greater or less difficulty depending on the circumstances, have been able to control and contain attempts to create internal disorder. For most of the century (with the notable exception of the period of strikes in South Wales in 1911), the armed forces have not been used to suppress popular unrest,[2] although they have been required to maintain essential services during strikes and on occasion to deal with extreme terrorist action (for example, the oc-

---

[1] *Conway* v. *Rimmer* [1968] A. C. 910, 982.
[2] See D. G. T. Williams, *Keeping the Peace*, pp. 32–5.

cupation of the Iranian embassy in London in May 1980). But in the 19th century and earlier, when there was less political freedom and police forces were weaker, the local magistrates were expected to call in detachments of soldiers to restore order when necessary. Today in Great Britain, conditions would indeed have the character of an emergency if it became necessary to invoke the aid of the armed forces for this purpose.

This section considers (a) the role of the troops in aiding the civil authorities to maintain law and order, and (b) the situation of martial law, when ordinary civil government has broken down and only military force can enable a form of rough justice to be maintained.

Use of the troops in assisting the police

By long tradition the British police do not as a general practice carry firearms, although today these are available to all police forces for use in situations of necessity. A decision to call in the troops to restore order was, in the past at least, a decision enabling firearms to be used to repress the disturbances. This use of the troops may be illustrated by a rather late example, the Featherstone riots in 1893.[3] When the police were engaged elsewhere, a small detachment of soldiers was summoned to protect a colliery against a riotous crowd which broke windows and set buildings on fire. As darkness was falling, a magistrate called on the crowd to disperse and he read the proclamation from the Riot Act. When the crowd did not disperse, the magistrate authorised the soldiers to fire and their officer decided that the only way to protect the colliery was to fire on the crowd. Two members of the crowd were killed. A committee of inquiry held that the action of the troops was justified in law.

When troops are thus used, what is the basis of their authority? Whatever may be the constitutional rules today that govern the decision that the armed forces should be called in,[4] their legal authority to act in a situation of riot seems to rest upon no statutory or prerogative powers of the Crown but simply on the duty of all citizens to aid in the suppression of riot and on the duty of the armed forces to come to the aid of the civil authorities.[5] In place of the common law rules on the use of force in the prevention of crime, section 3 of the Criminal Law Act 1967 now provides:

A person may use such force as is reasonable in the circumstances in the prevention of crime, or in effecting or assisting in the lawful arrest of offenders or suspected offenders or of persons unlawfully at large.

Thus, the use of firearms must be justified by the necessity of the situation and does not become legal by reason of the decision to call in the troops. Indeed, the use of excessive force or the premature use of firearms would render the officer in command and the individual soldiers personally responsible for death

---

[3]   Report of the Committee on the Disturbances at Featherstone, C. 7234, 1893; Wilson, *Cases,* p. 729. And see H. C. 236 (1908).

[4]   See authorities cited in note 10 *post.*

[5]   *Charge to Bristol Grand Jury* (1832) 5 C. & P. 261.

or injuries caused.[6] Issues of liability are decided by the criminal or civil courts after the event.

At a time before modern communications and the development of professional police, it was for the local magistrates (the civil power) to summon the military to their aid. The old learning is inapplicable today, for the magistrates have ceased to play a role in controlling operations designed to maintain the peace. Many of the old rules are solemnly repeated in the current edition of the Manual of Military Law, but the Manual strikes a more realistic note when it states:

It is to be expected that a disturbance grave enough to be beyond the power of the police to suppress would be a matter of national concern in which counter measures would be taken only under close control of the Government. It is most unlikely that a local military commander would be so cut off from superior command as to have to act on his own authority in so serious a matter.[7]

In 1976, the Commissioner of the Metropolitan Police, Sir Robert Mark, described what would happen today if the police ceased to be able to deal with threats to public order, for example, because of dangerous attacks from political terrorists.

In such situations, permission of the Home Secretary is sought by the chief officer of police to invoke military aid and the Minister of Defence, in consultation with the Home Secretary, who will have considered the views of the chief officer of police, will decide whether to authorise the ultimate sanction of force by such troops as he may make available. Such assistance was formerly sought by police from the magistracy rather than from the Home Office, but whatever the legal position the present practice reflects the emergence of a professional, well-organised police service which has inevitably assumed the primary responsibility for law and order ... The request to the Home Secretary having been approved, it is clearly desirable that both police and the army should then conform to exactly the same terms of engagement. There is no question of one service coming under command of the other. The police commander would simply indicate to the military commander the problem and the target and offer him whatever support he required whilst playing a containing or supporting role. The army commander would act in accordance with the joint police/army plan. He would not be under the command of the police commander but would act in conjunction with him under his duty at common law to come to the aid of the civil power. The joint objective would, of course, be to bring the operation to a successful conclusion, ideally without loss of life. But its achievement would clearly involve a voluntary, if temporary, restriction of the right of the police to complete freedom under the law in their operational decisions and actions. In such circumstances police, army, Home Office and Ministry of Defence must act in complete accord.[8]

These procedures came into operation when members of the Special Air Service Regiment were used in May 1980 to end the occupation by terrorists

---

[6]   *Lynch* v. *Fitzgerald* [1938] I.R. 382. And see *Farrell* v. *Secretary of State for Defence* [1980] 1 All E.R. 166.

[7]   *Manual of Military Law*, Pt. II, s. 5; M. Supperstone, *Brownlie's Law of Public Order and National Security*, app. 5.

[8]   Cmnd 6496, 1979, app. 9, p. 96 (reprinted in R. Mark, *Policing a Perplexed Society*, ch.2).

of the Iranian embassy in London. In such an emergency, the normal lines of control and responsibility must be modified. Whereas for operational purposes, police forces are not subject to direct political control, the army acts 'on the orders of its political masters to whom it is through its command structure accountable'.[9]

By contrast with 19th century practice, the 'civil power' that may call in the armed forces appears no longer to be the local magistracy, but the Home Secretary, acting on a request from a chief officer of police.[10] It is then for the Secretary of State for Defence to respond to the call. In such a situation, conventions of individual and collective responsibility of ministers must merge. It may be assumed that the decisions of both Cabinet ministers are taken through permanent machinery authorised by the Cabinet for dealing with civil emergencies, and serviced by the Civil Contingencies Unit of the Cabinet Office. In themselves, these arrangements for joint operations between police and army give no additional legal authority to police or army for interfering with the rights of citizens. In modern conditions, the proposition that to call in the troops makes possible the use of firearms needs to be qualified in two ways. First, the police have already had to train and equip themselves with firearms 'to deal with armed criminals and political terrorists not posing any extraordinary problem or capable of posing a limited threat'.[11] The occasions on which firearms may be carried are governed by police rules but in 1976 Sir Robert Mark argued that the discretion of the individual constable extended to cover the use of firearms: 'A jury or a police disciplinary inquiry may examine his actions but his use of a firearm does not differ in law from his use of a truncheon'.[12] Second, it is no longer correct, as was said in 1893, that a soldier can act only by using deadly weapons.[13] To call in the army to deal with civil unrest would indeed be of incalculable political significance. But the British army's experience in Northern Ireland suggests that there are many other ways of dealing with hostile crowds which are more effective and less deadly than firing into them — batons, riot shields, water cannon, rubber bullets and even C.S. gas[14] – and the armed forces do not have a monopoly of the use of C.S. gas.[15]

Use of the troops in Northern Ireland
The use of troops in Northern Ireland and their potential use against political

---

[9]   *Ibid.*, p. 94, and see ch. 23.
[10]   H. C. Deb., 8 Apr. 1976, col. 617. See also E. Bramall (1980) 128 *Jl. of Royal Society of Arts* 480; S. C. Greer [1983] P. L. 573; and R. Evelegh, *Peace Keeping in a Democratic Society*, pp. 11–21, 91–4.
[11]   Cmnd 6496, 1976, p. 95. On the Special Patrol Group in London and task forces in other police forces, see (1979) 2 *State Research* 130. And see Atomic Energy Authority (Special Constables) Act 1976; J. C. Woodliffe [1983] P.L. 440.
[12]   Cmnd. 6496, 1976, p. 95. In 1983, police officers who shot the wrong man (Stephen Waldorf) mistakenly believing him to be an armed and dangerous criminal, were acquitted by a jury of criminal liability; he was later paid substantial compensation by the police.
[13]   C. 7234, pp. 10, 12.
[14]   See Reports on medical and toxicological aspects of C.S. gas, Cmnd 4173, 1969; Cmnd 4775, 1975.
[15]   New guidelines for police use of C.S. gas and baton-rounds were issued by the Home Secretary after the Toxteth riots in 1981: H.C. Deb., 19 Oct. 1981, col. 31 (W.A.).

terrorists are of the kind which have been described by a military writer as low intensity operations.[16] Such use gives rise to formidable political and constitutional problems, not least in the identification of political groups whose activities may be described as subversive.[17] In 1975, the Home Office defined subversion as comprising activities 'which threaten the safety or well-being of the State, and are intended to undermine or overthrow parliamentary democracy by political, industrial or violent means'.[18] On this basis, since 1969 the scale of subversive activities in Northern Ireland has required the armed forces to share with the police a difficult and unenviable role in maintaining internal security.[19] Reference has been made already to the grave errors made in the adoption of interrogation in depth against selected internees.[20] In 1972, the Northern Ireland Court of Appeal decided that the Northern Ireland Parliament under the Government of Ireland Act 1920 had no legal authority to confer powers of arrest upon the armed forces; this decision led instantly to legislation which retrospectively conferred this power upon the Stormont Parliament.[21]

Regarding the use of firearms, difficult cases concerning the criminal liability of individual soldiers have come before the courts. Thus in 1971 a Marine commando was acquitted by a jury on charges of malicious wounding arising out of a single shot which he had fired into a crowd throwing stones and advancing towards him.[22] In 1976 the House of Lords refused to lay down a general rule governing the degree of force which it was reasonable for a soldier to use in exercising his power to stop and question a civilian whom he honestly and reasonably believed to be a potential terrorist; such a question was one of fact, not of law.[23]

Possibly the most controversial use of firearms occurred on Sunday, 30 January 1972 in Londonderry, when the use of paratroops against a crowd which had gathered on the occasion of an unlawful civil rights march led to shooting in which 13 civilians died. An inquiry by Lord Widgery, C.J. made public the Yellow Card instructions given to soldiers on the use of firearms and examined the difficulties inherent in these instructions and in the conduct of military operations against hostile sections of the civilian population.[24] But Lord Widgery's findings on the Londonderry affair were themselves challenged.[25]

Martial law

The term martial law may be given a variety of meanings. In former times,

---

[16] F. Kitson, *Low Intensity Operations.*

[17] See *e.g.* Kitson's definition at p. 3 of subversion as 'all illegal measures short of the use of armed force taken by one section of the people . . . to overthrow those governing the country . . . or to force them to do things which they do not want to do'; and note the reference to the role of law at pp. 69–70.

[18] H.C. Deb., 6 Apr. 1978, col. 618.

[19] See *e.g.* the critical study by R. Evelegh, *Peace Keeping in a Democratic Society.*

[20] Ch. 6.

[21] *R. (Hume et al.) v. Londonderry Justices* 1972 N.I.L.R. 91; Northern Ireland Act 1972.

[22] *The Times,* 31 Mar. 1971.

[23] *A.-G. for Northern Ireland's Reference (No. 1 of 1975)* [1977] A.C. 105. And see *Farrell's* case, note 6 *ante*; H.C. 262 (1983–4), app. B.

[24] H.C. 220 (1971–72); Wilson, *Cases,* p. 733.

[25] S. Dash, *Justice Denied.*

martial law included what is now called military law.[26] In international law, martial law refers to the powers exercised by a military commander in occupation of foreign territory. In the present context, martial law refers to an emergency amounting to a state of war when the military may impose restrictions and regulations upon citizens in their own country.[27] In such a situation of civil war or insurrection, the ordinary functioning of the courts gives way before the tasks of the military in restoring the conditions which make normal government possible. Unlike the use of armed forces for restoring order upon the occasion of riots, when the military are subject to direction by the civil authorities and to control by the courts if excessive force is used, under martial law the military authorities are (for the time being) deemed the sole judges of the steps that should be taken. These steps might involve taking drastic steps against civilians, for example, the removal of life, liberty or property without due process of law, but possibly accompanied by the creation of military tribunals to administer summary justice. Such tribunals are not to be confused with the courts-martial which regularly administer military law.

It would be wrong to state the principal aspects of martial law as if they were part of present day law, if only for the reason that within Great Britain occasions for the exercise of martial law have not arisen since at least 1800. Moreover the Petition of Right 1628 contains a prohibition against the issue by the Crown of commissions of martial law giving the army powers over civilians, at least in time of peace, and the meaning of this prohibition is far from clear today.[28] In times of national emergency today, Parliament prefers to give the civil and military authorities wide powers of governing by means of temporary statutory powers. It is submitted, therefore, that any discussion of the possible operation of martial law in Great Britain must assume that Parliament itself is prevented by the urgency of events from giving the necessary powers to the military authorities. If Parliament is sitting but refuses to pass emergency legislation, there would seem to be great difficulty, from a constitutional standpoint, in accepting that extraordinary powers of the military arise by process of common law.[29] Moreover, short of a military coup, or an extreme emergency in which human survival becomes the only criterion, it must be assumed that the government continues to control the armed forces and to be responsible for their use to Parliament. In Northern Ireland since 1969, at no time has the British government invoked the doctrine of martial law as a justification for exempting the actions of the forces from scrutiny in the courts; instead there has been reliance on statutory powers, or on the use of common law powers falling far short of a martial law situation.

An attempt to describe the doctrine of martial law must be based upon case-law arising out of the Boer War, the civil war in Ireland early in the 1920s, and incidents in the earlier history of British colonies. But only the future can tell whether this mingled case-law is applicable in Great Britain: and may we long remain in uncertainty.[30]

---

26   Ch. 23.
27   Keir and Lawson, *Cases in Constitutional Law*, ch. IIIC; Heuston, *Essays*, pp. 150–62; Wilson, *Cases*, pp. 735–8.
28   *Cf. Marais* v. *General Officer Commanding* [1902] A.C. 109, 115.
29   *Cf. Egan* v. *Macready* [1921] 1 I.R. 265, 274.
30   *Cf.* the argument in Dicey, ch. 8, that martial law is unknown to the law of England.

Position of the courts during martial law

If in a state of civil war or insurrection the administration of justice breaks down because the courts are unable to function, it follows as a matter of fact that the acts of the military in seeking to restore order cannot be called into question in the courts so long as this situation lasts. As the English Law Officers said in 1838 in relation to the power of the governor of Lower Canada to proclaim martial law, martial law 'can only be tolerated because, by reason of open rebellion, the enforcing of any other law has become impossible'.[31] If in such a situation the executive proclaims martial law, the proclamation does not increase the powers of the military but merely gives notice to the people of the course which the government must adopt to restore order. In 1838 the Law Officers considered that, when the regular courts were in operation, any persons arrested by the military must be delivered to the courts to be dealt with according to law; 'there is not, as we conceive, any right in the Crown to adopt any other course of proceeding'.[32]

In 1902, in the *Marais* case, the Privy Council significantly extended the doctrine of martial law by holding that a situation of martial law might exist though the civil courts were still sitting. During the Boer War martial law had been proclaimed over certain areas of Cape Colony: Marais, a civilian, sought in the Supreme Court at Cape Town to challenge the legality of his arrest and detention for breach of military rules in an area subject to martial law. Lord Halsbury, on behalf of the Judicial Committee, declared that where war actually exists, the ordinary courts have no jurisdiction over the military authorities, although there might often be doubt as to whether a situation of war existed, as opposed to a mere riot or other disturbance.[33] Once a war situation had been recognised to exist, the military would presumably be able to deal with the inhabitants of an area under martial law on the same footing as the population of a foreign territory occupied during a war between states, subject only to the possibility of being called to account for their acts in the civil courts after the resumption of normal government at a later date.[34]

Advantage of the *Marais* case was taken by the UK government during the serious disturbances in Ireland in 1920–1. Early in 1920 the Westminster Parliament passed the Restoration of Order in Ireland Act, which gave exceptional powers to the executive, created new offences, provided for civilians to be tried and sentenced by properly convened courts-martial and prescribed the maximum penalties that could be imposed. Yet in December 1920, martial law was proclaimed in areas of Ireland and the General Officer Commanding the army declared *inter alia* that any unauthorised person found in possession of arms would be subject to the death penalty. The General also established informal military courts for administering summary justice to those alleged to have committed the prohibited acts.

In *R. v. Allen*, the King's Bench Division in Ireland refused to intervene in the case of a death sentence imposed by such a military court on a civilian for possession of arms. The court held that a state of war existed in the area

---

[31] Opinion of J. Campbell and R. M. Rolfe, 16 Jan. 1838; Keir and Lawson, *op. cit.*, p. 231.
[32] *Ibid.*
[33] *Marais* v. *General Officer Commanding, ante.* And see *Tilonko* v. *A.-G. of Natal* [1907] A.C. 93.
[34] Page 554 *post.*

in question; that military acts could not therefore be questioned in the civil courts even though the latter were still operating; and that the army authorities could take the lives of civilians if they deemed it to be absolutely essential. It was immaterial that Parliament had not authorised the death penalty for unauthorised possession of arms.[35]

The decisions of other Irish courts were not all so favourable to the army. In *Egan* v. *Macready*, O'Connor M.R. distinguished the *Marais* case, holding that the Restoration of Order in Ireland Act 1920 created a complete code for military control of the situation which excluded the power of the army to impose the death penalty where Parliament had not granted this; he ordered the prisoner to be released by issuing habeas corpus.[36] In *R. (Garde)* v. *Strickland*, the court in strong terms asserted its power and duty to decide whether or not a state of war existed which justified the application of martial law, holding also that, so long as that state existed, no court had jurisdiction to inquire into the conduct of the army commander in repressing rebellion.[37] In *Higgins* v. *Willis*, in which an action was brought for wrongful destruction of a civilian's house, the court declared that the plaintiff had a right to have his case against the military decided by the courts as soon as the state of war had ceased.[38]

In the only decision by the House of Lords, *Re Clifford and O'Sullivan*, on facts similar to those in *R.* v. *Allen* it was held that the courts could not by issuing a writ of prohibition review the proceedings of a military tribunal set up under a proclamation of martial law.[39] This decision turned on the technical scope of the writ of prohibition, which was at that time considered to be available only against inferior bodies exercising judicial functions.[40] The House of Lords regarded the military tribunal in question, which was not a regularly constituted court-martial, as merely an advisory committee of officers to assist the commander-in-chief; moreover its duties had already been completed. The House expressly refrained from discussing the merits of other remedies that might be available, for example, a writ of habeas corpus. It followed that the army's decision to take the life of a citizen did not become subject to judicial control merely because an informal hearing had been given to the civilian by a military tribunal.

Position of the courts after martial law ends

After termination of the state of martial law, the courts have jurisdiction to review the legality of acts committed during the period of martial law. It is not possible to state with any certainty what standards will be applied by the courts in respect either of criminal or civil liability. First, there is no doubt that at common law many acts of the army which are necessary for dealing with civil war and insurrection will be justified; nor would there be liability at common law for damage to person or property inflicted accidentally in the course of

---

[35] [1921] 2 I.R. 241. For Cabinet discussion of martial law in Ireland, see T. Jones, *Whitehall Diary*, vol. 3, pt. I.
[36] [1921] 1 I.R. 265, criticised in Heuston, *Essays*, p. 158.
[37] [1921] 2 I.R. 317.
[38] [1921] 2 I.R. 386.
[39] [1921] 2 A.C. 570.
[40] Ch. 35.

actual fighting.[41] But what is not clear is whether the test should be that of strict necessity or merely *bona fide* belief in the necessity of the action, nor whether a stricter standard may be required in the case of some acts than others, nor where the burden of proof should lie. Secondly, there is uncertainty as to the legal effect of superior orders.[42] Thirdly, in the past it was usual after martial law for an Act of Indemnity to be passed giving retrospective protection to the armed forces. On the basis of *Wright* v. *Fitzgerald*[43] it would seem that in interpreting an Indemnity Act, the courts presume that Parliament does not intend to indemnify a defendant for merely wanton or cruel acts not justified by the necessities of the situation, but the extent of protection depends on the terms of the Indemnity Act, which may be both explicit and very wide.[44]

During the two world wars, the civil and criminal courts continued to function in Great Britain although their operation was subject to statutory restrictions. No state of martial law was declared. The Defence of the Realm Act 1914 did however authorise for a few months the trial of civilians by court-martial for offences against defence regulations. The Emergency Powers (Defence) (No. 2) Act 1940, passed under the threat of imminent invasion, gave authority for a system of special war zone courts to exercise criminal jurisdiction if, on account of military action, criminal justice had to be more speedily administered than in the ordinary courts. Such courts were never required to sit. In Northern Ireland since 1968, the ordinary civil and criminal courts have continued to function, although in dealing with terrorist offences the powers and procedures of the criminal courts have been much amended.[45]

B. Emergency powers in peace and war

While the Crown has some emergency powers under the prerogative, particularly in time of war or invasion, these powers are generally too uncertain for the government to rely on them.[1] During the two world wars, Parliament conferred exceptional powers on the executive for the conduct of the war and the maintenance of civilian life. During time of peace there is permanent statutory authority by which a state of emergency may be declared, and permanent machinery exists in the Civil Contingencies Unit of the Cabinet Office for enabling the government to respond rapidly in emergency situations, if necessary by the activation of regional emergency committees throughout the country.[2]

Emergency Powers Acts 1920 and 1964[3]

By the Emergency Powers Act 1920, as amended in 1964, a wide power to

---

[41] *Burmah Oil Co.* v. *Lord Advocate* [1965] A.C. 75; and ch. 13 C.

[42] Ch. 23.

[43] (1798) 27 St. Tr. 765, discussed by P. O' Higgins (1962) 25 M. L.R. 413.

[44] See the notorious example in *Phillips* v. *Eyre* (1870) L.R. 6 Q.B. 1 and *cf.* Indemnity Act 1920.

[45] N.I. (Emergency Provisions) Act 1978.

[1] Ch. 13 C.

[2] H.C. Deb., 15 Jan. 1979, col. 1318.

[3] G. S. Morris [1979] P.L. 317; K. Jeffery and P. Hennessy, *States of Emergency: British Governments and Strikebreaking since 1919*.

govern in emergency by means of statutory regulations is conferred on the executive, subject to the safeguard of parliamentary control. This power arises only when a state of emergency has been declared by royal proclamation. A proclamation of emergency may be issued if at any time it appears to the Crown that there have occurred, or are about to occur, events of such a nature as to be calculated to deprive the community, or any substantial part of it, of the essentials of life by interfering with the supply and distribution of food, water, fuel or light, or with the means of locomotion. Such events might include a strike in one or more major public utilities or industries, natural disasters or a serious nuclear accident. A proclamation can remain in force only for one month, though the emergency may be prolonged by the issue of a fresh proclamation. The proclamation must be forthwith communicated to Parliament. If Parliament is not sitting, it must be summoned to meet within five days.

So long as a proclamation is in force, regulations may be made by Order in Council for securing the essentials of life to the community. Such powers may be conferred on government departments, the armed forces and the police as may be deemed necessary for preserving peace or for securing and regulating the supply and distribution of necessities for maintaining the means of transport, 'and for any other purposes essential to the public safety and the life of the community' (1920 Act, section 2(1)). But the regulations may not impose compulsory military service or industrial conscription, nor make it an offence for anyone to take part in a strike or peacefully to persuade others to do so. Regulations may provide for the trial, by courts of summary jurisdiction, of persons guilty of offences against the regulations, subject to maximum penalties; but existing procedure in criminal cases may not be altered and no right to punish by fine or imprisonment without trial may be conferred. The regulations must be laid before Parliament and expire after seven days unless a resolution is passed by both Houses providing for their continuance.

The effectiveness of the Act was fully tested only on the occasion of the General Strike of 1926. Since 1945, proclamations of emergency have been issued on the occasion of major strikes by dockers, merchant seamen, miners and power workers. States of emergency were declared on five occasions by the Conservative government between 1970 and 1974. Whenever an emergency is declared, a complete set of emergency regulations is issued, whether or not it is expected that they will need to be used. It was under such regulations during the coal miners' strike and power crisis in 1972 that the use of electricity was severely controlled.[4] The Energy Act 1976 now provides alternative machinery for requiring energy to be conserved during an actual or threatened emergency affecting fuel or electricity supplies.[5]

The Emergency Powers Act 1964, section 2, gave permanent force to defence regulations originating in the second world war that enable members of the armed forces by order of the Defence Council, to be temporarily employed in agriculture or in 'urgent work of national importance'. This power has en-

---

[4]   For debates on emergency regulations, see *e.g.* H.C. Deb., 14 Feb. 1972, col. 33; 8 Aug. 1972, col. 1580; 15 Nov. 1973, col. 680.

[5]   And see Civil Aviation Act 1982, ss. 62, 63.

abled the government to require the armed forces to maintain essential services and public utilities which have been interrupted by strikes, notably during the firemen's strike in the winter of 1977–8 and the prison officers' strike in 1980.[6] The armed forces are never a satisfactory substitute for the workers on strike, but their work may reduce the impact of the strike upon the community.[7] The police have also been used for similar purposes, for example to provide emergency ambulance services.[8]

Emergency powers in time of war

Before the mid 19th century, it was the practice in times of national danger to pass what were often known as Habeas Corpus Suspension Acts.[9] Such Acts took various forms. Some prevented the use of habeas corpus for securing speedy trial or the right to bail in the case of persons charged with treason or other offences. Others conferred upon the executive wide powers of arrest and detention which would not normally have been acceptable. After the danger was over, it was often the practice to pass an Indemnity Act to protect officials retrospectively from liability for illegal acts which they might have committed. During the two world wars, habeas corpus was not suspended but extremely wide powers were conferred on the executive. The Defence of the Realm Acts 1914–5 empowered the Crown to make regulations by Order in Council for securing the public safety or for the defence of the realm. In *R.* v. *Halliday, ex parte Zadig* the House of Lords held that this general power was wide enough to support a regulation authorising the Secretary of State to detain persons without trial on the grounds of their hostile origins or associations.[10] Dissenting, Lord Shaw of Dunfermline declined to infer from the delegation of a general power to make regulations for public safety and defence that a man could be detained without trial and without being accused of any offence.

Wide however as were the powers of the executive, it was still possible to challenge defence regulations in the courts.

In *Attorney-General* v. *Wilts United Dairies Ltd*[11] an attempt by the Food Controller to impose a charge of two pence a gallon as a condition of issuing licences for the supply of milk was held invalid, on the ground that the Food Controller's power under a defence regulation to regulate the supply of milk did not confer power to impose charges upon the subject. Doubt was also expressed whether a regulation conferring such a power would have been within the general power to make regulations for the public safety or the defence of the realm.

In *Chester* v. *Bateson*[12] a defence regulation empowered the Minister of Munitions to declare an area in which munitions were manufactured to be a special area. The intended effect of such a declaration was to prevent any person without the consent of the minister from taking proceedings to recover possession of any dwellinghouse in the area, if a munition worker was living in it and duly paying rent. It was held that Par-

---

6 And see Imprisonment (Temporary Provisions) Act 1980.
7 C. Whelan (1979) 8 I.L.J. 222.
8 G.S. Morris (1980) 9 I.L.J. 1.
9 Dicey, pp. 229–37.
10 [1917] A.C. 260.
11 (1921) 37 T.L.R. 884; Wilson, *Cases*, p. 389.
12 [1920] 1 K.B. 829; Wilson, *Cases*, p. 387.

liament had not deliberately deprived the citizen of access to the courts and that the regulation was invalid, since it could not be shown to be a necessary or even reasonable way of securing the public safety or the defence of the realm.

Such decisions help to explain why it was considered necessary after the war to pass the wide Indemnity Act 1920 and a separate Act relating to illegal charges, the War Charges Validity Act 1925.

When war was declared in 1939, the Emergency Powers (Defence) Act 1939 empowered the making of regulations by Order in Council which appeared necessary or expedient for the public safety, the defence of the realm, the maintenance of public order, the efficient prosecution of any war in which His Majesty might be engaged and the maintenance of supplies and services essential for the life of the community. There followed a list of particular purposes for which regulations could be made, including the detention of persons in the interests of public safety or the defence of the realm. To avoid another *Wilts United Dairies* case, the Treasury was empowered to impose charges in connection with any scheme of control under Defence Regulations. Treasury regulations imposing charges required confirmation by an affirmative resolution of the House of Commons. Other regulations had to be laid before Parliament after they were made and could be annulled by negative resolution within 28 days.[13] Compulsory military service was imposed by separate National Service Acts and compulsory direction of labour to essential war work was authorised by the Emergency Powers (Defence) (No. 2) Act 1940.

Although access to the courts was not barred, the scope for judicial review of executive action was limited. Thus the courts could not consider whether a particular regulation was necessary or expedient for the purposes of the Act which authorised it.[14] The court could, however, hold an act to be illegal as being not authorised by the regulation relied upon to justify it.[15]

Special problems of judicial control arose in relation to the power of the executive to authorise detention without trial in the interests of public safety or the defence of the realm. Under Defence Regulation 18B, the Home Secretary was empowered to detain those whom he had reasonable cause to believe came within specified categories (including persons of hostile origin or association) and over whom it was necessary to exercise control. Persons detained could make objections to an advisory committee appointed by the Home Secretary. The Home Secretary had to report monthly to Parliament on the number of persons detained and the number of cases in which he had not followed the advice of the committee. It was open to a detainee to apply for habeas corpus, but such applications had little chance of success in view of the decision of the House of Lords in *Liversidge* v. *Anderson*.[16] In spite of a powerful dissenting judgement by Lord Atkin, the House took the view that the power to detain could not be controlled by the courts, if only because considerations of security

---

13 Ch. 33.
14 *R.* v. *Comptroller-General of Patents, ex p. Bayer Products* [1941] 2 K.B. 306. See also *Pollok School* v. *Glasgow Town Clerk* 1946 S.C. 373.
15 *E.g. Fowler & Co. (Leeds) Ltd* v. *Duncan* [1941] Ch. 450.
16 [1942] A.C. 206; and see C. K. Allen (1942) 58 L.Q.R. 232 and R. F. V. Heuston (1970) 86 L.Q.R. 33.

forbade proof of the evidence upon which detention was ordered. The words 'had reasonable cause to believe' only meant that the Home Secretary must have a belief which in his mind was reasonable. The courts would not enquire into the grounds for his belief, although apparently they might examine positive evidence of *mala fides* or mistaken identity.[17] Stress was laid upon the responsibility of the Home Secretary to Parliament. In only one case did a person who had been detained under the regulation secure his release by habeas corpus proceedings. His detention having been ordered on the ground that he was connected with a fascist organisation, he was wrongly informed that the order had been made on the ground of his being of hostile origins and association. The Divisional Court ordered his release, but the Home Secretary thereupon made a new order for his detention.[18]

Emergency powers since 1945

Although the Emergency Powers (Defence) Acts 1939–40 expired in 1946, post-war conditions did not permit all war-time controls to be ended, in particular rationing schemes and the control of industry. Economic difficulties in the late 1940s caused the Labour government to retain and even extend its powers under a series of Supplies and Services Acts.[19] These Acts authorised the government to make regulations to maintain and control essential supplies and services for broad economic and social purposes, but in fact these powers were little used. The Land Powers (Defence) Act 1958 replaced the Defence Regulations regarding the requisitioning of land and made permanent provision for the use of land for military purposes. Under the Emergency Laws (Re-enactment and Repeals) Act 1964, certain powers were made permanent, principally those dealing with the control of the terms of consumer credit transactions. It is curious that the present power of the Department of Trade to control imports into and exports from the United Kingdom still derives from temporary legislation that was enacted when war was declared in September 1939.[20]

C. Prevention of Terrorism (Temporary Provisions) Act 1984

Special powers to deal with threats to security have long been known in Northern Ireland. It was under the Civil Authorities (Special Powers) Act 1922 passed by the Northern Ireland Parliament that internment of suspected terrorists was introduced in 1971.[1] That Act was eventually replaced by the

---

[17] Lord Wright at 261. The majority decision in *Liversidge* v. *Anderson* cannot now be relied on as an authority, either on the point of construction or in its declaration of legal principle: *R.* v. *Home Secretary, ex p. Khawaja* [1984] A.C. 74, 110 (Lord Scarman) and see *e.g. Ridge* v. *Baldwin* [1964] A.C. 40, 73 (Lord Reid).

[18] *R.* v. *Home Secretary, ex p. Budd* [1942] 2 K.B. 14; *The Times*, 28 May 1941.

[19] *E.g.* Supplies and Services (Extended Purposes) Act 1947.

[20] Imports, Exports and Customs Powers (Defence) Act 1939; *cf. Willcock* v. *Muckle* [1951] 2 K.B. 844.

[1] For criticism of the 1922 Act, see Report of a Commission of Inquiry appointed by the National Council for Civil Liberties, 1936. See also H. Calvert, *Constitutional Law in Northern Ireland*, ch. 20 and *Emergency powers: a fresh start* (Fabian Tract 416), 1972.

Northern Ireland (Emergency Provisions) Act passed at Westminster in 1973, amended in 1975 and re–enacted in 1978.[2] It was only when serious bomb attacks were made by the IRA in Birmingham in 1974 that Parliament within a few hours passed the Prevention of Terrorism (Temporary Provisions) Act 1974 to give additional powers to the police and the government for dealing in Great Britain with suspected terrorists. The 1974 Act was re-enacted in 1976, after fuller consideration from Parliament than had been given to it in 1974.[3] A detailed review of the operation of the 1976 Act was undertaken in 1978 by Lord Shackleton and again in 1983 by Lord Jellicoe,[4] and the Act was re–enacted with modifications in 1984.

Part I of the 1984 Act restricts the freedom of association in Great Britain, making it an offence to belong to, collect money or invite support for, or to arrange or to speak to a meeting in support of, any proscribed organisation (section 1). The Act itself proscribes the IRA and the Irish National Liberation Army, but the Home Secretary may by order proscribe any other organisation that appears to him to be concerned in promoting or encouraging terrorism that is occurring in the United Kingdom and connected with affairs in Northern Ireland.[5] It is an offence to wear in public any item of dress or to display any article (for example, a badge) demonstrating support for a proscribed organisation (section 2).

Part II restricts the freedom of movement within the United Kingdom by authorising the Secretary of State to issue exclusion orders to those suspected of being concerned in the commission or instigation of terrorist acts. The Secretary of State may use these powers in such way as appears to him expedient to prevent acts of terrorism 'designed to influence public opinion or Government policy with respect to affairs in Northern Ireland' (section 3(1),(6)). An exclusion order may (a) prohibit persons from being in or entering Great Britain (but such an order may not be made against a British citizen who at the time is ordinarily resident in Great Britain and has been so resident for the preceding three years); (b) prohibit persons from being in or entering Northern Ireland (subject to a restriction similar to that in (a) in the case of British citizens ordinarily resident in Northern Ireland); and (c) prohibit any person who is not a British citizen from being in or entering the United Kingdom (sections 4–6). Where an exclusion order is served on a person, he may within 7 days submit written representations to the Secretary of State;[6] such representations are referred by the Secretary of State to a person nominated to act as an adviser (section 7). The adviser grants an interview to the person excluded if he requests one, but the final decision rests with the Secretary of State. An exclusion order requires the person named to be removed from Great

---

[2] The 1973 Act was preceded by the Diplock Report, Cmnd 5185, 1972 and the N.I. (Emergency Provisions) Amendment Act 1975 by the Gardiner Report, Cmnd 5847, 1975; Wilson, *Cases*, pp. 749–84.

[3] Supperstone, *op. cit.*, ch. 10.

[4] Cmnd 7324, 1978; Cmnd 8803, 1983. And see D. Bonner [1983] P.L. 224; C. P. Walker (1983) 46 M.L.R. 484.

[5] By s.14(1), 'terrorism' means the use of violence for political ends, and includes any use of violence for the purpose of putting the public or any section of the public in fear.

[6] When he is outside the United Kingdom, the period is 14 days: 1984 Act, s. 7.

Britain, Northern Ireland or the United Kingdom as the case may be (section 8). An exclusion order may be revoked at any time by the Secretary of State, and if not revoked earlier it expires after 3 years (when a fresh order may if necessary be made).

Under Part III of the Act, it is an offence to solicit, receive or make contributions for the support of acts of terrorism connected with Northern Ireland affairs (section 10). It is an offence to withhold information from the police which might be of material assistance in preventing such terrorist acts or in securing the arrest or conviction of any other person for such acts (section 11). Under Part IV of the Act, which applies to acts of terrorism connected with Northern Ireland and also terrorist acts in general (but not to terrorist acts connected solely with the United Kingdom or with parts of Great Britain), all persons entering or leaving Great Britain and Northern Ireland may be searched and examined with a view to determining whether they are concerned with such terrorism or are subject to an exclusion order (section 13). By section 12, a constable may arrest without warrant a person reasonably suspected of being (a) guilty of offences against the Act; (b) concerned in the commission or preparation of acts of terrorism; or (c) subject to an exclusion order. Such a person may be detained in right of the arrest for not more than 48 hours, but the Secretary of State may extend the detention for up to a further 5 days. A detained person need not be brought before a court. Thus the police may arrest on reasonable suspicion of terrorist involvement without there being suspicion of specific offences; the extension of detention for up to 7 days in all enables the police to make further investigations before deciding whether to charge a suspect.

The life of the 1984 Act is limited to 5 years, subject within that time to annual renewal by the Home Secretary with the approval of Parliament. In his review of the 1976 Act, Lord Jellicoe in 1983 concluded that if the legislation effectively reduced terrorism, it should be continued for as long as a substantial terrorist threat remains, but it must not make unacceptable inroads into civil liberties, and there must be safeguards to minimise scope for abuse.[7] Between 1974 and 1982, 5,555 people were detained under the Act in Great Britain, 89 per cent of whom were released without further action being taken, whether in the form of exclusion orders or criminal charges. The use of the Act in Great Britain fell sharply from a yearly average of 900 detained in 1975–9 to a yearly average of 250 in 1981–2. Between 1979 and 1982, 459 extensions of detention beyond 48 hours were granted.[8] Without these powers, Lord Jellicoe considered that the police would be seriously handicapped in dealing with terrorists, but he recommended that detainees should have access to legal advice and the right to communicate news of their detention to relatives or friends.[9]

The making of exclusion orders is the most extreme of the Act's powers in its effect on civil liberties. In 1974–82, 292 exclusion orders were made in a few cases excluding from Great Britain persons who had been resident there

---

[7] Cmnd 8803, 1983, ch. 1.
[8] Cmnd 8803, ch. 3 and annex D.
[9] See now the Police and Criminal Evidence Act 1984, part V; p. 484 *ante*.

for as much as 19 years.[10] But, in Lord Jellicoe's view, the exclusion system had materially contributed to public safety in the United Kingdom. The 1984 Act kept exclusion orders in being, while moderating the severity of the powers.

In view of the limited life of the Act and the need for annual renewal, it is still justifiable to consider the Act in the context of emergency powers, but events such as the Harrod's bombing in London in December 1983 mean that there is no immediate prospect of the Act being brought to an end. Since there appears to be little scope for judicial protection of those against whom the Act is applied,[11] political vigilance continues to be necessary in respect of these exceptional powers.

---

[10]   Cmnd 8803, 1983, pp. 64, 72; H.C. 230 (1982–3), p. 12; D. Bonner [1982] P. L. 262; C. P. Walker [1983] P.L. 537.

[11]   *Ex p. Lynch* [1980] N.I.L.R. 126; W. Finnie (1982) 45 M.L.R. 215. And see *McVeigh* v. *UK* (1981) 5 E.H.R.R. 71.

Chapter 30

State security

The maintenance of the security of the state is a primary duty of the government. But more than many other tasks of government, it may require to be performed under conditions of continuing secrecy and it is difficult to devise appropriate measures of democratic control. Today state security or more commonly national security is mentioned in over 30 statutes, nearly always in provisions which exclude security issues from public knowledge or scrutiny. Thus the Parliamentary Commissioner may not investigate action taken with the authority of the Secretary of State for the purposes of protecting the security of the state[1] and under the Immigration Act 1971, section 15(3), an alien who is deported on the ground that his deportation is in the interests of national security has not the usual right to appeal to a tribunal against the deportation order.[2] Under such legislation, a minister commonly has conclusive power to determine whether action was taken on grounds of national security.[3] The common law may at first sight appear to take little account of state necessity.[4] However, national security is a matter to which the courts in fact attach considerable importance.[5] This does not mean that the judges should abandon all their power to decide at the mere mention by an official of national security.[6] There is also the problem of how to secure parliamentary oversight of security measures. Since 1979, the Defence Committee of the House of Commons has reviewed aspects of state security, but parliamentary committees have been advised by the government not to inquire into the Security Service.[7]

This chapter examines the nature of the Security Service, security procedures applicable to the civil service, the Official Secrets Acts, the system of

---

[1] Parliamentary Commissioner Act 1967, sch. 3, para. 5. And see *e.g.* Contempt of Court Act 1981, s.10; Civil Aviation Act 1982, ss. 6, 67.

[2] Ch. 25 B.

[3] *E.g.* Race Relations Act 1976, ss. 42, 69(2).

[4] *Entick* v. *Carrington* (1765) 19 St. Tr. 1030.

[5] *E.g. Conway* v. *Rimmer* [1968] A.C. 910 at 955, 993; *A.-G.* v. *Jonathan Cape Ltd* [1976] Q.B. 752,768.

[6] *Chandler* v. *DPP* [1964] A.C. 763, 811. *Cf.* the *Hosenball* case, p. 457 *ante.*

[7] See H.C. 773 (1979–80); H.C. 242 (1982–3); H.C. Deb., 12 May 1983, col. 444 (W.A.).

'D' notices and the law relating to telephone tapping. All these topics are important in relation to state security; some of them, notably the Official Secrets Acts and telephone tapping, also have a wider significance.

The Security Service[8]

The Security Service is not established by statute[9] nor is it recognised by common law. Thus there is no mention of its existence in the Official Secrets Acts, which create offences relating to espionage. But in the year 1983–4, its operations were estimated to cost £71 million.[10] The cardinal principle of operations is that the Service is to be used solely for the purpose of the defence of the realm. It has been said that the Service does not exist to pry into any man's private conduct or business affairs nor into his political opinions except in so far as they are subversive, *i.e.* they would contemplate the overthrow of the government by unlawful means.[11] The members of the Service have no special powers of arrest or search such as the police have; in the eyes of the law they are ordinary citizens with no powers greater than anyone else. The Service is essentially an expert organisation charged with the task of countering espionage, subversion and sabotage. The absence of special powers and the small size of the Service have made essential close co-operation with the police forces, in particular with the Special Branch of the Metropolitan Police and other forces.[12] If, for example, a search warrant is required by the Security Service, it is granted to a constable.

At one time there was much misapprehension about ministerial responsibility for this Service. Since its purpose is the defence of the realm, it might have been supposed that responsibility should lie with the Secretary of State for Defence. Lord Denning's report in 1963 clarified the position. Ultimate responsibility is borne by the Prime Minister, to whom parliamentary questions about security are addressed and who is advised on security matters by the Secretary to the Cabinet.[13] But since 1952 the Security Service has been the primary responsibility of the Home Secretary, since its functions are closely allied to the responsibility of the Home Office in defending the realm against subversive activities and preserving law and order. There is a well-established convention that ministers 'do not concern themselves with the detailed information which may be obtained by the Security Services in particular cases, but are furnished with such information only as may be necessary for the determination of any issue on which guidance is sought'.[14] In 1979, during a debate that followed the disclosure that Anthony Blunt had been a Russian

---

8   See D. G. T. Williams, *Not in the Public Interest*, Pt. 2, and T. Bunyan, *The Political Police in Britain*, chs. 3, 4. The next two paragraphs are based mainly on Lord Denning's report into the Profumo affair, Cmnd 2152, 1963, Pt. II. And see Wilson, *Cases*, p. 681.

9   The Civil List and Secret Service Money Act 1782, ss. 24–9, repealed in 1967, authorised payments for the secret service. For the accounting procedure, see Epitome of Reports from the Committees of Public Accounts 1857–1937, H.C. 154 (1938), p. 203.

10   Supply Estimates for 1983–4, H.C. 237–II (1982–3).

11   *Cf.* p. 551, *ante.*

12   See H.C. Deb., 24 May 1978, col. 1715 and (1979) 2 *State Research* 121.

13   H. Wilson, *The Labour Government 1964–70*, p. 481.

14   Lord Denning's report, p. 80.

spy and had been granted immunity from prosecution by the Attorney-General in 1964, the Prime Minister stated that there was no need to change the relationship between the Security Service and ministers outlined in the Denning report; but she stressed the need for the Director-General of the Service to report to the Home Secretary and if necessary to the Prime Minister when information was secured indicating that a minister or senior public servant was a security risk.[15]

In 1964 there was set up by the Prime Minister the Security Commission, which at the Prime Minister's request investigates and reports upon the circumstances in which a breach of security is known to have occurred in the public service or there is good reason to believe that it has occurred. When a prosecution for breach of the Official Secrets Acts has been completed, the commission may examine any failure of departmental security procedures, and advise whether any change is desirable. Exceptionally, after two ministers resigned in 1973 because of acts of private immorality, the commission was asked to consider whether security had been endangered by these events.[16] The chairman of the commission is a judge and it may also include retired members of the civil service, the armed forces and the diplomatic service. In 1982, the commission completed a full review of security procedures in the public service and in 1983 reported on the security implications of the conviction for spying of a member of the staff at Government Communications Headquarters, Cheltenham.[17]

Security procedures in the civil service[18]

In chapter 15, a brief account was given of the two main procedures (the purge procedure and the positive vetting procedure) which exist to ensure the reliability of those whose work in the civil service is likely to bring them into contact with matters affecting state security. While the positive vetting procedure may be applied to candidates for appointment to the rank of under-secretary and above, there are many less senior appointments whose work may include handling particularly secret information (for example, clerks in the Ministry of Defence, typists in the Cabinet Office, architects working on defence installations). All members of the diplomatic service and of the police Special Branch are also subject to positive vetting.

In 1956, a conference of Privy Councillors reported that the main risk to state security came not from espionage by the professional agents of foreign powers but from communists and others subject to communist influence. The fact that a public servant was a communist not only barred his employment on secret duties but might also in some departments affect his chances of promotion. Close relationships with communist sympathisers (for example, through marriage) might justify removal from secret work. Similar safeguards were also needed in respect of persons outside government employment who

---

15 H.C. Deb., 21 Nov. 1979, col. 402.
16 Cmnd 5367, 1973.
17 Cmnd 8540, 1982; Cmnd 8876, 1983.
18 D. C. Jackson (1957) 20 M.L.R. 364; M. R. Joelson [1963] P.L. 51; Street, *Freedom, Individual and the Law*, ch. 9; Wilson, *Cases*, pp. 89–98.

were employed by government contractors on secret work.[19] In 1961, the report of the Radcliffe committee on security procedures in the public service viewed the position differently: it was not the activities of the Communist party in Great Britain which were the main threat to security but the intelligence and espionage services of the Soviet bloc. These services were prepared to take advantage of any form of sympathy, weakness or compulsion and did not select their instruments either necessarily or essentially on ideological grounds.[20] The committee recommended that the purge procedure and the possibility of an appeal should be extended to officers in civil service trade unions who were denied access to defence establishments or barred by a department from taking part in industrial negotiation with the department. In 1982, the Security Commission considered that the external threat from the Soviet bloc was undiminished, but that the internal threat from subversive groups of the extreme left and extreme right (mainly the former) had increased. These groups wished to overthrow democratic government by violent and other unconstitutional means, and might seek to publish information that would be injurious to national interests. The growth of computers also posed new security problems.[21]

The procedures which exist to ensure that unreliable individuals are not employed on work that involves access to secrets of importance to security are essentially not judicial procedures. They may be criticised for not providing the individual with the safeguards appropriate to judicial proceedings, in which a precise charge must be formulated and all the evidence given by witnesses in the presence of the individual and lawyers representing him.[22] If civil servants relied for their protection on these procedures alone, they would indeed be vulnerable to the malicious half-truths and gossip that typify a witch-hunt. The nature of the political background in Britain may help to explain why these administrative procedures serve their purpose without apparently leading to innumerable acts of injustice.[23] In this context, it is not possible to rely upon conviction and punishment for a specific offence after the event. Procedures such as positive vetting are thus intended to prevent breaches of security occurring. In 1983, the Security Commission recommended the introduction of polygraph screening on a trial basis for counter-intelligence examinations.[24]

In 1984, the government decided that the intelligence and monitoring operations performed by the Government Communications Headquarters at Cheltenham were so vital to national security that those working there should lose the statutory rights conferred on civil servants by the Employment Protection (Consolidation) Act 1978 and should be barred by new conditions of service from membership of a trade union. A similar position already applied to those working in M.I.5 and M.I.6. Despite much criticism of the govern-

19   Cmnd 9715, 1956. The purge procedure was extended to include the staff of government contractors, after a solicitor employed by ICI had been dismissed on request of the government: see H.L. Deb., 21 Jun. 1956, col. 1226.
20   Cmnd 1681, 1962.
21   Cmnd 8540, 1982.
22   Street, *op. cit.*, pp. 236–47. For comparable difficulties in deportation appeals involving national security, see p. 456 *ante*.
23   *Cf.* M. R. Joelson [1963] P.L. 51, 67–71.
24   Cmnd 8876, 1983. And see H.C. 242 (1982–3).

ment's decision, the great majority of staff at Cheltenham accepted the new conditions of service as well as a payment of £1,000 each.[25]

The Official Secrets Acts 1911–39[26]
The Official Secrets Acts 1911–39 serve two distinct but related purposes:

(*a*) to protect the interests of the state against espionage and other activities which might be useful to an enemy and therefore injurious to state security;
(*b*) to guard against the unauthorised disclosure of information which is held by servants of the state in their official capacity, whether or not the information has any direct reference to state security as such. The legal sanctions under (*b*) help to support the sanctions against espionage, since it may in a particular case be possible to prove unauthorised disclosure of information without being able to prove elements of espionage. They also serve to protect the corridors of power against disclosure of information and publicity which a government might find politically embarrassing or inconvenient. The Official Secrets Act 1911, on which later Acts have built, was passed rapidly through Parliament in circumstances in which ministers emphasised purpose (*a*) as the primary object of the Act and did not mention purpose (*b*). In 1972, the Franks committee on section 2 of the 1911 Act commented that new legislation should be introduced to separate the espionage laws from the general protection of official information.[27]

Section 1(1) of the 1911 Act creates a group of offences, mainly connected with espionage. It is an offence, punishable with 14 years' imprisonment,

if any person *for any purpose prejudicial to the safety or interests of the State* –
(*a*) approaches, inspects, passes over or is in the neighbourhood of, or enters any prohibited place within the meaning of this Act; or
(*b*) makes any sketch, plan, model, or note which . . . might be or is intended to be directly or indirectly useful to an enemy; or
(*c*) obtains, collects, records, or publishes or communicates to any other person any secret official code word or any sketch, plan, model, article, or note, or other document or information which . . . might be or is intended to be directly or indirectly useful to an enemy.

The italicised phrase caused difficulties when charges under section 1 were brought following a non-violent political demonstration against an RAF base, in *Chandler* v. *DPP*.[28]

Anti-nuclear demonstrators sought to immobilise an RAF bomber base by sitting down on the runway. They were arrested as they approached the base and charged with conspiring to enter a prohibited place for a purpose prejudicial to the safety or interests of the state, contrary to section 1 of the 1911 Act. The trial judge refused to allow the accused to bring evidence to show that it would be beneficial to the United Kingdom if the government's nuclear policy were abandoned. For a variety of inter-locking reasons, the House of Lords unanimously upheld the conviction. The demonstrators ad-

---

25   H.C. Deb., 25 Jan. 1983, col. 917; 1 Mar. 1984, col. 387 and see p. 283 *ante*.
26   Williams, *Not in the Public Interest*, Pt. 1; Bailey, Harris and Jones, *Civil Liberties: Cases and Materials*, ch. 6.
27   Cmnd 5104, 1972; p. 569 *post*.
28   [1964] A.C. 763; Wilson, *Cases*, p. 713.

mittedly wished to obstruct the use of the airbase and it was immaterial that they believed that such obstruction would ultimately benefit the country. The offences created by the 1911 Act, section 1 were not confined to spying but included sabotage and other acts of physical interference.

This decision was criticised,[29] but it seems impossible to argue that Parliament intended a spy who had passed military secrets to a foreign power to be able to establish as a defence that his purpose in so doing was to force the British government to change its policies. The outcome in *Chandler's* case would have been different if the demonstrators' intention had merely been to hold a protest meeting on the road outside the air-base, since the prosecution would have had to establish that to protest about nuclear policy was itself an act prejudicial to the interests of the state. In *Chandler's* case, Lord Devlin alone stressed that it was for the jury to decide all questions of fact, including the issue of the accused's purpose and its likely effect on the interests of the state. During an official secrets trial in 1978, the judge (Mars-Jones J.) indicated that the use of section 1 in situations that fell short of spying and sabotage could be oppressive.[30]

Section 2 of the 1911 Act created a plethora of over 2,000 different offences related to the misuse of official information.[31] In particular, by section 2(1) it is an offence punishable by two years' imprisonment,

if any person having in his possession or control ... any document or information ... which has been entrusted in confidence to him by any person holding office under Her Majesty ... communicates the ... document or information to any person, other than a person to whom he is authorised to communicate it, or a person to whom it is in the interests of the State his duty to communicate it.

Other offences include the unauthorised retention of documents, failure to take reasonable care of documents and, under section 2(2), the receipt of documents or information in breach of the Act unless the recipient proves that the communication to him was contrary to his desire. Section 2 plainly extends to the disclosure of information which bears no relation to national security, for the language is wide enough to cover any information which anyone holding an office, however humble, under the Crown receives in confidence. Thus it would be a breach of this section if, without authority, a tax inspector revealed the details of an individual's tax return or a social security official disclosed internal rules on the payment of social security benefits. In the former instance, section 2 protects the individual's privacy from intrusion; in the latter instance, section 2 protects the official system from public knowledge and criticism.

For the purposes of the Official Secrets Acts, a policeman holds office under the Crown and his disclosure of police information relating to crime, even if it is of no particular public interest, may be an offence.[32] A journalist who

---

29 D. Thompson [1963] P.L. 201; *cf.* Smith and Hogan, p. 789.
30 A. Nichol [1979] Crim. L.R. 284; C. Aubrey, *Who's Watching You?*
31 Cmnd 5104, 1972, p. 14.
32 *Lewis* v. *Cattle* [1938] 2 K.B. 454. Staff of bodies such as the Atomic Energy Authority, the Post Office and British Telecommunications are deemed officers of the Crown for this purpose: Atomic Energy Act 1954, sch. 3; Post Office Act 1969, sch. 4, para. 21; British Telecommunications Act 1981, sch. 3, para. 17.

receives such information is also guilty of an offence, and so may be his colleagues to whom he passes on the information. Disclosure contrary to section 2 is an offence whether or not it is for a purpose prejudicial to essential state interests.[33] Civil servants and others subject to the Acts are required to sign declarations acknowledging their duty to observe the Acts both on entering their employment and on leaving it. Their duty continues after they have retired from the public service.

The draconian width of section 2, which has been well described as a 'catch-all', is mitigated in two ways. First, as with all offences under the Official Secrets Acts, the consent of the Attorney-General in England (or the Lord Advocate in Scotland) is necessary before any prosecution is brought.[34] Secondly, the authorisation which prevents disclosure of information being an offence can be wholly informal and may be implicit in the circumstances of disclosure. Ministers and many senior civil servants, by what is known as the practice of self-authorisation, are able to decide for themselves how much information to disclose, at least in matters relating to their own duties.[35] Thus, when an off the record briefing is given to a journalist (for example, to enable him to 'leak' the contents of a Bill before it is published in Parliament) no breach of the Official Secrets Acts has occurred. More than once it has been stressed that section 2 of the 1911 Act is not to be blamed for the secrecy which is maintained about the decision-making process in government, since at any time ministers could decide to adopt a more open approach.[36] Nonetheless the present form of the 1911 Act often presents journalists with a real difficulty in knowing what they may safely publish.

Other provisions of the Official Secrets Acts which may be briefly mentioned include section 7 of the 1920 Act, under which it is an offence to attempt to commit any offence under the Acts or to endeavour to persuade another person to commit such an offence, or to aid and abet or to do *any act preparatory* to the commission of such an offence.[37] Under the 1920 Act, section 8, a court may exclude the public from the trial of an offence under the Acts if the prosecution applies for this on the ground that the publication of evidence would be prejudicial to national safety. The accused and his lawyers may not be excluded and the sentence must be delivered in open court. It was formerly the law that refusal on demand by a police inspector to disclose the source of information obtained in breach of the Acts was itself an offence[38] but by the Official Secrets Act 1939 this special power of interrogation is restricted to cases covered by section 1 of the 1911 Act and, except in cases of urgency, the consent of the Secretary of State is required.

Reform of the Official Secrets Act 1911, section 2

The operation of the Official Secrets Act 1911, section 2, was examined closely by a committee chaired by Lord Franks which reported in 1972.[39] The com-

---

33 *R. v. Fell* [1963] Crim. L.R. 207.
34 Official Secrets Act 1911, s. 8.
35 Cmnd 5104, 1972, p. 14.
36 *E.g.* Cmnd 4089, 1969, p. 11; Cmnd 5104, 1972, ch. 5.
37 See *R. v. Oakes* [1959] 2 Q.B. 350 and *R v. Bingham* [1973] Q.B. 870.
38 *Lewis* v. *Cattle ante.*
39 Cmnd 5104, 1972; Wilson, *Cases*, pp. 455–69.

mittee had been appointed after, but not because of, an unsuccessful prosecution of the *Sunday Telegraph* for publishing Foreign Office documents
relating to the Labour government's policy towards the Nigerian civil war.[40]
The committee reported that the present law was unsatisfactory and that section 2 should be repealed. Instead, there should be a new Official Information
Act, to protect only certain forms of information, namely:

(*a*) classified information relating to defence or internal security, or to foreign
relations, or to the currency or to the reserves, the unauthorised disclosure of
which would cause serious injury to the interests of the nation;
(*b*) information likely to assist criminal activities or to impede law
enforcement;
(*c*) Cabinet documents (in the interests of collective responsibility)[41];
(*d*) information which has been entrusted to the government by a private individual or concern (for example, for tax or social security purposes or in a
census).

The requirement that information of the kind specified in (*a*) must be classified would make necessary a new official system of classification of documents
which, unlike the existing system, would have legal consequences. Offences
under the new Act were proposed to include the communication by a Crown
servant contrary to his official duty of information subject to the Act; the communication by any person of information of the kinds set out in (*a*), (*b*) and
(*c*) which he reasonably believes has reached him as a result of a breach of
the Act; and the use of official information of any kind for purposes of private
gain. Prosecutions under the Act would require the consent of the Attorney-
General or in certain cases (for example, the use of official information for
purposes of private gain) of the Director of Public Prosecutions.

The Franks committee therefore recommended that the law should be narrowed and that protection of official information by criminal sanctions should
continue only where the public interest clearly required this. By 1984, however, no reform of the Official Secrets Acts had taken place, although other
weaknesses in the law became evident during the so–called ABC trial in
1978.[42] The nature of such a reform cannot satisfactorily be separated from
broad questions of open government, in particular the need for extending public access to official information.[43] In 1979 the Conservative government introduced not a Freedom of Information Bill but a Protection of Official
Information Bill. This sought inter alia to give absolute protection to information regarding security and intelligence, regardless of whether that information was already available to the public.[44] However, the Bill was abandoned
by the government because of the severe political reaction to the disclosure
that Anthony Blunt had been a Russian spy, a disclosure which could have
been criminal if the Bill had been enacted.

---

[40]   See J. Aitken, *Officially Secret*.
[41]   *Cf.* ch. 14 A.
[42]   Note 30 *ante*.
[43]   For the Labour government's position, see Cmnd 7285, 1978 and Cmnd 7520, 1979. See also
D. Leigh, *The Frontiers of Secrecy*; J. Michael, *The Politics of Secrecy*; R. Delbridge and M. Smith
(ed.), *Consuming Secrets*; and, on the problem of disclosure by public employees, Y. Cripps
[1983] P.L. 600.
[44]   H.L. Deb., 5 Nov. 1979, col. 612; *cf.* Cmnd 7285, 1978, para. 31.

'D' notices[45]

The freedom of the press is restricted by the Official Secrets Acts, but on some matters of special importance to security the government cannot afford to rely merely on criminal sanctions imposed after the event of publication. The system of 'D' notices is a form of extra-legal censorship which rests on agreement and co-operation between the government and the press. A 'D' notice is a formal letter of warning or request, sent by the secretary of the Services, Press and Broadcasting Committee to newspaper editors, news editors in broadcasting, editors of periodicals concerned with defence information, and selected publishers. The object is to request a ban on publication of specified subjects which relate to defence or national security. The system is essentially voluntary, based on mutual trust and confidence, and there are no legal sanctions to enforce disregard of a notice. The committee's chairman is the Permanent Under–Secretary in the Ministry of Defence, but it contains more press representatives than civil servants. It approves the form and content of 'D'notices on the proposal of the government department concerned. The secretary of the committee plays a key role in advising editors on the interpretation of notices. The importance of his role was shown in 1967 when the *Daily Express* published a report that copies of private cables and telegrams sent overseas from the United Kingdom were regularly made available to the security authorities, a practice authorised by the Official Secrets Act 1920, section 4. The Prime Minister, Mr Wilson, claimed that this article was a breach of a 'D' notice. An investigation by three Privy Councillors established that this was not the case but that there had been misunderstandings to which the secretary of the committee had contributed.[46] The Defence Committee of the House of Commons reviewed the 'D' notice system in 1980, and concluded (with reservations) that 'D' notices should be maintained, despite sharp divisions within the press about the value of the scheme which, judged in legal terms, is manifestly imperfect and imprecise.[47]

Interception of communications

In 1957 controversy arose over the practice of telephone tapping when it was revealed that the Home Secretary had disclosed to the chairman of the Bar Council information obtained by police tapping of telephones in the course of investigations relating to the association of a barrister (Marrinan) with a known criminal (Billy Hill). A committee of Privy Councillors, the Birkett committee, was appointed to inquire into the powers and practice of the executive in intercepting communications.[48] The committee's conclusions on the law were accepted as the basis for official practice thereafter, but growing disquiet about telephone tapping led in 1979 to a judicial ruling on the matter and to subsequent proceedings under the European Convention on Human Rights.

---

[45] . Williams, *Not in the Public Interest*, ch. 4; Cmnd 3309, 1967; H.C. 773 (1979–80); Cmnd 8129, 1981.

[46] Cmnd 3309 and 3312 (1967); P. Hedley and C. Aynsley, *The D-notice Affair*. In 1967, Prime Minister Wilson rejected the finding that no breach of a 'D' notice had occurred but he later admitted that his handling of the affair was wrong: *The Labour Government 1964–70*, pp. 478–82, 530–4.

[47] H.C. 773 (1979–80); J. Jaconelli [1982] P.L. 37.

[48] Cmnd 283, 1957; Wilson, *Cases*, p. 673.

The Crown's monopoly of the postal service derives from the prerogative, but for many years a series of Post Office Acts has regulated the service. As far back as 1663, a royal proclamation forbade the opening of any letters or packets except with the direct warrant of the Secretary of State. Since at least that date, the Secretary of State (now the Home Secretary) has from time to time authorised the interception of letters. It is today a criminal offence for any officer of the Post Office to open a postal packet except, *inter alia*, 'in obedience to an express warrant in writing under the hand of a Secretary of State'.[49] While the legislation does not expressly empower the Secretary of State to authorise the opening of postal packets, it implies that such a power is known to the law.[50] The Birkett committee reported that at no time had it been suggested with any authority that the exercise of the power to intercept postal packets was unlawful. The committee found that the power was used mainly to assist in the detection of certain forms of crime and the serious evasion of customs duty. It was exceptionally used on the request of the Security Service where there was a major subversive or espionage activity that was likely to injure the national interest and the material likely to be obtained by interception would be of direct use in providing necessary information for the Security Service. Warrants were issued on the personal authority of the Home Secretary and were subject to regular review.

As regards telephone tapping, the Birkett committee's verdict was unpersuasive. The committee found that messages had been intercepted by the Post Office as controllers of the telephone service ever since the introduction of the telephone. Before 1937 the Post Office had acted on the view that the practice was not contrary to law and did not require the authority of the Secretary of State. In 1937, the Home Office expressed the opinion that the power to authorise the interception of letters and telegrams by warrant of a Secretary of State was wide enough to include the interception of telephone messages. After 1937, telephones were tapped only when expressly authorised by warrant of the Home Secretary, by analogy with the interception of mail. But the legal basis of telephone tapping remained obscure: was the power derived from the application of Crown prerogative to a new technology, or had the power been obliquely recognised by statute?[51] The Birkett report in 1957 reached a feeble conclusion: 'it is difficult to resist the view that if there is a lawful power to intercept communications in the form of letters and telegrams, then it is wide enough to cover telephone communications as well'.[52] But it was only in 1979 that the law on telephone tapping was reviewed by a court.

Malone, a London antique dealer who had been accused of handling stolen goods, sued the police for a declaration that the police acted unlawfully in tapping his telephone on the authority of a warrant from the Home Secretary. Malone claimed that the tapping had infringed his rights of property, privacy, and confidentiality and also the right to respect 'for his private and family life, his home and his correspondence' (European Convention on Human Rights, article 8). Megarry V.-C. dismissed the action, holding inter alia that Malone's rights under common law had not been infringed; there was

---

[49]   Post Office Act 1953, s. 58(1); Post Office Act 1969, sch. 4, para. 2.
[50]   *Cf.* Street, *Freedom, Individual and the Law*, p. 49.
[51]   See *A.-G.* v. *Edison Telephone Co.* (1880) 6 Q.B.D. 244.
[52]   Cmnd 283, 1957, p. 15.

in English law no right of privacy and no user of a telephone could assume that his conversations were confidential. Tapping by the Post Office could be carried out for the police without any breach of the law, and therefore no statutory or common law power was required to justify it. Malone could not rely on the European Convention on Human Rights since, as a treaty that had not been given domestic effect by legislation, the Convention was not justiciable in English courts. However, the judge examined a decision of the European Court of Human Rights on telephone tapping in Germany,[53] and concluded that telephone tapping 'is a subject which cries out for legislation'.[54]

The judge's plea for legislation fell on deaf ears so far as the government was concerned. In 1980, the government described and upheld the existing administrative arrangements for phone tapping,[55] but to allay concern asked Lord Diplock to monitor the procedures for interception of communications carried out on behalf of the police, the Customs and Excise and the Security Service. In his first report, Lord Diplock concluded that, on the basis of the principles observed by the Secretary of State in issuing warrants, and of individual cases which he had examined, the procedures were justified and caused the minimum of interference with the individual's rights of privacy.[56]

Since responsibility for the telephone service had been transferred from the Post Office to British Telecommunications, and since the government in 1984 was seeking to 'privatise' that undertaking, legislation was all the more necessary. In February 1984, the House of Lords amended the Telecommunications Bill (against the wishes of the government) to lay down in statutory form arrangements for authorising interception.[57] This amendment was later withdrawn when the government undertook to introduce legislation on the subject in the 1984–5 session of Parliament. Probably the most compelling reason why telephone tapping should be placed on a statutory basis is that under the European Convention of Human Rights, interference with a person's private life, home and correspondence is justifiable in the interests of national security, public safety and prevention of crime only if the interference is in accordance with the law, and that law provides adequate safeguards against abuse.[58]

53   *Klass* v. *Germany* (1978) 2 E.H.R.R. 24.
54   *Malone* v. *Metropolitan Police Commissioner* [1979] Ch. 344; C. P. Walker [1980] P.L. 184, V. Bevan [1980] P.L. 431.
55   Cmnd 7873, 1980.
56   Cmnd 8791, 1980.
57   H.L. Deb., 21 Feb. 1984, col. 632. And see H.C. Deb., 1 Apr. 1981, cols. 321–72.
58   Note 53 *ante*; *Malone* v. *UK* (1982) 5 E.H.R.R. 385. On 2 Aug. 1984 the European Court of Human Rights held in *Malone* v. *UK* that telephone tapping in Britain lacked adequate guarantees against abuse and that Malone's right to privacy under article 8 of the Convention had been violated.

Chapter 31

Protection of human rights

A. Legislation against discrimination

The classical freedoms of contract and property, which in legal theory all persons may equally enjoy, are inherently likely to produce substantial social and economic inequality. The freedom of property owners to dispose of their property to whom they please, the freedom of employers to decide whom to employ, the power of trade unions to decide whom to admit to membership, the freedom of individuals to decide with whom they wish to associate for social purposes – all these freedoms make it possible that less powerful groups are barred from access to opportunities which other groups freely enjoy. In some legal systems, the provisions of a written constitution have been used to redress the balance, for example the 14th amendment of the United States constitution, which provides that no state shall deny to any person within its jurisdiction the equal protection of the laws. In the United Kingdom, where this method of achieving public goals has not been adopted as a legal and political technique, selective use has been made of legislation to deal with some forms of discrimination. Of one form of discrimination against minorities, a House of Commons committee said in 1975:

Race discrimination and race prejudice are still widespread. The fact that much of the discrimination and prejudice is covert, negligent, or unintentional does not make this less harmful, and it is aggravated by growing lack of confidence among the ethnic communities, especially the young – the second generation non-immigrant population. Consequently there is a risk of the communities becoming permanently alienated.[1]

Only in exceptional circumstances did the common law provide protection for members of minority racial groups.[2] The harm that might be done to society by racial discrimination is considered to justify legislative intervention into areas of individual decision, particularly those which have a public or corporate dimension and do not concern purely private matters. The first legislation against racial discrimination was the Race Relations Act 1965, but this

---

[1]   Report of Select Committee on Race Relations and Immigration, H.C. 448–I (1974–5) xxiii.
[2]   *Constantine* v. *Imperial Hotels Ltd* [1944] K.B. 693; *Scala Ballroom (Wolverhampton) Ltd* v. *Ratcliffe* [1958] 3 All E.R. 220.

Act, even as strengthened and extended by the Race Relations Act 1968, provided only limited protection. The categories of individuals who benefited and the types of discrimination outlawed were narrow. The means of enforcement under the Act, which denied victims a direct right of access to the courts, were unsatisfactory.

While the 1968 Act succeeded in some of its purposes (for example, to prevent publication of advertisements offering houses or jobs to white persons only), the Act's limitations coupled with an increased need to promote better race relations provided the reason why a new Act was passed in 1976. During the same period the movement aimed at securing increased rights for women gathered momentum and this culminated in the Sex Discrimination Act 1975. This Act has many features in common with the Race Relations Act 1976.

Race Relations Act 1976[3]

Compared with the 1968 Act, the 1976 Act provided greater protection against racial discrimination, increased the powers of enforcement agencies and gave greater rights to individuals to take proceedings against those committing acts of discrimination. Discrimination in a direct form is stated to occur when one person treats another less favourably than he treats or would treat other persons on grounds of colour, race, nationality or ethnic or national origins (sections 1, 3). This extends the formula used in the 1968 Act to include discrimination based on nationality.[4] Religious discrimination is not in itself prohibited, but the decision of the House of Lords in *Mandla* v. *Dowell Lee*[5] established that the Act does protect Sikhs. Until *Mandla* there had been doubt whether the Sikhs should be regarded as a racial rather than simply a religious group.[6]

The 1976 Act substantially extended the concept of discrimination when it outlawed what is known as indirect discrimination. This occurs where a person acts in a manner not in itself overtly discriminatory but where the effect of that action, intentional or not, is to discriminate. Thus, in terms of the 1976 Act, a person may apply to another a requirement or condition which he applies or would apply equally to persons of different racial groups (defined by reference to colour, race, nationality or ethnic or national origins) and which therefore does not directly or overtly discriminate. Such action becomes discrimination, however, when the condition imposed is such that the proportion of persons of the same racial group who can comply with it is considerably smaller than the proportion of other persons who can comply; and when the condition is not justifiable irrespective of racial considerations[7] and has a det-

---

3 For fuller accounts see I. A. Macdonald, *Race Relations and the New Law* and L. Lustgarten, *Legal Control of Racial Discrimination* (which concentrates on discrimination in employment). Works dealing with the earlier law include A. Lester and G. Bindman, *Race and Law* and B. A. Hepple, *Race, Jobs and the Law*.

4 Thus reversing *Ealing B C* v. *Race Relations Board* [1972] A.C. 342, decided under the 1968 Act.

5 [1983] 2 A.C. 548.

6 The same question arises in relation to Jewish people. See *Seide* v. *Gillette Industries Ltd* [1980] I.R.L.R. 427 and [1983] P.L. 4.

7 For the suggestion that justification may be based on reasons acceptable to right thinking people as sound and tolerable, see *Ojutiku* v. *Manpower Services Commission* [1982] I.C.R. 661 and *Clarke* v. *Eley (IMI) Kynoch Ltd* [1983] I.C.R. 165. See also *Perera* v. *Civil Service Commission* [1983] I.C.R. 428.

rimental effect on those who cannot comply. The *Mandla* case concerned the question of whether the headmaster of a private school was indirectly discriminating against Sikh boys when he imposed rules on school uniform which forbade turbans. Holding the rules to be discriminatory, the House of Lords interpreted the words 'can comply' to mean not 'can physically comply', but 'can in practice comply' or 'can consistently with the customs and cultural conditions of the racial group comply'.[8]

Discrimination is unlawful in the field of employment, except where being of a particular racial group is a genuine qualification for stated jobs (for example, the theatre) and except for employment in a private household (sections 4, 5). It is unlawful to dismiss an employee for refusal to carry out racially discriminatory instructions.[9] It is, further, unlawful to discriminate in the choice of partners for partnerships of six or more persons, admission to trade unions and professional organisations, granting of licences and qualifications for trades or vocations, vocational training and employment agency services (sections 10–14).

Discrimination is also unlawful in education and in the provision of goods, services and facilities to the public or a section of the public.[10] There are exceptions for residential accommodation in small premises and for the fostering or care of children in a person's home (section 23(2)). Associations which have more than 25 members may not discriminate as respects admission to membership or the treatment of associate members (section 25).[11] but an association whose main aim is to provide benefits to persons of a particular racial group may discriminate on grounds of race, nationality or ethnic or national origin but not as regards colour (section 26). Advertising in terms which suggest an intention to discriminate is unlawful, but it is now permissible to state that a job requires a member of a particular racial group (for example, a Chinese waiter for a Chinese restaurant) (section 29). Other conduct declared unlawful includes the adoption of discriminatory requirements or conditions (section 28), and instructing, inducing or aiding persons to commit unlawful discrimination (sections 30, 31, 33).

The Commission for Racial Equality replaced both the former Race Relations Board and the Community Relations Commission. Its chairman and members are appointed by the Home Secretary and its annual report to him is laid before Parliament.[12] Unlike the former Board, the Commission has power on its own initiative or when directed by the Home Secretary to carry out formal investigations, and for this purpose it may require evidence to be given to it (sections 48–52). Such investigations must not, however, be lightly undertaken. The Commission may not embark upon an investigation unless

---

[8] [1983] 2 A.C. 548 at 565–6 (Lord Fraser). This test was derived from that applied in the sex discrimination case of *Price* v. *Civil Service Commission* [1978] 1 All E.R. 1228.

[9] *Zarczynska* v. *Levy* [1979] 1 All E.R. 864; *Showboat Entertainment Centre Ltd* v. *Owens* [1984] 1 All E.R. 836.

[10] For advice from the Inland Revenue being treated as a service, see *Savjani* v. *Inland Revenue Commissioners* [1981] Q.B. 458.

[11] On the law before 1976, see *Race Relations Board* v. *Charter* [1973] A.C. 868 and *Race Relations Board* v. *Dockers' Labour Club* [1976] A.C. 285.

[12] For criticism of the C.R.E.'s effectiveness, see report of the House of Commons Home Affairs Committee, H.C. 46 (1981–2); see also Cmnd 8547, 1982 and [1984] P.L. 236.

it has a reasonable suspicion that acts of discrimination have occurred.[13] If discrimination is established, the Commission has power to issue a non-discrimination notice (against which there is a right of appeal)[14] and may within five years follow up such a notice by seeking an injunction from the county court or, in Scotland, an interdict from the sheriff court (sections 57–61). Enforcement in the employment field, however, takes the form of a complaint by the victim of discrimination to an industrial tribunal, from whom an appeal on a point of law lies to the Employment Appeal Tribunal.[15] When such a complaint is brought to a tribunal, the services of a conciliation officer are available. The tribunal may declare the rights of the parties in regard to the alleged discrimination, or order compensation to be paid, or recommend other steps to be taken by way of a remedy (sections 53–55).[16]

Complaints of discrimination outside employment may be brought by the victim before designated county courts. The court may award damages, including compensation for injury to feelings, but it is a defence to an action for damages based on indirect discrimination if the alleged discriminator proves that he did not intend to discriminate against the claimant on racial grounds (section 57(3)). The Commission for Racial Equality has power to assist complainants in pursuing their remedies in difficult or important cases (section 66).[17] The Act applies to service under the Crown and to the police. Government departments and ministers are required not to make discriminatory appointments to offices or posts which are not covered by the general rules against discrimination in the employment field (section 76).

The Sex Discrimination Act 1975
The structure of the Sex Discrimination Act 1975 resembles that of the Race Relations Act 1976, which was largely based upon the former Act. The 1975 Act makes it unlawful to discriminate on the grounds of sex (whether by preferring males to females, or *vice versa*) or marital status.[18] The Act is aimed at both direct and indirect discrimination.[19] The Act prohibits discrimination in employment, except where a person's sex is a 'genuine occupational qualification' (section 7) and subject to a number of special cases (for example, ministers of religion); in education, although single-sex schools and colleges may continue; and in the provision of goods, facilities and services,[20] including the management of rented accommodation. Discriminatory advertisements are unlawful. The Equal Opportunities Commission was created to enforce the

---

13 R. v. *Commission for Racial Equality, ex p. Hillingdon Council* [1982] A.C. 779, applied in *In re Prestige Group* [1984] 1 W.L.R. 335; and see *Home Office* v. *C.R.E.* [1982] Q.B. 385.
14 *C.R.E.* v. *Amari Plastics Ltd* [1982] Q.B. 265.
15 Page 710 *post.*
16 Problems may arise in both race and sex discrimination cases in relation to the discovery of confidential documents. See *Science Research Council* v. *Nassé* [1980] A.C. 1028.
17 As it did in the case of *Mandla* v. *Dowell Lee* [1983] 2 A.C. 548.
18 See *Peake* v. *Automotive Products Ltd* [1978] Q.B. 233 and *Ministry of Defence* v. *Jeremiah* [1980] Q.B. 87.
19 See *Price* v. *Civil Service Commission* [1978] 1 All E.R. 1228 and *Steel* v. *Union of Post Office Workers* [1978] 2 All E.R. 504.
20 See *Gill* v. *El Vino Co. Ltd* [1983] Q.B. 425 (discrimination to refuse service to women at a public bar).

Act. Those who are discriminated against have the same rights to seek individual remedies as under the Race Relations Act 1976.

Closely related to the Sex Discrimination Act 1975 is the Equal Pay Act 1970, which was amended by the 1975 Act and came into force at the same time. The two statutes overlap in relation to discrimination in respect of pay and other conditions of employment. The effect of Community law upon equal pay legislation has been notable, since Article 119 of the EEC Treaty as interpreted by the European Court of Justice has gone significantly further in protecting the rights of women than the equal pay legislation passed at Westminster.[21] In 1983, regulations were made under the European Communities Act 1972 which amended the Equal Pay Act 1970 and sought to bring national law into conformity with Community law.[22]

B. European Convention on Human Rights[1]

The protection of human rights, which is primarily a matter for the state in whose territory the rights may be enjoyed, cannot today be confined within national boundaries. The European Convention on Human Rights was signed at Rome in 1950, was ratified by the United Kingdom in 1951 and came into force amongst those states which had ratified it in 1953. The Convention is a treaty under international law and its authority derives solely from the consent of those states who have become parties to it. It was a direct result of the movement for co-operation in Western Europe which in 1949 created the Council of Europe. Inspiration for the Convention came from the wide principles declared in the United Nations Universal Declaration of Human Rights in 1948.[2] The Convention declares certain human rights which are or should be protected by law in each state. It also provides political and judicial procedures by which alleged infringements of these rights may be examined at an international level. In particular, the acts of public authorities may be challenged even though they are in accordance with national law. The Convention thus provides a constraint upon the legislative authority of national parliaments, including that at Westminster.[3]

The scope of the Convention

The Convention does not cover the whole field of human rights. It omits economic and social rights, over which considerable political controversy might arise, and is confined to certain basic rights and liberties which the framers of the Convention considered would be generally accepted in the liberal democracies of Western Europe. These rights and liberties include:

---

21 See *e.g. Macarthys Ltd* v. *Smith* [1981] Q.B. 180, *Garland* v. *British Rail Engineering Ltd* [1983] 2 A.C. 751.
22 See the Equal Pay (Amendment) Regulations S.I. 1983 No. 1794; also *EC Commission* v. *UK* [1982] I.C.R. 578; C. McCrudden (1983) 12 I.L.J. 197 and (1984) 13 I.L.J. 50; and H.L. Deb., 5 Dec. 1983, col. 929.

1   The extensive literature includes R. Beddard, *Human Rights and Europe;* J. E. S. Fawcett, *The Application of the European Convention on Human Rights;* F. G. Jacobs, *The European Convention on Human Rights;* F. Castberg, *The European Convention on Human Rights.*
2   See I. Brownlie, *Basic Documents on Human Rights*, p. 21.
3   Ch. 5 C.

the right to life (article 2);

freedom from torture or inhuman or degrading treatment or punishment (article 3);

freedom from slavery or forced labour (article 4);

the right to liberty and security of person (article 5) including the right of one who is arrested to be informed promptly of the reasons for his arrest and of any charge against him;[4]

the right to a fair trial by an impartial tribunal of a person's civil rights and obligations and of criminal charges against him (article 6), including the right to be presumed innocent of a criminal charge until proved guilty and the right to be defended by a lawyer and to have free legal assistance 'when the interests of justice so require';

the prohibition of retroactive criminal laws (article 7);

the right to respect for a person's private and family life, his home and correspondence (article 8);

freedom of thought, conscience and religion (article 9) and freedom of expression (article 10);

freedom of peaceful assembly and of association with others, including the right to form and join trade unions (article 11);

the right to marry and found a family (article 12).

Many of these rights are subject to exceptions or qualifications. Thus article 5 sets out the grounds on which a person may lawfully be deprived of his liberty; these include the lawful arrest of a person to prevent his entering the country without authority, and the lawful detention 'of persons of unsound mind, alcoholics or drug addicts or vagrants' (article 5(1)(*f*)).[5] So too the right to respect for private and family life under article 8 is protected from interference by a public authority

except such interference as is in accordance with the law and is necessary in a democratic society in the interests of national security, public safety or the economic well-being of the country, for the prevention of disorder or crime, for the protection of health or morals, or for the protection of the rights and freedoms of others.

Clearly it is essential that such restrictions should not be interpreted so widely that the protected right becomes illusory.

By article 14, the rights declared in the Convention are to be enjoyed

without discrimination on any ground such as sex, race, colour, language, religion, political or other opinion, national or social origin, association with a national minority, property, birth or other status.

Member states may derogate from most but not all of their obligations under the Convention in time of war or other public emergency (and the United Kingdom has done so in respect of Northern Ireland), but they must inform the Secretary-General of the Council of Europe of the measures taken and the reasons (article 15).[6] In general all persons benefit from the Conven-

---

[4] *Cf. Christie* v. *Leachinsky*, p. 478 *ante.*

[5] Compare the grounds for lawful detention set out in ch. 26 A.

[6] See *Lawless* v. *Ireland* (No. 3), 1 Jul. 1961, (Series A, No. 3), 1 E.H.R.R. 15; and *cf.* ch. 29.

tion regardless of citizenship but a state may restrict the political activities of aliens (article 16).

The scope of the Convention was extended by the first Protocol concluded as an addendum to the Convention in 1952, and ratified by the United Kingdom. By this protocol, every person is entitled to the peaceful enjoyment of his possessions (article 1); the right to education is protected and states must respect the right of parents to ensure education of their children in conformity with their own religious and philosophical convictions (article 2);[7] and the right to take part in free elections by secret ballot is declared (article 3).[8] The fourth Protocol to the Convention, concluded in 1963, guarantees freedom of movement within a state and freedom to leave any country; it also precludes a state from expelling or refusing to admit its own nationals. This protocol has not been ratified by the United Kingdom because our citizenship and immigration laws do not guarantee to all citizens the right to enter the United Kingdom.[9]

By article 1 of the Convention, states who are parties to it must secure to all within their jurisdiction the rights declared. Article 13 declares that everyone whose rights are violated 'shall have an effective remedy before a national authority, notwithstanding that the violation has been committed by persons acting in an official capacity'. While these articles undoubtedly impose an obligation on every state to ensure that its domestic law conforms to the Convention, it seems that a state is under no duty to incorporate the Convention itself within its domestic law.[10] In practice it is for each state to decide whether this should be done and, subject to review by the Convention institutions, how to provide an effective remedy for breaches of the Convention. In about half the states who are parties to the Convention (including Austria, Belgium, the Federal Republic of Germany, Italy, Luxembourg and the Netherlands) the Convention has been incorporated within the domestic law, but the effect of this is far from uniform.[11] Other states, including the United Kingdom, the Scandinavian countries and Ireland, have not incorporated the Convention within their domestic law. Successive British governments have maintained that human rights are already adequately protected by law in the United Kingdom. While incorporation could take various forms,[12] to be fully effective incorporation would have to enable British courts to apply the Convention if necessary in preference to existing rules of statute or common law. The constitutional implications will be discussed in section C of this chapter. At present, the Convention may not be applied directly by British courts; nor may litigants rely on the Convention as the basis for new rights.[13] The extent to which the Convention can be taken into account by the courts is uncertain,

---

[7]   The United Kingdom accepted this principle 'only so far as is compatible with provision of efficient instruction and training, and the avoidance of unreasonable public expenditure'; and see p. 637 post and Campbell and Cosans v. U.K. (post).
[8]   See Liberal Party v. UK (1980) 4 E.H.R.R. 106 (simple majority electoral system not a breach of Convention).
[9]   Ch. 25.
[10] Swedish Engine Drivers Union v. Sweden, 6 Feb. 1976 (Series A, No. 20), 1 E.H.R.R. 617, 631.
[11] A. Drzemczewski, European Human Rights Convention in Domestic Law.
[12] J. Jaconelli, Enacting a Bill of Rights, the Legal Problems, ch. 9.
[13] Malone v. Metropolitan Police Commissioner [1979] Ch. 344; Kaur v. Lord Advocate 1981 S.L.T. 322.

but it seems that in interpreting statutes passed since the United Kingdom ratified the Convention in 1951, the courts may take the Convention into account, and may presume that Parliament in legislating does not intend to infringe the Convention.[14] But the Convention does not prevail over clear statutory provisions to the contrary, and it may not be taken into account where no relevant legislation exists.[15] In exercising powers under the Immigration Act 1971, immigration officers are not required to take account of the Convention.[16]

Institutions and procedure

One novel feature of the Convention was the right which it gave to individuals to complain of breaches of the Convention by the states party to it. The enforcement procedure makes use both of the Committee of Ministers of the Council of Europe (a committee of political representatives of the member states) and of two institutions created by the Convention: (a) the European *Commission* of Human Rights, which in 1982 comprised 20 individual members, elected by the Committee of Ministers but in office acting independently; and (b) the European *Court* of Human Rights, comprising 20 judges elected by the Consultative Assembly of the Council of Europe. No two members of the Commission or the Court respectively may be citizens of the same state. In 1982, the Council of Europe had 21 member states, all of whom except Lichtenstein had ratified the Convention. They included Austria, Cyprus, Iceland, Malta, Norway, Sweden, Switzerland and Turkey as well as the ten members of the EEC.

The function of the *Commission* is to receive and inquire into alleged breaches of the Convention either (a) at the request of any state party to the Convention which alleges that another state has breached the Convention (article 24) (these are known as inter-state cases); or (b) where a state has recognised the competence of the Commission to receive such petitions, on the receipt of a petition from an individual or a non-governmental organisation alleging a violation of rights by the state in question (article 25). Although not all states have recognised the right of individuals to petition to the Commission, very many more petitions come to the Commission than inter-state cases. Thus between 1955 and the end of 1981, only 13 inter-state cases had been considered by the Commission but 9,620 cases had come to the Commission by individual petition.

When an individual petition is received, the Commission must first decide whether it is admissible under the Convention: thus the Commission may deal with a matter only after the applicant has exhausted all available domestic remedies and only if the petition is brought within six months of the final national decision (article 26). The Commission must also reject as inadmissible any petition which it considers incompatible with the Convention, manifestly ill-founded or an abuse of the right of petition (article 27). In fact only 255 of the 9,620 petitions received between 1955 and 1981 were declared admiss-

---

[14] *Garland* v. *British Rail Engineering Ltd* [1983] 2 A.C. 751.
[15] *Malone's* case, *ante*, at 379–80; *Kaur's* case *ante*.
[16] *R.* v. *Chief Immigration Officer, Heathrow Airport, ex p. Salamat Bibi* [1976] 3 All E.R. 843, reversing earlier decisions to the contrary.

ible. When a petition clears the hurdle of admissibility, the Commission must then investigate the facts fully and must offer its services to the parties with a view to securing a friendly settlement of the dispute (article 28). If such a settlement is not arranged, a secret report on the dispute is sent by the Commission to the state or states concerned and to the Committee of Ministers (article 31). Thereafter the matter may be dealt with finally by the Committee of Ministers, deciding by a two-thirds majority, or it may be brought within three months before the European Court of Human Rights.

A case may be brought before the *Court* only where the states concerned have accepted the compulsory jurisdiction of the Court (article 46) or expressly consented to the case coming to the Court (article 48). Only the Commission or a state concerned may refer a case to the Court: the individual applicant has no such right, although since January 1983 he has had the right to be represented in proceedings before the Court. The decision of the Court, usually given in a chamber of seven judges, is final. If the Court finds that action taken on behalf of a state has conflicted with the Convention, and if the domestic law of the state does not allow full reparation to be made, the Court 'shall, if necessary, afford just satisfaction to the injured party' (article 50), for example, by an award of compensation.

Cases involving the United Kingdom

From this brief account, it will be seen that enforcement of the Convention depends essentially upon a state recognising both the right of individual petition to the Commission and also the compulsory jurisdiction of the Court. It was in 1966 that the British government first made the two declarations necessary under articles 25 and 46; these declarations have since been renewed at intervals of several years.[17]

Since 1966 a wide variety of individual petitions have been brought against the UK government, and there have also been inter-state references to the Commission by the Republic of Ireland. In addition to innumerable decisions and opinions being given by the Commission, the Court between 1975 and mid 1984 decided 12 cases involving the United Kingdom. Later in 1984 other important cases were awaiting decision by the Court.[18] The first British case to reach the Court, *Golder* v. *United Kingdom*, concerned a refusal by the prison authorities to permit a convicted prisoner access to legal advice about a possible action in defamation against a prison officer. The Court held unanimously that this refusal infringed article 8 of the Convention (respect for private life and correspondence) and by a majority of 9 judges to 3 that the guarantee of a fair hearing in the determination of a person's civil rights (article 6(1)) included the right of access to a lawyer for advice about possible proceedings.[19] The Court held under article 50 that these conclusions gave 'just satisfaction' to Golder, and did not recommend the payment of compensation. In *Silver* v. *United King-*

---

[17] See *e.g. Yearbook of the European Convention on Human Rights* 1982, pp. 8, 18. The declarations extend to territories for whose foreign relations the United Kingdom is responsible, but not since 1981 to the Isle of Man: H.C. Deb., 18 Mar. 1981, col. 98 (W.A.).

[18] *E.g. Ashingdane* v. *U.K.* (1984) 6 E.H.R.R. 69.

[19] *Golder* v. *U.K.* 21 Feb. 1975 (Series A, No. 18) 1 E.H.R.R. 524; and see D. J. Harris (1974–5) 47 B.Y.I.L. 391.

dom, a similar infringement of a prisoner's rights was held to have occurred, and the Court also reviewed in detail the practice in British prisons of censoring prisoners' letters.[20]

Questions concerning the interpretation of article 3 of the Convention (which protects individuals against torture and inhuman or degrading treatment or punishment) arose in *Republic of Ireland* v. *United Kingdom* in relation to the interrogation of I.R.A. suspects,[21] in *Tyrer* v. *United Kingdom* in relation to the corporal punishment of juveniles in the Isle of Man[22] and in *Campbell and Cozans* v. *United Kingdom*. In the last case, the practice of corporal punishment in Scottish schools was held to infringe the right of parents to have their children educated in conformity with their philosophical convictions.[23] In *X* v. *United Kingdom* the Court held certain procedures for the compulsory detention of mental patients to infringe article 5.[24] In *Dudgeon* v. *United Kingdom*, legislation in Northern Ireland making homosexual conduct between adult males a crime was held to infringe the individual's right to respect for his private life under article 8.[25] The law of contempt of court was held to infringe freedom of expression under article 10 in *Sunday Times Ltd* v. *United Kingdom*,[26] but the English law on obscene publications survived scrutiny in *Handyside* v. *United Kingdom*.[27] In *Young, James and Webster* v. *United Kingdom* three former employees of British Railways, dismissed for refusing to join a trade union, established that their freedom of association had been infringed as a result of legislation on the closed shop passed by the Labour government in 1974 and 1976; they were awarded substantial compensation.[28]

These decisions have often led to changes in the law intended to prevent future infringements of the Convention; thus the Contempt of Court Act 1981 sought *inter alia* to bring the law of contempt into conformity with article 10, new prison rules were issued after the *Golder* and *Silver* cases, and the law of mental health was changed after *X* v. *United Kingdom*.

The procedure under the Convention is too elaborate to provide a prompt remedy to a person whose rights are infringed. Indeed, the Convention assumes that the primary protection of human rights is to be found in the national legal system. In respect of some states, such as Austria, cases coming to the Commission have revealed weaknesses (for example, excessive delays) in the system of criminal justice. The cases involving the United Kingdom have, by contrast, in a wide variety of situations raised the question whether legislation, official acts and judicial decisions always give adequate protection to the rights and liberties of minority groups in the United Kingdom. It should by now be beyond dispute that the United Kingdom ought to place on a permanent basis the right of individual petition to the Commission and the com-

---

[20] 25 Mar. 1983 (Series A, No. 61) 5 E.H.R.R. 347.
[21] 18 Jan. 1978 (Series A, No. 25) 2 E.H.R.R 25; p. 92 *ante*.
[22] 25 Apr. 1978 (Series A, No. 26) 2 E.H.R.R. 1.
[23] 25 Feb. 1982 (Series A, No. 48) 4 E.H.R.R. 293.
[24] 24 Oct. 1981 (Series A, No. 46) 4 E.H.R.R. 188; p. 474 *ante*.
[25] 23 Sep. 1981 (Series A, No. 45) 4 E.H.R.R. 149.
[26] 26 Apr. 1979 (Series A, No. 30) 2 E.H.R.R. 245; ch. 19 B.
[27] 7 Dec. 1976 (Series A, No. 24) 1 E.H.R.R. 737; ch. 27 B.
[28] 26 Jun. 1981 (Series A, No. 44) 4 E.H.R.R. 38; 18 Oct. 1982 (Series A, No. 55) 5 E.H.R.R. 201.

pulsory jurisdiction of the Court. There is also an increasingly strong argument to be made that the present legal status of the Convention in the United Kingdom is unsatisfactory and that the judges should be enabled to apply the Convention directly in their decisions.[29]

The European Convention on Human Rights and the EEC

For practical purposes, the European Convention on Human Rights is separate from the system of Community law. The Commission and Court of Human Rights both sit at Strasbourg under the Council of Europe umbrella and must not be confused with the EEC Commission at Brussels or the European Court of Justice at Luxembourg. The European Convention does not rank as a 'European Treaty' for the purposes of the European Communities Act 1972 and thus section 2(1) of the Act does not give it direct effect within United Kingdom law.[30] Indeed, in creating the EEC the Treaty of Rome made no express provision for the protection of human rights, although it created certain new rights in the economic and social field and provided machinery by which these rights could be enforced. But the lack of express protection for human rights has caused difficulties, particularly in German courts, which have been reluctant to accept that Community law should prevail over the protection for human rights which is a fundamental aspect of the German constitution.[31] By article 164 of the Treaty of Rome, however, the European Court of Justice must ensure the observance of the general principles of law in the interpretation and application of the Treaty. In a developing line of cases, that court has stated that respect for human rights forms part of the common legal traditions shared by members of the EEC.[32] As evidence of these general principles of law, the Court of Justice may look to the European Convention on Human Rights, especially since France ratified the Convention in 1974, the last member state of the EEC to do so. For the future it is desirable that the two systems should be brought more closely together, but for the present, the European Commission of Human Rights has no jurisdiction to entertain a complaint about a Community decision.[33]

C. A Bill of Rights for the United Kingdom?

The unwritten constitution lays emphasis on the virtues of the common law and the legislative supremacy of Parliament. It relies on the political process to secure that Parliament does not override the basic rights and liberties of the individual, nor remove from the courts the adjudication of disputes between

---

29   Section C *post*.
30   *Kaur* v. *Lord Advocate* 1981 S.L.T. 322; ch. 8 B.
31   See the decision of the German Constitutional Court in the *Internationale Handelsgesellschaft* case [1974] 2 C.M.L.R. 540; and U. Scheuner (1975) 12 C.M.L. Rev. 171.
32   See the *Internationale Handesgesellschaft* case [1972] C.M.L.R. 255, *Nold* v. *EC Commission* [1974] C.M.L.R. 338 and *Rutili* v. *French Minister of Interior* [1976] 1 C.M.L.R. 140. P. Pescatore (1970) 18 Am. Jl. of Comp. Law 343 and (1972) 9 C.M.L. Rev. 73; and E. Grabitz in (ed. St. J. Bates *et al.*) *In Memoriam J.D.B. Mitchell*, p. 194. E.C. Commission, *The Protection of Fundamental Rights in the European Community*, Bulletin Supp. 5/76, and Memorandum adopted on 4 Apr. 1979, Bulletin Supp. 2/79, on which see H.L. 362 (1979–80).
33   *Confédération Française Démocratique du Travail* v. *European Communities* [1979] 2 C.M.L.R. 229.

the citizen and the state arising out of the exercise of public powers. In the mid 1970s, a growing number of critics doubted the continuing effectiveness of the traditional British approach to individual liberties and advocated the creation of a new Bill of Rights.[1] These proposals were taken up and examined in governmental and parliamentary circles. Thus in 1977, the Standing Advisory Commission on Human Rights in Northern Ireland published a full study, recommending that the protection of rights in Northern Ireland would be best advanced by the creation of a Bill of Rights for the whole United Kingdom.[2] In 1978, a select committee of the House of Lords considered whether a Bill of Rights was desirable and, if so, what form it should take.[3] The committee was unanimous that if there were to be a Bill of Rights, it should be a Bill to incorporate the European Convention on Human Rights in UK law, but the committee was divided on whether a Bill of Rights was desirable. The House of Lords later approved a Bill proposed by the Liberal peer, Lord Wade, that sought to incorporate the European Convention in UK law.[4] However, the Conservative government after 1979 was not persuaded that a Bill of Rights was necessary or desirable, and Lord Wade's Bill made no progress in the Commons.

Many factors contributed to the movement for increasing constitutional protection for human rights. They included disillusionment with the parliamentary process and the electoral system; concern at the record of the United Kingdom under the European Convention on Human Rights; dissatisfaction with the performance of the courts in dealing with disputes between the citizen and public authorities; concern over the role of the state in economic and social affairs; concern over the future of Northern Ireland; and, especially in the late 1970s, the problem of how to devolve powers to parts of the United Kingdom while providing safeguards against abuse of these powers. In his Hamlyn lectures, Lord Scarman had called for the enactment of entrenched and fundamental laws protected by a Bill of Rights, 'a constitutional law which it is the duty of the courts to protect even against the power of Parliament'.[5]

No single Bill of Rights could be an answer to all these criticisms of the constitution. Moreover, there is a great variety of legal forms which a Bill of Rights could adopt. These include:

(a) a completely new written constitution for the United Kingdom, to include entrenched clauses devoted to fundamental rights and not liable to be overthrown by ordinary process of legislation;

(b) a Bill of Rights passed by Parliament intended to prevail over all earlier Acts of Parliament and judicial decisions, and which might also seek to entrench the rights declared in the Bill against subsequent Acts of Parliament;

---

[1]   See Lord Scarman, *English Law – the New Dimension*; Lord Hailsham, *The Times*, 12, 16, 19 and 20 May 1975 and *The Dilemma of Democracy*; Sir K. Joseph, *Freedom under the Law*; M. Zander, *A Bill of Rights?*; P. T. Wallington and J. McBride, *Civil Liberties and a Bill of Rights*; C. M. Campbell (ed.), *Do we need a Bill of Rights?*; H.W.R. Wade, *Constitutional Fundamentals*.

[2]   Cmnd 7009, 1977.

[3]   H.L. 176 (1977–8). And see *Legislation on Human Rights, a Discussion Document*, 1976 (Home Office).

[4]   H.L. Bill 54 (1980–1); H.L. Deb., 5 Dec. 1980, col. 533; 3 Feb. 1981, col. 1102; and see H.C. Deb., 8 May 1981, col. 419.

[5]   *English Law – the New Dimension*, p. 20.

(c) a Bill to incorporate within national law the European Convention on Human Rights and to empower British courts to give relief against breaches of the Convention;
(d) a Bill to declare certain principles which must be observed in the exercise of their powers by subordinate bodies (such as government departments and local authorities), but not applying to Parliament itself;
(e) a Bill to create rights not recognised by the common law, for example, the right to privacy or the freedom from improper discrimination.

Of these possibilities, (a) is the most innovatory; in a wholly new constitution, the powers of the legislature could clearly be limited by the constitution. By contrast, (e) is the least innovatory since it would merely follow legislation like the Sex Discrimination Act 1975. Scheme (d) would be relevant to the reform of administrative law but would not give rise to fundamental constitutional problems. What both (b) and (c) have in common is that, without creating a new constitution, they would seek to engraft on the present constitution an added power in the courts to give redress to the individual even against an Act of Parliament. Such an attempt would raise issues concerning the relation of the courts to the political process, including the special difficulties inherent in the attempt by a supreme Parliament to bind itself.[6]

In 1973, the report of the royal commission on the constitution gave scant attention to the legal protection of human rights.[7] Today such a commission would be bound to examine fully not only the need to fulfil Britain's obligations under the European Convention on Human Rights, but also the experience of other countries, within Europe and the Commonwealth. In recent years, notable developments in the constitutional protection of human rights have occurred in Canada.

The legal protection of human rights in Canada

In 1960, on the proposal of Prime Minister Diefenbaker, the Canadian Parliament enacted a Bill of Rights.[8] This Bill did not take the form of an amendment to the Canadian constitution and it applied solely to federal law. Section 1 of the Bill of Rights declared that certain human rights and fundamental freedoms had existed and should continue to exist in Canada 'without discrimination by reason of race, national origin, colour, religion or sex'. Those rights and freedoms included:

(a) the right of the individual to life, liberty, security of the person and enjoyment of property, and the right not to be deprived thereof except by due process of law;
(b) the right of the individual to equality before the law and the protection of the law.

By section 2, unless it was expressly declared by an Act of the Canadian parliament that a law should operate notwithstanding the Bill of Rights, every law of Canada had to be construed and applied so as not to abrogate, abridge or infringe the rights or freedoms protected in the Bill of Rights. In the leading case of *R. v. Drybones*,[9] the Supreme Court of Canada held by a majority of

---

6   Ch. 5 C.
7   Kilbrandon report, pp. 228–31.
8   The standard work is W. S. Tarnopolsky, *The Canadian Bill of Rights*.
9   [1970] S.C.R. 282, discussed in Tarnopolsky, *op. cit.*, ch. 4; V. S. MacKinnon [1973] P. L. 295; J. G. Sinclair (1970) 8 Osgoode Hall L. J. 549; P. Weiler, *In the Last Resort*, ch. 7.

6–3 that the effect of section 2 of the Bill of Rights was that a section of the pre-existing Indian Act, which discriminated against Indians by making it an offence for Indians to be found intoxicated anywhere outside an Indian reserve, was inoperative, because it conflicted with the individual's right to equality before the law. Accordingly the Bill of Rights 1960 was held to override an incompatible provision of an earlier Act of the Canadian Parliament.

Notwithstanding the *Drybones* case, the use made of the Bill of Rights 1960 by the Canadian courts was limited,[10] as was its constitutional status. One of the main elements in Prime Minister Trudeau's scheme for reforming the Canadian constitution in 1980–2 was to establish a constitutionally binding Charter of Rights and Freedoms.[11] The terms of the Charter may be read in the Canada Act 1982. The Charter seeks to guarantee certain fundamental freedoms (freedom of conscience and religion, freedom of thought and expression, freedom of peaceful assembly, freedom of association), democratic rights (related to the right of citizens to vote and the holding of elections), mobility rights (the right of citizens to enter, remain in and leave Canada), rights in relation to the system of law and justice (for example, the right not to be arbitrarily detained or imprisoned), rights to the equal protection and equal benefit of the law without discrimination, and rights in respect of the two official languages of Canada. By section 24 of the Charter, anyone whose guaranteed rights or freedoms have been infringed, may apply to a Canadian court 'for such remedy as the court considers appropriate and just in the circumstances'. By section 26, the guarantee in the Charter of certain rights and freedoms must not be taken as denying the existence of other rights or freedoms that exist in Canada. Two important limitations on the effect of the Charter must be noted. First, by section 1, the Charter guarantees the rights and freedoms specified 'subject only to such reasonable limits prescribed by law as can be demonstrably justified in a free and democratic society'. This appears to authorise legislative limits to be imposed on the guaranteed rights and freedoms, subject to review by the courts of the justification for such limits.[12] Second, by section 33, the Charter is not entrenched against either the federal parliament or provincial legislatures, whenever in new federal or provincial legislation it is expressly declared that the legislation shall operate notwithstanding a named right or freedom. This power of 'express legislative override' does not however apply to the rights guaranteed in respect of the two official languages of Canada. Given these two limiting factors, it remains to be seen whether the Supreme Court of Canada will come to exercise a jurisdiction on human rights comparable with that of the US Supreme Court. Whatever the Canadian experience of the Charter may be, it does not follow that similar legislation in the United Kingdom would produce similar results. But as we will now see, one favoured scheme in Britain not only provides for

---

[10] See *e.g. Brownridge* v. *R.* (1972) 28 D.L.R. (3d) 1, *A. –G. of Canada* v. *Lavell* (1973) 38 D.L.R. (3d) 481, *Hogan* v. *R.* [1975] 2 S.C.R. 574, *A. –G. of Canada* v. *Canard* [1976] 1 S.C.R. 170, *Miller and Cockriell* v. *R.* [1977] 2 S.C.R. 680.

[11] See App. A; and E. P. Belobaba and E. Gertner (ed.), *The New Constitution and the Charter of Rights* (1982, 4 Supreme Court L.R.).

[12] This section reproduces in a looser and more general form qualifying provisions that are found in articles 8–11 of the European Convention on Human Rights.

an express legislative override, but also goes further than this in seeking to maintain the legislative supremacy of Parliament.

A possible Bill of Rights for the United Kingdom

There are formidable legal and political problems in the enactment of a new Bill of Rights for the United Kingdom.[13] Some public lawyers reject the case for any constitutional change likely to give greater power to the judiciary. They believe that, in reviewing administrative decisions, the courts are already inclined to interfere in political disputes and should not be encouraged to extend this to the review of legislative decisions: political decisions should be made by democratically elected politicians, not by judges.[14] At the other extreme are those lawyers who, like Lord Scarman in his Hamlyn lectures in 1974, wish to see a new constitutional settlement, including the enactment of fundamental rights that may not be violated by ordinary process of legislation.[15] Between these two widely different opinions, the scheme favoured by the House of Lords in 1978–81 for incorporating the European Convention on Human Rights provides a compromise which both enables the United Kingdom to give better effect to its existing obligations under articles 1 and 13 of the Convention, and responds positively to the domestic movement for the greater protection of human rights. It is therefore worthwhile to examine briefly the contents of Lord Wade's Bill.[16]

By clause 1, the European Convention (together with protocols to the Convention that have been ratified by the British government) is declared to have the force of law in the United Kingdom and to be enforceable by action in UK courts. By clause 2, in the case of conflict arising between any laws existing *prior to* the passing of the new Bill of Rights and the terms of the Convention, the latter shall prevail. By clause 3, in the more difficult case of conflict arising between any statute enacted *after* the passing of the new Bill of Rights and the terms of the Convention, the later enactment shall be deemed to be subject to the Convention 'and shall be so construed unless such subsequent enactment provides otherwise or does not admit of any construction compatible with' the new Bill of Rights. (Thus, the possibility of *express* legislative override is recognised, as in the Canadian Charter of Rights and Freedoms; but, unlike the Canadian Charter, the Bill also recognises that there may be *implied* legislative override, where the terms of the later Act do not bear any interpretation that is compatible with the Convention.)[17] By clause 4, provision is made in war or other public emergency for the government to take measures derogating from the Convention, on the lines of article 15 of the Convention.

This proposal leaves many questions unanswered. Thus it would be for the courts to decide how the Convention should be given the force of law and the remedies that might be appropriate to an individual whose rights are infringed. It would also be for the courts to decide on the authority which should be

---

13   On some of the difficulties, see J. Jaconelli, *Enacting a Bill of Rights, the Legal Problems*.
14   See *e.g.* J. A. G. Griffith (1979) 42 M.L.R. 1; and *cf.* R. Dahrendorf (1977) 40 M.L.R. 1 and E. H. Reidel in (ed. St. J. Bates *et al.*) *In Memoriam, J. D. B. Mitchell*, p. 38.
15   Note 1 *ante*.
16   Note 4 *ante*.
17   On this matter, see H.L. 176, 1977–8, paras. 13–23; and *cf.* Cmnd 7009, 1977, pp. 69–71.

attached to decisions of the European Commission and Court of Human Rights. It may be questioned whether clause 3 goes far enough in seeking to entrench the new Bill of Rights against future legislative action, although a different view is that clause 3 provides a safety-valve which is a necessity both because of the legislative supremacy of Parliament and as a matter of political realities.[18] Another criticism is that the Bill does not provide for the possibility of future amendments to the European Convention; presumably fresh legislation at Westminster would be needed in such an event. Those who would have liked to see a new home-grown Bill of Rights may regret that Lord Wade's Bill is confined to incorporation of the European Convention.[19] Nonetheless the Bill would significantly add to the powers of the British courts, and would enable them to review existing provisions of the law from the standpoint of the European Convention, without attempting to confer on them the ultimate power to overrule Parliament.

While, therefore, it may be argued that Lord Wade's Bill does the minimum necessary to render the European Convention enforceable in UK courts, the Bill in 1984 remained the only scheme for empowering the courts to give greater protection to human rights for which broad political support might in the future be forthcoming. Such support did not exist in 1984. It remains to be seen whether future decisions of the European Court of Human Rights will influence government thinking in favour of incorporating the Convention.

---

[18] See note 17.
[19] Cf. Jaconelli, *op. cit.*, chs. 9, 10; and Wallington and McBride, *op. cit.*, app. 1. See also A. Lester [1984] P.L. 46.

a matter of interpretation. The Duncan & Commission had concluded that Human Rights Act may be interpreted either clause a question arises in settling accurately the bill of rights against it[...] legality [...]for although a literary citation probably provides a test when it is a matter of political choices. Another criticism is that the bill does not provide for the peaceful [...] of future amendment to this proposal. Commentators presumably feel it is important. What should be would be necessary so that there would [...] then likely to occur. Few home-grown bill of Rights may assert that Lord [...] quite a bit as confined to European Union of the European Convention. Furthermore, the bill would distinguish by add to Empowers of the panel, votes, and would enable these few systems presumably protection law from the developments of the European Convention, without challenge it could not then, the effect amounting to rare-ruple [...]

W.R. Alderley, during hearing, said that Lord Vane's Bill [...] the amount necessary to render the European Convention enforceable in UK to ensure in [...] Rights Act, the aim of the only. I am further support, using the context, for direct protection of human rights [...] which broad political support might in fact create its own value, such support and the basic [...] and if communities to give careful consideration to the European Court of Human Rights will influence government thinking in favour of incorporation of the Convention.

_____
Footnote:
Note 1. [illegible] [...] Wilkins and McBride [...]; see also A. Jones [illegible], P. [illegible]

Administrative law

Chapter 32

Development and nature of administrative law

Administrative law is a branch of public law which is concerned with the composition, powers, duties, rights and liabilities of the various organs of government which are engaged in administration. Or, more concisely, the law relating to public administration.[1] On this broad definition, administrative law includes not only the law relating to the structure of central and local government but also the law dealing with the social services, the public utilities (for example, water, gas, postal services, transport) and the control and regulation of private activities, whether for social, economic or environmental reasons (for example, immigration control, licensing and town planning). It would be impossible within a short space to give a coherent summary of this massive body of law. Indeed, many of these areas of law (for example, town planning, social security) are established areas of study in their own right. In Part III of this book, emphasis is placed on general aspects of administrative law which are important in all the specialised areas of government. They include delegated legislation; the judicial control of public authorities; and the liability of public authorities, notably the Crown, to be sued in contract or tort for damages. There will also be considered the nature and use of specialised tribunals, public inquiries and the Parliamentary Commissioner for Administration, all of which enable citizens to express their grievances and obtain remedies against official decisions without recourse to the ordinary courts.

Functions of administrative law
One important function of administrative law is to enable the tasks of government to be performed. Administrative agencies are created by law and equipped with powers to carry out public policies, drawn up within government and approved by Parliament.[2] A second function of the law is to govern

---

[1] Jennings, *Law and Constitution*, ch. 6. *Cf.* H.L.E. vol. 1, 'Administrative Law', para. 1. For further reading, see texts entitled *Administrative Law* by (respectively) P. P. Craig; D. L. Foulkes; J. F. Garner; and H. W. R. Wade; S. A. de Smith, *Judicial Review of Administrative Action* is an authoritative treatise on judicial control. See also J. Beatson and M. H. Matthews, *Administrative Law, Cases and Materials*; and C. Harlow and R. Rawlings, *Law and Administration*.

[2] Lord Parker of Waddington, *Recent Developments in the Supervisory Powers of the Courts over Inferior Tribunals*, (Lionel Cohen Lectures) 1959, p. 25.

the relations between various administrative agencies, for example, between a minister and a local authority[3], or between two local authorities.[4] The third function of the law is to govern the relations between an administrative agency and those individuals or private bodies over whose affairs the agency is entrusted with power. Thus the law serves as a control upon administration, since individuals may challenge the acts of an agency which adversely affect them, as being contrary to law, for example, by being beyond the powers of the agency.[5] Very often, however, the practising lawyer's attention focuses on the last of these three functions, regarding the sole purpose of administrative law as being to provide a remedy for his client's grievance. Such an approach leads to disappointment, when the individual is not able to obtain the remedy he wants without interfering with a public policy which is being pursued under the direct or indirect authority of Parliament.

An individual's rights are seldom absolute: thus a landowner whose estate is required for a new motorway does not have an absolute right to prevent the acquisition of his land for a purpose considered to be in the general interest of the community. Nor can a parent have an absolute right to send her child to a particular state school, regardless of whether or not that school is already full.[6] But this does not mean that the powers of public authorities should themselves be regarded as absolute. Few would dispute that individuals, local communities and minority groups should have some right to legal protection when confronted with the coercive powers of the state.

Administrative law serves to ensure that public authorities take their decisions in accordance with the law; it also is a means of promoting the accountability of public authorities and of securing some public participation in their decisions.[7]

The constitutional background to administrative law

Earlier chapters have described the structure of central government and the civil service; the responsibility of ministers to Parliament; local government; and the use of public corporations to control the nationalised industries and other public services. The legislative supremacy of Parliament is also relevant to administrative law, since there is no constitutional court which may hold that the statutory powers of an agency are contrary to the constitution. Notwithstanding the supremacy of Parliament, the courts impose standards of lawful conduct upon public authorities as a matter of common law, and it is arguable that the power to impose such standards is a constitutional fundamental. As has been said, the judges 'may be discovering a deeper constitutional logic than the crude absolute of statutory omnipotence'.[8]

In a modern legal system, the way that disputes arising out of administration are handled is of constitutional significance. Where, as in the Federal Republic of Germany, there are separate courts, one entrusted with inter-

---

3   *E.g. Secretary of State for Education* v. *Tameside MB* [1977] A.C. 1014, p. 634 *post.*
4   *E.g. Bromley B C* v. *Greater London Council* [1983] A.C. 768.
5   Chs. 34 and 35.
6   *Cf.* Education Act 1980, s. 6.
7   D. J. Galligan (1982) 2 *Ox. Jl. of Legal Studies* 257.
8   H. W. R. Wade, *Constitutional Fundamentals*, p. 68.

preting the constitution and one dealing with disputes between the citizen and the administration, a distinction between constitutional and administrative law can be based on the actual work done by the two courts. In the United Kingdom, however, it is impossible to draw a hard and fast line between constitutional and administrative law. Public law disputes are handled by the same courts and judges that have jurisdiction in matters of private law. Many leading disputes with an administrative background are settled on constitutional grounds and may have constitutional repercussions.[9] In *Congreve* v. *Home Office*, the Court of Appeal upheld a citizen's claim that the executive had no power to make him pay an extra £6 for a licence to watch colour television when he had already paid what was the lawful rate of £12 when he took out the licence.[10] It is immaterial whether this decision appears in digests of case-law under the heading of constitutional or administrative law. So too, an area of government administered by reliance on prerogative powers (for example, the issue of passports) or directly affecting a citizen's fundamental rights (for example, the control of immigration), may be treated as a branch of either constitutional or administrative law. Constitutional developments such as Britain's membership of the European Community and participation in the European Convention on Human Rights have many implications for administrative law. In general, enforcement of the criminal law falls outside the scope of administrative law, but administration of the police and the penal system often gives rise to legal disputes about the exercise of official powers. The powers and procedures of Parliament also fall outside administrative law, but the rules of public accounting directly affect the working of government departments[11] and so do parliamentary procedures for the scrutiny of delegated legislation.[12]

Administrative law and 'droit administratif'

The study of administrative law in Britain was for many years dominated by the comparison which Dicey drew between the system of administrative jurisdiction (*le contentieux administratif*) in France, under which a special hierarchy of administrative courts (notably the *Conseil d'Etat*) deals with most disputes concerning the exercise of administrative power, and the common law in England.[13] Dicey was at pains to contrast the disadvantages involved in a system of administrative courts handling disputes between officials and citizens with the advantages enjoyed in Britain through the absence of such a system. The common law, as Dicey saw it, subjected executive actions to control by the same courts and according to the same principles as governed the relationships between private citizens. Dicey concluded that the common law system gave the citizen better protection against arbitary action by the executive than the French system. Unfortunately, Dicey's denial that *droit admin-*

---

9 *E.g.* the *Tameside* case, n. 3 *ante*.

10 [1976] Q.B. 629.

11 See C. C. Turpin, *Government Contracts*.

12 Ch. 33.

13 Dicey, ch. 12 and app. 2. And see F. H. Lawson (1959) 7 *Political Studies* 109, 207; C. J. Hamson, *Executive Discretion and Judicial Control*; and L. N. Brown and J. F. Garner, *French Administrative Law*.

istratif existed in England led many lawyers to suppose that there was no such thing as administrative law in the United Kingdom.

Old beliefs die hard[14] but today there is plenty of evidence that administrative law in Britain has fully recovered from Dicey's denial of its existence. Senior judges in Britain are now well aware that their power to control the actions of public authorities is of great constitutional significance. Lord Diplock has described the rapid development of 'a rational and comprehensive system of administrative law' as having been 'the greatest achievement of the English courts' in his judicial lifetime.[15] Amongst those who contributed notably to this achievement were Lord Reid, the senior judge in the House of Lords between 1962 and 1974, and Lord Denning M. R. who presided over the Court of Appeal between 1962 and 1982. Despite these developments, there are many differences between the English and French approaches to administrative law.

The French system still lays emphasis on the use of separate administrative courts whereas the British system relies heavily upon the superior civil courts for reviewing the legality of administrative decisions and for supervising the work of specialised tribunals. In both systems, the essential principles of judicial control are judge-made and do not derive from either codes or statutes. But in France, a heavy price paid for a separate administrative jurisdiction is a complex area of law relating to the division of jurisdiction between the civil and the administrative courts (that is, between the private and the public sectors of law); questions of conflict must be settled by the *Tribunal des Conflits* or by legislation. Where the French system gains is that administrative courts may more readily develop rules of procedure (for example, regarding the obtaining of evidence from government departments) and rules of substantive liability (for example, regarding administrative contracts, or the state's liability for harm caused by official acts) which take account of the public law setting of the disputes. These rules may confer special duties upon the administration (for example, liability without fault in certain circumstances),[16] not merely immunities.

By contrast, the British approach, manifest in case-law and in the Crown Proceedings Act 1947, has been to apply general principles of liability in contract and tort to public bodies as well as to private citizens. It was by application of the general law of negligence that the liability of the Home Office was decided in respect of harm done by escaping Borstal boys.[17] In respect of the judicial control of official decisions however, special principles of law are necessary since the jurisdiction to review the validity of official acts has no counterpart in private law. In English law, special remedies developed for this purpose based on the old prerogative writs of certiorari, prohibition and mandamus. But without reform of the law, it was impossible to couple these

---

14   Mr Maudling, when Home Secretary, said in a debate on a clause of the Immigration Bill 1971: 'I have never seen the sense of administrative law in our country, because it merely means someone else taking the Government's decisions for them' (Standing Committee B, 25 May 1971, col. 1508).

15   *In re Racal Communications Ltd.* [1981] A.C. 374, 382 and *R.* v. *Inland Revenue Cmssrs., ex p. National Federation of Self-Employed* [1982] A.C. 617, 641.

16   C. R. Harlow, (1976) 39 M.L.R. 516.

17   *Dorset Yacht Co.* v. *Home Office* [1970] A.C. 1004; ch. 36.

public law remedies with remedies such as the declaration of right and the injunction, which serve both private and public law purposes.[18] Moreover, there have been periods, notably in the 1950s, when the British courts seemed reluctant to exercise jurisdiction over public authorities and forced the citizen to rely unduly heavily on political remedies. Since the mid 1960s, the judges have appeared more willing to play an active role in umpiring administrative law disputes: today they could not be accused of reluctance to find for the citizen against government. While gaps in legal protection for the citizen undoubtedly exist,[19] the British courts are capable of providing an effective, authoritative and timely remedy to individuals who challenge the legality of official acts.

Historical development

One casualty of the 17th century constitutional conflicts was the use of executive organs (the King's Council and the Court of Star Chamber) to enable the national government to control the acts of local officials such as the justices of the peace. The effect of the Bill of Rights in 1689 was to restrict prerogative powers and to make the King govern through Parliament. The common law courts were, with Parliament, regarded as a guarantee against a return to the despotism of Tudor or Stuart times. If the prerogative had not thus been curtailed, it is possible that our public law might have developed as a branch of the powers of the Sovereign. But it followed from the 17th century settlement that, when new powers of government were needed, they had to be obtained from Parliament.

In England, there was never a complete separation of the administration from the judiciary. In the justices of the peace, the enforcement of the criminal law and local administration (for example, regarding the poor law and the upkeep of highways and bridges) were inextricably blended. Administrative powers were usually exercised in judicial forms. The county justices, meeting in quarter sessions, continued to govern rural England until their administrative powers were transferred to the county councils created in 1888. During the 18th and early 19th centuries, there was little, if any, administrative or political control over the activities of the justices, but their exercise of power could be challenged in the Court of King's Bench by recourse to the prerogative writs.[20] Particularly in the period of reform after 1832, new local bodies were established by Parliament such as the poor law guardians, public health boards and school boards. They too were controlled on matters of law and jurisdiction by means of the prerogative writs. When modern local authorities were created and new departments of central government emerged, the Court of King's Bench extended its controlling jurisdiction to include them. In his famous lectures at Cambridge in 1887–8, Maitland argued for a broad approach to constitutional law that would include these new organs of government:

---

[18] Ch. 35.
[19] See *e.g. Hoffman-La Roche & Co.* v. *Secretary of State for Trade* [1975] A.C. 295, 359 (Lord Wilberforce).
[20] See E. G. Henderson, *Foundations of English Administrative Law*; and de Smith, *Judicial Review*, app. 1.

Year by year the subordinate government of England is becoming more and more important. The new movement set in with the Reform Bill of 1832: it has gone far already and assuredly it will go further. We are becoming a much governed nation, governed by all manner of councils and boards and officers, central and local, high and low, exercising the powers which have been committed to them by modern statutes.[21]

Since these bodies were exercising statutory powers, disputes about the limits of their power were settled by the courts, often but not invariably by recourse to the prerogative writs. Thus it was that judicial control, which originally served to check the powers of inferior courts, was adapted to review the exercise of statutory powers first by local authorities and then in the 20th century by ministers of the Crown.[22] It is a long step from reviewing the rate levied by county justices to pay for repairs to a bridge[23] to reviewing statutory regulations made by the Secretary of State for the Environment which seek to bind the whole community as if they had been enacted by Parliament.[24] Yet in both instances the constitutional principle is being invoked that it is ultimately for the courts to ensure that inferior courts, tribunals and other public agencies conform to due standards of legality.

Inevitably strains on the law have been imposed by the development of this jurisdiction. The work of the courts has been supplemented by the growth of the political responsibility of ministers to Parliament. Frequently Parliament has created special tribunals to which certain classes of dispute have been referred for adjudication. But the judges have been willing to adapt common law methods to changing conditions in government. The *ultra vires* doctrine has been refined to cope with more complex legislation; principles have been developed for controlling the exercise of discretionary powers; and the rules of natural justice have been developed and extended, although this process has often been unsystematic and haphazard in its results.

In Scotland, the detailed history of the law has been different but the general form of the development has been similar. After the abolition of the Privy Council for Scotland, following the Union with England in 1707, the Court of Session necessarily adopted a supervisory role comparable to that of the Court of King's Bench in England. Since the prerogative writs were never part of Scots law, and since a separate court of equity was never created, the remedies for controlling inferior tribunals and administrative agencies were obtained from the Court of Session by the procedures used for civil litigation between private parties. But the principles upon which judicial control was founded were remarkably similar to those developed in English law.[25] The sheriff court also exercised an important but more specific role in enabling many local administrative disputes to be settled judicially.[26] In the 20th century, much of the development in government has been by statute law which applies both in England and Scotland, and the response of the Scottish courts to it has been very similar to that of the English courts.

---

21   Maitland, *History*, p. 501.
22   *E.g. Board of Education* v. *Rice* [1911] A.C. 179 and *Local Government Board* v. *Arlidge* [1915] A.C. 120, on which see Dicey, app. 2.
23   *R.* v. *Glamorganshire Inhabitants* (1700) 1 Ld. Raym. 580.
24   *Daymond* v. *South West Water Authority* [1976] A.C. 609.
25   See *e.g. Moss' Empires Ltd* v. *Glasgow Assessor* 1917 S.C. (H.L.) 1.
26   *Brown* v. *Hamilton DC* 1983 S.L.T. 397.

Reform of administrative law

The explosion of government in the 20th century did not wait for lawyers and academic writers in Britain to acquire an understanding of administrative law. The first textbooks on the subject appeared only in the late 1920s.[27] At first a narrow approach was taken to the subject, confining it to delegated legislation and the exercise of judicial powers by administrative agencies. Only later was a broader definition of administrative law adopted as covering all administrative powers and duties as well as judicial control of the administration.

The development of administrative law in Britain since the 1920s has been much influenced by two committees appointed by the Lord Chancellor to inquire into aspects of the subject. The Committee on Ministers' Powers was appointed in 1929 at a time when a storm of criticism was being directed against departments by some judges and barristers, by prominent academic lawyers at Oxford and a small group of M.P.s. The appointment of the committee closely followed the publication of a strongly critical work, *The New Despotism*, by the Lord Chief Justice, Lord Hewart, who considered that the courts were losing their historic control over the activities of the executive. The terms of reference of the committee were

to consider the powers exercised by, or under the direction of (or by persons or bodies appointed specially by), Ministers of the Crown by way of (a) delegated legislation, and (b) judicial or quasi-judicial decision, and to report what safeguards were desirable or necessary to secure the constitutional principles of the sovereignty of Parliament and the supremacy of the law.

The committee, which vindicated the civil service from the charge of bureaucratic tyranny, analysed from the point of view of constitutional principle the legislative and judicial powers vested in ministers and made many recommendations to improve delegated legislation and administrative justice.[28] Though no government adopted its recommendations, its influence was seen in changes made in drafting Bills which conferred powers on departments, and in the establishment by the House of Commons in 1944 of a select committee to scrutinise delegated legislation.[29]

In 1955, at a time when the governmental machine was again under attack from sections of political opinion,[30] the Committee on Administrative Tribunals and Inquiries was appointed to consider and make recommendations on:

(a) The constitution and working of tribunals other than the ordinary courts of law, constituted under any Act of Parliament by a Minister of the Crown or for the purposes of a Minister's functions.
(b) The working of such administrative procedures as include the holding of an inquiry or hearing by or on behalf of a Minister on an appeal or as the result of objections or representations, and in particular the procedure for the compulsory purchase of land.

---

[27] W. A. Robson, *Justice and Administrative Law* and F. J. Port, *Administrative Law*.
[28] Cmd 4060, 1932.
[29] Ch. 33.
[30] The attack was intensified by the Crichel Down affair, p. 114 *ante*.

This committee, over which Sir Oliver Franks presided, reported in 1957.[31] Its terms of reference corresponded broadly to the second part of the terms of reference of the earlier committee but, unlike that committee, it found great difficulty in distinguishing formally between judicial and administrative decisions. Adopting a more pragmatic approach than its predecessor, it examined one by one the tribunals which fell within its terms of reference and inquired how far the characteristics of openness, fairness and impartiality applied to each. It also made recommendations for strengthening the public inquiry as a protection for citizens affected by town planning and compulsory purchase. The committee concluded that judicial control, whether by direct appeal to the courts or by review through the prerogative orders, should be maintained and where necessary extended. These recommendations led directly to the Tribunals and Inquiries Act 1958, which set up the Council on Tribunals, and to other action implementing the committee's report.[32]

The terms of reference of the Franks committee confined its attention to areas where recourse to a tribunal or a public inquiry was already available. The committee could not consider those areas of governmental power where neither safeguard existed.[33] Nor could the committee consider the provision of a redress for individuals suffering from maladministration. These two problems were examined in 1961 by a non-governmental committee appointed by Justice.[34] The report, *The Citizen and the Administration*, recommended (a) that, except where there are overriding considerations of government policy, a citizen should be entitled to appeal from a departmental decision on a matter of discretion to an impartial tribunal; rather than the creation of many new tribunals, a general tribunal should be created to hear miscellaneous appeals against discretionary decisions, and (b) that a Parliamentary Commissioner (Ombudsman) be appointed to investigate complaints of maladministration. Nothing came of the former recommendation, but the appointment of a Parliamentary Commissioner for Administration was first made in 1967. Notwithstanding this innovation, the English and Scottish Law Commissions, after a preliminary survey of the field, recommended in 1969 that a royal commission be appointed to examine administrative law in both English and Scottish law.[35] But the government decided against this and asked the two Law Commissions to study separately the effectiveness of administrative law remedies in the English and Scottish courts. The English Law Commission eventually produced a report which recommended important procedural reforms[36] and these were implemented between 1977 and 1981.[37]

The continuing refusal of governments to approve a general inquiry into administrative law led in 1979 to a further initiative being taken by Justice,

---

31   Cmnd 218, 1957.
32   Ch. 37A and B.
33   J. A. G. Griffith (1959) 22 M.L.R. 125.
34   For comment see I. M. Pedersen [1962] P.L. 15, J. D. B. Mitchell [1962] P.L. 82 and A. W. Bradley [1962] C.L.J. 82. Justice is the British section of the International Commission of Jurists.
35   Cmnd 4059, 1969.
36   Cmnd 6407, 1976; and see the Scottish Law Commission, *Remedies in Administrative Law*, Memorandum No. 14, 1971.
37   Ch. 35.

with All Souls College Oxford, to create a committee to review administrative law in the United Kingdom, under the chairmanship of Sir Patrick Neill Q. C. In 1985, the committee was expected to recommend *inter alia* that a permanent Administrative Review Commission be appointed for consultation and review of administrative procedures, that the grounds on which judicial review may be sought should be enacted in legislation and that reasons be given for all administrative decisions. But despite reforms in administrative law made in other Commonwealth countries,[38] there was no immediate likelihood of the committee's recommendations being adopted by government.

Law and the administrative process

The principle that government must be conducted according to law[39] means that for every act performed in the course of government there must be legal authority; or, as it is frequently put, that a public authority or official must act *intra vires*. Just as it is from statute or common law that a power must be shown to originate, so also will statute or common law determine how, by whom and for what purposes the power may be exercised. Thus the tax collector must be able to show, if challenged, that Parliament or a body entrusted by Parliament with the levying of taxation has conferred the power to collect taxes on holders of his office or on the department which he serves. Further, he must collect taxes only in accordance with the statutory rules as interpreted in the courts, and may levy tax only on those whom the law has made subject to being taxed.[40] The same applies to all officials and agencies whose acts or decisions directly affect the rights and duties of private individuals.

Yet it is not possible to describe the administrative process in terms of law alone. There are many administrative tasks (for example, budgeting, co-ordination and planning, resource management) to which law is not of primary relevance. Although law provides the framework for government, politicians and administrators are likely to view law not as an end in itself, but as a means to the achievement of social or economic policies. In areas of government such as taxation, the detailed rules may be found in statutes or in judicial decisions interpreting the statutes. But even here, exceptional circumstances may arise in which the revenue authorities exercise an extra-statutory discretion not to enforce payment of tax in a situation which neither Parliament nor the government can have foreseen.[41] The practice of granting extra-statutory concessions, while of long standing, would defeat the whole purpose of imposing taxes by law if it became at all extensive; but by the nature of a tax concession, it may escape challenge in a court of law.[42]

By contrast with taxation, in many areas of government the nature of the legal framework is deliberately skeletonic, so as to allow for wide discretion on the part of the department concerned in promoting policies which are

---

[38]   *E.g.* in Australia, the Administrative Decisions (Judicial Review) Act 1977.
[39]   Ch. 6.
[40]   *Daymond's* case *ante* (n. 24); and see the cases cited in ch. 16.
[41]   See *e.g.* Annual Report of Parliamentary Commissioner for 1970, H.C. 261 (1970–71) p. 36 (refusal to refund gaming licence duty to casino in Scotland).
[42]   But not judicial criticism: *Vestey* v. *Inland Revenue Cmssrs.* [1980] A.C. 1148, p. 624 *post*.

602   *Part III: Administrative law*

nowhere laid down in statutory rules. Thus the department responsible for grants to industry may wish to make selective grants to certain forms of industry or to discriminate between areas of high and low unemployment.[43] Wide discretion is found in many other areas of government, such as the control of immigration and the management of council housing. In principle, discretionary powers are subject to control by the courts. But in practice the exercise of discretion is often more closely controlled by departmental rules which lay down how officials should exercise their powers. This was the basis on which the means-tested scheme of supplementary benefits was administered until 1980, but in that year the scheme of administrative discretion exercised through departmental rules was changed into a scheme of entitlement based upon statutory regulations.[44]

The work of many officials can therefore be described as being concerned with the administration of government policies and the management of public business, rather than with the administration of the law as such. It is moreover often very difficult, if not impossible, to separate the administration of an existing policy from the making of new policy. For example, if under a scheme of grants to industry an application is received in respect of a new industrial process which has never before been grant-aided, the decision on whether to make a grant is likely to serve as a precedent within the department for future decisions coming from similar firms. Thus the process of administering policy gives rise to the formulation of a more detailed policy than had previously existed. When a decision of this kind is being taken the department will take into account factors such as the likely cost of making grants in all like cases. The practical consequences of such a decision will have a much greater effect on the outcome than any legal considerations, assuming that the law permits a wide range of possible decisions.

Decision-making within a department is a very different process from the process by which a court settles a dispute between two parties. A civil case, for example, is decided by the judge after hearing evidence and legal arguments brought before the court by the parties in an adversary procedure. After the exchange of written pleadings, the proceedings usually take place in public before the judge, in the presence of the parties and their lawyers. A reasoned decision is announced in open court. Usually, the decision when made can be challenged only by appeal to a higher court. The government has no political responsibility for the court's decision. By contrast, a departmental decision is typically taken in secret, without an adversary procedure. Often it is not known at what level in the department the decision has been taken, but the minister is responsible to Parliament for it. Political pressure may be brought to bear on the department both before and after the decision. Except where a statute so requires, reasons for the decision need not be given, although political pressure may bring about some explanation.

Although the two processes of administrative and judicial decision-making are different, it would be wrong to assume that one method is intrinsically superior to the other or to suppose that a department should always seek to adopt the methods of a court. Everything depends on the type of decision to

---

43   See *e.g. British Oxygen Co* v. *Board of Trade* [1971] A.C. 610.
44   Social Security Act 1980, amending Supplementary Benefits Act 1976.

be made and on the results which it is desired to achieve from a particular scheme.[45] In many cases, Parliament has provided that certain classes of decisions are taken not by civil servants in the department but by independent tribunals, which apply a modified form of judicial procedure in making decisions. In other cases, Parliament has provided that a stage of the administrative process should be exposed to view in the form of a public inquiry, while leaving the final decision in the hands of the minister or department.[46]

Powers, duties and discretion

The exercise of administrative functions normally involves the choice between two or more possible courses of action on the part of the administrator. Only rarely is there placed on him the duty of taking a specific course of action; for example, the duty of a local government official to produce council minutes for inspection by an elector.[47] But in general, administrative action involves the exercise of discretion. While it would be wrong to suppose that the law regulates all forms of official discretion,[48] there are many important principles of administrative law which govern the exercise of discretion. For administrative discretion, although it may be wide, is very rarely unlimited. Even where a statute confers a wide discretion on a minister, it is possible to seek a remedy in the courts on the ground that a particular decision is beyond his legal authority, for example because it seeks to achieve policies which are not authorised by the stature.[49]

If an Act which confers authority to administer a branch of government is analysed, it will often be found to confer a broad duty on the minister or on local authorities to fulfil certain broad policy objectives;[50] it may also confer narrower duties to act in specified situations; and it will also confer various powers which will promote the purposes of the Act. In administrative law, 'power' has two meanings, which are often not distinguished: (a) capacity to act in a certain way (for example, power to provide services, or to purchase land by agreement with the owner); (b) authority to infringe or to take away the rights of others (for example, power to acquire land compulsorily, whether or not the owner wishes to sell; power to license a trade or occupation). Powers, duties and discretion are often very closely related to each other. There may sometimes be a duty to exercise a discretion.[51] If a public authority is to fulfil the broad duties laid on it by Parliament, it must be equipped with powers which may adversely affect the rights of individuals. If use of these powers is challenged in the courts, the authority may seek to rely on its broad statutory duty as a justification for its action, while the individual may seek to show that the powers in question have not been lawfully exercised.

---

[45]   G. Ganz, [1972] P.L. 215, 299. *Cf. Local Government Board* v. *Arlidge* [1915] A.C. 120.
[46]   Ch. 37.
[47]   Local Government Act 1972, s. 228.
[48]   For a provocative discussion of official discretion, see K. C. Davis, *Discretionary Justice*. See also A. W. Bradley (1974) 13 J.S.P.T.L. 35 and J. Jowell [1973] P.L. 178.
[49]   *Padfield* v. *Minister of Agriculture* [1968] A.C. 997; *Congreve* v. *Home Office* [1976] Q.B. 629.
[50]   *E.g.* Education Act 1944, s. 1, which imposes a duty on the Secretary of State 'to secure the effective execution by local authorities, under his control and direction, of the national policy for providing a varied and comprehensive educational service in every area'.
[51]   *E.g. Ferguson* v. *Earl of Kinnoull* (1842) 9 Cl. & F. 251.

So the court may be faced with a dilemma. It is not easy to balance action taken on behalf of the public at large against the interests of a single individual whose rights, including the free enjoyment of his property, may be affected by the exercise of the public power.[52] The court is not concerned with the political merits of the policy adopted by the authority. At the same time, it must protect the individual from any attempt to override his rights except by due process of law. Thus a judge who reviews the legality of executive action has a different constitutional function from that of the administrative body whose decision he reviews. In practice serious questions may arise before a court as to where the dividing-line comes between matters that a public authority should decide and those that should be decided by the judges.[53]

These matters will be considered more fully in later chapters. In the rest of this chapter, we will consider two general matters, namely the classification of powers and the distinction between public and private law, which are relevant to the process of judicial control. The former topic is now in decline, in contrast with the increasing importance attached to the latter by some judges. But both topics contain many pitfalls for the unwary.

Classification of powers

Under a written constitution which is founded upon the separation of powers, it may be necessary for a court to decide whether legislative or executive action has improperly infringed the judicial power.[54] Although this is not the case in the United Kingdom, there are several purposes in administrative law for which attempts have been made to classify the powers of government as being legislative, administrative or judicial in character.[55] Thus under the Statutory Instruments Act 1946 in its application to earlier statutes, a distinction was drawn between instruments which were legislative and those which were executive in character.[56] The jurisdiction of the Parliamentary Commissioner for Administration applies to 'action taken in the exercise of administrative functions' by a government department, which may mean that he is not concerned with the functions of departments which are legislative in character.[57] Under the Crown Proceedings Act 1947, section 2(5), the Crown is not liable in respect of the acts of any person who is discharging responsibilities of a judicial nature vested in him.[58] There are also other purposes for which it may be necessary to decide whether a particular procedure may be described as judicial. Thus, absolute privilege at common law protects a witness who gives evidence at a statutory inquiry into a teacher's dismissal,[59]

---

[52]   E.g. *Pride of Derby Angling Association Ltd* v. *British Celanese Ltd* [1953] Ch. 149.

[53]   E.g. *Bromley B C* v. *Greater London Council* [1893] A.C. 768, p. 636 *post*. And see Lord Devlin, (1978) 41 M.L.R. 501.

[54]   *Liyanage* v. *R.* [1967] 1 A.C. 259; *Shell Co. of Australia Ltd* v. *Federal Commissioner of Taxation* [1931] A.C. 275. And ch. 4.

[55]   de Smith, *Judicial Review*, ch. 2. The term 'ministerial' commonly denotes not the powers of a minister, but any duty the performance of which involves no exercise of discretion or independent judgment *e.g.* the enforcement of a warrant issued for the non-payment of rates (de Smith, pp. 70–1).

[56]   Statutory Instruments Regulations 1947, regn. 2(1); ch. 33.

[57]   Parliamentary Commissioner Act 1967, s. 5 (1); ch. 37 D.

[58]   Ch. 36.

[59]   *Trapp* v. *Mackie* [1979] 1 All E.R. 489.

but the law of contempt of court does not extend to administrative tribunals, such as a local valuation court which decides disputes about the valuation of property under the rating system.[60] Under article 177 of the EEC Treaty, only a court or tribunal has power to refer questions for a preliminary ruling to the European Court of Justice and this would exclude an administrative body without judicial functions.[61]

Apart from these examples, there are two main purposes for which, at least in the past, emphasis has been placed on the classification of functions. First, arising out of the history of the prerogative writs outlined above, certiorari and prohibition were seen as means of jurisdictional control, by which to control inferior tribunals and other bodies which exercised jurisdiction or were required to act judicially. These writs were in fact used against many administrative bodies, yet to legitimise the intervention of the Court of King's Bench, administrative functions were often described as judicial. Secondly, the rules of natural justice were held to apply 'when administrative bodies were performing judicial functions and were therefore required to act judicially.[62]

While many governmental powers may be described without difficulty as legislative (for example, the power to make statutory regulations), administrative (for example, the power to place a contract for the delivery of supplies to a department) or judicial (for example, the valuation in a disputed case of land which has been compulsorily acquired), many powers are so classifiable only with difficulty and others defy such classification. The body upon whom the power is conferred affords no reliable test of the nature of the power. The Queen in Council, like the old county justices in England, exercises legislative, administrative and judicial powers. Laws are not always general in application; legislative form may be used to apply government policy in an individual case.[63] Government departments exercise both formal and informal powers of rule-making: when is the issue of a circular which delegates executive powers to be regarded as a legislative act?[64] How should we classify the decision to build a motorway,[65] the issuing or revocation of a licence,[66] or the dismissal of a chief constable?[67] Does a decision change its character from being judicial to administrative if it is vested in a government department instead of a court?[68]

Especially in the 1930s, many attempts were made to distinguish judicial and legislative functions from administrative functions. The motive was to bring the legislative and judicial powers of departments within a greater measure of judicial control. The attempts were not particularly successful. One school of thought argued that a tribunal which based its decisions on policy or expediency was legislating, and that the true distinction was between a judicial body which looked to existing legal rules to guide it and an admin-

---

[60]   *A.-G.* v. *B.B.C.* [1981] A.C. 303; p. 350 *ante.*
[61]   Ch. 8 A.
[62]   Ch. 34 B.
[63]   *Hoffman-La Roche & Co.* v. *Secretary of State for Trade* [1975] A.C. 295.
[64]   *Blackpool Corporation* v. *Locker* [1948] 1 K.B. 349.
[65]   *Bushell* v. *Secretary of State for the Environment* [1981] A.C. 75.
[66]   *Boulter* v. *Kent Justices* [1897] A.C. 556.
[67]   *Ridge* v. *Baldwin* [1964] A.C. 40.
[68]   *Local Government Board* v. *Arlidge* [1915] A.C. 120.

istrative body which, in effect, had power by the exercise of a wide discretion to make up its own rules for deciding a dispute.[69] In opposition to this approach, it was argued that there was no real distinction to be drawn between administrative and judicial functions, judicial administration being merely a specialised form of general administration.[70] In this period, the term 'quasi-judicial' came into vogue to describe a function which could not easily be classified as either judicial or administrative. It was used variously to describe judicial functions vested in a body which was not a court and also functions vested in a department which gave rise to a public inquiry. In the latter case, the term quasi-judicial was sometimes applied to the whole process of public inquiry and the resulting decision, and sometimes merely to the inquiry itself. Thus in 1935 it was said, 'Although the act of affirming a clearance area order is an administrative act, the consideration which must precede the doing of that act is of the nature of a quasi-judicial consideration'.[71] Today it seems best to avoid use of the term quasi-judicial wherever possible.[72]

In exercising their supervisory jurisdiction over public authorities, the courts were in the past often inclined to apply a classificatory label to a particular decision, and then, following the application of the label, to draw out certain consequences, for example, the availability of certiorari or the application of natural justice. This approach did not take full account of the historical development of judicial control and it often led to circular argument. Thus in *Nakkuda Ali* v. *Jayaratne*, the Privy Council held that a textile licensing controller had no duty to act judicially in revoking a dealer's licence because he was not required by statute to give a hearing to the dealer before deciding to revoke.[73] Moreover an earlier decision of the House of Lords had caused grave doubt to be cast upon 'quasi-judicial' used in relation to administrative powers.[74]

The heresy that a public authority's powers had to be described as 'judicial' before its decisions could be subject to judicial review was dispelled by the House of Lords in *Ridge* v. *Baldwin*. Lord Reid stated that in situations where officials and others had power to make decisions affecting the rights of individuals, the duty to act judicially could readily be inferred from the nature of the decision; it was not necessary to look for any express judicial element, such as the duty to give a formal hearing.[75] In the light of *Ridge* v. *Baldwin*, the courts today place much less emphasis on the classification of a power as judicial or quasi-judicial in considering the scope of judicial review. It is now well accepted that administrative functions are subject to the controlling juris-

---

69 See D. M. Gordon (1933) 49 L.Q.R. 94, 419; the meaning which Gordon applies to an 'administrative' tribunal does not conform with modern usage.
70 W. A. Robson, *Justice and Administrative Law*, ch. 1; and see Jennings, *Law and Constitution*, app. 1.
71 *Errington* v. *Minister of Health* [1935] 1 K.B. 249, 273 (Maugham L.J.).
72 de Smith, *Judicial Review*, p. 77. And see *R.* v. *Cmssn. for Racial Equality, ex p. Hillingdon BC* [1982] A.C. 779, 787.
73 [1951] A.C. 66.
74 *Franklin* v. *Minister of Town Planning* [1948] A.C. 87 criticised by H. W. R. Wade (1949) 10 C.L.J. 216; ch. 34 B.
75 [1964] A.C. 40; ch. 34 B.

diction of the courts without it being necessary for a court first to apply the appropriate label.[76] As has been said, 'it is the characteristics of the proceeding that matter, not the precise compartment or compartments into which it falls'.[77] The language of judicial, quasi-judicial and administrative functions may still be heard in some judgments[78] but the classification of functions has lost much of its earlier significance. Even where the rules of natural justice do not apply, administrative bodies are under a duty to act fairly.[79]

Private and public law

While the classification of functions as legislative, administrative or judicial has declined sharply in importance, a recent tendency, associated particularly with Lord Diplock, has been for administrative cases to be resolved in terms of whether the dispute in question falls within private or public law. We have seen that in France a distinction between public and private law is made in deciding whether a dispute should be settled by the *tribunaux administratifs* or by the civil courts. But in Britain the tradition has been that the superior civil courts exercise an undivided jurisdiction over all justiciable disputes, whether they concern private citizens or public authorities.[80] The term private law may indeed describe branches of the law which solely concern the rights of private individuals, just as public law can describe areas of the law governing public authorities. But no legal consequence need follow from these descriptions. Indeed many disputes today involve both the private rights of the individual (for example, his right of property) and the powers of a public authority (for example, compulsory purchase of land, and the control of development).

The recent judicial trend ascribes definite legal consequences to the public/private law distinction. These consequences are of two broad kinds, first as regards substantive legal rules, second as regards matters of procedure. An example of the former was *Town Investments Ltd.* v. *Department of the Environment*: in deciding whether offices in London occupied by goverment departments and the US navy were subject to counter-inflation legislation, the House of Lords held that the lease of the offices entered into by the Secretary of State for the Environment as lessee was governed by public law: 'expressed in the term of art in public law, the tenant was the Crown'.[81] Similarly, in a town planning case in the House of Lords, Lord Scarman invoked the distinction when he said, 'it is wrong to introduce into public administrative law concepts such as equitable estoppel which are essentially aids to the doing of justice in private law'.[82]

But the public/private law distinction has more often had implications of

---

[76] See *e.g. R.* v. *Hillingdon BC, ex p. Royco Homes Ltd* [1974] Q.B. 720; *R.* v. *Greater London Council, ex p. Blackburn* [1976] 3 All E.R. 184.

[77] *In re Pergamon Press Ltd* [1971] Ch. 388, 402 (Sachs L.J.).

[78] *E.g. R.* v. *Kent Police Authority, ex p. Godden* [1971] 2 Q.B. 662; *Glynn* v. *Keele University* [1971] 2 All E.R. 89; and *R.* v. *Secretary of State for the Environment, ex p. Ostler* [1977] Q.B. 122.

[79] *In re H.K. (an infant)* [1967] 2 Q.B. 617; ch. 34 B.

[80] For discussion of this tradition, see ch. 6 and J. D. B. Mitchell [1965] P.L. 95, arguing for the creation of a new public law jurisdiction.

[81] [1978] A.C. 359, 381 (Lord Diplock). And see C. Harlow (1977) 40 M.L.R. 728.

[82] *Newbury D C* v. *Sec. of State for Environment* [1981] A.C. 578, 617. And see ch. 34 C.

a procedural kind, related to matters such as the nature of the personal right or interest which an individual has to show in seeking a judicial remedy[83] and above all to the choice of procedure available in the High Court.[84] Adopting this approach, the House of Lords in 1983 made a complex analysis of a local authority's duties under the Housing (Homeless Persons) Act 1977. Some of these duties (for example, to inquire whether a family was homeless) were held to be essentially public law functions, but others (such as the duty to rehouse a family once it had been found to be homeless) were held to be private law duties. Although the public law and the private law duties concerned the same parties, they were said to be enforceable by different procedures in the courts.[85]

This approach to duties arising under a single Act of Parliament is over-elaborate and likely to lead to undue complexity of reasoning in future cases. It is submitted that many of the cases in which the distinction has been applied could have been more satisfactorily resolved on other grounds.[86] It is also doubtful whether a new and radical division in the 'seamless web' of the law should be based upon judicial views about choice of procedure. In *O'Reilly* v. *Mackman*, for example, a convicted prisoner's interest in ensuring that the prison authorities observed the law in deciding the period of remission he would receive was described by Lord Diplock as no more than a 'legitimate expectation' so far as private law was concerned, but a matter of 'sufficient interest' to him in public law to justify the prisoner in seeking a remedy in the courts.[87] Such a distinction is difficult to comprehend. However, in *Davy* v. *Spelthorne Borough Council*, the House of Lords held that an action in damages for negligence against a local council was 'an ordinary action for tort' which did not raise 'any issue of public law as a live issue';[88] in a separate judgment, Lord Wilberforce urged caution in use of the public/private law distinction:

'Before the expression 'public law' can be used to deny a subject a right of action in the court of his choice it must be related to a positive prescription of law, by statute or by statutory rules. We have not yet reached the point at which mere characterisation of a claim as a claim in public law is sufficient to exclude it from consideration by the ordinary courts'.[89]

---

[83]   *Gouriet* v. *Union of P.O. Workers* [1978] A.C. 435 and *R.* v. *Inland Revenue Comsrs., ex p. National Federn. of Self-Employed* [1982] A.C. 617; pp. 662, 666 *post.*

[84]   *O'Reilly* v. *Mackman* [1983] 2 A.C. 357 and *Cocks* v. *Thanet D C* [1983] 2 A.C. 286; p. 668 *post.*

[85]   *Cocks* v. *Thanet D C, ante.*

[86]   *Cf.* C. Harlow (1980) 43 M.L.R. 241; P. Cane [1981] P.L. 322, [1982] P.L. 202; G. Samuels (1983) 46 M.L.R. 558.

[87]   [1983] 2 A.C. at 275.

[88]   [1984] A.C. 262; and see P. Cane [1984] P.L. 16.

[89]   [1984] A.C. at 276.

Chapter 33

Delegated legislation

Although the legal source of administrative powers may be found either in common law or in statutes, the great bulk of domestic administration is today carried on under statutory powers. Government departments may indeed exercise powers derived from the royal prerogative, that is, from the common law powers of the Crown that are not shared with subjects.[1] As a source of administrative power, the prerogative predominates in foreign affairs and to a lesser extent in relation to defence and the armed forces. Scales of pay for the civil service as well as conditions of employment and rules of conduct are laid down by Order in Council or other instruments, issued under the prerogative or by virtue of the Crown's authority as employer. But there is no residual prerogative power in the Crown to impose obligations or restrictions upon the people.[2] For the vast area of public action which is a feature of the welfare state, it is almost exclusively in statute that the source of power lies. Nor does the prerogative have any relevance to activities of bodies such as local authorities or the boards of the nationalised industries.

The term statute law covers both Acts of Parliament and delegated legislation. Most delegated legislation, or as it is sometimes called subordinate legislation, is made in the form of statutory instruments. One function of legislation is to create the organs that are necessary if the tasks of government are to be performed, for example, by creating a new public corporation, providing for the appointment of its members and laying down the financial rules to which it must conform. A second function of legislation is to provide the powers that are needed if a public service is to be performed, and to lay down the principal rules for the operation of the service. It is in fact very rare for an Act to contain all the provisions which are essential if a complex service is to be provided. An Act may do no more than outline the main features of the scheme, leaving the details to be filled in by subordinate legislation. In consequence of the many tasks which central government performs today, the

---

[1]   Ch. 13 C.
[2]   In *R.* v. *Criminal Injuries Compensation Board, ex p. Lain* [1967] 2 Q.B. 864, it was held that the Crown had power under the prerogative to enact a scheme which conferred financial benefits upon victims of criminal violence: p. 249 *ante*.

bulk of statutory instruments is now formidable. In 1981 there were enacted 72 Public General Acts which were contained in 2276 pages. In the same year the total of statutory instruments issued was 1892; although many of these were local in effect, the published volumes of general instruments amounted to over 6500 pages.

Historical development

The formal process by which a Bill becomes an Act has never been the sole method of legislation. In the period before the legislative function of Parliament had become clearly established, it was difficult to distinguish between enactment by King in Parliament and legislation by the King in Council. Even when legislation by Parliament had become a distinct process, considerable power to legislate by proclamation remained with the Crown: in Tudor times these decrees were enforced through the agency of the Council and the Star Chamber. In 1539, by the Statute of Proclamations, royal power to issue proclamations 'for the good order and governance' of the country was recognised to exist and such proclamations were to be observed and enforced as if made by Act of Parliament. One reason given for the Act was that sudden occasions might arise when speedy remedies were needed which could not wait for the meeting of Parliament; the Act contained saving words for the protection of the common law, life and property. The repeal of the Statute in 1547 made little difference to the Tudor use of proclamations and only in the 17th century were the limits of the prerogative power to legislate defined.[3]

The modern doctrine of the supremacy of Parliament means both that such prerogative powers of legislation as still exist have survived by grace of Parliament, and also that any other legislative powers exercised within the country must be derived from the authority of Parliament. From early times there are instances of Parliament granting the task of legislating in specialised fields to subordinate authorities. In 1531 Parliament granted legislative powers to the Commissioners of Sewers, forerunners of the modern rivers and land drainage authorities. After 1689 the annual Mutiny Acts delegated power to the Crown to make regulations for the better government of officers and soldiers (Articles of War), but in general it was not until the period of social reform in the 19th century that delegation of wide legislative power became common. The first modern Factories Act in 1833 conferred power on the four factory inspectors appointed under the Act to make orders and regulations, breaches of which were punishable under the criminal law.[4] A very wide power that remained law for over a century was the power, first vested in the Poor Law Commissioners, 'to make and issue all such rules, orders and regulations for the management of the poor . . . and for carrying this Act into execution . . . as they shall think proper'.[5]

The late 19th century saw a great increase in the delegation of legislative power to government departments and other subordinate bodies, granted piecemeal as need arose. The resulting confusion of terms (including rules,

---

[3] Ch. 5 A.
[4] Labour of Children etc. in Factories Act 1833. See now Health and Safety at Work etc. Act 1974, ss. 15 and 80.
[5] Poor Law Amendment Act 1834, s. 15.

regulations, orders, byelaws, schemes and directions), the variety of procedures by which the powers were exercised, and the great difficulty of discovering what the law was, led to a system of official printing and publication in 1890 and to the Rules Publication Act 1893. This introduced the general expression, 'statutory rules and orders', helped to unify procedures and introduced a safeguard of prior publicity. During the first world war, the Defence of the Realm Acts granted power in very wide terms to the government to make regulations for the conduct of the war.[6]

In the period after 1918 many lawyers became aware for the first time of the wide legislative powers of government departments. The Committee on Ministers' Powers[7] concluded that unless Parliament was willing to delegate law-making powers, it would be unable to pass the kind or quantity of legislation which modern public opinion required. The committee drew attention to certain dangers in delegated legislation and suggested the introduction of greater safeguards against abuse. Subsequently the Statutory Instruments Act 1946 replaced the Rules Publication Act 1893 and made possible a greater uniformity of procedure. Parliamentary control has been improved by the annual appointment since 1944 of a scrutinising committee, first by the Commons and today by the Commons and Lords jointly. The general practice of delegated legislation has been reviewed by several parliamentary committees,[8] but the flood of subordinate legislation shows no sign of abating. In 1960–9, 830 general statutory instruments were made on average each year. In 1970–7, this had increased to 1182.[9]

Justification of delegated legislation

Delegated legislation is an inevitable feature of modern government for the following reasons:

1 Pressure upon parliamentary time. If Parliament attempted to enact all legislation itself, the legislative machine would break down, unless there was a radical alteration in the procedure for the consideration of Bills. The granting of legislative power to a department which is administering a public service can largely obviate the need for amending Bills. Although many statutory instruments are laid before Parliament, only rarely do they give rise to matters which need the consideration of either House, and in practice Parliament spends a very small proportion of its time on business connected with them.[10]

2 Technicality of subject-matter. Legislation on technical topics necessitates prior consultation with experts and interests concerned. The giving of

---

[6] Ch. 29 B.
[7] Page 599 *ante*.
[8] Reports of Select Committee on Delegated Legislation, H.C. 310 (1952–3); Joint Committee on Delegated Legislation, H.L. 184, H.C. 475 (1971–2) and H.L. 204, H.C. 468 (1972–3); Select Committee on Procedure, H.C. 588–I (1977–8), ch. 3.
[9] Report of Select Committee on Procedure, H.C. 588–I (1977–8), ch. 3.
[10] In 1970–1, the House of Commons and its committees spent 1187 hours on Government Bills (594 hours in the House itself) and the House spent 105 hours debating statutory instruments (Griffith, *Parliamentary Scrutiny of Government Bills*, p. 16 and H.C. 475 (1971–2) p. 52).

legislative power to ministers facilitates such consultation. Draft Bills are often regarded as confidential documents and their text is not disclosed until they have been presented to Parliament and read a first time. Thereafter they can only be altered by formal amendment at the committee or report stages. No such secretive custom need impede the preparation of delegated legislation. There is also a good reason for keeping out of the statute book highly technical provisions which do not involve questions of principle, and which only experts in the field concerned can readily understand.[11]

3 The need for flexibility.   When a major new social service is being established, it is not possible to foresee every administrative difficulty that may arise, nor to have frequent recourse to Parliament for amending Acts to make adjustments that may be called for after the scheme has begun to operate. Delegated legislation fills those needs. When the Social Security Act 1980 provided that the supplementary benefits scheme should be based on statutory rules rather than administrative discretion, a massive quantity of detailed regulations was published; inevitably the discovery of mistakes and defects in the scheme led to many subsequent amending regulations.

4 State of emergency.   In times of emergency a government may need to take action quickly and in excess of its normal powers. Many written constitutions include provision in times of emergency for the suspension of formal guarantees of individual liberty. Although the Crown still possesses an ill-defined residue of prerogative power capable of use in time of national danger, the Emergency Powers Act 1920 today makes permanent provision enabling the executive to legislate subject to parliamentary safeguards in the event of certain emergencies.[12] Following the unilateral declaration of independence by the Rhodesian government in 1965, Parliament granted exceptionally wide legislative powers enabling the Queen in Council to take all necessary steps to bring about the resumption of lawful government in Rhodesia.[13] Upon the resumption of direct rule of Northern Ireland by the British government in 1972, wide power to legislate for Northern Ireland was conferred on the Queen in Council.[14]

Exceptional types of delegated legislation
While much delegated legislation is essential, governments are often tempted to obtain from Parliament greater powers than they should be given. Criticism centres upon particular types of delegated legislation.

1 Matters of principle.   There is a clear threat to parliamentary government if power is delegated to legislate on matters of general policy, or if so wide a discretion is conferred that it is impossible to be sure what limit the legislature intended to impose. There is no formal limit to the delegation of legis-

---

[11]   J. A. G. Griffith (1951) 14 M.L.R. 279, 425.
[12]   Ch. 29 B.
[13]   Southern Rhodesia Act 1965; ch. 24.
[14]   Northern Ireland (Temporary Provisions) Act 1972 s.1(3) and schedule, para. 4; Northern Ireland Act 1974, schedule 1, para. 1.

lative powers, but it would be unacceptable except in war-time for power to be vested in the executive to make such regulations as might be expedient in the public interest. In practice, Acts of Parliament frequently confer legislative powers in wide terms. One reason for this is that if powers are phrased more narrowly, this will make it more likely that the department will need to seek increased powers from Parliament in future. A proposal that Parliament should adopt a policy of passing framework legislation, with all details left to delegated legislation, was rejected by the House of Commons Committee on Procedure in 1978, on the ground that this would further weaken parliamentary control.[15] Another reason against framework legislation is that if the power of the courts to declare delegated legislation *ultra vires* is to be of value, the delegated powers must be defined with reasonable precision. But there are few absolutes in this debate and legislative practice is often a compromise between different attitudes to delegation.

2 Delegation of taxing power. We have seen how vital to the development of parliamentary government was the insistence that Parliament alone could authorise taxation.[16] This insistence survives in an attenuated form, but modern pressures, particularly associated with the government's responsibility for the economy, have made it necessary for Parliament to delegate certain taxing powers to the government. In particular, the working of a tariff system has been found impracticable without delegation of the power to vary and impose import duties from time to time.[17] Since 1961 the government has also had power to vary certain classes of indirect taxation by order of the Treasury.[18] Each of these powers is subject to special parliamentary control in that orders imposing import duties or varying indirect taxation cease to have effect unless they are confirmed by a resolution of the House of Commons within a limited time.

3 Sub-delegation. When a statute delegates legislative power to a minister, exercisable by statutory instrument, it may be assumed that Parliament intends the statutory instrument itself to contain the rules. Is it a proper use of such powers for the instrument to sub-delegate legislative power, by authorising rules to be made by another body or by another procedure? The legal maxim, *delegatus non potest delegare*, means that a delegate may not sub-delegate his power, but the parent Act may always override this by expressly authorising sub-delegation. Thus the Emergency Powers (Defence) Act 1939 authorised sub-delegation and this sometimes resulted in legislative action at four removes from the parent Act. Without express authority in the parent Act, it is doubtful whether sub-delegation of legislative powers is valid. Where sub-delegation occurs, control by Parliament becomes more difficult. In 1978, the Joint Committee on Statutory Instruments criticised the recurring tendency of departments to seek to by-pass Parliament by omitting necessary detail from

---

[15]   H.C. 588-I (1977-8), ch. 2.
[16]   Ch. 5 A.
[17]   Import Duties Act 1958. The government's powers under this Act are much affected by British membership of EEC: European Communities Act 1972, s. 5.
[18]   Finance Act 1961, s. 9 and Finance Act 1964, s. 8.

statutory instruments and vesting a wide discretion in ministers to vary the rules without making further statutory instruments.[19] Under the European Communities Act 1972, sub-delegation is prohibited except for rules of procedure for courts or tribunals.[20]

4 Retrospective operation.   It follows from the supremacy of Parliament that Acts may have retrospective operation.[21] But in principle retrospective legislation is repugnant to the conception of the rule of law. If on occasions retrospective legislation is considered necessary, as in the case of the War Damage Act 1965, this should be done by Parliament itself and not through delegated legislation.[22]

5 Exclusion of the jurisdiction of the courts.   The power of the courts in reviewing delegated legislation is confined to declaring it *ultra vires*, whether on grounds of substance or procedure.[23] While control over the merits of delegated legislation is a matter for ministers and for Parliament, the possibility of control by the courts is important and should not be excluded. It should never be for a minister to determine the limits of his own powers.[24]

6 Authority to modify an Act of Parliament.   Sometimes power is delegated to modify a statute. Thus the reform of local government made necessary extensive alterations in numerous local Acts.[25] Particularly criticised has been the so-called 'Henry VIII clause' enabling a minister to modify the Act itself so far as necessary for bringing it into operation.[26] The Committee on Ministers' Powers recommended that this type of clause should never be used except for the purpose of bringing an Act into operation and should be subject to a time limit of one year from the passing of the Act. Some recent Acts dealing with schemes of social and industrial control have however included powers which enable a minister to broaden or narrow the scope of the schemes in the light of experience.[27]

The European Communities Act 1972 was notable not only for the introduction of Community law into the United Kingdom, which cannot easily be compared with the delegation of legislative power to ministers, but also for the very wide legislative powers which it conferred upon the government.[28] Section 2(2) authorises the making of Orders in Council and ministerial regulations to implement Community obligations of the United Kingdom, to

---

19 H.L. 51, H.C. 579 (1977–8), p. 10; and see *Customs and Excise Cmssrs.* v. *J. H. Corbitt (Numismatists)Ltd.* [1981] A.C. 22.
20 European Communities Act 1972 s.2(2) and sch. 2.
21 Ch. 5 B.
22 For examples, see C. K. Allen, *Law and Orders*, p. 204 and H.C. 70-ix (1970–1).
23 Page 622 *post*.
24 Yet under the Counter-Inflation Act 1973, sch. 3, para. 1, an order made under Part II of the Act 'may define any expressions used in the provisions under which it is made'. And see *Jackson* v. *Hall* [1980] A.C. 854.
25 *E.g.* Local Government Act 1972, s. 262; p. 384 *ante*.
26 M.P.R. pp. 36–8; C. T. Carr, *Concerning English Administrative Law*, pp. 41–7.
27 See Health and Safety at Work etc. Act 1974, ss. 15 and 80; Sex Discrimination Act 1975, s. 80, esp. sub-s. (3).
28 Ch. 8 B.

enable rights under the EEC treaties to be exercised and 'for the purpose of dealing with matters arising out of or related to any such obligations or rights'. Schedule 2 to the Act excludes certain matters from the general power, including the imposition of taxes, retroactive legislation, sub-delegation of legislative power (other than power to make rules of procedure for any court or tribunal) and the creation of new criminal offences punishable with imprisonment for more than two years or fines above stated amounts. But, subject to these limitations, Orders in Council or regulations under section 2(2) may make 'any such provision (of any such extent) as might be made by Act of Parliament' (section 2(4)). Subject only to schedule 2, this comes close to an attempt to confer legislative supremacy upon delegated legislation. The intention must have been to use the widest language possible so as to exclude the possibility of judicial review on grounds of *vires* in the case of instruments made under section 2(2). But it is doubtful whether this intention has been achieved; instruments under section 2(2)· are not valid if made to give effect to *future* Community obligations.[29]

Nomenclature

Despite the Statutory Instruments Act 1946, terminology is still at times confusing. The term 'statutory instrument' is a comprehensive expression to describe all forms of subordinate legislation subject to the 1946 Act.[30] Within the scope of the Act are many legislative powers conferred on ministers by Acts passed before the 1946 Act came into operation. As regards Acts passed after the 1946 Act came into operation, there are two categories of statutory instrument: (a) legislative powers conferred on the Queen in Council and stated in the parent Act to be exercisable by Order in Council; (b) legislative powers conferred on a minister of the Crown and stated in the parent Act to be exercisable by statutory instrument. The first of these, the statutory Order in Council, must be distinguished from prerogative Orders in Council, which are not statutory instruments at all, even though for convenience some of them are published as an appendix to the annual volumes of statutory instruments. One reason why some legislative powers are vested in the Queen in Council and others are vested in a named minister is that some powers may need to be exercised by any department of the government whereas others concern only one particular department; also the greater·formality of an Order in Council is thought appropriate to some classes of legislation. The expression 'statutory instrument' does not include local authority byelaws, nor does it include such acts as the confirmation of compulsory purchase orders by a minister. Moreover there are other kinds of rule made under statutory authority which are not statutory instruments, for example immigration rules under the Immigration Act 1971 and the civil service pension scheme made under the Superannuation Act 1972.[31]

Although statutory instrument is the generic term, a variety of names apply to different kinds of statutory instrument: rules, orders, regulations, warrants,

---

[29] H.L. Deb., 17 Feb. 1976, cols. 399–417 and H.L. 51, H.C. 169 (1977–8), pp. 17–18.
[30] The official abbreviation for statutory instruments made since 1 Jan. 1948 is S.I. followed by the year and number *e.g.* S.I. 1982 No. 252.
[31] See also *R.* v. *Clarke* [1969] 2 Q.B. 91 and H.C. 588-III (1977–8), apps. 22, 23.

schemes and even licences and directions. Several of these terms may be used in a single Act to distinguish different procedures applied to different powers. The argument for uniform practice in nomenclature is based on convenience. In practice, the term 'regulation' is used mainly for matters of wide general importance, such as social security regulations. Where the legislation deals with procedure, rules are generally enacted, for example, the Rules of the Supreme Court. With the term 'order' there is less uniformity; thus an Order in Council may bring into effect all or part of an Act of Parliament, and in town planning law a general development order contains detailed rules for the control of development.

Control of delegated legislation

'There is now general agreement over the necessity for delegated legislation; the real problem is how this legislation can be reconciled with the processes of democratic consultation, scrutiny and control'.[32] The process of subordinate legislation differs significantly from that of legislation by Bill; it is equally important that there should be effective forms of control. The existing means of control will be described under four headings: 1 consultation of interests; 2 control through parliamentary procedures; 3 publication; 4 challenge in the courts.

1 Consultation of interests.   Unlike the procedure of legislation by Bill, whereby the proposals are considered publicly in principle and in detail as the Bill passes through both Houses, most delegated legislation comes into force as soon as it is made public, either at once or after a short interval stated in the document itself. At one time the Rules Publication Act 1893 required 40 days' notice to be given in the *London Gazette* of a proposal to make rules of a permanent character. But this rule was repealed by the Statutory Instruments Act 1946.

There is therefore no general requirement of prior publicity, and an ordinary member of the public has little chance of getting to know about proposed statutory instruments.[33] But by an almost universal practice, the department proposing to make a new statutory instrument takes steps to ensure that the various interests particularly affected by the proposal are consulted. Some Acts of Parliament make this obligatory. Social security regulations must be submitted in draft to the Social Security Advisory Committee, whose disagreements, if any, with the Secretary of State must be reported to Parliament along with the regulations.[34] So too the Council on Tribunals must be consulted before rules of procedure for administrative tribunals and inquiries are made.[35] Several Acts do not specify the bodies to be consulted, leaving it to the minister to consult with such associations and bodies as appear to him to be affected.[36] Even where there are no express requirements, advantage may be gained from consulting trade organisations or interests likely to be affected

---

[32] Memorandum by the late Aneurin Bevan M.P. quoted in H.C. 310 (1952–3).

[33] J. F. Garner [1964] P.L. 105.

[34] Social Security Act 1980, ss. 9, 10 and schedule 3.

[35] Tribunals and Inquiries Act 1971, ss. 10, 11.

[36] *E.g.* Industrial Training Act 1964, s. 1(4) considered in *Agricultural Training Board* v. *Aylesbury Mushrooms Ltd* [1972] 1 All E.R. 280.

by the proposed legislation. Consultation helps to ensure that the contents of subordinate legislation are as acceptable as possible to the interests concerned, and also secures the benefits of specialised knowledge from outside government. In one or two exceptional instances, a ministry's legislative proposals must be published and the interests affected have the right to present their objections before an inspector appointed by the minister. But this form of inquiry is usually reserved for such matters as the ministerial confirmation of compulsory purchase orders.

2 Control by Parliament.[37]   Parliamentary control of delegated legislation originates in the fact that legislative powers derive from statute. There is therefore always some opportunity of giving consideration, at the committee stage of a Bill, to clauses delegating legislative power. But how effective is this control? The Ministers' Powers Committee recommended that all Bills conferring power to legislate should in each House be referred to a small standing committee to report whether there were any objections of principle to the proposals.[38] This recommendation has never been adopted and in 1953 a committee of the Commons considered that individual members and unofficial committees of members could be relied on to take close interest in any proposed delegation.[39]

A measure of general control over departmental legislation is provided by the political responsibility of a minister to Parliament for his department. Thus responsibility for regulations may be raised through questions to the minister, and during debates relating to his department. Parliament has also provided additional means of control specially for ministerial legislation. It must not, however, be forgotten that basic reasons for delegating legislative power are pressure on Parliament's time and the technical nature of the subjects; the very object of delegation would be frustrated if Parliament had to approve each instrument in detail. The procedure through which a statutory instrument must pass depends on the terms of the parent Act. The principal procedures are the following:

(a)   laying of draft instrument before Parliament, and requiring affirmative resolution before instrument can be 'made';

(b)   laying of instrument after it has been made, to come into effect only when approved by affirmative resolution;

(c)   laying of instrument that takes immediate effect, but requires approval by affirmative resolution within a stated period as a condition of continuance;

(d)   laying of instrument that takes immediate effect, subject to annulment by resolution of either House;

(e)   laying in draft, subject to resolution that no further proceedings be taken – in effect a direction to the minister not to 'make' the instrument;

(f)   laying before Parliament, with no further provision for control.

Finally, some statutory instruments are not required to be laid before Parliament at all.

---

[37]   Erskine May, ch. 23; J. E. Kersell, *Parliamentary Supervision of Delegated Legislation*; and reports cited in n. 8 *ante*.

[38]   M.P.R. pp. 67–8.

[39]   H.C. 310 (1952–3).

In cases (a)–(c) (positive procedure), an affirmative resolution of each House (or in the case of financial instruments, of the House of Commons alone) is needed if the instrument is to come into force or to remain in operation. In cases (d) and (e) (negative procedure), no action need be taken in either House unless there is some opposition to the instrument.

Of these procedures, by far the most common is case (d) (subject to annulment); the most frequent of the positive procedures is case (a). Under the positive procedure, it is the minister concerned who must secure the affirmative resolution and if necessary the government must allot time for the resolution to be discussed in Parliament within the course of ordinary business; under the negative procedure, it is for any member who so wishes to 'pray' that the instrument should be annulled. Consideration of 'prayers' is exempted business and, subject to a closure time of 11.30 p.m., may be taken after the normal close of business. Even so, a great weakness of the system is that time may not be found for debate of all the prayers for annulment which M. P.s may wish to raise.[40] In practice, the positive procedure is reserved for particularly important measures, for example, orders made by the Treasury varying indirect taxation, or regulations made under the Emergency Powers Act 1920.

A novel provision made by the European Communities Act 1972 was that a statutory instrument made under section 2(2) should be subject to annulment by a resolution of either House unless a draft of the instrument had been approved by each House before the instrument was made.[41] Thus the government may choose whether the negative or positive procedure should be used. Because of the fear that the choice of procedure would tend to favour the government, it is unlikely that this formula will become more general.[42] Both Labour and Conservative governments have been criticised for choosing the negative procedure for important measures modifying Acts of Parliament.[43]

One feature common to all these procedures is that neither House may amend a statutory instrument, except for very rare instances where amendment is expressly authorised by the parent Act.[44] If this were possible, it might involve the House in detailed consideration of matters which Parliament has delegated to a minister, and it would cause complications if each House introduced different amendments. Where a House is not satisfied with an instrument as it stands, the minister should withdraw it and start again.

The Statutory Instruments Act 1946 introduced some general provisions to promote uniformity of procedure. By section 4, where an instrument must be laid in Parliament after being made, it must in general be laid before it comes into operation; every copy of such an instrument must show on its face three dates, showing when it was made, laid, and came into operation respectively. What constitutes laying before Parliament is governed by the practice or direction of each House[45] and an instrument may be laid when Parliament is

---

40   A. Beith (1981) 34 *Parliamentary Affairs* 165.
41   European Communities Act 1972, sch. 2, para. 2.
42   H.C. 468 (1972–3), para. 49; Wilson, *Cases*, p. 374.
43   H.L. 51, H.C. 169 (1977–8), para. 36; H.C. 15-viii (1981–2); and see Cmnd 8600, 1982.
44   Emergency Powers Act 1920, s. 2(4) and Census Act 1920, s. 1(2).
45   Laying of Documents before Parliament (Interpretation) Act 1948, and see *R. v. Immigration Appeal Tribunal, ex p. Joyles* [1972] 3 All E.R. 213.

not sitting. The rule that an instrument be laid before it comes into operation is so clearly expressed that, although there is no judicial authority on the matter, it is submitted that failure to lay an instrument prevents it from coming into operation.[46] But the position is doubtful in the case of delegated legislation that is outside the 1946 Act. While under the 1946 Act an interval of one day between laying and operation is sufficient, in practice departments try to ensure that the interval is not less than 21 days.[47]

By section 5 of the 1946 Act, where an instrument is subject to annulment, as in procedure (*d*) above, there is a uniform period of 40 days during which a prayer for annulment may be moved, exclusive of any time during which Parliament is adjourned for more than four days or is prorogued or dissolved. Where, as in procedure (*e*), an instrument is laid in draft but subject to the negative procedure, there is a similar period of 40 days during which the resolution may be moved. In the case of instruments which need an affirmative resolution before they can come into operation (procedure (*b*)), no set period is provided as it is for the government in each case to decide how urgently the instrument is needed. Under procedure (*c*) the length of time during which the affirmative resolution must be secured is stated in the parent Act and varies from case to case. The Standing Orders of each House and an official publication, *Statutory Instrument Practice*, seek to ensure that proper laying procedures are observed.

Although a parent Act may expressly confine control of statutory instruments to the Commons, and this occurs in the case of fiscal measures, the House of Lords is usually granted the same powers of control as the Commons. Moreover, the procedure under the Parliament Acts 1911 and 1949 for by-passing the Lords applies only to Bills and not to statutory instruments. But it is extremely rare for the House of Lords to exercise its legal veto over subordinate legislation. When in 1968 the House rejected an order containing sanctions against the Rhodesian government made under the Southern Rhodesia Act 1965,[48] this caused the Labour government to propose that the power of the Lords to veto statutory instruments should be abolished.[49] Although the present power of veto could be abused as a means of harassing a government unpopular with the House of Lords, a reformed second chamber would provide a valuable safeguard against misuse by the executive of legislative powers.

When a vote is taken on a statutory instrument in the Commons, it is extremely rare for the government not to obtain a majority. On 24 July 1978, the minority Labour government was defeated in the Commons on regulations made under the Dock Work Regulation Act 1976. Both in 1972 and in 1982, the Conservative government was defeated on proposed new immigration rules, but modified rules were subsequently approved by the Commons in each case.[50]

---

[46] Cf. de Smith, *Judicial Review*, pp. 147–8 but see A.I.L. Campbell [1983] P.L. 43.
[47] H.L. 51, H.C. 169 (1977–8), pp. 11–12.
[48] On 18 Jun. 1968, the Southern Rhodesia (United Nations Sanctions) Order 1968 was rejected but on 18 Jul. 1968, an identical Order was approved.
[49] Cmnd 3799, 1969, pp. 22–3; Parliament (No. 2) Bill 1969, clauses 13–15. And see ch. 11 B.
[50] H.C. Deb., 22 Nov. 1972, col. 1343 and 15 Dec. 1982, col. 436.

Joint Committee on Statutory Instruments

All general statutory instruments laid before Parliament, as well as other statutory orders, come under scrutiny by the Joint Committee on Statutory Instruments, consisting of seven members appointed from each House. The members from the Commons also meet separately to scrutinise those instruments which are laid only in the Commons. The joint committee is advised by the Speaker's Counsel and by Counsel to the Lord Chairman of Committees.

The committee's duty is to consider whether the attention of the Houses should be drawn to an instrument on any of the following grounds, namely:

(*a*)   that it imposes a charge on the public revenues or contains provisions requiring payments to be made to the Exchequer or any government department or to any local or public authority in consideration of any licence or consent, or of any services to be rendered, or prescribes the amount of any such charge or payments;

(*b*)   that it is made in pursuance of an enactment containing specific provisions excluding it from challenge in the courts, either at all times or after the expiration of a specified period;

(*c*)   that is purports to have retrospective effect where the parent statute confers no express authority so to provide;

(*d*)   that there appears to have been unjustifiable delay in the publication or in the laying of it before Parliament;

(*e*)   that there appears to have been unjustifiable delay in sending a notification under the proviso to section 4(1) of the Statutory Instruments Act 1946, where an instrument has come into operation before it has been laid before Parliament;

(*f*)   that there appears to be a doubt whether it is *intra vires* or that it appears to make some unusual or unexpected use of the powers under which it was made;

(*g*)   that for any special reason its form or purport calls for elucidation;

(*h*)   that its drafting appears to be defective.

The committee may also report an instrument on any other ground which does not impinge on its merits or on the policy behind it. The committee is therefore concerned with the scrutiny of instruments on what are called technical grounds, that is, legal, constitutional and procedural matters. Under ground (*f*), the committee may express doubts about the *vires*, or legal validity, of an instrument, but the committee is not a court and is not able to give a binding decision on such an issue. That is a matter exclusively for the courts to determine. Before an adverse report on an instrument is made by the committee, the department concerned is given an opportunity to furnish orally or in writing such explanations as it may think fit. In practice, a senior official, and not the minister, offers the necessary explanation. Few instruments are reported to the two Houses in proportion to the total output of subordinate legislation, but the trend is for the number to increase.[51] The report by the committee on a particular instrument itself has no effect on the instrument, although it may encourage a member to table a prayer against the instrument. As well as its regular reports on instruments scrutinised, the committee may also issue special reports concerned with matters such as the drafting of

---

[54]   Between 1966 and 1972, the Commons committee examined 5496 instruments and reported 57 (H.C. 475, 1971–2, para. 54). In 1980–1 alone, the joint committee reported 80 instruments (H.C. 15–viii, 1981–2).

subordinate legislation and delays in publication.

It is not the function of this committee to examine the merits or policy of an instrument. These matters may be discussed by the whole House if a debate is held on an affirmative resolution or on a prayer for annulment. The impossibility of finding enough time in the Commons to debate the merits of instruments which M.P.s wished to discuss led in 1972 to a proposal that committees should be used to debate instruments on their merits.[52] For this purpose, one or more standing committees may now be appointed, on the lines of the standing committees used for the committee stage of Bills.[53] An instrument may be referred for debate to a standing committee on the proposal of a minister, unless 20 or more M. P.s object. In the committee, one and a half hours are allowed for considering each instrument.[54] After this consideration, a vote on the affirmative resolution or the prayer for annulment may be taken in the whole House without further debate. A debate in standing committee may be better than no debate at all, but in 1978 it was said by the Select Committee on Procedure to provide only vestigial control of statutory instruments and to be in need of comprehensive reform.[55]

In order that each House may inform itself about EEC secondary legislation, committees of the two Houses have been appointed which have functions comparable with those of the committees which deal with statutory instruments.[56]

3 Publicity. Although it is desirable that all legislation should be publicised before it takes effect, there are some matters, for example changes in indirect taxation, where the object of the legislation would be defeated if it had to be made known to the public in advance of enactment. This is recognised by the Statutory Instruments Act, which allows that for essential reasons a statutory instrument may come into operation even before it is laid before Parliament, with the safeguard that the Lord Chancellor and the Speaker must be provided with an immediate explanation. Apart from this, publicity is now secured by the following rules:

(*a*) A uniform procedure has been laid down for numbering, printing, publishing and citing statutory instruments.[57] An instrument classified as local by reason of its subject-matter and certain classes of general instrument certified by the authority which makes the instrument may be exempted from the requirements of printing and sale of the publication. Each year is published a collected edition of all general instruments made during the year which are still operative.

(*b*) The rule that where an instrument has to be laid before Parliament it must be laid before it comes into operation has already been mentioned.

(*c*) It is a defence in proceedings for contravention of a statutory instrument to prove that it had not been issued by H. M. Stationery Office at the date

---

52 H.C. 475 (1971–2), para. 123.
53 Ch. 11 B.
54 In the case of instruments concerning Northern Ireland, 2½ hours: H.C. S.O. 79.
55 H.C. 588–1 (1977–8), p. xxxiv.
56 Ch. 8 B.
57 Statutory Instruments Act 1946, s. 2.

of the alleged contravention, unless it is shown by the prosecutor that reasonable steps have been taken to bring the purport of the instrument to the notice of the public or of persons likely to be affected by it or of the person charged.[58] Thus ignorance of a statutory instrument is no defence but failure to issue it may in certain circumstances be a defence. This statutory defence is necessary because these instruments may otherwise operate without any warning of their enactment.

4 Challenge in the courts.   If made in accordance with the prescribed procedure, and if it is within the powers conferred by the parent Act, a statutory instrument is as much part of the law as the statute itself. The essential difference between statute and statutory instrument is that, unlike Parliament, a minister has not unlimited powers. Consequently, if a government department attempts to enforce a statutory instrument against an individual, whether by criminal or civil proceedings, the individual may as a defence question the validity of the instrument. The courts have power to decide this question even though the instrument has been approved by resolution of each House of Parliament.[59]

The validity of a statutory instrument may be challenged on two main grounds (a) that the content or substance of the instrument is *ultra vires* the parent Act, (b) that the correct procedure has not been followed in making the instrument. The chances of such a challenge succeeding may depend on the terms of the Act by which legislative power has been conferred. If a minister is given power to make such regulations as appear to him to be necessary or expedient for achieving a particular purpose, the minister is unlikely to be successfully challenged unless he uses the power for a totally different purpose. But even in such a case there is a judicial presumption that Parliament does not intend certain forms of legislation to be made unless by express words or by necessary implication it has clearly authorised them. The principles that no man should be deprived of access to the courts except by clear words of Parliament, and that there is no power to levy a tax without clear authority are illustrated by cases arising out of Defence Regulations made during the first world war.[60] That these basic constitutional principles can cut down the width of even such expressions as 'power to make such regulations as seem to the minister to be necessary' was illustrated in *Commissioners of Customs and Excise* v. *Cure and Deeley Ltd.*

The Finance (No. 2) Act 1940 empowered the Commissioners to make regulations providing for any matter for which provision appeared to them to be necessary for giving effect to the statutory provisions relating to puchase tax. Regulations were made under which, if proper tax returns were not submitted by manufacturers, the Commissioners might determine the amount of tax due, 'which amount shall be deemed

---

58   Statutory Instruments Act 1946, s. 3(2); *R.* v. *Sheer Metalcraft Ltd* [1954] 1 Q.B. 586; Wilson, *Cases*, p. 367. In (1974) 37 M.L.R. 510, D. J. Lanham argues that at common law delegated legislation must be published before it can come into force. But see A. I. L. Campbell [1982] P.L. 569, and in reply D. J. Lanham [1983] P.L. 395

59   *Hoffman-La Roche* v. *Secretary of State for Trade* [1975] A.C. 295.

60   *A.-G.* v. *Wilts United Dairies Ltd* and *Chester* v. *Bateson*, discussed in ch. 29 B. And see *Kerr* v. *Hood* 1907 S.C. 895.

to be the proper tax due', unless within seven days the tax-payer satisfied the Commissioners that some other sum was due. *Held* that the regulation was invalid in that it purported to prevent the tax-payer proving in a court the amount of tax actually due, and substituted for the tax authorised by Parliament some other sum arbitrarily determined by the Commissioners.[61]

By similar reasoning a court might declare invalid a statutory instrument which purported to have retrospective effect, or to sub-delegate legislative power, in the absence of clear authority from Parliament for such provisions. In 1973, the Court of Session declared *ultra vires* a regulation made by the Secretary of State for Scotland which without express authority from Parliament sought to remove from qualified teachers the right to continue teaching without first registering with a statutory Teaching Council.[62] In 1976, the House of Lords by 3–2 held *ultra vires* a regulation which authorised the levying of sewerage charges on houses not connected with public sewers,[63] and in 1982 the Home Secretary's power to make rules for the management of prisons was held not to permit him to make rules fettering a prisoner's right of access to the courts.[64] But in *McEldowney* v. *Forde*, which concerned the freedom of association in Northern Ireland, the House of Lords by 3–2 upheld a remarkably phrased ban on republican clubs imposed by the Northern Ireland Minister for Home Affairs.[65]

In reviewing the contents of delegated legislation, the courts do not lightly strike down a statutory instrument but they are now prepared to apply a test of unreasonableness where a regulation is so unreasonable that Parliament cannot be taken as having authorised it to be made under the Act in question.[66]

A serious procedural error by the department concerned could lead to an instrument being declared invalid. Thus where there was a duty to consult interested organisations before regulations were made, it was held that the mere sending of a letter to an organisation did not amount to consultation.[67] This does not mean that every minor procedural error would vitiate the statutory instrument; some procedural requirements are held to be directory (that is, of such a kind that failure to comply with them does not invalidate the instrument) and not mandatory or imperative.[68] Where either on grounds of substance or procedure an instrument is to some extent defective, this does not necessarily mean that the whole instrument is a nullity; it may still be operative to its lawful extent or be binding upon persons not affected by the defect of procedure.[69]

It was at one time believed that if the parent Act provided that regulations when made should have effect 'as if enacted in this Act', the courts were

---

[61] [1962] 1 Q.B. 340; Wilson, *Cases*, p. 392.

[62] *Malloch* v. *Aberdeen Corp.* 1974 S.L.T. 253; and see Education (Scotland) Act 1973.

[63] *Daymond* v. *South West Water Authority* [1976] A.C. 609.

[64] *Raymond* v. *Honey* [1983] A.C. 1.

[65] [1971] A.C. 632; Wilson, *Cases*, p. 395. And see D. N. MacCormick (1970) 86 L.Q.R. 171.

[66] *Maynard* v. *Osmond* [1977] Q.B. 240, *Cinnamond* v. *British Airports Authority* [1980] 2 All E.R. 368; *cf. Sparks* v. *Edward Ash Ltd.* [1943] K.B. 223, 230.

[67] The *Aylesbury Mushrooms* case, n. 36 *ante*.

[68] de Smith, *Judicial Review*, pp. 142–8 and p. 630 *post*.

[69] *Dunkley* v. *Evans* [1981] 3 All E.R. 285; the *Aylesbury Mushrooms* case, n. 36 *ante*.

precluded from inquiring into the validity of the regulations; but in 1931 the House of Lords were of the opposite opinion[70] and it is likely that this expression in the parent Act adds nothing to the binding effect of a properly made instrument. It is undesirable that the power of a court to rule on the validity of a statutory instrument should be excluded, however rarely the power may need to be used.

Byelaws
In chapter 21 the powers of local authorities to make byelaws have been described. Byelaws are a form of delegated legislation where the initiative is conferred on a local authority or some other public body. Central control is retained through the requirement of ministerial confirmation before a byelaw can take effect; the courts have also exercised a greater degree of control over byelaws than over ministerial regulations.[71]

Administrative rule-making
Legislation by statutory instrument is more flexible than legislation by Act of Parliament, since the law can be changed without need to wait for a Bill to pass through Parliament. Nonetheless, statutory instrument procedures are today complex and the instruments are expressed in formal language. In government business today many less formal methods of rule-making are used. Such methods are sometimes directly authorised by Act of Parliament but rules so made have a doubtful legal status (for example, the immigration rules made under the Immigration Act 1971).[72]

Depending on the parent Act, these rules may totally evade the procedures for parliamentary control described above. Most administrative rules are issued without direct statutory authority. This phenomenon was once described as 'administrative quasi-legislation'[73] when it was related to the practice of issuing the official interpretation of doubtful points in statutes and of stating concessions that would be made in individual cases. In 1944 Parliament was notified of a 20-page list of extra-statutory concessions given by the Inland Revenue in war-time.[74] The practice has continued on a widespread basis ever since, for the revenue authorities have often chosen to waive the application of over-harsh laws rather than to seek changes in the legislation. In 1979, the Inland Revenue's use of executive discretion rather than a statutory basis for assessing tax was described by the House of Lords as unconstitutional.[75] As Walton J. had said, 'One should be taxed by law, and not untaxed by concession'.[76]

In 1976–78, when the minority Labour government was seeking to pursue a non-statutory incomes policy, a wide range of government powers was used to bring pressure to bear on industry, including the awarding of government

---

[70] *Minister of Health* v. *R.* [1931] A.C. 494.
[71] Page 385 *ante*.
[72] See ch. 25 B.
[73] R. E. Megarry (1944) 60 L.Q.R. 125.
[74] Cmd 6559, 1944; and p. 293 *ante*.
[75] *Vestey* v. *I.R.C.* (No. 2) [1980] A.C. 1148.
[76] *Vestey* v. *I.R.C.* [1979] Ch. 177, 197. And see the *British Tax Encyclopedia*, part 6 and D. W. Williams [1979] *British Tax Review* 137.

contracts.[77] The use of such powers had a quasi-legislative effect but the policy collapsed when the House of Commons voted against it in December 1978.

In areas of local government, such as town planning and education, ministerial statements of policy and circulars to local authorities may have a practical effect which falls little short of modifying the law. On important matters of general policy where controversial issues are involved, government by circular is not a satisfactory substitute for legislation. Thus in 1965, 1970 and again in 1974 successive Secretaries of State for Education and Science issued circulars regarding the reorganisation of secondary education. But a legal obligation to adopt the policy of comprehensive secondary schools was created only by the Education Act 1976, which in turn was amended after the general election in 1979. Such circulars cannot however require the performance of unlawful acts.[78]

Informal rule-making is frequently adopted by departments in order that wide discretion vested in ministers by statute may be exercised by civil servants in a reasonably uniform manner. Some departments which rely on such rules make a practice of publishing them; others attempt to keep them secret, which causes problems when a person affected by application of the rules has a right of appeal to a tribunal, or wishes to know the reasons for a decision. The most absurd example of official secrecy occurred in the Compton Bassett case. Here, after the Crichel Down affair, the Treasury had notified Parliament of the rules regarding the disposal by departments of land which had been compulsorily acquired but was no longer needed; but when the rules were changed in 1966, the Treasury decided not to tell Parliament and insisted on keeping the text of the amendments secret.[79] Like any large organisation, a department may wish to give instructions to its staff on purely internal matters without publishing them. But it is contrary to both legal and democratic principles that rules which directly affect the interests of the citizen should not be published. Problems arising out of the application and interpretation of departmental rules have frequently come before the Parliamentary Commissioner for Administration, most notably in the Sachsenhausen case.[80]

The conclusion must be that while delegated legislation in the form of statutory instruments and byelaws has, not without difficulty, been accommodated within the legal system, many executive powers of rule-making present a continuing challenge to the notion of government according to law.

---

[77]   G. Ganz [1978] P.L. 333, R. B. Ferguson and A. C. Page [1978] P.L. 347, and T. C. Daintith [1979] C.L.P. 41; p. 294 *ante*.

[78]   *Royal College and Nursing* v. *D.H.S.S.* [1981] A.C. 800, *Gillick* v. *West Norfolk Health Authority* [1984] 1 All E.R. 365.

[79]   R. Gregory and P. Hutchesson, *The Parliamentary Ombudsman*, pp. 593–9.

[80]   Ch. 37 D.

Chapter 34

Judicial control of administrative action

Judicial control of administrative action raises some of the most difficult problems of public law. As we have already seen, many of the tasks of public authorities in administering public services (for example, planning for the future, making effective use of resources) are not of a character susceptible of adjudication in a court.[1] Control of these functions can only be a matter for administrative and political means. Yet public authorities have power to regulate private activities, by licensing and other controls, and to confer benefits and impose burdens upon individuals. While administrative and political control is of no less importance in these matters, the law is also relevant, for it serves to determine both the permitted extent of public powers and also the rights and duties of the individual. Where Parliament has provided an appeal to a tribunal or to an inferior court against an administrative decision, a further right of appeal or recourse to the superior courts generally follows: it is now well accepted that tribunals and inferior courts should be bound by decisions of the higher courts on matters of law and jurisdiction.[2] In many fields Parliament has provided no right of appeal against administrative decisions. Nonetheless the superior courts still exercise a residual controlling power on matters such as *vires*, which are relevant to the *legality* of official decisions. Judicial control cannot be a substitute for administrative or political control of the *merits* or *expediency* of official decisions. Nor are the judges responsible for the efficiency of the administration. But the courts ensure that decisions made on political or other grounds conform to the law and that certain basic standards of fair procedure are observed.

In affording protection against official decisions which contravene the current standards of lawful administration, the judges look both to the common law (for example, for its presumptions in favour of an individual's common law rights) and to Acts of Parliament, since the courts must ensure that the intentions of Parliament as may be inferred from its legislation are fulfilled. In a particular case, the extent of judicial control depends on a variety of factors: the power in question and its statutory context; the agency in whom

[1] Page 601 *ante.*
[2] Tribunals and Inquiries Act 1971, s. 13; ch. 37 A.

is vested the power; the existence of means of appealing from or challenging the decision; the effect of the decision on the individual who seeks a remedy in the court. There is in consequence a danger that judical control as a subject for study fragments into a large number of disparate branches of public law, such as immigration control, education and town planning. Nevertheless, some general principles have emerged and these are discussed in this chapter. These principles may be deduced from numerous judicial decisions interpreting individual statutes. Often study of the case-law does not reveal a definite answer to a new problem. Thus a decision of the court in a town planning case may or may not be relevant to a contested claim to social security benefit. A typical question that arises is whether a statute which limits judicial review of a compulsory purchase order is to be interpreted in the same way as a statute which seeks to exclude review of a tribunal's decision assessing compensation for the loss of property abroad.[3]

Judicial review of administrative action therefore involves the judges in the task of developing legal principles against a complex and often changing legislative and political background. This branch of the law is far from static and precedents must be used with great care. As Lord Diplock said in 1981, 'Any judicial statements on matters of public law if made before 1950 are likely to be a misleading guide to what the law is today'.[4] Moreover, while administration requires a sound legal basis, the most authoritative treatise on judicial review in English law opens with the words: 'Judicial review of administrative action is inevitably sporadic and peripheral. The administrative process is not, and cannot be, a succession of justiciable controversies'.[5] Judicial decisions may appear sporadic and peripheral when set against the whole work of government. But the general principles which emerge from the judicial process should be neither haphazard, incoherent nor contradictory.[6]

The legal solution to many administrative disputes inevitably involves judicial discretion. Even if the relevant general principles are clear, their application to a particular dispute is seldom clear cut. This fact, taken with the political impact that a judicial decision may have when it concerns the policy of a minister or large local authority, leads sometimes to criticism of the judges for their political bias.[7] A prominent instance of this occurred in 1981, when the cheap-fares policy for London of the (Labour) Greater London Council (GLC) was challenged in the courts by the (Conservative) Bromley Council. Some extravagant language used by two judges in the Court of Appeal (Lord Denning M. R. and Watkins L. J.) condemning the actions of the GLC fuelled the flames of political controversy, but that court's decision was upheld in more restrained terms by a unanimous House of Lords.[8] It is impossible for anyone to consider the cheap-fares issue without some social or political prejudice, but the record of proceedings in the House of Lords indicates that, given the

---

[3] See *R. v. Secretary of State for the Environment, ex p. Ostler* [1977] Q.B. 122; p. 672 *post*.

[4] *R. v. Inland Revenue Cmssrs., ex p. National Federation of Self Employed* [1982] A.C. 617, 640.

[5] de Smith, *Judicial Review*, p. 3.

[6] For a perceptive critique of the underlying theories, see D. J. Galligan (1982) 2 *Ox. Jl. of Legal Studies* 257.

[7] *E.g.* J. A. G. Griffith, *The Politics of the Judiciary*, chs. 3–7.

[8] *Bromley Council v. Greater London Council* [1983] A.C. 768; and see the sequel *R. v. London Transport Executive, ex p. GLC* [1983] Q.B. 484; J. Dignan (1983) 99 L.Q.R. 605.

existing legislation and the structure of government in London, there were weighty legal arguments against the manner in which the GLC had sought to carry out the Labour party's election pledge to secure lower fares in London. If the Conservative government and Parliament had so wished, amending legislation to validate the GLC's policy would have been a simple matter. The *Bromley* case does not provide a basis for extensive criticism of the judiciary for political bias. But there is some force in the view that British judges are more experienced in remedying instances of individual injustice, like the case of the probationer police-officer dismissed without a hearing by his chief constable,[9] than in evaluating the legality of social and economic policies.

Although the emphasis in this chapter is on English law, the principles of judicial review in the law of Scotland are very similar. Chapter 35 deals with the judicial remedies by which review may be obtained. These remedies are very different as between England and Scotland, although some statutory remedies are common to both systems. Because there has in the past been a close connection in English law between the grounds of review and the remedies, it will be necessary in the present chapter to make some reference to procedures that will be explained more fully in chapter 35.

A. Excess and abuse of powers

The ultra vires rule

When a power vested in a public authority is exceeded, acts done in excess of the power are invalid as being *ultra vires*. The *ultra vires* doctrine cannot be used to question the validity of an Act of Parliament; but it serves to control those who exceed the administrative discretion which an Act has given. The simplest instance of the rule is where an act is done in excess of a power to acquire private rights or to regulate private activities. Three examples may be given.

1   In *Sovmots Investments Ltd.* v. *Secretary of State for the Environment*, the Camden Borough Council in 1972 made a compulsory purchase order of 36 maisonettes for housing purposes, under the Housing Act 1957. These maisonettes formed part of the Centre Point complex of offices and shops, completed in 1966 but never occupied. Access to the maisonettes was obtained through the main building and they could be used as dwellings only if services such as electricity and water were provided from the rest of the building. Such ancillary rights and services were not specified in the purchase order. When the owners of Centre Point challenged the legality of the order, the Court of Appeal held that the 1957 Act authorised local authorities to acquire such rights over adjacent property as were necessary to enable flats and maisonettes to be occupied. But the House of Lords (Lord Russell dissenting) held that the council's powers of acquiring land for housing purposes were limited to those rights in land expressly conferred by statute, and could not be extended by necessary implication to include ancillary rights. Moreover, even if such rights could be so acquired, they had to be specified in the purchase order. The Centre Point order was accordingly quashed as being beyond the powers of the council.[1]

2   *Laker Airways Ltd* v. *Department of Trade* concerned the Civil Aviation Act 1971,

---

9   *Chief Constable of North Wales* v. *Evans* [1982] 3 All E.R. 141.

1   [1979] A.C. 144.

under which the Civil Aviation Authority (CAA) regulates the operation of scheduled services to and from the United Kingdom. The CAA was bound by objectives set out in section 3(1) of the 1971 Act to ensure that the publicly-owned British Airways had no monopoly of long-distance routes and that at least one other British airline could compete on each route. By section 3(2), the Secretary of State could give written guidance to the CAA regarding its functions. In 1972, the CAA granted Laker Airways a licence to run a cut-price service, Skytrain, between London and New York, but the US authorities delayed their consent. In 1975, the Secretary of State adopted a new policy, deciding that the British licence for Skytrain should be revoked and issuing 'guidance' whereby, except with the consent of British Airways, no more than one British airline should operate on long-distance routes. This 'guidance' was approved by resolution of each House of Parliament as required by the 1971 Act. *Held* (Court of Appeal) the Secretary of State's 'guidance' was *ultra vires*, since it conflicted with the 1971 Act by giving a monopoly position to British Airways. The power to issue guidance did not include power to alter the objectives set out in the Act.[2]

3   The Caravan Sites and Control of Development Act 1960 gave power to local authorities to grant licences for caravan sites 'subject to such conditions as the authority may think it necessary or desirable to impose ... in the interest of persons dwelling thereon in caravans, or of any other class of persons, or of the public at large'. An appeal against unduly burdensome conditions lay to the magistrates' court. Chertsey District Council issued a licence subject to conditions (*inter alia*) that individual site rents should be agreed with the council and that no premiums should be charged on incoming dwellers, that the dwellers should be granted security of tenure similar to that under the Rent Acts for controlled tenancies, that dwellers should be free to choose where they did their shopping and should not be restricted in the callers they had or in the formation of tenants' or political associations. The site-owner challenged these conditions as *ultra vires*. *Held* by the House of Lords that the Act of 1960 was restricted to granting powers to impose conditions relating to the use of the site; these conditions related to the contents of the agreements for letting caravans made with individual dwellers; despite the apparently very wide terms of the enabling Act, all the conditions were *ultra vires* and void.[3]

As these cases illustrate, the limits of an authority's power are often not obvious. Although, as in the caravan sites case, the courts sometimes cut down the scope of an apparently wide discretion, the powers of an authority include not only those expressly conferred by statute but also those which are reasonably incidental to those expressly conferred.[4]

By the Housing Act 1957, the 'general management, regulation and control' of council houses were vested in the local housing authority. A local authority arranged with an insurance company a scheme by which tenants could pay a small weekly premium, collected by the council together with the rent, for the insurance of their household goods. The scheme was held to be within the authority's statutory power of management.[5]

But, as we saw in the *Sovmots* case, the principle of implied powers does not apply to legislation that involves the compulsory acquisition of property.

2   [1977] Q.B. 643, discussed by G. R. Baldwin [1978] P.L. 57.
3   *Mixnam's Properties Ltd* v. *Chertsey UDC* [1965] A.C. 735, discussed by G. Ganz, (1964) 27 M.L.R. 611. See also *R.* v. *Hillingdon BC, ex p. Royco Homes Ltd* [1974] Q.B. 720.
4   In the case of local authorities, see Local Government Act 1972, s. 111; p. 382 *ante*.
5   *A.-G.* v. *Crayford UDC* [1962] Ch. 575.

Incorrect procedure

Where statute authorises a certain power to be exercised after a stated procedure has been followed, failure to observe the procedure may result in the purported exercise of the power being declared a nullity.

In *Ridge* v. *Baldwin*, the Brighton police committee summarily dismissed their chief constable following his trial at the Central Criminal Court on charges of conspiracy; his acquittal had been accompanied by serious criticism of his conduct by the trial judge. Disciplinary regulations made under the Police Act 1919 laid down a procedure by which formal inquiry had to be held into charges brought against a chief constable before he could be dismissed. The committee contended that this procedure did not apply to the power of dismissal under the Municipal Corporations Act 1882. The House of Lords held *inter alia* that the disciplinary regulations did apply, and 'inasmuch as the decision was arrived at in complete disregard of the regulations it must be regarded as void and of no effect'.[6]

But not every procedural error invalidates administrative action. In the past the courts have distinguished between procedural requirements which are mandatory (breach invalidates) and those which are directory (breach does not invalidate). But this distinction does not take account of whether there has been a total failure to observe the procedure, or substantial compliance with it; nor of whether the procedural defect caused any real prejudice to the individual.[7] In 1979, Lord Hailsham, commenting upon the distinction, suggested that the courts are faced with 'not so much a stark choice of alternatives but a spectrum of possibilities'. He continued, 'The jurisdiction is inherently discretionary, and the court is frequently in the presence of differences of degree which merge almost imperceptibly into differences of kind'.[8]

Abuse of discretionary powers[9]

The courts may intervene not only to prevent powers being exceeded but also to prevent them being abused. The justification for this is that the exercise of a discretion for an improper purpose or without taking into account all relevant considerations is regarded as failure to exercise the discretion lawfully. This does not mean that the courts may substitute their own decision for that of the body or person to whom a discretion has been entrusted.

In *Associated Provincial Picture Houses Ltd* v. *Wednesbury Corporation*, the local authority gave the company leave for Sunday cinema performances subject to the condition that no children under 15 should be admitted to Sunday performances, with or without an adult. The Sunday Entertainments Act 1932 gave a local authority power to sanction Sunday performances, 'subject to such conditions as the authority think fit to impose'. The Court of Appeal held that the local authority had not acted unreasonably or *ultra vires* in imposing the condition.[10]

---

6   [1964] A.C. 40, 117 (Lord Morris of Borth-y-Gest).
7   Compare *Coney* v. *Choyce* [1975] 1 All E.R. 979 (no prejudice caused by failure to notify school closure at school entrance) with *Bradbury* v. *London Borough of Enfield* [1967] 3 All E.R. 434 (complete failure to notify proposed changes in composition of schools).
8   *London and Clydesdale Estates Ltd.* v. *Aberdeen DC* [1979] 2 All E.R. 876, 883.
9   For a full account, see de Smith, *Judicial Review*, ch. 6.
10 [1948] 1 K.B. 223; Wilson, *Cases*, p. 408.

Lord Greene's judgment in this case is commonly cited today in decisions involving judicial review of powers for unreasonableness. What is often referred to as the *Wednesbury* test is the proposition that a court may interfere with the exercise of discretion for unreasonableness only when the authority has come to a conclusion 'so unreasonable that no reasonable authority could ever have come to it'. It is clear from Lord Greene's judgement that unreasonableness as a ground of review is closely related to other grounds such as irrelevant considerations, improper purposes and error of law. The meaning of 'unreasonable' was central to the decision of the House of Lords in the *Tameside* case.[11] Lord Diplock there said that 'unreasonable' denotes 'conduct which no sensible authority acting with due appreciation of its responsibilities would have decided to adopt', a formula which seems very likely to give rise to conflicting interpretations.

Where an authority has discretionary powers, control of the merits of its decisions is primarily a matter for political or administrative means. Sometimes by statute the decision of a local authority requires ministerial confirmation or is subject to an appeal to the minister. Exceptionally, when statute has provided a full right of appeal to a court against an official decision, the court may be able to apply its own view of the merits, provided it has due regard to the opinions of the authority which made the first decision.[12]

In some cases the language of the statute seeks to confer an absolute discretion on the administrator; where this is so the powers of the court are much reduced. Under the British Nationality Act 1981, the Home Secretary may if he thinks fit grant naturalisation to an alien who satisfies certain conditions. Even if these conditions are satisfied, naturalisation may be refused. The Home Secretary is not required to assign any reason for refusal, and his decision is not subject to appeal to or review in any court.[13] In the past, the courts were readier to accept that executive discretion was immune from judicial review than they are today. During the second world war power was given to the Home Secretary to detain anyone whom he had reasonable cause to believe was a person of hostile origin or association. In *Liversidge* v. *Anderson*, it was held by the House of Lords, Lord Atkin dissenting, that the court could not enquire into the grounds for the belief which led to the making of a detention order; the matter was one for executive discretion. In regard to such an issue, an objective test of reasonableness could not be applied, but only a subjective test. The statement of his belief by the Home Secretary was accepted as conclusive.[14] But *Liversidge* v. *Anderson* is an extreme example of judicial unwillingness to review executive discretion, best explained by wartime circumstances.[15] The present attitude of the courts to claims that a minister has unfettered discretion is shown by the decision of the House of Lords in *Padfield* v. *Minister of Agriculture*.

---

[11] Page 634 *post*.

[12] *Sagnata Investments Ltd* v. *Norwich Corp.* [1971] 2 Q.B. 614.

[13] British Nationality Act 1981, ss. 6(1), 44(2) and sch. 1; T. St. J. N. Bates [1982] P.L. 179.

[14] [1942] A.C. 206; p. 558 *ante*. Cf. *Nakkuda Ali* v. *Jayaratne* [1951] A.C. 66 and *R.* v. *Governor of Brixton Prison, ex p. Soblen* [1963] 2 Q.B. 243, p. 454 *ante*.

[15] See R. F. V. Heuston, (1970) 86 L.Q.R. 33, (1971) 87 L.Q.R. 161.

Under the Agricultural Marketing Act 1958, the milk marketing scheme included a complaints procedure by which a committee of investigation examined any complaint made about the operation of the scheme 'if the Minister in any case so directs'. Padfield, a farmer in south-east England, complained about the scheme of prices paid to farmers in that region by the Milk Marketing Board. The minister refused to direct that the complaint be referred to the committee of investigation, and claimed that he had an unfettered discretion in deciding whether or not to refer complaints to the committee. *Held* the minister would be directed to deal with the complaint according to law. The reasons given by the minister for his refusal were not good reasons in law and showed that he had not exercised his discretion in a manner which promoted the intention and objects of the Act of 1958. 'The policy and objects of the Act must be determined by construing the Act as a whole, and construction is always a matter of law for court'.[16]

The decision in *Padfield's* case was particularly significant in that the judges, after examining the reasons given by the Minister of Agriculture to see whether they conformed to the Act, were prepared to assume that he had no better reasons for his decision.[17] The willingness of the judges to impose limits upon the minister's discretion in *Padfield* matches the way in which they have frequently cut down the width of local authority discretions. Thus a local planning authority may grant planning permission 'subject to such conditions as they think fit', but the courts have severely limited the apparent width of this power.[18]

Some grounds on which the courts may hold that a power has been abused will now be described. It must be emphasised that these grounds overlap and are often not easily distinguished from each other.[19]

1 Irrelevant considerations.   Powers vested in a public authority must be exercised in accordance with the intention of Parliament as may be inferred from the Act in question. In a 19th-century case, local justices were held not to have exercised their discretion lawfully when they refused to order a parish to meet certain poor law expenses on the ground that the operation of the Act of Parliament was unjust.[20] In 1972, the Birmingham licensing planning committee was held to have taken extraneous considerations into account when it required a hotel company to make payments to brewery companies as a condition of the company receiving a licence for a new hotel.[21]

The court's power to rule that certain considerations are irrelevant may severely limit the scope of general words in a statute. For example, in deciding whether to grant a caravan licence under public health legislation, a public health authority could not take into account matters of local amenity, as these were relevant to town planning law.[22] But the courts do not always interpret

---

16   [1968] A.C. 997, 1030 (Lord Reid); Wilson, *Cases*, p. 560.
17   *Padfield* is criticised by R. C. Austin in [1975] C.L.P. 150 but Lord Denning M.R. considers it 'a landmark in our administrative law' ([1977] A.C. 1014, 1025).
18   E.g. *Hall and Co. Ltd.* v. *Shoreham-by-Sea UDC* [1964] 1 All E.R. 1. And see *Fawcett Properties Ltd.* v. *Bucks CC* [1961] A.C. 636; Wilson, *Cases*, p. 568.
19   See G. D. S. Taylor [1976] C.L.J. 272.
20   *R.* v. *Boteler* (1854) 4 B. & S. 969.
21   *R.* v. *Birmingham Licensing Planning Committee, ex p. Kennedy* [1972] 2 Q.B. 140.
22   *Pilling* v. *Abergele UDC* [1950] 1 K.B. 636; on different legislation, *cf.* the *Mixnam's Properties* case (n. 3 *ante*).

statutory discretion so narrowly.[23]

2 Improper purposes. The exercise of a power for an improper purpose is invalid. Improper purposes include, but are not restricted to, malice or personal dishonesty on the part of the officials or councillors making the decision; examples of this kind are rare. Most instances of improper purpose have arisen out of a mistaken interpretation by a public authority of what it is empowered to do, sometimes contributed to by an excess of zeal in the public interest. Thus a city council which was empowered to buy land compulsorily for the purpose of extending streets or improving the city could not validly buy land for the purpose of taking advantage of an anticipated increase in value of the land.[24] In *Congreve* v. *Home Office*, where the Home Office had threatened certain holders of television licences that their licences would be revoked by the Home Secretary if they did not each pay an extra £6, the Court of Appeal held that it was an improper exercise of the Home Secretary's discretionary power of revocation 'to use a threat to exercise that power as a means of extracting money which Parliament has given the Executive no mandate to demand'.[25]

Difficulty arises when the authority is motivated both by lawful and unlawful purposes.

The Westminster Corporation was empowered to construct public conveniences but not to provide pedestrian subways. Underground conveniences were designed so that the subway leading to them provided a means of crossing a busy street. It was sought to restrain the corporation from proceeding with the work on the ground that the real object was the provision of a crossing and not of public conveniences. The court refused to intervene. 'It is not enough to show that the corporation contemplated that the public might use the subway as a means of crossing the street. In order to make out a case of bad faith, it must be shown that the corporation constructed the subway as a means of crossing the street under colour and pretence of providing public conveniences not really wanted'.[26]

In such cases a distinction has sometimes been drawn between purpose and motive, so that where an exercise of power fulfils the purposes for which the power was given, it matters not that those exercising it were influenced by an extraneous motive. But the motive-purpose distinction is difficult to maintain, and it has sometimes given way to the test of what was the dominant purpose, or to the rather stricter rule, already outlined, that the presence of any extraneous or irrelevant considerations invalidates the decision.[27]

3 Error of law. An authority which is entrusted with a discretion must direct itself properly on the law or its decision may be declared invalid.

---

23 *E.g. Hanks* v. *Minister of Housing* [1963] 1 Q.B. 999, *Westminster Bank Ltd* v. *Beverley BC* [1971] A.C. 508 and *Roberton* v. *Secretary of State* [1976] 1 All E.R. 689 (risk of assassination of Prime Minister relevant to diversion of footpath on Chequers Estate).

24 *Municipal Council of Sydney* v. *Campbell* [1925] A.C. 338.

25 [1976] Q.B. 629, 662 (Geoffrey Lane L.J.).

26 *Westminster Corp.* v. *London and North Western Railway Co.* [1905] A.C. 426, 432 (Lord Macnaghten); *cf. Webb* v. *Minister of Housing* [1965] 2 All E.R. 193, discussed in [1965] C.L.J. 1.

27 De Smith, *Judicial Review*, pp. 325–33.

In *Perilly* v. *Tower Hamlets Borough Council*, the council wrongly believed that it was under a statutory duty to deal with applications for trading licences in the Petticoat Lane market in the strict order in which they were received; it therefore refused a licence to Perilly on the death of his mother, although she had had a pitch in the market for 30 years. The court quashed a licence which the council had granted to a newcomer to the market, and ordered that the licence be issued to Perilly.[28]

The notion of error of law goes much wider than a mere mistake of statutory interpretation. A minister commits an error of law if *inter alia* he acts when there is no evidence to support his action or if he comes to a conclusion to which, on the evidence, he could not reasonably have come.[29] These principles, developed by the courts in relation to town planning and compulsory purchase decisions, were highlighted in 1976 when a Labour Secretary of State for Education and a Conservative local council clashed over the reorganisation of secondary education.

Under the Education Act 1944, section 68, if the Secretary of State was satisfied that an education authority was proposing to act unreasonably, he could issue such directions to the authority as appeared to him expedient. When in May 1976 the newly elected Tameside council proposed, contrary to an earlier plan, to continue selection for entry to five grammar schools in the coming September, the Secretary of State directed the council to adhere to the earlier plan. The House of Lords refused to enforce this direction, holding that the direction was valid only if the Secretary of State had been satisfied that no reasonable authority could act as the council was proposing to. 'Unreasonable' in section 68 did not mean conduct which the Secretary of State thought was wrong. On the facts, there was no material on which the Secretary of State could have been satisfied that the council was acting unreasonably. The Secretary of State must therefore have misdirected himself as to the grounds on which he could act.[30]

Reliance on error of law as a ground for controlling discretion places the courts in a position of some strength *vis-à-vis* the administration since it is peculiarly for the courts to identify errors of law. As the *Tameside* case indicated, error of law is a sufficiently pliable concept to enable the judges, if they feel it is necessary, to make a very close scrutiny of the reasons for an official decision and also the facts on which it was based: We will be considering later in this chapter the difficult question of whether it has now become a general rule that a tribunal which makes an error of law in reaching a decision must in all circumstances be held to be exceeding its jurisdiction.

4 Unauthorised delegation. An authority to which the exercise of discretion has been entrusted by statute cannot delegate that exercise to another unless upon the construction of the statute it is clear that the delegation is authorised.

Barnard v. *National Dock Labour Board* concerned a statutory scheme for the registration of dock-workers, under which the disciplinary powers of the National Dock Labour

---

28   [1973] Q.B. 9; and see *R.* v. *Greater Birmingham Appeal Tribunal, ex p. Simper* [1974] Q.B. 543.
29   *Ashbridge Investments Ltd* v. *Minister of Housing* [1965] 3 All E.R. 371; *Coleen Properties Ltd* v. *Minister of Housing* [1971] 1 All E.R. 1049.
30   *Secretary of State for Education* v. *Tameside MB* [1977] A.C. 1014.

Board had to be delegated to local dock boards. The London dock board purported to delegate its disciplinary function to the port manager, who during a trade dispute suspended Barnard from work. *Held*, that disciplinary powers could not be lawfully delegated to the port manager; the purported suspension was declared a nullity.[31]

The rule against unauthorised delegation of powers might seem to require all powers vested in a minister to be exercised by him personally. That the courts have accepted the exigencies of departmental administration was shown in *Local Government Board* v. *Arlidge*:[32] powers and duties conferred on a minister may properly be exercised by officials in his department, whose decisions the minister can control and for whom he is responsible to Parliament.[33] But where a statutory duty is vested in one minister, he may not adopt a policy by which the decision is effectively made by another minister.[34] And, where a discretion is vested in a subordinate officer, it may not be taken away from him by orders from a superior.[35] Somewhat similar principles apply to statutory agencies. Thus the Police Complaints Board could not adopt a rule of taking no action on complaints which the Director of Public Prosecutions had decided should not lead to criminal proceedings;[36] but the Commission for Racial Equality may delegate to its staff the task of conducting formal investigations into alleged discrimination.[37] In local government, there is now very wide authority for the delegation by councils of their functions to committees, sub-committees and officers.[38]

5 Discretion may not be fettered. A discretion may not be surrendered, whether the surrender takes the form of contracting in advance to exercise it in a particular way or of pre-judging the way in which it shall be exercised. Thus licensing committees have full discretion in licensing matters, but it is their duty to hear all applications and to apply their minds in each case presented to them, whatever general policy they may have decided upon. Each applicant must have the opportunity of urging that the particular circumstances of his case should be taken into account before a decision is made.[39] A public authority may properly adopt a general policy and indicate to an applicant that the policy will be applied unless there is something exceptional in his case; but the authority may not adopt a rule that applications of a certain kind should always be refused.[40]

These principles apply to the exercise of discretionary powers vested in government departments. In practice it is often essential that departments should formulate policies and apply them.

---

[31] [1953] 2 Q.B. 18. And see de Smith, *Judicial Review*, pp. 298–309.

[32] [1915] A.C. 120, p. 645 *post*.

[33] *Carltona Ltd* v. *Commissioners of Works* [1943] 2 All E.R. 560; *Re Golden Chemical Products* [1976] Ch. 300. And ch. 15.

[34] *Lavender & Son Ltd* v. *Minister of Housing* [1970] 3 All E.R. 871; Wilson, *Cases*, p. 570.

[35] *Simms Motor Units Ltd* v. *Minister of Labour* [1946] 2 All E.R. 201.

[36] *R.* v. *Police Complaints Bd, ex p. Madden* [1983] 2 All E.R. 353.

[37] *R.* v. *Cmssn for Racial Equality, ex p. Cottrell & Rothon* [1980] 3 All E.R. 265.

[38] Page 387 *ante*.

[39] *R.* v. *Torquay Licensing Justices, ex p. Brockman* [1951] 2 K.B. 784.

[40] *R.* v. *Port of London Authority, ex p. Kynoch* [1919] 1 K.B. 176, 184 (dictum of Bankes L.J.). And see D. J. Galligan [1976] P.L. 332 and *R.* v. *Police Complaints Board, ex p. Madden, ante*.

Under a scheme for discretionary investment grants to industry, the Board of Trade applied a rule that grants could not be paid in respect of items costing less than £25 and refused to pay a grant to a firm which had spent over £4 million on gas cylinders costing £20 each: the House of Lords accepted that the department was entitled to make such a rule or policy, provided that it was prepared to listen to arguments for the exercise of individual discretion.[41]

In such a case, an individual may find it very difficult to persuade officials that he should receive preferential treatment. His right might be more realistically described as a right to ask that the general policy should be changed.[42]

Even so, public authorities are finding it difficult to adopt definite policies that do not, in the opinion of the courts, interfere with the proper exercise of discretion.[43]

6 Other grounds.   Some grounds of review apply particularly to local authorities. One controversial factor is that elected councils are expected to observe due standards of financial responsibility to the ratepayers, but the limits of this duty are difficult to determine. In *Roberts* v. *Hopwood*, the House of Lords held invalid a decision by the Poplar council in 1923 to pay a minimum wage of £4 per week to all adult employees, regardless of the work which they did, their sex and the falling cost of living; the judges considered that the council had exceeded its power to pay such wages as it saw fit, by making gifts or gratuities to its staff which it had no power to do.[44] Fifty years later, the principle that local authorities owe a fiduciary duty to their ratepayers as regards the management of local finance was again prominent in *Bromley Council* v. *Greater London Council*. The House of Lords held that the Greater London Council must exercise its powers in relation to fares on London transport with due regard to ordinary business principles; the decision that fares be cut by 25% had caused both a big increase in the subsidy payable by ratepayers and also a sharp loss in rate support grant paid from central goverment. The council was thus in breach of the fiduciary duty which it owned to London ratepayers.[45] But a modified scheme of subsidy for London fares later survived legal challenge[46] and in *Pickwell* v. *Camden Council* the court accepted as lawful a local pay settlement made by the council during national strikes which was more favourable to workers in Camden than was the national settlement.[47] Excessive expenditure on a lawful object may in extreme circumstances be restrained by the court; but much will depend on the decision-making process and on how the relevant considerations were taken into account.

The courts may declare invalid byelaws made by public authorities which they deem to be unreasonable, for example because they are manifestly oppres-

---

41   *British Oxygen Co.* v. *Board of Trade* [1971] A.C. 610; Wilson, *Cases*, p. 580. And see *Schmidt* v. *Home Secretary* [1969] 2 Ch. 149 and *Cumings* v. *Birkenhead Corp* [1972] Ch. 12.

42   *British Oxygen Co.* v. *Board of Trade, ante*, at 631 (Lord Dilhorne).

43   E.g. *A.-G. ex rel. Tilley* v. *Wandsworth BC* [1981] 1 W.L.R. 854, *R.* v. *Secretary of State for the Environment, ex p. Brent BC* [1982] Q.B. 593 and *R.* v. *Rochdale BC ex p. Crome Ring Mill Ltd.* [1982] 3 All E.R. 761.

44   [1925] A.C. 578. And see *Prescott* v. *Birmingham Corpn.* [1955] Ch. 210.

45   [1983] A.C. 768.

46   *R.* v. *London Transport Executive, ex p. GLC* [1983] Q.B. 484.

47   [1983] Q.B. 962, discussed by C. Crawford [1983] P.L. 248.

sive or are such that no reasonable authority could have made them.[48] But here too the word 'unreasonable' must be used with great care, as it has become a term of legal art.[49]

Failure to perform a statutory duty

We have so far been considering how a public authority may exceed its powers or misuse its discretion. A public authority may also act unlawfully if it fails to perform a duty imposed upon it by statute, for example to perform a public service or to grant a benefit to a specified class of individuals. The remedies appropriate for enforcing such a duty will be considered in the next chapter. A few comments on the problems of identifying an enforceable duty may be made here. In some cases, the statutory duty is clear and precise and is plainly enforceable by the persons concerned. Thus any elector for a local authority area is entitled to inspect the authority's minutes and to make copies or extracts of those minutes.[50] But there are many statutory duties which are more general in character and may not be clearly enforceable in the courts by private persons. Thus the Education Act 1944, section 76, obliges a local education authority to pay regard 'to the general principle that, so far as is compatible with the provision of efficient instruction . . . and the avoidance of unreasonable public expenditure, pupils are to be educated in accordance with the wishes of their parents'. How far does this statutory duty create enforceable rights in the parents of children of school age?

In *Watt* v. *Kesteven County Council*, the authority, which maintained no grammar school, secured places and paid fees for pupils entitled to secondary education at an independent school within their area. A Roman Catholic parent refused this facility and sent his two sons to a Catholic school in an adjacent county. The authority declined to pay the fees for attendance at this school, although it was recognised as efficient. *Held* by the Court of Appeal that the duty on the authority to make school places available was not enforceable by action by the parent, but only by the Minister of Education under his default powers.[51]

By contrast, under section 8 of the same Education Act, education authorities have a duty 'to secure that there shall be available for their area sufficient schools . . . for providing full time education' suitable to their pupils. In *Meade* v. *Haringey BC*, a local authority was faced with strike action by school caretakers and ancillary staff and decided that all schools should close until further notice. The Court of Appeal held that parents who suffered as a result of this decision to close the schools had a remedy in court, and that the council would be in breach of its duty if it decided to close the schools in sympathy with a trade union's claims at a time when the closure could reasonably have been avoided.[52]

---

[48] *Kruse* v. *Johnson* [1898] 2 Q.B. 91; *Cinnamond* v. *British Airports Authority* [1980] 2 All E.R. 368; p. 385 *ante*.

[49] *Secretary of State for Education* v. *Tameside MB* [1977] A.C. 1014; p. 634 *ante*.

[50] Local Government Act 1972, s. 228.

[51] [1955] 1 Q.B. 408, applied in *Bradbury* v. *London Borough of Enfield* [1967] 3 All E.R. 434 and *Cumings* v. *Birkenhead Corpn.* [1972] Ch. 12.

[52] [1979] 2 All E.R. 1016.

There are some statutory duties from which it is impossible to deduce a right of private enforcement, particularly where the duty is one which has no counterpart in the relations between two individuals, such as the duty of the Secretary of State for Education and Science to promote education and the progressive development of educational institutions. While there may be no judicial sanction for duties such as these, there may be a political sanction or some administrative remedy. The legislation may itself provide for enforcement when an authority is in default, for example where a housing authority delays unreasonably in carrying out its duty of selling council houses to its tenants.[53]

Finally, it must be noted that the statutory language is not always decisive of whether a public authority has a duty or a discretion on a certain matter. In some circumstances, the word 'may' used in legislation may be equivalent to 'must'.[54]

The concept of jurisdiction[55]

Our discussion so far of the *ultra vires* doctrine has been phrased in terms of powers, discretion and duties. In many cases however use is made of the language of jurisdiction. For historical reasons, as we saw in chapter 32, the concepts of *vires* (powers) and jurisdiction are very closely linked. Often it makes no difference whether a certain matter is regarded as being *ultra vires* or in excess of jurisdiction. But an inferior tribunal or a body such as a licensing authority may be said to have jurisdiction to hear and determine certain categories of questions, whether it be a claim for a social security benefit or a taxi-driver's licence. In the past these decisions were often taken in judicial form and they are still subject to control by the superior courts on jurisdictional grounds. This supervision does not seek to provide a fresh decision on the merits but to ensure that the body in question has observed the limits which are a condition of its power to make binding decisions. According to a famous dictum in *R. v. Nat Bell Liquors*,

'That supervision goes to two points: one is the area of the inferior judgment and the qualifications and conditions of its exercise; the other is the observance of the law in the course of its exercise.'[56]

Thus all tribunals and like bodies are subject in English law to control by the High Court on jurisdictional grounds, whether or not there is a statutory right of appeal from their decisions. While important differences exist between judicial review and remedies available by way of appeal, there is a wide overlap between the two, since many decisions made by a tribunal could give rise both to an appeal and to judicial review.[57] In the discussion which now

---

53   Housing Act 1980, s. 23; *R. v. Secretary of State for the Environment, ex p. Norwich Council* [1982] Q.B. 808.

54   *Padfield* v. *Minister of Agriculture* [1968] A.C. 997; de Smith, *Judicial Review*, pp. 283–5.

55   See de Smith, *Judicial Review*, ch. 3 and Wade, *Administrative Law*, ch. 9. For the position in Scots law, see A. W. Bradley (ed. Bates, Finnie, Usher and Wildburg) *In Memoriam – J. D. B. Mitchell*, ch. 1.

56   [1922] 2 A.C. 128, 156.

57   As in *R. v. Hillingdon BC, ex p. Royco Homes Ltd.* [1974] Q.B. 720.

follows, the inferior body whose decisions are under review will be described simply as a tribunal, but the principles involved also apply to many bodies (such as licensing authorities) which are not classified as tribunals for such purposes as supervision by the Council on Tribunals.[58]

The limits of a tribunal's jurisdiction

Tribunals have both a positive duty to decide the questions that the legislature intended them to decide and a negative duty to refrain from exceeding their jurisdiction. Many jurisdictional questions may arise at the outset of proceedings: for example, is the complaint one with which the tribunal may deal? has any essential prior procedure been observed?[59] are the members of the tribunal properly appointed? The first duty of a tribunal is to decide such preliminary matters, if questions about these are raised. But it is well established that no tribunal has power to decide conclusively the limits of its own jurisdiction.[60] Thus, if a tribunal refuses to 'hear and determine' a particular matter, saying that it falls outside its jurisdiction, that decision may be challenged in the High Court. So too can the decision of a tribunal to go ahead and decide a matter against the objection of one party. The aggrieved party may immediately request the High Court to intervene and prohibit further proceedings in excess of jurisdiction; or, if a decision on the merits has been made, the court may hold that the whole dispute was outside the tribunal's jurisdiction,[61] even if at the time the aggrieved party did not challenge the jurisdiction of the tribunal.[62]

Although it has been argued to the contrary,[63] jurisdictional control applies not just at the outset of a case but throughout the time that the matter is before the tribunal. Thus if a tribunal, after properly conducted proceedings, reaches a decision (such as to impose a penalty on one party) which is outside its power, the aggrieved person can have the decision quashed by the High Court as unlawful.

These rules maintain the principle that tribunals do not have unlimited jurisdiction. To give an illustration used in the House of Lords, a tribunal established by Parliament to give protection to wives against their husbands may not exceed its jurisdiction by interpreting 'wives' to include a woman who without marrying has been living with a man.[64] In practice very difficult questions may arise in distinguishing between (a) elements in a tribunal decision which amount to an excess of jurisdiction if they are, in the opinion of a superior court, decided incorrectly; and (b) elements in a tribunal decision which arguably may be incorrect but are none the less 'within jurisdiction' and can be put right only by an appeal on the merits, if one exists. One reason for these difficulties is that the courts have often gone far into the merits of

---

58 Ch. 37 A.
59 E.g. *R.* v. *Paddington Rent Tribunal, ex p. Bell Properties Ltd.* [1949] 1 K.B. 666.
60 See the famous passage in *R.* v. *Shoreditch Assessment Committee, ex p. Morgan* [1910] 2 K.B. 859, 880 (Farwell L.J.).
61 For the remedies, see ch. 35.
62 *Essex Congregational Union* v. *Essex CC* [1963] A.C. 808.
63 By D. M. Gordon, whose articles include (1931) 47 L.Q.R. 386, 557 and (1971) 34 M.L.R. 1. And see de Smith, *Judicial Review*, pp. 110–13.
64 Lord Pearce in *Anisminic Ltd.* v. *Foreign Compensation Commission* [1969] 2 A.C. 147, 194.

a decision to correct what they consider to be a mistake by a tribunal, while justifying their action on jurisdictional grounds.

An additional complication in English law comes from the remedy of certiorari. For historical reasons this remedy is available both to review matters affecting jurisdiction, and also to review errors of law which appear on the record of the tribunal's decision, whether or not those errors may be said to affect jurisdiction.[65]

Jurisdictional fact and law

What has been called the doctrine of jurisdictional fact and law provides one approach to the problem of distinguishing between jurisdictional and non-jurisdictional elements in a tribunal decision. Assume that by statute the Home Secretary is empowered to deport an alien when he deems this to be conducive to the public good.[66] If the Home Secretary proposes to use this power against X, believing X to be an alien, X's status may be said to be a collateral question, or a matter of jurisdictional fact, which X can ask the High Court to resolve. If X is found by the court not to be an alien, then the Home Secretary has no power to deport him. This means that the court can review the evidence relevant to X's nationality and may decide the matter for itself, whereas (assuming X is indeed an alien) the court will not interfere with the Home Secretary's discretionary decision that X should be deported unless it can be shown that the Home Secretary has abused his discretion.

Although this is a fundamental principle of law, its importance was virtually ignored by the House of Lords in 1980 in *R. v. Home Secretary, ex p. Zamir.*[67] Fortunately, that decision was overruled by the House three years later in *Khawaja's* case.[68] These cases both concerned the power of the Home Secretary under the Immigration Act 1971 to remove from the United Kingdom persons who were 'illegal entrants' under the Act. In *Zamir's* case, the House held that it was not a condition precedent of the power to remove that the immigration officer should satisfy the court that the individual was indeed an illegal entrant. This approach was tantamount to treating the individual's status as an illegal entrant as if it were a matter of Home Secretary's discretion. But in *Khawaja's* case, the House of Lords applied the principle that (in Lord Scarman's words) 'where the exercise of executive power depends upon the precedent establishment of an objective fact, the courts will decide whether the requirement has been satisfied'.[69] On this test it was not sufficient that the immigration officers believed Khawaja to be an illegal entrant; Khawaja's status as an illegal entrant was an objective fact which had to be established by evidence before the power to remove him could be exercised. This stricter test is particularly suitable when the individual's liberty is at stake.

Jurisdictional issues of this kind may involve the court not only in looking again at the evidence but also in reviewing the decisions on matters of law which were made by the tribunal. The difficulty of drawing the line between

---

[65]   Page 659 *post.*
[66]   An illustration used in *Khawaja's* case (*post*) by Lord Bridge.
[67]   [1980] A.C. 930.
[68]   *R. v. Home Secretary, ex p. Khawaja* [1984] A.C. 74.
[69]   [1984] A.C. at 110.

jurisdictional and non-jurisdictional matters is illustrated by the complex litigation in *Anisminic Ltd.* v. *Foreign Compensation Commission*.[70]

The tribunal in question was the Foreign Compensation Commission, created by the Foreign Compensation Act 1950. It had rejected a claim made by a British company (Anisminic) under a scheme for compensating British subjects who had lost property in Egypt during the Suez affair. The reason for rejection was that, on the commission's interpretation of the relevant Order in Council, it was fatal to the claim that Anisminic's assets in Egypt had been acquired by an Egyptian company, since the order required that any 'successor in title' to the British claimant had to be of British nationality. If Anisminic's action for judicial review was to succeed, it had to be established not only that the commission's interpretation of the order was erroneous, but also that the commission's decision rejecting the claim was a nullity, since the Foreign Compensation Act 1950 excluded the power of the High Court to review errors of law made within the jurisdiction of the commission. *Held* by a majority in the House of Lords, that the commission's interpretation of the Order in Council was wrong (since the Egyptian company was not Anisminic's 'successor in title'); and that this error had caused the commission to take into account a factor (the nationality of the Egyptian company) which was irrelevant to Anisminic's claim. Thus the commission had exceeded the limits of its jurisdiction and the decision was a nullity.

This decision has been much discussed.[71] The main issue for present purposes is whether the *Anisminic* case has established the rule that *all* errors of law made by a tribunal will cause the tribunal to exceed its jurisdiction. On a reading of the speeches in *Anisminic*, this does not seem to have been the intention of the judges, but in *Pearlman* v. *Keepers and Governors of Harrow School*, Lord Denning M. R. said that the distinction between an error which entails absence of jurisdiction and an error made within the jurisdiction was very fine and was being eroded. He submitted that the distinction should be abandoned and that the new rule should be that 'no court or tribunal has any jurisdiction to make an error of law on which the decision of the case depends'.[72] In supporting Lord Denning's view, Lord Diplock has said:

'The breakthrough made by *Anisminic* was that, as respects administrative tribunals and authorities, the old distinction between errors of law that went to jurisdiction and errors of law that did not was for practical purposes abolished.'[73]

But other judges, in the House of Lords and in the Judicial Committee, have maintained the traditional rule that tribunals may commit errors of law while remaining within their jurisdiction.[74] Lord Denning, unshaken in his view, has reasserted that administrative tribunals and other authorities exceed their jurisdiction if they make an error of law on which their decision depends.[75]

---

[70]   [1969] 2 A.C. 147; and see p. 671 *post*.
[71]   See H. W. R. Wade (1969) 85 L.Q.R. 198, B. C. Gould [1970] P.L. 358, L. H. Leigh [1980] P.L. 34.
[72]   [1979] Q.B. 56, 70; and see H. F. Rawlings [1979] P.L. 404.
[73]   *Re Racal Communications Ltd.* [1981] A.C. 374, 383 and see Lord Diplock [1974] C.L.J. 233, 243.
[74]   *Re Racal Communications Ltd.* at 390, and *South East Asia Fire Bricks* v. *Non-Metallic etc. Union* [1981] A.C. 363.
[75]   *R.* v. *Chief Immigration Officer, ex p. Kharrazi* [1980] 3 All E.R. 373.

The present state of the law is thus uncertain. There is much to be said for the view that all material decisions on points of law made by tribunals and other such bodies should be liable to scrutiny by the superior courts. Until this principle has been confirmed in legislation, it is salutary that the superior courts should be able to supervise the decisions of tribunals, even if for the time being they must justify their intervention on jurisdictional grounds.

We now turn to consider the doctrine of natural justice, which like the rules of *ultra vires* is central to judicial review of administrative action.

B. Natural justice

The requirements of natural justice are essentially unwritten rules of the common law; on many matters they have been embodied in enacted law, for example where statutory procedures enable an individual who disagrees with an official decision to appeal to a tribunal. As an unwritten principle, natural justice evolved largely through the control exercised by the central courts over bodies of inferior jurisdiction.[1] This control applied not only to justices of the peace but also to other bodies in relation to certain of their powers, for example, the power of the governing body of a corporation to deprive persons of membership or corporate office. The rules of natural justice were also applied to arbitrators, and to the disciplinary functions of professional bodies and voluntary associations. With the development of new governmental powers affecting an individual's property or livelihood, natural justice served to supplement the shortcomings of Victorian legislation. Public authorities were bound to observe natural justice in many of their functions, and it was for the courts to determine the limits of this obligation. The achievement of the courts in this difficult task will be considered later in this section. It is convenient first to illustrate the two main rules of natural justice with examples drawn from the ordinary courts themselves.

The rule against bias: no man a judge in his own cause

The essence of a fair judicial decision is that it shall have been made by an impartial judge. The rule against bias laid down in *R.* v. *Rand*[2] is that disqualification of a judge from acting in a particular case can arise in two ways: (a) where he has any direct pecuniary interest, however small, in the subject matter of inquiry – thus a judge who is a shareholder in a company appearing before him as a litigant must decline to hear the case, save by consent of all the parties;[3] (b) where, apart from direct pecuniary interest, there is a real likelihood that the judge would have a bias in favour of one of the parties. Where bias is alleged, the reviewing court does not decide whether the decision was in fact biased, but whether in the circumstances a reasonable possibility of bias was established. *R.* v. *Sussex Justices, ex parte McCarthy* is an extreme

---

[1] Pages 597–8 *ante*. For accounts of natural justice, see de Smith, *Judicial Review*, chs. 4 & 5; Wade, *Administrative Law*, chs. 13–15; G. A. Flick, *Natural Justice*; P. Jackson, *Natural Justice*.

[2] (1866) L.R. 1 Q.B. 230, approved in *R.* v. *Sunderland Justices* [1901] 2 K.B. 357; and see *Wildridge* v. *Anderson* (1897) 25 R. (J.) 27.

[3] *Dimes* v. *Grand Junction Canal (Proprietors of)* (1852) 3 H.L.C. 759. And see R. Cranston [1979] P.L. 237.

instance of the principle that justice should not only be done, but should manifestly be seen to be done.

The acting clerk to the justices was a member of a firm of solicitors who were to represent the plaintiff in civil proceedings as a result of a collision in connection with which the applicant was summoned for a motoring offence. The acting clerk retired with the bench but was not asked to advise the justices on their decision to convict the applicant. *Held* that, as the clerk's firm was connected with the case in the civil action, he ought not to advise the justices in the criminal matter and therefore could not, had he been required to do so, properly have discharged his duties as clerk. The conviction was accordingly quashed, despite the fact that the clerk had actually taken no part in the decision to convict.[4]

To disqualify a person from acting in a judicial capacity, an unreasonable suspicion of bias is not enough, particularly when further facts could readily have been verified.[5] According to recent case-law, a judicial decision must be set aside if there are grounds for a reasonable suspicion of bias on the part of one or more members of the tribunal, and it is not necessary that the reviewing court should decide that there was in fact a real likelihood of bias.

In *Metropolitan Properties Ltd* v. *Lannon*, a rent assessment committee had fixed the rent for three flats in one block of flats. The chairman of the committee was a solicitor who lived with his father in a second block of flats owned by the same property group. The chairman's firm was negotiating about rents with the landlords on behalf of his father and other tenants in the second block. *Held* that the decision of the committee must be quashed. 'No man can be an advocate for or against a party in one proceedings, and at the same time sit as a judge of that party in another proceeding.'[6]

There was also a reasonable suspicion of bias when a magistrate who was a member of an education committee and a school governor heard the prosecution of two farmers for having delivered short measure of vegetables to local schools.[7] But no reasonable suspicion of bias arises where the majority of members of a tribunal appointed to hear charges of professional misconduct are members of the profession in question.[8]

The right to a hearing: no man to be condemned unheard

It is equally fundamental to a just judicial decision that each party should have the opportunity of knowing the case against him and of stating his own case. Each party must have the chance to present his version of the facts and to make his submissions on the relevant rules of law. Each side must be able to comment on all material considered by the judge, and neither side must communicate with the judge behind the other's back. Although the written rules of court procedure are founded on these general principles, there is scope for the unwritten right to a hearing to operate even in the courts. Thus the High Court cannot order a solicitor personally to bear costs caused by his

---

[4] [1924] 1 K.B. 256; *cf. R.* v. *Rand (ante)*.
[5] *Cf. R.* v. *Camborne Justices, ex p. Pearce* [1955] 1 Q.B. 41.
[6] [1969] 1 Q.B. 577, 600; and see F. Alexis [1979] P.L. 143.
[7] *R.* v. *Altrincham Justices, ex p. Pennington* [1975] Q.B. 549.
[8] *Re S (a barrister)* [1981] 2 All E.R. 952.

misconduct unless he is given an opportunity to meet the complaint,[9] nor can a witness to proceedings for assault be bound over to keep the peace unless the magistrates give him an opportunity of being heard.[10] Yet the requirements of natural justice are not invariable: although a party to civil proceedings is normally entitled to know all the material considered by the judge, the nature of the High Court's ancient jurisdiction over children is such that in exceptional cases the judge may take into account confidential medical reports on the children which are not disclosed to the parents.[11] But the Court of Appeal acted in breach of natural justice when in a case concerning the wardship of children the court read and acted upon a letter by a social worker which the parties had not seen.[12]

Natural justice and administrative authorities

In what circumstances are bodies other than the courts bound to observe the rules of natural justice? It would be an exaggeration to suggest that natural justice must be observed whenever an official or public body exercises a legal power. The duty arises in a variety of situations whenever it is particularly important to an individual directly affected by the decision that a fair procedure should be observed. Therefore, if the exercise of power directly affects a man's rights, or his property, or his character, it is more likely to be subject to natural justice; so is a decision which follows a procedure involving the confrontation of two opposing views, in a manner comparable to that of litigation.[13] Thus a university may not deprive a senior member of his degrees or impose penalties upon a student without informing him of the charges brought against him and giving him an opportunity of answering them.[14] Nor can a trade union expel a member without giving him adequate notice of the charges giving rise to the penalty of expulsion.[15] The same principle was applied in the 19th century to action by a local authority under statutory powers directed against an individual's property.

In *Cooper* v. *Wandsworth Board of Works*, the plaintiff recovered from the board damages in trespass for demolishing his partly-built house. He had failed to notify his intention to build the house to the board, which by statute thereupon had power to demolish the building. *Held*, that the board should have given a hearing to the plaintiff before exercising their statutory power of demolition. 'Although there are no positive words in a statute requiring that the party shall be heard, yet the justice of the common law shall supply the omission of the legislature'.[16]

---

9   *Abraham* v. *Jutsun* [1963] 2 All E.R. 402. And see Rules of the Supreme Court, Order 62, rule 8(2).
10 *Sheldon* v. *Bromfield Justices* [1964] 2 Q.B. 573; *cf. R.* v. *Working Justices, ex p. Gossage* [1973] Q.B. 448.
11 *In re K (infants)* [1965] A.C. 201.
12 *B.* v. *W., Wardship: Appeal* [1979] 3 All E.R. 83.
13 See R. B. Cooke [1954] C.L.J. 14. *Cf. Durayappah* v. *Fernando* [1967] 2 A.C. 337, 349 and see G. D. S. Taylor (1975) 1 Monash Univ. Law Rev. 258.
14 *Dr Bentley's case* (1723) 1 Stra. 557; see also *Ceylon University* v. *Fernando* [1960] 1 All E.R. 631 and cases cited in n. 37 *post*.
15 *Annamunthodo* v. *Oilfield Workers' TU* [1961] A.C. 945; *cf. Breen* v. *AEU* [1971] 2 Q.B. 175.
16 (1863) 14 C.B. (N.S.) 180, 194 (Byles J.); Wilson, *Cases*, p. 587.

In a similar manner the rule against bias has been applied to local authorities. Thus a local authority's decision to grant planning permission for the development of certain land was quashed by the court on the ground that one of the councillors who had approved the granting of permission had acted as estage agent for the developer.[17] When an education sub-committee had confirmed the decision by the governors of a school to terminate a teacher's employment, the decision was quashed by the court because the fact that three members of the sub-committee were also governors of the school gave rise to the possibility of bias.[18] And when the Barnsley markets committee revoked a stall-holder's licence for a trivial and isolated misdemeanour, that decision was also quashed: not only did the committee hear the evidence of the market manager (who was in the position of a prosecutor) in the absence of the stall-holder, but the manager was present throughout the committee's deliberations.[19]

Natural justice and ministers' powers

The older instances of natural justice date from the period before the development of the present structure of government. Today the granting of new executive power is often accompanied by complex statutory procedures designed to reconcile administrative needs with safeguards for the individual. To what extent may additional unwritten rules of fair procedure be applied by the courts?[20] Does the rule that no man should be judge in his own cause continue to be relevant if the settlement of disputes arising from the execution of policy is entrusted to the minister whose department is responsible for maintaining that policy? There are some instances of governmental power where the courts have allowed little scope for natural justice, notably the powers of the Home Secretary in relation to aliens.[21] In 1915, in one of the earliest cases on public inquiries, the House of Lords in *Local Government Board* v. *Arlidge* held that the common law rules of natural justice required little more from a department than the carrying out in good faith of its usual procedures.

The Hampstead council had made a closing order in respect of a house which appeared unfit for human habitation. The owner appealed to the Local Government Board as prescribed by the Housing and Town Planning Act 1909. A public inquiry was held before a housing inspector and after receiving his report the board confirmed the closing order. Arlidge applied to the court to declare the decision invalid, on the grounds that the order of the board did not disclose which official of the board actually decided the appeal; that he, Arlidge, had not been heard orally by that official; and that he was not permitted to see the report of the inspector who conducted the public inquiry. The House of Lords rejected Arlidge's claims, holding that Parliament, having entrusted judicial duties to an executive body, must be taken to have intended it to follow the procedure which was its own and was necessary if it was to be capable of doing its work efficiently. So long as the officials dealt with the question referred to them without bias,

---

17 *R* v. *Hendon RDC, ex p. Chorley* [1933] 2 K.B. 696. And see p. 386 *ante*.
18 *Hannam* v. *Bradford Corp.* [1970] 2 All E.R. 690.
19 *R*. v. *Barnsley Council, ex p. Hook* [1976] 3 All E.R. 452.
20 See *Wiseman* v. *Borneman* [1971] A.C. 297, 308 (Lord Reid).
21 *Ex p. Venicoff* [1920] 3 K.B. 72; *Schmidt* v. *Home Secretary* [1969] 2 Ch. 149. For the immigration appeals system, see ch. 25 B.

and gave the parties an adequate opportunity of presenting the case, the board could follow its own established procedures, even though they were not those of a court of law.[22]

Similarly in *Board of Education* v. *Rice*, Lord Loreburn laid it down that in disposing of an appeal the Board of Education was bound to act in good faith and to listen fairly to both sides, since that was a duty which lay on everyone who decided anything. The board was not, however, bound to follow the procedure of a trial. It could obtain information in any way it thought best, always giving a fair opportunity to those who were parties in the controversy to correct or contradict any relevant statement prejudicial to their view.[23]

These two decisions of the House of Lords did not mean, however, that departments were totally freed from the duty to observe the essentials of fair procedure. In the 1930s, there was much litigation concerned with procedures for slum clearance and the compulsory purchase of land. In these cases, the courts found great difficulty in applying common law rules of natural justice to the duties of the minister. In the best-known of these cases, *Errington* v. *Minister of Health*, the court quashed a slum clearance order made by the Jarrow council: the facts were that, after the public inquiry into the order had been held, private discussions took place between council officials and civil servants, and a Whitehall official visited the houses affected in the presence of council officials but without informing the owner. The court held that an order made in such circumstances was in breach of natural justice and was not within the powers conferred by the Housing Act 1930.[24] In this and other cases, the courts attempted to distinguish between the judicial and administrative functions of the minister. Thus the judges accepted that the final decision of the minister could be based on matters of policy, and was thus administrative, but asserted that the department exercised judicial or quasi-judicial functions at the public inquiry stage.[25] This approach was called into question in *Franklin* v. *Minister of Town and Country Planning*.

The New Towns Act 1946 empowered the minister, after consultation with local authorities, to make a draft order designating the site of a proposed new town. If objections were made and not withdrawn, the minister was bound to arrange for a local public inquiry and to consider the report of the person holding the inquiry. While the Act was still a Bill, the minister made a public speech stating that Stevenage would be the first new town. When the Act had become law, he made a draft order designating Stevenage as a new town and a local inquiry was held into the objections received. Later the minister confirmed the draft order. The validity of this confirmation was challenged in the High Court. The House of Lords held (a) that there was no evidence that the minister had not genuinely considered the report of the inspector who held the inquiry; (b) that the inquiry was essentially into the objections received and the minister was not bound to call evidence in favour of the scheme at the inquiry.[26]

---

22 [1915] A.C. 120.
23 [1911] A.C. 179.
24 [1935] 1 K.B. 249; Wilson, *Cases*, p. 603. See also *Johnson & Co. (Builders) Ltd* v. *Minister of Health* [1947] 2 All E.R. 395; Wilson, *Cases*, p. 606.
25 This followed the analysis made in the Ministers' Powers Report, p. 599 *ante*.
26 [1948] A.C. 87; Wilson, *Cases*, p. 611.

The striking feature of the decision is that the House of Lords considered that at no stage was any judicial or quasi-judicial duty imposed on the minister, that his duty to consider the inspector's report was purely administrative and that talk of the rule against bias was irrelevant. It is difficult to reconcile this reasoning with cases such as *Errington* v. *Minister of Health*.[27] There is an obvious distinction between the confirmation by the minister of a scheme initiated by the local authority, and the procedure whereby it is for the minister alone to take the initiative and decide the issue in selecting a new town. In the latter case Parliament has expressly made the minister judge in his own cause, and this necessarily means that the rule against bias must be modified. But the common law conception of natural justice which required a man to be heard in defence of his property never depended on the two-tier situation of one authority confirming the proposals of another.[28] It may be best to explain the decision of the House of Lords in terms of a deliberate refusal to involve the courts in the task of assessing the merits of the pioneer project of a politically controversial new scheme of social control; for this, responsibility was owed to Parliament.[29]

The subsequent history of public inquiry procedures has turned not so much on the common law rules of natural justice, as on the reforms made following the Franks Report on Administrative Tribunals and Inquiries in 1957. These reforms, brought about by legislative and executive action, will be discussed in chapter 37. But these reforms have not been applied to all public inquiries; and common law rules of natural justice may still be relevant. In 1976, a decision of the Secretary of State for the Environment confirming a compulsory purchase order under the Housing Act 1957 was held to be in breach of natural justice, since it was based on an opinion formed by the inspector on a matter which had never been considered at the public inquiry.[30] But in *Bushell* v. *Secretary of State for the Environment*, which concerned the procedures at a controversial inquiry into a proposed motorway, the House of Lords adopted an approach which, as in *Franklin's* case, stressed the administrative character of the minister's decision and protected crucial aspects of the official process from full investigation at the inquiry.[31]

The present scope of natural justice
Although the application of natural justice to public inquiry procedures continues to present problems, the importance of natural justice in judicial review of administrative action in general has not been in doubt since the decision of the House of Lords in *Ridge* v. *Baldwin*.

---

[27] See H. W. R. Wade (1949) 10 C.L.J. 216 and *cf. Wednesbury Corp.* v. *Ministry of Housing* [1966] 2 Q.B. 275.

[28] *Ridge* v. *Baldwin* [1964] A.C. 40, 72–3 (Lord Reid).

[29] There is now direct parliamentary control over new town orders: New Towns Act 1981, s. 77(4).

[30] *Fairmount Investments Ltd* v. *Secretary of State for the Environment* [1976] 2 All E.R. 865.

[31] [1981] A.C. 75. Statutory rules of procedure for motorway inquiries have now been made: S.I. 1976 No 721.

In this case the Court of Appeal had held that the Brighton police committee were under no duty in natural justice to grant the chief constable a hearing before the committee exercised its power to dismiss 'any constable whom they think negligent in the exercise of his duty or otherwise unfit for the same';[32] in dismissing the plaintiff, 'the defendants were acting in an administrative or executive capacity just as they did when they appointed him'.[33] The House of Lords overruled this view: quite apart from the procedure laid down by the discipline regulations, natural justice required that a hearing should have been given before the committee exercised its power. The failure to give a hearing invalidated the dismissal, and the subsequent hearing given to Ridge's solicitor did not cure the earlier defect.[34]

This decision could have been regarded narrowly as an interpretation of a particular statute. But, as we have already seen[35] *Ridge* v. *Baldwin* established that natural justice was not confined to powers which were classified as judicial or quasi-judicial. Since 1964 the duty to observe natural justice has been applied in a very wide variety of situations. These situations include: the exercise of statutory powers relating to the continuation or termination of public employment, to the special benefit of police officers and school teachers;[36] powers of universities and other educational bodies relating to student discipline and status;[37] the expulsion by the National Executive Committee of the Labour party of a constituency association;[38] the granting of a licence to conduct a gaming establishment;[39] the revocation of a market-stall licence;[40] and the power to condemn food as unfit for human consumption.[41] The wide application of natural justice led Megarry J. in 1970 to remark that the courts were tending to apply the principles of natural justice to all powers of decision unless the circumstances indicated the contrary.[42] But on two occasions Megarry J. refused to impose a duty to give notice or a hearing before certain contractual powers were exercised,[43] nor does natural justice apply to the making of delegated legislation.[44]

The most notable advance has been that disciplinary powers exercised over prisoners by boards of prison visitors have become subject to scrutiny by the

---

32   Municipal Corporations Act 1882, s. 191(4).
33   [1963] 1 Q.B. 539, 576 (Harman L. J.).
34   [1964] A.C. 40; p. 630 *ante*; and see A. W. Bradley [1964] C.L.J. 83.
35   Page 606 *ante*.
36   *Hannam* v. *Bradford Corp.* [1970] 2 All E.R. 690; *R.* v. *Kent Police Authority, ex p. Godden* [1971] 2 Q.B. 662; *Malloch* v. *Aberdeen Corp.* [1971] 2 All E.R. 1278; *Chief Constable of North Wales* v. *Evans* [1982] 3 All E.R. 141.
37   *R.* v. *Aston University Senate, ex p. Roffey* [1969] 2 Q.B. 538; *Glynn* v. *Keele University* [1971] 2 All E.R. 89; and *Herring* v. *Templeman* [1973] 3 All E.R. 569. *Cf. Vidyodaya University Council* v. *Silva* [1964] 3 All E.R. 865, criticised in [1965] C.L.J. 3. See also P. M. Smith (1981) 97 L.Q.R. 610 and *Casson* v. *University of Aston* [1983] 1 All E.R. 88.
38   *John* v. *Rees* [1970] Ch. 345. And see *Lewis* v. *Heffer* [1978] 3 All E.R. 354.
39   *R.* v. *Gaming Board, ex p. Benaim and Khaida* [1970] 2 Q.B. 417.
40   *R.* v. *Barnsley Council, ex p. Hook* [1976] 3 All E.R. 452.
41   *R.* v. *Birmingham City Justices, ex p. Chris Foods Ltd* [1970] 3 All E.R. 945.
42   *Gaiman* v. *National Association for Mental Health* [1971] Ch. 317, 333.
43   *Gaiman's* case (council of management's power to expel members of company limited by guarantee) and *Hounslow Council* v. *Twickenham Garden Developments Ltd* [1971] Ch. 233 (architect's notice of contractor's default).
44   *Bates* v. *Lord Hailsham* [1972] 3 All E.R. 1019.

courts, although it is uncertain whether this also applies to the lesser disciplinary powers exercised by prison governors.[45] On an appeal from the Bahamas concerning a minister's refusal of an individual's constitutional right to citizenship, the Judicial Committee held that natural justice must be observed by any person who has legal authority to determine questions affecting the rights of individuals.[46] But this is not the sole indicator of natural justice, and a developing test is that natural justice must be observed when an individual has a 'legitimate expectation' of being heard.[47] On this basis aliens had no right to be heard before the Home Secretary decided not to extend their permitted stay in the country,[48] but the courts will give greater protection to those who are threatened by the revocation of an existing licence than to those who are merely applicants for the initial grant of a licence.[49] There is no absolute rule that natural justice does not apply in the case of preliminary investigations, inspections or suspensions pending a final decision, but the right to a hearing is often excluded because of the need for urgent action or because the individual's rights will be observed at a later stage in the procedure.[50] Considerations of national security may exclude natural justice.[51]

Natural justice and fairness

One consequence of the wide application of natural justice to administrative acts has been to make it virtually impossible to describe the content of the rules of natural justice except in very general terms. A *dictum* of Tucker L. J. has been frequently cited with approval:

> There are in my view no words which are of universal application to every kind of inquiry and every kind of domestic tribunal. The requirements of natural justice must depend on the circumstances of the case, the nature of the inquiry, the rules under which the tribunal is acting, the subject-matter that is being dealt with and so forth.[52]

If there is an 'irreducible minimum' at the core of natural justice, it may be expressed as (a) the right to be heard by an unbiased tribunal; (b) the right to have notice of charges of misconduct; and (c) the right to be heard in answer to those charges.[53] In practice natural justice goes much wider than this and this formulation provides no answer to such questions as whether the right to a hearing entitles the individual to an oral hearing, or merely to submit written representations.[54] There is no universal requirement that an individual is

---

45   *R.* v. *Board of Visitors of Hull Prison, ex p. St. Germain* [1978] Q.B. 678, and (No. 2) [1979] 3 All E.R. 545.

46   *A.-G.* v. *Ryan* [1980] A.C. 718.

47   *Schmidt* v. *Home Secretary* [1969] 2 Ch. 149; *Cinnamond* v. *British Airports Authority* [1980] 2 All E.R. 368. And see p. 283 *ante*.

48   *Schmidt* v. *Home Secretary* (*ante*).

49   *McInnes* v. *Onslow-Fane* [1978] 3 All E.R. 211.

50   *Wiseman* v. *Borneman* [1971] A.C. 297, *Furnell* v. *Whangarei High Schools Board* [1973] A.C. 660, *Norwest Holst Ltd.* v. *Secretary of State for Trade* [1978] Ch. 201, *Lewis* v. *Heffer* (*ante*).

51   *R.* v. *Home Secretary, ex p. Hosenball* [1977] 3 All E.R. 452. And see p. 283 *ante*.

52   *Russell* v. *Duke of Norfolk* [1949] 1 All E.R. 109, 118.

53   Lord Hodson in *Ridge* v. *Baldwin* [1964] A.C. 40 at 132.

54   De Smith, *Judicial Review*, p. 201 considers that there is a *prima facie* right to an oral hearing.

entitled to be represented by a lawyer at a hearing,[55] but many aspects of procedure are subject to natural justice. Thus natural justice may require an adjournment to be given.[56] The manner in which evidence is obtained by tribunals is subject to constraints of natural justice[57] but hearsay evidence is not necessarily excluded.[58] Natural justice may entitle a party to cross-examine those who give evidence against him[59] and even obtain the names of potential witnesses from the other side.[60] But in some contexts it is sufficient that the gist of allegations against an individual is made known to him, so that he has a chance to defend himself.[61] Once a decision has been taken, natural justice does not require reasons to be given, at least for decisions given by the Gaming Board or the Parole Board.[62]

In *Ridge* v. *Baldwin*, in rebutting the view that natural justice was so vague as to be meaningless, Lord Reid referred to the test of what a reasonable man would regard as fair procedure in particular circumstances.[63] One reason why analysis of the present content of natural justice is difficult is that the courts have since 1967 tended to rely heavily upon the concept of administrative fairness. In *Re H.K.*, which concerned the nature of the inquiry which should be made by an immigration officer when seeking to discover the true age of a potential immigrant who claimed to be under 16, Lord Parker C. J. said that good administration required that the immigration officer should act fairly: 'only to that limited extent do the so-called rules of natural justice apply, which in a case such as this is merely a duty to act fairly'.[64] Even where administrative authorities are not required to observe natural justice or to act judicially, they may nonetheless be required to act fairly.[65]

Thus an undertaking by a public authority to receive and consider representations may create a right to a hearing on the matters in question for, as Lord Fraser has said, 'when a public authority has promised to follow a certain procedure, it is in the interest of good administration that it should act fairly and should implement its promise, so long as implementation does not interfere with its statutory duty'.[66] The duty to act fairly is thus more widespread but may be less onerous than the duty to observe natural justice. Since many

---

55   *Pett* v. *Greyhound Racing Association Ltd* [1969] 1 Q.B. 125 and *(No. 2)* [1970] 1 Q.B. 46; *Enderby Town Football Club Ltd.* v. *Football Association Ltd* [1971] Ch. 591; *Maynard* v. *Osmond* [1977] Q.B. 240. *Cf. R.* v. *Home Secretary, ex p. Tarrant* [1984] 1 All E.R. 799.

56   *Hanson* v. *Church Cmssrs for England* [1978] Q.B. 823, *cf. Ostericher* v. *Secretary of State for the Environment* [1978] 3 All E.R. 82.

57   *R.* v. *Deputy Industrial Injuries Cmssr, ex p. Moore* [1965] 1 Q.B. 456, *Crompton* v. *General Medical Council* [1982] 1 All E.R. 35.

58   *T. A. Miller Ltd.* v. *Minister of Housing* [1968] 2 All E.R. 633.

59   *R.* v. *Board of Visitors, ex p. St. Germain* (No. 2) [1979] 3 All E.R. 545. *Cf. R.* v. *Cmssn for Racial Equality, ex p. Cottrell and Rothon* [1980] 3 All E.R. 265.

60   *R.* v. *Blundeston Board of Visitors, ex p. Fox-Taylor* [1982] 1 All E.R. 646.

61   *R.* v. *Gaming Board, ex p. Benaim and Khaida* [1970] 2 Q.B. 417, *Maxwell* v. *Dept. of Trade and Industry* [1974] Q.B. 523.

62   *R.* v. *Gaming Board (ante)*, *Payne* v. *Lord Harris of Greenwich* [1981] 2 All E.R. 842, *cf. McInnes* v. *Onslow-Fane (ante)*.

63   [1964] A.C. 40 at 65.

64   [1967] 2 Q.B. 617, 630 applied in *R.* v. *Home Secretary, ex p. Mughal* [1974] Q.B. 313.

65   *Pearlberg* v. *Varty* [1972] 2 All E.R. 6.

66   *A.-G. of Hong Kong* v. *Ng Yuen Shiu* [1983] A.C. 629, 638; and *R.* v. *Liverpool Corp., ex p. Liverpool Taxi Operators Assn.* [1972] 2 Q.B. 299.

judges often explain natural justice purely in terms of fairness,[67] it is now impossible from the case-law to discover where natural justice stops and fairness begins.

It is a welcome development that judges are prepared to review administrative acts generally on grounds of unfairness, but the notion of fairness depends a great deal upon the judges' intuitive perception of unfairness. Judicial discretion here, as in other areas of law, needs to be founded upon definite rules and principles if it is not to become arbitrary. It is submitted that, as with natural justice, control on grounds of fairness should be confined to matters of procedure and should not be widened to include issues relating to the substance of administrative decisions.[68]

Two difficulties related to the effects of a breach of natural justice may be briefly mentioned. The first is whether the failure by an authority to give a hearing to which the individual is entitled is cured by a full and fair hearing given later by an appellate body. In 1979 the Judicial Committee held that no absolute rule can be laid down on this matter; sometimes the appeal proceedings may take the form of a full rehearing and this may cure the earlier defect, but in other situations the individual may be entitled to a fair hearing at both stages. In intermediate cases, the court must decide 'whether, at the end of the day, there has been a fair result, reached by fair methods'.[69]

The second difficulty concerns the legal effect, if any, of a decision reached in breach of natural justice. When a breach of natural justice is established, then as in *Ridge* v. *Baldwin* the court may declare the decision in question to be void and a nullity. In *Durayappah* v. *Fernando*, however, the Judicial Committee held that failure to give a hearing when one was due made the decision voidable and not void.[70] This decision was plainly contrary to legal principle. In 1979 the Judicial Committee accepted that a decision reached in breach of natural justice was void rather than voidable, adding however that until it was declared to be void by a court it was capable of having some effect in law and could be the basis of an appeal to a higher body.[71]

C. Binding nature of official acts

In his dealings with government, the citizen often needs to know if he can rely on a statement made to him by an official or on an administrative decision which has been notified to him. In business and commercial affairs, an individual is entitled to hold another to his word when a *contract* has been

---

[67] See *e.g. Wiseman* v. *Borneman* [1971] A.C. 297 (especially Lord Morris); *Maxwell* v. *Department of Trade* [1974] Q.B. 523; and *Selvarajan* v. *Race Relations Board* [1976] 1 All E.R. 12. See also D. H. Clark [1975] P.L. 27 and C. P. Seepersad [1975] P.L. 242.

[68] *Cf. Maxwell* v. *Department of Trade (ante)* at 540, where Lawton L.J. remarked that there were two facets of fairness, what is done and how it is done. See now *Chief Constable of North Wales* v. *Evans (ante)*.

[69] *Calvin* v. *Carr* [1980] A.C. 574, discussed by M. Elliott (1980) 43 M.L.R. 66.

[70] [1967] 2 A.C. 337, criticised by H. W. R. Wade (1967) 83 L.Q.R. 499 and (1968) 84 L.Q.R. 95; see M. B. Akehurst (1968) 31 M.L.R. 2, 128 and D. Oliver [1981] C.L.P. 43.

[71] *Calvin* v. *Carr ante.*

[1] See P. P. Craig (1977) 93 L.Q.R. 398, A. W. Bradley [1981] C.L.P. 1 and M. Akehurst [1982] P.L. 613.

concluded between them. But official decisions like the issue of a licence, the granting of planning permission or the payment of a subsidy, usually do not take a contractual form. When is a citizen entitled to hold a public authority to its word, or to the word of one of its officials? Is an authority free to change its mind, or to disavow an official whose conduct has led the citizen to believe that the authority has made a certain decision? May a senior civil servant in Whitehall overrule what has been done by a regional office of the ministry?

These questions raise a wide variety of issues, and answers to them take diverse legal forms. It is not possible to treat informal advice, assurances about future conduct, misleading statements, properly taken decisions and errors in communicating decisions as if they all had the same legal effect[2]. Here it is possible only to outline a few of the situations which may arise, remembering that in this section we are not concerned with the general subject of judicial review of administrative action.

First, if an official agency takes a decision affecting the rights of the subject and then communicates it to the citizen, without qualifying it by words such as 'provisional' or 'subject to review', the agency has exercised its discretion in the matter and may not thereafter alter the decision to the subject's disadvantage.[3] This general principle applies only in the absence of express statutory guidance. Thus in tax and social security matters the statutes give express authority for reviewing decisions, for example when fresh information is available.[4] Some statues provide that when a decision has been made, for example to grant planning permission for development, it may be revoked only on payment of compensation.[5] Apart from such provision, a public authority which has conferred a continuing discretionary benefit upon an individual under a mistake of fact, may revoke the benefit for the future once it has discovered the true position.[6]

Second, an assurance about its future conduct given to citizens by a public authority may, on principles of fairness, be held to bind the authority where the assurance is compatible with the authority's statutory duties.[7] But other assurances, for example those relating to future executive action in the conduct of a war, may by their nature be incapable of having a binding effect.[8]

Third, an official who appears to the citizen to have authority to bind the agency may act as if he has such authority when in reality he has not. If in this situation the citizen relies on the official's statement to his detriment, the agency may be estopped (that is, barred) from denying the truth of the statement. In *Robertson* v. *Minister of Pensions*,[9] Denning J. applied the following principle:

---

2   *Cf.* M. A. Fazal [1972] P.L. 43.
3   *Re 56 Denton Road Twickenham* [1953] Ch. 51; and see G. Ganz [1965] P.L. 237.
4   *E.g.* Social Security Act 1975, ss. 96, 104.
5   Town and Country Planning Act 1971, s. 164.
6   *Rootkin* v. *Kent C. C.* [1981] 2 All E.R. 227.
7   R. v. *Liverpool Corp., ex p. Liverpool Taxi Operators' Association* [1972] 2 Q.B. 299 (undertaking to consult taxi owners before granting more licences) and *A.-G. of Hong Kong* v. *Ng Yuen Shiu* [1983] 2 A.C. 629 (undertaking to treat illegal immigrants on merits of each case).
8   The *Amphitrite* case, p. 690 *post*.
9   [1949] 1 K.B. 227. For the facts see page 279 *ante*.

Whenever government officers, in their dealings with a subject, take on themselves to assume authority in a matter with which the subject is concerned, he is entitled to rely on their having the authority which they assume. He does not know and cannot be expected to know the limits of their authority, and he ought not to suffer if they exceed it.[10]

This principle was soon buffeted by an unduly conservative House of Lords.[11] It may need certain qualifications in the interest of maintaining the rules of criminal law and the *ultra vires* doctrine. Should an official be able to authorise persons to commit criminal offences with impunity?[12] An estoppel (which is a rule of evidence) does not have the effect of enabling an agency to avoid performance of its statutory duties[13] or of conferring jurisdiction where none exists.[14] Subject to these considerations, there are good reasons why public authorities, including the Crown, should be subject to the operation of estoppel in administrative matters. It was said in *Southend Corporation* v. *Hodgson (Wickford) Ltd* that estoppel could not hinder the exercise of a statutory discretion[15] but on somewhat similar facts in *Lever Finance Ltd* v. *Westminster Council*, a local planning authority was held to be bound by a mistaken statement made on the telephone by a planning officer, in the exercise of his ostensible authority.[16] However, a growing tendency to rely on estoppel in planning matters was curbed by the Court of Appeal in *Western Fish Products Ltd.* v. *Penwith DC*, which criticised *Lever Finance* and asserted that no estoppel could prevent a statutory body exercising its discretion or performing its duty.[17] While this forceful decision is likely to hold sway in the area of planning, situations may arise in other contexts in which a public authority in exercising a discretion must take account of previous statements or assurances which have been given to the individual.[18]

Fourth, where the citizen reasonably relies on advice given by an official (for example, a social security clerk who wrongly advises a citizen that he is not eligible for a certain benefit so that the citizen loses his entitlement), the appropriate remedy seems to be to require the department to compensate the citizen for his loss, either as a matter of legal liability or by recourse to the Parliamentary Commissioner.[19] But it would scarcely be reasonable for a large company with abundant technical information and resources to rely on a junior civil servant's statement on a legal or technical matter.

Fifth, and most difficult, a department accurately informs the citizen what

---

10   *Falmouth Boat Construction Co.* v. *Howell* [1950] 2 K.B. 16, 26.
11   *Howell* v. *Falmouth Boat Construction Co.* [1951] A.C. 837. And see the strange case of *A.-G. for Ceylon* v. *Silva* [1953] A.C. 461.
12   *Cf. R.* v. *Arrowsmith* [1975] Q.B. 678 and authorities there cited.
13   *Maritime Electric Co.* v. *General Dairies Ltd* [1937] A.C. 610, *Rhyl UDC* v. *Rhyl Amusements Ltd* [1959] 1 All E.R. 257 and J. A. Andrews (1966) 29 M.L.R. 1.
14   *Essex Congregational Union* v. *Essex CC* [1963] A.C. 808.
15   [1962] 1 Q.B. 416, discussed in [1961] C.L.J. 139.
16   [1971] 1 Q.B. 222, discussed in [1971] C.L.J. 3.
17   [1981] 2 All E.R. 204.
18   *E.g. R.* v. *Inland Revenue Cmssrs, ex p. Preston* [1983] 2 All E.R. 300; and *The Times*, 16 Aug. 1984.
19   Chs. 36 and 37 D.

its present practice is (for example, in interpreting a statutory regulation which affects the citizen's business activities) but later after further consideration decides to alter its practice to the prejudice of the citizen, who may have taken the earlier information into account in planning his business. A department must be free for good reason to alter its practice for the future, unless to do so would be considered by a court to create inconsistency and thus be unfair to the individual.[20] But should it be free to apply the new practice to earlier transactions in respect of which official action may still be pending? This is one of the hidden problems of administrative discretion which are more likely to be answered by the Parliamentary Commissioner than by the courts.

---

[20]   *H.T.V. Ltd.,* v. *Price Commission* [1976] I.C.R. 170.

Chapter 35

Methods of judicial control

In chapter 34 we considered the principles which regulate the review of administrative action by the courts. We must now examine the procedures by which the courts exercise this jurisdiction. Review may take place indirectly, in the course of a prosecution or other enforcement proceedings initiated by a public authority; here the individual may wish to raise as a defence that the regulation or byelaw or decision which is sought to be enforced is *ultra vires*. So too, a civil action for damages may be based on an act which, unless authorised by statute, would be a tort or breach of contract (chapter 36). But in this chapter we will be concerned with the procedures which enable there to be direct review by a court of acts and decisions of public authorities. When such action is challenged by an individual, he will probably wish the court to provide one or more of the following forms of relief: (a) to quash, or set aside as a nullity, a decision that is *ultra vires* or in excess of jurisdiction; (b) to restrain the authority from acting *ultra vires* or in excess of jurisdiction; (c) to order the authority to perform its lawful duties; (d) to declare the rights and duties of the parties; (e) to order the authority to provide financial redress for loss or damage suffered; and (f) to secure temporary relief, pending the outcome of the proceedings. Despite the tortuous path which the development of this branch of English law has taken, it is arguable that the effect of recent reforms has been at long last to establish something approaching a comprehensive procedure for securing these different forms of relief.

The reforms referred to took place in the years 1977–82 and will be summarised below. The main effect has been that certain remedies which had long been available in the High Court – notably the prerogative orders (mandamus, prohibition and certiorari), injunctions and declarations – were for purposes of administrative law transformed into *forms of relief*[1] obtainable by a single procedure known as an application for judicial review. These changes in procedure were accompanied by judicial reorganisation so that, according to one expert view, without Parliament having directly authorised it, a specialised administrative court has been established.[2] Because of the

---

[1] Supreme Court Act 1981, s. 31 (1).
[2] L. Blom-Cooper [1982] P.L. 250, 260.

nature of the reforms, it was in 1984 difficult to say how much of the old law regarding individual remedies had been swept away and how much survived, albeit with modifications. For this reason, and since the reforms of 1977–82 cannot be understood without some knowledge of the earlier law, we must first examine the individual remedies themselves, before reviewing the present state of the law.

Thereafter this chapter will deal with statutory remedies created for the review of certain official decisions, the legislative exclusion of judicial review, and the very different system of remedies in Scots law. One omission is habeas corpus. This ancient writ is an important remedy against administrative action which takes away individual liberty; it was not included in the recent reforms and is discussed in chapter 26 B.

The prerogative orders[3]

The prerogative writs of mandamus, prohibition and certiorari (later restyled orders[4]) were the principal means by which the Court of King's Bench exercised jurisdiction over local justices and other bodies from the 17th century onwards.[5] Although the writs issued on the application of subjects from earliest times, the word 'prerogative' is apt because they were associated with the right of the Crown to ensure that justice was done by inferior courts and tribunals. They share with the writ of habeas corpus nomenclature (for example, *R.* v. *Bristol Council, ex parte Smith*) which indicates that the High Court has been moved to intervene against the defendant authority on the application of a private person; but the Crown as such plays no part in the proceedings. This background helps to explain important aspects of the prerogative orders (for example, the need for leave from the courts, the summary procedure, the nature of the applicant's interest, the discretionary nature of the remedy), since the orders were means of upholding the public interest in the administration of justice, rather than simply protecting the individual's rights.

Mandamus

Mandamus is an order from the High Court commanding a public authority or official to secure the performance of its or his public duty, in the performance of which the applicant has a sufficient legal interest. The order does not lie against the Crown. If a government department is acting as agent of the Crown and is responsible only to the Crown, having no duty to the subject, it is not subject to an order of mandamus.[6] However, mandamus does lie to enforce the performance of a duty which has been imposed by statute upon a minister or on a department or on named civil servants, provided that the applicant can show that the duty is one which is owed to him and not merely to the Crown.[7] This means that mandamus can be used to enforce the performance of many departmental duties in matters which directly affect the indi-

---

[3]   For a full account, see de Smith, *Judicial Review*, Pt. III.
[4]   Administration of Justice (Miscellaneous Provisions) Acts, 1933, s. 5 and 1938, s. 7.
[5]   De Smith, *Judicial Review*, app. 1; E. G. Henderson, *Foundations of English Administrative Law*.
[6]   *R.* v. *Lords of the Treasury* (1872) L.R. 7 Q.B. 387.
[7]   *R.* v. *Special Cmssrs for Income Tax* (1888) 21 Q.B.D. 313, 317.

vidual.[8] Mandamus does not lie if there is an alternative remedy in a domestic tribunal[9] nor in general if there is an effective and convenient remedy of another kind. Thus mandamus does not lie if a statute creates an obligation and provides a specific remedy for enforcing it, for example complaint to a minister.[10] But the court must decide whether the alternative remedy is sufficiently effective and convenient. Mandamus was obtained by a ratepayer to compel production of the accounts of a local authority for inspection, notwithstanding that the officers of the council concerned were liable to prosecution.[11] And mandamus was available to compel a chief officer of police to enforce the law against gaming and pornography at the request of a citizen, even though the citizen could have instituted a private prosecution of the wrongdoers.[12]

Mandamus will not lie if the authority has complete discretion whether to act or not. But there may be a duty to exercise a discretion, such as the duty of a tribunal to hear and determine a case within its jurisdiction. Thus the Home Secretary was required by mandamus to hear and determine the application made by the wife of a UK citizen for a certificate of patriality.[13] So too the duty of a tribunal to give reasons for its decisions under the Tribunals and Inquiries Act 1971, section 12, may be enforced by mandamus. Where a minister has power to give directions to a local authority, for example in the exercise of default powers, such a direction may be enforced by mandamus, provided that the court is satisfied that the direction is lawful.[14] Failure to comply with an order of mandamus constitutes contempt of court and is punishable accordingly.

Prohibition and certiorari

An order of prohibition issues primarily to prevent an inferior court or tribunal from exceeding its jurisdiction, or acting contrary to the rules of natural justice, where something remains to be done which can be prohibited. Certiorari served originally to bring a case or decision from an inferior court into the Court of King's Bench for review. In administrative law today it is a means of quashing decisions by inferior courts, tribunals and public authorities where there has been (a) an excess of jurisdiction or an *ultra vires* decision; (b) a breach of natural justice; or (c) an error of law on the face of the record.[15] Certiorari serves a purely negative purpose, since by setting aside a decision it prepares the way for a fresh decision to be taken.

As means of jurisdictional control, prohibition and certiorari cover broadly the same ground. The main difference is that certiorari quashes an order or decision already given, and prohibition prevents an order or decision being

---

8   *E.g. Padfield* v. *Minister of Agriculture* [1968] A.C. 997.
9   *R.* v. *Dunsheath, ex p. Meredith* [1951] 1 K.B. 127. *Cf.* other university cases cited on p. 648 ante.
10   *Pasmore* v. *Oswaldtwistle UDC* [1898] A.C. 387; Wilson, *Cases*, p. 628.
11   *R.* v. *Bedwelty UDC, ex p. Price* [1934] 1 K.B. 333.
12   *R.* v. *Metropolitan Police Cmssr, ex p. Blackburn* [1968] 2 Q.B. 118, *the same (No. 3)* [1973] Q.B. 241.
13   *R.* v. *Home Secretary, ex p. Phansopkar* [1976] Q.B. 606.
14   *Sec. of State for Education* v. *Tameside M. B.* [1977] A.C. 1014.
15   Page 659 *post.*

made which if made would be subject to certiorari.[16] It is convenient to seek both remedies in the same proceedings when a decision in excess of jurisdiction has already been made and other similar decisions have yet to be made.[17] Likewise certiorari and mandamus may be sought in the same proceedings, certiorari to quash a decision in excess of jurisdiction and mandamus to compel the tribunal to hear and determine the case according to law.[18]

The scope of both certiorari and prohibition, as well as mandamus, is confined to what may be described as the area of public law.[19] A non-statutory domestic tribunal, for example the Stewards of the Jockey Club, may not be controlled by the prerogative orders, but by an action for a declaration and by an injunction.[20] Nor do the prerogative orders apply in respect of purely contractual powers, for example the dismissal of an employee, even if the power is being exercised by a public authority[21] or the expulsion of a member by a trade union. But the prerogative orders would seem to lie in respect to statutory powers relating to an employee's status, even though there is a contractual element in the relationship.[22]

Despite the judicial origins of certiorari and prohibition, for many years they have been available against ministers, departments, local authorities and other bodies exercising administrative functions. During the 20th century, the courts have at times found difficulty in accepting such broad use of the remedies. For a period, a dictum of Atkin L. J. from *R. v. Electricity Commissioners, ex parte London Electricity Joint Committee* had special authority:

> Wherever any body of persons, having legal authority to determine the rights of subjects and having the duty to act judicially, act in excess of their legal authority, they are subject to the controlling jurisdiction of the King's Bench Division exercised in these writs.[23]

In this case the Electricity Commissioners were regarded as acting judicially in exercising functions of inquiry and recommendation concerning the reorganisation of the electricity industry, but some later judges took a narrower view of the duty to act judicially.[24] However, when a certificate granted by a legal aid committee was quashed by certiorari, it was said that where the decision is that of an administrative body, 'the duty to act judicially may arise in the course of arriving at that decision'.[25] Certiorari was not sought in *Ridge v. Baldwin*, but Lord Reid's analysis is as applicable to the prerogative orders as to natural justice, namely that a duty to act judicially may readily be

---

16   E.g. *R. v. Minister of Health, ex p. Davis* [1929] 1 K.B. 619 and *R. v. Minister of Health, ex p. Yaffe* [1930] 2 K.B. 98.
17   *R. v. Paddington Rent Tribunal, ex p. Bell Properties Ltd.* [1949] 1 K.B. 666.
18   E.g. *R. v. Paddington Valuation Officer, ex p. Peachey Property Corpn* [1966] 1 Q.B. 380 and *R. v. Hammersmith Coroner, ex p. Peach* [1980] Q.B. 21 (inquest into death of Blair Peach).
19   *Cf. R. v. Inland Revenue Commissioners, ex p. National Federation of Self-Employed* [1982] A.C. 617, 639 (Lord Diplock).
20   E.g. *Nagle* v. *Feilden* [1966] 2 Q.B. 633; *Law* v. *National Greyhound Club* [1983] 3 All E.R. 300.
21   *R. v. Post Office, ex p. Byrne* [1975] I.C.R. 221; *R. v. BBC, ex p. Lavelle* [1983] 1 All E.R. 241.
22   *Cf. Vine* v. *National Dock Labour Board* [1957] A.C. 488.
23   [1924] 1 K.B. 171, 205.
24   E.g. *R. v. Legislative Committee of Church Assembly, ex p. Haynes-Smith* [1928] 1 K.B. 411.
25   *R. v. Manchester Legal Aid Committee, ex p. Brand & Co.* [1952] 2 Q.B. 413, 429.

inferred where there is statutory authority to decide what an individual's rights should be.[26] But it is not always necessary to show that rights are at stake; thus certiorari issues against the Criminal Injuries Compensation Board, which has power to determine matters affecting individuals, even though their rights as such are not involved.[27] In this context Lord Parker C. J. said:

the exact limits of the ancient remedy by way of certiorari have never been, and ought not to be, specifically defined. They have varied from time to time, being extended to meet changing conditions ... We have ... reached the position when the ambit of certiorari can be said to cover every case in which a body of persons, of a public as opposed to a purely private or domestic character, has to determine matters affecting subjects provided always that it has a duty to act judicially.[28]

When in 1978 the Court of Appeal, reversing the Divisional Court, held that the disciplinary proceedings of boards of prison visitors were subject to the prerogative orders, both courts accepted that the board was required to act judicially.[29] Indeed, in the Divisional Court Lord Widgery C. J. said, 'One knows nowadays that it is not necessary to show a judicial act in order to get certiorari, but if the order is a judicial act it makes it that much easier to justify the making of the order'.[30] To avoid reopening outdated controversies, it should now be openly accepted that the prerogative orders are residual remedies for the control of administrative decisions, for example the decisions of a local planning authority[31] and the censorship policies of a cinema licensing authority,[32] as well as for controlling inferior tribunals generally.

Error of law on the face of the record
One important use of certiorari is as a means of ensuring that inferior tribunals and statutory bodies apply the law correctly, at least so far as the official record of their decision is concerned. The leading modern authority is *R.* v. *Northumberland Compensation Appeal Tribunal, ex parte Shaw.*[33] In this case the tribunal, set up to hear appeals as to the compensation payable to local government officers made redundant through the introduction of the National Health Service, had given reasons for its decision which were bad in law due to a wrong interpretation of the relevant statute. Such an error of law can be reviewed by certiorari, provided that the error is disclosed on the record of the decision. The availability of the remedy depends on the documents which form the record for this purpose.[34] These may include a written explanation of a decision made available later[35] and even affidavit evidence regarding the decision-making process.[36] A tribunal may misdirect itself as to the law

---

26 Pages 606, 648 *ante.*
27 *R.* v. *Criminal Injuries Compensation Board, ex p. Lain* [1967] 2 Q.B. 864.
28 *Lain's case (ante)*, p. 882.
29 *R.* v. *Board of Visitors of Hull Prison, ex p. St. Germain* [1978] Q.B. 678, [1979] Q.B. 425.
30 [1978] Q.B. 678, 689.
31 *R.* v. *Hillingdon BC, ex p. Royco Homes Ltd.* [1974] Q.B. 720.
32 *R.* v. *Greater London Council, ex p. Blackburn* [1976] 3 All E.R. 184.
33 [1952] 1 K.B. 388.
34 *Baldwin and Francis Ltd.* v. *Patents Appeal Tribunal* [1959] A.C. 663.
35 *R.* v. *Greater Birmingham Appeal Tribunal, ex p. Khan* [1979] 3 All E.R. 759.
36 *R.* v. *Southampton Justices, ex p. Green* [1976] Q.B. 11.

without disclosing error on the record. While a serious error may sometimes be revealed by inference from the decision itself, errors of law are more likely to be disclosed on the record if a tribunal gives reasons for its decision. The importance for this purpose of sufficiently full reasons being given is recognised in the Tribunals and Inquiries Act 1971. Section 12 imposes a duty on tribunals subject to the Act, and on ministers where a public inquiry has been or could have been held, to state the reasons for their decisions if requested at the time to do so; any statement of reasons is deemed to be part of the record, so that certiorari lies if reasons which are wrong in law are given.[37]

In accordance with the recommendation of the Franks committee, Parliament accepted the principle that there should be a right of appeal on law from administrative tribunals to the High Court.[38] Such an appeal gives the court wider scope than certiorari for error of law on the record; thus the practical effect of a statutory right of appeal on points of law is to supersede the use of certiorari for this purpose.

We have examined above the difficult issue of whether a distinction may still be drawn between errors of law within jurisdiction and errors of law which cause a tribunal to exceed its jurisdiction.[39] If it comes to be established that all errors of law go to jurisdiction, it will be possible to lay to rest the aged doctrine of error of law on the face of the record.

Locus standi and the prerogative orders (before 1978)

When an administrative body's decision is challenged by a private individual, the question arises whether that individual has sufficient interest in the decision to justify the court's intervention. Some would wish the courts to entertain a challenge to an authority's conduct from any member of the public. But English law has never openly recognised an *actio popularis*, and the applicant for a prerogative order has usually had to show a personal right or interest in the matter. According to the case-law, the nature of the right or interest required could vary with the particular remedy being sought.[40] Judicial attitudes have fluctuated. Thus in 1897 an applicant for mandamus had to show a specific legal right to performance of the duty in question,[41] but seventy years later a member of the public was allowed to seek mandamus in respect of police policies in London.[42] By 1976, the trend of judicial decisions appeared to be developing a single test of *locus standi* for all the prerogative orders,[43] and the reforms of 1978–82 reinforced that trend. Before coming to those reforms, we will consider two remedies, the injunction and the declaration, which unlike the prerogative orders are available in all branches of the law.

Injunctions[44]

An injunction may be claimed against a public authority or official, to restrain unlawful acts which are threatened or are being committed, for example to

37   *E.g. Re Poyser and Mills Arbitration* [1964] 2 Q.B. 467, and *ex p. Khan (ante)*.
38   Tribunals and Inquiries Act 1971, s. 13.
39   Pages 638–42 *ante*.
40   De Smith, *Judicial Review*, pp. 409–21, 550–3; S. M. Thio, *Locus Standi and Judicial Review*.
41   *R. v. Lewisham Union Guardians* [1897] 1 Q.B. 498.
42   *R. v. Metropolitan Police Cmssr, ex p. Blackburn* [1968] 2 Q.B. 118.
43   *R. v. Liverpool Corpn, ex p. Liverpool Taxi Operators' Assn* [1972] 2 Q.B. 299; and note 32 *ante*.
44   De Smith, *Judicial Review*, ch. 9.

restrain unlawful interference with private rights[45] or to restrain *ultra vires* action such as improper expenditure of local funds.[46] An important exception is that injunctions are not available against the Crown, nor against officers of the Crown where the effect would be to grant relief against the Crown which could not be obtained in proceedings directly against the Crown.[47] In place of an injunction against the Crown, the court may make an order declaring the rights of the parties, but no interim relief may be obtained.[48]

Where the injunction concerns private rights (for example, a property dispute or liability in private nuisance), the ordinary rules in the law of property or tort apply as to who may seek an injunction. But when the injunction concerns a matter of public right, (for example, the public nuisance caused by the obstruction of a highway) an injunction can be obtained by the Attorney-General, either at his own instance or at the instance of a relator (i.e. one who informs). A relator need have no personal interest in the subject-matter of the claim save his interest as a member of the public. The consent of the Attorney-General given to the proceedings prevents any objection being taken to the relator's standing in the matter.

There are two cases where a person can sue without joining the Attorney-General: (a) if interference with the public right also constitutes an interference with the plaintiff's private right; for example, where an obstruction upon a highway is also an interference with a private right of access to the highway;[49] (b) where no private right of the plaintiff is interfered with, but he suffers special damage peculiar to himself from the interference with a public right, for example, where as a result of a public nuisance a plaintiff's premises have been rendered unhealthy.[50]

A third exception, under the Local Government Act 1972, is that a local authority may institute proceedings affecting its area in its own name, even though the object of the proceedings is to enforce public rights which before the 1972 Act would have required the Attorney-General's consent to relator proceedings.[51]

Relator actions can be used to restrain unlawful action by a public authority, even though its validity could have been tested by certiorari.[52] They also enable a court to review decisions by a public authority which do not affect an individual's rights or interests closely enough to enable him to seek a prerogative order. One use of relator proceedings, that goes far outside the scope of administrative law, is to provide additional means of enforcing the criminal law, when existing penalties and procedures are inadequate to deter repeated breach.

In *Attorney-General* v. *Sharp*, the defendant was the owner of a fleet of omnibuses in Manchester; he had been prosecuted 48 times for breach of local regulations in plying for hire without a licence. The defendant continued to run his buses without a licence,

---

[45] E.g. *Pride of Derby Angling Assn,* v. *British Celanese Ltd* [1953] Ch. 149.

[46] *A.-G.* v. *Aspinall* (1837) 2 My. & Cr. 406.

[47] Crown Proceedings Act 1947, s. 21; ch. 36.

[48] *R.* v. *Inland Revenue Cmssrs, ex p. Rossminster Ltd* [1980] A.C. 952. On interlocutory relief against public authorities in general, see *Smith* v. *Inner London Education Authy* [1978] 1 All E.R. 411.

[49] *Boyce* v. *Paddington BC* [1903] 1 Ch. 109, *Barrs* v. *Bethell* [1982] Ch. 294.

[50] *Benjamin* v. *Storr* (1874) L.R. 9 C.P. 400.

[51] *Stoke-on-Trent Council* v. *B & Q (Retail) Ltd* [1984] 2 All E.R. 332.

[52] *A.-G.* v. *Tynemouth Corp.* [1899] A.C. 293.

since despite the fines he found it profitable to do so. *Held* that, since the rights of the public were involved and as the remedies provided by the local Act had proved ineffective, there was jurisdiction to grant an injunction at the instance of the Attorney-General by way of ancillary relief.[53]

In somewhat similar circumstances, relator proceedings have been used to enforce planning control and fire precautions against those who find it profitable to break the law.[54]

One important limitation on the use of relator proceedings is that the Attorney-General never consents to proceedings against departments of central government. Another important limitation is that he has absolute discretion in deciding whether consent should be given. Although he may be accountable to Parliament for his decisions, he cannot be required to justify them to the courts nor have the courts power to overrule his decisions. These questions, raised earlier in *Attorney-General, ex rel. McWhirter* v. *Independent Broadcasting Authority*,[55] were settled conclusively in 1977 in *Gouriet's* case.

The Union of Post Office Workers had asked its members to boycott South African mail for one week as a protest against apartheid. Gouriet, claiming that the boycott would be criminal conduct under the Post Office Act 1953, asked the Attorney-General to consent to proceedings for an injunction against the union. This consent was refused. Gouriet then obtained an interim injunction against the union from the Court of Appeal. Lawton and Ormrod L. JJ. held that the Attorney-General's refusal of consent was not subject to review by the courts but that Gouriet could as a member of the public seek a declaration that proposed action would be a breach of the criminal law, and if necessary an interim injunction to restrain it. Lord Denning M. R. went further, holding that the refusal of consent to relator proceedings could be reviewed by the courts, and if necessary would be overridden, indirectly, since the court could grant any citizen a declaration or an injunction to restrain criminal conduct. On appeal to the House of Lords, *held* that where the Attorney-General has refused his consent to relator proceedings, a private citizen who asserts that the public interest is affected by a threatened breach of the criminal law, may not go to the civil courts for a remedy, whether injunction or declaration. Public rights may be asserted in a civil action only by the Attorney-General as representing the public. The Attorney-General's discretion in relator proceedings may not be reviewed in the courts.[56]

In the circumstances of the *Gouriet* case, involving the use of an injunction to restrain potentially criminal conduct by a trade union, a difficult discretion had to be exercised in the public interest and it would have broken new constitutional ground for the Attorney-General's decision to be subject to judicial review. Yet in not dissimilar circumstances involving the imminent breach of a local authority's duty to maintain its schools, the court has been willing to assume jurisdiction.[57] The proposition that public rights can be asserted only by the Attorney-General must be applied with care in admin-

---

[53] [1931] 1 Ch. 121; and see *A.-G.* v. *Harris* [1961] 1 Q.B. 74 and n. 51 *ante*.

[54] *A.-G.* v. *Bastow* [1957] 1 Q.B. 514, *A.-G.* v. *Smith* [1958] 2 Q.B. 173, *A.-G.* v. *Chaudry* [1971] 3 All E.R. 938.

[55] [1973] Q.B. 629.

[56] *Gouriet* v. *Union of Post Office Workers* [1978] A.C. 435, criticised by P. P. Mercer [1979] P.L. 214.

[57] *Meade* v. *Haringey BC* [1979] 2 All E.R. 1016, p. 637 *ante*.

istrative law. The judges in *Gouriet* were not dealing with issues relating to the prerogative orders,[58] where consent to proceedings is given by the court. But the ruling in *Gouriet* is not confined to injunctions and applies also to proceedings brought for a declaration in respect of public rights.

The High Court may grant an injunction to restrain a person from acting in an office to which he is not entitled, and may also declare the office to be vacant. This procedure takes the place of the ancient procedure of an information in the nature of a writ of quo warranto.[59]

Declaratory judgments[60]

A declaratory judgment is one which is merely declaratory of the legal relationship of the parties and is not accompanied by any sanction or means of enforcement. The authority of a court's ruling on law is such that a declaratory judgment will normally serve to restrain both the Crown and public authorities from illegal conduct. Order 15, rule 16, of the Rules of the Supreme Court provides:

No action or other proceedings shall be open to objection on the ground that a merely declaratory judgment or order is sought thereby, and the Court may make binding declarations of right whether or not any consequential relief is or could be claimed.

It is an obvious convenience in many public law disputes to be able to have the law determined in its application to particular facts without seeking a coercive remedy. An important and early example arose in *Dyson* v. *Attorney-General*, where a taxpayer obtained a declaration against the Crown that the tax authorities had no power to request certain information from him on pain of a £50 penalty for disobedience.[61] The jurisdiction to grant declarations is as wide as the law itself, except that the judges may as a matter of discretion impose limits upon its use. Thus an action for a declaratory judgment must be based on a concrete case which has arisen. The courts will not give answers to questions propounded in the form of hypothetical cases and are reluctant to grant a bare declaration that can have no legal consequences.[62]

Nor will the court give an opinion on a point of law which is in issue in concurrent criminal proceedings.[63] But in administrative law the declaration may be available when other remedies are not and, before the reform of the prerogative orders, there were procedural advantages in declaratory proceedings (for example, in discovery of documents).[64] In *Pyx Granite Co. Ltd.* v. *Minister of Housing*, the House of Lords held that a statutory procedure for obtaining a decision on whether planning permission was needed for development did not exclude the owner's right to come to court for a declaration.[65]

---

[58] See *R.* v. *Inland Revenue Cmssrs, ex p. National Federation of Self-Employed* [1982] A.C. 617 (speeches of Lords Diplock, Scarman and Roskill).
[59] Supreme Court Act 1981, s. 30: *cf.* Local Government Act 1972, s. 92.
[60] De Smith, *Judicial Review*, ch. 10; I. Zamir, *The Declaratory Judgment* and [1977] C.L.P. 43.
[61] [1912] 1 Ch. 158.
[62] *Maxwell* v. *Dept of Trade* [1974] Q.B. 523.
[63] *Imperial Tobacco Ltd* v. *A.-G.* [1981] A.C. 718.
[64] *Vine* v. *National Dock Labour Board* [1957] A.C. 488.
[65] [1960] A.C. 260.

In the context of judicial review, the declaration was formerly considered to be both alternative to and in some respects preferable to the prerogative orders. Thus the judgment of a tribunal could be declared invalid as being in excess of jurisdiction.[66] But the declaration could not be used as a means of correcting errors of law on the face of the record of a tribunal's decision, after the time for seeking certiorari had expired.[67] Nor could the court by a declaration decide *de novo* a question entrusted by statute to a minister[68] or a special tribunal.[69] But where a tribunal has made findings of fact from which a decision in favour of the individual would be the only lawful outcome, the court may make a declaration accordingly.[70]

The usefulness of the declaration as a remedy was seriously limited when the court refused a declaration of right to someone who was in fact seriously prejudiced by an *ultra vires* decision of a local authority, on the ground that neither his common law nor his statutory rights were affected.[71] Comparison between the prerogative orders and the declaration as means of seeking judicial review has however been transformed by the reforms considered below, the need for which will now be outlined.

The need for reform before 1978
Amongst the main reasons for what was described by the Law Commission as 'the dilemma of the litigant seeking judicial review'[72] were the following:

1.   While two or more of the prerogative orders could be sought in the same proceedings, and an injunction and declaration could be sought together, the two classes of remedy could not be combined, nor could a litigant who made the wrong choice convert one procedure into the other. Damages could be sought with an injunction or declaration, but not with the prerogative orders.
2.   The rules of standing to sue differed as between the prerogative orders and injunctions/declarations; they also were liable to differ as between the various prerogative orders.
3.   The summary procedure used for the prerogative orders did not allow for discovery of documents, or other interlocutory procedure.
4.   Certiorari had to be sought within six months, but no fixed limit of time applied to the declaration.
5.   Leave from the court was required for prerogative order proceedings but not for injunctions/declarations; relator actions needed consent from the Attorney-General.
6.   The declaration lay in respect of all forms of official act, including delegated legislation, and against all public authorities, including the Crown. But a declaration could not quash a decision made by a tribunal within jurisdiction, nor could interim relief be obtained against the Crown.

---

66   *Anisminic Ltd.* v. *Foreign Compensation Cmssn*, p. 641 *ante*.
67   *Punton* v. *Ministry of Pensions* (No. 2) [1964] 1 All E.R. 448, and see P. Cane (1980) 43 M.L.R. 266.
68   *Healey* v. *Minister of Health* [1955] 1 Q.B. 221.
69   *Argosan·Finance Ltd* v. *Oxby* [1965] Ch. 390.
70   *Balfour* v. *Barty-King* [1979] 2 All E.R. 80.
71   *Gregory* v. *Camden BC* [1966] 2 All E.R. 196, criticised in [1966] C.L.J. 156.
72   Report on Remedies in Administrative Law, Cmnd 6407, 1976, p. 15.

There was the further factor that during the 1970s an increasing number of applications for prerogative orders led to a serious backlog of cases in the Divisional Court.[73]

To resolve these difficulties, the Law Commission proposed a draft Bill to create the procedure of application for judicial review. The Commission emphasised that the new procedure was not to be an exclusive remedy, and litigants would remain free to seek an injunction or declaration if they so chose. In the event the procedure was created by amending the Rules of the Supreme Court to provide a new Order 53.[74] This came into effect in January 1978 and was further amended in 1980 to allow for a single judge to hear matters previously heard by the Divisional Court of two or three judges.[75] The Supreme Court Act 1981, section 31, enacted the main features of the application for judicial review and the High Court's business was reorganised by forming a Crown Office list, to include applications under Order 53 and related administrative procedures.[76] A year later, the House of Lords in *O'Reilly* v. *Mackman* and *Cocks* v. *Thanet DC* gave added impetus to the reforms by holding that for most purposes of judicial review, application under Order 53 had become an exclusive remedy, contrary to the proposals of the Law Commission in 1976.[77]

Applications for judicial review under Order 53

By section 31 of the Supreme Court Act 1981 applications to the High Court for an order of mandamus, prohibition or certiorari (and for an injunction restraining a person from acting in a public office to which he is not entitled) must be made, in accordance with rules of court, by an application for judicial review. Neither the Act nor Order 53 sought to alter the existing scope of the prerogative orders at common law. The High Court now has a discretionary power (by section 31(2) of the 1981 Act) to make a declaration or grant an injunction whenever an application for judicial review has been made. In exercising this discretion the court must have regard *inter alia* to the nature of the matters in respect of which the prerogative orders apply and to the nature of the persons and bodies against whom the orders lie. Thus within what may be called the 'public law' field of the prerogative orders, declarations and injunctions may now be granted on an application for judicial review. But the Act leaves it entirely open whether within this field an application for judicial review is to be the sole means of obtaining an injunction or declaration.

Leave of the court is needed for every application for judicial review (section 31(3)). Since 1980 leave has usually been granted by a single judge without a hearing.[78] Once leave is obtained, the hearing of the application may take place before a single judge. Certain judges of the Queen's Bench Division have been designated for this purpose and to hear other cases on the 'Crown Office'

---

[73] See L. Blom-Cooper [1982] P.L. 250, 253.
[74] S.I. 1977 No. 1955, discussed by J. Beatson and M. H. Matthews (1978) 41 M.L.R. 437.
[75] S.I. 1980 No. 2000.
[76] Practice Direction [1981] 3 All E.R. 61.
[77] Page 668 *post*.
[78] Ord. 53, r. 3 (as amended in 1980).

list.[79] Appeals against a refusal of leave lie to a single judge in open court or the Divisional Court, thence to the Court of Appeal but not the House of Lords.[79a]

On an application for judicial review, the court may award damages if these have been sought by the applicant and the court is satisfied that damages could have been obtained by an action brought for the purpose (section 31(4)). But the substantive rules of liability in damages were not altered.[80]

The court may refuse to give leave or relief if it considers that there has been undue delay in making an application and if for stated reasons relief should not be granted (section 31(6)). By Order 53, an application for judicial review shall be made within three months unless there is good reason for extending the period; statutory time limits for review are not affected.

If the relief sought is prohibition or certiorari, the granting of leave for the application operates as a stay of the proceedings challenged; when other forms of relief are sought, the court may grant such interim relief as could be granted in an action begun by writ.[81] But the 1981 Act does not grant power to award interim relief against the Crown, as the Law Commission had recommended in 1976.

Procedural flexibility on an application for judicial review now exists in that the court may allow the discovery of documents, interrogatories, cross-examination of witnesses etc., but without prejudice to any privileges of the Crown.[82] When certiorari is sought, the court may both quash the decision under review and also remit it with a direction to the body in question to reach a fresh decision in accordance with the findings of the court (section 31(5)). When the relief sought is a declaration, injunction or damages, and the court does not consider this appropriate on an application for judicial review, the court may allow proceedings to be continued as if they had been begun by writ.[83]

The two most significant issues which have arisen in relation to applications for judicial review concern (a) standing to sue and (b) the exclusiveness or otherwise of the procedure.

Standing to apply for judicial review

At the stage when leave is sought for an application for judicial review, the court must not grant leave 'unless it considers that the applicant has a sufficient interest in the matter to which the application relates', (section 31(3)). The test of sufficient interest was recommended by the Law Commission as a formula which would allow for further development in the rules of standing. The test plainly allows the court a considerable discretion to decide what is to constitute 'sufficient interest'. To what extent did the test alter existing rules of locus standi?

In *R. v. Inland Revenue Commissioners, ex parte National Federation of Self-Employed and Small Businesses*, a body of taxpayers challenged arrangements made by the commissioners for levying tax on wages paid to casual employees on Fleet Street newspapers. For

---

[79]   L. Blom-Cooper [1982] P.L. 250, 259; note 75 *ante.*
[79a]   *In re Poh* [1983] 1 All E.R. 287.
[80]   Ch. 36.
[81]   Ord. 53, r. 10.
[82]   Ord. 53, r. 8.
[83]   Ord. 53, r. 9(5).

many years the employees had given fictitious names to evade tax, but the commissioners agreed with the employers and unions on a scheme for collecting tax in future and for two previous years, in return for an undertaking by the commissioners not to investigate any earlier years. The national federation, complaining that their members were never treated so favourably, applied under Order 53 for a declaration that the arrangement was unlawful, and a mandamus ordering the commissioners to collect tax as required by law. The Court of Appeal held, assuming the agreement to be unlawful, that the federation had sufficient interest in the matter for their application to be heard. The House of Lords *held* that the question of sufficient interest was not merely a preliminary issue to be decided when leave was being sought on an application for judicial review, but had to be resolved in relation to what was known by the court of the matter under review. On the evidence, the tax agreement was a lawful exercise of the commissioners' discretion. In general, unlike local ratepayers,[84] a taxpayer did not have an interest in challenging decisions concerning other taxpayers' affairs. In the circumstances, the national federation did not have sufficient interest to challenge the commissioners' decisions.[85]

The speeches in this case are notable because they contain many revealing statements about the significance of Order 53, and also because they include a perplexing diversity of opinions about the scope and function of the test of 'sufficient interest'. The summary above seeks to present in brief the views of three judges (Lords Wilberforce, Fraser and Roskill), although Lord Fraser also stressed that the test of sufficient interest was a logically prior question which had to be answered before any question of the merits arose. Lord Scarman paid lip-service to the existence of a test of standing separate from the merits, but his conclusion that the national federation had no sufficient interest because they had not shown that the tax authorities had failed in their duties, virtually eliminated any prior test of standing separate from the merits. Lord Diplock, who advocated an extremely broad test of standing, was alone in holding that the national federation had sufficient interest in the matter; in his view the federation's case simply failed on its merits. What emerges from the various speeches is that the judges were both reluctant to turn away the applicants without hearing at least something of their case, and unwilling to hold that the tax authorities were immune from judicial review. They also confirmed that the statements of principle made in *Gouriet* v. *Union of Post Office Workers*[86] are confined to relator actions. Indeed, it would seem that Order 53 provides a means of obtaining a declaration or injunction without the need for a relator action in any situation which falls within the scope of the prerogative orders.[86a]

Does Order 53 provide an exclusive remedy?

Although the House of Lords failed to sound a clear note in the *National Federation* case, the House in two later cases was unanimous in holding that litigants seeking judicial review of administrative action must proceed by application under Order 53. The need for a decision on the matter arose because neither the Supreme Court Act 1981 nor Order 53 expressly excluded

---

[84]   *Arsenal FC* v. *Ende* [1979] A.C. 1.
[85]   [1982] A.C. 617, discussed by P. Cane [1981] P.L. 322.
[86]   Page 662 *ante*.
[86a] And see S. Nott [1984] P.L. 22.

the individual's right in public law cases of bringing an action for an injunction or declaration, or an action for damages for breach of statutory duty. The issue had arisen in numerous cases concerning immigrants, prisoners, homeless persons and others, and judicial opinion was divided.[87]

In *O'Reilly* v. *Mackman*, convicted prisoners who had lost remission of sentence in disciplinary proceedings after riots at Hull prison sued for a declaration that the disciplinary awards were null and void because of breaches of natural justice.[88] The defendants applied to have the action struck out on the ground that the decisions of boards of visitors could be challenged only by an application for review under Order 53. *Held* (House of Lords) while the High Court had jurisdiction to grant the declarations sought, the prisoners' case was based solely on rights and obligations arising under public law. Order 53, by its requirement of leave from the court and by its time limit, protected public authorities against groundless or delayed attacks, and had removed previous defects in the system of remedies. In Lord Diplock's words, it would 'as a general rule be contrary to public policy, and as such an abuse of the process of the court, to permit a person seeking to establish that a decision of a public authority infringed rights to which he was entitled to protection under public law to proceed by way of ordinary action and by this means to evade the provision of Order 53 for the protection of such authorities'.[89]
And in *Cocks* v. *Thanet DC*, the House held that a person who seeks to challenge a decision by a local authority under the Housing (Homeless Persons) Act 1977 that he was not entitled to permanent accommodation must do so by application under Order 53, and not by suing in the country for a declaration and damages for breach of statutory duty.[90]

Although Lord Diplock in *O'Reilly's* case stated that neither the Supreme Court Act 1981 nor Order 53 established the application for judicial review as an exclusive remedy in public law matters, these two decisions left it in no doubt that the judges wished to carry further in this direction than either Parliament or the Law Commission had done the reforms associated with Order 53. As has already been indicated, the heavy reliance on the public law/private law distinction in *O'Reilly* and *Cocks* is unsatisfactory.[91] Indeed, the decisions could be better justified on the purely practical considerations mentioned by Lord Diplock in *O'Reilly*. As it is, the policy of channelling administrative law cases through Order 53 could lead to undue erosion in the rights of litigants. For example, a taxpayer who has a right of appeal to the High Court on a point of law, must be entitled to raise in his appeal all relevant points of law, including the illegality of any administrative directions on which his assessment was based; he should not be forced to take separate proceedings and seek the leave of the court under Order 53.[92]
Many other questions about the implications of these reforms remain to be

---

87   The decisions included: *Uppal* v. *Home Office, The Times*, 11 Nov. 1978, *Heywood* v. *Board of Visitors of Hull Prison* [1980] 3 All E.R. 594, *De Falco* v. *Crawley BC* [1980] Q.B. 460, *Lambert* v. *Ealing BC* [1982] 2 All E.R. 394.
88   See *R.* v. *Board of Visitors of Hull Prison, ex p. St Germain* [1978] Q.B. 678, p. 649 *ante*.
89   [1983] 2 A.C. 237, discussed by A. Grubb [1983] P.L. 190.
90   [1983] 2 A.C. 286. *Cf. Davy* v. *Spelthorne BC* [1984] A.C. 262, p. 608 *ante*.
91   Page 608 *ante*.
92   *Henry Moss of London Ltd.* v. *Customs and Excise Cmssrs* [1981] 2 All E.R. 86, criticised in [1981] P.L. 476.

answered. One early effect would seem to be a very considerable increase in the discretionary powers of the judges, but in the long term, given the changes in judicial organisation that have taken place, more consistent doctrines of judicial review of administrative action should evolve.[92a]

Statutory machinery for challenge

The technicalities of the prerogative and other remedies in their unreformed state often led in the past to legislation providing a simpler and quicker procedure for securing judicial review. Such legislation was always related to specific powers of government and usually included provisions excluding other forms of judicial review. An important example is provided by the standard procedure for the compulsory purchase of land. After a compulsory purchase order has been made by the local authority and, where objections have been raised by the owner concerned, an inquiry has been held into the order, the minister must decide whether to confirm the order. If he decides to confirm, there is a period of six weeks from the confirmation during which any person aggrieved by the purchase order may challenge the validity of the order in the High Court[93] on two grounds: (a) that the order is not within the powers of the enabling Act; or (b) that the requirements of the Act have not been complied with and that the objector's interests have been substantially prejudiced thereby.[94] These grounds have been interpreted as covering all grounds upon which judicial review may be sought, including in (a) matters affecting *vires*, abuse of discretion, and natural justice and in (b) observance of all relevant statutory procedures.[95] When an aggrieved person makes an application to the High Court for review, the court may make an interim order suspending the purchase order, either generally or so far as it affects the applicant's property. If the order is not challenged in the High Court during the six week period, the order is statutorily protected from challenge in the courts; any other form of judicial review of the order is excluded, whether before or after the confirmation of the order.[96]

This effective method of challenge was first provided by the Housing Act 1930 at a time when there was strong feeling against legislative attempts to exclude judicial review of ministers' actions altogether. Today it is found in the Housing Act 1957 in regard to clearance orders and in many other statutes relating to land.[97] Resort to this remedy has often enabled the High Court to give its entire attention to the principles of judicial review in issue, uncomplicated by the preliminary procedural and jurisdictional questions which may arise in regard to the prerogative orders.[98] The imposition of a time-limit on the right of challenge is necessary in order that if no objection is taken promptly the authorities concerned can proceed to put the decision into effect.

92a And see app. B.
93 Or in Scotland in the Court of Session.
94 Acquisition of Land Act 1981, s. 23 (consolidating earlier Acts).
95 *Ashbridge Investments Ltd* v. *Minister of Housing* [1965] 3 All E.R. 371 and *Coleen Properties Ltd* v. *Minister of Housing* [1971] 1 All E.R. 1049.
96 Acquisition of Land Act 1981, s. 25; pp. 670–2 *post*.
97 *E.g.* Town and Country Planning Act 1971, ss. 244, 275.
98 Examples include the cases of *Fairmount Investments Ltd*, p. 647 *ante*; *Sovmots Investments Ltd*, p. 628 *ante*; and *Bushell*, p. 647 *ante*.

Other statutory rights of appeal include the right to appeal to the High Court on matters of law from many administrative tribunals,[99] and the procedures for recourse to the High Court on points of law affecting planning decisions.[1] Although these statutory remedies are outside the scope of the application for judicial review under Order 53, they are heard in the High Court by the same judges.[2]

It is however necessary for an applicant to the court to bring himself within the scope of the procedure, and the question of *locus standi* depends on the statutory provisions. The six week right to challenge compulsory purchase orders and planning decisions is given to 'any person aggrieved'. This clearly includes the owner who objects to his land being compulsorily purchased but, in a planning case in 1961, it was held not to include neighbouring owners who had objected at a public inquiry to new development which they claimed would injure the amenity of their property; they were considered to have no legal interest that would render them aggrieved persons in law.[3] But in 1973, Ackner J. gave a more generous interpretation to the phrase 'person aggrieved', including within it the officers of an amenity association who had opposed new development at a public inquiry.[4] This decision was welcome, for those who take part in a public inquiry have a definite interest in ensuring that the decision which follows conforms to the law; for other purposes in planning, the interests of neighbours and other third parties are still not protected.[5] But local ratepayers have standing to challenge the rating valuation of any property in their local area.[6]

Statutory exclusion of judicial control[7]
There is a strong presumption that the legislature does not intend access to the courts to be denied. But where Parliament has appointed a specific tribunal for the enforcement of new rights and duties, it is necessary to resort to that tribunal in the first instance. Unless an appeal to the courts is provided by the statute, their jurisdiction is limited to the methods already discussed in this chapter. But many statutes have contained words designed to oust the jurisdiction of the courts. Such provisions have been interpreted by the judges so as to leave, if at all possible, their supervisory powers intact. At one time the prerogative orders were often excluded by name but even the express exclusion of certiorari was not effective against a manifest defect of jurisdiction or fraud committed by a party procuring an order of the court.[8] One frequently found clause was that a particular decision 'shall be final', but it is settled law that this does not restrict the power of the court to issue

---

99   Tribunals and Inquiries Act 1971, s. 13.
1   Town and Country Planning Act 1971, ss. 246, 247.
2   Note 76 *ante*.
3   *Buxton* v. *Minister of Housing* [1961] 1 Q.B. 278; *cf. Maurice* v. *London CC* [1964] 2 Q.B. 362.
4   *Turner* v. *Secretary of State for Environment* (1973) 72 L.G.R. 380.
5   *Gregory* v. *Camden BC*, note 71 *ante*.
6   *Arsenal FC* v. *Ende* [1979] A.C. 1.
7   De Smith, *Judicial Review*, ch. 7.
8   *Colonial Bank of Australasia* v. *Willan* (1874) 5 P.C. 417.

certiorari, either for jurisdictional defects or for error of law on the record.[9] Such a clause means simply that there is no right of appeal from the decision.

Another instance of a clause which does not deprive the courts of their supervisory jurisdiction is where it is stated that a statutory order when made shall have effect as if enacted in the Act which authorised it; the court may nonetheless hold the order to be invalid if it conflicts with the provisions of the Act.[10]

It is then only by an exceptionally strong formula that Parliament can effectively deprive the High Court or the Court of Session of supervisory jurisdiction over inferior tribunals and public authorities. Exclusion clauses today frequently accompany the granting of an express right to challenge the validity of an order or decision during a limited time. Thus the statute which permits challenge of a compulsory purchase order within six weeks of its confirmation provides that subject to the possibility of challenge in that time, 'a compulsory purchase order . . . shall not, either before or after it has been confirmed, made or given, be questioned in any legal proceedings whatsoever . . .'.[11]

In *Smith* v. *East Elloe Rural District Council* the plaintiff, whose land had been taken compulsorily for the building of council houses nearly six years previously, alleged that the making of the order had been caused by wrongful action and bad faith on the part of the council and its clerk. She submitted that the exclusion clause did not exclude the court's power in cases of fraud and bad faith. On this preliminary point of law, the House of Lords held by a bare majority that the effect of the Act was to protect compulsory purchase orders from judicial review except by statutory challenge during the six-week period. Although the validity of the order could no longer be challenged, the action against the clerk of the council for damages could proceed.[12]

A different attitude towards the scope of an exclusion clause was taken by the House of Lords in 1968 in a decision which we have already considered in relation to jurisdictional control.

In *Anisminic Ltd* v. *Foreign Compensation Commission*, the Foreign Compensation Act 1950, section 4(4), provided that the determination by the commission of any application made under the Act 'shall not be called in question in any court of law'. The commission was a judicial body responsible for distributing funds supplied by foreign governments as compensation to British subjects. It rejected a claim made by Anisminic for a reason which the company submitted was erroneous in law and exceeded the commission's jurisdiction. *Held*, by a majority in the House of Lords, section 4(4) did not debar a court from inquiring whether the commission had made in law a correct decision on the question of eligibility to claim. 'Determination' meant a real determination, not a purported determination. By taking into account a factor which in the view of the majority was irrelevant to the scheme, the commission's decision was a nullity. Lord Wilberforce said, 'What would be the purpose of defining by statute the limit of a tribunal's powers, if by means of a clause inserted in the instrument of definition, those limits could safely be passed?'[13]

---

[9]   *R.* v. *Medical Appeal Tribunal, ex p. Gilmore* [1957] 1 Q.B. 574.
[10] *Minister of Health* v. *R.* [1931] A.C. 494.
[11] Acquisition of Land Act 1981, s. 25.
[12] [1956] A.C. 736.
[13] [1969] 2 A.C. 147, 208 (and p. 641 *ante*). For the legislative sequel, see Foreign Compensation Act 1969, s. 3.

This decision is a striking example of the ability of the courts to interpret privative clauses in such a way as to maintain the possibility of judicial review. Although the authority of *Smith* v. *East Elloe RDC* was questioned in the *Anisminic* case, the former decision was not overruled: indeed, the issues involved in considering the finality which should be given to a compulsory purchase order are different from those involved in considering how far an award of compensation should be subject to review. In 1976, the Court of Appeal held that the statutory bar on attempts to challenge the validity of a purchase order after the six week period was absolute: an aggrieved owner was not allowed to bring such a challenge some months later, even though he alleged that the order had been vitiated by a breach of natural justice and good faith which he had only discovered after the six week period.[14] Even if the purchase order must stand, this should not prevent the owner from seeking compensation from those responsible for the alleged acts of bad faith.

Tribunals and Inquiries Act 1971, section 14

The Franks Committee in 1957 recommended that no statute should contain words purporting to oust the prerogative orders. Section 14 of the Tribunals and Inquiries Act 1971 (re-enacting the Tribunals and Inquiries Act 1958) provides that

any provision in an Act passed before 1st August 1958 that any order or determination shall not be called into question in any court, or any provision in such an Act which by similar words excludes any of the powers of the High Court, shall not have effect so as to prevent the removal of the proceedings into the High Court by order of certiorari or to prejudice the powers of the High Court to make orders of mandamus.

There is a corresponding provision to restrict exclusion of the supervisory jurisdiction of the Court of Session. This extension of supervisory power does not apply in three cases, namely (a) to discretionary decisions of the Secretary of State under section 26 of the British Nationality Act 1948,[15] (b) to an order or determination of a court of law, or (c) where an Act makes special provision for application to the High Court within a specified time, for example, the power to challenge a compulsory purchase order within six weeks of its confirmation. This means that section 14 of the 1971 Act has no effect on the decision in *Smith* v. *East Elloe RDC*.[16]

The effect of section 14 largely depends on the interpretation placed on the words 'order or determination'. To take one example from the Parliament Act 1911, section 3 provides that 'any certificate of the Speaker of the House of Commons . . . shall be conclusive for all purposes and shall not be questioned in any court of law'. Such a certificate would seem to be a determination within the meaning of section 14 of the Tribunals and Inquiries Act. But is that Act to be construed as setting aside the common law rule which prevents the courts from inquiring into any matter which is internal to the proceedings

---

14   *R.* v. *Secretary of State for the Environment, ex p. Ostler* [1977] Q.B. 122, discussed by N. P. Gravells (1978) 41 M.L.R. 383 and J. E. Alder (1980) 43 M.L.R. 670. And see *Hamilton* v. *Secretary of State for Scotland* 1972 S.L.T. 233.

15   See now British Nationality Act 1981, s. 44; p. 441 *ante.*

16   *Hamilton* v. *Secretary of State for Scotland, ante.*

of the House of Commons?[17] Perhaps guidance is to be found in the First Schedule to the Act which for other purposes lists the tribunals which come within the Act. These have one characteristic in common: they are concerned with disputes affecting the rights of the individual and not with such matters as the passage of legislation by Parliament.

One common form of statutory provision is not affected by section 14 of the 1971 Act. The jurisdiction of the courts may be restricted indirectly if a power is conferred upon an authority in terms which allow it to act 'if it is satisfied', 'if it thinks fit', 'if it appears to it', or 'if in its opinion'.[18] There has been a contrast in the attitude of the courts to such statutory formulae. The courts have always sought to retain their supervisory jurisdiction in face of statutes purporting to exclude review. On the other hand, they have sometimes been content to interpret literally words conferring discretionary powers on ministers.[19] More recent decisions indicate a more interventionist brand of judicial review.[20]

Remedies in Scots administrative law[21]

The prerogative orders have never been part of Scots law, except to the extent that they were introduced into Scotland by legislation for the purposes of revenue law, nor did a separate court of equity ever develop in Scotland. Apart from statutory remedies like the six-week right to challenge a compulsory purchase order, which apply both in Scotland and England, administrative law remedies in Scotland are essentially the same remedies as are available in private law to enforce matters of civil obligation. The most important of these remedies are: (a) the ancient remedy of *reduction*, by which any document (including decisions of tribunals, local byelaws, the dismissal of public servants and other disciplinary decisions) may be quashed as being in excess of jurisdiction, in breach of natural justice or in other ways contrary to law;[22] (b) the no less ancient remedy of *declarator*, from which the English declaration of right was derived; (c) the remedy of *interdict*, corresponding to both injunction and prohibition in English law; (d) the action for damages for breach of civil obligation; and (e) a summary remedy to enforce performance of statutory duties, comparable with but not identical to mandamus.[23] By contrast with the former English law, all relevant forms of relief may be sought in the same proceedings.[24]

Some important points of comparison with English law may be noted. First, it was established in *Watt* v. *Lord Advocate* that while the remedy of reduction may be used to quash decisions of tribunals which are in excess of their jurisdiction, it is not available (as certiorari is in English law) to review errors of

---

[17] Ch. 12 A. And *cf.* Scotland Act 1978, s. 17(4).

[18] For recent examples, see Housing (Homeless Persons) Act 1977.

[19] *E.g. Robinson* v. *Minister of Town and Country Planning* [1947] K.B. 702.

[20] *Commissioners of Customs and Excise* v. *Cure and Deeley Ltd* [1962] 1 Q.B. 340; *Padfield* v. *Minister of Agriculture* [1968] A.C. 997; *Durayappah* v. *Fernando* [1967] 2 A.C. 337. And see R. C. Austin [1975] C.L.P. 150.

[21] See Scottish Law Commission, Memorandum No. 14, *Remedies in Administrative Law*, 1971.

[22] See *e.g. Malloch* v. *Aberdeen Corp.* [1971] 2 All E.R. 1278; *Barrs* v. *British Wool Marketing Board* 1957 S.C. 72.

[23] Court of Session Act 1868, s. 91; *T. Docherty Ltd* v. *Burgh of Monifieth* 1971 S.L.T. 12.

[24] *E.g. Macbeth* v. *Ashley* (1874) L.R. 2 H.L. Sc. 352.

law made by a tribunal within jurisdiction.[25] However, in *Watt's* case the court held that the error of law in question had led the tribunal to exceed its jurisdiction, since it had caused a statutory entitlement to unemployment benefit to be withheld on an extraneous consideration. This decision revealed a difference between English and Scots law which could prejudice the rights of individuals wishing to pursue claims in Scotland. Since the social security scheme is meant to apply uniformly throughout Great Britain, a statutory right of appeal to the Court of Session (and to the English Court of Appeal) from the Social Security Commissioners was later provided.[26]

Second, in Scots law there is no direct equivalent to relator proceedings. The Lord Advocate has in this respect never assumed the role played by the Attorney-General. For this reason, and because Scots law does not favour the granting of an interdict by a civil court to restrain further criminal conduct, *Gouriet's* case[27] has no direct application in Scotland. The lack of relator proceedings is partly made good by broader rules on the individual's title and interest to sue, which permit individuals to sue directly to enforce many public rights.[28] In *Wilson* v. *Independent Broadcasting Authority* members of a group campaigning in the referendum on devolution had title and interest to sue for an interdict to restrain the showing of a series of political broadcasts which did not maintain a proper balance between the two sides. The judge, Lord Ross, could see 'no reason in principle why an individual should not sue in order to prevent a breach by a public body of a duty owed by that public body to the public'.[29] This statement of principle is to be welcomed, although it is not supported by all the cases.[30]

Third, difficult situations brought about by official failures may sometimes be resolved by the power of the Court of Session to exercise an extraordinary equitable jurisdiction in the form of the *nobile officium* of the court.[31]

Fourth, largely because the procedural difficulties relating to the prerogative orders did not exist in Scotland, the Scottish Law Commission decided after 1971 to discontinue its investigation of administrative law remedies. But this did not mean that Scottish procedures of civil litigation were ideal for the prompt resolution of disputes arising under social legislation such as the Housing (Homeless Persons) Act 1977. When in *Brown* v. *Hamilton DC* the House of Lords held that at common law the decisions of local authorities under that Act could be reviewed only in the Court of Session and not in the sheriff court, Lord Fraser remarked that there was a need in Scotland for a summary procedure in the Court of Session, possibly on the lines of the application for judicial review in English law.[32]

---

25   1979 S.C. 120, and see article by A. W. Bradley cited at p. 638, note 55 *ante*.

26   Social Security Act 1980, s. 14.

27   Page 662 *ante*.

28   *Duke of Atholl* v. *Torrie* (1852) 1 Macq. 65; *Ogston* v. *Aberdeen Tramways Co.* (1896) 24 R. 8.

29   1979 S.C. 351.

30   *D. & J. Nicol* v. *Dundee Harbour Trustees* 1915 S.C. (H.L.) 7; *Simpson* v. *Edinburgh Corp.* 1960 S.C. 313.

31   *Ferguson, Petitioners* 1965 S.C. 16.

32   1983 S.L.T. 397, 418 and see 1983 S.L.T. (News) 109. In June 1984, a working party (chairman, Lord Dunpark) recommended to the Lord President of the Court of Session that such a procedure be created.

Chapter 36

Liability of public authorities and the Crown[1]

In chapters 34 and 35, we examined the law that enables the courts to review the decisions of public authorities on grounds such as *ultra vires*, error of law and breach of natural justice. To complete this study of the judicial control of public authorities, we must now consider their position in relation to civil liability, in particular the law of tort and contract. In principle, public authorities in English law are subject to the same rules of liability in tort and contract as apply to private individuals and companies. There is no separate law of administrative liability for wrongful acts.[2] In practice, however, public authorities require powers to enable them to maintain public services and perform regulatory functions; these powers are generally not available to private individuals. Many new public works, such as motorways and power-stations, could not be created unless there was power in the public interest to override private rights that might be adversely affected. Parliament has often legislated to give public authorities special powers or protection.[3] The courts have also recognised in some contexts that the public interest may require a public authority to be treated differently from private individuals.

At several points in this chapter, the special position of the Crown will be emphasised. In the past, important distinctions were drawn between (a) the Crown, including departments of central government, and (b) other public bodies, such as local authorities and statutory corporations. While many of these distinctions have been removed, notably by the Crown Proceedings Act 1947, others still survive. This chapter deals in section A with the liability of public authorities and the Crown in tort, and in section B with contractual liability. Section C deals with other aspects of the law relating to the Crown, including such procedural immunities and privileges as survive and the rules of evidence relating to the non-disclosure of evidence in the public interest.

---

[1] H. W. R. Wade, *Administrative Law*, chs. 19–21; P. P. Craig, *Administrative Law*, chs. 15, 17, 18; H. Street, *Governmental Liability*; P. W. Hogg, *Liability of the Crown*; C. Harlow, *Compensation and Government Torts*; J. Beatson and M. H. Matthews, *Administrative Law, Cases and Materials*, chs. 12–14.

[2] As was stressed in Dicey's account of the 'rule of law': ch. 6 *ante*.

[3] *E.g.* Public Authorities Protection Act 1893, repealed in 1954.

Relevant aspects of the law in Scotland will be mentioned briefly in each section. Although the common law in Scotland regarding the position of the Crown differed from the law in England, the same broad approach to the liability of public authorities in general has been followed in both legal systems, especially since the Crown Proceedings Act 1947.

A. Liability of public authorities and the Crown in tort

Individual liability

In the absence of statutory immunity, every individual is liable for wrongful acts that he commits and for such omissions as give rise to actions in tort at common law or for breach of statutory duty. This applies even if an officer representing the Crown claims to be acting out of executive necessity.

In *Entick* v. *Carrington*[1] the King's Messengers were held liable in an action of trespass for breaking and entering the plaintiff's house and seizing his papers, even though they were acting in obedience to a warrant issued by the Secretary of State. This was held no defence as the Secretary had no legal authority to issue such a warrant.

Obedience to orders does not normally constitute a defence whether the orders are those of the Crown, a local authority,[2] a limited company or an individual employer.[3] The general principle that superior orders are no defence to an action in tort would, if unqualified, have placed too heavy a burden on many subordinate officials and would have impeded the administration of justice and government. At common law an officer of the court, such as a sheriff, who executes an order of the court, is protected from personal liability unless the order is on its face clearly outside the jurisdiction of the court.[4] Moreover it has been found necessary to provide statutory protection for certain classes of official. Thus certain statutes exempt the servants of a local authority from being sued in respect of acts done *bona fide* in the course of duty.[5] The Constables Protection Act 1750 protects constables who act in obedience to the warrant of a magistrate, though the magistrate acted without jurisdiction in issuing the warrant. Again, the Mental Health Act 1983, section 139, affords constables and hospital staff some protection against civil and criminal liability in respect of acts such as the compulsory detention of a mental patient, unless the act was done in bad faith or without reasonable care.[6] Under the Crown Proceedings Act 1947, section 10, a member of the armed forces may be immune from civil liability in respect of death or personal injury caused to another member of the armed forces while both are on duty.[7] The liability of the individual official will therefore turn both on the powers which he may exercise and also on the privileges and immunities which he may enjoy.

---

[1]   (1765) 19 St. Tr. 1030; p. 93 *ante.*
[2]   *Mill* v. *Hawker* (1875) L.R. 10 Ex. 92.
[3]   For the position of the armed forces, see ch. 23.
[4]   *The Case of the Marshalsea* (1613) 10 Co. Rep. 76a.
[5]   E.g. *Food and Drugs Act* 1955, s. 128; National Health Service Act 1977, s. 125. *Cf.* Town and Country Planning Act 1971, s.4(6).
[6]   On the earlier law, amended in 1982, see *R.* v. *Bracknell Justices ex p. Griffiths* [1976] A.C. 314; *Carter* v. *Metropolitan Police Commissioner* [1975] 2 All E.R. 33.
[7]   Page 679, *post.*

Vicarious liability of public authorities

While the individual liability of public officials was historically important in establishing that public authorities were themselves subject to the law, individual liability is not today a sufficient basis for the liability of large organisations. It is now essential to be able to sue an individual's employing authority, if only because the authority is a more substantial defendant: a successful plaintiff wants the certainty of knowing that he will in fact receive damages and costs awarded to him.

We examine below the process by which vicarious liability came to be imposed on the departments of central government. In cases not involving the Crown, it has long been the law that a public authority is, like any other employer, liable for the wrongful acts of its servants or agents committed in the course of their employment. It was established in 1866 that the liability of a public body whose servants negligently execute their duties is identical with that of a private trading company.

In *Mersey Docks and Harbour Board Trustees* v. *Gibbs*,[8] a ship and its cargo were damaged on entering a dock by reason of a mud bank left negligently at the entrance. The trustees were held liable and appealed to the House of Lords on the ground that they were not a company deriving benefit from the traffic, but a public body of trustees constituted by Parliament for the purpose of maintaining the docks. That purpose involved authority to collect tolls for maintenance and repair of the docks, for paying off capital charges and ultimately for reducing the tolls for the benefit of the public. It was held that these public purposes did not absolve the trustees from the duty to take reasonable care that the docks were in such a state that those who navigated them might do so without danger.

In spite of the argument that a corporation should not be liable for a wrongful act, since a wrongful act must be beyond its lawful powers and therefore not attributable to it, it is clear that a corporation is, like any other employer, liable for the torts of its employees acting in the course of their employment. Thus a hospital authority is liable for negligence in the performance of their professional duties by those physicians and surgeons who are employed by the authority.[9] Under general principles of vicarious liability, a public authority is not liable for acts committed by an employee who is acting outside the course of his employment 'on a frolic of his own'. Moreover, even where an official is appointed and employed by a local authority, the authority is not liable for acts which he commits under the control of a central authority or in the exercise of a distinct public duty imposed on him by the law.[10] There was formerly no vicarious liability in respect of police officers, but by statute the chief constable is now vicariously liable for their acts committed in the performance of their functions, and damages awarded against the police are paid out of police funds.[11]

---

[8]   (1866) L.R. 1 H.L. 93.
[9]   *Cassidy* v. *Minister of Health* [1951] 2 K.B. 343; R. F. V. Heuston and R. S. Chambers, *Salmond and Heuston on the Law of Torts*, pp. 432–3.
[10]   *Stanbury* v. *Exeter Corpn* [1905] 2 K.B. 838.
[11]   Police Act 1964, s.48; Police (Scotland) Act 1967, s.39; ch. 20.

Tortious liability of the Crown

There were two main rules which until 1948 governed the complicated law relating to the liability of the Crown: (a) the rule of substantive law that the King could do no wrong; (b) the procedural rule derived from feudal principles that the King could not be sued in his own courts. The survival of these rules into the 20th century meant that before 1948 the Crown could be sued neither in respect of wrongs that had been expressly authorised nor in respect of wrongs such as negligence committed by Crown servants in the course of their employment.[12] Nor were government ministers vicariously liable for the tortious acts of staff in their departments, since in law ministers and civil servants are alike servants of the Crown.[13] It became increasingly anomalous that this immunity of the Crown applied to the activities of central government. The rigour of the Crown's immunity was eased before 1948 by concession. Acting through the Treasury Solicitor, departments were often prepared to defend an action against a subordinate official and pay damages if he was found personally liable for a wrongful act. From this there developed the practice by which the Crown might nominate a defendant on whom a writ could be served. This practice was however disapproved by the House of Lords after the second world war, in a case in which the nominated defendant could not have been personally liable for the alleged tort.[14] It became urgently necessary for the law to be changed to permit the Crown to be sued in tort. As early as 1927, a draft Bill had been recommended by a government committee, but opposition from the armed services and the Post Office had prevented reform of the law.[15] The law was at last placed on a new basis by the Crown Proceedings Act 1947.

With certain important exceptions, the Crown Proceedings Act 1947 (which applies only to proceedings by and against the Crown in right of Her Majesty's Government in the United Kingdom)[16]established the principle that the Crown is subject to the same liabilities in tort as if it were a private person of full age and capacity, (a) in respect of torts committed by its servants or agents, (b) in respect of the duties which an employer at common law owes to his servants or agents, and (c) in respect of any breach of the common law duties of an owner or occupier of property (section 2(1)). The Crown is therefore vicariously liable for the torts of its servants or agents, for example, negligent driving by a Crown servant while in the course of his employment.

The Crown was also made liable for breach of a statutory duty, provided that the statute is one which binds the Crown as well as private persons (section 2(2)) such as the Occupiers' Liability Act 1957. The Act of 1947 imposes no liability enforceable by action in the case of statutory duties which bind only the Crown or its officers, such as the duty placed upon the Secretary for

---

12   See *e.g. Viscount Canterbury* v. *A.-G.* (1842) 1 Ph. 306 (negligence of Crown servants causing Houses of Parliament to burn down).

13   *Bainbridge* v. *Postmaster-General* [1906] 1 K.B. 178.

14   *Adams* v. *Naylor* [1946] A.C. 543. See also *Royster* v. *Cavey* [1947] 1 K.B. 204.

15   Cmd 2842, 1927. Some changes in the law relating to the Crown as litigant were made in the Administration of Justice (Miscellaneous Provisions) Act 1933 and the Limitation Act 1939.

16   On which see *Franklin* v. *A.-G.* [1974] Q.B. 185, *Tito* v. *Waddell (No. 2)* [1977] Ch. 106, *Mutasa* v. *A.-G.* [1980] Q.B. 114, *R.* v. *Secretary of State, ex p. Indian Assn of Alberta* [1982] Q.B. 892.

Education and Science by section 1 of the Education Act 1944, to promote the education of the people.

Although the general principle of Crown liability is established, the Act of 1947 elaborates this in some detail. Thus the vicarious liability of the Crown is restricted to the torts of its officers as defined in the Act (section 2(6)). This definition requires that the officer shall (a) be appointed directly or indirectly by the Crown and (b) be paid in respect of his duties as an officer of the Crown at the material time wholly out of the Consolidated Fund,[17] moneys provided by Parliament or a fund certified by the Treasury. This excludes, for example, the police.[18] There is also no vicarious liability for acts done by officers acting in a judicial capacity or in execution of judicial process (section 2(5)), nor for acts or omissions of a Crown servant unless apart from the Act the servant would have been personally liable in tort (section 2 (1)). The general law relating to indemnity and contribution applies to the Crown as if it were a private person (section 4). The Act does not authorise proceedings to be brought against the Sovereign in her personal capacity (section 40(1)) and does not abolish any prerogative or statutory powers of the Crown, in particular those relating to the defence of the realm and the maintenance of the armed forces (section 11(1)).

The principal exception from liability in tort relates to the armed forces. Neither the Crown nor a member of the armed forces is liable in tort in respect of acts or omissions causing death or personal injury which are committed by a member of the armed forces while on duty, where (a) the injured or killed was himself a member of the armed forces on duty at the time or, if not on duty as such, was on any land, premises, ship, aircraft or vehicle which was being used for the purposes of the armed forces, and (b) the injury is certified by the Secretary of State for the Social Services as attributable to service for purposes of pension entitlement (section 10). This certificate does not however guarantee an award of a pension unless the conditions for entitlement are fulfilled.[19]

A similar exception from liability formerly applied to the Post Office. The Act of 1947 provided that neither the Crown, nor an officer of the Crown (save at the suit of the Crown) could be held liable in tort for any act or omission in relation to a postal packet (unless it was a registered inland packet) or to a telephonic communication (section 9). Nor was there any liability in contract.[20] When in 1969 the Post Office ceased to be a government department and became a public corporation with a status like that of a nationalised industry, the existing limitations on the liability of the Post Office were continued, even though the Post Office was no longer part of the Crown.[21] Subject then to special rules for the armed forces and the Post Office, the Crown Proceedings Act 1947 in principle assimilated the tortious liabilities of the Crown to those of a private person. There are however many situations involving the potential liability of the government in which the analogy of private liability

---

[17] Ch. 16.
[18] Ch. 20.
[19] *Adams* v. *War Office* [1955] 3 All E.R. 245.
[20] *Triefus & Co. Ltd* v. *Post Office* [1957] 2 Q.B. 352.
[21] Post Office Act 1969, ss.6(5), 29, 30; British Telecommunications Act 1981, s.70.

is not helpful. In the case of some claims against the Crown, the courts may hold that the claims are non-justiciable;[22] but in other cases the courts may apply to governmental action rules derived from, for example, the ordinary law of negligence.[23]

In the law of Scotland, the position of the monarch in respect of Crown proceedings was not identical with the position in English law, the Court of Session being less willing than the English courts to grant the King immunity from being sued.[24] However, it was held in 1921 that the Crown was not vicariously liable for the wrongful acts of Crown servants.[25] Section 2 of the 1947 Act therefore established such liability in Scotland, although the terminology is necessarily modified. Thus 'tort' in the Act's application to Scotland means 'any wrongful or negligent act or omission giving rise to liability in reparation'.[26]

The Act of 1947 thus enabled the Crown to be sued in England in the law of torts, and in Scotland in the law of delict, or reparation. We will now consider some aspects of the substantive law governing the liability in tort of public authorities generally.

Statutory authority as a defence

Where the acts of a public authority interfere with an individual's rights (whether these concern property, contract or individual liberty), those acts will be unlawful unless legal authority for them exists. Such authority may be found either in legislation or in the common law established in decisions of the courts. Where Parliament expressly authorises something to be done, the doing of it in accordance with that authority cannot be wrongful. It will depend on the legislation whether compensation is payable for the rights which Parliament has authorised to be taken away. The undertaking of many public works affecting private rights of property (for example, the construction of nuclear installations, new roads, and reservoirs) is subject to detailed rules of compensation in the relevant legislation.[27] But often express provision for compensation is not made. It is then for the court in interpreting the legislation to decide what powers are authorised and whether any compensation is payable. Certain presumptions may be observed in such interpretation. In particular it is assumed that, when discretionary power is given to a public body, there is no intention to interfere with private rights, unless the power is expressed in such a way as to make interference inevitable.

In *Metropolitan Asylum District* v. *Hill*, hospital trustees were empowered by statute to build hospitals in London. A smallpox hospital was built at Hampstead in such a way as to constitute a nuisance at common law. *Held*, in the absence of express words or necessary implication in the statute authorising the commission of a nuisance, the

---

22   E.g. *Tito* v. *Waddell (No. 2)* and *Mutasa* v. *A.-G.* (note 16 *ante*).
23   E.g. *Dorset Yacht Co.* v. *Home Office* [1970] A.C. 1004; p. 685 *post*.
24   See J. D. B. Mitchell [1957] P.L. 304.
25   *MacGregor* v. *Lord Advocate* 1921 S.C. 847.
26   Crown Proceedings Act 1947, s.43 (*b*). And see *Keatings* v. *Secretary of State for Scotland* 1961 S.L.T. (Sh. Ct.) 63.
27   See *e.g.* Nuclear Installations Acts 1965 and 1969 (as amended by Energy Act 1983, Part II); Land Compensation Act 1973; Reservoirs Act 1975, ss.18, 28.

building of the hospital was unlawful. 'Where the terms of the statute are not imperative, but permissive, when it is left to the discretion of the persons empowered to determine whether the general powers committed to them shall be put into execution or not, . . . the fair inference is that the Legislature intended that discretion to be exercised in strict conformity with private rights and did not intend to confer licence to commit nuisance in any place which might be selected for the purpose'.[28]

If, however, the exercise of a statutory power, and *a fortiori* of a statutory duty, inevitably involves injury to private rights, or if express powers are given to do something in a particular way which must involve injury, for example, to construct a building upon a particular site for a particular purpose, there is no remedy unless the statute makes provision for compensation.[29]

In *Allen* v. *Gulf Oil Refining Ltd*, the House of Lords held by 4–1 that a local Act which envisaged the building of an oil refinery at Milford Haven, though it gave the company no express power to construct the refinery and did not define the site, did give authority for the construction and use of the refinery. Such authority protected the company against liability for nuisance caused to neighbouring owners which was the inevitable result of the construction of the refinery, even though the Act gave the owners no compensation for the loss of their rights.[30]

While the courts may, as in *Allen* v. *Gulf Oil Refining Ltd*, hold that the right to sue for nuisance has been taken away, the courts will rarely hold that the individual's right to sue in negligence has been taken away. Thus the negligent performance of a statutory duty may give rise to liability; and where the exercise of a statutory power necessarily involves injury to private rights, care must be taken not to aggravate the injury by negligent execution. As a leading dictum of Lord Blackburn put it,

'. . .no action will lie for doing that which the legislature has authorised, if it be done without negligence, although it does occasion damage to anyone; but an action does lie for doing that which the legislature has authorised, if it be done negligently.'[31]

Thus in a war-time case, where a car had crashed into an unlit street shelter, it was held that a local council's statutory power to erect air-raid shelters on the highway could be exercised only if the council took reasonable care to avoid injury to the public by providing such street lighting as was then permissible.[32] However, if a public authority which merely has a power to act, and not a duty, decides to take action but acts inefficiently, it is not liable unless the inefficiency causes extra damage to an individual: this was so held in 1941, in the difficult case of *East Suffolk Catchment Board* v. *Kent*, when the use by a river board of an ineffective method of removing flood water from a farmer's land was held to create no liability towards the farmer.[33] In the light

---

28   (1881) 6 App. Cas. 193, 212–3 (Lord Watson).
29   *Hammersmith Rly Co.* v. *Brand* (1869) L.R. 4 H.L. 171.
30   [1981] A.C. 1001.
31   *Geddis* v. *Proprietors of Bann Reservoir* (1878) 3 App. Cas 430, 455–6; and see *Lagan Navigation Co.* v. *Lambeg Bleaching Co.* [1927] A.C. 226, 246.
32   *Fisher* v. *Ruislip-Northwood UDC* [1945] K.B. 584.
33   [1941] A.C. 74. And see M. J. Bowman and S. H. Bailey [1984] P.L. 277.

of developments in the law since 1941, similar facts today might well be viewed differently.[34]

Statutory duties[35]

It was at one time the view that any person who could show that he had sustained harm from a failure to perform a duty imposed by Parliament could bring an action for damages against the person or body liable to perform it.[36] If this general principle applied today, it would be very important as a means of compelling public authorities to perform their statutory duties. But the remedy of damages is not available for every breach of statutory duty. Under the Education Act 1944, section 8, it is the duty of a local education authority to secure that there are available for their area sufficient schools for providing secondary education suitable to the requirements of senior pupils. In *Watt* v. *Kesteven County Council*, the Court of Appeal held that the duty imposed on the council by this section was not enforceable by action by a parent, but only by the Secretary of State for Education under his default powers; thus a Roman Catholic parent was not entitled to insist that the council should pay the fees for his children to attend a Catholic school in an adjacent county, even though the council was prepared to pay similar fees for the children to attend a non-Catholic independent school within its own area.[37]

The courts today would probably be equally reluctant to allow an action for damages by a parent to enforce the statutory duty of the Secretary of State for Education to promote education in England and Wales and the progressive development of educational institutions.[38] Such a duty is so broadly phrased that to prove damage to an individual resulting from breach of the duty would be very difficult. But it must not be assumed that the courts will never be prepared to enforce duties arising under the Education Act, whether by awarding damages or issuing injunctions or a declaration. Thus in *Meade* v. *London Borough of Haringey*, where a local authority had closed its schools for five weeks in sympathy with a trade union's wage claim on behalf of the school caretakers, the Court of Appeal held that the statutory remedy for a parent to complain to the Secretary of State for Education did not exclude the remedies usually available in the courts for breach of statutory duty in a situation in which the council had acted improperly.[39]

It is notoriously difficult to summarise all the factors that may be taken into account by a court in deciding whether a statutory duty should be judicially enforceable and, if so, whether an action for damages will lie. Many duties are laid on administrative bodies which the courts may consider are owed primarily to the public and are not enforceable by individuals. Thus in *Becker* v. *Home Office*, which involved the claim of a former prisoner that she had suffered

---

34   *Anns* v. *Merton Council* [1978] A.C. 728, at 756–7 (Lord Wilberforce) and 764–7 (Lord Salmon); p. 685 *post*. And see *Fellowes* v. *Rother DC* [1983] 1 All E.R. 513.

35   R. A. Buckley (1984) 100 L.Q.R. 204.

36   Dicta to this effect in *Couch* v. *Steel* (1854) 3 E. & B 402 were disapproved in *Atkinson* v. *Newcastle Waterworks Co.* (1877) 2 Ex. D. 441.

37   [1955] 1 Q.B. 408, applied in *Bradbury* v. *London Borough of Enfield* [1967] 3 All E.R. 434 and *Cumings* v. *Birkenhead Corpn* [1972] Ch. 12.

38   Education Act 1944 s.1.

39   [1979] 2 All E.R. 1016; P. Cane [1981] P.L. 11.

loss from a breach of statutory prison rules, the Court of Appeal held that the Prison Rules 1964 were intended to regulate the conduct of prisons but not to create rights in a prisoner. Lord Denning M.R. went so far as to say,

'If the courts were to entertain actions by disgruntled prisoners, the governor's life would be made intolerable. The discipline of the prison would be undermined . . . Even if [the Prison Rules] are not observed, they do not give rise to a cause of action'.[40]

One recurring problem is that legislation which creates new duties often does not provide any express remedy for securing that the duties are performed. Thus the Housing (Homeless Persons) Act 1977 imposed certain duties upon local housing authorities to respond to requests from homeless persons for the provision of housing. In one of the earlier cases under the Act, *Thornton* v. *Kirklees Council*, the Court of Appeal held that, since the Act imposed a duty on a housing authority for the benefit of a specified category of persons but prescribed no special remedy for breach of the duty, it was to be assumed that a civil action for damages lay for breach of that duty.[41] But in *Cocks* v. *Thanet Council*, *Thornton*'s case was given a restrictive interpretation by the House of Lords, which held that the primary remedy for an individual claiming to be entitled to assistance under the 1977 Act was to seek judicial review of the housing authority's decisions by application to the Divisional Court.[42] According to *Cocks* v. *Thanet Council*, an action seeking damages for breach of duty under the 1977 Act lies only when a council has decided that a homeless family is entitled to be re-housed, and then fails to provide them with a house.

An action for damages is evidently not available as a sanction for every statutory duty. Even where an Act recognises a private right in an individual, it may prescribe a remedy other than damages as the sole remedy for breach.[43] But the fact that a pecuniary penalty for breach is payable to the Crown does not normally exclude an action for damages, which serves the different purpose of compensating the injured person.[44] Where a statutory duty resembles an existing common law duty, and the individual suffers injury to person or property, a court may readily hold that damages are payable.[45] It is more difficult to decide the appropriate remedy in the case of statutory duties arising from public services or public powers of control.[46] In 1969 the English and Scottish Law Commissions recommended that the courts should in interpreting statutes assume that the remedy of damages is available for breach of statutory duty, unless Parliament expressly provides to the contrary.[47] Yet this recommen-

---

[40] [1972] 2 Q.B. 407, 418. The decision is consistent with *Arbon* v. *Anderson* [1943] K.B. 252 but not with recent decisions upholding prisoners' rights *e.g. R.* v. *Board of Visitors of Hull Prison, ex p. St. Germain* [1978] Q.B. 678; p. 649 *ante*.

[41] [1979] Q.B. 626, applying *Cutler* v. *Wandsworth Stadium Ltd* [1949] A.C. 398. And *cf. Lonrho Ltd* v. *Shell Petroleum Ltd (No. 2)* [1982] A.C. 173.

[42] [1982] 2 A.C. 286, following *O'Reilly* v. *Mackman* [1983] 2 A.C. 237, p. 668 *ante*.

[43] See *e.g. Atkinson* v. *Newcastle Waterworks Co. (ante). Cf. Read* v. *Croydon Corpn* [1938] 4 All E.R. 631.

[44] *Monk* v. *Warbey* [1935] 1 K.B. 75.

[45] *E.g. Reffell* v. *Surrey CC* [1964] 1 All E.R. 743.

[46] *E.g. A.G., ex rel. McWhirter* v. *IBA* [1973] Q.B. 629 and *Booth & Co. (International) Ltd* v. *National Enterprise Board* [1978] 3 All E.R. 624.

[47] H.C. 256 (1968–9), para. 38; Buckley, *op. cit.*, at p. 230.

dation did not take account of the characteristic relationships between government and the individual which are the concern of administrative law; in many of these instances damages might not be an appropriate remedy.

The great variety of duties imposed by statute helps to explain why there is no single form of judicial proceedings for enforcing public duties. Some are enforceable by civil proceedings brought by the Attorney-General in the public interest.[48] Some duties are enforceable by an order of mandamus, which may be obtained on an application for judicial review.[49] Others are enforceable only by recourse to statutory compensation.[50] In the case of the duty to repair the highway, an action formerly lay against a highway authority for misfeasance (for example, the defective filling of a trench) but not for non-feasance (that is, mere failure to repair).[51] This ancient distinction became unjustifiable in modern conditions. Highway authorities are today liable for failure to maintain a highway maintainable at the public expense, subject to the defence of reasonable care having been taken.[52] The courts had earlier shown their dislike for the non-feasance rule by their unwillingness to allow non-feasance to be a defence to actions concerning other public duties than the duty to repair highways.[53]

Developments in administrative liability[54]

In France, not only the judicial review of official decisions but also the power to hold the administration liable for wrongful acts committed in the course of public services are entrusted to separate administrative courts.[55] Under this system, rules of administrative liability have developed which differ from the ordinary rules of civil liability that apply between private persons. In English law, public authorities and officials are in principle subject to the same law of civil liability as are private individuals. One possible disadvantage of the English approach is that it requires a claim against a public authority to be based upon a particular tort (for example, negligence, nuisance or trespass to the person); and it has been questioned whether existing categories in the law of torts adequately cover all situations in which the acts or omissions of a public authority may cause harm to private persons.[56] A partial answer to these criticisms is that (to take an important example) the law of negligence is far from static, and recent developments have strengthened its application to public authorities. Thus in *Hedley Byrne & Co.* v. *Heller and Partners*, the House of Lords held that there might be liability for financial loss caused through reliance on a negligent mis-statement.[57] Although the case concerned a banker's

---

48   Page 660 *ante*.
49   Page 656 *ante*.
50   Note 27 *ante*.
51   See *e.g. Cowley* v. *Newmarket Local Board* [1892] A.C. 345.
52   Highways Act 1980, s.58; and see *Haydon* v. *Kent CC* [1978] Q.B. 343.
53   *Pride of Derby Angling Assn* v. *British Celanese Ltd* [1953] Ch. 149; *cf. Smeaton* v. *Ilford Corpn* [1954] Ch. 450.
54   B. C. Gould (1972) 5 *New Zealand Universities Law Review* 105; G. Ganz [1973] P.L. 84; C. Harlow (1976) 39 M.L.R. 516; J. McBride [1979] C.L.J. 323; and works cited in note 1 *ante*.
55   L. N. Brown and J. F. Garner, *French Administrative Law*, ch. 8.
56   H. W. R. Wade, *Administrative Law*, 3rd edn., p. 110.
57   [1964] A.C. 465.

reference given in the course of private business, the decision has far-reaching implications for public authorities. A person who relies to his detriment on inaccurate statements made to him by an official in the course of the latter's duties may now have a remedy both against the official and his employing authority.[58] In *Culford Metal Industries Ltd* v. *Export Credits Guarantee Department*, the department was liable in negligence for having given bad advice to an English company, which had caused the company to be uninsured when German contractors failed to pay the company for work carried out in Saudi Arabia.[59] If there can be liability for the giving of incorrect advice which leads to financial loss, then arguably there should also be liability for negligent delay in performing administrative functions which causes similar loss.[60] In practice, compensation for loss caused by such acts of maladministration may often be obtained through recourse to the Ombudsman.[61] Probably because of this, fewer claims reach the courts and the detailed rules of liability remain uncertain.

Although the Crown Proceedings Act 1947 in principle assimilated the tort liability of central government to that of a private person, the duties of the government may give rise to issues of liability which are not easily resolved by applying legal principles which relate to the acts of private individuals.

In *Dorset Yacht Co.* v. *Home Office*,[62] the Home Office was sued for the value of a yacht which had been damaged when seven Borstal boys absconded at night from a Borstal summer camp on an island in Poole harbour. The plaintiffs alleged that the boys were able to abscond because of the negligence of their officers. It was argued for the Home Office that the system of open Borstals would be jeopardised if any liability was imposed on the Home Office for the wrongful acts of those who absconded. The House of Lords held, Lord Dilhorne dissenting, that the Home Office was liable for the negligence of the officers; in the circumstances the officers owed a duty of care to the yacht owners, the damage to the yacht being reasonably foreseeable as the direct consequence of a failure to take reasonable care.

This decision has significance in the developing law of negligence, but its limits should be noted. It did not establish that the Home Office is liable regardless of negligence; nor does the case govern the situation in which it is alleged that an executive discretion (for example, to transfer a boy to an open Borstal) has been improperly exercised. Lord Diplock in the *Dorset Yacht* case suggested that questions of liability for the exercise of discretion were to be settled by applying the public law concept of *ultra vires* rather than the civil law concept of negligence.[63] The relationship between the two concepts arose again in *Anns* v. *Merton Council*.

Under the Public Health Act 1936, local authorities had power to make byelaws regulating the construction of new buildings and a power to inspect buildings during con-

---

58 *Ministry of Housing* v. *Sharp* [1970] 2 Q.B. 223.
59 *The Times*, 25 Mar. 1981.
60 Cf. *Revesz* v. *Commonwealth of Australia* (1951) 25 A.L.J. 179.
61 Ch. 37D; and see Harlow, *Compensation and Government Torts*, part IV.
62 [1970] A.C. 1004; and see C. J. Hamson [1969] C.L.J. 273, G. Semar [1969] P.L. 269, and M. A. Millner [1973] C.L.P. 260.
63 [1970] A.C 1004 at 1067.

struction to ensure conformity with byelaws. A block of maisonettes was built in London with inadequate foundations; this eventually led to serious structural damage. The occupiers alleged that the council's officials had negligently failed to make a proper inspection of the foundations. The House of Lords held that, although there was no statutory duty of inspection, a failure to inspect the foundations could be a breach of the duty of care which the council owed to future occupiers of the maisonettes. The council's liability could arise either from a failure by the council to exercise its discretion properly on the policy issue of whether inspections should take place, or from an 'operational' failure by officials in carrying out the council's policy that inspections should occur.[64]

Distinguishing between (a) the policymaking discretion and (b) the operational function of carrying out policy, Lord Wilberforce considered that the more 'operational' a power or duty might be, the easier it was to superimpose on it a common law duty of care. He stressed both that some discretion entered into many 'operational' functions, and that a public authority could be liable even for its policy decisions, if in reaching them it went outside the area of legitimate discretion. While the policy/operational distinction is sometimes helpful, it is submitted that it does not provide a clearcut or conclusive test of public liability, and that in many situations such liability can be determined without reference to it.[65]

It is not only in the law of negligence that difficult questions of administrative liability arise. English law appears strangely unwilling to accept that an individual should be indemnified for loss sustained by invalid administrative action.[66] Despite the reforms in the procedure of applying for judicial review, by which it is now possible to seek damages while at the same time seeking an order of certiorari or mandamus, there has been no change in the rules of liability.[67] When a trader's licence for a market-stall is cancelled in breach of natural justice, he may by certiorari recover his licence,[68] but he appears to have no legal right to be compensated for the intervening loss of income that he suffers unless, in exceptional circumstances, he could establish that the market authority had acted with malice against him.[69] The Judicial Committee affirmed in 1981 that a public authority's decision may be invalid, in the sense of being *ultra vires*, without giving rise to a right to damages for ensuing loss.

---

[64]   [1978] A.C. 728, affirming (on different grounds) *Dutton* v. *Bognor Regis UDC* [1972] 1 Q.B. 373. In Lord Salmon's view, the Merton council was liable for a negligent inspection, but not for a complete failure to inspect: [1978] A.C. at 762, 767.

[65]   See *e.g.* D. Oliver [1980] C.L.P. 269, citing *Bird* v. *Pearce* [1979] R.T.R. 369 and *Haydon* v. *Kent CC* [1978] Q.B. 343; *cf.* P. P. Craig (1978) 94 L.Q.R. 428 and *Administrative Law*. pp. 534–44.

[66]   *Hoffman-La Roche* v. *Secretary of State for Trade* [1975] A.C. 295, 358 (Lord Wilberforce). On the difficulties of securing restitution from public authorities, see P. B. H. Birks [1980] C.L.P. 191.

[67]   Page 666 *ante*. It seems that the right to sue public authorities in tort is not affected by recent developments in the procedure of application for judicial review: *Page Motors Ltd* v. *Epsom and Ewell BC* (1982) 80 L.G.R. 337, and P. Cane [1983] P.L. 202; *Davy* v. *Spelthorne BC* [1984] A.C. 262.

[68]   *R.* v. *Barnsley Council, ex p. Hook* [1976] 3 All E.R. 452; p. 645 *ante*.

[69]   *David* v. *Abdul Cader* [1963] 3 All E.R. 579, discussed in [1964] C.L.J. 4; and *Roncarelli* v. *Duplessis* (1959) 16 D.L.R. (2d) 689.

In *Dunlop* v. *Woollahra Council*, an owner of building land suffered financial loss when the local council imposed restrictions on the prospective development. The restrictions were later quashed as being *ultra vires*. *Held*, that the owner had no claim in damages for the loss resulting from the invalid restrictions. Moreover, the council had not acted negligently in imposing the restrictions, having taken legal advice before so doing. The council had acted in good faith and, in the absence of malice, could not be liable for the tort of abuse of public office.[70]

This decision, which discouraged several possible developments in administrative liability, reinforced the view of the English Law Commission in 1976 that an inquiry into the question of damages as a remedy for illegal administrative action was desirable.[71] Such an inquiry could also examine the argument that for some forms of injury caused to individuals by the operation of public services, there should be strict liability, that is, liability without proof of fault on the part of the authority concerned: it is wrong that a cyclist injured by an exploding gas main should not recover damages because she cannot prove that the Gas Board had been negligent.[72] In relation to such personal injury arising from the operation of public utilities, it would be a relatively simple matter to establish a scheme for no-fault compensation. But it would be much more difficult to establish a general scheme of compensation applying to the whole of government in respect of economic loss resulting from invalid administrative decisions.[73]

B. Contractual liability

In English law, the contracts of public authorities are in general subject to the same law that governs contracts between private persons.[1] There is no separate body of law governing administrative contracts, as there is in France.[2] There are however certain qualifications which must be made to this general statement. Contracts made on behalf of the Crown are subject to certain exceptional rules, which will be examined below together with relevant provisions of the Crown Proceedings Act 1947. Contracts made by statutory bodies such as local authorities are subject to the rules of *ultra vires*, both as regards matters of substance and matters of procedure. Thus a contract which it is beyond the power of a local authority to make (for example, because it conflicts with a statute which binds the authority) is void and unenforceable.[3] A contract made

---

[70] *Dunlop* v. *Woollahra Council* [1982] A.C. 158. And *cf. Takaro Properties Ltd* v. *Rowling* [1978] 2 N.Z.L.R. 314.

[71] Cmnd 6407, p. 4.

[72] *Dunne* v. *North Western Gas Board* [1964] 2 Q.B. 806; *cf. Dept of Transport* v. *North West Water Authority* [1983] 3 All E.R. 273.

[73] *Cf.* Craig, *Administrative Law*, pp. 550–4, 557–8; Harlow, *Compensation and Government Torts*, pp. 144–61.

[1] H. Street, *Governmental Liability*, ch. 3; J. D. B. Mitchell, *The Contracts of Public Authorities*; C. C. Turpin, *Government Contracts*; P. W. Hogg, *Liability of the Crown*, ch. 5 and see e.g. *Gibson* v. *Manchester Council* [1979] 1 All E.R. 972.

[2] Mitchell, *op. cit.*, ch. 4; L. N. Brown and J. F. Garner, *French Administrative Law*, pp. 125–30.

[3] *Rhyl UDC* v. *Rhyl Amusements Ltd* [1959] 1 All E.R. 257.

by a public authority is also void if it seeks to fetter the future exercise of the authority's discretionary powers.[4] Thus where a local planning authority in Cheshire agreed with Manchester University to discourage new development within the vicinity of the Jodrell Bank radio telescope, the purported agreement was without legal effect.[5] Moreover, a local authority remains free to exercise its power to make byelaws even though the effect of doing so may be to render the future performance of contracts it has made impossible or unprofitable for the contractor.[6] Other restraints may also apply to contracts of public authorities: thus the nationalised industries are subject to statutory duties regarding the terms on which they provide their services.[7] In the case of a local authority, its standing orders normally regulate the procedure by which contracts are placed and these may not be ignored by a council.[8] Where the officers of a local council purport to execute a contract in terms which have never been approved by the council, the contract is wholly void and not binding on the council.[9] A further control in the public interest is that contracts entered into by local authorities are subject to retrospective scrutiny by the system of local government audit.[10]

Contractual liability of the Crown

In English law before 1948, the Crown's immunity from being sued in the courts was not confined to liability in tort and extended to all other aspects of civil liability. But it had been for many years regarded as essential that the subject should be able to obtain judicial redress under a contract made with the Crown or government department. The petition of right was originally a remedy available only for the recovery of property from the Crown, but it became available to enforce contractual obligations. The practice was simplified by the Petitions of Right Act 1860. A petition of right lay in respect of any claim arising out of contracts by which the Crown could be bound, but not in respect of claims in tort. It lay also for the recovery of real property, for damages for breach of contract[11] and to recover compensation under a statute.[12] It was a condition precedent to the hearing of a petition by the court that it should be endorsed with the words *fiat justitia* by the Crown on the advice of the Home Secretary, who acted on the opinion of the Attorney-General. There was no appeal against the refusal of the *fiat*. A judgment in favour of a suppliant on a petition of right took the form of a declaration of the rights to which the suppliant was entitled and, being always observed by the Crown, was as effective as a judgment in an ordinary action.

---

4   *Ayr Harbour Trustees* v. *Oswald* (1883) 8 App. Cas. 623; *Trigg* v. *Staines UDC* [1969] 1 Ch. 10; *Dowty Boulton Paul Ltd* v. *Wolverhampton Corpn (No. 2)* [1973] Ch. 94. And see P. Rogerson [1971] P.L. 288.
5   *Stringer* v. *Minister of Housing* [1971] 1 All E.R. 65.
6   *William Cory & Son Ltd* v. *City of London* [1951] 2 K.B. 476.
7   E.g. *South of Scotland Electricity Board* v. *British Oxygen Co.* [1959] 2 All E.R. 225 (duty to avoid 'undue discrimination' in fixing tariffs).
8   *R.* v. *Hereford Corpn, ex p. Harrower* [1970] 3 All E.R. 460.
9   *North West Leicestershire DC* v. *East Midlands Housing Assn* [1981] 3 All E.R. 364.
10   Ch. 21.
11   *Thomas* v. *R.* (1874) L.R. 10 Q.B. 31.
12   *A.-G.* v. *De Keyser's Royal Hotel* [1920] A.C. 508.

By section 1 of the Crown Proceedings Act 1947, in all those cases where a petition of right was formerly required, it is now possible to sue the appropriate government department, or where no department is named for the purpose the Attorney-General, by ordinary process either in the High Court or in a county court. No prior *fiat* from the Crown is now required.

While the Petitions of Right Act 1860 was repealed by the Crown Proceedings Act 1947, it would appear to have been kept in being for the purpose of proceedings in matters of contract or property against the Sovereign personally.[13] Since the 1947 Act applies only to proceedings against the Crown in right of the government of the United Kingdom, a procedural problem faced holders of Rhodesian government stock in 1974 when they attempted to force the British government to pay arrears of interest that had accrued since 1965. Since the Petitions of Right Act 1860 had been repealed and Rhodesian matters lay outside the remedies provided by the 1947 Act, it was necessary for the stockholders to bring their petition in the pre-1860 form.[14]

In Scotland the petition of right procedure had never been part of the law, since it was always possible to sue the Crown as of right in the Court of Session on contractual claims or for the recovery of property.[15] Accordingly section 1 of the Crown Proceedings Act 1947 does not apply to Scotland.

In general the ordinary rules of contract apply to the Crown: thus an agent need only have ostensible authority to bind the Crown and there is no rule requiring the actual authority of the Crown.[16] Those who make contracts on behalf of the Crown, as its agents, are in accordance with the general rule not liable personally.[17] But the special position of the Crown in some respects must be noted. Statutory authority is not needed before the Crown can make a contract, but payments due under the Crown's contracts come from money provided by Parliament; if Parliament exceptionally provides that no money is payable to a certain contractor, he is barred from enforcing payments that would otherwise be due.[18] If a contract expressly provides that payments thereunder are to be conditional upon Parliament appropriating the money, the Crown is not liable if Parliament does not do so. But, in general, 'the prior provision of funds by Parliament is not a condition preliminary to the obligation of the contract'.[19] Payments due under contract are made out of the general appropriation for the class of service to which the contract relates, and not from funds specifically appropriated to a particular contract. Under the Crown Proceedings Act 1947, as will be seen, the court can do no more than declare the sum due, since no execution to enforce a judgment can be levied against Crown property. There is moreover a rule of law, the exact extent of which it is not easy to determine, that the Crown cannot bind itself so as to fetter its future executive action.

---

[13]   Crown Proceedings Act 1947, s.40(1); *Franklin* v. *A.-G.* [1974] Q.B. 185, 194.

[14]   *Franklin* v. *A.-G.* [1974] Q.B. 185; *Franklin* v. *R.* [1974] Q.B. 202.

[15]   J. D. B. Mitchell, *Constitutional Law*, p. 304.

[16]   But see *A.-G. for Ceylon* v. *Silva* [1953] A.C. 461 on the difficulties of establishing ostensible authority in relation to the Crown; Turpin, *op. cit.*, pp. 33–6.

[17]   *Macbeath* v. *Haldimand* (1786) 1 T.R. 172.

[18]   *Churchward* v. *R.* (1865) L.R. 1 Q.B. 173.

[19]   *New South Wales* v. *Bardolph* (1934) 52 C.L.R. 455, 510 (Dixon J.); Street, *op. cit.*, pp. 84–92 and Turpin, *op. cit.*, pp. 25–7.

In *Rederiaktiebolaget Amphitrite* v. *R.* a Swedish shipping company, Sweden being a neutral in the first world war, was aware that neutral ships were liable to be detained in British ports. They obtained an undertaking from the British government that a particular ship, if sent to this country with a special class of cargo, would not be detained. Accordingly the ship was sent with such a cargo, but the government withdrew their undertaking and refused clearance for the ship. On trial of a petition of right, it was held that the undertaking of the government was not enforceable as the Crown was not competent to make a contract which would have the effect of limiting its power of executive action in the future.[20]

It has been suggested that the defence of executive necessity only 'avails the Crown where there is an implied term to that effect or that is the true meaning of the contract';[21] or again that the defence has no application to ordinary commercial contracts made by the Crown. A preferable view is that the *Amphitrite* case illustrates a general principle that the Crown, or any other public authority, cannot be prevented by an existing contract from exercising powers which are vested in it either by statute or common law for the protection of the public interest.[22]

In *Commissioners of Crown Lands* v. *Page*, the Crown sued for arrears of rent due under a lease of Crown land that had been assigned to the defendant. The defence was that the land had been requisitioned by a government department and that this constituted eviction by the Crown as landlord. The Court of Appeal held that the arrears were payable. Devlin L.J. said: 'When the Crown, in dealing with one of its subjects, is dealing as if it too were a private person, and is granting leases or buying and selling as ordinary persons do, it is absurd to suppose that it is making any promise about the way in which it will conduct the affairs of the nation.'[23]

There are many other problems arising from government contracts to which the accepted principles of English law provide no answer, for example, the power of a department to place contracts and to remove a firm from its list of approved contractors.[24] This power was used by the Labour government in 1975–8 to require companies who were granted contracts to observe a non-statutory pay policy.[25] This is an outstanding example of a government's ability to achieve certain public goals without recourse to the formalities of legislation.[26]

While the awarding of contracts is not a matter for judicial review, government contracts are subject to the scrutiny of the Comptroller and Auditor-General. Much of the practice of central government in placing and administering contracts derives from rulings of the Public Accounts Committee.[27] In

---

20   [1921] 3 K.B. 500.
21   *Robertson* v. *Minister of Pensions* [1949] 1 K.B. 227, 237 (Denning J.).
22   Street, *op. cit.*, pp. 98–9; Mitchell, *Contracts of Public Authorities*, pp. 27–32, 52–65.
23   [1960] 2 Q.B. 274, 292; see also *William Cory & Son Ltd* v. *City of London* [1951] 2 K.B. 476.
24   Turpin, *op. cit.*, ch. 5 and pp. 233–8.
25   G. Ganz [1978] P.L. 333.
26   T. C. Daintith [1979] C.L.P. 41. Until it was rescinded by the House of Commons on 16 Dec. 1982, the Fair Wages Resolution had for many years required uniform conditions on fair wages to be included in all government contracts; and see R. W. Rideout, *Principles of Labour Law*, pp. 357–60.
27   Ch. 16.

view of the number and value of government contracts awarded each year, remarkably few disputes arising from such contracts reach the courts. Such disputes in practice are resolved by various forms of consultation, negotiation or arbitration. The Review Board for Government Contracts, which was established in 1969 under an agreement between the government and the Confederation of British Industry, regularly reviews such matters as the profit formula for non-competitive government contracts and it may also examine in relation to a particular contract a complaint by either party that the price paid is not 'fair and reasonable.'[28] Government contracts are excluded from the jurisdiction of the Parliamentary Ombudsman.[29]

Service under the Crown

Service under the Crown is another instance of the special contractual position of the Crown; for it is part of the prerogative that the Crown employs its servants at its pleasure, whether in the civil service or the armed forces. The Crown claims that its freedom to dismiss its servants at will is necessary in the public interest. Certainly the case-law suggests that the relationship between the Crown and its servants gives rise to few rights on the part of the servant against the Crown. Thus, in the absence of statutory provision,[30] no Crown servant has a remedy for wrongful dismissal.

In *Dunn* v. *R.*, Dunn claimed that he had been engaged in Crown service by the Consul General for the Niger Protectorate for a term of three years certain. His claim for damages for premature dismissal failed. Lord Herschell said: 'Such employment being for the good of the public, it is essential for the public good that it should be capable of being determined at the pleasure of the Crown, except in exceptional cases where it has been deemed to be more for the public good that some restriction should be imposed on the power to dismiss its servants.'[31]

Having failed in his petition of right, Dunn sued the servant of the Crown who had engaged him, for damages for breach of warranty of authority. It was held that no action lies against a Crown servant for breach of warranty of authority, but the decision can be supported on the narrower ground that Dunn must be deemed to have known that the officer who had engaged him had no power in law to engage him for a fixed period: *Dunn* v. *MacDonald*.[32]

The Crown's power to dismiss its servants at pleasure has sometimes been explained on the basis that a term to this effect is implied into every contract of employment made by the Crown. If this were so, the Crown's power to dismiss at pleasure could be excluded by an express term in the contract of employment, but the court may well disregard any such attempt to depart from the normal rule as a clog or fetter on the overriding power of the Crown.[33]

---

28 See *e.g.* Report of the Board on the 3rd General Review of the profit formula for non-competitive government contracts, 1980.
29 Ch. 37 D.
30 *E.g.* the rule that judges hold office during good behaviour, p. 334 *ante*; *Gould* v. *Stuart* [1896] A.C. 575 and *Reilly* v. *R.* [1934] A.C. 176; and see note 38 *post*.
31 [1896] 1 Q.B. 116; G. Nettheim [1975] C.L.J. 253.
32 [1897] 1. Q.B. 401.
33 *Terrell* v. *Secretary of State for the Colonies* [1953] 2 Q.B. 482.

Although a civil servant has no tenure of office as a matter of common law, in practice he has a very high degree of security. This security depends upon convention rather than law, and the collective agreements on wages and other conditions of service reached between the staff side and the employers' side in joint councils do not give rise to contractual rights.[34] Indeed it may be asked whether Crown service is a contractual relationship at all. Thus members of the armed forces cannot sue for arrears of pay, for no engagement between the Crown and members of the armed forces can be enforced by a court of law.[35] In respect of the civil service, despite earlier decisions to the contrary,[36] it now seems that the Crown may be liable to a civil servant for arrears of salary.[37] Many of the older arguments in favour of the Crown's privileged position as a civil employer have been superseded since 1971 when the statutory right to bring proceedings in an industrial tribunal for unfair dismissal was conferred on civil servants.[38] However the Crown has power in the interests of state security to exempt classes of civil servants from the application of what is now the Employment Protection (Consolidation) Act 1978. This power was used in 1984 to exempt the civilian staff of the Government Communications Headquarters at Cheltenham from the Act. At the same time, the government used the prerogative powers of the Crown to impose a new condition of service barring GCHQ staff from union membership.[39] Subject to the statutory remedy for unfair dismissal, the Crown retains its legal power to dismiss its servants at pleasure. In its employment practices, the Crown must not in general discriminate on racial or sexual grounds.[40]

C. The Crown in litigation: privileges and immunities

As we have already seen,[1] 'the Crown' is a convenient term in constitutional law for the collectivity that now comprises the Sovereign in her governmental capacity, ministers, civil servants and the armed forces. When the Sovereign governed in person, it was understandable that royal officials should benefit from many of the Sovereign's immunities and privileges. But despite the increase in the scale of government and the decline of personal government by the Sovereign, the personnel of central government continued to benefit from Crown status. The shield of the Crown extended to what was described not very satisfactorily as the general government of the country or 'the province of government',[2] but not to local authorities nor to many public corporations.

---

34   *Rodwell* v. *Thomas* [1944] K.B. 596; *cf. Riordan* v. *War Office* [1959] 3 All E.R. 552.
35   *Leaman* v. *R.* [1920] 3 K.B. 663; *Kynaston* v. *A.-G.* (1933) 49 T.L.R. 300.
36   *Mulvenna* v. *Admiralty* 1926 S.C. 842; *Lucas* v. *Lucas and High Commissioner for India* [1943] P. 68, criticised by D W. Logan (1945) 61 L.Q.R. 240; and see *Dudfield* v. *Ministry of Works, The Times*, 24 Jan. 1964.
37   *Kodeeswaran* v. *A.-G. of Ceylon* [1970] A.C. 1111; *cf. Sutton* v. *A.-G.* (1923) 39 T.L.R. 294 and *Cameron* v. *Lord Advocate* 1952 S.C. 165.
38   See now Employment Protection (Consolidation) Act 1978, s.138; and *e.g. Howard* v. *Department for National Savings* [1981] 1 All E.R. 674.
39   See H.C. Deb., 25 Jan. 1984, col. 917 and H.C. 238 (1983–4); p. 283, *ante*.
40   Sex Discrimination Act 1975, s.75; Race Relations Act 1976, s.85. Ch. 31 A.

1   Pages 229, 302 *ante*.
2   *Mersey Docks Trustees* v. *Cameron* (1861) 11 H.L.C. 443, 508; *B.B.C.* v. *Johns* [1965] Ch. 32.

Although the Crown Proceedings Act 1947 deprived government departments of their immunity from being sued, for several reasons it may still be necessary to know whether a public authority has Crown status.[3] It is good legislative practice for an Act which creates a new public body to state whether and to what extent it should enjoy Crown status,[4] but this does not always happen. Whether because of express legislation or judicial interpretation, a public agency may be regarded as having Crown status for some purposes, but not for others.

In regard to central government, the underlying concept of 'the Crown' has various legal consequences. Government contracts are concluded in the name of individual departments and ministers, acting expressly or impliedly for the Crown.

In *Town Investments Ltd* v. *Department of the Environment*, it had to be decided whether a rent-freeze imposed by counter-inflation legislation applied to two office-blocks in London, of which the Secretary of State for the Environment was the lessee 'for and on behalf of Her Majesty'; the offices were occupied by a variety of departments, and in part by the US navy. The House of Lords held (Lord Morris dissenting) that the Crown was the tenant and that the premises were occupied for the purpose of a business carried on by the Crown; the leases were therefore subject to the rent-freeze.[5]

While this decision took account of the practical realities of relations within central government, it revealed a striking anomaly in the effects of the legislation, namely that the Crown as tenant could take the benefit of the rent-freeze, whereas the Crown as landlord was not barred from increasing the rents which its tenants had to pay. The legal reasons for this inequity will now be examined.

Application of statutes to Crown[6]

As we have already seen, under the 1947 Act the Crown may be sued for breach of statutory duty. But nothing in the Act affects 'any presumption relating to the extent to which the Crown is bound by an Act of Parliament' (section 40(2)(*f*)). The rule that Acts do not bind the Crown, that is, that the Crown's rights and interests are not prejudiced by legislation unless a statute so enacts by express words or by necessary implication, significantly limits the extent of governmental liability for breach of statutory duty. It is by the operation of this rule, for example, that Crown property is in law exempt from local rates and taxation. Difficult questions may arise as to whether an official or a public authority is entitled to benefit from the presumption of Crown immunity.[7] Moreover the effect of the presumption is not always clear. In 1947 the Judicial Committee took a strict view of the test of 'necessary implication', holding that in the absence of express words the Crown is bound by a statute

---

3   *E.g.* liability to taxation and the criminal law; whether staff are Crown servants (*R.* v. *Barrett* [1976] 3 All E.R. 895). And see cases cited at pp. 251, 302 *ante*.

4   See *e.g.* Crown Agents Act 1979, s.1(5).

5   [1978] A.C. 359, discussed by C. Harlow (1977) 40 M.L.R. 728 and (1980) 43 M.L.R. 241, 244–5.

6   Street , *Governmental Liability*, ch. 6; Hogg, *Liability of the Crown*, ch. 7; Craig, *Administrative Law*, ch. 18(2).

7   See *e.g. Coomber* v. *Berkshire Justices* (1883) 9 App. Cas. 61; and note 3 *ante*.

only if the purpose of the statute would be 'wholly frustrated' if the Crown were not bound.[8] In 1981, Woolf J. held, interpreting section 75 of the Race Relations Act 1976, that the Act bound the Crown to the extent that the Commission for Racial Equality had power to conduct an investigation into alleged discrimination in the Home Office's system of immigration control.[9] Where an Act does not apply to the Crown or its servants acting in the course of duty, a Crown servant is not liable either civilly or criminally if he disregards the statute.[10] But these restrictive rules do not prevent the Crown deriving benefits from legislation. Even though the Crown is not named in an Act, the Crown may take advantage of rights conferred generally by the Act as in the *Town Investments* case, provided that the circumstances for the exercise of those rights exist.[11]

Procedure

Where the Act of 1947 enables proceedings to be brought against the Crown in English courts, whether in tort or contract or for the recovery of property, in principle the normal procedure of litigation applies. The action is brought against the appropriate department, the Minister for the Civil Service being responsible for publishing a list of departments and naming the solicitor for each department to accept process on its behalf; in cases not covered by the list, the Attorney-General may be made defendant. The trial follows that of an ordinary High Court or county court action except that:

(*a*) judgment against the department cannot be enforced by the ordinary methods of levying execution or attachment; but the department is required to pay the amount certified to be due as damages and costs (section 25);

(*b*) in place of an injunction or a decree of specific performance, remedies which are sanctioned by imprisonment for default, the court makes an order declaring the rights of the parties (section 21);[12] an interim declaration in place of an interim injunction may not be made;[13]

(*c*) there can be no order for restitution of property, but the court may declare the plaintiff entitled as against the Crown (section 21);

(*d*) in lieu of an order for the attachment of money owed by the Crown to a debtor, a judgment creditor may obtain an order from the High Court directing payment to himself and not to the debtor (section 27); for this purpose the Crown is within the jurisdiction of the English courts, even in respect of savings accounts held with the National Savings Bank, whose head office is in Glasgow.[14]

An action for a declaration may be brought against the Crown without

8   *Province of Bombay* v. *Municipal Corpn of Bombay* [1947] A.C. 58; and see *Re Automatic Telephone and Electric Co.'s Applications* [1963] 2 All E.R. 302.
9   *Home Office* v. *Commission for Racial Equality* [1982] Q.B. 385.
10   *Cooper* v. *Hawkins* [1904] 2 K.B. 164. See now Road Traffic Regulation Act 1984, s.130
11   Crown Proceedings Act 1947, s.31; and note 5 *ante*.
12   Attempts to obtain injunctions against ministers failed in *Merricks* v. *Heathcoat-Amory* [1955] Ch. 567 and *Harper* v. *Home Secretary* [1955] Ch. 238.
13   *International General Electric Co.* v. *Commissioners of Customs and Excise* [1962] Ch. 784; *R.* v. *Inland Revenue Commissioners, ex p. Rossminster Ltd* [1980] A.C. 952 (for differing views on the need for reform, see Lord Diplock at 1014–5 and Lord Scarman at 1027.)
14   *Brooks Associates Inc.* v. *Basu* [1983] 1 All E.R. 508.

claiming any consequential relief, for example where a wrong is threatened,[15] but not to determine purely hypothetical questions which may never arise; for example, as to whether there is a contingent liability to a tax.[16]

In private litigation, when the plaintiff seeks an interim injunction against the defendant to maintain the *status quo* pending the final decision of the case, the court will grant such a request only if the plaintiff gives an undertaking as to damages, so that the defendant's loss may be made good if the plaintiff's action ultimately fails. When the Crown is seeking to assert rights of property or contract, the Crown may be expected to give such an undertaking. But when the Crown takes proceedings to enforce the law, an undertaking as to damages is generally not appropriate.[17]

In Scotland, where civil procedure is very different from that in England, actions in respect of British or United Kingdom departments (like the Ministry of Defence or the Inland Revenue) may be brought against the Lord Advocate;[18] in respect of Scottish departments, actions are brought against the Secretary of State for Scotland.[19] The restrictions on the remedies which may be obtained against the Crown are broadly the same as in English law: thus a declarator but not interdict may be issued against the Crown or against ministers.[20] Actions may be raised by and against the Crown in either the Court of Session or the sheriff court.

Non-disclosure of evidence on grounds of public interest

Discovery of documents is a procedure in civil litigation by which a party may inspect all documents in the possession or control of his opponent which relate to the matters in dispute. Formerly it could not be used against the Crown. By section 28 of the 1947 Act, the court may order discovery against the Crown and may also require the Crown to answer interrogatories, that is, written questions to obtain information from the other party on material facts. But the Act expressly preserves the existing rule of law that the Crown may refuse to disclose any document or to answer any question on the ground that this would be injurious to the public interest; the Act even protects the Crown from disclosing the mere existence of a document on the same ground. Crown privilege, as the power of the Crown to withhold documentary evidence from the courts has been called, is not restricted to proceedings in which the Crown is a party and applies equally to civil proceedings between private individuals. The need for some power to protect documents from publication in the interests of state security was well illustrated by *Duncan* v. *Cammell Laird & Co.*[21] What is more difficult is to determine the extent of the power, the grounds on which it may be claimed, and the ability of the court to control the executive

---

[15] *Dyson* v. *A.-G.* [1912] 1 Ch. 158.

[16] *Argosam Finance Co.* v. *Oxby* [1965] Ch. 390; and see p. 664 *ante*.

[17] *Hoffman-La Roche & Co.* v. *Secretary of State for Trade* [1975] A.C. 295 (department seeking to compel company to observe price control for drugs.)

[18] Crown Suits (Scotland) Act 1857; Law Officers Act 1944, s.2; and see *Lord Advocate* v. *Argyll CC* 1950 S.C. 304.

[19] Reorganisation of Offices (Scotland) Act 1939, s.1(8).

[20] Before 1947, interdict was sometimes issued against ministers of the Crown: *Bell* v. *Secretary of State for Scotland* 1933 S.L.T. 519.

[21] [1942] A.C. 624.

in exercising this power. Subsequent history shows that these matters were not finally settled in *Duncan* v. *Cammell Laird & Co.*, as was once thought to be the case.

Early in 1939 a new naval submarine sank while on trial with the loss of 99 lives, including civilian workmen. Many actions in negligence were brought by the personal representatives against the company, who had built the submarine under contract with the Admiralty. In a test action, the company objected to the production of documents relating to the design of the submarine. The First Lord of the Admiralty directed the company not to produce the documents on the ground of Crown privilege, since disclosure would be injurious to national defence.

The House of Lords held that the documents should not be disclosed. Although a validly taken objection to disclosure was conclusive, and should be taken by the minister himself, the decision ruling out such documents was that of the judge. In deciding whether it was his duty to object, a minister should only withhold production where the public interest would otherwise be damnified, for example, where disclosure would be injurious to national defence or to good diplomatic relations, 'or where the practice of keeping a class of documents secret is necessary for the proper functioning of the public service'.[22]

On this basis, documents might be withheld either because the *contents* of those documents must be kept secret (as in *Duncan's* case itself) or on the much wider ground that they belonged to a *class* of documents which must as a class be treated as confidential, for example civil service memoranda and minutes, to guarantee freedom and candour of communication on public matters. Thereafter the practice developed of withholding documents simply on the minister's assertion that they belonged to a class of documents which it was necessary in the public interest for the proper functioning of the public service to withhold.[23] Where documents were withheld, oral evidence of their contents could not be given; and it seemed that the courts could not overrule the minister's objection if taken in correct form.

Concern at these unduly wide claims of privilege was eased by government concessions. In 1956 the Lord Chancellor stated that privilege would not be claimed in certain types of litigation for certain kinds of documents in a department's possession; these included factual reports about accidents involving government employees or government premises and, where the Crown or a Crown employee was being sued for negligence, medical reports by service or prison doctors. In 1962 the government stated that statements made to the police during criminal investigations would not be withheld where the police were sued for malicious prosecution or wrongful arrest, and that in other civil proceedings the question of whether statements to the police should be withheld would be left to the trial judge, subject in each case to the names of police informers not being revealed.[24] These concessions were not accompanied by any change in the law, and it was still considered that in English law the courts were bound by the minister's objection. By contrast, it was already established in Scotland that a court must take account of the minister's decision but is not

---

22   [1942] A.C. at 642.
23   See *Ellis* v. *Home Office* [1953] 2 Q.B. 135 and *Broome* v. *Broome* [1955] P. 190 for examples of the harsh operation of the rule.
24   See H.L. Deb., 6 Jun. 1956, col. 741–8 and 8 Mar. 1962, col. 1191.

bound by it and in exceptional circumstances may overrule it if the interests of justice so require.[25] After several decisions of the English Court of Appeal had cast doubt on the conclusiveness of the minister's objection,[26] in 1968 the House of Lords overruled an objection taken by the Home Secretary to the production of certain police reports. This established the principle that it is for the court to hold the balance between the public interest in the administration of justice and the public interest in the efficient conduct of government.

In *Conway* v. *Rimmer*[27] a former probationary constable sued a police superintendent for malicious prosecution after an incident of a missing electric torch which had led to the acquittal of the plaintiff on a charge of theft and to his dismissal from the police. The Home Secretary claimed privilege for (a) probationary reports on the plaintiff and (b) the defendant's report on the investigation into the incident. He certified that these were confidential reports within a class of documents production of which would be injurious to the public interest. *Held,* the court has jurisdiction to order the production of documents for which Crown privilege is claimed. The court will give full weight to a minister's view, but this need not prevail if the relevant considerations are such that judicial experience is competent to weigh them.

The House of Lords thus departed from the wide rule laid down in *Duncan* v. *Cammell Laird,* which it accepted had been properly decided on the facts. English law was thereby brought into line with Scots law, Lord Reid considering there to be no justification for the law on such a matter of public policy being different in the two countries.

Since *Conway* v. *Rimmer* enabled the courts to have the last word on ministerial objections to disclosure, the courts have the onerous duty of deciding when, on a balancing of the competing public interests, the withholding of evidence is justified. Subsequent cases have involved re-appraisal of this area of law, with the courts laying more stress on their conception of what the public interest requires than on the notion of Crown privilege. The issues arising have included (a) the use as evidence of material which is subject to the constraints of confidentiality; (b) the disclosure of documents relating to the formulation of government policy; and (c) the grounds which must be shown before the court will inspect documents. In the brief account of this case-law which follows, emphasis will be given to decisions of the House of Lords since 1972. Continuing development in the law remains likely.[28]

In *Rogers* v. *Home Secretary,*[29] the House of Lords refused to order production of a secret police report to the Gaming Board about an applicant for a gaming licence, holding that the report fell into a class of documents which should not be disclosed. The judgments emphasised that power to withhold evidence on grounds of public interest was not a privilege of the Crown as such and that 'Crown privilege' was a misnomer. In *Alfred Crompton Amusement Machines Ltd* v. *Commissioners of Customs and Excise,* the House refused to order production of documents supplied in confidence to the Commissioners by other taxpayers.

---

[25]   *Glasgow Corp.* v. *Central Land Board* 1956 S.C. (H.L.) 1; *Whitehall* v. *Whitehall* 1957 S.C. 30.

[26]   Including *Merricks* v. *Nott-Bower* [1965] 1 Q.B. 57 and *In re Grosvenor Hotel London (No 2)* [1965] Ch. 1210; D. H. Clark (1967) 30 M.L.R. 489.

[27]   [1968] A.C. 910; D. H. Clark (1969) 32 M.L.R. 142.

[28]   See Lord Mackay of Clashfern (1983) 2 *Civil Justice Quarterly* 337.

[29]   [1973] A.C. 388.

Lord Cross said that where the considerations for and against disclosure were evenly balanced, the court should uphold a claim to privilege on the ground of public interest 'and trust to the head of the department concerned to do whatever he can to mitigate the ill-effects of non-disclosure'.[30] But in *Norwich Pharmacal Co.* v. *Commissioners of Customs and Excise*, the Commissioners were ordered in the interests of justice to produce information which identified the importers of a patented chemical compound, and their claim of privilege was rejected.[31]

In *D.* v. *National Society for the Protection of Cruelty to Children*, the House of Lords held that public interest as a ground for non-disclosure of confidential material was not confined to the efficient functioning of government departments.[32] In that case, the Court of Appeal had ordered the NSPCC to reveal the identity of someone who had informed the society of a suspected case of child battering. The society, established by royal charter, had a statutory responsibility to take proceedings for the care of children. The House of Lords held, by analogy with the rule protecting the identity of police informers from disclosure, that the names of informants to the society should be immune from disclosure. It was emphasised that confidentiality as such is not a separate head of privilege, 'but it may be a very material consideration to bear in mind when privilege is claimed on the ground of public interest'.[33]

Confidential material in the form of statements to the police during a statutory investigation into a complaint against the police was protected by the Court of Appeal from disclosure.[34] The court considered that such statements should be immune as a 'class' against disclosure, since disclosure for the purposes of civil litigation was likely to impede the future investigation of complaints. In two linked cases, *Science Research Council* v. *Nassé* and *British Leyland U K Ltd* v. *Nyas*,[35] the issue was whether on an employee's complaint of unlawful discrimination, the employers must produce confidential reports on other employees. The House of Lords held that such reports were not covered by public interest immunity, and that the court or tribunal had power at its discretion to order production, after having inspected the reports. Lord Scarman suggested that public interest immunity should be restricted 'to what must be kept secret for the protection of government at the highest levels and in the truly sensitive areas of executive responsibility'.[36] However, the language of public interest immunity was used in *Campbell* v. *Tameside Council*, where a teacher had been assaulted by an 11 year old pupil and wished to see psychologists' reports held by the council; the Court of Appeal ordered discovery after inspecting the reports, since the public interest in the adminis-

---

30 [1974] A.C. 405 (claims to professional privilege by the Commissioners' solicitors were also upheld).
31 [1974] A.C. 133.
32 [1978] A.C. 171.
33 Lord Cross, [1974] A.C. 405 at 433, cited by Lord Simon, [1978] A.C. 171 at 239.
34 *Neilson* v. *Laugharne* [1981] Q.B. 736; *Hehir* v. *Metropolitan Police Commissioner* [1982] 2 All E.R. 335 (privilege may not be waived by police).
35 [1980] A.C. 1028; ch. 31A.
36 [1980] A.C. at 1088.

tration of justice outweighed any harm to the public service resulting from production of the reports.[37]

In *Conway* v. *Rimmer*, Lord Reid had expressed the opinion that Cabinet minutes and documents concerned with policy-making within departments were protected against disclosure, in order that the inner working of the government machine should not be exposed to ill-informed and biased criticism.[38] In *Burmah Oil Co. Ltd* v. *Bank of England*,[39] the House of Lords had for the first time to consider the extent to which such high-level documents should be protected from disclosure.

In 1975 the Burmah Oil company had with government approval agreed to sell its holdings in BP stock to the Bank of England as part of an arrangement protecting the company from liquidation. Later the company sought to have the sale set aside as unconscionable and inequitable. It therefore wished to see documents held by the bank, including (a) ministerial communications and minutes of meetings attended by ministers and (b) communications between senior civil servants relating to policy matters. The Crown contended that it was 'necessary for the proper functioning of the public service' that the documents be withheld. The House of Lords held that the Crown's claim of immunity was not conclusive. If it was likely (or reasonably probable) that the documents contained matter that was material to the issues in the case, the court might inspect them to determine where the balance lay between the competing public interests. Having inspected the documents, the House ordered that they be not produced since they did not contain material necessary for disposing fairly of the case. Lord Wilberforce dissented from the decision to inspect; in his view, it was a plain case of 'public interest immunity properly claimed on grounds of high policy'.[40]

In the *Burmah. Oil* case, judicial opinion had moved far beyond the position in *Conway* v. *Rimmer*. Lord Wilberforce's views were more favourable to the government's claims than those of the other judges, but even he envisaged that there might be circumstances in which a high-level governmental interest must give way before the interests of justice.[41] It would seem that even Cabinet papers are not immune from disclosure in an exceptional case where the interests of justice so require.[42] In the Watergate tapes case, it was the public interest in criminal justice that led the US Supreme Court to order President Nixon to deliver his tapes to the special investigator.[43]

Apart from such exceptional circumstances, did the *Burmah Oil* decision mean that the judges should regularly inspect and if necessary order the production of documents relating to policy-making within government departments? This power was exercised by McNeill J. in *Williams* v. *Home Office*,[44] But in *Air Canada* v. *Secretary of State for Trade*[45] the House of Lords upheld the

---

[37] [1982] Q.B. 1065.
[38] [1968] A.C. 910, 952; see also Lord Upjohn at 993.
[39] [1980] A.C. 1090; D. G. T. Williams [1980] C.L.J. 1.
[40] [1980] A.C. at 1117.
[41] [1980] A.C. at 1113.
[42] As in the Australian case of *Sankey* v. *Whitlam* (1978) 21 A.L.R. 505. See also *Air Canada* v. *Secretary of State for Trade* [1983] 2 A.C. 394, 432 (Lord Fraser); I. G. Eagles [1980] P.L. 263.
[43] *Nixon* v. *US* (1974) 418 U.S. 683.
[44] [1981] 1 All E.R. 1151.
[45] [1983] 2 A.C. 394.

Secretary of State's claim for immunity and refused to inspect the documents. The majority (Lords Fraser, Wilberforce and Edmund-Davies) held that for a court to exercise the power of inspection, it was not sufficient that the documents *might* contain information relevant to the issues in dispute; the party seeking access to the documents must show that it was reasonably probable that the documents were likely to help his case. A speculative belief to this effect was not enough. The minority (Lords Scarman and Templeton) did not consider that the applicant must show that disclosure of the documents would materially assist his case, but he must show that the documents were likely to be necessary for fairly disposing of the issues in dispute; on the facts of the case, Air Canada had failed to do this.

The majority view in *Air Canada* emphasises that even where the applicant is seeking judicial review of a policy decision, the litigation has an adversary character, and the court does not have an inquisitorial power to inspect relevant documents held within government. While the *Air Canada* case does not call into question the power of the courts to override executive claims to privilege, it makes more severe the obstacle which an applicant for discovery has to surmount if he is to persuade the court to exercise its powers.

The power of the courts to order discovery of documents in the course of litigation exists to promote the administration of justice, not to increase the opportunities for public criticism of government decisions. This is one reason why in *Home Office* v. *Harman*, the House of Lords by a majority held a solicitor to be in contempt of court who had shown to a journalist copies of Home Office documents that had been made available to her for use in litigation, even though these documents had been read out in open court.[46]

[46]   *Home Office* v. *Harman* [1983] 1 A.C. 280 and ch. 19 B.

Chapter 37
Administrative justice

The title of this chapter might seem a contradiction in terms: there are such marked differences between the way in which decisions are made by civil servants and ministers on the one hand, and by the courts on the other, that the two systems, administration and justice, should be kept quite separate. However, as we have seen in relation to the judicial control of administrative action, there is a strong tendency in public law in Britain for principles derived from the work of the courts, such as the doctrine of natural justice,[1] to be applied to administrative decisions. The same tendency applies to the development of institutions within government. In his seminal book, *Justice and Administrative Law*, first published in 1928, Professor Robson described the extent to which 'trial by Whitehall' had developed in the British constitution. He argued that the judicial powers given to administrative bodies served to promote the welfare of society and that administrative justice could become 'as well-founded and broad-based as any other kind of justice now known to us and embodied in human institutions'.[2]

In this chapter we will examine institutions and procedures concerned with an extensive area of public decision-making that lies somewhere between the world of government departments on one hand and that of the law courts on the other. This territory is liable to become a battle-ground as competing interests from the administrative and legal worlds struggle to occupy it. In one sector of the disputed territory that was formerly under strong departmental influence, namely administrative tribunals, the judicial model of decision-making now holds sway. The British system of tribunals, today best referred to without the adjective 'administrative', will be outlined in section A of this chapter. In another sector, that of public inquiries (considered in section B), government departments still exercise the dominant influence over the procedures and the eventual decisions that are made. Again, when things go wrong in government, impartial means are needed for discovering what happened so that those responsible may be called to account and democratic trust

---

[1] Ch. 34 B.
[2] W. A. Robson, *Justice and Administrative Law*, p. 515. And see W. A. Robson [1979] C.L.P. 107.

may be restored. In section C will be described one constitutional device, the 'tribunal of inquiry' appointed under the Tribunals of Inquiry (Evidence) Act 1921, that allows formal techniques of judicial investigation to be applied to scandals and disasters of special importance. By contrast, section D is concerned with the ombudsman. The mission of this relatively new office is to investigate individual complaints about governmental action and to remedy injustice that official errors have caused, but the ombudsman carries out his mission by 'informal' means which owe little to traditional court procedures. Before we examine these sectors of administrative justice separately, a brief discussion of the role of tribunals and inquiries may be helpful.

When Parliament authorises new forms of social service or state regulation, it is inevitable that questions and disputes will arise out of the application of the legislation. There are three main ways in which such questions and disputes may be settled: (a) by conferring new jurisdiction on one or other of the ordinary courts; (b) by creating new machinery in the form of special tribunals; (c) by empowering the appropriate minister to make the decisions. In the last case, Parliament may be content with the normal process of departmental decision or may require the minister to observe a special procedure, for example to hold a public inquiry, before the decision is made. There are important distinctions to be drawn between decisions made by a tribunal and departmental decisions involving a public inquiry. In the past, these distinctions have not always been appreciated, but at least since the report of the Franks committee,[3] it has been accepted that tribunals and inquiries differ in their constitutional status and functions. The distinction is still liable to be misunderstood. On the one hand, the appearance of tribunals as part of the administrative structure is deceptive, for the typical tribunal exercises functions which are essentially judicial in character, although of a specialised nature. Indeed most tribunals could today be regarded as specialised courts. As the Franks committee stated,

We consider that tribunals should properly be regarded as machinery provided by Parliament for adjudication rather than as part of the machinery of administration. The essential point is that in all these cases Parliament has deliberately provided for a decision outside and independent of the Department concerned.[4]

On the other hand, the public inquiry, while it grants citizens affected by official proposals some safeguard against ill-informed and unreasoned decisions, is essentially a step in a complex process which leads to a departmental decision for which a minister is responsible to Parliament. Granted the distinction between tribunals and inquiries, why should they be treated together under a single heading of administrative justice? Probably the best answer, based on the conclusions of the Franks committee, is that both with tribunals and inquiries the ordinary departmental procedures are not considered enough to protect the individual's interests. All powers of government should be exercised fairly – but principles of openness, fairness and impartiality must be maintained with special care whenever Parliament does not leave it to a de-

---

3   Page 599 *ante*.
4   Cmnd 218, 1957, p. 9.

partment to make its decision in the manner it thinks best. Moreover, developments in real life often overtake textbook distinctions. We will discover in section B that the holding of some public inquiries may today lead directly to a decision being made by the official who conducts the inquiry, not by the department concerned; thus a new form of 'tribunal' is developing under the guise of an inquiry.

A. Tribunals[1]

Reasons for creation of tribunals

For many centuries Britain has had specialised courts in addition to the courts of general jurisdiction. Medieval merchants had their courts of pie poudre; the tin miners of Devon and Cornwall had their courts of Stannaries.[2] The growth of the welfare state led to the creation of many procedures for the settlement of disputes. The National Insurance Act of 1911, which created the first British social insurance scheme, provided for the adjudication of disputes by new administrative agencies. The present social security scheme includes a complex and virtually self-contained structure for the settlement of disputes concerning the benefit or pension payable to claimants.

The creation of special tribunals has from time to time been considered, particularly by lawyers, to endanger the position of the judiciary and the authority of the law administered in the ordinary civil and criminal courts.[3] The right of access to the courts is indeed an important safeguard for the citizen, but the machinery of the courts is not suited for settling every dispute which may arise out of the work of government. There are two broad reasons for this. First, modern government gives rise to many disputes which cannot be solved by applying objective legal principles or standards and depend ultimately on what is desirable in the public interest as a matter of social policy. Although there is a danger in over-simplifying the distinction between law and policy, decisions which depend on broad issues of national policy should be made by ministers responsible for their decisions to Parliament; but where it is possible to formulate the relevant criteria of decision as a body of statutory principles, it may be desirable to vest the power to decide either in the courts or in a specially created tribunal.[4] In some fields, such as town planning, governments have been anxious to retain power to decide in the hands of the department concerned. In some fields, notably the regulation of civil aviation, a special agency such as the Civil Aviation Authority exists with power to develop policies through the mechanism of licensing, but with ultimate control being retained by the minister, to whom appeals against the Authority's decisions may

---

[1] See report of the Franks committee, Cmnd 218, 1957, Parts II and III; W. A. Robson, *Justice and Administrative Law*, ch. 3; R. M. Jackson, *The Machinery of Justice*, ch. 6; R. E. Wraith and P. G. Hutchesson, *Administrative Tribunals*; J. A. Farmer, *Tribunals and Government*.

[2] See *R.* v. *East Powder Justices, ex p. Lampshire* [1979] Q.B. 616.

[3] See *e.g.* L. Scarman, *English Law – the New Dimension*, Part III.

[4] For the debate on justiciability when the Restrictive Practices Court was created in 1956, see H.C. Deb., 6 Mar. 1956, cols. 1927 ff.; G. Marshall in (ed.) A. G Guest, *Oxford Essays in Jurisprudence*, pp. 282–7; and R. Stevens [1964] P.L. 221. And for the theoretical issues, see J. Jowell [1973] P.L. 178.

be brought.[5] In other fields, such as social security, the principles applicable have been laid down in statutes or in statutory instruments, and the duty of applying them has been vested in a hierarchy of tribunals, for whose individual decisions no minister is politically responsible, and which the government can control only by amending the relevant statutory rules. Here the relationship between minister and tribunal approaches that which exists between the government and the ordinary judiciary. Where this is the case, tribunals exist not because they are required to exercise a political discretion which could not be entrusted to the courts but because (and this is the second broad reason for the existence of tribunals) the tribunals can do the work of adjudication more efficiently than the courts.[6]

This bold claim can be justified on several practical grounds. As Professor Street said in relation to claims for social security benefit, 'For these cases we do not want a Rolls-Royce system of justice'.[7] Practical factors that have favoured the setting up of tribunals include the following: the desire for a procedure which avoids the formality of the ordinary courts; the need, in implementing a new social policy, for the speedy, cheap and decentralised determination of a large number of individual cases; the need for expert and specialised knowledge on the part of the tribunal which a court with a wide general jurisdiction might not acquire; and the fact that without being transformed in character the courts could not cope with the case-load that is now borne by social security tribunals, industrial tribunals and the like. One important characteristic of tribunals compared with the courts is that the legal profession does not have a monopoly of the right to represent those appearing before tribunals. This fact alone makes tribunals more accessible to the public than the courts, since an individual's case may often be presented effectively by a trade union official, an accountant, a surveyor, a doctor, a social worker or a friend.

A further reason for preferring tribunals to the courts may be found in the apparent reluctance of some members of the legal profession, including the judiciary, to adapt the individualistic tradition of the common law to modern conceptions of social justice. Some judges have interpreted social legislation too narrowly; indeed, the principles of statutory interpretation often do not give a sufficient guide to the court in determining the intention of Parliament.[8] The department responsible for administering a social policy has often preferred special machinery for the adjudication of disputes, designed for a particular task, rather than have disputes settled in the ordinary courts.

The necessity for administrative justice should not however lead to the creation of tribunals for their own sake when the ordinary courts could well take the decisions in question. In the view of the Franks committee, 'a decision should be entrusted to a court rather than to a tribunal in the absence of special considerations which make a tribunal more suitable'.[9] Moreover,

---

5   See *Laker Airways Ltd* v. *Department of Trade* [1977] Q.B. 643; G. R. Baldwin [1978] P.L. 57 and (1980) 58 *Public Administration* 287.
6   *Cf.* the distinction between 'policy-oriented' and 'court-substitute' tribunals: B. Abel-Smith and R. Stevens, *In Search of Justice*, pp. 220–1 and Farmer, *op. cit.* ch. 8.
7   *Justice in the Welfare State*, p. 3.
8   See English and Scottish Law Commissions, *The Interpretation of Statutes*, H.C. 256 (1968–9).
9   Cmnd 218, p. 9.

granted the need for specialised tribunals, the essential merits of the court system should so far as is practicable be incorporated in the tribunal system. Thus the desire of a department to provide new tribunals must not be permitted to conflict with the principle of independent decisions being made in accordance with the law. In particular, the appointment and dismissal of members of tribunals must not be solely in the hands of the department concerned. Again, there is danger as well as merit in informal procedures. If all the rules of evidence observed in courts also bound tribunals, it would be impossible for tribunals to reach decisions simply and speedily. Some tribunals follow procedures that are essentially inquisitorial rather than adversary, but minimum standards of evidence and proof must be observed by tribunals if justice is to be done.[10] One safeguard lies in the appointment to tribunals of legally qualified chairmen, another in maintaining in all cases the right to legal representation – although if this right is to benefit those who most need it, legal aid or assistance must be extended to tribunals.[11] A further safeguard is the right of appeal, either to a higher tribunal or to the ordinary courts: in particular, it should always be possible to challenge in the superior courts a tribunal's ruling on points of law, and tribunals should always give reasons for their decisions.

Since the Franks report of 1957, acceptance of many of these principles has removed much earlier distrust of tribunals. But there will inevitably continue to be tension between the attitudes of those who believe that tribunals should come to resemble courts in all but name, and those who insist that tribunals must be flexible, informal and accessible to the ordinary person in a way in which the courts are not. Indeed, some would argue that it is the courts which must learn from tribunals, rather than vice versa.

Classification of tribunals

It is not easy to classify the many tribunals which exercise judicial functions in relation to specific branches of government, nor to draw a sharp line between those bodies which may by classed as tribunals and those which may not. A list of tribunals under the supervision of the Council on Tribunals is published annually in the council's report. In the report for 1982–3, this list included agricultural land tribunals, the Civil Aviation Authority and the Director General of Fair Trading in their licensing functions, education appeal committees (dealing with allocation of pupils to schools), immigration adjudicators and the Immigration Appeal Tribunal, industrial tribunals, the two Lands Tribunals, mental health review tribunals, National Health Service family practitioner committees, the Comptroller-General of Patents, war pensions appeal tribunals, rating valuation courts, rent assessment committees, social security appeal tribunals and the Social Security Commissioners, the general and special commissioners of income tax, traffic commissioners, value-added tax tribunals and, in Scotland, children's hearings and the Crofters Commission.

---

[10] See *e.g. R.* v. *Deputy Industrial Injuries Cmssr ex p. Moore* [1965] 1 Q.B. 456; and *cf.* H. W. R. Wade, *Administrative Law*, p. 803.

[11] See 33rd Report of Lord Chancellor's Advisory Committee on Legal Aid for 1982–3 (H.C. 137, 1983–4), pp. 194–209.

It is possible to group these tribunals by their subject-matter, for example, (a) social security and social services (b) land, property and housing (c) economic activities, licensing and taxation (d) others, including industrial and immigration tribunals.[12] But it is more useful to analyse tribunals in terms of the general considerations which are discussed below: thus in some tribunals the parties are private individuals (landlord/tenant, employer/employee) but in many tribunals a citizen is in dispute with a government department. Moreover, some bodies which are not subject to the Council on Tribunals have strong claims to be regarded as tribunals. These include the Criminal Injuries Compensation Board, the Foreign Compensation Commission, the Gaming Board, legal aid committees, the Parole Board and the many professional discipline committees. From the names of all these diverse bodies, there is evidently no invariable legislative practice of calling a tribunal a tribunal! Nor does the fact that a tribunal is styled a court by Parliament mean that it has all the attributes of a court, such as the power to commit for contempt of court.[13]

Problems of classification and terminology point to the lack of a planned system of tribunals. One solution to the organisation of administrative justice might be to create a series of higher administrative courts or tribunals, each covering a range of related jurisdictions. On matters of social security, the Social Security Commissioners serve as a national appeal tribunal within a variety of different adjudication structures. There has also been a definite policy of concentrating disputes relating to the valuation of land on the Lands Tribunal, and those relating to employment on industrial tribunals. Many attempts to resist the proliferation of tribunals have been made by the Council on Tribunals,[14] not always with success, for the department concerned with new legislation can often discover reasons for establishing a newer and more suitable tribunal than any which exist. One limiting factor is that many tribunals, especially at the local level, depend on part-time service from their members; to vest too wide a jurisdiction in one tribunal might over-burden these members. The Franks committee rejected the general principle that tribunal service should be based on whole-time salaried employment. There are in fact notable exceptions to that principle (for example, the Social Security Commissioners, the Lands Tribunal and the full-time chairmen of industrial tribunals), especially at the national or appellate level.

General considerations

Tribunals are concerned with a wide range of activities but certain questions are of general application. (a) What is the composition of the tribunal? Tribunals are not composed of government officials. Often they are constituted of lay members of the public, sometimes coming from groups such as employers' organisations and trade unions. But in certain tribunals specialist qualifications are required (for example, in medicine or in land valuation) and

---

12   *Cf.* Cmnd 218, 1957, Part III; Wraith and Hutchesson, *op. cit.*, ch. 2; and Farmer, *op. cit.*, chs. 7 and 8.
13   *A.-G.* v. *B.B.C.* [1981] A.C. 303; ch. 19B. See also N.Y. Lowe and H.F. Rawlings [1982] P.L. 418 and Contempt of Court Act 1981, s.19.
14   See *e.g.* reports of Council on Tribunals for 1974–5, p. 9; 1978–9, p. 12; 1981–2, p. 14.

membership may involve a full-time salaried appointment; frequently provision is made for a legally qualified chairman. (b) Who appoints the members of the tribunal and who has power to dismiss? Usually appointments are made for a fixed period of years, either by the minister concerned, by the Lord Chancellor, or by both minister and Lord Chancellor jointly; in general dismissal now requires the concurrence of the Lord Chancellor.[15] (c) What are the powers and jurisdiction of the tribunal? In particular, how extensive is the tribunal's discretion? Many tribunals, like the Lands Tribunal and the commissioners of income tax, exercise strictly judicial functions. Some, like the Civil Aviation Authority, base their decisions on wider aspects of policy, exercising regulatory functions in a judicial form. (d) What procedure is followed by the tribunal and how formal is it? Are hearings in public or in private, and do individuals appearing before it have the right of legal representation? In 1984, legal aid was available before the Lands Tribunal, the Commons Commissioners and the Employment Appeal Tribunal; legal assistance by way of representation was available before mental health review tribunals. Legal advice and assistance without representation could be obtained in connection with all tribunal proceedings.[16] (e) Are the tribunal's decisions final, or is there the right to appeal, whether on law, on fact, or on the merits? The Franks committee considered that the ideal appeal structure took the form of a general appeal from the tribunal of first instance to an appellate tribunal; that as a matter of principle appeal should not lie from a tribunal to a minister; and that all decisions of tribunals should be subject to review by the courts on points of law.[17] The structure of social security appeals complies broadly with this pattern but many other tribunals depart from it. (f) Are the tribunal's decisions published and, if so, do they have authority as binding or persuasive precedents for future tribunals? (g) What is the relation between the tribunal and the department with whose work it is associated? What opportunities are there for the department to influence the work of the tribunal other than by formal legislation?

The structure of some leading tribunals will now be outlined, together with one professional disciplinary tribunal. The tribunals chosen for this purpose do not include tribunals that have already been mentioned in earlier chapters, namely the commissioners of income tax, the immigration appeals structure and mental health tribunals.[18]

Social security appeals[19]

In common with the income tax system, the social security system requires each year millions of decisions directly affecting the financial position of individuals to be taken by civil servants. Whenever a decision is taken that ad-

---

[15] Page 711 *post.*
[16] Legal Aid Act 1979, adding s.2A to Legal Aid Act 1974; S.I. 1982, No. 1592. And see Legal Aid Act 1974, s.2.
[17] Cmnd 218, 1957, p. 25.
[18] See respectively, pp. 292, 452 and 474.
[19] Social Security Act 1975, part III as amended; Health and Social Services and Social Security Adjudications Act 1983, sch. 8. On the earlier system, see H. Street, *Justice in the Welfare State,* ch. 1; Farmer, *Tribunals and Government,* ch. 4; R. Micklethwait, *The National Insurance Commissioners.*

versely affects an individual (for example, when a claim to benefit is refused or when less benefit is paid than an individual has claimed), it is important that he or she should be able to appeal against it, if only because such decisions must be founded upon a sound legal base, not upon the arbitrary decision of an official. As we have already seen, the right of appeal to an independent authority was recognised in the National Insurance Act 1911. When after 1945 the social security scheme became more complex as new benefits were provided, the adjudication procedures also became more diverse and elaborate. An important distinction formerly existed between the structure of appeals for contributory benefits under national insurance (such as unemployment benefit and retirement pension) and that for non-contributory means-tested benefits, notably supplementary benefits. The large element of official discretion in the supplementary benefit scheme before 1980 was one reason for this difference, but during the 1970s there was extensive criticism of the supplementary benefit tribunals.[20] The reform of supplementary benefits in 1980, when the role of official discretion was much reduced in favour of detailed regulations governing entitlement to benefit, paved the way for an important reform in tribunal structure.[21] The following account outlines the main forms of adjudication that now exist.

Claims for benefit in most areas of social security (such as child benefit, unemployment benefit and supplementary benefit) are decided in the first instance by an adjudication officer appointed by the Secretary of State for the Social Services. These officers are full-time civil servants, mostly working in local DHSS offices, and may have other duties in addition to adjudication of claims. They act subject to advice from a chief adjudication officer. From an adjudication officer's decision, there is a right of appeal to a social security appeal tribunal. This tribunal, which sits locally, comprises two members, representing employed earners, employers and other insured persons, together with a chairman who, after a transitional period from 1984 in which existing lay chairmen may continue to sit for certain appeals, must be a qualified lawyer of five years' standing. The chairman is selected to sit by the President of Social Security and Medical Appeal Tribunals, from a panel of lawyers appointed by the Lord Chancellor or, in Scotland, by the Lord President of the Court of Session. From the appeal tribunal's decision, an appeal may be brought (subject in some cases to leave being granted and, in supplementary benefit cases, only on points of law) to the Social Security Commissioners, who are senior barristers, advocates or solicitors appointed by the Crown and sitting in London, Edinburgh and Cardiff. Normally an appeal is heard by a single Commissioner, but the Chief Commissioner may direct that an appeal involving a question of law of special difficulty should be heard by a tribunal of three Commissioners.[22] Formerly there was no right of appeal from a Commissioner's decision, but in English law such a decision could be reviewed by certiorari[23] and in Scotland it could be set aside if it was in excess of juris-

---

20   E.g. K. Bell, *Research Study on Supplementary Benefit Appeal Tribunals*; M. Adler and A. W. Bradley, *Justice, Discretion and Poverty*; A. W. Bradley (1976) 27 N.I.L.Q. 96.

21   S.I. 1984 No. 451 (made under the Act of 1983 cited in note 19).

22   Social Security Act 1975, s.116.

23   E.g. *R. v. Chief National Insurance Commissioner, ex p. Connor* [1981] Q.B. 758.

diction.[24] Since 1980, there has been an appeal with leave on a point of law from a Social Security Commissioner to the Court of Appeal in England, and to the Inner House of the Court of Session in Scotland.[25] Selected decisions of Social Security Commissioners are published and bind all adjudication officers and local tribunals, although the law they lay down may be changed at any time by Act of Parliament or by fresh regulations made by the Secretary of State under his delegated powers.

Some questions on which a social security claim may depend (for example, a claimant's contribution record) are reserved for decision by the Secretary of State, and are not decided by a tribunal. From such a decision, there is a right of appeal on law to the High Court or Court of Session.[26] Various medical questions (for example, the extent of disablement caused by an industrial injury or disease) are decided either by an adjudicating medical practitioner employed by the DHSS or by a medical board formed by two such practitioners, with an appeal to a medical appeal tribunal, consisting of two independent medical members sitting with a legal chairman. From the medical appeal tribunal, appeal lies on a point of law to the Social Security Commissioners.[27] Special procedures also exist in relation to claims for attendance allowance and mobility allowance, with an appeal on points of law to the Social Security Commissioners.[28]

The present structure of social security appeals may appear complex, but it is a considerably simpler system than was formerly the case. In 1984 was created the office of President of Social Security and Medical Appeal Tribunals, to whom was transferred from the DHSS responsibility for administering the social security appeal tribunals. One reason for this transfer was to enhance the visible independence of local tribunals from their parent department. It is too early to evaluate the effects of these changes, but it may be hoped that the introduction of the presidential system in social security appeal tribunals and the requirement of legally-qualified chairmen will not mean that the local tribunals become inaccessible to the claimant or unduly legalistic in their style of operation. On the basis of the most recent statistics the social security appeal tribunals will decide about 100,000 cases each year; the Social Security Commissioners decide around 4,500 appeals.[29]

Lands Tribunal

The Lands Tribunal Act 1949 authorised two Lands Tribunals, one for Scotland and one for the rest of the United Kingdom.[30] The latter tribunal has jurisdiction over a variety of matters relating to the valuation of property, including the assessment of compensation for compulsory acquisition of land and rating appeals from the local valuation courts. The jurisdiction can be enlarged

---

24 *Watt* v. *Lord Advocate* 1979 S.C. 120.
25 Social Security Act 1980, s.14.
26 Social Security Act 1975, s.94.
27 Social Security Act 1975, s.112.
28 Social Security Act 1975, ss.105–6; S.I. 1984 No. 451, parts X, XI.
29 Report of Council on Tribunals for 1982–3, app. C.
30 The Lands Tribunal in Scotland was established only in 1971, to deal with matters arising under the Conveyancing and Feudal Reform (Scotland) Act 1970 and also with valuation of land for planning, compulsory purchase and tax purposes.

by Order in Council. The President of the Lands Tribunal, who must have held judicial office or be a barrister of at least 7 years' standing, is like the other members appointed by the Lord Chancellor. These members must be barristers, solicitors or persons qualified by professional experience in the valuation of land. There is no fixed composition for the tribunal; this is varied according to the particular case as the president may determine. Thus a single surveyor may sit, or the president together with members who are lawyers and surveyors. On the application of any party a case may be stated on a point of law for determination by the Court of Appeal;[31] otherwise the decision of the Lands Tribunal is final.

The composition of the Lands Tribunal ensures that it has access to expertise both in legal and valuation matters. While procedure before the tribunal can be as formal and elaborate as litigation in the courts, particularly when large sums of money are at stake, the tribunal may adopt a simpler procedure in smaller cases. Legal aid is available before the tribunal. In 1982, the Lands Tribunal for Scotland disposed of 308 cases; the Lands Tribunal for the rest of the United Kingdom disposed of 1369 cases, 661 after a hearing.

Industrial tribunals[32]

Industrial tribunals were first established under the Industrial Training Act 1964 to determine disputes arising from the imposition on certain industries of a levy to meet the expenses of industrial training boards. They rapidly acquired a wide jurisdiction, which now includes disputes under the Equal Pay Act 1970 and many issues under the Employment Protection (Consolidation) Act 1978, in respect of such matters as guarantee payments, facilities for trade union activities, maternity pay, redundancy payments and (in practice the most numerous) unfair dismissal. The tribunals also deal with allegations of discrimination in relation to employment, under the Sex Discrimination Act 1975 and the Race Relations Act 1976.[33] An industrial tribunal consists of a lawyer chairman and two lay members drawn from panels representing each side of industry. The tribunals are organised on the presidential system. The two presidents of industrial tribunals, in England and Scotland respectively, are responsible for overseeing the administration of the tribunals, convening conferences of chairmen and members, and representing the tribunals in their relations with the Department of Employment, the Council on Tribunals and other bodies. Many of the chairmen hold full-time, permanent posts. Associated with the tribunals, but separate from them, is an advisory and conciliation service. In 1982, the tribunals disposed of over 42,500 cases, nearly 17,000 being decided after a hearing.

When the Industrial Relations Act 1971 was in force between 1971 and 1974, appeals on questions of law from industrial tribunals went to the controversial National Industrial Relations Court, although it was not these appeals which gave rise to the controversy.[34] Appeals on law now lie to the

---

[31]   See *R. v. Lands Tribunal, ex p. City of London Corpn* [1982] 1 All E.R. 892.
[32]   See Employment Protection (Consolidation) Act 1978, part VIII and sch. 9; B. A. Hepple and P. O'Higgins, *Encyclopedia of Labour Relations Law*, part 1, ch. 22.
[33]   Ch. 31 A.
[34]   Page 337 *ante.*

Employment Appeal Tribunal, a body comparable to the Restrictive Practices Court.[35] It consists of nominated judges of the High Court and the Court of Session, one of whom is appointed by the Lord Chancellor to be president of the tribunal, sitting with lay persons with special knowledge or experience of industrial relations. The tribunal is a superior court of record but conducts its business with less formality than the High Court and lawyers have no monopoly of representation.

Solicitors Disciplinary Tribunal

The Solicitors Disciplinary Tribunal appointed under the Solicitors Act 1974 is an example of a tribunal which exercises disciplinary powers over a profession under the authority of statute. It is established for the purpose of hearing applications against solicitors, either to strike them off the roll or to compel them to answer allegations made against them by clients. This tribunal is appointed by the Master of the Rolls. For hearing of applications there sits a board of two members who are practising solicitors, and one lay person. The tribunal may order a solicitor to be struck off the roll, suspend him from practice, impose a financial penalty on him, or order him to pay costs. It acts as a judicial body, hearing formal applications by complainants, administering oaths and generally conducting its procedure as a court of law. It hears applications in private but makes public its decisions. Every order of the tribunal must be prefaced by a statement of its findings on the facts of the case. Appeals lie to the High Court or to the Master of the Rolls.[36] The existence of the tribunal does not deprive the High Court of its disciplinary jurisdiction over solicitors, as officers of the court, but when conduct of a solicitor is deserving of punishment, the court generally leaves the matter to be dealt with under the 1974 Act.[37]

Tribunals and Inquiries Act 1971

The main conclusions of the Franks committee on the status of tribunals have already been mentioned. The committee also made detailed recommendations for improving existing tribunals, which were largely adopted. Thus in the national insurance field, the right of legal representation was recognised in all cases and the principle of public hearings was established. Other recommendations were implemented by the Tribunals and Inquiries Act 1958, which was re-enacted in 1971: the chairmen of certain tribunals are now selected by the minister concerned from a panel of persons approved by the Lord Chancellor (section 7), a provision that should help to ensure that chairmen are either legally qualified or have suitable alternative experience; in the case of most tribunals the minister's power to terminate membership of a tribunal can only be exercised with the concurrence in England and Wales of the Lord Chancellor, and in Scotland of the Lord President of the Court of Session (section 8); appeals on points of law lie from certain tribunals to the High Court or the Court of Session (section 13); and all tribunals are under a duty, if re-

---

[35] Employment Protection (Consolidation) Act 1978, s.135 and sch. 11; p. 330 *ante*.
[36] Solicitors Act 1974, ss.46–9; and see S.I. 1975 No. 727. *Cf.* Solicitors (Scotland) Act 1958, ss.5–9.
[37] *R. & T. Thew Ltd* v. *Reeves (No. 2)* [1982] Q.B. 1283.

quested on or before the giving or notification of the decision, to give reasons for their decision, such reasons whether written or oral being deemed to form part of the record for the purpose of review by certiorari (section 12).[38] In practice, many rules of procedure for particular tribunals require reasons to be given in every case.[39]

Council on Tribunals[40]

The Tribunals and Inquiries Act 1971 also continued in being the Council on Tribunals, first established under the 1958 Act. The members of the Council (in number between ten and fifteen) are appointed by the Lord Chancellor and the Lord Advocate (in respect of Scotland),[41] and the Council has a Scottish committee. The council is under a duty to keep under review the constitution and working of a large number of tribunals, that is, those originally named in the First Schedule to the 1958 Act and also those subsequently included by statutory instrument made by the Lord Chancellor and the Lord Advocate (section 15). The Lord Chancellor and the Lord Advocate have power to ask the council to consider and report on matters concerning any tribunal other than ordinary courts of law. In one instance, concerning those administrative procedures which involve a statutory inquiry, the council may itself take the initiative on a matter determined to be of special importance.[42] The council's functions are essentially advisory; it has no power to interfere with the decision of a tribunal in a particular case, although it may comment on the way in which tribunals operate. The council has no executive powers: the Franks Committee's recommendation that members of tribunals should be appointed by the council was not accepted by the government, and the council merely has power to make to the appropriate minister general recommendations on the appointment of tribunal members (section 5).

The council makes an annual report to the Lord Chancellor and the Lord Advocate, and other reports by the council are made to these ministers. The council may take the initiative in reporting on any tribunal placed under its general supervision, but it does not follow that any action will be taken on the report to the Lord Chancellor. The council has no rule-making powers but must be consulted before any procedural rules are made for any tribunals subject to their supervision (section 10) or for any procedures involving a statutory inquiry (section 11). Often the council is consulted by the government on proposed legislation to create new tribunals.

The council undoubtedly serves to remind departments of the qualities of fairness, openness and impartiality which the Franks committee stressed that tribunals should possess. Its extensive work on procedural rules gives detailed expression to those qualities. With limited resources, it has done little to promote research into the conduct of tribunals and it has neither the resources

---

[38] Page 659 *ante*.
[39] *E.g.* Social Security (Adjudication) Regulations 1984 No. 451, regs 19(2), 26(4), 34(4), 63(2). But *cf.* report of Council on Tribunals for 1981–2, pp. 22–3.
[40] H. W. R. Wade [1960] P.L. 351; J. F. Garner [1965] P.L. 321; D. C. M. Yardley [1980] J.S.W.L. 265; D. G. T. Williams [1984] P.L. 73; C. Harlow and R. Rawlings, *Law and Administration*, ch. 6.
[41] S.I. 1972 No. 2002.
[42] Section B, *post*.

nor the power to investigate complaints about particular tribunals,[43] a limitation which it now admits.[44] It has often drawn attention to the problem of a backlog of cases building up in particular tribunals, for example in immigration appeals. Where a department does not accept the council's advice, there is little that the council can do except publish the fact in its annual report.

In 1980, the Council on Tribunals published a special report examining its own functions, recommending *inter alia* that it should be granted power to act as an advisory body over the whole area of administrative adjudication, that its right to be consulted about relevant legislation should be clearly defined and that its resources should be strengthened.[45] Although the government agreed that a 'code' for consultation between the council and departments should be prepared, all the other proposals made by the council were peremptorily rejected.[46]

B. Public inquiries

We have seen that the Franks committee concluded that tribunals should be regarded as machinery for adjudication rather than as part of the machinery of administration. The same conclusion is not applicable to public inquiries, whose role is too deeply embedded in the whole process of government and administration to permit them to be transplanted into the world of adjudication. We have already examined the attitude of the courts to inquiries in the context of natural justice.[1] Cases such as *Local Government Board* v. *Arlidge*, *Errington*'s case and *Franklin*'s case[2] illustrate the difficulties found by the courts in reviewing ministers' decisions made following a public inquiry, particularly over the extent to which holding an inquiry may be regarded as a judicial or quasi-judicial function. As seen by the Franks committee in 1957, the 'administrative' view was to regard the inquiry as a step leading to a ministerial decision in the exercise of discretion, for which the minister was responsible only to Parliament. By contrast, on the 'judicial' view, the inquiry appeared 'to take on something of the nature of a trial and the inspector to assume the guise of a judge', so that the ensuing decision must be based directly upon the evidence presented at the inquiry.[3]

The Franks committee rejected these two extreme interpretations. In the committee's view, the objects of the inquiry procedures were (a) to protect the interests of the citizens most directly affected by a governmental proposal by granting them a statutory right to be heard in support of their objections; and (b) to ensure that thereby the minister would be better informed of the whole facts of the case before the final decision was made. To ensure a reasonable

---

[43] See R. Lister, *Council Inaction*, 1975 (Child Poverty Action Group Report).
[44] Cmnd 7805, 1980, ch. 7.
[45] Cmnd 7805, 1980.
[46] Report of Council on Tribunals for 1980–1, p. 7; and for 1981–2, app. C.

[1] Ch. 34B. And see generally R. E. Wraith and G. B. Lamb, *Public Inquiries as an Instrument of Government*.
[2] Page 645–7 *ante*.
[3] Cmnd 218, 1957, p. 58.

balance between the conflicting interests concerned, and to see that Parliament's intention in requiring the public inquiry procedure to be observed was fulfilled, the committee recommended (a) that the individual should know in good time before the inquiry the case he would have to meet; (b) that any relevant lines of policy laid down by the ministry should be disclosed at the inquiry; (c) that the inspectors who conduct inquiries should be under the control of the Lord Chancellor, and not under that of the minister directly concerned with the subject-matter of their work; (d) that the inspector's report should be published together with the letter from the minister announcing the final decision; (e) that the decision letter should contain full reasons for the decision, including reasons to explain why the minister had not accepted recommendations of the inspector; (f) that it should be possible to challenge a decision made after a public inquiry in the High Court, on the grounds of jurisdiction and procedure.[4]

Except for the recommendation that the corps of inspectors should be transferred to the Lord Chancellor's Department, these recommendations were accepted by the government and initially brought into force by administrative action.[5] Moreover, the Council on Tribunals was given power to consider and report on matters arising out of the conduct of statutory inquiries; this allows an individual who is dissatisfied with some aspect of a particular inquiry to complain to the council. In this context, 'statutory inquiry' includes both an inquiry or hearing held by or on behalf of a minister in pursuance of a duty imposed by any statutory provision, and also what is known as a discretionary inquiry, that is an inquiry initiated by a minister other than in pursuance of a statutory duty where such an inquiry is designated for this purpose by statutory instrument.[6]

Rules of procedure for public inquiries

Under the Tribunals and Inquiries Act 1971, section 11, the Lord Chancellor (or the Lord Advocate, in the case of Scotland) may, after consulting the Council on Tribunals, make rules regulating the procedure at statutory inquiries. Rules have been made in respect of inquiries held for many purposes, including inquiries into local authorities' compulsory purchase orders, appeals against the refusal of planning permission and proposals for the construction of motorways and power stations.[7] In the case of compulsory purchase inquiries, at least 42 days' notice of the inquiry must be given to the local authority and to every owner of an interest in the land affected who has objected to the making of the compulsory purchase order. At least 28 days before the inquiry, the local authority must send to every objector and to central departments a written statement of the reasons for the order. Both objectors and the local authority have a right to appear at the inquiry and to be represented,

---

4   Cmnd 218, Part IV.
5   Ministry of Housing circular 9/58, 27 Feb. 1958; and see report of Council on Tribunals for 1963, app. A.
6   Tribunals and Inquiries Act 1971, s. 19; and see S.I. 1975 No. 1379, S.I. 1976 No. 293 and S.I. 1983 No. 1287.
7   See respectively S.I. 1976 No. 746; S.I. 1974 No. 419, 420; S.I. 1976 No. 721; and S.I. 1981 No. 1841.

either by a lawyer or some other person. Objectors must be informed of the views of any government departments which support the order, and departmental representatives are required to attend the inquiry in order that they may give evidence about departmental policy. Some observance is paid to the traditional doctrine of ministerial responsibility by the provision that the inspector may disallow a question put to such a representative if in the inspector's opinion it is 'directed to the merits of government policy'. Subject to the rules, procedure at the inquiry is determined by the inspector. The degree of formality may be expected to depend on the circumstances of the inquiry, particularly the extent of legal representation. The inspector may visit the land alone before or during the inquiry, but if he visits it after the inquiry, notice must be given to the local authority and to the objectors, who have the right to accompany him. The inspector's report must include his findings of fact and his recommendations, if any; it will be published when the minister's decision is notified to the parties.[8]

One important rule deals with the situation where the minister, after considering the inspector's report, either differs from the inspector on a finding of fact, or, after the close of the inquiry, 'receives any new evidence, including expert evidence on a matter of fact, or takes into consideration any new issue of fact, not being a matter of government policy, which was not raised at the inquiry'. In such a case, if the minister proposes not to follow the inspector's recommendation because of this new material, the local authority and objectors must be informed and they have the right to require the inquiry to be reopened. The background to this lies in what was known as the chalk-pit affair.[9]

At an inquiry into a planning authority's refusal of permission for the digging of chalk in North Essex, neighbouring owners brought evidence to show that their land would be seriously harmed if this were permitted. On the strength of this evidence the inspector recommended that permission should not be given. Subsequently the Ministry of Housing consulted privately with the Ministry of Agriculture about this, and later granted planning permission, *inter alia* on the ground that the chalk workings would not harm neighbouring land. The neighbouring owners tried unsuccessfully to seek a remedy in the High Court, and then complained to the Council on Tribunals about this apparent abuse of inquiry procedure. Although the government refused to admit that anything improper had occurred, following pressure from the Council on Tribunals the Lord Chancellor finally accepted the council's view on the point of principle and agreed to make the rules of procedure already quoted.

One effect of the statutory rules for inquiries is to give the individuals most closely affected by compulsory purchase and planning proposals better legal protection, since the rules are enforceable in the courts. In circumstances such as those in *Errington v. Minister of Health*,[10] the landowner could now base his challenge to the purchase order on the failure to comply with the statutory rules. But rules of procedure have not been made for all public inquiries.[11]

---

[8] When this requirement of publication applies, *Local Government Board* v. *Arlidge*, p. 645 *ante*, is to this extent reversed.

[9] See J. A. G. Griffith (1961) 39 *Public Administration* 369; and *Buxton* v. *Minister of Housing* [1961] 1 Q.B. 278.

[10] Page 646 *ante*.

[11] *Fairmount Investments Ltd* v. *Secretary of State for Environment* [1976] 2 All E.R. 865; and see *Bushell's* case, p. 718 *post*.

Although the rules define those who are entitled to statutory notice of an inquiry and to take part in it, they invariably give the inspector a discretion to allow members of the public to appear at the inquiry, call evidence and cross-examine other witnesses. In practice, community associations and other interest groups are always permitted to take part. Although such persons and organisations are not statutory parties, by taking part in the inquiry they acquire a right to come to the court to enforce the rules of procedure.[12]

Similar rules have been made for many public inquiries in Scotland. Two differences may be noted. The person appointed to conduct an inquiry is known as the reporter, which may describe his duties more accurately than the term 'inspector'. After the inquiry, the reporter must circulate to all the parties a draft of that part of his proposed report which contains the summary of the evidence and his findings of fact, in order that inaccuracies may be corrected.[13]

The part played by the Council on Tribunals in the preparation of these rules and the steps it has taken to secure the more frequent award of costs to those taking part in inquiries, at least for owners who successfully object to the compulsory purchase of their land, indicate the value of the council in continuing the work begun by the Franks committee. But in circumstances of serious abuse, the courts have the power to give an effective remedy to an owner which the council lacks.[14] Moreover, the council has neither the legal powers nor the resources properly to investigate complaints about inquiries. If someone is aggrieved by the improper conduct of an inquiry, or by the acts of the department related to the inquiry, he may instead take the complaint to the ombudsman (the Parliamentary Commissioner for Administration) who can conduct a full investigation into allegations of maladministration.[15]

Developments in the use of public inquiries
The public inquiry continues to be an important step in the process by which certain decisions are made, especially those concerning the use of land for developments of environmental significance.[16] Although the Franks committee had sought to steer a middle course between the 'judicial' and 'administrative' views of the inquiry, its report led inevitably to greater legalisation. Increased involvement of the legal profession in inquiries was one aspect of the pressure on the planning process that led to delays and over-centralisation of decisions on many local issues during the 1960s and early 1970s. Because of dissatisfaction with lengthy and expensive inquiries into statutory development plans,[17] together with a desire for broader public participation, planning law now provides for the holding of an *examination in public* into a 'structure plan'.[18]

---

12   Turner v. *Secretary of State for Environment* (1973) 72 L.G.R. 380.
13   See S.I. 1976 No. 1559.
14   Note the rebuff suffered by the Council on Tribunals in the Packington Estate case, discussed in [1966] P.L. 1 and illumined in R. Crossman, *Diaries of a Cabinet Minister*, I, pp. 450–1, 456–7, 467–8, 528.
15   Section D *post*.
16   For a group of case-studies, see R. Gregory, *The Price of Amenity*.
17   The Greater London Development Plan inquiry lasted 22 months and dealt with 28,000 objections: Report of the Panel of Inquiry into the G.L.D.P., 1973, vol. 1, p. 3.
18   Town and Country Planning Act 1971, s.9(3)–(8) inserted by Town and Country Planning (Amendment) Act 1972, s.3(1); M. Grant, *Urban Planning Law*, ch. 3B.

The examination is conducted by a panel appointed by the Secretary of State and deals only with such aspects of the plan as the department considers should be examined publicly. Those who take part are selected by the department from amongst objectors to the plan, and other parties. The procedure thus contrasts sharply with a public inquiry, at which everyone interested may bring forward evidence on all relevant matters. However, earlier stages in the making of a structure plan involve public consultation and participation, and this may be more effective than a public inquiry in discovering the state of public opinion in a locality.[19] So far as 'local plans' are concerned (as distinct from structure plans), a public inquiry is held before an inspector appointed by the Secretary of State, but he reports not to central government but to the local authority that prepared the plan. That authority will not necessarily wish to alter its earlier proposals, even if recommended to do so by the inspector.[20]

As regards the control of development, recent government policy has been to reduce delay by transferring the power to decide planning appeals from the Secretary of State to the inspectorate. Since 1981, all appeals in respect of applications for planning permission and all appeals against enforcement notices may be decided by an inspector.[21] An inspector's decision is subject to review in the courts as if it were the decision of a minister, but the Secretary of State is not responsible to Parliament for the decision. The fact that an inspector at a planning appeal now has power to decide and not merely to recommend, gives added significance to the proceedings before him. An important development in procedure that also saves time is that most planning appeals are now decided not after a formal inquiry, but by a simpler, non-statutory procedure based on the exchange of written representations between the parties.[22] Where this procedure is used, however, the public at large have less scope for effective participation than at an inquiry.[23]

While the transfer of power to decide planning appeals has been possible because in most cases national issues do not arise, the role of the inquiry in matters of national importance continues to be controversial. During the 1970s government policy in promoting a national network of motorways led to stormy scenes at motorway inquiries, as local objectors came to realise that the proceedings at an inquiry might have little effect where the Department of Transport had already decided that a new motorway was needed. There was also uncertainty about the scope of the inquiries and the rights of objectors.[24] In 1978, a review of highway procedures made detailed proposals for improving the assessment of need for new trunk roads and for restoring public confidence in the inquiry system.[25] So far as the courts were concerned, the

---

[19] And see L. T. Bridges (1979) 2 *Urban Law and Policy* 241.

[20] Grant, *op. cit.*, ch. 3C. And see M. J. Bruton *et al.* [1980] J.P.L. 374, [1982] J.P.L. 276.

[21] But the Secretary of State may retain power to decide particular appeals, and appeals concerning operational land of statutory undertakings go jointly to the Secretary of State and the relevant minister: S.I. 1981 No. 804; Grant, *op. cit.*, ch. 13C.

[22] Grant, *op. cit.*, ch. 13D.

[23] For the rule that inquiries must in general be held in public, see Planning Inquiries (Attendance of Public) Act 1982.

[24] See P. H. Levin (1979) 57 *Public Administration* 21.

[25] Cmnd 7133, 1978; report of Council on Tribunals for 1977–8, p. 25 and app. C; and Levin, *op. cit.*, pp. 35–42.

history of motorway inquiries culminated in the case of *Bushell* v. *Secretary of State for the Environment*.[26]

During a lengthy inquiry held concerning two sections of new motorway near Birmingham, the inspector allowed the objectors to bring evidence challenging departmental estimates of future traffic growth, but refused to allow civil servants to be cross-examined on the matter. After the inquiry but before the minister took his decision, the department revised its traffic estimates, but the minister did not allow the inquiry to be re-opened for examination of the new estimates. The objectors claimed that natural justice entitled them (a) to cross-examine officials on the traffic predictions and (b) to a re-opening of the inquiry. The House of Lords upheld the motorway orders, holding that natural justice had not been infringed. The judges stressed that an inquiry was quite unlike civil litigation. An inspector had wide discretion to disallow cross-examination if it would serve no relevant purpose. The methods of predicting future traffic growth were an essential element in national policy for motorways, and were not suitable for investigation at local inquiries. Lord Edmund-Davies, dissenting, held that the objectors had been denied 'a fair crack of the whip'.[27]

This decision was a sharp reminder of the fact that a public inquiry into a controversial proposal put forward by a government department is only part of a broader political process. In this process, it is not possible to expect the minister concerned to assume a cloak of judicial impartiality and detachment.

The strain placed upon the inquiry in relation to proposals of outstanding national importance is also evident in inquiries such as that conducted (exceptionally) by a High Court judge into the proposal by British Nuclear Fuels Ltd to establish a nuclear fuel reprocessing plant at Windscale[28] and the marathon Sizewell B inquiry conducted in 1982-4 into the proposal by the Central Electricity Generating Board to build a PWR nuclear power station in Suffolk. Lengthy and expensive as such inquiries are, and difficult as it is for interest groups to take part, they afford a means of scrutinising in public the technical and environmental aspects of a proposal and of ventilating issues of public concern. This scrutiny does not always lead to a reversal of government policies, but it would be rash to suppose that better decisions would be made if there were no public inquiries. Could the system be improved? In 1971, legislation was passed enabling an *ad hoc* Planning Inquiry Commission to be appointed to inquire into matters of national or regional importance or involving important technical or scientific issues.[29] Such a commission has never been set up. In 1978, a non-governmental committee proposed a new procedure for the investigation of projects with major national implications; this involved a two-stage 'project inquiry' conducted by an impartial committee, followed if necessary by a local inquiry into issues relating to a specific site.[30] But these proposals were not accepted by the government.

One serious weakness in the system of inquiries is the lack of financial provision for enabling objectors to present their case at major public inquiries.

---

26   [1981] A.C. 75. And see *Lovelock* v. *Minister of Transport* (1980) 78 L.G.R. 576.
27   [1981] A.C. at 118.
28   See the Parker Report 1978; H.C. Deb., 6 Mar. 1978, col. 981, 22 Mar. 1978, col. 1537 and 15 May 1978, col. 111; and P. McAuslan (1979) 2 *Urban Law and Policy* 25.
29   Town and Country Planning Act 1971, ss.47-9.
30   Outer Circle Policy Unit (with Justice and the Council for Science and Society), *The Big Public Inquiry*.

In some instances a successful objector may recover costs of appearing at an inquiry, but only rarely are costs paid to third party objectors; it is wrong that it should be the Secretary of State, advised by officials, who decides whether objectors who have made out a strong case at an inquiry of public concern should be reimbursed their costs.[31]

C. Tribunals of inquiry

Tribunals and inquiries are both part of the ordinary structure of administrative justice and many thousands of decisions are made each year by recourse to these procedures. The 'tribunal of inquiry' is a much rarer happening, barely twenty having been appointed since the Tribunals of Inquiry (Evidence) Act 1921 was passed. In the 19th century, parliamentary committees were occasionally appointed to inquire into matters of public concern, for example allegations of corruption amongst government servants or politicians. The use of such committees was discredited in 1913 when a parliamentary committee investigated the conduct of members of the Liberal government in the Marconi Company affair and in reaching its conclusions produced three conflicting reports.[1] Under the 1921 Act, when both Houses of Parliament resolve that it is expedient that a tribunal be appointed to inquire into a matter of urgent public importance, a tribunal may be appointed by Her Majesty or by a Secretary of State. The instrument of appointment may confer on the tribunal all the powers of the High Court, or in Scotland the Court of Session, with regard to the examination of witnesses and production of documents. Where a person summoned as a witness before the tribunal fails to attend or refuses to answer any question which the tribunal may legally require him to answer, or commits any other contempt, the chairman of the tribunal may report the matter to the High Court or the Court of Session for inquiry and punishment. This power resulted in 1963 in the imprisonment of two journalists who refused to disclose their sources of information to a tribunal investigating the circumstances in which the Admiralty employed a spy on secret work.[2]

Tribunals of inquiry are appointed to investigate serious allegations of corruption or improper conduct in the public service, or to investigate a matter of public concern which requires thorough and impartial investigation to allay public anxiety and may not be dealt with by ordinary civil or criminal processes. In the former category fall the tribunals appointed in 1936 to inquire into a leakage of Budget secrets, in 1948 to investigate bribery of ministers and civil servants, in 1957 to investigate the premature disclosure of information relating to the raising of the bank rate, in 1971 to investigate circumstances relating to the collapse of the Vehicle and General Insurance Company, and in 1978 to investigate the disastrous financial operations of the Crown Agents in 1968–74.[3] In the latter category falls the tribunal of inquiry into the Aberfan

---

[31] Report of Council on Tribunals, Cmnd 2471, 1965; Wraith and Lamb, *op. cit.*, pp. 277–95.

[1] See F. Donaldson, *The Marconi Scandal*.

[2] A.-G. v. *Mulholland & Foster* [1963] 2 Q.B. 477; p. 344 *ante*.

[3] See Cmd 5184, 1936; Cmd 7616, 1948; Cmnd 350, 1957; H.C. 133 (1971–2); H.C. 364 (1981–2). And see G. W. Keeton, *Trial by Tribunal*.

coal tip disaster in 1966 and the tribunal which inquired into the 'Bloody Sunday' shootings in Londonderry in 1972.[4]

The task of a tribunal of inquiry is to investigate certain allegations or events with a view to producing an authoritative and impartial account of the facts, attributing responsibility or blame where it is necessary to do so. It is not the duty of tribunals of inquiry to make decisions as to what action should be taken in the light of their findings of fact. The chairman of the tribunal is normally a senior judge, assisted by one or two additional members who are often eminent lawyers. Exceptionally, the 'Bloody Sunday' inquiry was conducted by Lord Chief Justice Widgery sitting alone. The matter to be inquired into is presented publicly to the tribunal by a Law Officer or senior counsel, instructed by the Treasury Solicitor, whose duty it is to call all relevant witnesses, whether or not suspicion has fallen upon them. The tribunal usually allows witnesses to be legally represented and their costs may be met *ex gratia* out of public funds. There may be cross-examination of the witnesses by counsel appearing at the tribunal and witnesses may be questioned by members of the tribunal. Because of the inquisitorial nature of the proceedings, it is difficult to provide the same facilities to a witness for answering an accusation as he would have if a criminal charge were brought against him. Thus the tribunal proceedings may result in severe criticism of a witness who has not been called on to meet definite charges and may not have an adequate opportunity of answering accusations against him.[5] The Attorney-General may, however, inform a witness that no criminal proceedings will be brought against him in respect of matters arising out of his evidence.

In 1966, a royal commission on tribunals of inquiry under the chairmanship of Salmon L. J. reported that tribunals of inquiry should be appointed only in cases of vital public importance, but that it was necessary to retain the possibility of inquisitorial procedure.[6] The commission did not favour changes such as a preliminary inquiry or a subsequent right of appeal. Sittings in private were to be discouraged. Emphasis was laid upon the protection of persons whose reputations might be involved; for example, a witness should be told beforehand of any allegations affecting him and he should be entitled to legal representation, to cross-examine those giving evidence adverse to him and to call relevant witnesses. The dual role of the Attorney-General as a member of the government and as independent counsel to the tribunal should be avoided by the appointment of another Queen's Counsel to act for the tribunal.

In 1966, at the time of the Aberfan disaster, concern arose about the permissible extent of press comment on the disaster, having regard to the uncertain operation of the *sub judice* rule once the tribunal of inquiry had been appointed. In 1969 a departmental committee, also chaired by Salmon L. J., examined the rules of contempt of court in relation to tribunals of inquiry.[7]

---

4   H.C. 553 (1966–7); and H.C. 220 (1971–2).
5   This criticism was made of the tribunal of inquiry which investigated the collapse of the Vehicle and General Insurance Company and found a senior civil servant to have been negligent in his work: H.C. 133 (1971–2) p. 116 *ante.*
6   Cmnd 3121, 1966; Wilson, *Cases*, p. 552.
7   Cmnd 4078, 1969. And see Cmnd 5313, 1973.

When the law of contempt of court was reformed in 1981, the changes then made were in general extended to tribunals of inquiry; in particular, the proceedings of such a tribunal are deemed to be 'active' from the time at which the tribunal is appointed until its report is presented to Parliament.[8]

The public procedures of a tribunal of inquiry were not considered suitable for a review of events leading to the outbreak of the Falklands Islands hostilities that involved access to many secret Cabinet, diplomatic and intelligence documents; instead, a committee of privy councillors was appointed.[9]

D. Parliamentary Commissioner for Administration

Until 1967, the main safeguards for the citizen against oppressive or faulty government were the following: judicial review of administrative action, through remedies described in chapter 35; the right of appeal to a tribunal against an administrative decision; the opportunity of taking part in a public inquiry held before a ministry's decision was made; redress by parliamentary means with the aid of an M. P.; and a request for administrative review of a decision already taken. Although, as we have seen, each may be effective in particular situations, each has its limitations.[1] For example, many discretionary decisions affecting the individual are made without the possibility of recourse to a tribunal or inquiry. Judicial review is often uncertain, expensive, and liable to be cumbrous in procedure; it is more effective in protecting established common law rights than interests which arise from social or economic legislation. Parliamentary procedures are not well suited to the impartial finding of facts nor to the resolution of disputes according to sound principles of administration.

To give further protection to the citizen, the office of Parliamentary Commissioner for Administration was created in 1967. Although it derived from the Ombudsman in Scandinavian countries and in New Zealand,[2] the British model was designed to fit within existing British institutions, without detracting from existing remedies. While the Parliamentary Commissioner has close links with the executive, the office is designed as an extension of Parliament; and it has virtually no links with the judicial system. As Sir Cecil Clothier, then the Commissioner, said in 1984:

'The office of Parliamentary Commissioner stands curiously poised between the legislative and the executive, while discharging an almost judicial function in the citizen's dispute with his government; and yet it forms no part of the judiciary.'[3]

On one view, the essence of the ombudsman idea for the ordinary person is accessibility, flexibility and informality. On another view, the ombudsman

---

[8]   Contempt of Court Act 1981, s.20; and see pp. 346–7, 349–50 *ante*.

[9]   Pages 244, 266 *ante*. and *cf.* the abortive proposals for a joint parliamentary committee into the Rhodesian oil sanctions affair, headed by a Lord of Appeal in Ordinary: H.C. Deb., 1 Feb. 1979, col. 1709 ff. and H.L. Deb., 8 Feb. 1979, col. 849 ff.

[1]   *Cf. The Citizen and the Administration* (the Whyatt Report) p. 600 *ante*; and Cmnd 2767, 1965.

[2]   On comparative aspects, see ed. D. C. Rowat, *The Ombudsman*; W. Gellhorn, *Ombudsmen and Others*; F. Stacey, *Ombudsmen Compared*.

[3]   Report for 1983 (H.C. 322, 1983–4), p. 1.

provides an authoritative means of 'judging' the behaviour of officials, thus helping to maintain standards of administration that are publicly acceptable. In the British version of the ombudsman, the latter view often seems to prevail over the former.

Status and jurisdiction[4]

The Parliamentary Commissioner is appointed by the Crown and holds office during good behaviour, although he may be removed by the Crown following addresses by both Houses (section 1). By a practice dating from 1977, the government consults the chairman of the House of Commons select committee on the Parliamentary Commissioner before making an appointment.[5] The Commissioner's salary is charged on the Consolidated Fund (section 2). He appoints his own staff, subject to Treasury consent as to numbers and conditions of service (section 3).His staff in practice are mostly recruited from the ranks of the civil service. The three ombudsmen who served between 1967 and 1979 all had civil service careers; the fourth ombudsman, Sir Cecil Clothier (1979–84), was a practising Queen's Counsel before his appointment.

The main task of the Commissioner is to investigate the complaints of citizens who claim to have suffered injustice in consequence of maladministration by government departments in the exercise of their administrative functions (section 5). His area of jurisdiction is closely defined by the 1967 Act, the Second Schedule of which lists the departments of central government subject to investigation. This list may be amended by Order in Council (section 4) – a power which is exercised whenever departments are abolished or created.

The Commissioner has no jurisdiction over authorities which are not departments of the central government, for example, local authorities, the police, and the nationalised industries, the reason for this being that ministers are not responsible to Parliament for their decisions. He may, however, investigate complaints about the way in which central departments have discharged their functions in these various fields. His jurisdiction is further limited by the exclusion of many matters for which ministers are responsible to Parliament (section 5(3) and Third Schedule). They include:

(*a*) action taken in matters certified by a Secretary of State to affect relations or dealings between the UK government and any other government, or international organisation;
(*b*) action taken outside the UK by any officer representing or acting under the authority of the Crown;[6]
(*c*) the administration of dependent territories outside the UK;
(*d*) action taken by a Secretary of State under the Extradition Act 1870 or the Fugitive Offenders Act 1967;

---

4   References in the text are to the Parliamentary Commissioner Act 1967. For a full account, see R. Gregory and P. G. Hutchesson, *The Parliamentary Ombudsman*. And see Wilson, *Cases*, pp. 172–197; K. C. Wheare, *Maladministration and its Remedies*; C. Harlow and R. Rawlings, *Law and Administration*, ch. 7; I. Pugh (1978) 56 *Public Administration* 127; A. W. Bradley [1980] C.L.J. 304.
5   Cmnd 6764, 1977.
6   The acts of British consuls abroad, other than honorary consuls, are now within the Commissioner's jurisdiction, if the complainant is resident or has a right of abode in the UK: Parliamentary Commissioner (Consular Complaints) Act 1981; S.I. 1979 No. 915.

(*e*) action taken by or with the authority of the Secretary of State for investigating crime or protecting the security of the state, including action so taken with respect to passports;

(*f*) the commencement or conduct of civil or criminal proceedings before any court in the UK, court martial or international court;

(*g*) any exercise of the prerogative of mercy;

(*h*) action taken on behalf of the central government by hospital boards and other authorities in the National Health Service;

(*i*) matters relating to contractual or other commercial transactions on the part of central government;[7]

(*j*) appointments, discipline and other personnel matters in relation to the civil service and the armed forces, and decisions of ministers and departments in respect of other branches of the public service (for example, teachers' pensions);

(*k*) the grant of honours, awards or privileges within the gift of the Crown.

In respect of each restriction, different policy considerations arise. It was these restrictions which led in Parliament to criticism that the legislation sought to carve up areas of possible grievances in an arbitrary way.[8] Those restrictions which have been most criticised are in (*i*) and (*j*) above. The government has power by Order in Council to revoke any of these restrictions (section 5(4)), but despite frequent recommendations from the House of Commons committee that the restriction on personnel matters in (*j*) should be revoked, successive governments have refused to do so.[9]

Another limitation is that the Commissioner may not normally investigate any action in respect of which the complainant has or had a right of recourse to a tribunal or a remedy by proceedings in any court of law, although he may do so if in a particular case the citizen could not reasonably be expected to exercise his right (section 5(2)). If a citizen is dissatisfied with a decision about a social security benefit, or an award of compensation on a compulsory purchase of land, he clearly should appeal to the relevant tribunal. But the Commissioner often accepts that a complainant cannot be reasonably expected to embark on the hazardous course of litigation.

There is no rule that the complainant must be a British citizen, but in general either he must be resident in the United Kingdom or have been present in the United Kingdom or on a British ship or aircraft when the offending action occurred, or the action concerned must relate to rights or obligations arising in the United Kingdom (section 6(4)).

There is also a time bar: the Commissioner may investigate a complaint only if it is made to an M. P. within twelve months from the date when the citizen first had notice of the matter complained of, except where special circumstances justify the Commissioner in accepting a complaint made after a longer interval (section 6(3)).

---

[7] This is subject to an exception for transactions relating to compulsorily purchased land and other land brought under threat of compulsory powers. But for this exception, a latter-day Crichel Down affair (p. 114 *ante*) would be outside the Commissioner's jurisdiction.

[8] H.C. Deb., 18 Oct. 1966, col. 67 (Quintin Hogg M.P.) *Cf.* report by Justice, *Our Fettered Ombudsman*, 1977.

[9] See *e.g.* H.C. 615, 1977–8; and Cmnd 7449, 1979. Some aspects of employment relating to overseas development are now within jurisdiction: S.I. 1983 No. 1707.

It is for the Commissioner to determine whether a complaint is duly made under the Act; in practice many complaints identify the injustice that has been suffered more closely than the maladministration which caused it.[10] The Commissioner has an express discretion to decide whether to investigate a complaint.[11] But the Act does not protect the Commissioner if he takes up a complaint on a matter outside his jurisdiction. Thus if he began to investigate a complaint about the dismissal of a civil servant, or the actions of a local authority, it is doubtful whether a person could be held liable for obstruction or contempt for refusing to supply information to the Commissioner (section 9). His rulings on the extent of his powers may involve difficult constitutional issues, for example regarding the extent to which he may investigate the acts of court officials.[12]

Procedure

One important feature of the ombudsman idea is that the ombudsman should be accessible to the individual. But in Britain the citizen has no right to present his complaint to the Parliamentary Commissioner. In the first instance, a complaint of maladministration must be addressed by the person who claims to have suffered injustice to an M. P. (section 5(1)). It is for the M. P. to decide whether to refer the complaint to the Commissioner. Usually a citizen will send the complaint to his constituency M. P. but the Act does not require this. When the Commissioner receives a complaint from a private person that is clearly investigable, he may send it with the complainant's agreement to his M. P., saying that he is prepared to investigate it if the M. P. wishes him to do so.[13] When the Commissioner receives a complaint from an M. P. he must first decide whether it falls within his jurisdiction. If so, and if he decides to conduct an investigation, he must give the department concerned and any person named in the complaint an opportunity of commenting on any allegations made (section 7(1)). The investigation must be carried out in private (section 7(2)); normally an officer of the Commissioner's staff examines the relevant department files. The Commissioner has wide powers of compelling ministers and officials to produce documents and has the same powers as the High Court in England or the Court of Session in Scotland to compel any witness to give evidence before him (section 8). The Commissioner's investigation is not restricted by the doctrine of Crown privilege (section 8(3)). The only documents which are statutorily privileged are those certified by the Secretary of the Cabinet, with the approval of the Prime Minister, to relate to proceedings of the Cabinet or a committee of the Cabinet (section 8(4)).

When the investigation is complete, the Commissioner must send to the M.P. concerned a report of the results of the investigation (section 10(1)). If the Commissioner considers that injustice was caused through maladministration and has not been remedied, he may lay a special report before Parliament (section 10(3)). Such a report and other communications relating to an investigation are absolutely privileged in the law of defamation (section 10(5)).

---

10 Cf. R. v. *Local Commissioner for Administration, ex p. Bradford Council* [1979] Q.B.287, 313.
11 S. 5(5), 1967 Act. And see *In re Fletcher's Application* [1970] 2 All E.R. 527.
12 Report of P.C.A. for 1979, H.C. 402 (1979–80), p. 34.
13 Report of P.C.A. for 1978, H.C. 205 (1978–9), p. 4.

A minister has no power to veto an investigation, but he may give notice to the Commissioner that publication of certain documents or information would be prejudicial to the safety of the state or against the public interest and this notice binds the Commissioner in making his report (section 11(3)).

The Commissioner has no executive powers. Thus he cannot alter a departmental decision or award compensation to a citizen, although he may suggest an appropriate remedy. But a minister will be under a strong obligation to accept the Commissioner's findings and take necessary corrective action. Circumstances might arise in which a report would have such controversial political implications that a minister could come under pressure not to accept the recommendations.[14] To give support to the Commissioner in such a situation, and to watch over his work, a select committee is appointed by the House of Commons to examine the reports he lays in Parliament. This committee takes evidence from the departments concerned and reports to the House on the Commissioner's work. The committee has been successful in helping to ensure the provision by departments of adequate remedies and the improvement of defective procedures, but not in efforts to remove limits upon the ombudsman's jurisdiction.[15]

The Commissioner's case-work

What is meant by the phrase, 'injustice to the person aggrieved in consequence of maladministration' (section 10(3))? No definition and no illustrations of maladministration and injustice are given in the Act. Maladministration includes such defects as 'neglect, inattention, delay, incompetence, ineptitude, perversity, and arbitrariness'[16] but other examples of maladministration may be found in the Commissioner's published reports. They include failure to give effect to assurances given to a citizen[17]; incorrect advice about social security or tax matters; excessive delay in operating a free veterinary service for farmers;[18] dilatory enforcement of regulations against asbestosis;[19] failure to make departmental policy known in the press[20] and even the making of misleading statements by a minister in Parliament.[21] In 1984, Home Office officials were criticised severely for having failed to deal promptly with complaints from a prisoner that his conviction for murder had been based on evidence from a forensic scientist whose evidence in other trials was known to be incompetent and unreliable.[22]

Even if maladministration has occurred, this does not in itself mean that injustice has thereby been caused to the individual. Conversely, injustice or

---

14   In 1975, the government was supported by the Commons in rejecting the Commissioner's finding that the government could not be absolved of all responsibility for holidaymakers' losses arising from the collapse of the Court Line group: H.C. Deb., 6 Aug. 1975, col. 532.
15   R. Gregory [1982] P.L. 49.
16   H.C. Deb., 18 Oct. 1966, col. 51 (R. H. S. Crossman M.P.).
17   See A. W. Bradley [1981] C.L.P. 1, 8–11.
18   Report of P.C.A. for 1970, H.C. 261 (1970–1) p. 10.
19   3rd report of P.C.A., H.C. 259 (1975–6), p. 189.
20   7th report of P.C.A., H.C. 680 (1974–5).
21   5th report of P.C.A., H.C. 498 (1974–5).
22   4th report of P.C.A., H.C. 191 (1983–4).

hardship may exist which has been caused not by maladministration, but, for example, by an Act of Parliament or a judicial decision.

One difficult matter has been the relation between maladministration and discretionary decisions. Unlike the New Zealand ombudsman, who is empowered to find that a discretionary decision was wrong, the Commissioner may not question the merits of a discretionary decision taken without maladministration (section 12(3)). Where administrative errors have been made in the procedures leading to a discretionary decision, the Commissioner can report accordingly. But what is the position where a discretionary decision has caused manifest hardship to the individual, but no identifiable administrative defect has occurred in the procedures leading up to it? The Commissioner is now willing in such a case to infer an element of maladministration from the very decision itself. Similarly he is now prepared to inquire into harsh decisions which may have been based on the over-rigorous application of departmental policies.[23]

To give a detailed example of the Commissioner's investigations, the Sachsenhausen case was the first occasion on which he found a department to be seriously at fault.[24]

Under the Anglo-German Agreement of 1964, the German government provided £1 million for compensating UK citizens who suffered from Nazi persecution during the second world war. Distribution of this money was left to the discretion of the UK government and in 1964 the Foreign Secretary (then Mr Butler) approved rules for the distribution. Later the Foreign Office withheld compensation from twelve persons who claimed to be within these rules because of their detention within the Sachsenhausen concentration camp. Pressure from many M.P.s failed to get this decision reversed and a complaint of maladministration was referred to the Parliamentary Commissioner. By this time the whole of the £1 million had been distributed to other claimants. After extensive investigations, the Commissioner reported that there were defects in the administrative procedure by which the Foreign Office reached its decisions and subsequently defended them, and that this maladministration had damaged the reputation of the claimants. When this report was debated in the Commons, the Foreign Secretary (Mr George Brown) assumed personal responsibility for the decisions of the Foreign Office, which he maintained were correct. He nonetheless made available an additional £25,000 in order that the claimants might receive the same rate of compensation as successful claimants of the fund.[25]

It may be commented that at no time were legal rights of the claimants involved, for the Foreign Office rules were not enforceable in law, and there was no possibility of a judicial remedy.[26] Parliamentary pressure alone, without the report of the Commissioner, would not have been successful. Indeed, the report was based on information about the Foreign Office decisions which traditional parliamentary procedures could not have discovered. The case well illustrates the fact that the Commissioner may investigate the conduct of min-

---

23   1st report of P.C.A., H.C. 9 (1968–9); 2nd report from select committee on P.C.A., H.C. 350 (1967–8), and see G. Marshall [1973] P.L. 32.

24   3rd report of P.C.A., H.C. 54 (1967–8); 1st report from select committee on P.C.A., H.C. 258 (1967–8); G. K. Fry [1970] P.L. 336; and Gregory and Hutchesson, *op. cit.*, ch. 11.

25   H.C. Deb. 5 Feb., 1968, cols. 105–117.

26   See *Rustomjee* v. *R.* (1876) 2 Q.B.D.. 69; p. 314 *ante*.

isters as well as civil servants (section 4(4)). In retrospect, it appears that the Foreign Office erred in deciding to distribute the money itself, rather than entrusting this to the Foreign Compensation Commission, a judicial body for whose decisions the Foreign Secretary is not responsible.[27]

In the five years 1979–83, an average of about 860 complaints were referred by M.P.s to the Commissioner each year. Of these over 70% were rejected as being outside his jurisdiction (for example, because no central department was involved or because a personnel matter from the civil service or armed forces was involved). In 40% of the cases which were fully investigated, the complaints of maladministration were found to be wholly justified, and in another 23% of the cases partly justified. The remedies which departments provide include *ex gratia* compensation; the remission of tax where under-payment has arisen through official error; the payment of arrears of pensions and benefits that have been wrongly withheld; and revised procedures to prevent repetition of mistakes. In one case in 1982, £57,000 was paid by the Department of Industry to compensate for the 'shoddy treatment' of a company's application for industrial assistance.[28] The granting of a remedy to one complainant may well lead to the same being done for others similarly placed.[29] The Commissioner has no power to compel a department to provide a remedy; but where injustice caused by maladministration has not been remedied, he may lay a report before Parliament (section 10(3)). The first such report in 1978 led to a government decision to introduce legislation enabling the injustice to be remedied.[30]

A continuing problem is to secure adequate publicity for the British ombudsman's reports. In addition to his annual reports, he occasionally lays in Parliament a report on an investigation which he considers to be of general interest; and he also publishes a quarterly selection of reports on his investigations, in an anonymised form. But these reports seldom lead to headlines in the press.

Commissioners for the National Health Service and local government

The ombudsman experiment has been copied in other areas of government.[31] As we have seen, complaints about the National Health Service were excluded from the jurisdiction of the Parliamentary Commissioner. A scheme of Health Service Commissioners for England, Wales and Scotland respectively was later introduced.[32] Complaints about the acts of health authorities and other bodies may be referred directly to the appropriate Commissioner by a member of the

---

[27] Report from select committee on P.C.A., H.C. 385 (1968–9). And see *Anisminic Ltd* v. *Foreign Compensation Commission* (p. 641 *ante*) and [1968] C.L.J. 42.

[28] 2nd report of P.C.A. (H.C. 150, 1982–3) p. 50; and see C. Harlow, *Compensation and Government Torts*, part 4.

[29] *E.g.* 4th report of P.C.A., H.C. 312 (1977–8).

[30] 6th report of P.C.A., H.C. 598 (1977–8); Local Government, Planning and Land Act 1980, s.113; [1982] P.L. at pp. 61–3.

[31] For Northern Ireland, see the Parliamentary Commissioner (N.I.) Act 1969, and the Commissioner for Complaints (N.I.) Act 1969; and H.C. 254 (1979–80).

[32] National Health Service Act 1977, Part V; National Health Service (Scotland) Act 1978, Part VI.

public. But he may not investigate action taken in connection with the diagnosis of illness or the treatment of a patient which, in the opinion of the Commissioner, was taken solely in the exercise of clinical judgement. Many aspects of the Health Service Commissioners are modelled directly on the Parliamentary Commissioner Act 1967; in practice the Parliamentary Commissioner also holds the three posts of Health Service Commissioner. As such, his reports are considered by the House of Commons committee on the Parliamentary Commissioner.

So far as local government is concerned, there have also been created Commissions for Local Administration in England and in Wales (of which the Parliamentary Commissioner is an *ex officio* member) and a Commissioner for Local Administration in Scotland.[33] Again the scheme resembles the Parliamentary Commissioner model, with certain differences. Individuals may complain to the Commissioner for Local Administration for their area regarding alleged maladministration by local authorities, joint boards, police authorities (other than the Home Secretary) and water authorities. The normal channel of complaints is via a member of the authority complained against, but a Commissioner may accept a complaint if he is satisfied that a member refused to refer a complaint to the Commissioner when requested to do so. A Commissioner may not investigate complaints about action which affects all or most of the inhabitants in the area of a local authority, nor complaints about such matters as public passenger transport, the provision of entertainments and markets, nor complaints which relate to the giving of instruction or the internal organisation, management and discipline of local authority schools. Reports on cases investigated are sent to the local authority and to the complainant. To watch over the work of the Commissions and to receive their general reports, special bodies representing local authorities have been appointed. The greatest number of complaints have related to housing and town planning.[34] If a Commissioner's report that injustice has been caused by maladministration is not accepted by the council concerned, his only power is to issue a further report to this effect. Since there are no parliamentary means of ensuring compliance with a Local Commissioner's report, there is a strong case to be made for imposing a legal obligation on a council to provide a remedy in such circumstances.[35]

Although there are statutory provisions which enable the various Commissioners to co-operate with each other,[36] it would take an exceptional citizen to know how and to whom he could refer his complaints about officialdom. From the individual's viewpoint, a uniform and simple right of access to all ombudsmen is highly desirable; and this could be the first step to establishing a single system of ombudsmen to investigate complaints of maladministration

---

33   Local Government Act 1973, Part III; Local Government (Scotland) Act 1975, Part II. And see Local Government Act 1978 (local authorities may pay compensation for injustice caused by maladministration).

34   See generally N. Lewis and B. Gateshill, *The Commission for Local Administration*; report by Justice, *The Local Ombudsman* (1980); D. Foulkes [1978] P.L. 264; D. C. M. Yardley [1983] P.L. 522.

35   *Cf.* Commissioner for Complaints (Northern Ireland) Act 1969, s.7.

36   *E.g.* Local Government Act 1974, s.33.

against all public authorities. If such a system were to be established, it would have to be decided whether it should be extended in scope (for example, whether the nationalised industries should be brought within the system).[37] Attention would also need to be given to the relationships that should exist between the system of ombudsmen and other forms of public remedy for individual grievances, notably the remedies that may be obtained through recourse to the courts.[38]

---

[37] See report by Justice, *The Citizen and the Public Agencies*, 1976.
[38] *Cf.* A. W. Bradley [1980] C.L.J. 304, 320–32.

and all public authorities. Whether a citizen were to have access to the judge or to the ombudsman, and whether the particular grievance should be brought within the system would also need to be given to the relationship that should exist between the system of ombudsmen and other forms of public remedy for individual grievances, notably the remedies that may be obtained through recourse to the courts.

Appendix A
The Canadian constitutional controversy, 1981–2

The Dominion of Canada was created when the Westminster Parliament passed the British North America Act 1867, giving effect to a scheme agreed within Canada for a federal union of four provinces. Under the Act, legislative and executive powers for Canada were divided between the federal parliament and the provincial parliaments. Since 1867, the allocation of powers has formed an important part of Canadian constitutional law. Until 1949 the Judicial Committee of the Privy Council was the final court of appeal on constitutional disputes; since then, appeals have lain to the Supreme Court of Canada.

Although the 1867 Act provided for other territories to be admitted to the federal union of Canada, it contained no provision for its own amendment. As an Act of the Westminster Parliament, it could be amended only by a further Act passed at Westminster. Between 1871 and 1964, fourteen British North America Acts were passed, amending the 1867 Act.

Early in Canada's history it came to be accepted that the Westminster Parliament should not interfere in Canada's domestic affairs. The following conventions developed to govern the amendment procedure:

(a) that Westminster would amend the 1867 Act only upon a formal request from Canada, and that such a request would be granted;
(b) that the request from Canada would be approved for forwarding to London by a joint address to the Crown from both houses of the Canadian parliament;
(c) that no amendment of the 1867 Act would be made by Westminster solely on the request of a Canadian province.

Since amendments to the 1867 Act could modify the federal/provincial allocation of powers, the provincial governments had a strong interest in taking part in the process. They therefore claimed that it was also a convention:

(d) that the federal parliament would not request an amendment directly affecting federal-provincial relationships without prior consultation and agreement with the provinces.

Of (d) an official report stated, 'this principle did not emerge as early as others, but since 1907, and particularly since 1930, has gained increasing

recognition and acceptance. The nature and the degree of provincial participation in the amending process, however, have not lent themselves to easy
definition'.[1] As an instance of the principle in (*d*), before Westminster was
asked in 1940 to transfer power to legislate on unemployment insurance from
the provinces to the federal parliament, all provinces were consulted and gave
their consent to the proposal.[2]

By the Statute of Westminster 1931,[3] Canada's equality of status with the
United Kingdom was confirmed as a matter of law, except so far as the 1867
Act was concerned. Power to amend the 1867 Act could have been conferred
in 1931, but because no agreement had been reached in Canada about the
amendment procedure, section 7 of the 1931 Statute excluded amendments to
the 1867 Act from the scope of the Statute. In 1949, when limited power to
amend the 1867 Act was conferred on the federal parliament, power to affect
the position of the provinces was excluded.[4]

After 1945, numerous attempts to reach a unanimous agreement on constitutional reform were made by the federal government and the provinces, but
without success. In 1980, the Trudeau government decided to wait no longer
for provincial agreement. It proposed a scheme to end the power of Westminster to legislate for Canada, to create a new Charter of Rights binding both
provincial and federal legislatures, and to establish a complex formula for
constitutional amendment. When eight of the ten provinces opposed the
scheme, the crucial question arose in Canada whether the federal authorities
were entitled to request Westminster to enact the Trudeau scheme, against so
much provincial opposition.

Differing opinions on this matter were obtained from the courts in three
provinces (Manitoba, Newfoundland and Quebec),[5] and these were taken on
appeal to the Supreme Court of Canada. The Supreme Court was unanimous
only in holding that the Trudeau proposals directly affected the legislative
rights and privileges of the provinces. The judgments dealt separately with the
issues of law and convention. By 7 to 2, the court held that it was *lawful* for
the Trudeau scheme to be submitted to Westminster without provincial agreement. The majority held that there was no legal rule which limited the power
of the Canadian parliament to adopt resolutions seeking amendment of the
1867 Act. 'What is desirable as a political limitation does not translate into
a legal limitation, without expression in imperative constitutional text or
statute'.[6] There was no process by which constitutional conventions 'crystal-
lised into law'. The two dissenting judges (Martland and Ritchie JJ.) held that
the dominant principle in Canadian constitutional law was federalism, and
that provincial rights had never been restricted without the agreement of the
provinces. The two houses of the Canadian parliament could request Westminster to make amendments only by observing the principle of federalism; in
the circumstances they were attempting to exercise a power they did not possess.

[1] G. Favreau, *The Amendment of the Constitution of Canada*, 1965, p. 15.
[2] British North America Act 1940.
[3] Ch. 24.
[4] British North America Act 1949 (No. 2).
[5] *References re Amendment of the Constitution of Canada* (1981) 117 D.L.R. (3d) 1, 118 D.L.R. (3d) 1
and 120 D.L.R. (3d) 385.
[6] *Reference re Amendment of the Constitution of Canada* (*Nos. 1, 2, and 3*) (1982) 125 D.L.R. (3d) 1, 29.

On the issue of constitutional convention, by 6 to 3 the court held that the proposed request to Westminster infringed the convention that legislation affecting provincial rights must have provincial support. In deciding that this convention existed, the court adopted the test for the existence of conventions laid down by Sir Ivor Jennings,[7] asking three questions: (*a*) what are the precedents? (*b*) did the actors in the precedents believe that they were bound by a rule? and (*c*) is there a reason for the rule? The majority concluded that it would be *unconstitutional* (i.e. in breach of convention) if the Trudeau scheme went forward. The minority (Laskin C. J., Estey and McIntyre JJ.) doubted whether a court should express a view about extra-legal matters, such as an alleged breach of convention. They could discover no clear convention regarding the degree of provincial support that was needed. Before the existence of a convention could be recognised, the parties concerned must regard it as binding upon them, and the federal government had never accepted that provincial consent was required.

The Supreme Court dealt only with the procedures to be followed in Canada and did not examine what Westminster should do if faced with a request for legislation which was opposed by eight provinces. As a sovereign legislature Westminster was in legal theory free to do as it pleased, but in reality was Westminster bound by the conventions of British/Canadian relations to give effect to every proposal for amendment coming from Ottawa? This matter was examined in depth at Westminster by the House of Commons Select Committee on Foreign Affairs. The committee reported that, while the functions of Westminster were strictly limited and must be exercised in accordance with Canadian wishes, Westminster had a duty to act as guardian of the federal principle in Canada and should not give automatic approval to any request coming from the federal parliament that was opposed by substantial provincial opinion.[8] This report ran contrary to the Canadian government's position, but was consistent with what the majority of the Supreme Court had to say on the issue of convention.

The Supreme Court's decision forced further negotiations to take place in Canada, as a result of which all provinces except Quebec agreed to support a modified version of the federal scheme. Despite continuing protests from Quebec,[9] the Canadian parliament resolved that the modified scheme be transmitted to Westminster. The House of Commons Committee on Foreign Affairs reported that it now saw no reason for opposing the proposals.[10] In due course the Canada Act 1982 received the royal assent. Section 1 gave the force of law in Canada to the attached Constitution Act 1982, which included a Canadian Charter of Rights and Freedoms and provided for future amendment of the constitution.[11] Section 2 provided that no Act of the UK Parliament passed after the Constitution Act came into force should extend to Canada as part

---

7   *Law and the Constitution*, p. 136.

8   H.C. 42 (1980–1), and H.C. 295 (1980–1).

9   See *Re A.-G. of Quebec* and *A.-G. of Canada* (1982) 140 D.L.R. (3d) 385.

10   H.C. 128 (1981–2).

11   See J. B. Laskin [1981] P.L. 340 and [1982] P.L. 549; D. C. McDonald, *Legal Rights in the Canadian Charter of Rights and Freedoms*; W. Tarnopolsky and G. Beaudouin, *The Canadian Charter of Rights and Freedoms, a Commentary.*

of its law. Subsequently the Canada Act 1982 was challenged in British courts by Canadian minority groups, but without success.[12]

The decision of the Canadian Supreme Court to deal separately with the law and with the conventions reflects the distinction between legal and non-legal rules discussed in chapter 2. It is therefore almost paradoxical that the court did rule on the existence and content of a constitutional convention.[13] However, the case had reached the court by a reference procedure which enables Canadian courts to give wide-ranging advisory opinions. It was more-over a political necessity that the court should not confine itself to issues of strict legality, since the prospect of Westminster attempting to resolve the dispute was unattractive to all concerned.

Throughout the controversy, the common view (endorsed by the Supreme Court) was that in law Westminster retained full legislative sovereignty for Canada, regardless of any prior procedures in Canada. The political realities were very different,[14] and this was reflected in the preamble to the Canada Act 1982, which emphasised that the Act was being passed solely at the request of Canada.

The manner in which the Canadian Supreme Court handled this remark-able controversy was instrumental in securing that further political nego-tiations achieved a greater measure of agreement. But the theoretical relationship between legislative sovereignty and constitutional conventions is probably more subtle and less clearcut than the separate judgments indicate.

---

12   *R. v. Foreign Secretary, ex p. Indian Association of Alberta* [1982] Q.B. 892; *Manuel v. A.-G.* [1982] 3 All E.R. 822.

13   R. Brazier and St. J. Robilliard [1982] P.L. 28.

14   *Cf.* the argument advanced in (ed.) N. E. Eastham and B. Krivy, *The Cambridge Lectures 1981*, ch. 21 (A. W. Bradley).

This appendix notes developments occurring during or before December 1984; the order of paragraphs corresponds with the chapters to which they relate.

1 The Representation of the People Bill, which received its second reading in the House of Commons on 10 December 1984, proposed changes in the franchise and electoral law. It was prepared not after a Speaker's conference on electoral law (cf. page 169), but after a review of the legislation made by the Home Affairs Committee of the Commons (see H.C. 32 (1982–3) and Cmnd 9140, 1984). The Bill proposed that at parliamentary and European Assembly elections, British citizens who were resident abroad on the qualifying date and made an overseas elector's declaration, would have the right to vote in respect of the UK constituency in which they had previously been registered; this right would continue for seven years after a British citizen ceased to reside in the United Kingdom. The Bill also proposed to change the rules of postal and proxy voting, and to widen the categories of those entitled to vote by post (cf. page 152). The Bill sought to raise the deposit payable by candidates at parliamentary elections from £150 to £1,000, and to lower the minimum share of the constituency vote needed to retain the deposit from 12½ per cent to 5 per cent. The Bill also proposed to change the Meeting of Parliament Act 1797 (page 172) so that, should the Sovereign die after a dissolution and before the general election, polling day and the meeting of the new Parliament would be delayed for 14 days and the former Parliament would not reassemble. The Bill was later amended to provide for an election deposit of £500 and to restrict overseas voting rights to five years in duration.

The Elections (Northern Ireland) Bill, which had its third reading in the Commons on 6 December 1984, sought to strengthen safeguards against impersonation at elections in Northern Ireland, requiring electors to produce documentary proof of their identity before voting.

2 In *Council of Civil Service Unions* v. *Minister for the Civil Service* [1984] 3 All E.R. 935, the House of Lords upheld the government's decision to remove from a section of the civil service the right to belong to a trade union, but broke new ground in holding that the exercise of prerogative power was sub-

ject to judicial review (see pages 255, 283 and 692). The majority (Lords Scarman, Diplock and Roskill) held that the controlling factor in determining whether the exercise of executive power is subject to judicial review is the justiciability of its subject matter, not whether the source of the power is the prerogative. Powers derived from or exercised directly under the prerogative might, depending on the subject matter, be reviewed on grounds of error of law, unreasonableness and procedural impropriety. This decision was much influenced by recent developments in administrative law, and also relied on *R. v. Criminal Injuries Compensation Board, ex p. Lain* (page 249). The majority accepted that many prerogative acts, for example concerning foreign affairs or defence, were inherently unsuitable for judicial review, but did not consider that this applied to control of the civil service.

The decision that GCHQ staff should lose the right to union membership had not been taken directly by the Crown but under a power to regulate the civil service conferred on the Minister for the Civil Service by a prerogative instrument, the Civil Service Order in Council 1982 (page 276). Lords Fraser and Brightman agreed that the use of such delegated power was reviewable with reference to the scope and limits of the delegation, but differed from the majority in leaving open the question of whether powers exercised directly under prerogative were immune from judicial review.

The judges were unanimous in holding that GCHQ staff had had a legitimate expectation of being consulted before the decision taking away union rights was made. However, it was established that the decision not to consult the unions was based on national security, a consideration which was held to override procedural fairness.

3 On an appeal from Northern Ireland, *McC. (a Minor)* v. *Mullan* [1984] 3 All E.R. 908, the House of Lords held three justices of the peace liable in damages for having acted outside their jurisdiction in passing a custodial sentence upon an unrepresented juvenile without having first informed him of his right to legal aid. In giving the principal judgment, Lord Bridge rejected Lord Denning's approach in *Sirros* v. *Moore* (page 340), which sought to assimilate the immunity of judges in inferior courts to that of judges in the superior courts. While the liability of members of inferior courts for acts done in excess of jurisdiction was strongly affirmed by the Lords, a majority considered *obiter* that the old common law liability of justices who acted within jurisdiction but maliciously and without reasonable and probable cause could no longer arise.

4 In *Secretary of State for Defence* v. *Guardian Newspapers Ltd* [1984] 3 All E.R. 601, the House of Lords by a majority upheld the decision of the Court of Appeal that under section 10 of the Contempt of Court Act 1981 (page 344), the Guardian newspaper must return the copy of a secret memorandum which had been 'leaked' to it by a civil servant. The House held that section 10 required the Crown to show on the balance of probabilities that disclosure of the material was necessary in the interests of national security. In the view of the majority (Lords Diplock, Roskill and Bridge), the Crown had established this, not because of the contents of the document in question but because whoever had leaked it might in future leak other classified documents, with more serious consequences. Lords Fraser and Scarman dissented, holding that the

Crown's evidence was not enough, in terms of the 1981 Act, to satisfy the court that disclosure of the source was 'necessary' in the interests of national security.

5 The object of the Prosecution of Offences Bill, which received a second reading in the House of Lords on 29 November 1984, was to create a new structure for the prosecution of offences in England and Wales, giving effect to the government's policy outlined in Cmnd 9074, 1983 (page 359). Under the Bill would be established a Crown Prosecution Service headed by the Director of Public Prosecutions, whose functions would be exercised under the superintendence of the Attorney-General. These functions would include the duty of conducting all criminal proceedings instituted on behalf of the police, and advising the police about the institution of criminal proceedings, the arrest and detention of suspects, and the exercise of powers of entry, search and seizure. In practice the D.P.P.'s functions would be exercised by lawyers appointed to act under his direction as Crown Prosecutors or prosecuting officers. Private individuals would still be able to institute prosecutions, subject as now to the power of the D.P.P. to take over a private prosecution. The D.P.P. would report annually to the Attorney-General, and his report would be laid before Parliament. The Prosecution of Offences Bill also included a controversial proposal enabling the Attorney-General to refer to the Court of Appeal for an advisory opinion any Crown Court conviction where in the Attorney-General's view a different sentence ought to have been imposed from that in fact awarded; this clause was later rejected by the Lords.

6 The government's detailed proposals for reforming local government in Greater London and the six metropolitan counties (page 377) were preceded by the Local Government (Interim Provisions) Act 1984. As amended against government wishes by the House of Lords, the Act provided that the term of office for which existing councillors had been elected should be extended until the councils themselves were abolished on 1 April 1986. The Act also imposed certain temporary restraints upon the freedom of the seven councils to make decisions in the interim period. (See also H.L. Deb., 18 Dec. 1984, col. 561).

The Local Government Bill, which sought to give detailed effect to the White Paper *Streamlining the Cities* (Cmnd 9063, 1983) received a second reading in the Commons on 4 December 1984. Part I of the Bill proposed to abolish the metropolitan county councils and the Greater London Council with effect from 1 April 1986. Parts II to IX of the Bill, together with the Bill's 17 schedules, provided for the re-allocation of the functions of the abolished councils (mainly to the metropolitan district councils and the London boroughs); the replacement of the Inner London Education Authority by a directly elected authority; the creation of joint authorities (nominated by borough and district councils) with responsibility for police, fire and passenger transport functions in the six metropolitan areas and fire and civil defence in London; and for many other matters including finance, property and staffing.

New restraints upon the financial autonomy of local authorities in England and Wales were created by the Rates Act 1984 (page 393). This Act empowered the Secretary of State for the Environment to 'rate-cap'; that is, to designate a local authority as one restricted in any financial year to levying a

rate no higher than a prescribed maximum amount (expressed as a figure of the rate in the pound). Notice of such designation must be served on the authority and a report laid before the House of Commons. The Secretary of State will determine the amount to be prescribed after determining the total level of permitted expenditure for the authority. The Rates Act 1984 also provided for the eventual designation of all local authorities (with exemptions for good behaviour) as being subject to 'capping' by the imposition of maximum rate levels.

7   *Reynolds* v. *Metropolitan Police Commissioner* [1984] 3 All E.R. 649 concerned (*inter alia*) the common law extension of police powers of search and seizure under a search warrant that had been confirmed by cases such as *Chic Fashions (West Wales) Ltd* v. *Jones* (page 487). The Court of Appeal held that police acting on a search warrant under the Forgery Act 1913 were entitled to remove for examination documents which there was reasonable cause to believe might be evidence of any offence, but they were bound to return promptly any documents found on further scrutiny to be of no evidential value (cf. Police and Criminal Evidence Act 1984, section 19; page 488). In *Collins* v. *Wilcock* [1984] 3 All E.R. 374, a policewoman was held to have used unlawful force when she laid hold of the arm of a woman suspected of being a prostitute, in order to detain her for the purpose of cautioning her (cf. *Kenlin* v. *Gardner* and *Donnelly* v. *Jackman*, page 482). But in *Lodwick* v. *Saunders, The Times*, 4 Dec. 1984, the court upheld the power of the police at common law to detain a vehicle which had been stopped under statutory powers and was suspected of being stolen.

8   As regards the admissibility of improperly obtained evidence (pages 489–90), the Police and Criminal Evidence Act 1984, section 78, provides that in any criminal proceedings the court may refuse to allow prosecution evidence to be given if it appears to the court that, in all the circumstances, including those in which the evidence was obtained, to admit the evidence would have such an adverse effect on the fairness of the proceedings that it should not be admitted. This section, which does not alter any rule of law requiring the exclusion of evidence such as confessions which have been obtained by oppression (page 484), vests in English courts a discretion broadly analogous to that exercised by Scottish courts (page 489). But it is difficult to predict the effect of such a broad discretion. By contrast, a proposal by Lord Scarman, acceptable to the House of Lords but not to the government, specified the tests that the court would have to apply in excluding improperly obtained evidence (see H.L. Deb., 31 Jul. 1984, col. 653 and H.C. Deb., 29 Oct. 1984, col. 1011).

9   The Video Recordings Act 1984 (page 520) establishes a scheme for the censorship of video recordings, under which it is an offence (subject on summary conviction to a fine not exceeding £20,000) to supply (whether or not for reward) any recording for which no classification certificate has been issued. Certain recordings are exempt from this requirement (for example, those concerned with sport, religion or music and those designed to be educational) and so are certain kinds of supply (for example, if the recording is for transmission by the BBC or the IBA). Although not specified in the Act, members and

officers of an enlarged British Board of Film Censors (page 522) are to be designated by the Home Secretary as the classifying authority; designation is subject to an adverse vote in either House of Parliament and it is a condition of designation that there is an adequate right of appeal against an adverse classification decision. In classifying video recordings, the designated authority must have special regard to the likelihood of certified recordings being viewed in the home; it may hold that a video work unsuitable for general viewing (with or without advice as to the desirability of parental guidance), is suitable only for viewing by persons over 18 and (in this event) that the recording shall be supplied only in a licensed sex shop, or is wholly unsuitable for viewing. Supply in breach of the classification conditions is an offence.

10 During much of 1984, discussion of public order (see chapter 28) was dominated by the prolonged coal-strike which led in parts of Great Britain to bitter confrontation between police and striking miners. Although numerous criminal charges arose out of the disturbances (see H.C. Deb., 14 Dec. 1984, col. 637, W.A.), by December 1984 the government's longstanding review of the law of public order had not been completed. An inquiry established by the National Council for Civil Liberties into the role of the police, police authorities and the criminal courts relating to the strike, produced a first report, *Civil Liberties and the Miners' Dispute*, which sought to identify the freedoms and liberties infringed in the events related to the strike, and called for a parliamentary or judicial inquiry into these matters. In *Moss* v. *McLachlan* (*The Times*, 29 Nov. 1984), the Divisional Court held that the police had reasonable grounds for apprehending an imminent breach of the peace when they stopped a group of striking miners in their cars from moving along a motorway with the apparent intention of conducting mass picketing at nearby collieries. In the court's view, if the police honestly and reasonably formed the opinion that there was a real risk of breach of the peace occurring in close proximity both in place and time, they were justified in taking reasonable preventive action, for example by restricting freedom of movement, and they were acting in execution of their duty when they turned back the miners. The guarded terms of this decision left scope for argument about the extent of police preventive powers in other situations (cf. pages 540–5).

11 Judicial review of administrative action gave rise to a strong flow of cases throughout 1984. As regards the grounds of review, *Findlay* v. *Home Secretary* [1984] 3 All E.R. 801 concerned a decision by the Home Secretary to tighten up policies for granting parole to prisoners serving life sentences for murder and other long sentences for violence or drug trafficking; *inter alia*, the House of Lords held that the Home Secretary was entitled to have a policy regarding the discretion to grant parole and that he had not fettered this discretion by adopting a policy which required exceptional circumstances or compelling reasons to be shown before parole would in certain situations be granted (cf. pages 635–6). In *R.* v. *Greater Manchester Coroner, ex p. Tal* [1984] 3 All E.R. 240, the Divisional Court held that judicial review of inferior courts and tribunals extended to errors of law within jurisdiction and was not confined to excess of jurisdiction or error of law on the face of the record; Robert Goff L. J. said unequivocally, 'Since *Anisminic*, the requirement that an error of law within the jurisdiction

must appear on the face of the record is now obsolete' (cf. pages 640–1, 659–60). As regards natural justice, in *Mahon* v. *Air New Zealand Ltd* [1984] A.C. 808, the Judicial Committee quashed certain findings of fact made by a royal commission that had investigated the causes of an air disaster, on grounds that included failure by the commission to base these findings on evidence with some probative value, and breach of the duty of fairness owed to those whose interests might be adversely affected (cf. pages 649–51).

The widening scope of judicial review was apparent in *R.* v. *Home Secretary, ex p. McAvoy* [1984] 3 All E.R. 417, when Webster J. was prepared to review a decision by the Home Secretary removing an unconvicted prisoner from one prison to another, but not to scrutinise the operational or security reasons for the move. But in *R.* v. *Deputy Governor of Camphill Prison, ex p. King* [1984] 3 All E.R. 897, the Court of Appeal held that a prison governor's disciplinary decisions were not open to judicial review (cf. page 649). Lawton L. J. said, 'The courts are not concerned with supervising the exercise of statutory powers of management but with preventing the misuse of public law.' This unsatisfactory reasoning was not the only difficulty caused by judicial attempts to define the phenomenon of 'public law' (cf. pages 607–8). Thus in respect of public sector employment, the Court of Appeal held in *R.* v. *East Berkshire Health Authority, ex p. Walsh* [1984] 3 All E.R. 425 that the dismissal of a nursing officer by a health authority (which was bound by statute to contract with employees on prescribed terms) did not give rise to an application for judicial review under Order 53 (see pages 665–9), but only to private law remedies. But in *R.* v. *Home Secretary, ex p. Benwell* [1984] 3 All E.R. 854, Hodgson J. held that a prison officer could challenge his dismissal by applying under Order 53, since the statutory code of discipline for prison officers imported a sufficient 'public law' element into the dismissal.

The exclusive character of Order 53 proceedings in a public law context that was stressed in *O'Reilly* v. *Mackman* (page 668), was considered again by the House of Lords in *Wandsworth Council* v. *Winder* [1984] 3 All E.R. 976: when a council sued the tenant of a council flat for non-payment of rent, the tenant raised a defence that rent increases made by the council were *ultra vires*, even though he could have applied for judicial review of the increases under Order 53; this defence was held not to be an abuse of process, since the tenant's private law rights were affected by the council's decision.

In *Steeples* v. *Derbyshire CC* [1984] 3 All E.R. 468, Webster J. granted a neighbouring owner and ratepayer a declaration that planning permission given by a local authority to itself was *ultra vires* and in breach of natural justice. This suggested that *Gregory* v. *Camden BC* (page 664) was no longer of authority. However, *Steeples* had been decided in 1981, well before *O'Reilly* v. *Mackman*, and much of the judge's reasoning cannot stand with the approach of the House of Lords in that case.

The effect of alternative remedies upon judicial review under Order 53 was considered in *R.* v. *Epping General Commissioners, ex p. Goldstraw* [1983] 3 All E.R. 257 and *R.* v. *Huntingdon DC, ex p. Cowan* [1984] 1 All E.R. 58.

12 As regards the liability of public authorities and the Crown, the House of Lords held in *Peabody Donation Fund (Governors)* v. *Lindsay Parkinson and Co. Ltd* [1984] 3 All E.R. 529 that a local authority in London owed no duty of care to

the owners and developers of building land to use enforcement powers under public health legislation so as to ensure an adequate drainage scheme for new houses, even though the authority might reasonably have foreseen that failure to do so would result in economic loss to the plaintiffs (cf. *Anns* v. *Merton Council*, pages 685–6). In *Trawnik* v. *Lennox*, *The Times*, 14 Dec. 1984, the Court of Appeal held that residents of the British sector of Berlin could not sue the Attorney-General concerning anticipated nuisance from the use by British troops of a firing range near their houses. The primary reason for this decision was that the Crown could be liable in tort only if sued under the Crown Proceedings Act 1947; one difficulty in the plaintiffs' way was a certificate issued by the Foreign Secretary under section 40(3) of the 1947 Act, declaring that any liability of the Crown alleged in the action arose otherwise than in respect of Her Majesty's government in the United Kingdom (cf. page 678 and cases cited at note 16). In *Buckley* v. *Law Society* (*No.* 2) [1984] 3 All E.R. 313, Megarry V.-C. held that the Law Society was entitled in the public interest to refuse to disclose the identity of persons informing the Society about solicitors suspected of dishonesty, the principle in *D.* v. *N.S.P.C.C.* (page 698) extending to the Law Society's statutory functions.

Bibliography

ABEL-SMITH, B., & STEVENS, R., *In Search of Justice*, 1968
ADLER, M., & BRADLEY, A. W. (ed.), *Justice, Discretion and Poverty*, 1976
AITKEN, J., *Officially Secret*, 1971
ALDERMAN, R. K., & CROSS, J. A., *The Tactics of Resignation*, 1967
ALDERSON, J. C., *Policing Freedom*, 1979
ALEXANDER, A., *The Politics of Local Government in the United Kingdom*, 1982
ALLEN, C. K., *Laws and Orders*, 3rd edn, 1965
ALLEN, C. K., *Law in the Making*, 7th edn, 1964
AMERY, L. S., *Thoughts on the Constitution*, 2nd edn, 1953
ANDREWS, J. A. (ed.), *Welsh Studies in Public Law*, 1970
ANSON, W. R., *The Law and Custom of the Constitution*, vol. I, *Parliament* (ed. M. L. Gwyer), 5th edn, 1922; vol. II, *The Crown* (ed. A. B. Keith), 4th edn, 1935
ARLIDGE, A., & EADY, D., *The Law of Contempt*, 1982
ARMSTRONG, W. (ed.), *Budgetary Reform in the United Kingdom*, 1980
ARNSTEIN, W. L., *The Bradlaugh Case*, 1965
AUBREY, C., *Who's Watching You?*, 1981
AUSTIN, J., *The Province of Jurisprudence Determined* (ed. H. L. A. Hart), 1954

BAGEHOT, W., *The English Constitution* (introdn R. H. S. Crossman), 1963
BAILEY, S. H., CROSS, C. A., & GARNER, J. F., *Cases and Materials in Administrative Law*, 1977
BAILEY, S. H., HARRIS, D. J., & JONES, B. L., *Civil Liberties: Cases and Materials*, 1980
BALDWIN, R., & KINSEY, R., *Police Powers and Politics*, 1982
BARKER, A. (ed.), *Quangos in Britain*, 1982
BARNETT, J., *Inside the Treasury*, 1982
BASSETT, R. G., *1931: Political Crisis*, 1958
BATES, T. St. J. N., et al., *In Memoriam J. D. B. Mitchell*, 1983
BEATSON, J., & MATTHEWS, M. H., *Administrative Law, Cases and Materials*, 1983
BEBR, G., *Judicial Control of the European Communities*, 1965
BEDDARD, R., *Human Rights and Europe*, 2nd edn, 1980
BEDI, S. D., *Extradition in International Law and Practice*, 1966
BEER, S. H., *Treasury Control*, 2nd edn, 1957
BELL, K., *Research Study of Supplementary Benefit Appeal Tribunals*, (H.M.S.O.), 1975
BELOBABA, E. P., & GERTNER, E., *The New Constitution and the Charter of Rights*, 1982
BENTHAM, J., *Handbook of Political Fallacies* (ed. H. A. Larrabee), 1962
BERGER, R., *Impeachment*, 1973
BERKELEY, H., *The Power of the Prime Minister*, 1968
BIRCH, A. H., *Representative and Responsible Government*, 1964
BIRRELL, D., & MURIE, A., *Policy and Government in Northern Ireland: Lessons of Devolution*, 1980
BLACKSTONE, *Commentaries on the Laws of England*, 10th edn, 1787; 14th edn, 1803
BLOM-COOPER, L. J., & DREWRY, G., *Final Appeal*, 1972

BOGDANOR, V., *Devolution*, 1979
BOGDANOR, V., *Multi-party Politics and the Constitution*, 1983
BOGDANOR, V., *The People and the Party System*, 1981
BORRIE, G. J., & LOWE, N. V., *The Law of Contempt*, 2nd edn, 1983
BRIDGE, J. W., LASOK, D., *et al.*, *Fundamental Rights*, 1973
BRIDGES, Lord, *The Treasury*, 2nd edn, 1966
BRINKHORST, L. J., & SCHERMERS, H. G., *Judicial Remedies in the European Communities*, 2nd edn, 1978
BROMHEAD, P. A., *The House of Lords and Contemporary Politics, 1911–1957*, 1958
BROMHEAD, P. A., *Private Members' Bills in the British Parliament*, 1956
BROWN, R. G. S., & STEEL, D. R., *The Administrative Process in Britain*, 2nd edn, 1979
BROWN, L. N., & GARNER, J. F., *French Administrative Law*, 3rd edn, 1983
BROWN, L. N., & JACOBS, F. G., *The Court of Justice of the European Communities*, 2nd edn, 1983
BROWNLIE, I., *Basic Documents on Human Rights*, 2nd edn, 1981
BRYCE, J., *Studies in History and Jurisprudence*, 1901
BUNYAN, T., *The Political Police in Britain*, 1976
BUTLER, D. (ed.), *Coalitions in British Politics*, 1978
BUTLER, D., *Governing without a Majority: Dilemmas for Hung Parliaments in Britain*, 1983
BUTLER, D., & HALSEY, A. H. (ed.), *Policy and Politics*, 1978
BUTLER, D. E., *The Electoral System in Britain since 1918*, 2nd edn, 1963
BYRNE, T., *Local Government in Britain*, 1981

CALVERT, H., *Constitutional Law in Northern Ireland*, 1968
CALVERT, H. (ed.), *Devolution*, 1975
CAMPBELL, A., *Common Market Law*, 1969 & 1973
CAMPBELL, C. M. (ed.), *Do we need a Bill of Rights?*, 1980
CARR, C., *Concerning English Administrative Law*, 1941
CARTWRIGHT, T. J., *Royal Commissions and Departmental Committees in Britain*, 1975
CASTBERG, F., *The European Convention on Human Rights*, 1974
CHAPMAN, L., *Your Disobedient Servant*, rev. edn, 1979
CHESTER, D. N., *The Nationalization of British Industry, 1945–51*, 1975
CHESTER, D. N., & BOWRING, N., *Questions in Parliament*, 1962
CHITTY, J., *Prerogatives of the Crown*, 1820
CHUBB, B., *The Control of Public Expenditure*, 1952
CLARKE, R., *New Trends in Government*, 1971
COLLINS, L., *European Community Law in the United Kingdom*, 2nd edn, 1980
COOMBES, D., *The Member of Parliament and the Administration*, 1966
COSGROVE, R. A., *The Rule of Law: Albert Venn Dicey, Victorian Jurist*, 1980
COWEN, D. V., *The Foundations of Freedom*, 1961
COX, B., *Civil Liberties in Britain*, 1975
CRAIES, W. F., *Statute Law* (ed. S. G. C. Edgar), 7th edn, 1971
CRAIG, P. P., *Administrative Law*, 1983
CRICK, B., *The Reform of Parliament*, 2nd edn, 1968
CRITCHLEY, T. A., *The Conquest of Violence*, 1970
CRITCHLEY, T. A., *A History of the Police in England and Wales*, 2nd edn, 1978
CROMBIE, J., *Her Majesty's Customs and Excise*, 1962
CROSS, C. A., *Principles of Local Government Law*, 6th edn, 1981
CROSS, R., *Evidence*, 5th edn, 1979
CROSS, R., *Precedent in English Law*, 3rd edn, 1977
CROSS, R., *Statutory Interpretation*, 1976
CROSSMAN, R.H.S., *The Diaries of a Cabinet Minister* (vol. I), 1975

DAALDER, H., *Cabinet Reform in Britain, 1914–1963*, 1964
DALE, W., *The Modern Commonwealth*, 1983
DALYELL, T., *Devolution, The End of Britain?*, 1977
DASH, S., *Justice Denied*, 1972
DAVIES, K., *Law of Compulsory Purchase and Compensation*, 4th edn, 1984
DAVIES, K., *Local Government Law*, 1983
DAVIS, K. C., *Discretionary Justice*, 1969
DELBRIDGE, R., & SMITH, M. (ed.), *Consuming Secrets*, 1982

DENNING, Lord, *What next in the Law?*, 1982
d'ENTREVES, A. P., *The Notion of the State*, 1967
de SMITH, S. A., *Constitutional and Administrative Law* (ed. H. Street & R. Brazier), 4th edn, 1981
de SMITH, S. A., *Judicial Review of Administrative Action* (ed. J. M. Evans), 4th edn, 1980
de SMITH, S. A., *The New Commonwealth and its Constitutions*, 1964
DEVLIN, Lord, *The Criminal Prosecution in England*, 1960
DICEY, A. V., *The Law of the Constitution* (ed. E. C. S. Wade), 10th edn, 1959
DICEY, A. V., & RAIT, R. S., *Thoughts on the Union between England and Scotland*, 1920
DONALDSON, A. G., *Some Comparative Aspects of Irish Law*, 1957
DONALDSON, F., *The Marconi Scandal*, 1962
DONALDSON, G., *Edinburgh History of Scotland*, vol. 3, *James V–VII*, 1965
DRZEMCZEWSKI, A., *European Human Rights Convention in Domestic Law*, 1983
DWORKIN, R., *Taking Rights Seriously*, 1977

EASTHAM, N. E., & KRIVY, B., *The Cambridge Lectures 1981*, 1982
EDWARDS, J. Ll. J., *The Law Officers of the Crown*, 1964
EHLERMANN, C. D., *The Role of the Legal Service of the Commission in the Creation of Community Law*, 1981
ELCOCK, H., & WHEATON, M., *Local Government*, 1982
ELLIOTT, M. J., *The Role of Law in Central-Local Relations*, 1981
ELTON, G. R., *Studies in Tudor and Stuart Politics and Government* (2 vols), 1974
ERSKINE MAY, *Parliamentary Practice (The Law, Privileges, Proceedings and Usage of Parliament)* (ed. Sir C. Gordon), 20th edn, 1983
EVANS, G. (ed.), *Labour and the Constitution, 1972–1975*, 1977
EVANS, J. M., *Immigration Law*, 2nd edn, 1983
EVATT, H. V., *The King and His Dominion Governors*, 1936
EVELEGH, R., *Peace Keeping in a Democratic Society*, 1978
EWING, K. D., *Trade Unions, the Labour Party and the Law*, 1983
EWING, K. D., & FINNIE, W., *Civil Liberties in Scotland*, 1982

FARMER, J. A., *Tribunals and Government*, 1974
FARRAR, J. H., *Law Reform and the Law Commission*, 1974
FAVREAU, G., *The Amendment of the Constitution of Canada*, 1965
FAWCETT, J. E. S., *The Application of the European Convention on Human Rights*, 1969
FAWCETT, J. E. S., *The British Commonwealth in International Law*, 1963
FERGUSON, W., *Edinburgh History of Scotland*, vol. 4, *1689 to the Present*, 1968
FINER, S. E. (ed.), *Adversary Politics and Electoral Reform*, 1975
FINER, S. E., *Anonymous Empire*, 2nd edn, 1966
FLICK, G. A., *Natural Justice*, 1979
FORD, P. & G. (ed.), *Luke Graves Hansard's Diary, 1814–1841*, 1962
FORSEY, E. A., *The Royal Power of Dissolution of Parliament in the British Commonwealth*, 1943
FORSYTH, W., *Cases and Opinions on Constitutional Law*, 1869
FOULKES, D. L., *Administrative Law*, 5th edn, 1982
FREEMAN, E. A., *The Growth of the English Constitution*, 1872
FRIEDMANN, W. G., *Law in a Changing Society*, revised 1964
FRIEDMANN, W. G. (ed.), *Public and Private Enterprise in Mixed Economies*, 1974
FRIEDMANN, W. G., & GARNER, J. F. (ed.), *Government Enterprise*, 1970
FRYDE, E. B., & MILLER, E. (ed.), *Historical Studies of the English Parliament 1399–1603*, 1970
FULLER, L. L., *The Morality of Law*, 1964

GARNER, J. F., *Administrative Law*, 5th edn, 1979
GELLHORN, W., *Ombudsmen and Others*, 1966
GHAI, Y. P., & McAUSLAN, J. P. W. B., *Public Law and Political Change in Kenya*, 1970
GORDON, G. H., *Criminal Law of Scotland*, 2nd edn, 1978
GORDON, P., *Policing Scotland*, 1980
GOSTIN, L. O., *A Human Condition*, 1975, 1977
GOUGH, J. W., *Fundamental Law in English Constitutional History*, 1955
GRANT, J. P. (ed.), *Independence and Devolution, the Legal Implications for Scotland*, 1976
GRANT, M., *Urban Planning Law*, 1982
GREGORY, R., *The Price of Amenity*, 1971

GREGORY, R., & HUTCHESSON, P. G., *The Parliamentary Ombudsman*, 1975
GREY, Earl, *Parliamentary Government*, 1864
GRIFFITH, J. A. G., *Central Departments and Local Authorities*, 1966
GRIFFITH, J. A. G. (ed.), *From Policy to Administration*, 1976
GRIFFITH, J. A. G., *Parliamentary Scrutiny of Government Bills*, 1974
GRIFFITH, J. A. G., *Politics of the Judiciary*, 2nd edn, 1981
GUEST, A. G. (ed.), *Oxford Essays in Jurisprudence*, 1961

HAGUE, D. C., MACKENZIE, W. J. M., & BARKER, A. (ed.), *Public Policy and Private Interests*, 1975
HAILSHAM, Lord, *The Dilemma of Democracy*, 1978
HAMSON, C. J., *Executive Discretion and Judicial Control*, 1954
HANHAM, H. J., *The Nineteenth Century Constitution, 1815–1914*, 1969
HANSON, A. H., *Parliament and Public Ownership*, 1961
HANSON, A. H., & WALLES, M. J., *Governing Britain*, 3rd edn, 1980
HANSON, L., *The Government and the Press, 1695–1763*, 1936
HARLOW, C., *Compensation and Government Torts*, 1982
HARLOW, C., & RAWLINGS, R., *Law and Administration*, 1984
HARMAN, H., & GRIFFITH, J. A. G., *Justice Deserted*, 1979
HART, H. L. A., *The Concept of Law*, 1961
HART, H. L. A., & HONORE, A. M., *Causation in the Law*, 1959
HARTLEY, T. C., *The Foundations of European Community Law*, 1981
HARTLEY, T. C., & GRIFFITH, J. A. G., *Government and Law*, 2nd edn, 1981
HARTLEY-BOOTH, V. E., *British Extradition Law and Procedure*, 1980
HAYEK, F. A., *The Constitution of Liberty*, 1963
HAYEK, F. A., *The Road to Serfdom*, 1944
HEARN, W. E., *The Government of England*, 1867
HECLO, H., & WILDAVSKY, A., *The Private Government of Public Money*, 1974
HEDLEY, P., & AYNSLEY, C., *The D-Notice Affair*, 1967
HENDERSON, E. G., *Foundations of English Administrative Law*, 1963
HENLEY, D., *et al.*, *Public Sector Accounting and Financial Control*, 1984
HEPPLE, B. A., *Race, Jobs and the Law in Britain*, 2nd edn, 1970
HEPPLE, B. A., & O'HIGGINS, P., *Encyclopaedia of Labour Relations Law*, 1972
HERBERT, A. P., *Uncommon Law*, 1935
HERMAN, V., & LODGE, J., *The European Parliament and the European Community*, 1978
HEUSTON, R. F. V., *Essays in Constitutional Law*, 2nd edn, 1964
HEUSTON, R. F. V., *Lives of the Lord Chancellors 1885–1940*, 1964
HOGG, P. W., *Liability of the Crown*, 1971
HOLDSWORTH, W., *A History of English Law* (14 vols.), 1923–64
HOOD PHILLIPS, O., *Constitutional and Administrative Law*, 6th edn, 1978
HOOD PHILLIPS, O., *Reform of the Constitution*, 1970
HOWARD, C., *Australian Federal Constitutional Law*, 2nd edn, 1972
HUNNINGS, N. M., *Film Censors and the Law*, 1967

JACKSON, P., *Natural Justice*, 2nd edn, 1979
JACKSON, R. M., *The Machinery of Justice in England*, 7th edn, 1977
JACOBS, F. G., *The European Convention on Human Rights*, 1975
JACOBS, F. G., & DURAND, A., *References to the European Court: Practice and Procedure*, 1975
JACONELLI, J., *Enacting a Bill of Rights, the Legal Problems*, 1980
JEFFERY, K., & HENNESSY, P., *States of Emergency: British Governments and Strikebreaking since 1919*, 1983
JENKINS, R., *Mr Balfour's Poodle*, 1954
JENNINGS, I., *Cabinet Government*, 3nd edn, 1959
JENNINGS, I., *The Law and the Constitution*, 5th edn, 1959
JENNINGS, I., *Parliament*, 2nd edn, 1957
JENNINGS, I., *The Sedition Bill Explained*, 1934
JOHNSON, N., *In Search of the Constitution*, 1977
JOHNSON, N., *Parliament and Administration; the Estimates Committee 1945–65*, 1966
JOHNSTON, A., *The Inland Revenue*, 1965
JONES, J. M., *British Nationality Law*, 2nd edn, 1956
JONES, T., *Whitehall Diary*, vol. 3 (ed. R. K. Middlemas), 1971
JOSEPH, K., *Freedom under the Law*, 1975

KAPTEYN, P. J. G., & VERLOREN VAN THEMAAT, P., *Introduction to the Law of the European Communities*, 1973

KEATING, M. J., & MIDWINTER, A., *The Government of Scotland*, 1983

KEETON, G. W., *Trial by Tribunal*, 1960

KEIR, D. L., & LAWSON, F. H., *Cases in Constitutional Law*, 6th edn, 1979

KEITH-LUCAS, B., & RICHARDS, P. G., *The History of Local Government in the 20th Century*, 1978

KELLAS, J. G., *The Scottish Political System*, 1973

KERMODE, D. G., *Devolution at Work: A Case Study of the Isle of Man*, 1979

KERR, J., *Matters for Judgment*, 1979

KERSELL, J. E., *Parliamentary Supervision of Delegated Legislation*, 1960

KITSON, F., *Low Intensity Operations*, 1971

LASOK, D., *et al.* (ed.), *Fundamental Duties*, 1980

LASOK, D., & BRIDGE, J. W., *Law and Institutions of the European Communities*, 3rd edn, 1982

LATHAM, R. T. E., *The Law and the Commonwealth*, 1949

LAUNDY, P., *The Office of Speaker*, 1964

LAWRENCE, R. J., *The Government of Northern Ireland*, 1965

LEIGH, D., *The Frontiers of Secrecy*, 1980

LEIGH, L. H., *Police Powers in England and Wales*, 1975

LESTER, A., & BINDMAN, G., *Race and Law*, 1972

LEVY, H. P., *The Press Council*, 1967

LEWIS, C., *State and Diplomatic Immunity*

LEWIS, N., & GATESHILL, B., *The Commission for Local Administration*, 1978

LIKIERMAN, J. A., *Cash Limits and External Financing Limits*, 1981

LIPSTEIN, K., *The Law of the European Community*, 1974

LUSTGARTEN, L., *Legal Control of Racial Discrimination*, 1980

McDONALD, D. C., *Legal Rights in the Canadian Charter of Rights and Freedoms*, 1982

MacDONALD, I. A., *Immigration Law and Practice in the United Kingdom*, 1983

MacDONALD, I. A., *Race Relations and the New Law*, 1977

MacDONALD, I. A., & BLAKE, N., *The New Nationality Law*, 1982

McILWAIN, C. H., *Constitutionalism, Ancient and Modern*, 1947

McILWAIN, C. H., *The High Court of Parliament*, 1910

MACKENZIE STUART, A. J., *The European Communities and the Rule of Law*, 1977

MACKINTOSH, J. P., *The British Cabinet*, 3rd edn, 1977

MACKINTOSH, J. P., *The Devolution of Power*, 1968

MACKINTOSH, J. P., *Specialist Committees in the House of Commons – have they failed?* (rev.), 1980

McNAIR, Lord, *Law of Treaties*, 2nd edn, 1961

McNAIR, Lord, & WATTS, A. D., *The Legal Effects of War*, 4th edn, 1966

MAITLAND, F. W., *The Constitutional History of England*, 1908

MALLORY, J. R., *The Structure of Canadian Government*, 1971

Manual of Military Law, 9th edn, 1968

MARGACH, J., *The Abuse of Power*, 1978

MARK, R., *In the Office of Constable*, 1978

MARK, R., *Policing a Perplexed Society*, 1977

MARKESINIS, B. S., *The Theory and Practice of Dissolution of Parliament*, 1972

MARSHALL, G., *Constitutional Conventions*, 1984

MARSHALL, G., *Constitutional Theory*, 1971

MARSHALL, G., *Parliamentary Sovereignty and the Commonwealth*, 1957

MARSHALL, G., *Police and Government*, 1965

MARSHALL, G., & MOODIE, G. C., *Some Problems of the Constitution*, 5th edn, 1971

MATHIJSEN, P. S. R. F., *A Guide to European Community Law*, 3rd edn, 1980

MEGARRY, R. E., & WADE, H. W. R., *The Law of Real Property*, 4th edn, 1975

MICHAEL, J., *The Politics of Secrecy*, 1982

MICKLETHWAIT, R., *The National Insurance Commissioners*, 1976

MIDDLEMAS, K., & BARNES, J., *Baldwin*, 1969

MIERS, D. R., & PAGE, A. C., *Legislation*, 1982

MILL, J. S., *Representative Government*, 1861

MILLER, C. J., *Contempt of Court*, 1976

MILLER, J. BENNETT, *Administrative and Local Government Law in Scotland*, 1961

MILLER, J. D. B., *Survey of Commonwealth Affairs: Problems of Expansion and Attrition, 1953–1969*, 1974
MILLETT, J. D., *The Unemployment Assistance Board*, 1940
MILNE, D., *The Scottish Office*, 1957
MITCHELL, J. D. B., *Constitutional Law*, 2nd edn, 1968
MITCHELL, J. D. B., *The Contracts of Public Authorities*, 1954
MOORE, R., & WALLACE, T., *Slamming the Door*, 1975
MOORE, W. H., *Act of State in English Law*, 1906
MORGAN, J. P., *The House of Lords and the Labour Government, 1964–1970*, 1975
MORRIS, A. (ed.), *The Growth of Parliamentary Scrutiny by Committee*, 1970
MORRISON, H., *Government and Parliament*, 3rd edn, 1964
MOSLEY, R. K., *The Story of the Cabinet Office*, 1969
MUNRO, C. R., *Television, Censorship and the Law*, 1979

NICOLSON, H., *King George V*, 1952
NOEL, E., *The European Community: How it Works*, 1979
NORMANTON, E. L., *The Accountability and Audit of Governments*, 1966
NORTON, P., *The Commons in Perspective*, 1981
NORTON, P., *Constitution in Flux*, 1982
NORTON, P., *Dissension in the House of Commons 1945–1974*, 1975; *1974–1979*, 1980

O'CONNELL, D. P., & RIORDAN, A., *Opinions on Imperial Constitutional Law*, 1971
O'HIGGINS, P., *Cases and Materials on Civil Liberties*, 1980
O'HIGGINS, P., *Censorship in Britain*, 1972

PAINE, T., *Rights of Man* (ed. H. Collins), 1969
PALLEY, C., *The Constitutional History and Law of Southern Rhodesia 1888–1965*, 1966
PANNICK, D., *Judicial Review of the Death Penalty*, 1982
PARRIS, H., *Constitutional Bureaucracy*, 1969
PARRY, A., & HARDY, S., *EEC Law*, 2nd edn, 1981
PARRY, C. (ed.), *British Digest of International Law*
PARRY, C., *Nationality and Citizenship Laws of the Commonwealth*, 2 vols., 1957–60
PATERSON, A., *The Law Lords*, 1982
POLYVIOU, P. G., *The Equal Protection of the Laws*, 1980
POLYVIOU, P. G., *Search and Seizure: Constitutional and Common Law*, 1982
PORT, F. J., *Administrative Law*, 1929

REDLICH, J., & HIRST, F. W., *The History of Local Government in England* (ed. B. Keith-Lucas), 2nd edn, 1970
REID, G., *The Politics of Financial Control*, 1966
RENTON, R. W., & BROWN, H. H., *Criminal Procedure* (ed. G. H. Gordon), 5th edn, 1983
RICHARDS, P. G., *Parliament and Conscience*, 1970
RICHARDS, P. G., *Patronage in British Government*, 1963
RIDEOUT, R. W., *Principles of Labour Law*, 4th edn, 1983
RILEY, P. W. J., *The Union of England and Scotland*, 1978
ROBERTS, C., *The Growth of Responsible Government in Stuart England*, 1966
ROBERTS-WRAY, K., *Commonwealth and Colonial Law*, 1966
ROBERTSON, G., *Obscenity*, 1979
ROBERTSON, G., *The People against the Press*, 1983
ROBINSON, A., *Parliament and Public Spending – The Expenditure Committee 1970–6*, 1978
ROBSON, W. A., *Justice and Administrative Law*, 3rd edn, 1951
ROBSON, W. A., *Nationalised Industry and Public Ownership*, 2nd edn, 1962
ROGALY, J., *Grunwick*, 1977
ROLPH, C. H., *The Trial of Lady Chatterley*, 1961
ROSEVEARE, H., *The Treasury*, 1969
ROWAT, D. C., *The Ombudsman*, 2nd edn, 1968
RUBINSTEIN, A., *Jurisdiction and Illegality*, 1965

SALMOND, J. W., & HEUSTON, R. V. F., *The Law of Torts*, 18th edn, 1981
SAWER, G., *Federation under Strain*, 1977

SCARMAN, Lord, *English Law – The New Dimension*, 1974

SCHREINER, O. D., *The Contribution of English Law to South African Law and the Rule of Law in South Africa*, 1967

SHARPE, R. J., *The Law of Habeas Corpus*, 1976

SHEARER, I. A., *Extradition in International Law*, 1971

SIMPSON, A. W. B. (ed.), *Oxford Essays in Jurisprudence* (Second Series), 1973

SINGER, P., *Democracy and Disobedience*, 1973

SMELLIE, K. B., *A History of Local Government*, 4th edn, 1968

SMITH, J. C., & HOGAN, B., *Criminal Law*, 5th edn, 1983

SORENSEN, M. (ed.), *Manual of Public International Law*, 1968

STACEY, F., *Ombudsmen Compared*, 1978

STEEL, D., *A House Divided; the Lib-Lab Pact and the Future of British Politics*, 1980

STEEL, D., *No Entry*, 1969

STEPHEN, J. F., *Digest of Criminal Law*, 1877

STEPHEN, J. F., *History of the Criminal Law of England* (3 vols.), 1883

STEVENS, R., *Law and Politics: the House of Lords as a judicial body, 1800–1976*, 1979

STEWART, J. D., *British Pressure Groups*, 1956

STREET, H., *Freedom, the Individual and the Law*, 5th edn, 1982

STREET, H., *Governmental Liability*, 1953

STREET, H., *Justice in the Welfare State*, 2nd edn, 1975

SUMMMERS, R. (ed.), *Essays in Legal Philosophy*, 1968

SUPPERSTONE, M., *Brownlie's Law of Public Order and National Security*, 2nd edn, 1981

TARNOPOLSKY, W. S., *The Canadian Bill of Rights*, 2nd edn, 1975

TARNOPOLSKY, W., & BEAUDOUIN, G. A., *The Canadian Charter of Rights and Freedoms, a Commentary*, 1982

TASWELL-LANGMEAD, T. P., *English Constitutional History* (ed. T.F.T. Plucknett), 11th edn, 1960

TERRY, C. S., *The Scottish Parliament 1603–1707*, 1905

THIO, S. M., *Locus Standi and Judicial Review*, 1971

THOMAS, D., *A Long Time Burning*, 1969

THOMPSON, E. P., *Whigs and Hunters: the Origin of the Black Act*, 1975

THOMPSON, E. P., *Writing by Candlelight*, 1980

TURACK, D. C., *The Passport in International Law*, 1972

TURPIN, C. C., *Government Contracts*, 1972

USHER, J. A., *European Court Practice*, 1983

VALLAT, F., *International Law and the Practitioner*, 1966

VILE, M. J. C., *Constitutionalism and the Separation of Powers*, 1967

WADE, H. W. R., *Administrative Law*, 5th edn, 1982

WADE, H. W. R., *Constitutional Fundamentals*, 1980

WALKER, D. M., *The Scottish Legal System*, 4th edn, 1976

WALKER, P. GORDON, *The Cabinet*, rev. 1972

WALKLAND, S. A., & RYLE, M. (ed.), *The Commons Today*, 1981

WALLINGTON, P. T., & McBRIDE, G., *Civil Liberties and a Bill of Rights*, 1976

WEILER, P., *In the Last Resort*, 1974

WHEARE, K. C., *Maladministration and its Remedies*, 1973

WHEARE, K. C., *Modern Constitutions*, 2nd edn, 1966

WHEARE, K. C., *The Constitutional Structure of the Commonwealth*, 1960

WHEARE, K. C., *The Statute of Westminster and Dominion Status*, 5th edn, 1953

WHEELER–BENNETT, J., *King George VI*, 1958

WHITLAM, G., *The Truth of the Matter*, 1979

WILLIAMS, D. G. T., *Not in the Public Interest*, 1965

WILLIAMS, D. G. T., *Keeping the Peace*, 1967

WILLIAMS, E. N., *The 18th Century Constitution, 1688–1815*, 1960

WILLIAMS, O. C., *History of Private Bill Procedure*, 2 vols., 1949

WILLSON, F. M. G., *The Organization of British Central Government, 1914–1964*, 2nd edn, 1968

WILSON, G. P., *Cases and Materials on Constitutional and Administrative Law*, 2nd edn, 1976

WILSON, G. P., *Cases and Materials on the English Legal System*, 1973
WILSON, H., *The Governance of Britain*, 1976
WILSON, H., *The Labour Government, 1964–70*, 1974
WILSON, S. S., *The Cabinet Office to 1945*, 1975
WOLFE, J. N. (ed.), *Government and Nationalism in Scotland*, 1969
WADE, H. W. R., *...*, Government and Nationalism in Scotland, 1969
WRAITH, R. E., & HUTCHESSON, P. G., *Administrative Tribunals*, 1973
WRAITH, R. E., & LAMB, G. B., *Public Inquiries as an Instrument of Government*, 1971
WYATT, D., & DASHWOOD, A., *The Substantive Law of the EEC*, 1980

YARDLEY, D. C. M., *Principles of Administrative Law*, 1981
YOUNG, H., *The Crossman Affair*, 1976
YOUNG, T., *Incitement to Disaffection*, 1976

ZAMIR, I., *The Declaratory Judgment*, 1962
ZANDER, M., *A Bill of Rights?*, 2nd edn, 1980

Index

Constitutional and administrative law